Basque Country, Navarra & La Rioja
Pages 118–139

Aragón
Pages 230–245

Catalonia
Pages 210–229

San Sebastián
(Donostia)

Iruña
(Pamplona)

Zaragoza

Lleida

Barcelona

EASTERN
SPAIN

Barcelona
Pages 140–199

THE BALEARIC ISLANDS

uenca

Palma de
Mallorca

Valencia

lbacete

Alacant
(Alicante)

Murcia

The Balearic Islands
Pages 510–531

Almería

THE CANARY ISLANDS

Valencia and Murcia
Pages 246–267

The Canary Islands
Pages 532–555

THE CANARY ISLANDS

Santa Cruz
de Tenerife

Las Palmas
de Gran Canaria

EYEWITNESS TRAVEL

SPAIN

DK Penguin Random House

Project Editor Nick Inman
Art Editors Jaki Grosvenor, Janis Utton
Editors Catherine Day, Lesley McCave, Seán O'Connell
Designers Susan Blackburn, Dawn Davies-Cook,
Joy Fitzsimmons, Helen Westwood

Main Contributors
John Ardagh, David Baird, Mary-Ann Gallagher, Vicky Hayward,
Adam Hopkins, Lindsay Hunt, Nick Inman, Paul Richardson, Martin Symington,
Nigel Tisdall, Roger Williams

Photographers
Max Alexander, Joe Cornish, Neil Lukas, Neil Mersh, John Miller,
Kim Sayer, Linda Whitwam, Peter Wilson

Illustrators
Stephen Conlin, Gary Cross, Richard Draper, Isidoro González-Adalid Cabezas
(Acanto Arquitectura y Urbanismo S.l.), Claire Littlejohn, Maltings
Partnership, Chris Orr & Assocs, John Woodcock

Printed and bound in China

First American Edition, 1996
Published in the United States
by DK Publishing, 345 Hudson Street
New York, New York 10014
17 18 10 9 8 7 6 5 4 3

Reprinted with revisions 1997, 1999, 2000, 2001, 2002, 2003, 2004,
2005, 2006, 2007, 2008, 2009, 2010, 2011, 2013, 2014, 2016

Copyright 1996, 2016 © Dorling Kindersley Limited, London
A Penguin Random House Company

Published in the UK by Dorling Kindersley Limited.

A catalog record for this book is available from the Library of Congress.

ISSN 1542-1554
ISBN 978-1-4654-4020-4

Floors are referred to throughout in accordance with European usage; ie the
"first floor" is one floor up.

MIX
Paper from
responsible sources
FSC™ C018179
www.fsc.org

**The information in this
DK Eyewitness Travel Guide is checked regularly.**
Every effort has been made to ensure that this book is as up-to-date as possible
at the time of going to press. Some details, however, such as telephone numbers,
opening hours, prices, gallery hanging arrangements and travel information, are
liable to change. The publishers cannot accept responsibility for any consequences
arising from the use of this book, nor for any material on third party websites, and
cannot guarantee that any website address in this book will be a suitable source of
travel information. We value the views and suggestions of our readers very highly.
Please write to: Publisher, DK Eyewitness Travel Guides, Dorling Kindersley,
80 Strand, London WC2R 0RL, UK, or email: travelguides@dk.com.

Front cover main image: The white town of Arcos de la Frontera, Andalusia

◀ Plaza de Cibeles at Christmas time, Madrid

Contents

How to Use This Guide **6**

King Alfonso X the Learned

Introducing Spain

Discovering Spain **10**

Putting Spain on
the Map **18**

A Portrait of Spain **22**

Spain Through the Year **44**

The History of Spain **50**

Northern Spain

Introducing
Northern Spain **78**

Galicia **88**

Asturias and
Cantabria **104**

The Basque Country,
Navarra and La Rioja **118**

Barcelona

Introducing
Barcelona **142**

Old Town **146**

Eixample **162**

Montjuïc **172**

Further Afield **178**

Barcelona Street
Finder **183**

Shopping and
Entertainment
in Barcelona **190**

Eastern Spain

Introducing Eastern
Spain **202**

Catalonia **210**

Aragón **230**

Valencia and Murcia **246**

Madrid

Introducing Madrid **270**

Old Madrid **272**

Statue of Alfonso XII, Madrid

Bourbon Madrid **286**

Further Afield **304**

Madrid Street Finder **311**

Shopping and
Entertainment in
Madrid **320**

Madrid Province **330**

Central Spain

Introducing Central
Spain **340**

The impressive 15th-century Belmonte Castle

Castilla y León **350**

Castilla-La Mancha **382**

Extremadura **404**

Southern Spain

Introducing Southern
Spain **420**

Seville **430**

Seville Street Finder **451**

Shopping and
Entertainment in
Seville **458**

Andalusia **462**

Spain's Islands

Introducing Spain's
Islands **508**

The Balearic Islands **510**

The Canary Islands **532**

Travellers' Needs

Where to Stay **558**

Where to Eat and Drink **576**

Shopping **606**

Entertainment **608**

Outdoor Activities and
Specialist Holidays **610**

Survival Guide

Practical Information **616**

Travel Information **626**

General Index **636**

Phrase Book **671**

Iglesia de Santa María
del Naranco in Asturias

HOW TO USE THIS GUIDE

This guide helps you to get the most from your visit to Spain. It provides detailed practical information and expert recommendations. Introducing Spain maps the country and sets it in its historical and cultural context. The five regional sections, plus Barcelona and Madrid, describe important sights, using maps, photographs and illustrations. Features cover topics from food and wine to fiestas and beaches. Restaurant and hotel recommendations can be found in *Travellers' Needs*. The *Survival Guide* has tips on everything from transport to using the telephone system.

Barcelona, Madrid and Seville

These cities are divided into areas, each with its own chapter. For Barcelona and Madrid, a last chapter, *Further Afield*, covers peripheral sights. Madrid Province, surrounding the capital, has its own chapter. All sights are numbered and plotted on the chapter's area map. Information on each sight is easy to locate, as it follows the numerical order on the map.

Sights at a Glance lists the chapter's sights by category: Churches and Cathedrals, Museums and Galleries, Streets and Squares, Historic Buildings, Parks and Gardens.

All pages relating to Madrid have green thumb tabs. Barcelona's are pink and Seville's are red.

A locator map shows where you are in relation to other areas of the city centre.

1 Area Map
For easy reference, sights are numbered and located on a map. City centre sights are also marked on Street Finders: Barcelona (*pages 183–9*); Madrid (*pages 311–19*); Seville (*pages 451–7*).

2 Street-by-Street Map
This gives a bird's-eye view of the key areas in each chapter.

Stars indicate the sights that no visitor should miss.

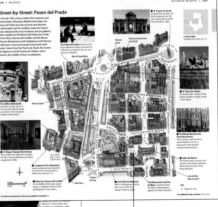

A suggested route for a walk is shown in red.

3 Detailed information
The sights in the three main cities are described individually. Addresses, telephone numbers, opening hours, admission charges, tours, photography and wheelchair access are also provided, as well as public transport links.

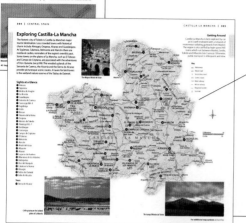

1 Introduction

The landscape, history and character of each region is outlined here, showing how the area has developed over the centuries and what it has to offer to the visitor today.

Spain Area by Area

Apart from Barcelona, Madrid and Seville, the country has been divided into 12 regions, each of which has a separate chapter. The most interesting cities, towns and villages, and other places to visit, are numbered on a *Regional Map*.

2 Regional Map

This shows the road network and gives an illustrated overview of the whole region. All interesting places to visit are numbered and there are also useful tips on getting to, and around, the region by car and public transport.

Fiesta boxes highlight the best traditional fiestas in the region.

Each area of Spain can be quickly identified by its colour coding, shown on the inside front cover.

3 Detailed information

All the important towns and other places to visit are described individually. They are listed in order, following the numbering on the Regional Map. Within each town or city, there is detailed information on important buildings and other sights.

For all top sights, a Visitors' Checklist provides the practical information you will need to plan your visit.

4 Spain's top sights

These are given two or more full pages. Historic buildings are dissected to reveal their interiors. The most interesting towns or city centres are shown in a bird's-eye view, with sights picked out and described.

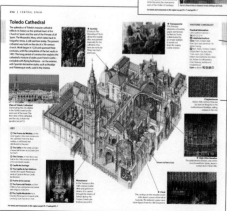

INTRODUCING SPAIN

Discovering Spain   10–17

Putting Spain on the Map   18–21

A Portrait of Spain   22–43

Spain Through the Year   44–49

The History of Spain   50–75

DISCOVERING SPAIN

The following tours have been designed to take in as many of Spain's highlights as possible, while keeping long-distance travel to a minimum. First come three 2-day tours exploring Spain's most enticing cities: Madrid, Barcelona and Seville. These itineraries can be combined to form a week-long tour (all three cities are linked by fast AVE trains). Extra suggestions are provided for those who want to extend their stay to 10 days.

A one-week itinerary of Bilbao and the Basque Lands and a themed 10-day tour of Northern Spain follow. Next comes a one-week itinerary of the Mediterranean coast, from Barcelona to Cartagena via Valencia. Finally, we've created a tour that combines Madrid with the three great cities of old Al Andalus: Seville, Córdoba and Granada. Pick, combine and follow your favourite tours, or simply dip in and out and be inspired.

Madrid and Moorish Spain: Granada, Córdoba and Seville

- Soak up the electric atmosphere of the Spanish capital, Madrid, admiring the world-class art museums and being spoiled for choice when it comes to shopping and eating.

- Be seduced by Seville, an enchanting city of narrow whitewashed streets, with its La Giralda bell tower and the opulent palace of the Real Alcázar.

- Explore delightfully preserved Andalusian towns like Carmona and Écija, with their fine palaces and churches.

- Marvel at the Mezquita in Córdoba and get lost in the maze of the old Jewish Quarter.

- Drive through rolling hills and olive groves to take in a string of pretty villages, from Montilla to Priego de Córdoba, enjoying fresh local wines with dinner.

- Visit Granada's extraordinary palace of Alhambra, surrounded by the scented gardens of the Generalife and the spirit of Al Andalus. Tuck into tasty tapas, and listen to flamenco in a hilltop cave.

Key

— Madrid and Moorish Spain
— Bilbao and the Basque Lands
— Wild Spain
— Barcelona and the Mediterranean Coast

La Giralda
The bell tower of the Seville Cathedral, formerly a minaret, is World Heritage-listed.

◀ *Pier in the Prince's Garden at Aranjuez Castle, by Gianni Dagli Orti*

Wild Spain: Cantabria, Asturias and Galicia

- Visit enchanting fishing villages-cum-resorts, and the Cantabrian capital of Santander.

- Wander the perfectly preserved historic town of Santillana del Mar, and see prehistoric cave art at Cuevas de Altamira.

- Hike the lofty peaks and valleys of spectacular Parque Nacional de los Picos de Europa.

- Hang out in bustling Gijón, then head east along the craggy Costa Verde to discover idyllic villages and secret coves.

- Spend a day in Roman-walled Lugo, heading on to stone-and-granite Santiago de Compostela.

Bilbao and the Basque Lands

- Be dazzled in Bilbao by the spectacular Museo Guggenheim, then shop at the city's chic boutiques.

- Visit the city of Gernika-Lumo's poignant ancient oak, one of few places to survive the 1937 bombing.

- Meander the wild and beautiful Costa Vasca, sampling the day's catch at enchanting seaside towns.

- Soak up the beach glamour of San Sebastián and enjoy some of the best tapas in the world.

- Inland, visit scenic Santuario de Loiola and hilltop Santuario de Arantzazu.

- Stroll around delightful Vitoria, the Basque capital.

- Explore the historic wine-producing town of Haro, taking in a few bodegas.

Barcelona and the Mediterranean Coast by Train

- Get lost in Barcelona's Gothic Quarter, admire Gaudí's fairy-tale architecture, shop and eat to your heart's content, then relax on the fabulous city beaches.

- Stroll around Sitges, one of the prettiest (and liveliest) towns on the Med, then head to Tarragona to visit a slew of Roman remains.

- Relax in lovely Peníscola, piled up on a promontory almost completely surrounded by the sea, then head to dazzling Valencia, fusing old and new with flair.

- Spend a day in vibrant Alicante (Alacant), chock-full of fantastic art museums, and with a castle atop a crag boasting great coastal views.

- Tour traditional Murcia, taking in its Baroque architecture and old-world spirit. Then on to old Cartagena, stuffed with Punic and Roman remains.

2 Days in Madrid

Tapas, flamenco, art, monuments and museums – the capital has the lot.

- **Arriving** Barajas Airport is 13 km (8 miles) from the city centre, linked by metro, bus (local and express) and taxi.

Day 1
Morning Begin at the Plaza Mayor, the huge arcaded square in Madrid's historic heart (*p277*), then take a stroll around the surrounding cobbled streets. Head into the pretty 19th-century Mercado de San Miguel (located just off the square) for a gourmet lunch at one of the many chic tapas bars.

Afternoon Visit the Prado (*pp296–9*), Spain's biggest museum. Highlights include the superlative *Las Meninas* by Velázquez, and a host of his works for the Spanish Habsburg monarchs. The charming gardens at the sumptuous Hotel Ritz by Belmond just next door are ideal for a post-museum cocktail.

> **To extend your trip...**
> Head into the Guadarrama mountains north of Madrid, visiting ancient Segovia (*pp368–9*) and the walled city of Ávila (*pp366–7*).

Playa Mayor, Madrid's grand arcaded square

Day 2
Morning Stroll along the Gran Vía (*pp284–5*), Madrid's glittering answer to New York's Broadway, admiring the turn-of-the-20th-century theatres, as well as some of the city's first skyscrapers. The street is now a shopping mecca, packed with flagship stores. Relax at one of the arty restaurants in Malasaña (*p308*).

Afternoon Head to the Museo Nacional Centro de Arte Reina Sofía (*pp302–3*), a superb contemporary art museum, to admire Picasso's powerful *Guernica* and works by Gaudí, Miró and Dalí, among others. In the evening, take a tour of the lively tapas bars around the Plaza de Santa Ana.

2 Days in Barcelona

Be enchanted by the city's medieval quarter, Modernista monuments, gourmet cuisine and city beaches.

- **Arriving** El Prat Airport is 18 km south of the city centre, with regular train and bus connections.

Day 1
Morning Get lost in the beautiful stone labyrinth of Barcelona's Gothic Quarter (*Barri Gòtic*, *pp148–9*). Visit the remarkable ruins of the ancient Roman colony of Barcino, still visible beneath the Conjunt Monumental de la Plaça del Rei (home to the Barcelona History Museum, *pp150–51*). Then explore the magnificent Barcelona Cathedral (*pp152–3*), especially its enchanting cloister. There are dozens of excellent places in the area for a quick bite to eat.

Afternoon Wander down the city's most famous promenade, Las Ramblas (*pp154–5*), to the Port Vell (*p160*), now a marina full of yachts and pleasure boats. Then head to the traditional fishermen's neighbourhood of Barceloneta (*p160*), strolling through the unbelievably narrow streets packed with old-fashioned tapas bars. If you're feeling tired take a late-afternoon siesta on

Barcelona's busy, tree-lined pedestrian thoroughfare, Las Ramblas

For practical information on travelling around Spain, see pp626–35

the beach before dining on traditional paella at one of the seafront restaurants.

Day 2
Morning Spend the morning at Gaudí's spectacular (and still unfinished) Sagrada Família (pp170–71). Admire the awesome façades, and take the lift up to the upper galleries for vertiginous city views. Stroll up to the nearby Hospital de la Santa Creu i de Sant Pau (p169), set in an enchanting complex of Modernista pavilions. Enjoy a lazy lunch in the Eixample neighbourhood.

Afternoon Wander down the fashionable Passeig de Gràcia (p164), which is lined with scores of top international designer boutiques and flagship stores of famous high-street brands. This street is as famous for its Modernista architecture as it is for its shopping, and is crowned by two of Gaudí's most celebrated buildings, the Casa Batlló (p168) and La Pedrera (p169), both of which must be visited. Round out the day with a tapas tour of the Eixample neighbourhood's many bars.

To extend your trip…
Visit enchanting, medieval Girona (pp218–19), then head to the glorious Costa Brava (p221) for a couple of days' hiking or simply lazing on the beach.

---

2 Days in Seville

The spirit of Al Andalus lives on in Seville's whitewashed lanes, intricately tiled mansions and ornate courtyards – the perfect place to enjoy authentic Spanish pleasures like flamenco and fino.

- **Arriving** San Pablo Airport is 10 km (6 miles) northeast of the city centre. Take a bus or taxi to the city. From Madrid Airport, the high-speed AVE train to Seville takes 2 hours 20 minutes.

Day 1
Morning Start with a visit to Seville's most recognizable landmark, La Giralda (pp440–41), the exquisite minaret-cum-bell tower attached to the vast cathedral. The tomb of Christopher Columbus can be found inside the cathedral, along with a wealth of lavish artworks, but the highlight is the extraordinary views from the top of La Giralda. Then head to the sumptuous Real Alcázar (pp444–5), a magnificent royal palace richly decorated with elaborate tiles and stucco work.

Afternoon Cool off with a gentle stroll in the charming Parque María Luisa (pp448–9), with its colourfully tiled benches and tinkling fountains. There are a couple of fascinating museums to explore, full of archaeological artifacts and traditional Andalusian folk art. Enjoy a traditional dinner and perhaps some flamenco in the vibrant Triana neighbourhood (p450).

Day 2
Morning Visit the enticing Barrio Santa Cruz, an enchanting warren of narrow lanes lined with ivory houses sporting geranium-filled balconies. Spend some time in the fascinating Archivo de Indias (p443), a handsome 16th-century building that contains the historical records of Spain's colonization of the Americas. Take a look at the paintings in the Hospital de los Venerables (p443), then delight in the Casa de Pilatos (pp442–3), a breathtaking palace with a beautiful garden.

Afternoon Admire the superb art collection in the Museo de Bellas Artes (p434), housed in a handsome 17th-century convent set around a charming courtyard. Take in the fabulous shops along the nearby Calle Sierpes, many of which sell gorgeous flamenco dresses and mantilla shawls. For dinner, there is a great choice of tapas bars in the area.

To extend your trip…
Drive east, via Carmona and Écija, or travel by train to Córdoba (pp482–5) to visit the remarkable Mezquita.

Mudéjar architecture and intricate stucco work at the Real Alcázar, Seville

Bilbao and the Basque Lands

- **Duration** 7 days.
- **Airports** Arrive and depart from Bilbao Airport.
- **Transport** This tour must be done by car.
- **Booking ahead** Bilbao: Guggenheim tickets (www. guggenheim-bilbao.es), any of the Michelin-starred restaurants.

Day 1: Bilbao
The vast, spectacular Museo Guggenheim (pp124–5) deserves a day to itself. Admire the gleaming curves of Frank Gehry's magnificent design from the banks of the river, and don't miss Jeff Koons' flower-covered *Puppy* at the entrance. Afterwards, stroll along the banks of the river, then enjoy an evening in the atmospheric tapas bars of the city's Old Town (*Casco Viejo, p122*).

Day 2: Bilbao and Gernika
Spend the morning at Bilbao's other fantastic art museum, the Museo de Bellas Artes (*p122*), which displays works by Basque, Spanish and international artists. The museum overlooks the city's most beautiful public park, perfect for a stroll. Have lunch in a local café, and then drive to Gernika-Lumo (pp122–3). Bombed on the orders of General Franco in 1937, this town now contains a poignant peace museum.

Day 3: Along the Coast to San Sebastián (Donostia)
Explore the spectacular Costa Vasca (*p123*), with its plunging cliffs and beautiful bays. Stop off at a string of enchanting towns, such as Lekeitio, Zumaia, Zarautz and pretty little Getaria, barely changed in centuries. Any of these towns are ideal for a seafood lunch by the beach.

Day 4: San Sebastián
Stroll around the narrow streets surrounding the magnificent Basilica de Santa María in San Sebastián's beautiful Old Town (*pp126–7*), then visit the Museo de San Telmo, set in a 16th-century monastery. After lunch in one of the celebrated traditional tapas bars, hike up the Monte Urgell to enjoy the views, then head to the Playa de la Concha, a crescent of golden sand curving round an idyllic bay. For dinner, splash out on one of the many Michelin-starred restaurants (*see p585*).

Day 5: Oñati and the Santuario de Loiola
From San Sebastián, drive inland through verdant countryside to the Santuario de Loiola (*p128*), a lavish 18th-century complex built on the site where the founder of the Jesuits, San Ignacio de Loyola, was born in the 1490s. Continue to the elegant little university town of Oñati (*p128*), which boasts a few handsome Renaissance buildings. You could also visit the nearby Santuario de Arantzazu (*p128*),

A pretty street in San Sebastián's Old Town leads to the Basilica de Santa Maria

an unattractive modern construction from the 1950s, which nonetheless enjoys a sublime mountain setting.

Day 6: Vitoria
Explore the vibrant Basque capital of Vitoria (Gasteiz) (*p130*), beginning with the charming Plaza de la Virgen Blanca. Don't miss the older of Vitoria's two cathedrals, the handsome Gothic Catedral de Santa María. After lunch, visit the fascinating Museo de Arqueologia y Naipes (BIBAT), an archaeology museum which also contains a curious collection of historic playing cards.

Day 7: Haro and back to Bilbao
Return to Bilbao, but first stop off in Haro (*p132*), capital of the Rioja Alta region, to pick up some of the area's world-famous wines and perhaps enjoy a tasting or two. It's a perfect place for lunch, with a host of lively tapas bars serving great food to match the wonderful local wines.

Frank Gehry's sleek and gleaming Museo Guggenheim, a spectacular structure of glass, titanium and limestone

For practical information on travelling around Spain, see pp626–35

Wild Spain: Cantabria, Asturias and Galicia

- **Duration** 10 days, or add this itinerary to Bilbao and the Basque Lands for a 17-day tour covering a large swathe of Northern Spain.

- **Airports** The nearest is in Santander, also a major ferry port with services from the UK. The airport is 5 km (3 miles) from the city centre, and linked by bus.

- **Transport** This tour is designed to be done by car.

The verdant valleys and majestic mountains of the Parque Nacional de los Picos de Europa

Day 1: Castro Urdiales and Lardeo
Enjoy two of Cantabria's prettiest and most popular beach resorts, Castro Urdiales (p117) and Laredo (p117). Each has a delightful Old Quarter and some spectacular beaches. Though the town beaches get busy in summer, you'll find breathtaking, emptier stretches on either side of the towns.

Day 2: Santander
Next up is the Cantabrian capital Santander (p117), which was completely rebuilt in the 1940s after a devastating fire destroyed its historic heart. Still an atmospheric port city, it has good seafood restaurants and some wonderful beaches.

Day 3: Santillana del Mar and the Cuevas de Altamira
Drive west to Santillana del Mar (p116), which, despite its name, is not on the coast but set a few kilometres inland. It is an enchanting and beautifully preserved town, replete with churches, palaces and mansions. Then visit the Cuevas de Altamira (p116), site of prehistoric cave art just a couple of kilometres from Santillana del Mar. Although you can't visit the original caves, the paintings have been re-created in the excellent museum.

Day 4: Cangas de Onís and Covadonga
Stroll around the ancient Asturian capital of Cangas de Onís (p111), which enjoys a spectacular mountain backdrop. Nearby Covadonga (p112) is also worth a visit, a charming mountain town that is the main gateway to the stunning Parque Nacional de los Picos de Europa.

Day 5: Parque Nacional de los Picos de Europa
You could spend weeks in this national park (p112). In one day you can at least enjoy a fantastic hike, some rock climbing or simply a picnic among some of the most spectacular mountain scenery Spain has to offer.

Day 6: Gijón
Continue west to Gijón (p109), a port city with a charming old town piled up on a narrow isthmus. It has some great restaurants, long beaches and a few museums, which are worth visiting.

Beachcombers soak up the sun at Playa del Camello, Santander

Day 7: Oviedo
Spend a day in handsome Oviedo (pp110–11), a historic city gathered around a splendid, Gothic cathedral. Famous across Spain for its vibrant cultural life, it has Pre-Romanesque churches located on the hills overlooking the city.

Day 8: Costa Verde
Head west along the coast road which skirts the glorious Costa Verde (pp108–9). With its cliffs and coves, verdant hills and picturesque villages, this is easily one of Spain's loveliest and least spoiled stretches of coastline. Stop off and explore charming towns like Castropol, Luarca and Cudillero.

Day 9: Lugo
Cross the border into Galicia, and aim for the ancient city of Lugo (p103). Once an important Roman settlement, Lugo is still ringed by spectacular and remarkably intact Roman walls, which you can climb to enjoy fabulous views. Within the walls, the old city is a charming jumble of narrow streets and pretty squares – perfect for a wander.

Day 10: Santiago de Compostela
End your journey in the magical city of Santiago de Compostela (pp94–7) – the goal of pilgrims for more than 1,000 years. An enchanting city built of cool grey stone, it is dominated by its magnificent cathedral, said to contain the bones of St James.

Barcelona and the Mediterranean Coast by Train

- **Duration** 7 days.
- **Airports** Arrive in Barcelona's El Prat Airport, depart from Murcia's San Javier Airport.
- **Transport** This tour is exclusively by train. There is a choice of services on this route, from the plush, expensive Talgos to inexpensive regional and local trains. Most journey times are around an hour – check timetables and prices on www.renfe.com.
- **Booking Ahead** Barcelona: Sagrada Família tickets.

Charming, balconied stone terraces in Barcelona's Gothic Quarter

Day 1: Barcelona
Choose a day from the 2 Days in Barcelona itinerary on pp12–13.

Day 2: Sitges and Tarragona
Take an early train to Sitges (*p228*) and enjoy the morning strolling around this enchanting seaside town. Enjoy a seafood lunch, then catch a train to Tarragona (*pp228–9*), once the capital of an important Roman province and replete with Roman monuments. Enjoy a seafood dinner by the port.

Day 3: Peníscola and Valencia
In the morning, all aboard to Benicarló-Peníscola, the station for Peníscola (*p251*). Take a taxi to the historic quarter, a whitewashed maze piled up on a promontory and crowned with a castle. Have a lazy lunch by the beach, then ride the rails back to Valencia (*pp254–7*) in time for an evening tapas bar crawl around the charming historic quarter.

Day 4: Valencia
Spend the day sightseeing in Valencia, beginning with a visit to the cathedral (*pp254–5*), where you can climb the bell tower for tremendous views. In the afternoon, head to the City of Arts and Sciences (*p257*) to take in the interactive science museum or the Oceanografic, Europe's biggest aquarium. For dinner, enjoy a genuine paella – invented in Valencia.

Day 5: Alicante (Alacant)
Enjoy the train journey south through the hills to Alicante (*pp264–5*), a vibrant seaside city that offers great shopping and nightlife as well as a lively cultural scene. Take in fabulous views from the clifftop Castillo de Santa Bárbara and wander around the winding streets of the Old Town. Tuck into some tapas in the Old Quarter.

Day 6: Murcia
Another relatively short journey brings you to Murcia (*p266*), the handsome capital of the Murcia region. Its centre is dominated by the vast Gothic cathedral, completed in 1467 and later given a sumptuous Baroque façade. The 19th-century casino, a sort of Spanish social club, is also worth a visit for its dazzling and eclectic decoration. Much of the city centre is pedestrianized, and Murcia's pretty squares are crammed with great tapas bars.

> **To extend your trip…**
> Reward yourself with some relaxing beach time and swimming in the warm, tranquil waters of the Mar Menor (*p266*).

Day 7: Cartagena
The culmination of your trip, the port city of Cartagena (*p267*), is an hour's train journey from Murcia. One of the oldest cities in Spain, it preserves a slew of remarkable Phoenician, Roman and Moorish monuments, including a spectacular Roman theatre and a lofty castle (now home to a history museum), which enjoys fabulous panoramic views.

Tarragona's Roman amphitheatre, overlooking the Mediterranean

For practical information on travelling around Spain, see pp626–35

Madrid and Moorish Spain: Granada, Córdoba and Seville

- **Duration** 10 days.
- **Airports** Arrive in Madrid's Barajas Airport, depart from Granada Airport.
- **Transport** High-speed AVE train from Madrid to Seville; hire car for the rest of the trip.
- **Booking Ahead** Granada: entry tickets to Alhambra.

Days 1 and 2: Madrid
See the 2 Days in Madrid itinerary on p12.

Days 3 and 4: Seville
Take the high-speed AVE train from Atocha station to Seville. *Experience the best of the city with the 2 Days in Seville itinerary on p13.*

Day 5: Carmona and Écija
Hire a car for the rest of your journey. Drive east of Seville, stopping first at Carmona (*p480*), an aristocratic town tucked behind Moorish city walls. Continue east to Écija (*p481*), famous for extreme heat and a distinctive skyline punctured by the silhouettes of 11 Baroque church spires. Spend a night here.

Day 6: Córdoba
Córdoba (*pp482–5*) is less than an hour's drive east of Écija. At its heart is the vast 8th-century

Mezquita (*pp484–5*), a masterpiece of Islamic art, where you can easily spend a couple of hours. Then head into the narrow lanes of the former Jewish Quarter, and visit the enchanting Palacio de Viana, an aristocratic mansion set around several elegant courtyards. Enjoy supper on one of Córdoba's enchanting squares.

Day 7: Córdoba
Begin your day with breakfast on the Plaza de La Corredera, a handsome 17th-century square that hosts a daily market. Visit the Alcázar de los Reyes Cristianos and its blissful gardens (*p482*). Choose one of Córdoba's many museums to visit in the afternoon, or simply explore the maze of streets, including the Callejón de las Flores, famous for its beautiful flowers. Visit the Plaza de Tendillas for dinner options.

Day 8: Montilla to Montefrío
Drive through beautiful Andalusian countryside to Granada, taking in several attractive villages. First of these is Montilla (*p486*), a celebrated wine town, followed by Aguilar de la Frontera, wrapped around an octagonal square. Continue through hills and orchards to Priego de Córdoba (*p486*), packed with breathtaking Baroque architecture, and then to Montefrío (*pp486–7*), a tumble of chalk-white buildings crowned by the remnants of a

Terracotta-and-white-striped arches top countless columns inside the Mezquita

Moorish fortress. Spend the night in either Priego de Córdoba or Montefrío.

Day 9: Granada
Press on to Granada (*pp490–96*), just a short drive from Montefrío. The spirit of old Al Andalus is strongest here, thanks to the presence of the hauntingly beautiful Alhambra Palace, which crowns the city. An old Moorish neighbourhood spills down the hill opposite the Alhambra, its narrow lanes lined with craftshops, bathhouses and cafés. Stop for lunch here, then head up to explore the vast Alhambra palace and fortress complex (*pp494–5*) and the Generalife gardens (*p496*), where the Nasrid rulers made their attempt to recreate paradise on earth. Top off the day with a tapas bar crawl – a must in Granada.

Day 10: Granada
Visit the splendid Gothic cathedral (*p490*), constructed by order of the Catholic Monarchs (Ferdinand and Isabella) after the fall of Granada in 1492. They also ordered the construction of the nearby Capilla Real (*p490*), which contains their elaborate tombs and those of their daughter and her husband. Take a look at the cultural centre in the 16th-century Corral del Carbón (*p490*), which displays local crafts. In the evening, take in a flamenco show in one of the caves in Sacromonte (*p493*).

Portico and pool of the Partal, part of the Alhambra palace complex

Portsmouth,
Plymouth ↑

Putting Spain on the Map

Spain, in southwestern Europe, covers the greater part of the
Iberian Peninsula. The third-largest country in Europe, it includes
two island groups – the Canaries in the Atlantic and the Balearics
in the Mediterranean – and two small territories in North Africa.
Its southernmost point faces
Morocco across a
strait, making
Spain a bridge
between
continents.

*Bay of
Biscay*

*Atlantic
Ocean*

Ortigueira
Ferrol
A Coruña
N634
Avilés
Gijón
Oviedo
Santander
Llanes
ASTURIAS
CANTABRIA
A8
A8
A8
A67

Santiago de
Compostela
Lugo
A6
AP9
A66
Miranda de Eb

GALICIA
AP53
Ponferrada
León
Palencia
Burgos
A231
A231

Pontevedra
Ourense
A52
A52
Benavente
CASTILLA Y LEÓN
Valladolid
Peñafiel
Aranda
Duero

Vigo
A3
Zamora
A11
A66
A62
A1

Braga
A7
Vila Real
Salamanca
A66
A6
Segovia

Porto
A24
A50
Ávila
Guadalaja
MADRID

Aveiro
A62
Ciudad Rodrigo
A66
Madrid

Coimbra
A25
Plasencia
Talavera
de la Reina
Aranjuez
A5

Leiria
A17
A23
Coria
Castelo
Branco
Toledo
CASTILLA-L

A66
A5
Cáceres
Trujillo
N502

PORTUGAL
A8
A1
Santarem
Badajoz
A5
Mérida
N430
EXTREMADURA
Tormel
Ciudad Real
A43

Lisbon
Setúbal
A6
Evora
Zafra
A41
Puertollano
Valdepeñas

Beja
A66
N502
N432
Linares
A4
A44
Úb

Córdoba
Jaén

Lagos
A2
Sevilla
A4
ANDALUSIA
A45

Huelva
A49
A92
Estepa
A92
Gran
A45

Faro
A22
AP4
A45

Jerez de la
Frontera
Málaga
Mot

Cádiz
A381
A7
Marbella

A48
Algeciras

Tangier
Ceuta
Melilla

↙ *Canary Islands*

Key

═══ Motorway
─── Major road
─── International border
∙∙∙∙ Regional border
-- - Ferry route

For map symbols *see back flap*

The Canary Islands

Cádiz, Huelva

Lanzarote

Arrecife

Puerto del Rosario

Santa Cruz de la Palma

Tenerife

La Palma

Santa Cruz de Tenerife

Fuerteventura

Las Palmas de Gran Canaria

San Sebastián

La Gomera

Los Cristianos

Valverde

Gran Canaria

El Hierro

Biarritz

San Sebastián

bao

PAÍS

ASCO

Vitoria (Gasteiz)

Pamplona

NAVARRA

Pau

Tarbes

FRANCE

oño

RIOJA

Soria

Tudela

Huesca

Jaca

ARAGÓN

Zaragoza

Calatayud

Alcañiz

Lleida

La Seu de Urgell

ANDORRA

CATALUÑA

Vic

Manresa

Perpignan

Figueres

Girona

Barcelona

Genoa, Livorno, Civitavecchia

Sitges

Tarragona

M e d i t e r r a n e a n
S e a

Tortosa

Benicarló

Teruel

Cuenca

Benicàssim

Castellón de la Plana

Ciudadela

Menorca

Alcudia

Mahón

Sagunto

Requena

PAÍS VALENCIANO

Valencia

Palma

Mallorca

Albacete

Gandia

Xábia

Ibiza

Ibiza

ISLAS BALEARES

Hellin

Elda

Benidorm

Alicante

MURCIA

Murcia

Huéscar

Lorca

Cartagena

Águilas

Mojácar

Almería

Melilla, Nador
Ghazaouet

Europe and North Africa

NORWAY

SWEDEN

ESTONIA

LATVIA

LITHUANIA

NORTH SEA

DENMARK

REP. OF IRELAND

UNITED KINGDOM

NETHERLANDS

BELGIUM

GERMANY

POLAND

BELARUS

UKRAINE

CZECH REP.

SLOVAKIA

ATLANTIC OCEAN

FRANCE

SWITZ.

AUSTRIA HUNGARY

ROMANIA

BOSNIA HERZ.

SERBIA

MONTEN.

BULGARIA

MAC.

ITALY

PORTUGAL

Madrid

SPAIN

GREECE

MOROCCO

TUNISIA

ALGERIA

LIBYA

Canary Islands

0 kilometres 100
0 miles 50

Regional Spain

Spain has a population of 47 million and receives more than 40 million
visitors a year. It covers an area of 504,780 sq km (194,900 sq miles).
Madrid is the largest city, followed by Barcelona and Valencia. The
country is dominated by a central plateau drained by the Duero, Tagus
(Tajo) and Guadiana rivers. This book divides Spain into 15 areas, but
officially it has 17 independent regions called *comunidades autónomas*.

Getting Around

Spain's regional capitals
and islands are linked by
regular flights and there
is a shuttle service
between Madrid and
Barcelona. The TALGO
and AVE high-speed
trains provide fast rail
services and are backed
up by regional and local
rail networks. Some
motorways have
expensive tolls, but are
fast. The Balearic
and Canary islands are
served by regular ferries.

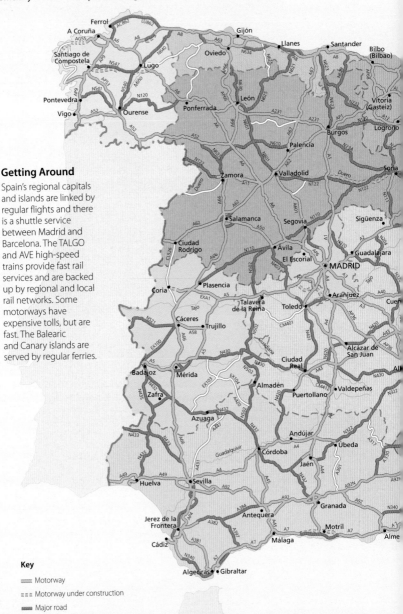

Key

- ▬▬ Motorway
- ▪▪▪ Motorway under construction
- ▬▬ Major road
- ▭▭ Minor road

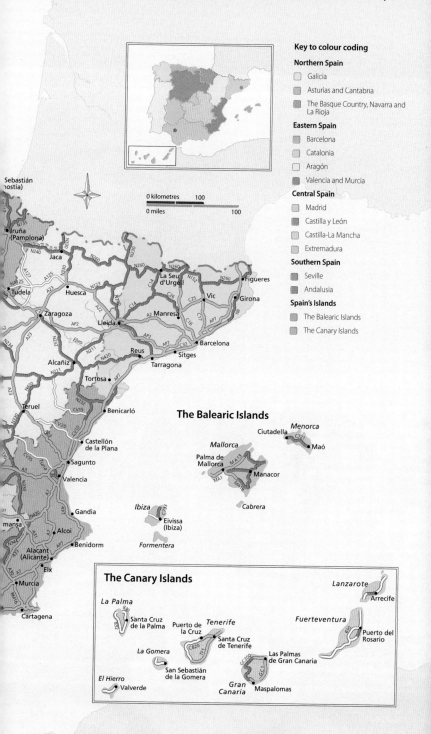

Key to colour coding

Northern Spain
- Galicia
- Asturias and Cantabria
- The Basque Country, Navarra and La Rioja

Eastern Spain
- Barcelona
- Catalonia
- Aragón
- Valencia and Murcia

Central Spain
- Madrid
- Castilla y León
- Castilla-La Mancha
- Extremadura

Southern Spain
- Seville
- Andalusia

Spain's Islands
- The Balearic Islands
- The Canary Islands

0 kilometres 100
0 miles 100

Sebastián
ostia)

Iruña
(Pamplona)

Jaca

Tudela

Huesca

La Seu
d'Urgell

Figueres

Vic

Girona

Zaragoza

Lleida

Manresa

Alcañiz

Reus

Barcelona

Sitges

Tortosa

Tarragona

Teruel

Benicarló

Castellón
de la Plana

Sagunto

Valencia

mansa

Gandia

Alcoi

Benidorm

Alacant
(Alicante)

Elx

Murcia

Cartagena

The Balearic Islands

Menorca

Ciutadella

Mallorca

Maó

Palma de
Mallorca

Manacor

Ibiza

Eivissa
(Ibiza)

Cabrera

Formentera

The Canary Islands

Lanzarote

Arrecife

La Palma

Santa Cruz
de la Palma

Puerto de
la Cruz

Tenerife

Fuerteventura

Santa Cruz
de Tenerife

Puerto del
Rosario

La Gomera

Las Palmas
de Gran Canaria

El Hierro

San Sebastián
de la Gomera

Valverde

*Gran
Canaria*

Maspalomas

A PORTRAIT OF SPAIN

The familiar images of Spain – flamenco dancing, bullfighting, tapas bars and solemn Easter processions – do no more than hint at the diversity of the country. Spain has four official languages, two major cities of almost equal importance and a greater range of landscapes than any other European country. These remarkable contrasts make Spain an endlessly fascinating country to visit.

Separated from the rest of Europe by the Pyrenees, Spain reaches south to the coast of North Africa. It has both Atlantic and Mediterranean coastlines, and includes two archipelagos – the Balearics and the Canary Islands.

The climate and landscape vary from snowcapped peaks in the Pyrenees, through the green meadows of Galicia and the orange groves of Valencia, to the desert of Almería. Madrid is the highest capital in Europe, and Spain its most mountainous country after Switzerland and Austria. The innumerable sierras have always hindered communications. Until railways were built it was easier to move goods from Barcelona to South America than to Madrid.

In early times, Spain was a coveted prize for foreign conquerors, including the Phoenicians and the Romans. During the Middle Ages, much of it was ruled by the Moors, who arrived from North Africa in the 8th century. It was reconquered by Christian forces, and unified at the end of the 15th century. A succession of rulers tried to impose a common culture, but Spain remains as culturally diverse as ever. Several regions have maintained a strong sense of their own independent identities. Many Basques and Catalans, in particular, do not consider themselves to be Spanish. Madrid may be the nominal capital, but it is closely rivalled in commerce, the arts and sport by Barcelona, the capital city of Catalonia.

Landscape with a solitary cork tree near Albacete in Castilla-La Mancha

◄ Flamenco dancing in Seville

Peñafiel Castle in the Duero Valley (Castilla y León), built between the 10th and 13th centuries

The Spanish Way of Life

The inhabitants of this very varied country have few things in common, except for a natural sociability and a zest for living. Spaniards commonly put as much energy into enjoying life as they do into their work. The stereotypical "mañana" (leave everything until tomorrow) is a myth, but time is flexible in Spain and many people bend their work to fit the demands of their social life, rather than let themselves be ruled by the clock. The day is long in Spain and Spanish has a word, *madrugada*, for the time between midnight and dawn, when city streets are often still lively.

"Vinegar Face" in Pamplona's Los Sanfermines fiesta

Spaniards are highly gregarious. In many places people still go out in the evening for the *paseo*, when the streets are crowded with strollers. Eating is invariably communal and big groups often meet up for tapas or dinner. Not surprisingly, Spain has more bars and restaurants per head than any other country in Europe. Underpinning Spanish society is the extended family.

Traditionally, the state in Spain has been very inefficient at providing public services – although this has improved in the last 30 years. The Spanish have therefore always relied on their families and personal connections, rather than institutions, to find work or seek assistance in a crisis. This attitude has sometimes led to a disregard for general interests – such as the environment – when they have conflicted with private ones.

Most Spaniards place their family at the centre of their lives. Three generations may live together under one roof, or at least see each other often. Even lifelong city-dwellers refer fondly to their *pueblo* – the town or village where their family comes from and where they return

Tables outside a café in Madrid's Plaza Mayor

whenever they can. Children are adored in Spain and, consequently, great importance is attached to education. The family in Spain, however, is under strain as couples increasingly opt for a higher income and better lifestyle rather than a large family. One of the most striking transformations in modern Spain has been in the birth rate, from one of the highest in Europe, at 2.72 children for every woman in 1975, to 1.3 children for every woman in 2014. Catholicism is still a pervasive influence over Spanish society,

The windmills and castle above Consuegra, La Mancha

Virgin of Guadalupe in Extremadura

although church attendance among those under 35 has been declining and now stands at below 10 per cent. The images of saints watch over some shops, bars and lorry drivers' cabs. Church feast days are marked by countless traditional fiestas, which are enthusiastically maintained in modern Spain.

Sport and the Arts

Spanish cultural life has been experiencing a rejuvenation. Spanish-made films – notably those of cult directors Pedro Almodóvar and Alejandro Amenábar – have been able to compete with Hollywood for audiences, and the actress Penélope Cruz won an Oscar in 2009. The overall level of reading has risen, and contemporary literature has steadily gained a wider readership. The performing arts have been restricted by a lack of facilities, but major investments have provided new venues, regional arts centres and new symphony orchestras. The country has produced many remarkable opera singers, including

A matador plays a bull in the Plaza de Toros de la Maestranza, Seville

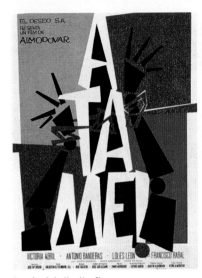

Poster for a Pedro Almodóvar film

Montserrat Caballé, Plácido Domingo and José Carreras. Spain has also excelled in design, particularly evident in the interior furnishings shops of Barcelona.

Spaniards are the most avid TV-watchers in Europe after the British. There are two state-owned TV channels in Spain, as well as a growing number of private channels and regional TV stations thanks to digital platforms. Sports are one of the mainstays of TV programming. Spanish sportsmen and women have been very successful – for example, tennis player Rafael Nadal and Formula 1 driver Fernando Alonso. Such role models have encouraged participation in sport and more facilities have been provided to meet this demand. Most popular are basketball and, above all, soccer.

Bullfighting has enjoyed renewed popularity since the late 1980s. For aficionados, a *corrida* provides a link to Spain's roots, and the noise, colour and crowd are as much of an attraction as the bullfight itself. In Catalonia, however, bullfighting was banned in 2012.

Spain Today

Since the mid-20th century, Spain has undergone more social change than any-where in western Europe. Until the 1950s, Spain was predominantly a poor, rural country, in which only 37 per cent of the population lived in towns of over 10,000 people. By the 1990s, the figure was 65 per cent. As people flooded into towns and cities, many rural areas became depopulated. The 1960s saw the beginning of spectacular economic growth, partly due to a burgeoning tourist industry. In that decade, car ownership increased from 1 in 100 to 1 in 10.

A farmer with his crop of maize hanging to dry on the outside of his house in the hills of Alicante

Beach near Tossa de Mar on the Costa Brava

After the death of dictator General Franco in 1975, Spain became a constitutional monarchy under King Juan Carlos I. Felipe VI acceded to the throne following his father's abdication in 2014. The post-Franco era, up until the mid-1990s, was dominated by the Socialist Prime Minister Felipe González. As well as presiding over major improvements in roads, education and health services, the Socialists increased Spain's international standing. The PSOE could not continue forever, however, and in 1996 revelations of a series of scandals lost the PSOE the election. Spain joined the European Community in 1986, triggering a spectacular increase in the country's prosperity. The country's fortunes seemed to peak in the extraordinary year of 1992, when Barcelona staged the Olympic Games and Seville hosted a world fair, Expo '92.

With the establishment of democracy, the 17 autonomous regions of Spain have acquired considerable powers. Several have their own languages, which are officially given equal importance to Spanish (strictly called Castilian). A number of Basques favour independence, and the Basque terrorist group ETA was a constant thorn in the side of Spanish democracy until 2011, when they declared a cessation of hostilities.

During the 1980s Spain enjoyed an economic boom as service industries and manufacturing expanded. Even so, GDP remains below the European Union average, and growth halted in 2009's economic downturn, with the unemployment rate at around 25 per cent in 2015. Agriculture is an important industry, but, while it is highly developed in some regions, it is inefficient in others. Tourism provides approximately ten per cent of the country's earnings. Most tourists still come for beaches. But, increasingly, foreign visitors are drawn by Spain's rich cultural heritage and spectacular countryside. Anyone who knows this country, however, will tell you that it is the Spanish people's capacity to enjoy life to the full that is Spain's biggest attraction.

King Felipe VI

Demonstration for Catalan independence

Architecture in Spain

Spain has always imported its styles of architecture: Moorish from North Africa, Romanesque and Gothic from France and Renaissance from Italy. Each style, however, was interpreted in a distinctively Spanish way, with sudden and strong contrasts between light and shady areas; façades alternating between austerity and extravagant decoration; and thick walls pierced by few windows to lessen the impact of heat and sunlight. Styles vary from region to region, reflecting the division of Spain before unification. The key design of a central patio surrounded by arcades has been a strong feature of civil buildings since Moorish times.

The 15th-century Casa de Conchas in Salamanca (see p365)

Romanesque and Earlier (8th–13th Centuries)

Romanesque churches were mainly built in Catalonia and along the pilgrim route to Santiago (see p87). Their distinctive features include round arches, massive walls and few windows. Earlier churches were built in Pre-Romanesque (see p110) or Mozarabic (see p355) style.

Round arch

Multiple apses

The Romanesque Sant Climent, Taüll (p215)

Moorish (8th–15th Centuries)

The Moors (see pp56–7) reserved the most lavish decoration for the interior of buildings, where ornate designs based on geometry, calligraphy and plant motifs were created in azulejos (tiles) or stucco. They made extensive use of the horseshoe arch, a feature inherited from the Visigoths (see pp54–5). The greatest surviving works of Moorish architecture (see pp426–7) are in Southern Spain.

The Salón de Embajadores in the Alhambra (see p494) has exquisite Moorish decoration.

Gothic (12th–16th Centuries)

Gothic arched window

Gothic was imported from France in the late 12th century. The round arch was replaced by the pointed arch which, because of its greater strength, allowed for higher vaults and taller windows. External buttresses were added to prevent the walls of the nave from leaning outwards. Carved decoration was at its most opulent in the Flamboyant Gothic style of the 15th century. After the fall of Granada, Isabelline, a late Gothic style, developed. Meanwhile, Moorish craftsmen working in reconquered areas created the highly decorative hybrid Christian-Islamic style Mudéjar (see p59).

Rose window

Tracery

Pointed arch

Flying buttress

The nave of León Cathedral (see pp358–9), built in the 13th century, is supported by rib vaulting and is illuminated by the finest display of stained glass in Spain.

Sculptural decoration above the doorways of León Cathedral's south front depicted biblical stories for the benefit of the largely illiterate populace.

Renaissance (16th Century)

Around 1500 a new style was introduced to Spain by Italian craftsmen and Spanish artists who had studied in Italy. The Renaissance was a revival of the style of ancient Rome. It is distinguished by its sense of symmetry and the use of the round arch, and Doric, Ionic and Corinthian columns. Early Spanish Renaissance architecture is known as Plateresque because its fine detail resembles ornate silverwork (*platero* means "silversmith").

The Palacio de las Cadenas in Úbeda (*see p501*) has a severely Classical façade.

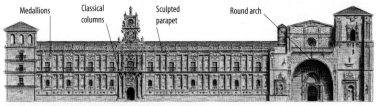

Medallions | Classical columns | Sculpted parapet | Round arch

The Hostal de San Marcos in León (*see p357*), one of Spain's finest Plateresque buildings

Baroque (17th–18th Centuries)

Baroque was driven by a desire for drama and movement. Decoration became extravagant, with exuberant sculpture and twisting columns. Although the excessive Baroque style of Churrigueresque is named after the Churriguera family of architects, it was their successors who were its main exponents.

The ornamentation on the Baroque façade of Valladolid University (*see p370*) is concentrated above the doorway.

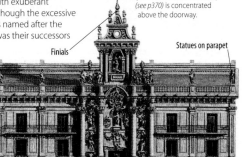

Finials | Statues on parapet

The façade of the Museo de Historia in Madrid (*pp308–9*)

Modern (Late 19th Century onwards)

Modernisme (*see pp144–5*), a Catalan interpretation of Art Nouveau, is seen at its best in Barcelona. Its architects experimented with a highly original language of ornament. In recent decades, Spain has seen an explosion of bold, functionalist architecture in which the form of a building reflects its use and decoration is used sparingly.

Torre de Picasso in Madrid (*p310*)

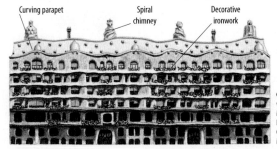

Curving parapet | Spiral chimney | Decorative ironwork

Casa Milà, in Barcelona (*see p169*), was built in 1910 by Modernisme's most famous and best-loved architect, Antoni Gaudí, who drew much of his inspiration from nature.

Vernacular Architecture

As well as its cathedrals and palaces, Spain has a great variety of charming vernacular buildings. These have been constructed by local craftsmen to meet the practical needs of rural communities and to take account of local climate conditions, with little reference to formal architectural styles. Due to the high expense involved in transporting raw materials, builders used whatever stone or timber lay closest to hand. The three houses illustrated below incorporate the most common characteristics of village architecture seen in different parts of Spain.

A cave church in Artenara *(see p549)*, on Gran Canaria

Stone House

The climate is wet in the north and houses like this one in Carmona *(see p115)*, in Cantabria, are built with overhanging eaves to shed the rain. Wooden balconies catch the sun.

Detail of stonework

Family and farm often share rural houses. The ground floor is used to stable animals, or store tools and firewood.

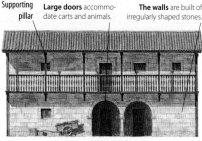

Supporting pillar

Large doors accommodate carts and animals.

The walls are built of irregularly shaped stones.

Timber-Framed House

Spain, in general, has few large trees and wood is in short supply. Castilla y León is one of the few regions where timber-framed houses, such as this one in Covarrubias *(see p374)*, can be found. These houses are quick and cheap to build. The timber frame is filled in with a coarse plaster mixed from lime and sand, or adobe (bricks dried in the sun).

Half-timbered wall

The ends of the beams supporting the floorboards are visible.

Stone plinths below upright timbers provide protection from damp.

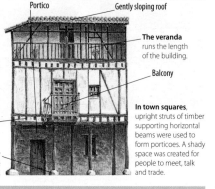

Portico

Gently sloping roof

The veranda runs the length of the building.

Balcony

In town squares, upright struts of timber supporting horizontal beams were used to form porticoes. A shady space was created for people to meet, talk and trade.

Whitewashed House

Houses in the south of Spain – often built of baked clay – are regularly whitewashed to deflect the sun's intense rays. Andalusia's famous white towns *(see pp472–3)* exemplify this attractive form of architecture.

Clay-tiled roof

Windows are small and few in number, and deeply recessed, in order to keep the interior cool.

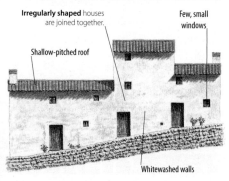

Irregularly shaped houses are joined together.

Few, small windows

Shallow-pitched roof

Whitewashed walls

The Plaza Mayor

Almost every town in Spain centres on a main square, the *plaza mayor*, like this one in Pedraza de la Sierra *(see p369)*, near Segovia. More than a market square, it acts as a focus for local life. It is usually overlooked by the church, the town hall, shops and bars and the mansions of aristocratic families.

Town hall *(ayuntamiento)*

Medieval porticoes beneath the buildings provided shade for shops and markets.

Church

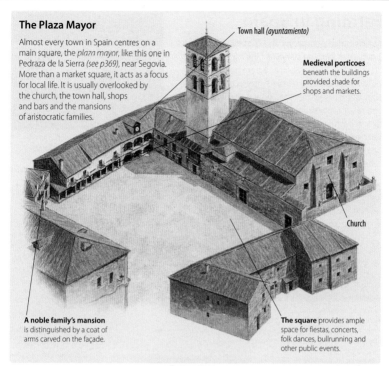

A noble family's mansion is distinguished by a coat of arms carved on the façade.

The square provides ample space for fiestas, concerts, folk dances, bullrunning and other public events.

Rural Architecture

A variety of distinctive buildings dots the countryside.

Where the rock is soft and the climate hot, subterranean dwellings have been excavated. Insulated from extremes of temperature, they provide a comfortable place to live.

Hórreos, granaries raised on stone stilts to prevent rats climbing up into the grain, are a common sight in Galicia (where they are stone-built) and Asturias (where they are made of wood). In fields you will often see shelters for livestock or for storing crops, such as the *teitos* of Asturias.

Windmills provided power in parts of Spain where there was little running water but plentiful wind, like La Mancha and the Balearic Islands.

Almost everywhere in the Spanish countryside you will come across *ermitas*, isolated chapels or shrines dedicated to a local saint. An *ermita* may be opened only on the patron saint's feast day.

Cave houses in Guadix near Granada *(see p497)*

Teito in Valle de Teverga in Asturias *(see p109)*

Hórreo, a granary, on the Rías Baixas *(see p99)* in Galicia

Windmill above Consuegra *(see p398)* in La Mancha

Farming in Spain

Spain's varied geography and climate have created a mosaic of farming patterns ranging from lush dairylands to stony hillsides where goats graze. Land can be broadly divided into *secano*, or dry cultivation (used for olives, wheat and vines), and much smaller areas of *regadío*, irrigated land (planted with citrus trees, rice and vegetables). Farming in many parts is a family affair relying on traditional, labour-intensive methods, but it is becoming increasingly mechanized.

The high rainfall and mild summers of Northern Spain make it suitable for dairy farming. Farms are often small, especially in Galicia, one of the country's most under-developed regions. Crops such as maize and wheat are grown in small quantities.

Plains of cereals make up much of the farmland of the central *meseta* of Spain. Wheat is grown in better-watered, more fertile western areas; barley is grown in the drier south.

Cork oaks thrive in Extremadura and western Andalusia.

MADRID

SEVILLA

Sheep grazed on the rough pastures of Central Spain are milked to make cheese, especially *manchego*, which is produced in La Mancha *(see p343).*

	Jul–Aug Wheat harvested in Central Spain	**Sep** Rice harvest in Eastern Spain. Grape harvest at its height	**Oct** Maize harvested in Northern Spain	**Dec–Mar** Olives for making oil picked
			Oct–Nov Table olives picked	
Spring	**Summer**		**Autumn**	**Winter**
Mar–Apr Orange trees in blossom on Mediterranean coast			**Nov–Dec** Oranges picked	**Feb** Almond trees in blossom
Jun–Aug Haymaking in Northern Spain		**Sep** Start of wild mushroom season	**Dec** Pigs are slaughtered when cold weather arrives	

Oranges, lemons and clementines are grown on the irrigated coastal plains beside the Mediterranean. The region of Valencia is the prime producer of oranges.

BARCELONA•

Wine is produced in many parts of Spain (*see pp580–81*). The country's best sparkling wine grapes are grown in Catalonia.

Rice is grown in the Ebro delta, in the Marismas del Guadalquivir, around L'Albufera near Valencia and also at Calasparra in Murcia.

| 0 kilometres | 200 |
| 0 miles | 100 |

Olive trees are planted in long, straight lines across large swathes of Andalusia, especially in the province of Jaén. Spain is the world's leading producer of olive oil.

Cork oaks are stripped of their bark every 10 years

Crops from Trees

The almond, orange and olive create the three most characteristic landscapes of rural Spain, but several other trees provide important crops. Wine corks are made from the bark of the cork oak. Tropical species, such as avocado and cherimoya, a delicious creamy fruit little known outside Spain, have been introduced to the so-called Costa Tropical of Andalusia (*see p487*); and bananas are a major crop of the Canary Islands. Elsewhere, peaches and loquats are also grown commercially. Figs and carobs – whose fruit is used for fodder and as a substitute for chocolate – grow semi-wild.

Almonds grow on dry hillsides in many parts of Spain. The spring blossom can be spectacular. The nut, enclosed by a fleshy green skin, is used in a variety of sweetmeats, including the Christmas treat *turrón* (*see p191*).

Olive trees grow slowly and often live to a great age. The fruit is harvested in winter and either pickled in brine, for eating as a snack, or to extract the oil, which is widely used in Spanish cuisine.

Sweet oranges are grown in dense, well-irrigated groves near the frost-free coasts. The sweet smell of orange blossom in springtime is unmistakable. Trees of the bitter orange are often planted for shade and decoration in parks and gardens.

Spain's National Parks

Few other countries in western Europe have such unspoiled scenery as Spain, or can boast tracts of wilderness where brown bears live and wolves hunt. More than 200 nature reserves protect a broad range of ecosystems. The most important areas are the 13 national parks, the first of which was established in 1918. Natural parks *(parques naturales)*, regulated by regional governments, are also vital to the task of conservation.

Clear mountain river, Ordesa

Mountains

Much of Spain's finest scenery is found in the mountains. Rivers have carved gorges between the peaks of the Picos de Europa. Ordesa and Aigüestortes share some of the most dramatic landscapes of the Pyrenees, while the Sierra Nevada has an impressive range of indigenous wildlife.

Chamois are well adapted to climbing across slopes covered in scree. They live in small groups, always alert to predators, and feed on grass and flowers.

Eagle owls are Europe's largest owl, easily identified by their large ear tufts. At night they hunt small mammals and birds.

Rough terrain in the Picos de Europa

Wetlands

Wetlands include coastal strips and freshwater marshes. Seasonal floods rejuvenate the water, providing nutrients for animal and plant growth. These areas are rich feeding grounds for birds. Spain's best-known wetland is Doñana. Catalonia's Delta de l'Ebre *(see p229)* and Tablas de Daimiel, in La Mancha, are much smaller.

Lynx, endangered by hunting and habitat loss, can occasionally be spotted in Doñana *(see pp468–9)*.

Black-winged stilts, with their long, straight legs, are adept at stalking tiny freshwater crustaceans.

Laguna del Acebuche, Parque Nacional de Doñana

Islands

Cabrera, off Mallorca, is home to rare plants, reptiles and seabirds, such as Eleonara's falcon. The surrounding waters are important for their marine life.

Lizards are often found in rocky terrain and on cliff faces.

Cabrera archipelago, Balearic Islands

National Parks

- Mountains
- Wetlands
- Islands
- Woods and Forests
- Volcanic Landscapes

Mountains

① Picos de Europa *pp112–13*
② Ordesa y Monte Perdido *pp236–7*
③ Aigüestortes y Estany de Sant Maurici *p215*
④ Sierra Nevada *p489*

Wetlands

⑤ Tablas de Daimiel *p403*
⑥ Doñana *pp468–9*

Islands

⑦ Archipiélago de Cabrera *p521*
⑧ Illa de Ons *p99*

Woods and Forests

⑨ Cabañeros *p391*
⑩ Garajonay *p537*

Volcanic Landscapes

⑪ Caldera de Taburiente *p536*
⑫ Teide *pp542–3*
⑬ Timanfaya *pp552–3*

VISITORS' CHECKLIST

All but one of the national parks are managed by the Ministerio de Medio Ambiente. **Tel** 915 46 81 11. 🔲 **magrama.gob.es/es/red-parques-nacionales** Parque Nacional d'Aigüestortes y Estany de Sant Maurici is administered jointly with Catalonia's Department of Environment. **Tel** 973 69 61 89. Most of Spain's national parks have visitors' centres, often called Centros de Interpretació.

Woods and Forests

Deciduous broad-leaved forests grow in the northwest of Spain, and stands of Aleppo and Scots pine cover many mountainous areas. On the central plateau there are stretches of open woodland of evergreen holm oak and cork oak in the Parque Nacional de Cabañeros. Dense, lush *laurisilva* woodland grows in the Parque Nacional de Garajonay, on La Gomera, one of the smaller Canary Islands.

Parque Nacional de Garajonay

Black vultures are the largest birds of prey in Europe, with an enormous wingspan of over 2.5 m (8 ft).

Hedgehogs, common in woodlands, root among fallen leaves and grass to find worms and slugs.

Volcanic Landscapes

Three very different parks protect parts of the Canary Islands' amazing volcanic scenery. Caldera de Taburiente on La Palma is a volcanic crater surrounded by woods. Mount Teide in Tenerife has unique alpine flora, and Lanzarote's Timanfaya is composed of barren but atmospheric lava fields.

Rabbits are highly opportunistic, quickly colonizing areas in which they can burrow. In the absence of predators, populations may increase, damaging fragile ecosystems.

Canaries belong to the finch family of songbirds. The popular canary has been bred from the wild serin, native to the Canaries.

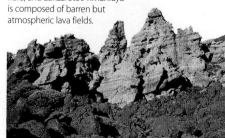

Colonizing plant species, Mount Teide (Tenerife)

Spanish Art

Three Spanish painters stand out as milestones in the history of Western art. Diego de Velázquez was a 17th-century court portrait painter and his *Las Meninas* is a seminal work. Francisco de Goya depicted Spanish life during one of its most violent periods. The prolific 20th-century master, Pablo Picasso, is recognized as the founder of modern art. To these names must be added that of El Greco – who was born in Crete but who lived in Spain, where he painted religious scenes in an individualistic style. The work of these and Spain's many other great artists can be seen in world-renowned galleries, especially the Prado *(see pp296–9).*

In his series *Las Meninas* (1957), Picasso interprets the frozen gesture of the five-year-old Infanta Margarita. Altogether, Picasso produced 44 paintings based on Velázquez's canvas. Some of them are in Barcelona's Museu Picasso *(see p157).*

The king and queen, reflected in a mirror behind the painter, may be posing for their portrait.

Self-portrait of Velázquez

Religious Art in Spain

The influence of the Catholic Church on Spanish art through the ages is reflected in the predominance of religious imagery. Many churches and museums have Romanesque altarpieces or earlier icons. El Greco *(see p395)* painted from a highly personal religious vision. Baroque religious art of the 17th century, when the Inquisition *(see p278)* was at its height, often graphically depicts physical suffering and spiritual torment.

The Burial of the Count of Orgaz by El Greco (see p394)

Las Meninas (1656)

In Velázquez's painting of the Infanta Margarita and her courtiers, in the Prado *(see pp296–9),* the eye is drawn into the distance where the artist's patron, Felipe IV, is reflected in a mirror.

| 1285–1348 Ferrer Bassá | 1390–1410 Pere Nicolau | The Saviour *by José de Ribera* | 1598–1664 Francisco de Zurbarán |
| | 1363–95 Jaume Serra | 1428–1460 Luis Daimau | 1591–1652 José de Ribera |

1300	**1400**	**1500**
	1388–1424 Luis Borrassa	1474–95 Bartolomé Bermejo	1565–1628 Francisco Ribalta
		1450–1504 Pedro Berruguete	
Virgin and Child *by Ferrer Bassá*	1427–52 Bernat Martorell	1541–1614 El Greco	1599–1660 Diego de Velázquez

José Nieto, the queen's chamberlain, stands in the doorway in the background of the painting.

Court jester

Modern Art

The early 20th-century artists Joan Miró *(see p176)*, Salvador Dalí *(see p219)* and Pablo Picasso *(see p157)* all belonged to the Paris School. More recent artists of note include Antonio Saura and Antoni Tàpies *(see p168)*. Among many great Spanish art collections, the Museo Reina Sofia in Madrid *(see pp302–3)* specializes in modern art. Contemporary artists are accorded great prestige in Spain. Their work is to be seen in town halls, banks and public squares, and many towns have a museum dedicated to a local painter.

Salvador Dalí's painting of the *Colossus of Rhodes* (1954)

Collage (1934) by Joan Miró

The Family of King Charles IV
was painted in 1800 by Francisco de Goya *(see p243)*, nearly 150 years after *Las Meninas*. Its debt to Velázquez's painting is evident in its frontal composition, compact grouping of figures and in the inclusion of a self-portrait.

The Holy Children with the Shell *by Murillo*

1893–1983 Joan Miró

1881–1973 Pablo Picasso

1904–89 Salvador Dalí

1746–1828 Francisco de Goya

1863–1923 Joaquín Sorolla

1923–2012 Antoni Tàpies

1700 **1800** **1900**

1642–93 Claudio Coello

1887–1927 Juan Gris

1618–82 Bartolomé Esteban Murillo

Jug and Glass *(1916) by Juan Gris*

1930–1998 Antonio Saura

Literary Spain

The best-known work of Spanish literature, *Don Quixote* is considered the first modern novel, but Spain has produced many major works over the last 2,000 years. The Roman writers Seneca, Lucan and Martial were born in Spain. Later, the Moors developed a flourishing, but now little-known, literary culture. Although Spanish (Castilian) is the national tongue, many enduring works have been written in the Galician and Catalan regional languages. Basque literature, hitherto an oral culture, is a more recent development. Many foreign writers, such as Alexandre Dumas, Ernest Hemingway and Karel Capek, have written accounts of their travels in Spain.

Middle Ages

As the Roman empire fell, Latin evolved into several Romance languages. The earliest non-Latin literature in Spain derives from an oral tradition that arose before the 10th century. It is in the form of *jarchas*, snatches of love poetry written in Mozarab, the Romance language that was spoken by Christians living under the Moors.

In the 12th century, the first poems appeared in Castilian. During the next 300 years, two separate schools of poetry developed. The best-known example of troubadour verse is the anonymous epic, *El Cantar del Mío Cid*, which tells of the heroic exploits of El Cid *(see p374)* during the Reconquest. Works of clerical poetry – for example, Gonzalo de Berceo's *Milagros de Nuestra Señora*, relating the life of the Virgin – convey a moral message.

Spanish literature evolved in the 13th century after Alfonso X the Learned *(see p59)* replaced Latin with Castilian Romance (later called Spanish) as the official language.

Alfonso X the Learned
(1221–84)

Under his supervision a team of Jews, Christians and Arabs wrote scholarly treatises. The king himself was a poet, writing in Galician Romance.

The first great prose works in Spanish appeared in the 14th and 15th centuries. *El Libro de Buen Amor,* by an ecclesiastic, Juan Ruiz, is a tale of the love affairs of a priest, interleaved with other stories. Fernando de Rojas uses skilful characterization in *La Celestina* to tell a tragic love story about two nobles and a scheming go-between. This was an age in which tales of chivalry were also popular.

The prolific Golden Age dramatist, Félix Lope de Vega

Golden Age

The 16th century hailed the start of Spain's Golden Age of literature. But it was also a period of domestic strife. This found expression in the picaresque novel, a Spanish genre originating with the anonymous *El Lazarillo de Tormes*, a bitter reflection on the misfortunes of a blind man's guide.

Spiritual writers flourished under the austere climate of the Counter-Reformation. St John of the Cross's *Cántico Espiritual* was influenced by Oriental erotic poetry and the Bible's *Song of Songs*.

The 17th century saw the emergence of more great talents. The life and work of Miguel de Cervantes *(see p337)* straddles the two centuries of the Golden Age. He published his masterpiece, *Don Quixote*, in 1615. Other important writers of the time include Francisco de Quevedo and Luis de Góngora.

Corrales (public theatres) appeared in the 17th century, opening the way for Lope de Vega *(see p294)*, Calderón de la Barca and other dramatists.

Don Quixote's adventures portrayed by José Moreno Carbonero

18th and 19th Centuries

Influenced by the French Enlightenment, literature in the 18th century was seen as a way to educate the people. Such was the aim, for instance, of Leandro Fernández de Moratín's comedy *El Sí de las Niñas*. This period saw the development of journalism as well as the emergence of the essay as a literary form. Romanticism had a short and late life in Spain. *Don Juan Tenorio*, a tale of the legendary irrepressible Latin lover by José Zorrilla, is the best-known Romantic play.

The satirical essayist Larra stands out from his contemporaries at the beginning of the 19th century. Towards the end of the century, the novel became a vehicle for realistic portrayals of Spanish society. Benito Pérez Galdós, regarded by many to be Spain's greatest novelist after Cervantes, studied the human condition in his *Episodios*

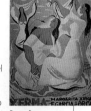

José Zorrilla (1817–93)

Nacionales. The heroine in Clarín's *La Regenta* is undone by the reactionary prejudices of provincial town society.

20th Century

Writers at the turn of the century, including Pío Baroja *(see p68)*, Miguel de Unamuno and Antonio Machado, described Spain as falling behind the rest of Europe. Ramón María del Valle-Inclán wrote highly satirical plays that created the foundations of modern Spanish theatre. In poetry, the Nobel Prize winner, Juan Ramón Jiménez, strived for pureness of form.

The so-called "Generation of 27" combined European experimental art with Spain's traditional literary subjects. The best-known of them is the poet and playwright Federico García Lorca who was executed by a Fascist firing squad in 1936 *(see p71)*. He drew on the legends and stereotypes of his native Andalusia to make universal statements in his poems and plays, such as *Yerma*. In the aftermath of the Civil War, many intellectuals who had backed the Republic were forced into exile. The Franco regime tried to create its own propagandist culture. Yet the finest literature of the period was written in spite of the political climate. Camilo José Cela's *La Colmena*, a description of everyday life in the hungry, postwar city of Madrid, set a mood of social realism that inspired other writers.

Poster for a Lorca play

Since the 1960s, the novel has become increasingly popular due to the emergence of writers like Joan Benet, Julio Llamazares, Antonio Muñoz Molina, José Manuel Caballero Bonald, Juan Marsé and the best-selling Carlos Ruiz Zafón.

The 20th and 21st centuries have also witnessed a surge of great Spanish literature from Latin America. Prominent authors include Jorge Luis Borges, José Ángel Mañas, Javier Marías and Gabriel García Márquez.

Camilo José Cela, Nobel Prize-winning novelist, by Alvaro Delgado

The Art of Bullfighting

Bullfighting is a sacrificial ritual in which men (and also a few women) pit themselves against an animal bred for the ring. In this "authentic religious drama", as poet García Lorca described it, the spectator experiences vicariously the fear and exaltation felt by the matador. Although a growing number of Spaniards oppose it on grounds of cruelty, and it was banned in Catalonia in 2012, it is still popular. Many Spaniards see talk of banning bullfighting as striking at the essence of their being, for they regard the *toreo*, the art of bullfighting, as a noble part of their heritage. Bullfights today, however, are often debased by practices that weaken the bull, especially shaving its horns.

Plaza de Toros de la Maestranza, Seville. This ring is regarded, with Las Ventas in Madrid, as one of the top venues for bullfighting in Spain.

The matador wears a *traje de luces* (suit of lights), a colourful silk outfit embroidered with gold sequins.

The passes are made with a *muleta*, a scarlet cape stiffened along one side.

Well treated at the ranch, the *toro bravo* (fighting bull) is specially bred for qualities of aggressiveness and courage. As aficionados of bullfighting point out in its defence, the young bull enjoys a full life while it is being prepared for its 15 minutes in the ring. Bulls must be at least four years old before they fight.

The Bullfight

The *corrida* (bullfight) has three stages, called *tercios*. In the first one, the *tercio de varas*, the matador and *picadores* (horsemen with lances) are aided by *peones* (assistants). In the *tercio de banderillas*, *banderilleros* stick pairs of darts in the bull's back. In the *tercio de muleta* the matador makes a series of passes at the bull with a *muleta* (cape). He then executes the kill, the *estocada*, with a sword.

The matador plays the bull with a *capa* (red cape) in the *tercio de varas*. *Peones* will then draw the bull towards the *picadores*.

Horses are now padded.

Picadores goad the bull with steel-pointed lances, testing its bravery. The lances weaken the animal's shoulder muscles.

The Bullring

The *corrida* audience is seated in the *tendidos* (stalls) or in the *palcos* (balcony), where the *presidencia* (president's box) is situated. Opposite are the *puerta de cuadrillas*, through which the matador and team arrive, and the *arrastre de toros* (exit for bulls). Before entering the ring, the matadors wait in a corridor (*callejón*) behind *barreras* and *burladeros* (barriers). Horses are kept in the *patio de caballos* and the bulls in the *corrales*.

Key

- Tendidos
- Palcos
- Presidencia
- Puerta de cuadrillas
- Arrastre de toros
- Callejón
- Barreras
- Burladeros
- Patio de caballos
- Corrales

Plan of a typical bullring

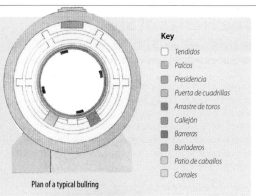

Banderillas, barbed darts, are thrust into the bull's already weakened back muscles.

Manolete is regarded by most followers of bullfighting as one of the greatest matadors ever. He was eventually gored to death by the bull Islero at Linares, Jaén, in 1947.

The bull may go free if it shows courage – spectators wave white handkerchiefs, asking the *corrida* president to let it leave the ring alive.

José Tomás is one of Spain's leading matadors today. He is famous for his purist approach and for his natural and elegant style with both the *capa* and the *muleta*.

The bull weighs about 500 kg (1,100 lbs).

Banderilleros enter to provoke the wounded bull in the *tercio de banderillas*, sticking pairs of *banderillas* in its back.

The matador makes passes with the cape in the *tercio de muleta*, then lowers it and thrusts in the sword for the kill.

The estocada recibiendo is a difficult kill, rarely seen. The matador awaits the bull's charge rather than moving to meet it.

The Fiestas of Spain

On any day of the year there is a fiesta happening somewhere in Spain – usually more than one. There isn't a village, town or city in the country which doesn't honour its patron saint, the Virgin or the changing seasons with processions, bullrunning, fireworks, re-enacted battles, some ancestral rite or a *romería* – a mass pilgrimage to a rural shrine. Whatever the pretext, a fiesta is a chance for everyone to take a break from normal life (most shops and offices close) and let off steam, with celebrations sometimes going on around the clock.

Many *romerías* wind through the countryside during the year

Spring Fiestas

The end of winter and the start of spring are marked by Valencia's great fire festival, Las Fallas *(see p259)*, in which huge papier-mâché sculptures are set alight in a symbolic act of burning the old in order to make way for the new.

Alcoi's mock battles between costumed armies of Moors and Christians in April *(see p259)* are the most spectacular of the countless fiestas which commemorate the battles of the Reconquest. Seville's April Fair *(see p435)*, is the biggest celebration held in Andalusia.

During the festival of Los Mayos, on 30 April and the following days, crosses are decorated with flowers in parts of Spain.

Easter

Most communities observe Easter in some form with pomp and solemnity. It is heralded by the Palm Sunday processions. The most impressive of these is in Elx, where intricate sculptures are woven from blanched leaves cropped from the most extensive forest of palm trees in Europe *(see p265)*.

The best Semana Santa (Easter Week) processions are held in Seville *(see p435)*, Granada, Málaga, Murcia and Valladolid. Brotherhoods of robed men carry *pasos*, huge sculptures depicting the Virgin, Christ or scenes of the Passion, through the streets. They are accompanied by people dressed as biblical characters or penitents, in tall conical hats. In some towns passion plays are acted out. In others, people carry heavy crosses. Sometimes the centuries-old ritual of self-flagellation can be witnessed.

Summer Fiestas

The first major fiesta of the summer is Pentecost (also known as Whitsun), in May or June, and its most famous celebration is at El Rocío *(see p467)*, where many thousands of people gather in a frenzy of religious devotion.

At Corpus Christi (in May or June) the consecrated host is carried in procession through many cities in an ornate silver monstrance. The route of the procession is often covered with a carpet of flowers. The main Corpus Christi celebrations take place in Valencia, Toledo and Granada.

On Midsummer's Eve (La Víspera de San Juan), bonfires are lit all over, especially in the areas along the Mediterranean coast, to herald the celebration of St John the Baptist on 24 June.

The Brotherhood of Candlemas, Semana Santa (Easter Week) in Seville

During Los Sanfermines *(see p136)* in Pamplona in July, young people run through the streets in front of six bulls.

The Virgin of Carmen, who is revered as the patron of fishermen, is honoured in many ports on 16 July.

The important Catholic holiday of Assumption Day, 15 August, is marked by a huge number and variety of fiestas.

Autumn Fiestas

There are few fiestas in autumn, but in most wine regions the grape harvest is fêted. The annual pig slaughter has become a jubilant public event in some villages, especially in Extremadura. In Galicia it is traditional to roast chestnuts on street bonfires.

On All Saints' Day, 1 November, people remember the dead by visiting cemeteries to lay flowers, especially chrysanthemums, on graves.

Christmas and New Year

Nochebuena (Christmas Eve) is the main Christmas celebration, when families gather for an evening meal before attending Midnight Mass, known as *misa del gallo* (Mass of the rooster). During the Christmas period, *belenes* (crib scenes) of painted figurines abound. You may also see a "living crib", peopled by costumed actors. Spain's "April Fools' Day" is 28 December, when people play practical jokes on each other. Clown-

The losers end up in the harbour in Dénia's July fiesta *(see p259)*

like characters may make fun of passers-by.

To celebrate New Year's Eve *(Noche Vieja)*, crowds gather beneath the clock in Madrid's central square, the Puerta del Sol *(see p276)*, after a midnight celebration at home with their families. Traditionally people eat 12 grapes, one on each chime of midnight, to bring good luck for the year.

Epiphany, on 6 January, is celebrated with parades of the Three Kings in villages and towns the evening before.

Winter Fiestas

Animals hold centre stage in a variety of fiestas on 17 January, the Day of St Anthony, patron saint of animals, when pets and livestock are blessed by priests. St Agatha, the patron saint of married women, is honoured

on 5 February, when women, for once, are the protagonists of many fiestas. In Zamarramala (Segovia), for example, women take over the mayor's privileges and powers for this particular day *(see p372)*.

St Anthony's Day in Villanueva de Alcolea (Castellón province)

Carnival

Carnival, in February or early March (depending on the date of Easter), brings a chance for a street party as winter comes to an end and before Lent begins. The biggest celebrations are held in Santa Cruz de Tenerife *(see p540)* – comparable with those of Rio de Janeiro – and in Cádiz *(see p467)*. Carnival was prohibited by the Franco regime because of its licentiousness and frivolity. It ends on or after Ash Wednesday with the Burial of the Sardine, a "funeral" in which a mock sardine, representing winter, is ritually burned or buried.

A spectacularly costumed choir singing during Carnival in Cádiz

SPAIN THROUGH THE YEAR

Festivals, cultural events and sports competitions crowd the calendar in Spain. Even small villages have at least one traditional fiesta, lasting a week or more, when parades, bullfights and fireworks displays replace work (*see pp42–3*). Many rural and coastal towns celebrate the harvest or fishing catch with a gastronomic fair at which you can sample local produce.

Music, dance, drama and film festivals are held in Spain's major cities throughout the year. Meanwhile, the country's favourite outdoor sports – football, basketball, cycling, sailing, golf and tennis – culminate in several national and international championships. It is a good idea to confirm specific dates of events with the local tourist board as some vary from year to year.

Spring

Life in Spain moves outdoors with the arrival of spring, and terrace cafés begin to fill with people. The countryside is at its best as wild flowers bloom, and irrigation channels flow to bring water to the newly sown crops. The important Easter holiday is a time of solemn processions throughout the country.

Feria del Caballo (Festival of the Horses) in Jerez de la Frontera

March

International Vintage Car Rally *(usually first Sun)*, from Barcelona to Sitges. More than 60 vintage cars make this annual 45-km (28-mile) journey.
Las Fallas *(15–19 Mar)*, Valencia *(see p259)*. This spectacular fiesta also marks the start of the bull-fighting *(see pp40–41)* season.
Fiestas *(end Feb or mid-Mar)*, Castellón de la Plana. All in honour of Mary Magdalene.

April

Spanish Motorcycle Grand Prix *(Apr/early May)*, Jerez de la Frontera race track.

Religious Music Week *(Easter week, from Passion Sat)*, Cuenca.
Trofeo Conde de Godó *(mid- to late Apr)*, Barcelona. Spain's international tennis championship.
Moors and Christians *(21–24 Apr)*, Alcoi *(see p262)*. This colourful costumed event celebrates the Christian victory over the Moors in 1276.

April Fair *(2 weeks after Easter)*, Seville. Exuberant Andalusian fiesta *(see p435)*.
Feria Nacional del Queso *(late Apr/early May)*, Trujillo (Cáceres). A festival celebrating Spanish cheese *(see p411)*.

May

Dos de Mayo *(2 May)*, Madrid. Music, fireworks and dancing in the streets in remembrance of the 1808 rebellion against Napolean's occupation.
Feria del Caballo *(first week)*, Jerez de la Frontera. Horse fair showing Andalusia at its most traditional, with fine horses and beautiful women in flamenco dresses.
Fiestas de San Isidro *(8–15 May)*, Madrid *(see p294)*. Bullfights at Las Ventas bullring are the highlights of the taurine year.
Spanish Formula One Grand Prix *(May/Jun)*, Montmeló circuit, Barcelona. International motor race.

Onlookers lining the street during the Vuelta Ciclista a España *(p46)*

San Sebastián, one of the most popular resorts on the north coast

Summer

August is Spain's big holiday season. The cities empty as Spaniards flock to the coast or to their second homes in the hills. Their numbers are swelled by millions of foreign tourists, and beaches and camp sites are often full to bursting. As the heat starts in the centre and south, entertainment often takes place only in the evening, when the temperature has dropped. In late summer the harvest begins and there are gastronomic

The pouring and tasting of cider in Asturias's Cider Festival

fiestas everywhere to celebrate food and drink, from the fishing catches of the north coast to the sausages of the Balearic Islands.

June
International Festival of Music and Dance *(Jun–Jul)*, Granada. Classical music and ballet staged in the Alhambra and the Generalife.
Grec Arts Festival *(late Jun–Aug)*, Barcelona. Both Spanish and international theatre, music and dance.
A Rapa das Bestas *(Jun, Jul, Aug)*, Pontevedra, La Coruña and Lugo provinces (Galicia). Wild horses are rounded up so that their manes and tails can be cut *(see p102)*.
Classical Theatre Festival *(end Jun–Aug)*, Mérida. Staged in the Roman theatre and amphitheatre *(see p414)*.

July
Guitar Festival *(timing varies)*, Córdoba. From classical to flamenco *(see pp428–9)*.
International Classical Theatre Festival of Almagro *(Jul)*. Spanish and classical repertoire in one of the oldest theatres in Europe *(see p403)*.

Blues Cazorla *(Jul)*, Cazorla (Jaén). Largest blues festival in Spain, held over three days.
Cider Festival *(second weekend)*, Nava (Asturias). Includes traditional cider-pouring competitions.
International Jazz Festivals in San Sebastián *(third week)*, Getxo *(first week)* and Vitoria *(mid-Jul)*.
Pyrenean Folklore Festival *(late Jul/early Aug, odd years)*, Jaca (Aragón). Folk costumes, music and dance.
Certamen Internacional de Habaneras y Polifonía *(late Jul–early Aug)*, Torrevieja (Alicante). Musical competition of 19th-century seafarers' songs.

August
International Festival of Santander *(Aug)*. Celebration of music, dance and theatre.
Copa del Rey MAPFRE *(end Jul/first week Aug)*, Palma de Mallorca. Sailing competition, presided over by King Felipe VI.
Descent of the Río Sella *(first Sat)*. Canoe race in Asturias from Arriondas to Ribadesella *(see p111)*.
Assumption Day *(15 Aug)* The Assumption is celebrated throughout the country.

Participants in the Descent of the Río Sella canoe race

Semanas Grandes *(mid-Aug)*, Bilbao and San Sebastián. "Great Weeks" of sporting and cultural events.
Misteri d'Elx *(14–15 Aug; also 29 Oct–1 Nov during Medieval Festival)*, Elx *(see p265)*. Unique liturgical drama featuring spectacular special effects.

Vines and the village of Larouco in the Valdeorras wine region of Galicia *(see p82)* in autumn

Autumn

Autumn usually brings rain after the heat of summer, and, with the high tourist season over, a large number of resorts practically close down. Harvest festivities continue, however, and the most important celebrations are in honour of the grape. The first pressings are blessed and, in some places, wine is served for free.

Wild mushrooms

In woodland areas, freshly picked wild mushrooms start to appear in various dishes on local restaurant menus. The hunting season begins in the middle of October and runs until February. Autumn is also the start of the new drama and classical music seasons in the major cities of Spain.

September

Vuelta Ciclista a España *(Sep)*. Annual bicycle race around Spain.

Grape Harvest *(mid-Sep)*, Jerez de la Frontera. Celebration of the new crop in the country's sherry capital.

San Sebastián Film Festival *(mid- to late Sep)*. Gathering of film-makers *(see p127)*.

Festival de la Mercé *(17–24 Sep)*, Barcelona. Free concerts and folkloric events.

Bienal de Arte Flamenco *(early Sep–early Oct, even years only)*, Seville. Top flamenco artists perform.

October

Día de la Hispanidad *(12 Oct)*. Spain's national holiday marks Columbus's discovery of America in 1492. The biggest celebration in the country is the exuberant fiesta of Día del Pilar in Zaragoza *(see p243)*, which marks the end of the bullfighting year.

Moors and Christians *(mid-Oct)*, Callosa d'en Sarria (Alicante). Parades in honour of the local madonna.

Saffron Festival *(last weekend)*, Consuegra (Toledo).

Driving down the fairway at one of Spain's golfing championships

November

All Saints' Day *(1 Nov)*. This marks the start of the *matanza* (pig slaughter) in rural Spain.

Os Magostos *(11 Nov)*. Chestnut-harvest fairs abound in Galicia.

Latin American Film Festival *(mid-Nov for one week)*, Huelva *(see p466)*.

National Flamenco Competition *(mid-Nov for two weeks)*, Córdoba. Song, dance and guitar performances.

Lana Turner on centre-stage at the San Sebastián Film Festival

Public Holidays

Besides marking the national holidays below, each region (*comunidad autónoma*) celebrates its own holiday, and every town and village has at least one other fiesta each year. If a holiday falls on a Tuesday or a Thursday, some people also choose to take holidays on the intervening Monday or Friday, making a long weekend called a *puente* (bridge).

Año Nuevo *(New Year's Day)* (1 Jan)
Día de los Tres Reyes *(Epiphany)* (6 Jan)
Jueves Santo *(Maundy Thursday)* (Mar/Apr)
Viernes Santo *(Good Friday)* (Mar/Apr)
Día de Pascua *(Easter Sunday)* (Mar/Apr)
Día del Trabajo *(Labour Day)* (1 May)
Asunción *(Assumption Day)* (15 Aug)
Día de la Hispanidad *(National Day)* (12 Oct)
Todos los Santos *(All Saints' Day)* (1 Nov)
Día de la Constitución *(Constitution Day)* (6 Dec)
Inmaculada Concepción *(Immaculate Conception)* (8 Dec)
Navidad *(Christmas Day)* (25 Dec)

Assumption Day in La Alberca (Salamanca)

Winter

Winter varies greatly from region to region. In the mountains, snowfalls bring skiers to the slopes; while in lower areas, olive and orange picking are in full swing. The higher parts of Central Spain can become very cold. Andalusia, the east coast and the Balearic Islands have cool nights but often sunny days. The winter warmth of the Canary Islands brings the high tourist season. Christmas is a special time of celebration – an occasion for families to reunite, share food and attend religious celebrations.

Skiers in the Sierra de Guadarrama, north of Madrid (see p333)

"El Gordo", the largest Spanish lottery prize, being drawn

December

El Gordo *(22 Dec)*. Spain's largest lottery prize, "the Fat One", is drawn.
Noche Buena *(24 Dec)* is a family Christmas Eve, followed by Midnight Mass.
Santos Inocentes *(28 Dec)*, Spain's version of April Fools' Day, when people play tricks.
Noche Vieja *(31 Dec)*. New Year's Eve is most celebrated in Madrid's Puerta del Sol.

January

Día de los Tres Reyes *(6 Jan)*. On the eve of the Epiphany, the Three Kings parade through town, throwing sweets to the children.
La Tamborrada *(19–20 Jan)*, San Sebastián. Drumming en masse in traditional costume.

Canary Islands International Music Festival *(Jan–Feb)*.

Classical concerts are held on La Palma and Tenerife.

February

La Endiablada *(2–3 Feb)*, Almonacid del Marquesado (Cuenca). Townsfolk dress as devils in honour of San Blas.
ARCO *(mid-Feb)*, Madrid. International contemporary art fair.
Pasarela Cibeles (Fashion Week) *(mid-Feb)*, Madrid. Women's and men's fashion shows in the capital.
Carnival *(Feb/Mar)*. Final fiesta before Lent, with colourful costumes. Those in Santa Cruz de Tenerife and Cádiz are among the best.

4 8 | INTRODUCING SPAIN

The Climate of Spain

Spain's large landmass, with its extensive high plateaus and mountain ranges, and the influences of the Mediterranean and Atlantic, produce a wide range of climatic variation, especially in winter. The north is wettest year-round, the eastern and southern coasts and the islands have mild winters, while winter temperatures in the interior are often below freezing. Summers everywhere are hot, except in upland areas.

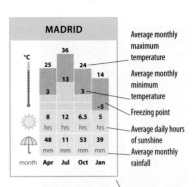

MADRID

Average monthly maximum temperature
Average monthly minimum temperature
Freezing point
Average daily hours of sunshine
Average monthly rainfall

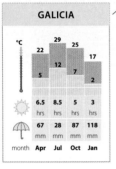

ASTURIAS AND CANTABRIA

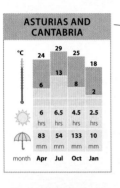

GALICIA

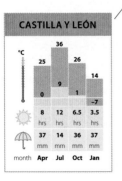

CASTILLA Y LEÓN

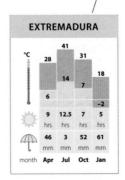

EXTREMADURA

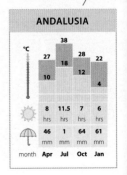

ANDALUSIA

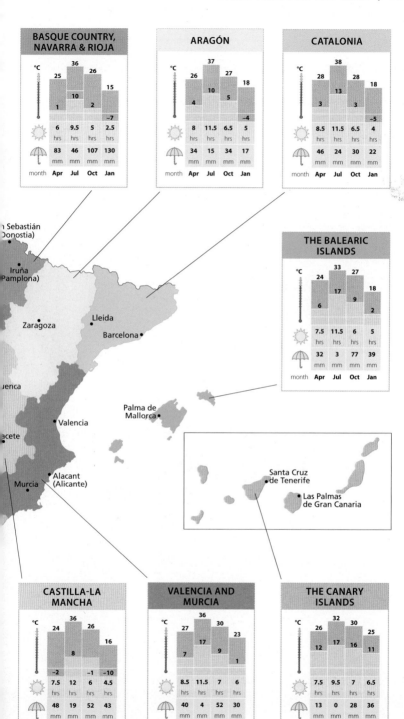

BASQUE COUNTRY, NAVARRA & RIOJA

°C			
25	36	26	15
1	10	2	-7

6 hrs	9.5 hrs	5 hrs	2.5 hrs
83 mm	46 mm	107 mm	130 mm

| month | **Apr** | **Jul** | **Oct** | **Jan** |

ARAGÓN

°C			
26	37	27	18
4	10	5	-4

8 hrs	11.5 hrs	6.5 hrs	5 hrs
34 mm	15 mm	34 mm	17 mm

| month | **Apr** | **Jul** | **Oct** | **Jan** |

CATALONIA

°C			
28	38	28	18
3	13	3	-5

8.5 hrs	11.5 hrs	6.5 hrs	4 hrs
46 mm	24 mm	30 mm	22 mm

| month | **Apr** | **Jul** | **Oct** | **Jan** |

THE BALEARIC ISLANDS

°C			
24	33	27	18
6	17	9	2

7.5 hrs	11.5 hrs	6 hrs	5 hrs
32 mm	3 mm	77 mm	39 mm

| month | **Apr** | **Jul** | **Oct** | **Jan** |

San Sebastián (Donostia)

Iruña (Pamplona)

Zaragoza

Lleida

Barcelona

Cuenca

Valencia

Palma de Mallorca

Albacete

Alacant (Alicante)

Murcia

Santa Cruz de Tenerife

Las Palmas de Gran Canaria

CASTILLA-LA MANCHA

°C			
24	36	26	16
-2	8	-1	-10

7.5 hrs	12 hrs	6 hrs	4.5 hrs
48 mm	9 mm	52 mm	43 mm

| month | **Apr** | **Jul** | **Oct** | **Jan** |

VALENCIA AND MURCIA

°C			
27	36	30	23
7	17	9	1

8.5 hrs	11.5 hrs	7 hrs	6 hrs
40 mm	4 mm	52 mm	30 mm

| month | **Apr** | **Jul** | **Oct** | **Jan** |

THE CANARY ISLANDS

°C			
26	32	30	25
12	17	16	11

7.5 hrs	9.5 hrs	7 hrs	6.5 hrs
13 mm	0 mm	28 mm	36 mm

| month | **Apr** | **Jul** | **Oct** | **Jan** |

THE HISTORY OF SPAIN

The Iberian Peninsula, first inhabited around 800,000 BC, has long been subject to foreign influences. From the 11th century BC it was colonized by sophisticated eastern Mediterranean civilizations, starting with the Phoenicians, then the Greeks and Carthaginians.

The Romans arrived in 218 BC to fight the Carthaginians, thus sparking off the Second Punic War. They harvested the peninsula's agricultural and mineral wealth and established cities with aqueducts, temples and theatres.

With the fall of the Roman Empire in the early 5th century AD, Visigothic invaders from the north assumed power. Their poor political organization, however, made them easy prey to the Moors from North Africa. In the 8th century, the peninsula came almost entirely under Moorish rule. Europe's only major Muslim territory, the civilization of Al Andalus excelled in mathematics, geography, astronomy and poetry. In the 9th and 10th centuries Córdoba was Europe's leading city.

From the 11th century, northern Christian kingdoms initiated a military reconquest of Al Andalus. The marriage, in 1469, of Fernando of Aragón and Isabel of Castile, the so-called Catholic Monarchs, led to Spanish unity. They took Granada, the last Moorish kingdom, in 1492. Columbus discovered the Americas in the same year, opening the way for the Spanish conquistadors, who plundered the civilizations of the New World.

The succeeding Habsburg dynasty spent the riches from the New World in endless foreign wars. Spain's decline was exacerbated by high inflation and religious oppression. Although the Enlightenment in the late 18th century created a climate of learning, Spain's misfortunes continued into the next century with an invasion by Napoleon's troops and the loss of her American colonies. A new radicalism began to emerge, creating a strong Anarchist movement. The political instability of the late 19th and early 20th centuries led to dictatorship in the 1920s and a republic in the 1930s, which was destroyed by the Spanish Civil War. Victorious General Franco ruled by repression until his death in 1975. Since then Spain has been a constitutional monarchy.

Bullfighting in Madrid's Plaza Mayor in the 17th century

◀ Moors paying homage to Fernando and Isabel, the 15th-century Catholic Monarchs

Prehistoric Spain

The Iberian Peninsula was first inhabited by hunter-gatherers around 800,000 BC. They were eclipsed by a Neolithic farming population from 5000 BC. First in a wave of settlers from over the Mediterranean, the Phoenicians landed in 1100 BC, to be followed by the Greeks and Carthaginians. Invading Celts mixed with native Iberian tribes (forming the Celtiberians). They proved a formidable force against the Romans, the next conquerors of Spain.

Spain in 5000 BC

☐ Neolithic farming settlements

Iron Dagger (6th century BC)
Weapons, like this dagger from Burgos, represent the later Iron Age, in contrast to earlier metal objects which were for domestic use.

Small silver bottle

The 28 bracelets have perforations and moulded decorations.

Stone Age Man
This skull belongs to a Palaeolithic man, who hunted deer and bison with tools made of wood and stone.

Incised geometric pattern

La Dama de Elche
Dating from the 4th century BC, this stone statue is a fine example of Iberian art. Her austere beauty reveals traces of Greek influence.

The Villena Treasure

Discovered in 1963 during works in Villena, near Alicante, this Bronze Age find consists of 66 dazzling objects mostly of gold, including bowls, bottles and jewellery (see p264). The treasure dates from around 1000 BC.

800,000 BC *Homo erectus* arrives in Iberian Peninsula

300,000 BC Tribes of *Homo erectus* live in hunting camps in Soria and Madrid

35,000 BC Cro-Magnon man evolves in Spain

2500 BC Los Millares (*p505*) is inhabited by early metal-workers with belief in the afterlife

1800–1100 BC Civilization of El Argar, an advanced agrarian society, flourishes in southeast Spain

| 800,000 BC | | 2500 | 2000 |

500,000 BC Stones used as tools by hominids (probably *Homo erectus*)

100,000–40,000 BC Neanderthal man in Gibraltar

5000 BC Farming begins in Iberian Peninsula

18,000–14,000 BC Drawings by cave dwellers at Altamira (Cantabria), near Ribadesella (Asturias) and at Nerja (Andalusia)

Bison cave drawing, Altamira

Greek Ceramic Vase
The Greek colonizers brought new technology, including the potter's wheel, as well as refined artistic ideals. Ceramics, such as this 6th-century-BC vase depicting the Labours of Hercules, provided sophisticated models.

Where to See Prehistoric Spain

The most famous cave paintings in Spain are at Altamira *(see p116)*. There are dolmens in many parts of the country; among the largest are those at Antequera *(see p479)*. The Guanches – the indigenous inhabitants of the Canary Islands – left behind more recent remains *(see p551)*.

La Naveta d'es Tudons is one of the many prehistoric stone monuments scattered across the island of Menorca *(see p531)*.

An excavated Celtic village, with its round huts, can be seen near A Guarda in Pontevedra *(see p100)*.

The largest of the treasure's five bottles, made of silver, stands 22.5 cm (9 in) high.

Bowls of beaten gold may have originated in southwest Spain.

Brooches with separate clasps

The smaller pieces are of unknown use.

Astarte (8th century BC)
Worship of Phoenician deities was incorporated into local religions. One of the most popular was the fertility goddess Astarte, shown on this bronze from the kingdom of Tartessus.

Phoenician gold ornament

1100 BC Phoenicians believed to have founded modern-day Cádiz

600 BC Greek colonists settle on northeast coast of Spain

228 BC Carthaginians occupy south-east Spain

1500	1000	500

1200 BC The "talaiotic" people of Menorca erect three unique types of stone building: *taulas*, *talaiots* and *navetas*

Taula in Menorca

775 BC Phoenicians establish colonies along the coast near Málaga

300 BC *La Dama de Elche* is carved *(p300)*

700 BC Semi-mythical kingdom of Tartessus thought to be at its height

Carthaginian glass necklace

Romans and Visigoths

The Romans came to Spain to fight the Carthaginians and take possession of the region's huge mineral wealth. Later, Hispania's wheat and olive oil became mainstays of the empire. It took 200 years to subdue the peninsula, which was divided in three provinces: Tarraconensis, Lusitania and Baetica. In time, cities with Roman infrastructure developed. The fall of the empire in the 5th century left Spain in the hands of the Visigoths, invaders from the north. Politically disorganized, they fell victim to the Moors in 711.

Spain (Hispania) in 5 BC

- ☐ Tarraconensis
- ☐ Lusitania
- ☐ Baetica

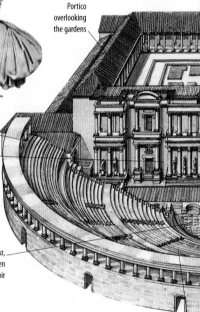

Trajan *(AD 53–117)*
Trajan was the first Hispanic Roman emperor (AD 98–117). He improved public administration and expanded the empire.

Portico overlooking the gardens

Good acoustics at every level

A Classical façade served as a backdrop for tragedies. Additional scenery was used for comedies.

Seneca *(4 BC–AD 65)*
Born in Córdoba, the Stoic philosopher Seneca lived in Rome as Nero's adviser.

The *orchestra,* a semicircular open space for the choir

Visigothic Relief
This crude Visigothic stone carving, based on a Roman relief, is in the 7th-century church of Quintanilla de las Viñas, near Burgos *(p374)*.

The auditorium seated over 5,000. The audience was placed according to social status.

218 BC Scipio the Elder lands with a Roman army at Emporion *(p220)*. The Second Punic War begins	**c.200 BC** Romans reach Gadir (modern Cádiz) after driving Carthaginians out of Hispania		**26 BC** Emerita Augusta (Mérida) is founded and soon becomes capital of Lusitania
	155 BC Lusitanian Wars begin. Romans invade Portugal		**19 BC** Augustus takes Cantabria and Asturias, ending 200 years of war

200 BC	**100**	**AD 1**	**AD 100**

| **219 BC** Hannibal takes Saguntum *(p253)* for Carthaginians | **133 BC** Celt-Iberian Wars culminate in destruction of Numantia, Soria *(p381)* | **61 BC** Julius Caesar, governor of Hispania Ulterior, begins final conquest of northern Portugal and Galicia | **AD 74** Emperor Vespasian grants Latin status to all towns in Hispania, completing proce of Romanization |
| *Hannibal* | | **82–72 BC** Roman Civil War. Pompey founds Pompaelo (Pamplona) in 75 BC | |

Gladiator Mosaic

Mosaics were used as decoration both indoors and out. Themes range from mythical episodes to portrayals of daily life. This 4th-century AD mosaic shows gladiators in action and has helpful labels to name the fighters and show who is dead or alive.

Where to See Roman Spain

Like Mérida, Tarragona (see pp228–9) has extensive Roman ruins, and Itálica (see p480) is an excavated town. A magnificent Roman wall rings Lugo in Galicia (see p103). Built in Trajan's rule, the bridge over the Tagus at Alcántara (see p414) has a temple on it.

Emporion, a Roman town, was built next to a former Greek colony in the 3rd century BC. The ruins include grand villas and a forum (see p220).

The gardens were used as a foyer during intervals by the Hispanic nobility, dressed in elegant togas.

Stage building in granite and marble

Scaena, the platform on which the actors performed

Segovia's Roman aqueduct (see pp368–9), a huge monument with 163 arches, dates from the end of the 1st century AD.

Roman Theatre, Mérida

Theatre was an extremely popular form of entertainment in Hispania. This reconstruction shows the theatre at Mérida (see p414), built in 16–15 BC.

Visigothic Cross

Although Visigothic kings seldom ruled long enough to make an impact on society, the early Christian Church grew powerful. Fortunes were spent on churches and religious art.

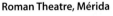

Mosaic from Mérida

415 Visigoths establish their court at Barcelona

409 Vandals and their allies cross Pyrenees into Tarraconensis

446 Romans attempt to win back rest of Hispania

476 Overthrow of the last Roman emperor leads to end of Western Roman Empire

200	300	400	500

258 Franks cross Pyrenees into Tarraconensis and sack Tarragona

312 Christianity officially recognized as religion under rule of Constantine, the first Christian emperor

The Codex Vigilianus, *a Christian manuscript*

589 Visigothic King Reccared converts from Arianism to Catholicism at Third Council of Toledo

Al Andalus: Muslim Spain

The arrival of Arab and Berber invaders from North Africa, and their defeat of the Visigoths, gave rise to the most brilliant civilization of early medieval Europe. These Muslim settlers, often known as the Moors, called Spain "Al Andalus". A rich and powerful caliphate was established in Córdoba and mathematics, science, architecture and the decorative arts flourished. The caliphate eventually broke up into small kingdoms or *taifas*. Meanwhile small Christian enclaves expanded in the north.

Spain in AD 750
Extent of Moorish domination

Water Wheel
Moorish irrigation techniques, such as the water wheel, revolutionized agriculture. New crops, including oranges and rice, were introduced.

The palace, dating from the 11th century, was surrounded by patios, pools and gardens.

Astrolabe
Perfected by the Moors around AD 800, the astrolabe was used by navigators and astronomers.

Remains of a Roman amphitheatre

Silver Casket of Hisham II
In the Caliphate of Córdoba, luxury objects of brilliant craftsmanship were worked in ivory, silver and bronze.

Fortified entrance gate

Curtain walls with watchtowers

711 Moors, led by Tariq, invade Spain and defeat Visigoths at battle of Guadalete

732 Moors' advance into France is halted by Charles Martel at Poitiers

778 Charlemagne's rearguard defeated by Basques at Roncesvalles (*p138*)

785 Building of great mosque at Córdoba begins

Charlemagne (742–814)

750	800	850

722 Led by Pelayo, Christians defeat Moors at Covadonga (*p113*)

756 Abd al Rahman I proclaims independent emirate in Córdoba

744 Christians under Alfonso I of Asturias take León

Pelayo (718–37)

c.800 Tomb of St James (Santiago) is supposedly discovered at Santiago de Compostela

822 Abd al Rahman II begins 30-year rule marked by patronage of the arts and culture

Puerta de Sabbath in Córdoba's Mezquita
Wealth and artistic brilliance were lavished on mosques, especially in Córdoba (*see pp484–5*). Calligraphy was a major element in decoration.

Where to See Moorish Spain

The finest Moorish buildings are in Andalusia, mainly in the cities of Córdoba (*see pp482–3*) and Granada (*see pp490–96*). Almería (*see p505*) has a large, ruined *alcazaba* (castle). In Jaén (*see p497*) there are Moorish baths. Further north, in Zaragoza, is the castle-palace of La Aljafería (*see p241*).

Medina Azahara (*see p481*), sacked in the 11th century but partly restored, was the final residence of Córdoba's caliphs.

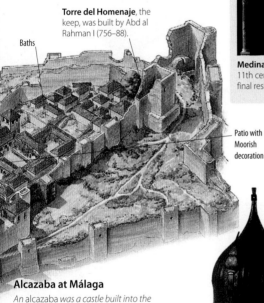

Torre del Homenaje, the keep, was built by Abd al Rahman I (756–88).

Baths

Patio with Moorish decoration

Alcazaba at Málaga

An alcazaba was a castle built into the ramparts of a Moorish city, often protected by massive concentric walls. In Málaga (see p478) – the principal port of the Moorish kingdom of Granada – the vast Alcazaba was built in the 8–11th centuries on the site of a Roman fortress, and incorporated massive curtain walls and fortified gates.

Moorish Sword
A fine example of late Moorish craftsman-ship, this sword has a golden pommel. The blade is inscribed with Arabic writing.

Warrior Helmet
Practical as well as ornate, this Islamic nobleman's helmet, made of iron, gold and silver, incorporates inscriptions, a coat of arms and chain mail.

905 Emergent Navarra becomes Christian kingdom under Sancho I

976 Al Mansur, military dictator, usurps caliphal powers and sacks Barcelona. Córdoba Mezquita finished

1010 Medina Azahara sacked by Berbers

| 900 | 950 | 1000 |

913 Christian capital is established at León

936 Building of Medina Azahara palace starts near Córdoba

Bronze stag from Medina Azahara

1013 Caliphate of Córdoba breaks up. Emergence of *taifas*: small, independent Moorish kingdoms

The Reconquest

The infant Christian kingdoms in the north – León, Castile, Navarra, Aragón and Catalonia – advanced south gradually in the 11th century, fighting in the name of Christianity to regain land from the Moors. After the fall of Toledo in 1085, the struggle became increasingly a holy war. Militant North African Muslims – Almoravids and Almohads – rallied to the Moorish cause and ultimately took over Al Andalus in the 12th century. As the Christians pushed further south, soon only Granada remained under Moorish control.

Spain in 1173
☐ Christian kingdoms
▨ Al Andalus

Golden Goblet
The exquisite goblet (1063) of Doña Urraca, daughter of Alfonso VI, shows the quality of medieval Christian craftsmanship.

Fernando I
Fernando formed the first Christian power bloc in 1037 by uniting Léon with Castile, which was emerging as a major military force.

Armies of Castile, Aragón and Navarra

The Almohads fight until the bitter end, although many comrades lay slain.

Alhambra, Palace of the Nasrids
Moorish art and architecture of singular beauty continued to be produced in the Nasrid kingdom of Granada. Its apogee is the exquisite Alhambra *(see pp494–5)*.

Las Navas de Tolosa
The Christian victory over the Almohads in the Battle of Las Navas de Tolosa (1212) led to Moorish Spain's decline. The army of Muhammad II al Nasir was no match for the forces of Sancho VII of Navarra, Pedro II of Aragón and Alfonso VIII of Castile. A stained-glass window in Roncesvalles (see p138) depicts the battle.

1037 León and Castile united for first time under Fernando I

1065 Death of Fernando I precipitates fratricidal civil war between his sons

1086 Almoravids respond to pleas for help from Moorish emirs by taking over *taifas* (splinter states)

Uniforms of military orders

1158 Establishment of the Order of Calatrava, the first military order of knights in Spain

1050	**1100**	**1150**	**1200**

El Cid

1085 Toledo falls to Christians under Alfonso VI of Castile

1094 The legendary El Cid *(see p374)* captures Valencia

1137 Ramón Berenguer IV of Catalonia marries Petronila of Aragón, uniting the two kingdoms under their son, Alfonso II

1147 Almohads arrive in Al Andalus and make Seville their capital

1143 Portugal becomes separate kingdom

1212 Combined Christian forces defeat Almohads at battle of Las Navas de Tolosa

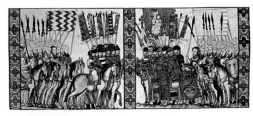

Cantigas of Alfonso X (1252–84)
This detail of a manuscript by Alfonxo X portrays the confrontation between Moorish and Christian cavalry. Alfonso the Learned encouraged his scholars to master Arab culture and translate ancient Greek manuscripts brought by the Moors.

Sancho VII of Navarra leads the Christian forces.

St James (Santiago)
Known as the Moor-slayer, St James is said to have miraculously intervened at the Battle of Clavijo in 844. This powerful figurehead is the patron saint of Spain.

Where to See Mudéjar Spain

The Mudéjares – Muslims who remained in territories under Christian occupation – created a distinctive architectural style distinguished by its ornamental work in brick, plaster and ceramics. Aragón, particularly Zaragoza (see pp240–41) and Teruel (see pp244–5), boasts some of the finest Mudéjar buildings. Seville's Reales Alcázares is an exquisitely harmonious collection of patios and halls built under Pedro I (see pp444–5).

The Mudéjar tower of Teruel Cathedral combines both brick and colourful ceramics to highly decorative effect.

Santa María la Blanca (see p395), a former synagogue and church, shows the fusion of cultures in medieval Toledo.

1215 Foundation of Salamanca University

1230 Fernando III reunites Castile and León

Crest of Castile and León

1250 Toledo at its height as a centre of translation and learning, influenced by Alfonso X the Learned

1232 Granada becomes capital of future Nasrid kingdom. Building of the Alhambra begins

1385 Portuguese defeat Castilians at Aljubarrota, crushing King Juan's aspirations to throne of Portugal

1388–9 Treaties end Spanish phase of Hundred Years' War

1250   **1300**   **1350**   **1400**

1386 Invasion of Galicia by the English, ended by Bayonne Treaty

1401 Work starts in Seville on what was then the world's largest Gothic cathedral

Alfonso X

The Catholic Monarchs

The foundation of the Spanish nation-state was laid by Isabel I of Castile and Fernando II of Aragón *(see p74)*. Uniting their lands in military, diplomatic and religious matters, the "Catholic Monarchs", as they are known, won back Granada, the last Moorish kingdom, from Boabdil. The Inquisition gave Spain a reputation for intolerance, yet in art and architecture brilliant progress was made and the voyages of Columbus opened up the New World.

Spain's Exploration of the New World

▮ Route of Columbus's first voyage

Tomb of El Doncel (15th century)
This effigy of a page who died in the fight for Granada combines ideals of military glory and learning *(see p386)*.

Alhambra

Boabdil, the grief-stricken king, moves forward to hand over the keys to Granada.

The Inquisition
Active from 1478, the Inquisition *(see p278)* persecuted those suspected of heresy with increasing vigour. This member of the Brotherhood of Death took victims to the stake.

Baptizing Jews
After the Christian reconquest of Granada, Jews were forced to convert or leave Spain. The *conversos* (converted Jews) were often treated badly.

The Fall of Granada (1492)

This romantic interpretation by Francisco Pradilla (1846–1921) reflects the chivalry of Boabdil, ruler of Granada, as he surrenders the keys of the last Moorish kingdom to the Catholic Monarchs, Fernando and Isabel, following ten long years of war.

1454 Enrique IV, Isabel's half-brother, accedes to throne of Castile

1465 Civil war erupts in Castile

1478 Papal bull authorizes Castilian Inquisition with Tomás de Torquemada as Inquisitor General

Torquemada

1450	1460	1470	1480

1451 Birth of Isabel of Castile

Fernando and Isabel on 15th-century gold coin

1469 Marriage of Fernando and Isabel in Valladolid unites Castile and Aragón

1474 Death of Enrique IV leads to civil war; Isabel triumphs over Juana la Beltraneja, Enrique's supposed daughter, to become queen

1479 Fernando becomes Fernando II of Aragón

Columbus Arriving in the Americas
The Catholic Monarchs financed Columbus's daring first voyage partly because they hoped for riches in return, but also because they expected him to convert infidels.

Boabdil
As the forlorn king left Granada, his mother reputedly said, "Don't cry as a child over what you could not defend as a man".

Fernando of Aragón

Isabel, queen of Castile, witnesses the surrender of Granada, surrounded by a glittering entourage.

Where to See Gothic Architecture in Spain

Spain has many great Gothic cathedrals, especially in Seville (*pp440–41*), Burgos (*pp376–7*), Barcelona (*pp152–3*), Toledo (*pp396–7*) and Palma de Mallorca (*pp524–5*). Secular buildings from this era include commodity exchanges like La Lonja in Valencia (*p255*) and castles (*pp348–9*).

León cathedral (*pp358–9*) has a west front covered in statuary. Here Christ is seen presiding over the Last Judgment.

Crown of Isabel
Worn at the surrender, Isabel's crown is now in her final resting place, the Capilla Real in Granada (*see p490*).

Cardinal Cisneros

1494 Treaty of Tordesillas divides the New World territories between Portugal and Spain

1496 Foundation of Santo Domingo, on Hispaniola, first Spanish city in the Americas

1509 Cardinal Cisneros' troops attack Oran in Algeria and temporarily occupy it

1490

1500

1510

1492 Fall of Granada after ten-year war. Columbus reaches America. Expulsion of Jews from Spain

1502 Unconverted Moors expelled from Spain

Columbus's ship, the Santa María

1504 Following death of Isabel, her daughter Juana la Loca becomes queen of Castile with Fernando as regent

1516 Death of Fernando

1512 Annexation of Navarra, leading to full unification of Spain

The Age of Discovery

Following Columbus's arrival in the Bahamas in 1492, the conquistadors went into Central and South America, conquering Mexico (1519), Peru (1532) and Chile (1541). In doing so, they destroyed Indian civilizations. In the 16th century, vast quantities of gold and silver flowed across the Atlantic to Spain. Carlos I and his son Felipe II spent some of it on battles to halt the spread of Protestantism in Europe, and in the Holy War against the Turks.

Spanish Empire in 1580
☐ Dominions of Felipe II

Mapping the World
This 16th-century German map reflects a new world, largely unknown to Europe before the era of conquistadors.

Galleons were armed with cannons as a defence against pirates and rival conquerors.

The lookout
was essential for spotting enemies and making landfall.

Aztec Mask
In their great greed and ignorance, the Spanish destroyed the empires and civilizations of the Aztecs in Mexico and the Incas in Peru.

Forecastle

Seville
Granted the trading monopoly with the Americas, Seville, on the banks of the Guadalquivir, was Europe's richest port in the early 16th century.

1519 Magellan, Portuguese explorer, leaves Seville under Spanish patronage to circumnavigate the globe

1520–21 Revolt by Castilian towns when Carlos I appoints foreigner, Adrian of Utrecht, as regent

1532 Pizarro takes Peru with 180 men and destroys Inca Empire

1554 International Catholic alliance created by marriage of future king Felipe II with Mary Tudor of England

Pizarro

| 1520 | 1530 | 1540 | 1550 |

1519 Conquest of Mexico by Cortés. Carlos I crowned Holy Roman Emperor Charles V

Conquistador Hernán Cortés

1540 Father Bartolomé de las Casas writes book denouncing the oppression of Indians

Bartolomé de las Casas

Defeat of the Spanish Armada
Spain's self-esteem suffered a hard blow when its "invincible" 133-ship fleet was destroyed in an attempt to invade Protestant England in 1588.

New World Crops

Not only did Spain profit from the gold and silver brought across the ocean from the Americas, but also from an amazing range of new crops. Some, including potatoes and maize, were introduced for cultivation in Spain, while others, such as tobacco and cacao, were mainly grown in native soil. Cocoa, from cacao beans, gained favour as a drink.

Cacao plant

Peruvian with exotic New World fruit

Armour of Felipe II
Felipe II (1556–98) was a cunning administrator, who claimed to rule the world with paper rather than military might.

Flag of Spain (until 1785)

Storage space for New World treasures

Spanish Galleon

Although sturdily built to carry New World treasure back to Spain, these ships were hard to manoeuvre except with the wind behind. They were often no match for smaller, swifter pirate vessels.

Carlos I (1516–56) During his tumultuous 40-year reign, Carlos I (Holy Roman Emperor Charles V) often led his troops on the battlefield.

1557 First of a series of partial bankruptcies of Spain

1561 Building of El Escorial, near Madrid, begins

El Escorial
(see pp334–5)

1588 Spanish Armada fails in attack on England

1560

1561 Madrid becomes capital of Spain

1568 Moriscos (converted Moors) in the Alpujarras (Granada) rebel against high taxes and persecution

1570

1571 Spanish victory over Turks in naval battle of Lepanto

1569 Bible published for first time in Castilian

1580

1580 Portugal unites with Spain for the next 60 years

1590

The Golden Age

Spain's Golden Age was a time of great artistic and literary achievement led by the painters – El Greco and Velázquez (*see pp36–7*) – and writers (*see pp38–9*), especially Cervantes and the prolific dramatists Lope de Vega and Calderón de la Barca. This brilliance occurred, however, against a background of economic deterioration and ruinous wars with the Low Countries and France. Spain was gradually losing its influence in Europe and the reigning house of Habsburg entered irreversible decline.

The Spanish Empire in Europe in 1647
☐ Spanish territories

Don Quixote and Sancho Panza
Cervantes' satire on chivalrous romance, *Don Quixote*, contrasts the fantasy of the main character with his servant's realism.

A clock is a reminder of the inevitable passage of time.

The knight is dressed in mid-17th-century fashion.

Money represents worldly wealth.

Duke of Lerma
This bronze statue depicts the Duke of Lerma (c.1550–1625), a favourite of King Felipe III.

The Knight's Dream (1650)
This painting, attributed to Antonio de Pereda, is on a familiar Golden Age theme: human vanity. A young gentleman sits asleep beside a table piled with objects symbolizing power, wealth and mortality. The pleasures of life, we are told, are no more real than a dream.

Felipe III

1600 Capital temporarily moves to Valladolid

1609 Felipe III orders the expulsion of the Moriscos

1619 Construction of Plaza Mayor, Madrid

1621 Low Countries war resumes after 12-year truce

1625 Capture of Breda, Netherlands, after one-year siege

1643 Fall of Count-Duke Olivares. Spain heavily defeated by France at Battle of Rocroi

1600	1610	1620	1630	1640

1605 Publication of first of two parts of Cervantes' *Don Quixote*

1609 Lope de Vega publishes poem on the art of comic drama

1622 Velázquez moves from Seville to Madrid to become court painter the following year

Lope de Vega (1562–1635)

1640 Secession of Portugal, amalgamated with Spain since 1580

Fiesta in the Plaza Mayor in Madrid
This famous square *(see p277)* became the scene for pageants, royal celebrations, bullfights and executions, all overlooked from the balconies.

Seville School of Art

Seville's wealth, together with the patronage of the Church, made it a centre of the arts, second only to the royal court. Velázquez, who was born in Seville, trained under the painter Pacheco. Sculptor Juan Martínez Montañés and painters Zurbarán and Murillo created great works which are displayed in the Museo de Bellas Artes *(see p434)*.

San Diego de Alcalá Giving Food to the Poor (c.1646) by Murillo

An angel warns that death is near.

The banner says, "It [death] pierces perpetually, flies quickly and kills".

A mask symbolizes the Arts.

Expulsion of the Moriscos
Although they had converted to Christianity, the last Moors were still expelled in 1609.

Weapons represent power.

The skull on the book shows Death triumphant over Learning.

Surrender of Breda
Spain took the Dutch city of Breda on 5 June 1625 after a year-long siege. The event was later painted by Velázquez.

1652 Spanish troops regain Catalonia, following 12-year war with France

Calderón de la Barca

1669 Calderón de la Barca's last work, *La Estátua de Prometeo*, is published

1683–4 Louis XIV attacks Catalonia and Spanish Netherlands

1650	1660	1670	1680	1690	1700

1648 Holland achieves independence from Spain by Treaty of Westphalia, ending the Thirty Years' War

1659 Peace of the Pyrenees signed with France. Louis XIV marries Felipe IV's daughter María Teresa, leading to Bourbon succession in Spain

Coin from the reign of Felipe IV

1700 Death of Carlos II brings Habsburg line to an end. Felipe V, the first Bourbon king, ascends the throne

Bourbons to First Republic

The War of the Spanish Succession ended in triumph for the Bourbons, who made Spain a centralized nation. Their power was at its height during the reign of the enlightened despot Carlos III. But the 19th century was a troubled time. An invasion by revolutionary France led to the War of Independence (Peninsular War). Later came the Carlist Wars – caused by another dispute over the succession – liberal revolts and the short-lived First Republic.

Spain in 1714
☐ Domain after Treaty of Utrecht

The Enlightenment
The Enlightenment brought new learning and novel projects. On 5 July 1784 this Montgolfier balloon rose above Madrid.

Spanish rebel faces death in a gesture of crucifixion.

A Franciscan friar is among the innocent victims.

Queen María Luisa
The dominating María Luisa of Parma, portrayed by Goya, forced her husband Carlos IV to appoint her lover, Manuel Godoy, prime minister in 1792.

Battle of Trafalgar
The defeat of the Franco-Spanish fleet by the British admiral, Lord Nelson, off Cape Trafalgar in 1805 was the end of Spanish sea power.

Hundreds of lives were taken in the executions, which lasted several days.

1702–14 War of the Spanish Succession. Spain loses Netherlands and Gibraltar by Treaty of Utrecht

1724 Luis I (son of Felipe V) gains throne when his father abdicates, but dies within a year; Felipe V reinstated

1767 Carlos III expels Jesuits from Spain and Spanish colonies

1700	1720	1740	1760	17

1714 Siege and reduction of Barcelona by Felipe V

Felipe V, the first Bourbon king (1700–24)

Count of Floridablanca (1728–1808)

1762–3 British government declares war on Spanish over colonies in America

1782 Count of Floridablanca helps to recover Menorca from Britain

Carlos III Leaving Naples
When Fernando VI died without an heir in 1759, his half-brother Carlos VII of Naples was put on the Spanish throne as Carlos III. His enlightened reign saw the foundation of academies of science and art and the beginning of free trade.

French soldiers, operating on orders from Marshal Murat, execute Spanish patriots.

General Prim (1814–70)
General Prim was one of 19th-century Spain's most influential figures. He forced the abdication of Isabel II, and pursued liberal policies until assassinated in Madrid.

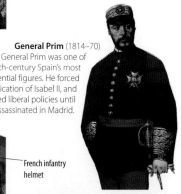

French infantry helmet

The 3rd of May in Madrid by Goya (1814)
On 2 May 1808, in reaction to Napoleon's occupation of Spain, the people of Madrid rose in vain against the occupying French forces. The next day the French army took its revenge by executing hundreds of people, both rebels and bystanders. These events sparked off the War of Independence.

Baroque Magnificence
The sacristy of the Monasterio de la Cartuja in Granada is typical of Spanish Baroque, more sumptuous than anywhere else in Europe.

1805 Battle of Trafalgar. Nelson defeats French and Spanish at sea

1809 Wellington's troops join with Spanish to triumph over French at Talavera

Duke of Wellington

1841–3 María Cristina, followed by General Espartero, acts as regent for Isabel II

1868 Revolution under General Prim forces Isabel II into exile. Amadeo I is king for three years from 1870

| 1800 | 1820 | 1840 | 1860 |

1808–14 Joseph Bonaparte on throne. War of Independence

1812 Promulgation of liberal constitution in Cádiz leads to military uprising

1824 Peru is the last South American country to gain independence

1833–9 First Carlist War

1836 Mendizábal seizes monastic property for the Spanish state

1847–9 Second Carlist War

Carlist soldiers

Republicans and Anarchists

Spain's First Republic lasted only a year (1873) and consumed four presidents. The late 19th century was a time of national decline, with Anarchism developing in reaction to rampant political corruption. The loss of Cuba, in 1898, was a low point for Spain, although there was a flurry of literary and artistic activity in the following years. The country's increasing instability was briefly checked by the dictatorship of Primo de Rivera. Spanish politics, however, were becoming polarized. Alfonso XIII was forced to abdicate and the ill-fated Second Republic was declared in 1931.

The Legacy of Spanish Colonization in 1900
☐ Spanish-speaking territories

Anarchist Propaganda
Anarchism was idealistic, though often violent. This poster states, "Anarchist books are weapons against Fascism".

Workers unite, calling for radical social reform.

Pío Baroja
Baroja (1872–1956) was one of the most gifted novelists of his day. He was too original to be grouped with the writers of the Generation of 1898, who tried to create a national renaissance after the loss of Spain's colonies.

Power to the People

Political protest was rife under the Second Republic, as shown by this Communist demonstration in the Basque Country in 1932. Industrial workers banded together, forming trade unions to demand better pay and working conditions, and staging strikes. The Spanish Communist Party developed later than the Anarchists, but eventually gained more support.

1873
Declaration of First Republic, lasting only one year

First Republic's last president, Emilio Castelar (1832–99)

1888 Universal Exhibition in Barcelona creates new buildings and parks, such as the Parc de la Ciutadella

1897 Prime Minister Cánovas del Castillo assassinated by an Italian Anarchist

| 1870 | 1880 | 1890 | 1900 |

1875 Second Bourbon restoration puts Alfonso XII on throne

Alfonso XII and Queen María

1893 Anarchists bomb opera-goers in the Barcelona Liceu

1898 Cuba and Philippines gain independence from Spain following the Spanish-American War

1870–75 Third Carlist War

Tragic Week
Led by Anarchists and Republicans, workers in Barcelona took to the streets in 1909 to resist a military call-up. The reprisals were brutal.

Universal Exhibitions
In 1929, Seville and Barcelona were transformed by exhibitions promoting art and industry. The fairs brought international recognition.

The banner appeals for working-class solidarity.

Picasso
Born in Málaga in 1881, the artist Pablo Picasso spent his formative years as a painter in the city of Barcelona (see p157) before moving to Paris in the 1930s.

Cuban War of Independence
Cuba began its fight for freedom in 1895, led by local patriots such as Antonio Maceo. In the disastrous campaign, Spain lost 50,000 soldiers and most of its navy.

The Garrotte
Convicted Anarchists were executed by the garrotte – an iron collar that brutally strangled the victim while crushing the neck.

1912 Prime Minister José Canalejas murdered by Anarchists in Madrid

Second Republic election poster

1921 Crushing defeat of Spanish army at Anual, Morocco

1931 Proclamation of Second Republic with a two-year coalition between Socialists and Republicans

1933 General election returns right-wing government

1910	1920	1930

1909 Semana Trágica (Tragic Week) in Barcelona. Workers' revolt against conscription for Moroccan Wars quashed by Government troops

1923 Primo de Rivera stages victorious coup to become military dictator under Alfonso XIII

1930 Primo de Rivera resigns after losing military support

1931 Republicans win local elections, causing Alfonso XIII to abdicate

1934 Revolution of Asturian miners suppressed by army under General Franco

Civil War and the Franco Era

Nationalist generals rose against the government in 1936, starting the Spanish Civil War. The Nationalists, under General Franco, were halted by the Republicans outside Madrid, but with support from Hitler and Mussolini they inched their way to victory in the north and east. Madrid finally fell in early 1939. After the war, thousands of Republicans were executed in reprisals. Spain was internationally isolated until the 1950s, when the United States brought her into the Western military alliance.

Spain on 31 July 1936
☐ Republican-held areas
▨ Nationalist-held areas

Franco's Ideal World
Under Franco, Church and State were united. This poster shows the strong influence of religion on education.

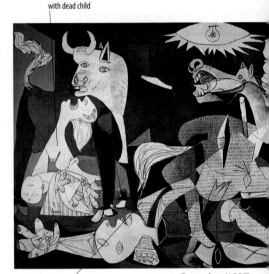

Anguished mother with dead child

Composition reflecting total chaos

Guernica (1937)
On behalf of advancing Nationalists, the Nazi Condor Legion bombed the Basque town of Gernika-Lumo (see pp122–3) on 26 April 1937 – a busy market day. This was Europe's first air raid on civilians, and it inspired Picasso's shocking Guernica *(see p303). Painted for a Republican Government exhibition in Paris, it is full of symbols of disaster.*

Nationalist Poster
A Nationalist poster adorned with Fascist arrows reads "Fight for the Fatherland, Bread and Justice".

1936 Republican Popular Front wins the general election on 16 January. On 17 July, Nationalist generals rise against Republicans

1938 On 8 January, Republicans lose battle for Teruel in bitter cold

1939 In March, Madrid, Valencia and Alicante fall in quick succession to Franco's troops

1945 By end of World War II, Spain is diplomatically and politically isolated

1947 Spain declared monarchy with Franco as regent

| 1935 | 1940 | 1945 | 1950 |

1936 Nationalists declare Franco head of state on 29 September

1937 On 26 April, Nazi planes bomb Basque town of Guernica (Gernika-Lumo)

1939 Franco declares end of war on 1 April and demands unconditional surrender from Republicans

1938 On 23 December, Nationalists bomb Barcelona

1953 Deal with US permits American bases on Spanish soil in exchange for aid

Soldiers surrendering to Nationalist troops

Garcia Lorca

Federico García Lorca (1898–1936) was Spain's most brilliant dramatist and lyric poet of the 1920s and 1930s. His homosexuality and association with the Left, however, made him a target for Nationalist assassins. He was shot by an ad hoc firing squad near his home town of Granada.

Scene from Lorca's play *Blood Wedding*

Anarchist Poster
Anarchists fought for the Republic, forming agricultural collectives behind the lines. Their influence waned when they were discredited by the Communist Party.

A wounded horse representing the Spanish people

Witnesses to the massacre stare in wonder and disbelief.

Crucifixion gesture

The flower is a symbol of hope in the midst of despair.

The Hungry Years
Ration cards illustrate the post-war period when Spain nearly starved. Shunned by other nations, the country received aid from the US in 1953 in return for accepting military bases.

Spanish Refugees
As the Nationalists came closer to victory, thousands of artists, writers, intellectuals and other Republican supporters fled Spain into indefinite exile.

1962 Tourism on the Mediterranean coast is boosted by official go-ahead

Sunbathers

1969 Franco declares Prince Juan Carlos his successor

1973 ETA assassinates Admiral Carrero Blanco, Franco's hard-line prime minister

1955	1960	1965	1970	1975

1959 Founding of ETA, Basque separatist group

1955 Spain joins United Nations

Franco's funeral, 23 November 1975

1970 "Burgos trials" of the regime's opponents outrage world opinion

1975 Death of Franco results in third Bourbon restoration as Juan Carlos is proclaimed king

Modern Spain

Franco's death left Spain's political future hanging in the balance. But few people wanted to preserve the old regime and the transition from dictatorship to democracy proved surprisingly swift and painless. The previously outlawed Socialist Workers' Party, under Felipe González, won the general election in 1982 and set about modernizing Spain. Considerable power has since been devolved to the regions. For many years a major threat facing central government was the persistent violence of ETA, the Basque separatist organization. Spain's international relations have been strengthened by its membership of NATO and the European Union.

Spain Today

▢ Spain

▨ Other European Union states

Coup d'Etat, 23 February 1981
Civil Guard colonel, Antonio Tejero, held parliament at gunpoint for several hours. Democracy survived because King Juan Carlos refused to support the rebels.

Castilla y León's modern pavilion was one of EXPO's 150 pavilions built to innovative designs.

Hi-tech floodlight

Anti-NATO Protest Rally
When Spain joined NATO in 1982, some saw it as a reversal of Socialist ideals. To others it represented an improvement in Spain's international standing.

Expo '92
Over 100 countries were represented at the Universal Exposition, which focused world attention on Seville in 1992. The many pavilions displayed scientific, technological and cultural exhibits.

Spanish royal family

1981 Military officers stage attempted coup d'etat to overthrow democracy

1983 Semi-autonomous regional governments are established to appease Basque Country and Catalonia

1992 Barcelona Olympics and Seville Expo '92 place Spain firmly within community of modern European nations

1998 ETA, the Basque separatist terrorist group, announces a ceasefire that lasts a year

1980	1985	1990	1995

1977 First free elections return centrist ovemment under Adolfo Suárez. Political parties, including Communists, are legalized

1982 Landslide electoral victory brings Socialist Workers' Party (PSOE), under Felipe González, to power. Football World Cup held in Spain

1986 Spain joins EC (now EU) and NATO

1992 Spain celebrates quincentenary of Columbus's voyage to America

1994/5 Corruption scandals rock the long-serving government

1996 In the gen election on 3 M González loses t coalition led by

Tourism
From 1959 to 1973 the number of annual visitors to Spain grew from 3 million to 34 million, transforming once-quiet coasts and islands.

Felipe González Elected
In 1982 the Spanish Socialist Workers' Party (PSOE) leader was elected prime minister. González transformed Spain during his 13 years in power.

Leaning blue tower rises above Andalusia's pavilion.

Ana Belén
Spanish women enjoyed much greater freedom and opportunity upon the advent of democracy. In a 1980s opinion poll, they voted the singer and actress Ana Belén the woman they most admired.

El País
Founded in Madrid in 1976, the liberal daily *El País* is the best-selling newspaper in Spain. During the transition to democracy it had a great influence on public opinion.

A monorail carried visitors around the site.

Barcelona Olympic Games
The opening ceremony of the Barcelona Olympics included stunning displays of music, dance and colourful costumes.

...bi, Barcelona ...ympic Mascot

2004 José Luis Rodríguez Zapatero of the Spanish Socialist Party comes into power on 14 March

2008 José Luis Rodríguez Zapatero of the Spanish Socialist Party is re-elected on 9 March

2011 Mariano Rajoy of the Popular Party comes into power on 20 November

Mariano Rajoy

2005	2010	2015	2020

...Spain celebrates ...rs of democracy ...ign of Juan Carlos I

2004 Madrid is hit by the worst terrorist attacks in Spain's modern history in March. Bombs detonated on the city's trains killed 191 people

2014 King Juan Carlos I abdicates in favour of his son, Felipe VI

2011 ETA announces a permanent ceasefire

Rulers of Spain

Spain became a nation-state under Isabel and Fernando, whose marriage eventually united Castile and Aragón. With their daughter Juana's marriage, the kingdom was delivered into Habsburg hands. Carlos I and Felipe II were both capable rulers, but in 1700 Carlos II died without leaving an heir. After the War of the Spanish Succession, Spain came under the French Bourbons, who have ruled ever since – apart from an interregnum, two republics and Franco's dictatorship. The current Bourbon king, Felipe VI, a constitutional monarch, is respected for his social work and his support of democracy.

1665–1700 Carlos II

1479–1516 Fernando, King of Aragón

1474–1504 Isabel, Queen of Castile

1516–56 Carlos I of Spain (Holy Roman Emperor Charles V)

1598–1621 Felipe III

1400	1475	1550	1625
Independent Kingdoms		**Habsburg Dynasty**	
1400	1475	1550	1625

1469 Marriage of Isabel and Fernando leads to unification of Spain

1504–16 Juana la Loca (with Fernando as regent)

1621–65 Felipe IV

Fernando and Isabel, the Catholic Monarchs

Unification of Spain

In the late 15th century the two largest kingdoms in developing Christian Spain – Castile, with its military might, and Aragón (including Barcelona and a Mediterranean empire) – were united. The marriage of Isabel of Castile and Fernando of Aragón in 1469 joined these powerful kingdoms. Together the so-called Catholic Monarchs defeated the Nasrid Kingdom of Granada, the last stronghold of the Moors (see pp60–61). With the addition of Navarra in 1512, Spain was finally unified.

1700–24 Felipe

1556–98 Felipe II

1843–68 Isabel II reigns, following the regency of her mother María Cristina (1833–41) and General Espartero (1841–3)

1724 Luis I reigns after Felipe V's abdication, but dies within a year

1871–3 Break in Bourbon rule: Amadeo I of Savoy

1939–75 General Franco Head of State

1814–33 First Bourbon restoration, following French rule: Fernando VII

1931–9 Second Republic

2014 Felipe VI

1759–88 Carlos III

1875–85 Second Bourbon restoration: Alfonso XII

| '00 | 1775 | 1850 | 1925 | 2000 |

Bourbon Dynasty | Bourbon | Bourbon

| '00 | 1775 | 1850 | 1925 | 2000 |

1808–13 Break in Bourbon rule: Napoleon's brother, Joseph Bonaparte, rules as José I

1746–59 Fernando VI

1724–46 Felipe V reinstated as king upon the death of his son, Luis I

1902–31 Alfonso XIII

1886–1902 María Cristina of Habsburg-Lorraine as regent for Alfonso XIII

1788–1808 Carlos IV

1873–4 First Republic

1868–70 The Septembrina Revolution

1975–2014 Third Bourbon restoration: Juan Carlos I

NORTHERN
SPAIN

Introducing Northern Spain   **78–87**

Galicia   **88–103**

Asturias and Cantabria   **104–117**

The Basque Country, Navarra
  and La Rioja   **118–139**

Introducing Northern Spain

Increasing numbers of visitors are discovering the quiet, sandy beaches and deep green landscapes of Northern Spain. The Atlantic coast, from the Pyrenees to the Portuguese border, is often scenic but at its most attractive in the cliffs and *rías* of Galicia. Inland, the mild, wet climate has created lush meadows and broad-leaved forests, making this area ideal for a peaceful, rural holiday. The famous medieval pilgrimage route to the city of Santiago de Compostela crosses Northern Spain, its way marked by magnificent examples of Romanesque architecture. Plentiful seafood and dairy produce, and the outstanding red wines of La Rioja, add to the pleasure of a tour through this part of Spain.

Oviedo *(see pp110–11)* has a number of Pre-Romanesque churches, most notably the graceful Santa María del Naranco, and a fine Gothic cathedral.

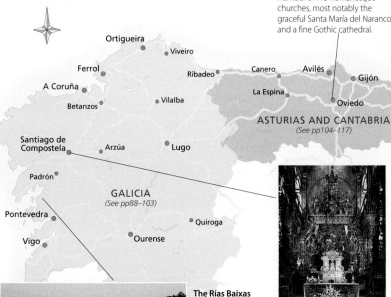

Ortigueira

Viveiro

Ferrol

Ribadeo

Canero   Avilés

A Coruña

La Espina   Gijón

Betanzos   Vilalba

Oviedo

ASTURIAS AND CANTABRIA
(See pp104–117)

Santiago de Compostela   Arzúa   Lugo

Padrón

GALICIA
(See pp88–103)

Pontevedra

Quiroga

Vigo   Ourense

Santiago de Compostela
(see pp94–5) attracts thousands of pilgrims and tourists each year. Its majestic cathedral was one of the most important shrines in medieval Christendom.

The Rías Baixas
(see p99) is one of Spain's prettiest coastlines. Scattered around its pretty towns and villages are many quaint *hórreos*, grain stores, raised on stone stilts.

| 0 kilometres | 50 |
| 0 miles | 50 |

The Picos de Europa mountain range *(see pp112–13)* dominates the landscape of Asturias and Cantabria. Rivers have carved deep gorges through the mountains and there are many footpaths through a variety of spectacular scenery.

◀ Fog-covered Asturias at dawn

Santillana del Mar
(see p116), with its well-preserved medieval streets, is one of the most picturesque towns in Spain. The Convento de Regina Coeli houses a small museum containing a collection of painted wooden figures and other works of religious art.

San Sebastián *(see p126)*, the most elegant holiday resort in the Basque Country, is sited around a beautiful horseshoe bay of golden sandy beaches. The city hosts international arts events, including Spain's premier film festival.

nes
Panes
Santander
Laredo
Torrelavega
Bilbao
San Sebastián
Eibar
Andoain
Llodio
Zumárraga
Reinosa
Corconte
Vitoria
(Gasteiz)
THE BASQUE COUNTRY,
NAVARRA AND
LA RIOJA
(See pp118–39)
Pamplona
Miranda de Ebro
Logroño
Calahorra
Torrecilla
en Cameros
Tudela

Pamplona *(see pp136–7)*, the capital of Navarra since the 9th century, is best known for its annual fiesta, Los Sanfermines. The highlight of each day of riotous celebration is the *encierro*, in which bulls stampede through the streets of the city.

The Monasterio de Leyre *(see p139)*, founded in the early 11th century, was built in a lonely but attractive landscape. The monastery was once the burial place of the kings of Navarra and its crypt is among the finest examples of early Romanesque art in Spain.

The Flavours of Northern Spain

The wild, wet north of Spain is as famous for its rain as it is for its culinary excellence. The rain keeps the pastures lush and green – perfect dairy farming terrain – and the Atlantic provides an incredible variety of seafood. The Basques, in particular, are celebrated chefs, and the region boasts some of the finest restaurants in Europe, along with gastronomic societies (called *txokos*) in every village. Inland and in the remoter regions you'll find old-fashioned country cooking – roast lamb and tender young beef, slow-cooked stews – and traditionally made cheeses.

Idiazábal cheese

Pulpo a la gallega, Galicia's signature dish

Galicia

The westernmost tip of Spain, battered by the Atlantic into a series of plunging *rías*, is famous for its wealth of seafood – from staples like dried and salted cod *(bacalao)* to unusual delicacies like barnacles *(percebes)*, which look like tiny dinosaur feet. Every bar will serve up a plate of *pulpo a la gallega* or a dish of *pimientos del Padrón* (one in

every dozen has a spicy kick). Inland, you'll find tender veal, free-range chicken and delicate soft cheeses such as delicious *tetilla*.

Asturias and Cantabria

The bay-pocked coastline provides delicious fresh fish, often served simply grilled (try the fabulous sardines offered in almost every port) or slowly simmered in casseroles. Inland,

the lush green pastures form Spain's dairy country – most Spanish milk, cream and some of its finest cheeses come from this region. Try Asturian Cabrales, a pungent blue cheese, best accompanied by a glass of local cider. The mountains provide succulent meat and game, often traditionally stewed with beans, as in the celebrated Asturian dish of *fabada*.

Fish and seafood from the waters of Northern Spain

Clams · Red mullet · Mackerel · Oysters · Elvers · Baby octo[pus]

Regional Dishes and Specialities

Unsurprisingly, seafood rules supreme along the coastline, from the ubiquitous octopus in a piquant sauce served in Galicia, to the extraordinary spider crabs, which are a sought-after delicacy in the Basque Lands. The verdant pastures and rich farmland provide a wealth of fresh vegetables, including Navarra's justly famous asparagus, along with all kinds of wonderful cheeses. Slow-cooked stews, an Asturian speciality, are particularly good in the mountains, along with tender lamb and outstanding game in season. The renowned wines from La Rioja are excellent, but those of adjoining Navarra are less pricey and often equally interesting. The crisp whites of Galicia and the Basque Lands are the perfect accompaniment to the fresh seafood, and throughout the north you'll find powerful liqueurs flavoured with local herbs.

Cherries

Bacalao al Pil Pil Salted cod is slowly cooked with olive oil, chilli and garlic to create this classic Basque dish.

Array of *pintxos* laid out in a bar in the Basque Country

Basque Country

The Basque Country is a paradise for gourmets, renowned throughout Spain for the excellence of its natural produce and the creative brilliance of its chefs. Basque cuisine leans towards seafood, of which there is a dazzling variety: humble salted cod and hake (made extraordinary with delicious sauces) are most common, but sought-after delicacies include elvers (baby eels) and spider crab. Basque wines, drunk young and tart, are the perfect counterpoint. Bar counters groan with platters of *pintxos* (crusty bread with gourmet toppings), each one of them a miniature work of art, and the Basques also make wonderful cheeses, including delicate, smoky Idiazábal.

Navarra and La Rioja

The fertile farmland of landlocked Navarra produces a spectacular array of fruit and vegetables such as asparagus, artichokes, cherries, chestnuts and peppers (often hung in pretty strings to dry and used

Red peppers strung up to dry in the sun outside a house

to flavour *embutidos*, or cured meats). In the Navarrese mountains, lamb is the most popular meat and you will find *cordero al chilindrón* (lamb stew) featuring on almost every menu. In season, you'll also find richly flavoured game, including partridge, hare and pheasant.

Tiny La Rioja is Spain's most famous wine region, producing rich, oaky reds and whites *(see pp82–3)*. The cuisine of La Rioja borrows from the neighbouring Basque Country and Navarra, with lamb featuring heavily, along with seafood and top-quality local vegetables.

On the Menu

Angulas a la Bilbaína Baby eels cooked in olive oil with garlic – a Basque delicacy.

Cocido Montañés Cantabrian stew of pork, spicy sausage, vegetables – and a pig's ear.

Fabada Asturiana Asturian beans stewed with cured meats and pork.

Pimientos del Padrón A *Gallego* dish of green peppers fried in olive oil with rock salt.

Pulpo a la Gallega Octopus, cooked until tender in a spicy paprika sauce.

Trucha a la Navarra Trout, stuffed with ham and quickly grilled or fried.

Empanada Gallega The perfect picnic snack, these golden pastries are stuffed with all kinds of fillings.

Chilindrón de Cordero A rich, hearty stew from the mountains of Navarra, this is made with succulent lamb.

Leche Frita "Fried milk" is a scrumptious, custardy dessert from Cantabria. Simple but utterly delicious.

Wines of Northern Spain

Spain's most renowned wine region, La Rioja, is best known for its red wines, matured to a distinctive vanilla mellowness. Some of the most prestigious bodegas were founded by émigrés from Bordeaux, and Rioja reds are similar to claret. La Rioja also produces good white and rosé wines. Navarra reds and some whites have improved dramatically, thanks to a government research programme. The Basque region produces a tiny amount of the tart *txakoli* (*chacolí*). Larger quantities of a similar wine are made further west in Galicia, whose best wines are full-bodied whites, particularly from the Albariño grape.

Repairing barrels in Haro, La Rioja

Ribeiro, a popular wine of Galicia, is slightly fizzy. It is often served in white porcelain bowls (*cuencos*).

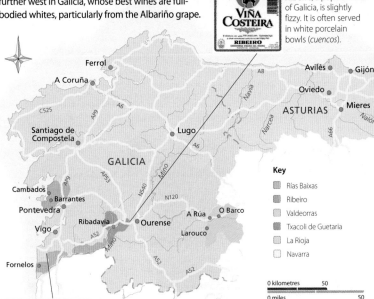

Key
- Rías Baixas
- Ribeiro
- Valdeorras
- Txacoli de Guetaria
- La Rioja
- Navarra

0 kilometres 50
0 miles 50

Lagar de Cervera is from Rías Baixas, a region known for producing Spain's most fashionable white wines.

Wine village of El Villar de Álava in Rioja Alta

Wine Regions

The wine regions of Northern Spain are widely dispersed. Cradled between the Pyrenees and the Atlantic are the important regions of Rioja and Navarra. Wines from La Rioja are divided into the DOs (denominations of origin) of Rioja Alavesa, Rioja Alta and Rioja Baja, divided by the Río Ebro. The river also cuts through the wine region of Navarra. To the north are some of the vineyards of the Basque Country: the minuscule Txakoli de Guetaria region. In the far west lie the four wine regions of rugged, wet Galicia: Rías Baixas, Ribeiro, Valdeorras and Ribeira Sacra.

Gathering the grape harvest in the traditional way in Navarra

Remelluri, one of the single-estate "Château" Riojas, from the vineyards of Rioja Alavesa, is soft and not too oaky.

Chivite, from a family bodega in Navarra, is made entirely from Tempranillo and aged in the barrel, resulting in a style similar to Rioja.

Viña Ardanza
is blended, as are most red Riojas. The best, like this reserva, are aged for two or more years in American oak casks.

Key Facts about Wines of Northern Spain

 La Rioja and Navarra are influenced by both Mediterranean and Atlantic weather systems. The hillier, northwestern parts receive some Atlantic rain, while the hot Ebro plain has a Mediterranean climate. The Basque region and Galicia are both cool, Atlantic regions with high rainfall. Soils everywhere are stony and poor, except in the Ebro plain.

Grape Varieties

The great red grape of La Rioja and Navarra is Tempranillo. In Rioja it is blended with smaller quantities of Garnacha, Graciano and Mazuelo, while in Navarra Cabernet Sauvignon is permitted and blends well with Tempranillo. Garnacha, also important in Navarra, is used for the excellent *rosados* (rosés). Whites of Navarra and Rioja are made mainly from the Viura grape. Galicia has many local varieties, such as Albariño, Godello, Loureira and Treixadura.

Good Producers

Rías Baixas: Fillaboa, Palacio de Fefiñanes, Terras Gauda, Santiago Ruiz. *Ribeiro:* Viña Costeira. *La Rioja:* Baigorri, Bodegas Riojanas (Canchales, Monte Real), CVNE (Imperial, Viña Real Oro), Marqués de Cáceres, Marqués de Murrieta, Marqués de Riscal, Martínez Bujanda, Remelluri, La Rioja Alta (Barón de Oña). *Navarra:* Bodega de Sarría, Guelbenzu, Julián Chivite (Gran Feudo), Magaña, Ochoa, Príncipe de Viana.

Forests of the North

Much of Spain was once blanketed by a mantle of trees. Today, just ten per cent of the original cover remains, mostly in the mountainous north, where rainfall is high and slopes too steep for cultivation. Large areas of mixed deciduous forest – mainly beech, Pyrenean oak and chestnut, with some ash and lime – dominate the landscape, particularly in Cantabria and the Basque Country. The undergrowth of shrubs and flowering plants provides habitats for many insects, mammals and birds. The forests are also the refuge of Spain's last brown bears (see p108).

Forest in Northern Spain in autumn

Regeneration of the forest

Dead materials – leaves, twigs and the excrement and bodies of animals – are broken down by various organisms on the forest floor, especially fungi, bacteria and ants. This process releases nutrients which are absorbed by trees and other plants, enabling them to grow.

Fly agaric mushrooms

Lichens grow slowly and are sensitive to pollution. Their presence in a forest often indicates that it is in good health.

The stag beetle takes its name from the huge antler-like mandibles of the male. Despite their ferocious appearance, these beetles are harmless to humans.

Millipede and fungus on a woodland floor

Beech Forest

Beech leaf and mast

Beech, the dominant species in the Cantabrian mountains and Pyrenees, grows on well-drained soils. Some trees retain their distinctive copper-red leaves through the winter. Beech mast (nuts) are collected to feed to pigs.

The thick crown shuts out light, inhibiting undergrowth.

Long, thin orange buds

Male golden orioles, among the most colourful European birds, are hard to spot because they spend much of their time in the thick cover provided by old woodlands. Females and juveniles are a duller yellow-green with a brownish tail.

Beech martens are nocturnal. By day, they sleep in a hollow tree or another animal's abandoned nest. At night they feed on fruit, birds and small mammals.

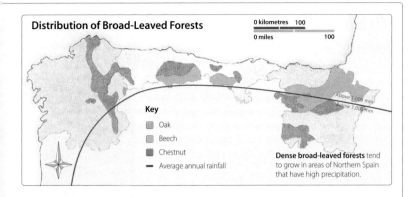

Distribution of Broad-Leaved Forests

0 kilometres 100
0 miles 100

Key
- Oak
- Beech
- Chestnut
- Average annual rainfall

Above 1,000 mm
Below 1,000 mm

Dense broad-leaved forests tend to grow in areas of Northern Spain that have high precipitation.

Chestnut Forest

Leaf and chestnut

Chestnut trees grow on well-drained acidic soils. They have slender yellow flowers and in summer produce their fruit, which is eaten by wild boar, dormice, squirrels and mice. The wood is hard and durable but splits easily.

Oak Forest

Oak leaf and acorn

Three main species of oak tree – pedunculate, Pyrenean and the evergreen holm oak – dominate the ancient woodlands of the north. Over 300 species of animal, such as wild boar, squirrels and nuthatches, feed off oaks.

Large leaves have sharp, serrated edges.

Few massive, spreading branches

Grey twigs ending in numerous buds

Deep spiral ridges on trunk

The pipistrelle bat is a nocturnal species common in woodlands. It catches and eats small insects in flight. Larger insects are taken to a perch. The bat hibernates in winter in a hollow tree or cave.

The jay, a member of the crow family, is a common but somewhat shy woodland bird with a distinctively raucous cry. It can be identified in flight by its white rump, black tail and above all by its bright-blue wing patch.

Blue tits feed mainly in the tree canopy of broad-leaved woods and rarely come down to the ground. The male and female have similar, distinctive plumage. They may raise the back feathers of the crown if alarmed.

Red squirrels bury large numbers of acorns during autumn to last through winter, since these diurnal creatures do not hibernate. Many of the acorns are left to sprout into seedlings.

The Road to Santiago

According to legend the body of Christ's apostle James was brought to Galicia. In AD 813 the relics were supposedly discovered at Santiago de Compostela, where a cathedral was built in his honour *(see pp96–7)*. In the Middle Ages half a million pilgrims a year flocked there from all over Europe, crossing the Pyrenees at Roncesvalles *(see p138)* or via the Somport Pass *(see p234)*. They often donned the traditional garb of cape, long staff and curling felt hat adorned with scallop shells, the symbol of the saint. The various routes, marked by the cathedrals, churches and hospitals built along them, are still used by travellers today.

19th-century painting of the Pórtico da Gloria of Santiago Cathedral

Astorga *(see p356),* once a Roman city, was an important halt on the pilgrim route in the Middle Ages. The museum within its cathedral has a collection of gold and silver plate including a 13th-century gold filigree cross.

A certificate is given to pilgrims covering 100 km (62 miles) of the route on foot, or 200 km (125 miles) on horseback.

O Cebreiro *(see p103)* has a 9th-century church and some of the ancient *pallozas* the pilgrims often used for shelter.

León was one of the main pilgrim stops. Its cathedral *(see pp358–9)* contains one of Spain's finest collections of stained glass.

Ribadeo

Oviedo

A Coruña

Maritime Route

Vilar de Donas

Santiago de Compostela

Ligonde

Portuguese Route

↓ Porto Lisboa

Vigo • • Tui

Silver Route

O Cebreiro

Villafranca del Bierzo

Ponferrada's huge Templar castle stands close to the town centre *(see p355).*

Ponferrada

Astorga

Hospital de Órbigo

León

Sahagún

Salamanca

0 kilometres   50
0 miles   50

Romanesque Church Architecture

Carved capital

The Romanesque style of architecture *(see p28)* was brought to Spain from France during the 10th and 11th centuries. As the pilgrimage to Santiago became more popular, many glorious religious buildings were constructed along its main routes. Massive walls, few windows, round heavy arches and barrel vaulting are typical features of Romanesque architecture.

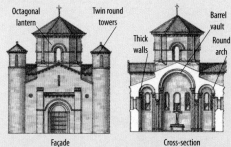

Octagonal lantern

Twin round towers

Façade

Barrel vault

Thick walls

Round arch

Cross-section

San Martín de Frómista *(see p372)*, built in the 11th century, is the only complete example of the "pilgrimage" style of Romanesque. The nave and aisles are almost the same height and there are three parallel apses.

Parallel apses

Nave

Aisle

Floorplan

Pamplona's *(see pp136–7)* Gothic cathedral was one of the pilgrims' first stops after crossing the Pyrenees at Roncesvalles.

Santo Domingo de la Calzada's *(see p132)* pilgrim hospital is now a parador.

Puente la Reina (see p135) *takes its name from the 11th-century humpbacked bridge (puente), built for pilgrims and still used by pedestrians.*

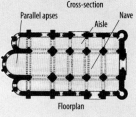

Frómista preserves one of the finest Romanesque churches on the French route.

Santander

San Sebastián (Donostia)

↗ Paris

Northern Route

Bilbo (Bilbao)

Orreaga (Roncesvalles)

Valcarlos

↗ Le Puy Vézelay

↗ Arles

Iruña (Pamplona)

Aragonese Route

Lizarra (Estella)

Puente la Reina

Sangüesa

Jaca

San Juan de Ortega

Nájera

French Route

Logroño

San Juan de la Peña

Frómista

Burgos

Santo Domingo de la Calzada

Routes to Santiago

Several traditional pilgrimage roads converge on Santiago de Compostela. The main road from the Pyrenees is known as the French Route, with the Aragonese Route as a variation.

Burgos has a magnificent Gothic cathedral *(see pp376–7)*.

GALICIA

Lugo · A Coruña · Pontevedra · Ourense

Remote in the northwest corner of the peninsula, Galicia is the country's greenest region. In its hilly interior, smallholdings are farmed by traditional methods. Galicia is Spain's main seafaring region – three of its four provinces have an Atlantic coastline, and its cuisine is based on superb seafood. The Galicians, whose origins are Celtic, are fiercely proud of their culture and language.

Much of Galicia still has a medieval quality. Some inland farms are divided into plots too tiny or steep for tractors to work, so oxen and horses are used for ploughing. Grain is stored in quaint, pillared granaries called *hórreos*. The misty, emerald countryside abounds with old granite villages and is dotted with *pazos* – traditional stone manor houses.

The discovery of the supposed tomb of St James the Apostle, in the 9th century, confirmed medieval Santiago de Compostela as Europe's most important religious shrine after St Peter's in Rome. Pilgrims and tourists still follow this ancient route of pilgrimage across Northern Spain. The Galician coast is incised by many fjord-like rías; the loveliest of these are the Rías Baixas in the west. Elsewhere it juts defiantly into the Atlantic in rocky headlands, such as Cabo Fisterra, Spain's most westerly point. Many people still make a living from the sea. Vigo in Pontevedra is the most important fishing port in Spain.

Galicia's official language, used on most signs, is *Gallego*. It has similarities to the language of Portugal, which borders Galicia to the south. The Celtic character of this haunting land is still evident in the Galicians' favourite traditional instrument, the bagpipes.

Staple crops – maize, cabbages and potatoes – growing on the harsh land around Cabo Fisterra

◀ Grand spiral staircase in the Convento de San Domingos de Bonaval, Santiago de Compostela

Exploring Galicia

Santiago de Compostela is Galicia's major tourist attraction. This beautiful city is the centrepiece of a region with many fine old towns, especially Betanzos, Mondoñedo, Lugo and Pontevedra. The resorts along the coastline of the wild Rías Altas, with their backdrop of forest-covered hills, offer good bathing. The Rías Baixas, the southern part of Galicia's west coast, has sheltered coves and sandy beaches, and excellent seafood in abundance. Travelling through the interior, where life seems to have changed little in centuries, is an ideal way to spend a peaceful, rural holiday.

Musicians dressed in traditional costumes playing in Pontevedra

Sights at a Glance

1. Rías Altas
2. Mondoñedo
3. Betanzos
4. A Coruña
5. Costa da Morte
6. Santiago de Compostela
   pp94–7
7. Padrón
8. A Toxa
9. Pontevedra
10. Vigo
11. Baiona
12. A Guarda
13. Tui
14. Celanova
15. Verín
16. Ourense
17. Monasterio de Ribas de Sil
18. Monasterio de Oseira
19. Vilar de Donas
20. Lugo
21. O Cebreiro

The isolated monastery at Ribas de Sil

0 kilometres   25

0 miles   15

Getting Around

The region's main airports are at A Coruña, Santiago de Compostela and Vigo. A network of motorways connects Verín, Vigo, A Coruña and O Cebreiro, but traffic along the coast can be heavy. Rail lines link Galicia's major cities, and towns along the north coast are served by the RENFE line *(see p629)*. Coach services run between the major cities.

Cabo Ortegal

RÍAS ALTAS

①

n Andrés e Teixido

deira

Ortigueira

O Barqueiro

Cervo

LU862

Viveiro

Burela

AC116

Ferreira

Foz

Oviedo

N634

Ribadeo

Jarón

AG64

Vegadeo

Fene

51

As Pontes de García Rodríguez

A8

Pontedeume

Cabreiros

🏛🏯 ② **MONDOÑEDO**

Porto da Xesta 590m

A Pontenova

Embalse do Eume

Vilalba

N634

N640

BETANZOS

🏯

Miño

Meira

A6

Baamonde

Eo

NVI

A Fonsagrada

Guitiriz

Rábade

Curtis-Estación

Monasterio Sobrado Los Monjes

Friol

LUGO ⑳ 🏯🏯🏛

Navia de Suarna

rzúa

Nadela

Melide

⑲ **VILAR DE DONAS**

O Corgo

Guntín

NVI

Becerreá

Palas de Rei

G A L I C I A

A Golada

Sarria

Samos

Pedrafita do Cebreiro

N540

A6

N640

Embalse de Belesar

🏯🏛 ㉑

Lalín

O CEBREIRO

O Castro

Chantada

Ponferrada León

🏯 ⑱ **MONASTERIO DE OSEIRA**

Monforte de Lemos

N525

N120

Quiroga

Brués

⑰ **MONASTERIO DE RIBAS DE SIL**

O Barco

N120

Carballiño

AG53

A Rúa

Castro Caldelas

🏛🏯 ⑯ **OURENSE**

Puebla de Trives

Ribadavia

Embalse de Prada

ortegada

N525

Bidei

A Veiga

LANOVA ⑭

Allariz

Viana do Bolo

🏯

Vilar de Barrio

Bande

Xinxo de Limia

Embalse das Portas

A Gudiña

Limia

A52

Valladolid

Monterrei

N525

⑮ **VERÍN**

P O R T U G A L

↓ *Vila Real*

Calvary in Pontevedra's Praza de la Herrería

Key

━━ Motorway

= = Motorway under construction

━━ Major road

═══ Minor road

━━ Scenic route

▬▬ Main railway

---- Minor railway

▬▬ International border

▬▬ Regional border

For additional map symbols *see back flap*

Carved coat of arms on a housefront in Mondoñedo

❶ Rías Altas

Lugo & A Coruña. 🚉 Ribadeo.
🚌 Viveiro. 🛈 Foz, 982 13 24 26.
🗓 Tue.

Deep *rías* are interspersed with coves and headlands along the beautiful north coast from Ribadeo to A Coruña. Inland are hills covered with forests of pine and eucalyptus. Many of the small resorts and fishing villages are charming.

The lovely, winding **Ría de Ribadeo** forms the border with Asturias. To the west of it is the small fishing port of **Foz**, which has two good beaches. Nearby, the 10th-century Iglesia de San Martín de Mondoñedo, standing alone on a hill, contains carvings of biblical scenes on its transept capitals – note the story of Lazarus. **Viveiro**, a summer holiday resort 35 km (22 miles) away, is a handsome old town surrounded by Renaissance walls and gateways, typically Galician glassed-in balconies or *galerías*, and a Romanesque church. Near the pretty fishing village of O Barqueiro is the headland of Estaca de Bares, with its lighthouse and wind turbines.

Westward along the coast, the lovely **Ría de Ortigueira** leads to the fishing port of the same name, characterized by neat white houses. Around this area there are also many wild and unspoiled beaches.

High cliffs rise out of the sea near the village of **San Andrés de Teixido**, whose church is the focal point for pilgrims on 8 September. According to legend, those who fail to visit the church in their lifetime will come back to it as an animal in the afterlife. The village of **Cedeira**, which sits on a quiet bay, is a rich summer resort with neat lawns, modern houses with *galerías*, and a long, curving beach.

❷ Mondoñedo

Lugo. 🗺 4,000. 🚌 🛈 Plaza de la Catedral 34, 982 50 71 77. 🗓 Thu.
🗓 As Quendas (1 May), Nuestra Señora de los Remedios (2nd Sun in Sep), San Lucas (18 Oct).

This delightful town is set in a fertile inland valley. Stately houses with carved coats of arms and *galerías* are in the main square. This is dominated by the **cathedral**, a building of golden stone with a Romanesque portal, a 16th-century stained-glass rose window, 17th-century cloisters and 18th-century Baroque towers. A statue in a chapel in the cathedral, Nuestra Señora la Inglesa, was rescued from St Paul's Cathedral in London. The **Museo Diocesano**, entered through the cathedral, contains works by Zurbarán and El Greco.

🏛 Museo Diocesano
Plaza de la Catedral. **Tel** 982 52 10 06.
Open 11am–2pm, 4–7pm daily. 🗓

❸ Betanzos

A Coruña. 🗺 13,500. 🚉 🚌 🛈 Plaza de Galicia 1, 981 77 66 66. 🗓 Tue, Thu & Sat. 🗓 San Roque (14–25 Aug).

The handsome town of Betanzos lies in a fertile valley slightly inland. Its broad main square has a replica of the Fountain of Diana at Versailles. In its steep narrow streets are fine old houses and Gothic churches. The **Iglesia de Santiago**, built in the 15th century by the tailors' guild, has a statue of St James on horseback above the door. The **Iglesia de San Francisco**, dated 1387, has statues of wild boars and a heraldic emblem of Knight Fernán Pérez de Andrade, whose 14th-century tomb is inside the church. For centuries his family were the overlords of the region.

Environs
20 km (12 miles) north is the large, though pretty, fishing village of **Pontedeume**, with its narrow, hilly streets. Its medieval bridge still carries the main road to the large industrial town of **Ferrol**, to the north. Originally a medieval port, Ferrol became an important naval base and dockyard town in the 18th century, and its Neo-Classical buildings survive from that time. General Franco *(see pp70–71)* was born in Ferrol in 1892.

Ornate tomb in the Iglesia de San Francisco in Betanzos

Pavement cafés in Betanzos' Plaza de García Hermanos

For hotels and restaurants in this region see p562 and pp582–3

Stone cross standing above the perilous waters of the Costa da Morte

❹ A Coruña

A Coruña. 246,000.
🛈 Plaza de María Pita, 981 92 30 93.
📷 Fiestas de María Pita (Aug).
🌐 **turismocoruna.com**

This proud city and busy port has played a sizable role in Spanish maritime history. Felipe II's doomed Armada sailed from here to England in 1588 (see p63). Today, the sprawling industrial suburbs contrast with the elegant town centre, which is laid out on an isthmus leading to a headland. The **Torre de Hércules**, Europe's oldest working lighthouse, is a famous local landmark. Built by the Romans and rebuilt in the 18th century, it still flashes across the deep. Climb its 242 steps for a wide ocean view.

On the large, arcaded Plaza de María Pita, the city's main square, is the handsome town hall. The sea promenade of **La Marina** is lined with tiers of glass-enclosed balconies or galerías. Built as protection against the strong winds, they explain why A Coruña is often referred to as the City of Glass. The peaceful, tiny Plazuela da las Bárbaras is enchanting.

A Coruña has several fine Romanesque churches, such as the **Iglesia de Santiago**, with a carving of its saint on horseback situated beneath the tympanum, and the **Iglesia de Santa María**. This church, featuring a tympanum carved with the Adoration of the Magi, is one of the best-preserved 12th-century buildings in Galicia.

The quiet Jardín de San Carlos contains the tomb of the Scottish general Sir John Moore, who was killed in 1809 as the British army evacuated the port during Spain's War of Independence from France (see p67).

The lofty Torre de Hércules lighthouse at A Coruña

❺ Costa da Morte

A Coruña. 🚌 A Coruña, Malpica.
🛈 Plaza de María Pita, A Coruña, 981 92 30 93. 📷 Fiesta de la Virgen del Carmen (16 Jul).
🌐 **turismocostadamorte.com**

From Malpica to Fisterra the coast is wild and remote. It is called the "Coast of Death" because of the many ships lost in storms or smashed on the rocks by gales over the centuries. The headlands are majestic. There are no coastal towns, only simple villages, where fishermen gather gastronomic percebes (barnacles), destined for the region's restaurants.

One of the most northerly points of the Costa da Morte, **Malpica**, has a picturesque fishing port. Laxe has good beaches and safe bathing. **Camariñas**, one of the most appealing places on this coast, is a fishing village where women make bobbin-lace in the streets. Beside the lighthouse on nearby Cabo Vilán, a group of futuristic wind turbines, tall and slender, swirl in graceful unison – a haunting sight.

To the south is Corcubión, exuding a faded elegance, and lastly, **Cabo Fisterra** "where the land ends". This cape, with its lighthouse, is a good place to watch the sun go down over the Atlantic.

❻ Street-by-Street: Santiago de Compostela

In the Middle Ages Santiago de Compostela was Christendom's third most important place of pilgrimage *(see pp86–7)*, after Jerusalem and Rome. Around the Praza do Obradoiro is an ensemble of historic buildings that has few equals in Europe. The local granite gives a harmonious unity to the mixture of architectural styles. With its narrow streets and old squares, the city centre is compact enough to explore on foot. Two other monuments worth seeing are the Convento de San Domingos de Bonaval, to the east of the centre and the Colegiata Santa Maria la Real del Sar, a 12th-century Romanesque church, located to the east of the city.

RÚA DE XERUSAL

RÚA DA TRO

0 metres 100
0 yards 100

★ Monasterio de San Martiño Pinario
The Baroque church of this monastery has a huge double altar and an ornate Plateresque façade with carved figures of saints and bishops.

RUELA DO VAI DE DEUS

RÚA DE SAN FRANCISCO

PRAZA DA INMACULADA

Pazo de Xelmírez

★ Hostal de los Reyes Católicos
Built by the Catholic Monarchs as an inn and hospital for sick pilgrims, and now a parador, this magnificent building has an elaborate Plateresque doorway.

PRAZA DO OBRADOIRO

Praza do Obradoiro
This majestic square is one of the world's finest and the focal point for pilgrims arriving in the city. The cathedral's Baroque façade dominates the square.

The Pazo de Raxoi, with its Classical façade, was built in 1772 and houses the town hall.

San Paio de Antealtares
This is one of the oldest monasteries in Santiago. It was founded in the 9th century to house the tomb of St James, now in the cathedral.

VISITORS' CHECKLIST

Practical Information
A Coruña. 95,000.
santiagoturismo.com
Calle Rúa do Vilar 63, 981 55 51 29. Wed (cattle), Thu.
Semana Santa (Easter Week), Santiago Day (25 Jul).

Transport
10 km (6 miles) north.
Calle Hórreo s/n, 902 32 03 20. Praza de Camilo Díaz Baliño s/n, 981 54 24 16.

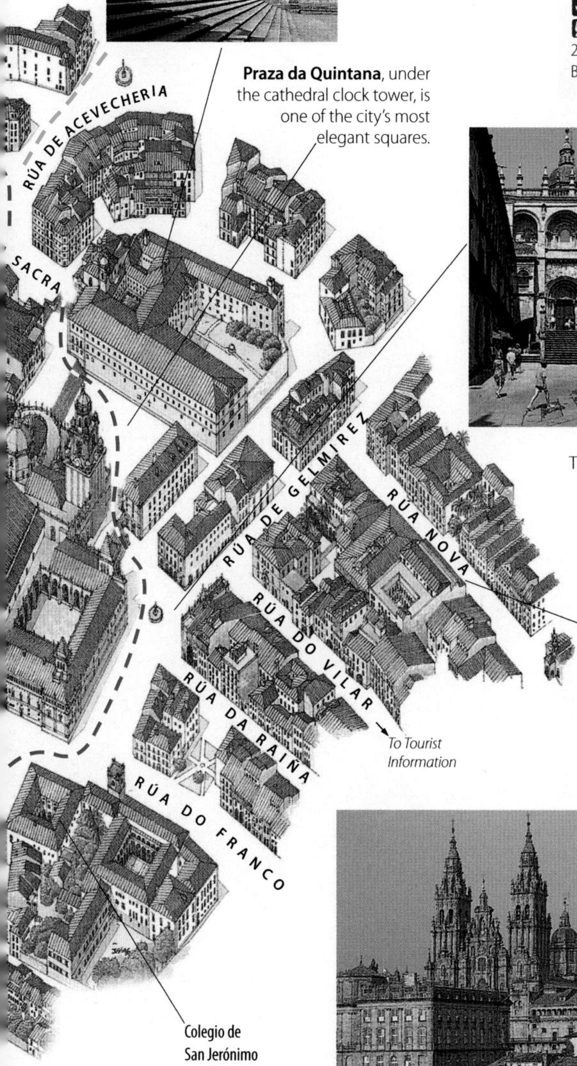

Praza da Quintana, under the cathedral clock tower, is one of the city's most elegant squares.

RÚA DE ACEVECHERIA

SACRA

Praza das Praterias
The Silversmiths' Doorway of the cathedral opens onto this charming square with a stone fountain in the centre.

RÚA DE GELMIREZ

RÚA NOVA

RÚA DO VILAR

RÚA DA RAIÑA

Rúa Nova is a handsome arcaded old street leading from the cathedral to the newer part of the city.

→ To Tourist Information

RÚA DO FRANCO

Colegio de San Jerónimo

★ **Cathedral**
This grand towering spectacle has welcomed pilgrims to Santiago for centuries. Though the exterior has been remodelled over the years, the core of the building has remained virtually unchanged since the 11th century.

Key
— Suggested route
— Pilgrims' route

Santiago Cathedral

With its twin Baroque towers soaring high over the Praza do Obradoiro, this monument to St James is a majestic sight, as befits one of the great shrines of Christendom *(see pp86–7)*. The present building dates from the 11th–13th centuries and stands on the site of the 9th-century basilica built by Alfonso II. Through the famous Pórtico da Gloria is the same interior that met pilgrims in medieval times. The choir, designed by Maestro Mateo, has been completely restored.

"Passport" – proof of a pilgrim's journey

★ West Façade
The richly sculpted Baroque Obradoiro façade was added in the 18th century.

★ Pórtico da Gloria
The sculpted Doorway of Glory, with its statues of apostles and prophets, is 12th century.

KEY

① **Cathedral Museum** items, including a version of Goya's *The Swing*, are on display, as well as the cathedral's cloister, chapterhouse, library, reliquary chapel and crypt.

② **The Santo dos Croques** (Saint of Bumps) has greeted pilgrims since the 12th century. Touching this statue with the forehead is said to impart luck and wisdom.

③ **Pazo de Xelmírez**

④ **Statue of St James**

⑤ **The twin towers** are the cathedral's highest structures at 74 m (243 ft).

⑥ **The** *botafumeiro*, a giant censer, is swung high above the altar by eight men during important services.

⑦ **Mondragón Chapel** (1521) contains fine wrought-iron grilles and vaulting.

⑧ **Clock Tower**

⑨ **Cloisters**

⑩ **Chapterhouse**

VISITORS' CHECKLIST

Practical Information
Praza do Obradoiro.
Tel 981 58 35 48.
Open 7am–8:30pm daily.
🕊 7:30am, 8:30am, 9am,
10am, 11am, noon, 1pm, 6pm,
7:30pm. 📷 rooftops and Pazo
de Xelmírez (tickets and bookings
in museum, 981 57 56 09).
♿ Museum: **Open** daily.
Closed Sun pm, 1 & 6 Jan,
Easter Fri pm, Easter Sat pm, 25
Jul, 15 Aug, 25 Dec. ♻

High Altar
Visitors can pass behind the ornate high altar to embrace the silver mantle of the 13th-century statue of St James.

★ **Porta das Praterias**
The 12th-century Silversmiths' Doorway is rich in bas-relief sculptures of biblical scenes.

Crypt
The relics of St James and two disciples are said to lie in a tomb in the crypt, under the altar, in the original 9th-century foundations.

❼ Padrón

A Coruña. 🏔 8,700. 🚌 🚐
ℹ️ Avenida Compostela, 627 21 07
77. 🚩 Sun. 🎎 Santiago (24–25 Jul).

This quiet town on the Río Ulla,
known for its piquant green
peppers, was a major seaport
until it silted up. Legend has
it the boat carrying the body
of St James to Galicia *(see p86)*
arrived here. The supposed
mooring stone, or *padrón*, lies
below the altar of the church
by the bridge.

The leafy avenue beside the
church features in the poems of
one of Galicia's greatest writers,
Rosalía de Castro (1837–85).
Her home, where she spent
her final years, has been
converted into a **museum**.

Environs

The estuary town of Noia (Noya)
lies on the coast 20 km (12
miles) west. Its Gothic church
has a finely carved portal. East
of Padron is Pazo de Oca, a
manor house, with a crenellated
tower, idyllic gardens and a lake.

🏛 **Museo Rosalia de Castro**
La Matanza. **Tel** 981 81 12 04.
Open Tue–Sun. 🦽 ♿

The picturesque gardens and lake of Pazo de Oca

❽ A Toxa

Near O Grove, Pontevedra. 🚌 ℹ️ Praza
do Corgo, O Grove, 986 73 14 15. 🚩 Fri.

A tiny pine-covered island
joined to the mainland by a
bridge, A Toxa (La Toja) is one
of the most stylish resorts in
Galicia. The *belle époque* palace-
hotel *(see p562)* and luxury
villas add to the island's elegant
atmosphere. A Toxa's best-
known landmark is the small
church covered with scallop
shells. Across the bridge is
O Grove (El Grove), a thriving
family resort and fishing port
on a peninsula, with holiday
hotels and flats alongside
glorious beaches.

Scallop-covered roof of the church on A Toxa island

❾ Pontevedra

Pontevedra. 🏔 82,000. 🚍 🚐
ℹ️ Casa da Luz, Praza da Verdura s/n,
986 09 08 90. 🚩 1st, 8th, 15th & 23rd
of each month. 🎎 Fiestas de la
Peregrina (2nd week in Aug).
🌐 **visit-pontevedra.com**

Pontevedra lies inland, at the
head of a long *ría* backed by
green hills. The delightful old
town is typically Galician and has
a network of cobbled alleys and
tiny squares with granite calvaries,
flower-filled balconies and excellent tapas bars. On the south
side of the Old Town are the
Gothic Ruinas de San Domingos,
now part of the **Museo de
Pontevedra**, with Roman steles
and Galician coats of arms and
tombs. To the west, the 16th-
century **Iglesia de Santa María
la Mayor** contains a magnificent
Plateresque *(see p29)* façade.

On the **Praza de la Leña**,
two 18th-century mansions,
along with two other buildings
in the adjacent streets, form
the Museo de Pontevedra, one
of the best museums in Galicia.
The Bronze Age treasures are
superb. Among the paintings
are 15th-century Spanish
primitives, canvases by
Zurbarán and Goya, and on
the top floor a collection by
Alfonso Castelao, a Galician
artist and Nationalist who
forcefully depicted the
misery endured by his people
during the Spanish Civil War.

🏛 **Museo de Pontevedra**
Calle Pasantería 2–12. **Tel** 986 80 41
00. **Open** 10am–9pm Tue–Sat,
11am–2pm Sun. Ruinas de San
Domingos close at 2pm in winter
and on Sun. 🌐 **museo.depo.es**

Rías Baixas

This southern part of Galicia's west coast consists of four large *rías* or inlets between pine-covered hills. The beaches are good, the scenery is lovely, the bathing safe and the climate much milder than on the wilder coast to the north. Though areas such as Vilagarcía de Arousa and Panxón have become popular holiday resorts, much of the Rías Baixas (Rías Bajas) coastline is unspoiled, such as the quiet stretch from Muros to Noia. This part of the coastline provides some of Spain's most fertile fishing grounds. Mussel-breeding platforms are positioned in neat rows along the *rías*, looking like half-submerged submarines, and in late summer the women harvest clams.

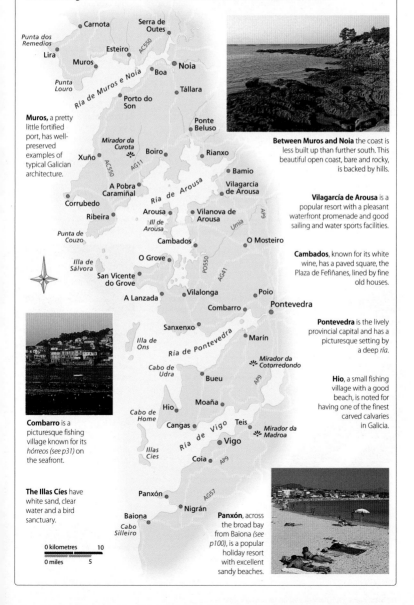

Muros, a pretty little fortified port, has well-preserved examples of typical Galician architecture.

Between Muros and Noia the coast is less built up than further south. This beautiful open coast, bare and rocky, is backed by hills.

Vilagarcía de Arousa is a popular resort with a pleasant waterfront promenade and good sailing and water sports facilities.

Cambados, known for its white wine, has a paved square, the Plaza de Fefiñanes, lined by fine old houses.

Pontevedra is the lively provincial capital and has a picturesque setting by a deep *ría*.

Hio, a small fishing village with a good beach, is noted for having one of the finest carved calvaries in Galicia.

Combarro is a picturesque fishing village known for its *hórreos (see p31)* on the seafront.

The Illas Cíes have white sand, clear water and a bird sanctuary.

Panxón, across the broad bay from Baiona *(see p100)*, is a popular holiday resort with excellent sandy beaches.

0 kilometres 10
0 miles 5

Cannons on the battlements of Monterreal fortress, Baiona

⑩ Vigo

Pontevedra. 📊 295,000. ✈ 🚌 🚊 ℹ️ Cánovas del Castillo 3, 986 22 47 57. 🚌 Wed, Sun. 🎭 Cristo de los Afligidos (3rd weekend in Jul), Cristo de la Victoria (1st week in Aug). 🌐 **turismodevigo.org**

Galicia's largest town is also the biggest fishing port in Spain. It is situated in an attractive setting near the mouth of a deep *ría* spanned by a high suspension bridge, and is surrounded by wooded hills. Vigo is not noted for its old buildings but does have striking modern sculptures such as Juan José Oliveira's horses statue in the Praza de España. The oldest part of the town, Barrio del Berbes, is near the port and used to be the sailors' quarter. Its cobbled alleys are full of bars and cafés where you can find some of the finest tapas. The Mercado de la Piedra, better known by its Galician name Mercado de A Pedra, is located near the port and sells reasonably priced fish and shellfish.

⑪ Baiona

Pontevedra. 📊 12,000. 🚊 ℹ️ Paseo Ribeira, 986 68 70 67. 🚌 Mon in Sabaris (nearby). 🎭 Santa Liberata (20 Jul), Virgen de la Anunciada (2nd Sun in Aug). 🌐 **turismodebaiona.com**

The *Pinta*, one of the caravels from the fleet of Christopher Columbus, arrived at this small port on 1 March 1493, bringing the first news of the discovery of the New World. Today Baiona (Bayona), which is sited on a broad bay, is a popular summer resort, its harbour a mix of pleasure and fishing boats. The 12th- to 17th-century **Iglesia Antigua Colegiata de Santa María** is Romanesque with Cistercian influences. Symbols on the arches indicate the local guilds that helped build the church.

A royal fortress once stood on Monterreal promontory, to the north of town. Sections of its defensive walls remain, but the interior has been converted into a smart parador *(see p562)*. A walk around the battlements offers superb views of the coast.

On the coast a short distance to the south is a huge granite and porcelain statue of the **Virgen de la Roca** sculpted by Antonio Palacios in 1930. Visitors can climb up inside the statue.

Bronze sculpture by Oliveira in Vigo's Praza de España

⑫ A Guarda

Pontevedra. 📊 10,500. 🚊 ℹ️ Plaza del Reloj 1, 986 61 45 46. 🚌 Sat. 🎭 Virgen del Carmen (16 Jul), Monte de Santa Tecla (2nd week Aug). 🌐 **aguarda.es**

The little fishing port of A Guarda (La Guardia) is famous for seafood and is particularly well-known for its lobsters.

On the slopes of Monte de Santa Tecla are the remains of a Celtic settlement of some 100 round stone dwellings dated around 600–200 BC. The **Museo de Monte de Santa Tecla** sits on a nearby hilltop.

Environs

About 10 km (6 miles) north, the tiny Baroque **Monasterio de Santa María** stands by the beach at Oia. Semi-wild horses roam the surrounding hills and, in May and June, are rounded up for branding in a series of day-long fiestas *(see p102)*.

🏛 Museo de Monte de Santa Tecla

A Guarda. **Tel** 986 61 45 46. **Open** Tue–Sun. 🎫 for hilltop access (free Mon).

Circular foundations of Celtic dwellings at A Guarda

⑬ Tui

Pontevedra. 📊 17,000. 🚌 🚊 ℹ️ Calle Colon 2, 986 60 17 89. 🚌 Thu. 🎭 San Telmo (first weekend after Easter).

Spain's main frontier town with Portugal, Tui (Tuy) stands on a hillside above the Río Miño. Its graceful old streets curve up to an old quarter and the 12th-century hilltop **cathedral**. The two countries were often at war during the Middle Ages, and as a result the church is built in the style

Unloading the catch in Spain's largest fishing port, Vigo

of a fortress, with towers and battlements. It has a cloister and choir stalls and a richly decorated west porch.

Nearby is the **Iglesia de San Telmo**, dedicated to the patron saint of fishermen, whose Baroque ornamentation shows a Portuguese influence. Near the cathedral is an iron bridge, the **Puente Internacional**, built by Gustave Eiffel in 1884 to stretch across the river to Valença do Minho in Portugal.

The Romanesque **Iglesia de Santo Domingo**, beside the Parque de la Alameda, has ivy-covered cloisters and tombs with carved effigies. The church overlooks the river, which is used in August for the Descent of the Río Miño, a festive canoe race.

Fishing in Spain

The Spanish eat more seafood per head than any other European nation except Portugal. The country has Europe's largest fishing fleet in terms of catch. However, with the fishing industry in crisis, there are only about 5,000 boats that land Spain's catch of fish and shellfish. Much of this is caught offshore, where octopus, mackerel, clams and lobster are plentiful. The stocks in the seas around Spain have become depleted by overfishing and an oil spill in 2002, forcing deep-sea trawlers to travel as far as Canada and Iceland.

⑭ Celanova

Ourense. 🚅 5,600. 🚌 ℹ️ Plaza Mayor 1, 988 43 22 01. 🚆 Thu. 🎪 San Roque (15 Aug).

On the main square of this little town is the massive **Monasterio de San Salvador**, also known as the Monasterio de San Rosendo, after its founder. Founded during the 10th century and later rebuilt, it is mainly Baroque, though one of its two lovely cloisters is Renaissance. The enormous church of this Benedictine monastery has an ornate altarpiece and

Ceramic tiled floor of the Iglesia de San Miguel

Gothic choir stalls. In the garden is the 10th-century Mozarabic **Iglesia de San Miguel**.

Environs
At **Santa Comba de Bande**, 26 km (16 miles) to the south, is an even older little church. The features of this 7th-century Visigothic *(see pp54–5)* church include a lantern turret and a horseshoe arch that has carved marble pillars.

⑮ Verín

Ourense. 🚅 14,600. 🚌 ℹ️ Avda San Lazaro 26–28, 988 41 16 14. 🚆 3rd, 11th & 23rd of month. 🎪 Carnival (Feb), Santa María (15 Aug).

Though it stands amid vineyards, Verín produces more than wine. Its mineral springs have given it a thriving bottled water industry. The town has many old houses with arcades and glass balconies (*galerías*). The **Castillo de Monterrey**, built during the wars with Portugal, is 3 km (2 miles) to the west. Inside its three rings of walls are two 15th-century keeps, an arcaded courtyard and a 13th-century church with a carved portal. The castle once housed a monastery and hospital, and is now open to visitors Wed–Sun.

The Castillo de Monterrey, standing high above the town of Verín

The outrageous costumes of *Os Peliqueiros* in Laza

Galicia's Fiestas

Os Peliqueiros *(Carnival, Feb/Mar)*, Laza (Ourense). Dressed up in grinning masks and outlandish costumes, with cowbells tied to their belts and brandishing sticks, Os Peliqueiros take to the streets on Carnival Sunday. They are licensed to lash out at onlookers, who are forbidden to retaliate. On Carnival Monday morning, a battle takes place, with flour, water and live ants used as ammunition. Laza's carnival comes to an end on the Tuesday with a reading of the satirical "Donkey's Will" and the burning of an effigy.

Flower pavements *(Corpus Christi, May/Jun)*, Ponteareas (Pontevedra). The streets of the town along which the Corpus Christi procession passes are carpeted with intricate designs made from brightly coloured flower petals.

A Rapa das Bestas *(Jun–Aug)*, Oia (Pontevedra). Semi-wild horses are rounded up by local farmers for their manes and tails to be cut. What was once a chore is now a popular fiesta.

St James's Day *(25 Jul)*, Santiago de Compostela. On the night before, there is a firework display in the Praza do Obradoiro. The celebrations are especially wild in a holy year (when 25 July falls on a Sunday).

⑯ Ourense

Ourense. 🅜 107,000. 🚆 🚌
🛈 Isabel la Católica 2, 988 36 60 64.
📅 7th, 17th & 26th of each month.
🎎 Os Maios (1–3 May), Fiestas de Ourense (end Jun).

The old quarter of Ourense was built around the city's well-known thermal springs, Fonte das Burgas. Even today, these spout water at a temperature of 65°C (150°F) from three fountains.

This old part of the town is the most interesting, particularly the small area around the arcaded Plaza Mayor. Here the **cathedral**, founded in 572 and rebuilt in the 12th–13th centuries, has a vast gilded reredos by Cornelis de Holanda. On the triple-arched doorway are carved figures reminiscent of the Pórtico da Gloria at Santiago *(see p96)*. Nearby is the elegant 14th-century cloister, the **Claustro de San Francisco**.

Another landmark is the 13th-century **Puente Romano**, a seven-arched bridge which crosses the Río Miño, north of the town. It is built on Roman foundations and is still used by traffic.

Environs

The towns of **Allariz**, 25 km (16 miles) south, and **Ribadavia**, to the west, have old Jewish quarters with narrow streets and Romanesque churches. Ribadavia is also noted for its Ribeiro wines – a dry white and a port-like red *(see pp82–3)* – and has a wine museum.

Ornate Gothic reredos in the cathedral at Ourense

⑰ Monasterio de Ribas de Sil

Ribas de Sil, Ourense. **Tel** 988 01 01 10. **Open** daily.

Near its confluence with the Miño, 28 km (17 miles) from Ourense, the Río Sil carves a deep curving gorge in which dams form two reservoirs of dark-green water. A hairpin road winds to the top of the gorge, where the Romanesque Gothic Monasterio de Ribas de Sil is situated high on a crag above the chasm. Restored and converted into a charming parador, it has an enormous glass wall in one of the three cloisters, and fine views.

The Río Sil winding its way through the gorge

The grandiose Monasterio de Oseira surrounded by the forests of the Valle de Arenteiro

⑱ Monasterio de Oseira

Oseira, Ourense. **Tel** 988 28 20 04.
Open 10am–noon Mon–Sat, 3:30–6:30pm daily (guided visits only). ⬚ compulsory.
W **mosteirodeoseira.org**

This monastery stands on its own in a wooded valley near the hamlet of Oseira, named after the bears (*osos*) that once lived in this region. It is a grey building with a Baroque façade dating from 1709. On the doorway is a statue of the Virgin as nurse, with St Bernard kneeling at her feet. The interior of the 12th- to 13th-century church is typically Cistercian in its simplicity.

Fresco of a *dona* in the monastery at Vilar de Donas

⑲ Vilar de Donas

Lugo. ⓜ 80. ⓘ Palas de Rey, Avda de Compostela 47, 982 38 07 40. Church: **Open** Easter–Oct: 11am–2pm, 3:30–6:30pm Tue–Sun; rest of the year: ask for key. ⬚ ⓕ San Antonio (13 Jun), San Salvador (6 Aug).

This hamlet on the Road to Santiago (*see pp86–7*) has a small church, San Salvador, just off the main road. Inside are tombs of some of the Knights of the Order of Santiago. Also inside are frescoes painted by the nuns who lived here until the 15th century.

The Cistercian **Monasterio Sobrado de los Monjes**, to the northwest, has a medieval kitchen and chapterhouse, and a church with unusual domes.

⑳ Lugo

Lugo. ⓜ 98,000. ⓔ ⓔ ⓘ Plaza del Campo 11, 982 25 16 58. ⓔ Tue & Fri. ⓕ San Froilán (4–12 Oct). **W** **lugo.gal**

Capital of Galicia's largest province, Lugo was also an important centre under the Romans. Attracted to the town by its thermal springs, they constructed what is now the finest surviving **Roman wall** in Spain. The wall, which encircles the city, is about 6 m (20 ft) thick and 10 m (33 ft) high with ten gateways. Six of these give access to the top of the wall, from where there is a good view of the city.

Inside the wall, the Old Town is lively, with pretty squares. In the **Praza de Santo Domingo** is a black statue of a Roman eagle, built to commemorate Augustus's capture of Lugo from the Celts in the 1st century BC. The large, Romanesque **cathedral** is modelled on that of Santiago. It features an elegant Baroque cloister, and a chapel containing the alabaster statue of Nuestra Señora de los Ojos Grandes (Virgin of the Big Eyes). The **Museo Provincial** exhibits local Celtic and Roman finds, while the **Museo Interactivo da Historia de Lugo** presents the city's history with

high-tech exhibits in a striking modern building.

Environs
The stone hamlet of Santa Eulalia, situated in open country to the west, conceals a curious building, discovered in 1924: a tiny temple, with lively, bright frescoes of birds and leaves. Though its exact purpose is unknown, it is thought to be an early Christian church and has been dated at around the 3rd century AD.

🏛 Museo Provincial
Praza da Soedade. **Tel** 982 24 21 12.
Open Jul & Aug: Mon–Sat (am only Sat); Sep–Jun: daily (am only Sun). ♿
W **museolugo.org**

🏛 Museo Interactivo da Historia de Lugo
Parque da Milagrosa. **Tel** 982 25 16 58.
Open 11am–1:30pm & 5–7:30pm Tue–Sat, 4–8pm Sun. **W** **lugo.es/ws/mihl**

㉑ O Cebreiro

Lugo. ⓜ 1,150. ⓔ ⓘ 982 36 70 25. ⓕ Santa Maria Real (8 Sep), Santo Milagro (9 Sep).

In the hills in the east of Galicia, close to the border with León, is one of the most unusual villages on the Road to Santiago. Its 9th-century church was supposedly the scene of a miracle in 1300 when the wine was turned into blood and the bread into flesh. Nearby, there are several *pallozas*, round thatched stone huts of a Celtic design. Some have been restored, and are now part of a **folk museum**.

🏛 Museo Etnográfico
O Cebreiro. **Tel** 982 36 70 25. **Open** Tue–Sun.

Painted gourd in O Cebreiro's museum

ASTURIAS AND CANTABRIA

Asturias · Cantabria

The spectacular Picos de Europa massif sits astride the border between Asturias and Cantabria. In this rural region cottage crafts are kept alive in villages in remote mountain valleys and forested foothills. There are many ancient towns and churches, and pretty fishing ports on the coasts. Cave paintings, such as those at Altamira, were made by people living here about 35,000 years ago.

Asturias is proud that it resisted invasion by the Moors. The Reconquest of Spain is held to have begun in 718 when a Moorish force was defeated by Christians at Covadonga in the Picos de Europa. The Christian kingdom of Asturias was founded in the 8th century, and in the brilliant, brief artistic period that followed many churches were built around the capital, Oviedo. Some of these Pre-Romanesque churches still stand. Today, Asturias is a province and a principality under the patronage of the heir to the Spanish throne. In the unspoiled Asturian countryside cider is produced and a quaint language, known as *Bable* or *Asturiano*, is spoken.

Cantabria centres on Santander, its capital, a port and an elegant resort. It is a mountainous province with a legacy of Romanesque churches in isolated spots. It also has well-preserved towns and villages such as Santillana del Mar, Carmona and Bárcena Mayor.

Mountains cover more than half of both provinces, so mountain sports are a major attraction. Expanses of deciduous forests remain in many parts, some sheltering Spain's last wild bears. Along the coasts are pretty fishing ports and resorts, such as Castro Urdiales, Ribadesella and Comillas, and sandy coves for bathing. Both the coastal plains and uplands are ideal for quiet rural holidays.

Peaceful meadow around Lago de la Ercina in the Picos de Europa massif

◄ The scenic Costa Verde, Asturias, with lush meadows reaching down to the shoreline

Exploring Asturias and Cantabria

The most obvious attraction in this area is the group of mountains that straddles the two provinces – the Picos de Europa. These jagged peaks offer excellent rock climbing and rough hiking, and in certain parts can be explored by car or bicycle. These and several other nature reserves in the area are home to rare species of flora and fauna, including the capercaillie and brown bear. The coast offers many sandy coves for bathing. Santander and Oviedo are lively university cities with a rich cultural life. There are innumerable unspoiled villages to explore, especially the ancient town of Santillana del Mar. Some of the earliest examples of art exist in Cantabria, most notably at Altamira, where the cave drawings and engravings are among the oldest to be found in Europe.

Typical flower-covered balcony in the village of Bárcena Mayor

A view along the crowded beach of Playa del Camello, Santander

Sights at a Glance

1. Taramundi
2. Castro de Coaña
3. Costa Verde
4. Teverga
5. Avilés
6. Gijón
7. Oviedo
8. Valdediós
9. Ribadesella
10. Cangas de Onís
11. *Parque Nacional de los Picos de Europa pp112–13*
12. Potes
13. Comillas
14. Valle de Cabuérniga
15. Alto Campoo
16. Cuevas de Altamira
17. Santillana del Mar
18. Puente Viesgo
19. Santander
20. Laredo
21. Castro Urdiales

Cantabrian dairy farmers loading hay onto their cart

Getting Around

The main road through the region is the A8. Most other major roads follow the directions of the valleys and run north to south. Minor roads are generally good but can be slow and winding. The private RENFE railway, which follows the coast from Bilbao to Ferrol in Galicia, is both useful and scenic. Brittany Ferries services (one to three times a week) link Santander with Plymouth and Portsmouth. Asturias has a small international airport near Avilés.

Key

— Motorway

= = Motorway under construction

▬ Secondary road

— Minor road

— Scenic route

▬ Main railway

— Minor railway

▬ Regional border

△ Summit

Carved figure in the
Convento de Regina Coeli,
Santillana del Mar

For additional map symbols *see back flap*

Craftsman making knife blades in a forge at Taramundi

❶ Taramundi

Asturias. 🏠 750. 🚹 Calle Solleiro 14, 985 64 68 77. 🗓 San José (19 Mar). 🅦 taramundi.net

Situated in the remote Los Oscos region, this small village houses a rural tourism centre which organizes forest tours in four-wheel drive vehicles and has several hotels and holiday cottages to rent. Taramundi has a tradition of wrought-iron craftsmanship. Iron ore was first mined in the area by the Romans. There are approximately 13 forges in and around the village, where craftsmen can still be seen making traditional knives with decorated wooden handles.

Environs
About 20 km (12 miles) to the east, at **San Martín de Oscos**, there is an 18th-century palace. At **Grandas de Salime**, 10 km (6 miles) further southeast, the Museo Etnográfico has displays showing local crafts, traditional life and farming.

🏛 **Museo Etnográfico**
Esquios. **Tel** 985 97 96 40.
Open daily. 🅿 🦽

❷ Castro de Coaña

Asturias. 🚌 5 km (3 miles) from Navia. **Tel** 985 97 84 01. **Open** Wed–Sun.

One of the best-preserved prehistoric sites of the Cantabrian area, Castro de Coaña was later occupied by the Romans. Set on a hillside in the Navia Valley are the remains of its fortifications and the stone foundations of

oval and rectangular dwellings, some of which stand head high. Inside can be found hollowed-out stones which are thought to have been used for crushing corn.

The museum on the site displays many of the finds that have been unearthed at Castro de Coaña. Among the interesting remains on display are pottery, tools and Roman coins.

Circular stone foundations of dwellings at Castro de Coaña

❸ Costa Verde

Asturias. ✈ 🚉 Avilés. 🚌 Oviedo, Gijón. 🚹 Avilés, Calle Ruiz Gomez 21, 985 54 43 25.

The aptly named "green coast" is a succession of attractive sandy coves and dramatic cliffs, punctuated by deep estuaries and numerous fishing villages. Inland, there are lush meadows, and pine and eucalyptus forests, backed by mountains. This stretch of coastline has been less spoiled than most in Spain; the resorts tend to be modest in size, like the hotels.

Two pretty fishing ports, **Castropol** and **Figueras**, stand by the eastern shore of the Ría de Ribadeo, forming the border with Galicia. To the east are other picturesque villages such as Tapia de Casariego and Ortiguera, in a small rocky cove. Following the coast, **Luarca** lies beside a church and a quiet cemetery on a headland, and has a neat little harbour packed with red, blue and white boats. The village of **Cudillero** is even more delightful – outdoor cafés and excellent seafood restaurants crowd the tiny plaza beside the port, all of which are squeezed into a narrow cove. Behind, white cottages are scattered over the steep hillsides.

Further along the coast is the rocky headland of Cabo de Peñas where, in the fishing village of **Candás**, bullfights are held on the sand at low tide on 14 September. East of Gijón, **Lastres** is impressively located below a cliff, and **Isla** has a broad open beach. Beyond Ribadesella is the

The Brown Bear

The population of Spain's brown bears *(Ursus arctos)* has dwindled from about 1,000 at the beginning of the 20th century to about 250 today. Hunting by man and the destruction of the bear's natural forest habitat have caused the decline. But now, protected by nature reserves such as Somiedo, where most of the bears in Asturias are found, together with new conservation laws, this magnificent omnivore is increasing in numbers again.

One of the remaining bears in the forests of Asturias

Church and cemetery overlooking the sea from the headland at Luarca

lively town of **Llanes**. Among the attractions of this old fortified seaport, with its dramatic mountain backdrop, are ruined ramparts and good beaches.

❹ Teverga

Asturias. 🗺 1,900. 🚌 La Plaza.
ℹ️ Dr García Miranda s/n, San Martin de Teverga, 985 76 42 93. **Open** 15 Jun–15 Sep: Tue–Sun; rest of year: Sat & Sun only. **W** tevergaturismo.com

This area is rich in scenery, wildlife and ancient churches. Near the southern end of the Teverga gorge is **La Plaza**. Its church, Iglesia de San Pedro de Teverga, is a fine example of Romanesque architecture. West of La Plaza is **Villanueva**, with its Romanesque Iglesia de Santa María. The 20-km (12-mile) Senda del Oso path skirts the edge of a bear enclosure.

Environs
The large **Parque Natural de Somiedo** straddles the mountains bordering León. Its high meadows and forests are a sanctuary for wolves, brown bears and capercaillies, as well as a number of rare species of wild flowers.

The park has 4 glacial lakes, and is peppered with herdsmen's traditional thatched huts, known as *teitos (see p31)*.

❺ Avilés

Asturias. 🗺 81,700. ✈️ 🚆 🚌 ℹ️ Calle Ruíz Gómez 21, 985 54 43 25. 🗓 Mon. 🎭 San Agustín (last week Aug).

Avilés became the capital of Asturias' steel industry in the 1800s and is still ringed by big factories. Even though it is sometimes criticized for having little to offer the visitor, the town

hides a medieval heart of some character, especially around the Plaza de España. The **Iglesia de San Nicolás Bari** is decorated with frescoes and has a Renaissance cloister. The **Iglesia de Padres Franciscanos** contains a fine 14th-century chapel and holds the tomb of the first Governor of the US state of Florida. All around are arcaded streets. The international airport outside Avilés serves all Asturias.

❻ Gijón

Asturias. 🗺 278,000. 🚆 🚌
ℹ️ Puerto Deportivo, Espigón Central de Fomento, 985 34 17 71. 🗓 Sun. 🎭 Semana Negra (mid-Jul), La Virgen de Begoña (15 Aug). **W** gijon.info

The province's largest city, this industrial port has been much rebuilt since the Civil War when it was bombarded by the Nationalist navy. The city's most famous son is Gaspar Melchor de Jovellanos, an eminent 18th-century author, reformer and diplomat.

Gijón's Old Town is on a small isthmus and headland. It centres on the arcaded Plaza Mayor and the 18th-century **Palacio de Revillagigedo**, a Neo-Renaissance folly now housing a cultural centre. The beach is popular in summer.

🏛 Palacio de Revillagigedo/ Centro Cultural Cajastur
Plaza del Marqués 2.
Tel 985 34 69 21. **Open** Tue–Sun for temporary exhibitions. ♿

The pretty 12th-century Iglesia de San Pedro at La Plaza

❼ Oviedo

Asturias. 🅰 225,000. 🚊 🚌 ℹ️ Plaza de la Constitución 4, 984 08 60 60. ⛴ Thu, Sat & Sun. 🎭 San Mateo (14–21 Sep). 🌐 **turismoviedo.es**

Oviedo, a university city and the cultural and commercial capital of Asturias, stands on a raised site on a fertile plain. The nearby coal mines have made it an important industrial centre since the 19th century. It retains some of the atmosphere of that time, as described by Leopoldo Alas ("Clarín") in his great novel *La Regenta (see p39)*.

In and around Oviedo are many Pre-Romanesque buildings. This style flourished in the 8th–10th centuries and was confined to a small area of the kingdom of Asturias, one of the few enclaves of Spain not invaded by the Moors.

The nucleus of the medieval city is the stately Plaza Alfonso II, bordered by a number of handsome old palaces. On this square is situated the Flamboyant Gothic **cathedral** *(see p28)* with its high tower and asymmetrical west façade. Inside are tombs of Asturian kings and a majestic 16th-century gilded reredos. The cathedral's supreme treasure is the Cámara Santa, a restored 9th-century chapel containing statues of Christ and the apostles. The chapel also houses many works of 9th-century Asturian

Cross of Angels in the treasury of Oviedo Cathedral

art including two crosses and a reliquary – all made of gold, silver and precious stones.

Also situated in the Plaza Alfonso II is the **Iglesia de San Tirso**. This church was originally constructed in the 9th century, but subsequent restorations have left the east window as the only surviving Pre-Romanesque feature.

Sited behind the cathedral is the **Museo Arqueológico**, housed in the old Benedictine monastery of San Vicente, with its fine cloisters. It contains local prehistoric, Romanesque and Pre-Romanesque treasures.

The **Museo de Bellas Artes**, in Velarde Palace, has a good range of Asturian and Spanish paintings, such as Carreño's portrait of Carlos II *(see p74)* and others by Greco, Goya, Dalí, Miró and Picasso.

Two of the most magnificent Pre-Romanesque churches are on Mount Naranco, to the

Santa María del Naranco

This church, on Mount Naranco, was originally built as a summer palace for Ramiro I in the 9th century. It is one of the finest examples of Pre-Romanesque or Asturian architecture, a style characterized by the slender proportions of its buildings and their original and graceful ornamentation.

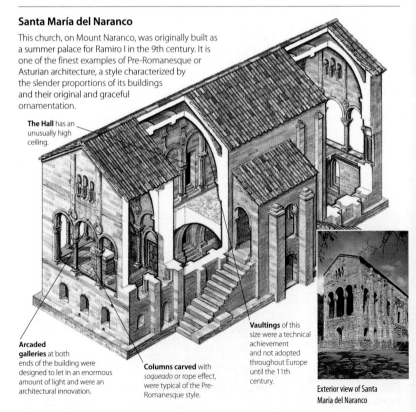

The Hall has an unusually high ceiling.

Arcaded galleries at both ends of the building were designed to let in an enormous amount of light and were an architectural innovation.

Columns carved with *soqueado* or rope effect, were typical of the Pre-Romanesque style.

Vaultings of this size were a technical achievement and not adopted throughout Europe until the 11th century.

Exterior view of Santa María del Naranco

Church overlooking the sea at Ribadesella

north. **Santa María del Naranco** has a large barrel-vaulted hall on the main floor and arcaded galleries at either end. Some of the intricate reliefs on the door jambs of the nearby **San Miguel de Lillo** show acrobats and animal tamers in a circus.

The early 9th-century church of **San Julián de los Prados** stands on the road leading northeast out of Oviedo. The largest of Spain's surviving Pre-Romanesque churches, it is noted for the frescoes which cover all of its interior.

Ⅲ Museo Arqueológico
Calle San Vicente 3. **Tel** 985 20 89 77.
Open Wed–Sun. ♿

Ⅲ Museo de Bellas Artes
Calle Santa Ana 1. **Tel** 985 21 30 61.
Open Tue–Sun. ♿

❽ Valdediós

Asturias. 🏘 150. 🛈 Monasterio de Santa María, 985 89 23 24. Monastery **Open** 11am–1:30pm, 4:30–7pm Tue–Sun (11am–1pm Nov–Apr).

Set alone in a field near this hamlet, the tiny 9th-century **Iglesia de San Salvador** is a jewel of Pre-Romanesque art. Its ceiling has vivid Asturian frescoes, and by the portal are recesses where pilgrims slept. The church in the **Monasterio de Santa María** next door is 13th-century Cistercian, with cloisters from the 16th century.

Environs
To the north, the resort town of **Villaviciosa** lies amid apple orchards. In nearby **Amandi**, the hilltop Iglesia de San Juan has a 13th-century portal and delicate carvings and friezes.

Iglesia de San Salvador de Valdediós in its idyllic setting

❾ Ribadesella

Asturias. 🏘 6,000. 🚉 🚌 🛈 Paseo Princesa Letizia, 985 86 00 38. ☀ Wed. 🎎 Descent of the Río Sella (first Sat of Aug). 🖥 **ribadesella.es**

This enchanting little seaside town bestrides a broad estuary. On one side is the lively old seaport full of tapas bars below a clifftop church. Across the estuary is a holiday resort. A multicoloured flotilla of kayaks arrives here from Arriondas (upstream) in an international regatta that is held every year on the first Saturday in August.

On the edge of town is the **Cueva de Tito Bustillo**. This cave is rich in stalactites but is best known for its many prehistoric drawings, which were discovered in 1968, some dating from around 18,000 BC. These include red and black pictures of stags and horses. To protect the paintings, only 360 visitors are allowed in per day; tickets are given out from 10am every day and should be booked in advance. There is a museum on the site.

🏛 Cueva de Tito Bustillo
Ribadesella. **Tel** 985 86 12 55.
Open Apr–Nov: Wed–Sun (free Wed).

❿ Cangas de Onís

Asturias. 🏘 6,500. 🚌 🛈 Avenida Covadonga 1, 985 84 80 05. ☀ Sun. 🎎 San Antonio (13 Jun), Cheese Festival (12 Oct). 🖥 **cangasdeonis.com**

Cangas de Onís, one of the gateways to the Picos de Europa *(see pp112–13)*, is where Pelayo, the 8th-century Visigothic nobleman and hero of the Reconquest, set up his court. The town has a Romanesque bridge and the 8th-century chapel of Santa Cruz.

Environs
About 3 km (2 miles) east in Cardes is the **Cueva del Buxu**, which has engravings and rock-drawings over 10,000 years old. Only 25 visitors are allowed daily, and no visitors under 7.

🏛 Cueva del Buxu
Tel 608 17 54 67 (mobile). 🎦 Wed–Sun. 🎎 reservations essential; call 3–5pm Wed–Sun (free Wed).

⓫ Parque Nacional de los Picos de Europa

These beautiful mountains were reputedly christened the "Peaks of Europe" by returning sailors for whom this was often the first sight of their homeland. The range straddles three regions – Asturias, Cantabria and Castilla y León – and has diverse terrain. In some parts, deep winding gorges cut through craggy rocks, while elsewhere verdant valleys support orchards and dairy farming. The celebrated creamy blue cheese Cabrales *(see p80)* is made here. The Picos offer rock climbing and upland hiking as well as a profusion of flora and fauna. Tourism in the park is well organized.

Covadonga
The Neo-Romanesque basilica, built between 1886 and 1901, stands on the site of Pelayo's historic victory.

Lago de la Ercina
Together with the nearby Lago Enol, this lake lies on a wild limestone plateau above Covadonga and below the peak of Peña Santa.

Desfiladero de los Beyos
This deep, narrow gorge with its high limestone cliffs winds spectacularly for 10 km (6 miles) through the mountains. Tracing the route of the Río Sella below, it carries the main road from Cangas de Onís to Riaño.

KEY

① **Desfiladero del Río Cares** is a deep gorge formed by the River Cares in the heart of the Picos. A dramatic footpath follows the gorge, passing through tunnels and across high bridges up to 1,000 m (3,280 ft) above the river.

② **Bulnes**, one of the remotest villages in Spain, enjoys fine views of Naranjo de Bulnes and can now be accessed by an underground funicular railway from Puente Poncebos as well as by foot.

③ **Naranjo de Bulnes**, with its tooth-like crest, is in the heart of the massif. At 2,519 m (8,264 ft), it is one of the highest summits in the Picos de Europa.

Key

═══ Major road

═══ Minor road

– – – Footpath

──── National park boundary

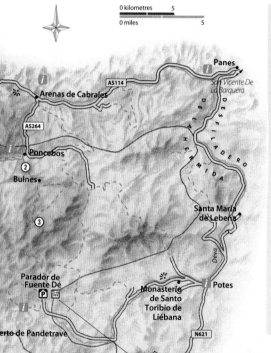

A dramatic view of the mountains of the Picos de Europa

VISITORS' CHECKLIST

Practical Information
ℹ️ Casa Dago, Avda Covadonga 43, Cangas de Onís, 985 84 86 14. **Tel** 942 73 66 10.
ⓦ **magrama.gob.es/es/red-parques-nacionales/nuestros-parques/picos-europa**
Fuente Dé cable car: **Open** Jul–Sep: 9am–8pm daily, Oct–Jun: 10am–6pm daily.

Transport
🚌 Oviedo to Cangas de Onís.

Pelayo the Warrior

A statue of this Visigothic nobleman who became king of Asturias guards the basilica at Covadonga. It was close to this site, in 722, that Pelayo and a band of men – though vastly outnumbered – are said to have defeated a Moorish army. The victory inspired Christians in the north of Spain to reconquer the peninsula *(see pp58–9)*. The tomb of the warrior is in a cave which has become a shrine, also containing a painted image of the Virgin.

Pelayo's statue

Fuente Dé Cable Car
The 900-m (2950-ft) ascent from Fuente Dé takes visitors up to a wild rocky plateau pitted with craters. From here there is a spectacular panorama of the Picos' peaks and valleys.

For hotels and restaurants in this region see pp562–3 and pp583–4

Statue of the Virgin, San Vicente de la Barquera

Asturias and Cantabria's Fiestas

La Vijanera *(first Sun of the year)*, Silió (Cantabria). This is a costumed parade which dates back to pre-Roman times, and celebrates the triumph of good over evil.

La Folía *(second Sun after Easter)*, San Vicente de la Barquera (Cantabria). The statue of the Virgen de la Barquera is said to have arrived at San Vicente in a boat with no sails, oars or crew. Once a year, it is put in a decorated fishing boat, which sails at the head of a procession to bless the sea. Groups of young girls, called *picayos*, stand on the shore singing traditional songs. La Folía usually takes place on the second Sunday after Easter, depending on local tides.

Fiesta del Pastor *(25 Jul)*, near Cangas de Onís (Asturias). Regional dances are performed on the shores of Lake Enol in the Picos de Europa National Park.

Battle of the Flowers *(last Fri of Aug)*, Laredo (Cantabria). Floats adorned with flowers are paraded through this small resort. A flower-throwing free-for-all follows the procession.

Nuestra Señora de Covadonga *(8 Sep)*, Picos de Europa (Asturias). Huge crowds converge on the shrine of Covadonga *(see p112)* to pay homage to the patron saint of Asturias.

⑫ Potes

Cantabria. 🏔 1,500. 🛈 Calle Independencia 12, 942 73 07 87. 🚌 Mon. 🎉 Ntra. Sra. de Valmayor (15 Aug), Santísima Cruz (14 Sep).

A small ancient town, with old balconied houses lining the river, Potes is the main centre of the eastern Picos de Europa. It is situated in the broad Valle de Liébana, whose fertile soil yields prime crops of walnuts, cherries and grapes. A potent spirit called *orujo* is made in the town. The **Torre del Infantado**, in the main square, is a defensive tower built in the 15th century.

Environs

Between Potes and the coast runs a gorge, the **Desfiladero de la Hermida**. Halfway up it is **Santa María de Lebeña**, a 10th-century Mozarabic church.

West of Potes is the monastery church of **Santo Toribio de Liébana**, one of the most revered spots in the Picos de Europa. Founded in the 7th century, it became known

throughout Spain a century later when it received reputedly the largest fragment of the True Cross. An 8th century monk, St Beatus of Liébana, wrote the *Commentary on the Apocalypse*. The restored Romanesque monastic buildings were rebuilt in the 1200s, and are now occupied by Franciscan monks.

⑬ Comillas

Cantabria. 🏔 2,400. 🛈 Plaza Joaquín del Piélago 1, 942 72 25 91. 🚌 Fri. 🎉 El Cristo (16 Jul). Palacio Sobrellano: **Open** Mar–Oct: 9:30am–2:30pm, 3:30–6:30pm daily (to 7:30pm mid-Jun–mid-Sep); Nov–Feb: 9:30am–3:30pm daily. 🎨

This pretty resort is known for its buildings by Catalán Modernista architects *(see pp144–5)*. Antonio López y López, the first Marquis of Comillas, hired Joan Martorell to design the Neo-Gothic **Palacio Sobrellano** (1881), now a museum. Comilla's best-known

Stone bridge and houses in the ancient town of Potes

Surviving Classical columns among the ruins of the Roman town of Julióbriga, near Reinosa

monument is Gaudí's *(see p168)* **El Capricho**, now a restaurant. It was designed from 1883 to 1889 and is a Mudéjar-inspired fantasy with a minaret-like tower covered in green and yellow tiles. Another Modern-ista building is the **Universidad Pontificia**, on a hilltop overlooking the sea. It was designed by Joan Martorell to plans by Domènech i Montaner *(see p144).*

Wall tile on the façade of El Capricho

Environs
The fishing port of **San Vicente de la Barquera** has arcaded streets, ramparts and the Gothic Romanesque church of Nuestra Señora de los Ángeles.

⓮ Valle de Cabuérniga

Cantabria. 🚌 Bárcena Mayor.
🛈 Ayuntamiento de Cabuerniga, 942 70 60 01.

Two exceptionally picturesque towns, notable for their superb examples of rural architecture, draw visitors to the Cabuérniga Valley. A good road takes you to the once-remote **Bárcena Mayor**. Its cobbled streets are furnished with old lamps and filled with boutiques, and restaurants serving regional dishes. The pretty houses have flower-covered balconies and cattle byres.

Carmona is an old, unspoiled village approximately 20 km (12 miles) to the northwest of Bárcena Mayor. Its solid stone houses, with pantiled roofs and wooden balconies, are typically Cantabrian *(see p30)*. Woodcarv-ing, the traditional craft of the region, is still practised in this village, where men work outside their houses on a variety of artifacts including bowls, fiddles, *albarcas* (clogs) and chairs. The 13th-century Palacio de los Mier, a manor house in the centre of the village, has been restored and is now a hotel.

The extensive, wild beech woods near **Saja** have been designated a nature reserve.

Traditional balconied houses in Bárcena Mayor

⓯ Alto Campoo

Cantabria. 🚡 1,900. 🚊 🚌 Reinosa.
🛈 Estación de Montaña, 942 77 92 23 (am only); Reinosa, 942 75 52 15.
⛪ San Sebastián (20 Jan, Reinosa).

Sited high in the Cantabrian mountains, this winter resort lies below the Pico de Tres Mares (2,175 m/7,000 ft), the "Peak of the Three Seas", so called because the rivers rising near it flow into the Mediterranean, the Atlantic and the Bay of Biscay. The Río Ebro, one of Spain's longest rivers, rises in this area and its source, at Fontíbre, is a beauty spot. A road and a chair lift reach the summit of Tres Mares for a breathtaking panorama of the Picos de Europa and other mountain chains. The resort is small, with 23 pistes totalling 32 km (20 miles) in length, and has few facilities for après-ski.

Environs
Reinosa, some 26 km (16 miles) to the east of Alto Campoo, is a handsome market town with old stone houses. Further southeast is Retortillo, a hamlet where the remains of **Julióbriga**, a town built by the Romans as a bastion against the wild tribes of Cantabria, can be seen.

The main road south out of Reinosa leads to **Cervatos**, where the former collegiate church has erotic carvings on its façade. This novel device was meant to deter the villagers from pleasures of the flesh.

At **Arroyuelo** and **Cadalso**, to the southeast, are two churches built into rock faces in the 8th and 9th centuries.

One of the many paintings of bison at Altamira

⑯ Cuevas de Altamira

Cantabria. **Tel** 942 81 80 05. 🚌 Santillana del Mar. Caves: **Closed** to the public, check website for details. Museum: **Open** 9:30am–6pm Tue–Sat (to 8pm May–Oct), 9:30am–3pm Sun. **Closed** 1 & 6 Jan, 1 May, 28 Jun, 24, 25 & 31 Dec. 🚏 advance booking advisable, 902 24 24 24 (free every Sat from 2pm & Sun). ♿ 🏷 **W** museodealtamira.mcu.es

These caves contain some of the world's finest examples of prehistoric art. The earliest engravings and drawings, discovered in 1879, date back to around 30,000 BC *(see p53)*. Public entry to the caves is very restricted, but the on-site museum contains a replica of the caves. Similar sites that remain open to the public are found at nearby Puente Viesgo, Ribadesella *(see p111)* in Asturias and at Nerja *(see p487)* in Andalusia.

⑰ Santillana del Mar

Cantabria. 🏠 4,000. 🚌 🚺 Calle Jesus Otero 20, 942 81 88 12. 🎪 Santa Juliana (28 Jun), San Roque (16 Aug). **W** santillanadelmarturismo.com

Set just inland, belying its name, this town is one of the prettiest in Spain. Its ensemble of 15th- to 18th-century stone houses survives largely intact.

The town grew up around a monastery, which was an important pilgrimage centre, the Romanesque **La Colegiata**. The church houses the tomb of the local early medieval martyr St Juliana, and contains a 17th-century painted reredos and a carved south door. In its lovely cloisters, vivid biblical scenes have been sculpted on the capitals. On the town's two main cobbled streets there are houses built by local noblemen. These have either fine wooden galleries or iron balconies, and coats of arms inlaid into their stone façades. In the past, farmers used the open ground floors as byres for stabling their cattle.

In the enchanting **Plaza Mayor**, in the centre of town, is a mansion-turned-parador.

Carved figure of Christ in the Convento de Regina Coeli

The **Museo Diocesano** is housed in the restored Convento de Regina Coeli, east of the town centre, and has a collection of painted carvings of religious figures.

🏛 **Museo Diocesano**
El Cruce. **Tel** 942 84 03 17. **Open** Tue–Sun. 🚏

⑱ Puente Viesgo

Cantabria. 🏠 2,800. 🚌 🚺 Calle Manuel Pérez Mazo 2, 942 59 81 05 (town hall). 🎪 La Perolá (20 Jan), San Miguel (28–29 Sep).

This spa village is best known for **El Monte Castillo**, a complex of caves dotted around the limestone hills above the town. Decorated by prehistoric man, it is thought the late Palaeolithic cave dwellers used the deep interior as a sanctuary. They left drawings of horses, bison and other animals, and some 50 hand prints. The colours used to create the images were made from minerals in the cave.

Environs
The lush Pas valley, to the southeast, is home to transhumant dairy farmers, the Pasiegos. In the main town of **Vega de Pas**, you can buy two Pasiego specialities – *sobaos*, or sponge cakes, and *quesadas*, a sweet which is made from milk, butter and eggs. In **Villacarriedo** there is a handsome 18th-century mansion, with two Baroque façades of carved stone hiding a medieval tower.

🏠 **El Monte Castillo**
Puente Viesgo. **Tel** 942 59 84 25. **Open** Wed–Sun (mid-Jun–mid-Sep: Tue–Sun; Nov–Feb: am only). 🚏 🏷

Main façade of La Colegiata in Santillana del Mar

The Palacio de la Magdalena in Santander

⑲ Santander

Cantabria. 🏘 176,000. ✈ 🚆 🚌 🚢
ℹ Jardines de Pereda s/n, 942 20 30
00. 🚢 Mon–Thu. 🎡 Santiago (25 Jul).
🌐 **turismodecantabria.com**

Cantabria's capital, a busy port, enjoys a splendid site near the mouth of a deep bay. The town centre is modern – after being ravaged by fire in 1941 it was reconstructed. The **cathedral** was rebuilt in Gothic style, but retains its 12th-century crypt. The **Museo de Bellas Artes** houses work by Goya as well as other artists of the 19th and 20th centuries. The town's **Museo de Prehistoria y Arqueología** displays finds from caves at Altamira and Puente Viesgo *(see opposite)*, such as Neolithic axe heads, and Roman coins, pottery and figurines. The **Museo Marítimo** has rare whale skeletons and 350 species of local fish.

The town extends along the coast around the Península de la Magdalena, a headland on which there is a park, a small zoo and the **Palacio de la Magdalena** – a summer palace built for Alfonso XIII in 1912, reflecting the resort's popularity at the time with the Royal Family.

The seaside suburb of **El Sardinero**, north of the headland, is a smart resort with a long graceful beach, backed by gardens, elegant cafés and a majestic white casino. In July and August El Sardinero plays host to a major theatre and music festival.

🏛 **Museo de Bellas Artes**
Calle Rubio 6. **Tel** 942 20 31 20.
Open Tue–Sun. 🎫

🏛 **Museo de Prehistoria y Arqueología**
Calle Casimiro Sainz 4. **Tel** 942 20
71 09. **Open** Wed–Sun. 🚻 🎫

🏛 **Museo Marítimo**
C/ San Martin de Bajamar.
Tel 942 27 49 62. **Open** Tue–Sun.

⑳ Laredo

Cantabria. 🏘 11,800. 🚌 **ℹ** Alameda
Miramar, 942 61 10 96. 🎡 Batalla de
Flores (last Fri of Aug), Carlos V's last
landing (3rd week in Sep).

Its long, sandy beach has made Laredo one of Cantabria's most popular bathing resorts. The attractive Old Town has narrow streets with balconied houses leading up to the 13th-century **Iglesia de Santa María de la Asunción**, with its Flemish altar and bronze lecterns. One of the highlights of the year in Laredo is the colourful Battle of the Flowers, which takes place in August *(see p114)*.

㉑ Castro Urdiales

Cantabria. 🏘 32,000. 🚌 **ℹ** Parque
Armestoy Avda de la Constitución s/n,
942 87 15 12. 🚢 Thu. 🎡 San Pelayo
(26 Jun), Coso Blanco (1st Fri of Jul), San
Andrés (30 Nov). Iglesia: **Open** daily.

Castro Urdiales, a busy fishing town and popular holiday resort, is built around a picturesque harbour. Above the port, on a high promontory, stands the pinkish Gothic **Iglesia de Santa María**, as big as a cathedral. Beside it the restored castle, said to have been built by the Knights Templar, has been converted into a lighthouse. Handsome glass-fronted houses, or *galerías*, line the promenade. The small town beach often becomes crowded, but there are bigger ones to the west, such as the Playa de Ostende.

Environs
Near the village of **Ramales de la Victoria**, 40 km (25 miles) south, are prehistoric caves containing etchings and engravings, reached by a very steep mountain road.

Small boats moored in the harbour at Castro Urdiales

THE BASQUE COUNTRY, NAVARRA AND LA RIOJA

Vizcaya · Guipúzcoa · Álava · La Rioja · Navarra

Green hills meet Atlantic beaches in the Basque Country, land of an ancient people of mysterious origin. Navarra, also partly Basque, was a powerful medieval kingdom. The beautiful western Pyrenees form part of its charming countryside. The vineyards of La Rioja, to the south, produce many of Spain's finest wines.

The Basques are a race apart – they will not let you forget that theirs is a culture different from any in Spain. Although the Basque regional government enjoys considerable autonomy, there is a strong separatist movement seeking to sever links with the government in Madrid.

The Basque Country (Euskadi is the Basque name) is an important industrial region. The Basques are great deep-sea fishermen and fish has a major role in their imaginative cuisine, regarded by many as the best in Spain.

Unrelated to any other tongue, the Basque language, *Euskara,* is widely used on signs and most towns have two names; the fashionable resort of San Sebastián, for example, is officially known as Donostia – San Sebastián. *Euskara* is also spoken in parts of Navarra, which is counted as part of the wider (unofficial) Basque Country. Many of its finest sights – the towns of Olite and Estella, and the monastery of Leyre – date from the Middle Ages, when Navarra was a kingdom straddling the Pyrenees. Pamplona, its capital, is best known for its daredevil bullrunning fiesta, which is held in July.

As well as its vineyards and bodegas, La Rioja is a region of market gardens. Among its many historic sights are the cathedral of Santo Domingo de la Calzada and the monasteries of San Millán de la Cogolla and Yuso.

Basque farmhouse near Gernika-Lumo in the Basque Country

◀ Beautiful yellow fields of La Rioja in summertime

Exploring the Basque Country, Navarra and La Rioja

These green, hilly regions have diverse attractions. The Pyrenees in Navarra offer skiing in winter and climbing, caving and canoeing the rest of the year. The cliffs of the Basque Country are broken by rocky coves, *rías*, and wide bays with beaches of fine yellow sand, interspersed with fishing villages. Inland, minor roads wind through wooded hills, valleys and gorges, past lonely castles and isolated homesteads. In La Rioja, to the south, they cross vineyards, passing villages and towns clustered round venerable churches and monasteries.

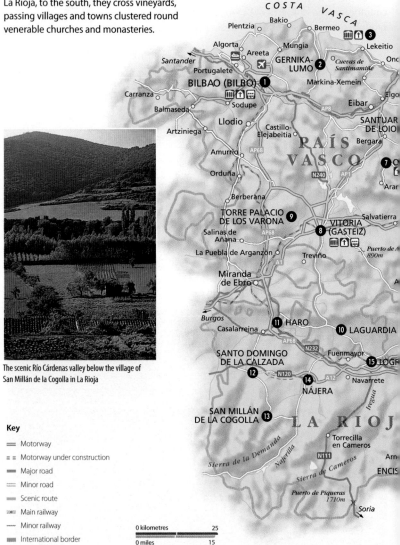

The scenic Río Cárdenas valley below the village of San Millán de la Cogolla in La Rioja

Key

- ▬▬ Motorway
- ═ ═ Motorway under construction
- ▬▬ Major road
- ═══ Minor road
- ▬▬ Scenic route
- ▭▬▭ Main railway
- ─── Minor railway
- ▓▓▓ International border
- ▬▬ Regional border

0 kilometres 25
0 miles 15

For additional map symbols *see back flap*

Sights at a Glance

1. Bilbao (Bilbo)
2. Gernika-Lumo
3. Costa Vasca
4. San Sebastián (Donostia)
5. Hondarribia (Fuenterrabía)
6. Santuario de Loiola
7. Oñati
8. Vitoria (Gasteiz)
9. Torre Palacio de los Varona
10. Laguardia
11. Haro
12. Santo Domingo de la Calzada
13. San Millán de la Cogolla
14. Nájera
15. Logroño
16. Enciso
17. Tudela
18. Monasterio de La Oliva
19. Ujué
20. Olite
21. Puente la Reina
22. Estella (Lizarra)
23. Pamplona (Iruña)
24. Las Cinco Villas del Valle de Bidasoa
25. Elizondo
26. Roncesvalles (Orreaga)
27. Valle de Roncal
28. Monasterio de Leyre
29. Castillo de Javier
30. Sangüesa

Getting Around

The main road in the north is the A8 (E5). The A68 AP68 (E804) runs southwards from Bilbao via Haro and follows the Ebro Valley. Motorway spurs extend to Vitoria and Pamplona. The rail network connects the cities and the larger towns, and most towns are served by coach. Bilbao has an international airport. In the Basque Country, signs are in both Basque and Castilian.

The fashionable Playa de Ondarreta, one of San Sebastián's three beaches

Buildings overlooking the Río Nervión in Bilbao

❶ Bilbao

Vizcaya. 🗺 354,000. ✈ 🚊 🚌 ⛴
ℹ Plaza Ensanche 11, 944 79 57 60.
🎉 Santiago (25 Jul), La Asunción
(15 Aug), Semana Grande (late Aug).
🌐 **bilbao.net/bilbaoturismo**

Bilbao (Bilbo) is the centre of Basque industry, an important port and the largest Basque city. It is surrounded by high, bare hills. Its suburbs spread 16 km (10 miles) along the Río Nervión (Nerbioi) to its estuary. The river between Las Arenas and the fishing port of Portugalete is crossed via the **Puente Colgante** (a UNESCO World Heritage Site). This iron transporter bridge, built in 1888, has a suspended cabin for cars and passengers. On the east bank of the estuary is Santurtzi (Santurce), from where ferries sail to the UK (see p627).

Bilbao has flourished as an industrial city since the mid-19th century, when iron ore

began to be extracted from deposits northwest of the city. Soon, steelworks and chemical factories became a major part of the local landscape. In the last two decades, however, many of the old shipyards and factories have been replaced by parks, riverside walks, pavement cafés and striking new architecture.

The city's medieval heart, the *casco viejo*, was built in the 14th century. Here, amid alleys lively with *pintxos* bars, is the arcaded Plazuela de Santiago and the **Catedral Basílica de Santiago**. The **Museo Vasco** displays Basque art, folk artifacts and photographs of Basque life. In the cloister is the Idol of Mikeldi, an animal-like carving dating from the 3rd to 2nd century BC.

In the newer town is the large **Museo de Bellas Artes** (Museum of Fine Art), one of Spain's best art museums. It displays art ranging from 12th-century Basque and Catalan pieces to works by modern artists of international fame, including Vasarely, Kokoschka, Bacon, Delaunay and Léger. There are also paintings by Basque artists.

The jewel in the area's cultural crown is the **Museo Guggenheim Bilbao** (see pp124–5). The museum is part of a redevelopment of the city which includes the expansion of its port and the metro system, designed in a futuristic style by Norman Foster. Another striking building is the **Palacio de la Música y Congresos Euskalduna**, designed to resemble a ship.

The **Alhóndiga**, a century-old wine warehouse, was converted into a cultural centre in 2010. It boasts design shops and restaurants, a library, a fabulous pool and a rooftop terrace.

West of the city, a funicular railway ascends to the village of La Reineta and a panorama across the dockyards.

🏛 **Museo Vasco**
Plaza Miguel de Unamuno 4. **Tel** 94 415 54 23. **Open** Tue–Sun. **Closed** public hols. 🍴 (except Thu). ♿

🏛 **Museo de Bellas Artes**
Plaza del Museo 2. **Tel** 94 439 60 60. **Open** Tue–Sun. 🍴 (except Wed). 📷 ♿

🎭 **Palacio de la Música y Congresos Euskalduna**
Avenida Abandoibarra 4. **Tel** 94 403 50 00. **Open** for concerts. 🍴 📷 ♿

🎭 **Alhóndiga**
Plaza Arriquibar 4. **Tel** 94 401 40 14.
🌐 **alhondigabilbao.com**

❷ Gernika-Lumo

Vizcaya. 🗺 16,000. 🚌 🚌 ℹ Artekalea 8, 94 625 58 92. 🎉 Aniversario del Bombardeo de Guernica (26 Apr), San Roque (14–18 Aug).

This little town is of great symbolic significance to the Basques. For centuries, Basque leaders met in democratic assembly under an oak on a hillside here. On 26 April 1937 Gernika-Lumo (Guernica) was the target of the world's first saturation bombing raid, carried out by Nazi aircraft at the request of General Franco. Picasso's powerful painting (see pp70–71) of this outrage can be seen in Madrid (see p303).

The town has since been rebuilt and is rather dull. But in a garden, inside a pavilion and closely guarded, is the 300-year-old petrified trunk of the oak tree, the *Gernikako Arbola*, or Oak of Gernika, symbol of the ancient roots of the Basque people. Younger oaks, nurtured from its acorns, have been planted beside it. The Basque people make visits to this ancient tree as if on a pilgrimage. The **Casa de Juntas**, nearby, is a former

Zuloaga's *Condesa Mathieu de Noailles* (1913), Bilbao Museum of Fine Art

Basque fishermen depicted in the stained-glass ceiling of the Casa de Juntas in Gernika-Lumo

chapel where the parliament of the province of Vizcaya reconvened in 1979, when the Basque provinces regained their autonomy. In one room a stained-glass ceiling depicts the Oak of Gernika with Basque citizens debating their rights.

The Europa Park, next door, has peace sculptures by Henry Moore and Eduardo Chillida.

Environs

Five km (3 miles) northeast of Gernika, near Kortézubi (Cortézubi), are the **Cuevas de Santimamiñe**. On the walls of a small chamber are charcoal drawings of animals made by cave dwellers around 11,000 BC. Discovered in 1917, the drawings cannot be seen, but replicas are projected on the walls at the entrance. For conservation reasons the caves are closed to the public, but a 3D simulation in the nearby hermitage offers an impressive virtual reproduction. Guided visits last 90 minutes and must be booked in advance.

Casa de Juntas
C/ Allende Salazar. **Tel** 94 625 11 38.
Open daily. **Closed** 1 & 6 Jan, 16 Aug, 24, 25 & 31 Dec. 📷 book ahead. ♿

Cuevas de Santimamiñe
Kortézubi. **Tel** 944 65 16 57.
Open Tue–Sun. 📷 📷 book ahead.

❸ Costa Vasca

Vizcaya & Guipúzcoa. 🚉 Bilbao.
🚌 Bilbao. 🛈 Getxo, 94 491 08 00.

The Basque country's 176 km (110 miles) of coastline is heavily indented: rugged cliffs alternate with inlets and coves, backed by wooded hills. Some of the fishing villages are overdeveloped, but the scenery inland is attractive.

There are good beaches north of **Algorta** (near Bilbao). **Plentzia** is a pleasant estuary town with a marina. Eastwards on the coast is **Bakio**, a large fishing village. Beyond it the BI3101, a dramatic corniche road, winds high above the sea past the tiny island hermitage, San Juan de Gaztelugatxe, and Matxitxaco, a headland light-

Anglers on the quayside at Lekeitio, a port on the Costa Vasca

house. It passes Bermeo, a port with a fishery museum, the **Museo del Pescador**, and Mundaka, a small surfing resort. On the serene Ría de Guernica there are two sandy beaches, **Laida** and **Laga**.

At the fishing port of **Lekeitio**, old Basque houses line the seafront below the 15th-century church of Santa María. One long beach, good for swimming, sweeps round the village of **Saturrarán** and the old port of **Ondarroa**. The Lekeitio–Ondarroa road is lined with pines.

Zumaia is a beach resort with an old quarter. In the **Espacio Cultural Ignacio Zuloaga**, the former home of the well-known Basque painter who lived from 1870 to 1945, colourful studies of Basque rural and maritime life are on display. **Getaria**, along the coast, is spread steeply around a fishing port, and has lively cafés and the 14th-century Iglesia de San Salvador. **Zarautz**, once a fashionable resort, has sizable beaches and elegant mansions.

Museo del Pescador
Plaza Torrontero 1. **Tel** 94 688 11 71.
Open Tue–Sun. **Closed** public hols.
📷 (free last Thu of the month). ♿

Espacio Cultural Ignacio Zuloaga
Santiago Etxea 4, Zumaia. **Tel** 943 86 23 41. **Open** Apr–Sep: 4–8pm Wed–Sun; other times by appt. 📷 📷

Bilbao: Museo Guggenheim

The Museo Guggenheim Bilbao is the jewel in the city's cultural crown. The building itself is a star attraction: a mind-boggling array of silvery curves by the American architect Frank Gehry, which are alleged to resemble a ship or a flower. The Guggenheim's collection represents an intriguingly broad spectrum of modern and contemporary art, and includes works by Abstract Impressionists such as Willem de Kooning and Mark Rothko. Most of the art shown here is displayed as part of an ongoing series of temporary exhibitions and shows from the permanent collections of the Guggenheim museums in New York, Venice and Berlin.

View from the City
Approaching along the Calle de Iparraguirre, the Guggenheim stands out amid traditional buildings.

★ Titanium façade
Rarely used in buildings, titanium is more usually used for aircraft parts. In total 60 tons were used, but the layer is only 3 mm (0.1 inches) thick.

Arcelor Gallery
Dominated by Richard Serra's *The Matter of Time*, this gallery is the museum's largest. The fish motif, seen in the flowing shape, is one of architect Frank Gehry's favourites.

★ Atrium
The space in which visitors to the museum first find themselves is the extraordinary 60-m- (165-ft-) high atrium. It serves as an orientation point and its height makes it a dramatic setting for exhibiting large pieces.

VISITORS' CHECKLIST

Practical Information
Avenida Abandoibarra 2. **Tel** 944 35 90 00. **w** guggenheim-bilbao.es **Open** 10am–8pm Tue–Sun (daily Jul & Aug). Art After Dark: 10pm–1am one Fri a month. booking online advisable, especially during high season.

Transport
Moyua. 1, 10, 11, 13, 18, 27, 38, 48, 71.

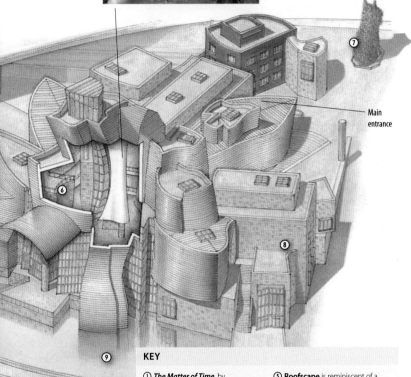

Main entrance

KEY

① *The Matter of Time*, by sculptor, Richard Serra, was created in hot-rolled steel. It is over 30 m (100 ft) long.

② **Nerua** is the museum's Michelin-starred restaurant.

③ **The Puente de la Salve** was incorporated into the design of the building, which extends underneath it.

④ **The tower**, on the far side of the bridge, was designed to resemble a sail. It is not an exhibition space.

⑤ **Roofscape** is reminiscent of a ship, with the Guggenheim's prow-like points and metallic material.

⑥ **Second-floor balcony**

⑦ *Puppy*, by American artist Jeff Koons, is a 13-m (43-ft) West Highland terrier with a coat of flowers watered by an internal irrigation system. It has become a favourite icon of the city

⑧ **Café**

⑨ **Water garden beside the River Nervión**

San Sebastián's Playa de Ondarreta, with its view across the bay

❹ San Sebastián

Guipúzcoa. 🏠 186,000.
✈ Hondarribia (22 km). 🚌 🚉
🛈 Alameda del Bulevard 8, 943 48 11
66. 🅰 Sun. 🎭 San Sebastián (20 Jan);
Semana Grande (week of 15 Aug).
W sansebastianturismo.com

Gloriously situated on a neat, shell-shaped bay, San Sebastián (Donostia) is the most elegant and fashionable Spanish seaside resort. At either end of the bay is a tower-topped hill – Monte Urgull in the east and Monte Igueldo in the west. Between the two, in the mouth of the bay, lies a small island, the Isla de Santa Clara.

San Sebastián became a smart resort in the late 19th century. It still has many luxury shops and one of Spain's grandest hotels, the María Cristina (see p564), but San Sebastián is now primarily a family resort.

The city is renowned for its great summer arts festivals. The theatre festival is held in May; jazz festivals are held in July; a classical music festival, in August; and the San Sebastián International Film Festival, in September. The Semana Grande in August is the city's principal fiesta.

Cuisine plays a huge part in local life: many Basque men here belong to gastronomic clubs where they gather to cook, eat, drink and talk. Women are invited to such meetings, but they don't take part in the food preparation.

The Old Town

San Sebastián's fascinating Old Town (Parte Vieja) is wedged between the bay and the Río Urumea. The alleys, packed with restaurants and tapas bars, are intensely animated at night. In the local fish market, stalls piled high with delicacies testify to the key role of fish in the town.

The heart of the Old Town is the **Plaza de la Constitución**, a handsome, arcaded square. The numbers on the balconies date from when the square was used as a bullring – organizers sold a ticket for each numbered place. Nearby are the impressively reverent **Basílica de Santa Maria** and the 16th-century church of **Iglesia de San Vicente**.

Monte Urgull rises behind the Old Town. On the summit are a statue of Christ and the ruined **Castillo de Santa Cruz de la Mota**, with old cannons.

Beaches

San Sebastián's two principal beaches follow the bay round to **Monte Igueldo**. The **Playa de Ondarreta** is the more fashionable of the two, while the **Playa de la Concha** is the larger. Between them is the **Palacio Miramar**, built in 1889 by the Basque architect José Goicoa, to designs by Selden Wornum, a British architect. The palace, built for Queen María Cristina, established San Sebastián as an aristocratic resort. The gardens are open to the public.

At the water's edge near the Playa de Ondarreta is a striking group of modern iron sculptures, The Comb of the Winds by Eduardo Chillida. A road and a funicular railway, built in 1912, lead to the top of Monte Igueldo, where there is a small amusement park.

To the east of the Playa de la Concha is the surfer's favourite, **Playa de Zurriola**, with surf schools and shops, overlooked by the hill, **Monte Ulía**.

🐟 Aquarium

Plaza Carlos Blasco de Imaz 1.
Tel 943 44 00 99. **Open** Easter–Jun & Sep: 10am–8pm daily (to 9pm Sat & Sun); Jul–Aug: 10am–9pm daily; Oct–Easter: 10am–7pm (to 8pm Sat & Sun). **Closed** 1 & 20 Jan, 25 Dec. 🐟 🎥 🛆

This remodelled aquarium boasts a 360-degree underwater tunnel, where visitors can view over 5,000 fish, including four species of shark. Tickets allow entry to a Naval Museum, with exhibits of Basque naval history.

The Comb of the Winds by Eduardo Chillida

For hotels and restaurants in this region see pp563–4 and pp585–6

Josep Maria Sert's murals of Basque life in the Museo de San Telmo

Kursaal

Avenida de Zurriola 1. **Tel** 943 00 30 00. 🚗 📷 ♿ 🅿 ♿ **W** **kursaal.org**

These giant cubes stand out as the most prominent feature on Zurriola beach, especially when lit up at night. Designed by Rafael Moneo, the cubes contain large auditoriums, for most of the year home to conferences and concerts.

🏛 Museo de San Telmo

Plaza Zuloaga 1. **Tel** 943 48 15 80. **Open** 10am–8pm Tue–Sun. **Closed** 1 & 20 Jan, 25 Dec. 🚗 (free Tue). 📷 ♿

This is a large museum in a 16th-century monastery below Monte Urgull. In the cloister is a collection of Basque funerary columns dating from the 15th–17th centuries.

The museum also contains displays of furniture, tools and other artifacts, and paintings by local Basque artists: 19th-century works by Antonio Ortiz Echagüe,

modern paintings by Ignacio Zuloaga, portraits by Vicente López and masterpieces by El Greco. The chapel holds 11 murals by the Catalan artist Josep Maria Sert, depicting Basque legends, culture and the region's seafaring life.

Environs

5 km (3 miles) east of San Sebastián is **Pasai Donibane**, a picturesque fishing village consisting of a jumble of houses built along one cobbled main street, which has some good fish restaurants.

Around 8 km (5 miles) south of San Sebastián is the interesting medieval town of **Hernani**, which has been awarded the status of Cultural Interest Site. The forests surrounding the town are dotted with prehistoric remains, including dolmens, megalithic monuments and burial mounds.

The waterfront of the tiny fishing village of Pasaia Donibane

Old balconied houses in the upper town, Hondarribia

❺ Hondarribia

Guipúzcoa. 🏘 16,500. 🚆 🚌 ℹ️ Arma Plaza 9, 943 64 36 77; Minatera, 9 Puerto Deportivo, 934 64 54 58. 🎉 La Kutxa Entrega (25 Jul), Alarde (6–8 Sep). **W** **bidasoaturismo.com**

Hondarribia (Fuenterrabía), the historic town at the mouth of the Río Bidasoa, was attacked by the French over many centuries. The upper town is protected by 15th-century walls and entered via their original gateway, the handsome **Puerta de Santa María**. They enclose alleys of old houses with carved eaves, balconies and coats of arms.

The streets cluster round the church of **Nuestra Señora de la Asunción y del Manzano**, with its massive buttresses, tall Baroque tower and, inside, a gold reredos. At the town's highest point is the 10th-century **castle**, now a parador (see p564).

Hondarribia has seafront cafés in La Marina, its lively fishermen's quarter. It is also a seaside resort, with beaches stretching to the north.

Environs

A hill road climbs westwards to the shrine of the Virgin of Guadalupe. Further along this road are panoramic views of the coast and the mountains. From the **Ermita de San Marcial**, which stands on a hill 9 km (6 miles) to the south, there are views of the Bidasoa plain straddling the border – the French towns are neatly white, the Spanish ones are greyer.

San Sebastián Film Festival

This festival, founded in 1953, is one of the five leading European annual film festivals. It is held in late September, drawing more than 200,000 spectators. The special Donostia Prize is awarded as a tribute to the career of a star or director: winners have included Meryl Streep, Ian McKellen and Woody Allen. Visiting celebrities have included Quentin Tarantino, Ethan Coen and Bertrand Tavernier. Prizes also go to individual new films. An early winner was Hitchcock's *Vertigo*. The festival's website is www.sansebastianfestival.com.

Benicio Del Toro receiving an award

The Renaissance façade of the former Basque university in Oñati

❻ Santuario de Loiola

Loiola, Guipúzcoa. **Tel** 943 02 50 00.
🚌 **Open** 10am–1pm, 3:30–7pm
(to 8pm in summer) daily.
🌐 santuariodeloyola.org

Saint Ignatius of Loiola (San Ignacio de Loyola), founder of the Jesuits, was born in the 1490s in the Santa Casa (holy house), a stone manor near Azpeitia. In the 1600s it was enclosed by the Basílica de San Ignacio, and the rooms in which the aristocratic Loiola family lived were converted into chapels. The Chapel of the Conversion is where Ignatius, as a young soldier, recovered from a war injury and had a profound religious experience.

A diorama depicts episodes in the saint's life: dedicating his life to Christ at the Monastery of Montserrat (see pp222–3); writing his *Spiritual Exercises* in a cave at Manresa; his imprisonment by the Inquisition; and his pilgrimage to the Holy Land. The basilica, built from 1681 to 1738, has a Churrigueresque dome and a circular nave with rich carvings.

❼ Oñati

Guipúzcoa. 🚹 11,000. 🚌 ℹ️ C/ San Juan 14, 943 78 34 53. 🚐 Sat. 🎭 Corpus Christi (May/Jun), San Miguel (29 Sep–1 Oct). 🌐 oinati.org

This historic town in the Udana Valley has a distinguished past. In the First Carlist War, 1833–9 (see p67), it was a seat of the court of Don Carlos, brother of King Fernando VII and pretender to the throne. Its former **university**, built in about 1540, was for centuries the only one in the Basque Country. It has a Renaissance façade, decorated with statues of saints, and an elegant patio.

In the Plaza de los Fueros is the **Iglesia de San Miguel**, a Gothic church with a stone cloister in Gothic-Flemish style. It contains the tomb of Bishop Zuázola of Ávila, the founder of the university. Opposite is the Baroque **town hall** (ayuntamiento).

Environs

A mountain road ascends 9 km (6 miles) to the **Santuario de Arantzazu**, below the peak of Aitzgorri. In 1469 it is believed a shepherd visualized the Virgin here. Over the door of the church, built in the 1950s, are sculptures of the apostles by Jorge Oteiza.

🏛️ **Universidad de Sancti Spiritus**
Avenida de la Universidad Vasca.
Tel 943 78 34 53. **Open** daily for guided tours (phone Oñati tourist information in advance). 🎨

The imposing Santuario de Loiola, with its Churrigueresque cupola

The Founding of the Jesuit Order

The Society of Jesus was founded in Rome in 1539 by Saint Ignatius and a group of priests who were dedicated to helping the poor. Pope Paul III soon approved the order's establishment, with Ignatius as Superior General. The order, which grew wealthy, vowed military obedience to the pope and became his most powerful weapon against the Reformation. Today, there are approximately 20,000 Jesuits working, mainly in education, in 112 countries.

Saint Ignatius of Loiola

Basque Culture

The Basques may be Europe's oldest race. Anthropologists think they could be descended from Cro-Magnon people, who lived in the Pyrenees 40,000 years ago. The dolmens and carved stones of their ancestors are evidence of the Basques' pagan roots.

Long isolated in their mountain valleys, the Basques preserved their unique language, myths and art for millennia, almost untouched by other influences. Many families still live in the isolated, chalet-style stone *caseríos*, or farmhouses, built by their forebears. Their music and high-bounding dances are unlike those of any other culture, and their cuisine is varied and imaginative.

The *fueros*, or ancient Basque laws and rights were suppressed under General Franco, but since the arrival of democracy in 1975 the Basques have had their own parliament and police force, having won great autonomy over their own affairs.

The Basque Region

▨ *Areas of Basque culture*

The national identity is symbolized by the region's flag: *La Ikurriña*. The white cross symbolizes Christianity. The green St Andrew's Cross commemorates a battle won on his feast day.

Bertsolaris are bards. They improvise witty, sometimes humorous songs, whose verses relate current events or legends. *Bertsolaris* sing, unaccompanied, to gatherings in public places, such as bars and squares, often in competition. This oral tradition has preserved Basque folklore, legends and history. No texts were written in *Euskara* (Basque) until the 16th century.

The Basque economy has always relied on fishing and associated industries, such as ship-building and agriculture. In recent history, heavy industries have made this region prosperous.

Traditional sports are highly respected in Basque culture. In pelota, teams hit a ball at a wall, then catch it with a wicker scoop or their hands. Sports involving strength, such as log-splitting and weight-lifting, are the most popular.

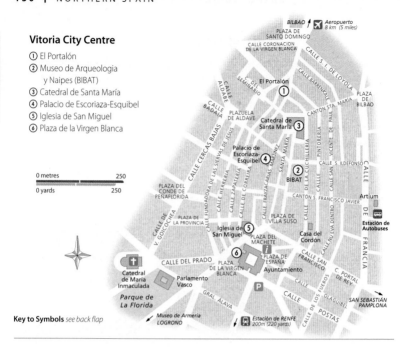

Vitoria City Centre

① El Portalón
② Museo de Arqueologia
   y Naipes (BIBAT)
③ Catedral de Santa María
④ Palacio de Escoriaza-Esquibel
⑤ Iglesia de San Miguel
⑥ Plaza de la Virgen Blanca

0 metres   250
0 yards   250

Key to Symbols *see back flap*

❽ Vitoria

Álava. 🔊 240,000. 🚉 🚌
ℹ️ Plaza de España 1, 945 16 15 98.
🗓️ Thu. 🎺 Romería de San
Prudencio (27–28 Apr), Fiestas
de la Virgen Blanca (4–9 Aug).
🆆 vitoria-gasteiz.org/turismo

Vitoria (Gasteiz), the seat of
the Basque government,
was founded on a hill – the
province's highest point and the
site of an ancient Basque town,
Gasteiz. Vitoria's oldest part,
El Campillo, was rebuilt in 1200
after a fire. The city later grew
rich on the iron and wool trades.

The old town focuses on the
Plaza de la Virgen Blanca, with
its monument to a battle fought
nearby in 1813, when the British

Duke of Wellington defeated
the French. Around the plaza
are old houses with *miradores*
(glazed balconies).

On the hillside above the
plaza is the Gothic **Iglesia de
San Miguel**. An outside niche
contains a statue of the Virgen
Blanca (White Virgin), Vitoria's
patron saint. A big festival *(see
p136)* starts before her feast day,
which is on 5 August. On the wall
of San Miguel facing the **Plaza
del Machete** there is a recess
with a replica of the machete
on which the city's rulers swore
to uphold the laws or be slain.

The Old Town has several
Renaissance palaces, including
the 16th-century **Palacio de
Escoriaza-Esquibel**, with its

Plateresque *(see p29)* patio.
Around it is a charming area
of alleys linked by steep steps.

The city has two cathedrals.
The oldest is the Gothic **Catedral
de Santa María**, with a sculpted
west porch. Close by, in Calle
Correría, a street of old houses,
is **El Portalón**, a merchant's
house and hostel from the 15th
century. The building, which is
full of Basque country furniture
and art, is now a restaurant.

Among the city's later architectural gems are an arcaded
street, **Los Arquillos**, and the
adjoining **Plaza de España**, also
arcaded. They were built in the
late 18th century to link the Old
Town with the new quarter then
being built. South of the old town
is the Neo-Gothic **Catedral Nueva
de María Inmaculada**, begun in
1907 and finished in 1973.

🏛️ Artium
Calle de Francia 24. **Tel** 945 20 90 20.
Open Tue–Sun. 🅿️ ♿ 🆆 artium.org
Artium, the Basque Museum
of Contemporary Art, occupies
a striking white building and
contains one of Spain's largest
collections of modern and
contemporary art. The focus
is mainly on Spanish artists like
Dalí, Miró, Tàpies and Chillida.

The quiet Plaza de España in the centre of Vitoria

For hotels and restaurants in this region see pp563–4 and pp585–6

The Gothic west door of Vitoria's Catedral de Santa María

🏛 Museo de Arqueología y Naipes (BIBAT)

Palacio de Bendaña, C/ Cuchillería 54. **Tel** 945 20 37 00. **Open** Tue–Sun. 🚹

Vitoria's archaeology museum is set in a stunning purpose-built edifice and features 1,500 pieces, including prehistory artifacts and Roman sculptures found at Álava. Visitors can experience multimedia projections and sound effects.

The grandson of Heraclio Fournier, who founded a playing cards factory in Vitoria in 1868, also displays his collection of more than 6,000 items in this museum. The oldest exhibits are late 14th-century Italian cards. Among the many sets of tarot cards are some designed by Salvador Dalí in the 1980s.

🏛 Museo de Armería

Paseo Fray Francisco 3. **Tel** 945 18 19 25. **Open** Tue–Sun. 🚹 phone 945 18 19 18 for guided tours. 🚹

The weapons here range from prehistoric axes to 20th-century pistols. Medieval armour and an exhibit on the 1813 battle of Vitoria are also on display.

🏛 Museo de Arte Sacro

Catedral Nueva de María Inmaculada, Calle Monseñor Cadena y Eleta s/n. **Tel** 945 15 06 31. **Open** 10am–2pm, 4–6:30pm Tue–Fri, 10am–2pm Sat, 11am–2pm Sun & public hols. 🚹 call ahead. 🚹

The design of this museum is considerate to the surrounding cathedral. Exhibits of religious art are displayed in sections related to their medium.

❾ Torre Palacio de los Varona

Villanañe, Álava. **Tel** 945 35 30 40. **Open** 11am–2pm, 4–7pm Tue–Sat, 11am–2pm Sun (winter: Sat & Sun only). 🚹 🚹

The small town of Villanañe hosts a beautiful example of medieval civil architecture, the best-preserved 14th-century fortified military building in the region – now a museum displaying original furniture. The upper rooms are decorated with colourful 17th-century wallpaper, while some of the floors are made with traditional Manisse porcelain tiles.

Environs

On the A2622 Pobes–Tuesta road are the **Salinas de Añana**, a group of saltpans fed by mineral springs. The nearby village of **Tuesta** boasts a Romanesque church. Inside are capitals carved with historical scenes, and a medieval wood sculpture of St Sebastián.

❿ Laguardia

Álava. 🔼 1,500. 🚹 Calle Mayor 52, 945 60 08 45. 🚹 Tue. 🚹 San Juan and San Pedro (23–29 Jun).

This little wine town is the capital of La Rioja Alavesa, a part of southern Álava province where Rioja wines *(see pp82–3)* have been produced for centuries. It is a fertile, vine-clad plain, sheltered by high hills to the north. There are fine panoramic views from the road that climbs up to the Herrera pass. Laguardia is a medieval hill town, its encircling ramparts, towers and fortified gateways visible from afar. Along its steep, narrow cobbled streets there are many **bodegas** (wine cellars), offering wine tastings and tours throughout the year. It is usually necessary to make a booking in advance. The Gothic **Iglesia de Santa María de los Reyes** has an austere façade and a richly embellished inner portal that has retained its original colouring.

Vineyards near Laguardia, capital of La Rioja Alavesa, a wine-producing region since the Middle Ages

⓫ Haro

La Rioja. ⛰ 11,500. 🚌 🚃 ℹ️ Plaza de la Paz, 941 30 35 80. 🗓 Tue & Sat. 🍷 Wine Battle (29 Jun), San Juan, San Felices, San Pedro (24–29 Jun), Virgen de la Vega (8 Sep). 🌐 **haro.org**

A graceful town on the Río Ebro, Haro has a lively old quarter with wine taverns and mansions. It is crowned by the hilltop **Iglesia de Santo Tomás**, a Gothic church with a Plateresque *(see p29)* portal.

Haro is the centre for the vineyards and bodegas of the Rioja Alta wine region, which is higher and cooler than the Rioja Baja *(see pp82–3)*. The clay soil and the climate – Haro is sheltered by a sierra to the north – create the conditions in which the famous regional wines are produced. Many bodegas run tours and tastings. To join one, you need to book ahead at the bodega. There may be a small charge. The charming cafés in the Old Town offer local wines and tapas at low prices and a convivial atmosphere.

A wine-throwing orgy is the climax of the area's fiesta *(see p136)* held every June.

Tomb of St Dominic in the cathedral of Santo Domingo de la Calzada

Rows of Rioja vines on the rolling hills near Haro

⓬ Santo Domingo de la Calzada

La Rioja. ⛰ 6,700. 🚃 ℹ️ Calle Mayor 33, 941 34 12 38. 🗓 Sat. 🍷 Fiestas del Santo (25 Apr–15 May), Día del Patron (12 May).

This town on the Road to Santiago de Compostela *(see pp86–7)* is named after the 11th-century saint who built bridges and roads *(calzadas)* to help pilgrims. Santo Domingo also founded a hospital, which now serves as a parador *(see p564)*. Miracles performed by the saint are recorded in carvings on his tomb in the town's part-Romanesque, part-Gothic **cathedral**, and in paintings on the wall of the choir. The most obvious and bizarre record is a sumptuously decorated cage set in a wall in which, for centuries, a live cock and hen have been kept. The cathedral has a carved walnut reredos at the high altar, the last work, in 1541, of the artist Damià Forment. The restored 14th-century **ramparts** of the town are also worth seeing.

The Cock and Hen of St Dominic

A live cock and hen are kept in the cathedral of Santo Domingo de la Calzada as a tribute to the saint's miraculous life-giving powers. Centuries ago, it is said, a German pilgrim refused the advances of a local girl, who denounced him as a thief. He was hanged as a consequence, but later his parents found him alive on the gallows. They rushed to a judge, who said, dismissively, "Nonsense, he's no more alive than this roast chicken on my plate". Whereupon, the chicken stood up on the plate and crowed.

The cock and hen in their decorated cage

⓭ San Millán de la Cogolla

La Rioja. 🅰 250. 🚌 from Logroño.
ℹ Monasterio de Yuso (open Tue–Sun), Portería de Yuso, Piso de Abajo, 941 37 30 49; Monasterio de Suso, 941 37 30 82 (book ahead). 📷 compulsory. 🎉 Traslación de las Reliquias (26 Sep), San Millán (12 Nov). 🌐 **monasteriodeyuso.org**

This village grew up around two monasteries. On a hillside above the village is the **Monasterio de San Millán de Suso**. It was built in the 10th century on the site of a community founded by St Emilian, a shepherd hermit, in 537. The church, hollowed out of pink sandstone, has Romanesque and Mozarabic features. It contains the carved alabaster tomb of St Emiliano.

Below it is the **Monasterio de San Millán de Yuso**, built between the 16th and 18th centuries. The part-Renaissance church has Baroque golden doors and a Rococo sacristy with 17th-century paintings.

In the treasury there is a collection of ivory plaques. They were once part of two 11th-century jewelled reliquaries, which were plundered by French troops in 1813.

Medieval manuscripts are also displayed in the treasury. Among them is a facsimile of one of the earliest known texts in Castilian Romance (see p38). It is a commentary by a 10th-century Suso monk on a work by San Cesáreo de Arles, the *Glosas Emilianenses*.

The Monasterio de San Millán de Yuso in the Cárdenas Valley

Cloister of the Monasterio de Santa María la Real, Nájera

⓮ Nájera

La Rioja. 🅰 8,500. 🚉 ℹ Plaza de San Miguel 10, 941 36 00 41. 🚌 Thu. 🎉 San Prudencio (28 Apr), Santa María la Real (16–19 Sep).

The Old Town of Nájera, west of Logroño, was the capital of La Rioja and Navarra until 1076, when La Rioja was incorporated into Castile. The royal families of Navarra, León and Castile are buried in the **Monasterio de Santa María la Real**. It was founded in the 11th century beside a sandstone cliff where a statue of the Virgin was found in a cave. A 13th-century Madonna can be seen in the cave, beneath the carved choir stalls of the 15th-century church.

The 12th-century carved tomb of Blanca of Navarra, the wife of Sancho III, is the finest of many royal sarcophagi.

🏛 **Monasterio de Santa María la Real**
Plaza Santa María 1, Nájera.
Tel 941 36 10 83. **Open** Tue–Sun. 📷

⓯ Logroño

La Rioja. 🅰 152,000. 🚉 🚌 ℹ Escuelas Trevijano, C/ Portales 50, 941 29 12 60. 🎉 San Bernabé (11 Jun), San Mateo (21 Sep). 🌐 **lariojaturismo.com**

The capital of La Rioja is a tidy, modern city of wide boulevards and smart shops. It is the commercial centre of a fertile plain where quality vegetables are produced, in addition to Rioja wines. In Logroño's pleasant old quarter on the Río Ebro is the Gothic **cathedral**, with twin towers. Above the south portal of the nearby **Iglesia de Santiago el Real**, which houses an image of the patron saint Our Lady of Hope, is an equestrian statue of St James as Moorslayer (see p59).

Environs
About 50 km (30 miles) south of Logroño, the N111 winds through the dramatic **Iregua Valley**, through tunnels, to the Sierra de Cameros.

The ornate Baroque west door of Logroño Cathedral

⓰ Enciso

La Rioja. 🅰 160. 🚌 from Logroño. ℹ Plaza Mayor, 941 39 60 05. 🎉 San Roque (16 Aug).

Near this remote hill village west of Calahorra is Spain's "Jurassic Park". Signposts point to the *huellas de dinosaurios* (dinosaur footprints). Embedded in rocks overhanging a stream are the prints of many giant, three-toed feet, up to 30 cm (1 ft) long. They were made around 150 million years ago, when dinosaurs moved between the marshes of the Ebro Valley, at that time a sea, and these hills. Prints can also be seen at other locations in the area.

Environs
Arnedillo, 10 km (6 miles) to the north, is a spa with thermal baths once used by Fernando VI. In **Autol**, to the east, there are two unusual limestone peaks.

The intricately carved portal of Tudela Cathedral

⓱ Tudela

Navarra. 🗺 35,500. 🚉 🚌
ℹ️ Plaza Fueros 5, 948 84 80 58.
🗓 Sat. 🎉 Santa Ana (26–30 Jul).

Navarra's second city is the great commercial centre of the vast agricultural lands of the Ebro Valley in Navarra, the Ribera. Much of Tudela consists of modern developments, but its origins are ancient. Spanning the Ebro is a 13th-century bridge with 17 irregular arches. The Old Town has two well-preserved Jewish districts.

The **Plaza de los Fueros** is old Tudela's main square. It is surrounded by houses with wrought-iron balconies. On some of their façades are paintings of bullfights, a reminder that the plaza was formerly used as a bullring.

The **cathedral**, begun in 1194, exemplifies the religious toleration under which Tudela was governed after the Reconquest.

It is Early Gothic, with a carved portal depicting the Last Judgment. There is a Romanesque cloister, and beside the cathedral sits a 9th-century chapel that is thought to have once been a synagogue.

Environs
To the north is the **Bárdenas Reales**, an arid area of limestone cliffs and crags. About 20 km (12 miles) west of Tudela is the spa town of **Fitero**, with the 12th-century Monasterio de Santa María.

⓲ Monasterio de La Oliva

Carcastillo, Navarra. **Tel** 948 72 50 06.
🚌 from Pamplona. **Open** daily. 🎟
🌐 monasteriodelaoliva.org

French Cistercian monks built this small monastery on a remote plain in the 1100s. The church is simple but adorned with rose windows.

One of the cloisters in the Monasterio de La Oliva

The serene cloister, dating from the 14th and 15th centuries, adjoins a 12th-century chapter-house. The church also has a 17th-century tower. Today, the monks survive by selling local honey and cheese, their own wine, and by accepting paying guests (see p561).

⓳ Ujué

Navarra. 🗺 198. ℹ️ Plaza Municipal, 948 73 90 46. 🎉 Virgen de Ujué (Sun after 25 April). 🌐 ujue.es

An unspoiled hill village, Ujué commands a high spur at the end of a winding road. It has quaint façades, cobbled alleys and steep steps. The impressive and austere **Iglesia de Santa María** is in Gothic style, with a Romanesque chancel and an exterior lookout gallery. The ruined fortifications around the church offer views of the Pyrenees.

On the Sunday after 25 April, pilgrims in black capes visit the Virgin of Ujué, whose Romanesque image is displayed in the church.

⓴ Olite

Navarra. 🗺 3,900. 🚉 🚌 ℹ️ Plaza de Teobaldos 10, 948 74 17 03. 🗓 Wed. 🎉 Medieval Markets (late Aug), Exaltación de la Santa Cruz (13–19 Sep). 🌐 olite.es

The historic town of Olite was founded by the Romans and later chosen as a royal residence by the kings of Navarra. Parts of the town's old walls can be seen. They enclose a delightful

---

The Kingdom of Navarra

Navarra emerged as an independent Christian kingdom in the 10th century, after Sancho I Garcés became king of Pamplona. Sancho III the Great expanded the kingdom, and at his death, in 1035, Navarra stretched all the way from Ribagorza in Aragón to Valladolid. Sancho VI the Wise, who reigned 1150–94, recognized the independent rights (fueros) of many towns. In 1234, Navarra passed by marriage to a line of French rulers. One, Carlos III, the Noble, built Olite Castle. His grandson, Carlos de Viana, wrote The Chronicle of the Kings of Navarra in 1455. In 1512 Navarra was annexed by Fernando II of Castile, as part of united Spain, but it kept its own laws and currency until the 1800s.

Prince Carlos de Viana, Carlos III's grandson

jumble of steep, narrow streets and little squares, churches and the **Monasterio de Santa Clara**, begun in the 13th century. The houses along the Rúa Cerco de Fuera and the Rúa Mayor were built between the 16th and 18th centuries.

The castle, the **Palacio Real de Olite**, was built in the early 15th century by Carlos III, and has earned Olite its nickname "the Gothic town". It was heavily fortified, but was brilliantly decorated inside by Mudéjar artists with *azulejos* (ceramic tiles) and marquetry ceilings. The walkways were planted with vines and orange trees, and there was an aviary and a lions' den.

During the War of Independence (*see pp66–7*) the castle was burned to prevent it falling into French hands. Since 1937, however, it has been restored to a semblance of its former glory. Part of it houses a parador (*see p564*).

Today, the castle is a complex of courtyards, passages, large halls, royal chambers, battlements and turrets. From the "windy tower", monarchs could watch tournaments.

Adjoining the castle is a 13th-century former royal chapel, the **Iglesia de Santa María**, with its richly carved Gothic portal.

Olite is in the Navarra wine region (*see pp82–3*) and the town has several bodegas.

🏠 **Palacio Real de Olite**
Plaza de Carlos III. **Tel** 948 74 00 35.
Open daily. ♿ 🎫

The five-arched, medieval pilgrims' bridge at Puente la Reina

㉑ Puente la Reina

Navarra. 🏘 2,900. 🛈 C/ Mayor 105, 948 34 13 01 (closed Jan & Feb). 🚌 Sat. 🎉 Santiago (24–30 Jul).

Few towns along the Road to Santiago de Compostela (*see pp86–7*) evoke the past as vividly as Puente la Reina. The town takes its name from the graceful, humpbacked pedestrian bridge over the Río Arga. The bridge was built for pilgrims during the 11th century by royal command.

On Puente la Reina's narrow main street is the **Iglesia de Santiago**, which has a gilded statue by the west door showing the saint as a pilgrim. On the edge of town is the **Iglesia del Crucifijo**, another pilgrim church which was built in the 12th century by the Knights Templar. Contained within the church is a Y-shaped wooden crucifix of a

Distinctive crucifix in Puente la Reina

sorrowful Christ with arms upraised, which is said to have been a gift from a German pilgrim in the 14th century.

Environs
Isolated in the fields about 5 km (3 miles) to the east is the 12th-century **Iglesia de Santa María de Eunate**. This octagonal Romanesque church may once have been a cemetery church for pilgrims, as human bones have been unearthed here. Pilgrims would shelter beneath the church's external arcade.

West of Puente la Reina is the showpiece hill village of **Cirauqui**. It is also charming, if rather over-restored. Chic little balconied houses line tortuously twisting alleys linked by steps. The Iglesia de San Román, built in the 13th century on top of the hill, has a sculpted west door.

The battlements and towers of the Palacio Real de Olite

Basque Country, Navarra and La Rioja's Fiestas

Los Sanfermines *(6–14 Jul)*, Pamplona (Navarra). In the famous *encierro* (bullrunning) six bulls are released at 8am each morning to run from their corral through the narrow, cobbled streets of the Old Town. On the last night of this week-long, nonstop festival, crowds with candles sing Basque songs in the main square. The event gained worldwide fame after Ernest Hemingway described it in his novel, published in 1926, *The Sun Also Rises*.

Bulls scattering the runners in Pamplona

Wine Battle *(29 Jun)*, Haro (La Rioja). People dressed in white clothes squirt each other with wine from leather drinking bottles in the capital of the Rioja Alta wine region.
Danza de los Zancos *(22 Jul and last Sat of Sep)*, Anguiano (La Rioja). Dancers on stilts, wearing ornate waistcoats and yellow skirts, hurtle down the stepped alley from the church to the main square.
La Virgen Blanca *(5 Aug)*, Vitoria (Álava). A dummy holding an umbrella (the *celedón*) is lowered from San Miguel church to a house below – from which a man in similar dress emerges. The mayor fires a rocket and the crowds in the square light cigars.

Pilgrims drinking from the wine tap near the monastery at Irache

㉒ Estella

Navarra. 🏠 14,000. 🚌 ℹ️ Calle de San Nicolás 1, 948 55 63 01. 🕐 Thu. 🎉 San Andrés (first week in Aug). 🌐 estellaturismo.com

In the Middle Ages Estella (Lizarra) was the centre of the royal court of Navarra and a major stopping point on the pilgrims' Road to Santiago de Compostela *(see pp86–7)*. The town was a stronghold of the Carlists *(see p67)* in the 19th century. A memorial rally is held here on the first Sunday of May every year.

The most important monuments in Estella are sited on the edge of town, across the bridge over the Río Ega. Steps climb steeply from the arcaded Plaza de San Martín to the remarkable **Iglesia de San Pedro de la Rúa**, built on top of a cliff from the 12th to 14th century. It features a Cistercian Mudéjar-influenced, sculpted doorway. The carved capitals are all that now remain of the Romanesque cloister, which was destroyed when a castle overlooking the church was blown up in 1592. The **Palacio de los Reyes de Navarra** (now a museum), on the other side of the Plaza de San Martín, is a rare example of civil Romanesque architecture.

In the town centre, on Plaza de los Fueros, **Iglesia de San Juan Bautista** has a Romanesque porch. The north portal of the **Iglesia de San Miguel** has Romanesque carvings of St Michael slaying a dragon.

Environs
The **Monasterio de Nuestra Señora de Irache**, 3 km (2 miles) southwest of Estella, was a Benedictine monastery which sheltered pilgrims on their way to Santiago. The church is mainly Transitional Gothic in style, but it has Romanesque apses and a cloister in Plateresque style. It is capped by a remarkable dome.

A bodega next to the monastery provides pilgrims with wine from a tap in a wall.

A small road branches off the NA120 north of Estella and leads to the **Monasterio de Iranzu**, built in the 12th–14th century. The austerity of its church and cloisters is typically Cistercian.

The Lizarraga Pass, further up the NA120, offers views of attractive beech woods.

㉓ Pamplona

Navarra. 🏠 198,000. ✈️ 🚌 🚆 ℹ️ Calle San Saturnino 2, 948 42 07 00. 🎉 Sanfermines (6–14 Jul), San Saturnino (29 Nov). 🌐 turismodepamplona.es

The old fortress city of Pamplona (Iruña) is said to have been founded by the Roman general Pompey. In the 9th century it became the capital of Navarra. This fairly busy city explodes into even more life in July during the fiesta of **Los Sanfermines**, with its daredevil bullrunning.

From the old **city walls** *(murallas)* you can get a good overview of Pamplona. The nearby **cathedral**, which is built in ochre-coloured stone, looks down on a

Stone tracery in the elegant cloister of Pamplona cathedral

The impressive Neo-Classical façade of the Palacio del Gobierno de Navarra

loop in the Río Arga. It was built on the foundations of its 12th-century predecessor, and is mainly Gothic in style, with twin towers and an 18th-century façade. Inside there are lovely choir stalls and the alabaster tomb of Carlos III and Queen Leonor.

The southern entrance to the cloister is the carved, medieval Puerta de la Preciosa. The cathedral priests would gather here to sing an antiphon (hymn) to La Preciosa (Precious Virgin) before the night service.

The Museo Diocesano in the cathedral's 14th-century kitchen and refectory displays Gothic altarpieces, polychrome wood statues from all over Navarra, and a French 13th-century reliquary of the Holy Sepulchre.

West of the cathedral is the Old Town, cut through with many alleys. The Neo-Classical **Palacio del Gobierno de Navarra** lies in the Plaza del Castillo and is the seat of the Navarrese government (not open to the public). Outside, a statue of 1903 shows a symbolic woman upholding the *fueros* (historic laws) of Navarra (*see p134*). North of the palace is the medieval **Iglesia de San**

Sculpture in Pamplona depicting the *encierro*

Saturnino, built on the site where St Saturninus is said to have baptized some 40,000 pagan townspeople, and the Baroque **town hall** (*ayuntamiento*).

Beneath the old town wall, in a 16th-century hospital with a Plateresque doorway, is the **Museo de Navarra**. This is a museum of regional archaeology, history and art. Exhibits include Roman mosaics and an 11th-century, Islam-inspired ivory casket. There are murals painted during the 14th–16th centuries, a portrait by Goya, and a collection of paintings by Basque artists.

To the southeast is the city's massive 16th-century **citadel**, erected in Felipe II's reign. It is designed with five bastions in a star shape. Beyond it are the spacious boulevards of the new town, and also the university's green campus.

🏛 **Museo de Navarra**
Cuesta de Santo Domingo s/n.
Tel 948 42 64 92.
Open Tue–Sun. 🏛 ♿

🏛 **Palacio de Navarra**
Avenida Carlos III 2.
Tel 848 42 71 27.
Open by appointment. ♿

Pamplona City Centre

① Museo de Navarra
② City walls
③ Cathedral
④ Town Hall
⑤ Iglesia de San Saturnino
⑥ Palacio de Navarra

Key

Bullrunning route

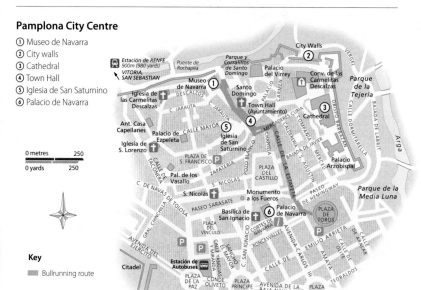

Basque houses in the picturesque town of Etxalar, Valle de Bidasoa

㉔ Las Cinco Villas del Valle de Bidasoa

Navarra. 🚆 Pamplona, San Sebastián. 🚹 948 63 12 22 (Easter week & summer; 948 59 23 86 rest of year). 🌐 turismo.navarra.es; 🌐 baztan-bidasoa.com

Five attractive Basque towns lie in or near this valley, the most northerly being **Bera** (Vera). The houses in **Lesaka** have wooden balconies under deep eaves. The road south passes hills dotted with white farmsteads to reach **Igantzi**, (Yanci), with its red-and-white houses. **Arantza** is the most remote town. Since the 12th century, pigeons have been caught in huge nets strung across a pass above **Etxalar** (Echalar). At the summit of La Rhune on the French border is a great view of the Pyrenees.

㉕ Elizondo

Navarra. 🚗 3,000. 🚌 🚹 Palacio de Arizkunenea, 948 58 12 79 (closed winter). ⛴ Thu. 🎯 Santiago (25 Jul).

This is the biggest of a string of typical Basque villages in the very beautiful valley of Baztán. By the river are noble houses bearing coats of arms.

    Arizkun, further up the valley, has old fortified houses and a 17th-century convent. The **Cueva de Brujas**, in Zugarramurdi, was once a meeting place for witches.

The forested countryside around Roncesvalles

Canopy over the Virgin and Child in the Colegiata Real, Roncesvalles

㉖ Roncesvalles

Navarra. 🚗 24. 🚹 Antiguo Molino s/n, 948 76 03 01. 🎯 Día de la Virgen de Roncesvalles (8 Sep). 🌐 roncesvalles.es

Roncesvalles (Orreaga), on the Spanish side of a pass through the Pyrenees, is a major halt on the Road to Santiago (see pp86–7). Before it became associated with the pilgrim's way, Roncesvalles was the site of a major battle in 778, in which the Basques of Navarra slaughtered the rearguard of Charlemagne's army as it marched homeward. This event is described in the 12th-century French epic poem The Song of Roland.

    The 13th-century **Colegiata Real**, which has served travellers down the centuries, has a silver-plated Virgin and Child below a high canopy. In the graceful chapterhouse, off the cloister, is the white tomb of Sancho VII the Strong (1154–1234), looked down upon by a stained-glass window of his great victory, the battle of Las Navas de Tolosa (see pp58–9). Exhibits in the church museum include "Charlemagne's chessboard", an enamelled reliquary which is so called because of its chequered design.

㉗ Valle de Roncal

Navarra. 🚌 from Pamplona. 🚹 Paseo Julian Gayarre s/n, Roncal, 948 47 52 56; Isaba, 948 89 32 51. 🌐 vallederoncal.es

Running perpendicular to the Pyrenees, this valley is still largely reliant on sheep, and the village of **Roncal** is known for its cheeses. Because of the valley's relative isolation, the inhabitants have preserved their own identity, and local costumes are worn during fiestas. The ski resort of **Isaba**, further up the valley, has a museum of local history and life. A spectacular road winds from Isaba to the tree-lined village of Ochagavia in the parallel **Valle de Salazar**. To the north, the **Selva de Irati**, one of Europe's largest woodlands, spreads over the Pyrenees into France, below snowy Monte Ori at 2,017 m (6,617 ft).

Colourful balconies of houses in the village of Roncal

㉘ Monasterio de Leyre

Yesa, Navarra. **Tel** 948 88 41 50.
Yesa. **Open** daily. Chants: 7:30am, 9am, 7pm and 9:10pm daily.
Closed 1 Jan, 25 Dec.
W monasteriodeleyre.com

The monastery of San Salvador de Leyre is situated high above a reservoir, alone amid grand scenery, backed by limestone cliffs. The abbey has been here since the 11th century, when it was a great spiritual and political centre. Sancho III and his successors made it the royal pantheon of Navarra. The monastery began to decline in the 12th century. It was abandoned from 1836 until 1954, when it was restored by the Benedictines, who turned part of it into a hotel. To see the monastery, you must join one of the tours run every morning and afternoon.

The big 11th-century church has a Gothic vault and three lofty apses. On its west portal are weather-worn carvings of strange beasts, as well as biblical figures. The Romanesque crypt has unusually short columns with chunky capitals. The monks' Gregorian chant *(see p380)* during services is wonderful to hear.

㉙ Castillo de Javier

Javier, Navarra. **Tel** 948 88 40 24.
from Pamplona. **Open** daily.
W santuariojaviersj.org

St Francis Xavier, the patron saint of Navarra, a missionary and a priest of the Jesuit order *(see p128)*, was born in this 13th-century castle in 1506. It has since been restored and is now a Jesuit spiritual centre. Of interest are the saint's bedroom and a museum in the keep devoted to his life. In the oratory is a 13th-century polychrome Christ on the cross and a macabre 15th-century mural of grinning skeletons entitled *The Dance of Death*.

Crucifix in the oratory of the Castillo de Javier

㉚ Sangüesa

Navarra. 5,000. C/ Mayor 2, 948 87 14 11 (closed Mon in winter).
Fri. San Sebastián (11 Sep).
W sanguesa.es

Since medieval times this small town beside a bridge over the Río Aragón has been a stop on the Aragonese pilgrimage route to Santiago *(see pp86–7)*.

The richly sculpted south portal of the **Iglesia de Santa María la Real** is a 12th- and 13th-century treasure of Romanesque art *(see p28)*. It has many figures and details depicting the Last Judgment and society in the 13th century.

The Gothic **Iglesia de Santiago** and the 12th- to 13th-century Gothic **Iglesia de San Francisco** are also worth seeing. On the main street the 16th-century **town hall** *(ayuntamiento)* and the square beside it stand on sites that were once part of the medieval palace of the Prince of Viana and a residence of the kings of Navarra. The library beside the square is housed in what remains of the palace and is open to the public.

Environs
To the north of Sangüesa there are two deep, narrow gorges. The most impressive is the **Hoz de Arbayún**, whose limestone cliffs are inhabited by colonies of vultures. It is best seen from the NA178 north of Domeño. The **Hoz de Lumbier** can be seen from a point on the A21.

The roughly carved columns in the crypt of the Monasterio de Leyre

BARCELONA

Introducing Barcelona	**142–145**
Old Town	**146–161**
Eixample	**162–171**
Montjuïc	**172–177**
Further Afield	**178–182**
Barcelona Street Finder	**183–189**
Shopping in Barcelona	**190–193**
Entertainment in Barcelona	**194–199**

Introducing Barcelona

Barcelona, one of the Mediterranean's busiest ports, is more than the capital of Catalonia. In culture, commerce and sport it not only rivals Madrid, but also considers itself on a par with the greatest European cities. The success of the 1992 Olympic Games, staged in the Parc de Montjuïc, confirmed this to the world. Although there are plenty of historical monuments in the Old Town (Ciutat Vella), Barcelona is best known for the scores of buildings in the Eixample left by the artistic explosion of Modernisme *(see pp144–5)* in the decades around 1900. Always open to outside influences because of its location on the coast, not too far from the French border, Barcelona continues to sizzle with creativity: its bars and the public parks speak more of bold contemporary design than of tradition.

Casa Milà *(see p169)*, also known as La Pedrera, is the most avant-garde of all the works of Antoni Gaudí *(see p168)*. Barcelona has more Art Nouveau buildings than any other city in the world.

0 kilometres		1
0 miles	0.5	

AVINGUDA DEL PARAL·LEL

Las Ramblas

MONTJUÏC
(see pp172–77)

RONDA DEL LITORAL

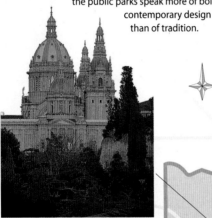

Palau Nacional *(see p176)*, on the hill of Montjuïc, dominates the fountain-filled avenue built for the 1929 International Exhibition. It now houses the Museu Nacional d'Art de Catalunya, which covers 1,000 years of Catalan art and includes a splendid Romanesque section.

Montjuïc Castle *(see p177)* is a massive fortification dating from the 17th century. Sited on the crest of the hill of Montjuïc, it offers panoramic views of the city and port, and forms a sharp contrast to the ultramodern sports halls built nearby for the 1992 Olympic Games.

Christopher Columbus surveys the waterfront from the top of a 60-m (200-ft) column *(see p160)* in the heart of the Port Vell (Old Port). From the top, visitors can look out over the promenades and quays that revitalized the area.

◀ Entrance to Park Güell, Barcelona, with Gaudí's mosaic balcony in foreground

The Sagrada Família
(see pp170–71), Gaudí's unfinished masterpiece, begun in 1882, rises above the streets of the Eixample. Its polychromatic ceramic mosaics and sculptural forms inspired by nature are typical of his work.

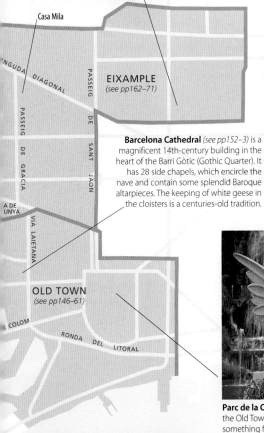

Casa Mila

EIXAMPLE
(see pp162–71)

Barcelona Cathedral *(see pp152–3)* is a magnificent 14th-century building in the heart of the Barri Gòtic (Gothic Quarter). It has 28 side chapels, which encircle the nave and contain some splendid Baroque altarpieces. The keeping of white geese in the cloisters is a centuries-old tradition.

OLD TOWN
(see pp146–61)

Parc de la Ciutadella *(see p158)*, between the Old Town and the Vila Olímpica, has something for everyone. The gardens full of statuary offer relaxation, the boating lake and the zoo are fun, while the museum within its gates covers natural history.

Las Ramblas *(see pp154–5)* is the most famous street in Spain, alive at all hours of the day and night. A stroll down its length to the seafront, taking in its palatial buildings, shops, cafés and street vendors, makes a perfect introduction to Barcelona life.

Gaudí and Modernisme

Towards the end of the 19th century a new style of art and architecture, Modernisme, a variant of Art Nouveau, was born in Barcelona. It became a means of expression for Catalan nationalism and counted Josep Puig i Cadafalch, Lluís Domènech i Montaner and, above all, Antoni Gaudí i Cornet *(see p168)* among its major exponents. Barcelona's Eixample district *(see pp162–71)* is full of the highly original buildings that they created for their wealthy clients.

All aspects of decoration in a Modernista building, even interior design, were planned by the architect. This door and its tiled surround are in Gaudí's 1906 Casa Batlló *(see p168)*.

A dramatic cupola covers the central salon, which rises through three floors. It is pierced by small round holes, inspired by Islamic architecture, giving the illusion of stars.

Upper galleries are richly decorated with carved wood and cofferwork.

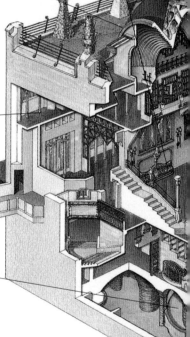

The spiral carriage ramp is an early sign of Gaudí's predilection for curved lines. He would later exploit this to the full in the wavy façade of his masterpiece, the Casa Milà (La Pedrera) *(see p169)*.

1859 Civil engineer Ildefons Cerdà i Sunyer submits proposals for expansion of Barcelona

1878 Gaudí graduates as an architect

1900 Josep Puig i Cadafalch builds Casa Amatller *(see p168)*

1903 Lluís Domènech i Montaner builds Hospital de la Santa Creu i de Sant Pau *(see p169)*

Hospital detail

| 1850 | 1865 | 1880 | 1895 | 1910 | 1925 |

1883 Gaudí takes over design of Neo-Gothic Sagrada Família *(see pp170–71)*

Detail of Sagrada Família

1888 Barcelona Universal Exhibition gives impetus to Modernisme

1905 Domènech i Montaner builds Casa Lleó Morera *(see p168)*. Puig i Cadafalch builds Casa Terrades *(see p169)*

1912 Casa Milà completed

1926 Gaudí dies

Bizarrely decorated chimneys became one of the trademarks of Gaudí's later work. They reach a fantastic extreme on the gleaming, hump-backed roof of the Casa Batlló.

Elaborate wrought-iron lamps light the grand hall.

Ceramic tiles decorate the chimneys.

Gaudí's Materials

Gaudí designed, or collaborated on designs, for almost every known medium. He combined bare, undecorated materials – wood, rough-hewn stone, rubble and brickwork – with meticulous craftwork in wrought iron and stained glass. Mosaics of ceramic tiles were used to cover his fluid, uneven forms.

Stained glass, Sagrada Família *(see pp170–71)*

Mosaic of ceramic tiles, Park Güell *(see p182)*

Detail of iron gate, Casa Vicens *(see p168)*

Ceramic tiles on El Capricho *(see p115)*

Parabolic arches, used extensively by Gaudí, show his interest in Gothic architecture *(see p28)*. These arches form a corridor in his 1890 Col·legi de les Teresianes, a convent school in the west of Barcelona.

Escutcheon alludes to the Catalan coat of arms.

Palau Güell (1889)

Gaudí's first major building in the centre of the city *(see p155)* established his international reputation for outstandingly original architecture. Built for his lifelong patron, the industrialist Eusebi Güell, the mansion stands on a small plot of land in a narrow street, making the façade difficult to view. Inside, Gaudí creates a sense of space by using carved screens, galleries and recesses. His unique furniture is also on display.

Organic forms inspired the wrought iron around the gates to the palace. Gaudí's later work teems with wildlife, such as this dragon, covered with brightly coloured tiles, which guards the steps in the Park Güell.

OLD TOWN

The Old Town, traversed by the city's most famous avenue, Las Ramblas, is one of the most extensive medieval city centres in Europe. The Barri Gòtic contains the cathedral and a maze of streets and squares. Across from the Via Laietana, the El Born neighbourhood is dominated by the Santa Maria del Mar church and is replete with 14th-century mansions. This area is bounded by the leafy Parc de la Ciutadella, home to the city's zoo. The revitalized seafront is a stimulating mix of old and new. Trendy shops and restaurants make up the fashionable marina, contrasted with the old maritime neighbourhood of Barceloneta and the modern Olympic port.

Sights at a Glance

Museums and Galleries

2 Museu Frederic Marès
4 Museu d'Idees i Invents de Barcelona (MIBA)
9 Museu d'Art Contemporani
14 Museu Picasso
18 Museu de la Xocolata
21 Castell dels Tres Dragons
22 Museu Martorell
29 Museu Marítim and Drassanes

Streets and Districts

8 El Raval
10 Las Ramblas
13 El Born
16 Carrer Montcada
25 Barceloneta

Harbour Sights

24 Port Olímpic
26 Port Vell
28 Golondrinas

Churches

7 Cathedral (pp152–3)
15 Basílica de Santa Maria del Mar

Historic Buildings

1 Casa de l'Ardiaca
3 Conjunt Monumental de la Plaça del Rei
5 Ajuntament
6 Palau de la Generalitat
11 Palau de la Música Catalana
12 La Llotja
17 Mercat del Born

Monuments

19 Arc del Triomf
27 Monument a Colom

Parks and Gardens

20 Parc de la Ciutadella
23 Zoo de Barcelona

See also Barcelona Street Finder maps 2, 5, 6

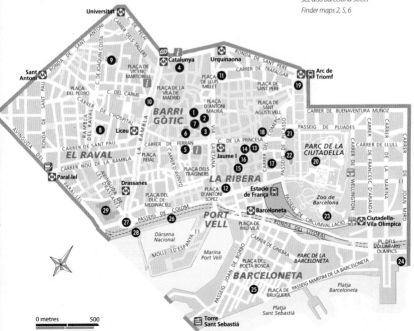

◄ The glorious, Gothic interior of Barcelona Cathedral

For map symbols see back flap

Street-by-Street: Barri Gòtic

The Barri Gòtic (Gothic Quarter) is the true heart of Barcelona. The oldest part of the city, it was the site chosen by the Romans in the reign of Augustus (27 BC–AD 14) on which to found a new *colonia* (town), and has been the location of the city's administrative buildings ever since. The Roman forum was on the Plaça de Sant Jaume, where now stand the medieval Palau de la Generalitat, Catalonia's parliament, and the Casa de la Ciutat, Barcelona's town hall. Close by are the Gothic cathedral and royal palace, where Columbus was received by Fernando and Isabel on his return from his voyage to the New World in 1492 *(see p61)*.

❶ Casa de l'Ardiaca
Built on the Roman city wall, the Gothic-Renaissance archdeacon's residence now houses Barcelona's historical archives.

To Plaça de Catalunya

SANT SEVER

PIETA

❼ ★ Cathedral
The façade and spire are 19th-century additions to the original Gothic building. Among the artistic treasures inside are medieval Catalan paintings.

SANT DOMÈNEC DEL CALL

SANT HONORAT

CARRER DEL BISBE

❻ Palau de la Generalitat
The seat of Catalonia's governor has superb Gothic features, which include the chapel and a stone staircase rising to an open-air, arcaded gallery.

PLAÇA DE SANT JAUME

CARRER DE FERRAN

To Las Ramblas

CARRER DE LA CIUTAT

❺ Ajuntament
Barcelona's town hall was built in the 14th and 15th centuries. The façade is a Neo-Classical addition. In the entrance hall stands *Three Gypsy Boys* by Joan Rebull (1899–1981), a 1976 copy of a sculpture he originally created in 1946.

❹ MIBA
The Museu d'Idees i Invents de Barcelona (MIBA) is a collection of fascinating inventions.

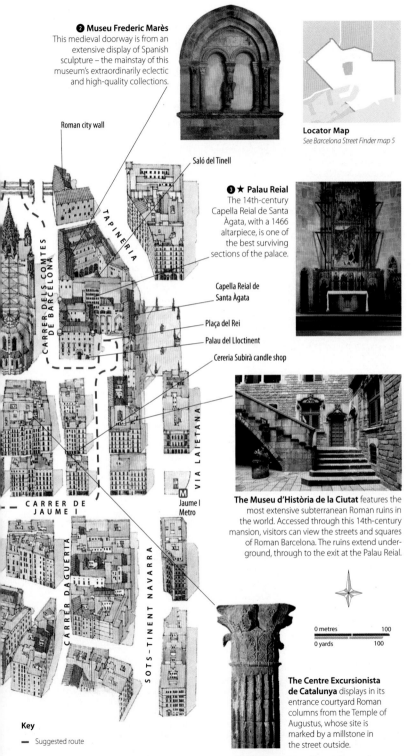

❷ Museu Frederic Marès
This medieval doorway is from an extensive display of Spanish sculpture – the mainstay of this museum's extraordinarily eclectic and high-quality collections.

Roman city wall

Saló del Tinell

Locator Map
See Barcelona Street Finder map 5

❸ ★ Palau Reial
The 14th-century Capella Reial de Santa Àgata, with a 1466 altarpiece, is one of the best surviving sections of the palace.

Capella Reial de Santa Àgata

Plaça del Rei

Palau del Lloctinent

Cereria Subirà candle shop

TAPINERIA

CARRER DELS COMTES DE BARCELONA

CARRER DE JAUME I

CARRER D'AGUERIA

SOTS–TINENT NAVARRA

VIA LAIETANA

Ⓜ Jaume I Metro

The Museu d'Història de la Ciutat features the most extensive subterranean Roman ruins in the world. Accessed through this 14th-century mansion, visitors can view the streets and squares of Roman Barcelona. The ruins extend underground, through to the exit at the Palau Reial.

| 0 metres | 100 |
| 0 yards | 100 |

The Centre Excursionista de Catalunya displays in its entrance courtyard Roman columns from the Temple of Augustus, whose site is marked by a millstone in the street outside.

Key

— Suggested route

For additional map symbols *see back flap*

Decorated marble letterbox, Casa de l'Ardiaca

❶ Casa de l'Ardiaca

Carrer de Santa Llúcia 1. **Map** 5 B2.
Tel 93 256 22 55. 🚇 Jaume I. **Open**
9am–8.45pm Mon–Fri (to 7:30pm
Jul–Sep), 9am–1pm Sat. **Closed** Sat
Jul–Sep, public hols. 🌐 **bcn.
cat/arxiu/arxiuhistoric**

Standing beside what was
originally the Bishop's
Gate in the Roman wall is
the Archdeacon's House.
It was built in the 12th
century, but its present
appearance dates from
around 1500 when it
was remodelled and
a colonnade added. In
1870 this was extended
to form the Flamboyant
Gothic *(see p28)* patio
around a fountain. The Modernista
architect Domènech i Montaner
(1850–1923) added the fanciful
marble letterbox, carved with
three swallows and a tortoise,
beside the Renaissance portal.
Upstairs is the Arxiu Històric de
la Ciutat (City Archives). Visitors
are only allowed into the courtyard and the entrance hall, which
occasionally hosts art exhibitions.

❷ Museu Frederic Marès

Plaça de Sant Iu 5. **Map** 5 B2. **Tel** 93 256
35 00. 🚇 Jaume I. **Open** 10am–7pm
Tue–Sat, 11am–8pm Sun. 🌐 (free first
Sun of each month & every Sun from
3pm). ♿ 📷 🌐 **museumares.bcn.cat**

The sculptor Frederic Marès i
Deulovol (1893–1991) was also
a traveller and collector, and this
museum is a monument to his
eclectic taste. The building is part
of the Royal Palace complex and

Virgin, Museu
Frederic Marès

was occupied by 13th-century
bishops, 14th-century counts
of Barcelona, 15th-century
judges and 18th-century
nuns, who lived here
until they were expelled in
1936. Marès, who had a
small apartment in the
building, opened this
museum in 1948. It is
one of the most fasci-
nating in the city and
has a notable collection
of Romanesque and
Gothic religious art. On
the ground and first
floors there are stone
sculptures and two
complete Romanesque
portals. Exhibits on the
three floors above range
from clocks, crucifixes, costumes,
antique cameras, pipes, tobacco
jars and postcards to an amusement room full of toys.

❸ Conjunt Monumental de la Plaça del Rei

Plaça del Rei. **Map** 5 B2. **Tel** 93 256
21 22. 🚇 Jaume I. **Open** 10am–7pm
Tue–Sat, 10am–8pm Sun. **Closed** 1
Jan, 1 May, 24 Jun, 25 Dec. 🌐 (free
first Sun of each month & every Sun
from 3pm.) 📷 by appointment.
🌐 **museuhistoria.bcn.cat**

The Conjunt Monumental de
la Plaça del Rei refers to the
ensemble of buildings on the
square, including the **Palau Reial**
(Royal Palace), which was the
residence of the count-kings of
Barcelona from its foundation in
the 13th century, and the royal
chapel. It can be visited as part
of the **Museu d'Història de
Barcelona**. The complex also
includes the 14th-century Gothic
Saló del Tinell, a vast room with
arches spanning 17 m (56 ft). This
is where Isabel and Fernando
(see p74) received Columbus on
his return from America. It is also
where the Holy Inquisition sat.

On the right, built into the
Roman city wall, is the royal
chapel, the Capella Reial de Santa
Àgata, with an altarpiece (1466)
by Jaume Huguet. Its bell tower is
formed by part of a watchtower
on the Roman wall. Stairs on the
right lead to the 16th-century
tower of Martí the Humanist (who
reigned 1396–1410), the last of
Barcelona's count-kings.

Hebrew tablet

Barcelona's Early Jewish Community

From the 11th to the 13th centuries, Jews
dominated Barcelona's commerce and culture,
providing doctors and founding the first seat
of learning. But in 1243, 354 years after they
were first documented in the city, violent anti-
Semitism led to the Jews being consigned to a
ghetto, El Call. Ostensibly to provide protection,
the ghetto had only one entrance, which led into
the Plaça de Sant Jaume. Jews were heavily taxed by the monarch,
who viewed them as "royal serfs"; but in return they also received
privileges, as they handled most of Catalonia's lucrative trade with
North Africa. However, official and popular persecution finally led
to the disappearance of the ghetto in 1401, 91 years before Judaism
was fully outlawed in Spain *(see p61)*.

Originally there were three synagogues. The main one, Sinagoga
Mayor at No. 5 Carrer de Marlet, is said to be the oldest in Europe
and can be visited. A 14th-century Hebrew tablet that reads "Holy
Foundation of Rabbi Samuel Hassardi, His soul will rest in Heaven"
is embedded in the wall.

The main attraction of the Museu d'Història is located underground. Entire streets of old Barcino are accessible via a lift and walkways suspended over the ruins of Roman Barcelona. The site was found when the Casa Clariana-Padellàs, the Gothic building from which you enter, was moved here stone by stone in 1931. The water and drainage systems, baths, homes with mosaic floors and even the old forum are among some of the most extensive and complete subterranean Roman ruins in the world.

❹ Museu d'Idees i Invents Barcelona (MIBA)

Carrer de la Ciutat 7. **Map** 5 A2. **Tel** 93 332 79 30. 🚇 Jaume I, Liceu. **Open** 10am–2pm, 4–7pm Mon–Fri, 10am–8pm Sat, 10am–2pm Sun & public hols. ♿ 🎧 📷 📷
🌐 **mibamuseum.com**

This small museum contains a diverse collection of brilliant inventions, ranging from useful (water purifiers) to bizarre (a mop that doubles as a microphone). A swirling slide links the galleries, and there's a great hands-on invention area for children.

❺ Ajuntament

Plaça de Sant Jaume 1. **Map** 5 A2. **Tel** 934 02 70 00. 🚇 Jaume I, Liceu. **Open** 10am–1:30pm Sun & public hols; 10am–8pm 12 Feb, 23 Apr & 30 May, or by appointment (934 02 70 00).
📷 11am in English. ♿ 🌐 **bcn.cat**

The magnificent 14th-century city hall faces the Palau de la Generalitat. Flanking the entrance are statues of Jaime (Jaume) I, who granted the city rights to elect councillors in 1249, and Joan Fiveller, who levied taxes on court members in the 1500s.

Inside is the huge council chamber, the 14th-century Saló de Cent, built for the city's 100 councillors. The Saló de les Cròniques, on the first floor, was commissioned for the 1929 International Exhibition and decorated by Josep-Marià Sert with murals of momentous events in Catalan history.

❻ Palau de la Generalitat

Plaça de Sant Jaume 4. **Map** 5 A2. **Tel** 93 402 46 00. 🚇 Jaume I. **Open** 10am–1:30pm 2nd & 4th Sun of the month; 10am–8pm 23 Apr, 11 & 24 Sep (carry your passport). ♿ 📷 by appt. 🌐 **gencat.cat**

Since 1403, the Generalitat has been the seat of the Catalonian

The Italianate façade of the Palau de la Generalitat

Governor. Above the entrance, in its Renaissance façade, is a statue of Sant Jordi (St George) the patron saint of Catalonia – and the Dragon. The late Catalan-Gothic courtyard is by Marc Safont (1416).

Among the fine interiors are the Gothic chapel of Sant Jordi, also by Safont, and Pere Blai's Italianate Saló de Sant Jordi. At the back, one floor above street level, lies the *Pati dels Tarongers*, the Orange Tree Patio, by Pau Mateu, which has a bell tower built by Pere Ferrer in 1568.

The Catalan president has offices here as well as in the Casa dels Canonges. The two buildings are connected by a bridge across Carrer del Bisbe, built in 1928 and modelled on the famous Bridge of Sighs in Venice.

The magnificent council chamber, the Saló de Cent, in the Ajuntament

❼ Barcelona Cathedral

This compact Gothic cathedral, with a Romanesque chapel (Capella de Santa Llúcia) and beautiful cloister, was begun in 1298 under Jaime (Jaume) II, on the foundations of a site dating back to Visigothic times. It was not finished until the late 19th century, when the main façade was completed. A white marble choir screen, sculpted in the 16th century, depicts the martyrdom of St Eulàlia, the city's patron. Next to the font, a plaque records the baptism of six Caribbean Indians, whom Columbus brought back from the Americas in 1493.

Nave Interior
The Catalan-style Gothic interior has a single wide nave with 28 side chapels. These are set between the columns supporting the vaulted ceiling, which rises to 26 m (85 ft).

KEY

① **The Capella del Santíssim Sagrament** houses the 16th-century Christ of Lepanto crucifix.

② **The main façade** was not completed until 1889, and the central spire until 1913. It was faithfully based on the original 1408 plans of the French architect Charles Galters.

③ **The twin octagonal bell towers** date from 1386–93. The bells were installed in this tower in 1545.

④ **The Sacristy Museum** has a small treasury. Pieces include an 11th-century font, tapestries and liturgical artifacts.

⑤ **Porta de Santa Eulàlia, entrance to Cloisters**

⑥ **Capella de Santa Llúcia**

★ **Choir Stalls**
The top tier of the beautifully carved 15th-century stalls contains the coats of arms (1518) of the 12 knights of the Order of Toisón del Oro.

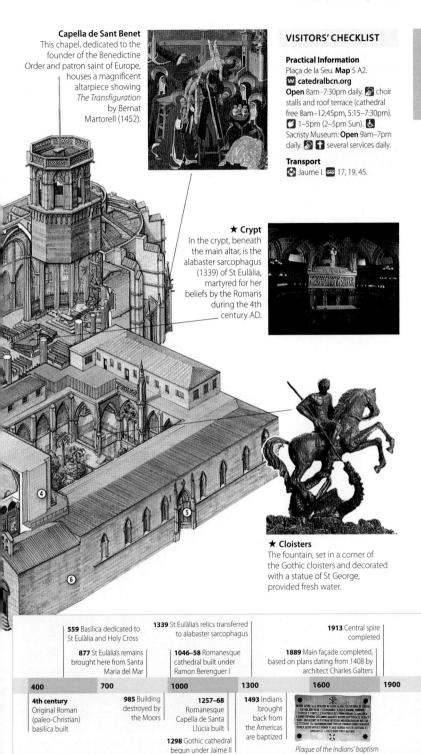

Capella de Sant Benet
This chapel, dedicated to the founder of the Benedictine Order and patron saint of Europe, houses a magnificent altarpiece showing *The Transfiguration* by Bernat Martorell (1452).

VISITORS' CHECKLIST

Practical Information
Plaça de la Seu. **Map** 5 A2.
ⓦ catedralbcn.org
Open 8am–7:30pm daily. 🎵 choir stalls and roof terrace (cathedral free 8am–12:45pm, 5:15–7:30pm).
📷 1–5pm (2–5pm Sun). ♿
Sacristy Museum: **Open** 9am–7pm daily. 🎵 🕆 several services daily.

Transport
🚇 Jaume I. 🚌 17, 19, 45.

★ Crypt
In the crypt, beneath the main altar, is the alabaster sarcophagus (1339) of St Eulàlia, martyred for her beliefs by the Romans during the 4th century AD.

★ Cloisters
The fountain, set in a corner of the Gothic cloisters and decorated with a statue of St George, provided fresh water.

559 Basilica dedicated to St Eulàlia and Holy Cross

877 St Eulàlia's remains brought here from Santa Maria del Mar

1339 St Eulàlia's relics transferred to alabaster sarcophagus

1046–58 Romanesque cathedral built under Ramon Berenguer I

1913 Central spire completed

1889 Main façade completed, based on plans dating from 1408 by architect Charles Galters

400	700	1000	1300	1600	1900

4th century Original Roman (paleo-Christian) basilica built

985 Building destroyed by the Moors

1257–68 Romanesque Capella de Santa Llúcia built

1298 Gothic cathedral begun under Jaime II

1493 Indians brought back from the Americas are baptized

Plaque of the Indians' baptism

❽ El Raval

Map 2 F3. Catalunya, Liceu.

The district of El Raval lies to the west of Las Ramblas and includes the old red-light area near the port, which was once known as the Barri Xinès (Chinese Quarter).

From the 14th century, the city hospital was in Carrer de l'Hospital, which still has some herbal and medicinal shops. Gaudí was brought here after being fatally hit by a tram in 1926. The buildings now house the Biblioteca de Catalunya (Catalonian Library), but the elegant former dissecting room has been fully restored.

Towards the port in Carrer Nou de la Rambla is Gaudí's Palau Güell (see p145). At the end of Sant Pau is the city's most complete former Romanesque church, the 12th-century Sant Pau del Camp, with a charming cloister featuring exquisitely carved capitals.

❾ Museu d'Art Contemporani

Plaça dels Àngels 1. **Map** 2 F2. **Tel** 93 412 08 10. Universitat, Catalunya. **Open** 11am–7:30pm Mon–Fri (to 8pm Jun–Sep), 10am–9pm Sat, 10am–3pm Sun. **Closed** 1 Jan, 25 Dec. guided tour times change according to the exhibits; check calendar on website. **macba.cat** Centre de Cultura Contemporània: Montalegre 5. **Tel** 93 306 41 00. **cccb.org**

This dramatic, glass-fronted building was designed by the American architect Richard Meier. Its light, airy galleries act as the city's contemporary art mecca. The permanent collection of predominantly Spanish painting, sculpture and installation from the 1950s onwards is complemented by temporary exhibitions by foreign artists like US painter Susana Solano and South African photojournalist David Goldblatt.

Next to the MACBA, a remodelled 18th-century hospice houses the **Centre de Cultura Contemporània**, a lively arts centre that hosts major arts festivals and regular shows.

❿ Las Ramblas

The historic avenue of Las Ramblas (Les Rambles in Catalan) is busy around the clock, especially in the evenings and at weekends. Newsstands, caged bird and flower stalls, tarot readers, musicians and mime artists throng the wide, tree-shaded central walkway. Among its famous buildings are the Liceu Opera House, the huge Boqueria food market and some grand mansions.

Exploring Las Ramblas

The name of this long avenue, also known as Les Rambles, comes from the Arabic *ramla*, meaning "the dried-up bed of a seasonal river". The 13th-century city wall followed the left bank of such a river that flowed from the Collserola hills to the sea. Convents, monasteries and the university were built on the other bank in the 16th century. As time passed, the riverbed was filled in and those buildings demolished, but they are remembered in the names of the five consecutive Rambles that make up the great avenue between the Port Vell and Plaça de Catalunya.

Palau Güell: C/ Nou de la Rambla 3–5. **Map** 2 F3. **Tel** 93 472 57 75. Liceu. **Open** 10am–8pm Tue–Sun (free Apr–Oct: 5–8pm Sun & Nov–Mar: 2:30–5:30pm Sun). **Closed** 1 & 6–13 Jan, 25 & 26 Dec. **palauguell.cat** Museu de Cera: Pg de la Banca 7. **Map** 2 F4. **Tel** 93 317 26 49. Drassanes. **Open** 10am–1:30pm, 4–7:30pm Mon–Fri, 11am–2pm, 4:30–8:30pm Sat, Sun & public hols.

The monument to Columbus at the bottom of the tree-lined Ramblas

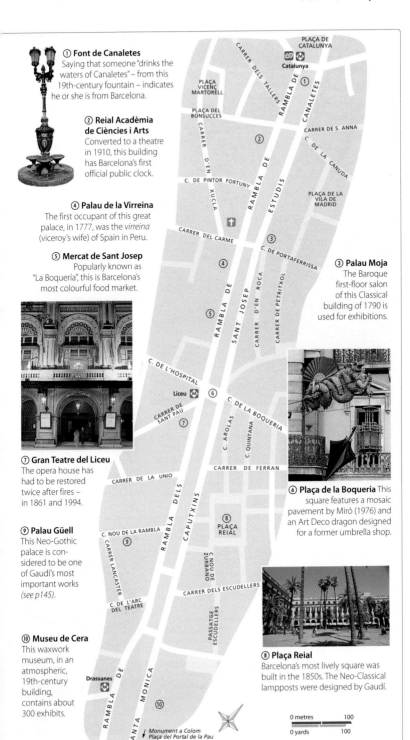

① Font de Canaletes
Saying that someone "drinks the waters of Canaletes" – from this 19th-century fountain – indicates he or she is from Barcelona.

② Reial Acadèmia de Ciències i Arts
Converted to a theatre in 1910, this building has Barcelona's first official public clock.

④ Palau de la Virreina
The first occupant of this great palace, in 1777, was the *virreina* (viceroy's wife) of Spain in Peru.

⑤ Mercat de Sant Josep
Popularly known as "La Boquería", this is Barcelona's most colourful food market.

⑦ Gran Teatre del Liceu
The opera house has had to be restored twice after fires – in 1861 and 1994.

⑨ Palau Güell
This Neo-Gothic palace is considered to be one of Gaudí's most important works *(see p145).*

⑩ Museu de Cera
This waxwork museum, in an atmospheric, 19th-century building, contains about 300 exhibits.

③ Palau Moja
The Baroque first-floor salon of this Classical building of 1790 is used for exhibitions.

⑥ Plaça de la Boquería This square features a mosaic pavement by Miró (1976) and an Art Deco dragon designed for a former umbrella shop.

⑧ Plaça Reial
Barcelona's most lively square was built in the 1850s. The Neo-Classical lampposts were designed by Gaudí.

PLAÇA DE CATALUNYA
Catalunya
CARRER DELS TALLERS
RAMBLA DE CANALETES
PLAÇA VICENÇ MARTORELL
PLAÇA DEL BONSUCCES
CARRER DE S. ANNA
C. DE LA CANUDA
CARRER D'EN XUCLA
C. DE PINTOR FORTUNY
RAMBLA DE ESTUDIS
PLAÇA DE LA VILA DE MADRID
CARRER DEL CARME
C. DE PORTAFERRISSA
CARRER D'EN ROCA
CARRER DE PETRITXOL
RAMBLA DE SANT JOSEP
C. DE L'HOSPITAL
Liceu
C. DE LA BOQUERIA
CARRER DE SANT PAU
C. AROLAS
C. QUINTANA
CARRER DE FERRAN
CARRER DE LA UNIO
RAMBLA DELS CAPUTXINS
PLAÇA REIAL
C. NOU DE LA RAMBLA
CARRER LANCASTER
C. NOU DE ZURBANO
CARRER DELS ESCUDELLERS
C. DE L'ARC DEL TEATRE
PASSATGE ESCUDELLERS
Drassanes
RAMBLA DE SANTA MONICA
Monument a Colom
Plaça del Portal de la Pau

0 metres   100
0 yards   100

Glorious stained-glass dome, Palau de la Música Catalana

❶ Palau de la Música Catalana

Carrer Palau de la Música 4–6. **Map** 5 B1. **Tel** 932 95 72 00. 🚇 Urquinaona. **Open** 10am–3:30pm daily (to 6pm Easter & Jul, 9am–8pm Aug); and for concerts. 🅿 ♿ limited. 📷 in English on the hour, 10am–3pm. 🌐 **palaumusica.org**

This is a real palace of music, a Modernista celebration of tilework, sculpture and glorious stained glass. It is the only concert hall in Europe lit by natural light. Designed by Lluís Domènech i Montaner, it was completed in 1908. Although a few extensions have been added, the building still retains its original appearance. The elaborate red-brick façade is hard to appreciate fully in the confines of the narrow street. It is lined with mosaic-covered pillars topped by busts of the great composers Palestrina, Beethoven and Bach. The large stone sculpture of St George and other figures at the corner of the building portrays an allegory from Catalan folksong by Miquel Blay.

But it is the interior of the building that is truly inspiring. The auditorium is lit by a huge inverted dome of stained glass depicting angelic choristers. The sculptures of composers Wagner and Clavé on the proscenium arch that frames the stage area were designed by Domènech but finished by Pau Gargallo. The stunning "Muses of the Palau", the group of 18 highly stylized, instrument-playing maidens, are the stage's backdrop. Made of terracotta and trencadís (pieces of ceramic), the muses have become the building's most admired feature.

The work of Josep Anselm Clavé (1824–74) in promoting Catalan song led to the creation of the Orfeó Català choral society in 1891, a focus of Catalan nationalism and the inspiration behind the Palau.

Although the Orfeó is now based at the more state-of-the-art L'Auditori on Carrer de Lepant (see p195), there is a concert at the Palau nearly every night; it is the main venue for the city's jazz and guitar festivals, and world music, flamenco and symphony orchestras regularly grace its flamboyant stage.

The Palau's new era began with the completion of the work carried out by the top local architect Oscar Tusquets. An underground concert hall and an outdoor square for summer concerts were added, consolidating the Palau's reputation as Barcelona's most loved music venue.

⓬ La Llotja

Carrer del Consolat de Mar 2. **Map** 5 B3. **Tel** 93 547 88 49. 🚇 Barceloneta, Jaume I. **Closed** to the public (except twice a year, days vary).

La Llotja (meaning "commodity exchange") was built in the 1380s as the headquarters of the Consolat de Mar. It was remodelled in Neo-Classical style in 1771 and housed the city's stock exchange until 1994, the original Gothic hall acting as the main trading room. It can still be seen through the windows.

The upper floors housed the Barcelona School of Fine Arts from 1849 to 1970, attended by Pablo Picasso and Joan Miró. It is now occupied by the local chamber of commerce.

Statue of Poseidon in the courtyard of La Llotja

⑬ El Born

Map 5 B3. ⓜ Jaume I.

Named for the jousting sessions that once took place in its central boulevard, El Born is a tiny pocket of the La Ribera district. The village-like atmosphere of the neighbourhood makes it popular with local residents and young urbanites. Trendy bars, fashion and design shops are juxtaposed with medieval architecture. The 14th-century mansions of Carrer Montcada have remained intact and now house high-calibre galleries and museums, while the tiny, pedestrianized streets and squares fanning out from the Mercat del Born are the centre of the city's café culture. The numerous bars and restaurants are a magnet for revellers, much to the annoyance of the full-time residents who voice their complaints visually through the banners hanging from El Born's balconies.

⑭ Museu Picasso

Carrer Montcada 15–23. **Map** 5 B2. **Tel** 932 56 30 00. ⓜ Jaume I. **Open** 9am–7pm Tue–Sun (to 9:30pm Thu). 🎟 (free under age 18, over 65, 1st Sun of month & every Sun after 3pm). 🎫 11am Sun in English (except Aug), book in advance at 93 256 3022. ♿ 🖥 **museupicasso.bcn.cat**

One of Barcelona's most popular attractions, the Picasso Museum is housed in five adjoining medieval palaces on Carrer Montcada: Berenguer d'Aguilar, Baró de Castellet, Meca, Mauri and Finestres.

It opened in 1963 showing works donated by Jaime Sabartes, a friend of Picasso. Following Sabartes' death in 1968, Picasso himself donated paintings, including early examples. These were complemented by graphic works, left in his will, and 141 ceramic pieces given by his widow, Jacqueline.

The strength of the 4,200-piece collection is Picasso's early works. These show how, even at the ages of 15 and 16, he was painting major works, such as *The First Communion* (1896) and *Science and Charity* (1897). The most famous work is his series of 44 paintings, *Las Meninas*, which was inspired by Velázquez's masterpiece.

⑮ Basílica de Santa Maria del Mar

Plaça Sta Maria 1. **Map** 5 B3. **Tel** 93 310 23 90. ⓜ Jaume I. **Open** 9am–1pm, 5–8:30pm Mon–Sat, 10am–2pm, 5–8pm Sun. 🏛 roof terrace. 🎫 in English on the hour, summer: 1–3pm Mon–Fri, 2pm & 3pm Sat & Sun; winter: 1–5pm Mon–Fri, 1–4pm Sat & Sun.

This is the city's only example of a church entirely in the Catalan Gothic style. It took just 55 years to build, with money donated by merchants and shipbuilders. The speed gave it a unity of style both inside and out. The west front has a 15th-century rose window of the Coronation of the Virgin. More stained glass, from the 15th–18th centuries, lights the nave and aisles.

The choir and furnishings were burned in the Civil War (*see p71*), adding to the sense of space and simplicity. The church has great acoustics for concerts.

A wedding service in the Gothic interior of Santa Maria del Mar

Pablo Picasso, *Self-Portrait* in charcoal (1899–1900)

Pablo Picasso in Barcelona

Picasso (1881–1973) was born in Málaga and was almost 14 when he came to Barcelona, where his father had found a job in the city's art academy. Picasso enrolled, and was a precocious talent among his contemporaries. He was a regular visitor to Els Quatre Gats, an artists' café still in existence in Carrer Montsió, where he held his first exhibition. He also exhibited in Sala Parks, a gallery still functioning in Carrer Petritxol. The family lived in Carrer Mercé and Picasso had a studio in Carrer Nou de la Rambla. It was among the prostitutes of Carrer d'Avinyò that he found inspiration for the work that many art historians see as the wellspring of modern art, *Les Demoiselles d'Avignon* (1906–7). Picasso left Barcelona for Paris in his early twenties and initially returned several times. After the Civil War his opposition to Franco kept him in France, but he designed a frieze for Barcelona's College of Architects in 1962 and was persuaded to allow the city to open a museum of his work, which it did the following year.

Renaissance-style 17th-century façades lining Carrer Montcada

⑯ Carrer Montcada

Map 5 B3. ⬢ Jaume I. Museu dels Cultures del Món: at No. 12. **Tel** 93 256 23 00. **Open** 10am–7pm Tue–Sat, 10am–8pm Sun. ⬛

The most authentic medieval street in the city is a narrow lane, overshadowed by gargoyles and roofs that almost touch overhead. The Gothic palaces that line it date back to Catalonia's expansion in the 13th century. Almost all of the buildings were modified over the years, particularly during the 17th century. Only Casa Cervelló-Guidice at No. 25 retains its original façade.

The **Museu dels Cultures del Món** (Museum of World Cultures), in the Nadal and Marqués de Lió 16th-century palaces at No. 12, imaginatively displays more than 700 exhibits from around the world.

At No. 22 is one of the city's best-known champagne and *cava* bars, the cheerful El Xampanyet.

The cosy, cottage-like confines of *cava* bar El Xampanyet

⑰ Mercat del Born

Map 5 C3. ⬢ Jaume I, Barceloneta.

This covered market, with its ornate ironwork and crystal roof, was inspired by the original Les Halles in Paris and it was Barcelona's principal wholesale market until the early 1970s, when it outgrew its location. The street names in the vicinity reflect what went on in Barcelona's former mercantile hub: L'Argenteria was lined with silversmiths, Flassaders was where you went for a woven blanket and Vidrieria was once lit up with glass-blowers' torches. A few of these establishments remain, but they are now outnumbered by chic fashion and interiors boutiques.

While the market was being remodelled, extensive ruins of the 18th-century city were discovered beneath its foundations. These ruins are now the focal point of the new cultural centre, complemented by exhibitions, talks and screenings. Much of this area was razed after Barcelona fell to the French-Spanish forces during the War of Succession (*see p66*), with particularly heavy losses in El Born. This key event in Catalonia's history is remembered each year on 11 September, with activities focused on a monument dedicated to those who died in 1714, located near the market.

⑱ Museu de la Xocolata

Comerç 36. **Map** 5 C2. ⬢ Jaume I, Arc de Triomf. **Tel** 93 268 78 78. **Open** 10am–7pm Mon–Sat (to 8pm 15 Jun–15 Sep), 10am–3pm Sun & pub hols. **Closed** 1 & 6 Jan, 1 May, 25 & 26 Dec. ⬛ ⬛ ⬛ **W** museuxocolata.cat

Founded by Barcelona's chocolate- and pastry-makers' union, this museum celebrates the history of one of the most universally loved foodstuffs: from the discovery of cocoa in South America to the invention of the first chocolate machine in Barcelona. This confectionery tale is told through old posters, photographs and footage.

The real thing is displayed in a homage to the art of the *mona*. This was a traditional Easter cake that over the centuries evolved into an edible sculpture. Every year, pâtissiers compete to create the most imaginative piece, decorating their chocolate versions of well-known buildings or folk figures with jewels, feathers and other materials. The museum shop sells – you guessed it – all manner of chocolate goods.

The pink brick façade of the late 19th-century Arc del Triomf

⑲ Arc del Triomf

Passeig Lluís Companys. **Map** 5 C1. ⬢ Arc de Triomf.

The main gateway to the 1888 Universal Exhibition, which filled the Parc de la Ciutadella, was designed by Josep Vilaseca i Casanovas. It is built of brick in Mudéjar (*see p59*) style, with sculpted allegories of crafts, industry and business. The frieze by Josep Reynés on the main façade represents the city welcoming foreign visitors. Visitors can climb to the viewing terrace at the top of the arch during the 48h Open House Barcelona festival, usually held at the end of October.

⑳ Parc de la Ciutadella

Passeig de Picasso, 21. **Map** 5 D2. ⬢ Barceloneta, Ciutadella-Vila Olímpica, Arc de Triomf. **Open** 8am–dusk daily. ⬛

This popular park has a boating lake, orange groves and parrots living in the palm trees. It was once the site of a massive star-shaped citadel, built for Felipe V between 1715 and 1720 following a 13-month siege of the city. The fortress was intended to house soldiers to keep law and order, but was never used for this purpose. Converted into a prison, the citadel became notorious during the Napoleonic occupation *(see p67)* and, during the 19th-century liberal repressions, it was hated as a symbol of centralized power. In 1878, under General Prim, whose statue stands in the middle of the park, it was pulled down and the park given to the city, to become, in 1888, the venue of the Universal Exhibition *(see pp68–9)*. Three buildings survived: the Governor's Palace, now a school; the chapel; and the arsenal, occupied by the Catalan parliament.

The park offers more cultural and leisure activities than any other in the city and is particularly popular on Sunday afternoons, when people gather to play instruments, dance and relax, or visit the museum and zoo. A variety of works by Catalan sculptors such as Marès, Arnau, Carbonell, Clarà, Llimona, Fuxà, Gargallo and Dunyach can be seen, alongside work by modern artists such as Tàpies and Botero.

The gardens in the Plaça de Armes were laid out by French landscape gardener Jean Forestier and centre on a cascade based around a triumphal arch. It was designed by architect Josep Fontseré, with the help of Antoni Gaudí, then still a young student.

Modernist exterior of the Castell dels Tres Dragons

㉑ Castell dels Tres Dragons

Passeig de Picasso. **Map** 5 C2. 🚇 Arc de Triomf, Jaume I. **Closed** to the public.

At the entrance to the Parc de la Ciutadella is the Castell dels Tres Dragons (Castle of the Three Dragons), named after a play by Frederic Soler. A fine example of Modernista architecture *(see pp144–5)*, the combination of visible iron supports and exposed red brickwork were radical innovations at the time.

It was built by Lluís Domènech i Montaner for the 1888 Universal Exhibition and was later used as a workshop for Modernista design. Once part of the Museu de Ciències Naturals, the Castell now houses a laboratory for the museum and is open only to researchers.

㉒ Museu Martorell

Parc de la Ciutadella. **Map** 5 C3. **Tel** 93 319 69 12. 🚇 Arc de Triomf, Jaume I. **Closed** for renovations.

Part of the Museu de Ciències Naturals, the Museu Martorell is Barcelona's oldest museum. It opened in 1882 and was the first building in the city to be constructed expressly for the purpose of housing a museum. Beside it is the Hivernacle, a glasshouse by Josep Amargós, and the Umbracle, a conservatory by the park's architect, Josep Fontseré. Both date from 1884 and were designed for the 1888 Universal Exhibition.

㉓ Zoo de Barcelona

Parc de la Ciutadella. **Map** 6 D3. **Tel** 902 457 545. 🚇 Ciutadella-Vila Olímpica. **Open** 10am–5pm daily (Mar–mid-May & mid-Sep–Oct to 6pm; mid-May–mid-Sep: to 7pm). 🅿️ ♿ 🌐 **zoobarcelona.cat**

The animals in this zoo, laid out in the 1940s, are separated by moats instead of bars. Dolphin and whale shows are held in one of the aquariums. All the aquatic creatures here will eventually move to a designated marine zoo, but plans are currently on hold due to budget cuts. The zoo has pony rides, electric cars and a train. Roig i Soler's 1885 sculpture by the entrance, *The Lady with the Umbrella*, has become a symbol of the city.

Ornamental cascade in the Parc de la Ciutadella designed by Josep Fontseré and Antoni Gaudí

Smart boats and the twin skyscrapers at the Port Olímpic

❷❹ Port Olímpic

Map 6 F4. 🚇 Ciutadella-Vila Olímpica.

The most dramatic rebuilding for the 1992 Olympics was the demolition of the old industrial waterfront and the laying out of 4 km (2 miles) of promenade and pristine sandy beaches. Suddenly Barcelona seemed like a seaside resort. At the heart of the project was a 0.6 sq km (¼ sq mile) new estate of 2,000 apartments and parks called Nova Icària. The area is still popularly known as the Vila Olímpica because the buildings originally housed the Olympic athletes.

On the seafront there are twin 44-floor blocks, two of Barcelona's tallest skyscrapers, one occupied by offices and the other by the Hotel Arts (see p565). They stand beside a bustling marina, which was also built for 1992. The marina is the setting for several restaurants and bars.

❷❺ Barceloneta

Map 5 B5. 🚇 Barceloneta.

Barcelona's fishing "village", which lies on a triangular tongue of land jutting into the sea just below the city centre, is renowned for its fish restaurants and port-side cafés.

Barceloneta was built by the architect and military engineer Juan Martín de Cermeño in 1753 to rehouse people made homeless by the construction of a large fortress, La Ciutadella (see pp158–9). Since then it has housed largely workers and

fishermen. Laid out on a grid system with narrow houses of two or three floors, the area has a friendly air.

In the small Plaça de la Barceloneta, is the Baroque church of Sant Miquel del Port, also by Cermeño. The large central square is dominated by a contemporary covered market.

Today, the remnants of Barceloneta's fishing fleet are based in the nearby industrial docks by a small clock tower. On the opposite side of this harbour is the Torre de Sant Sebastià, terminus of the cable car that runs across the port, via the World Trade Centre, to Montjuïc. Ricardo Bofill's sail-shaped Hotel W is a landmark on Barceloneta beach.

❷❻ Port Vell

Map 5 B4. 🚇 Barceloneta, Drassanes Aquàrium: **Tel** 93 221 74 74.
Open Jun & Sep: 9:30am–9:30pm daily; Jul–Aug: 9:30am–11pm daily; Oct–May: 9:30am–9pm Mon–Fri, 9:30am–9:30pm Sat, Sun & public hols.
🅿 ♿ ⚧ 🆆 **aquariumbcn.com**

The city's leisure port is at the foot of Las Ramblas, just beyond the old customs house. This was built in 1902 at the Portal de la Pau, the former maritime entrance to the city, where steps lead into the water. To the south, the Moll de Barcelona, with a World Trade Centre, serves as the passenger pier for visiting cruise ships. In front of the customs house, Las Ramblas is linked to the yacht clubs on the Moll d'Espanya by a swing

bridge and pedestrian jetty. The Moll d'Espanya (moll meaning "quay, wharf or pier") has a shopping and restaurant complex, the Maremagnum, plus an IMAX cinema and the largest aquarium in Europe.

The Moll de la Fusta (Timber Wharf), with terrace cafés, has red structures inspired by van Gogh's painting of the bridge at Arles. At the end of the wharf stands El Cap de Barcelona (Barcelona Head), a 20-m (66-ft) sculpture by Pop artist Roy Lichtenstein.

❷❼ Monument a Colom

Plaça del Portal de la Pau. **Map** 2 F4.
Tel 93 302 52 24. 🚇 Drassanes. **Open** 9am–8:30pm daily (to 7:30pm Oct–Feb). **Closed** 1 & 6 Jan, 25 & 26 Dec. ♿

The Columbus Monument in the Portal de la Pau (the "Gate of Peace") was designed by Gaietà Buigas for the 1888 Universal Exhibition.

The 60-m (200-ft) cast-iron monument marks the spot where Columbus stepped ashore in 1493 after discovering America, bringing with him six Caribbean Indians. He was accorded a state welcome by the Catholic Monarchs in the Saló del Tinell (see p150). The Indians' conversion to Christianity is commemorated in the cathedral (see pp152–3).

There is a small viewing platform at the top of the monument, where a 7-m (24-ft) bronze statue of Columbus points out to sea.

Fishing boat moored at the quayside of Barceloneta

A *golondrina* departing from the Plaça del Portal de la Pau

㉘ Golondrinas

Plaça del Portal de la Pau. **Map** 2 F5. **Tel** 93 442 31 06. 🚇 Drassanes. **Open** times vary – phone ahead. 🌐 **w** lasgolondrinas.com

Sightseeing trips around the harbour can be made on small double-decker boats called *golondrinas* ("swallows"). They moor beside the steps of the Plaça del Portal de la Pau in front of the Columbus Monument. Tours last around half an hour. The boats go out beneath the steep, castle-topped hill of Montjuïc towards the industrial port.

An alternative one-and-a-half-hour trip in modern catamarans takes in Barcelona Harbour, the commercial port and beaches.

㉙ Museu Marítim and Drassanes

Avinguda de les Drassanes. **Map** 2 F4. **Tel** 93 342 99 20. 🚇 Drassanes. **Open** 10am–8pm daily (partially open due to refurbishment, check website for details). **Closed** 1 & 6 Jan, 25 & 26 Dec. 🌐 free Sun after 3pm. ♿ **w** mmb.cat

The great galleys that made Barcelona a major seafaring power were built in the sheds of the Drassanes (shipyards), which now house the maritime museum. These royal dry docks are the largest and most com-plete surviving medieval complex of their kind in the world. They were founded in the mid-13th century, when dynastic

marriages uniting the kingdoms of Sicily and Aragón meant that better maritime communications between the two became a priority. Three of the yards' four original corner towers survive.

Among the vessels to slip from the Drassanes' vaulted halls was the *Real*, flagship of Don Juan of Austria, Charles V's illegitimate son, who led the Christian fleet to victory against the Turks at Lepanto in 1571 *(see p63)*. The museum's showpiece is a full-scale replica decorated in red and gold. A restored century-old schooner, the *Santa Eulàlia*, is moored in the Port Vell and can be visited.

The *Llibre del Consulat de Mar*, a book of nautical codes and practice, is a reminder that Catalonia was once the arbiter of Mediterranean maritime law. The expertise of its sailors is also evident in the collection of Pre-Columbian charts and maps, including one of 1439 that was used by Amerigo Vespucci.

Stained-glass window in the Museu Marítim

(see p63)

Barcelona's Fiestas

La Mercè *(24 Sep)*. The patroness of Barcelona, Nostra Senyora de la Mercè (Our Lady of Mercy), whose church is near the port, is honoured for a week around 24 September with Masses, concerts and dances. The biggest events are the *correfoc* – a wild procession of people dressed as devils and monsters, dancing with fireworks – and the *piro musical* – an impressive firework display with music held at the Font Màgica in Montjuïc.

Firework display during the fiesta of La Mercè

Els Tres Tombs *(17 Jan)*. Horsemen, dressed in top hats and tails, ride three times through the streets in honour of St Anthony, the patron saint of animals.
Dia de Sant Ponç *(11 May)*. Stalls along Carrer Hospital sell herbs, honey and candied fruit on the day of the patron saint of beekeepers and herbalists.
La Diada *(11 Sep)*. Catalonia's "national" day is an occasion for singing the Catalan anthem and separatist demonstrations.
Festa Major *(varies)*. Each district hosts its own *festa* in which streets compete to outdo each other in the inventiveness and beauty of their decorations. The most spectacular take place in the neighbourhood of Gràcia.

EIXAMPLE

Barcelona claims to have the greatest collection of Art Nouveau buildings of any city in Europe. The style, known in Catalonia as Modernisme, flourished after 1854, when it was decided to pull down the medieval walls to allow the city to develop into what had previously been a construction-free military zone.

The designs of the civil engineer Ildefons Cerdà i Sunyer (1815–76) were chosen for the new expansion (*eixample*) inland. These plans called for a rigid grid system of streets, but at each intersection the corners were chamfered to allow the buildings there to overlook the junctions or squares. The few exceptions to

this grid system include the Diagonal, a main avenue running from the wealthy area of Pedralbes down to the sea, and the Hospital de la Santa Creu i de Sant Pau by Modernista architect Domènech i Montaner (1850–1923). He hated the grid system and deliberately angled the hospital to look down the diagonal Avinguda de Gaudí towards Antoni Gaudí's church of the Sagrada Família, the city's most spectacular Modernista building *(see pp170–71)*. The wealth of Barcelona's commercial elite, and their passion for all things new, allowed them to give free rein to the age's most innovative architects in designing their residences as well as public buildings.

Sights at a Glance

Museums and Galleries
❷ Fundació Antoni Tàpies

Churches
❻ *Sagrada Família pp170–71*

Modernista Buildings
❶ Illa de la Discòrdia
❸ Casa Milà "La Pedrera"

❹ Casa Terrades "Casa de les Punxes"
❺ Hospital de la Santa Creu i de Sant Pau

See also Barcelona Street Finder maps 3, 4, 5

◀ Aerial view of apartment block Casa Milà, designed by Gaudí

For map symbols *see back flap*

Street-by-Street: Quadrat d'Or

The hundred or so city blocks centring on the Passeig de Gràcia are known as the Quadrat d'Or, "Golden Square", because they contain so many of Barcelona's best Modernista buildings *(see pp144–5)*. This was the area within the Eixample favoured by the wealthy bourgeoisie, who embraced the new artistic and architectural style with enthusiasm, not only for their residences, but also for commercial buildings. Most remarkable is the Illa de la Discòrdia, a single block containing houses by Modernisme's most illustrious exponents. Many interiors can be visited by the public, revealing a feast of stained glass, ceramics and ornamental ironwork.

Diagonal Metro

Vinçon home decor store *(see pp192–3)*

Passeig de Gràcia, the Eixample's main avenue, is a showcase of highly original buildings and smart shops. The graceful street lamps are by Pere Falqués (1850–1916).

❷ **Fundació Tàpies**
Topped by Antoni Tàpies' wire sculpture *Cloud and Chair*, this 1879 building by Domènech i Montaner houses a wide variety of Tàpies' paintings, graphics and sculptures.

RAMBLA DE CATALUNYA

PASSEIG DE GRÀCIA

Casa Amatller

Museu del Perfum

Casa Ramon Mulleras

❶ ★ **Illa de la Discòrdia**
In this city block, three of Barcelona's most famous Modernista houses vie for attention. All were created between 1900 and 1910. This ornate tower graces the Casa Lleó Morera by Domènech i Montaner.

To Plaça de Catalunya

Casa Batlló

Casa Lleó Morera

Passeig de Gràcia Metro

The Palau Baró de Quadras was designed by Puig i Cadafalch in 1904. The façade, in Neo-Gothic style, is highly ornate and covered with distinctive sculptures. This carving adorns the doorway.

Locator Map
See Barcelona Street Finder map 3

AVINGUDA DIAGONAL

CARRER DE PAU CLARIS

CARRER DE PROVENÇA

Casa Thomas

CARRER DE MALLORCA

To Sagrada Família

CARRER DEL BRUC

CARRER DE ROGER DE LLÚRIA

ER DE VALÈNCIA

CARRER D'ARAGÓ

Palau Ramon de Montaner

❹ Casa Terrades "Les Punxes"
Built in red brick with carved stone ornamentation, this 1905 house by Puig i Cadafalch echoes the Gothic buildings of northern Europe, and was the Modernista architect's largest work.

❸ ★ Casa Milà "La Pedrera"
Gaudí put all his architectural daring into this, his most famous house. The result is a remarkable wave-like façade and a roofscape of chimneys and vents resembling abstract sculptures.

| 0 metres | 100 |
| 0 yards | 100 |

Key

— Suggested route

For additional symbols *see back flap*

Sumptuous interior of the Casa Lleó Morera, Illa de la Discòrdia

❶ Illa de la Discòrdia

Passeig de Gràcia, between Carrer d'Aragó and Carrer del Consell de Cent. **Map** 3 A4. 🚇 Passeig de Gràcia. Casa Lleó Morera: **Tel** 93 676 27 33. 📷 guided tours only (no high heels), book in advance online or at the Palau de la Virreina (see p197); 11am Mon–Sat in English. 🖥 **casalleomorera. com** Casa Amatller: **Tel** 93 216 01 75. **Open** 10am–6pm daily. **Closed** 2 weeks in Jan, 25 & 26 Dec. 📷 guided tours only (no high heels), book online. 🖥 **amatller.org** Casa Batlló: **Tel** 93 216 03 06. **Open** 9am–9pm daily. 📷 ♿ 🖥 **casabatllo.es**

The most famous group of Modernista (see pp144–5) buildings in Barcelona amply illustrates the range of styles involved in the movement. The block in which they stand has been dubbed the Illa de la Discòrdia, "Block of Discord", owing to the startling visual argument between them.

The three most famous houses, on Passeig de Gràcia, were remodelled from existing houses early in the 20th century, but named after their original owners.

No. 35 is **Casa Lleó Morera** (1902–6), the first residential work of Lluís Domènech i

Montaner. The ground floor was gutted to create a shop in 1943, but the Modernista interiors upstairs still exist.

At No. 41 is **Casa Amatller**, designed by Puig i Cadafalch in 1898. Its façade is a harmonious blend of styles, featuring Moorish and Gothic windows. The stepped gable roof is dotted with tiles. Inside the wrought-iron main doors is a fine stone

staircase beneath a stained-glass roof. The Amatller family apartments are being restored; check the website before planning a visit. The rest of the building is occupied by the **Institut Amatller d'Art Hispanic**.

The third house is Gaudí's **Casa Batlló** (1904–6). Its façade has heavily tiled walls and curving iron balconies pierced with holes to look like masks or skulls. The humpbacked, scaly-looking roof is thought to represent a dragon, with St George (the patron saint of Catalonia) as a chimney.

❷ Fundació Antoni Tàpies

Carrer d'Aragó 255. **Map** 3 A4. **Tel** 93 487 03 15. 🚇 Passeig de Gràcia. **Open** 10am–8pm Tue–Sun & public hols (to 6:30pm in winter). **Closed** 1 & 6 Jan, 25 Dec. 📷 📷 by appt (93 207 58 62). ♿ 🖥 **fundaciotapies.org**

Antoni Tàpies (1923–2012) was one of Spain's foremost contemporary artists. Inspired by Surrealism, his abstract work was executed in a variety of materials, including concrete and metal (see p164). Only a small part of the collection can be shown at one time, and exhibits rotate regularly. There are also excellent temporary exhibitions. All are housed in the first domestic building in Barcelona to be built with iron (1880), designed by Domènech i Montaner.

Antoni Gaudí (1852–1926)

Born in Reus (Tarragona) into a family of artisans, Gaudí was the leading exponent of Catalan Modernisme. Following a stint as a blacksmith's apprentice, he studied at Barcelona's School of Architecture. Inspired by a nationalistic search for a romantic medieval past, his work was supremely original. His first major achievement was the Casa Vicens (1888) at No. 24 Carrer de les Carolines. But his most celebrated building is the extravagant church of the Sagrada Família (see pp170–71), to which he devoted his life from 1914. He gave all his money to the project and often went from house to house begging for more, until his death a few days after being run over by a tram.

Decorated chimneypot, Casa Vicens

◀ Extraordinary sculptured and ceramic-encrusted chimneys of Gaudí's Casa Milà

The rippled façade of Gaudí's apartment building, Casa Milà

The towers and gables are influenced in particular by north European Gothic architecture. However, the deeply carved, floral stone ornament of the exterior, in combination with red brick as the principal building material, are typically Modernista.

❾ Hospital de la Santa Creu i de Sant Pau

Carrer de Sant Antoni Maria Claret 167. **Map** 4 F2. **Tel** 93 291 90 00. 🚇 Hospital de Sant Pau. Grounds: **Open** 10am–6:30pm Mon–Sat (to 4:30pm Nov–Mar), 10am–2:30pm Sun. **Closed** 1 & 6 Jan, 25 & 26 Dec. ♿ 🎫 (free first Sun of month). 🎧 in English at noon & 1pm. 🌐 santpaubarcelona.org

❸ Casa Milà

Passeig de Gràcia 92. **Map** 3 B3. **Tel** 90 220 21 38. 🚇 Diagonal. **Open** 9am–8pm daily (Nov–Feb: to 6:30pm). **Closed** 7–13 Jan, 25 Dec. 🎫 (temporary exhibitions free.) 🌐 lapedrera.com

Usually called "La Pedrera" ("the stone quarry"), the Casa Milà is Gaudí's greatest contribution to Barcelona's civic architecture, and his last work before he devoted himself entirely to the Sagrada Família *(see pp170–71)*.

Built 1906–12, "La Pedrera" completely departed from the established construction principles of the time and, as a result, the building was strongly attacked by Barcelona's intellectuals.

Gaudí designed this corner apartment block, eight storeys high, around two circular courtyards. The intricate ironwork balconies, by Josep Maria Jujol, are like seaweed against the wave-like walls of white undressed stone. There are no straight walls in the building.

The Milà family had an apartment on the first floor. The top floor now houses the **Gaudí Museum**. Regular guided tours take in the extraordinary roof, where the multitude of sculpted air ducts and chimneys are so sinister they have been dubbed the *espanta-bruixes*, the witch-scarers.

❹ Casa Terrades

Avinguda Diagonal 416. **Map** 3 B3. 🚇 Diagonal. **Closed** to public.

This freestanding, six-sided apartment block by Modernista architect Puig i Cadafalch gets its nickname, "Casa de les Punxes" (House of the Points), from the spires on its six corner turrets, which are shaped like witches' hats. It was built between 1903 and 1905 by converting three existing houses on the site and is an eclectic mixture of medieval and Renaissance styles.

Spire on the main tower, Casa Terrades

Lluís Domènech i Montaner began designing a new city hospital in 1902. Totally innovative in concept, his scheme consisted of 26 Mudéjar-style pavilions set in large gardens, as he disliked huge wards and believed that patients would recover better amid fresh air and trees. All the connecting corridors and service areas were hidden underground. Also believing art and colour to be therapeutic, he decorated the pavilions profusely. The turreted roofs were tiled with ceramics, and the reception pavilion embellished with sculptures by Pau Gargallo and mosaic murals.

Statue of the Virgin, Hospital de la Santa Creu i de Sant Pau

❻ Sagrada Família

Europe's most unconventional church, the Temple Expiatori de la Sagrada Família, is an emblem of a city that likes to think of itself as individualistic. Crammed with symbolism inspired by nature and striving for originality, it is Gaudí's *(see pp144–5)* greatest work. In 1883, a year after work had begun on a Neo-Gothic church on the site, the task of completing it was given to Gaudí, who changed everything, extemporizing as he went along. It became his life's work and he lived like a recluse on the site for 14 years. He is buried in the crypt. At his death, only one tower on the Nativity façade had been completed, but work resumed after the Civil War and several more have since been finished to his original plans. Work continues today, financed by public subscription.

Bell Towers
Eight of the 12 spires, one for each apostle, have been built. Each is topped by Venetian mosaics.

The Finished Church

Gaudí's initial ambitions have been kept over the years, using various new technologies to achieve his vision. Still to come is the central tower, which is to be encircled by four large towers representing the Evangelists. Four towers on the Glory (south) façade will match the existing four on the Passion (west) and Nativity (east) façades. An ambulatory – like an inside-out cloister – will run round the outside of the building.

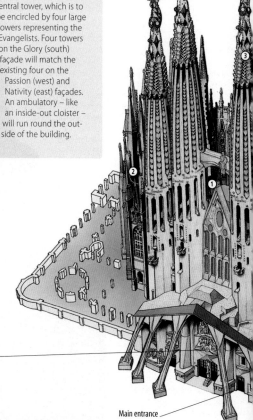

Main entrance

★ Passion Façade
This bleak façade was completed from 1986 to 2000 by artist Josep Maria Subirachs. A controversial work, its sculpted figures are angular and often sinister.

Spiral Staircases
The steep stone staircases – 370 steps in each – are closed to the public. The views from the upper galleries are reachable via lift only.

VISITORS' CHECKLIST

Practical Information
C/ Sardenya. **Map** 4 E3. **Tel** 93 513 20 60. **w** sagradafamilia.org
Open daily. Apr–Sep: 9am–8pm; Oct–Mar: 9am–7pm; Nov–Feb: 9am–6pm (to 2pm 1 & 6 Jan, 25 & 26 Dec). timed tickets only, advance booking advisable. in English 11am, 1pm & 3pm daily (also noon daily May–Oct). numerous services daily.

Transport
Sagrada Família. 19, 43, 51.

★ Nativity Façade
The most complete part of Gaudí's church, finished in 1930, has doorways which represent Faith, Hope and Charity. Scenes of the Nativity and Christ's childhood are embellished with symbolism, such as doves representing the congregation.

★ Crypt
The crypt, where Gaudí is buried, was begun by the original architect, Francesc de Paula Villar i Lozano, in 1882. This is where services are held. On the lower floor a museum traces the careers of both architects and the church's history.

KEY

① **The altar canopy** was designed by Gaudí.

② **The apse** was the first part of the church Gaudí completed. Stairs lead down from here to the crypt below.

③ **Towers with lift**

④ **The nave** contains a forest of fluted pillars that support four galleries above the side aisles; a large number of skylights let in both natural and artificial light.

MONTJUÏC

The hill of Montjuïc, rising to 213 m (699 ft) above the commercial port on the south side of the city, is Barcelona's biggest recreation area. Its museums, art galleries, gardens and nightclubs make it a popular place in the evenings as well as during the day.

There was probably a Celtiberian settlement here before the Romans built a temple to Jupiter on their Mons Jovis, which may have given Montjuïc its name – though another theory suggests that a Jewish cemetery on the hill inspired the name Mount of the Jews.

The absence of a water supply meant that there were few buildings on Montjuïc until the castle was erected on the top in 1640.

The hill finally came into its own as the site of the 1929 International Fair. With great energy and flair, buildings were erected all over the north side, with the grand Avinguda de la Reina Maria Cristina, lined with huge exhibition halls, leading into it from the Plaça d'Espanya. In the middle of the avenue is the Font Màgica (Magic Fountain), which is regularly illuminated in colour. Above it is the Palau Nacional, home of the city's historic art collections. The Poble Espanyol is a crafts centre housed in copies of buildings from all over Spain. The last great surge of building on Montjuïc was for the 1992 Olympic Games, which left Barcelona with international-class sports facilities.

Sights at a Glance

Historic Buildings
8 Castell de Montjuïc

Modern Architecture
4 Pavelló Mies van der Rohe
9 Estadi Olímpic de Montjuïc

Museums and Galleries
1 Fundació Joan Miró
2 Museu Arqueològic
3 Museu Nacional d'Art de Catalunya
6 CaixaForum

Squares
7 Plaça d'Espanya

Theme Parks
5 Poble Espanyol

See also Barcelona Street Finder maps 1, 2

0 metres 500
0 yards 500

◀ Spectators admiring the light show at the Font Màgica (Magic Fountain)   **For map symbols** *see back flap*

Street-by-Street: Montjuïc

Montjuïc is a spectacular vantage point from which to view the city. It has a wealth of art galleries and museums, an amusement park and an open-air theatre. The most interesting buildings lie around the Palau Nacional, where Europe's greatest Romanesque art collection is housed. Montjuïc is approached from the Plaça d'Espanya between brick pillars based on the campanile of St Mark's in Venice, which give a foretaste of the eclecticism of building styles. The Poble Espanyol illustrates the traditional architecture of Spain's regions, while the Fundació Joan Miró is boldly modern.

④ Pavelló Mies van der Rohe
This statue by Georg Kolbe *(see p177)* stands serenely in the steel, glass, stone and onyx pavilion built in the Bauhaus style as the German contribution to the 1929 International Exhibition.

⑤ ★ Poble Espanyol
Containing replicas of buildings from many regions, this "village" provides a fascinating glimpse of vernacular styles.

③ ★ Museu Nacional d'Art de Catalunya
Displayed in the National Palace, the main building of the 1929 International Exhibition is Europe's finest collection of early medieval frescoes. These were a great source of inspiration for Joan Miró *(see p176)*.

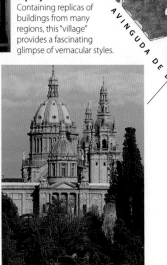

To Montjuïc castle and Olympic stadium

| 0 metres | | 100 |
| 0 yards | | 100 |

Fountains and cascades descend in terraces from the Palau Nacional. Below them is the Font Màgica (Magic Fountain). In the evening, from Thursday to Sunday (October to April: Friday and Saturday), its jets are programmed to a multicoloured music and light show. This marvel of water-and-electrical engineering was originally built by Carles Buigas (1898–1979) for the 1929 International Exhibition.

Locator Map
See Barcelona Street Finder map 1

aça d'Espanya

Museu Etnològic displays artifacts from Oceania, Africa, Asia and Latin America.

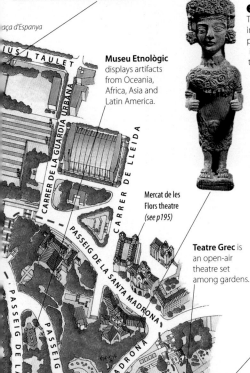

❷ **Museu Arqueològic**
The museum displays important finds from prehistoric cultures in Catalonia and the Balearic Islands. The *Dama de Ibiza*, a 4th-century sculpture, was found in Ibiza's Carthaginian necropolis *(see p515)*.

Mercat de les Flors theatre *(see p195)*

Teatre Grec is an open-air theatre set among gardens.

❶ ★ **Fundació Joan Miró**
This tapestry by Joan Miró hangs in the centre he created for the study of modern art. In addition to Miró's works in various media, the modern building by Josep Lluís Sert is of architectural interest.

CARRER DE LA GUARDIA URBANA
CARRER DE LLEIDA
PASSEIG DE LA SANTA MADRONA
PASSEIG DE LA SANTA MADRONA
AVINGUDA DE MIRAMAR

To Montjuïc castle and cable car

Key
— Suggested route

Flame in Space and Naked Woman (1932) by Joan Miró

❶ Fundació Joan Miró

Parc de Montjuïc. **Map** 1 B3. **Tel** 93 443 94 70. 🚇 Espanya, then bus 150, 55 or Paral.lel, then Montjuïc funicular. **Open** 10am–7pm Tue, Wed, Fri & Sat (Jul–Sep: to 8pm), 10am–9:30pm Thu, 10am–2:30pm Sun & public hols. **Closed** 1 Jan, 25 & 26 Dec. 🎦 ♿ 🅆 fundaciomiro-bcn.org

Joan Miró (1893–1983) studied at the fine art school at La Llotja *(see p156)*. From 1919, he spent much of his time in Paris. Though opposed to Franco, he returned to Spain in 1940 and lived mainly in Mallorca, where he died.

An admirer of primitive Catalan art and Gaudí's Modernisme *(see pp144–5)*, Miró always remained a Catalan painter but developed a Surrealistic style, with vivid colours and fantastical forms suggesting dream-like situations.

In 1975, after the return of democracy to Spain *(see p72)*, his friend, the architect Josep Lluís Sert, designed the stark, white building to house a permanent collection of paintings, sculptures and tapestries lit by natural light. Miró himself donated the works and some of the best pieces on display include his *Barcelona Series* (1939–44), a set of 50 black-and-white lithographs. Periodic exhibitions of other artists' work are also held.

❷ Museu Arqueològic

Passeig Santa Madrona 39–41. **Map** 1 B3. **Tel** 93 423 21 49. 🚇 Espanya, Poble Sec. **Open** 9:30am–7pm Tue–Sat, 10am–2:30pm Sun & public hols. **Closed** 1 Jan, 25 & 26 Dec. 🎦 (free last Sun of month, 23 Apr, 18 May, 11 & 24 Sep and for under 16s & over 65s). ♿ 🅆 mac.cat

Housed in the Renaissance-inspired 1929 Palace of Graphic Arts, the museum shows artifacts from prehistory to the Visigothic period (AD 415–711). Highlights are finds from the Greco-Roman town of Empúries *(see p220)*, Iberian silver treasure and Visigothic jewellery.

❸ Museu Nacional d'Art de Catalunya

Parc de Montjuïc, Palau Nacional. **Map** 1 B2. **Tel** 93 622 03 60. 🚇 Espanya. 🚌 55, 150. **Open** 10am–8pm Tue–Sat (to 6pm Oct–Apr), 10am–3pm Sun & pub hols. **Closed** 1 Jan, 1 May, 25 Dec. 🎦 🍽 ♿ 📷 by appt (93 622 03 75), free 1st Sun of month & Sat from 3pm. 🅆 mnac.cat

The austere **Palau Nacional** was built for the 1929 International Exhibition, but in 1934 it was used to house an art collection that has since become the most important in the city.

The museum has probably the world's greatest display of Romanesque *(see p28)* items, centred around a series of magnificent 12th-century frescoes taken from Catalan Pyrenean churches. The most remarkable are the wall paintings from Sant Climent de Taüll *(see p28)* and from Santa Maria de Taüll *(see p215)*.

The expanding Gothic collection covers the whole of Spain but particularly Catalonia, and a collection of notable Baroque and Renaissance works hails from all over Europe.

A fine collection of modern art includes Modernista furniture by Gaudí *(see pp144–5)*, and paintings by Picasso, Ramon Casas and Salvador Dalí. The museum offers a rare opportunity to view more than a millennium of Catalan artistic activity in a single location.

12th-century *Christ in Majesty*, Museu Nacional d'Art de Catalunya

Morning by Georg Kolbe (1877–1945), Pavelló Mies van der Rohe

❹ Pavelló Mies van der Rohe

Avinguda Francesc Ferrer i Guàrdia 7. **Map** 1 A2. **Tel** 93 423 40 16. 🚇 Espanya. 🚌 13, 150. **Open** 10am–8pm daily (to 6pm in winter). **Closed** 1 Jan, 25 Dec. 🅿 under 16s free. 📷 noon Sat. 🌐 **miesbcn.com**

The modern, simple lines of the glass and polished stone German Pavilion must have shocked visitors to the International Exhibition in 1929. Designed by Ludwig Mies van der Rohe (1886–1969), director of the avant-garde Bauhaus school, it includes his *Barcelona Chair*, now an icon of Modernism. The building was demolished after the exhibition, but a replica was built on the centenary of his birth.

❺ Poble Espanyol

Avinguda Francesc Ferrer i Guàrdia 13. **Map** 1 A2. **Tel** 93 508 63 00. 🚇 Espanya. 🚌 50, 150. **Open** 9am–8pm Tue–Thu & Sun (to 8pm Mon, 3am Fri, 4am Sat). 🅿 ♿ 🌐 **poble-espanyol.com**

The popular Poble Espanyol (Spanish Village) was built for the 1929 International Exhibition to display Spanish architectural styles and crafts.

Building styles from all over Spain are illustrated by 116 houses arranged on streets radiating from a main square. The village was refurbished at the end of the 1980s.

Resident artisans produce crafts including hand-blown glass,

ceramics, Toledo damascene (*see p394*) and Catalan canvas sandals. There are also bars, restaurants, nightclubs and a flamenco *tablao (see pp196–7)*.

❻ CaixaForum

Avinguda Francesc Ferrer i Guàrdia 6–8. **Map** 1 B2. **Tel** 93 476 86 00. 🚇 Espanya. 🚌 13, 50. **Open** 10am–8pm daily (Jul & Aug: to 11pm Wed). **Closed** 1 & 6 Jan, 25 Dec. 🅿 ♿ 🌐 **obrasocial.lacaixa.es**

This collection of 700 works by Spanish and international artists is housed in the Antiga Fàbrica Casaramona, a restored textile mill (1911) in Modernista style, built by Josep Puig i Cadafalch. The permanent exhibition here is Joseph Beuys' *Espai de Dolor* (Chamber of Pain).

❼ Plaça d'Espanya

Avinguda de la Gran Via de les Corts Catalanes. **Map** 1 B1. 🚇 Espanya. Fountain Show: May–Sep: 9–11:30pm Thu–Sun; Oct–Apr: 7–9pm Fri & Sat.

The fountain in the middle of this road junction, the site of public gallows until 1715, is by Josep Maria Jujol, one of Gaudí's followers. The 1899 bullring is by Font i Carreras. Catalans have never taken to bullfighting, and the arena was converted into Las Arenas shopping centre by British architect Richard Rogers.

On the Montjuïc side of the roundabout is the Avinguda de la Reina Maria Cristina, flanked by two brick campaniles, modelled on the bell towers of St Mark's in Venice. The avenue leads up to Carles Buigas's *Font*

Màgica (Magic Fountain) in front of the Palau Nacional.

❽ Castell de Montjuïc

Parc de Montjuïc. **Map** 1 B5. **Tel** 93 329 86 53. 🚇 Paral·lel, then funicular & cable car. 🚌 150 from Plaça Espanya. **Open** 10am–8pm daily (to 6pm Oct–Mar). 🅿 (free Sun from 3pm & for under 16s).

The summit of Montjuïc is occupied by an 18th-century castle, first built in 1640 but destroyed by Felipe V in 1705. The present fortress was built for the Bourbon family. During the War of Independence the castle was captured by the French, and after the Civil War it became a prison, where the Catalan leader Lluís Companys was executed in 1940. It is now a peace museum, with further exhibits on the castle's history.

❾ Estadi Olímpic de Montjuïc

Passeig Olímpic 17–19. **Map** 1 A4. **Tel** 93 426 20 89. 🚇 Espanya, Poble Sec. 🚌 50, 61, 125. Open for events. Museum: **Open** 10am–6pm Tue–Sat, 10am–2:30pm Sun (Apr–Sep: to 8pm Tue–Sat). 🅿 📷 ♿

The Neo-Classical façade has been preserved from the stadium, built by Pere Domènech i Roura for the 1936 Olympics, cancelled at the onset of the Civil War. It was refitted for the 1992 Olympics.

Nearby are the **Palau Sant Jordi** indoor stadium, by Arata Isozaki, swimming pools by Ricardo Bofill and the **Museu Olímpic i de l'Esport**, which covers all aspects of sport.

View from Palau Nacional downhill towards the Plaça d'Espanya

FURTHER AFIELD

The radical redevelopment of Barcelona's outskirts in the late 1980s and early 1990s gave it a wealth of new buildings, parks and squares. The city's main station, Sants, was rebuilt and the neighbouring Parc de l'Espanya Industrial and Parc de Joan Miró were created, containing lakes, modern sculpture and futuristic architecture.

The Plaça de Glòries is being remodelled to contain the design museum and a park. In the west of the city, where the streets start to climb steeply, are the historic royal palace and monastery of Pedralbes, and Gaudí's famous Park Güell, dating from 1910. Beyond is the Serra de Collserola, the city's closest rural area. Two funiculars provide an exciting way of reaching its heights, which offer superb views of the city. Tibidabo, the highest point, with a funfair, the Neo-Gothic church of the Sagrat Cor and a modern steel-and-glass communications tower, is a favourite place among Barcelonans for a day out.

Sights at a Glance

Museums and Galleries
❸ Camp Nou (Experience Tour & Museum)
❻ Museu Blau
❽ Cosmocaixa – Museu de la Ciència

Historic Buildings
❹ Monestir de Santa Maria de Pedralbes

Modern Buildings
❺ Torre de Collserola

Parks and Gardens
❶ Parc de Joan Miró
❷ Parc de l'Espanya Industrial
❾ Park Güell

Theme Parks
❼ Tibidabo

Key
▨ Barcelona city centre
▭ Motorway
▭ Major road
▭ Minor road

0 km 1
0 miles 1

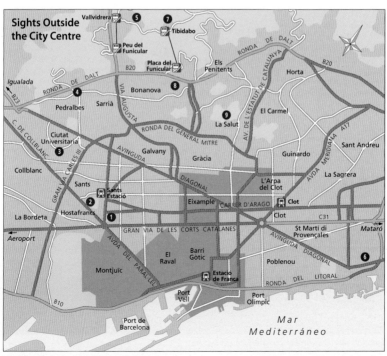

◀ Tibidabo theme park with Barcelona in the background

For additional map symbols *see back flap*

Dona i Ocell (1983) by Joan Miró in the Parc de Joan Miró

❶ Parc de Joan Miró

Carrer d'Aragó 1. 🚇 Tarragona.

Barcelona's 19th-century slaughterhouse *(escorxador)* was transformed in the 1980s into this unusual park, hence its alternative name, Parc de l'Escorxador.

It is constructed on two levels, the lower of which is popular with kids because of its open areas, fringed with shady paths and palm trees. The upper level is paved and dominated by a 1983 sculpture by Joan Miró *(see p176)* entitled *Dona i Ocell* (Woman and Bird). Standing 22 m (72 ft) high in the middle of a pool, its surface is coated with colourful pieces of glazed tile. There are also several play areas for kids.

❷ Parc de l'Espanya Industrial

Plaça de Joan Peiró. 🚇 Sants-Estació.

This modern park, designed by the Basque architect Luis Peña Ganchegui, owes its name to the textile mill that used to stand on the 5-hectare (12-acre) site.

Laid out in 1986 as part of Barcelona's policy to provide more open spaces, the park has canals and a rowing lake – with a statue of Neptune at its centre. Tiers of steps rise around the lake like an amphitheatre and on one side, a row of 10 futuristic watchtowers serves as public viewing platforms and lamp standards.

Six contemporary sculptors are represented in the park, among them Andrés Nagel, whose huge metal dragon incorporates a children's slide.

❸ Camp Nou (Experience Tour & Museum)

Avda de Aristides Maillol. **Tel** 90 218 99 00. 🚇 Maria Cristina, Collblanc. **Open** late Mar–mid-Oct, Christmas & Easter hols: 9:30am–7:30pm daily; mid-Oct–late Mar: 10am–6:30pm Mon–Sat, 10am–2:30pm Sun; reduced hours on public hols & match days. **Closed** 1 & 6 Jan, 25 Dec. 🅿 📷 of the stadium. ♿ 🌐 fcbarcelona.com

Camp Nou, Europe's largest football stadium, is home to the city's famous football club, Barcelona FC (Barça, as it is known locally). Founded in 1899, it is one of the world's richest soccer clubs, and has more than 100,000 members.

Line of watchtowers in the Parc de l'Espanya Industrial

The stadium is a magnificent, sweeping structure, built in 1957 to a design by Francesc Mitjans. An extension was added in 1982 and it can now comfortably seat 100,000 fans.

The club's popular museum is a glossy interactive experience, with touch-screen panels detailing the club's history and their many victories. There are also paintings and sculptures of famous club footballers commissioned for an exhibition held in celebration of the club in 1985 and 1987. *Blau-grana* (blue-burgundy) are the colours of Barça's strip. The club's flags were used as an expression of local nationalist feelings during the Franco dictatorship, when the Catalan flag was banned.

As well as hosting its own high-profile matches (mainly at weekends), Camp Nou also accommodates affiliated local soccer clubs and promotes a number of other sports.

Camp Nou stadium, the prestigious home of the Futbol Club Barcelona

For hotels and restaurants in this area see p565 and pp587–8

❹ Monestir de Santa Maria de Pedralbes

Baixada del Monestir 9. **Tel** 93 256 34 34. 🚇 Reina Elisenda or bus 22, 63, 64, 78. **Open** Apr–Sep: 10am–2pm Tue–Fri, 10am–7pm Sat, 10am–8pm Sun; Oct–Mar: 10am–2pm Tue–Fri, 10am–5pm Sat & Sun. 📷 by appt. **Closed** 1 Jan, Good Friday, 1 May, 24 Jun, 25 Dec. 🎫 (free first Sun of month, every Sun from 3pm and for under 16s; combined ticket with the Museu d'Història de Barcelona (see p150) also available). ♿ ground floor only. 🌐 **monestirpedralbes.bcn.cat**

Approached through an arch in its walls, the monastery of Pedralbes still has the air of a living enclosed community. This is heightened by its furnished cells, kitchens, infirmary and refectory. But the nuns of the Order of St Clare moved to an adjoining building in 1983. The monastery was founded in 1326 by Elisenda de Montcada de Piños, fourth wife of Jaime II of Catalonia and Aragón. Her tomb lies between the church and the cloister. On the church side her effigy is dressed in royal robes; on the other, as a nun.

The monastery is built around a cloister. The rooms encircling the cloister include a dormitory, a refectory, a chapterhouse, an abbey and day cells. Artworks and liturgical ornaments, pottery and furniture are on display.

The most important room in the monastery is the Capella (chapel) de Sant Miquel, with murals of the *Passion* and the

Madonna of Humility, Monestir de Santa Maria de Pedralbes

Life of the Virgin, both painted by Ferrer Bassa in 1346, when Elisenda's niece, Francesca Saportella, was abbess.

❺ Torre de Collserola

Carretera de Vallvidrera al Tibidabo. **Tel** 93 211 79 42. 🚇 Peu de Funicular, then Funicular de Vallvidrera & bus 111. **Open** times vary; check website for latest information. **Closed** 1 & 6 Jan, 25, 26 & 31 Dec. 🎫 ♿ 🌐 **torredecollserola.com**

In a city that enjoys thrills, the ultimate ride is offered by

the communications tower near Tibidabo mountain *(see p182)*. A glass-sided lift swiftly reaches the top of this 288-m- (944-ft-) tall structure standing on the summit of a 445-m (1,460-ft) hill.

The tower was designed by English architect Norman Foster for the 1992 Olympic Games. Needle-like in form, it is a tubular steel mast on a concrete pillar. There are 13 levels. The top one has an observatory with a powerful telescope, and a public viewing platform with a 360-degree view encompassing Barcelona, the sea and the mountains.

❻ Museu Blau

Plaça Leonardo da Vinci 4–5, Parc del Fòrum. **Tel** 93 256 22 00. 🚇 El Maresme Fòrum. 🚌 7, 36, 43, 99, H16. **Open** 10am–7pm Tue–Sat, 10am–8pm Sun. 🎫 free first Sun of month, every Sun from 3pm, under-16s. ♿ 🌐 **museublau.bcn.cat**

Museu Blau is the city's science museum with a collection that is more than 100 years old. Exhibited across two floors are 3 million specimens in the fields of mineralogy, palaeontology, zoology and botany. Previously located in the Parc de la Ciutadella *(see pp158–9)*, the museum is now housed in the Parc del Fòrum in a modern, innovative building designed by architects Herzog & de Meuron. The same team also conceived the permanent Planet Life exhibition, which is a fascinating journey through the history of life on earth. The Biography of the Earth section illustrates the evolution of life from the first microbes to the present day, while Earth Today comprehensively details the variety of life forms sharing the planet. Independent "Islands of Science" are spaced throughout Planet Life, which focus on specific topics, such as sexuality and genetics. There are also temporary exhibitions, a Media Library and a Science Nest for children up to age 6 at weekends, where images and sound effects recreate different natural surroundings.

Barcelona v Real Madrid

FC Barcelona

Real Madrid

Més que un club is the motto of Barcelona FC: "More than a club". More than anything else it has been a symbol of the struggle of Catalan nationalism against the central government in Madrid. To fail to win the league is one thing. To come in behind Real Madrid is a complete disaster. Each season the big question is which of the two teams will win the title. Under the Franco regime in a memorable episode in 1941, Barça won 3–0 at home. At the return match in Madrid, the crowd was so hostile that the police and referee "advised" Barça to prevent trouble. Demoralized by the intimidation, they lost 11–1. Loyalty is paramount: one Barça player who left to join Real Madrid received death threats.

Merry-go-round, Tibidabo

❼ Tibidabo

Plaça del Tibidabo 3–4. **Tel** 93 211 79 42. 🚇 Avda Tibidabo, then Tramvia Blau or Bus 196 & Funicular. 🚌 111, T2A from Plaça de Catalunya. Amusement Park: **Open** variable – check website for times. **Closed** Oct–Jun: Mon–Fri. ♿ Temple del Sagrat Cor: **Tel** 93 417 56 86. **Open** 10am–8pm daily. ♿ 🖥 tibidabo.cat

The heights of Tibidabo are reached by the Tramvia Blau (Blue Tram) and a funicular railway. The name, inspired by Tibidabo's views of the city, comes from the Latin *tibi dabo* (I shall give you) – a reference to the Temptation of Christ when Satan took him up a mountain and offered him the world spread at his feet.

The hugely popular Parc d'Atraccions first opened in 1908. While the old rides retain their charm, new ones have been added over the years, including the thrilling Dragon Khan rollercoaster. The hilltop location at 517 m (1,696 ft) adds to the thrill. The Museu d'Automates is a display of automated toys, jukeboxes and gaming machines.

Tibidabo is crowned by the Temple Expiatori del Sagrat Cor (Church of the Sacred Heart), built with religious zeal but little taste by Enric Sagnier between 1902 and 1911. A lift takes you up to the feet of an enormous figure of Christ.

Just a short bus ride away is another viewpoint worth visiting – the Torre de Collserola (see p181).

❽ Cosmocaixa – Museu de la Ciència

Carrer Isaac Newton 196. **Tel** 93 212 60 50. 🚇 Avinguda del Tibidabo, then Tramvia Blau. 🚌 17, 22, 58, 196. **Open** 10am–8pm Tue–Sun (daily Jul–Aug & public hols). **Closed** 1 & 6 Jan, 25 Dec. 🎟 (free 5–8pm Tue–Fri, 6–8pm Sat, Sun & public hols, first Sun of every month). ♿

This excellent science museum is located in a striking Modernista building. Exhibits include the Flooded Forest, which allows visitors to explore the Amazonian rainforest both above and below the waterline. A science lab is one of several great areas for children.

❾ Park Güell

Carrer d'Olot. **Tel** 010 (from Barcelona). 🚇 Lesseps, Vallcarca. 🚌 24, 32, 92, H6. **Tel** 90 220 03 02. **Open** late Mar–early May & early Sep–end Oct: 8am–8pm daily (to 9:30pm early May–early Sep); end Oct–late Mar: 8:30am–6:15pm daily, last entry 30 min before closing. 🎟 timed tickets only. 🎫 ♿ Casa-Museu Gaudí: **Tel** 93 219 38 11. **Open** Apr–Sep: 10am–8pm daily (to 6pm Oct–Mar). **Closed** 1 Jan. 🎟 combined ticket with the Sagrada Família also available.

A UNESCO World Heritage Site, the Park Güell is Antoni Gaudí's *(see pp144–5)* most colourful creation. He was commissioned in the 1890s by Count Eusebi Güell to design a garden city on 20 hectares (50 acres) of the family estate. Little of the grand design for decorative public buildings and 60 houses became reality. What we see today was completed between 1910 and 1914, and the park opened in 1922. The so-called "Monumental Area", home to most of Gaudí's surviving creations in the park, requires an admission ticket, but the green expanses around the edge of this area are free to explore.

The Room of a Hundred Columns is a cavernous hall of 84 crooked pillars that is brightened by glass and ceramic mosaics; it was intended as the marketplace for the estate. Above it is the Gran Plaça Circular, an open space with a snaking balcony of coloured mosaics that offers stunning views of the city and is said to have the world's longest bench.

Two pavilions at the entry are by Gaudí, but the Casa-Museu Gaudí, a gingerbread-style house where Gaudí lived from 1906 to 1926, was built by Francesc Berenguer.

Mosaic-encrusted chimney by Gaudí at the entrance of the Park Güell

BARCELONA STREET FINDER

The map references given with the sights, shops and entertainment venues described in the Barcelona section of the guide refer to the street maps on the following pages. Map references are also given for Barcelona hotels *(see pp564–5)*, and for bars and restaurants *(see pp586–8)*. The schematic map below shows the area of Barcelona covered by the *Street Finder*. The symbols used for sights and other features and services are listed in the key at the foot of the page.

0 kilometres   2
0 miles   1

Key to Street Finder

Major sight	Funicular railway station
Place of interest	Tram station
Other building	Tourist information
Main railway station	Hospital with casualty unit
Local (FGC) railway station	Police station
Metro station	Church
Coach station	Railway line
Cable-car station	Pedestrianized street

Scale of Map Pages

0 metres   250
0 yards   250

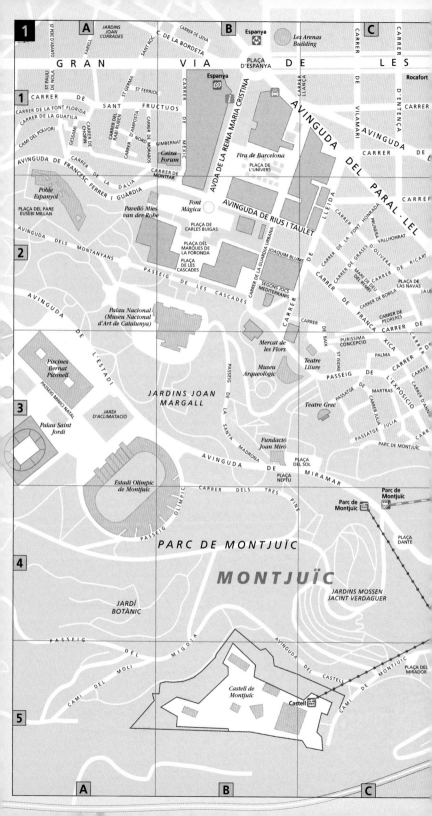

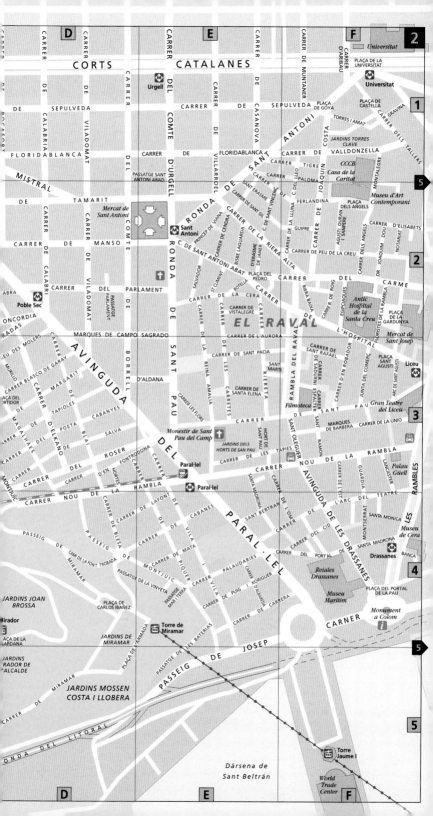

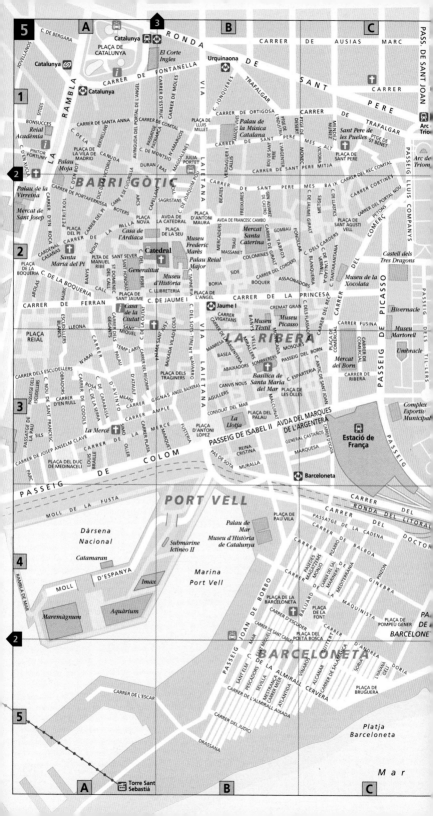

SHOPPING IN BARCELONA

Barcelona is known for its style and sophistication, and can be neatly divided into distinctive shopping districts – Passeig de Gràcia for designer stores and old shops with beautiful Modernista frontages, Barri Gòtic for eclectic antiques and boutiques, El Born for serious fashion divas, and El Raval for markets, quirky designs and museum shops. These categories are not fixed, but do provide a useful rule of thumb, and help define the city when time is limited. There are many food markets as well – 44 in all – and a scattering of flea markets such as the modern Els Encants and the charming Sant Cugat antiques fair. There is something for everyone in Barcelona – from high-street fashion and unique boutiques to local shops selling traditional crafts. All shops close on Sundays, except Maremagnum.

Some of the beautifully displayed confectionery at Escribà

Markets

Barcelona has an impressive range of markets selling a wide variety of things. Everyone should explore **La Boqueria** on Las Ramblas, one of the the most spectacular food markets in Europe. The small and lively Plaça del Pi is also home to a food market selling cheese, honey and sweets. It is held on the first and third Friday, Saturday and Sunday of each month.

On Sunday mornings, coin and stamp stalls are set up in the Plaça Reial, while antiques are sold in Plaça Nova on Thursdays. The city's main flea market, **Encants Vells**, takes place on Monday, Wednesday, Friday and Saturday. It offers a variety of goods including jewellery and clothing.

In December, a Christmas street market is held near the cathedral, where Christmas trees, figurines and other decorative items are sold.

Food and Drink

Barcelonans are proud of their culinary heritage, and rightly so. The land produces superlative vegetables and fruits, flavourful meats and a huge array of cheeses. The bountiful sea offers fresh fish and other seafood, and the wine-growing regions of the Penedès and the Priorat make some of the best vintages in the world. As if all this wasn't enough, chocolate shops, candy makers and patisseries also do their best to complete the feast.

La Boqueria food market is the obvious place to start a gastronomical journey, but Barcelona's numerous specialist food shops are not to be ignored either.

OlisOliva, in the Mercat Santa Caterina in El Born, stocks a superb selection of olive oils and a range of beauty products such as soaps and lotions. Around the corner, **La Botifarrería de Santa María** stocks wonderful artisan charcuterie and a lip-smacking selection of home-made sausages. These include inventive combinations such as pork and cuttlefish, beef and beetroot, and lamb and wild mushroom. **Casa Gispert** is the stop for top-grade dried fruit and nuts, as well as coffee toasted in-house. The fabulous **Formatgeria La Seu** is a walk-in dairy where you can choose from a great seasonal collection of cheeses made by small producers.

Xocoa is the trendiest of the many chocolate-makers in the city, with its retro packaging and fun shapes, including chocolate CDs and giant keys. **Escribà Pastisseries** is more extravagant, with magnificently sculpted cakes and life-size chocolate models of famous personalities. **Cacao Sampaka** is an innovative sweet shop that stocks amazing off-the-wall fillings such as anchovy, black olive and blue cheese, as well as more familiar herb, spice and floral flavours.

Casa Colomina is ideal for those who want to sample

Mouthwatering fruit stalls in La Boqueria market

traditional Spanish sweets such as turrón (nougat made with almonds). **Caelum**, where all the sweetmeats are made by nuns, sells lovely yemas (a sweet made with egg yolks) and mazapans (marzipan treats) and other tasty confections. **Papabubble**, a gorgeous wood-panelled shop, adds modern touches to old-fashioned sweets. You can watch the sweet chefs preparing these handmade concoctions.

For some of the best bread in town, visit **Bopan** near Rambla de Catalunya. This smart café has its own versions of many different types of bread, from Continental favourites to African specialities.

In El Born, **Vila Viniteca** sells a formidable range of Spanish and Catalan wines. Among more than 7,500 labels here you can find cheap and cheerful table wines, as well as decadently expensive Priorats and Riojas. Also remember that leaving Barcelona without a bottle of the nation's beloved Catalan champagne, cava, would be verging on the sacrilegious. The delightfully old-fashioned grocery store **Colmado Múrria** sells a wonderful range of conserves, wines, oils and other deli items.

Department Stores and Galerías

The Plaça Catalunya branch of **El Corte Inglés**, the largest department store chain in Spain, is a Barcelona landmark. It is a handy place with everything under one roof, including plug adaptors and services such as photographic development. There are other branches around the city.

The *galerías* (fashion malls), built mostly during the 1980s, are hugely popular. **Bulevard Rosa** on the Passeig de Gràcia has hundreds of stores selling clothes and accessories. On the Avinguda Diagonal is **L'Illa**, a large, lively shopping mall containing chain stores as well as specialist retailers. The **Maremagnum** shopping centre

Menswear department in Adolfo Domínguez

has all the usual Spanish chains and is open daily, including Sundays and holidays.

High Street and Sports Fashion

Ubiquitous Spanish fashion houses Zara and Mango have stores all over the city, with both flagships on the Passeig de Gràcia. They are great for good-value basics, workwear and fashionable party dresses. Both also offer a decent menswear range.

Those looking for more upmarket buys can rely on **Massimo Dutti** and **Adolfo Domínquez**. Both labels offer classically styled, elegant and fairly affordable clothing for men and women.

For more individualized fashion, try one of the smaller, independent shops in El Born and the Barri Gòtic. Carrer Flassaders and the lanes that lead off it in El Born are a particularly good hunting ground for cutting-edge fashion boutiques.

Custo Barcelona is one of the city's most famous design labels. Several branches of this store are in the Old Town, and are piled high with the trademark bright prints and daringly mismatched coats and skirts.

For outlets, head to Calle Girona, where several of them are clustered.

Finally, football fans can head for FC Barcelona's official store, the **Botiga del Barça**. It stocks every conceivable item of merchandise related to the team, including stripes, scarves, boots, balls and keychains.

Spanish and International Designer Labels

For stylish and original women's clothing, especially feminine-yet-contemporary dresses, and footwear by Spanish and European designers, try **Como Agua de Mayo** in the Born area.

The Barri Gòtic has several stores that stock a range of top designer labels, and this is where you'll find seasonal collections from Vivienne Westwood, Dolce & Gabbana and many others.

Host to big designer labels such as Gucci, Chanel and Carolina Herrera, Avenida Diagonal and the Passeig de Gràcia are where fashionistas like to go shopping. Passeig de Gràcia is home to **Loewe**, which stocks sleek luxury luggage, and is also a reputed name in fashion.

The stylishly sparse display of furniture at Vinçon *(see p192)*

Second-Hand and Vintage Fashion

The diminutive Carrer Riera Baixa in El Raval is home to many interesting second-hand stores. Once a theatre, the vintage shop **Lailo** sells whimsical collectibles such as costumes from the Liceu opera house and 1950s bathing suits. Plenty of vintage items can also be found on nearby Carrer Tallers: at **Flamingos**, which has a fabulous interior, the clothing is sold by weight, and bargains can always be found.

Jewellery, Bags and Accessories

Barcelona has plenty of tiny, Aladdin's Cave-type shops to help put together the perfect outfit. **Joid'Art** has top-quality silver pieces at good prices, both imported and by local designers. Visit **Minu Madhu** for embroidered jackets, patchwork scarves, appliqué handbags and hand-painted silk kerchiefs in sumptuous textures and colours.

Take a bit of the city's streetlife home – literally – with a Demano handbag. Recycled polyester PVC from banners and placards is transformed into bags in this endeavour by three designers and the city hall. The innovative and eco-friendly range is available from stockists all over town.

Ulleres M. Assumpta is a tiny shop selling retro-style and vintage artisan glasses and sunglasses, including its own original designs.

Hats and Shoes

Patterned leather shoes and decorative soles from the cult Mallorcan shoemaker, **Camper**, can be purchased at numerous branches around the city. **Vialias** is a home-grown Barcelona outfit selling beautifully stylish leather women's shoes and cool unisex trainers. **La Manual Alpargatera** is another cult classic, beloved by Sardana dancers (see p229) and celebrities alike for its exquisite, individually fitted espadrilles and straw hats.

Cherry Heel, with several branches around town, has a fantastic selection of luxury footwear, with brands like Le Silla and Rupert Sanderson.

For the best in designer sports shoes, head to **Czar** in the Born. Their hip selection includes Puma, Paul Smith, Rizzo, Fluxa and Le Coq Sportif.

For trendily old-fashioned hats, go to **Sombrerería Obach** where you will find classics ranging from Basque berets to stetsons and hand-woven Montecristi Panamas.

Books and Music

Arguably the finest specialist travel bookshop in Spain, **Altaïr** stocks a stupendous range of maps, travel guides and coffee-table books for anyone who loves to live on the move. If you are simply looking for some holiday reading, try **Casa del Llibre**, the city's biggest bookstore for books and magazines in English.

Barcelona has also become a hot spot for music collectors, largely due to Sonár, the city's annual electronica festival. **Wah Wah Discos** and **Discos Revolver** are good for stocking up on the latest club tunes and old vinyl, while **FNAC** has a wide variety of books, CDs and DVDs.

Unusual Gifts and Knick-Knacks

Barcelona is a wonderful city for unearthing intriguing knick-knacks and one-of-a-kind gifts. **Sabater Hnos. Fábrica de Jabones** sells home-made soaps, which come in all shapes and smells, from traditional lavender to delicious chocolate.

Cereria Subirà is the city's oldest shop, and sells a phenomenal array of decorative and votive candles in a variety of beautiful designs.

Arlequí Màscares specializes in superb hand-painted, papier-mâché folk masks such as Italian Commedia dell'Arte masks, glossy French party masks, Japanese Noh masks and many others.

Arts and Antiques

Antiques aficionados will be delighted by what Barcelona has to offer. Equivalent to an antiques shopping mall, the Bulevard dels Antiquaris, in Passeig de Gràcia, is home to over 70 shops filled with vintage relics and every sort of antique imaginable. These range from ancient coins to tin drums and 19th-century candelabra.

Carrer del Call in the Barri Gòtic is another such hub with plush shops, including **L'Arca de l'Àvia**, which sells antique lace, dolls and fine furniture. **Heritage** is a purveyor of semi-precious stone jewellery and antique silks. Also check out the several **Artur Ramón** shops on Carrer de la Palla for 18th- and 19th-century ceramics, and 14th-century paintings.

Sala Parés, the city's oldest and most prestigious gallery, exhibits Catalan artists, both past and present. For pictures that won't break the bank, try the **Boutique Galería Picasso** for prints, lithographs and posters of works by the great Spanish masters, Picasso, Dalí and Miró.

Interiors

L'Appartement is an eclectic gallery and shop that exhibits and sells furniture ranging from funky lamps to stylish folding armchairs. **Zara Home** has four basic styles in its collection: classic, ethnic, contemporary and white, all at very reasonable prices. **Siesta**, which used to be a haberdashery, is today a boutique and art gallery. It still maintains the original wood-and-glass cabinets, now filled with unique ceramics and contemporary jewellery by local artists.

Vinçon is the star among Barcelona's design stores, and a favourite with fans of gizmos and gadgets. Housed in a 1900s apartment, it is filled with everything from French Le Creuset cookware to straight-edged tumblers and Coderch lighting.

DIRECTORY

Markets

La Boqueria
Las Ramblas 101.
Map 5 A2.

Encants Vells
Plaça de les Glóries
Catalanes. **Map** 4 F5.

Food and Drink

Bopan
Rambla de Catalunya 119.
Map 3 A3.
Tel 932 37 35 23.

La Botifarrería de Santa María
Carrer Santa María 4.
Map 5 B3.
Tel 933 19 97 84.

Cacao Sampaka
C/ Consell de Cent 292.
Map 3 A4.
Tel 932 72 08 33.

Caelum
C/ Palla 8. **Map** 5 A2.
Tel 933 02 69 93.

Casa Colomina
Carrer de Portaferrissa, 8.
Map 5 A2.
Tel 934 12 25 11.

Casa Gispert
C/ Sombrerers 23.
Map 5 B3.
Tel 933 19 75 35.

Colmado Múrria
C/ Roger de Llúria 85.
Map 3 B4.
Tel 932 15 57 89.

Escribà Pastisseries
Las Ramblas 83. **Map** 5
A1. **Tel** 933 01 60 27.

Formatgeria La Seu
C/ Dagueria 16. **Map** 5 B3.
Tel 934 12 65 48.

OlisOliva
Avenida Francesc Cambó
153–155. **Map** 5 B2.
Tel 932 68 11 47.

Papabubble
C/ Ample 28. **Map** 5 A3.
Tel 932 68 86 25.

Vila Viniteca
C/ Agullers 7. **Map** 5 B3.
Tel 902 32 77 77.

Xocoa
C/ Vidrería 4. **Map** 5 B2.
Tel 933 19 79 05.

Department Stores and Galerías

Bulevard Rosa
Passeig de Gràcia 55.
Map 3 A4.
Tel 932 15 83 31.

El Corte Inglés
Plaça de
Catalunya 14.
Map 5 B1.
Tel 933 06 38 00.

L'Illa
Avinguda
Diagonal 557.
Tel 934 44 00 00.

Maremagnum
Moll d'Espanya 5.
Map 5 A4.
Tel 932 25 81 00.

High Street and Sports Fashion

Adolfo Domínguez
Passeig de Gràcia 32.
Map 3 A4.
Tel 619 660 277.

Botiga del Barça
Ronda Universitat 37.
Map 5 A1.
Tel 933 18 64 77.

Custo Barcelona
Plaça de les Olles 7.
Map 5 B3.
Tel 932 68 78 93.

Massimo Dutti
Portal de L'Angel 16.
Map 5 A1.
Tel 933 01 89 11.

Spanish and International Designer Labels

Como Agua de Mayo
C/ Argenteria 4.
Map 5 B3.
Tel 933 10 64 41.

Loewe
Passeig de
Gràcia 35.
Map 3 A4.
Tel 932 16 04 00.

Second-Hand and Vintage Fashion

Flamingos
C/ Tallers 31, El Raval.
Map 2 F1.
Tel 93 182 43 87.

Lailo
C/ Riera Baixa 20.
Map 2 F2.
Tel 934 41 37 49.

Jewellery, Bags and Accessories

Joid'Art
Plaça Sta. María 7. **Map** 5
B3. **Tel** 933 10 10 87.

Minu Madhu
C/ Sta. María 18. **Map** 5
B3. **Tel** 933 10 27 85.

Ulleres M. Assumpta
C/ Ramalleres 3. **Map** 2 F2.
Tel 933 18 29 96.

Hats and Shoes

Camper
C/ Elizabets 9. **Map** 2 F2.
Tel 933 42 41 41.

Cherry Heel
Passeig del Born 36.
Map 3 C5.
Tel 932 95 62 64.

Czar
Passeig del Born 20.
Map 5 C3.
Tel 933 10 72 22.

La Manual Alpargatera
C/ Avinyó 7. **Map** 5 A3.
Tel 933 01 01 72.

Sombrerería Obach
Carrer del Call 2. **Map** 5
A2. **Tel** 933 18 40 94.

Vialis
C/ Vidrieria 15. **Map** 5 B3.
Tel 933 19 94 91.

Books and Music

Altaïr
Gran Via 616. **Map** 3 A4.
Tel 933 42 71 71.

Casa del Llibre
Passeig de Gràcia 62. **Map**
3 A4. **Tel** 932 72 34 80.

Discos Revolver
Tallers 11. **Map** 5 A1.
Tel 934 12 62 48.

FNAC
Plaça de Catalunya 4.
Map 3 A4.
Tel 933 44 18 00.

Wah Wah Discos
C/ Riera Baixa 14.
Map 2 F2.
Tel 934 42 37 03.

Unusual Gifts and Knick-Knacks

Arlequí Màscares
Plaça St Josep Oriol 8. **Map**
5 A2. **Tel** 933 17 24 29.

Cereria Subirà
Baixada Llibreteria 7. **Map**
5 A2. **Tel** 933 15 26 06.

Sabater Hnos. Fábrica de Jabones
Pl Sant Felip Neri 1,
Barri Gòtic. **Map** 5 B2.
Tel 933 01 98 32.

Arts and Antiques

L'Arca de l'Àvia
C/ Banys Nous 20. **Map** 5
A2. **Tel** 933 02 15 98.

Artur Ramón
C/ Palla 23. **Map** 5 A2.
Tel 933 02 59 70.

Boutique Galería Picasso
C/ Tapinería 10. **Map** 5 B2.
Tel 933 10 49 57.

Heritage
C/ Banys Nous 14. **Map** 5
A2. **Tel** 933 17 85 15.

Sala Parés
C/ Petritxol 5. **Map** 5 A2.
Tel 933 18 70 20.

Interiors

L'Appartement
C/ Enric Granados 44.
Map 3 A4.
Tel 934 52 29 04.

Siesta
Ferlandina, 18. **Map** 2 F2.
Tel 933 17 80 41.

Vinçon
Passeig de Gràcia 96.
Map 3 A3.
Tel 932 15 60 50.

Zara Home
Rambla de Catalunya 71.
Map 3 A4.
Tel 934 87 49 72.

ENTERTAINMENT IN BARCELONA

Barcelona has one of the most colourful and alternative live arts scenes in Europe, offering a variety of entertainment, from the spectacular Modernista masterpiece the Palau de la Música and the gilded Liceu opera house, to small independent theatres hosting obscure Catalan comedies and dark Spanish dramas. But there's also much to see simply by walking around the city. Street performances you may stumble upon range from the human statues on Las Ramblas to excellent classical, ragtime and jazz buskers in the squares. In addition, there are a series of weekend-long musical and arts fiestas that run throughout the year, many of which now attract international performers from all over Europe and beyond.

The magnificent interior of the Palau de la Música Catalana

Entertainment Guides

The most complete guide to what's going on each week in Barcelona is the Catalan-language *Time Out*, out every Thursday. This guide also includes cinema listings. The Friday *La Vanguardia* features the entertainment supplement *Què Fem?* Barcelona's free English-language magazine, *Metropolitan*, also offers details of cultural events going on in town.

Seasons and Tickets

Theatre and concert seasons for the main venues run from September to June, with limited programmes at other times. The city's varied menu of entertainment reflects its rich, multicultural artistic heritage. In summer, the city hosts the Barcelona **Festival del Grec**, a showcase of international music, theatre and dance, held at open-air venues. There is also a wide variety of concerts to choose from during the **Festa de la Mercè**, held in September. The **Festival del Sónar**, which takes place in June, has become Europe's biggest electronic music festival, drawing musicians from around the world. The **Clàssics als Parcs**, held in June and July, presents classical music in serene surroundings.

The simplest way to get theatre and concert tickets is to buy them at the box office, although tickets for many theatres can also be bought from branches of Catalunya Caixa and La Caixa savings banks, or online through **Ticketmaster**. Tickets for the Grec festival are sold at **tourist offices** and at the **Palau de la Virreina**.

Theatre and Dance

Most theatre in Barcelona is performed in Catalan and English-language productions are still in short supply. However, many Catalan and Spanish shows are well worth seeing, regardless of language constraints. There are some good independent theatre groups, such as Els Comediants and La Cubana. They offer a thrilling mélange of theatre, music, mime and elements from traditional Mediterranean fiestas. Also staged at the tiny **LLantiol Teatre** in El Raval is a weekly repertoire of alternative shows, comedy, magic and other off-the-cuff performances designed to attract a mixed crowd, from the city's growing expatriate community to local arts lovers. Similarly, the **L'Antic Teatre** in La Ribera is a laid-back cultural centre and bar with a scruffy, but pleasant, summer roof-terrace and a small restaurant. It hosts a number of alternative production companies and also shows films outside on the terrace throughout the summer.

Las Ramblas and Paral.lel are the main hubs of the city's bigger and more mainstream theatres. The **Teatre Tívoli** is a

Outrageous stage show at one of Barcelona's many clubs

The façade of the modern Teatre Nacional de Catalunya

gargantuan theatre where high-quality productions, dance and musical recitals by Catalan, Spanish and international stars are held. The **Teatre Poliorama** on Las Ramblas, meanwhile, is known more for musicals, occasional operas and contemporary flamenco performances. The **Teatre Apolo** is good for big-bang musicals such as Queen's *We Will Rock You* and ABBA's *Mamma Mia!*

For serious theatre-lovers, the **Teatre Nacional de Catalunya** (TNC) is an imposing, columned affair designed by the Catalan architect Ricard Bofill, with state-of-the-art facilities and a weighty line-up of Spanish and Catalan directors. Good for avant-garde performances, contemporary dance and music is the **Mercat de les Flors**, a converted flower market in the Montjuïc area that is known as Barcelona's "City of Theatre". This is the same part of town that contains Barcelona's drama school and the **Teatre Lliure**, home to the most prestigious Catalan-language theatre company.

Modern dance has always been popular in Barcelona and performances can often be caught at the city's main theatres. The **Teatre Victòria** on Avinguda del Paral.lel is good for ballet and more classical dance productions, as is the **Liceu** opera house.

Opera and Classical Music

Opera and classical music are loved by Catalans who lap it up with near-religious reverence. Indeed, many of the great artists of the 20th century were locals, including the celebrated cellist Pau Casals and opera singers José Carreras and Montserrat Caballé.

The city of Barcelona is also home to some of the most spectacular venues in the world, including the glamorous, gilded **Gran Teatre del Liceu**, which first opened its doors in 1847. The opera house has been a continuing beacon of Catalan arts for more than 150 years, with a rich and dramatic history of fire and bomb attacks. It burned down for the third time in 1994, but careful renovations have restored it to its former glory. Despite its misfortunes, it has sustained a stellar line-up of the greatest composers in the world. Among them are Puccini and Tchaikovsky, as well as Catalan composers such as Felip Pedrell, Vives and Enric Granados. Sergei Diaghilev's Russian ballets were also staged here.

The whimsical fancy of the **Palau de la Música Catalana** is another of Barcelona's architectural triumphs *(see p156)*. A jewel-bright vision by the Modernista master Lluís Domènech i Montaner, this sublime concert hall has a dedicated audience, and performers who vie to play here. This is also the main venue for the city's jazz and guitar festivals, as well as national and international symphony orchestras.

Both venues, the Gran Teatre del Liceu and Palau de la Música Catalana, can be visited on interesting daytime guided tours, but booking tickets for an evening production remains by far the best way to experience the ambience.

Modern, but no less important as a shrine to the Catalan arts scene, **L'Auditori de Barcelona** was built to accommodate growing demands for better facilities and to attract ever greater numbers of world-class musicians. It began primarily as a place for classical concerts and orchestral recitals, but has since begun to embrace giants of jazz, pop and rock.

It is also worth keeping abreast of regular choral music that is performed at the city's churches and cathedrals. Most notable among these are the **Església Santa Maria del Pi**, the main cathedral on Plaça del Pi, and the **Basílica Santa Maria del Mar**, particularly around Christmas and Easter.

Packed house at the gigantic Nou Camp stadium

Sports

The undoubted kings of sport in Catalonia are **FC Barcelona**, known locally as Barça. They have the largest football stadium in Europe, Camp Nou *(see p180)*, and a fanatical following.

Tickets for Barça home matches in the national league *(La Liga)*, the King's Cup *(Copa del Rey)* and Champions League can be purchased at the FC Barcelona ticket offices (in person or by telephone) or, perhaps most conveniently, they can be bought online through the club website or Ticketmaster. Barcelona also has a high-ranking basketball team.

Amusement Park

In summer, Barcelona's giant amusement park on the summit of **Tibidabo** (see p182) is extremely busy and is usually open till the early hours on weekends. Getting there by tram, funicular or cable car is even more fun.

Film

Directors such as Alejandro Amenábar (*The Sea Inside* and *Agora*), Catalan writer and director Isabel Coixet (*My Life Without You* and *Elegy*) and, of course, Spain's bad boy of film, Pedro Almodóvar (*All About My Mother* and *The Skin I Live In*) have revitalized Spanish cinema. Woody Allen's *Vicky Cristina Barcelona* (2008) brought the city to an even wider audience. Today, Barcelona has become the venue for many independent film festivals. The biggest event of the year is the International Film Festival in Sitges, which is held in October.

Most cinemas dub films in Spanish or Catalan, but there are an increasing number of VO (original version) venues that screen Hollywood blockbusters as well as independent art-house movies.

The **Icària Yelmo Cineplex** is the town's biggest multiscreen VO complex, built around a US-style mall, with a variety of fast-food eateries and shops. The **Renoir Floridablanca**, on the edge of El Raval and the Eixample, screens a range of European and international movies, usually with Spanish or Catalan subtitles. In Gràcia, **Verdi** and **Verdi Park** feature good independent movies, with an interesting selection of foreign films. Escape the summer heat at outdoor film screenings held in the gardens next to the Castell de Montjuïc (see p177). A band plays before the film, and there are also beer stands. You can rent deckchairs, and many people bring a picnic.

The two-screen **Méliès** is a gem showcasing art-house movies, Hollywood classics, B&W horrors and anything by Fellini or Alfred Hitchcock. At the **Phenomena** cinema, you can catch cult classics, from *Casablanca* to *The Big Lebowski*. It's worth knowing that the prices for movie tickets are lower for weekend matinées. Some cinemas offer midnight and early-hour screenings.

Live Music: Rock, Jazz and Blues

In terms of popular music, Barcelona may not compare to London, whose endless clubs, pubs, stadiums and music emporiums make it one of the best places for live music. However, it doesn't do too badly, given its size. The city attracts a star-studded cast that ranges from pop stars such as Kylie Minogue and Madonna to contemporary jazz musicians such as the Brad Mehldau Quartet, hip-hoppers, rappers and world groove mixers, country singers and good old-fashioned rock-and-rollers.

Barcelona has a clutch of tiny, intimate venues, including the cellar-like **Jamboree**, attracting a number of jazz heavyweights as well as more experimental outfits. Later on it becomes a club.

Another good bet is the **Jazz Sí Club**, a more obscure destination but much beloved by aficionados of the genre. It doubles up as a jam session space for students from the nearby music school. The narrow, crowded and smoky **Harlem Jazz Club** is one of the city's longest surviving clubs for alternative and lesser-known jazz troupes.

One of the two major venues for pop and rock maestros is **Bikini** Barcelona's very own Studio 54. It opened in 1953, preceding the New York icon by a year. This veteran of the scene, which is open from midnight onwards, is still going strong with a robust line-up of big-name bands and a cocktail of different club nights. The other, **Razzmatazz**, arguably the city's most important live music venue, has played host to big-name pop bands such as the Arctic Monkeys, Noel Gallagher's High Flying Birds and James Morrison. Club sessions go on until dawn in some clubs, including Razz Club and The Loft, next door. This trendy venue also holds rock and jazz concerts several nights a week.

Barcelona boasts an architectural masterpiece to host visiting bands: Arata Isozaki's flying saucer, **Palau Sant Jordi**, on Montjuïc, houses extravaganzas like Disney on Ice, the Rolling Stones and Madonna.

One of the city's most popular smaller venues is **Sala BeCool**, which puts on live bands and club nights focused on electronic music.

For a touch of unbeatable glam, **Luz de Gas** is a glitzy ballroom that oozes old-fashioned atmosphere with its lamp-lit tables and chandeliers and features lists of bands and shows that enjoyed their heyday here in the 1970s and 1980s. It's not quite cabaret, but gets close, though not as close as the infamous **El Cangrejo**. This club features outrageous drag cabaret, with shockingly attired queens in full make-up and sequins miming along to numbers by Sara Montiel (the Spanish sex symbol) and back-chatting with the crowd.

Flamenco

Aside from the **Ciutat Flamenco Festival** in May, one of the best places to catch a flamenco show is **El Tablao de Carmen**, a stylish restaurant serving both Catalan and Andalusian dishes. The venue is named after Carmen Amaya, a famous dancer who performed for King Alfonso XIII in 1929, in the very spot where it now stands. Various dinner and show packages are available.

Another good place is **Tablao Cordobés**, in Las Ramblas since 1970 and decorated by the restorers of the Alhambra in Granada. You can have dinner or a drink while watching a show.

For a less formal ambience, **Los Tarantos** (above Jamboree) is an atmospheric nightspot with live flamenco and Latin music every night of the week.

DIRECTORY

Festivals

Barcelona Festival del Grec
Tel 010. Contact any tourist office. 🅦 grec.bcn.cat

Classics als Parcs
Tel 010. 🅦 bcn.es/parcsijardins

Festa de la Mercè
See p161.

Festival del Sónar
Palau de la Virreina.
🅦 sonar.es

Tickets

Palau de la Virreina
Las Ramblas 99. **Map** 5 A1. **Tel** 933 16 10 00.

Ticketmaster
🅦 ticketmaster.es

Tourist Office
Plaça de Catalunya.
Map 5 A1.
Tel 932 85 38 34.
🅦 barcelonaturisme.com

Theatre and Dance

L'Antic Teatre
C/ Verdaguer i Callís 12.
Map 5 B1.
Tel 933 15 23 54.

Llantiol Teatre
C/ Riereta 7. **Map** 2 E2.
Tel 933 29 90 09.

Mercat de les Flors
C/ de Lleida 59. **Map** 1 B2.
Tel 934 26 18 75.
🅦 mercatflors.cat

Teatre Apolo
Av del Paral.lel 59. **Map** 1 B1. **Tel** 934 41 90 07.
🅦 teatreapolo.com

Teatre Lliure
Plaça Margarida Xirgu 1.
Tel 932 89 27 70.
🅦 teatrelliure.com

Teatre Nacional de Catalunya (TNC)
Plaça de les Arts 1.
Tel 933 06 57 00.
🅦 tnc.cat

Teatre Poliorama
Las Ramblas 115. **Map** 5 A1. **Tel** 933 17 75 99.
🅦 teatrepoliorama.com

Teatre Tívoli
C/ Casp 8–10. **Map** 3 B5.
Tel 934 12 20 63.
🅦 grupbalana.com

Teatre Victòria
Av del Paral.lel 67–9. **Map** 1 B1. **Tel** 933 29 91 89.
🅦 teatrevictoria.com

Opera and Classical Music

L'Auditori de Barcelona
C/ de Lepant 150. **Map** 4 E1. **Tel** 932 47 93 00.
🅦 auditori.cat

Basílica Santa Maria del Mar
Plaça de Santa Maria.
Map 5 B3.
Tel 933 10 23 90.

Església Santa Maria del Pi
Plaça del Pi. **Map** 5 A2.
Tel 933 18 47 43.

Gran Teatre del Liceu
Las Ramblas 51–9. **Map** 2 F3. **Tel** 934 85 99 00.
🅦 liceubarcelona.cat

Palau de la Música Catalana
C/ Palau de la Música 4–6. **Map** 5 B1.
Tel 902 44 28 82.
🅦 palaumusica.org

Sports

FC Barcelona
Camp Nou, Avda Aristides Maillol. **Tel** 934 96 36 00.
🅦 fcbarcelona.com

Amusement Park

Tibidabo
Plaça del Tibidabo, 3.
Tel 932 11 79 42.
🅦 tibidabo.cat

Film

Icària Yelmo Cineplex
C/ Salvador Espriu 61.
Map 6 E4.
Tel 902 22 09 22.
🅦 yelmocines.es

Méliès
C/ Villarroel 102. **Map** 2 E1. **Tel** 934 51 00 51.
🅦 cinesmelies.net

Phenomena
C/ de Sant Antoni Maria Claret 168. **Map** 4 F1. **Tel** 932 52 77 43.
🅦 phenomena-experience.com

Renoir Floridablanca
C/ Floridablanca 135.
Map 1 C1.
Tel 934 26 33 37.
🅦 cinesrenoir.com

Verdi
C/ Verdi 32. **Map** 3 B1.
Tel 932 38 78 00.
🅦 cines-verdi.com

Verdi Park
C/ Torrijos 49. **Map** 3 C2.
Tel 932 38 78 00.
🅦 cines-verdi.com

Live Music: Rock, Jazz and Blues

Bikini
Deu i Mata 105.
Tel 933 22 08 00.
🅦 bikinibcn.com

El Cangrejo
C/ Montserrat 9. **Map** 2 F4. **Tel** 933 01 29 78.

Harlem Jazz Club
C/ Comtessa de Sobradiel 8.
Tel 933 10 07 55.
🅦 harlemjazzclub.es

Jamboree
Plaça Reial 17. **Map** 5 A3.
Tel 933 19 17 89.
🅦 masimas.com

Jazz Sí Club
C/ Requesens 2.
Tel 933 29 00 20.
🅦 tallerdemusics.com

Luz de Gas
C/ Muntaner 246. **Map** 2 F1. **Tel** 932 09 77 11.
🅦 luzdegas.com

Palau Sant Jordi
Passeig Olímpic 5–7.
Map 1 B4.
Tel 934 26 20 89.

Razzmatazz
C/ Pamplona 88. **Map** 4 F5. **Tel** 933 20 82 00.
🅦 salarazzmatazz.com

Sala BeCool
Plaça Joan Llongueras 5.
Tel 933 62 04 13.
🅦 salabecool.com

Flamenco

Ciutat Flamenco Festival
🅦 ciutatflamenco.com

Tablao Cordobés
Ramblas 35.
Map 5 A2.
Tel 933 17 57 11.
🅦 tablaocordobes.com

El Tablao de Carmen
Poble Espanyol, Avda Francesc Ferrer i Guàrdia, 13. **Map** 1 B1.
Tel 933 25 68 95.
🅦 tablaodecarmen.com

Los Tarantos
Plaça Reial 17. **Map** 5 A3.
Tel 932 04 12 10.
🅦 masimas.com/en/tarantos

Nightlife

Barcelona has one of the most varied nightlife scenes, with something for everybody. Old-fashioned dance halls rub shoulders with underground drum and bass clubs and trashy techno discos, and club-goers are either glammed up or grunged out. Each *barri* (neighbourhood) offers a different flavour, while clubs and bars with outdoor terraces enliven the beachfront during the summer months.

Nightlife

In the summer the beaches become party havens when the *xiringuitos* (beach bars) spring back into life. Wander from Platja de Sant Sebastià in Barceloneta, all the way to Bogatell (a few kilometres beyond the Hotel Arts) and you'll find people dancing barefoot on the sand to the tune of Barcelona's innumerable DJs. Way uptown (above the Diagonal), the city's most glamorous terraces morph into social hubs while the Barri Gòtic – lively at the best of times – becomes one massive street party throughout the summer. If you want to hang with the locals, the demolition of some of El Raval's less salubrious streets has meant that the neighbourhood has become much safer and easier to move about. The underground vibe, however, remains steadfastly intact with tiny hole-in-the-wall-style bars where folks drink and boogie till the early hours. Similarly Gràcia has a bohemian, studenty ambience. If it's an alternative scene you seek Poble Sec has a handful of "ring-to-enter" joints and the city's only serious drum and bass club, **Plataforma**. The city also has a thriving and friendly gay scene, most notably within the Eixample Esquerra, also known as the Gay Eixample, boasting numerous late-night drinking holes, discotheques, saunas and cabarets.

Barri Gòtic

The Plaça Reial is overrun with tourists banging on tin drums and whooping it up, but if you're looking for more grown-up fun, check out **Marula Café**.

This slinky club focuses on danceable funk and R&B, and it also has a small stage for live concerts. The tiny but ultra-hip **Macarena** is one of the city's most prestigious clubs. It majors in electronica and features the city's best DJs, renowned international artists and new talent. Jazz lovers shouldn't miss the daily concerts at **Jamboree**, one of Spain's mythical jazz clubs. Later, the venue becomes one of the most popular funk and hip-hop discos in town. The nightclub **The Apartment** is one of the newest on the lively Carrer Escudellers and features big-name DJs and regular live gigs.

El Raval

Designer clubs proliferate in Barcelona these days. With slinky red, black and white decor and a specially designed underlit bar, **Zentraus** is one of the best-looking clubs in the neighbourhood. A restaurant until midnight or so, the tables are cleared away once the DJ sessions get under way. **Moog** is more extreme, with blaring, heart-pumping techno for aficionados of the genre. The stark industrial interior gives it the character of a New York nightclub in the mid-1990s. Likewise, the state-of-the-art sound system ensures a thumping, ear-bleedingly good night out. Going back in time, check out the old-school ambience of **El Cangrejo**, where in 1924 the famous *copla* singer Carmen Amaya made her debut. On Friday and Saturday nights you can see drag shows here (the best ones are by Carmen de Mairena) followed

by pop revival DJ sessions. Other nights feature a 1970s and 1980s music theme.

Port Vell and Port Olímpic

Beach parties aside, this area continues to be a hub for creatures of the night. The Port Olímpic itself is nothing but bars and boats, while **Maremagnum** has a clutch of music bars and cocktail bars. **Catwalk** is one of the few clubs in Barcelona playing hip-hop and R&B. **C.D.L.C.**, in front of the Hotel ArtsV, still draws celebrities staying nearby, while neighbouring **Shôko**, with an Oriental theme, gets the crowd overflow.

Eixample

One of the city's best-loved discos, **City Hall**, is a multiple space and terrace, where you can pick and choose your groove according to your mood. It has different themes every night from Saturday night-fever discos to Sunday chill-outs. **Ommsessions Club**, in the Hotel Omm, is one of Barcelona's most glamorous addresses, beloved by models and fashionistas. Salsa fans should head to **Antilla**, where live music is combined with salsa classes and exotic cocktails. **Dow Jones** is Barcelona's "drinks stock exchange", where the prices of drinks rise and fall throughout the evening according to demand.

Montjuïc

Barcelona's mega-clubs are located away from the city centre and from anyone trying to sleep. Most of them are only open on Friday and Saturday nights. The big boys are based in Poble Espanyol, where folks can party until the sunrise. **La Terrrazza** is a summer club that hosts rave-like parties under the stars. It takes its name from the giant terrace it occupies. **The One** features a state-of-the-art sound system and top international DJs. Also in Poble Espanyol is **Upload**, another mega-club, which combines club nights with burlesque dinner shows and other events.

Poble Sec

The most alternative nightlife has come to roost in the "dry village", though in name only. The bars are wet and the music is happening. **Apolo** is another old-fashioned music hall, though it attracts a more independent breed of DJ and performer. Expect anything from soulful gypsy folk singers from Marseille, to the legendary purveyor of deep funk, Keb Darge. Further into the village, **Mau Mau** is an alternative club and cultural centre with a firm eye on what's new and happening. This could mean local DJs, Japanese musicians such as the cultish Cinema Dub Monks, alternative cinema, and multimedia art installations. If it's of the here and now, chances are Mau Mau's on it. At the other end of the spectrum, head to tiny **Tinta Roja** for low lights, romance and tango shows (from Thursday to Sunday nights) in a bar which recalls the Buenos Aires of the 1940s.

Gràcia and Tibidabo

Gràcia has a laid-back, alternative vibe, and its narrow streets are packed with bars and cafés. This isn't the neighbourhood to find big clubs, but it is the ideal place to enjoy a few drinks and watch the world go by. **Bobby Gin** is one of Gràcia's trendiest addresses and prides itself on preparing the best gin and tonics in town: speciality concoctions include the Ginfonk, with rose infusion, lime and strawberries. The friendly **Eldorado**, on the lively Plaça del Sol, manages to combine café, bar, club and games room (with table football, pool and pinball). Spanish music and 1980s pop dominate in what is just one of many relaxed "music bars". The **Atlantic** club in Tibidabo is set in a beautiful Modernista mansion with its own gardens, while the **Mirablau** offers unparalleled views over the city from its perch near the Tramvia Blau stop, halfway up Tibidabo.

DIRECTORY

Barri Gòtic

The Apartment
C/ Escudellers 5, Barri Gòtic. **Map** 5 A3.
Tel 93 252 69 40.

Jamboree
Plaça Reial 17, Barri Gòtic. **Map** 5 A3. **Tel** 93 319 17 89. [W] masimas.com

Macarena
C/ Nou de Sant Francesc 5. **Map** 5 A3.
Tel 93 301 30 64.
[W] macarenaclub.com

Marula Café
C/ Escudellers 49, Barri Gòtic. **Map** 5 A3.
Tel 93 318 76 90.
[W] marulacafe.com

El Raval

El Cangrejo
C/ Montserrat 9. **Map** 2 F4. **Tel** 93 301 29 78.

Moog
C/ L'Arc del Teatre 3, El Raval. **Map** 2 F4.
Tel 93 319 1789.
[W] masimas.com

Zentraus
Rambla de Raval 41, El Raval. **Map** 2 F3.
Tel 93 443 80 78.
[W] zentraus.cat

Port Vell and Port Olímpic

Catwalk
C/ Ramon Trias Fargas 2–4, Port Olímpic.
Map 6 E4.
Tel 93 224 07 40.
[W] clubcatwalk.net

C.D.L.C.
Passeig Marítim 32, Port Olímpic.
Map 6 E4.
Tel 93 224 04 70.
[W] cdlcbarcelona.com

Shôko
Passeig Marítim 36, Port Olímpic. **Map** 6 E4.
Tel 93 225 92 00.
[W] shoko.biz

Eixample

Antilla
Carrer d'Aragó 141–3.
Tel 93 451 45 64.
[W] antillasalsa.com

City Hall
Rambla de Catalunya 2–4, Eixample.
Map 3 A3.
Tel 93 233 33 33.
[W] cityhallbarcelona.com

Dow Jones
C/ Bruc 97. **Map** 3 B4.
Tel 93 420 35 48.

Ommsessions Club
Hotel Omm, C/ Rosselló 265. **Map** 3 B3.
Closed in summer.
Tel 93 445 40 00.
[W] hotelomm.es/nightclub

Montjuïc

The One
Poble Espanyol, Avinguda Francesc Ferrer i Guàrdia 13. **Map** 1 A2.
Tel 902 90 92 89.

La Terrrazza
Poble Espanyol, Avda Ferrer i Guàrdia 13.
Map 1 A1. **Tel** 93 272 49 80 / 687 969 825.
[W] laterrrazza.com

Upload
Poble Espanyol, Avinguda Francesc Ferrer i Guàrdia 13. **Map** 1 B1.
Tel 932 28 98 08.
[W] uploadbarcelona.com

Poble Sec

Apolo
C/ Nou de la Rambla 113, Poble Sec. **Map** 2 D4.
Tel 93 441 40 01.
[W] sala-apolo.com

Mau Mau
C/ d'en Fontrodona 35, Poble Sec. **Map** 2 D3.
Tel 93 441 80 15.
[W] maumaunderground.com

Plataforma
C/ Nou de la Rambla 145.
Map 2 D4. **Tel** 93 329 00 29. [W] tintaroja.cat

Tinta Roja
C/ Creu dels Molers 17, Poble Sec. **Map** 2 D3.
Tel 93 443 32 43.
[W] tintaroja.cat

Gràcia and Tibidabo

Atlantic
Avinguda del Tibidabo 56, Tibidabo. **Tel** 93 418 20 18. [W] atlanticbarcelona.com

Bobby Gin
C/ Francisco Giner 47, Gràcia. **Map** 3 B2.
Tel 93 368 18 92.
[W] bobbygin.com

Eldorado
Plaça del Sol 4, Gràcia.
Map 3 B1.

Mirablau
Plaça Doctor Andreu, Tibidabo. **Tel** 93 418 58 79. [W] mirablaubcn.com

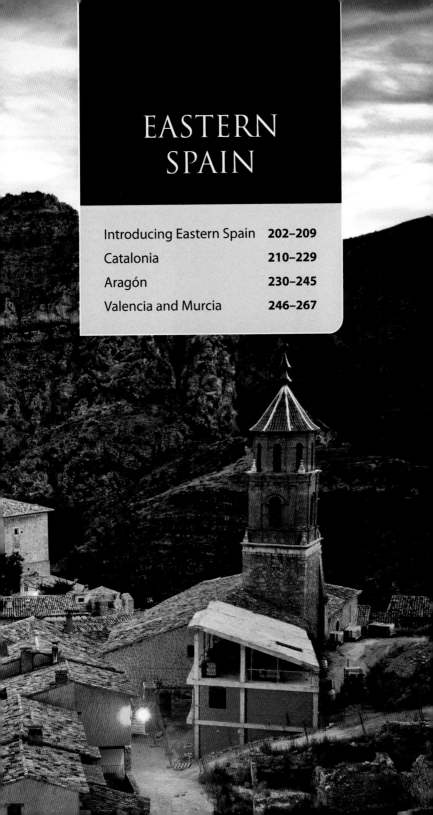

EASTERN SPAIN

Introducing Eastern Spain   **202–209**

Catalonia   **210–229**

Aragón   **230–245**

Valencia and Murcia   **246–267**

Introducing Eastern Spain

Eastern Spain covers an extraordinary range of climates and landscapes, from the snowbound peaks of the Pyrenees in Aragón to the beaches of the Costa Blanca and Costa Cálida, popular for their winter warmth and sunshine. The region has a wealth of historical sights including ancient monasteries near Barcelona, magnificent Roman ruins in Tarragona, Mudéjar churches and towers in Aragón and the great cathedrals of Valencia and Murcia. Away from the busy coasts, the countryside is often attractive but little visited.

Ordesa National Park (see pp236–7) in the Pyrenees has some of the most dramatic mountain scenery in Spain. It makes excellent walking country.

Zaragoza (see pp240–41) has many striking churches, especially the cathedral, the Basílica de Nuestra Señora del Pilar, and the Mudéjar-style Iglesia de la Magdalena.

Valencia (see pp254–7) is Spain's third-largest city. It has an old centre of narrow streets overlooked by venerable houses and monuments, such as the Miguelete, the cathedral's conspicuous bell tower. The city hosts a spectacular festival, Las Fallas, in March.

| 0 kilometres | 50 |
| 0 miles | 50 |

Murcia Cathedral (see p266), built in the 14th century, has a Baroque façade and belfry, and two ornate side chapels – one in Late Gothic style and the other Renaissance. The cathedral museum houses Gothic altarpieces and other fascinating exhibits.

Jaca

Hues

Almudévar

Gallur

Zaragoza

Calatayud

ARAGON
(See pp230–45)

Calamocha

Montalbán

Alfambra

Teruel

Chelva

Sagu

Requena

Valenci

VALENCIA AND MURCIA
(See pp246–67)

X

A

Jumilla

Elda

Alica

Cieza

Elche

Caravaca de La Cruz

Murcia

Alhama de Murcia

San Javier

Lorca

Mazarrón

Cartagena

Águillas

◀ Picturesque town of Albarracín, surrounded by stony hills, Teruel province

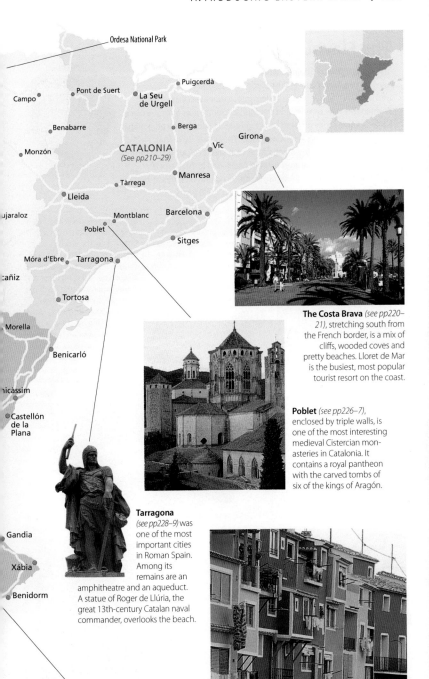

Ordesa National Park

Campo
Pont de Suert
La Seu de Urgell
Puigcerdà
Benabarre
Berga
Monzón
Girona
CATALONIA
(See pp210–29)
Vic
Tàrrega
Manresa
Lleida
ujaraloz
Montblanc
Barcelona
Poblet
Sitges
Móra d'Ebre
Tarragona
cañiz
Tortosa
Morella
Benicarló
nicàssim
Castellón de la Plana
Gandia
Xábia
Benidorm

The Costa Brava *(see pp220–21)*, stretching south from the French border, is a mix of cliffs, wooded coves and pretty beaches. Lloret de Mar is the busiest, most popular tourist resort on the coast.

Poblet *(see pp226–7)*, enclosed by triple walls, is one of the most interesting medieval Cistercian monasteries in Catalonia. It contains a royal pantheon with the carved tombs of six of the kings of Aragón.

Tarragona *(see pp228–9)* was one of the most important cities in Roman Spain. Among its remains are an amphitheatre and an aqueduct. A statue of Roger de Llúria, the great 13th-century Catalan naval commander, overlooks the beach.

The Costa Blanca *(see pp262–5)* is an attractive coast, as well as a popular holiday destination. Calp is overshadowed by a huge rock, the Penyal d'Ifach. In La Vila Joiosa, a line of houses has been painted in striking colours to make them visible to sailors at sea.

The Flavours of Eastern Spain

The current stars of Spain's culinary firmament are Catalans like Ferran Adriá or Carme Ruscalleda, whose creativity and innovation have brought them international acclaim. Fashionable new eateries and traditional country inns alike still place the emphasis firmly on fresh local ingredients. Along with adjoining Murcia and Catalonia, Valencia produces a huge array of fruit, vegetables, seafood, meat and game, all heaped colourfully in local markets. Rice is the key ingredient in paella and its many local variations. In landlocked Aragón, country cooking includes dishes that recall the Arabic occupation more than 1,000 years ago.

Valencian rice

Fresh octopus lie on the ice of a fish-seller's stall

Catalonia

The incredible variety of fresh produce in Catalonia is a reflection of the varied landscape – the Mediterranean provides all manner of fish and shellfish, the inland plains offer a wealth of vegetables and fields of golden rice, and the mountains contribute meat, game and wild mushrooms (a Catalan obsession). Spain's finest chefs create culinary fireworks in their celebrated restaurants, but Catalan cuisine, even at its most experimental, is essentially simple and relies on the wonderful freshness of its produce.

Aragón

In landlocked, mountainous Aragón, the emphasis is firmly on meat – particularly lamb, but also beef, rabbit and free-range chicken, often served simply grilled or slowly simmered in earthenware pots. There is also much excellent charcuterie, including hams and cured sausages, some flavoured with spices, which are often used to flavour the hearty stews popular in the mountainous north. River trout and eels are regularly found on local menus and, perhaps unusually so far

A range of fresh vegetables grown in eastern Spain

Labels: Artichokes, Onions, Aubergines (eggplants), Celery, Capers, Tomatoes, Green beans

Regional Dishes and Specialities

The lush Mediterranean coastline, backed by fertile plains and cool mountains, offers an extraordinary abundance of fresh produce here. From the sturdy stews of land-locked Aragón and the traditional cured meats of inland Murcia, to the celebrated seafood paellas and other rice dishes of Valencia, this is a region that dazzles with the variety of its cuisine. Spring and summer bring tiny broad beans, asparagus, and all manner of other vegetables and fruits. In autumn and winter, the annual pig slaughter is followed by the preparation of hams and cured meats, mushrooms proliferate on shady hills, and gamey stews keep out the winter cold. Seafood remains a constant, whether in *zarzuela de mariscos* (a rich shellfish stew) or the Murcian favourite of sea bream baked in a salty crust.

Candied fruits

Suquet de peix A Catalan stew of fresh, firm-fleshed fish, flavoured with tomatoes, garlic and toasted almonds.

Spectacular harvest of wild autumn mushrooms in a local market

north, the ancient Arabic heritage can still be tasted in exquisite local sweets and desserts, from candied fruits to heavenly *guirlache*, made from almonds and sugar.

Valencia

Valencia, the "Orchard of Spain", is magnificently lush and fertile. Most famous for its oranges, it also produces countless other fruits and vegetables, partnered in local recipes with Mediterranean seafood and mountain lamb, rabbit and pork. In spring, hillsides blaze with cherry and almond blossom and, in autumn, the golden rice fields are spectacular. Spain's signature dish, paella, is a Valencian invention – the local plump *bomba* rice is perfect for soaking up juices.

Murcia

Tiny, arid Murcia is almost a desert in parts but, thanks to irrigation methods introduced by the Arabs more than 1,000 years ago, it has become one of the largest fruit- and vegetable-growing regions in

An *embutidos* (cured meats) producer shows off his wares

Europe. The mountainous hinterland is famous for its flavoursome *embutidos* (cured meats), especially *morcilla* (black pudding/blood sausage) and *chorizo* (spicy, paprika-flavoured cured sausage), along with its excellent rice, which has earned its own DO *(denominación de origen)*. Along the coast, you can enjoy a wide range of fresh Mediterranean seafood, including sea bream baked in a salt crust, or lobster stew from the Mar Menor. The area's Arabic heritage lingers particularly in the desserts, flavoured with saffron, pine nuts and delicate spices.

ON THE MENU

Arroz Negro A Valencian rice dish; squid ink gives the distinctive dark colour.

Caldero Murciano Fishermen's stew, flavoured with saffron and plenty of garlic.

Dorada a la Sal Sea bream baked in a salty crust to keep the fish moist and succulent.

Fideuá A paella made with shellfish and tiny noodles instead of rice.

Guirlache An Aragonese sweet, made of toasted whole almonds and buttery caramel.

Migas con Tropezones Crusty breadcrumbs fried with garlic, pork and spicy cured sausage.

Paella In Spain's best-known dish, ingredients include saffron, round *bomba* rice, and meat, fish and shellfish.

Lentejas al estilo del Alto Aragón Lentils are slowly cooked with garlic, chunks of ham and black sausage.

Crema Catalana This hugely popular dessert is an eggy custard topped with a flambéed sugar crust.

Wines of Eastern Spain

Spain's eastern seaboard offers a wide spread of wines of different styles. Catalonia deserves pride of place, and here the most important region is Penedès, home of *cava* (traditional-method sparkling wine) and some high-quality still wine. In Aragón, Cariñena reds can be good, and Somontano, in the Pyrenees, has fine, international-style varietals. Valencia and Murcia provide large quantities of easy-drinking reds, whites and *rosados* (rosés). Most notable among these are the rosés of Utiel-Requena, the Valencian Moscatels and the strong, full-bodied reds made in Jumilla.

Cabernet Sauvignon vines

Somontano has had remarkable success due to the cultivation of international grape varieties such as Chardonnay and Pinot Noir.

Monastery of Poblet and Las Murallas vineyards in Catalonia

| 0 kilometres | | 100 |
| 0 miles | 50 | |

Key Facts about Wines of Eastern Spain

Location and Climate
The climate of Eastern Spain varies mainly with altitude – low-lying parts are hot and dry; it also gets hotter the further south you go. The wine regions of Catalonia have a Mediterranean climate along the coast, which becomes drier futher inland. The middle Penedès is a favoured location with a range of climates which suits many grape varieties. Somontano has a cooler, altitude-tempered climate. Valencia and Murcia can be, in contrast, unrelentingly hot.

Grape Varieties
The most common native red grape varieties planted in much of Eastern Spain are Garnacha, Tempranillo – which is called Ull de Llebre in Catalonia – Monastrell and Cariñena. Bobal makes both reds and, to a greater extent, rosés in Utiel-Requena. For

whites, Catalonia has Parellada, Macabeo and Xarel·lo (the trio most commonly used for *cava*), while in Valencia, Merseguera and Moscatel predominate. In the regions furthest to the southeast, Airén and Pedro Ximénez are sometimes found. French grape varieties, such as Chardonnay, Merlot, Cabernet Sauvignon and Sauvignon Blanc, flourish in the regions of Penedès, Costers del Segre and Somontano.

Good Producers
Somontano: Viñas del Vero, Viñedos del Altoaragón. **Alella**: Marqués de Alella, Parxet. **Penedès**: Codorníu, Conde de Caralt, Freixenet, Juvé y Camps, Masía Bach, Mont-Marçal, René Barbier, Miguel Torres. **Costers del Segre**: Castell del Remei, Raimat. **Priorato**: Cellers Scala Dei, Masía Barril. **Valencia**: Vicente Gandia. **Utiel-Requena**: C. Augusto Egli. **Alicante**: Gutiérrez de la Vega. **Jumilla**: Asensio Carcelén (Sol y Luna), Bodegas Vitivino.

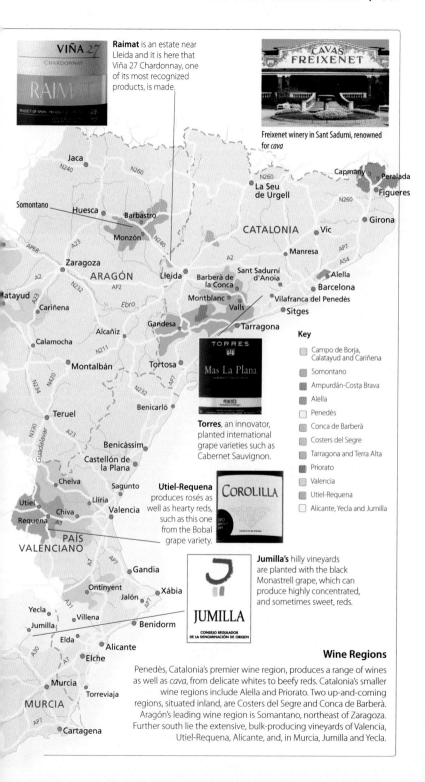

Raimat is an estate near Lleida and it is here that Viña 27 Chardonnay, one of its most recognized products, is made.

Freixenet winery in Sant Sadurni, renowned for *cava*

Torres, an innovator, planted international grape varieties such as Cabernet Sauvignon.

Utiel-Requena produces rosés as well as hearty reds, such as this one from the Bobal grape variety.

Jumilla's hilly vineyards are planted with the black Monastrell grape, which can produce highly concentrated, and sometimes sweet, reds.

Key

- Campo de Borja, Calatayud and Cariñena
- Somontano
- Ampurdán-Costa Brava
- Alella
- Penedès
- Conca de Barberà
- Costers del Segre
- Tarragona and Terra Alta
- Priorato
- Valencia
- Utiel-Requena
- Alicante, Yecla and Jumilla

Wine Regions

Penedès, Catalonia's premier wine region, produces a range of wines as well as *cava*, from delicate whites to beefy reds. Catalonia's smaller wine regions include Alella and Priorato. Two up-and-coming regions, situated inland, are Costers del Segre and Conca de Barberà. Aragón's leading wine region is Somontano, northeast of Zaragoza. Further south lie the extensive, bulk-producing vineyards of Valencia, Utiel-Requena, Alicante, and, in Murcia, Jumilla and Yecla.

Flowers of the Matorral

The *matorral*, a scrubland rich in wild flowers, is the distinctive landscape of Spain's eastern Mediterranean coast. It is the result of centuries of woodland clearance, during which the native holm oak was felled for timber and to provide land for grazing and cultivation. Many colourful plants have adapted to the extremes of climate here. Most flower in spring, when hillsides are daubed with pink and white cistuses and yellow broom, and the air is perfumed by aromatic herbs such as rosemary, lavender and thyme. Buzzing insects feed on the abundance of nectar and pollen.

The century plant's flower stalk can reach 10 m (32 ft).

Spanish broom is a small bush with yellow flowers on slender branches. The black seed pods split when dry, scattering the seeds on the ground.

Aleppo pine   Rosemary

Jerusalem sage, an attractive shrub which is often grown in gardens, has tall stems surrounded by bunches of showy yellow flowers. Its leaves are greyish-white and woolly.

Rose garlic has round clusters of violet or pink flowers at the end of a single stalk. It survives the summer as the bulb familiar to all cooks.

Foreign Invaders

Several plants from the New World have managed to colonize the bare ground of the *matorral*. The prickly pear, thought to have been brought back by Christopher Columbus, produces a delicious fruit which can be picked only with thickly gloved hands. The rapidly growing century plant, a native of Mexico which has tough spiny leaves, sends up a tall flower shoot only when it is 10–15 years old, after which it dies.

Prickly pear in fruit

Flowering shoots of the century plant

Common thyme is a low-growing aromatic herb, which is widely cultivated for use in the kitchen.

The mirror orchid, a small plant that grows on grassy sites, is easily distinguished from other orchids by the brilliant metallic blue patch inside the lip, fringed by brown hairs.

Temp °C/F												Rainfall in/mm

— Temperature   ▪ Rainfall

Most plants found in the *matorral* come into bloom in the warm, moist spring. The plants protect themselves from losing water during the dry summer heat with thick leaves or waxy secretions, or by storing moisture in bulbs or tubers.

Wildlife of the Matorral

The animals that live in the *matorral* are most often seen early in the morning, before the temperature is high. Countless insects fly from flower to flower, providing a source of food for birds. Smaller mammals, such as mice and voles, are active only at night, when it is cooler and there are few predators around.

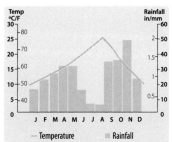

Holm oaks are very common in Eastern Spain. The leaves are tough and rubbery to prevent water loss.

The strawberry tree is an evergreen shrub with glossy serrated leaves. Its edible, strawberry-like fruit turns red when ripe.

Tree heather

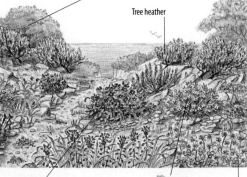

Ladder snakes feed on small mammals, birds and insects. The young are identified by a black pattern like the rungs of a ladder, but adults are marked with two simple stripes.

Scorpions hide under rocks or wood by day. When disturbed, the tail is curled quickly over the body in a threatening gesture. The sting, lethal to small animals, can cause some irritation to humans.

The Dartford warbler, a skulking bird that has dark plumage and a cocked tail, sings melodiously during its mating display. Males are more vividly coloured than females.

The swallow-tail butterfly is one of the most conspicuous of the great many insects living in the *matorral*. Bees, ants and grasshoppers are also extremely common.

Grey-leaved cistus, growing on sunny sites, has crumpled petals and bright yellow anthers.

Narrow-leaved cistus exudes a sticky aromatic gum used in perfumes.

Star clover is a low-growing annual whose fruit develops into a star-shaped seed head. Its flowers are often pale pink.

CATALONIA

Lleida · Andorra · Girona · Barcelona province · Tarragona

Catalonia is a proud nation-within-a-nation, which was once, under the count-kings of Barcelona-Aragón, one of the Mediterranean's great sea powers. It has its own semi-autonomous regional government and its own language, Catalan, which is used in place names, menus and on road signs throughout the region.

The Romans first set foot on the Iberian Peninsula at Empúries on Catalonia's Costa Brava ("wild coast"). They left behind them great monuments, especially in and Around Tarragona, the capital of their vast province of Tarraconensis. Later, Barcelona emerged as the region's capital, economically and culturally important enough to rival Madrid. In the 1960s the Costa Brava became one of Europe's first mass package-holiday destinations. Although resorts such as Lloret de Mar continue to draw the crowds, former fishing villages such as Cadaqués remain relatively unspoiled on this naturally attractive coast.

Inland, there is a rich artistic heritage to be explored. Catalonia has several spectacular monasteries, especially Montserrat, its spiritual heart, and Poblet. There are also many medieval towns, such as Montblanc, Besalú and Girona – which contain a wealth of monuments and museums.

In the countryside there is a lot to seek out, from the wetland wildlife of the Río Ebro delta to the vineyards of Penedès (where most of Spain's sparkling wine is made). In the high Pyrenees rare butterflies brighten remote mountain valleys, and little hidden villages encircle exquisite Romanesque churches.

Aigüestortes i Estany Sant Maurici National Park in the central Pyrenees, in the province of Lleida

◀ Boats shelter in Tossa de Mar's horseshoe bay on the Costa Brava

Exploring Catalonia

Catalonia includes a long stretch of the Spanish
Pyrenees, whose green, flower-filled valleys hide
picturesque villages with Romanesque churches.
The Parc Nacional d'Aigüestortes and Vall d'Aran
are paradises for naturalists, while Baqueira-
Beret offers skiers reliable snow. Sun-lovers can
choose between the rugged Costa Brava or the
long sandy stretches of the Costa Daurada.
Tarragona is rich in Roman monuments. Inland
are the monasteries of Poblet and Santes Creus
and the well-known vineyards of Penedès.

Isolated houses in the countryside around
La Seu d'Urgell

Key

- ▬▬ Motorway (highway)
- ▬▬ Other highway
- ▬▬ Main road
- ▬▬ Minor road
- ▬▬ Scenic route
- ➤━➤ Main railway
- ▬▬ Minor railway
- ▬▬ International border
- ▬▬ Regional border
- △ Summit

Getting Around

A tunnel near Puigcerdà
has made the central
Catalan Pyrenees easily
accessible. Buses, more
frequent in summer,
connect most towns.
The main north–south
railway hugs the coast
from Blanes southwards.
Other lines run from
Barcelona through Vic,
Lleida and Tortosa.

For additional map symbols *see back flap*

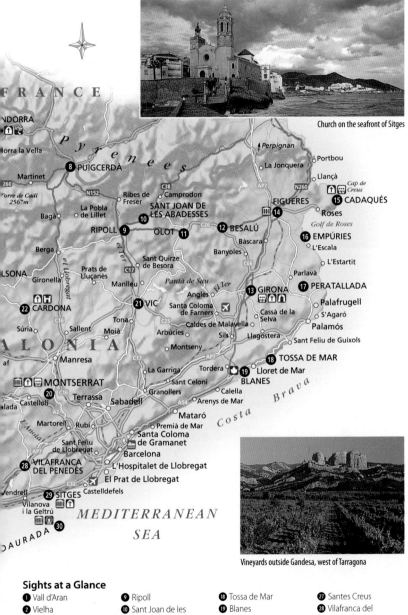

Church on the seafront of Sitges

FRANCE

NDORRA

Pyrenees

Perpignan

Portbou

La Jonquera

Llançà

Cap de Creus

8 PUIGCERDÀ

Martinet

Torre de Cadí 2567m

Ribes de Freser

Camprodon

La Pobla de Lillet

SANT JOAN DE LES ABADESSES

FIGUERES

15 CADAQUÉS

Roses

Golf de Roses

Bagà

RIPOLL **9**

OLOT **11**

12 BESALÚ

16 EMPÚRIES

Berga

Bàscara

L'Escala

Banyoles

L'Estartit

Sant Quirze de Besora

Parlavà

LSONA

Prats de Lluçanès

Pantà de Sau

Gironella

Manlleu

GIRONA **13**

17 PERATALLADA

Angles

Palafrugell

22 CARDONA

VIC **21**

Santa Coloma de Farners

Cassà de la Selva

S'Agaró

Súria

Tona

Caldes de Malavella

Palamós

Sallent

Moià

Arbúcies

Sils

Llagostera

Sant Feliu de Guíxols

Manresa

Montseny

18 TOSSA DE MAR

La Garriga

Tordera

19 Lloret de Mar

BLANES

Sant Celoni

Calella

Costa Brava

20 MONTSERRAT

Granollers

Arenys de Mar

Terrassa

Sabadell

Mataró

Costa Brava

Castellolí

Premià de Mar

Martorell

Rubí

Santa Coloma de Gramanet

Sant Feliu de Llobregat

Barcelona

28 VILAFRANCA DEL PENEDÈS

L'Hospitalet de Llobregat

Vendrell

El Prat de Llobregat

29 SITGES Castelldefels

Vilanova i la Geltrú

MEDITERRANEAN SEA

DAURADA

30

Vineyards outside Gandesa, west of Tarragona

Sights at a Glance

1 Vall d'Aran
2 Vielha
3 Baqueira-Beret
4 Vall de Boí
5 Parc Nacional d'Aigüestortes
6 Andorra
7 La Seu d'Urgell
8 Puigcerdà

9 Ripoll
10 Sant Joan de les Abadesses
11 Olot
12 Besalú
13 Girona
14 Figueres
15 Cadaqués
16 Empúries
17 Peratallada

18 Tossa de Mar
19 Blanes
20 Montserrat pp222–3
21 Vic
22 Cardona
23 Solsona
24 Lleida
25 Monestir de Poblet pp226–7
26 Montblanc

27 Santes Creus
28 Vilafranca del Penedès
29 Sitges
30 Costa Daurada
31 Tarragona
32 Tortosa
33 Delta de l'Ebre
Barcelona see pp142–3

The Vall d'Aran, surrounded by the snowcapped mountains of the Pyrenees

Butterflies of the Vall d'Aran

A huge variety of butterflies and moths is found high in the mountains and valleys of the Pyrenees. In particular, the isolated Vall d'Aran is the home of several unique and rare sub-species. The best time of year to see the butterflies is between May and July.

Grizzled Skipper *(Pyrgus malvae)*

Clouded Apollo *(Parnassius mnemosyne)*

Checkered Skipper *(Carterocephalus palaemon)*

❶ Vall d'Aran

Lleida N230. 🚌 Vielha. 🛈 Vielha, 973 64 01 10. 🌐 visitvaldaran.com

This Valley of Valleys – *aran* means "valley" – is a beautiful 600-sq-km (230-sq-mile) haven of forests and flower-filled meadows, surrounded by towering mountain peaks.

The Vall d'Aran was formed by the Riu Garona, which rises in the area and flows out to France as the Garonne. With no proper link to the outside world until 1924, when a road was built over the Bonaigua Pass, the valley was cut off from the rest of Spain for most of the winter. Snow still blocks the narrow pass from November to April, but today access is easy through the Túnel de Vielha from El Pont de Suert.

The fact that the Vall d'Aran faces north means that it has a climate similar to that found on the Atlantic coast. Many rare wild flowers and butterflies flourish in the perfect conditions created by the damp breezes and shady slopes. It is also a noted habitat for many species of narcissus.

Tiny villages have grown up beside the Riu Garona, often around Romanesque churches, notably at **Bossòst**, **Salardú**, **Escunhau** and **Arties**. The valley is also ideal for outdoor sports such as skiing and is popular with walkers.

❷ Vielha

Lleida. 🏔 2,000. 🚌 🛈 Carrer Sarriulèra 10, 973 64 01 10. 🌐 Thu. 🎉 Fiesta de Vielha (8 Sep), Feria de Vielha (8 Oct).

Now a modern ski resort, the capital of the Vall d'Aran preserves relics of its medieval past. The Romanesque church of **Sant Miquel** has an octagonal bell tower, a tall, pointed roof and a superb wooden 12th-century crucifix, the *Mig Aran Christ*. It once formed part of a larger carving, since lost, which represented the Descent from the Cross. The **Museu dera Vall d'Aran** is a museum devoted to Aranese history and folklore.

🏛 **Museu dera Vall d'Aran**
Carrer Major 26. **Tel** 973 64 18 15. **Open** Tue–Sun. **Closed** public hols. 🚻 ♿

Mig Aran Christ (12th-century), Sant Miquel church, Vielha

❸ Baqueira-Beret

Lleida. 🏔 100. 🚡 Baqueira-Beret,
902 415 415. 🎿 Romería de Nuestra
Señora de Montgarri (2 Jul).
🌐 baqueira.es

This ski resort, one of Spain's best,
is popular with both the public
and the Spanish royal family.
There is reliable winter snow
cover and a choice of over 40
pistes at altitudes from 1,520 m
to 2,470 m (4,987 ft to 8,104 ft).

Baqueira and Beret were
separate mountain villages
before skiing became popular,
but now form a single resort.
The Romans took full advantage
of the thermal springs located
here; nowadays they are
appreciated by tired skiers.

❹ Vall de Boí

Lleida N230. 🚉 La Pobla de Segur.
🚌 Pont de Suert. 🚹 Barruera, 973
69 40 00. 🌐 vallboi.com

This small valley on the edge of
the Parc Nacional d'Aigüestortes
is dotted with tiny villages,
many of which are built around
Catalan Romanesque churches.

Dating from the 11th and
12th centuries, these churches
are distinguished by their tall
belfries, such as the **Església
de Santa Eulàlia** at Erill-la-Vall,
which has six floors.

The two churches at Taüll,
Sant Climent (see p28) and
Santa Maria, have superb
frescoes. Between 1919 and
1923 the originals were taken
for safekeeping to the Museu
Nacional d'Art de Catalunya in
Barcelona (see p176) and replicas
now stand in their place. You
can climb the towers of Sant
Climent for superb views of
the surrounding countryside.

Other churches in the area
worth visiting include those
at **Coll**, for its fine ironwork,
Barruera, and **Durro**, which
has another massive bell tower.

At the head of the valley is the
hamlet of **Caldes de Boí**, popular
for its thermal springs and the
nearby ski station, Boí-Taüll. It is
also a good base for exploring
the Parc Nacional d'Aigüestortes,
the entrance to which is only
5 km (3 miles) from here.

The tall belfry of Sant Climent church at
Taüll in the Vall de Boí

❺ Parc Nacional d'Aigüestortes

Lleida. 🚉 La Pobla de Segur. 🚌 Pont
de Suert, La Pobla de Segur. 🚹 Boí,
973 69 61 89; Espot, 973 62 40 36.
🌐 parcsnaturals.gencat.cat/es/
aiguestortes

The pristine mountain scenery
of Catalonia's only national
park (see pp34–5) is among
the most spectacular to be
seen in the Pyrenees.

Established in 1955, the park
covers an area of 102 sq km
(40 sq miles). Its full title is Parc
Nacional d'Aigüestortes i Estany
de Sant Maurici, named after the
lake (estany) of Sant Maurici in
the east and the Aigüestortes
(literally, "twisted waters") area in
the west. The main access towns

are Espot, to the east, and Boí, to
the west. Dotted around the park
are waterfalls and the sparkling,
clear waters of around 150 lakes
and tarns which, in an earlier
era, were scoured by glaciers
to depths of up to 50 m (164 ft).

The finest scenery is around
Sant Maurici lake, which lies
beneath the twin shards of the
Serra dels Encantats (Mountains
of the Enchanted). From here,
there is a variety of walks,
particularly along the string
of lakes that lead north to
the towering peaks of Agulles
d'Amitges. To the south is the
dramatic vista of Estany Negre,
the highest and deepest tarn
in the park.

Early summer in the lower
valleys is marked by a mass of
pink and red rhododendrons,
while later in the year wild lilies
bloom in the forests of fir, beech
and silver birch.

The park is also home to a
variety of wildlife. Chamois (also
known as izards) live on mountain screes and in the meadows,
while beavers and otters can
be spotted by the lakes. Golden
eagles nest on mountain ledges,
and grouse and capercaillie are
found in the woods.

During the summer the park
is popular with walkers, while
in winter, the snow-covered
mountains are ideal for cross-
country skiing.

A crystal-clear stream, Parc Nacional d'Aigüestortes

The Catalan Language

Catalan has now fully recovered from the ban it suffered under Franco's dictatorship and has supplanted Castilian (Spanish) as the language in everyday use all over Catalonia. Spoken by more than 9.5 million people, it is a Romance language akin to the Provençal of France. Previously it was suppressed by Felipe V in 1717 and only officially resurfaced in the 19th century, when the Jocs Florals (medieval poetry contests) were revived during the rebirth of Catalan literature. A leading figure of the movement was the poet Jacint Verdaguer (1845–1902).

Catalonia's national emblem

⑥ Andorra

Principality of Andorra. 77,000. Andorra la Vella. Plaça de la Rotonda, Andorra la Vella, 376 73 00 03. andorra.ad

Andorra occupies 464 sq km (179 sq miles) of the Pyrenees between France and Spain. In 1993, it became fully independent and held its first ever democratic elections. Since 1278, it had been an autonomous feudal state under the jurisdiction of the Spanish bishop of La Seu d'Urgell and the French Count of Foix (a title adopted by the President of France). These are still the ceremonial joint heads of state.

Andorra's official language is Catalan, though French and Castilian are also spoken. The currency changed from the peseta to the euro in 2002.

For many years Andorra has been a tax-free paradise for shoppers, reflected in the crowded shops of the capital, **Andorra la Vella**. Les Escaldes (near the capital), as well as Sant Julià de Lòria and El Pas de la Casa (near the Spanish and French borders), have also become shopping centres.

Most visitors never see Andorra's rural charms, which match those of other parts of the Pyrenees. The region is excellent for walkers. One of the main routes leads to the **Cercle de Pessons**, a bowl of lakes in the east, and past Romanesque chapels such as **Sant Martí** at La Cortinada. In the north is the picturesque Sorteny Valley, where traditional farmhouses have been converted into snug restaurants.

⑦ La Seu d'Urgell

Lleida. 13,000. Avinguda Valls d'Andorra 33, 973 35 15 11. Tue & Sat. Festa Major (Aug).

This ancient Pyrenean town was made a bishopric by the Visigoths in the 6th century. Feuds between the bishops of Urgell and the Counts of Foix over land ownership led to the emergence of Andorra in the 13th century.

The 12th-century **cathedral** has a much-venerated Romanesque statue of Santa Maria d'Urgell. The **Museu Diocesà** contains medieval works of art and manuscripts, including a 10th-century copy of St Beatus of Liébana's *Commentary on the Apocalypse (see p114)*.

Museu Diocesà
Plaça del Deganat. **Tel** 973 35 32 42. **Open** daily. **Closed** public hols.

Carving, La Seu d'Urgell cathedral

⑧ Puigcerdà

Girona. 9,000. Carrer Querol 1, 972 88 05 42. Sun. Festa de l'Estany (third Sun of Aug). puigcerda.com

Puig is Catalan for "hill". Although Puigcerdà sits on a relatively small hill compared with the encircling mountains, which rise to 2,900 m (9,500 ft), it nevertheless has a fine view

right down the beautiful Cerdanya Valley, watered by the trout-filled Riu Segre. Puigcerdà, very close to the French border, was founded in 1177 by Alfonso II as the capital of Cerdanya, which shares a past and its culture with the French Cerdagne. The Spanish enclave of **Llívia**, an attractive little town with a medieval pharmacy, lies 6 km (4 miles) inside France.

Cerdanya is the largest valley in the Pyrenees. At its edge is the nature reserve of **Cadí-Moixeró**, which has a population of alpine choughs.

Portal of Monestir de Santa Maria

⑨ Ripoll

Girona. 11,000. Plaça Abat Oliba, 972 70 23 51. Sat. Festa Major (11–12 May). ripoll.cat/turisme

Once a tiny mountain base from which raids against the Moors were made, Ripoll is now best known for the **Monestir de Santa Maria**, built in AD 888. The town has been called "the cradle of Catalonia", as the monastery was both the power base and cultural centre of Guifré el Pélos (Wilfred the Hairy), founder of the 500-year dynasty of the House of Barcelona. He is buried in the monastery.

In the later 12th century, the huge west portal gained a series of intricate carvings, which are perhaps the finest Romanesque carvings in Spain. They depict historical and biblical scenes. The two-storey cloister is the only other part of the original monastery to have survived wars and anti-clerical purges. The rest is a 19th-century reconstruction.

The medieval town of Besalú on the banks of the Riu Fluvià

⑩ Sant Joan de les Abadesses

Girona. 🏔 3,600. 🚍 ℹ️ Plaza de Abadía 9, 972 72 05 99. 🚌 Sun. 🎭 Festa Major (second Sun of Sep). 🌐 santjoandelesabadesses.cat

A fine, 12th-century Gothic bridge arches over the Riu Ter to this unassuming market town, whose main attraction is its **monastery**.

Founded in AD 885, it was a gift from Guifré, first count of Barcelona, to his daughter, the first abbess. The church is unadorned except for a superb wooden calvary, *The Descent from the Cross*. Made in 1150, it looks modern; part of it, a thief, was burned in the Civil War and replaced with such skill that it is hard to tell which is new. The monastery's museum has Baroque and Renaissance altarpieces.

12th-century calvary, Sant Joan de les Abadesses monastery

Environs
To the north is **Camprodon**, a small town full of grand houses, and shops selling local produce. The region is especially noted for its *embutits* (charcuterie).

⑪ Olot

Girona. 🏔 32,000. 🚍 ℹ️ Hospici 8, 972 26 01 41. 🚌 Mon. 🎭 Corpus Christi (Jun), Festa del Tura (8 Sep). 🌐 turismeolot.com

This small market town is at the centre of a landscape pockmarked with the conical hills of extinct volcanoes. But it was an earthquake in 1474 which last disturbed the town, destroying its medieval past.

During the 18th century the town's textile industry spawned the "Olot School" of art: finished cotton fabrics were printed with drawings, and in 1783 the Public School of Drawing was founded.

Much of the school's work, which includes sculpted saints and paintings such as Joaquim Vayreda's *Les Falgueres*, is in the **Museu Comarcal de la Garrotxa**, housed in an 18th-century hospice. There are also pieces by Modernista sculptor Miquel Blay, whose damsels support the balcony at No. 38 Passeig Miquel Blay.

🏛 **Museu Comarcal de la Garrotxa**
C/ Hospici 8. **Tel** 972 27 11 66. **Open** Tue–Sun. **Closed** 1 Jan, 25 Dec. 🎟 ♿

⑫ Besalú

Girona. 🏔 2,300. 🚍 ℹ️ C/ del Pont 1, 972 59 12 40. 🚌 Tue. 🎭 Sant Vicenç (22 Jan), Festa Major (last weekend of Sep). 🎫 🌐 besalu.cat

A magnificent medieval town, with a striking approach across a fortified bridge over the Riu Fluvià, Besalú has two fine churches. These are the Romanesque **Sant Vicenç** and **Sant Pere**, the sole remnant of Besalú's Benedictine monastery. It was founded in AD 948, but pulled down in 1835.

In 1964 a **mikvah**, a ritual Jewish bath, was discovered. It was built in 1264 and is one of only three of that period to survive in Europe. The tourist office organizes guided visits to all the town's attractions.

To the south, the sky-blue lake of **Banyoles**, where the 1992 Olympic rowing contests were held, is ideal for picnics.

Sausage shop in the mountain town of Camprodon

Girona Old Town

① Església de Sant Pere de Galligants
② Banys Àrabs
③ Església de Sant Feliu
④ Catedral
⑤ Museu d'Art
⑥ Museu d'Història de Girona
⑦ Museu d'Història dels Jueus

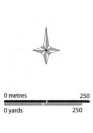

| 0 metres | 250 |
| 0 yards | 250 |

Key to Symbols *see back flap*

⑬ Girona

Girona. 🗺 97,000. ✈ 🚉 🚌
🛈 Rambla de la Llibertat 1, 972 22
65 75. 🏛 Tue, Sat. 🎭 Sant Narcís
(late Oct). 🌐 **girona.cat/turisme**

This handsome town puts on its best face beside the Riu Onyar, where tall, pastel-coloured buildings rise above the water. Behind them, in the Old Town, the Rambla de la Llibertat is lined with busy shops and street cafés.

The houses were built in the 19th century to replace sections of the city wall damaged during a seven-month siege by French troops in 1809. Most of the rest of the ramparts, first raised by the Romans, are still intact and have been turned into the **Passeig Arqueològic** (Archaeological Walk), which runs around the city.

The walk starts on the north side of the town, near the **Església de Sant Pere de Galligants** (St Peter of the Cock Crows). The church now holds the city's archaeological collection.

From here a narrow street into the old part of town passes through the north gate, where huge Roman foundation stones are still visible. They mark the route of the Via Augusta, the road that originally ran from Tarragona to Rome. The most popular place of devotion for the people of Girona is the **Església de Sant Feliu**. The church, begun in the 14th century, was built over the tombs of St Felix and St Narcissus, both patrons of the city. Next to the high altar are eight Roman sarcophagi embedded in the apse wall.

Despite their name, the nearby **Banys Àrabs** (Arab Baths), lit by a fine octagonal lantern, were built in the late 12th century, about 300 years after the Moors had left.

🏛 Museu d'Història dels Jueus

Carrer de la Força 8. **Tel** 972 21 67 61.
Open 10am–6pm Tue–Sat (Jul & Aug: to 8pm; Sep–Jun: to 2pm). **Closed** 1 & 6 Jan, 25 & 26 Dec. 🔲 📷 ♿
🌐 **girona.cat/call**

Amid the maze of alleyways and steps in the Old Town is the former, partially restored, Jewish quarter of El Call. The Museu d'Història dels Jueus gives a history of Girona's Jews, who were expelled in the late 15th century.

🏰 Cathedral

Open Apr–Oct: 10am–7:30pm daily; Nov–Mar: 10am–6:30pm daily. 🔲 free Sun. 🌐 **catedraldegirona.org**

The style of Girona Cathedral's solid west face is pure Catalan Baroque, but the rest of the building is Gothic. The single nave, built in 1416 by Guillem

Painted houses crowded along the bank of the Riu Onyar in Girona

For hotels and restaurants in this region see pp565–7 and pp588–90

Bofill, is the widest Gothic span in Christendom. Behind the altar is a marble throne known as "Charlemagne's Chair" after the Frankish king whose troops took Girona in 785. In the chancel is a 14th-century jewel-encrusted silver and enamel altarpiece. In the museum are Romanesque paintings and statues such as a 14th-century statue of the Catalan king, Pere the Ceremonious, and a 10th-century illuminated copy of St Beatus of Liébana's *Commentary on the Apocalypse.*

The collection's most famous item is a large, well-preserved 11th- to 12th-century tapestry, called *The Creation.*

Tapestry of *The Creation*

🏛 Museu d'Art

Pujada de la Catedral 12. **Tel** 972 41 27 77. **Open** Tue–Sun. **Closed** 1 & 6 Jan, 25 & 26 Dec. 🅿 ♿ 📷 by appt. 🌐 museuart.com

This former episcopal palace is one of Catalonia's best art galleries, with works ranging from the Romanesque period to the 20th century. Items from churches destroyed through war or neglect give an idea of church interiors long ago. Highlights are 10th-century carvings, a silver-clad altar from the church at Sant Pere de Rodes and a 12th-century beam from Cruïlles.

🏛 Museu d'Història de Girona

Carrer de la Força 27. **Tel** 972 22 22 29. **Open** 10:30am–6:30pm Tue–Sat (to 5:30pm Oct–Apr), 10:30am–1:30pm Sun. 📷

This museum is housed in a former convent. Parts of the cemetery are preserved, including the recesses where the bodies of members of the Capuchin Order were placed while decomposing. The collection includes old Sardana (*see p229*) instruments.

⓮ Figueres

Girona. 🚂 45,000. 🚌 🚆 ℹ Plaça del Sol, 972 50 31 55. 🛒 Thu. 🎉 Santa Cruz (3 May), San Pedro (29 Jun). 🌐 visitfigueres.cat

Figueres is in the north of the Empordà (Ampurdán) region, the fertile plain that sweeps inland from the Gulf of Roses. Every Thursday, the market here fills with fruit and vegetables from the area.

The **Museu del Joguet** (Toy Museum) is housed on the top floor of the old Hotel de Paris, on the Rambla, Figueres' main street. Inside are exhibits from all over Catalonia. At the lower end of the Rambla is a statue of Narcís Monturiol i Estarriol (1819–85), claimed to be the inventor of the submarine.

A much better known son of the town is Salvador Dalí, who founded the **Teatre-Museu Dalí** in 1974. The most visited museum in Spain after the Prado, the galleries occupy Figueres' old main theatre. Its roof has an eye-catching glass dome. Not all the work shown is by Dalí, and none of his best-known works are here. But the

Rainy Taxi, a monument in the garden of the Teatre-Museu Dalí

displays, including *Rainy Taxi* – a black Cadillac being sprayed by a fountain – are a monument to the man who, fittingly, is buried here.

🏛 Museu del Joguet

Carrer Sant Pere 1. **Tel** 972 50 45 85. **Open** daily. 📷 ♿

🏛 Teatre-Museu Dalí

Plaça Gala-Salvador Dalí. **Tel** 972 67 75 00. **Open** Jun–Sep: daily; Oct–May: Tue–Sun. **Closed** Mon Oct–May, 1 Jan, 25 Dec. 📷 🌐 salvador-dali.org

The Art of Dalí

Salvador Dalí i Domènech was born in Figueres in 1904 and mounted his first exhibition at the age of 15. After studying at the Escuela de Bellas Artes in Madrid, and dabbling with Cubism, Futurism and Metaphysical painting, the young artist embraced Surrealism in 1929, becoming the movement's best-known painter. Never far from controversy, the self-publicist Dalí became famous for his hallucinatory images – such as *Woman – Animal Symbiosis* – which he described as "hand-painted dream photographs". Dalí's career also included writing and film-making, and established him as one of the 20th century's greatest artists. He died in his home town in 1989.

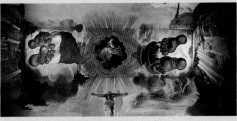

Ceiling fresco in the Wind Palace Room, Teatre-Museu Dalí

⓯ Cadaqués

Girona. 🔼 3,000. 🚌 ℹ️ Carrer Cotxe 1, 972 25 83 15. 🔷 Mon. 🎏 Festa Major de Verano (first week of Sep), Santa Esperança (18 Dec).
W visitcadaques.org

This pretty resort is overlooked by the Baroque **Església de Santa Maria**. In the 1960s it was dubbed the "St Tropez of Spain", due to the young crowd that sought out Salvador Dalí in nearby Port Lligat. The house where he lived from 1930 until his death in 1989 is known as the **Casa-Museu Salvador Dalí**. Visitors can see the painter's workshop, the library, private bedrooms, garden area and swimming pool. Book in advance, as visits are permitted only in small numbers. In summer, a "bus-train" takes visitors there from Cadaqués.

🏛️ **Casa-Museu Salvador Dalí**
Port Lligat. **Tel** 972 25 10 15. Reservations required, email pllgrups@fundaciodali.org **Open** Tue–Sun (daily mid-Jun–mid-Sep). **Closed** 1 Jan, 7 Jan–early Feb, 25 Dec. 🎫 **W** salvador-dali.org

⓰ Empúries

Girona. 🚌 L'Escala. **Tel** 972 77 59 76. **Open** from 10am, closing time varies with season; check website. 🏃 ruins. 🎫 25 Jun–15 Sep: 11:30am daily in English. **W** mac.cat

The ruins of this Greco-Roman town *(see p55)* are beside the sea. Three settlements were built between the 7th and 3rd centuries BC: the old town (Palaiapolis);

An excavated Roman pillar in the ruins of Empúries

the new town (Neapolis); and the Roman town. The **old town** was founded by the Greeks in 600 BC as a trading port. It was built on what was a small island, and is now the site of the hamlet of Sant Martí de Empúries. In 550 BC this was replaced by a town on the shore which the Greeks named Emporion, meaning "trading place". In 218 BC, the Romans landed at Empúries and built a city next to the new town.

A nearby museum exhibits some of the site's finds, but the best are in Barcelona's Museu Arqueològic *(see p176)*.

⓱ Peratallada

Girona. 🔼 400. ℹ️ C/ Unió 3, Ajuntament de Forallac, Vullpellac (972 64 55 22). 🎏 Fira de les Herbes (last weekend in Apr or first in May), Festa Major (6 & 7 Aug), Medieval Market (first weekend in Oct). **W** forallac.cat

This tiny village is stunning and only a short inland trip from the Costa Brava. With Pals and Palau Sator it forms part of the "Golden Triangle" of medieval villages. Its mountaintop position gives some dramatic views of the area. A labyrinth of cobbled streets wind up to the well-conserved castle and lookout tower, whose written records date from the 11th century. Both counts and kings made doubly sure of fending off any attackers by constructing a sturdy wall enclosing the entire village that even today limits the nucleus from further expansion, ensuring it retains its medieval character.

Looking south along the Costa Brava from Tossa de Mar

⓲ Tossa de Mar

Girona. 🔼 6,000. 🚌 ℹ️ Avinguda Pelegrí 25, 972 34 01 08. 🔷 Thu. 🎏 Festa Major d'Hivern (22 Jan), Festa Major d'Estin (29 Jun–2 Jul).
W infotossa.com

At the end of a corniche, the Roman town of Turissa is one of the prettiest along the Costa Brava. Above the New Town is the **Vila Vella** (Old Town), a protected national monument. In the old town, the **Museu Municipal** has a collection of local archaeological finds and modern art including *The Flying Violinist*, by the artist Marc Chagall.

🏛️ **Museu Municipal**
Plaça Pintor Roig i Soler 1. **Tel** 972 34 07 09. **Open** Jun–Sep: daily. 🎫

⓳ Blanes

Girona. 🔼 40,000. 🚉 🚌 ℹ️ Passeig de Catalunya 21, 972 33 03 48. 🔷 Mon. 🎏 El Bilar (6 Apr), Sta Ana (late Jul). **W** visitblanes.net

The working port of Blanes has one of the longest beaches on the Costa Brava, but the highlight of the town is the **Jardí Botànic Marimurtra**. These fine gardens, designed by Karl Faust in 1928, are spectacularly sited above cliffs. There are 7,000 species of Mediterranean and tropical plants.

🌿 **Jardí Botànic Marimurtra**
Passeig Carles Faust 9. **Tel** 972 33 08 26. **Open** daily. **Closed** 1 & 6 Jan, 24 & 25 Dec. 🎫 ♿ **W** marimurtra.cat

The Costa Brava

The Costa Brava ("wild coast") runs for some 200 km (125 miles) from Blanes northwards to the region of Empordà (Ampurdán), which borders France. It is a mix of pine-backed sandy coves, golden beaches and crowded, modern resorts. The busiest resorts – Lloret de Mar, Tossa de Mar and La Platja d'Aro – are to the south. Sant Feliu de Guíxols and Palamós are still working towns behind the summer rush. Just inland there are medieval villages to explore, such as Peralada, Peratallada and Pals. Wine, olives and fishing were the mainstays of the area before the tourists came in the 1960s.

Cadaqués retains an air of seclusion, as it is accessible only by a steep road. It has an arty atmosphere and its small, stony beaches remain unspoiled and less crowded than others.

L'Estartit is a good base for the Illes Medes, a former pirates' lair, which now form a marine reserve with clear waters perfect for skin diving.

Palamós is a working port with modern hotels to the south, and secluded beaches and coves lapped by clear water to the north.

La Platja d'Aro's long and sandy beach is lined with modern hotel blocks. It is one of the most popular resorts on the coast.

Tossa de Mar has a golden beach and a small cove beneath the fortified Old Town.

Roses lies at the head of a sweeping bay. Its sandy beach, the longest on the Costa Brava, has become a mecca for lovers of water sports.

L'Escala is a small resort, popular mainly with local tourists. It has fine beaches and a small port where fishing nets dry in the sun.

Begur is a hilltop town just inland. It has good views of the coast, and small coves are tucked at its feet.

Llafranc, a white-washed resort, with a promenade leading to neighbouring Calella, is one of the coast's most pleasant resorts.

Llançà
Port de la Selva · Cap de Creus
Parc Natural del Cap de Creus
Peralada
Cadaqués
Castelló d'Empúries · C260 · Roses
Fortià · Empuriabrava
Parc Natural dels Aiguamolls de l'Empordà
L'Escala
Punta del Milà
L'Estartit
Illes Medes · Riu Ter
Torroella de Montgrí
Peratallada · Pals · Begur
C66
Palafrugell
Llafranc
Calella de Palafrugell
Palamós
Platja d'Aro
S'Agaró
Sant Feliu de Guíxols
Llagostera
C35
Tossa de Mar
Tordera
Lloret de Mar
Blanes
Malgrat de Mar

0 kilometres 10
0 miles 10

Lloret de Mar has more hotels than anywhere else on the coast. But there are unspoiled beaches nearby, such as Santa Cristina.

⑳ Monestir de Montserrat

The "Serrated Mountain" *(mont serrat)*, its highest peak rising to 1,236 m (4,055 ft), is a magnificent setting for Catalonia's holiest place, the Monastery of Montserrat, which is surrounded by chapels and hermits' caves. A chapel was first mentioned in the 9th century, the monastery was founded in the 11th century and in 1811, when the French attacked Catalonia in the War of Independence *(see p67)*, it was destroyed and the monks killed. Rebuilt and repopulated in 1844, it was a beacon of Catalan culture during the Franco years. Today Benedictine monks live here. Visitors can hear the Escolania singing the *Salve Regina* and the *Virolai* (Marian and Montserrat hymns) in the basilica at 1pm and 7pm Monday to Friday, 6:45pm Monday to Thursday and noon and 6:45pm on Sundays, except in the summer and during the Christmas period.

The Way of the Cross
This path passes 11 statues representing the Stations of the Cross. It begins near the Plaça de l'Abat Oliba.

KEY

① **Funicular to the holy site of Santa Cova**

② **The Museum** has a collection of 19th- and 20th-century Catalan paintings and many Italian and French works. It also displays liturgical items from the Holy Land.

③ **Plaça de Santa Maria's** focal points are two wings of the Gothic cloister built in 1476. The modern monastery façade is by Françesc Folguera.

④ **Gothic cloister**

⑤ **The Black Virgin** *(La Moreneta)* looks down from behind the altar. Protected behind glass, her wooden orb protrudes for pilgrims to touch.

⑥ **The rack railway** *(La Cremallera)*, follows the course of a historic rail line built in 1880.

⑦ **Cable car to Aeri de Montserrat station**

View of Montserrat
The complex includes cafés and a hotel. A second funicular transports visitors to nature trails above the monastery.

★ Basilica Façade

Agapit Vallmitjana sculpted Christ and the apostles on the basilica's Neo-Renaissance façade. It was built in 1900 to replace the Renaissance façade of the original church, consecrated in 1592.

VISITORS' CHECKLIST

Practical Information
Montserrat, Barcelona province.
Tel 938 77 77 77.
 montserratvisita.com
Basilica: **Open** 7:30am–8pm daily.
from 7:30am daily.
Museum: **Open** 10am–5:45pm
daily.

Transport
Aeri de Montserrat, then cable car; Monistrol-Enllaç, then La Cremallera rack railway.
from Barcelona.

Basilica Interior
The sanctuary in the domed basilica is adorned by a richly enamelled altar and paintings by Catalan artists.

★ The Virgin of Montserrat

The small wooden statue of La Moreneta (the dark one) is the soul of Montserrat. It is said to have been made by St Luke and brought here by St Peter in AD 50. Centuries later, the statue is believed to have been hidden from the Moors in the nearby Santa Cova (Holy Cave). Carbon dating suggests, however, that the statue was carved around the 12th century. In 1881 Montserrat's Black Virgin became patroness of Catalonia.

The blackened Virgin of Montserrat

Inner Courtyard
On one side of the courtyard is the baptistry (1958), with sculptures by Carles Collet. Pilgrims may approach the Virgin through a door to the right.

❷ Vic

Barcelona. 🚗 40,900. 🚌 🚆
ℹ️ Plaça del Pes, 93 886 20 91.
🕐 Tue, Sat & Sun. 🎭 Mercat del
Ram (Sat before Easter), Sant Miquel
(28 Jun–7 Jul), Música Viva (mid-Sep),
Mercat Medieval (6–10 Dec).
🌐 **victurisme.cat**

Market days are the best time to
go to this small country town.
This is when the renowned local
sausages *(embotits)* are piled
high in the large Gothic Plaça
Major, along with other produce
from the surrounding plains.

In the 3rd century BC Vic was
the capital of an ancient Iberian
tribe, the Ausetans. The town was
then colonized by the Romans –
the remains of a Roman temple
survive today. Since the 6th
century the town has been a
bishop's see. In the 11th century,
Abbot Oliva commissioned the
El Cloquer tower, around which
the cathedral was built in the
18th century. The interior of the
cathedral is covered with vast
murals by Josep Maria Sert
(1876–1945). They are painted
in reds and golds, and represent
scenes from the Bible.

Adjacent to the cathedral is
the **Museu Episcopal de Vic**,
which has one of the best
collections of Romanesque
artifacts in Catalonia. Its large
display of mainly religious art
and relics includes bright,
simple murals and wooden
sculptures from rural churches.
Also on display are 11th- and
12th-century frescoes.

Cardona dominating the surrounding area from its hilltop site

🏛 **Museu Episcopal**
Plaça Bisbe Oliba. **Tel** 938 86 93 60.
Open Tue–Sun. **Closed** 1 & 6 Jan,
Easter Sun, 25 & 26 Dec. ♿ 🎫 📷

❷ Cardona

Barcelona. 🚗 5,100. 🚆 ℹ️ Avinguda
Rastrillo, 93 869 27 98. 🕐 Sun.
🎭 Festa Major (2nd last Sun of Sep).
🌐 **cardona.cat**

The 13th-century castle of the
dukes of Cardona, constables
to the crown of Aragón, is set
on the top of a hill. The castle
was rebuilt in the 18th century
and is now a parador. Beside
the castle is an early 11th-
century church, the **Església
de Sant Vicenç**, where the
dukes are buried.

The castle gives views of the
town below and of the Mon-
tanya de Sal (Salt Mountain),
a huge salt deposit beside the
Riu Cardener which has been
mined since Roman times.

❷ Solsona

Lleida. 🚗 9,200. 🚆 ℹ️ Carrer Castell
20, 973 48 00 50. 🕐 Tue & Fri.
🎭 Carnival (Feb); Corpus Christi
(May/Jun), Festa Major (8–11 Sep).
🌐 **solsonaturisme.com**

Nine towers and three gateways
remain of Solsona's fortifications.
Inside the walls is an ancient
town of noble mansions. The
cathedral has a black stone
Virgin. The **Museu Diocesà
i Comarcal** contains
Romanesque paintings
and archaeological finds.

🏛 **Museu Diocesà i Comarcal**
Plaça Palau 1. **Tel** 973 48 21 01. **Open**
Tue–Sun. **Closed** 1 Jan, 25 & 26 Dec. ♿

❷ Lleida

Lleida. 🚗 138,400. 🚌 🚆 ℹ️ Carrer
Major 31 bis, 973 70 03 19. 🕐 Thu &
Sat. 🎭 Sant Anastasi (11 May), Sant
Miquel (29 Sep). 🌐 **lleidatur.com**

Dominating Lleida (Lérida),
the capital of Catalonia's only
landlocked province, is **La Suda**,
a large, ruined fort taken from
the Moors in 1149. The old
cathedral, **La Seu Vella**,
founded in 1203, is situated
within the walls of the fort,
high above the town. It was
transformed into barracks by
Felipe V in 1707 but today,
sadly, is desolate. It remains
imposing, however, with
Gothic windows in the cloister.

A lift descends from the Seu
Vella to the Plaça de Sant Joan
in the town below. This square is
at the midpoint of a busy street
sweeping round the foot of the

Twelfth-century altar frontal, Museu Episcopal de Vic

hill. The new cathedral is here, as are manorial buildings such as the rebuilt 13th-century town hall, the **Paeria**.

㉕ Poblet

See pp226–7.

㉖ Montblanc

Tarragona. 🚹 7,300. 🚃 🚌
🛈 Antiga Església de Sant Francesc, 977 86 17 33. 🖻 Tue, Fri. 🎭 Setmana Medieval (2 weeks in Apr), Festa Major (8–9 Sep). 🌐 **montblanc medieval.org**

The medieval grandeur of Montblanc lives on within its walls, said to be Catalonia's finest piece of military architecture. At the **Sant Jordi** gate, St George allegedly slew the dragon. The **Museu Comarcal de la Conca de Barberà** has displays on local crafts.

🏛 **Museu Comarcal de la Conca de Barberà**
Carrer Josa 6. **Tel** 977 86 03 49.
Open Tue–Sun & public hols. 🎫

㉗ Santes Creus

Tarragona. 🚹 150. 🚌 🛈 Plaça de Sant Bernat 1, 977 63 81 41. 🖻 Sat & Sun. 🎭 Sta Llúcia (13 Dec).

Home to the the prettiest of the "Cistercian triangle" monasteries is the tiny village of Santes Creus. The other two, Vallbona

de les Monges and Poblet *(see pp226–7)*, are nearby. The **Monestir de Santes Creus** was founded in 1150 by Ramón Berenguer IV *(see p58)* during his reconquest of Catalonia. The Gothic cloisters are decorated with figurative sculptures, a style first permitted by Jaime II, who ruled from 1291 to 1327. His finely carved tomb, along with that of other nobles, is in the 12th-century church.

🏛 **Monestir de Santes Creus**
Tel 977 63 83 29. **Open** Tue–Sun.
Closed 1 & 6 Jan, 25 & 26 Dec. 🎫 (free Tue). 📷 ♿

㉘ Vilafranca del Penedès

Barcelona. 🚹 38,700. 🚃 🚌
🛈 Carrer Cort 14, 93 818 12 54.
🖻 Sat. 🎭 Festa Major (29 Aug– 2 Sep). 🌐 **turismevilafranca.cat**

This busy market town is set in Catalonia's main wine-producing region *(see pp206–7)*. The **Vinseum** (Wine Museum), in a 14th-century palace, documents the history of the area's wine trade. Local bodegas can be visited for wine tasting.

Eight km (5 miles) to the north is **Sant Sadurní**, the capital of Spain's sparkling wine, *cava* *(see pp580–81)*.

🏛 **Vinseum**
Plaça Jaume I. **Tel** 93 890 05 82.
Open Tue–Sun & public hols. 🎫

Anxaneta climbing to the top of a tower of casters

Catalonia's Fiestas

Human Towers *(various dates and locations)*. The province of Tarragona is famous for its *castellers* festivals, where teams of men stand on each other's shoulders in an effort to build the highest human tower. Each tower, which can be up to seven people high, is topped by a small child called the *anxaneta*. *Castellers* can be seen in action in many towns, especially Vilafranca del Penedès and Valls.
Dance of Death *(Maundy Thu)*, Verges (Girona). Men dressed as skeletons perform a macabre dance.
St George's Day *(23 Apr)*. Lovers give each other a rose and a book on the day of Catalonia's patron saint. The book is in memory of Cervantes, who died on this day in 1616.
La Patum *(Corpus Christi, May/Jun)*, Berga (Barcelona province). Giants, devils and bizarre monsters parade through the town.
Midsummer's Eve *(23 Jun)*. Celebrated all over Catalonia with bonfires and fireworks.

Monestir de Santes Creus, surrounded by poplar and hazel trees

㉕ Monestir de Poblet

The Monastery of Santa Maria de Poblet is a haven of tranquillity and a resting place of kings. It was the first and most important of three Cistercian monasteries, known as the "Cistercian triangle" *(see p225)*, that helped to consolidate power in Catalonia after it had been recaptured from the Moors by Ramon Berenguer IV. The monastery was abandoned and fell into disrepair as a result of the Ecclesiastical Confiscations Act of 1835. Restoration, now largely complete, began in 1930 and monks returned in 1940.

Library
The Gothic scriptorium was converted into a library in the 17th century, when the Cardona family donated its book collection.

KEY

① **Royal doorway**

② ④ **Museum**

③ **Wine cellar**

⑤ **Former kitchen**

⑥ **The 12th-century refectory** is a vaulted hall with an octagonal fountain and a pulpit.

⑦ **The dormitory** is reached by stairs from the church. The vast 87-m (285-ft) gallery dates from the 13th century.

⑧ **San Esteve cloister**

⑨ **Parlour cloister**

⑩ **New sacristy**

⑪ **The Abbey Church**, large and unadorned, with three naves, is a typical Cistercian building.

⑫ **Baroque church façade**

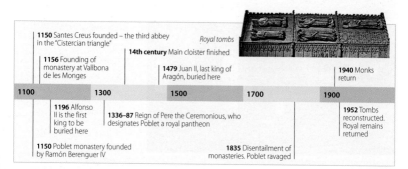

1150 Santes Creus founded – the third abbey in the "Cistercian triangle"		*Royal tombs*	**14th century** Main cloister finished		
	1156 Founding of monastery at Vallbona de les Monges		**1479** Juan II, last king of Aragón, buried here		**1940** Monks return
1100	**1300**		**1500**	**1700**	**1900**
	1196 Alfonso II is the first king to be buried here	**1336–87** Reign of Pere the Ceremonious, who designates Poblet a royal pantheon			**1952** Tombs reconstructed. Royal remains returned
1150 Poblet monastery founded by Ramón Berenguer IV			**1835** Disentailment of monasteries. Poblet ravaged		

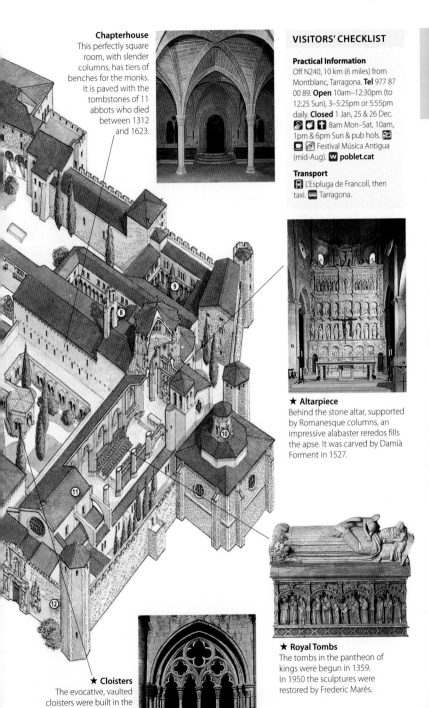

Chapterhouse
This perfectly square room, with slender columns, has tiers of benches for the monks. It is paved with the tombstones of 11 abbots who died between 1312 and 1623.

VISITORS' CHECKLIST

Practical Information
Off N240, 10 km (6 miles) from Montblanc, Tarragona. **Tel** 977 87 00 89. **Open** 10am–12:30pm (to 12:25 Sun), 3–5:25pm or 5:55pm daily. **Closed** 1 Jan, 25 & 26 Dec. 🅿️ 📷 🚻 8am Mon–Sat, 10am, 1pm & 6pm Sun & pub hols. 🎫 📷 🎵 Festival Música Antigua (mid-Aug). **W** poblet.cat

Transport
🚉 L'Espluga de Francolí, then taxi. 🚌 Tarragona.

★ Altarpiece
Behind the stone altar, supported by Romanesque columns, an impressive alabaster reredos fills the apse. It was carved by Damià Forment in 1527.

★ Royal Tombs
The tombs in the pantheon of kings were begun in 1359. In 1950 the sculptures were restored by Frederic Marès.

★ Cloisters
The evocative, vaulted cloisters were built in the 12th and 13th centuries and were the centre of monastic life. The capitals are beautifully decorated with carved scrollwork.

Palm trees lining the waterfront at Sitges

㉙ Sitges

Barcelona. ㎍ 29,100. 🚂 🚌 🚹 C/ Sínia Morera 1, 93 810 93 40. 🚢 Thu. 🎭 Carnival (Feb–Mar), Festa Major (22–27 Aug). 🌐 sitgestur.cat

There are no less than nine beaches to choose from at this seaside town. It has a reputation as a gay resort but is just as popular with all. Lively bars and restaurants line its main boulevard, the Passeig Marítim, and there are many examples of Modernista architecture among the 1970s apartment blocks. Modernista artist Santiago Rusiñol (1861–1931) spent much time here and bequeathed his quirky collection of ceramics, sculptures, painting and ornate ironwork to the **Museu Cau Ferrat**. It lies next to Sitges's landmark, the 17th-century church of **Sant Bartomeu i Santa Tecla**, which juts out proudly on a promontory.

🏛 **Museu Cau Ferrat**
Carrer Fonollar. **Tel** 938 94 03 64. **Open** Tue–Sun. 🎫 🎦

㉚ Costa Daurada

Tarragona. 🚂 🚌 Calafell, Sant Vicenç de Calders, Salou. 🚹 Tarragona, 977 23 03 12. 🌐 costadaurada.info

The long, sandy beaches of the Costa Daurada (Golden Coast) run along the shores of Tarragona province. **El Vendrell** is one of the area's active ports. The **Museu Pau Casals** in Sant Salvador (El Vendrell) is dedicated to the famous cellist. **Port Aventura**, south of Tarragona, is one of Europe's largest theme parks and has many exotically themed attractions, such as Polynesia and Wild West. **Cambrils** and **Salou** are the liveliest resorts – the rest are low-key, family holiday spots.

🏛 **Museu Pau Casals**
Avinguda Palfuriana 67.
Tel 977 68 42 76. **Open** Tue–Sun. 🎫

🎡 **Port Aventura**
Avinguda de l'Alcalde Pere Molas, km 2, Vila-seca. **Tel** 902 20 22 20.
Open mid-Mar–6 Jan. 🎫 🚹

㉛ Tarragona

Tarragona. ㎍ 140,100. 🚅 🚂 🚌 🚹 Carrer Major 39, 977 25 07 95. 🚢 Tue, Thu & Sun. 🎭 Sant Magí (19 Aug), Santa Tecla (23 Sep). 🌐 tarragonaturisme.cat

Tarragona is now a major industrial port, but it has preserved many remnants of its Roman past. As the capital of Tarraconensis, the Romans used it as a base for the conquest of the peninsula in the 3rd century BC *(see pp54–5)*.

The avenue of Rambla Nova ends on the clifftop Balcó de Europa, in sight of the ruins of the **Amfiteatre Romà** and the ruined 12th-century church of **Santa Maria del Miracle**.

Nearby is the Praetorium, a Roman tower that was converted into a palace in medieval times. It now houses the **Pretori i Circ Romans**. This displays Roman and medieval finds, and gives access to the cavernous passageways of the excavated Roman circus, built in the 1st century AD. Next to the Praetorium is the **Museu Nacional Arqueològic**, containing the most important collection of Roman artifacts in Catalonia. It has an extensive collection of bronze tools and beautiful mosaics, including a

The remains of the Roman amphitheatre, Tarragona

Head of Medusa. Among the most impressive remains are the huge Pre-Roman stones on which the Roman wall is built. An archaeological walk stretches 1 km (half a mile) along the wall.

Behind the wall lies the 12th-century **cathedral**, built on the site of a Roman temple. This evolved over many centuries, as seen from the blend of styles of the exterior. Inside is an alabaster altarpiece of St Tecla, carved by Pere Joan in 1434. The 13th-century cloister has Gothic vaulting, but the doorway is Romanesque.

In the west of town is a 3rd- to 6th-century Christian cemetery *(ask about opening times in the archaeological museum)*.

Ruins of the Palaeo-Christian Necropolis

Environs
The **Aqüeducte de les Ferreres** lies just outside the city, next to the A7 motorway. This 2nd-century aqueduct was built to bring water to the city from the Riu Gaià, 30 km (19 miles) to the north. The **Arc de Berà**, a 1st-century triumphal arch on the Via Augusta, is 20 km (12 miles) northeast on the N340.

The bustling, provincial town of **Reus** lies inland from Tarragona. Although its airport serves the Costa Daurada, it is often overlooked by holiday-makers. However there is some fine Modernista architecture to be seen here, notably some early work by Antoni Gaudí who was born in Reus. The Pere Mata Psychiatric Institute was designed by Domènech i Montaner before his master-piece, the Hospital de la Santa Creu i de Sant Pau *(see p169)*.

🏛 Pretori i Circ Romans
Plaça del Rei. **Tel** 977 22 17 36.
Open Tue–Sun. 📷

🏛 Museu Nacional Arqueològic de Tarragona
Plaça del Rei 5. **Tel** 977 23 62 09.
Open Tue–Sun. 📷 (senior citizens and under 18s free). ♿ 🌐 **mnat.es**

❷ Tortosa

Tarragona. 🔼 34,500. ℹ️ Rambla Felip Pedrell 3, 977 44 96 48. 🚍 Mon. 🎪 Nostra Senyora de la Cinta (Aug/Sep). 🌐 **tortosaturisme.cat**

A ruined castle and medieval walls are clues to Tortosa's historical importance. Sited at the lowest crossing point on the Riu Ebre (Río Ebro), it has been strategically significant since Iberian times. The Moors held the city from the 8th century until 1148. The old Moorish castle, known as La Zuda, is all that remains of their defences. It has been renovated as a parador. The Moors also built a mosque in 914. Its foundations were used for the cathedral, on which work began in 1347. Although not completed for 200 years, the style is Gothic.

Tortosa was badly damaged in 1938–9 during one of the fiercest battles of the Civil War *(see pp68–71)*, when the Ebre formed the front line between the opposing forces.

❸ Delta de L'Ebre

Tarragona. 🚆 Aldea. 🚍 Deltebre, Aldea. ℹ️ Deltebre, 977 48 93 09. 🌐 **turismedeltebre.com**

The delta of the Riu Ebre is a prosperous rice-growing region and wildlife haven. Some 70 sq km (27 sq miles) have been turned into a nature reserve, the **Parc Natural del Delta de L'Ebre**. In Deltebre there is an information centre and an interesting **Eco-Museu**, with an aquarium containing species found in the delta.

The main towns in the area are **Amposta** and **Sant Carles de la Ràpita**, both of which serve as good bases for exploring the reserve.

The best sites for seeing wildlife are along the shore, from the Punta del Fangar in the north to the Punta de la Banya in the south. Everywhere is accessible by car except Illa de Buda. Flamingoes breed on this island, and other waterbirds, such as avocets, can be seen from tourist boats that leave from Riumar and Deltebre.

🏛 Eco-Museu
Carrer Martí Buera 22. **Tel** 977 48 96 79. **Open** Tue–Sun. **Closed** 1 & 6 Jan, 25 & 26 Dec. 📷 ♿ 🌐

The Sardana

Catalonia's national dance is more complicated than it appears. The success of the Sardana depends on all of the dancers accurately counting the complicated short- and long-step skips and jumps, which accounts for their serious faces. Music is provided by a *cobla*, an 11-person band consisting of a leader playing a three-holed flute *(flabiol)* and a little drum *(tabal)*, five woodwind players and five brass players. When the music starts, dancers join hands and form circles. The Sardana is performed during most local fiestas *(see p225)* and at special day-long gatherings called *aplecs*.

A group of Sardana dancers captured in stone

ARAGÓN

Zaragoza · Huesca · Teruel

Stretching almost half the length of Spain, and bisected by the Ebro, one of the country's longest rivers, Aragón takes in a wide variety of scenery, from the snowcapped summits of Ordesa National Park in the Pyrenees to the dry plains of the Spanish interior. This largely unsung and undervisited region contains magnificent Mudéjar architecture and many unspoiled medieval towns.

From the 12th to 15th centuries Aragón was a powerful kingdom, or (more accurately) a federation of states, including Catalonia. In its heyday, in the 13th century, its dominions stretched across the Mediterranean as far as Sicily. By his marriage to Isabel of Castile and León in 1469, Fernando II of Aragón paved the way for the unification of Spain.

After the Reconquest, Muslim architects and craftsmen were treated more tolerantly here than elsewhere, and they continued their work in the distinctive Mudéjar style, building with elaborate brickwork and patterned ceramic decoration. Their work can be seen in churches all over Aragón and there are outstanding examples in the cities of Teruel and the capital, Zaragoza, Spain's fifth-largest city, which stands on the banks of the Ebro.

The highest peaks of the Pyrenees lie in Huesca province. Some of the region's finest sights are in the Pyrenean foothills, which are crossed by the Aragonese variation of the pilgrims' route to Santiago de Compostela. Probably the most spectacular of them is the monastery of San Juan de la Peña – half-concealed beneath a rock overhang – which was founded in the 9th century.

The climate of the region varies as much as the landscape: winters can be long and harsh and summers hot.

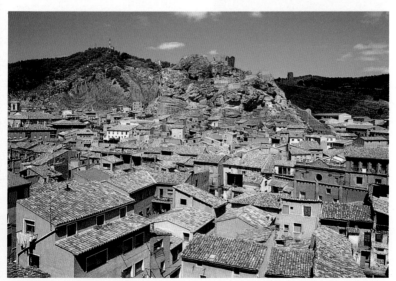

A view of the rooftops and medieval walls of Daroca

◀ Moorish arches inside the Aljafería Palace, Zaragoza

Exploring Aragón

The landscapes of Aragón range from the high Pyrenees, north of Huesca, through the desiccated terrain around Zaragoza to the forested hills of Teruel province. The cities of Teruel and Zaragoza have some of the most striking Mudéjar monuments in Spain. There are many small, picturesque preserved towns in the region. Ordesa National Park contains stunning mountain scenery, but it can only be visited fully after the snow melts in spring, and even then much of it has to be explored on foot. Pretty Los Valles offers less dramatic but equally enjoyable landscapes and is a popular tourist destination. Other attractive places include the impressively sited Castillo de Loarre and Monasterio de San Juan de la Peña, and the waterfalls of Monasterio de Piedra.

The Puerto de Somport, near Panticosa

Sights at a Glance

1. Sos del Rey Católico
2. Los Valles
3. Puerto de Somport
4. *Parque Nacional de Ordesa pp236–7*
5. Benasque
6. Ainsa
7. Jaca
8. Monasterio de San Juan de la Peña
9. Agüero
10. Castillo de Loarre
11. Huesca
12. Alquézar
13. Santuario de Torreciudad
14. Graus
15. Tarazona
16. Monasterio de Veruela
17. Zaragoza
18. Calatayud
19. Monasterio de Piedra
20. Daroca
21. Fuendetodos
22. Alcañiz
23. Valderrobres
24. Sierra de Gúdar
25. Mora de Rubielos
26. Teruel
27. Albarracín
28. Rincón de Ademuz

Getting Around

Zaragoza is linked by motorway to the Basque Country, Navarra, Madrid and Barcelona. Major roads link the region's main cities with each other, and Teruel with Valencia. Many minor roads have been improved and may be fast and uncongested in the flatter, central areas. The principal railway lines run from Zaragoza to Madrid and Barcelona, both of which are linked by high-speed AVE trains, and to Valencia. Coaches are infrequent, except between the main population centres. Zaragoza has a small international airport.

Key

═══ Motorway

═ ═ Motorway under construction

▬▬ Major road

═══ Minor road

▬▬ Scenic route

▬▭▬ Main railway

─── Minor railway

▦▦ International border

▬▬ Regional border

△ Summit

0 kilometres 20

0 miles 20

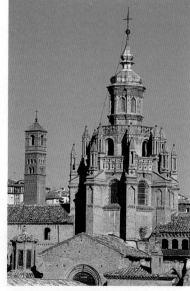

Mudéjar tower of Iglesia de Santa Magdalena, Tarazona

The town hall, Sos del Rey Católico

❶ Sos del Rey Católico

Zaragoza. 🏛 650. 🚌 ℹ️ Palacio de Sada, Plaza Hispanidad s/n, 948 88 85 24 (closed Mon & Tue in winter). 🛍 Fri. 🎭 Fiesta Mayor (third week of Aug). 📷 to Palacio de Sada. 🌐 oficinaturismososdelrey catolico.com

Fernando of Aragón – the so-called "Catholic King" who married Isabel of Castile, thereby uniting Spain *(see pp60–61)* – was born in this small town in 1452, thus its distinguished royal name.

The **Palacio de Sada**, the king's reputed birthplace, with a beautiful inner courtyard, is among the town's grandest stone mansions. It stands in a small square amid a maze of narrow cobbled streets. At the top of the town are the remnants of a castle and the **Iglesia de San Esteban**. The church's font and carved capitals are noteworthy, as are the 13th-century frescoes in two of the crypt's apses. From here there are fine views over the surrounding hills.

The Gothic-arched **Lonja** (commodities exchange) and the 16th-century **town hall** *(ayuntamiento)* are located on the adjacent main square.

Environs
The "Cinco Villas" are five towns recognized by Felipe V for their loyalty during the War of the Spanish Succession *(see p66)*. Sos del Rey Católico is the most appealing of these. The others are Ejea de los Caballeros, Tauste, Sádaba and **Uncastillo**. The latter, 20 km (12 miles) to the southeast, has a fortress and a Romanesque church, the Iglesia de Santa María.

❷ Los Valles

Huesca. 🚉 Jaca. 🚌 from Jaca to Hecho. ℹ️ Museum of Contemporary Art, Pallar d'Agustin, Hecho (Jun–Sep), 974 37 55 05.

The delightful valleys of Ansó and Hecho, formed by the Veral and Aragón Subordán rivers respectively, were once isolated due to poor road links, enabling their villages to retain traditional customs and a local dialect called *Cheso*. Now the area's crafts and costumes have made it popular with tourists. The Pyrenean foothills and forests above the valleys are good for walking, fishing and cross-country skiing.

Ansó lies in the prettiest valley, which becomes a shadowy gorge where the Río Veral and the road next to it squeeze between vertical crags and through rock tunnels. Many of its buildings have stone façades and steep, tiled roofs. The Gothic church (16th century) has a museum dedicated to local costume. Pieces of modern sculpture lie scattered beside the tourist

information office of **Hecho**, from an open-air festival previously held in the village. The bucolic village of **Siresa**, which contains the 11th-century church of San Pedro, lies to the north of Hecho.

❸ Puerto de Somport

Huesca. 🚌 Somport, Astun or Jaca. ℹ️ Pl Ayuntamiento 1, Canfranc, 974 37 31 41 (closed Sep–Jun: Sun & Mon).

Just inside the border with France, the Somport Pass was for centuries a strategic crossing point for the Romans and Moors, and for medieval pilgrims en route to Santiago de Compostela *(see pp86–7)*. Today the austere scenery is specked with holiday apartments built for skiing. **Astún** is modern and well organized, while **El Formigal**, to the east, is a stylish, purpose-built resort. Non-skiers can enjoy the scenery around the Panticosa gorge. **Sallent de Gállego** is popular for rock climbing and fishing.

Steep, tiled roofs of Hecho, with a typical pepper-pot chimney

Rough and craggy landscape around Benasque

❹ Parque Nacional de Ordesa

See pp236–7.

❺ Benasque

Huesca. 🗺 2,200. 🛈 Calle de San Sebastián 5, 974 55 12 89. 🚌 Tue. 🎉 San Pedro (29 Jun), San Marcial (30 Jun). 🌐 turismobenasque.com

Tucked away in the northeast corner of Aragón, at the head of the Esera Valley, the village of Benasque presides over a ruggedly beautiful stretch of Pyrenean scenery. Although the village has expanded greatly to meet the holiday trade, a sympathetic use of wood and stone has resulted in buildings which complement the existing older houses. A stroll through the old centre filled with aristocratic mansions is a delight.

The most striking buildings in Benasque are the 13th-century **Iglesia de Santa María Mayor**, and the **Palacio de los Condes de Ribagorza**. The latter has a Renaissance façade.

Above the village rises the Maladeta massif. There are magnificent views from its ski slopes and hiking trails. Several local mountain peaks, including **Posets** and **Aneto**, exceed 3,000 m (9,800 ft).

Environs

For walkers, skiers and climbers, the area around Benasque has a great deal to offer. The neighbouring resort of **Cerler** was developed with care from a rustic village into a popular base for skiing and other winter sports.

At Castejón de Sos, 14 km (9 miles) south of Benasque, the road passes through the **Congosto de Ventamillo**, a scenic rocky gorge.

❻ Aínsa

Huesca. 🗺 2,200. 🚌 🛈 Cruce de Carreteras, Avda Pirinaica 1, 974 50 07 67. 🚌 Tue. 🎉 San Sebastián (20 Jan), Fiesta Mayor (14 Sep).

The capital of the kingdom of Sobrarbe in medieval times, Aínsa has retained its charm. The Plaza Mayor, a broad cobbled square, is surrounded by neat terraced arcades of brown stone. On one side stands the belfry of the **Iglesia de Santa María** – consecrated in 1181 – and on the other the restored castle.

❼ Jaca

Huesca. 🗺 13,000. 🚉 🚌 🛈 Plaza de San Pedro 11, 974 36 00 98. 🚌 Fri. 🎉 La Victoria (first Fri of May), Santa Orosia y San Pedro (25–29 Jun). 🌐 jaca.es

Jaca dates back as far as the 2nd century AD. In the 8th century the town bravely repulsed the Moors – an act which is commemorated in the festival of La Victoria – and in 1035 became the first capital of the kingdom of Aragón. Jaca's 11th-century **cathedral**, one of Spain's oldest, is much altered inside. Traces of its original splendour can be seen on the restored south porch and doorway, where carvings depict biblical scenes. The dim nave and chapels are decorated with ornate vaulting and sculpture. A **museum** of sacred art, in the cloisters, contains a collection of Romanesque and Gothic frescoes and sculptures from local churches. The streets that surround the cathedral form an attractive quarter.

Sculpture in Jaca Cathedral

Jaca's only other significant tourist sight is its 16th-century **citadel**, a fort decorated with corner turrets, on the edge of town. Today the town serves as a principal base for the Aragonese Pyrenees.

The arcaded main square of Aínsa with the Iglesia de Santa María

⊙ Parque Nacional de Ordesa

Within its borders the Parque Nacional de Ordesa y Monte Perdido combines all the most dramatic elements of Spain's Pyrenean scenery. At the heart of the park are four glacial canyons – the Ordesa, Añisclo, Pineta and Escuain valleys – which carve the great upland limestone massifs into spectacular cliffs and chasms. Most of the park is accessible only on foot: even then, snow during autumn and winter makes it inaccessible to all except those with specialist climbing equipment. In high summer, however, the crowds testify to the park's well-earned reputation as a paradise for walkers and nature lovers alike.

Valle de Ordesa
The Río Arazas cuts through forested limestone escarpments, providing some of Ordesa's most popular walks.

Torla
This village, at the gateway to the park, huddles beneath the forbidding slopes of Mondarruego. With its core of cobbled streets and slate-roofed houses around the church, Torla is a popular base for visitors to Ordesa.

Pyrenean Wildlife

Ordesa is a spectacle of flora and fauna, with many of its species unique to the region. Trout streams rush along the valley floor, where slopes provide a mantle of various woodland harbouring creatures such as otters, marmots and capercaillies (large grouse). On the slopes, flowers burst out before the snow melts, with gentians and orchids sheltering in crevices and edelweiss braving the most hostile crags. Higher up, the Pyrenean chamois is still fairly common; but the Ordesa ibex, or mountain goat, became extinct in 2000. Attempts to resurrect it by cloning have had little success so far. The rocky pinnacles above the valley are the domain of birds of prey, among them the huge bearded vulture.

Spring gentian (*Gentiana verna*)

0 kilometres 2
0 miles 2

Key
= Major road
= Minor road
- - Footpath
━ Spanish/French border
━ National park boundary

For hotels and restaurants in this region see p567 and pp590–91

View from Parador de Bielsa
The parador, at the foot of Monte Perdido, looks out at stunning sheer rock faces streaked by waterfalls.

Parador de Biesla
ᴾ
ᴾᴱ PERDIDO
▲
,355 M
,008 FT)
VALLE DE PINETA
Cinca
Bielsa
Sierra de Las Tucas
efugio de Góriz
Cascada
Cola de Caballo
Vellos
Cañon de Añisclo
Revilla
Garganta de Escuan
Escuaín
Bielsa
Tella
Nerin
Bestué
Vellos
Puértolas

Cola de Caballo
The 70-m (230-ft) "Horse's Tail" waterfall makes a scenic stopping point near the northern end of the long hike around the Circo Soaso. It provides a taste of the spectacular scenery found along the route.

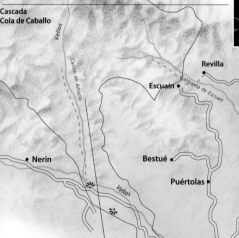

Hikers in Ordesa National Park

Cañon or Garganta de Añisclo
A wide path leads along this beautiful, steep-sided gorge, following the wooded course of the turbulent Río Vellos through dramatic limestone scenery.

Tips for Walkers

Several well-marked trails follow the valleys and can be easily tackled by anyone reasonably fit, though walking boots are a must. The mountain routes may require climbing gear, so check first with the visitors' centre and get a detailed map. Pyrenean weather changes rapidly – beware of ice and snow early and late in the season. Overnight camping is permitted, but only for a single night above certain altitudes.

For additional map symbols *see back flap*

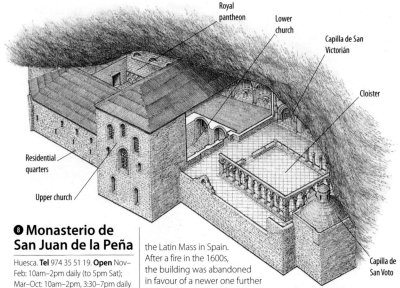

Royal pantheon

Lower church

Capilla de San Victorián

Cloister

Residential quarters

Upper church

Capilla de San Voto

❽ Monasterio de San Juan de la Peña

Huesca. **Tel** 974 35 51 19. **Open** Nov–Feb: 10am–2pm daily (to 5pm Sat); Mar–Oct: 10am–2pm, 3:30–7pm daily (to 8pm Jun–Aug). **Closed** 1 Jan, 25 Dec. 🅿 🖭 🎦 🖥 🔟 **monasterio sanjuan.com**

Set under a bulging rock, this monastery was an early guardian of the Holy Grail *(see p255)*. In the 11th century it underwent reformation in Cluniac style, and was the first monastery to introduce the Latin Mass in Spain. After a fire in the 1600s, the building was abandoned in favour of a newer one further up the hillside. This was later sacked by Napoleon's troops. It now houses a hotel and interpretation centre.

The church of the old monastery is on two floors. The lower one is a primitive rock-hewn crypt built in the early 10th century. The upper floor contains an 11th-century church with a simple triple apse hollowed out of the side of the cliff. The Romanesque pantheon contains the stacked tombs of the early Aragonese kings. The exterior cloister is San Juan de la Peña's *pièce de résistance*, the capitals of its columns carved with biblical scenes.

❾ Agüero

Huesca. 🅰 150. 🛈 San Jaime 1, 974 38 04 89. 🎭 San Blas (3 Feb), San Roque (16 Aug). 🔟 **aytoaguero.es**

The picturesque setting of this attractive village, clustered against a dramatic crag of eroded pudding stone, amply rewards a brief detour from the main road. The most important reason for visiting Agüero, however, is to see the 12th-century **Iglesia de Santiago**. This Romanesque church is reached by a long stony track leading uphill just before the village.

The capitals of the columns in this unusual triple-naved building are carved with fantastical beasts as well as scenes from the life of Jesus and the Virgin Mary. The beautiful carvings on the doorway display biblical events, including scenes from the Epiphany and Salome dancing ecstatically. The lively, large-eyed figures are attributed to the mason responsible for the superb carvings in the monastery at San Juan de la Peña.

❿ Castillo de Loarre

Loarre, Huesca. **Tel** 974 34 21 61. 🚆 Ayerbe. 🚌 from Huesca. **Open** daily. **Closed** Nov–Feb: Mon, 1 Jan, 25 Dec. 🅿 🎦 🔟 **castillodeloarre.es**

The ramparts of this fortress stand majestically above the road from Ayerbe. The fortress is so closely moulded around the contours of a rock that in poor visibility it could be easily mistaken for a natural outcrop. It was used as a set for Ridley Scott's film *Kingdom of Heaven* (2005). On a clear day, the hilltop setting is stupendous, with clear views of the surrounding orchards and reservoirs of the Ebro plain.

Village of Agüero, situated under a rocky crag

Inside the curtain walls lies a complex founded in the 11th century on the site of what had originally been a Roman settlement. It was later remodelled under Sancho I (Sancho Ramírez) of Aragón, who established a religious community here, placing the complex under the rule of the Order of St Augustine.

Within the castle walls is a Romanesque church with carved capitals, a chequered frieze and alabaster windows.

Sentry paths, iron ladders and flights of steps ramble precariously around the castle's towers, dungeons and keep.

The formidable Castillo de Loarre looming above the surrounding area

Altarpiece by Damià Forment, in Huesca Cathedral

⑪ Huesca

Huesca. ⚐ 52,000. 🚆 🚌 🚹 Plaza López Allué, 974 29 21 70. 🛒 Tue, Thu & Sat. 🎭 San Vicente (22 Jan), San Lorenzo (9–15 Aug).
🔲 huescaturismo.com

Founded in the 1st century BC, the independent state of Osca (present-day Huesca) had a senate and an advanced education system. From the 8th century, the area grew into a Moorish stronghold. In 1096 it was captured by Peter of Aragón and was the region's capital until 1118, when the title passed to Zaragoza.

Huesca is now the provincial capital. The pleasant old town has a Gothic **cathedral**. The eroded west front is surmounted by an unusual wooden gallery in Mudéjar style. Above the nave is slender-ribbed star vaulting studded with golden bosses. There is an alabaster altarpiece by the master

sculptor, Damià Forment. On the altarpiece, a series of Crucifixion scenes in relief are highlighted by illumination.

Opposite the cathedral is the Renaissance **town hall** (ayuntamiento). Inside hangs La Campana de Huesca, a gory 19th-century painting depicting the town's most memorable event: the beheading of a group of troublesome nobles in the 12th century by order of King Ramiro II. The massacre occurred in the former Palacio de los Reyes de Aragón, later the university and now the superb **Museo de Huesca**, containing archaeological finds and a collection of art.

🏛 Museo de Huesca

Plaza de la Universidad 1. **Tel** 974 22 05 86. **Open** 10am–2pm, 5–8pm Tue–Sat, 10am–2pm Sun & pub hols. **Closed** 1 & 6 Jan, 24, 25 & 31 Dec. ♿

⑫ Alquézar

Huesca. ⚐ 300. 🚹 C/ Arrabal s/n, 974 31 89 40. 🎭 San Sebastián (20 Jan), San Ipolito (12 Aug). 🌐

This Moorish village attracts much attention because of its spectacular setting. Its main monument, the stately 16th-century **collegiate church**, dominates a hill jutting above the strange rock formations of the canyon of the Río Vero. Inside, the church's cloisters have capitals carved with biblical scenes. Next to it is the chapel built after Sancho I recaptured Alquézar from the Moors. Nearby are the ruined walls of the original alcazár, which gives the village its name.

⑬ Santuario de Torreciudad

Huesca. **Tel** 974 30 40 25. 🚌 to El Grado from Barbastro. **Open** daily. ♿
🔲 torreciudad.org

This shrine was built to honour the devotion of the founder of the Catholic lay order of Opus Dei – San Jose María Escrivá de Balaguer – to the Virgin. It occupies a promontory with picturesque views over the waters of the **Embalse de El Grado** at Torreciudad. The huge church is made of angular red brick in a stark, modern design.

Inside, the elaborate modern altarpiece of alabaster, sheltering a glittering Romanesque Virgin, is in contrast to the bleak, functional nave.

Environs
The town of **Barbastro**, 30 km (18 miles) to the south, has an arcaded plaza mayor and a 16th-century cathedral with an altar by Damià Forment.

The ruins of Alquézar Castle, rising above the village

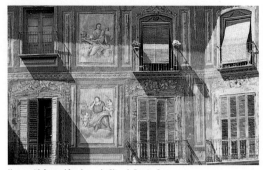
Houses with frescoed façades on the Plaza de España, Graus

⑭ Graus

Huesca. 🗺 3,400. 🚌 ℹ️ Plaza de la Compañía 1, 974 54 08 74. 🚌 Mon. 🎇 San Antonio (19 Jan), Santa Agneda (5 Feb), San Miguel (29 Sep–1 Oct). 🌐 **turismograus.com**

In the heart of Graus's old town is the unusual **Plaza de España**, surrounded by stone arcades and columns. It has brightly frescoed half-timbered houses and a 16th-century city hall. The home of the infamous Tomás de Torquemada *(see p60)* is in the narrow streets of the old quarter. At fiesta time, Graus is a good spot to see Aragonese dancing.

Environs
About 20 km (12 miles) north-east, the hill village of **Roda de Isábena** is the smallest village in Spain to boast a cathedral. Dating from 1067, this striking building has a 12th-century cloister off which is a chapel with 13th-century frescoes. North of the village is the picturesque Isábena valley.

⑮ Tarazona

Zaragoza. 🗺 10,700. 🚌 ℹ️ Plaza San Francisco 1, 976 64 00 74. 🚌 every other Thu. 🎇 San Atilano (27 Aug–1 Sep). 🌐 **tarazona.es**

Mudéjar towers stand high above the earth-coloured, mottled pantiles of this ancient bishopric. On the outskirts of the Old Town is the **cathedral**, all turreted finials and pierced brickwork with Moorish cloister tracery and Gothic tombs. In the upper town on the other side of the river, more churches, in typical Mudéjar

style, can be found amid the maze of narrow hilly streets. More unusual perhaps are the former bullring, now a circular plaza enclosed by houses, and the splendid Renaissance **town hall** *(ayuntamiento)*. The town hall, built of golden stone, has a façade carved with mythical giants and a frieze showing Carlos V's homage to Tarazona.

⑯ Monasterio de Veruela

Vera de Moncayo, Zaragoza.
Tel 976 64 90 25. 🚌 Vera de Moncayo. **Open** Wed–Mon. 🎨 🎭 by appt. ♿ 🌐 **visitveruela.com**

This Cistercian retreat, set in the green Huecha Valley near the Sierra de Moncayo, is one of the greatest monasteries in Aragón. Founded in the 12th century by French monks, the huge abbey church has a mixture of Roman-esque and Gothic features. Worn green and blue Aragonese tiles line the floor of its handsomely

vaulted triple nave. The well-preserved cloisters sprout exuberantly decorated beasts, heads of human beings and foliage in the Gothic style *(see p28)*. The plain, dignified chambers make a suitable venue for art exhibitions in the summer.

Environs
In the hills to the west the small **Parque Natural de Moncayo** rises to a height of 2,315 m (7,600 ft). Streams race through the woodland of this nature reserve, abound with birdlife. A tortuous potholed road leads to a chapel at 1,600 m (5,250 ft).

⑰ Zaragoza

Zaragoza. 🗺 666,000. ✈ 🚌 🚌 ℹ️ Plaza del Pilar, 976 20 12 00. 🚌 Wed & Sun. 🎇 San Valero (29 Jan), Cincomarzada (5 Mar), San Jorge (23 Apr), Virgen del Pilar (12 Oct). 🌐 **zaragoza.es/turismo**

A Celtiberian settlement called Salduba existed on the site of the present city; but it is from the Roman settlement of Cesaraugusta that Zaragoza takes its name. Its location on the fertile banks of the Río Ebro ensured its ascendancy, now Spain's fifth-largest city and the capital of Aragón.

Damaged during the War of Independence *(see p66)*, the city was largely rebuilt, but the old centre retains some interesting buildings. Most of the main sights are grouped around Plaza del Pilar. The most impressive of them is the **Basílica de Nuestra Señora del Pilar**, with its huge

Entrance and tower of the Monasterio de Veruela

church sporting 11 brightly tiled cupolas. Inside, the Santa Capilla (Lady Chapel) by Ventura Rodríguez contains a small statue of the Virgin on a pillar amid a blaze of silver and flowers. Her skirt-like *manta* is changed every day, and pilgrims pass behind the chapel to kiss an exposed part of the pillar. The basílica also has frescoes by Goya.

Nearby, on the square, stand the **town hall** *(ayuntamiento)*, the 16th-century Renaissance **Lonja** (commodities exchange) and the **Palacio Arzobispal**.

Occupying the east end of the square is Zaragoza's cathedral, **La Seo**, displaying a great mix of styles. Part of the exterior is faced with typical Mudéjar brick and ceramic decoration, and inside are a fine Gothic reredos and splendid Flemish tapestries.

Close by is the flamboyant Mudéjar bell tower of the **Iglesia de la Magdalena**, and remains of the Roman forum. Parts of the **Roman walls** can also be seen at the opposite side of the Plaza del Pilar, near the **Mercado de Lanuza**, a market with sinuous ironwork in Art Nouveau style.

The **Museo Camón Aznar** in the Pardo's Palace exhibits the

Some of the cupolas of the Basílica de Nuestra Señora del Pilar

eclectic collection of a wealthy local art historian, whose special interest was Goya. The top floor contains a collection of his etchings. Minor works by artists of other periods can be seen, as well as contemporary art. The **Museo de Zaragoza** has a Goya room and archaeological artifacts.

The **Museo Pablo Gargallo** is a showroom for the Aragonese sculptor after whom it is named, who was active at the beginning of the 20th century. One of the most important monuments in Zaragoza lies on the busy road to Bilbao. The **Aljafería** is an enormous Moorish palace built in the 11th century. A courtyard of lacy arches surrounds a sunken

garden and a small mosque. The **CaixaForum**, a cultural centre set in a contemporary building, hosts Spain's best touring exhibitions as well as talks, screenings and family activities.

🏛 **Museo Camón Aznar**

Calle Espoz y Mina 23. **Tel** 976 39 73 87. **Open** Tue–Sun. 🎧 ♿

🏛 **Museo de Zaragoza**

Plaza de los Sitios 6.
Tel 976 22 21 81. **Open** Tue–Sun. ♿

🏛 **Museo Pablo Gargallo**

Plaza de San Felipe 3.
Tel 976 72 49 22. **Open** Tue–Sun.

🏛 **CaixaForum**

Avenida Anselmo Clavé 4.
Tel 976 76 82 00. **Open** daily.

Zaragoza City Centre

① Roman walls
② Mercado de Lanuza
③ Museo Pablo Gargallo
④ Basílica de Nuestra Señora del Pilar
⑤ Museo Camón Aznar
⑥ Lonja
⑦ La Seo (Cathedral)
⑧ Palacio Arzobispal

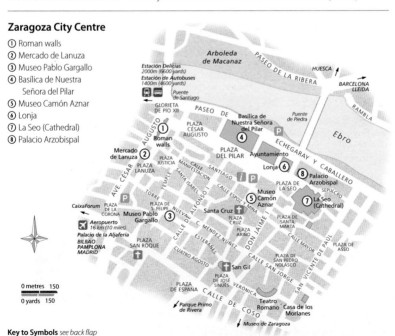

0 metres   150
0 yards   150

Key to Symbols *see back flap*

Gateway through the medieval walls of Daroca

🔞 Calatayud

Zaragoza. 🚗 21,900. 🚆 🚌
🛈 Plaza de Santa Teresa 3, 976 88
63 22. 🕐 Tue. 🎉 San Roque (14–17
Aug), Virgen de la Peña (6–10 Sep).
🌐 turismocatalayud.com

The huge Moorish fortress and
minaret-like church towers are
visible from miles around. Only
ruins are left of the 8th-century
Arab castle of the ruler, Ayub,
which gave the town its name.
The church of **Santa María la
Mayor** has a Mudéjar tower
and an elaborate façade in
the Plateresque style. The
17th-century church of **San
Juan Real** holds Goya paintings.
 The ruins of the Roman settlement of **Bílbilis** are east of
Calatayud, near Huérmeda.

🔟 Monasterio de Piedra

3 km (2 miles) south of Nuévalos,
Zaragoza. **Tel** 976 87 07 00.
🚆 Calatayud. 🚌 from Zaragoza.
Open daily. 🐾 🎉 ♿
🌐 monasteriopiedra.com

Built on the site of a Moorish
castle conquered by Alfonso II
of Aragón and given to

Cistercian monks in the 12th
century, this monastery was
damaged in the 19th century
and subsequently rebuilt. Some
of the 12th-century buildings
remain, including the chapterhouse, refectory and hostel.
 In the damp cellars, the monks
once distilled strong potions of
herbal liqueur. This was allegedly
the first place in Europe where
drinking chocolate, from Mexico,
was made *(see p63)*, and there is
now a chocolate exhibition.
 The park in which the monastery stands is a nature reserve
full of grottoes and waterfalls.
A hotel is now located in the
old monastery buildings.

🟡 Daroca

Zaragoza. 🚗 2,200. 🛈 Calle Mayor
44, 976 80 01 29. 🕐 Thu. 🎉 Santo
Tomás (7 Mar). 🎉 (of village).

An impressive array of battlemented medieval walls stretches
approximately 4 km (2 miles)
around this old Moorish
stronghold. Although parts of the
walls have decayed, some of the
114 towers and gateways are still
a remarkable sight, particularly
from the main road to Zaragoza.
 The **Colegial de Santa María**,
a church in the Plaza España,
houses the Holy Cloths from the
Reconquest *(see pp58–9)*. After a
surprise attack by the Moors in
1239, priests celebrating Mass
bundled the consecrated bread
into the linen sheets used for
the altar. Upon being unwrapped,
the cloths were miraculously
stained with blood.

Environs
The agricultural town of
Monreal del Campo, 42 km
(26 miles) south of Daroca,
has a saffron museum. Towards
Molina de Aragón, 20 km
(12 miles) from Daroca, is the
Laguna de Gallocanta, a lake
and wildlife refuge.

🟡 Fuendetodos

Zaragoza. 🚗 150. 🛈 Calle Cortes de
Aragón 7, 976 14 38 67. 🎉 San Roque
(last Sat of May), San Bartolomé
(24 Aug). 🌐 fuendetodos.org

This small village was the
birthplace of one of Spain's
best-known artists of the
late 18th and early 19th
centuries, Francisco de Goya.

Interior of Goya's cottage in Fuendetodos

Castle-parador above Alcañiz

The **Casa-Museo de Goya** is a neat cottage said to have been the painter's home. It has been restored and furnished in a style appropriate for the period.

Environs

Lying 14 km (9 miles) east of Fuendetodos is **Belchite**, the site of one of the most horrific battles of the Spanish Civil War *(see pp70–71)*, for control of the strategic Ebro Valley. Remains of the old, shell-torn town have been left tottering as a monument to the horrors of war.

In **Cariñena**, 25 km (16 miles) west of Fuendetodos, bodegas offer the opportunity to sample and buy the excellent, full-bodied red wine for which the region is justly renowned *(see pp206–7)*.

Casa-Museo de Goya
Calle Zuloaga 3. **Tel** 976 14 38 30.
Open 11am–2pm, 4–7pm
Tue–Sun.

② Alcañiz

Teruel. 16,300. Calle Mayor 1, 978 83 12 13. Tue. Fiestas Patronales (8–13 Sep). **w** alcaniz.es

Two buildings rise above the town of Alcañiz. One is the **castle**, once the headquarters of the Order of Calatrava. This historic building has been converted into a parador. The keep, the Torre del Homenaje, has a collection of 14th-century frescoes depicting the conquest of Valencia by Jaime I.

The other building is the **Iglesia de Santa María**. This church, on the sloping Plaza de España, has a Gothic tower and a Baroque façade.

On the same square are the elegantly galleried **Lonja** (commodities exchange), with its lacy Gothic arches, and the **town hall** *(ayuntamiento)*, with one Mudéjar and one Renaissance façade.

Aragón's Fiestas

Las Tamboradas *(Maundy Thursday and Good Friday)*, Teruel province. During Easter Week, brotherhoods of men wearing long black robes beat drums in mourning for Christ. Las Tamboradas begins with "the breaking of the hour" at midnight on Thursday in Híjar. The Tamborada in Calanda begins the following day at midday. The solemn drum rolls continue for several hours. Aching arms and bleeding hands are considered to be signs of religious devotion.

Young drummer in Las Tamboradas, Alcorija

Carnival *(Feb/Mar)*, Bielsa (Huesca). The protagonists of this fiesta, known as *Trangas*, have rams' horns on their heads, blackened faces and teeth made of potatoes. They are said to represent fertility.
Romería de Santa Orosia *(25 Jun)*, Yebra de Basa (Huesca). Pilgrims in folk costume carry St Orosia's skull to her shrine.
Día del Pilar *(12 Oct)*, Zaragoza. Aragón's distinctive folk dance, the *jota*, is performed everywhere during the city's festivities in honour of its patroness, the Virgin of the Pillar *(see pp240–41)*. On the Día del Pilar there is a procession with cardboard giants, and a spectacular display of flowers dedicated to the Virgin.

Francisco de Goya

Self-Portrait by Goya

Born in Fuendetodos in 1746, Francisco de Goya specialized in designing cartoons for the tapestry industry *(see p310)* in his early life, and in decorating churches such as Zaragoza's Basílica del Pilar with vivacious frescoes. In 1799 he became painter to Carlos IV, and depicted the king and his wife María Luisa with unflattering accuracy *(see p37)*. The invasion of Madrid by Napoleon's troops in 1808 *(see pp66–7)* and its attendant horrors had a profound and lasting effect on Goya's temperament, and his later works are imbued with cynical despair and isolation. He died in Bordeaux in 1828.

Alcalá de la Selva Castle, overlooking the town

⑳ Valderrobres

Teruel. 🏔 2,200. 🚍 *i* Avda Cortes de Aragón 7, 978 89 08 86. 🚌 Sat. 🎉 San Roque (mid-Aug). 🌐 valderrobres.es

Just inside Aragón's border with Catalonia, the town of Valderrobres overlooks the trout-filled Río Matarraña. Dominating the town is the **castle**, formerly a palace for Aragonese royalty. Below it stands the imposing Gothic **Iglesia de Santa María la Mayor**, with a huge rose window in Catalan Gothic style. The arcaded plaza has a pleasing late 16th-century town hall *(ayuntamiento)*.

Environs
Near Valderrobres is the mountain peak of **La Caixa**. At 14 km (9 miles) are the mountain passes of Beceite.

🏰 **Castillo de Valderrobres**
Tel 679 63 44 38. **Open** Tue–Sun (Oct–Jun: Fri–Sun & public hols). 🎫 🎫

⑳ Sierra de Gúdar

Teruel. 🚉 Mora de Rubielos. 🚍 Alcalá de la Selva. *i* C/ Diputación 2, Mora de Rubielos, 978 80 05 29. 🌐 sierradegudar.com

This range of hills, northeast of Teruel, is a region of pine woods, jagged limestone outcrops and scrub-covered slopes. At 2,028 m (6,653 ft), **Peñarroya** is the highest point. Nearby Valdelinares, Spain's highest village, is a ski station. From the access roads there are panoramic views of the hills. Especially noteworthy are the views from the towns of **Linares**

de Mora and **Alcalá de la Selva**, which has a castle set against a backdrop of rock faces. Its Gothic-Renaissance church, with shell motifs and twisted columns, shelters the shrine of the Virgen de la Vega.

⑳ Mora de Rubielos

Teruel. 🏔 1,650. *i* C/ Diputación 2, 978 80 05 29. 🚌 Mon & Fri. 🎉 San Miguel (28 Sep–1 Oct).

Dominated by one of the best-preserved castles in Aragón, Mora de Rubielos displays the remains of the old walled city with its bridges and a medieval old town. There is a fine 17th-century town hall as well as the **collegiate church** of Santa María.

Environs
Rubielos de Mora, lying 14 km (9 miles) to the southeast, is worth exploring simply for its well-preserved stone and timber buildings. Among the balconied houses is an Augustinian convent with a Gothic reredos.

⑳ Teruel

Teruel. 🏔 34,200. 🚉 🚍 *i* C/ San Francisco 1, 978 64 14 61. 🚌 Thu. 🎉 Día del Sermón de las Tortillas (Tue of Easter week), La Vaquilla del Ángel (mid-Jul), Feria del Jamón (mid-Sep). 🌐 teruelversionoriginal.es

This industrial town has been the scene of much desperate fighting throughout the centuries. It began with the Romans, the first to capture and civilize Celtiberian Turba.

During the Reconquest the town became a strategic frontier prize. In 1171 Alfonso II recaptured Teruel for Christian Spain, but many Muslims continued to live peacefully in the city, which they embellished with beautiful Mudéjar towers. The last mosque was closed only at the height of the Inquisition *(see p278)*, in 1502. More recently, during the terrible, freezing winter of 1937, the bitterest battle of the Civil War *(see pp70–71)* was fought here. There were many thousands of casualties.

The old quarter is home to the wedge-shaped Plaza del Torico, with a monument of a small bull,

Tiled towers and rooftops of Teruel Cathedral

Balconied café above Albarracín's main square

the city's emblem. Within walking distance lie the five remaining Mudéjar towers. Most striking are those of **San Salvador** and **San Martín**, both dating back to the 12th century. The latter has multi-patterned brickwork studded with blue and green ceramics.

Beside the **Iglesia de San Pedro** are the tombs of the famous Lovers of Teruel. The **cathedral** has more colourful Mudéjar work, including a lantern dome of glazed tiles, and a tower completed in the 17th century. The dazzling coffered ceiling is painted with lively scenes of medieval life.

The **Museo Provincial**, one of Aragón's best museums, is housed in an elegant mansion. It has a large collection of ceramics, testifying to an industry for which Teruel has long been known. North of the centre is the **Acueducto de los Arcos**, a 16th-century aqueduct.

🏛 **Museo Provincial**
Placa Fray Anselmo Polanco 3.
Tel 978 60 01 50. **Open** Tue–Sun. ♿

㉗ Albarracín

Teruel. 🚶 1,100. 🚌 ℹ️ C/ San Antonio 2, 978 71 02 62. 🗓 Wed. 🎉 Los Mayos (30 Apr–1 May), Fiestas Patronales (8–17 Sep). 🌐 albarracin.org

It is easy to see why this picturesque town earned an international award for historical preservation. A dramatic cliff above the Río Guadalaviar is the perfect setting for this attractive cluster of mellow pink buildings. Standing on a ridge behind the

town are the defensive walls and towers which date from Muslim times.

There is a good view of the town from below the **Palacio Episcopal** (Bishop's Palace). Inside the neighbouring 16th-century **cathedral**, which is topped by a belfry, there is a Renaissance carved wooden altarpiece depicting scenes from the life of St Peter. The treasury museum contains 16th-century Brussels tapestries and enamelled chalices.

Some of Albarracín's sturdy beamed and galleried houses have an unusual two-tier structure. The ground floor is limestone, and the overhanging upper storey is covered in rough coral-pink plasterwork. Many have been restored to their

medieval form. Just outside the town are the caves of Navazo and Callejón, with their prehistoric rock paintings. Reproductions can be seen in Teruel's Museo Provincial.

Environs
In the surrounding **Montes Universales**, which rise to 1,935 m (6,348 ft), is the source of the Tagus, one of Spain's longest rivers. From fertile cereal plains to crumbling rocks, this area is a colourful mixture of poplars, junipers and thick pine woods, with poppies in spring. At **Cella**, northeast of Albarracín, the Río Jiloca has its source.

㉘ Rincón de Ademuz

Valencia. 🚶 2,600. 🚌 Ademuz. ℹ️ Fuente Vieja 10, Ademuz, 978 78 22 67. 🗓 Wed. 🎉 Fiestas de Agosto (15 Aug), Fiestas de la Virgen del Rosario (early Oct).

This remote enclave south of Teruel belongs to the Comunidad Valenciana (*see p247*), but is effectively an island of territory, stranded between the borders of Aragón and Castilla-La Mancha. The area has not prospered in modern times, but still has an austere charm and some peaceful tracts of country scattered with red rocks.

The Lovers of Teruel

According to legend, in 13th-century Teruel two young people, Diego de Marcilla and Isabel de Segura, fell in love and wished to marry. However, her wealthy family forbade the match because he was poor. Diego was given five years in which to make his fortune. When he returned to Teruel, laden with wealth, he found Isabel already married. Diego died of a broken heart and Isabel, full of despair, died the following day. The Bodas de Isabel de Segura, a festival held in mid-February, includes a re-enactment of the events.

Isabel de Segura   Diego de Marcilla

VALENCIA AND MURCIA

Castellón · Valencia · Alicante · Murcia

Today, the central region of Spain's eastern Mediterranean coast is an important holiday destination – the beaches of the Costa Blanca, the Costa del Azahar and the Costa Cálida draw millions of tourists annually. Centuries ago, Muslim settlers made these regions bloom, and the fertile fields and citrus groves of the coastal plains are still Spain's citrus orchard and market garden.

These productive lands have been occupied for more than 50,000 years. The Greeks, Phoenicians, Carthaginians and Romans all settled here before the Moors arrived, trading the products of land and sea.

The provinces of Castellón, Valencia and Alicante (which make up the Comunidad Valenciana) were reconquered from the Moors by a Catalan army. The language these troops left behind them developed into a dialect, *Valenciano*, which is widely spoken and increasingly seen on signposts. Murcia, to the south, is one of Spain's smallest autonomous regions.

The population is concentrated on the coast where the historic towns and cities of Valencia, Alicante and Cartagena have been joined by modern package holiday resorts, such as Benidorm and La Manga del Mar Menor. Inland, where tourism has barely reached, the landscape rises into the chains of mountains that stand between the coast and the plateau of Central Spain. The scenery inland ranges from picturesque valleys and hills in the Maestrat, in the north of Castellón, to the semi-desert terrain around Lorca in southern Murcia.

The warm climate encourages outdoor life and exuberant fiestas. Most famous of these are Las Fallas of Valencia; the mock battles between Moors and Christians staged in Alcoi; and the lavish, costumed Easter processions in Murcia and Lorca.

Hill terraces of olive and almond trees ascending the hillsides near Alcoi

◀ Gulls on the beach at Peníscola, Costa del Azahar

Exploring Valencia and Murcia

The coasts of Valencia and Murcia are popular for seaside holidays and ideal for water sports almost all year round. Principal resorts include Benidorm, Benicàssim, La Manga del Mar Menor and Oropesa. Some coastal towns such as Peníscola, Gandia, Dénia, Alicante (Alacant) and Cartagena have charming old quarters, castles and other sites well worth visiting. Close to the sea are several scenic nature reserves: the freshwater lagoon of L'Albufera, and, on the Costa Blanca, the saltpans of Santa Pola and the striking limestone crag of the Penyal d'Ifach. Inland, the region offers excursions to such undiscovered beauty spots as El Maestrat and the mountains around Alcoi, as well as the undervisited historic towns of Xàtiva and Lorca. The two regional capitals, Valencia and Murcia, are both lively university cities with fine cathedrals and numerous museums.

Fishing nets strung out in the lagoon of L'Albufera

Getting Around

The region's principal roads are the A7/AP7/E15 motorway and the N332 along the coast. Other motorways connect Valencia with Madrid, A3 (E901), and Alicante with Madrid, N330 A31. There are main rail lines from Alicante, Valencia and Murcia to Madrid and Barcelona, but the rest of the rail network is rather fragmented and buses are often quicker than trains. A scenic narrow-gauge railway line along the Costa Blanca connects Dénia to Alicante via Benidorm. The region's international airports are at Alicante and Valencia.

Key

- ▬ Motorway
- ▬ Major road
- ▬ Minor road
- ▬ Scenic route
- ▭ Main railway
- — Minor railway
- ▬ Regional border
- △ Summit

For additional map symbols *see back flap*

Lemon groves outside Dénia

Sights at a Glance

1. El Maestrat
2. Morella
3. Peníscola
4. Costa del Azahar
5. Vilafamés
6. Castelló de la Plana
7. Onda
8. Coves de Sant Josep
9. Alto Turia
10. Sagunt
11. Monasterio de El Puig
12. *Valencia pp254–7*
13. L'Albufera
14. Xàtiva
15. Gandia
16. Dénia
17. Xàbia
18. Penyal d'Ifac
19. Guadalest
20. Alcoi
21. Benidorm
22. Novelda
23. Alicante (Alacant)
24. Illa de Tabarca
25. Elx (Elche)
26. Orihuela
27. Torrevieja
28. Murcia
29. Mar Menor
30. Cartagena
31. Costa Cálida
32. Lorca
33. Caravaca de la Cruz

0 kilometres   25

0 miles   20

One of the many coves on Xàbia's rugged coast

The unbroken medieval wall surrounding the historic hilltop town of Morella in El Maestrat

❶ El Maestrat

Castellón & Teruel. 🚌 Morella.
ℹ️ Plaza de San Miguel, Morella, 964 18 52 42. 🌐 comarcamaestrazgo.es

Crusading warlords of the Knights Templar and the Knights of Montesa – known as *maestres* (masters) – gave their name to this lonely upland region. To rule over this frontier land, which straddles the border between Valencia and Aragón, they built fortified settlements in dramatic defensive positions, often on rocky crags. The best preserved of them is **Morella**, the principal town. **Forcall**, not far from Morella, has two 16th-century mansions on its

The Torre de la Sacristía, in the restored village of Mirambel

porticoed square. To the south, the village of **Ares del Maestre** is spectacularly sited beneath a 1,318-m- (4,300-ft-) high rock.

Cantavieja is the main town in the Aragonese part of El Maestrat (where it is known as El Maestrazgo). It has a pretty arcaded square. The walled village of **Mirambel**, nearby, has been restored to its medieval condition.

There are several spooky but fascinating shrines to the Virgin in El Maestrat, notably the cave of La Balma at **Zorita**, which is reached via a rocky ledge.

The scenery in most parts is striking: fertile valleys alternate with breathtaking cliffs and bare, flat-topped mountains overflown by eagles and vultures. Tourism is developing very slowly here: there are few places to stay and the roads can be windy and slow.

❷ Morella

Castellón. 🏔 2,600. 🚌 ℹ️ Plaza de San Miguel, 964 17 30 32. 🚍 Sun. 🎉 Fiestas Patronales (mid–late Aug). 🌐 morellaturistica.com

Built on a high, isolated outcrop and crowned by a ruined castle, Morella cuts a dramatic profile. Its unbroken medieval walls retain six gates, which lead into a fan-shaped

maze of streets and steep, tapering alleys, many of which are shaded by the eaves of ancient houses. The main street is lined with shady porticoes. In the upper part of town is the **Basílica de Santa María la Mayor**. Its unique raised choir loft is reached by a finely carved spiral staircase.

NESTA CASA OBRO SAN VICENTE FERRER EL PRODIGIOS/
HA GLORE LA RESURRECCION DE UN NIÑO QUE SU MADRE
ENAJENADA HABIA DESCUARTIZADO Y GUISADO E/
BSEQUIO AL SANTO (1414)

Morella's Miracle

A plaque on the wall of Morella's Calle de la Virgen marks the house in which St Vincent Ferrer is said to have performed a bizarre miracle in the early 15th century. A housewife, distraught at having no meat to offer the saint, cut up her son and put him in the cooking pot. When St Vincent discovered this, he reconstituted the boy – except for one of his little fingers, which his mother had eaten to see if the dish was sufficiently salted.

❸ Peníscola

Castellón. 🚇 7,000. 🚌 ℹ️ Paseo Marítimo, 964 48 02 08. 🚢 Mon. 🎭 Fiestas Patronales (2nd week Sep). 🌐 peniscola.es

The fortified Old Town of Peníscola clusters around the base of a castle built on a rocky promontory, surrounded on three sides by the sea. This labyrinth of narrow winding streets and white houses is enclosed by massive ramparts. These are entered by either the Fosch Gate – reached by a ramp from the Plaza del Caudillo – or through the San Pedro Gate, from the harbour. Some visitors are drawn to the town because the 1961 Hollywood blockbuster *El Cid* was filmed there.

The **Castell del Papa Luna** was built on the foundations of an Arab fortress in the late 13th century by the Knights Templar. Their cross is carved above the door. It later became the residence of the papal pretender Pedro de Luna, cardinal of Aragón. He was elected Pope Benedict XIII during the Great Schism that split the Catholic Church at the end of the 14th century. Although he was deposed by the Council of Constance in 1414, he continued to proclaim his right to the papacy until his death as a nonagenarian in 1423.

🏰 Castell del Papa Luna
Calle Castillo. **Tel** 964 48 00 21. **Open** daily. **Closed** 1 & 6 Jan, 9 Sep, 9 Oct, 25 Dec. 🎫 📷

Sunset view of the beach and old town of Peníscola

❹ Costa del Azahar

Castellón. 🚉 Castelló de la Plana. 🚌 Castelló de la Plana. ℹ️ Castelló de la Plana, 964 35 86 88. 🌐 turismodecastellon.com

The "Orange Blossom Coast" of Castellón province is named after the dense citrus groves of the coastal plain. The three principal resorts are Oropesa, Peníscola and Benicàssim, where handsome old villas stand beside modern hotels and other tourist amenities. Alcossebre also has a popular beach. Vinaròs – the most northerly point – and Benicarló are key fishing ports supplying prawns and date mussels to local restaurants.

Sculpture in the Casa del Batlle

❺ Vilafamés

Castellón. 🚇 2,000. ℹ️ Plaza del Ayuntamiento 2, 964 32 99 70. 🚢 Fri. 🎭 San Miguel (late Mar), Patronales (mid-Aug).

This medieval town climbs from a flat plain along a rocky ridge to the restored round keep of its castle. The older, upper part of the town is a warren of sloping streets.

A 15th-century mansion houses the **Museo de Arte Contemporáneo de Vilafamés**. The artworks on display date from 1959 to the present.

🏛️ Museo de Arte Contemporáneo de Vilafamés
Casa del Batlle, Calle Diputación 20. **Tel** 964 32 91 52. **Open** Tue–Sun. 📷

Castelló de la Plana's planetarium, close to the beach

❻ Castelló de la Plana

Castellón. 🚇 180,000. 🚉 🚌 ℹ️ Plaza de la Hierva s/n, 964 35 86 88. 🚢 Mon. 🎭 Fiesta de la Magdalena (3rd Sun of Lent). 🌐 castellonturismo.com

Originally founded on high ground inland, the capital of Castellón province was relocated nearer to the coast in the 13th century.

The city centre, the Plaza Mayor, is bordered by the market, the cathedral, the town hall and **El Fadrí**, a 58-m- (190-ft-) high octagonal bell tower begun in 1590 and finished in 1604.

The **Museo de Bellas Artes** contains a collection of artifacts dating from the middle Palaeolithic era, paintings from the 14th to the 19th centuries and modern ceramics from the region. Most of the older works come from the nearby convents, because the government seized many church possessions in the 19th century. An important collection of paintings attributed to Francisco de Zurbarán is also on display here.

In **El Planetari** there are demonstrations of the night sky, the solar system and the nearest stars. Two rooms hold temporary exhibits.

🏛️ Museo de Bellas Artes
Avda Hermanos Bou 28. **Tel** 964 72 75 00. **Open** 10am–8pm Tue–Sat, 10am–2pm Sun. 📷 by appt. 🔔 📷

🔭 El Planetari
Paseo Marítimo 1, Grao. **Tel** 964 28 29 68. **Open** Oct–Jun: 11am–2pm, 4:30–8pm Tue–Sat, 11am–2pm Sun; Jul & Aug: 11am–1:45pm, 5–8:45pm Tue–Sat, 11am–2pm Sun. 📷 (planetarium). 🔔

❼ Onda

Castellón. 🏔 25,700. 🚌 🛈 Calle
Ceramista Peyró, 964 60 28 55.
🛒 Thu. 🎭 Feria del Santísimo
Salvador (5 & 6 Aug). 🌐 onda.es

Onda, home to a thriving
ceramics industry, is overlooked
by a ruined **castle**, which was
known to its Moorish founders
as the "Castle of the Three
Hundred Towers". The castle
houses a museum of local history.

However, the main reason
to visit Onda is to take a look
at the **Museo de Ciencias
Naturales El Carmen**, a natural
history museum belonging to
a Carmelite monastery.

The collection was begun in
1952 by the monks for their
own private scientific study. It
was only opened to the public
a decade later. The clever use
of subdued lighting lends
dramatic effect to the 10,000
plant and animal specimens
which are exhibited over three
floors. Objects include large
stuffed animals placed in
naturalistic settings, butterflies
and other insects, shells, fossils,
minerals and grisly, preserved
anatomical specimens.

**🏛 Museo de Ciencias Naturales
El Carmen**
Carretera de Tales. **Tel** 964 60 07 30.
Open Sat & Sun.
Closed 20 Dec–7 Jan. 🎫

Two butterfly exhibits in the
Museo El Carmen

Boat ride through the winding Coves de
Sant Josep

❽ Coves de Sant Josep

Vall d'Uixó, Castellón. **Tel** 964 69 05 76.
🚌 Vall d'Uixó. **Open** daily.
Closed 1 & 6 Jan, 25 Dec. 🎫 🎥
compulsory. 🌐 riosubterraneo.com

The caves of St Joseph were
first explored in 1902. The
subterranean river that formed
them and that still flows through
them, has been charted for
almost 3 km (2 miles). However,
only part of this distance can be
explored on a visit.

Boats take visitors along the
serpentine course of the river.
You may have to duck to avoid
projections of rock on the way.
Sometimes the narrow caves
open out into large chambers
such as the *Sala de los Murcié-
lagos* (Hall of the Bats – the bats
left when the floodlights were
installed). The water is at its
deepest – 12 m (39 ft) – in the
Lago Azul (Blue Lake). You can
explore a further 250 m (820 ft)
along the *Galería Seca* (Dry
Gallery) on foot. The caves are
often closed after heavy rain.

❾ Alto Turia

Valencia. 🚌 Chelva. 🛈 CV35
Valencia–Ademúz km 73, 96 163 50 84.

The attractive wooded hills of
the upper reaches of the Río
Turia in Valencia (Alto Turia) are
popular with hikers and day-
trippers. **Chelva**, the main town,
has an unusual clock on its
church, which shows not only
the hour but the day and month

as well. The town is overlooked
by the **Pico del Remedio**
(1,054 m/3,458 ft), from the
summit of which there is a fine
panoramic view of the region. In
a valley near Chelva, at the end
of an unsurfaced but drivable
track, are the remains of a Roman
aqueduct, **Peña Cortada**.

The most attractive and
interesting village in Alto Turia is
Alpuente, situated above a dry
gorge. Between 1031 and 1089,
when it was captured by El Cid
(*see p374*), Alpuente was the
capital of a small *taifa*, a Moorish
kingdom. In the 14th century
it was still important enough
for the kingdom of Valencia's
parliament to meet here. The
town hall is confined to a small
tower over a 14th-century
gateway, which was later
extended in the 16th century
by the addition of a rectangular
council chamber.

Requena, to the south is
Valencia's main wine town.
Further south, Valencia's other
principal river, the Xúquer
(Júcar), carves tremendous
gorges near Cortes de Pallas
on its way past the **Muela
de Cortes**. This massive, wild
plateau and nature reserve is
crossed by one small road and
a lonely dirt track.

La Tomatina

The highpoint of the annual
fiesta in Buñol (Valencia) is a
sticky food fight on the last
Wednesday of August, which
attracts thousands of visitors
dressed in their worst clothes.
Lorry loads of ripe tomatoes are
provided by the town council
at 11am for participants to hurl
at each other. No one in range
of the combatants is spared:
foreigners and photographers
are prized targets.

The battle originated in 1944.
Some say it began with a fight
between friends. Others say
irreverent locals pelted civic
dignitaries with tomatoes
during a procession. Increasing
national and international
press coverage means that
more people attend, and
more tomatoes are
thrown, every year.

Sagunt's ruined fortifications, added to by successive rulers of the town

⑩ Sagunt

Valencia. 🗺 66,000. 🚏 🚌 ℹ️ Pl
Cronista Chabret, 962 65 58 59. 🚢
Wed. 🎭 Fallas (15–19 Mar), Fiestas
(Jul–Aug). 🌐 turismo.sagunto.es

Sited near the junction of two
Roman roads, Sagunt (Sagunto)
played a crucial role in Spain's
ancient history.

In 219 BC, Hannibal, the
Carthaginian commander in
southern Spain, stormed and
sacked Rome's ally Saguntum.
All the inhabitants of the town
were said to have died in
the assault, the last throwing
themselves on to bonfires
rather than fall into the
hands of Hannibal's troops.
The incident sparked off the
Second Punic War, a disaster for
the Carthaginians, which ended
with Rome's occupation of the
peninsula (see pp54–5).

The town still contains several
reminders of the Roman
occupation, including the
1st-century-AD **Roman theatre**.
Built out of limestone in a natural
depression on the hillside above
the town, it has been controver-
sially restored using modern
materials. The theatre is now used
as a venue for music, plays and
Sagunt's annual theatre festival.

The ruins of the **castle**,
sprawling along the crest of
the hill above the modern-day
town, mark the original site of
Saguntum. Superimposed on
each other are the excavated
remains of various civilizations,
including the Iberians, the
Carthaginians, the Romans
and the Moors. The ruins of
the castle are divided into
seven divisions, the highest
being La Ciudadela, and the
most important Armas.

🏛 **Castillo de Sagunt**
Open Tue–Sun. **Tel** 962 66 62 01.

⑪ Monasterio de El Puig

El Puig, Valencia. **Tel** 961 47 02 00. 🚏
🚌 El Puig. **Open** Tue–Sat. 🎭
🕐 only, 10am, 11am, noon, 4pm,
5pm. 🌐 monasteriodelpuig.es.tl

This Mercedarian monastery
was founded by King Jaime I
of Aragón, who conquered
Valencia from the Moors in the
13th century. The monastery is
now home to a collection of
paintings from between the
16th and 18th centuries and
the **Museo de la Imprenta y
de la Obra Gráfica** (Museum
of Printing and Graphic Art).
The museum commemorates
the printing of the first book in
Spain – thought to have been in
Valencia in 1474 – and illustrates
the development of the printing
press. Exhibits include printers'
blocks and a copy of the smallest
printed book in the world.

Revellers throwing tomatoes at each other in the annual fiesta of La Tomatina

⑫ Valencia

Spain's third-largest city is sited in the middle of the *huerta*: a fertile plain of orange groves and market gardens, which is one of Europe's most intensively farmed regions. With its warm coastal climate, Valencia is known for its exuberant outdoor living and nightlife. In March the city stages one of Spain's most spectacular fiestas, Las Fallas *(see p259)*, in which giant papier-mâché sculptures are burned in the streets. Modern Valencia is a centre for trade and manufacturing, notably ceramics. A ferry service connects the city with the Balearic Islands.

Flowers in honour of Valencia's patroness, Virgen de los Desamparados

Exploring Valencia

Valencia stands on the course of the Río Turia. The city centre and the crumbling old quarter of El Carmen are on the right bank. Most of the monuments are within walking distance of the Plaza del Ayuntamiento, the triangular main square, which is presided over by the town hall.

The city was founded by the Romans in 138 BC and later conquered by the Moors. It was captured by El Cid *(see p374)* in 1096, retaken by the Moors, and finally recaptured by Jaime I, the Conqueror, in 1238, to become absorbed into the kingdom of Aragón. The three finest

buildings in Valencia were built during its economic and cultural heyday in the 14th and 15th centuries: the Torres de Serranos, a gateway that survived the demolition of the medieval walls in the 19th century, La Lonja and the cathedral.

🏛 Palau de la Generalitat

Plaza de Manises. **Tel** 963 86 34 61.
Open 9am–2pm Mon–Fri and by appt only.

This palace, which is now used by the Valencian regional government, was built in Gothic style between 1482 and 1579 but added to in the 17th and 20th centuries. It surrounds an enclosed stone patio from which two staircases ascend to splendidly decorated rooms.

The larger of the two Salas Doradas (Golden Chambers), on the mezzanine level, has a multicoloured coffered ceiling and tiled floor. The walls of the parliament chamber are decorated with frescoes.

🏛 Basílica de la Virgen de los Desamparados

Pl de la Virgen. **Tel** 963 91 92 14.
Open 8am–2pm, 4:30–9pm daily.

The statue of Valencia's patroness, the Virgin of the Helpless, stands above an altar in this 17th-century church, lavishly adorned with flowers and candles. She is honoured during Las Fallas by La Ofrenda ("the Offering"), a display of flowers in the square outside the church.

🏛 Cathedral

Plaza de la Reina. **Tel** 963 91 81 27.
Open 20 Mar–31 Oct: 10am–6:30pm Mon–Fri, 10am–5:30pm Sat, 2–5:30pm Sun & public hols; Nov–19 Mar: 10am–5:30pm Mon–Sat. 🏛 includes entry to the museum. Museo: **Open** as above. Miguelete: **Open** daily. 🏛 🎫

Built originally in 1262, the cathedral has been added to over the ages, and its three doorways are all in different styles. The oldest is the Romanesque Puerta del Palau, but the main entrance is the 18th-century Baroque portal, the Puerta de los Hierros.

A unique court meets on Thursdays at noon in front of the Gothic Puerta de los Apóstoles. For about 1,000 years, the

The Miguelete, the cathedral's bell tower on Plaza de la Reina

Water Tribunal has settled disputes between farmers over irrigation in the *huerta*.

Inside the cathedral, a chapel holds an agate cup, claimed to be the Holy Grail and formerly kept in the San Juan de la Peña *(see p238)*. Behind the main altar are some 15th-century frescoes.

The cathedral's bell tower, the **Miguelete**, is Valencia's main landmark and popular for the views it offers from the top. The cathedral also houses a museum.

La Lonja

Plaza del Mercado. **Tel** 963 52 54 78 ext. 4153. **Open** Tue–Sun (daily mid-Mar–mid-Oct).

An exquisite Late Gothic hall, built between 1482 and 1498 as a commodities exchange, La Lonja now hosts cultural events. The outside walls are decorated with gargoyles and other grotesque figures. The ceiling of the transactions hall features star-patterned vaulting, supported by spiral columns.

Mercado Central

Plaza del Mercado 6. **Tel** 963 82 91 00. **Open** 7am–3pm Mon–Sat.

This huge iron, glass and tile Art Nouveau building,

Ornate toilet sign outside Valencia's Mercado Central

with its parrot and swordfish weathervanes, opened in 1928 and is one of the largest and most attractive markets in Europe. Every morning its 350 or so stalls are filled with a bewildering variety of food.

Museo Nacional de Cerámica Gonzalez Martí

Poeta Querol 2. **Tel** 963 51 63 92. **Open** Tue–Sun. **Closed** 1, 6 & 22 Jan, 1 May, 24, 25 & 31 Dec. (free Sat pm & Sun).

Spain's Ceramics Museum is housed in the mansion of Marqués de Dos Aguas, an 18th-century fantasy of coloured plasterwork. The

doorway is edged by a carving by Ignacio Vergara. The exhibits include prehistoric, Greek and Roman ceramics and pieces by Picasso.

Colegio del Patriarca

Calle Nave 1. **Tel** 963 51 41 76. **Open** 11am–1:30pm daily. **Closed** Aug.

This seminary was built in 1584. The walls and ceiling of the church are covered with frescoes by Bartolomé Matarana. During Friday morning Mass, the painting above the altar, *The Last Supper* by Francisco Ribalta, is lowered to reveal a sculpture of the Crucifixion by an anonymous 15th-century German artist.

Valencia City Centre

1. Palau de la Generalitat
2. Basílica de la Virgen de los Desamparados
3. Cathedral
4. La Lonja
5. Mercado Central
6. Museo Nacional de Cerámica Gonzalez Martí
7. Colegio del Patriarca
8. Jardines del Río Turia
9. Museo de Bellas Artes
10. Torres de Serranos
11. Instituto Valenciano de Arte Moderno (IVAM)
12. Estación del Norte

0 metres   250
0 yards   250

Key to Symbols *see back flap*

The Palau de la Música, Valencia's prestigious concert hall

Beyond the Centre

The centre of the city is bordered by the Gran Vía Marqués del Túria and the Gran Vía Ramón y Cajal. Beyond these lie the 19th-century suburbs laid out on a grid plan.

The best way to get around beyond the centre is by the metro, one line of which is a tramway to the beaches of El Cabañal and La Malvarrosa. The port area, redeveloped for the 2007 America's Cup, is full of bars and restaurants.

🌳 Jardines del Río Túria

Where once there was a river there is now a 10-km- (6-mile-) long strip of gardens, sports fields and playgrounds crossed by 19 bridges. In a prominent position above the riverbed stands the Palau de la Música, a concert hall built in the 1980s. The centrepiece of the nearby children's playground is the giant figure of Gulliver pinned to the ground and covered with steps and slides. Jardín de Cabecera aims to recreate the

Ecce Homo by Juan de Juanes in the Museo de Bellas Artes

Túria River's original landscape, with a lake, beach, waterwheel, waterfall and riverside wood.

The best of Valencia's other public gardens stand near the banks of the river. The largest of them, the Jardines del Real – known locally as Los Viveros – occupy the site of a royal palace which was torn down in the Peninsular War. The Jardín Botánico, created in 1802, is planted with 7,000 species of shrubs and trees.

🏛 Museo de Bellas Artes

Calle San Pío V 9. **Tel** 963 87 03 00. **Open** 11am–5pm Mon, 10am–7pm Tue–Sun. **Closed** 1 Jan, Good Fri, 25 Dec. ♿ 🎧 by appt.

An important collection of 2,000 paintings and statues dating from the 14th to the 19th centuries is housed in this former seminary, which was built between 1683 and 1744.

Valencian art dating from the 14th and 15th centuries is represented by a series of golden altarpieces by Alcanyis, Pere Nicolau and Maestro de Bonastre. Velázquez's self-portrait and works by Bosch, El Greco, Murillo, Ribalta, Van Dyck and the local Renaissance painter Juan de Juanes hang on the first floor. On the top floor there are six paintings by Goya and others by important 19th- and 20th-century Valencian artists: Ignacio Pinazo, Joaquín Sorolla and Antonio Muñoz Degrain. A large collection of the latter's hallucinatory coloured paintings are gathered together in one room, among them the disturbing *Amor de Madre*.

🏯 Torres de Serranos

Plaza de los Fueros. **Tel** 963 91 90 70. **Open** Tue–Sun. **Closed** 1 Jan, 1 May, 25 Dec. 🎫 (free Sun).

Erected in 1391 as a triumphal arch in the city's walls, this gateway combines defensive and decorative features. Its two towers combine battlements and delicate Gothic tracery.

🏛 Instituto Valenciano de Arte Moderno (IVAM)

Calle Guillem de Castro 118. **Tel** 963 86 30 00. **Open** 10am–7pm Tue–Sun. 🎫 (free Sun). 🎧 by appointment. 📷 🏠 ♿ 🖥 ivam.es

The Valencian Institute of Modern Art is one of Spain's most highly respected spaces for displaying contemporary art. The core of its permanent collection is formed of work by Julio Gonzalez, arguably one of the most important 20th-century sculptors. All art forms are represented in its temporary exhibitions, with emphasis on photography and photomontage. One of the eight galleries, Sala Muralles, incorporates a stretch of the old city walls.

Art Nouveau-style column in the Estación del Norte

🚉 Estación del Norte

Calle Xátiva 24. **Tel** 902 32 03 20 (RENFE). **Open** daily.

Valencia's local railway station was built from 1906 to 1917 in a style inspired by Austrian Art Nouveau. The exterior is decorated with orange and orange-blossom flower motifs, while, inside, ceramic murals and stained glass in the foyer and cafeteria depict the life and crops of the *huerta* and L'Albufera *(see p258).*

The hemispherical IMAX cinema at the Ciutat de les Arts i de les Ciències

🏛 Ciutat de les Arts i de les Ciències

Avenida Autovia del Saler 1–7. **Tel** 902 10 00 31. Museum **Open** 10am–6pm or 7pm daily (to 9pm 1 Jul–15 Sep). 🌊 🌊 🖥 🏛 ♿ 🚾 cac.es

The futuristic complex of the City of Arts and Sciences stands at the seaward end of the Río Túria gardens. It is made up of five stunning buildings, four of them designed by Valencian architect Santiago Calatrava.

The Palau de les Arts, the final building to be added to the complex, has a concert hall with four performance spaces including an open-air theatre. On the other side of the Puente de Monteolivete is L'Hemisfèric, an architectural pun by Calatrava on the theme of vision, consisting of a blinking eye. The "eyeball" is an auditorium equipped as an IMAX cinema and planetarium. Next to this is the Museu de les Ciènces Príncipe Felipe, a science museum contained within a structure of glass and gleaming white steel arches. The displays inside are mainly geared towards visiting school parties. Opposite the museum is L'Umbracle, a giant pergola of parabolic arches covering the complex's car park.

The last part of the "city" is an aquarium, the Oceanografic, designed by architect Felix Candela as a series of lagoons and pavillions linked up by bridges and tunnels.

🏛 Museo de Historia de Valencia

Carrer Valencia 42, Mislata. **Tel** 963 701 105. **Open** Tue–Sun. 🌊 (free Sat & Sun). ♿

Valencia's history museum is housed in the 19th-century cistern that used to supply the city with water, now an atmospheric labyrinth of pillars and arches. The displays tell the story of the city's development, from its foundations by the Romans to the present day. In each section there is a "time machine", a full-sized screen on which a typical scene of daily life is reproduced in the language of the visitor's choice.

El Cabañal and La Malvarrosa Beaches

To the east of the city, the beaches of El Cabañal and La Malvarrosa are bordered by a broad and lively esplanade about 2 km (1 mile) long. Although these two former fishermen's districts were carelessly developed in the 1960s and 1970s, they retain some quaint, traditional houses tiled on the outside to keep them cool in summer. The light of La Malvarrosa inspired the Impressionist painter Joaquín Sorolla (see p309). The Paseo de Neptuno, near the port, is lined with restaurants, many of which specialize in paella. The revamped port district and marina also feature many modern hotels.

Environs

The farmed plain of the *huerta* is a maze of fields planted with artichokes and *chufas*, the raw ingredient of *horchata*.

Manises, near the airport, is famous for its ceramics, which are sold in shops and factories. There is also a ceramics museum.

Horchata, Valencia's Speciality

In summer, the bars and cafés of Valencia offer a thirst-quenching drink unique to the area. *Horchata*, a sweet, milky drink produced mainly in the nearby town of Alboraia, is made from *chufas* (earth almonds). It is served semi-frozen or in liquid form and usually eaten with *fartons* – soft, sweet breadsticks – or *rosquilletas* – crunchy biscuit sticks. The oldest *horchatería* in the city centre is Santa Catalina, off the Plaza de la Virgen.

Painted tiles showing woman serving *horchata*

Fishing boats on the shore of the freshwater lake, L'Albufera

⑬ L'Albufera

Valencia. 🚌 ℹ️ Carretera del Palmar,
Racó de l'Olla, 961 62 73 45. 🇼 **citma.**
gva.es/va/web/pn-l-albufera

A freshwater lake on the coast
just south of Valencia, L'Albufera
is one of the prime wetland
habitats for birds in Eastern Spain.

It is cut off from the sea by a
wooded sandbar, the Dehesa,
and fringed by a network of
paddy fields, which produce
a third of Spain's rice.

L'Albufera is fed by the Río
Turia and connected to the sea
by three channels, which are
fitted with sluice gates to control the water level. The lake
reaches a maximum depth of
2.5 m (8 ft), and is gradually
shrinking because of natural
silting and the reclamation of
land. In the Middle Ages the
lake encompassed an area
over ten times its present size.

Over 250 species of birds –
including large numbers of
egrets and herons – have been
recorded in the lake's reedbeds
and marshy islands, the *matas*.
L'Albufera was declared a nature
reserve in 1986. Many birds can
be seen with binoculars from
the shores of the lake.

A visitors' centre at Racó de
l'Olla provides information on
the ecology of lake, the paddy
fields and the Dehesa.

⑭ Xàtiva

Valencia. 🚹 29,300. 🚊 🚌
ℹ️ Alameda de Jaime I 50, 962 27
33 46. 🚆 Tue & Fri. 🎉 Las Fallas (16–
19 Mar); Fira de Agosto (14–20 Aug).

Along the narrow ridge of
Mount Vernissa, above Xàtiva,
run the ruins of a once-grand
castle of 30 towers. It was
largely destroyed by Felipe V
in the War of the Spanish
Succession *(see p66)*. Felipe
also set fire to the town, which
continues to wreak its revenge
in an extraordinary way – by
hanging Felipe's full-length
portrait upside down in the
Museo Municipal.

Until the attack, Xàtiva was
the second town of the kingdom of Valencia. It is thought to

Felipe V's full-length portrait hanging
upside down in Xàtiva

have been founded by the
Iberians. Under the Moors it
became prosperous, and in the
12th century it was the first
European city to make paper.

Among the sights in the
streets and squares of the Old
Town are a former hospital with
a Gothic-Renaissance façade,
and a Gothic fountain in the
Plaça de la Trinidad.

The oldest church in Xàtiva is
the **Ermita de San Feliú** (Chapel
of St Felix) on the road up to the
fortress. It dates from around
1262 and is hung with a number
of 14th- to 16th-century icons.

🏰 Castillo de Xàtiva
Subida del Castillo. **Tel** 962 27 42 74.
Open Tue–Sun. 🅿️

🏛️ Museo Municipal
Carrer de la Corretgeria 46. **Tel** 962 27
65 97. **Open** Tue–Sun. 🅿️ ♿

⑮ Gandia

Valencia. 🚹 78,000. 🚊 🚌 ℹ️ Avda
Marqués de Campo, 962 87 77 88.
🚆 Thu, Sat. 🎉 Las Fallas (16–19 Mar).
🇼 **gandiaturismo.com**

In 1485, Rodrigo Borja (who
became Pope Alexander VI) was
granted the title of Duchy of
Gandia. He founded the Borgia
clan and, together with his
children, was later implicated
in murder and debauchery.

For hotels and restaurants in this region see pp567–8 and p591

Rodrigo's great-grandson later redeemed the family name by joining the Jesuit order. He was canonized as St Francis Borja by Pope Clement X in 1671.

The house in which he was born, the **Palau Ducal** (Duke's Palace), is now owned by the Jesuits. Its simple Gothic courtyard belies the ornate chambers within, especially the Baroque Golden Gallery. The small patio's tiled floor depicts the elements of earth, air, fire and water.

Palau Ducal
C/ Duc Alfons el Vell 1. **Tel** 962 87 14 65. **Open** daily.

The ornate and gilded interior of the Palau Ducal, Gandia

⑯ Dénia

Alicante. 41,600. C/ Dr Manuel Lattur 1, 966 42 23 67. Mon & Fri. Fiestas Patronales (early Jul). **denia.net**

This town was founded as a Greek colony. It takes its name from the Roman goddess Diana – a temple in her honour was excavated here. In the 11th century it became the capital of a short-lived Muslim kingdom, whose dominion extended from Andalusia to the Balearic Islands.

It is now a fishing port and holiday resort. The town centre spreads around the base of a low hill. A large **castle**, once an Arab fortress, on its summit overlooks the harbour. The entrance gate, the Portal de la Vila, survives, but it was altered in the 17th century. The Palacio

del Gobernador (Governor's House), within the castle, contains an archaeological **museum**, which shows the development of Dénia from 200 BC to the 18th century.

North of the harbour is the sandy beach of Las Marinas. To the south is the rocky and less-developed Las Rotas beach, which is good for snorkelling.

Castillo de Dénia
C/ San Francisco. **Tel** 966 42 06 56. **Open** daily. **Closed** 1 Jan, 25 Dec.

⑰ Xàbia

Alicante. 31,000. Plaza de la Iglesia 4, 965 79 43 56. Thu. San Juan (24 Jun), Moros Y Cristianos (third weekend of Jul), Bous a la Mar (first week of Sep). **xabia.org**

Pirates and smugglers once took advantage of the hiding places afforded by the cliffs, caves, inlets and two rocky islands along the coastline of Xàbia (also known as Jávea).

The town centre is perched on a hill on the site of an Iberian settlement. Many buildings here are made from the local Tosca sandstone. The 16th-century **Iglesia de San Bartolomé** was fortified to serve as a refuge in times of invasion. Missiles could be dropped on to attackers via openings over the door.

The seafront at Cabo de San Antonio is overlooked by ruined 17th- and 18th-century windmills. The bay is filled with modern developments, but the beaches are free of high-rise apartment blocks.

Entrance to the Gothic Iglesia de San Bartolomé in Xàbia

The ceremonial burning of Las Fallas on St Joseph's Day

Valencia and Murcia's Fiestas

Las Fallas (15–19 Mar). Huge papier-mâché monuments (fallas) are erected in the crossroads and squares of Valencia around 15 March and ceremonially set alight on the night of the 19th, St Joseph's Day. Costing thousands of euros each, the fallas depict satirical scenes. During the fiesta, known as Les Falles in Valencian, the city echoes to the sound of firecrackers.

Good Friday, Lorca (Murcia). The "blue" and "white" brotherhoods compete to outdo each other in pomp and finery during a grand procession of biblical characters.

Moors and Christians (21–24 Apr), Alcoi (Alicante). Two costumed armies march into the city, where they perform ceremonies and fight mock battles in commemoration of the Reconquest.

Bous a la Mar (early Jul), Dénia (Alicante). People dodge bulls on the quay until one or the other falls into the sea (see p43).

Misteri d'Elx (11–15 Aug), Elx (Alicante). This choral play, in the Iglesia de Santa María, has spectacular special effects.

La Tomatina (last Wed of Aug), Buñol (Valencia). Thousands of participants pelt each other with ripe tomatoes (see pp252–3).

The Costa Blanca

Less hectic than the Costa del Sol *(see pp476–7)* and with warmer winters than the Costa Brava *(see p221)*, the Costa Blanca occupies a prime stretch of Spain's Mediterranean coastline. Alicante, with its airport and mainline railway station, is the arrival and departure point for most tourists. Between Alicante and Altea there are long stretches of sandy beach, which have been heavily built up with apartment blocks and hotels. North of Altea there are more fine beaches, but they are broken by cliffs and coves. South from Alicante, as far as the resort of Torrevieja, the scenery is drier and more barren, relieved only by the wooded sand dunes of Guardamar del Segura.

Gandia marks the southern end of the Costa de Valencia, whose extensive beaches of fine sand and shallow water are popular with the Spanish.

Dénia's Las Marinas beach is a flat, sandy strip lined by hotels. The rocky Les Rotes beach is good for snorkelling.

El Grau

Gandia

Platja d'Oliva

Oliva

N332

Xàbia's busiest beach is El Arenal. Most of the resort's coastline is punctuated by cliffs and coves.

Pego

AP7

Dénia

Cap de Sant Antoni

Ondara

Gata de Gorgos

Xàbia

Cap Martí

Altea is a resort with an unspoiled, whitewashed old town on a hilltop. Beneath it is a long, shingle beach.

Benissa

Cap de la Nau

Moraira

AP7

N332

Calp

Polop

Altea

Finestrat

l'Albir

Benidorm's liveliest beach, Levante, has been voted one of the ten best beaches in the world. Poniente is further from the town centre.

Santa Pola is still a working fishing port, but its long, sandy beaches are very popular.

Busot

AP7

N332

Benidorm

La Vila Joiosa

Coveta Fumà

CV800

Mutxamel

El Campello

Sant Joan d'Alacant

Platja de Sant Joan has a long strip of seamless sand bordered by a road and a narrow-gauge railway, which gives easy access to the beach.

A31

A70

AP7

N332

Platja de Sant Joan

Cap de las Huertas

Alicante

Torrellano

Elx

Els Arenals del Sol

0 kilometres		20
0 miles	10	

The Illa de Tabarca attracts day-trippers for its natural beauty and clear waters, good for snorkelling.

Santa Pola

Platja del Pinet

Illa de Tabarca

Guardamar del Segura has one of the coast's least busy beaches. It is bordered by windswept sand dunes covered with aromatic pine woods.

Guardamar del Segura

N332

La Mata

Torrevieja

Torrevieja is a very popular package holiday resort with sweeping, sandy beaches to the south. It has been highly developed in recent years.

Alicante's city centre is served by the popular Postiguet beach. Nearby are vast, sandy beaches, such as La Albufereta and Sant Joan.

◀ Burning papier-mâché dragon at Las Fallas festival, Valencia

⑱ Penyal d'Ifac

Calp, Alicante. 🚊 Calp. 🚌 Calp.
i Avenida de los Ejércitos Españoles,
30, Calp, 965 83 75 96. Limited access
in Jul & Aug.

When viewed from afar, the
rocky outcrop of the Penyal d'Ifac
seems to rise vertically out of the
sea. One of the Costa Blanca's
most dramatic sights, this 332-m-
(1,089-ft-) tall block of limestone
looks virtually unclimbable.
However, a short tunnel, built in
1918, allows walkers access to the
gentler slopes on its seaward side.

Allow about 2 hours for
the round trip, which starts at
the visitors' centre above Calp
harbour. It takes you up gentle
slopes covered with juniper
and fan palm, with the waves
crashing below. As you climb,
and at the exposed summit,
there are spectacular views of a
large stretch of the Costa Blanca.
On a clear day you can see the
hills of Ibiza *(see pp514–17)*.

The Penyal d'Ifac is also home
to 300 types of wild plant, including several rare species. Migrating
birds use it as a landmark, and
the salt flats below it are an
important habitat for them. The
rock was privately owned
until 1987, when the regional
government acquired it and
turned it into a nature reserve.

Situated below the rock
is the Iberian town of Calp,
renowned for its beaches.

The magnificent limestone rock Penyal d'Ifac

⑲ Guadalest

Alicante. 👥 226. *i* Avenida de
Alicante, 96 588 52 98. 🎭 Fiestas de
San Gregorio (1st week of Jun), Virgen
de la Asunción (14–17 Aug).
🌐 **guadalest.es**

Despite drawing coach loads
of day-trippers from Benidorm,
this pretty mountain village
remains relatively unspoiled.
This is largely because its older
part is accessible only on foot
by a single entrance: a sloping
tunnel cut into the rock on
which the castle ruins and the
church's distinctive belfry are
precariously perched.

Guadalest was founded by
the Moors, who carved the
surrounding hillsides into

terraces and planted them
with crops. These are still
irrigated by the original ditches
constructed by the Moors.

From the **castle** there are
fine views of the surrounding
mountains. Access to the castle
is through the Casa Orduña.

The intriguing **Museo de
Microminiaturas**, displays a
microscopic version of Goya's
Fusilamiento 3 de Mayo painted
on a grain of rice; his *The Naked
Maja (see p297)*, painted on the
wing of a fly; and a sculpture
of a camel passing through
the eye of a needle.

🏛 **Museo de Microminiaturas**
Plaza San Gregorio 14. **Tel** 965 88 50 62.
Open summer: 10am–7pm daily (to
9pm Aug); winter: 10am–6pm daily. 🎟

The belfry of Guadalest, perched on
top of a rock

⑳ Alcoi

Alicante. 👥 59,600. 🚊 🚌 *i* Plaça
de Espanya, 14, 965 53 71 55. 🛍 Wed
& Sat. 🎭 Mercado Medieval (mid- to
late Mar), Moors and Christians
(23 Apr). 🌐 **alcoiturisme.com**

Sited at the confluence of three
rivers and surrounded by high
mountains, Alcoi is an industrial
city. But it is best known for its
mock battles between Moors and
Christians *(see p259)* and its *pela-
dillas* – almonds coated in sugar.

On the slopes above it is **Font
Roja**, a nature reserve offering
pleasant walks, and a shrine
marked by a towering statue
of the Virgin Mary.

Environs

To the north of Alcoi is the **Sierra
de Mariola**, a mountain range
famed for its herbs. The best
point of access is the village of
Agres. A scenic route runs from
here to the summit of Mont
Cabrer at 1,390 m (4,560 ft).
It passes two ruined *neveras*
– pits once used to store ice
for preserving fish and meat.

The bullring of **Bocairent**,
10 km (6 miles) west of Agres,
was carved out of rock in 1813.
A nearby cliff is pockmarked
with **Les Covetes dels Moros**
("The Moors' Caves"), but their
origin remains a mystery.

㉑ Benidorm

Alicante. 🏛 69,100. 🚉 🚌 🛈 Plaza Canalejas, El Torrejó, 965 85 13 11. 🏪 Wed & Sun. 🎉 Las Fallas (16–19 Mar), Virgen del Carmen (16 Jul), Moros y Cristianos (late Sep, early Oct), Fiestas Patronales (second weekend in Nov). 🌐 visitbenidorm.es

With forests of skyscrapers overshadowing its two long beaches, Benidorm is more reminiscent of Manhattan than the obscure fishing village it once was in the early 1950s.

Benidorm boasts more accommodation than any other resort on the Mediterranean, but its clientele has changed since the 1980s, when its name was synonymous with "lager louts". A huge public park and open-air auditorium used for cultural events, the **Parque de l'Aigüera**, is emblematic of the face-lift Benidorm has gone through. The town now attracts more elderly holiday-makers from the north of Spain than English youths. Even so, beyond the splendid sandy beaches, the top attractions are still said to be sex, sun, nightclubs and "English" pubs.

A park on a promontory between the Levante and Poniente beaches, the **Balcón del Mediterráneo**, ends in a giant waterspout – a single-jet fountain. From here there is a panoramic view of the town. A short way out

The old town of Altea, dominated by its domed church

Main staircase with floral lamp in the Casa Modernista, Novelda

to sea is the Illa de Benidorm, a wedge-shaped island served by ferries from the harbour. The island has been converted into a nature reserve for seabirds.

Environs
La Vila Joiosa (Villajoyosa), to the south, is much older than Benidorm. Its principal sight is a line of brightly painted houses that overhang the riverbed. They were painted in such vivid colours, it is said, so that their fishermen owners would be able to identify their homes when they were out at sea.

The older part of **Altea**, to the north of Benidorm, stands on a hill above modern beachfront developments. It is a delightful jumble of white houses, narrow streets and long flights of steps around a blue-domed church.

㉒ Novelda

Alicante. 🏛 27,000. 🚉 🚌 🛈 Calle Mayor 6, 965 60 92 28. 🏪 Wed & Sat. 🎉 Santa María Magdalena (19–25 Jul). 🌐 novelda.es

The industrial town of Novelda is dominated by its many marble factories. But it is the exquisitely preserved Art Nouveau house, the **Casa Modernista**, that is of special interest. It was built in 1903 and and rescued from demolition in 1970. The building's three floors are furnished in period style. There are few straight lines or functional shapes and almost every inch of wall space has some floral or playful motif.

Environs
Villena's museum has a collection of Bronze Age gold objects, the **Tesoro de Villena** (see pp52–3).

🚌 **Casa Modernista**
Calle Mayor 24. **Tel** 965 60 02 37. **Open** 10am–2pm Tue–Fri. 🎟 by appt.

🏛 **Tesoro de Villena**
Plaza de Santiago 1. **Tel** 965 80 11 50. **Open** Tue–Sun am. ♿ ♿

㉓ Alicante

Alicante. 🏛 332,000. ✈ 🚉 🚌 🚢 🛈 Explanada de España 1, 965 14 70 38. 🏪 Thu & Sat. 🎉 Hogueras (20–24 Jun). 🌐 alicanteturismo.com

A port and seaside resort built around a natural harbour, Alicante (Alacant) is the principal city of the Costa Blanca. Both the Greeks and Romans established settlements here. In the 8th century the Moors refounded the city under the shadow of Mount Benacantil. Its summit is now occupied by the **Castillo de Santa Bárbara**, which dates from the 16th century. Its top battlements offer a view over the whole city.

The focus of the city is the **Explanada de España**, a palm-lined promenade along the waterfront. The 18th-century **town hall** (ayuntamiento) is worth seeing for the Salón Azul (Blue Room). A metal disc on the marble staircase is used as a reference point in measuring the sea level all around Spain. A fine

Yachts moored in Alicante harbour, beside the Explanada de España

collection of 20th-century art can be seen at the **Museo de Arte Contemporáneo (MACA)**. Local artist Eusebio Sempere (1924–85) assembled works by Dalí, Miró, Picasso (*see pp36–7*) and others.

🏰 **Castillo de Santa Bárbara**
Playa del Postiguet. **Tel** 965 92 77 15.
Open daily. 🎦 (for elevator only). 🎟️
🌐 **castillodesantabarbara.com**

🏛️ **Ayuntamiento**
Plaza del Ayuntamiento 1. **Tel** 965 14 91 00. **Open** 9am–2pm Mon–Fri.

🏛️ **Museo de Arte Contemporáneo (MACA)**
Plaza de Santa María 3.
Tel 965 21 31 56. **Open** 10am–8pm Tue–Sat, 10am–2pm Sun. **Closed** 1 & 6 Jan, 1 May, 25 Dec & local hols. 🦽
🌐 **maca-alicante.es**

㉔ Illa de Tabarca

Alicante. 🚢 from Santa Pola/Alicante. 🛈 Santa Pola, 966 69 22 76.

The best point of departure for the Illa de Tabarca is Santa Pola. This small, flat island is divided into two parts: a stony, treeless area of level ground known as *el campo* (the countryside), and a walled settlement, which is entered through three gateways. The settlement was laid out on a grid plan in the 18th century, on the orders of Carlos III, to deter pirates.

Tabarca is a popular place to swim or snorkel and it can get crowded in the summer.

Fish and salt have long been important to the economy of Santa Pola. A Roman fish salting works has been excavated here, and outside the town are some modern saltpans.

㉕ Elx

Alicante. 🚶 230,000. 🚉 🚌
🛈 Parque Municipal, 966 65 81 96.
🏪 Mon & Sat. 🎭 Misteri d'Elx (14–15 Aug). 🌐 **visitelche.com**

The forest of over 300,000 palm trees that surrounds Elx (Elche) on three sides is said to have been planted by the Phoenicians around 300 BC. Part of it has been enclosed as a private garden called the **Huerto del Cura**. Some of the palms – one with a trunk which has divided into eight branches – are dedicated to notable people, like the Empress Elizabeth of Austria, who visited here in 1894.

The first settlement in the area, around 5000 BC, was at La Alcudia, where a 5th-century BC Iberian stone bust of a priestess, *La Dama de Elche* (*see p52*), was discovered in 1897. The original is in Madrid, but there are several replicas scattered around Elx.

The blue-domed Baroque church, the **Basílica de Santa María**, was built in the 17th century to house the **Misteri d'Elx** (*see p45*). Next to it is **La Calahorra**, a Gothic tower, which is a surviving part of the city's defences.

A clock on the roof next to the town hall has two 16th-century mechanical figures, which strike the hours on bells.

🌴 **Huerto del Cura**
Porta de la Morera 49.
Tel 965 45 19 36. **Open** daily. 🎟️ 🦽
🎟️ 🌐 **huertodelcura.com**

🏛️ **La Calahorra**
Calle Uberna. **Closed** to the public.

㉖ Orihuela

Alicante. 🚶 83,400. 🚉 🚌 🛈 Plaza Marqués de Rafal 5, 965 30 46 45. 🏪 Tue. 🎭 Moros y Cristianos (10–17 Jul).
🌐 **orihuelaturistica.es**

In the 15th century Orihuela was prosperous enough for Fernando and Isabel to stop and collect men and money on their way to do battle against the Moors at Granada. The Gothic **cathedral** houses Velázquez's *The Temptation of St Thomas Aquinas* in its museum. Among the exhibits in the **Museo San Juan de Dios** archaeological museum is a processional float bearing a 17th-century statue of a she-devil, *La Diablesa*.

🏛️ **Museo San Juan de Dios**
Calle del Hospital. **Tel** 966 74 31 54.
Open Tue–Sun. 🦽 🎟️

La Diablesa, Orihuela

㉗ Torrevieja

Alicante. 🚶 91,400. 🛈 Paseo Vista Alegre, 965 70 34 33. 🏪 Fri.
🎭 Habaneras (22–30 Jul).
🌐 **turismodetorrevieja.com**

During the 1980s, Torrevieja grew at a prodigious rate as thousands of Europeans purchased homes here. Before tourism, the town's source of income was sea salt. The salt-works are the most productive in Europe and the second most important in the world.

The *habaneras* festival celebrates Cuban music brought back by salt exporters.

Capilla del Junterón, Murcia

❷❽ Murcia

Murcia. 📍 439,700. 🚊 🚌 ℹ️ Plaza Cardenal Belluga, Ayuntamiento Building, 968 35 87 49. 📅 Thu. 🎭 Semana Santa (Easter Week). 🌐 **turismodemurcia.es**

A regional capital and university city on the River Segura, Murcia was founded in 825 by the Moors, following successful irrigation of the surrounding fertile plain.

The pedestrianized Calle de la Trapería, linking the cathedral and the former marketplace (now the Plaza Santo Domingo), is the city's main street.

On it stands the **Casino**, a gentlemen's club founded in 1847. It is entered through an Arab-style patio, fashioned on the royal chambers of the Alhambra. The huge ballroom has a polished parquet floor and is illuminated by five crystal chandeliers. Visitors can take a tour of the interior and splash out on a meal in the fine restaurant.

Work on the **cathedral** began in 1394 over the foundations of Murcia's central mosque, and it was finally consecrated in 1467. The large tower was added much later and constructed in stages from the 16th to the 18th centuries. The architect Jaime Bort built the main, Baroque façade between 1739 and 1754.

The cathedral's finest features are two exquisitely ornate side chapels. The first, the Capilla de los Vélez, is in Late Gothic style and was built between 1490 and 1507. The second, the Renaissance Capilla del Junterón, dates from the early 16th century.

The **cathedral museum** displays grand Gothic altarpieces, a frieze from a Roman sarcophagus and the third-largest monstrance in Spain.

Francisco Salzillo (1707–83), one of Spain's greatest sculptors, was born in Murcia, and a museum in the Iglesia de Jesús (Church of Jesus) exhibits nine of his *pasos* – sculptures on platforms. These are carried through the streets on Good Friday morning. The figures are so lifelike that a fellow sculptor is said to have told the men carrying a paso: "Put it down, it will walk by itself."

The **Museo Etnológico de la Huerta de Murcia**, 7 km (4.5 miles) out of Murcia, stands beside a large waterwheel – a 1955 copy in iron of the original 15th-century wooden wheel. The galleries display agricultural and domestic items, some of them 300 years old. A traditional, thatched Murcian farmhouse forms part of the museum.

🎰 **Casino**
Calle Trapería 18. **Tel** 968 21 53 99. **Open** 10:30am–7:30pm daily. 🔲 ♿ 📷

🏛️ **Museo Etnológico de la Huerta de Murcia**
Avda Príncipe, Alcantarilla. **Tel** 968 89 38 66. **Open** Museum: Thu–Sun; Gardens: Tue–Sun. **Closed** Aug & public hols. ♿

❷❾ Mar Menor

Murcia. ✈️ San Javier. 🚊 to Cartagena, then bus. 🚌 La Manga. ℹ️ La Manga, 968 14 61 36. 🌐 **marmenor.es**

The elongated, high-rise holiday resort of La Manga,

Arab-style patio, Murcia Casino

built on a long, thin, sandy strip, separates the Mediterranean and the Mar Menor, literally the "Smaller Sea".

Really a large lagoon, the sheltered Mar Menor can be 5°C (9°F) warmer than the Mediterranean in summer. Its high mineral concentrations first drew rest-cure tourists in the early 20th century. They stayed at the older resorts of Santiago de la Ribera and **Los Alcázares**, which still have pretty wooden jetties.

From either La Manga or Santiago de la Ribera you can make a ferry trip to the **Isla Perdiguera**, one of the five islands in the Mar Menor.

These days the region is very built-up, but to escape the crowds head to the **Parque Regional de Calblanque**. Its dunes and beaches are wild and unspoilt.

The resort of Los Alcázares on the edge of the Mar Menor

View of the domes and spires of Cartagena's town hall from the seafront

③⓪ Cartagena

Murcia. 🏙 218,200. ✈ San Javier. 🚉
🚌 🛳 ℹ Palacio Consistorial, Plaza
del Ayuntamiento 1, 968 12 89 55. 🛒
Wed. 🎭 Semana Santa (Easter Week),
Carthaginians and Romans (last two
weeks Sep). 🌐 **cartagenaturismo.es**

The first settlement founded in
the natural harbour of Cartagena
was constructed in 223 BC by
the Carthaginians, who called it
Quart Hadas (New City). After
conquering the city in 209 BC,
the Romans renamed it *Carthago
Nova* (New Carthage). Although
the city declined in importance
in the Middle Ages, its prestige
increased in the 18th century
when it became a naval base.

The park surrounding the ruins
of the **Castillo de la Concepción**,
Cartagena's castle, has views over
the impressive Roman theatre
and its museum, the **Museo del
Teatro Romano**. The city hall is
at the end of the Calle Mayor, a
street with handsome buildings
and balconies. Excavations in the
city include a Roman street and
the **Muralla Bizantina** (Byzantine
Wall), built between 589 and 590.
The **Museo Nacional de Arqueología Marítima** has treasures
from Greek and Roman wrecks.

🏛 **Museo del Teatro Romano**
Plaza del Ayuntamiento 9.
Tel 968 52 51 49. 🎫 📷 ♿
🌐 **teatroromanocartagena.org**

🏛 **Muralla Bizantina**
Calle Doctor Tapia Martínez.
Tel 968 50 79 66. **Open** Tue–Sat.

🏛 **Museo Nacional de
Arqueología Marítima**
Paseo Alfonso XII. **Tel** 968 12 11 66.
Open Tue–Sun. 🎫 free Sat pm & Sun.

③① Costa Cálida

Murcia. 🚉 Murcia. 🚌 Murcia.
ℹ C/ Antonio Cortijos, Águilas,
968 49 32 85. 🌐 **murciaturistica.es**

The most popular resorts of
Murcia's "Warm Coast" are around
the Mar Menor. Between Cabo
de Palos and Cabo Tinoso the
few small beaches are dwarfed
by cliffs. The resorts of the southern part of the coast are relatively
quiet. There are several fine
beaches at Puerto de Mazarrón;
and at nearby Bolnuevo the
wind has eroded soft rocks into
strange shapes. The growing
resort of Águilas marks the
southern limit of the coast,
at the border with Andalusia.

③② Lorca

Murcia. 🏙 91,700. 🚉 🚌
ℹ Convento de Merced, Puerta de
San Ginés, 968 44 19 14. 🛒 Thu.
🎭 Semana Santa (Easter Week),
Feria (3rd week of Sep), Día de San
Clemente (23 Nov). 🌐 **lorca.es**
🌐 **lorcaturismo.es**

The farmland around Lorca
is a fertile oasis in one of
Europe's most arid areas.
Lorca was an important
staging post on the Vía
Heraclea, as witnessed
by the Roman milepost
standing in a corner of
the Plaza San Vicente.
During the wars
between Moors and
Christians in the 13th
to 15th centuries, Lorca
became a frontier town
between Al Andalus and
the Castilian territory of

Murcia. Its castle dates from this
era, although only two of its
original 35 towers remain. In
2011, the city was hit by Spain's
worst earthquake for more than
50 years. The castle was badly
damaged but it has since been
repaired – there is now a parador
inside. After Granada fell the
town lost its importance and,
except for one surviving gateway,
its walls were demolished.

The central Plaza de España
is lined with handsome stone
buildings. One side of the square
is occupied by the **Colegiata
de San Patricio** (Church of St
Patrick), built between 1533 and
1704, the only church in Spain
dedicated to the Irish saint.

③③ Caravaca de
la Cruz

Murcia. 🏙 26,400. ℹ Calle de las
Monjas 17, 968 70 24 24. 🛒 Mon, 3rd
Sun of month (crafts). 🎭 Vera Cruz
(1–5 May). 🌐 **caravaca.org**

A town of ancient churches,
Caravaca de la Cruz's fame lies
in its castle, which houses the
Santuario de la Vera Cruz
(Sanctuary of the True Cross).
This is where a double-armed
cross is said to have appeared
miraculously in 1231 – 12 years
before the town was seized by
Christians. The highlight of the
Vera Cruz fiesta is the Race of
the Wine Horses, which
commemorates the lifting of a
Moorish siege of the castle and
the appearance of the cross.
The cross was dipped in wine,
which the thirsty defenders
then drank and recovered
their fighting strength.

Environs
Just to the north, among
the foothills on Murcia's
western border, is the
village of **Moratalla**, a
jumble of steep streets
and stone houses lying
beneath a 15th-century
castle. **Cehegín**, east of
Caravaca, is a partially
preserved 16th- and
17th-century town.

Roman milepost topped by a statue
of St Vincent, Lorca

INTRODUCING MADRID

Introducing Madrid   270–271

Old Madrid   272–285

Bourbon Madrid   286–303

Further Afield   304–310

Madrid Street Finder   311–319

Shopping in Madrid   320–323

Entertainment in Madrid   324–329

Madrid Province   330–337

Introducing Madrid

Spain's capital, a city of over three million people, is situated close to the geographical centre of the country, at the hub of both road and rail networks. Because of its distance from the sea and its altitude – 660 m (2,150 ft) – the city endures cold winters and hot summers, making spring and autumn the best times to visit. Madrid's attractions include three internationally famous art galleries, a royal palace, grand public squares and many museums filled with the treasures of Spain's history. The city is surrounded by its own small province, the Comunidad de Madrid, which takes in the Sierra de Guadarrama and one of Spain's most famous monuments, the palace of El Escorial.

The Palacio Real *(see pp280–81)*, the royal palace built by Spain's first Bourbon kings, dominates the western part of Old Madrid. Its lavishly decorated chambers include the throne room.

The Plaza Mayor *(see p277)*, Old Madrid's great 17th-century square, has been a focal point of the city since the days when it was used as a public arena for bullfights, trials by the Inquisition and executions *(see p278)*. An equestrian statue of Felipe III stands in the middle of the square.

PLAZA DE ESPAÑA

GRAN VIA

PLAZA DEL CALLAO

GRAN

CALLE DE BAILEN

OLD MADRID
(See pp272–85)

PUERTA DEL SOL

CALLE DE SEGOVIA

PLAZA MAYOR

CALLE

Madrid Province
(see pp330–37)

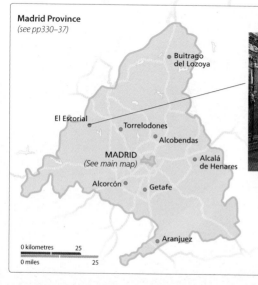

- Buitrago del Lozoya
- El Escorial
- Torrelodones
- Alcobendas
- **MADRID** *(See main map)*
- Alcalá de Henares
- Alcorcón
- Getafe
- Aranjuez

0 kilometres   25
0 miles   25

El Escorial *(see pp334–5)*, the massive, architecturally austere monastery-palace built by Felipe II, has some sumptuous apartments decorated with great works of art. Marble sarcophagi in the octagonal Royal Pantheon contain the mortal remains of many Spanish monarchs.

◀ Aerial view of Gran Via, Madrid's main shopping street

The Museo Thyssen-Bornemisza
(see pp292–3), one of the most important privately assembled art collections in the world, was sold to Spain in 1993. The early 19th-century palace houses works by Titian, Rubens, Goya, van Gogh and Picasso.

0 metres   500
0 yards   500

The Plaza de Cibeles *(see p290)*, one of the city's most impressive squares, is ringed by distinctive buildings, including Madrid´s former main post office. The building, with sculptures on its white façade, is now a cultural centre and the headquarters of the city council.

PLAZA DE COLÓN

PASEO DE RECOLETOS

PLAZA DE CIBELES   CALLE DE   ALCALÁ

CALÁ

BOURBON MADRID
(See pp286–303)

PLAZA DE CANOVAS DEL CASTILLO

PASEO DEL PRADO

ATOCHA

The Parque del Retiro *(see p301)* has leafy paths and avenues, and a boating lake overlooked by a majestic colonnade. It is an ideal place in which to relax between visits to the great art galleries and museums of Bourbon Madrid.

The Museo del Prado
(see pp296–9) is one of the world's greatest art galleries. It has important collections of paintings by Velázquez and Goya, whose statues stand outside the main entrances.

GOYA

The Museo Nacional Centro de Arte Reina Sofía *(see pp302–3)*, an outstanding museum of 20th-century art, is entered by highly original exterior glass lifts. Inside, the star exhibit is *Guernica*, Picasso's famous painting *(see p303)*.

OLD MADRID

When Felipe II chose Madrid as his capital in 1561, it was a small Castilian town of little real significance. In the following years, it was to grow into the nerve centre of a mighty empire.

According to tradition, it was the Moorish chieftain Muhammad ben Abd al Rahman who established a fortress above the Río Manzanares. Magerit, as it was called in Arabic, fell to Alfonso VI of Castile between 1083 and 1086. Narrow streets with houses and medieval churches began to grow up on the higher ground behind the old Arab *alcázar* (fortress), which was replaced by a Gothic palace in the 15th century. When this burned down in 1734, it was replaced by the present Bourbon palace, the Palacio Real.

The population had scarcely reached 20,000 when Madrid was chosen as capital, but by the end of the century it had more than trebled. The 16th-century city is known as the "Madrid de los Austrias", after the reigning Habsburg dynasty. During this period royal monasteries were endowed and churches and private palaces were built. In the 17th century, the Plaza Mayor was added and the Puerta del Sol, the "Gate of the Sun", became the spiritual and geographical heart not only of Madrid but of all Spain.

Sights at a Glance

Historic Buildings
- ⑨ *Palacio Real pp280–81*

Museums and Galleries
- ⑭ Real Academia de Bellas Artes de San Fernando

Churches and Convents
- ② Colegiata de San Isidro
- ⑤ Iglesia de San Nicolás de Bari
- ⑦ Catedral de la Almudena
- ⑩ Monasterio de la Encarnación
- ⑬ Monasterio de las Descalzas Reales

Streets, Squares and Parks
- ① Puerta del Sol
- ③ Plaza de la Villa
- ④ Plaza Mayor
- ⑥ Plaza de Oriente
- ⑧ Campo del Moro
- ⑪ Plaza de España
- ⑫ Gran Vía

See also Madrid Street Finder, maps 1, 2, 3, 4, 7

◄ Elegant stone fountain in Campo del Moro park with the Palacio Real behind

For map symbols *see back flap*

Street-by-Street: Old Madrid

Stretching from the charming Plaza de la Villa to the busy Puerta del Sol, the compact heart of Old Madrid is steeped in history and full of interesting sights. Trials by the Inquisition *(see p278)* and executions were once held in the Plaza Mayor. This porticoed square is Old Madrid's finest piece of architecture, a legacy of the Habsburgs *(see pp64–5)*. Other buildings of note are the Colegiata de San Isidro and the Palacio de Santa Cruz. For a more relaxing way of enjoying Old Madrid, sit in one of the area's numerous cafés or browse among the stalls of the Mercado de San Miguel.

❹ ★ Plaza Mayor
This beautiful 17th-century square competes with the Puerta del Sol as the focus of Old Madrid. The arcades at the base of the three-storey buildings are filled with cafés and craft shops.

The Mercado de San Miguel is housed in a 19th-century building with wrought-iron columns. The market has several excellent places to stop for a snack.

To Palacio Real

CALLE MAYOR

PLAZA COMMANDANTE MORENAS

PLAZA DE LA VILLA

CORDÓN

PUÑONROSTRO

CUCHILLEROS

Old Town Hall *(ayuntamiento)*

Casa de Cisneros

Arco de Cuchilleros

❸ ★ Plaza de la Villa
The 15th-century Torre de los Lujanes is the oldest of several historic buildings standing on this square.

The Basílica Pontificia de San Miguel is an imposing 18th-century church with a beautiful façade and a graceful interior. It is one of very few churches in Spain inspired by the Italian Baroque style.

0 metres 100
0 yards 100

For hotels and restaurants in this area see p568 and pp591–2

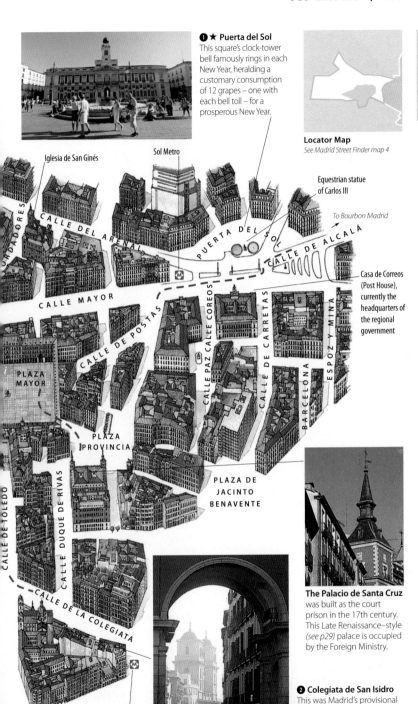

❶ ★ Puerta del Sol
This square's clock-tower bell famously rings in each New Year, heralding a customary consumption of 12 grapes – one with each bell toll – for a prosperous New Year.

Locator Map
See Madrid Street Finder map 4

Iglesia de San Ginés

Sol Metro

Equestrian statue of Carlos III

To Bourbon Madrid

CALLE DE LOS BORDADORES

CALLE DEL ARENAL

PUERTA DEL SOL

CALLE DE ALCALÁ

Casa de Correos (Post House), currently the headquarters of the regional government

CALLE MAYOR

CALLE DE POSTAS

CALLE PAZ

CALLE COREOS

CALLE DE CARRETAS

BARCELONA

ESPOZ Y MINA

PLAZA MAYOR

PLAZA PROVINCIA

PLAZA DE JACINTO BENAVENTE

CALLE DE TOLEDO

CALLE DUQUE DE RIVAS

CALLE DE LA COLEGIATA

Tirso de Molina Metro

The Palacio de Santa Cruz
was built as the court prison in the 17th century. This Late Renaissance–style *(see p29)* palace is occupied by the Foreign Ministry.

❷ Colegiata de San Isidro
This was Madrid's provisional cathedral until La Almudena was completed *(see p279)*. It is named after the city's patron, St Isidore, a local 12th-century farmer.

Key

— Suggested route

Kilometre Zero, the centre of Spain's road network, Puerta del Sol

❶ Puerta del Sol

Map 4 F2. 🔲 Sol.

Crowded and noisy with chatter and policemen's whistles, the Puerta del Sol makes a fitting centre for Madrid. This is one of the city's most popular meeting places, and huge crowds converge here on their way to the shops and sights in the old part of the city.

The square marks the site of the original eastern entrance to the city, once occupied by a gatehouse and castle. These disappeared long ago and in their place came a succession of churches. In the late 19th century the area was turned into a square and became the centre of café society.

Today the "square" is shaped like a half-moon. A recent addition is the modern glass train station in front of the statue of Carlos III. The southern side of the square is edged by an austere red-brick building, originally the city's post office, built in the 1760s under

The bronze bear and strawberry tree of Madrid, Puerta del Sol

Carlos III. In 1847 it became the headquarters of the Ministry of the Interior. The clock tower, which gives the building much of its identity, was added in 1866. During the Franco regime *(see pp70–71)*, the police cells beneath the building were the site of many human rights abuses. In 1963, Julián Grimau, a member of the underground Communist Party, allegedly fell from an upstairs window and miraculously survived, only to be executed soon afterwards.

The building is now home to the regional government and is the focus of many festive events. At midnight on New Year's Eve crowds fill the square to eat a grape on each stroke of the clock, a tradition supposed to bring good luck for the year. Outside a symbol on the ground marks Kilometre Zero, considered the centre of Spain's huge road network.

The buildings opposite are arranged in a semicircle and contain modern shops and cafés. At the start of Calle Alcalá is a bronze statue of the symbol of Madrid – a bear reaching for the fruit of a *madroño* (strawberry tree).

The Puerta del Sol has witnessed many important historical events. On 2 May 1808 the uprising against the occupying French forces began here, but the crowd, pitted against the well-armed French troops, was crushed *(see p67)*. In 1912 the liberal prime minister José Canalejas was assassinated in the square and, in 1931, the Second Republic *(see p69)* was proclaimed from the balcony of the Ministry of the Interior.

❷ Colegiata de San Isidro

Calle Toledo 37. **Map** 4 E3. **Tel**: 91 369 20 37. 🔲 La Latina. **Open** daily 9am–1pm, 7–9pm.

The Colegiata de San Isidro was built in the Baroque style *(see p29)* for the Jesuits in the mid-17th century. This twin-towered church served as Madrid's cathedral until La Almudena *(see p279)* was completed in 1993.

After Carlos III expelled the Jesuits from Spain in 1767 *(see p66)*, Ventura Rodríguez was commissioned to redesign the interior of the church. It was then rededicated to Madrid's patron saint, St Isidore, and two years later the saint's remains were moved here from the Iglesia de San Andrés. San Isidro was returned to the Jesuits during the reign of Fernando VII (1814–33).

Altar in the Colegiata de San Isidro

❸ Plaza de la Villa

Map 4 D3. 🔲 Ópera, Sol.

The much-restored and much-remodelled Plaza de la Villa is one of the most atmospheric spots in Madrid. Some of the city's most historic secular buildings are situated around this square.

The oldest building is the early 15th-century Torre de los Lujanes, with its Gothic portal and Mudéjar-style horseshoe arches. François I of France was allegedly imprisoned in it following his defeat at the Battle of Pavia in 1525. The Casa de Cisneros was built in 1537 for

Portal of the Torre de los Lujanes

the nephew of Cardinal Cisneros, founder of the historic University of Alcalá (see pp336–7). The main façade, on the Calle de Sacramento, is an excellent example of the Plateresque style (see p29).

Linked to this building, by an enclosed bridge, is the Old Town Hall (ayuntamiento). Designed in the 1640s by Juan Gómez de Mora, architect of the Plaza Mayor, it exhibits the same combination of steep roofs with dormer windows, steeple-like towers at the corners and an austere façade of brick and stone. Before construction was finished – more than 30 years later – the building had acquired handsome Baroque doorways. A balcony was later added by Juan de Villanueva, the architect of the Prado (see pp296–9), so that the royal family could watch Corpus Christi processions passing by.

❹ Plaza Mayor

Map 4 E3. 🔯 Sol.

The Plaza Mayor forms a splendid rectangular square, all balconies and pinnacles, dormer windows and steep slate roofs. The square, with its theatrical atmosphere, is very Castilian in character. Much was expected to happen here and a great deal did – bullfights, executions, pageants and trials by the Inquisition (see p278) – all watched by crowds, often in the presence of the reigning king and queen. The canonization of Madrid's patron, St Isidore, took

place here in 1622. One year earlier, in 1621, the execution of Rodrigo Calderón, secretary to Felipe III, was held here. Although hated by the Madrid populace, Calderón bore himself with such dignity on the day of his death that the phrase "proud as Rodrigo on the scaffold" survives to this day. Perhaps the greatest occasion of all, however, was the arrival here – from Italy – of Carlos III in 1760.

The square was started in 1617 and built in just two years, replacing slum houses. Its architect, Juan Gómez de Mora, was successor to Juan de Herrera, designer of Felipe II's austere monastery-palace, El Escorial (see pp334–5). Gómez de Mora echoed the style of his master, softening it slightly. The square was later reformed by Juan de Villanueva. The fanciest part of the arcaded construction

is the Casa de la Panadería (bakery). Its façade, now crudely reinvented, is decorated with allegorical paintings. Madrid's main tourist office is sited here.

The equestrian statue in the centre is of Felipe III, who ordered the square's construction. Started by the Italian Giovanni de Bologna and finished by his pupil Pietro Tacca in 1616, the statue was moved here in 1848 from the Casa de Campo (see p306). Today the square is lined with cafés, and is the venue for a collectors' market on Sundays (see pp320–21). The square's southern exit leads into Calle de Toledo towards the streets where the Rastro, Madrid's flea market (see p306), is held. A flight of steps in the southwest corner takes you under the Arco de Cuchilleros to the Calle de Cuchilleros, and some mesones, traditional restaurants.

Allegorical paintings on the Casa de la Panadería, Plaza Mayor

The Spanish Inquisition

The Spanish Inquisition was set up by Fernando and Isabel in 1478 to create a single, monolithic Catholic ideology in Spain. Protestant heretics and alleged "false converts" to Catholicism from the Jewish and Muslim faiths were tried, to ensure the religious unity of the country. Beginning with a papal bull, the Inquisition was run like a court, presided over by the Inquisitor-General. However, the defendants were denied counsel, not told the charges facing them and tortured to obtain confessions. Punishment ranged from imprisonment to beheading, hanging or burning at the stake. A formidable system of control, it gave Spain's Protestant enemies a major propaganda weapon by contributing to the *Leyenda Negra* (Black Legend) which lasted, along with the Inquisition, into the 18th century.

A Protestant heretic appears before the royal family, his last chance to repent and convert.

A convicted defendant, forced to wear a red *sanbenito* robe, is led away to prison.

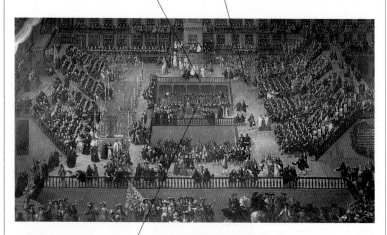

Those who have refused to confess are sentenced in public by day, and then executed before nightfall.

Auto-da-Fé in the Plaza Mayor

This painting by Francisco de Ricci (1683) depicts a trial, or auto-da-fé – literally, "show of faith" – held in Madrid's main square on 30 June 1680. Unlike papal inquisitions elsewhere in Europe, it was presided over by the reigning monarch, Carlos II, accompanied by his queen.

Torture was widely used by the Inquisitors and their assistants to extract confessions from their victims. This early 19th-century German engraving shows a man being roasted on a wheel.

The Procession of the Flagellants (c.1812) by Goya shows the abiding influence of the Inquisition on the popular imagination. The penitents in the picture are wearing the tall conical hats of heretics tried by the Inquisition. These hats can still be seen in Easter Week processions (see p42) throughout Spain.

❺ Iglesia de San Nicolás de Bari

Plaza de San Nicolás 1. **Map** 3 C2. **Tel** 91 559 40 64. Ⓜ Ópera. **Open** 8:30am–1pm, 5:30–8:30pm Mon, 8:30–9:30am, 6:30–8:30pm Tue–Sat, 10am–1:45pm, 6:30–8:45pm Sun. Groups should call in advance.

The first mention of the church of San Nicolás is in a document of 1202. Its brick tower, with horseshoe arches, is the oldest surviving ecclesiastical structure in Madrid. It is thought to be 12th-century Mudéjar in style, and may have originally been the minaret of a Moorish mosque.

❻ Plaza de Oriente

Map 3 C2. Ⓜ Ópera.

During his days as king of Spain, Joseph Bonaparte *(see p67)* carved out this stirrup-shaped space from the jumble of buildings to the east of the Palacio Real *(see pp280–81)*, providing the view of the palace enjoyed today.
   The square was once an important meeting place for state occasions; kings, queens and dictators all made public appearances on the palace balcony. The statues of early kings that stand here were originally intended for the palace roof, but proved too heavy. The equestrian statue of Felipe IV in the centre of the square is by Italian sculptor Pietro Tacca, and

View of the Catedral de la Almudena and the Royal Palace

is based on drawings by Velázquez. Across the square is the imposing Teatro Real, or Teatro de la Ópera, inaugurated in 1850 by Isabel II.

❼ Catedral de la Almudena

Calle Bailén 8–10. **Map** 3 C2. **Tel** 91 542 22 00. Ⓜ Ópera. **Open** 9am–8:30pm daily (10am–9pm Jul & Aug); Museum & Dome: 10am–2:30pm Mon–Sat. 🅿 ♿ ⓦ **catedraldelaalmudena.es**

Dedicated to the city's patron, the cathedral was begun in 1883 and completed over a century later. The Neo-Gothic grey and white façade is similar to that of the Palacio Real, which stands opposite. The crypt houses a 16th-century image of the Virgen de la Almudena. The dome offers grand views of the city.
   Further along the Calle Mayor is the site of archaeological excavations of the remains of Moorish and medieval city walls.
   The first royal wedding took place here between Prince Felipe and Letizia Ortiz in May 2004.

❽ Campo del Moro

Paseo Virgen del Puerto s/n. **Map** 3 A2. **Tel** 91 454 88 00. Ⓜ Ópera, Príncipe Pío. **Open** Oct–Mar: 10am–6pm daily; Apr–Sep: 10am–8pm daily. **Closed** 1 & 6 Jan, 1 & 15 May, 12 Oct, 9 Nov, 24, 25 & 31 Dec and for official functions. ⓦ **patrimonionacional.es**

The Campo del Moro (the "Field of the Moor") is a pleasing park, rising steeply from the Río Manzanares to offer one of the finest views of the Palacio Real *(see pp280–81)*.
   The park has a varied history. In 1109 a Moorish army led by Ali ben Yusuf bivouacked here, hence the name. It went on to become a jousting ground for Christian knights. In the late 19th century it was used as a lavish playground for royal children. Around the same time it was landscaped in what is described as English style, with winding paths, grass and woodland, fountains and statues. It was reopened to the public in 1931 under the Second Republic *(see p69)*, closed again under Franco, and not reopened until 1978.

Equestrian statue of Felipe IV, by Pietro Tacca, Plaza de Oriente

❾ Palacio Real

Madrid's vast and lavish Royal Palace was built to impress. The site, on a high bluff over the Río Manzanares, had been occupied for centuries by a royal fortress, but after a fire in 1734, Felipe V commissioned a truly palatial replacement. Construction lasted 17 years, spanning the reign of two Bourbon monarchs, and much of the exuberant decor reflects the tastes of Carlos III and Carlos IV *(see p75)*. The palace was used as a residence by the royal family until the abdication of Alfonso XIII in 1931 and is still used today for state occasions. A new museum of royal collections, being built next to the palace, is due to open in 2016.

★ Dining Room
This gallery was decorated in 1879. With its chandeliers, ceiling paintings and tapestries, it evokes the grandeur of regal Bourbon entertaining.

★ Porcelain Room
The walls and ceiling of this room, built on the orders of Carlos III, are entirely covered in royal porcelain from the Buen Retiro factory. Most of the porcelain is green and white, and depicts cherubs and wreaths.

First floor

The Hall of Columns, once used for royal banquets, is decorated with 16th-century bronzes and Roman imperial busts.

★ Gasparini Room
Named after its Neapolitan designer, the Gasparini Room is decorated with lavish Rococo chinoiserie. The adjacent antechamber, with painted ceiling and ornate chandelier, houses Goya's portrait of Carlos IV.

Key to Floorplan

- ☐ Exhibition rooms
- ☐ Entrance rooms
- ☐ Carlos III rooms
- ☐ Chapel rooms
- ☐ Carlos IV rooms

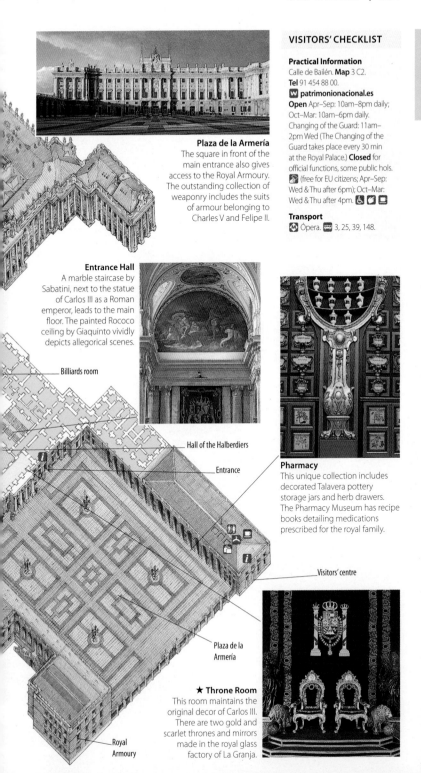

Plaza de la Armería
The square in front of the main entrance also gives access to the Royal Armoury. The outstanding collection of weaponry includes the suits of armour belonging to Charles V and Felipe II.

Entrance Hall
A marble staircase by Sabatini, next to the statue of Carlos III as a Roman emperor, leads to the main floor. The painted Rococo ceiling by Giaquinto vividly depicts allegorical scenes.

Billiards room

Hall of the Halberdiers

Entrance

Pharmacy
This unique collection includes decorated Talavera pottery storage jars and herb drawers. The Pharmacy Museum has recipe books detailing medications prescribed for the royal family.

Visitors' centre

Plaza de la Armería

★ Throne Room
This room maintains the original decor of Carlos III. There are two gold and scarlet thrones and mirrors made in the royal glass factory of La Granja.

Royal Armoury

Entrance to the Convento de la Encarnación

⑩ Monasterio de la Encarnación

Plaza de la Encarnación 1. **Map** 4 D1.
Tel 91 454 88 00. 🚇 Ópera, Santo
Domingo. **Open** 10am–2pm,
4–6:30pm Tue–Sat, 10am–3pm Sun &
public hols. **Closed** 1 & 6 Jan, Easter,
1 & 15 May, 27 Jul, 9 Nov, 24, 25 &
31 Dec. 🎟 (free Wed and Thu after
4pm for EU residents). ♿ 📷
🌐 patrimonionacional.es

Standing in a delightful tree-
shaded square, this tranquil
Augustinian convent was
founded in 1611 for Margaret
of Austria, wife of Felipe III. The
architect, Juan Gómez de Mora,
also built the Plaza Mayor *(see
p277)* and the façade clearly
reveals his work.

Still inhabited by nuns, the
convent has the atmosphere
of old Castile, with its blue and
white Talavera tiles, wooden
doors, exposed beams and
portraits of royal benefactors.
Inside is a collection of
17th-century art, with paintings
by José de Ribera and Vincente
Carducho lining the walls.
Polychromatic wooden statues
include *Cristo Yacente* (*Lying
Christ*), by Gregorio Fernández.

The convent's main attraction
is the reliquary chamber with a
ceiling painted by Carducho. It
is used to store the skulls and
bones of saints. There is also
a phial containing the dried
blood of St Pantaleon. According to a popular myth, the
blood liquefies each year on
27 July, the anniversary of the
saint's death. Should the blood

fail to liquefy, it is said that
disaster will befall Madrid. The
church was rebuilt by Ventura
Rodríguez after a fire in 1767.

⑪ Plaza de España

Map 1 C5. 🚇 Plaza de España.

One of Madrid's busiest traffic
intersections and most popular
meeting places is the Plaza de
España, which slopes down
towards the Palacio Real *(see
pp280–81)* and the Sabatini
Gardens. In the 18th and
19th centuries the square was
occupied by military barracks,
built here because of the
square's close proximity to
the palace. However, further
expansion of Madrid resulted
in its becoming a public space.

The square acquired its
present appearance during the
Franco period *(see pp70–71)*,
with the construction, on the
northern side, of the massive
Edificio España between 1947
and 1953. Across the square
is the Torre de Madrid (1957),
known as *La Jirafa* (The Giraffe),

which, for a while, was the
tallest concrete structure in
the world. The most attractive
part of the square is its centre,
occupied by a massive stone
obelisk built in 1928. In front
of it is a statue of the author
Cervantes *(see p337)*. Below him,
Don Quixote *(see pp398–9)* rides
his horse Rocinante while the
plump Sancho Panza trots
alongside on his donkey. On
the left-hand side is Dulcinea,
Don Quixote's sweetheart.

⑫ Gran Vía

Map 2 D5. 🚇 Plaza de España, Santo
Domingo, Callao, Gran Vía.

A main traffic artery of the
modern city, the Gran Vía
was inaugurated in 1910. Its
construction was executed in
three phases, spanned several
decades and required the
demolition of large numbers of
run-down buildings and small
lanes between the Calle de
Alcalá and the Plaza de España.
This road-building scheme soon
became the subject of a

Stone obelisk with statue of Miguel de Cervantes, Plaza de España

◀ Night-time traffic on the Gran Vía, seen from the Plaza de España

One of the many 1930s buildings lining the Gran Vía

zarzuela – a comic opera – that most madrileño of art forms *(see p326)*. Nowadays, the Gran Vía is at the centre of city life and, following a restoration programme, has become an architectural showpiece.

The most interesting buildings are clustered at the Alcalá end, starting with the Corinthian columns, high-level statuary and tiled dome of the Edificio Metrópolis *(see p288)*.

A temple with Art Nouveau mosaics on its upper levels crowns No. 1 Gran Vía. One striking feature of buildings at this end of the street is colonnaded galleries on the upper floors, imitating medieval Aragonese and Catalan architecture. Another is the fine wrought-iron balconies and carved stone details, such as the gargoyle-like caryatids at No. 12. This part of the Gran Vía has a couple of old-world Spanish shops.

On the Red de San Luis, an intersection of four major roads, is the Telefónica building. The first skyscraper to be erected in the capital, built between 1926 and 1929, it caused a sensation. Beyond here, the Gran Vía becomes much more American in character, with cinemas, tourist shops and many cafés.

Opposite Callao metro station, on the corner of the Calle Jacometrezo, is another well-known building, the Art Deco Capitol cinema, built in the 1930s.

⑬ Monasterio de las Descalzas Reales

Plaza de las Descalzas 3. **Map** 4 E2. **Tel** 91 454 88 00. Ⓜ Sol, Callao. **Open** 10am–2pm, 4–6:30pm Tue–Sat, 10am–3pm Sun & public hols. **Closed** 1 & 6 Jan, Easter, 1 & 15 May, 9 Nov, 24, 25 & 31 Dec. 🎫 🎥 (free Wed & Thu after 4pm for EU residents). Ⓦ **patrimonionacional.es**

Madrid's most notable religious building has a fine exterior in red brick and granite, and one of the few surviving examples of 16th-century architecture.

Around 1560, Felipe II's sister, Doña Juana, decided to convert the original medieval palace which stood here into a convent for nuns and women of the royal household. Her high rank, and that of her fellow nuns, accounts for the massive store of art and wealth of the Descalzas Reales (Royal Barefoot Sisters).

The stairway has a fresco of Felipe IV's family looking down, as if from a balcony, and a fine ceiling by Claudio Coello and his pupils. It leads up to a first-floor cloister, ringed with chapels containing works of art relating to the lives of the former nuns. The main chapel houses Doña Juana's tomb. The Sala de Tapices has a series of tapestries, one woven in 1627 for Felipe II's daughter, Isabel Clara Eugenia. Another,

Decorated chapel, Monasterio de las Descalzas Reales

The Triumph of the Eucharist, is based on cartoons by Rubens. The tapestries hang in the cloister on Good Friday and Corpus Christi. Major paintings on show include works by Brueghel the Elder, Titian and Zurbarán.

Fray Pedro Machado by Zurbarán

⑭ Real Academia de Bellas Artes de San Fernando

Calle Alcalá 13. **Map** 7 A2. **Tel** 91 524 08 64. Ⓜ Sevilla, Sol. **Open** 10am–3pm Tue–Sun. **Closed** some public hols. 🎫 (free Wed). 🎥 by appt. ♿ Ⓦ **realacademiabellas artessanfernando.com/en**

Famous former students of this arts academy, housed in an 18th-century building by Churriguera *(see p29)*, include Dalí and Picasso. Its art gallery's collection includes works such as drawings by Raphael and Titian. Among the old masters are paintings by Rubens and Van Dyck. Spanish artists from the 16th to the 19th centuries are well represented, with works by Ribera, Murillo, El Greco and Velázquez. One of the highlights is Zurbarán's *Fray Pedro Machado*, typical of the artist's paintings of monks.

An entire room is devoted to Goya, a former director of the academy. On show here are his painting of a relaxed Manuel Godoy *(see p66)*, the *Burial of the Sardine (see p43)*, the grim *Madhouse*, and a self-portrait painted in 1815.

BOURBON MADRID

To the east of Old Madrid, there once lay an idyllic district of market gardens known as the Prado, the "Meadow". In the 16th century a monastery was built and later the Habsburgs extended it to form a palace, of which only fragments now remain; the palace gardens are now the popular Parque del Retiro (see p301). The Bourbon monarchs chose this area to expand and embellish the city in the 18th century. They built grand squares with fountains, a triumphal gateway, and what was to become the Museo del Prado, one of the world's greatest art galleries. A more recent addition to the area is the Museo Nacional Centro de Arte Reina Sofía, a collection of modern Spanish and international art.

Sights at a Glance

Historic Buildings
1. Hotel Ritz by Belmond
12. Real Academia de la Historia
13. Teatro Español
14. Ateneo de Madrid
15. Congreso de los Diputados
16. Café Gijón
22. Estación de Atocha

Museums and Galleries
3. Museo Thyssen-Bornemisza pp292–3
6. Biblioteca Nacional de España
7. Museo Nacional de Artes Decorativas
8. Salón de Reinos
10. Museo del Prado pp296–9
11. Casa-Museo de Lope de Vega
19. Museo Arqueológico Nacional
23. Museo Nacional Centro de Arte Reina Sofía pp302–3

Monuments
5. Puerta de Alcalá

Churches
9. Iglesia de San Jerónimo el Real

Streets, Squares and Parks
2. Plaza Cánovas del Castillo
4. Plaza de Cibeles
17. Plaza de Colón
18. Calle de Serrano
20. Parque del Retiro
21. Real Jardín Botánico

See also Madrid Street Finder, maps 5, 6, 7, 8

◀ Memorial to the victims of the 2004 terrorist attacks, Parque del Retiro

For map symbols see back flap

Street-by-Street: Paseo del Prado

In the late 18th century, before the museums and lavish hotels of Bourbon Madrid took shape, the Paseo del Prado was laid out and soon became a fashionable spot for strolling. Today the Paseo's main attraction lies in its museums and art galleries. Most notable are the Museo del Prado (just south of the Plaza Cánovas del Castillo) and the Museo Thyssen-Bornemisza, both displaying world-famous collections. Among the grand monuments built under Carlos III are the Puerta de Alcalá, the Fuente de Neptuno and the Fuente de Cibeles, which stand in the middle of busy roundabouts.

The Paseo del Prado, based on the Piazza Navona in Rome, was built by Carlos III as a centre for the arts and sciences in Madrid.

The Edificio Metrópolis
(see p285), on the corner of Gran Vía and Calle de Alcalá, was built in 1910. Its façade is distinctively Parisian.

❸ ★ **Museo Thyssen-Bornemisza**
This excellent art collection occupies the Neo-Classical Villahermosa Palace, completed in 1806.

Banco de España Metro

Banco de España

❶ **Congreso de los Diputados**
Spain's parliament witnessed the transition from dictatorship to democracy *(see pp72–3)*.

❷ **Plaza de Cánovas del Castillo**
In the middle of this large square stands a sculpted fountain of the god Neptune in his chariot.

Hotel Palace

To Museo del Prado

0 metres 100
0 yards 100

5 ★ Puerta de Alcalá
Sculpted from granite, this former gateway into the city is especially beautiful when floodlit at night.

Palacio de Linares

Palacio de Comunicaciones and City Hall

PLAZA DE LA INDEPENDENCIA

CALLE DE ALCALÁ

PLAZA DE CIBELES

ALFONSO XI

CALLE DE MONTALBAN

CALLE DE ALFONSO XII

CALLE DE

PLAZA DE LA LEALTAD

CALLE ANTONIO MAURA

RUIZ DE ALARCÓN

CALLE FELIPE IV

MORETO

Locator Map
See Madrid Street Finder maps 7, 8

4 ★ Plaza de Cibeles
A fountain with a statue of the Roman goddess Cybele stands in this square.

7 The Museo Nacional de Artes Decorativas
This museum, near the Retiro, was founded in 1912 as a showcase for the Spanish manufacturing industry.

8 Salón de Reinos
The former army museum, this section of the Palacio del Buen Retiro may form part of the Prado Museum.

Casón del Buen Retiro *(see p296)*

1 Hotel Ritz by Belmond
With its *belle époque* interior, this is one of the most elegant hotels in Spain.

The Monumento del Dos de Mayo commemorates the War of Independence against the French *(see p67)*.

Key

— Suggested route

For additional map symbols *see back flap*

❶ Hotel Ritz by Belmond

Plaza de la Lealtad 5. **Map** 7 C3.
Tel 91 701 67 67. 🚇 Banco de España.
📶 ♿ 🅦 ritz.es

A few minutes' walk from the Prado, this hotel is said to be Spain's most extravagant. It was part of the new breed of hotels constructed as luxury accommodation for the wedding guests of Alfonso XIII in 1906.

Its opulence *(see p569)* is reflected in its prices. Each of the 158 rooms is beautifully decorated in a different style, with carpets made by hand at the Real Fábrica de Tapices *(see p310)*.

At the start of the Civil War *(see pp70–71)* the hotel was converted into a hospital, and it was here that the Anarchist leader Buenaventura Durruti died of his wounds in 1936.

The Fuente de Neptuno

❷ Plaza Cánovas del Castillo

Map 7 C3. 🚇 Banco de España.

This busy roundabout is named after Antonio Cánovas del Castillo, one of the leading statesmen of 19th-century Spain *(see p68)*, who was assassinated in 1897.

Dominating the plaza is the Fuente de Neptuno – a fountain with a statue depicting Neptune in his chariot, being pulled by two horses. The statue was designed in 1777 by Ventura Rodríguez as part of Carlos III's scheme to beautify eastern Madrid.

Visitors admiring the works of art in the Museo Thyssen-Bornemisza

❸ Museo Thyssen-Bornemisza

See pp292–3.

❹ Plaza de Cibeles

Map 7 C1. 🚇 Banco de España.
Casa de América exhibition room:
Tel 91 595 48 00. **Open** 11am–8pm
Mon–Sat, 11am–3pm Sun. **Closed**
Aug & public hols. 📷 11am, noon,
1pm Sat & Sun. 🅦 casamerica.es

The Plaza de Cibeles is one of Madrid's best-known and most beautiful landmarks.

The Fuente de Cibeles stands in the middle of the busy traffic island at the junction of the Paseo del Prado and the Calle de Alcalá. This sculpted fountain is named after Cybele, the Greco-Roman goddess of nature, and shows her sitting in her lion-drawn chariot. Designed by José Hermosilla and Ventura Rodríguez in the late 18th century, it is considered a symbol of Madrid. Around the square rise four important buildings. The most impressive are the town hall, where the mayor has his office, and the main post office, the Palacio de Comunicaciones, also home to a cultural centre, CentroCentro. Its appearance – white, with high pinnacles – is often likened to a wedding cake. It was built between 1905 and 1917 on the site of former gardens.

On the northeast side is the stone façade of the Palacio de Linares, built by the Marquis of Linares at the time of the second Bourbon restoration of 1875 *(see p68)*. Once threatened with demolition, the palace was reprieved and converted into the Casa de América, and now hosts art exhibitions by Latin American artists as well as theatrical performances and lectures. Take a break in the palace gardens and try one of Le Cabrera's excellent cocktails *(see p593)*.

In the northwest corner of the Plaza de Cibeles, surrounded by attractive gardens, is the heavily guarded Army Headquarters, which is housed in the buildings of the former Palacio de Buenavista. Commissioned by the Duchess of Alba in 1777, construction was twice delayed by fire.

On the opposite corner is the Banco de España, constructed between 1884 and 1891. Its design was inspired by the Venetian Renaissance style, with delicate ironwork adorning the roof and windows. Much-needed renovation work has returned the bank to its late 19th-century magnificence.

The Fuente de Cibeles, with the Palacio de Linares in the background

Central arch of the Puerta de Alcalá

❼ Museo Nacional de Artes Decorativas

Calle Montalbán 12. **Map** 8 D2.
Tel 91 532 64 99. 🚇 Retiro, Banco de
España. **Open** 9:30am–3pm Tue–Sat
(& 5–8pm Thu), 10am–3pm Sun.
Closed public hols. 🎟 (free Thu pm &
Sun). 📷 Sun (except Jul & Aug).
🌐 **mnartesdecorativas.mecd.es**

Housed in the 19th-century
Palacio de Santoña near the
Parque del Retiro, the National
Museum of Decorative Arts
contains an interesting collection of furniture and objets
d'art. The exhibits are mainly
from Spain and date back as far
as Phoenician times.

There are also some excellent
ceramics from Talavera de
la Reina *(see p390)*, and
ornaments from the Far East.

Refurbishment work may
affect some rooms.

❽ Salón de Reinos

Calle Méndez Núñez 1. **Map** 8 D2.
🚇 Retiro, Banco de España.
Closed for refurbishment.

The Salón de Reinos (Hall
of Kingdoms) is one of the
two remaining parts of the
17th-century Palacio del Buen
Retiro and gets its name from
the shields of the 24 kingdoms
of the Spanish monarchy,
part of the decor supervised
by court painter Velázquez
(see p36). In the time of Felipe
IV, the Salón was used for
diplomatic receptions and
official ceremonies.

Impressive façade of the Salón de Reinos

❺ Puerta de Alcalá

Map 8 D1. 🚇 Retiro.

This ceremonial gateway is
the grandest of the monu-
ments erected by Carlos III
in his attempt to improve the
looks of eastern Madrid. It was
designed by Francesco Sabatini
to replace a smaller Baroque
gateway, which had been built
by Felipe III for the entry into
Madrid of his wife, Margarita
de Austria.

Construction of the gate
began in 1769 and lasted nine
years. It was built from granite
in Neo-Classical style, with a
lofty pediment and sculpted
angels. It has five arches –
three central and two
outer rectangular ones.

Until the mid-19th century
the gateway marked the city's
easternmost boundary. It now
stands in the busy Plaza de la
Independencia, and is best
seen when floodlit at night.

❻ Biblioteca Nacional de España

Paseo de Recoletos 20–22. **Map** 6 D5.
Tel 91 580 78 00. **Open** 9am–9pm
Mon–Sat, 9am–2pm Sun. **Closed**
public hols. 📷 5pm Tue & Fri, noon
Sat. ♿ 🌐 **bne.es**

King Philip V of Spain founded
the National Library in 1712.
Since then, it has been
mandatory for printers to
submit a copy of every book
printed in Spain. Currently
it holds some 28 million
publications, plus a large
number of maps, musical
scores and audiovisual
records. Jewels include a first-
edition *Don Quixote* and two
handwritten codes by da Vinci.

A museum looks at the
history of the library as well
as the evolution of writing,
reading and media systems.
The library also holds regular
exhibitions, talks and concerts.

❸ Museo Thyssen-Bornemisza

This magnificent museum is based on the collection assembled by Baron Heinrich Thyssen-Bornemisza and his son, Hans Heinrich, the preceding baron. In 1992 it was installed in Madrid's 18th-century Villahermosa Palace, and was sold to the nation the following year. From its beginnings in the 1920s, the collection was intended to illustrate the history of Western art, from Italian and Flemish primitives, through to 20th-century Expressionism and Pop Art. The museum's collection, consisting of more than 1,000 paintings, includes masterpieces by Titian, Goya, van Gogh and Picasso. Carmen Thyssen's collection of mainly Impressionist art opened to the public in 2004. It is regarded by many critics as the most important private art collection in the world.

★ **The Virgin of the Dry Tree** (c.1465)
This tiny painted panel is by Bruges master Petrus Christus. The letter A hanging from the tree stands for "Ave Maria".

Hotel Room (1931)
Edward Hopper's painting is a study of urban isolation. The solitude is made less static by the suitcases and the train timetable on the woman's knee.

Key to Floorplan

- ☐ Ground floor
- ☐ First floor
- ☐ Second floor
- ☐ Temporary exhibitions
- ☐ Non-exhibition space

Gallery Guide

The galleries are arranged around a covered central courtyard, which rises the full height of the building. The top floor starts with early Italian art and goes through to the 17th century. The first floor continues the story with 17th-century Dutch works and ends with German Expressionism. The ground floor is dedicated to 20th-century paintings.

★ **Harlequin with a Mirror**
The figure of the harlequin was a frequent subject of Picasso's. The careful composition in this 1923 canvas, which is thought by some to represent the artist himself, is typical of Picasso's "Classical" period.

Portrait of Baron Thyssen-Bornemisza
This informal portrait of the previous baron, against the back-ground of a Watteau painting, was painted by Lucian Freud.

For hotels and restaurants in this area see pp568–9 and pp592–3

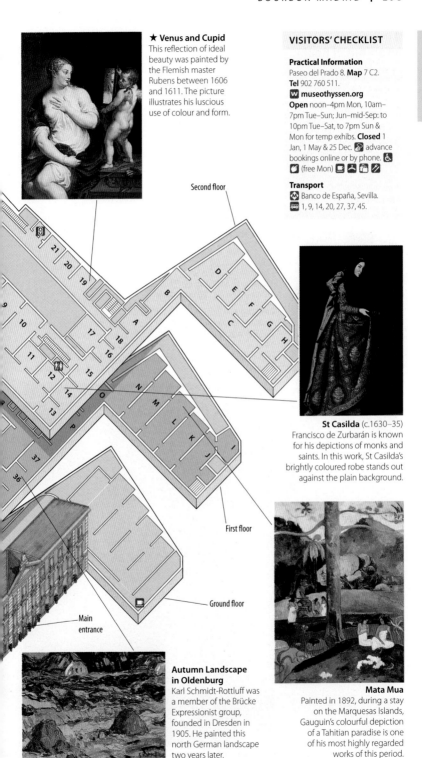

★ Venus and Cupid
This reflection of ideal beauty was painted by the Flemish master Rubens between 1606 and 1611. The picture illustrates his luscious use of colour and form.

VISITORS' CHECKLIST

Practical Information
Paseo del Prado 8. **Map** 7 C2.
Tel 902 760 511.
🆆 museothyssen.org
Open noon–4pm Mon, 10am–7pm Tue–Sun; Jun–mid-Sep: to 10pm Tue–Sat, to 7pm Sun & Mon for temp exhibs. **Closed** 1 Jan, 1 May & 25 Dec. 🦽 advance bookings online or by phone. ♿
🎟 (free Mon) 🔲 📷 🏠 ⃠

Transport
🚇 Banco de España, Sevilla.
🚍 1, 9, 14, 20, 27, 37, 45.

Second floor

First floor

Ground floor

Main entrance

St Casilda (c.1630–35)
Francisco de Zurbarán is known for his depictions of monks and saints. In this work, St Casilda's brightly coloured robe stands out against the plain background.

Autumn Landscape in Oldenburg
Karl Schmidt-Rottluff was a member of the Brücke Expressionist group, founded in Dresden in 1905. He painted this north German landscape two years later.

Mata Mua
Painted in 1892, during a stay on the Marquesas Islands, Gauguin's colourful depiction of a Tahitian paradise is one of his most highly regarded works of this period.

❾ Iglesia de San Jerónimo el Real

Calle del Moreto 4. **Map** 8 D3.
Tel 91 420 30 78. Ⓜ Banco de España.
Open 10am–1pm, 5–8pm Mon–Fri
(Apr–Sep: 6–8pm); weekends: open
for ceremonies. ♿

Built in the 16th century for
Queen Isabel, but since
remodelled, San Jerónimo is
Madrid's royal church. From the
17th century it became virtually
a part of the Retiro palace which
once stood here (see p301). The

Castizos during San Isidro

Madrid's Fiestas

San Isidro (15 May). Madrid's
great party around 15 May
is in honour of St Isidore,
the humble 12th-century
farmworker who became the
city's patron. With a *corrida*
every day, this is Spain's
biggest bullfighting event.
Throughout the city there are
also art exhibitions, open-air
concerts and fireworks.
Many people dress in *castizo*
(see p306) folk costume
for the occasion.
The Passion (Easter
Saturday), Chinchón. A
passion play is performed
in the town's atmospheric
arcaded Plaza Mayor.
Dos de Mayo (2 May). This
holiday marks the city's
uprising against Napoleon's
troops in 1808 (see p67).
New Year's Eve. The nation
focuses on the Puerta del
Sol (see p276) at midnight
as crowds gather to swallow
a grape on each chime
of the clock.

church was originally attached
to the Hieronymite monastery.
The cloister and part of the
atrium now form part of a
building at the Prado Museum.

The marriage of Alfonso XIII
and Victoria Eugenia of Batten-
berg took place here in 1906,
as did King Juan Carlos I's
coronation in 1975.

❿ Museo del Prado

See pp296–9.

⓫ Casa-Museo de Lope de Vega

Calle Cervantes 11. **Map** 7 B3.
Tel 91 429 92 16. Ⓜ Antón Martín.
Open 10am–6pm Tue–Sun.
Closed some public hols. 📷 📹 only
(available in English). 🆆 madrid.org

Félix Lope de Vega, a leading
Golden Age writer (see p38),
moved into this house in 1610.
Here he wrote over two-thirds
of his plays, thought to total
almost 1,000. Meticulously

Félix Lope de Vega

restored in 1935 using
some of Lope de Vega's own
furniture, the house gives a
great feeling of Castilian life
in the early 17th century. A
dark chapel with no external
windows occupies the centre,
separated from the writer's
bedroom by only a barred
window. The small garden
at the rear is planted with
the flowers and fruit trees
mentioned by the writer in
his works. He died here in 1635.

Statue of Goya in front of the Prado

Sunlit balcony of the magnificent Teatro Español

⑫ Real Academia de la Historia

Calle León 21. **Map** 7 A3.
Tel 91 429 06 11. 🚇 Antón Martín.
✉ **Closed** to the public. 🌐 rah.es

The Royal Academy of History is an austere brick building built by Juan de Villanueva in 1788. Its location, in the so-called Barrio de las Letras (Writers' Quarter), is apt.

In 1898, the intellectual and bibliophile, Marcelino Menéndez Pelayo, became director of the academy, living here until his death in 1912. The library holds more than 200,000 books.

The building is closed to the public and can only be viewed from the outside.

⑬ Teatro Español

Calle del Príncipe 25. **Map** 7 A3.
Tel 91 360 14 80. 🚇 Sol, Sevilla.
Open performances from 7pm Tue–Sun. 🎭 ♿ 🌐 teatroespanol.es

Dominating the Plaza Santa Ana is the Teatro Español, one of Madrid's oldest and most beautiful theatres. From 1583 many of Spain's finest plays, by leading dramatists of the time such as Lope de Rueda, were first performed in the Corral del Príncipe, which originally stood on this site. In 1802 this was replaced by the Teatro Español. The Neo-Classical façade, with pilasters and medallions, is by Juan de Villanueva. Engraved

on it are the names of great Spanish dramatists, including that of celebrated writer Federico García Lorca (see p39).

⑭ Ateneo de Madrid

Calle del Prado 21. **Map** 7 B3.
Tel 91 429 17 50. 🚇 Antón Martín, Sevilla. **Open** by appt 10am–1pm Mon–Fri; Library: 9am–12:45am Mon–Sat, 9am–9:45pm Sun. 📷 only.
🌐 ateneodemadrid.com

Formally founded in 1835, this learned association is similar to a gentlemen's club in atmosphere, with a grand stairway and panelled hall hung with the portraits of famous fellows. Closed down during past periods of repression and dictatorship, it is a mainstay of liberal thought in Spain. Many leading Socialists are members, along with writers and other Spanish intellectuals.

Carving on the façade of the Ateneo de Madrid

⑮ Congreso de los Diputados

Plaza de las Cortes. **Map** 7 B2.
Tel 91 390 65 25. 🚇 Sevilla.
Open 9am–2:30pm Mon & Fri (also July), 10:30am–12:30pm Sat. 📷 ♿
🌐 congreso.es

This imposing yet attractive building is home to the Spanish parliament, the Cortes. Built in the mid-19th century, it is characterized by Classical columns, heavy pediments and guardian bronze lions. It was here, in 1981, that Colonel Tejero of the Civil Guard held the deputies at gunpoint on national television, as he tried to spark off a military coup (see p72). His failure was seen as an indication that democracy was now firmly established in Spain.

Bronze lion guarding the Cortes

⑯ Café Gijón

Paseo de Recoletos 21. **Map** 5 C5.
Tel 91 521 54 25. 🚇 Banco de España.
Open 7:30am–1:30am Mon–Fri, 8am–2am Sat & public hols, 8am–1:30am Sun. ♿ 🌐 cafegijon.com

Madrid's café life (see pp324–5) was one of the most attractive features of the city from the turn of the 20th century, right up to the outbreak of the Civil War. Of the many intellectuals' cafés which once thrived, only the Gijón survives. Today the café continues to attract a lively crowd of literati. With its cream-painted wrought-iron columns and black and white tabletops, it is perhaps better known for its atmosphere and emanating history than for its appearance.

⑩ Museo del Prado

The Prado Museum contains the world's greatest assembly of Spanish painting – especially works by Velázquez and Goya – ranging from the 12th to 19th centuries. It also houses impressive foreign collections, particularly of Italian and Flemish works. The Neo-Classical building was designed in 1785 by Juan de Villanueva on the orders of Carlos III, and it opened as a museum in 1819. The Spanish architect Rafael Moneo has constructed a new building, over the adjacent church's cloister, where the temporary exhibitions are located. The Casón del Buen Retiro, now the Prado library, can be visited with a guided tour on Sundays.

★ Velázquez Collection
The Triumph of Bacchus (1629), Velázquez's first portrayal of a mythological subject, shows the god of wine (Bacchus) with a group of drunkards.

Second floor

The Martyrdom of St Philip
(c.1639) José de Ribera was influenced by Caravaggio's dramatic use of light and shadow, known as chiaroscuro, as seen in this work.

The Adoration of the Shepherds (1612–14)
This dramatic work shows the elongated figures and swirling garments typical of El Greco's style. It was painted during his late Mannerist period for his own funerary chapel.

First floor

Ticket office

Goya entrance (upstairs)

The Garden of Delights (c.1505) Hieronymus Bosch (El Bosco in Spanish), one of Felipe II's favourite artists, is especially well represented in the Prado. This enigmatic painting depicts Paradise and Hell.

Key to Floorplan

- ▢ Spanish painting
- ▢ Flemish and Dutch painting
- ▢ Italian painting
- ▢ French painting
- ▢ German painting
- ▢ British painting
- ▣ Sculpture
- ▣ Decorative arts
- ▢ Non-exhibition space

The Three Graces (c.1635)
This was one of the last paintings by the Flemish master Rubens, and was part of his own collection. The women dancing in a ring the Graces – are the daughters of Zeus, and represent Love, Joy and Revelry.

Ground
floor

★ **Goya Collection**
In *The Clothed Maja* and *The Naked Maja* (both c.1800), Goya tackled the taboo subject of nudity, for which he was later accused of obscenity.

Murillo
entrance

The Dolphin's Treasure is a spectacular collection of decorative objects from the 16th and 17th centuries.

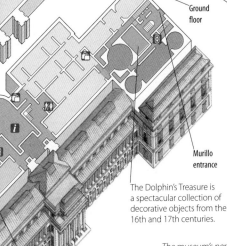

Velázquez
entrance

Gallery Guide

The museum's permanent collection is arranged chronologically over three main floors. Classical sculpture is on the ground floor, Velázquez on the first floor, and the extensive Goya collection across the Murillo side of all three floors. The permanent collection is accessed via the Velázquez and Goya entrances. Visitors to the temporary exhibitions should use the Jerónimos entrance.

The Annunciation
Fra Angelico's work of c.1425–8 is a high point of Italy's early Renaissance, as illustrated by the detailed architectural setting.

Casón del
Buen Retiro
Jerónimos
Building
Underground link
Villanueva Building
CALLE DE MORETO
Jerónimos
entrance
CALLE DE FELIPE IV
PASEO DEL PRADO

Changes at the Prado

The Jerónimos Building houses temporary exhibitions and Renaissance sculptures, as well as a shop, restaurant, café, auditorium and cloakroom. In the future the Salón de Reinos *(see p291)* may also become part of the Prado.

Museum buildings

Exploring the Prado's Collection

The importance of the Prado is founded on its royal collections. The wealth of foreign art, including many of Europe's finest works, reflects the historical power of the Spanish crown. The Low Countries and parts of Italy were under Spanish domination for centuries. The 18th century was an era of French influence, following the Bourbon accession to the Spanish throne. The Prado is worthy of repeated visits, but if you go only once, see the Spanish works of the 17th century.

St Dominic of Silos Enthroned as Abbot (1474–7) by Bermejo

Spanish Painting

Right up to the 19th century, Spanish painting focused on religious and royal themes. Although the limited subject matter was in some ways a restriction, it also offered a sharp focus that seems to have suited Spanish painters.

Spain's early medieval art is represented somewhat sketchily in the Prado, but there are some examples, such as the anonymous mural paintings from the Holy Cross hermitage in Maderuelo, which show a Romanesque heaviness of line and forceful characterization.

Spanish Gothic art can be seen in the Prado in the works of Bartolomé Bermejo and Fernando Gallego. The sense of realism in their paintings was borrowed from Flemish masters of the time.

Renaissance features began to emerge in the works of painters such as Pedro de Berruguete, whose auto-da-fé is both chilling and lively. St Catherine, by Fernando Yáñez de la Almedina, shows the influence of Leonardo da Vinci, for whom Yáñez probably worked while training in Italy.

What is often considered as a truly Spanish style – with its highly wrought emotion and deepening sombreness – first started to emerge in the 16th century in the paintings of the Mannerists. This is evident in Pedro Machuca's fierce *Descent from the Cross* and in the *Madonnas* of Luis de Morales, "the Divine". The elongation of the human figure in Morales' work is carried to a greater extreme by Domenikos Theotocopoulos, who is better known as El Greco *(see p395)*. Although many of his master-pieces remain in his adopted town of Toledo, the Prado has

Saturn Devouring One of his Sons (1820–23) by Francisco de Goya

an impressive collection, including *The Nobleman with his Hand on his Chest*.

The Golden Age of the 17th century was a productive time for Spanish art. José de Ribera, who lived in (Spanish) Naples, followed Caravaggio in comb-ining realism of character with the techniques of chiaroscuro (use of light and dark) and tenebrism (large areas of dark colours, with a shaft of light). Another master who used this method was Francisco Ribalta, whose *Christ Embracing St Bernard* is here. Zurbarán, known for still lifes and portraits of saints and monks, is also represented in the Prado.

This period, however, is best represented by the work of Diego de Velázquez. As Spain's leading court painter from his late twenties until his death, he produced scenes of heightened realism, royal portraits, and religious and mythological paintings. Examples of his art are displayed in the Prado. His greatest work is perhaps *Las Meninas (see p36)*, in Room 12.

Another great Spanish painter, Goya, revived Spanish art in the 18th century. He first specialized in cartoons for tapestries, then became a court painter. His work went on to embrace the horrors of war, as seen in *The 3rd of May in Madrid (see p67)*, and culminated in a sombre series known as *The Black Paintings*.

Still Life with Four Vessels (c.1658–64) by Francisco de Zurbarán

Flemish and Dutch Painting

Spain's long connection with the Low Countries naturally resulted in an intense admiration for the so-called Flemish primitives. Many exceptional examples of Flemish and Dutch art now hang in the Prado. *St Barbara*, by Robert Campin, has a quirky intimacy, while Rogier van der Weyden's *The Descent from the Cross* is an unquestioned masterpiece. Most notable of all, however, are Hieronymus Bosch's weird and eloquent inventions. The Prado has some of his major paintings, including *The Temptation of St Anthony* and *The Haywain*. Works from the 16th century include *The Triumph of Death* by Bruegel the Elder. There are nearly 100 canvases by the 17th-century Flemish painter Peter Paul Rubens, including *The Adoration of the Magi*. The most notable Dutch painting on display is Rembrandt's *Artemisia*, a portrait of the artist's wife. Other Flemish and Dutch artists featured at the Prado are Antonis Moor, Anton Van Dyck and Jacob Jordaens, considered one of the finest portrait painters of the 17th century.

Italian Painting

The Prado is the envy of many museums, not least for its vast collection of Italian paintings. Botticelli's dramatic wooden panels telling *The Story of Nastagio degli Onesti*, a vision of a knight forever condemned to hunt down and kill his own beloved, were

David Victorious over Goliath (c.1600) by Caravaggio

commissioned by two rich Florentine families and are a sinister high point.

Raphael contributes the superb *Christ Falls on the Way to Calvary* and the sentimental *The Holy Family of the Lamb. Christ Washing the Disciples' Feet*, an early work by Tintoretto, is a profound masterpiece and reveals the painter's brilliant handling of perspective.

Caravaggio had a profound impact on Spanish artists, who admired his characteristic handling of light, as seen in *David Victorious over Goliath*. Venetian masters Veronese and Titian are also very well represented. Titian served as court painter to Charles V, and few works express the drama of Habsburg rule so deeply as his sombre painting *The Emperor Charles V at Mühlberg*. Also on display are works by Giordano and Tiepolo, the master of Italian Rococo, who painted *The Immaculate Conception* as part of a series intended for a church in Aranjuez.

French Painting

Marriages between French and Spanish royalty in the 17th century, culminating in the Bourbon accession to the throne in the 18th century, brought French art to Spain. The Prado has eight works attributed to Poussin, among them his serene *St Cecilia* and *Landscape with St Jerome*. The magnificent *Landscape with the Embarkation of St Paula Romana at Ostia* is the best work here by Claude Lorrain. Among the 18th-century artists featured are Antoine Watteau and Jean Ranc. *Felipe V* is the work of the royal portraitist Louis-Michel van Loo.

St Cecilia (c.1635) by the French artist Nicolas Poussin

German Painting

Although German art is not especially well represented in the Prado, there are a number of paintings by Albrecht Dürer, including his classical depictions of Adam and Eve. His lively *Self-Portrait* of 1498, painted at the age of 26, is undoubtedly the highlight of the small but valuable German collection in the museum. Lucas Cranach is also featured and works by the late 18th-century painter Anton Raffael Mengs include some magnificent portraits of Carlos III.

The Descent from the Cross (c.1430) by Rogier van der Weyden

One of the many Roman mosaics at the Museo Arqueológico Nacional

⑰ Plaza de Colón

Map 6 D5. 🔼 Serrano, Colón.
Teatro Fernán Gómez Centro
de Arte: **Tel** 91 436 25 40.
🌐 teatrofernangomez.com

This large square, one of
Madrid's undisputed focal
points, is dedicated to 15th-
century explorer Christopher
Columbus (Colón in Spanish).

It is overlooked by huge
tower blocks, built in the 1970s
to replace the 19th-century
mansions which stood here.

On the south side of the
square is a palace housing
the National Library and
Archaeological Museum.
The Post-Modernist
skyscraper of the Heron
Corporation towers over
the Plaza de Colón from
the far side of the Paseo
de la Castellana.

The real feature of the
square, however, is the pair
of monuments dedicated
to the discoverer of the
Americas. The prettiest,
and oldest, is a Neo-Gothic
spire erected in 1885, with
Columbus at its top, pointing west. Carved reliefs on
the plinth give highlights of
his discoveries. Across the
square is the second, more
modern monument –
a cluster of four large
concrete shapes
inscribed with
quotations about
Columbus's journey
to America (see p61).

Constantly busy with
traffic, the plaza may
seem an unlikely venue
for cultural events.

Beneath it, however, is
an extensive complex,
the Teatro Fernán Gómez
Centro de Arte. Formerly
known as the Centro
Cultural de la Villa, this
centre is now named after
the Spanish cinema and
theatre actor, director and
writer Fernando Fernán
Gómez, who died in
Madrid in 2007. Exhibitions
are held in its prestigious
halls. The complex also
includes lecture rooms,
a theatre and a café.

⑱ Calle de Serrano

Map 8 D1. 🔼 Serrano.

Named after the 19th-century
politician Francisco Serrano y
Dominguez, Madrid's smartest
shopping street runs north
from the Plaza de la
Independencia, in the district
of Salamanca, to the Plaza
del Ecuador, in the district
of El Viso. Calle de Serrano is
lined with attractive shops
(p320) – many specializing
in expensive luxury items –
housed in old-fashioned
mansion blocks. Several
of the country's top
designers, including
Adolfo Domínguez and
Purificación García, have
boutiques towards the
north, near the ABC
Serrano (see p321) and the
Museo Lázaro Galdiano (see
p309). Branches of the Italian
shops Versace, Gucci and
Armani, as well as the
French Chanel, can be
found on the Calle de José
Ortega y Gasset. Lower
down the Calle de Serrano,
towards Serrano metro
station, are two branches
of Spain's famous depart-
ment store El Corte Inglés.

On the Calle de Claudio
Coello, which runs
parallel with Serrano,
there are several lavish
antique shops, in
keeping with the
area's upmarket
atmosphere. Under
Juan Bravo's bridge
is the **Museo de Arte**

Statue of Columbus,
Plaza de Colón

Público de Madrid, an open-
air sculpture museum (Paseo
de la Castellana 40).

⑲ Museo Arqueológico Nacional

Calle Serrano 13. **Map** 6 D5.
Tel 91 577 79 12. 🔼 Serrano.
🚌 5, 14, 21, 27, 45. **Open** 9:30am–
8pm Tue–Sat, 9:30am–3pm Sun.
🌐 man.es

Founded by Isabel II in 1867,
Madrid's archaeological
museum, which recently
reopened after extensive and
impressive restoration work,
houses a collection that consists
mainly of material uncovered
during excavations all over Spain,
as well as important pieces from
Egypt, ancient Greece and the
Etruscan civilization.

Highlights of the earliest finds
include an exhibition on the
ancient civilization of El Argar
in Andalusia (see p52), and a
display of jewellery uncovered
at the Roman settlement of
Numantia, near Soria (see p381).

Other exhibited pieces are
devoted to the period between
Roman and Mudéjar Spain.
Iberian culture is also represented, with two notable funerary
sculptures – La Dama de Elche
(see p52) and La Dama de Baza.
The Roman period is illustrated
with some impressive mosaics,
including one from the 3rd
century. The underside of
this 1,800-year-old work
shows a combat between two
gladiators, Simmachius and
Maternus; the upper register
displays Simmachius' victory.

Outstanding pieces from the
Visigothic period include several
splendid 7th-century gold votive
crowns from Toledo province.

On show from the Islamic
era is well-preserved pottery
uncovered from Medina
Azahara in Andalusia (see
p481) and metal objects.

Romanesque exhibits at
the museum include an ivory
crucifix carved in 1063 for
Fernando I of Castilla-León,
and the Madonna and Child
from Sahagún, considered
a masterpiece of Spanish art.

⓴ Parque del Retiro

Map 8 E3. **Tel** 91 530 00 41. 🚇 Retiro, Ibiza, Atocha. **Open** 6am–10pm (Apr–Oct: 6am–midnight). ♿

The Retiro Park, in Madrid's smart Jerónimos district, takes its name from Felipe IV's royal palace complex, which once stood here. Today, all that is left of the palace is the **Casón del Buen Retiro** *(see p296)* and the **Salón de Reinos** *(see p291)*.

Used privately by the royal family from 1632, the park became the scene of elaborate pageants, bullfights and mock naval battles. In the 18th century it was partially opened to the public, provided visitors were formally dressed, and in 1869 it was fully opened. Today, the Retiro remains one of the most popular places for relaxing in Madrid.

A short stroll from the park's northern entrance down the tree-lined avenue leads to the pleasure lake, where rowing boats can be hired. On one side of the lake is a half-moon colonnade in front of which an equestrian statue of Alfonso XII rides high on a column. Opposite, portrait painters and fortune-tellers ply their trade.

To the south of the lake are two palaces. The Neo-Classical **Palacio de Velázquez** and the **Palacio de Cristal** (Crystal Palace) were built by Velázquez Bosco in 1883 and 1887 respectively and regularly hold contemporary art exhibitions.

Statue of Bourbon King Carlos III in the Real Jardín Botánico

㉑ Real Jardín Botánico

Plaza de Murillo 2. **Map** 8 D4. **Tel** 91 420 30 17. 🚇 Atocha, Banco de España. **Open** 10am–dusk daily. **Closed** 1 Jan, 25 Dec. ♿ ♿ 🌐 **rjb.csic.es**

South of the Prado *(see pp296–9)*, and a suitable place for resting after visiting the gallery, are the Royal Botanical Gardens. Inspired by Carlos III, they were designed in 1781 by Gómez Ortega, Francesco Sabatini and Juan de Villanueva, architect of the Prado.

Interest in the plants of South America and the Philippines took hold during the Spanish Enlightenment *(see p66)*, and the neatly laid out beds offer a huge variety of flora, ranging from trees to herbs.

㉒ Estación de Atocha

Plaza del Emperador Carlos V. **Map** 8 D5. **Tel**: 902 24 02 02. 🚇 Atocha RENFE. **Open** 5am–1am daily. ♿ 🌐 **renfe.com**

Madrid's first railway service, from Atocha to Aranjuez, was inaugurated in 1851. Forty years later Atocha station was replaced by a new building, which was extended in the 1980s. The older part, built of glass and wrought iron, now houses an indoor palm garden. Next to it is the terminus for high-speed AVE trains to Seville, Toledo, Córdoba, Zaragoza, Lleida, Barcelona, Málaga, Valencia, Valladollid and France *(see p628)*.

The Ministerio de Agricultura, opposite, is a splendid late 19th-century building.

Entrance of Madrid's Estación de Atocha, busy with travellers

Monument of Alfonso XII (1901), facing the Retiro's boating lake

㉓ Museo Nacional Centro de Arte Reina Sofía

The highlight of this museum, commonly referred to as the Museo Reina Sofía, of 20th-century art is Picasso's *Guernica*. There are, however, other major works by influential artists, including Miró and Dalí. The collection is housed in Madrid's former General Hospital, built in the late 18th century. Major extensions, designed by Jean Nouvel, were inaugurated in 2005. The Nouvel Building includes the Collection 3: From Revolt to Postmodernity, a library, a bookshop, a café and auditoriums that host various events such as film screenings, lectures and concerts.

Portrait II (1938)
Joan Miró's huge work shows elements of Surrealism, but was painted more than 10 years after his true Surrealist period ended.

Nouvel building

★ **Woman in Blue** (1901)
Picasso disowned this work after it won only an honourable mention in a national competition. Decades later it was located and acquired by the Spanish state.

Landscape at Cadaqués
Salvador Dalí was born in Figueres in Catalonia. He became a frequent visitor to the town of Cadaqués, on the Costa Brava *(see p220–21)*, where he painted this landscape in the summer of 1923.

Key to Floorplan

☐ Exhibition space

▨ Non-exhibition space

Self-Portrait (Accident)
Alfonso Ponce de León's disturbing work, painted in 1936, prefigured his death in a car crash later that same year.

★ **The Gathering at Pombo Café** (1920)
José Gutiérrez Solana depicts a gathering of
intellectuals *(tertulia)* in a famous café in
Madrid, which no longer exists.

Glass lift

Entrance

VISITORS' CHECKLIST

Practical Information
Calle Santa Isabel 52. **Map** 7 C5.
Tel 91 774 10 00.
🌐 **museoreinasofia.es**
Open 10am–9pm Mon, Wed–
Sat, 10am–2:30pm Sun. **Closed** 1
& 6 Jan, 1 & 15 May, 9 Nov, 24, 25
& 31 Dec, some pub hols. 🅿
(free after 7pm Mon, Wed–Sat).
🚫♿📷🚭🍽🛗🛍🎧

Transport
Ⓜ Atocha. 🚌 6, 14, 19, 27,
45, 55, 86.

Gallery Guide

*The permanent collection is in
the Sabatini Building. Collection 1
on the second floor displays
works dating from 1900 to 1945,
and includes rooms dedicated
to important movements such
as Cubism and Surrealism;
Collection 2 on the fourth floor
has works dating from 1945 to
1968, including representatives
of Pop Art, Minimalism and
more recent tendencies.
Collection 3: From Revolt to
Postmodernity (1962–1982) is
located in the Nouvel Building.*

Visitors admiring *Guernica*

★ Picasso's Guernica

The most famous single work of the 20th
century, this Civil War protest painting *(see
pp70–71)* was commissioned by the Spanish
Republican government in 1937 for a Paris
exhibition. The artist found his inspiration in
the mass air attack of the same year on the
Basque town of Gernika-Lumo *(see pp122–3)*,
by German pilots flying for the Nationalist air
force. The painting hung in a New York
gallery until 1981, reflecting the artist's wish
that it should not return to Spain until
democracy was re-established. It was
moved here from the Prado in 1992.

Toki-Egin (Homenaje a San Juan de la Cruz) (1990)
In his abstract sculptures, Eduardo Chillida used a variety of
materials, such as wood, iron and steel, to convey strength.

FURTHER AFIELD

Several of Madrid's best sights, including some interesting but little-known museums, lie outside the city centre. The axis of modern Madrid is the Paseo de la Castellana, a long, wide avenue lined by skyscraper offices and busy with traffic. A journey along it gives a glimpse of Madrid as Spain's commercial and administrative capital. La Castellana skirts the Barrio de Salamanca, an upmarket district of stylish boutiques, named after the 19th-century aristocrat who built it, the Marquis de Salamanca. The districts around Old Madrid, especially Malasaña and La Latina, offer a more typically authentic *madrileño* atmosphere. On Sundays, some of the old streets are crowded with bargain hunters at the sprawling second-hand market, El Rastro. If you need to escape from the bustle of the city for a while, west of Old Madrid, across the Río Manzanares, is Madrid's vast, green recreation ground, the Casa de Campo, with its pleasant pine woods, boating lake, amusement park and zoo.

Sights at a Glance

Historic Buildings
6 Templo de Debod
9 Palacio de Liria
16 Real Fábrica de Tapices

Churches and Convents
5 Ermita de San Antonio de la Florida

Museums and Galleries
7 Museo de América
8 Museo Cerralbo
11 Museo de Historia de Madrid
12 Museo Sorolla
13 Museo Lázaro Galdiano

Streets, Squares and Parks
1 El Rastro
2 La Latina
3 Plaza de la Paja
4 Casa de Campo
10 Malasaña
14 Paseo de la Castellana
15 Plaza de Toros de Las Ventas
17 Parque de El Capricho

Key
▨ Madrid city centre
▢ Parks and open spaces
═ Motorway
▬ Major road
═ Minor road

0 kilometres ⸻ 2
0 miles ⸻ 1

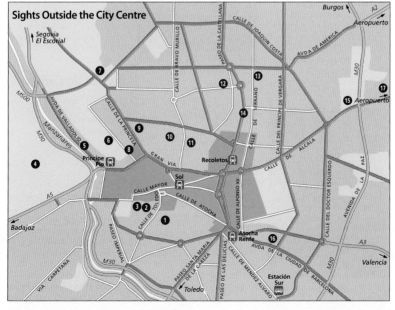

Sights Outside the City Centre

◀ Detail of the Plaza de Toros, with its ornate tilework decoration

For additional map symbols *see back flap*

❶ El Rastro

Calle Ribera de Curtidores. **Map** 4 E4.
🚇 La Latina, Tirso de Molina.
Open 10am–3pm Sun & public hols.

Madrid's celebrated flea market
(see p321), established in the
Middle Ages, has its hub in
the Plaza de Cascorro and
sprawls downhill towards the
Río Manzanares. The main street
is the Calle Ribera de Curtidores,
or "Tanners' Riverbank", once the
centre of the slaughterhouse
and tanning industry.

Although some people claim
that the Rastro has changed
a great deal since its heyday
during the 19th century, there
are still plenty of madrileños, as
well as tourists, who shop here.
They come in search of a bargain
from the stalls which sell a huge
range of wares – anything from
new furniture to second-hand
clothes. The wide range of
goods and the lively crowds in
the Rastro make it an ideal way
to spend a Sunday morning. It is
also worth making a stop at the
Galerías Piquer (Calle Ribera de
Curtidores 29) and the Plaza
General Vara del Rey.

The Calle de Embajadores is
the market's other main street.
It runs down past the Baroque
façade of the Iglesia de San
Cayetano, designed by José
Churriguera and Pedro de
Ribera. Its interior has been
restored since fire destroyed
it during the Civil War.

Further along the street is the
former Real Fábrica de Tabacos
(the Royal Tobacco Factory), begun
as a state enterprise in 1809. It is
partly occupied by an unofficial
and alternative cultural centre.

❷ La Latina

Map 4 D4. 🚇 La Latina.

The district of La Latina, together
with the adjacent Lavapiés, is
considered to be the heart of
castizo Madrid. This term is used
to describe the culture of the traditional working classes of Madrid
– that of the true madrileño.

La Latina runs along the city's
southern hillside from the Plaza
Puerta de Moros, southwards
through the streets where the
Rastro is held. To the east it
merges with Lavapiés. La Latina's
steep streets are lined with tall,
narrow houses, renovated to
form an attractive neighbourhood. There are old-fashioned
and trendy bars around the
Plaza del Humilladero as well
as in the Lavapiés district.

Bottles of wine for sale in an old-style bar
in Lavapiés

❸ Plaza de la Paja

Map 4 D3. 🚇 La Latina.

Once the focus of medieval
Madrid, the area around the
Plaza de la Paja – literally
Straw Square – is extremely
atmospheric and many
interesting buildings are
located on the square.

Climbing upwards from the
Calle de Segovia, a glimpse
left along the Calle Príncipe
Anglona yields a view of the
Mudéjar-style brick tower
of the Iglesia de San Pedro,
dating from the 14th century.

Interior of San Francisco el Grande

Up past the fountain, the Plaza
de la Paja ends with the harsh
stone walls of the Capilla del
Obispo, or Bishop's Chapel,
belonging originally to the
adjoining Palacio Vargas. The
superb Plateresque altarpiece
is by Francisco Giralte. Up to
the left, the Baroque, cherub-
covered dome of the Iglesia
de San Andrés stands out.

Nearby is a small cluster of
interlinked squares, ending in
the Plaza Puerta de Moros, a
reminder of the Muslim community which once occupied
the area. From here, a right turn
leads to the domed bulk of
San Francisco el Grande, an
impressive landmark. Inside the
church is a painting by Goya
and his brother-in-law Francisco
Bayeu. The choirstalls were
moved here from the monastery
of El Paular (see pp332–3).

❹ Casa de Campo

Avenida de Portugal. **Tel** 91 463 63 34.
🚇 Batán, Lago, Príncipe Pío, Casa de
Campo. **Closed** partially to cars.
🅦 esmadrid.com

This former royal hunting
ground, stretching over 1,740 ha
(4,300 acres), lies in southwestern Madrid. Its wide range of
amenities make it a popular
daytime recreation area. Attractions include a boating lake, a
zoo, and an amusement park –
the Parque de Atracciones.
Sports enthusiasts can make
use of the swimming pool and
jogging track. In the summer
the park is also used as a venue
for rock concerts.

Some of the curios on display at the Rastro
flea market

engineers involved in the project. The temple is carved with shallow reliefs, and stands in a line with two of its original three gates on high ground above the Río Manzanares, in the gardens of the Parque del Oeste. From the park there are sweeping views over the Casa de Campo to the Guadarrama mountains.

The park is the site of the former Montaña barracks, which were stormed by the populace at the start of the Civil War in 1936. Further west, below the brow of the hill, is an attractive rose garden.

Egyptian temple of Debod, with two of its original gateways

⑦ Museo de América

Avenida de los Reyes Católicos 6. **Tel** 91 549 26 41. Ⓜ Moncloa. **Open** 9:30am–3pm Tue–Sat (to 7pm Thu), 10am–3pm Sun. **Closed** some public hols. 🅿️ (free Sun). ♿ 📷 by appt. 🌐 **museodeamerica.mcu.es**

This museum houses artifacts related to Spain's colonization of parts of the Americas. Many of the exhibits, which range from prehistoric times to the present, were brought back to Europe by early explorers of the New World (see pp62–3).

The collection is arranged on the first and second floors, and individual rooms are given a cultural theme such as society, communication and religion. There is documentation of the Atlantic voyages by the first explorers, and examples of the objects which they found. The highlight of the museum is perhaps a war helmet belonging to the Tlingit people of North America. It depicts a wolf, the lineage motif and protector spirit, and was worn as a symbol of power and strength during battle. Also worth seeing are the solid gold funereal ornaments from Colombia, the Treasure of the Quimbayas (AD 500–1000), and the collection of contemporary folk art from some of Spain's former American colonies.

⑤ Ermita de San Antonio de la Florida

Glorieta San Antonio de la Florida 5. **Tel** 91 547 79 37. Ⓜ Príncipe Pío. **Open** 9:30am–8pm Tue–Sun. **Closed** public hols. 🅿️ ♿ 🌐 **esmadrid.com**

Goya enthusiasts should not miss a visit to the Neo-Classical Ermita de San Antonio de la Florida, built during the reign of Carlos IV. The present church stands on the site of two previous ones, and is dedicated to St Anthony. It is named after the pastureland of la Florida, on which the original church was built.

Goya took four months, in 1798, to paint the cupola. It depicts the resurrection of a murdered man who rises in order to prove the innocence of the falsely accused father of St Anthony. The characters in it are everyday people of the late 18th century: lurking, low-life types and lively *majas* (see p297)

– shrewd but elegant women. The fresco is considered by many art critics to be among Goya's finest works.

Goya's tomb is housed in the chapel. His remains were brought here from Bordeaux, where he died in exile in 1828 (see p243).

⑥ Templo de Debod

Paseo de Pintor Rosales. **Map** 1 B5. **Tel** 91 366 74 15. Ⓜ Ventura Rodríguez, Plaza de España. **Open** 9:30am–8pm Sat & Sun; Apr–Sep: 10am–2pm, 6–8pm Tue–Fri; Oct–Mar: 9:45am–1:45pm, 4:15–6:15pm Tue–Fri. **Closed** public hols & afternoons in Aug. 🌐 **esmadrid.com**

The Egyptian temple of Debod, built in the 2nd century BC, was rescued from the area flooded by the Aswan Dam and given to Spain as a tribute to Spanish

Piece of the Treasure of the Quimbayas

🟦 Museo Cerralbo

C/ Ventura Rodríguez 17. **Map** 1 C5.
Tel 91 547 36 46. 🚇 Plaza de España,
Ventura Rodríguez. **Open** 9:30am–3pm
Tue–Sat (also 5–8pm Thu), 10am–3pm
Sun. **Closed** some public hols. 🎫
(free Sun, after 5pm Thu & 2pm Sat).
🖂 📷 W **enmuseocerralbo.mcu.es**

This 19th-century mansion
near the Plaza de España is
a monument to Enrique de
Aguilera y Gamboa, the 17th
Marquis of Cerralbo. A com-
pulsive collector of art and
artifacts, he bequeathed his
lifetime's collection to the
nation in 1922, stipulating that
the exhibits be arranged exactly
as he left them. They range from
Iberian pottery to 18th-century
marble busts.

One of the star exhibits is
El Greco's magnificent *The
Ecstasy of Saint Francis of Assisi*.
There are also paintings by
Ribera, Zurbarán, Alonso
Cano and Goya.

The focal point of the main
floor is the ballroom, lavishly
decorated with mirrors. A large
collection of weaponry is on
display on this floor.

🟦 Palacio de Liria

Calle la Princesa 20. **Tel** 91 547 53 02.
🚇 Ventura Rodríguez. **Open** 10am–
noon Fri. 📷 obligatory. 🖂

The lavish but much-restored
Palacio de Liria was completed
by Ventura Rodríguez in 1780.
Once the residence of the Alba
family, and still owned by the
Duke, it can be visited by a
maximum of 15 people at one
time and by appointment only.

The palace houses the Albas'
outstanding collection of art,
and Flemish tapestries. There
are paintings by Titian, Rubens
and Rembrandt. Spanish art is
particularly well represented,
with major works by Goya,
such as his 1795 portrait of
the Duchess of Alba, as well as
examples of work by El Greco,
Zurbarán and Velázquez.

Behind the palace is the
Cuartel del Conde-Duque,
the former barracks of the
Count-Duke Olivares, Felipe IV's
minister. They were built in
1720 by Pedro de Ribera, who
adorned them with a Baroque
façade. The barracks now house
a cultural centre.

Rooftops in the Malasaña district

🟦 Malasaña

Map 2 F5. 🚇 Tribunal, Bilbao.

A feeling of the authentic old
Madrid pervades this district of
narrow, sloping streets and tall
houses. For some years it was
the centre of the *movida*, the
frenzied nightlife which began
after the death of Franco.

A walk along the Calle San
Andrés leads to the fashionable
area, Plaza del Dos de Mayo.
In the centre is a monument
to artillery officers Daoíz and
Velarde, who defended the
barracks which stood here at
the time of the uprising against
the French in 1808 *(see p67)*.

On Calle de la Puebla is the
Iglesia de San Antonio de los
Alemanes. The church was
founded by Felipe III in the
17th century as a hospital for
Portuguese immigrants, and
was later given over for use by
German émigrés. Inside, the
walls are decorated with 18th-
century frescoes by Giordano.

Nearby is the neighbourhood
of Conde Duque, a lively area
with a great cultural scene.

🟦 Museo de Historia de Madrid

Calle de Fuencarral 78. **Map** 5 A4.
Tel 91 701 18 63. 🚇 Tribunal.
Open 9:30am–8pm Tue–Sun. ♿
W **esmadrid.com**

The History Museum is worth
visiting just for its Baroque
doorway *(see p29)* by Pedro
de Ribera, arguably the finest

Main staircase of the exuberant Museo Cerralbo

in Madrid. Housed in the former hospice of St Ferdinand, the museum was inaugurated in 1929.

It holds a series of bird's-eye views and maps of Madrid. Among them is Pedro Teixeira's map of 1656, thought to be the oldest of the city. There is also a model of Madrid, made in 1830 by León Gil de Palacio.

Modern exhibits include a reconstruction of the collage-filled study of Ramón Gómez de la Serna, a key figure of the literary gatherings in the Café de Pombo (see p303).

Baroque façade of the Museo de Historia, by Pedro de Ribera

⑫ Museo Sorolla

Paseo del General Martínez Campos 37. **Map** 5 C1. **Tel** 91 3,10 15 84. ⊠ Rubén Darío, Iglesia, Gregorio Marañón. **Open** 9:30am–8pm Tue–Sat, 10am–3pm Sun. **Closed** public hols. ⊠ (free Sat after 2pm, Sun). Ⓦ **museosorolla.mcu.es**

The former studio-mansion of Valencian Impressionist painter Joaquín Sorolla has been left virtually as it was when he died in 1923.

Although Sorolla is perhaps best known for his brilliantly lit Mediterranean beach scenes, the changing styles of his paintings are well represented in the museum, with examples of his gentle portraiture and a series of works representing people from different parts of Spain. Also on display are various objects amassed during the artist's lifetime, including Spanish tiles and ceramics. The

Sorolla's former studio in the Museo Sorolla

house, constructed in 1910, has an Andalusian-style garden designed by Sorolla himself.

⑬ Museo Lázaro Galdiano

Calle Serrano 122. **Map** 6 E1. **Tel** 91 561 60 84. ⊠ Rubén Darío, Gregorio Marañón. **Open** 10am–4:30pm Mon & Wed–Sat, 10am–3pm Sun. **Closed** public hols. ⊠ (free for last hour). Ⓒ by appt. Ⓦ **flg.es**

This art museum is housed in the former mansion-home of the editor and financier José Lázaro Galdiano, and consists of his private collection of fine and applied art, bequeathed to the nation in 1947.

Charles V's fob watch

The collection ranges from the 6th to the 20th century and contains items of exceptional quality, ranging from less familiar Goya portraits to a mass of fob watches, including a cross-shaped pocket watch worn by Charles V. Among the most beautiful objects are a series of Limoges enamels, miniature sculptures, and The Saviour, a portrait attributed to a student of Leonardo da Vinci. The museum features paintings by English artists Constable, Turner, Gainsborough and Reynolds, as well as 17th-century paintings by the likes of Spanish painters Madrazo, Zurbarán, Ribera, Murillo and El Greco.

La Movida

With Franco's death in 1975 came a new period of personal and artistic liberty that lasted until the mid-1980s. For some, this translated into the freedom to stay out late, drinking and sometimes sampling drugs. The phenomenon was known as la movida, "the action", and it was at its most intense in Madrid. Analysts at the time saw it as having serious intellectual content, and la movida has had many lasting cultural effects on art, music and literature, like the emergence of satirical film director Pedro Almodóvar.

Poster for Almodóvar's Women on the Verge of a Nervous Breakdown

Torre de Picasso towering over the Paseo de la Castellana

⑭ Paseo de la Castellana

Map 6 D3. 🚇 Santiago Bernabéu, Cuzco, Plaza de Castilla, Gregorio Marañón, Colón.

The busy traffic artery which cuts through eastern Madrid has several parts. Its southernmost portion – the Paseo del Prado *(see pp288–9)* – starts just north of the Estación de Atocha *(see p301)*. The oldest section, it dates from the reign of Carlos III, who built it as part of his embellishment of eastern Madrid. At the Plaza de Cibeles, the avenue becomes the Paseo de Recoletos, which boasts stylish cafés, including the Café Gijón *(see p295)*.

The Plaza de Colón marks the start of the Paseo de la Castellana. This northernmost section has several examples of modern architecture, including the huge grey Nuevos Ministerios building. East of the square is the Estadio Bernabéu, home of Real Madrid Football Club *(see p181)*. At the north end, in Plaza de Castilla, you can find the two Puerta de Europa buildings, built at an angle as if leaning toward each other.

⑮ Plaza de Toros de Las Ventas

Calle Alcalá 237. **Tel** 913 56 22 00. 🚇 Ventas. **Open** for bullfights & concerts. 📷 🎫 by appt. (915 56 92 37). Museo Taurino: **Tel** 917 25 18 57. **Open** Mar–Oct: 9:30am–2:30pm Mon–Fri, 10am–1pm Sun; Nov–Feb: 9:30am–2:30pm Mon–Fri. 🌐 **lasventastour.com**

Whatever your opinion of bullfighting, Las Ventas is undoubtedly one of the most

beautiful bullrings in Spain. Built in 1929 in Neo-Mudéjar style, it replaced the city's original bullring which stood near the Puerta de Alcalá. With its horseshoe arches around the outer galleries and the elaborate tilework decoration, it makes a lovely venue for the *corridas* held during the bullfighting season, from May to October. The statues outside are monuments to two renowned Spanish bullfighters: Antonio Bienvenida and José Cubero.

Adjoining the bullring is the Museo Taurino. Memorabilia includes portraits and sculptures of famous matadors, as well as the heads of several bulls killed during fights at Las Ventas. Visitors can view close up the tools of the bullfighter's trade: capes and *banderillas* – sharp darts used to wound the bull *(see pp40–41)*. For some people, the gory highlight of the exhibition is the blood-drenched *traje de luces* worn by the legendary Manolete during his fateful bullfight at Linares in Andalusia in 1947.

⑯ Real Fábrica de Tapices

Calle Fuenterrabía 2. **Map** 8 F5. **Tel** 914 34 05 51. 🚇 Menéndez Pelayo. **Open** 10am–2pm Mon–Fri, last entry 30 minutes before closing. **Closed** public hols & Aug. 📷 🎫 only. 🌐 **realfabricadetapices.com**

Founded by Felipe V in 1721, the Royal Tapestry Factory is the sole survivor of several factories which were opened by the Bourbons *(see pp66–7)* during the 18th century. In 1889 the factory was relocated to this building just south of the Parque del Retiro.

Visitors can see the making of the carpets and tapestries by hand, a process which has changed little. Goya and his brother-in-law Francisco Bayeu created drawings, or cartoons, which were the models for tapestries made for the royal family. Some of the cartoons are on display here; others can be seen in the Museo del Prado *(see pp296–9)*. Some of the tapestries can be seen at El Pardo *(see p336)* and at El Escorial *(see pp334–5)*. Nowadays one of the factory's main tasks is making and repairing the carpets decorating Hotel Ritz by Belmond *(see p290)*.

⑰ Parque de El Capricho

Paseo de la Alameda de Osuna s/n. **Tel** 915 88 01 14. 🚇 Alameda de Osuna. **Open** Apr–Sep: 9am–9pm Sat (to 6:30pm Oct–Mar).

This lesser-known, remote park is one of the most unique and charming examples of a landscape garden in Spain. Built in the Romantic style on the whim of a duchess in the late 18th century, it displays both Italian and French influences. The plantlife is abundant, particularly in spring, when the garden comes to life with the groves of lilacs and cascading roses. Other interesting places include an artificial canal that leads to a lake with ducks and swans, the reed-covered boathouse known as the Casa de Cañas, the Casino del Baile (Dance Casino), a small temple, a modest palace with a beautiful ballroom, an unusual beehouse and underground bunkers dating back to the Civil War.

Plaza de Toros de Las Ventas, Madrid's beautiful bullring

MADRID STREET FINDER

The map references given with the sights, shops and entertainment venues described in the Madrid section of the guide refer to the street maps on the following pages. Map references are also given for Madrid hotels *(see pp568–9)*, and

for bars and restaurants *(pp591–3)*. The schematic map below shows the area of Madrid covered by the *Street Finder*. The symbols used for sights and other features are listed in the key at the foot of the page.

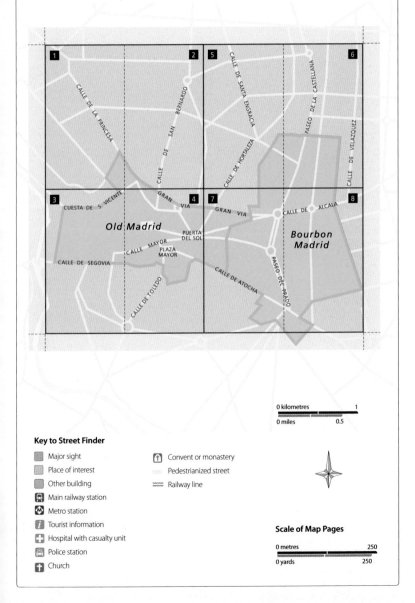

0 kilometres 1
0 miles 0.5

Key to Street Finder

Major sight

Place of interest

Other building

Main railway station

Metro station

Tourist information

Hospital with casualty unit

Police station

Church

Convent or monastery

Pedestrianized street

Railway line

Scale of Map Pages

0 metres 250
0 yards 250

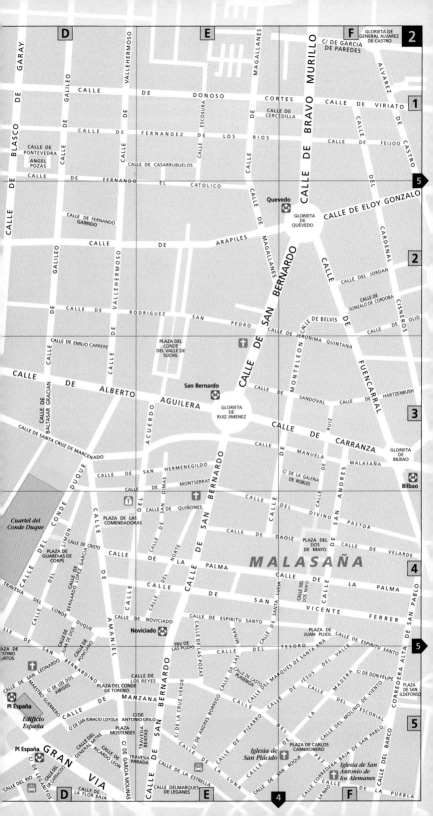

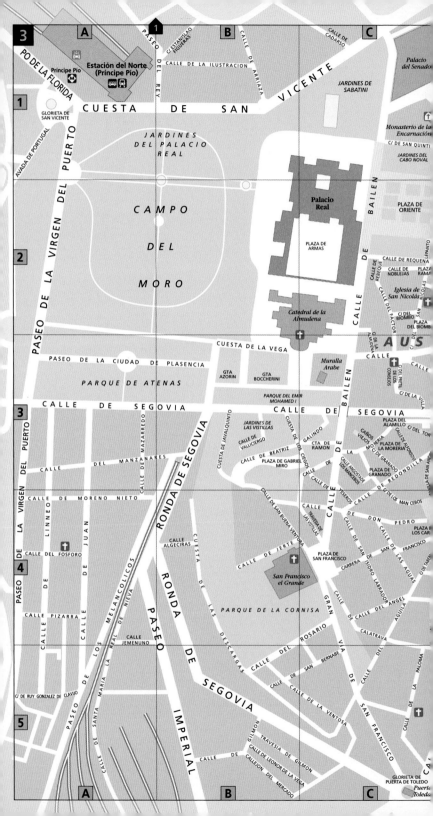

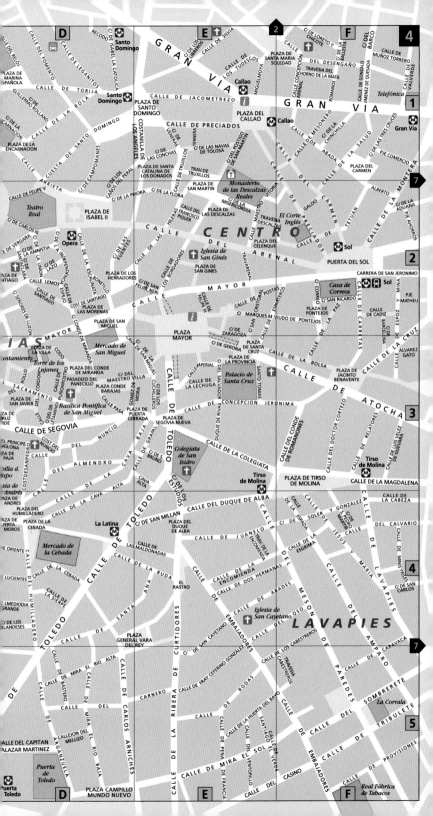

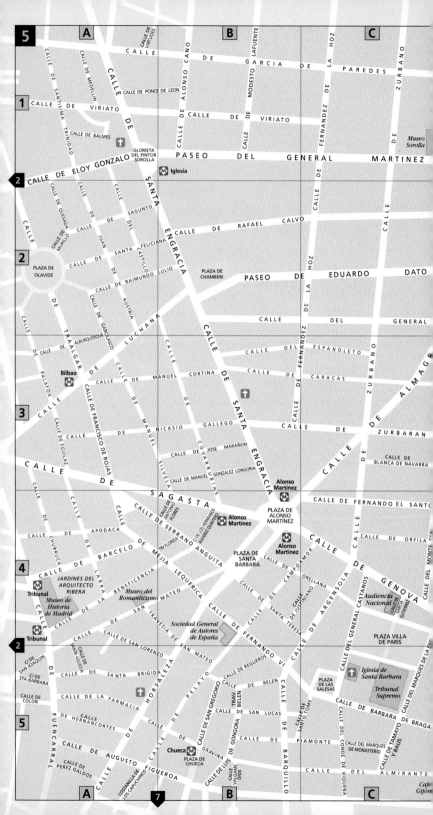

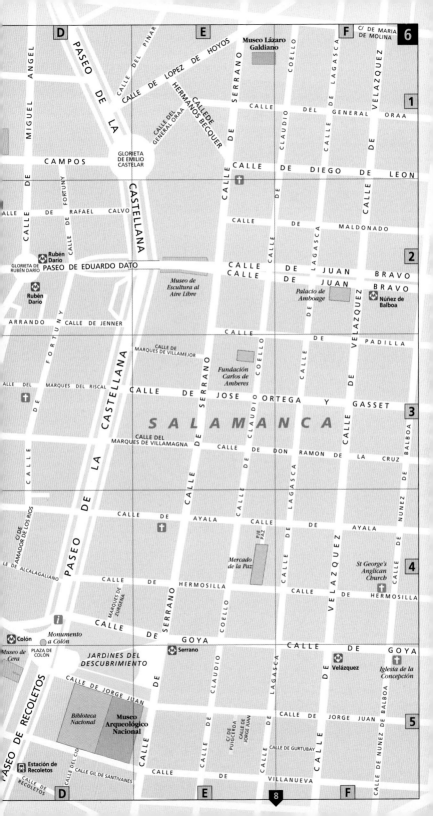

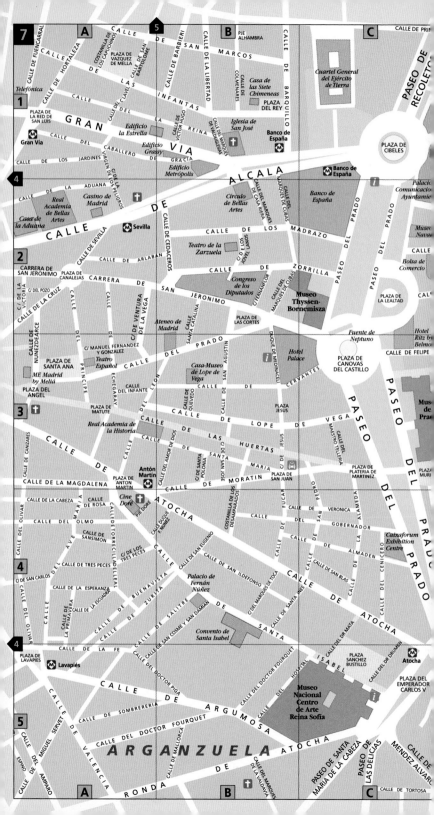

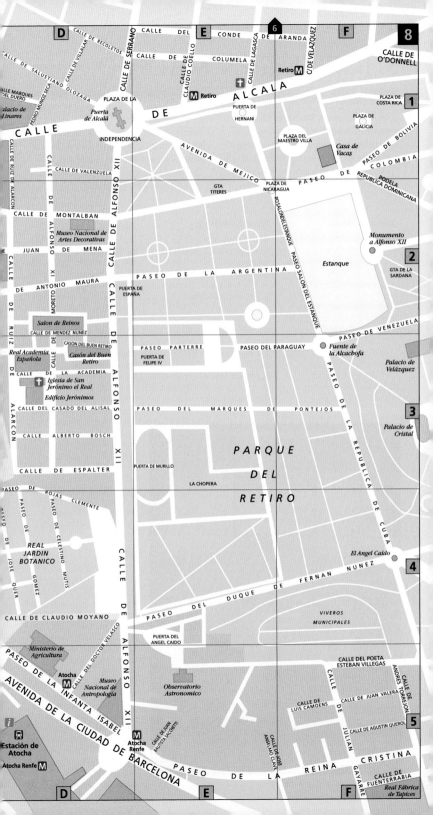

SHOPPING IN MADRID

Madrid is a shoppers' paradise, where designer stores compete for attention with small, quirky shops. Madrid still has more independent and family-run shops than most European capitals, so it should not be hard to pick up some truly original gifts. There are two main shopping hearts in the city – the crowded and popular streets around the pedestrianized Preciados and the Puerta del Sol, and Calle de la Princesa and adjacent streets. The Salamanca district is host to designer brands as well as upmarket antiques, while for the latest streetware visit the Chueca district. The colourful food markets dotted around the city are well worth a visit.

Opening Hours

Most shops in Madrid are open from 10am to 2pm and 5pm to 8:30pm Monday–Friday, though larger stores tend to stay open during lunch and close at 10pm. Small shops often close on Saturday afternoon. Shopping centres, department stores and big shops are permitted to open on Sundays, and the downtown shops around Sol open on Sundays, too. Many small shops close for a month (usually August) in the summer.

Food and Drink

Madrid is a paradise for gourmet food shopping. Strongly scented saffron, matured ewe's cheese or a fruity extra-virgin olive oil all make ideal gifts. Spain has a deep-rooted tradition of pork products, ranging from whole hams to sausages of every shape and size. The best and most expensive ham is Ibérico, from the small, black-hoofed Iberian pig. In Old Madrid, branches of **Museo del Jamón** have an enormous range of Spanish hams, cheeses and cured sausages. **La Chinata** is famous for its selection of olive oils and gourmet products. The department store El Corte Inglés has its own department dedicated to gourmet delicacies, as well as a supermarket for more general groceries. There are smaller delicatessens in nearly every district. In the Salamanca area, visit **Mantequerías Bravo**, famous for its excellent cheeses, preserves and sweets, and **Petra Mora**, a paradise for sophisticated palates.

If you are looking for good wine, head to **Bodega Santa Cecilia**, an outlet with a long history of selling Spanish and international wines. It also organizes tasting sessions. **Lavinia**, in the Salamanca district, is said to be Europe's biggest wine shop, with more than 1,500 brands available. For a truly authentic madrileño souvenir, try **La Violeta**, famous for its fragrant violet sweets.

Markets

A favourite local activity is shopping at the street, or flea, markets, where you can spend a pleasant few hours browsing for antiques, second-hand clothes, pottery, handicrafts and furniture. Some markets are focused on only one item, such as the Sunday-morning stamp, postcard and coin market under the arches of Plaza Mayor, or the Cuesta de Moyano at the Atocha end of Paseo de Prado, where stalls selling second-hand books are set up daily. The legendary El Rastro Sunday flea market (see p306). is a must for any visitor to Madrid, not only for the variety of goods to be found, from antiques to trendy

The enticing frontage of the Museo del Jamón

Inside one of the many antique shops in the streets around El Rastro

garments, but also for its lively atmosphere. It gets really crowded from noon onwards, with bargain hunters rubbing shoulders with those out to enjoy a pre-lunch apéritif at the numerous bars of the La Latina area. Be careful, however, as pickpockets frequent the market.

The best place for paintings is the street market in Plaza del Conde de Barajas, near Plaza Mayor on Sunday mornings, organized by the art association Taller Abierto.

It is worth visiting the colourful Mercado de San Miguel in Plaza San Miguel. Set up in a refurbished early 20th-century building, the market stalls and bars offer an array of produce and delicious delicatessen items, including traditional cured meats and Spanish cheeses. Mercado de San Antón in Chueca, Mercado de San Ildefonso in Malasaña or the trendy Platea in Plaza de Colón are other renovated markets with the same mix of stalls and bars.

Annual Fairs

February has become the "art month" in Madrid, with contemporary art fairs such as ARCO, Just Mad and Art Madrid. Whether you want to buy or simply browse, these and other events provide a great opportunity to catch up on the latest trends in the art world.

In the week prior to Madrid's Fiesta de San Isidro (see p44) which begins on 15 May, you can buy earthen cookware and wine jugs at the Feria de la Cerámica held in the Plaza de

las Comendadoras in the colourful district of Malasaña. The Feria del Libro, held in May–June, is an impressive outdoor bookfair. Hundreds of stalls are set up in the Parque del Retiro, and publishers and bookshop owners exhibit their wares for two weeks, with book signings taking place as well.

On the Plaza de España, the Feria de Artesanos takes place every December, selling all kinds of crafts, making it ideal for Christmas shopping. Throughout December, the Plaza Mayor is the venue for a traditional Christmas fair – the Mercado de Artículos Navideños, where festive bric-a-brac can be picked up.

Antiques and Arts

The commercial galleries and antiques shops of Madrid are all conveniently located along the streets of Serrano, Velázquez, Jorge Juán and Claudio Coello; in the Salamanca area, around Alonso Martínez; and on Doctor Fourquet street behind the Museo Reina Sofía. For cutting-edge Spanish art, head to the **Juana de Aizpuru** gallery, considered to be one of Madrid's top galleries for contemporary art.

Antique shops can also be found in El Rastro flea market, mainly along Calle de la Ribera de Curtidores. **Antigüedades Palacios** sells collectors' items such as furniture, paintings and European ceramics.

For specialist antique outlets, ranging from 18th-century lacquered furniture and ceramics, to Spanish paintings from the 16th to 18th centuries, visit

Coll & Cortés, **Portuondo**, **Cotanda**, **Codosero**, **María Gracia Cavestany** and **Theotokopoulos**. There are also opportunities for pricier antique shopping along the streets of the Prado, Santa Catalina (**Alcocer**) and Cervantes, near Plaza de Santa Ana. In Madrid, art and antiques auctions are held by both Spanish and international firms, including Durán, Goya, Segre, Ansorena and Alcalá.

Shopping Centres and Department Stores

Among the best shopping centres, or *centros comerciales*, are the tempting and expensive malls of the elegant Salamanca neighbourhood. **El Jardín de Serrano** is a high-quality *galleria*, housed in two restored 19th-century palaces that stocks fashion, jewellery, gifts and accessories. **ABC Serrano** has a range of shops that includes home furniture as well as designer fashions and gifts.

If you want more variety at a cheaper price, visit the huge **La Vaguada** in the north, or **El Corte Inglés**, a national institution with branches throughout the city. The latter also has a travel agency and offers services such as photo development and shoe repairs. Also good value for money are the shops in the **Príncipe Pío** shopping centre, located in the former Northern Railway Station. Shops, restaurants and cinemas sit under the original glass and iron roof.

Sunday morning in the busy Rastro flea market

Fashion

The Spanish chain stores **Zara** and **Bimba y Lola** have become international phenomena, offering easy-to-wear clothes for women at very good prices. Zara also caters to men and children. Both stores have branches all over the city. For upmarket fashion there are many well-known Spanish designers, such as **Purificacion Garcia**, who have their own shops in Madrid, mainly in the elegant Salamanca district or on the Calle de Jorge Juan.

Those in favour of a more unusual or original look should try **Ágatha Ruiz de la Prada's** creations (for kids and adults).

For high-quality designer menswear, check out **Roberto Verino**, **Custo Barcelona**, **Adolfo Domínguez** or **Caramelo**. These shops also offer women's clothes. Another popular, reasonably priced Spanish chain store for men is **Springfield**. At the top end of the market is the **Loewe** store for men, where a silk tie with a Spanish art motif makes a stylish gift.

The lively Chueca and Malasaña districts are the best places for the latest in street-wear, with offbeat local designers and second-hand shops on almost every corner. Some outlets also sell international brands at reduced prices.

Shoes and Leather Goods

Madrid is a haven for those with a shoe fetish. You will find every type of shoe here, from the traditional espadrille sold at **Antigua Casa Crespo** to the popular Majorcan Camper shoes. Try **Pretty Ballerinas** for beautiful ballerina shoes and pumps, while for sophistication, opt for the elegant **Farrutx**. If you are looking for trendy leather goods, head to **Malababa**. Make a trip to Bravo for some of the best national and international labels. Chic shoes, sandals and handbags with an innovative touch are available at **Cristina Castañer**. For a classical look, try **Carmina** or the Majorcan **Meermin**. For trainers or other budget buys, visit the shops along Calle de Fuencarral, or go to **Los Guerrilleros** in Calle Montera, near Puerta del Sol. The well-heeled will also want to check out the range of shoe outlets in the Chueca area, along Calle Augusto Figueroa.

Spain undoubtedly produces some of the best-quality leather in the world. The ultimate in bags and leather goes under the prestigious label of **Loewe**, whose products are sold all over the world. Another impressive (and perhaps more budget-friendly) national brand is **Salvador Bachiller**, where you will discover quality leather and exclusively designed bags, suitcases, wallets and other accessories.

Jewellery

In Calle Serrano and Gran Vía you will find both small shops, stacked with trays of gold studs, chains and bracelets, and grand, more exclusive jewellers. Man-made "Majorica" pearls, as well as the cultivated variety, can be found all over the city, including at the high-end department store El Corte Inglés.

The innovative Catalan **Tous** on Calle Serrano is popular among the young for its ubiquitous teddy-bear logo. If you are interested in original, simple designs, visit the acclaimed jeweller **Joaquín Berao** on Calle Lagasca. His shop resembles an art gallery devoted to tastefully designed pieces. For Spanish designs, visit **Aristocrazy** and the beautiful atelier of **Andrés Gallardo**. Museum shops are also a good place to shop for designer jewellery. Look out for original pieces from Verili, sold at the main museums in the city.

Crafts and Design

Traditional crafts such as woven baskets or embroidered linen are hard to find in Madrid and those that are available often tend to be Asian imports. However, lovely and inexpensive ceramics are widely available, though sometimes the more colourful pieces are from Morocco. A wide choice of ceramics can be found at **Cántaro**, near the Plaza de España. Well stocked in regional styles, the shop also carries so-called "extinct" ceramics – traditional styles of pottery no longer regularly produced. Many shops around Puerta del Sol stock embroidered tablecloths and shawls, but be aware that the authentic pieces can be quite expensive. The Spanish firm **PeSeta** makes artisanal fabric goods in their atelier.

In the Plaza Mayor, adjoining the Arco de Cuchilleros, is **El Arco Artesanías**, which sells handmade modern Spanish crafts, such as pottery, glassware and ironwork.

For contemporary design, head to **Deleite**, where you'll find Spanish, Portuguese and Nordic-inspired home goods, from artisanal porcelain jewellery to coat hangers.

Books and Music

The giant French-owned **FNAC** book and video store has an extensive selection of books and magazines in English and other languages, as do **Machado** and the **Casa del Libro**. A little further afield, **Booksellers** stocks English classics, though only a limited selection of new books. The second-hand bookstalls of the Mercado del Libro near the Parque del Retiro are good for cheap paperbacks and, some-times, rare volumes. The libraries of the Círculo de Bellas Artes (see p327) and the Museo Reina Sofía (see pp302–3) have a great collection of books as well. Art books can be found at one of the best specialist art book-shops, **Gaudí**, near Chueca.

For all types of music, go to the FNAC or one of the El Corte Inglés branches, either in Calle de Preciados or Paseo de la Castellana.

For flamenco enthusiasts, the specialist **El Flamenco Vive** store on Calle del Conde de Lemos stocks a fantastic range of flamenco kit, including the widest selection of books, guitars and CDs in the world.

DIRECTORY

Food and Drink

Bodega Santa Cecilia
C/ Blasco de Garay 74.
Map 2 D1.
Tel 914 45 52 83.

La Chinata
Calle Mayor 44. **Map** 4 D2.
Tel 911 52 20 08.

Lavinia
C/ de José Ortega y
Gasset 16. **Map** 6 F3.
Tel 914 26 06 04.

Mantequerías Bravo
C/ de Ayala 24. **Map** 6 E4.
Tel 915 76 02 93.

Museo del Jamón
Carrera de San
Jerónimo 6. **Map** 7 A2.
Tel 915 21 03 46.

Petra Mora
C/ de Ayala 21. **Map** 6 E4.
Tel 915 76 14 03.

La Violeta
Plaza Canalejas 6. **Map** 7
A2. **Tel** 915 22 55 22.

Antiques and Arts

Alcocer
Calle de Santa Catalina 5.
Map 7 B2.
Tel 914 29 79 19.

**Antigüedades
Palacios**
Plaza General Vara del
Rey 14. **Map** 4 E4.
Tel 915 27 31 70.

Codosero
Calle de Lagasca 36. **Map**
6 F5. **Tel** 914 31 55 81.

Coll & Cortés
Calle de Justiniano 3.
Map 5 B4.
Tel 913 10 05 82.

Cotanda
Calle de Lagasca 96. **Map**
6 F2. **Tel** 917 81 30 01.

Juana de Aizpuru
C/ Barquillo 44. **Map** 5 B5.
Tel 913 10 55 61.

**María Gracia
Cavestany**
C/ Ayala 6. **Map** 6 E4.
Tel 915 77 76 32.

Portuondo
Calle Castelló 85.
Tel 914 35 36 20.

Theotokopoulos
C/ Alcalá 97. **Map** 8 F1.
Tel 915 75 84 66.

Shopping Centres and Malls

ABC Serrano
C/ Serrano 61. **Map** 6 E2.
Tel 915 77 50 31.
🖥 abcserrano.com

El Corte Inglés
C/ Preciados 1–3. **Map** 4
F2. **Tel** 913 79 80 00.
🖥 elcorteingles.es
One of several branches.

El Jardín de Serrano
C/ Goya 6–8. **Map** 6 E4.
Tel 915 77 00 12.
🖥 jardindeserrano.es

Príncipe Pío
Estación del Norte. **Map** 3
A1. **Tel** 917 58 00 40.
🖥 ccprincipepio.com

La Vaguada
Av Monforte de Lemos 36.
Tel 917 30 10 00.
🖥 enlavaguada.com

Fashion

Adolfo Domínguez
C/ Serrano 96. **Map** 6 E2.
Tel 915 76 70 53.

**Ágatha Ruiz de la
Prada**
C/ Serrano 27.
Map 6 E4.
Tel 913 19 05 01.

Bimba y Lola
C/ Serrano 22.
Map 5 E5.
Tel 915 76 11 03.
One of several branches.

Caramelo
C/ Serrano 19. **Map** 6 E4.
Tel 914 35 01 77.

Custo Barcelona
Fuencarral 29. **Map** 5 A5.
Tel 913 60 46 36.
🖥 custo-barcelona.com

Loewe
C/ Serrano 26. **Map** 6 E4.
Tel 915 77 60 56.

Purificacion Garcia
C/ Serrano 28. **Map** 6 E5.
Tel 914 35 80 13.

Roberto Verino
C/ Serrano 33. **Map** 6 E4.
Tel 914 26 04 75.

Springfield
C/ Fuencarral 107.
Map 2 F3.
Tel 914 47 59 94.
One of several branches.

Zara
Gran Vía 34. **Map** 4 F1.
Tel 915 21 12 83.

Shoes and Leather Goods

Antigua Casa Crespo
C/ del Divino Pastor 29.
Map 2 F4.
Tel 915 21 56 54.

Bravo
C/ Serrano 42. **Map** 6 E4.
Tel 914 35 27 29.
One of several branches.

Camper
C/ de la Princesa 75.
Map 1 B2. **Tel** 902 36
45 98. 🖥 camper.es

Carmina
Calle de Claudio
Coello 73. **Map** 6 E3.
Tel 915 76 40 90.

Cristina Castañer
C/ del Almirante 24.
Map 5 C5. **Tel** 915 23
72 14. 🖥 castaner.com

Farrutx
C/ Serrano 7. **Map** 8 D1.
Tel 915 76 94 93.

Jocomomola
C/ Argensola 13.
Map 5 C5.
Tel 915 75 00 55.

Los Guerrilleros
C/ Montera 25.
Map 4 F2.
Tel 915 21 59 29.

Malababa
Calle Santa Teresa 5. **Map**
5 B4. **Tel** 912 03 59 51.

Meermin
Calle de Claudio
Coello 20. **Map** 6 E5.
Tel 914 31 21 17.

Pretty Ballerinas
C/ de Lagasca 30. **Map** 6
F4. **Tel** 914 31 95 09.
🖥 prettyballerinas.
com

Salvador Bachiller
Gran Vía 65. **Map** 2 D5.
Tel 915 59 83 21.

Jewellery

Andrés Gallardo
Conde de Romanones 5,
Patio. **Tel** 911 56 91 10.
🖥 andresgallardo.es

Aristocrazy
C/ Serrano 46. **Map** 6 E4.
Tel 914 35 11 38.
🖥 aristocrazy.com

Joaquín Berao
C/ Lagasca 44. **Map** 6 E5.
Tel 915 77 28 28.

Tous
C/ Serrano 46. **Map** 6 E4.
Tel 914 31 92 42.

Crafts and Design

El Arco Artesanías
Plaza Mayor 9. **Map** 4 E3.
Tel 913 65 26 80.
🖥 elarcoartesania.com

Cántaro
Calle de la Flor Baja 8.
Map 2 D5.
Tel 915 47 95 14.

Deleite
Calle Castelló 5.
Tel 687 08 88 43.
🖥 deleitedesign.com

PeSeta
Calle de Noviciado 9.
Map 2 E4.
Tel 915 21 14 04.

Books and Music

Booksellers
C/ Fernández de la Hoz
40. **Tel** 914 42 79 59.

Casa del Libro
Gran Vía 29. **Map** 4 F1.
Tel 902 02 64 02.
🖥 casadellibro.com

El Flamenco Vive
C/ del Conde de Lemos 7.
Map 4 D2.
Tel 915 47 39 17.

FNAC
C/ Preciados 28. **Map** 4
E1. **Tel** 915 95 62 00.
🖥 fnac.es

Gaudí
C/ Colón, 4. **Map** 5 A5.
Tel 913 08 18 29.

Machado
C/ Marqués de Casa Riera 2.
Map 7 B2.
Tel 913 10 17 05.

ENTERTAINMENT IN MADRID

As a major European capital, Madrid takes its arts and entertainment very seriously, hosting the finest and most diverse dance, music and theatre productions from around the world. Vibrant art, music and film festivals are held around the year, supplemented by a pulsating nightlife, raucous street parties and lively cafés.

Even traditional art forms, such as flamenco, bullfighting and Madrid's version of the operetta, *zarzuela*, are characterized by flamboyance and spectacle. Football is also a major draw, and Real Madrid is a hugely celebrated team. Between fiestas, flamenco, football and much more, the revelry never stops in Madrid.

Madrid's Teatro Real *(see p326)*

Entertainment Guides

Madrid's entertainment guides are mostly in Spanish. *Guía del Ocio*, a handy weekly guide to what's on in the city, comes out every Thursday and can be bought from kiosks. Three daily newspapers have entertainment supplements on Friday: *El Mundo*, *ABC* and *El País*.

The English-language monthly, *InMadrid* (www. inmadrid.com), publishes cultural listings and reviews of the latest bars and clubs. It is available in bookshops, record stores and Barajas Airport information office.

Information on forthcoming events can also be obtained from one of the **tourist information offices** in the city, where English will be spoken. The tourist board also publishes *Es Madrid*, a free, bilingual brochure.

Seasons and Tickets

There is always something going on in Madrid's theatres and stadiums, but the cultural season is at its peak from September to June. May's Fiesta de San Isidro, Madrid's patron saint festival, and the Festival de Otoño a Primavera, a music, theatre and dance festival held from October to June, attract many big Spanish and international names. Tickets can be bought from **Entradas.com** or **Telentrada.com**.

In July and August, Madrid hosts Veranos de la Villa (book through tourist offices), a special programme that includes art exhibitions, jazz, opera, flamenco, cinema and drama at various venues.

Tickets for a number of events can be bought at **FNAC** and **El Corte Inglés** stores and websites. Many other reliable internet sites also sell tickets. Check the websites of venues too, since many of them offer online booking services.

Cafés, Bars and Terraces

Madrid's social life revolves around an endless array of cafés, bars and summer terraces.

These venues are perfect places to relax and people-watch. Especially popular areas for *terraceo* (doing the rounds of various terraces) are Plaza de Santa Ana, Paja, Chueca and Dos de Mayo. The glamorous crowd often spend evenings strolling down avenues, such as Paseo de Recoletos and Rosales, stopping now and then to nip into a terrace bar or café.

Madrid has retained many of its old grand cafés. **Café Comercial**, a city landmark, is an excellent meeting place with its early 20th-century ambience. **Café del Círculo de Bellas Artes**, housed in a cultural foundation, is an institution in itself. It is ideal for coffee or lunch after spending a day pursuing cultural interests. Of the literary cafés, the famous **Café Gijón** *(see p295)* should not be missed. For delicious tea and cakes, visit **Mamá Framboise** and **Pomme Sucre** near Alonso Martínez.

In the evening, it is almost essential to head to a *taberna*, where you can order a *ración*,

Dancing the night away at the Joy Madrid Discoteque *(see p328)*

Exterior of the historic Café Gijón

the more substantial version of tapas, and accompany it with a good local wine. Go for a *taberna* crawl and visit the the older and most interesting establishments, such as **Taberna Antonio Sánchez**, which is well-known for its history and the quality of its tapas. **Bodega La Ardosa** is popular with both tourists and locals, and **Taberna Maceiras** is favoured for its Galician wines and other specialities.

Bullfighting

Although bullfighting (see pp40–41) is not as popular as it used to be in many other parts of Spain, it continues to thrive in Madrid. The **Plaza de Toros de las Ventas** is the most important ring in the world, holding *corridas* every Sunday from March to October. In May, during the Fiesta de San Isidro, there are *corridas* every day, with some of the biggest names participating in the spectacle.

The Las Ventas box office is open on Fridays from 10am to 2pm and from 5pm to 7pm. You can also purchase tickets from abroad through the **Taquilla Toros** website, and collect them at the box office up to two hours before the fight.

Football

Madrid is very proud of its team, **Real Madrid** (see p181), and the players are celebrities in Spain. With a capacity of 80,000, their home stadium Santiago Bernabéu is one of the greatest theatres of the game. Tickets can be bought on the phone, or through the team's official website.

For those wishing to visit the stadium, guided tours are conducted on Mondays and Saturdays between 10am and 7pm (10:30am to 6:30pm on Sundays and holidays); on days when there are matches, times vary. Tickets can be bought at the box office and online with no need to book in advance.

Real Madrid's rivals, **Atlético de Madrid**, are based at the Vicente Calderón stadium.

Dance

Madrid's dance scene has come a long way in recent years, with international companies and local talent performing regularly around the city. Madrid is the home of Spain's prestigious Ballet Nacional de España and the more contemporary Compañía Nacional de Danza, for many years directed by the world-famous dancer and chore-ographer Nacho Duato. Víctor Ullate's Ballet de la Comunidad de Madrid presents a more avant-garde mix of classical and contemporary dance.

A good time to experience Madrid's rich dance tradition is around April, when the annual En Danza festival takes place. Both Spanish and international dancers perform at this time in various theatres and other venues in and around Madrid.

Two major venues hosting dance are the **Teatros del Canal** and the **Teatro Real** (where opera is usually performed). Smaller venues such as **La Casa Encendida** and **Cuarta Pared** present alternative dance performances.

Details can usually be found in the entertainment listings or on the individual venue's website.

Flamenco

Although flamenco originated in Andalusia (see pp428–9), Madrid is often seen as its spiritual home and some of the best flamenco dancers and musicians regularly perform here. The scene is sparklingly vibrant, and interpretations of the art range from the traditional to the daringly innovative, inspired by dancers such as Joaquín Cortés. The big Suma Flamenca festival is held every year in June.

Most *tablaos* (flamenco venues) offer drinks and dinner with the show. Sometimes, however, the show may feature only singing and not the familar rhythmic dancing.

Café de Chinitas and **Corral de la Moreria** are among the older and better tablaos in town, but are somewhat touristy. Also well worth a visit are **La Taberna de Mister Pinkleton** and **Casa Patas**.

Mixed flamenco and pop bars such as **Cardamomo** are full of boisterous young people, but are a fun way of experiencing the sound and feel of flamenco. Two bars that feature regular, spontaneous performances are the atmospheric **Candela** and **Las Tablas**. Note that as these places are frequented by local flamenco aficionados, visitors should be respectful of the art.

Take into account that although bars are fun and a good introduction to the art of flamenco, some of the best dance troupes, singers and players usu-ally perform at the city's theatres.

Las Ventas bullring on the day of a bullfight

Classical Music, Opera and Zarzuela

Madrid's Auditorio Nacional de Música is home to Spain's national orchestra, Orquesta Nacional, as well as its national choir, Coro Nacional de España. With two concert halls, the auditorium also hosts many high-profile performances.

The illustrious **Teatro Real** is best known as the home of the city's opera company. It also houses Orquesta Sinfónica de Madrid, Spain's oldest orchestra with a rich history dating back to more than a century. The magnificent Real is the best place to watch top-class international and national opera performances. Tickets for a show can be bought at a maximum of two weeks in advance by phone or from the website and can be collected at the box office up to half an hour before the show begins.

The **Teatro Monumental** is the main venue for the excellent Orquesta Sinfónica y Coro de RTVE, the orchestra and choir of Spain's state television and radio company. The **Centro Cultural Conde Duque** hosts classical concerts among many other art events. **Fundación Juan March** holds free classical concerts every Saturday morning (book online).

Those who want to experience a Spanish, especially a *madrileño*, take on the operetta, should definitely make time to see a *zarzuela* being performed. The origins of this lively form of musical-drama-cum-social-satire can be traced back to early 17th-century Madrid, and the tradition is still going strong. With both spoken and sung parts as well as dancing, the *zarzuela* can be comic, ribald and even romantic. It is always enjoyable to watch.

The best productions are usually staged at the **Teatro de la Zarzuela**. Other theatres also host *zarzuela* performances occasionally. Check listings for details.

Look our for details on free, outdoor concerts in the papers. The Teatro Real normally opens the opera season with a live transmission of the first show on massive video screens in Plaza de Oriente.

Rock, Jazz and World Music

Madrid's music scene is eclectic and energetic, mixing top international pop stars with independent local bands performing at a variety of venues. Madrid's increasingly multicultural mix has ensured an explosion of Latin American and African sounds recently, as well as interesting fusions of both with more familiar Spanish sounds. In the 1980s, the heady days of *la movida (see p309)* gave birth to Spanish pop, and the momentum continues to this day with Madrid remaining the centre of the country's music scene.

For rock music, **Sala la Riviera**, located next to the Manzanares river, has an excellent and well-deserved reputation. It has hosted major international stars such as Bob Dylan, Patti Smith, the Cranberries and guitarist Joe Satriani, among countless others. **Honky Tonk**, in the Chamberí district, often has performances from local bands, so keep an eye out for posters advertising events, some of which are free.

Siroco has devoted itself to discovering new alternative and indie bands, and also doubles as a club with live music performances.

One of Europe's best jazz clubs, **Café Central**, with its Art Deco elegance, is one place that should not be missed. Also popular is the lively **Populart** jazz and blues venue.

Musicians from all over the world and of a range of musical genres can be heard at **El Sol**. One of the most important clubs of the Movida Madrileña *(see p309)*, El Sol is the only one that continues to promote the underground style of music of the 1980s.

There are plenty of other well-reputed live-music venues in the city. The best way to keep abreast of the latest events is to check out weekly listings and to keep an eye out for adverts on the street.

Theatre

Madrid has a theatrical tradition that stretches back to the Golden Age of the 17th century, with writers such as Lope de Vega and Calderón de la Barca creating a canon of work that is still performed today.

One of the most prestigious theatres in the city, the **Teatro de la Comedia** is traditionally home to the Compañía Nacional de Teatro Clásico, which stages classic works by Spanish playwrights. However, since the Comedia is under renovation, the company is now performing at the **Teatro Pavón** (until further notice).

Another one of the most highly regarded theatres is the **Teatro María Guerrero**, which presents Spanish modern drama, as well as foreign plays.

For contemporary and alternative theatre, Madrid has a thriving network of fringe venues such as **Cuarta Pared**. **Teatro Español** also puts on excellent productions.

For musicals, try **Teatro Nuevo Apolo**, **Teatro Lope de Vega** or **Teatro Caser Calderón**. Other venues such as **Teatro la Latina** and **Teatro Muñoz Seca** do comedy productions.

A wide range of Spanish and international theatrical talent take part in the annual Festival de Otoño a Primavera from October to June.

Cinema

Spanish cinema *(see p196)* has earned great international acclaim in recent years. For those with a grasp of the language, Spanish film is a rewarding experience, especially enjoyed at one of the grand film theatres along Gran Vía, such as **Capitol**, which has screened films since the early 1900s.

Non-Spanish movies can be seen in their original-language versions at **Verdi**, **Ideal**, **Golem** and **Renoir**. Screenings will be found listed in newspapers and listings magazines. Note that tickets cost less on the *día del espectador*, which is usually on Monday or Wednesday.

DIRECTORY

Tourist Offices

Comunidad de Madrid Tourist Office
C/ Duque de Medinacelli 2. **Map** 7 B3.
Tel 914 29 49 51.

Municipal Tourist Office
Pl Mayor 27. **Map** 4 E3.
Tel 914 54 44 10.

Tickets

El Corte Inglés
Tel 902 40 02 22.
w elcorteingles.com

Entradas.com
Tel 902 48 84 88.

FNAC
Tel 902 10 06 32.
w fnac.es

Tel Entrada
Tel 902 10 12 12.
w telentrada.com

Cafés, Bars and Terraces

Bodega La Ardosa
C/ Colón 13. **Map** 5 A5.
Tel 915 21 49 79.

Café Comercial
Glorieta de Bilbao 7. **Map** 2 F3. **Tel** 915 21 56 55.

Café del Círculo de Bellas Artes
C/ Alcalá 42. **Map** 7 B2.
Tel 913 60 54 00.

Café Gijón
Paseo de Recoletos 21.
Map 7 C1.
Tel 915 21 54 25.

Mamá Framboise
Calle de Fernando VI 23.
Map 5 B5.
Tel 913 91 43 64.

Pomme Sucre
Calle Barquillo 49. **Map** 5 B5. **Tel** 913 08 31 85.

Taberna Antonio Sánchez
C/ de Mesón de Paredes 13. **Map** 4 F5.
Tel 915 39 78 26.

Taberna Maceiras
C/ Huertas 66. **Map** 7 B3.
Tel 914 29 58 18.

Bullfighting

Taquilla Toros
w taquillatoros.com

Las Ventas
C/ Alcalá 237.
Tel 913 56 22 00.
w las-ventas.com

Football

Atlético de Madrid
Estadio Vicente Calderón, Paseo de la Virgen del Puerto 67.
Tel 902 26 04 03.
w clubatletico demadrid.com

Real Madrid
Estadio Santiago Bernabéu, C/ Concha Espina 1. **Tel** 913 98 43 00.
w realmadrid.es

Dance

La Casa Encendida
Ronda de Valencia 2.
Tel 902 43 03 22.

Teatros del Canal
C/ Cea Bermúdez 1. **Map** 3 B1. **Tel** 913 08 99 99.

Flamenco

Café de Chinitas
C/ Torija 7. **Map** 4 D1.
Tel 915 47 15 02.

Candela
C/ Olmo 2. **Map** 7 A4.
Tel 914 67 33 82.

Cardamomo
C/ Echegaray 15. **Map** 7 A2. **Tel** 913 69 07 57.

Casa Patas
C/ Cañizares 10. **Map** 7 A3. **Tel** 913 69 04 96.

Corral de la Morería
C/ de la Morería 17.
Map 3 C3.
Tel 913 65 84 46.

La Taberna de Mister Pinkleton
C/ de los Cuchilleros 7.
Map 4 E3. **Tel** 913 64 02 63. w latabernade misterpinkleton.com

Las Tablas
Pl de España 9. **Map** 1 C5.
Tel 915 42 05 20.

Classical Music Opera and Zarzuela

Auditorio Nacional de Música
C/ del Príncipe de Vergara 146.
Tel 913 37 01 40.
w auditorionacional. mcu.es

Centro Cultural Conde Duque
C/ del Conde Duque 11.
Map 2 D4.
Tel 915 48 73 26.

Fundación Juan March
Calle de Castelló 77.
Tel 914 35 42 40.
w march.es

Teatro Caser Calderón
C/ Atocha 18. **Map** 4 F3.
Tel 902 00 66 17.

Teatro de la Zarzuela
C/ de los Jovellanos 4.
Map 7 B2. **Tel** 915 24 54 00. w teatrodela zarzuela.mcu.es

Teatro Monumental
C/ Atocha 65. **Map** 7 A3.
Tel 914 20 37 97.

Teatro Real
Pl de Oriente. **Map** 4 D2.
Tel 915 16 06 00.
w teatro-real.com

Rock, Jazz and World Music

Café Central
Pl del Ángel 10. **Map** 7 A3. **Tel** 913 69 41 43.
w cafecentral madrid.com

Honky Tonk
C/ de Covarrubias 24.
Map 5 B3.
Tel 914 45 61 91.

Populart
C/ Huertas 22. **Map** 7 A3.
Tel 914 29 84 07.
w populart.es

Sala La Riviera
Paseo Virgen del Puerto s/n. **Tel** 913 65 24 15.

Siroco
C/ de San Dimas 3. **Map** 2 E4. **Tel** 915 93 30 70.

El Sol

C/ Jardínes 3. **Map** 7 A1.
Tel 915 32 64 90.
w elsolmad.com

Theatre

Cuarta Pared
C/ del Ercilla 17.
Tel 915 17 23 17.
w cuartapared.es

Teatro de la Comedia
C/ del Príncipe 14. **Map** 7 A2. **Tel** 915 21 49 31.

Teatro Español
C/ Príncipe 25. **Map** 7 A2.
Tel 913 60 14 84.

Teatro la Latina
Pl de la Cebada 2. **Map** 4 D4. **Tel** 913 65 28 35.

Teatro Lope de Vega
Gran Vía 57. **Map** 4 E1.
Tel 915 47 20 11.

Teatro María Guerrero
C/ de Tamayo y Baus 4.
Map 5 C5.
Tel 913 10 29 49.

Teatro Muñoz Seca
Pl del Carmen 1. **Map** 4 F1. **Tel** 915 23 21 28.

Teatro Nuevo Apolo
Pl Tirso de Molina 1. **Map** 4 F3. **Tel** 913 69 06 37.

Teatro Pavón
C/ de Embajadores 9.
Map 4 E4.
Tel 915 39 64 43.

Cinema

Capitol
Gran Vía 41. **Map** 4 E1.
Tel 902 33 32 31

Golem
C/ de Martín de los Heros 14. **Map** 1 A1.
Tel 915 59 38 36.

Ideal
C/ del Doctor Cortezo 6.
Map 4 F3.
Tel 913 69 25 18.

Renoir
C/ de Martín de los Heros 12. **Map** 1 C5.
Tel 915 41 41 00.

Verdi
C/ Bravo Murillo 28.
Tel 914 47 39 30.

Nightlife

Madrid's reputation as the city that never sleeps persists, despite recent political measures for earlier closing times. In fact, people from Madrid are known as *gatos* (cats) around Spain because of their nocturnal habits. The best nightlife is concentrated around specific districts, each with its own unique atmosphere and a wealth of places for people to get down to one of Madrid's best talents: *la marcha* (partying). Things hot up first in the Huertas area, moving on to Malasaña, Bilbao, Lavapiés and Chueca into the early hours of the morning. You don't need to go to a club for dancing as *madrileños* also dance to DJs and live music in smaller clubs, called *pubs* – all sorts of musical tastes are catered to more than amply *(see p326)*. Expect to find places crowded from Thursday to Sunday. Also prepare for late nights because things don't get going for *gatos* until midnight.

Santa Ana and Huertas

With many tapas bars, cafés and terraces, the Huertas area is the perfect place to begin preparing for the wild night ahead. The atmosphere is made by the crowd, which is a heady amalgam of ages, looks and origins. If you want to stay in one area, this is a good choice.

There are several little bars overlooking the lively Plaza de Santa Ana. Pop into any one of them to begin the night. **Viva Madrid** attracts a vivacious crowd of locals and foreigners. **Cardamomo**, a famous club, is a mandatory stop for any bar crawl. There is live flamenco at least once a week.

For late-night dancing, try the house DJs at **Joy Madrid Discoteque**. Near Atocha, you will find the spectacular seven-floor **Kapital**, which features every kind of music, and a rooftop bar that allows drinkers to gaze at the starlit sky. **Populart**, also a hugely popular club, features live jazz and occasional shows by Latin and world music bands. Note that weekends can get very crowded.

It is a local tradition to end the night with hot chocolate and *churros* (dough sticks) in one of the cafés around Plaza del Sol. The **Chocolatería San Ginés** is a great place for chocolate gorging: it's open 24 hours.

If the chocolate fix leaves you buzzing, check out **Bash**, which plays house and electronica on Friday and Saturday nights, taking the straight/gay mix of clubbers through to 6am the next day.

Alonso Martínez and Bilbao

This is one of the city's most animated areas. You will find hundreds of great haunts that play music ranging from R&B to Spanish pop.

To begin with, try some of the local bars around Plaza de Santa Bárbara, such as the **Cervecería Santa Bárbara**, the perfect place to start the night with a *caña* (beer). Later on (if you can get past the queues), try the glamorous club **Alegoría**, with its eclectic decor and pop music, where you can dance until late with the beautiful people, or **El Junco**, a dance and concert venue with the best jazz, funk and soul music in the capital. Alternatively, you can head for **Teatro Barceló**, formerly known as Pacha, one of Madrid's most famous discotheques. There are also plenty of live-music venues around, such as **Clamores**, one of Madrid's many temples of jazz music. However, note that areas such as Huertas are more active during weekdays.

Argüelles and Moncloa

This area is a favourite haunt of students, thanks to its proximity to the halls of residence of one of Madrid's major universities.

The "basements of Argüelles" are huge double-storeyed patios with several bars and discotheques. The atmosphere is fresh and young.

Another popular district is Moncloa, which has a more mature crowd, as well as several places where you can listen to local Spanish pop and dance tunes, such as nightclub **Lasal**, which is also a venue for concerts.

Chueca

The Chueca district dominates Madrid's gay scene. As well as having a large resident gay community, there are plenty of trendy late-night bars and clubs where gays and non-gays party together. In fact, what sets Chueca apart from other gay neighbourhoods in the world is the *mezcla*, the tolerant gay/straight mix.

The heart of the area is the Plaza de Chueca, packed with crowds visiting the terraces in the summer. Close by are mixed bars such as **Acuarela**, with its camp, religious-artifact decor. The Gay Pride Week in late June or July focuses around this area, though there are also plenty of well-established gay bars elsewhere in the city.

Malasaña

Malasaña was the centre of *la movida* in the Madrid of the 1980s *(see p309)*, and still has an alternative flavour that attracts many young bohemian types. The hub of this cosmopolitan district is the Dos de Mayo square, where you can have a *caña* on the terrace of the **El 2D** bar. However, the characteristic atmosphere of the area is changing rapidly into a more design-driven space. Some examples are the **La Huida**, **Circo** and **Kike Keller** bars, which have cultivated a revolutionary, arty atmosphere. **Bar & Co** is a typical Malasaña venue, where local bands play weekly. You can relax there after 3am if you don't feel like clubbing.

Tupperware, a fusion of past and present, is a rock bar with an ultra pop decor, where you can also listen to garage, indie and pop music.

Lavapiés

Once the Jewish quarter of Madrid, the narrow streets of Lavapiés are rich with an eclectic mix of races and cultures. One of the most fascinating and diverse districts in town, the locals' old habit of sitting outside their doors on summer nights continues, as does the multiracial crowd on the terraces of Calle de Argumosa. A vibrant fusion of artists, immigrants, hipsters and squatters results in some of the most brilliant music, art, food, alternative theatre and nightlife in the city.

La Escalera de Jacob and **La Victoria** hold concerts, theatre performances and intercultural workshops. The endearingly eccentric bar, **La Colonia de San Lorenzo**, offers exhibitions and film screenings.

La Latina

Still the best district in town for cosy little hideaways and tapas bars, La Latina is an especially good place to go on Sundays after wandering around the Rastro flea market (see p306). For an excellent cocktail, or coffee and cake in the morning, head to **Delic**, and for a cultural experience try **Anti Café**, where you can listen to unique DJs, poetry and drama. For a taste of the traditional, visit **Taberna Almendro**, a classic from before La Latina became a fashionable nightlife area. Another worthwhile bar is **Taberna del Tempranillo**, which also serves a variety of Spanish wines, cheeses and ham. In the exquisite **María Pandora** bar, you can try a selection of champagnes and cavas, surrounded by books and antiques. Afterwards, you can dance until late at **Berlín Cabaret**, a modern nightclub that runs a 1930s cabaret every night.

Azca

With a skyline punctuated by the highest buildings, this is one of the most modern areas in town. Near the Paseo de la Castellana and the Santiago Bernabéu stadium, this financial district has a multitude of clubs and bars doing brisk business in basements.

If visitors feel the urge to dance, Avenida de Brasil is the stretch to head for, full of large clubs, though they tend to be a little overcrowded.

Nearby, in the Chamartín area, you will find another hardcore clubbing scene, which vibrantly unfolds late at night.

DIRECTORY

Nightlife Venues

El 2D
Calle Velarde 24.
Map 2 F4.
Tel 914 48 64 72.

Acuarela
C/ Gravina 10.
Map 5 B5.
Tel 915 22 21 43.

Alegoría
C/ Villanueva 2.
Map 6 D5.
Tel 915 57 27 85.

Anti Café
C/ Unión 2.
Map 4 D2.
Tel 915 41 76 57.

Bar & Co
C/ Barco 34. **Map** 2 F5.
Tel 915 31 77 54.

Bash
Plaza de Callao 4. **Map** 4
E1 **Tel** 915 31 01 32.

Berlín Cabaret
Costanilla de San Pedro
11. **Tel** 913 66 20 34.

Cardamomo
C/ De Echegaray 15.
Map 7 A3.
Tel 913 69 07 57.

Cervecería Santa Bárbara
Pl Santa Bárbara 8.
Tel 913 19 04 49.

Chocolatería San Ginés
Pasadizo de San Ginés,
C/ Arenal 11.
Map 4 E2.
Tel 913 65 65 46.

Clamores
C/ Alburquerque 14.
Map 5 A3.
Tel 914 45 79 38.

Circo
C/ Corredera Baja de San
Pablo 21.
Map 2 F5.

La Colonia de San Lorenzo
C/ Salitre 38. **Map** 7 A5.
Tel 673 63 84 98.

Delic
Pl De La Paja s/n.
Map 4 D3.
Tel 913 64 54 50.

La Escalera de Jacob
C/ de Lavapiés 11.
Map 4 F4.
Tel 695 26 35 09.

La Huida
C/ Colón 11. **Map** 5 A5.

Joy Madrid Discoteque
C/ Arenal 11.
Map 4 E2.
Tel 913 66 37 33.

El Junco
Plaza de Santa Bárbara 10.
Map 5 B4.
Tel 913 19 20 81.

Kapital
C/ Atocha 125.
Map 7 C4.
Tel 914 20 29 06.

Kike Keller
C/ Corredera Baja de San
Pablo 17.
Map 2 F5.

Lasal
C/ Guzmán el Bueno 98.
Tel 686 41 09 90.

María Pandora
Pl Gabriel Miró 1.
Map 3 B3.
Tel 913 64 00 39.

Populart
C/ Huertas 22.
Map 7 A3.
Tel 914 29 84 07.

Taberna Almendro
C/ Almendro 22.
Map 4 D3.
Tel 913 65 42 52.

Taberna del Tempranillo
C/ de la Cava Baja 38.
Tel 913 64 15 32.

Teatro Barceló
C/ de Barceló 11.
Map 5 A4.
Tel 914 47 01 28.

Tupperware
C/ Corredera
Alta de San Pablo 26.
Tel 625 52 35 61.

La Victoria
Calle Santa Isabel 40.
Map 7 B4.
Tel 915 28 64 57.

Viva Madrid
C/ Manuel Fernández
González 7.
Tel 914 20 35 96.

MADRID PROVINCE

Madrid province (the Comunidad de Madrid) sits high on Spain's central plateau. There is plenty of superb scenery and good walking country in the sierras to the north, which are a refuge for city dwellers who go there to ski in winter or cool down during the torrid summers. In the western foothills of these mountains stands El Escorial, the royal palace-cum-monastery built by Felipe II,

from which he ruled his empire. Close by is the Valle de los Caídos, the war monument erected by Franco. The smaller royal palace of El Pardo is on the outskirts of Madrid, and south of the city is the 18th-century summer palace of Aranjuez, set in lush parkland. Historic towns include Alcalá de Henares, which has a Renaissance university building, and Chinchón, where taverns cluster around a picturesque arcaded market square.

Sights at a Glance

Towns and Cities

2 Buitrago del Lozoya
7 Manzanares el Real
9 Alcalá de Henares
10 Chinchón

Historic Buildings

3 Monasterio de Santa María de El Paular
5 Santa Cruz del Valle de los Caídos
6 El Escorial pp334–5
8 Palacio de El Pardo
11 Palacio Real de Aranjuez

Mountain Ranges

1 Sierra Norte
4 Sierra Centro de Guadarrama

Key

	Madrid city
	Madrid province
═══	Motorway
▬▬	Major road
──	Minor road

0 kilometres 25
0 miles 20

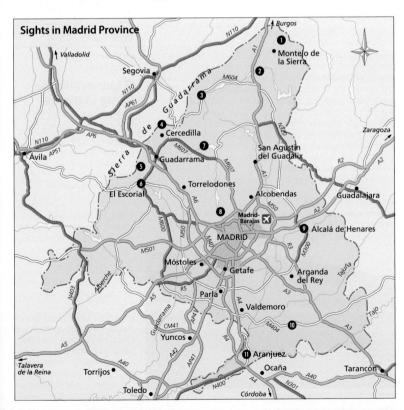

Sights in Madrid Province

◄ Snow-covered peaks of the Sierra Centro de Guadarrama   For additional map symbols *see back flap*

The village of Montejo de la Sierra in the Sierra Norte

❶ Sierra Norte

Madrid. 🚌 Montejo de la Sierra.
ℹ️ Calle Real 64, Montejo, 91 869
70 58. 🌐 sierradelrincon.org

The black slate hamlets of the Sierra Norte, which were once known as the Sierra Pobre (Poor Sierra), are located in the most attractively rural part of Madrid province.

At **Montejo de la Sierra**, the largest village in the area, an information centre organizes riding, the rental of traditional houses *(see p559)*, and visits to the nearby nature reserve of the **Hayedo de Montejo de la Sierra**. This is one of the most southern beech woods *(see p84)* in Europe, and a relic of a previous era, when climatic conditions here were more suitable for the beech. From Montejo, you can drive on to picturesque hamlets such as **La Hiruela** or **Puebla de la Sierra**, both in lovely walking country.

The drier southern hills slope down to the **Embalse de Puentes Viejas**, a reservoir where summer chalets cluster around artificial beaches. On the eastern edge of the sierra is the village of **Patones**, which is thought to have escaped invasion by the Moors and Napoleon's troops because of its isolated location.

❷ Buitrago del Lozoya

Madrid. 🗺️ 2,000. 🚌 ℹ️ Calle Tahona
19, 91 868 16 15. 🗓️ Sat. 🎉 La
Asunción and San Roque (15–16 Aug),
Cristo de los Esclavos (14–15 Sep).

Picturesquely sited above a meander in the Río Lozoya is the walled town of Buitrago del Lozoya. Founded by the Romans, it was fortified by the Arabs, and became an important market town in medieval times. The 14th-century Gothic-Mudéjar castle is in ruins, although the gatehouse, arches and stretches of the original Arab wall have survived. The castle is currently being restored and is closed to the public.

The town walls retain a charming atmosphere and can be visited for a fee.

The church of **Santa María del Castillo**, dating from the 14–15th century, has a Mudéjar tower and ceilings which were moved here from the old hospital. The **town hall** *(ayuntamiento)*, in the newer part of Buitrago, preserves a 16th-century processional cross. In the basement is the **Museo Picasso**. The prints, drawings and ceramics were collected by the artist's friend, Eugenio Arias.

🏛️ **Museo Picasso**
Plaza de Picasso 1. **Tel** 91 868 00 56.
Closed Mon, Sun pm. 🌐 **madrid. org/museo_picasso**

Altarpiece in the Monasterio de Santa María de El Paular

❸ Monasterio de Santa María de El Paular

Southwest of Rascafría on M604.
Tel 91 869 14 25. 🚌 Rascafría.
Open check the website for current tour times. 📷 obligatory.
Closed some public hols.
🌐 **monasteriopaular.com**

Founded in 1390 as Castile's first Carthusian monastery, Santa María de El Paular stands on the site of a medieval royal hunting lodge. Although it is mainly Gothic in style, Plateresque and Renaissance features were added later. The monastery was abandoned in 1836, when government minister Mendizábal ordered the sale of church goods *(see p67)*. It fell into disrepair until its restoration in the 1950s. Today the complex comprises a working Benedictine monastery, church and private hotel.

The church's delicate alabaster altarpiece, attributed to Flemish

Buitrago del Lozoya, standing next to the river

craftsmen, dates from the 15th century. Its panels depict scenes from the life of Jesus. The lavish Baroque *camarín* (chamber), behind the altar, was designed by Francisco de Hurtado in 1718. The cloister has impressive paintings by Vicente Carducho.

Every Sunday, the monks sing an hour-long Gregorian chant. If they are not busy, they will show you the cloister's Mudéjar brick vaulting and double sun-clock.

The monastery is a good starting point for exploring the towns of **Rascafría** and **Lozoya**. To the southwest is the nature reserve **Lagunas de Peñalara**.

❹ Sierra Centro de Guadarrama

Madrid. 🚊 Puerto de Navacerrada, Cercedilla. 🚌 Navacerrada, Cercedilla. 🛈 Navacerrada, 918 56 00 06. 🌐 sierraguadarrama.info

The central section of the Sierra de Guadarrama was little visited until the 1920s, when the area was first linked by train to Madrid. Today, the granite slopes are planted with pines and specked by holiday chalets. Villages such as **Navacerrada** and **Cercedilla** have grown into popular resorts for skiing, mountain-biking, rock climbing and horse riding. Walkers wanting to enjoy the pure mountain air can follow marked routes from Navacerrada.

The **Valle de la Fuenfría**, a nature reserve of wild forests, is best reached via Cercedilla. It has a well-preserved stretch of the original Roman road, as well as several picnic spots and marked walking routes.

The gigantic cross at Valle de los Caídos

❺ Santa Cruz del Valle de los Caídos

North of El Escorial on M600. **Tel** 91 890 56 11. 🚌 from El Escorial. **Open** Crypt: 10am–6pm Tue–Sun; (Apr–Sep: 10am–7pm). **Closed** some pub hols. 🎫 (free from 3pm Wed & Thu for EU citizens; from 4pm Apr–Sep).

General Franco had the Holy Cross of the Valley of the Fallen built as a memorial to those who died in the Civil War *(see pp70–71)*. The vast cross is located some 13 km (8 miles) north of El Escorial *(see pp334–5)*, and dominates the surrounding countryside. Some Spanish people find it too chilling a symbol of the dictatorship to be enjoyable, while for others its sheer size is rewarding.

The cross is 150 m (490 ft) high and rises above a basilica carved 250 m (820 ft) deep into the rock by prisoners. A number of them died during the 20-year-plus project. Access to the cross is currently closed to visitors for safety reasons.

Next to the basilica's high altar is the plain white tombstone of Franco, and, opposite, that of José Antonio Primo de Rivera, founder of the Falange Española Party. A further 40,000 coffins of soldiers from both sides in the Civil War lie here out of sight, including those of two unidentified victims.

Navacerrada pass in the Sierra de Guadarrama

❻ El Escorial

Felipe II's imposing grey palace of San Lorenzo de El Escorial stands out against the foothills of the Sierra de Guadarrama to the northwest of Madrid. It was built between 1563 and 1584 in honour of St Lawrence, and its unornamented severity set a new architectural style, known as Herreriano, which became one of the most influential in Spain. The interior was conceived as a mausoleum and contemplative retreat rather than a splendid residence. Its artistic wealth, which includes some of the most important works of art of the royal Habsburg collections, is concentrated in the museums, chapterhouses, church, royal pantheon and library. In contrast, the royal apartments are sober, with incongruous interiors.

★ **Royal Pantheon**
The funerary urns of Spanish monarchs line the marble mausoleum.

KEY

① **Patio de los Reyes**

② **The Alfonso XII College**
was founded by monks in 1875 as a boarding school.

③ **Bourbon Palace**

④ **Architectural Museum**

⑤ **Sala de Batallas**

⑥ **The Basílica's altarpiece** is the highlight of this huge decorated church. The chapel houses a superb marble sculpture of the Crucifixion by Cellini.

⑦ **The Royal Apartments**, on the second floor of the palace, consist of Felipe II's modestly decorated living quarters. His bedroom opens directly onto the high altar of the basilica.

⑧ **The Patio de los Evangelistas** is a temple by Herrera. The Jardín de los Frailes makes a nice walk.

⑨ **The Monastery** was founded in 1567, and has been run by Augustinian monks since 1885.

Main entrance

Entrance to Basilica only

★ **Library**
This impressive array of 40,000 books incorporates Felipe II's personal collection. On display are precious manuscripts, including a poem by Alfonso X the Learned. The 16th-century ceiling frescoes are by Tibaldi.

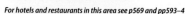

For hotels and restaurants in this area see p569 and pp593–4

★ **Museum of Art**
One of the highlights here is
The Calvary, by 15th-century
Flemish artist Rogier van
der Weyden, though it is
currently being restored by
the Prado museum.

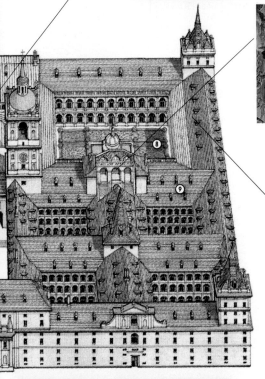

**The Glory of the Spanish
Monarchy by Luca Giordano**
This beautiful fresco, above the
main staircase, depicts Charles V
and Felipe II, and scenes of the
building of the monastery.

Chapterhouses
On display here is Charles
V's portable altar. The
ceiling frescoes depict
monarchs and angels.

The Building of El Escorial
When chief architect Juan Bautista de
Toledo died in 1567, he was replaced
by Juan de Herrera, royal inspector of
monuments. The plain architectural style
of El Escorial is called *desornamentado*,
literally, "unadorned".

Climber resting on a rock face of La Pedriza, near Manzanares el Real

❼ Manzanares el Real

Madrid. 🗻 7,200. 🚌 ℹ️ C/ del Cura, 639 17 96 02 (Fri, Sat & Sun mornings). 🛒 Tue & Fri. 🎉 Fiesta de Verano (early Aug), Cristo de la Nave (14 Sep). 🖥️ manzanareselreal.org

The skyline of Manzanares el Real is dominated by its restored 15th-century castle. Although the castle has some traditionally military features, such as double machicolations and turrets, it was used mainly as a residence by the Dukes of Infantado. Below the castle is a 16th-century church, a Renaissance portico and fine capitals. Behind the town, bordering the foothills of the Sierra de Guadarrama, is **La Pedriza**, a mass of granite screes and ravines, very popular with climbers. It now forms part of an attractive nature reserve.

Environs
Colmenar Viejo, 12 km (7.5 miles) southeast of Manzanares, has a Gothic-Mudéjar church.

❽ Palacio de El Pardo

El Pardo, northwest of Madrid off the A6. **Tel** 91 376 15 00. 🚌 601 from Moncloa. **Open** Oct–Mar: 10am–6pm daily; Apr–Sep: 10am–8pm daily **Closed** for royal visits & public hols. 🎟️ (free from 3pm Wed & Thu for EU residents; from 5pm Apr–Sep). 🖥️ patrimonionacional.es

This royal hunting lodge and palace, set in parkland just outside Madrid's city limits, boasts General Franco among its former residents. A tour takes visitors round the moated palace's Habsburg wing and the identical 18th-century extension, designed by Francesco Sabatini.

The Bourbon interior is heavy with frescoes, gilt mouldings and tapestries, many made to designs by Goya *(see p310)*. Today the palace hosts visiting heads of state and royal guests. Surrounding the palace and the 18th-century village of El Pardo is a vast forest of holm oak. The area is popular for picnicking, and game animals still run free.

Façade of Colegio de San Ildefonso in Alcalá de Henares

❾ Alcalá de Henares

Madrid. 🗻 204,000. 🚊 🚌 ℹ️ Callejón Santa María, 91 889 26 94. 🛒 Mon, Wed. 🎉 Feria de Alcalá (late Aug). 🗺️ weekend city tours. 🖥️ turismoalcala.es

At the heart of a modern industrial town is one of Spain's most renowned university quarters. Founded in 1499 by

Lavish 18th-century tapestry inside the Palacio de El Pardo

Cardinal Cisneros, Alcalá's **university** became one of the foremost places of learning in 16th-century Europe. The most historic college, **San Ildefonso**, survives. Former students include Golden Age playwright Lope de Vega *(see p294)*. In 1517 the university produced Europe's first polyglot bible, with text in Latin, Greek, Hebrew and Chaldean.

Alcalá's other sights are the cathedral, the **Casa-Museo de Cervantes**, birthplace of the Golden Age author, and the restored 19th-century neo-Moorish **Palacio de Laredo**.

🏛 **Casa-Museo de Cervantes**
Calle Mayor 48. **Tel** 91 889 96 54.
Open 10am–6pm Tue–Sun. **Closed** some public hols.

⑩ Chinchón

Madrid. 🄫 5,300. 🚌 ❶ Plaza Mayor 6, 91 893 53 23. 🄫 Sat. 🎊 Semana Santa (Easter Week), San Roque (12–18 Aug). 🗓 🌐 ciudad-chinchon.com

Chinchón is arguably Madrid province's most picturesque town. The 15th- to 16th-century, typically Castilian, porticoed **Plaza Mayor** has a splendidly theatrical air. It comes alive for the Easter passion play, acted out by the townspeople *(see p294)*, and during the August bullfights. The 16th-century church, perched above the square, has an altar painting by Goya, whose brother was a priest here. Just off the square is the 18th-century Augustinian

Chinchón's unique porticoed Plaza Mayor

monastery, which has been converted into a **parador** with a peaceful patio garden. A ruined 15th-century castle is on a hill to the west of town. Although it is closed to the public, there are views of Chinchón and the countryside from outside it.

Chinchón is a popular weekend destination for *madrileños*, who come here to sample the excellent chorizo and locally produced *anís (see p581)* in the town's many taverns.

⑪ Palacio Real de Aranjuez

Plaza de Parejas, Aranjuez. **Tel** 91 891 07 40. 🚉 🚌 **Open** Tue–Sun. **Closed** some public hols. 🎟 (free from 3pm Wed & Thu for EU residents; from 5pm Apr–Sep). ⚅ 🗓
🌐 patrimonionacional.es

The Royal Summer Palace and Gardens of Aranjuez grew up around a medieval hunting lodge standing beside a natural weir, the meeting point of the Tagus and Jarama rivers.

Today's palace of brick and white stone was built in the 18th century and later redecorated

by the Bourbons. A guided tour takes you through numerous Baroque rooms, among them the Chinese Porcelain Room, the Hall of Mirrors and the Smoking Room, modelled on the Alhambra in Granada. It is worth visiting Aranjuez to walk in the 3 sq km (1 sq mile) of shady royal gardens which inspired Joaquín Rodrigo's *Concierto de Aranjuez*. The Parterre Garden and the Island Garden survive from the original 16th-century palace.

Between the palace and the River Tagus is the 18th-century Prince's Garden, decorated with sculptures, fountains and lofty trees from the Americas. In the garden is the Casa de Marinos (Sailors' House), a museum housing the launches once used by the royal family for trips along the river. At the far end of the garden is the Casa del Labrador (Labourer's Cottage), a decorative royal pavilion built by Carlos IV.

The town's restaurants are popular for the exceptional quality of their asparagus and strawberries. In summer, a 19th-century steam train, built to carry strawberries, runs between here and the capital.

Miguel de Cervantes

Miguel de Cervantes Saavedra, Spain's greatest literary figure *(see p38)*, was born in Alcalá de Henares in 1547. After fighting in the naval Battle of Lepanto (1571), he was held captive by the Turks for more than five years. In 1605, when he was almost 60 years old, the first of two parts of his comic masterpiece *Don Quixote (see p399)* was published to popular acclaim. He continued writing novels and plays until his death in Madrid on 23 April 1616, the same date that Shakespeare died.

Gardens surrounding the Royal Palace at Aranjuez

CENTRAL
SPAIN

Introducing Central Spain   **340–349**

Castilla y León   **350–381**

Castilla–La Mancha   **382–403**

Extremadura   **404–417**

Introducing Central Spain

Much of Spain's vast central plateau, the *meseta*, is covered with wheat fields or dry, dusty plains, but there are many attractive places to explore. Central Spain's mountains, gorges, forests and lakes are filled with wildlife. A deep sense of history permeates the towns and cities of the tableland, reflected in some stunning architecture: the Roman ruins of Mérida, the medieval mansions of Cáceres, the Gothic cathedrals of Burgos, León and Toledo, the Renaissance grandeur of Salamanca, and castles almost everywhere.

León Cathedral *(see pp358–9)*, an outstanding Gothic building, was completed during the 14th century. As well as many glorious windows of medieval glass, it has superb carved choir stalls depicting biblical scenes and everyday life.

Salamanca *(see pp362–5)* is the site of some of the finest Renaissance and Plateresque architecture in Spain. Among the city's most notable buildings are the university, its façade a mass of carved detail; the old and new cathedrals (built side by side); and the handsome Plaza Mayor, built in warm golden sandstone.

Museo Nacional de Arte Romano in Mérida *(see pp414–15)* houses Roman treasures. The city has a well-preserved Roman theatre still in use.

Cistierna

Ponferrada

León

Astorga

Saha

Puebla de Sanabria

CASTILLA Y LEO?
(See pp350–81)

Benavente

Zamora

Tordesillas

Salamanca

Ciudad Rodrigo

Béjar

Plasencia

Talave de la Re

Navalmoral de la Mata

Cáceres

Trujillo

EXTREMADURA
(See pp404–17)

Herrera del Duque

Badajoz

Mérida

Zafra

Llerena

0 kilometres   50

0 miles   50

◄ Historic city of Toledo, Castilla-La Mancha

Burgos Cathedral *(see pp376–7)* is the work of some of the great medieval architects and artists, and it is full of treasures from all periods. This Baroque fresco of the coronation of the Virgin covers the domed ceiling of the sacristy.

Segovia *(see pp368–9)* extends along a rocky spur that divides two rivers. The city's landmarks are the Alcázar *(see pp348–9)* – a castle with distinctive fairy-tale towers – and the Roman aqueduct, built in the 1st century AD, which towers 29 m (95 ft) above a busy urban square.

Oña

Burgos

Palencia

Peñafiel   Aranda de Duero   Soria

adolid

valo

Medinaceli

Sigüenza   Maranchón

Segovia

ila   MADRID   Guadalajara

Madrid   Cañaveras

Getafe

Aranjuez

Tarancón   Cuenca

Toledo

CASTILLA-LA MANCHA
(See pp382–403)   Alarcón

Consuegra   San Clemente

Tormelloso

Ciudad Real   Manzanares   Albacete

Almagro

Valdepeñas

Puertollano   Hellín

Cuenca's Old Town *(see pp388–9)* was built on a ridge high above two gorges. One of the picturesque but precariously sited "Hanging Houses" is now home to a museum of abstract art.

Toledo Cathedral *(see pp396–7)*, with its exuberant sculptured decoration, is a great medieval building in a city of monuments. Toledo's architectural wealth stems from a fusion of Jewish, Christian and Muslim cultures.

The Flavours of Central Spain

Madrid is famous for its extremes of temperature – a climate that has given rise to the rueful local saying "nine months of winter and three months of hell". The surrounding regions suffer the same extremes, and their traditional cuisines reflect both the wintry cold and the dusty, scorched terrain. Meat predominates as roasts and stews and in warming soups, thickened with beans and pulses, which thrive despite the weather. Cured hams, spicy sausages and pungent cheeses are excellent accompaniments to the strong local wine. The finest ham is from Extremadura, where black-footed (*pata negra*) pigs forage freely among the oaks.

Manchego cheese

A chef preparing *gambas al ajillo*, a popular tapas dish

Madrid

Restaurants in Madrid, as befits the Spanish capital, offer cuisine from every corner of the country. Curiously, considering its distance from the ocean, the capital is famed for its seafood, flown in freshly every day. *Madrileños* appreciate every part of an animal, particularly when it comes to pork, and Madrid menus may feature brains, ears, pigs' trotters, and *callos a la madrileña* (tripe) is a classic local dish. Sturdy stews, such as the celebrated *cocido madrileño*, keep out the bitter winter cold. The *tapeo* – a bar crawl between tapas bars – is an institution in the city, and each bar has its own speciality dish.

Castilla y Leon

Spread out high on a plain, searingly hot in summer, and bitingly cold in winter, Castilla y León is famous for its roasted meats, served in *asadores* (grillhouses). The most celebrated local dish is *cochinillo* (suckling pig), but pork, chicken, game in season and lamb are also popular. These are often combined with local pulses and lentils in

Pinto beans
White (butter) beans
Black beans
Castillian garbanzos (chickpeas)
Red (kidney) beans
Armuña lentils
Beans and pulses, key ingredients in the cooking of Central Spain

Regional Dishes and Specialities

The cuisine of Spain's often wild and remote interior is characterized by warming soups and stews; traditionally made hams, cured meats and cheeses; plenty of filling beans and pulses; and flavourful fruit and vegetables. On the high plains of Castilla y León, locals keep out the winter cold with succulent roasted meats, and Extremaduran ham is the best you'll taste. In Don Quixote country, a glass of robust local wine and a chunk of Manchegan cheese is sheer delight. Fancy restaurants with fashionable food are few and far between, but welcoming, old-fashioned inns offer simple and tasty home cooking. Madrid, of course, is the exception: here you'll find every possible cuisine, along with excellent seafood, which is harder to find anywhere else in this landlocked region.

Fresh figs

Cocido Madrileño This rich stew is traditionally eaten in stages: first the broth, then vegetables and finally the meat.

Plucking the stamens from crocus flowers to make saffron

hearty soups and stews, which are given extra flavour with local *embutidos* (cured meats). The region also produces delicious cheeses such as soft Burgos, often served with honey, *membrillo* (quince jelly) or nuts for dessert. Local wines are robust and simple, a good accompaniment to the strong flavours of the regional cuisine of Castilla y León.

Castilla-La Mancha

This is Don Quixote country: empty, flat, dusty and scattered with windmills. Local inns and taverns serve traditional country cooking, with plenty of hearty soups, substantial casseroles and simply grilled local meat, poultry and seasonal game. Manchegan *gazpacho*, unlike its cold, vegetable-soup *andaluz* namesake, is a hefty stew made with whatever meat is available. A common accompaniment to it is *pisto*, a ratatouille-like dish made with a range of tasty, fresh local vegetables. The Arabs brought with them saffron, which is still grown around Consuegra, and their influence also lingers on in Toledo's famous marzipan sweets and the fragrant Alajú almond soup from Cuenca.

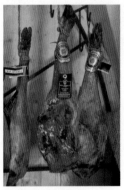

Cured hams hanging in an *embutidos* shop

Extremadura

Wild, beautiful Extremadura sees few visitors and, in many places, life continues virtually untouched by the 21st century. Endless rolling fields dotted with holm oak shelter the acorn-fed, black-footed pigs that make Spain's most highly prized hams *(jamón Ibérico)*. Thanks to the deeply rooted hunting tradition, partridge, hare and wild boar regularly feature on local menus along with river fish such as tench and trout. There are some delicious cheeses, as well as perfumed local honey and wonderful fruit, particularly cherries, peaches and figs.

On the Menu

Chocolate con Churros
The typical Spanish breakfast – thick hot chocolate with sugary strips of fried batter for dipping, originated in Madrid.

Cochinillo The speciality of Segovia: 21-day-old suckling pig, roasted until so tender it can be cut with a plate.

Gazpacho Manchego
Sometimes called a *galiano*, this is a rich stew traditionally made with hare and partridge.

Macarraca Extremaduran salad of chopped ripe tomatoes with peppers, onion and garlic.

Tortilla de Patata A simple potato omelette, now a staple in restaurants all over Spain.

Albóndigas Meatballs – sturdy and comforting country fare from the high plain of Castilla y León.

Migas Extremeñas Crumbs of country bread are fried up with peppers, pork and chorizo or cured sausage.

Yemas A delicious treat from Ávila, these lemony, custardy cakes are made with egg yolks and sugar.

Wines of Central Spain

The wines of Central Spain originate in either the small, high-quality regions of northwest Castilla y León or in the vast wine-producing plains of La Mancha and Valdepeñas. Ribera del Duero has become Spain's most fashionable red wine region, with its aromatic, rich yet fine reds made from Tinto Fino grapes (the local name for Tempranillo) and, more recently, lighter, fruity wines. Rueda makes a good white wine, made from the Verdejo grape. La Mancha and Valdepeñas both produce lots of simple white wine, and reds which can be mellow and fruity.

Harvesting Viura grapes at Rueda

Artesian well for irrigating vines in La Mancha

Toro makes the most powerful and fiery of all red wines from the ubiquitous Tempranillo grape.

Traditional earthenware *tinaja*, still used for fermenting wine

Key Facts about Wines of Central Spain

Location and Climate
Ribera del Duero, Rueda and Toro are all high-lying areas with extreme climates – very hot summer days combined with cool nights, and cold winters. The marked difference of temperature between day and night helps to preserve the acidity in the grapes. Both La Mancha and Valdepeñas are extremely hot and dry areas. In recent years, droughts have caused a severe shortage of grapes, though 2013 saw more rain and a better yield.

Grape Varieties
The Tempranillo grape – also known as Tinto Fino, Tinto del Toro and Cencibel – produces nearly all the best red wines of Central Spain. Cabernet Sauvignon is permitted in some regions; it is used in some Ribera del Duero wines and occasionally surfaces as a single varietal, as at the estate of the Marquis of Griñón in Méntrida. Verdejo, Viura and Sauvignon Blanc are used for white Rueda. The white Airén grape predominates in the vineyards of Valdepeñas and La Mancha.

Good Producers
Toro: Fariña (Gran Colegiata). **Rueda:** Álvarez y Diez, Los Curros, Marqués de Riscal, Sanz. **Ribera del Duero:** Alejandro Fernández (Pesquera), Boada, Hermanos Pérez Pascuas (Viña Pedrosa), Ismael Arroyo (Valsotillo), Vega Sicilia, Victor Balbás. **Méntrida:** Marqués de Griñón. **La Mancha:** Fermín Ayuso Roig (Estola), Vinícola de Castilla (Castillo de Alhambra). **Valdepeñas:** Casa de la Viña, Félix Solís, Luis Megía (Marqués de Gastañaga), Los Llanos.

COLEGIATA
TINTO
1985

Villafranca del Bierzo
Cacabelos
Leó
Ponferrada
A6
A52
Benavente
Zamora
Duero
A66
Salamanca
A62
Ciudad Rodrigo
A66
Coria
Plasencia
A66
A5
EXTREMADURA
Cáceres
Trujillo

0 kilometres   100
0 miles   50

Vineyard near Moral de Calatrava in Valdepeñas

Pesquera is made by Alejandro Fernández, the second most notable producer in the Ribera del Duero region, after Vega Sicilia.

Key

- Bierzo
- Cigales
- Toro
- Rueda
- Ribera del Duero
- Vinos de Madrid
- Méntrida
- La Mancha
- Valdepeñas
- Almansa

Marqués de Griñón is an intense Cabernet Sauvignon wine with a deep colour, made on a vast estate outside Toledo. Although officially a *vino de mesa* (see p581), its quality is as high as a DO wine.

Señorío de los Llanos is produced in Valdepeñas. Its fine reds – made from Cencibel (Tempranillo) and aged in oak – are of excellent value.

Wine Regions

The wine regions of Ribera del Duero, Toro and Rueda are situated on remote, high plateaus, straddling the Río Duero. To the northwest lies the isolated region of Bierzo, whose wines have more in common with neighbouring Valdeorras in Galicia. Some wine is produced around Madrid, and southwest of the capital is the largely undistinguished region of Méntrida. Most of Central Spain's wine is produced in La Mancha – the world's largest single wine region – and in the smaller enclave of Valdepeñas, which produces a great deal of *vino de mesa*.

Birds of Central Spain

The vast and varied wild habitats of Central Spain are home to the richest avifauna in the peninsula. White storks' nests are a common sight on the church towers and chimneypots of towns. Grebes, herons and shovelers can be seen in the marshlands; the distinctive hoopoe is often spotted in woods; and grasslands are the nesting grounds of bustards and cranes. The mountains and high plains are the domain of birds of prey such as the imperial eagle, peregrine falcon and vultures. Deforestation, changing agricultural practices and hunting have all taken their toll in recent decades. Today, almost 160 bird species are the subject of conservation initiatives.

Migration Routes

— Cranes
— Storks
— Raptors
— Wildfowl

Marshland and Wet Meadow

Wetlands, such as Lagunas de Ruidera *(see p401)*, on the edge of the plains of La Mancha, are vital feeding grounds for a wide range of waterfowl, some of which may remain in Spain throughout the year. Other migratory species use such sites as stopover points to feed, rest and build up enough energy to enable them to complete their journeys.

Woodland and Scrub

Habitats in areas of woodland, such as the Parque Nacional de Cabañeros *(see p391)*, and scrub support many species, such as rollers and woodpeckers, throughout the year. Food is plentiful and there are many places to roost and nest. Early in the morning is the best time for spotting some of the rarer species, such as the bluethroat.

Little egrets are recognized by their snow-white plumage and graceful slow flight. They feed largely on frogs, snails and small fish.

Rollers are commonly found in woodland, often nesting in tree stumps or holes left by woodpeckers. Their food includes grasshoppers, crickets and beetles.

Shovellers feed on the water surface with a characteristic shovelling motion. The male has brightly coloured plumage but the female is a dull brown.

Hoopoes can be easily identified by their striking plumage and by the crest which can be raised if the bird is alarmed. They feed on ground insects.

Storks

Both the white and the (much rarer) black stork breed in Spain. They can be recognized in flight by their slow, steady wingbeats and may occasionally be seen soaring on thermals, usually during migrations. During the breeding season they put on elaborate courtship displays, which involve "dancing", wing-beating and bill-clapping. Their large nests, made of branches and twigs and lined with grasses, are constructed on roofs, towers, spires and chimneypots, where they are easy to watch. They feed on insects, fish and amphibians. Stork populations are threatened by wetland reclamation and the use of pesticides.

The endangered black stork

Nesting on a monastery roof

Grassland and Field

Many of Spain's natural grasslands have been ploughed over to plant cereals and other crops. Remaining vestiges are rich in wild grasses and flowers and are vital habitats for species such as bustards and larks.

Cranes perform elegant courtship dances and are also stately birds in flight, their long necks extended to the limit. They are omnivores, feeding on amphibians, crustaceans, plants and insects.

Great bustards nest in shallow depressions formed in open grassland and cultivated fields. Spain is home to half of the world's population.

Mountain and High Plain

Some of Spain's most spectacular birds of prey live in mountain ranges, such as the Sierra de Gredos *(see p366)*, and the high plains of Central Spain. The broad wingspans of eagles and vultures allow them to soar on currents of warm air as they scan the ground below for prey and carrion.

Imperial eagles, with their vast wingspan of 2.25 m (7 ft), are extremely rare – only around 300 pairs are left in the whole of Spain.

Griffon vultures, a gregarious species, nest in trees and on rocky crags, often using the same place from year to year. Their broad wingspans can exceed 2 m (6 ft).

The Castles of Castile

The greatest concentration of Spain's 2,000 castles is in Castilla y León (now part of Castile), which derived its name from the word *castillo*, or castle. In the 10th and 11th centuries this region was the battleground between Moors and Christians. Villages and towns were fortified as protection against one side or the other. Most of the surviving castles in Castile, however, were built as noble residences after the area had been reconquered and there was no longer a military purpose for them. Fernando and Isabel *(see pp60–61)* banned the building of new castles at the end of the 15th century; many existing ones were converted to domestic use.

Coca Castle *(see p369)*, a classic Mudéjar design in brick

La Mota Castle *(see p370)*, at Medina del Campo, near Valladolid, was originally a Moorish castle but was rebuilt after 1440 and later became the property of Fernando and Isabel. The square-shaped Torre del Homenaje has twin bartizan turrets at its corners and machicolations beneath its battlements. Great curtain walls surround the castle.

Patio de armas (courtyard)

Bartizan turrets

The Torre de Juan II contained the dungeons.

The barbican, with the coat of arms of the Catholic Monarchs carved over the gate, contains the portcullis and guards' watchrooms.

Belmonte Castle *(see p398)* was built in the 15th century as the stronghold of the quarrelsome Marquis of Villena, Juan Pacheco. Late Gothic in style, it has a sophisticated, hexagonal ground plan, with a triangular bailey.

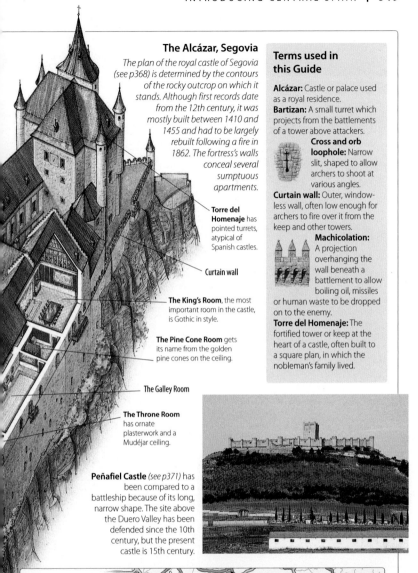

The Alcázar, Segovia

The plan of the royal castle of Segovia (see p368) is determined by the contours of the rocky outcrop on which it stands. Although first records date from the 12th century, it was mostly built between 1410 and 1455 and had to be largely rebuilt following a fire in 1862. The fortress's walls conceal several sumptuous apartments.

Torre del Homenaje has pointed turrets, atypical of Spanish castles.

Curtain wall

The King's Room, the most important room in the castle, is Gothic in style.

The Pine Cone Room gets its name from the golden pine cones on the ceiling.

The Galley Room

The Throne Room has ornate plasterwork and a Mudéjar ceiling.

Terms used in this Guide

Alcázar: Castle or palace used as a royal residence.

Bartizan: A small turret which projects from the battlements of a tower above attackers.

Cross and orb loophole: Narrow slit, shaped to allow archers to shoot at various angles.

Curtain wall: Outer, windowless wall, often low enough for archers to fire over it from the keep and other towers.

Machicolation: A projection overhanging the wall beneath a battlement to allow boiling oil, missiles or human waste to be dropped on to the enemy.

Torre del Homenaje: The fortified tower or keep at the heart of a castle, often built to a square plan, in which the nobleman's family lived.

Peñafiel Castle *(see p371)* has been compared to a battleship because of its long, narrow shape. The site above the Duero Valley has been defended since the 10th century, but the present castle is 15th century.

The Castles of Castilla y León

Some of Central Spain's finest surviving castles can be visited today. A few, such as Ciudad Rodrigo *(see p361)*, have been turned into luxurious paradors.

Palencia

Torrelobatón

Zamora

Tordesillas

Valladolid

Simancas

Cuéllar

Peñaranda de Duero

Aranda de Duero

Peñafiel

Calatañazor

Gormaz

Berlanga de Duero

Buen Amor

La Mota

Coca

Pedraza

Salamanca

Arévalo

Turégano

Segovia

Ávila

Ciudad Rodrigo

0 kilometres   100
0 miles   50

CASTILLA Y LEÓN

León · Zamora · Salamanca · Ávila · Segovia
Valladolid · Palencia · Burgos · Soria

Awesome expanses of ochre plains stretch to hills crowned with the castles that cover this vast region. Through Spain's history, these central provinces have had a major influence on its language, religion and culture. Their many historic cities preserve some of the country's most magnificent architectural sights.

The territories of the two rival medieval kingdoms of Castile and León, occupying the northern half of the great plateau in the centre of Spain, now form the country's largest region, or *comunidad autónoma*.

Castile and León were first brought together under one crown in 1037 by Fernando I, but the union was not consolidated until the early 13th century. The kingdom of Castile and León was one of the driving forces of the Reconquest. El Cid, the legendary hero, was born near Burgos.

Wealth pouring in from the wool trade and the New World, reaching a peak in the 16th century, financed the many great artistic and architectural treasures that can be seen today in the cities of Castilla y

León. Burgos has an exuberantly decorated Gothic cathedral. León Cathedral is famous for its wonderful stained glass. At the heart of the monumental city of Salamanca is the oldest university in the peninsula. Segovia's aqueduct is the largest Roman structure in Spain and its Alcázar is the country's most photographed castle. Ávila is surrounded by an unbroken wall, built by Christian forces against the Moors. In Valladolid, the regional capital, a superb collection of multicoloured sculpture is displayed in a magnificent 15th-century building.

Beyond the cities, in Castilla y León's varied countryside, there are many attractive small towns which preserve outstanding examples of the region's vernacular architecture.

Cereal fields and vineyards covering the fertile Tierra de Campos in Palencia province

◀ The fairy-tale Alcázar castle in moonlight, Segovia

Exploring Castilla y León

Covering the northern part of Central Spain's vast tableland,
Castilla y León has a huge variety of sights. Many – the University
of Salamanca, the Alcázar and aqueduct of Segovia, the medieval
walls of Ávila, the monastery at Santo Domingo de Silos, and the
great cathedrals of Burgos and León – are well-known. Other
historic towns and villages worthy of a detour include Ciudad
Rodrigo, Covarrubias, Pedraza de la Sierra and Zamora. This
region also has beautiful mountainous countryside in the
Sierra de Francia, Sierra de Bejar and Sierra de Gredos.

Sights at a Glance

1 El Bierzo
2 Villafranca del Bierzo
3 Ponferrada
4 Puebla de Sanabria
5 Astorga
6 Cueva de Valporquero
7 *León pp357–9*
8 Zamora
9 Ciudad Rodrigo
11 *Salamanca pp362–5*
12 Sierra de Gredos
13 Ávila
14 La Granja de San Ildefonso
15 Segovia
16 Pedraza de la Sierra
17 Sepúlveda
18 Castillo de Coca
19 Medina del Campo
20 Tordesillas
21 Valladolid
22 Medina de Rioseco
23 Palencia
24 Frómista
25 Aguilar de Campoo
26 Briviesca
27 Covarrubias
28 *Burgos pp374–7*
29 Lerma
30 Monasterio de Santo Domingo
de Silos
31 Peñaranda de Duero
32 El Burgo de Osma
33 Soria
34 Medinaceli

Tours

10 Sierra de Francia and
Sierra de Bejar

Getting Around

Madrid makes a convenient springboard for touring in Castilla y León. The major cities of the region are connected by rail, but the coach is often a quicker alternative. If you intend on exploring rural areas or small towns, it is advisable to hire a car.

Sunflowers growing in Burgos province

Key

- ▬▬ Motorway
- ▬ ▬ Motorway under construction
- ▬▬ Major road
- ▬ Secondary road
- ▬ Scenic route
- ▬▬ Main railway
- — Minor railway
- ▬▬ International border
- ▬▬ Regional border
- △ Summit

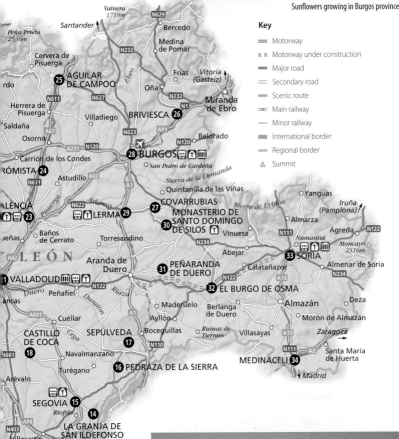

Peñaranda de Duero castle

❶ El Bierzo

León. 🚉 Ponferrada. 🚌 Ponferrada.
𝑖 C/ Gil y Carrasco, Ponferrada, 987
42 42 36. **W** ccbierzo.com

This northwestern region of León province was at one time the bed of an ancient lake. Sheltered by hills from the worst extremes of Central Spain's climate, its sun-soaked, alluvial soils make for fertile orchards and vineyards. Over the centuries, the area has also yielded rich mineral pickings including coal, iron and gold. Many hiking routes and picnic spots are within reach of the main towns of Ponferrada and Villafranca del Bierzo.

In the eastern section, you can trace the course of the old Road to Santiago (*see pp86–7*) through the **Montes de León**, past the pilgrim church and medieval bridge of Molinaseca. Turning off the road at the remote village of El Acebo, you pass through a deep valley where there are signs pointing to the **Herrería de Compludo**, a water-powered 7th-century ironworks. The equipment still works and is demonstrated regularly, although the site is currently closed for restoration.

The **Lago de Carucedo**, to the southwest of Ponferrada, is an ancient artificial lake. It acted as a reservoir in Roman times, a by-product of a vast gold-mining

A palloza in the Sierra de Ancares

operation. Using slave labour, millions of tonnes of alluvium were washed from the hills of Las Médulas by a complex system of canals and sluice gates. The ore was then panned, and the gold dust collected on sheep's wool. It is estimated that more than 500 tonnes of precious metal were extracted between the 1st and 4th centuries AD. These ancient workings lie within a memorable landscape of wind-eroded crags, and hills pierced by tunnels and colonized by gnarled chestnut trees. You can best appreciate the area from a viewpoint at Orellán, which is reached via a rough, steep track. **Las Médulas**, a village south of Carucedo, is another place to go for a fine view.

To the north of the A6 highway lies the Sierra de Ancares, a wild region of rounded, slate mountains marking the borders of Galicia and Asturias. Part of it now forms the **Reserva Nacional de los Ancares Leoneses**, an attractive nature reserve. The heathland is home to deer, wolves, brown bears and capercaillies.

Several villages high in the hills contain *pallozas* – primitive, pre-Roman stone dwellings. One of the most striking collections can be found in isolated **Campo del Agua**, in the west.

🏛 **Herrería de Compludo**
Compludo. **Tel** 987 42 42 36.
Closed for restoration. 🖼

✂ **Las Médulas**
Tel 987 42 07 08. **Open** 11am–2pm,
4–8pm daily (Oct–Mar: to 6pm).
Closed public hols. 🖼 🎥
W fundacionlasmedulas.org

❷ Villafranca del Bierzo

León. 🏔 3,500. 🚌 **𝑖** Avenida Díez
Ovelar 10, 987 54 00 28. 🚍 Tue.
🎺 Santo Tirso (28 Jan), Spring Fiesta
(1 May), Fiesta del Cristo (14 Sep).
W villafrancadelbierzo.org

Emblazoned mansions line the ancient streets of this delightful town. The solid, early 16th-century, drum-towered castle is still inhabited. Near the Plaza Mayor a number of imposing

Craggy, tree-clad hills around the ancient gold workings near the village of Las Médulas

churches and convents compete for attention. Particularly worth seeing are the fine sculptures adorning the north portal of the simple, Romanesque **Iglesia de Santiago** (open Jul–mid-Sep). At the church's Puerta del Perdón (Door of Mercy), pilgrims who were too weak to make the final gruelling hike across the hills of Galicia could obtain dispensation. Also sample the local speciality, cherries in *aguardiente*, a spirit.

Environs
One of the finest views over El Bierzo is from **Corullón**, to the south. This village with grey stone houses is set in a sunny location above the broad, fertile basin of the Río Burbia where the vines of the Bierzo wine region flourish *(see pp82–3)*. Two churches, the late 11th-century San Miguel and the Romanesque San Esteban, are worth a visit. Down in the valley, the Benedictine monastery at **Carracedo del Monasterio** stands in splendour. Founded in 990, it was once the most powerful religious community in El Bierzo.

Puerta del Perdón of Villafranca's Iglesia de Santiago

❸ Ponferrada

León. 68,700. C/ Gil y Carrasco 4, 987 42 42 36. Wed & Sat. Virgen de la Encina (8 Sep).
W ponferrada.org/turismo/en

A medieval bridge reinforced with iron *(pons ferrata)*, erected for the benefit of pilgrims on their way to Santiago de Compostela, gave this town its name. Today, prosperous from

The imposing Templar castle of Ponferrada

both iron and coal deposits, Ponferrada has expanded into a sizable town.

Most of its attractions are confined to the small old quarter. Ponferrada's majestic **castle** was constructed between the 12th and 14th centuries by the Knights Templar to protect pilgrims. During the Middle Ages it was one of the largest fortresses in northwest Spain.

Standing on the main square is the Baroque **town hall** *(ayuntamiento)*. One entrance to the square, one of the gateways of the medieval wall, is straddled by a tall clock tower. Nearby is the Renaissance **Basílica de la Virgen de la Encina**. The older **Iglesia de Santo Tomás de las Ollas** is hidden away in the town's village-like northern suburbs. Mozarabic, Romanesque and Baroque elements combine in the architecture of this simple church. The 10th-century apse has beautiful horseshoe arches. Ask at the nearest house for the key. The neighbour will open it for you.

Environs
A drive through the idyllic **Valle de Silencio** (Valley of Silence), south of Ponferrada, follows a poplar-lined stream past several bucolic villages. The last and most beautiful of these is **Peñalba de Santiago**. Its

10th-century Mozarabic church has horseshoe arches above its double portal.

❹ Puebla de Sanabria

Zamora. 1,500. Castillo de Puebla de Sanabria s/n, 980 62 07 34. Fri. Candelas (Feb), Las Victorias (8–9 Sep).
W pueblasanabria.com

This attractive old village lies beyond the undulating broom and oak scrub of the Sierra de la Culebra. A steep cobbled street leads past stone and slate houses with huge, overhanging eaves and walls bearing coats of arms, to a hilltop church and castle.

The village has become the centre of a popular inland holiday resort based around the largest glacial lake in Spain, the **Lago de Sanabria**, now a nature park. Among the many activities available are fishing, walking and water sports.

Most routes beckon visitors to Ribadelago, but the road to the quaint hill village of **San Martín de Castañeda** gives better views. There's a small visitors' centre for the nature reserve in San Martín's restored monastery. The village is very traditional – you may see cattle yoked to carts, and women dressed completely in black.

The 12th-century church and 15th-century castle of Puebla de Sanabria

The nave of Astorga Cathedral

❺ Astorga

León. ⚏ 11,900. 🚉 🚌 🅸 Plaza Eduardo de Castro 5. **Tel** 987 61 82 22. 🔷 Tue. 🎭 Roman Festival (end Jun); Santa Marta (late Aug). 🌐 **ayuntamientodeastorga.com**

The Roman town of Asturica Augusta was a strategic halt on the Vía de la Plata (Silver Road), a Roman road linking Andalusia and northwest Spain. Later it came to form a stage on the pilgrimage route to Santiago (*see pp86–7*).

Soaring above the ramparts in the upper town are Astorga's two principal monuments, the cathedral and the Palacio Episcopal. The **cathedral** was built between the 15th and the 18th centuries and displays a variety of architectural styles ranging from its Gothic apse to the effusive Baroque of its two towers, which are carved with various biblical scenes. The gilt altarpiece by

Gaspar Becerra is a masterpiece of the Spanish Renaissance. Among the many fine exhibits in the cathedral's museum are the 10th-century carved casket of Alfonso III the Great, the jewelled Reliquary of the True Cross and a lavish silver monstrance studded with enormous emeralds.

Opposite the cathedral is a fairy-tale building of multiple turrets and quasi-Gothic windows. The unconventional **Palacio Episcopal** (Bishop's Palace) was designed at the end of the 19th century by Antoni Gaudí, the highly original Modernista architect (*see p168*), for the incumbent bishop, a fellow Catalan, after a fire in 1887 had destroyed the previous building. Its bizarre appearance as well as its phenomenal cost so horrified the diocese that no subsequent bishops ever lived in it. Today it houses an assembly of medieval religious art devoted to the history of Astorga and the pilgrimage to Santiago. Roman relics, including coins unearthed in the Plaza Romana, are evidence of Astorga's importance as a Roman settlement. The palace's interior is decorated with Gaudí's ceramic tiles and stained glass.

Reliquary of the True Cross

🏛 Palacio Episcopal
Plaza Eduardo de Castro. **Tel** 987 61 68 82. **Open** Tue–Sun. **Closed** Mon, Sun pm, public hols. 🌀

❻ Cueva de Valporquero

León. **Tel** 987 57 64 08. **Open** mid-Oct–Dec & Mar–mid-May: 10am–5pm Thu–Sun, public hols; mid-May–mid-Oct: 10am–6pm daily. 🌀

This complex of limestone caves – technically a single cave with three separate entrances – is directly beneath the village of Valporquero de Torío. The caves were formed in the Miocene period between 5 and 25 million years ago. Severe weather conditions in the surrounding mountains make the caverns inaccessible between December and Easter. Less than half of the huge system, which stretches 3,100 m (10,200 ft) under the ground, is open to the public. Guided tours take parties through an impressive series of galleries in which lighting picks out the beautiful limestone concretions. Iron and sulphur oxides have tinted the rocks many subtle shades of red, grey and black. The vast Gran Rotonda, covering an area of 5,600 sq m (18,350 sq ft) and reaching a height of 20 m (65 ft), is the most stunning.

As the interior is cold, and the surface often slippery, it is advisable to wear warm clothes and sturdy shoes.

Illuminated stalactites hanging from the roof of one of the chambers in the Cueva de Valporquero

❼ León

León. ▨ 131,700. 🚉 🚌 ℹ Plaza de San Marcelo s/n, 987 87 83 36. 🏠 Wed & Sat. 🎭 San Juan and San Pedro (21–29 Jun), San Froilán (5 Oct). **W** leon.es

Founded as a camp for the Romans' Seventh Legion, León became the capital of a kingdom in the Middle Ages. As such it played a central role in the early years of the Reconquest *(see pp58–9)*.

The city's most important building – apart from its great **cathedral** *(see pp358–9)* – is the **Colegiata de San Isidoro**, built into the Roman walls which encircle the city. A separate entrance leads through to the Romanesque **Panteón Real** (Royal Pantheon), the last resting place of more than 20 monarchs. It is superbly decorated with carved capitals and 12th-century frescoes illustrating a variety of biblical and mythical subjects, as well as scenes of medieval life.

The alleyways in the picturesque old quarter around the Plaza Mayor are interspersed with bars and cafés, decrepit mansions and churches. Two well-preserved palaces stand near to the Plaza de Santo Domingo: the **Palacio de los Guzmanes**, with its elegantly arcaded Renaissance patio, and Antoni Gaudí's unusually restrained **Casa de Botines**.

The **Hostal de San Marcos** is a fine example of Spanish Renaissance architecture

Frescoes in Colegiata de San Isidoro showing medieval seasonal tasks

(see p29). Founded during the 12th century as a monastery lodging pilgrims going to Santiago, the present building was begun in 1513 as the headquarters of the Knights of Santiago. The main hall has a fine 16th-century coffered ceiling. A parador now occupies the main part of the Hostal. The **Museo de León** has many treasures, including a haunting little ivory crucifix, the *Cristo de Carrizo*.

The **MUSAC**, Museo de Arte Contemporáneo de Castilla y León, has a radical, interactive approach to exhibiting contemporary art.

Environs

Around 30 km (20 miles) east of León is the **Iglesia de San Miguel de Escalada**. Dating from the 10th century, it is one of the finest surviving churches built by the Mozarabs – Christians influenced by the Moors. It has Visigothic panels and stately horseshoe arches resting on carved capitals. At **Sahagún**, 70 km (40 miles) southeast of León, are the Mudéjar churches of San Tirso and San Lorenzo, with triple apses and belfries. A colossal ruined castle overlooks the Río Esla beside **Valencia de Don Juan**, 40 km (25 miles) south of León.

🏛 **Museo de León**
Plaza Santo Domingo 8. **Tel** 987 23 64 05. **Open** Tue–Sun. **Closed** Mon, Sun pm. 🎫 (free Sat & Sun).

🏛 **MUSAC**
Avenida de los Reyes Leoneses 24. **Tel** 987 09 00 00. **Open** Tue–Sun. ♿ 🎫 📷 (free 6pm Sun). **W** musac.es

The Maragatos

Astorga is the principal town of the Maragatos, an ethnic group of unknown origin, thought to be descended from 8th-century Berber invaders. By marrying only among themselves, they managed to preserve their customs through the centuries and keep themselves apart from the rest of society. The demise of their traditional trade of mule-driving, however, changed their way of life and the Maragatos have adapted to contemporary life, although their typical gastronomy and craftwork still survive.

Maragatos dressed in traditional costume

León Cathedral

The master builders of this Spanish Gothic cathedral *par excellence (see p28)* were inspired by French techniques of vaulting and buttressing. The present structure of golden sandstone, built on the site of King Ordoño II's 10th-century palace, was begun in the mid-13th century and completed less than 100 years later. It combines a slender but very high nave with the huge panels of stained glass which are its most magnificent feature. Although the cathedral has survived for 700 years, today there is concern about air pollution attacking the soft stone.

Cathedral Museum
Pedro de Campaña's panel, *The Adoration of the Magi*, is one of the many magnificent treasures displayed in the museum.

KEY

① **The West Rose Window** is largely 14th-century and depicts the Virgin and Child, surrounded by 12 trumpet-blowing angels.

② **The silver reliquary** is an ornate chest dating from the 16th century.

③ **The 13th- to 14th-century** cloister galleries are decorated with Gothic frescoes by Nicolás Francés.

④ **The altarpiece** includes five original panels created by Gothic master Nicolás Francés.

⑤ **The choir** has two tiers of 15th-century stalls. Behind it is the carved and gilded retrochoir, in the shape of a triumphal arch.

Entrance

★ **13th-Century Carvings**
Among the Gothic carvings on the front of León's cathedral, above the Puerta de la Virgen Blanca, is one depicting a scene from the Last Judgment.

For hotels and restaurants in this region see pp569–70 and pp594–5

Inside the Cathedral

The plan of the building is a Latin cross. The tall nave is slender but long, measuring 90 m (295 ft) by 40 m (130 ft) at its widest. To appreciate the dazzling colours of the stained glass it is best to visit on a sunny day.

VISITORS' CHECKLIST

Practical Information
Plaza de Regla.
Tel 987 87 57 70.
Open Oct–Apr: 9:30am–1:30pm & 4–7pm Mon–Sat, 9:30am–2pm Sun; May–Sep: hours vary, check website for details. ⓘ 9am, noon, 1pm & 6pm daily, plus 11am & 2pm Sun. ✉ ♿
Museum: **Open** Mon–Sat, check website for details. ♿ ✉
ⓦ catedraldeleon.org

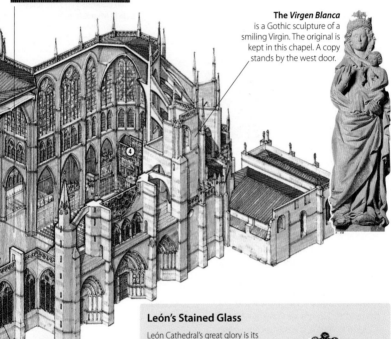

The *Virgen Blanca* is a Gothic sculpture of a smiling Virgin. The original is kept in this chapel. A copy stands by the west door.

León's Stained Glass

León Cathedral's great glory is its magnificent glasswork. The 125 large windows and 57 smaller, round ones date from every century from the 13th to the 20th. They cover an enormous range of subjects. Some reveal fascinating details about medieval life: *La Cacería*, in the north wall, depicts a typical hunting scene, while the rose window in the Capilla del Nacimiento shows pilgrims worshipping at the tomb of St James in Santiago de Compostela in Galicia *(see pp96–7)*. Restoration work can be viewed from an elevated platform on a guided tour.

A large window in the south wall

★ **Stained Glass**
The windows, covering an area of 1,900 sq m (20,400 sq ft), are the outstanding feature of the cathedral.

❽ Zamora

Zamora. ⚄ 65,300. 🚃 🚌 🛈
Avenida Príncipe de Asturias 1, 980 53
18 45. 🛒 Tue. 🎭 Semana Santa
(Easter Week), San Pedro (23–29 Jun).
🌐 **turismocastillayleon.com**

Little remains of Zamora's past as an important strategic frontier town. In Roman times, it was on the Vía de la Plata *(see p356)*, and during the Reconquest was fought over fiercely. The city has now expanded far beyond its original boundaries, but the old quarter contains a wealth of Romanesque churches.

The ruins of the **city walls**, built by Alfonso III in 893, are pierced by the Portillo de la Traición (Traitor's Gate), through which the murderer of Sancho II passed in 1072. The 16th-century **parador** *(see p570)* is in an old palace with a Renaissance courtyard adorned with coats of arms.

Two other palaces, the **Palacio de los Momos** and the **Palacio del Cordón**, have ornately carved façades and windows. Zamora's

Peaceful gardens of the Colegiata de Santa María in Toro

most important monument is its unique **cathedral**, a 12th-century structure built in Romanesque style but with a number of later Gothic additions. The building's most eye-catching feature is its striking, scaly, hemispherical dome. Inside, there are superb iron grilles and Mudéjar pulpits surround Juan de Bruselas' 15th-century choir

stalls. The allegorical carvings of nuns and monks on the misericords and armrests were once considered risqué. The museum, off the cloisters, has a collection of 15th- and 16th-century Flemish tapestries. These illustrate biblical passages and classical and military scenes.

Nearby, several churches exhibit features characteristic of Zamora's architectural style, notably multi-lobed arches and heavily carved portals. The best are the 12th-century **Iglesia de San Ildefonso** and the **Iglesia de la Magdalena**.

Another reason for visiting Zamora is for its lively Easter Week celebrations, when elaborate *pasos* (sculpted floats) are paraded in the streets. Otherwise they can be admired in the **Museo de Semana Santa**.

Environs
The 7th-century Visigothic church of **San Pedro de la Nave**, 23 km (14 miles) northwest of Zamora, is Spain's oldest church. Carvings

❿ Sierra de Francia and Sierra de Béjar

These attractive schist hills buttress the western edges of the Sierra de Gredos *(see p366)*. Narrow roads wind their way through picturesque chestnut, olive and almond groves, and quaint rural villages of wood and stone. The highest point of the range is La Peña de Francia, which, at 1,732 m (5,700 ft), is easily recognizable from miles around. The views from the peak, and from the roads leading up to it, offer a breathtaking panorama of the surrounding empty plains and rolling hills.

① La Peña de Francia
Atop the windswept peak is a 15th-century Dominican monastery sheltering a blackened statue of the Virgin and Child dating from 1890.

② La Alberca
This pretty and much-visited village sells local honey, hams and handicrafts. On 15 August each year it celebrates the Assumption with a traditional mystery play performed in costume.

③ Las Batuecas
The road from La Alberca careers down into a green valley, past the monastery where Luis Buñuel made his film *Tierra sin Pan* (Land without Bread).

Key

▬ Tour route
═══ Other roads

The unmistakable peak of La Peña de Francia

Fish-scale tiling on dome of Zamora Cathedral

adorn its capitals and friezes. **Toro**, 30 km (18 miles) east of Zamora, is at the heart of a wine region *(see pp344–5)*. The highlights of its **Colegiata de Santa María** are the Gothic west portal and a fine 16th-century Hispano-Flemish painting, *La Virgen de la Mosca*. In 1476, the forces of Isabel I *(see pp60–61)* secured a victory over the Portuguese at Toro, confirming her succession to the Castile throne.

❾ Ciudad Rodrigo

Salamanca. 🏔 13,600. 🚌 🚍
ℹ Plaza Mayor 27, 923 49 84 00.
🗓 Tue, Sat. 🎭 San Sebastián (20 Jan), Carnaval del Toro (before Lent), Easter week, Charrada (mid-Jul).

Despite its lonely setting – stranded on the country's western marches miles from anywhere – this lovely old town is well worth a detour. Its frontier location inevitably gave rise to fortification, and its robust 14th-century castle is now an atmospheric **parador**. The prosperous 15th and 16th centuries were Ciudad Rodrigo's heyday. During the War of Independence *(see pp66–7)*, the city, then occupied by the French, was besieged for two years before falling to the Duke of Wellington's forces.

The golden stone buildings within the ramparts are delightful. The main monument is the **cathedral** (closed Mon pm), whose belfry still bears the marks of shellfire from the siege. The exterior has a shapely curved balustrade and accomplished portal carvings. Inside, it is worth seeing the cloisters and the choir stalls, carved with lively scenes by Rodrigo Alemán. In the adjacent 16th-century **Capilla de Cerralbo** (Cerralbo Chapel; *only open to tourists in the summer*) is a 17th-century altarpiece. Off the chapel's south side is the arcaded Plaza del Buen Alcalde.

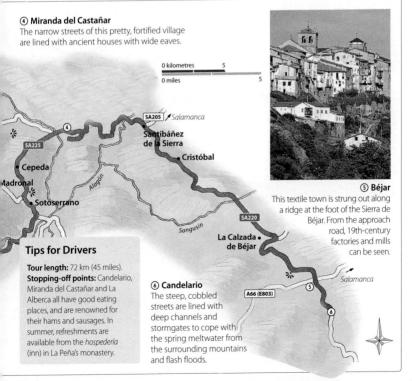

④ Miranda del Castañar
The narrow streets of this pretty, fortified village are lined with ancient houses with wide eaves.

0 kilometres   5
0 miles   5

SA205 ⟋ *Salamanca*

Santibáñez de la Sierra
● **Cristóbal**
④
SA225
● **Cepeda**
Madroñal
● **Sotoserrano**
Alagón
Sangusín
SA220
La Calzada de Béjar ●
A66 (E803)
Salamanca
⑤

⑤ Béjar
This textile town is strung out along a ridge at the foot of the Sierra de Béjar. From the approach road, 19th-century factories and mills can be seen.

Tips for Drivers

Tour length: 72 km (45 miles).
Stopping-off points: Candelario, Miranda del Castañar and La Alberca all have good eating places, and are renowned for their hams and sausages. In summer, refreshments are available from the *hospedería* (inn) in La Peña's monastery.

⑥ Candelario
The steep, cobbled streets are lined with deep channels and stormgates to cope with the spring meltwater from the surrounding mountains and flash floods.

For additional map symbols *see back flap*

⓫ Street-by-Street: Salamanca

The great university city of Salamanca is Spain's finest showcase of Renaissance and Plateresque architecture. Founded as an Iberian settlement in pre-Roman times, the city fell to Hannibal in 217 BC. Pre-eminent among its artists and master craftsmen of later years were the Churriguera brothers *(see p29)*. Their work can be seen in many of Salamanca's golden stone buildings, notably in the Plaza Mayor. Other major sights are the two cathedrals and the 13th-century university, one of Europe's oldest and most distinguished.

The Casa de las Conchas is easily identifiable from the stone scallop shells that stud its walls. It is now a library.

The Palacio de Monterrey is a Renaissance mansion.

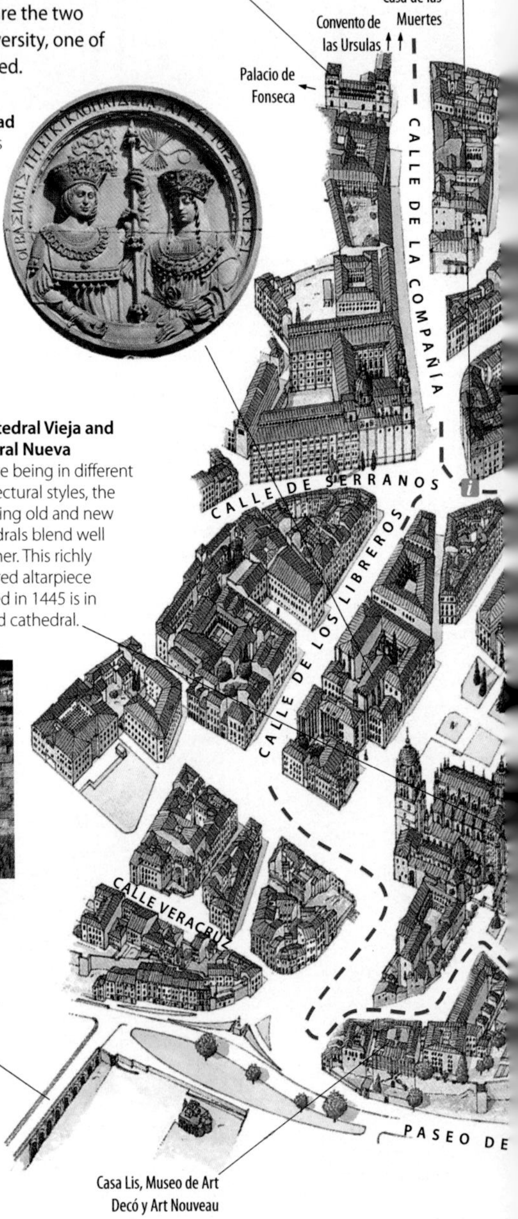

Casa de las Muertes

Convento de las Ursulas

Palacio de Fonseca

CALLE DE LA COMPAÑIA

★ Universidad
In the centre of the university's elaborate façade is this medallion, carved in relief, which depicts the Catholic Monarchs.

★ Catedral Vieja and Catedral Nueva
Despite being in different architectural styles, the adjoining old and new cathedrals blend well together. This richly coloured altarpiece painted in 1445 is in the old cathedral.

CALLE DE SERRANOS

CALLE DE LOS LIBREROS

Puente Romano
The Roman bridge across the Río Tormes, built in the 1st century AD, retains 15 of its original 26 arches. It provides an excellent view of the city.

CALLE VERACRUZ

0 metres 100
0 yards 100

Casa Lis, Museo de Art Decó y Art Nouveau

PASEO DE

★ **Plaza Mayor**
This 18th-century square is one of Spain's largest and grandest. On the east side is the Royal Pavilion, decorated with a bust of Felipe V, who built the square.

Key

— Suggested route

VISITORS' CHECKLIST

Practical Information
Salamanca. 🚗 152,000.
ℹ Plaza Mayor 32, 923 21 83 42.
📅 Sun. 🎭 San Juan de Sahagún (10–12 Jun), Virgen de la Vega (8–15 Sep).
w salamanca.es

Transport
✈ 15 km (9 miles) east.
🚉 Paseo de la Estación, 902 32 03 20. 🚌 Avda de Filiberto Villalobos 71, 923 23 67 17.

PLAZA MAYOR

PLAZA CORRILLO

MAYOR

CALLE DE SAN PABLO

CALLE DEL CONSUELO

GRAN VIA

PLAZA DEL CONCILIO DE TRENTO

ARROYO SANTO DOMINGO

RECTOR ESPERABÉ

Torre del Clavero
This 15th-century tower still has its original turrets. They are adorned with the coats of arms of its founders, and Mudéjar trelliswork.

Iglesia-Convento de San Esteban
The Plateresque façade of the church is carved with delicate relief. Above the door is a frieze decorated with medallions and coats of arms.

Convento de las Dueñas
Sculptures on the capitals of the beautiful two-storey cloister show demons, skulls and tormented faces, which contrast with serene carvings of the Virgin.

For additional map symbols *see back flap*

Exploring Salamanca

The majority of Salamanca's monuments are located inside the city centre, which is compact enough to explore on foot. The university, the Plaza Mayor, and the old and new cathedrals are all unmissable.

🏛 Catedral Vieja and Catedral Nueva

Tel 923 28 11 23. **Open** 10am–7:30pm daily (Oct–Mar: to 5:30pm).
w catedralsalamanca.org

The new cathedral (built during the 16th–18th centuries) did not replace the old, but was built beside it. It combines a mix of styles, being mainly Gothic, with Renaissance and Baroque additions. The west front has elaborate Late Gothic stonework.

The 12th- to 13th-century Romanesque old cathedral is entered through the new one. The highlight is a 53-panel altarpiece, painted in lustrous colours by Nicolás Florentino. It frames a statue of Salamanca's patron saint, the 12th-century Virgen de la Vega, crafted in Limoges enamel. In the vault above is a fresco depicting scenes from the Last Judgment, also by Florentino.

The 15th-century Capilla de Anaya (Anaya Chapel) contains the superb 15th-century alabaster tomb of Diego de Anaya, an archbishop of Salamanca.

Façade of Salamanca University, on the Patio de las Escuelas

🏛 Universidad

Calle Libreros. **Tel** 923 29 44 00.
Open daily. **Closed** 1 & 6 Jan, 25 Dec and for official functions.
w usal.es

The university was founded by Alfonso IX of León in 1218, making it the oldest in Spain. The 16th-century façade of the Patio de las Escuelas (Schools Square) is a perfect example of the Plateresque style (see p29). Opposite is a statue of Fray Luis de León, who taught theology here. His former lecture room is preserved in its original style. The Escuelas Menores building houses a huge zodiac fresco, The Salamanca Sky.

🏛 Plaza Mayor

This magnificent square was built by Felipe V to thank the city for its support during the War of the Spanish Succession (see p66). Designed by the Churriguera brothers (see p29) in 1729 and completed in 1755, it was once used for bullfights, but nowadays is a delightful place to stroll or shop. Within the harmonious blend of arcaded buildings and cafés are the Baroque town hall and, opposite, the Royal Pavilion, from where the royal family used to watch events in the square. The Plaza Mayor is built of warm golden sandstone, and is especially resplendent at dusk.

Royal Pavilion in Salamanca's beautiful Plaza Mayor

🏛 Iglesia-Convento de San Esteban

Plaza del Concilio de Trento s/n.
Tel 923 21 50 00. **Open** 10am–2pm, 4–7pm daily. **Closed** public hols.

The 16th-century church of this Dominican monastery has an ornamented façade. The relief on the central panel, completed by Juan Antonio Ceroni in 1610, depicts the stoning of St Stephen, to whom the monastery is dedicated. Above is a frieze with figures of children and horses.

The interior is equally stunning. The ornate altarpiece, of twisted gilt columns decorated with vines, is the work of José Churriguera and dates from 1693. Below it is one of Claudio Coello's last paintings, another representation of the martyrdom of St Stephen.

The double-galleried Claustro de los Reyes, completed in Plateresque style in 1591, has capitals that are carved with the heads of the prophets.

Salamanca's double cathedral, towering over the city

Sculpted shells on the walls of the Casa de las Conchas

⊞ Casa de las Conchas

Calle de la Compañía 2. **Tel** 923 26 93 17. **Open** daily. Library: **Open** 9am–9pm Mon–Fri, 9am–2pm Sat.

This mansion's name – House of the Shells – derives from the stone scallop shells that cover its walls. They are a symbol of the Order of Santiago, one of whose knights, Rodrigo Arias Maldonado, built the mansion in the early 1500s. He also adorned it with his family's coat of arms. It now houses a public library.

⊡ Convento de las Dueñas

Pl del Concilio de Trento 1. **Tel** 923 21 54 42. **Open** 10am–1:30pm, 4–7pm Mon–Sat. **Closed** pub hols.

The main feature of this Dominican convent, beside San Esteban, is its Renaissance double cloister, whose tranquil gardens seem strangely at odds with the grotesques carved on the capitals. The cloister also preserves tiled Moorish arches.

⊞ Casa Lis Museo Art Nouveau y Art Deco

Calle Gibraltar 14. **Tel** 923 12 14 25. **Open** Tue–Sun. (free Thu am).

This important art collection, housed in a 19th-century building, includes paintings, jewellery and furniture from all over Europe. Individual rooms are devoted to porcelain and Limoges enamel, and stained-glass work by Lalique.

⊡ Colegio de Fonseca or de los Irlandeses

Calle de Fonseca 4. **Tel** 923 29 45 70. **Open** daily.

The Archbishop of Toledo, Alfonso de Fonseca, built this Renaissance palace in 1521, and the coat of arms of the Fonseca family appears over the main entrance. Its name arises from the fact that it became a seminary for Irish priests at the end of the 19th century. The interior Italianate courtyard has a first-floor gallery and a chapel. Today it is used as a hotel, restaurant and university premises.

⊡ Convento de las Úrsulas

C/ de las Úrsulas 2. **Tel** 923 21 98 77. **Open** Tue–Sun. **Closed** last Sun of month.

In the church of this convent is the carved tomb of its founder, Alonso de Fonseca, the powerful 16th-century Archbishop of Santiago. The museum includes fine paintings by Luis de Morales.

⊞ Casa de las Muertes

Calle Bordadores. **Closed** to the public. The House of the Dead takes its name from the small skulls that embellish its façade. Grotesques and other figures also feature, and there is a cornice decorated with cherubs. The façade is a

Skull carving on the façade of the Casa de las Muertes

wonderfully accomplished example of the early Plateresque style.

The adjacent house is where author and philosopher Miguel de Unamuno died in 1936. The Casa-Museo de Unamuno, next door to the university, contains information about his life.

⊞ Torre del Clavero

Plaza de Colón. **Closed** to the public. The tower is the last vestige of a palace that once stood here. It was built around 1480 and is named after a former resident, the key warden (clavero) of the Order of Alcántara.

Tower opposite Casa de las Muertes

Environs

Northwest of the city, the Río Tormes leads through the fortified old town of **Ledesma**, across lonely countryside to the Arribes del Duero, a series of massive reservoirs near to the Portuguese border.

Dominating the town of **Alba de Tormes**, 20 km (12 miles) east of Salamanca, is the Torre de la Armería, the only remaining part of the castle of the Dukes of Alba. The Iglesia de San Juan was built in the 12th century in Romanesque style. The Iglesia-Convento de las Madres Carmelitas was founded by St Teresa of Ávila in 1571, and is where her remains are now kept.

The castle of **Buen Amor**, 24 km (15 miles) to the north, was founded in 1227. Later, it was used by the Catholic Monarchs while fighting Juana la Beltraneja (see p60). Today it is a hotel but can still be visited.

⑫ Sierra de Gredos

Ávila. 🚌 Navarrendonda.
ℹ️ Navarrendonda, C/ del Río s/n,
920 34 80 01. 🌐 turismoavila.com

This great mountain range, west of Madrid, has abundant wildlife, especially ibex and birds of prey. Some parts have been developed to cater for weekenders who come skiing, fishing, hunting or hiking. Tourism here isn't a recent phenomenon – Spain's first parador opened in Gredos in 1928. Despite this, there are many traditional villages off the beaten track.

The slopes on the south side of the range, extending into Extremadura, are fertile and sheltered, with pinewoods, and apple and olive trees. The northern slopes, in contrast, have a covering of scrub and a scattering of granite boulders.

A single main road, the N502, crosses the centre of the range via the Puerto del Pico, a pass at 1,352 m (4,435 ft), leading to Arenas de San Pedro, the largest town of the Sierra de Gredos. On this road is the castle of **Mombeltrán**, built at the end of the 14th century.

Near Ramacastañas, south of the town of Arenas de San Pedro, are the limestone caverns of the **Cuevas del Águila**.

The sierra's highest summit, the Pico Almanzor (2,592 m/ 8,500 ft) dominates the west. Around it lies the **Reserva Nacional de Gredos**, protecting the mountain's wildlife. Near

The Toros de Guisando near El Tiemblo in the Sierra de Gredos

El Tiemblo, in the east, stand the **Toros de Guisando**, four stone statues resembling bulls, believed to be of Celtiberian origin (see pp52–3).

⑬ Ávila

Ávila. 🏔 59,000. 🚉 🚌 ℹ️ Avenida de Madrid 39, 920 35 00 00. Walls: **Open** Tue–Sun (also Mon in summer). 🎭 🍷 Fri. 🎉 San Segundo (2 May); Sta Teresa (15 Oct). 🌐 avilaturismo.com

At 1,131 m (3,710 ft) above sea level, Ávila de los Caballeros ("of the Knights") is the highest provincial capital in Spain. In winter access roads can be blocked with snow. The centre of the city is encircled by the finest-preserved **medieval walls** in Europe. The walls are open to visitors (except Monday and in low season). One of the best views of the walls is from Los Cuatro Postes (Four Posts) on the road

to Salamanca. Built in the 11th century, the walls are over 2 km (1 mile) long. They are punctuated by 88 sturdy turrets, on which storks can be seen nesting in season. The ground falls away very steeply from the walls on three sides, making the city practically impregnable. The east side, however, is relatively flat, and therefore had to be fortified more heavily. The oldest sections of the wall are here. They are guarded by the most impressive of the city's nine gateways, the **Puerta de San Vicente**. The apse of the **cathedral** also forms part of the walls. The cathedral's war-like (and unfinished) exterior, decorated with beasts and scaly wild men, is an unusual design. The interior is a mixture of Romanesque and Gothic styles using an unusual mottled red and white stone. Finer points to note are the

Tuna in Ávila

The superbly preserved 11th-century walls, punctuated with 88 cylindrical towers, which encircle Ávila

carvings on the retrochoir and, in the apse, the tomb of a 15th-century bishop known as El Tostado, "the Tanned One", because of his dark complexion.

Many churches and convents in Ávila are linked to St Teresa, who was born in the city. The **Convento de Santa Teresa** was built on the site of her home within the walls and she also lived for more than 20 years in the **Monasterio de la Encarnación** outside the walls. There is even a local sweetmeat, *yemas de Santa Teresa*, named after the saint.

The **Basílica de San Vicente**, also located just outside the eastern walls, is Ávila's most important Romanesque church, distinguished by its ornamented belfry. It was begun in the 11th century but has some Gothic features which were added later. The west doorway is often compared to the Pórtico da Gloria of Santiago Cathedral

Beautiful gardens and palace of La Granja de San Ildefonso

Cloisters of the Real Monasterio de Santo Tomás in Ávila

(see pp96–7). Inside, the carved tomb of St Vincent and his sisters depicts their hideous martyrdom in detail. Another Romanesque-Gothic church worth seeing is the **Iglesia de San Pedro**.

Some way from the centre is the **Real Monasterio de Santo Tomás**, with three cloisters. The middle one, carved with the yoke and arrow emblem of the Catholic Monarchs, is the most beautiful. The last cloister leads to a museum displaying chalices and processional crosses. The church contains the tomb of Prince Juan, the only son of Fernando and Isabel. In the sacristy lies another historic figure: Tomás de Torquemada, head of the Inquisition *(see p60)*.

In Ávila, you may see groups of *tunas* – students dressed in traditional costume walking the town's streets while singing songs and playing guitars.

St Teresa of Jesus

Teresa de Cepeda y Ahumada (1515–82) was one of the Catholic Church's greatest mystics and reformers. When aged just 7, she ran away from home in the hope of achieving martyrdom at the hands of the Moors, only to be recaptured by her uncle on the outskirts of the city. She became a nun at 19 but rebelled against her order. From 1562, when she founded her first convent, she travelled around Spain with her disciple, St John of the Cross, founding more convents for the followers of her order, the Barefoot Carmelites. Her remains are in Alba de Tormes near Salamanca *(see p365)*.

Statue of St Teresa in the cathedral museum

⓮ La Granja de San Ildefonso

Segovia. **Tel** 921 47 00 19. 🚌 from Madrid or Segovia. **Open** 10am–8pm Tue–Sun (to 6pm Oct–Mar); gardens open until dusk. **Closed** 1, 6 & 23 Jan, 1 May, 24, 25 & 31 Dec. 🅿 (free from 3pm Wed & Thu for EU residents; from 5pm Apr–Sep). 📷 🆆 patrimonionacional.es

This sumptuous royal pleasure palace is set against the backdrop of the Sierra de Guadarrama mountains, standing on the site of the old Convento de Jerónimos.

In 1720, Felipe V embarked on a project to create a fine palace. A succession of different artists and architects contributed to the rich furnishings inside and the splendid gardens without.

A guided tour meanders through countless impressive salons decorated with ornate objets d'art and Classical frescoes against settings of marble, gilt and velvet. Huge glittering chandeliers, produced locally, hang from the ceiling. In the private apartments there are superb tapestries. The church is adorned in lavish high Baroque style, and the Royal Mausoleum contains the tomb of Felipe V and his queen.

In the gardens, stately chestnut trees, clipped hedges and statues frame a complex series of pools. On 30 May, 25 July and 25 August each year all of the spectacular fountains are set in motion. Between May and July, four fountains run every Wednesday and Saturday at 5:30pm, and Sunday at 1pm.

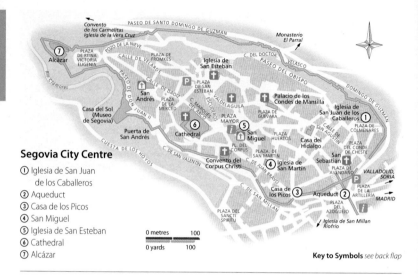

Segovia City Centre

① Iglesia de San Juan
   de los Caballeros
② Aqueduct
③ Casa de los Picos
④ San Miguel
⑤ Iglesia de San Esteban
⑥ Cathedral
⑦ Alcázar

| 0 metres | 100 |
| 0 yards | 100 |

Key to Symbols *see back flap*

⓯ Segovia

Segovia. 🕮 54,900. 🚆 🚍
🛈 Plaza del Azoguejo 1, 921 46
67 20. 🛒 Thu & Sat. 🎉 San Pedro
(29 Jun), San Frutos (25 Oct).
🌐 turismodesegovia.com

Segovia is the most spectacularly sited city in Spain. The old
town is set high on a rocky
spur and surrounded by the
Río Eresma and Río Clamores.
It is often compared to a ship –
the Alcázar on its sharp crag
forming the prow, the pinnacles
of the cathedral rising like
masts, and the aqueduct trailing
behind like a rudder. The view
of it from the valley below at
sunset is magical.

The **aqueduct**, in use until the
late 19th century, was built at
the end of the 1st century AD
by the Romans, who turned the
ancient town into an important
military base.

The **cathedral**, dating from
1525 and consecrated in 1678,
is the last great Gothic church
in Spain. It was built to replace
the old cathedral, which was
destroyed in 1520 during the
revolt of the Castilian towns
(see p62). The cloister, however,
survived and was rebuilt on the
new site. The pinnacles, flying
buttresses, tower and dome
form an impressive silhouette,
while the interior is light and
elegantly vaulted. Ironwork

grilles enclose the side chapels.
The chapterhouse museum,
with a coffered ceiling, houses
17th-century Brussels tapestries.

At the city's western end is the
Alcázar *(see pp348–9)*. Rising
sheer above crags with a multitude of gabled roofs, turrets and
crenellations, it appears like the
archetypal fairy-tale castle. The
present building is mostly a
fanciful reconstruction following
a fire in 1862. It contains a museum of weaponry and a series
of elaborately decorated rooms.
Climb the keep for great views.

Notable churches include the
Romanesque **San Juan de los**

Caballeros, which features an
outstanding sculptured portico,
San Martín with its beautiful
arcades and capitals, and
San Miguel, where Isabel the
Catholic was crowned Queen
of Castille. Just inside the city
walls, **Casa de los Picos** has a
unique façade adorned with
diamond-shaped stones.

Environs
The vast palace of **Riofrío**,
11 km (7 miles) to the southwest, is located in a deer park.
It was built as a hunting lodge
in 1752, and has richly
decorated rooms.

The imposing Gothic cathedral of Segovia

Segovia's Aqueduct

Water channel

Slots used to support blocks of ashlar

Arches reach a maximum height of 29 m (95 ft).

Water from the Río Frío flowed into the city, filtered through a series of tanks along the way.

Two tiers of arches – a total of 728 m (2,400 ft) in length – were needed to cope with the ground's gradient.

In this niche a statue of the Virgin Mary replaces an earlier inscription relating to the founding of the aqueduct.

Segovia's distinctive Alcázar, towering over the city

🏠 Alcázar de Segovia
Plaza de la Reina Victoria Eugenia.
Tel 921 46 07 59. **Open** daily.
Closed 1 & 6 Jan, 25 Dec. 🌐 (free for EU residents 3rd Tue of each month).
♿ 📷 📶 **alcazardesegovia.com**

🏛 Palacio de Riofrío
Tel 921 47 00 19. **Open** Tue–Sun.
🌐 (free for EU res Wed pm & Thu pm). 📶 **patrimonionacional.es**

⑯ Pedraza de la Sierra

Segovia. 🗺 500. ℹ️ C/ Real 3, 921 50 86 66 (closed Mon & Tue). 🎉 Nuestra Señora la Virgen del Carrascal (8 Sep).

The aristocratic little town of Pedraza de la Sierra is perched high over rolling countryside. Within its medieval walls, old streets lead to the porticoed **Plaza Mayor** (see p31). The huge **castle**, standing on a rocky outcrop, was owned by Basque artist Ignacio Zuloaga (1870–1945). The castle museum shows

some of his works. On the first and second Saturdays in July, concerts are held in Plaza Mayor.

Environs
The main sight at **Turégano**, 30 km (19 miles) west, is a large hilltop castle with the 15th-century Iglesia de San Miguel.

⑰ Sepúlveda

Segovia. 🗺 1,300. ℹ️ C/ Santos Justo y Pastor 8, 921 54 04 25 (closed Mon Jul–Sep; Mon, Tue Oct–Jun). 🎉 Wed. 🎉 Los Toros (last week of Aug).

Spectacularly sited on a slope above the Río Duratón, this picturesque town offers views of the Sierra de Guadarrama. Parts of its medieval walls and castle survive. Of its several Romanesque churches, the **Iglesia del Salvador**, behind the main square, is notable for possessing one of the oldest atria in Spain (1093).

Environs
Winding through a canyon haunted by griffon vultures is the Río Duratón, 7 km (4 miles) west of Sepúlveda. This area of striking beauty has been designated the **Parque Natural de las Hoces del Duratón**.
Ayllón, 45 km (28 miles) northeast of Sepúlveda, has an arcaded main square and the Plateresque (see p29) Palacio de Juan de Contreras of 1497.
The Iberian and Roman ruins at **Tiermes**, 28 km (17 miles) further southeast, have been partially excavated, and finds can be seen in Soria's Museo Numantino (see p381).

⑱ Castillo de Coca

Coca, Segovia. **Tel** 617 57 35 54. **Open** daily. **Closed** 15 days in Jan, 1st Tue of each month. 🌐 📷

Built in the late 15th century for the influential Fonseca family, Coca castle is one of Castilla y León's most memorable fortresses. It was used more as a residential palace than a defensive castle, although its turrets and battlements are a fine example of Mudéjar military architecture. The complex moated structure comprises three concentric walls around a massive keep. It is now a forestry school, with a display of Romanesque woodcarvings.

Environs
The 14th-century castle of **Arévalo** in Avila, 26 km (16 miles) southwest, is where Isabel I spent her childhood. The porticoed Plaza de la Villa is surrounded by some attractive half-timbered houses.

Massive keep of the 15th-century Castillo de Coca

⑲ Medina del Campo

Valladolid. 🚹 21,600. 🚉 🚌
ℹ️ Plaza Mayor 48, 983 81 13 57.
🅿️ Sun. 🎭 San Antolín (1–8 Sep).
🌐 medinadelcampo.es

Medina became wealthy in medieval times on the proceeds of huge sheep fairs and is still an important agricultural centre today. The vast brick Gothic-Mudéjar **Castillo de la Mota** (see p348), on its outskirts, began as a Moorish castle but was rebuilt in 1440. The town transferred the castle's ownership to the Crown in 1475. Isabel I and her daughter Juana "la Loca" ("the Mad") both stayed here. Later, it served as a prison – Cesare Borja was incarcerated here from 1506 to 1508. In a corner of the Plaza Mayor stands the modest house where Isabel died in 1504.

Environs
Towering over the plains, some 25 km (16 miles) to the south of Medina del Campo, are the walls of **Madrigal de las Altas Torres**, which owes its name to the hundreds of bastions that marked the old wall; only 23 remain. In 1451 Isabel was born here in a palace that later became the Monasterio de las Agustinas in 1527.

🏰 **Castillo de la Mota**
Tel 983 81 00 63. **Open** Tue–Sun pm.
Closed pub hols. 📷 only.
🌐 castillodelamota.es

⑳ Tordesillas

Valladolid. 🚹 9,000. 🚌 ℹ️ Casas del Tratado, 983 77 10 67 (closed Mon).
🅿️ Tue. 🎭 Fiestas de la Peña (mid-Sep). 🌐 tordesillas.net

This pleasant town is where the historic treaty between Spain and Portugal was signed in 1494, dividing the lands of the New World (see p60). A fateful oversight by the Spanish map-makers left the immense prize of Brazil to Portugal.

The town's main place to visit is the **Monasterio de Santa Clara**. It was constructed by

Castillo de la Mota at Medina del Campo

Alfonso XI around 1340 and then converted by his son Pedro the Cruel into a stunning residence for his mistress, María de Padilla. Pining for her native Andalusia, she had the convent decorated with fine Moorish arches, baths and tiles. Most impressive are the beautiful patio and the main chapel. There is a fantastic display of royal musical instruments, including the portable organ of Juana "la Loca".

In the old quarter, the **Iglesia de San Antolín** now houses a fascinating religious art museum, which displays paintings as well as a collection of liturgical objects.

🏛️ **Monasterio de Santa Clara**
Tel 983 77 00 71. **Open** Tue–Sun.
🎭 (free Wed pm & Thu pm for EU citizens). 🌐 patrimonionacional.es

🏛️ **Iglesia de San Antolín**
Calle Postigo. **Tel** 983 77 09 80.
Open Tue–Sun. 🎭

Moorish patio in the Monasterio de Santa Clara, Tordesillas

㉑ Valladolid

Valladolid. 🚹 311,500. 🚉 🚌 ℹ️
Glass Pavilion, Acera de Recoletos, 983 21 93 10. 🅿️ Wed, Sat, Sun. 🎭 Easter week, San Pedro Regalado (13 May), Virgen de San Lorenzo (8 Sep).
🌐 info.valladolid.es

The Arabic city of Belad-Walid (meaning "Land of the Governor") is located at the confluence of the Río Esgueva and Río Pisuerga. Although it has become sprawling and industrialized, Valladolid has some of Spain's best Renaissance art and architecture.

Fernando and Isabel (see pp60–61) were married in the Palacio Vivero in 1469 and, following the completion of the Reconquest in 1492, they made Valladolid their capital. Less spectacularly, Columbus died here, alone and forgotten, in 1506. In 1527 Felipe II was born in the Palacio de los Pimentel. José Zorrilla, who popularized the legendary Don Juan in his 1844 play (see p39), was also born in the city.

The Baroque façade (see p29) of the city's 15th-century **university** was begun in 1715 by Narciso Tomé. He later created the Transparente of Toledo Cathedral (see p397).

The **Iglesia de San Pablo** has a spectacular façade, embellished with angels and coats of arms in Plateresque style. Among the other noteworthy churches are **Santa María la Antigua**, with its Romanesque belfry, and the **Iglesia de Las Angustias**, where Juan de Juni's fine sculpture of the Virgen de los Cuchillos (Virgin of the Knives) is on display.

🏛 Casa de Cervantes
C/ Rastro s/n. **Tel** 983 30 88 10.
Open Tue–Sun. **Closed** pub hols.
🖼 (free Sun am).
🌐 **museocasacervantes.mcu.es**

The author of *Don Quixote* (*see p38*) lived in this simple house with whitewashed walls from 1603 to 1606. The rooms contain some of Cervantes' original furnishings.

🏛 Cathedral
Calle Arribas 1. **Tel** 983 30 43 62.
Closed Mon. 🖼 (Oct–Jun: free Thu).
🗓 by appt.

Work started on the unfinished cathedral in 1580 by Felipe II's favourite architect, Juan de Herrera, but lost momentum over the centuries. Churrigueresque (*see p29*) flourishes on the façade are in contrast to the sombre, square-pillared interior, whose only redeeming flamboyance is a Juan de Juni altarpiece. The Museo Diocesano inside, however, contains some fine religious art and sculpture.

🏛 Museo Nacional de Escultura
Cadenas de S Gregorio 1, 2 & 3. **Tel** 983 25 03 75. **Open** Tue–Sun. **Closed** Sun pm, public hols. 🖼 (free Sat pm & Sun). 🌐 **museoescultura.mcu.es**

This permanent art collection in the 15th-century Colegio de San Gregorio consists mainly of wooden religious sculptures from the 13th to 18th centuries.

Façade of Colegio de San Gregorio, Valladolid

Berruguete's *Natividad*, in Museo Nacional de Escultura, Valladolid

They include Juan de Juni's emotive depiction of the burial of Christ and *Recumbent Christ* by Gregorio Fernández. An Alonso Berruguete altarpiece, and walnut choir stalls by Diego de Siloé and other artists, are among the other fine works to be found here.

The building itself is worthy of attention, particularly the Plateresque staircase, the chapel by Juan Güas, and the patio of twisted columns and delicate basket arches. The façade is a fine example of Isabelline (*see p28*) sculpture, portraying a melee of naked children scrambling about in thorn trees and strange beasts.

The nearby 16th-century Palacio de Villena displays the valuable Belén Napolitano (Naples Christmas crib).

🏛 Patio Herreriano Museo de Arte Contemporáneo Español
Calle Jorge Guillén 6. **Tel** 983 36 27 71.
Open Tue–Sun. **Closed** Sun pm. 🖼
♿ 🌐 **museopatioherreriano.org**

This private collection of contemporary Spanish art opened in 2002, housed in the former Monastery of San Benito with its fine cloisters. More than 800 works by 200 Spanish artists are displayed, including work by Joan Miró, Eduardo Chillida, Antoni Tàpies and Miquel Barceló.

Environs
The moated grey castle that dominates the village of **Simancas**, 11 km (7 miles) southwest of Valladolid, was

converted by Charles V into Spain's national archive. The Visigothic church in the village of Wamba, 15 km (9 miles) to the west, contains the tomb of King Recceswinth.

An unusual long, narrow 15th-century **castle** on a ridge overlooks the wine town of Peñafiel, 60 km (40 miles) east of Valladolid (*see p349*).

㉙ Medina de Rioseco
Valladolid. 🚗 5,000. 🚌 🛈 Paseo de San Francisco, 983 72 03 19 (closed Mon). 🍴 Wed. 🎉 Easter week; San Juan (24 Jun), Virgen del Castillviejo (8 Sep). 🌐 **medinaderioseco.com**

During the Middle Ages this town grew wealthy from the profitable wool trade, enabling it to commission leading artists, mainly of the Valladolid school, to decorate its churches. The dazzling star vaulting and superb woodwork of the **Iglesia de Santa María de Mediavilla**, in the centre of town, are evidence of this. Inside, the Los Benavente Chapel is a tour de force, with a colourful stucco ceiling by Jerónimo del Corral (1554), and an altarpiece by Juan de Juni.

The interior of the **Iglesia de Santiago** is stunning, with a triple altarpiece designed by the Churriguera brothers of Salamanca (*see p29*).

The ancient buildings on Medina de Rioseco's main street, the Calle de la Rúa, are supported on wooden pillars, forming shady porticoes.

Altarpiece by Juan de Juni, Iglesia de Santa María de Mediavilla

Castilla y León's Fiestas

El Colacho *(Sun after Corpus Christi, May/Jun)*, Castrillo de Murcia (Burgos). Babies born during the previous 12 months are dressed in their best Sunday clothes and laid on mattresses in the streets. Crowds of people, including the anxious parents, watch as *El Colacho* – a man dressed in a bright red and yellow costume – jumps over the babies in order to free them from illnesses, especially hernias. He is said to represent the Devil fleeing from the sight of the Eucharist. This ritual is thought to have originated in 1621.

El Colacho jumping over babies in Castrillo de Murcia

St Agatha's Day *(Sun closest to 5 Feb)*, Zamarramala (Segovia). Every year two women are elected as mayoresses to run the village on the day of St Agatha, patron saint of married women. They ceremonially burn a stuffed figure representing a man.
Good Friday, Valladolid. The procession of 28 multi-coloured sculptures, which depict various scenes of the Passion, is one of the most spectacular in Spain.
Fire-walking *(23 Jun)*, San Pedro Manrique (Soria). Men, some carrying people on their backs, walk barefoot over burning embers. It is said that only local people can do this without being burned.

The beautiful carved retrochoir of Palencia Cathedral

㉓ Palencia

Palencia. 81,200. 🚗 🚌 ℹ️ Calle Mayor 31, 979 70 65 23. 🕐 Tue, Wed. 📅 Virgen de la Calle (2 Feb). 🌐 **palencia-turismo.com**

In medieval times, Palencia was a royal residence and the site of Spain's first university, founded in 1208. The city gradually diminished in importance following its involvement in the failed revolt of the Castilian towns of 1520 *(see p62)*.

Although Palencia has since expanded considerably on profits from coal and wheat, its centre, by the old stone bridge over the Río Carrión, remains almost village-like.

The city's main sight is the **cathedral**, known as *La Bella Desconocida* (the Unknown Beauty). It is especially worth a visit for its superb works of art, many the result of Bishop Fonseca's generous patronage. The retrochoir, exquisitely sculpted by Gil de Siloé and Simon of Cologne, and the two altarpieces, are also noteworthy. The altarpiece above the high altar was carved by Philippe de Bigarny early in the 16th century. The inset panels are by Juan de Flandes, Isabel I's court painter. Behind the high altar is the Chapel of the Holy Sacrament, with an altarpiece dating from 1529 by Valmaseda. In this chapel, high on a ledge to the left, is the colourful tomb of Doña Urraca of Navarra. Below the retrochoir, a Plateresque *(see p29)* staircase leads down to the fine Visigothic crypt.

Environs
Baños de Cerrato, 12 km (7 miles) to the south, boasts the tiny Visigothic Iglesia de San Juan Bautista, founded in 661. It is alleged to be the oldest intact church in Spain. Carved capitals and horseshoe arches decorate the interior.

㉔ Frómista

Palencia. 820. 🚗 🚌 ℹ️ Calle del Arquitecto Aníbal 2, 979 81 01 80. 🕐 Fri. 📅 San Telmo (week after Easter). 🌐 **fromista.es**

This town on the Road to Santiago de Compostela *(see pp86–7)* is the site of one of Spain's purest Romanesque churches. The **Iglesia de San Martín** is the highlight of the town, partly due to a restoration in 1904, leaving the church, dating from 1066, entirely Romanesque in style. The presence of Pagan and Roman motifs suggest it may have pre-Christian origins. Nearby, the **Iglesia de San Pedro** has notable Renaissance and Gothic sculptures.

Environs
Carrión de los Condes, 20 km (12 miles) to the northwest, is also on the Road to Santiago. The frieze on the door of the Iglesia de Santiago depicts not religious figures but local artisans. There are carvings of bulls on the façade of the 12th-century Iglesia de Santa María del Camino. The Monasterio de San Zoilo has a Gothic cloister and now operates as a hotel.

Interior of the Iglesia de San Juan Bautista at Baños de Cerrato

Posada of the Monasterio de Santa María la Real, Aguilar de Campoo

Located at **Gañinas**, 20 km (12 miles) to the northwest (just south of Saldaña), is the Roman villa, **La Olmeda**. It has a number of mosaics, including a hunting scene. Finds are shown in the archaeological museum in the Iglesia de San Pedro in Saldaña.

🏛 Villa Romana La Olmeda

Pedrosa de la Vega. **Tel** 979 11 99 97. **Open** Tue–Sun. **Closed** 1 & 6 Jan, 24, 25 & 31 Dec. 🎫 includes museum. 📷

🟤 Aguilar de Campoo

Palencia. 🔼 7,300. 🚉 🚌 **ℹ** Paseo de la Cascajera, 10, 979 12 36 41 (closed Mon & Sun pm). 🗓 Tue. 🎭 San Juan y San Pedro (23–29 Jun), Virgen del Llano (1st Sun in Sep). 🌐 aguilardecampoo.com

Situated between the parched plains of Central Spain and the lush foothills of the Cantabrian Mountains is the old fortified town of Aguilar de Campoo. In the centre of its ancient porticoed main square is the bell tower of the **Colegiata de San Miguel**. In this church is a mausoleum containing the tomb of the Marquises of Aguilar. Ask at the priest's house for the key.

Among the other places of interest are the **Ermita de Santa Cecilia**, and the restored Romanesque-Gothic **Monasterio de Santa María la Real**, which has a friendly *posada* (inn).

Environs

Six km (4 miles) south, at **Olleros de Pisuerga**, is a church built in a cave. From the parador at **Cervera de Pisuerga**, 25 km (15 miles) northwest of Aguilar, there are stunning views, and tours of the **Reserva Nacional de Fuentes Carrionas**. This is a rugged region overlooked by Curavacas, a 2,540-m (8,333-ft) peak.

🟤 Briviesca

Burgos. 🔼 7,700. 🚉 🚌 **ℹ** Calle Santa María Encimera 1, 947 59 39 39. 🗓 first Sat of month. 🎭 Feria de San José (19 Mar), Santa Casilda (9 May). 🌐 turismo-briviesca.com

This walled town, in the northeast of Burgos province, has an arcaded main square and several mansions. The best known of its churches is the **Convento de Santa Clara**, with its 16th-century walnut reredos carved with religious scenes. In 1387 Juan I of Aragón created the title Príncipe de Asturias for his son, Enrique, in the town. The **Santuario de Santa Casilda**, situated outside Briviesca, has a collection of votive objects.

Environs

Oña, 25 km (15 miles) north, is an attractive town. A Benedictine monastery was founded here in 1011.

Overlooking a fertile valley, 20 km (12 miles) further northeast, is the little hilltop town of **Frías**. Its castle overlooks cobbled streets and pretty old houses. Crossing the Río Ebro is a fortified medieval bridge, still with its central gate tower.

At **Medina de Pomar**, 30 km (20 miles) north of Oña, there is a 15th-century castle, once the seat of the Velasco family. Inside are the ruins of a palace with fine Mudéjar stucco decoration and Arabic inscriptions.

The medieval bridge over the Río Ebro at Frías, with its central gate tower

Flemish triptych inside the collegiate church in Covarrubias

㉗ Covarrubias

Burgos. 🅰 630. 🚌 🚹 C/ Monseñor Vargas, 947 40 64 61 (closed Sun pm, Mon; Mon–Wed in winter). 🚲 Tue. 🎪 San Cosme and San Damián (26– 27 Sep).

Named after the reddish caves on its outskirts, Covarrubias stands on the banks of the Río Arlanza. Medieval walls surround the charming old centre with its arcaded half-timbered houses (*see p30*). The distinguished **collegiate church** (closed Tue) shows the historical importance of Covarrubias: here is the tomb of Fernán González, first independent Count of Castile, and one of the great figures in Castilian history. By uniting several fiefs against the Moors in the 10th century, he started the rise in Castilian power that ensured the resulting kingdom of Castile would play a leading role in the unification of Spain. The church museum contains a Flemish triptych of the Adoration of the Magi, attributed to the school of Gil de Siloé, and a 17th-century organ.

Environs
A short distance east along the Río Arlanza lies the ruins of the 11th-century Romanesque monastery of San Pedro de Arlanza. At Quintanilla de las Viñas, 24 km (15 miles) north of Covarrubias, is a ruined 7th-century Visigothic church. The reliefs on the columns of the triumphal arch are remarkable, depicting sun and moon symbols that may be pagan.

㉘ Burgos

Burgos. 🅰 180,000. ✈ 🚌 🚹 Plaza de Alonso Martínez 7, 947 20 31 25. 🚲 Wed, Fri, Sat & Sun. 🎪 San Lesmes (30 Jan); Pedro and San Pablo (29 Jun). 🌐 **turismoburgos.org**

Founded in 884, Burgos has played a significant political and military role in Spanish history. It was the capital of the united kingdoms of Castile and León from 1073 until losing that honour to Valladolid after the fall of Granada in 1492 (*see pp60–61*). During the 15th and 16th centuries, Burgos grew rich from the wool trade and used its riches to finance most of the great art and architecture which can be seen in the city today. Less auspiciously, Franco chose Burgos as his Civil War headquarters (*see pp70–71*).

The city's strategic location on the main Madrid–France highway and on the route to Santiago (*see pp86–7*) ensure many visitors; but even without this Burgos would justify a long detour. Despite its size and extremes of climate, it is one of most agreeable provincial capitals in Castilla y León.

Approach via the bridge of Santa María, which leads into the old quarter through the restored **Arco de Santa María**, a gateway carved with statues of various local worthies. The main bridge into the city, however, is the Puente de San Pablo, where a statue commemorates the city's hero, El Cid. Not far from the bridge stands the **Casa del**

Cordón, a 15th-century palace (now a bank) which has a Franciscan cord motif carved over the portal. A plaque declares that this is where the Catholic Monarchs welcomed Columbus on his return, in 1497, from the second of his famous voyages to the Americas.

The lacy, steel-grey spires of the **cathedral** (*see pp376–7*) are a prominent landmark from almost anywhere in the city. On the rising ground behind it stands the restored **Iglesia de San Nicolás**, whose main feature is a superb altarpiece by Simon of Cologne (1505). Other churches worth visiting are the **Iglesia de San Lorenzo**, with its superb Baroque ceiling, and the **Iglesia de San Esteban**, which houses the **Museo del Retablo**, open to the public during summer. The **Iglesia de Santa Águeda** is the place where El Cid made King Alfonso VI swear that he played no part in the murder of his elder brother, King Sancho II (*see p360*).

The Arco de Santa María in Burgos, adorned with statues and turrets

El Cid (1043–99)

Rodrigo Díaz de Vivar was born into a noble family in Vivar del Cid, north of Burgos, in 1043. He served Fernando I, but was banished from Castile after becoming embroiled in the fratricidal squabbles of the king's sons, Sancho II and Alfonso VI. He switched allegiance to fight for the Moors, then changed side again, capturing Valencia for the Christians in 1094, ruling the city until his death. For his heroism he was named El Cid, from the Arabic *Sidi* (Lord). He was a charismatic man of great courage, but it was an anonymous poem, *El Cantar de Mío Cid*, in 1180, that immortalized him as a romantic hero of the Reconquest (*see pp58–9*). The tombs of El Cid and his wife, Jimena, are in Burgos Cathedral.

Statue of El Cid in Vivar del Cid

Burgos City Centre

① Iglesia de San Esteban
② Iglesia de San Nicolás
③ Iglesia de Santa Águeda
④ Cathedral
⑤ Iglesia de San Lorenzo
⑥ Arco de Santa María
⑦ Casa del Cordón
⑧ Museo de Burgos
⑨ Museo de la
    Evolución Humana

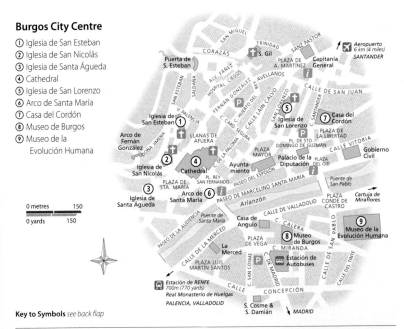

Key to Symbols *see back flap*

Across the river, the palace of the Casa de Miranda houses the archaeological section of the **Museo de Burgos**, with finds from the Roman city of Clunia. Nearby, the **Casa de Angulo** contains the Fine Arts section, whose prize exhibits are Juan de Padilla's tomb by Gil de Siloé, and a Moorish casket in enamelled ivory. Also nearby is the **Museo de la Evolución Humana**, which exhibits fossils from the site of the Sierra de Atapuerca, dating from some 780,000 years ago. A combined entrance ticket includes the museum, the **Yacimientos de**

Sculpted tomb of Juan de Padilla by Gil de Siloé, in Museo de Burgos

Atapuerca, the site of Europe's earliest settlement (on the outskirts of Burgos), and a bus to the site.

Two religious houses, on the outskirts of Burgos, are worth visiting. Just west of the city is the **Real Monasterio de Huelgas**, a late 12th-century Cistercian convent founded by Alfonso VIII. One of the most interesting parts is the **Museo de Ricas Telas**, a textile museum of ancient fabrics from the convent's royal tombs. In the Capilla de Santiago is a curious wooden figure of St James holding a sword, with which, according to tradition, royal princes were dubbed Knights of Santiago.

To the east of Burgos is the **Cartuja de Miraflores**, a Carthusian monastery founded during the 15th century. The church includes two of Spain's most notable tombs, attributed to Gil de Siloé. One holds the bodies of Juan II and Isabel of Portugal; the other contains that of their son, Prince Alfonso. The altarpiece by Gil de Siloé, allegedly gilded with the first consignment of gold brought back to Spain from the New World, is spectacular.

Polychrome altarpiece by Gil de Siloé, in Cartuja de Miraflores

🏛 **Museo de Burgos**
Calle Miranda, 13. **Tel** 947 26 58 75.
Open Tue–Sun. 🅿 (free Sat & Sun).
♿ partial.

🏛 **Museo de la Evolución Humana**
Paseo Sierra de Atapuerca. **Tel** 902 02 42 46. **Open** Tue–Sun. 🅿 (ticket offers combined entry to Yacimientos de Atapuerca and transport).

⛪ **Real Monasterio de Huelgas**
Calle de los Compases. **Tel** 947 20 16 30. **Open** Tue–Sun. **Closed** Some pub hols. 🅿 📷 (free Wed & Thu pm).

⛪ **Cartuja de Miraflores**
Ctra Burgos-Cardeña, km 3.
Tel 947 26 34 25. **Open** daily except Wed (Nov–Feb).

Burgos Cathedral

Spain's third-largest cathedral was founded in 1221 by Bishop Don Mauricio under Fernando III. The ground plan – a Latin cross – measures 84 m (92 yards) by 59 m (65 yards). Its construction was carried out in stages over three centuries and involved many of the greatest artists and architects in Europe. The style is almost entirely Gothic, and shows influences from Germany, France and the Low Countries. First to be built were the nave and cloisters, while the intricate, crocketed spires and the richly decorated side chapels are mostly later work. The architects cleverly adapted the cathedral to its sloping site, incorporating stairways inside and out.

West Front
The lacy, steel-grey spires soar above a sculpted balustrade depicting Castile's early kings.

★ Golden Staircase
This elegant Renaissance staircase by Diego de Siloé (1519–22) links the nave with a tall door (kept locked) at street level.

KEY

① **Capilla de la Presentación** (1519–24) is a funerary chapel with a star-shaped, traceried vault.

② **Capilla de Santa Tecla**

③ **Tomb of El Cid**

④ **Capilla de Santa Ana** features an altarpiece (1490) by the sculptor Gil de Siloé. The central panel shows St Anne with St Joachim.

⑤ **Lantern**

⑥ **Capilla de San Juan Bautista and museum**

⑦ **Interpretation Centre**

⑧ **Capilla de la Visitación**

⑨ **Reception and Information Centre**

⑩ **Capilla del Santísimo Cristo**

Puerta de Santa María

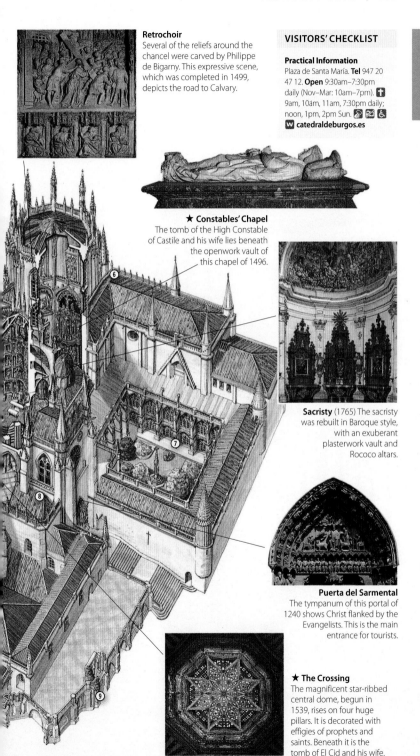

Retrochoir
Several of the reliefs around the chancel were carved by Philippe de Bigarny. This expressive scene, which was completed in 1499, depicts the road to Calvary.

VISITORS' CHECKLIST

Practical Information
Plaza de Santa María. **Tel** 947 20 47 12. **Open** 9:30am–7:30pm daily (Nov–Mar: 10am–7pm). 9am, 10am, 11am, 7:30pm daily; noon, 1pm, 2pm Sun.
w catedraldeburgos.es

★ Constables' Chapel
The tomb of the High Constable of Castile and his wife lies beneath the openwork vault of this chapel of 1496.

Sacristy (1765) The sacristy was rebuilt in Baroque style, with an exuberant plasterwork vault and Rococo altars.

Puerta del Sarmental
The tympanum of this portal of 1240 shows Christ flanked by the Evangelists. This is the main entrance for tourists.

★ The Crossing
The magnificent star-ribbed central dome, begun in 1539, rises on four huge pillars. It is decorated with effigies of prophets and saints. Beneath it is the tomb of El Cid and his wife.

㉙ Lerma

Burgos. 🅐 2,900. 🚇 🚌 🛈 Calle
Audiencia 6, 947 17 70 02 (closed
Mon, except Aug). 🛒 Wed.
🎉 Nuestra Señora de la Natividad
(8 Sep). 🌐 citlerma.com

The grandiose appearance of
this town is largely due to the
ambition of the notorious first
Duke of Lerma (see p64), Felipe
III's corrupt favourite and
minister from 1598 to 1618.
He misused vast quantities of
Spain's new-found wealth on
new buildings in his home town
– all strictly Classical in style,
in accordance with prevailing
fashion. At the top of the town,
the **Palacio Ducal**, built in 1605
as his residence, has been
transformed into a parador.

There are good views over
the Río Arlanza from the archways near to the **Convento de
Santa Clara** and also from the
Colegiata de San Pedro church,
which has a bronze statue of
the Duke's uncle.

The narrow, sloping streets of the Old Town
of Lerma

Gregorian Plainchant

At regular intervals throughout the
day, the monks of Santo Domingo
de Silos sing services in plainchant,
an unaccompanied singing of Latin
texts in unison. The origins of chant
date back to the beginnings of
Christianity, but it was Pope Gregory
I (590–604) who codified this
manner of worship. It is an ancient
and austere form of music which
has found a new appeal with
modern audiences. In 1994 a
recording of the monks became
a surprise hit all over the world.

Manuscript for an 11th-century
Gregorian chant

Cloisters of the Monasterio de Santo
Domingo de Silos

㉚ Monasterio de Santo Domingo de Silos

Santo Domingo de Silos (Burgos).
Tel 947 39 00 49. 🚌 from Burgos.
Open 10am–1pm, 4:30–6pm Tue–
Sun. **Closed** pub hols. 🔲 🛈 9am,
7pm Mon–Sat, 11am & 7pm Sun.
🌐 abadiadesilos.es

St Dominic gave his name to
the monastery he built in 1041
over the ruins of an abbey
destroyed by the Moors. It is
a place of spiritual and artistic
pilgrimage – its tranquil setting
has inspired countless poets.

Others come to admire the
beautiful Romanesque cloisters,
whose capitals are sculpted in a
variety of designs, both symbol-
istic and realistic. The carvings on
the corner piers depict various
scenes from the Bible and the
ceilings are coffered in Moorish
style. The body of St Dominic
rests in a silver urn, supported
by three Romanesque lions, in

a chapel in the north gallery.
The old pharmacy, just off the
cloister, has a display of jars from
Talavera de la Reina (see p390).

The Benedictine community
holds regular services in Gregorian chant in the Neo-Classical
church by Ventura Rodríguez.
The monastery offers accommodation for male guests.

Environs

To the southwest lies the
Garganta de la Yecla (Yecla
Gorge), where a path leads
to a narrow fissure cut by
the river. To the northeast, the
peaks and wildlife reserve of
the **Sierra de la Demanda**
extend over into La Rioja.

The 15th-century castle of Peñaranda
de Duero

㉛ Peñaranda de Duero

Burgos. 🅐 580. 🚌 🛈 C/ Trinquete
7. **Tel** 947 55 20 63 (closed Mon,
Sun pm). 🛒 Fri. 🎉 Santiago
(25 Jul), Santa Ana (26 Jul),
Virgen de los Remedios (8 Sep).
🌐 penarandadeduero.es

The castle of Peñaranda was
built during the Reconquest (see
pp58–9) by the Castilians, who
had driven the Moors back
south of the Río Duero. From
its hilltop site, there are views
down to one of the most
charming villages in old Castile,
where pantiled houses cluster
around a huge church. The
main square is lined with porticoed, timber-framed buildings
and the superb Renaissance
Palacio de Avellaneda. Framing
its main doorway are various

Curtain walls and drum towers of Berlanga de Duero castle

heraldic devices, and inside is a patio with fine decorated ceilings. On Calle de la Botica is a 17th-century **pharmacy**.

Environs
In **Aranda de Duero**, 18 km (10 miles) to the west, the **Iglesia de Santa María**, has an Isabelline façade *(see p28)*.

Palacio de Avellaneda
Plaza Condes de Miranda 1. **Tel** 947 55 20 13. **Open** 10am–2pm, 4–8pm Tue–Sun. only (every 30 min).

❸❷ El Burgo de Osma

Soria. 5,250. Plaza Mayor 9, 975 36 01 16 (closed Wed except in high season). Sat. Virgen del Espino and San Roque (14–19 Aug).

The most interesting sight in this attractive village is the **cathedral**. Although it is mostly Gothic (dating from 1232), with Renaissance additions, the tower is Baroque (1739). Its treasures include a Juan de Juni altarpiece and the tomb of the founder, San Pedro de Osma. The museum has a valuable collection of illuminated manuscripts and codices.

Porticoed buildings line the streets and the Plaza Mayor, and storks nest on the Baroque Hospital de San Agustín.

Environs
Overlooking the Río Duero at **Gormaz**, 12 km (7 miles) south, is a massive castle with 28 towers. There are also medieval fortresses at **Berlanga de Duero**, 20 km (12 miles) further

southeast, and at **Calatañazor**, 25 km (16 miles) northeast of El Burgo de Osma, near to where the Moorish leader al Mansur was killed in 1002 *(see p57)*.

❸❸ Soria

Soria. 40,150. C/ Medinaceli 2, 975 21 20 52. Thu. San Juan (24 Jun). **sorianitelaimaginas.com**

Castilla y León's smallest provincial capital stands on the banks of the Río Duero. Soria's stylish, modern parador is named after the poet Antonio Machado (1875–1939, *see p39*), who wrote in praise of the town and the surrounding plains. Many of the older buildings are gone, but among those remaining are the imposing **Palacio de los Condes de Gómara**, and the **Concatedral de San Pedro**, both built in the 16th century.

The **Museo Numantino**, opposite the municipal gardens, displays a variety of finds from the nearby Roman ruins of Numantia and Tiermes *(see p369)*. Across the Duero is the ruined

monastery of **San Juan de Duero**, with a 13th-century cloister of interlacing arches.

Environs
North of Soria are the ruins of **Numantia**, whose inhabitants endured a year-long Roman siege in 133 BC before defiantly burning the town and themselves *(see p54)*. To the northwest is the Sierra de Urbión, a range of pine-clad hills with a lake, the **Laguna Negra de Urbión**.

Museo Numantino
Paseo del Espolón 8. **Tel** 975 22 14 28. **Open** Tue–Sun. (free Sat & Sun).

❸❹ Medinaceli

Soria. 820. Campo San Nicolás, 975 32 63 47. Beato Julián de San Agustín (28 Aug), Cuerpos Santos (13 Nov). **medinaceli.es**

Only a triumphal arch remains of Roman Ocilis, perched on a high ridge over the Río Jalón. Built in the 1st century AD, it is the only one in Spain with three arches. It has been adopted as the symbol for ancient monuments on Spanish road signs.

Environs
Lying just to the east are the red cliffs of the Jalón gorges. On the Madrid–Zaragoza road is the Cistercian monastery of **Santa María de Huerta**, founded in the 12th century. Its glories include a 13th-century Gothic cloister and the superb, crypt-like Monks' Refectory.

Monasterio de Santa María de Huerta
Tel 975 32 70 02. **Open** daily. **Closed** 24 Aug.

Decorative arches in the cloister of the monastery of San Juan de Duero

CASTILLA-LA MANCHA

*Guadalajara · Cuenca · Toledo ·
Albacete · Ciudad Real*

La Mancha's empty beauty, its windmills and medieval
castles, silhouetted above the sienna plains, was
immortalized by Cervantes in Don Quixote's epic
adventures. Its brilliantly sunlit, wide horizons are one of
the classic images of Spain. This scarcely visited region has
great, scenic mountain ranges, dramatic gorges and the two
monument-filled cities of Toledo and Cuenca.

You will always find a castle nearby in this
region – as the name Castilla suggests.
Most were built in the 9th–12th centuries,
when the region was a battleground
between Christians and Moors. Others
mark the 14th- and 15th-century frontiers
between the kingdoms of Aragón and
Castile. Sigüenza, Belmonte, Alarcón,
Molina de Aragón and Calatrava la
Nueva are among the most impressive.

Toledo, which was the capital of
Visigothic Spain, is an outstanding
museum city. Its rich architectural and
artistic heritage derives from a coa-
lescence of Muslim, Christian and Jewish
cultures with medieval and Renaissance
ideas and influences.

Cuenca is another attractive city. Its
Old Town is perched above converging
gorges; on two sides it spills down
steep hillsides. Villanueva de los Infantes,
Chinchilla, Alcaraz and Almagro are
towns of character built between the
16th and 18th centuries. Ocaña and
Tembleque each has a splendid
plaza mayor (main square).

La Mancha's plains are brightened by
natural features of great beauty in its two
national parks – the Tablas de Daimiel, and
Cabañeros, within the Montes de Toledo.
Rimming the plains are beautiful upland
areas: the olive groves of the Alcarria;
Cuenca's limestone mountains; and the
peaks of the Sierra de Alcaraz. The wine
region of La Mancha is the world's largest
expanse of vineyards. Around Consuegra
and Albacete fields turn mauve in autumn
as the valuable saffron crocus blooms.

Windmills above Campo de Criptana on the plains of La Mancha

◀ Hanging Houses over the Huécar ravine in Cuenca, Castilla-La Mancha

Exploring Castilla-La Mancha

The historic city of Toledo is Castilla-La Mancha's major tourist destination. Less crowded towns with historical charm include Almagro, Oropesa, Alcaraz and Guadalajara. At Sigüenza, Calatrava, Belmonte and Alarcón there are medieval castles, reminders of the region's eventful past. Some towns on the plains of La Mancha, such as El Toboso and Campo de Criptana, are associated with the adventures of Don Quixote *(see p399)*. The wooded uplands of the Serranía de Cuenca, the Alcarria and the Sierra de Alcaraz provide picturesque scenic routes. A haven for bird lovers is the wetland nature reserve of the Tablas de Daimiel.

The village of Alcalá del Júcar

Sights at a Glance

1. Atienza
2. Sigüenza
3. Molina de Aragón
4. La Alcarria
5. Guadalajara
6. Serranía de Cuenca
7. *Cuenca pp388–9*
8. Segóbriga
9. Uclés
10. Illescas
11. Talavera de la Reina
12. Oropesa
13. Montes de Toledo
14. *Toledo pp392–7*
15. Templeque
16. Consuegra
17. Campo de Criptana
18. El Toboso
19. Belmonte
20. Alarcón
21. Alcalá del Júcar
22. Albacete
24. Alcaraz
25. Lagunas de Ruidera
26. Villanueva de los Infantes
27. Valdepeñas
28. Viso del Marqués
29. Calatrava la Nueva
30. Almagro
31. Tablas de Daimiel
32. Valle de Alcudia

Tours

23. Sierra de Alcaraz

Cattle grazing on the isolated plains of La Mancha

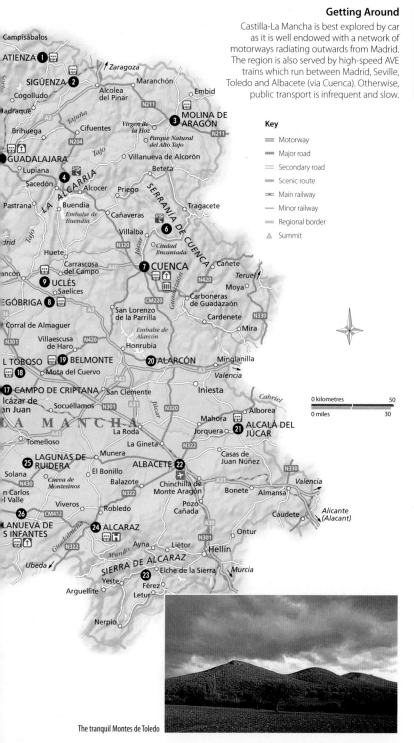

Castilla-La Mancha is best explored by car as it is well endowed with a network of motorways radiating outwards from Madrid. The region is also served by high-speed AVE trains which run between Madrid, Seville, Toledo and Albacete (via Cuenca). Otherwise, public transport is infrequent and slow.

Key

═══ Motorway

▄▄▄ Major road

═══ Secondary road

▬▬▬ Scenic route

▬■▬ Main railway

──── Minor railway

▬▬▬ Regional border

△ Summit

Campisábalos

ATIENZA ❶

SIGÜENZA ❷

Maranchón

Embid

Alcolea del Pinar

Cogolludo

Madraque

Brihuega

Cifuentes

Virgen de la Hoz

MOLINA DE ARAGÓN ❸

Parque Natural del Alto Tajo

GUADALAJARA

Lupiana

Sacedón

LA ALCARRIA ❹

Alcocer

Priego

Villanueva de Alcorón

Beteta

Pastrana

Buendía

Embalse de Buendía

Cañaveras

Tragacete

SERRANÍA DE CUENCA ❻

Villalba

Huete

Ciudad Encantada

Cañete

Carrascosa del Campo

CUENCA ❼

Teruel

UCLÉS ❾

Saelices

Moya

SEGÓBRIGA ❽

San Lorenzo de la Parrilla

Carboneras de Guadazaón

Corral de Almaguer

Cardenete

Villaescusa de Haro

Embalse de Alarcón

Honrubia

Mira

EL TOBOSO ⓳ BELMONTE

Mota del Cuervo ⓲

ALARCÓN ⓴

Minglanilla

CAMPO DE CRIPTANA ⓱

San Clemente

Iniesta

Valencia

Alcázar de San Juan

Socuéllamos

LA MANCHA

La Roda

Mahora

ALCALÁ DEL JÚCAR ㉑

Tomelloso

La Gineta

Jorquera

Casas de Juan Núñez

LAGUNAS DE RUIDERA ㉕

Munera

ALBACETE ㉒

Solana

Cueva de Montesinos

El Bonillo

Balazote

Chinchilla de Monte Aragón

Bonete

Almansa

Valencia

San Carlos del Valle

Viveros

Robledo

Pozo Cañada

Caudete

Alicante (Alacant)

VILLANUEVA DE LOS INFANTES ㉖

ALCARAZ ㉔

Ayna

Liétor

Ontur

Hellín

Úbeda

SIERRA DE ALCARAZ

Elche de la Sierra ㉓

Murcia

Arguellite

Yeste

Férez

Letur

Nerpio

The tranquil Montes de Toledo

For additional map symbols see back flap

❶ Atienza

Guadalajara. 🏠 500. 🚌 Cervantes 22, 949 39 92 93 (closed Mon–Fri). 🚍 Fri. 🎪 La Caballada (Pentecost Sun). 🌐 **visitclm.com**

Rising high above the valley it once protected, Atienza contains vestiges of its medieval past. Crowning the hill is a ruined 12th-century castle. The arcaded Plaza Mayor and the Plaza del Trigo are joined by an original gateway. The **Museo de San Gil**, a religious art museum, is in the church of the same name. The **Iglesia de Santa María del Rey**, at the foot of the hill, displays a Baroque altarpiece.

Environs
Campisábalos, to the west, has an outstanding 12th-century Romanesque church. The **Hayedo de Tejera Negra**, further west, is a nature reserve of beech woods.

🏛 **Museo de San Gil**
C/ San Gil. **Tel** 949 39 90 41.
Open Sat & Sun; by appt weekdays. 🎫

❷ Sigüenza

Guadalajara. 🏠 5,000. 🚉 🚌 🚩 Calle Serrano Sanz 9, 949 34 70 07. 🚍 Sat. 🎪 San Vicente (22 Jan), San Juan (24 Jun), Fiestas Patronales (mid-Aug). 🌐 **siguenza.es**

Dominating the hillside town of Sigüenza is its impressive castle-parador. The **cathedral** is Romanesque, with later additions such as the Gothic-Plateresque cloisters. In one of the chapels is the Tomb of El

Semi-recumbent figure of El Doncel on his tomb in Sigüenza Cathedral

Doncel, built for Martín Vázquez de Arce, Isabel of Castile's page *(see p60)*. He was killed in battle against the Moors in 1486. The sacristy has a ceiling carved with flowers and cherubs.

❸ Molina de Aragón

Guadalajara. 🏠 4,000. 🚌 🚩 Calle de las Tiendas, 949 83 20 98. 🚍 Thu. 🎪 Día del Carmen (16 Jul), Ferias (30 Aug–5 Sep). 🌐 **turismomolinaaltotajo.com**

Molina's attractive medieval quarter is at the foot of a hill next to the Río Gallo. The town was disputed during the Reconquest and captured from the Moors by Alfonso I of Aragón in 1129. Many monuments were destroyed during the War of Independence *(see p67)*, but the 11th-century hilltop castle preserves seven original towers. It is possible to visit the Romanesque-Gothic **Iglesia de Santa Clara**.

Environs
West of Molina is the **Virgen de la Hoz** chapel, set in a rust-red ravine. Further southwest is a nature reserve, the **Parque Natural del Alto Tajo**.

Arab ramparts above Molina de Aragón's Old Town

❹ La Alcarria

Guadalajara. 🚌 Guadalajara. 🚩 Palacio Ducal, Plaza de la Hora, Pastrana, 949 37 06 72. 🌐 **visitclm.com**

This vast stretch of undulating olive groves and fields east of Guadalajara is still evocative of Camilo José Cela's *(see p39)* classic book *Journey to the Alcarria*. Driving through the rolling hills, it seems that little has changed since this account of the hardship of Spanish rural life was written in the 1940s.

Towards the centre of the Alcarria are three immense, adjoining reservoirs called the **Mar de Castilla** (Sea of Castile). The first reservoir was built in

Olive groves in La Alcarria in the province of Guadalajara

1946, and holiday homes have subsequently sprung up close to the shores and on the outskirts of villages.

In the historic ducal town of **Pastrana**, 45 km (28 miles) southeast of Guadalajara, is one of the prettiest towns in the Alcarria. The town developed alongside the **Palacio Mendoza**, and by the 17th century was larger and more affluent than Guadalajara. The **Iglesia Colegiata de la Asunción** contains four 15th-century Flemish tapestries and paintings from El Greco's school.

Brihuega, 30 km (19 miles) northeast of Guadalajara, has a pleasant old centre.

❺ Guadalajara

Guadalajara. 🚹 84,800. 🚆 🚌
🛈 Plaza Aviación Militar Española, 949 88 70 99. 🚌 Tue, Sat. 🎉 Virgen de la Antigua (Sep). 🔲 **guadalajara.es**

Guadalajara's history is largely lost within the modern city, although traces of its Renaissance splendour survive. The **Palacio de los Duques del Infantado**, built between the 14th and 17th centuries by the powerful Mendoza dynasty, is an outstanding example of Gothic-Mudéjar architecture *(see p28)*. The main façade and patio are adorned with carving. The restored palace now houses the Museo Provincial. Among the churches in the town is the **Iglesia de Santiago**, with a Gothic-Plateresque chapel by Alonso de Covarrubias.

Detail of the façade of the Palacio de los Duques del Infantado

Sculpted rock figures in Ciudad Encantada

The 15th-century **Iglesia de San Francisco** is home to the mausoleum of the Mendoza family; it cannot, however, be visited. The cathedral is built on the site of a mosque.

Environs
At **Lupiana**, 11 km (7 miles) east of Guadalajara, is the two-storey Monasterio de San Bartolomé, founded in the 14th century.

🏛 **Palacio de los Duques del Infantado**
Avenida del Ejército. **Tel** 949 21 33 01.
Open daily; museum: Tue–Sun. ♿

❻ Serranía de Cuenca

Cuenca. 🚌 Cuenca. 🛈 Plaza Mayor 1, Cuenca, 969 24 10 51.
🔲 **serraniaaltadecuenca.es**

To the north and east of Cuenca stretches the vast *serranía*, a mountainous area of forests and pastures dissected by deep gorges. Its two most popular beauty spots are the **Ciudad Encantada** (Enchanted City), where the limestone has been eroded into spectacular shapes, and the moss-clad waterfalls and rock pools of the **Nacimiento del Río Cuervo** (Source of the River Cuervo).

The main river flowing through the area, the Júcar, carves a gorge near Villalba de la Sierra. The viewpoint of the **Ventano del Diablo** gives the best view of the gorge.

Between Beteta and Priego, to the north, is another spectacular river canyon, the **Hoz de Beteta**, where the Río Guadiela has cut its way through the surrounding cliffs. There are good views from the convent of **San Miguel de las Victorias**. A small road leads to the 18th-century royal spa of **Solán de Cabras**.

In the emptier eastern and southern tracts is **Cañete**, a pretty, fortified old town with a parish church displaying 16th-century paintings. To the southeast of Cañete are the eerie ridgetop ruins of the abandoned town of **Moya**.

➐ Street-by-Street: Cuenca

Cuenca's picturesque Old Town sits astride a steeply sided spur which drops precipitously on either side to the deep gorges of the Júcar and Huécar rivers. Around the Moorish town's narrow, winding streets grew the Gothic and Renaissance city, its monuments built with with the profits of the wool and textile trade. The main sight is the cathedral, one of the most original works of Spanish Gothic, with Anglo-Norman influences. One of the picturesque Hanging Houses, which jut out over the Huécar ravine, has been converted into the excellent Museum of Abstract Art.

The Plaza de la Merced
buildings contrast with the modern Museo de las Ciencias (Science Museum).

Museo de las Ciencias

CALLE DE SANTA MARIA

CALLE MOSEN DIEGO DE VALERA

CALLE DE ALFONSO VIII

Torre Mangana
This ruined lookout tower at the top of the town is all that remains of an Arab fortress. There are wonderful panoramic views from the top.

Ayuntamiento

Museo de Cuenca
The collection, covering prehistory up to the 17th century, includes an excellent exhibition on Roman Cuenca.

Key

━ Suggested route

★ Museo de Arte Abstracto
Spain's abstract art museum is inside one of the Hanging Houses. It contains works by the movement's leading artists, including Antoni Tàpies and Eduardo Chillida.

Plaza Mayor
This café-lined, arcaded square is in the heart of the Old Town. The 18th-century Baroque town hall (*ayuntamiento*), built with arches, stands at the south end.

VISITORS' CHECKLIST

Practical Information
Cuenca. 🏠 57,000.
🌐 **cuenca.es**
ℹ Plaza Mayor 1, 969 24 10 51.
🚌 Tue. Museo Diocesano:
Open Tue–Sun. 🏛 Museo de Arte Abstracto: **Open** Tue–Sun.
🏛 Museo de las Ciencias:
Open Tue–Sun. 🏛 🏛
Museo de Cuenca: **Open** Tue–Sat, Sun am. 🏛

Transport
🚉 Calle Mariano Catalina, 902 32 03 20. 🚌 Calle Fermín Caballero 20, 969 22 70 87.

The Iglesia de San Miguel, perched over the Júcar gorge, was built in the Romanic style.

0 metres 50
0 yards 50

PLAZA MAYOR

SEVERO CATALINA

CALLE DE SAN PEDRO

CALLE DE JULIÁN ROMERO

CALLE DE OBISPO VALERO

To Parador de Cuenca

★ **Hanging Houses**
The 14th-century beamed Casas Colgadas were once used as a summer residence for the royal family.

Museo Diocesano
The cathedral's treasures, which are housed in the Palacio Episcopal, include paintings by El Greco.

★ **Cathedral**
Highlights of the 12th- to 18th-century building are the decorated altar, chapterhouse and the side chapels.

Remains of a Roman building in Segóbriga

❽ Segóbriga

Saelices, Cuenca, CM-310, km 58.
Tel 629 75 22 57. **Open** Tue–Sun.
Museum: **Closed** some public hols.
🅿 📷 by appt. **W** visitclm.com

The small ruined Roman city of Segóbriga, near the town of Saelices, is located in open, unspoiled countryside close to the Madrid–Valencia motorway. The Romans who lived here exploited the surrounding area, growing cereals, felling timber and mining minerals.

Many parts of the city can be explored. The 1st-century theatre – which has a capacity of 2,000 people – is sometimes used for performances today. Segóbriga also had a necropolis, an amphitheatre, a temple to Diana and public baths. The quarries which supplied the stone to build the city can also be seen.

Nearby, a small **museum** has some of the site's finds, although the best statues are in Cuenca's Museo Arqueológico (see p388).

❾ Monasterio de Uclés

Uclés, Cuenca. **Tel** 969 13 50 58.
Open 10am–6pm daily (till 8pm Jul & Aug). **Closed** 1 & 6 Jan, 25 Dec. 🅿
W visitclm.com

The small village of Uclés, to the south of the Alcarria, is dominated by its impressive castle-monastery, nicknamed "El Escorial de La Mancha" for the similarity of its church's profile to that of El Escorial (see pp334–5). Originally an impregnable medieval fortress, Uclés became the monastery seat of the Order of Santiago

from 1174, because of its central location. The austere building you see today is mainly Renaissance but overlaid with Baroque detail. It has a magnificent carved wooden ceiling and staircase.

❿ Illescas

Toledo. 🚆 23,500. 🚌 🚖 ℹ Plaza Mercado 14, 925 51 10 51. 🕑 Thu.
🎉 Fiesta de Milagro (11 Mar), Virgen de la Caridad (31 Aug). **W** illescas.es

Illescas was the summer location for Felipe II's court. While there is little to see of its Old Town, the 16th-century **Hospital de la Caridad**, near the Iglesia de Santa María (12th–13th century and renovated in the 15th), has an important art collection, including five late El Grecos (see p395). The subjects of three of these are the Nativity, the Annunciation and the Coronation of the Virgin.

Ceramics in Talavera workshop

⓫ Hospital de la Caridad

Calle Cardenal Cisneros 2. **Tel** 925 54 00 35. **Open** Mon–Sat. 🅿 ♿

⓫ Talavera de la Reina

Toledo. 🚆 89,000. 🚌 🚖 ℹ
C/ Ronda del Cañillo 22, 925 82 63 22.
🕑 Wed & 1st Sat of month. 🎉 Las Mondas (Sat after Easter), Feria de San Isidro (15–18 May), Virgen del Prado (8 Sep), Feria de San Mateo (20–23 Sep). **W** talavera.org

A ruined 15th-century bridge across the Tagus marks the entrance to the old part of this busy market town. From the bridge you can walk past the surviving part of the Moorish and medieval wall to the 12th-century **collegiate church**. It has a small but beautiful Gothic cloister, and 18th-century belfry.

Talavera's ceramic workshops still produce the blue and yellow *azulejos* (tiles) which have been a trademark of the town since the 16th century; but nowadays they also make domestic and decorative objects.

A good selection of *azulejos* can be seen in the large **Ermita de la Virgen del Prado** by the river. Many of the interior walls have superb 16th- to 20th-century tile friezes of religious scenes.

Housed in a 17th-century convent, the **Museo Ruiz de Luna** houses the private Talavera pottery collection and personal works of ceramist Juan Ruiz de Luna.

Part of a frieze of tiles in Talavera's Ermita del Virgen del Prado

Traditional embroidery work in Lagartera, near Oropesa

⑫ Oropesa

Toledo. 🖼 2,900. 🚉 ℹ Calle Hospital 10, 925 43 02 01. 🚌 Mon & Thu. 🎉 Virgen de Peñitas (8–10 Sep), Beato Alonso de Orozco (19 Sep).
🌐 oropesadetoledo.org

Oropesa's medieval and Renaissance splendour as one of Toledo's satellite communities has left a charming old quarter at the centre of today's small farming town. A circular Ruta Monumental starts from the massive, mainly 15th-century **castle** on the top of the hill. A Renaissance extension – thought to be the work of Juan de Herrera, co-architect of El Escorial *(see pp334–5)* – was added to the castle in the 16th century by the wealthy and influential Álvarez family. Part of the castle has been converted into a parador.

The Ruta Monumental continues around the town, taking in a number of churches, convents, a small ceramics museum and the town hall which presides over the main square.

Environs

The area around Oropesa is excellent for buying handicrafts. **Lagartera**, just to the west of the town, is famous for the embroidery and lacework by the women in the village, and **El Puente del Arzobispo**, 12 km (7 miles) south of Oropesa, is a good source of painted ceramics and esparto (grass-weaving) work. **Ciudad de Vascos**, further southeast, is a ruined 10th-century Arab city in splendid countryside around Azután.

⑬ Montes de Toledo

Toledo. 🚉 Pueblo Nuevo del Bullaque. ℹ Parque Nacional de Cabañeros, 926 78 32 97. 🅿
🌐 turismocabaneros.com

To the southwest of Toledo a range of low mountains sweeps towards Extremadura. In medieval times the Montes de Toledo were owned by bishops and the kings. They cover some 1,000 sq km (386 sq miles).

The attractive nature reserve of the **Parque Nacional de Cabañeros** *(see pp34–5)* encloses a sizable area of woodland and pastures used for grazing sheep. The easiest access to the park is from **Pueblo Nuevo del Bullaque**. From here it is possible to make four-hour guided trips in Land Rovers, during which you may spot wild boar, deer and imperial eagles. In the pasturelands stand *chozos*, conical refuges for shepherds.

In the eastern foothills of the Montes de Toledo is **Orgaz**, with a parish church which contains works by El Greco. Nearby villages, such as **Los Yébenes** and **Ventas con Peña Aguilera**, are known for their leather goods and restaurants serving game.

On the plains stands the small church of **Santa María de Melque**, believed to date back to the 8th century. Close by is the Templar castle of **Montalbán**, a vast but ruined 12th-century fortress. Nearer to Toledo, at **Guadamur**, there is another handsome castle.

A *chozo* (shepherd's cabin) in the Parque Nacional de Cabañeros

Castilla-la Mancha's Fiestas

La Endiablada *(2–3 Feb)* Almonacid del Marquesado (Cuenca). At the start of the two-day-long "Fiesta of the Bewitched", men and boys, gaudily dressed as "devils", with cowbells strapped to their backs, gather in the house of their leader, the *Diablo Mayor*. They accompany the images of the Virgen de la Candelaria (Virgin of Candlemas) and St Blaise in procession. As the devils dance alongside the floats bearing the saints' images, they ring their bells loudly and incessantly.

One of the so-called "devils" in La Endiablada fiesta

Romería del Cristo del Sahúco *(Whit Monday, May/Jun)*, Peñas de San Pedro (Albacete). A cross-shaped coffin bearing a figure of Christ is carried 15 km (9 miles) here from its shrine by men dressed in white.
La Caballada *(Whit Sunday, early Jun)*, Atienza (Guadalajara). Horsemen follow the route across country taken by the 12th-century muleteers of Atienza, who are said to have saved the boy King Alfonso VIII of Castile from his uncle, Fernando II.
Corpus Christi *(May/Jun)*, Toledo. One of Spain's most dramatic Corpus Christi *(see p42)* processions. The cathedral monstrance *(see p396)* is paraded in the streets, whose walls are adorned with 48 17th-century Flemish tapestries.

⑭ Street-by-Street: Toledo

Picturesquely sited on a hill above the River Tagus is the historic centre of Toledo. Behind the old walls lies much evidence of the city's rich history. The Romans built a fortress on the site of the present-day Alcázar. The Visigoths made Toledo their capital in the 6th century AD, and left behind several churches. In the Middle Ages, Toledo was a melting pot of Christian, Muslim and Jewish cultures, and it was during this period that the city's most outstanding monument – its cathedral – was built. In the 16th century the painter El Greco came to live in Toledo, and today the city is home to many of his works.

Puerta Cristo de la Luz

The Iglesia de San Román, of Visigothic origin, now contains a museum relating the city's past under the Visigoths.

CARDENAL LORENZANA

CALLE DE SAN ROMÁN

CALLE DE ALFONSO X

CALL

CALLE DE ALFONSO XII

CALLE DE LA TRINIDAD

CALL

★ Iglesia de Santo Tomé
This church, with a beautiful Mudéjar tower, houses El Greco's masterpiece, *The Burial of the Count of Orgaz (see p36)*.

To Sinagoga de Santa María la Blanca and Monasterio de San Juan de los Reyes

To Sinagoga del Tránsito and Casa-Museo de El Greco

Archbishop's Palace
Spread over a large block, with façades on three streets, this 16th-century palace features an austere Renaissance design.

0 metres   100
0 yards   100

The Puerta de Sol has a double Moorish arch and two towers.

Mezquita del Cristo de la Luz
This mosque, one of the city's two remaining Muslim buildings, dates from around AD 1000.

To Estación de Autobuses and Estación de RENFE

VISITORS' CHECKLIST

Practical Information
Toledo. 🚇 84,000.
🌐 toledo-turismo.com
ℹ Plaza del Consistorio 1, 925 25 40 30. 🏛 Tue. 🎉 Easter, Corpus Christi (May/Jun), Virgen del Sagrario (15 Aug). Iglesia de San Román: **Open** Tue–Sun am. 🎭

Transport
🚉 Paseo de la Rosa, 902 32 03 20. 🚌 Avenida de Castilla-La Mancha, 925 21 58 50.

★ **Museo de Santa Cruz**
The museum's fine arts collection includes among its exhibits this 15th-century zodiac tapestry from Flanders.

The Plaza de Zocodover
is named after the market which was held here in Moorish times. It is still the city's main square, with many cafés and shops.

PLAZA DE ZOCODOVER

ALFILERITOS

E DEL HOMBRE DE PALO

CALLE DEL COMERCIO

CUESTA DE CARLOS V

SIXTO RAMÓN PARRO

RDENAL CISNEROS

Key
— Suggested route

★ **Cathedral**
Built on the site of a Visigothic cathedral and a mosque, this impressive structure is one of the largest cathedrals in Christendom *(see pp396–7)*. The Flamboyant Gothic high-altar reredos (1504) is the work of several artists.

Alcázar
The National Army Museum is housed here. In the central patio is a replica of the statue Carlos V y el Furor.

Toledo Cathedral rising above the rooftops of the medieval part of the city

Exploring Toledo

Toledo is easily reached from Madrid by rail, bus or car, and is then best explored on foot. To visit all the main sights you need at least two days, but it is possible to walk around the medieval and Jewish quarters in a long morning. To avoid the heavy crowds, go midweek and stay for a night, when the city is at its most atmospheric.

🏠 Alcázar

Calle Unión s/n. **Tel** 925 23 88 00. **Open** Thu–Tue. 🏛 (free Sun). 🎟

Charles V's fortified palace stands on the site of former Roman, Visigothic and Muslim fortresses. Its severe square profile suffered damage by fire three times before being almost completely destroyed in 1936, when the Nationalists survived a 70-day siege by the Republicans. Restoration followed the original plans and the siege headquarters have been preserved as a monument to Nationalist heroism. The former National Museo del Ejército was transferred from Madrid to this building, making the Alcázar the main army museum in Spain.

The Borbón-Lorenzana Library (open to the public) contains 100,000 books and manuscripts from the 16th to 19th centuries.

🏛 Museo de Santa Cruz

Calle Miguel de Cervantes 3. **Tel** 925 22 14 02. **Open** 10am–7pm Mon–Sat, 10am–2:30pm Sun. 🌐 patrimoniohistoricoclm.es

This museum is housed in a 16th-century hospital founded by Cardinal Mendoza. The building has some Renaissance architectural features, including the main doorway, staircase and cloister. The four main wings, laid out in the shape of a Greek cross, are dedicated to the fine arts. The collection is especially strong in medieval and Renaissance tapestries, paintings and sculptures. There are also works by El Greco, including one of his last paintings, *The Virgin of the*

The Virgin of the Immaculate Conception by El Greco (1613) in the Museo de Santa Cruz

Immaculate Conception (1613), still in its original altarpiece. Decorative arts on display include two typically Toledan crafts: armour and damascened swords, made by inlaying blackened steel with gold wire. Damascene work, such as plates and jewellery (as well as swords), is still produced in the city.

🏠 Iglesia de Santo Tomé

Plaza del Conde 4. **Tel** 925 25 60 98. **Open** daily. 🎟 🌐 santotome.org

Visitors come here mainly for El Greco's masterpiece, *The Burial of the Count of Orgaz (see p36)*. The Count paid for much of the 14th-century building that stands today. The painting, commissioned in his memory by a parish priest, depicts the miraculous appearance of St Augustine and St Stephen at his burial, to raise his body to heaven. It has never been moved from the setting for which it was painted, nor restored. Nevertheless, it is remarkable for its contrast of glowing and sombre colours. In the foreground, allegedly, are the artist and his son (both looking out), as well as Cervantes. The church is thought to date back to the 11th century, and its tower is a fine example of Mudéjar architecture.

Nearby is the **Pastelería Santo Tomé**, a good place to buy locally made marzipan.

🕎 Sinagoga de Santa María la Blanca

Calle de los Reyes Católicos 4.
Tel 925 22 72 57. **Open** daily.
Closed 1 Jan, 25 Dec. 🎫 🚻

The oldest and largest of the city's original synagogues, this monument dates back to the 12th–13th century. In 1405 it was taken over as a church by San Vincente Ferrer after the expulsion of the Jews. Restoration has returned it to its original beauty – carved stone capitals and wall panels stand out against white horseshoe arches and plasterwork. In the main chapel is a Plateresque altarpiece. In 1391 a massacre of Jews took place on this site, a turning point after years of religious tolerance in the city.

Mudéjar arches in the Sinagoga de Santa María la Blanca

🕎 Sinagoga del Tránsito, Museo Sefardí

C/ Samuel Leví. **Tel** 925 22 36 65.
Open Tue–Sun (Sun am only).
Closed public hols. 🎫 (free Sat pm & Sun). 🖥 **museosefardi.mcu.es**

The most elaborate Mudéjar interior in the city is hidden behind the humble façade of this former synagogue, built in the 14th century by Samuel Ha-Leví, the Jewish treasurer to Pedro the Cruel. The interlaced frieze of the lofty prayer hall fuses Islamic, Gothic and Hebrew geometric motifs below a wonderful coffered ceiling.

The synagogue houses a museum of Sephardi (Spanish Jewish) culture. The items on display date from both before and after the Jews' expulsion from Spain in the late 15th century (see p61).

Ornate ceiling in the Monasterio de San Juan de los Reyes

🏛 Monasterio de San Juan de los Reyes

Calle de los Reyes Católicos 17. **Tel** 925 22 38 02. **Open** daily. **Closed** 1 Jan, 25 Dec. 🎫 🚻 (ground floor only).
🖥 **sanjuandelosreyes.org**

A wonderful mixture of architectural styles, this monastery was commissioned by the Catholic Monarchs in honour of their victory at the battle of Toro in 1476 (see p361). It was originally intended to be their burial place, but they were actually laid to rest in Granada (see p490). Largely the work of Juan Guas, the church's main Isabelline structure was completed in 1496. Although it was badly damaged by Napoleon's troops in 1808 (see p67), it has been restored to its original splendour with features such as a Gothic cloister (1510), which has a multicoloured Mudéjar ceiling. Near to the church is a stretch of the Jewish quarter's original wall.

🏛 Museo del Greco

Paseo del Tránsito. **Tel** 925 22 36 65.
Open Tue–Sun. **Closed** Mon, Sun pm.
🎫 (free Sat pm, Sun). 🚻
🖥 **museodelgreco.mcu.es**

This museum is located in the heart of the Jewish quarter, in a house near to the one in which El Greco lived. It has a wide collection of his works. Canvases on display include *View of Toledo*, a detailed depiction of the city at the time, and the superb series *Christ and the Apostles*. Underneath the museum, on the ground floor, is a domestic chapel with a fine Mudéjar ceiling and a collection of art by painters of the Toledan School.

🏛 Iglesia de Santiago del Arrabal

Calle Real del Arrabal.
Closed to the public.

Close to the Puerta Antigua de Bisagra, this is one of Toledo's most beautiful Mudéjar monuments. It can be easily identified by its tower, which dates from the 12th-century Reconquest (see pp58–9). The church, which was built slightly later, has a beautiful woodwork ceiling and an ornate Mudéjar pulpit, but only the exterior of the building can be visited.

🕎 Puerta Antigua de Bisagra

When Alfonso VI conquered Toledo in 1085, he entered in through this gateway, alongside El Cid. It is the only gateway in the city to have kept its original 10th-century military architecture. The huge towers are topped by a 12th-century Arab gatehouse.

El Greco

Born in Crete in 1541, El Greco ("the Greek") came to Toledo in 1577 to paint the altarpiece in the convent of Santo Domingo el Antiguo. Enchanted by the city, he stayed here, painting religious portraits and altarpieces for other churches. Although El Greco was trained in Italy and influenced by masters such as Tintoretto, his works are closely identified with the city where he settled. He died in Toledo in 1614.

Domenikos Theotocopoulos, better known as El Greco

Toledo Cathedral

The splendour of Toledo's massive cathedral reflects its history as the spiritual heart of the Church in Spain and the seat of the Primate of all Spain. The Mozarabic Mass, which dates back to Visigothic times, is still said here today. The present cathedral was built on the site of a 7th-century church. Work began in 1226 and spanned three centuries, until the completion of the last vaults in 1493. This long period of construction explains the cathedral's mixture of styles: pure French Gothic – complete with flying buttresses – on the exterior; with Spanish decorative styles, such as Mudéjar and Plateresque work, used in the interior.

★ Sacristy
El Greco's *The Denuding of Christ*, above the marble altar, was painted especially for the cathedral. Also here are works by Titian, Van Dyck and Goya.

View of Toledo Cathedral
Dominating the city skyline is the Gothic tower at the west end of the nave. The best view of the cathedral, and the city, is from the parador *(see p571)*.

KEY

① **The Puerta del Mollete**, on the west façade, is the main entrance to the cathedral. From this door, *mollete*, or soft bread, was distributed to the poor.

② **The belfry** in the tower contains a heavy bell known as *La Gorda* ("the Fat One").

③ **The Cloister**, on two floors, was built in the 14th century on the site of the old Jewish market.

④ **Capilla de Santiago**

⑤ **The Capilla de San Ildefonso** contains the superb Plateresque tomb of Cardinal Alonso Carrillo de Albornoz.

⑥ **Puerta de los Leones**

⑦ **The Puerta del Perdón**, or Door of Mercy, has a tympanum decorated with religious characters.

⑧ **The Capilla Mozárabe** has a beautiful Renaissance ironwork grille, carved by Juan Francés in 1524.

Monstrance
In the Treasury is the 16th-century Gothic silver and gold monstrance. It is carried through the streets of Toledo during the Corpus Christi celebrations *(see p391)*.

★ **Transparente**
This Baroque altarpiece of marble, jasper and bronze, by Narciso Tomé, is illuminated by an ornate skylight. It stands out from the mainly Gothic interior.

VISITORS' CHECKLIST

Practical Information
Calle Cardenal Cisneros 1.
Tel 925 22 22 41.
 catedralprimada.es
Open 10am–6:30pm daily (from 2pm Sun), last entry 1 hr before closing.
 8am, 10am, 10:30am, 5:30pm, 6:30pm Mon–Sat, 8am, 9am, 11am, noon, 1pm, 5:30pm, 6:30pm Sun (Catholic); 9am Mon–Sat, 9:45am Sun (Mozarabic).
Choir, Treasury, Sacristy and Chapterhouse:
Open as above.

Chapterhouse
Above 16th-century frescoes by Juan de Borgoña is this multicoloured Mudéjar ceiling, unique in the city.

Entrance via Puerta Llana

★ **High Altar Reredos**
The polychrome reredos, one of the most beautiful in Spain, depicts scenes from Christ's life.

★ **Choir**
The carvings on the wooden lower stalls depict scenes of the fall of Granada. The alabaster upper ones show figures from the Old Testament.

Windmills on the ridge above Consuegra, overlooking the plains of La Mancha

⓯ Tembleque

Toledo. 🏛 2,300. 🚹 Plaza Mayor 1, 925 14 55 53. 🚌 Wed. 🎎 Jesús de Nazareno (23–27 Aug).
🌐 visitclm.com

The stone Plaza Mayor *(see p31)* at Tembleque dates from the 17th century. It is decorated with the red cross of the Knights Hospitallers, the military order which once ruled the town.

Environs
Ocaña, 30 km (20 miles) north of Tembleque, centres on the huge yet elegant, late 18th-century *plaza mayor*, one of the largest town squares in Spain, after Madrid and Salamanca.

⓰ Consuegra

Toledo. 🏛 11,000. 🚍 🚹 Avenida Castilla-La Mancha, 925 47 57 31. 🚌 Sat. 🎎 Consuegra Medieval (mid-Aug), La Rosa de Azafrán (last weekend Oct).

Consuegra's 11 windmills *(see p31)* and restored castle stand on a ridge, overlooking the plains of La Mancha. One windmill is set in motion every year during the town's festival to celebrate the autumn harvest of saffron *(see p342)*. During the fiesta, pickers compete to see who can strip petals from the saffron crocus the fastest.

Environs
About 4 km (2 miles) from Consuegra, on the road to **Urda**, is a Roman dam. An old restaurant at **Puerto Lápice**, off the A4 20 km (13 miles) south of Consuegra, claims to be the inn in which Don Quixote was "knighted" by the landlord.

⓱ Campo de Criptana

Ciudad Real. 🏛 14,800. 🚍 🚹 Sierra de los Molinos s/n, 926 56 22 31 (closed Mon & Sun pm). 🚌 Tue. 🎎 Virgen de Criptana (Easter Mon), Cristos de Villejos (first Thu in Aug), Ferias (23–28 Aug).

The remaining ten windmills of what was once La Mancha's largest group – 32 – stand on a hillcrest in the town. Three are 16th-century and have their original machinery intact. One is the tourist information office, and three others are museums.

Environs
More windmills stand above **Alcázar de San Juan** and **Mota del Cuervo**, a good place to buy *queso manchego*, local sheep's cheese *(see p343)*.

⓲ El Toboso

Toledo. 🏛 2,200. 🚹 Antonio Machado s/n, 925 56 82 26 (closed Mon). 🚌 Wed. 🎎 Carnival (17–20 Jan), Cervantes Day (23 Apr), San Agustín (27–30 Aug). 🌐 eltoboso.es

Of all the villages of La Mancha claiming links to Don Quixote, El Toboso has the clearest ties.

It was chosen by Cervantes as the birthplace of Dulcinea, Don Quixote's sweetheart. The **Casa de Dulcinea**, the home of Doña Ana Martínez Zarco, on whom Dulcinea was allegedly based, has been refurbished in its original 16th-century style.

The French army allegedly refused to attack the village during the War of Independence *(see pp66–7)*.

🏠 **Casa de Dulcinea**
Tel 925 19 72 88. **Open** Tue–Sun.
🎫 (free Sat & Sun). ♿

⓳ Belmonte

Cuenca. 🏛 2,200. 🚍 🚹 Avenida Luis Pinedo, 967 17 07 41. 🚌 Mon. 🎎 San Bartolomé (24 Aug), Virgen de Gracia (Sep). 🌐 visitclm.com

Belmonte's magnificent 15th-century **castle** *(see p348)* is one of the best preserved in the region. It was built by Juan Pacheco, Marquis of Villena, after Enrique IV gave him the town in 1456. Inside it has decorative carved coffered ceilings, and Mudéjar plasterwork. The **collegiate church** is especially remarkable for its richly

Belmonte's splendid 15th-century castle

decorated chapels and Gothic choirstalls, which were brought here from Cuenca Cathedral *(see p389)*. There is also outstanding ironwork, a Renaissance reredos and the font at which the Golden Age poet Fray Luis de León (1527–91) was baptized.

Environs

Two villages near Belmonte also flourished under the Marquis of Villena. The church at **Villaescusa de Haro**, 6 km (4 miles) to the northeast, has an outstanding 16th-century reredos. **San Clemente**, some 40 km (25 miles) further southeast, clusters around two near-perfect Renaissance squares. There is a Gothic alabaster cross in the Iglesia de Santiago Apóstol.

🏛 **Castillo de Belmonte**
Tel 678 64 92 20. **Open** Tue–Sun. 🖼

The castle of Alarcón, which has been converted into a state-run parador

⑳ Alarcón

Cuenca. 🗺 200. 🚉 Calle Posadas 6, 969 33 03 01. 🎭 San Sebastián (20 Jan), Fiesta del Emigrante (Aug), Cristo de la Fe (14 Sep). 🌐 visitclm.com

Perfectly preserved, the fortified village of Alarcón guards a narrow loop of the Río Júcar from on top of a rock. As you drive through its defences, you may have the impression of entering a film set for a medieval epic.

The village dates back to the 8th century. It became a key military base for the Reconquest *(see pp58–9)* and was recaptured from the Moors by Alfonso VIII in 1184 following a nine-month siege. It was later acquired by

The chalk cliffs of Alcalá del Júcar, honeycombed with tunnels

the Marquis of Villena. Alarcón has dramatic walls and three defensive precincts. The small, triangular **castle**, high above the river, has been turned into a parador, preserving much of its medieval atmosphere.

The **Iglesia de Santa María** is a Renaissance church with a fine portico and an altarpiece attributed to the Berruguete school. The nearby **Iglesia de Santísima Trinidad** is in Gothic-Plateresque style *(see p29)*.

㉑ Alcalá del Júcar

Albacete. 🗺 1,350. 🚉 Avenida de los Robles 1, 967 47 30 90 (Sat & Sun only). 🚌 Sun. 🎭 San Lorenzo (7–15 Aug). 🌐 alcaladeljucar.net

Where the Río Júcar runs through the chalk hills to the northeast of Albacete, it cuts a deep, winding gorge, the Hoz de Júcar, along which you can

drive for a stretch of 40 km (25 miles). Alcalá del Júcar is dramatically sited on the side of a spur of rock jutting out into the gorge. The town is a warren of steep alleys and flights of steps. At the top of the town, below the castle, houses have been extended by digging caves into the soft rock. Some of these have been transformed into tunnels cut from one side of the spur to the other.

Environs

To the west, the gorge runs past fertile orchards to the Baroque **Ermita de San Lorenzo**. Further on is the picturesque village of **Jorquera**, which was an independent state for a brief period during the Middle Ages, refusing to be ruled by the Crown. It retains its Arab walls. A collection of shields is on display in the Casa del Corregidor.

Don Quixote's La Mancha

Cervantes *(see p337)* doesn't specify where his hero was born, but several places are mentioned in the novel. Don Quixote is knighted in an inn in Puerto Lápice, believing it to be a castle. His sweetheart, Dulcinea, lives in El Toboso. The windmills he tilts at, imagining them to be giants, are thought to be those at Campo de Criptana. Another adventure takes place in the Cueva de Montesinos *(see p401)*.

Illustration from a 19th-century edition of *Don Quixote*

㉒ Albacete

Albacete. 172,500.
Plaza del Altozano, 967 63 00 04 (closed Sun pm). Tue. Virgen de los Llanos (8 Sep). **W** albaceteturistico.es

This provincial capital is not without its attractions. The excellent **Museo de Albacete** is located in a pleasant park and has exhibits ranging from Iberian sculptures and unique Roman amber and ivory dolls to 20th-century paintings. The **cathedral**, begun in 1515 and devoted to San Juan Bautista, has Renaissance altarpieces.

Albacete, also known for its daggers and jackknives, crafted here since Muslim times, holds an agricultural fair, every year.

Museo de Albacete
Parque Abelardo Sánchez. **Tel**: 967 22 83 07. **Open** Tue–Sun (Jul–mid-Sep: am only). (free Sat & Sun).

The castle of Chinchilla de Monte Aragón, overlooking the town

Environs
Chinchilla de Monte Aragón, 12 km (7 miles) to the southeast, has a well-preserved old quarter. Above the town is the shell of its 15th-century castle (closed to the public).

Almansa, 70 km (43 miles) further east, is dominated by another imposing castle, which is of Moorish origin.

㉔ Alcaraz

Albacete. 1,600. Calle Mayor 3, 967 38 08 27 (closed Mon). Wed. Canto de Los Mayos (30 Apr–1 May), La Romería de la Virgen (26 Aug, 8 Sep), Feria (4–9 Sep). **W** alcaraz.es

An important Arab and Christian stronghold, Alcaraz's military power waned after the Reconquest but its economy flourished around its (now defunct) carpet-making industry.

Standing in the attractive Renaissance Plaza Mayor are the

㉓ Sierra de Alcaraz

Where the Sierras of Segura and Alcaraz push northwards into the southeastern plains of La Mancha, they form spectacular mountains, broken up by dramatic gorges and fertile valleys. The source of the Río Mundo is a favourite beauty spot. Nearby Riópar, perched on the side of the mountain, has a 15th-century parish church. Among the less-explored villages, Letur, Ayna, Yeste and Liétor are especially picturesque. Their narrow, winding streets and craft traditions clearly reflect their Muslim origins.

⑤ **Source of the Río Mundo**
The river begins as a waterfall, inside the Cueva de Los Chorros, and tumbles down a dramatic cliff face into a bubbling spring at the bottom.

0 kilometres 5
0 miles 5

Key
━━ Tour route
══ Other roads

④ **Yeste**
The village of Yeste, which stands at the foot of the Sierra de Ardal, is crowned by a hilltop Arab castle. It was reconquered under Fernando III, and was later ruled by the Order of Santiago.

"twin towers" of **Tardón** and **Trinidad**, and an 18th-century commodity exchange, the **Lonja del Corregidor**, with Plateresque decoration. The square is surrounded by lively, narrow streets. On the outskirts of the town are the castle ruins and surviving arch of a Gothic aqueduct. Alcaraz makes a good base for touring the sierras of Alcaraz and Segura.

The "twin towers" of Tardón and Trinidad on Alcaraz's main square

㉕ Lagunas de Ruidera

Ciudad Real. 🚌 Ruidera. 🛈 Calle Redondilla 14, Ruidera (Sep–Jun: Wed–Sun, Jul–Aug: daily), 926 52 50 34. 🌐 lagunasderuidera.es

Once nicknamed "The Mirrors of La Mancha", the 15 inter-connected lakes which make up the Parque Natural de las Lagunas de Ruidera stretch for 39 km (24 miles) through a valley. They allegedly take their name from a story in *Don Quixote (see p399)* in which a certain Mistress Ruidera, her daughters and her nieces are said to have been turned into lakes by a magician.

La Mancha's lakes have recovered well from the recent years' falling water table, and are especially worth visiting for their wealth of wildlife, which includes great and little bustards, herons and many types of duck. The wildlife has increasingly come

One of the lakes in the Parque Natural de las Lagunas de Ruidera

under threat due to the number of tourists, and the development of holiday chalets on the lakes' shores. Near one of the lakes, the Laguna de San Pedro, is the **Cueva de Montesinos**, a deep, explorable cave which was also used as the setting for an episode in *Don Quixote*.

To the northwest, the lakes link up with the Embalse de Peñarroya reservoir.

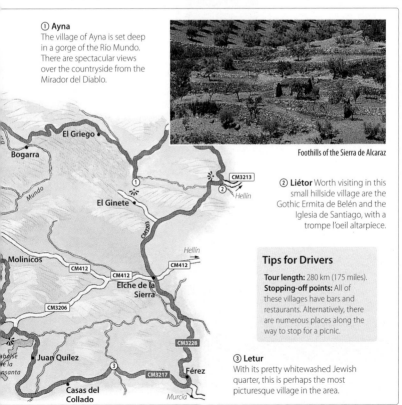

① Ayna
The village of Ayna is set deep in a gorge of the Río Mundo. There are spectacular views over the countryside from the Mirador del Diablo.

Foothills of the Sierra de Alcaraz

El Griego
Bogarra
Mundo
El Ginete
Molinicos
CM412
CM412
CM412
CM412
Hellín
CM503
CM3213
Hellín
Elche de la Sierra
CM3206
CM3228
Juan Quílez
CM3217
Férez
Casas del Collado
Murcia

② Liétor
Worth visiting in this small hillside village are the Gothic Ermita de Belén and the Iglesia de Santiago, with a trompe l'oeil altarpiece.

Tips for Drivers
Tour length: 280 km (175 miles).
Stopping-off points: All of these villages have bars and restaurants. Alternatively, there are numerous places along the way to stop for a picnic.

③ Letur
With its pretty whitewashed Jewish quarter, this is perhaps the most picturesque village in the area.

㉖ Villanueva de los Infantes

Ciudad Real. 🏔 5,800. 🚌 ℹ️ Plaza Mayor 3, 926 36 13 21. 🚃 Fri. 🎭 Cruz de Mayo (2–3 May), Ferias (late Aug), Fiesta del Pimiento (1st week of Sep). **W infantes.org**

Villanueva's Old Town, which centres on the graceful Neo-Classical Plaza Mayor, is one of the most attractive in La Mancha. Many buildings on the square have wooden balconies and arcades. Also on the square is the **Iglesia de San Andrés**, which has a Renaissance façade. Inside are a Baroque altarpiece and organ, as well as the (now empty) tomb of the Golden Age author Francisco de Quevedo. He lived and died in the **Convento de los Domínicos**.

Environs
The village of **San Carlos del Valle**, 25 km (15 miles) to the northwest, has an 18th-century square and galleried houses of rust-red stone.

㉗ Valdepeñas

Ciudad Real. 🏔 31,200. 🚆 🚌 ℹ️ Plaza de España, 926 31 25 52. 🚃 Thu. 🎭 Grape Harvest (1–8 Sep). **W valdepenas.es**

Valdepeñas is the capital of La Mancha's vast wine region, the world's largest expanse of vineyards, producing vast quantities of red wine (see pp344–5). This largely modern town comes alive for its wine

festival in September. In the network of older streets around the café-lined Plaza de España are the **Iglesia de la Asunción** and the municipal museum.

Valdepeñas has over 30 bodegas, 10 of which can be visited. One of them has been converted into the **Museo del Vino**, illustrating the various stages of wine production.

🏛 **Museo del Vino**
Calle Princesa 39. **Tel** 926 32 11 11. **Open** Tue–Sat & Sun am. 🖼

Courtyard of the Palacio del Viso in Viso del Marqués

㉘ Viso del Marqués

Ciudad Real. 🏔 2,750. 🚌 ℹ️ Calle Real 39, 926 33 68 15 (closed Sun pm & Mon). 🚃 Tue. 🎭 San Andrés (second Sun of May), Feria (24–28 Jul). **W visodelmarques.es**

The small village of Viso del Marqués in La Mancha is the unlikely setting of the **Palacio del Viso**, a grand Renaissance

mansion commissioned in 1564 by the Marquis of Santa Cruz, the admiral of the fleet that defeated the Turks at Lepanto in 1571 (see p63). One of the main features of the house is a Classical patio. Inside, the main rooms are decorated with Italian frescoes.

Environs
About 25 km (16 miles) northeast is Spain's oldest bullring at **Las Virtudes**. It was built in 1641 next to a 14th-century church, which has a Churrigueresque altarpiece.

🏛 **Palacio del Viso**
Plaza del Pradillo 12. **Tel** 926 33 75 18. **Open** Tue–Sun am. **Closed** some public hols. 🖼 📷

㉙ Calatrava la Nueva

Ciudad Real. Aldea del Rey. **Tel** 926 69 31 19. **Open** Tue–Sun. 🖼 **W visitclm.com**

Magnificent in its isolated hilltop setting, the ruined castle-monastery of Calatrava la Nueva is reached by a stretch of original medieval road.

It was founded in 1217 by the Knights of Calatrava, Spain's first military-religious order (see p58), to be their headquarters. The complex is of huge proportions, with a double patio and a church with a triple nave. The church has been restored and is illuminated by a beautiful rose window above the entrance. After the Reconquest, the

Expanse of vineyards near Valdepeñas

Calatrava la Nueva castle-monastery, dominating the plains of La Mancha

building continued to be used as a monastery until it was abandoned in 1802 following fire damage.

Opposite the castle are the ruins of a Muslim frontier fortress, **Salvatierra**, which was captured from the Moors by the Order of Calatrava in the 12th century.

⚉ Almagro

Ciudad Real. 🅼 9,100. 🚊 🚌
ℹ️ Plaza Mayor 1, 926 86 07 17.
🗓️ Wed. 🎭 Virgen de las Nieves (5 Aug), San Bartolomé (23–24 Aug).
🆆 ciudad-almagro.com

Almagro was disputed during the Reconquest, until the Order of Calatrava captured it and built the castle of Calatrava la Nueva to the southwest of the town. The rich architectural heritage of the atmospheric Old Town is partly the legacy of the Fugger brothers, the Habsburgs' bankers who settled in nearby Almadén during the 16th century.

The town's main attraction is its colonnaded stone plaza, with enclosed, green balconies. On one side is a 17th-century courtyard-theatre the **Corral de Comedias** – where a drama festival is held for the Festival de Teatro Clásico every summer.

Other monuments worth seeing include the Fuggers' Renaissance warehouse and former university, and also the castle, which has been converted into a parador.

Environs

To the northwest is **Ciudad Real**, founded by Alfonso X the Learned in 1255. Its sights include the Iglesia de San Pedro and the Mudéjar gateway, the Puerta de Toledo.

Raised walkway in the Parque Nacional de Las Tablas de Daimiel

⚉ Tablas de Daimiel

Ciudad Real. 🚌 Daimiel. ℹ️ Daimiel, Calle Santa Teresa s/n, 926 26 06 39 (closed Mon). 🎫 book in advance.
🆆 lastablasdedaimiel.com

The marshy wetlands of the Tablas de Daimiel, northeast of Ciudad Real, are the feeding and nesting grounds of a huge range of aquatic and migratory birds. Despite being national parkland since 1973, in recent years they became an ecological cause célèbre due to the growing threat from the area's lowering water table. They are now fully recovered.

One corner of the park is open to the public, with walking routes to islets and observation towers. Breeding birds here include great crested grebes and mallards. Otters and red foxes are also found in the park.

⚉ Valle de Alcudia

Ciudad Real. 🚌 Fuencaliente.
ℹ️ 926 47 02 88 (closed Mon).

Alcudia's lush lowlands, which border the Sierra Morena foothills to the south, are among Central Spain's most unspoiled countryside. The area is used largely as pastureland. In late autumn it is filled with sheep, whose milk makes the farmhouse cheese for which the valley is known.

The mountain village of **Fuencaliente** has thermal baths that open in the summer. Further north, **Almadén** is the site of a large mercury mine with a museum. **Chillón**, to the northwest, has a Late Gothic church.

Small isolated farmhouse in the fertile Valle de Alcudia

EXTREMADURA

Cáceres · Badajoz

Of all the Spanish regions, far-flung Extremadura – "the land beyond the River Douro" – is the most remote from the modern world. Green sierras run southwards through rolling hills strewn with boulders. Forests and reservoirs shelter rare wildlife. The towns, with their atmospheric old quarters, have a romantic, slow-paced charm. In winter, storks nest on their spires and bell towers.

The finest monuments in Extremadura are the ruins of ancient settlements scattered across the region. Many are exceptionally well preserved. Some of Spain's finest Roman architecture is to be seen in Mérida, capital of the Roman province of Lusitania, which has an aqueduct and a magnificent theatre. Other Classical remains dot the countryside – notably a Tartessan temple at Cancho Roano and a Roman bridge at Alcántara. Smaller finds are displayed in Badajoz museum.

Modern development has bypassed the old town of Cáceres, whose ancient walls, winding streets and nobles' mansions are still marvellously intact. Trujillo, Zafra and Jerez de los Caballeros have medieval and Renaissance quarters; and there are small, splendidly decorated cathedrals in Plasencia, Coria and Badajoz.

The castles and stout walls of Alburquerque and Olivenza mark frontiers embattled through history. Many cathedrals and monasteries were built in the troubled times during and after the Reconquest by the large military-religious orders which then governed the region for the Crown.

Extremadura was the birthplace of many conquistadors and emigrants to the New World; the riches they found there financed a surge of building. Guadalupe monastery, in the eastern hills, is the most splendid monument to the region's New World ties.

View over the rooftops of the historic town of Cáceres

◄ Typical pastures of the Extremadura region

Exploring Extremadura

Extremadura is ideal for nature lovers and those who want to get off the beaten track to discover the old Spain. It offers beautiful driving and walking country in its northern sierras and valleys, and exceptional wildlife in Monfragüe Natural Park. Some of the best Roman ruins in Spain can be found throughout Extremadura, especially in the regional capital, Mérida. The walled old town of Cáceres, with its well-preserved Jewish quarter, and the monasteries of Guadalupe and Yuste, are other historic sights not to be missed. To the south, the Templar towns in the Sierra Morena, such as Jerez de los Caballeros, have fine old buildings, while the small, historic towns of Coria, Zafra and Llerena all make charming bases for excursions.

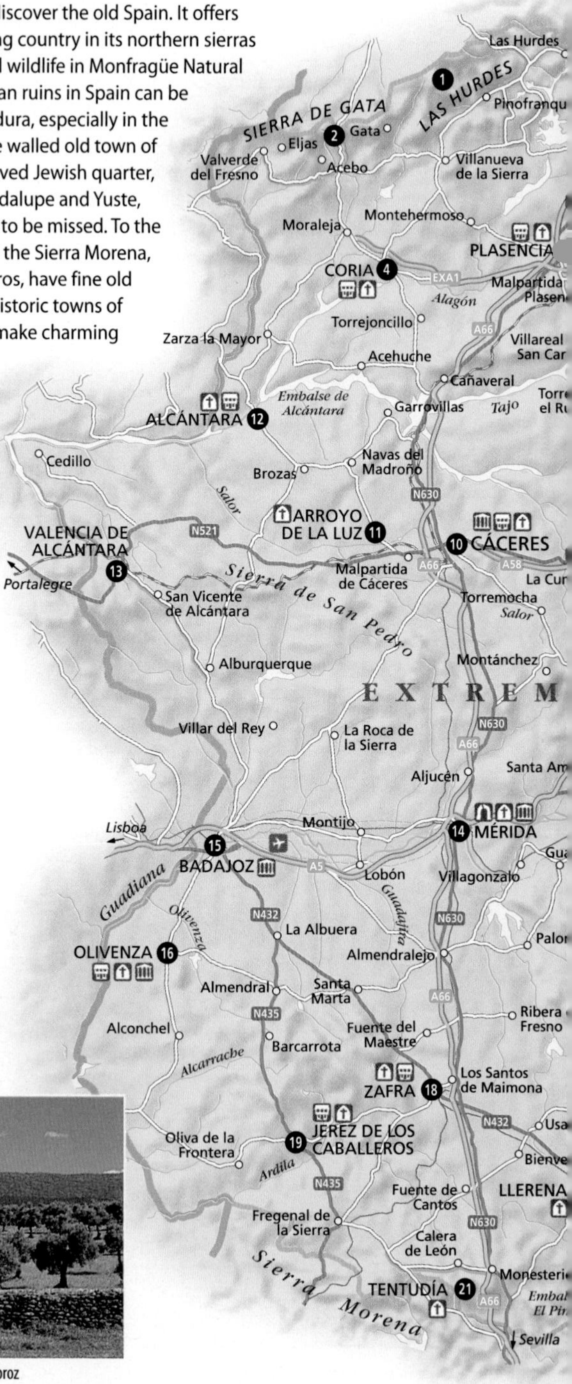

Sights at a Glance

1. Las Hurdes
2. Sierra de Gata
3. Hervás
4. Coria
5. Plasencia
6. Monasterio de Yuste
7. Parque Natural de Monfragüe
8. Guadalupe
9. Trujillo
10. Cáceres *pp412–13*
11. Arroyo de la Luz
12. Alcántara
13. Valencia de Alcántara
14. Mérida
15. Badajoz
16. Olivenza
17. Cancho Roano
18. Zafra
19. Jerez de los Caballeros
20. Llerena
21. Tentudía

Orchards near Hervás in the Valle del Ambroz

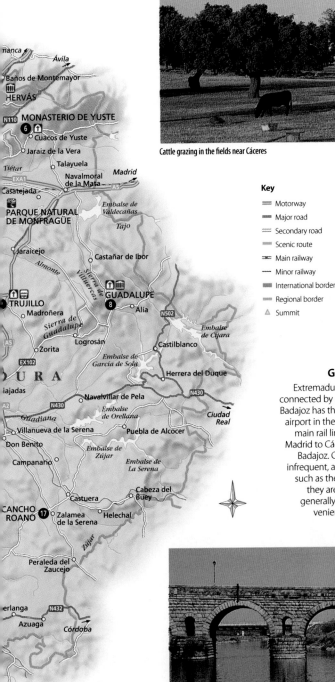

Cattle grazing in the fields near Cáceres

ñanca
Ávila
Baños de Montemayor
HERVÁS
N110 MONASTERIO DE YUSTE
6
Cuacos de Yuste
Jaraiz de la Vera
Tiétar
Talayuela
EXA1
Navalmoral
de la Mata
Madrid
A5
Casatejada
Embalse de Valdecañas
**PARQUE NATURAL
DE MONFRAGÜE**
Tajo
Jaraicejo
Castañar de Ibor
Almonte
Sierra de Villuercas
TRUJILLO
GUADALUPE
8
Madroñera
Alía
Sierra de Guadalupe
Logrosán
N502
Embalse de Cijara
A5
Zorita
Castilblanco
EX102
Embalse de García de Sola
Herrera del Duque
URA
iajadas
Navalvillar de Pela
N430
A2
N430
Embalse de Orellana
Ciudad Real
Guadiana
Villanueva de la Serena
Puebla de Alcocer
Don Benito
Embalse de Zújar
Campanario
Embalse de La Serena
Cabeza del Buey
**CANCHO
ROANO** 17
Castuera
Zalamea
de la Serena
Helechal
Zújar
Peraleda del
Zaucejo
erlanga
N432
Azuaga
Córdoba

0 kilometres   25
0 miles   15

Key
— Motorway
— Major road
— Secondary road
— Scenic route
— Main railway
— Minor railway
— International border
— Regional border
△ Summit

Getting Around

Extremadura is not very well connected by air or rail services. Badajoz has the only (domestic) airport in the region, while the main rail link is the line from Madrid to Cáceres, Mérida and Badajoz. Coach services are infrequent, and in many areas, such as the northern sierras, they are nonexistent. It is generally much more convenient to travel by car.

Roman bridge crossing the Río Guadiana at Mérida

For additional map symbols *see back flap*

Beehives, a common sight in Las Hurdes

❶ Las Hurdes

Cáceres. 🚌 Pinofranqueado, Caminomorisco, Nuñomoral. *i* Caminomorisco, 927 43 53 29. **W** todohurdes.com

Las Hurdes' slate mountains, goats and beehives were memorably caught in the 1932 Luis Buñuel film *Tierra sin Pan (Land without Bread)*. The area's legendary poverty disappeared with the arrival of roads in the 1950s, but the black slopes, riverbeds and hill terraces remain.

From Pinofranqueado or Vegas de Coria, roads climb past picturesque "black" villages like Batuequilla, Fragosa, and El Gasco, which sits under an extinct volcano. The more developed **Lower Hurdes** area, crossed by the Río Hurdano and the main access route (EX204), is dotted with camp sites and restaurants.

❷ Sierra de Gata

Cáceres. 🚌 Cáceres. *i* San Martín de Trevejo, 927 51 45 85. **W** sierradegata.org

There are 40 hamlets in the Sierra de Gata, scattered between olive groves, orchards and fields. The area has retained its charm by conserving hunters' paths for woodland walking, and its local crafts, most notably lace-making. In the lowland towns of **Valverde de Fresno** and **Acebo**, the local dialect, *chapurriau*, is still spoken. On the higher slopes, **Eljas**, **Gata** and **Villamiel** have remains of medieval fortresses. The old granite houses have family crests on the front and distinctive outside staircases.

Coat of arms on a house front in Acebo

❸ Hervás

Cáceres. 🚶 4,200. *i* C/ Braulio Navas 4, 927 47 36 18. 🚌 Sat. 🎊 Las Ferias Cristo de la Salud (14–16 Sep). **W** hervas.es

Sitting at the top of the wide Valle del Ambroz, Hervás is known for its medieval Jewish quarter, with its whitewashed houses. The tiny streets, dotted with taverns and craft workshops, slope down towards the Río Ambroz. Just off the main plaza is the **Museo Pérez Comendador-Leroux**, named after the town's noted 20th-century sculptor and his wife, whose work is exhibited here.

The next town up towards the Béjar pass is **Baños de Montemayor**, whose name comes from its sulphurous baths, which date back to Roman times. These were revived in the early 1900s and are open to the public. At **Cáparra**, southwest of Hervás, four triumphal arches stand on the Roman road, the Vía de la Plata *(see p356)*.

🏛 **Museo Pérez Comendador-Leroux**

C/ Asensio Neila 5. **Tel** 927 48 16 55. **Open** pm Tue; Wed–Fri; am Sat, Sun. 🗺

Traditional lace-making in one of the villages of the Sierra de Gata

Ancient wall and olive groves in the Valle del Ambroz

④ Coria

Cáceres. ⚐ 13,000. 🚌 ℹ️ Plaza de San Pedro 1, 927 50 80 00. 🕐 Thu. 🎭 Día de la Virgen (2nd Mon in May), San Juan (23–29 Jun). 🆆 turismo.coria.org

Coria's walled old town, perched above the Río Alagón, boasts a Gothic-Renaissance **cathedral** with rich Plateresque carving, and the 16th-century **Convento de la Madre de Dios**, which has a fine Renaissance cloister.

Forming part of the town walls, which are a Muslim and medieval patchwork, are an imposing castle tower, and four gates, two of which date back to Roman times. The gates are closed for the fiesta of San Juan in June for night-time bull-running. Situated below the old town is the **Puente Seco**, or Puente Viejo, a Roman bridge.

⑤ Plasencia

Cáceres. ⚐ 41,000. 🚉 🚌 ℹ️ Santa Clara 4, 927 42 38 43. 🕐 Tue. 🎭 Ferias (6–8 Jun). 🆆 plasencia.es

Plasencia's golden-grey walls, rising above a curve in the banks of the Río Jerte, tell of the town's past as a military bastion. Nowadays Plasencia is best known for its Tuesday market, dating back to the 12th century.

A short walk away are the town's two cathedrals, which are built back-to-back. The 15th- to 16th-century **Catedral**

Nueva has a Baroque organ and carved wooden choir stalls. The Romanesque **Catedral Vieja**, next to it, has a museum with works by Ribera, and a late 14th-century Bible.

The **Museo Etnográfico y Textil Pérez Enciso**, housed in a 14th-century hospital, has displays of crafts and costumes.

The rest of the Jerte Valley has pockets of outstanding beauty, such as the **Garganta de los Infiernos**, a nature reserve with dramatic, rushing waterfalls.

🏛 **Museo Etnográfico y Textil Pérez Enciso** Plaza del Marqués de la Puebla. **Tel** 927 42 18 43. **Open** Wed–Sun.

⑥ Monasterio de Yuste

Cuacos de Yuste (Cáceres). **Tel** 927 17 21 97. **Open** Tue–Sun. **Closed** some pub hols. 🎟 (free from 3pm Wed & Thu for EU res; from 5pm Apr–Sep). 🆒 🆆 patrimonionacional.es

The Hieronymite monastery of Yuste, where Charles V *(see p63)* retired from public life in 1557 and died a year later, is remarkable for its simplicity and its lovely setting in the wooded valley of La Vera.

The church's Gothic and Plateresque cloisters and the austere palace are open to visitors. Just below it is **Cuacos de Yuste**, the most unspoiled of La Vera's old villages, where peppers hang outside the houses.

Paprika peppers hanging up around a door in Cuacos de Yuste

A *Carantoña*, during the fiesta of St Sebastian, Acehuche

Extremadura's Fiestas

Carantoñas *(20–21 Jan)*, Acehúche (Cáceres). During the fiesta of St Sebastian, the *Carantoñas* take to the streets of the town dressed up in animal skins, with their faces covered by grotesque masks designed to make them look terrifying. They represent the wild beasts which are said to have left the saint unharmed.

Pero Palo *(Carnival Feb/Mar)*, Villanueva de la Vera (Cáceres). In this ancient ritual a wooden figure dressed in a suit and representing the devil is paraded around the streets and then destroyed – except for the head, which is reused the year after.

Los Empalaos *(Maundy Thursday)*, Valverde de la Vera (Cáceres). Men do penance by walking in procession through the town with their arms outstretched and bound to wooden plough beams.

La Encamisá *(7–8 Dec)*, Torrejoncillo (Cáceres). Riders on horseback, covered in white cloth, parade around town, where bonfires are set alight for the occasion.

Los Escobazos *(7 Dec)*, Jarandilla de la Vera (Cáceres). At night, the town is illuminated by bonfires in the streets, and torches are made from burning brooms.

❼ Parque Natural de Monfragüe

Cáceres. 🚌 Villarreal de San Carlos.
ℹ️ Villarreal de San Carlos, 927 19 91
34. 🌐 **turismoextremadura.com**

To the south of Plasencia, rolling hills drop from scrubby peaks through wild olive, cork and holm oak woods to the dammed Tagus and Tiétar river valleys. In 1979, some 500 sq km (200 sq miles) of these hills were granted natural park status in order to safeguard the area's outstandingly varied wildlife species, which includes a large proportion of Spain's protected bird species (*see pp346–7*).

The many species of bird which breed here include the black-winged kite, black vulture

Birdwatchers in the Parque Natural de Monfragüe

and, most notably, the black stork, as well as more common aquatic species on and near the water. Mammals living here include the lynx, red deer and wild boar. At **Villarreal de San**

Carlos, a hamlet founded in the 18th century, there is parking and an information centre. An ideal time to visit the park is September, when many migrating birds stop off here.

❽ Guadalupe

Cáceres. 🔼 2,000. 🚌 ℹ️ Pl Santa
María de Guadalupe, 927 15 41 28.
Monasterio: **Tel** 927 36 70 00. **Open**
daily. 🅿️ 🕐 only. 🍷 Wed. 🎉 Cruz
de Mayo (3 May), La Virgen y Día de la
Comunidad (8 Sep).
🌐 **monasterioguadalupe.com**

This village grew around the magnificent Hieronymite **Monasterio de Guadalupe**, founded in 1340. The main square has shops that sell handmade ceramics and beaten copper cauldrons, both traditional monastic crafts.

The turreted towers of the monastery, which is set in a deep wooded valley, help give it a fairy-tale air. According to legend, a shepherd found a wooden image of the Virgin Mary here in the early 14th century. The monastery grew to splendour

under royal patronage, acquiring schools of grammar and medicine, three hospitals, an important pharmacy and one of the largest libraries in Spain.

The 16th-century *hospedería* where royalty once stayed was destroyed by fire; the 20th-century reconstruction is now a hotel run by the monks. The old hospital has been converted into a parador. In the car park is a plaque commemorating Spain's first human dissection, which took place here in 1402.

By the time the New World was discovered, the monastery was very important and in 1496 was the site of the baptism of some of the first native Caribbeans brought to Europe by Columbus (*see pp60–61*).

The monastery was sacked by Napoleon in 1808. It was refounded by Franciscans a

century later. It is a major centre of Catholicism, visited by thousands of pilgrims.

Guided tours (in Spanish only) begin in the museums of illuminated manuscripts, embroidered vestments and fine art. They continue to the choir and the magnificent Baroque sacristy, nicknamed "the Spanish Sistine Chapel", because of Zurbarán's portraits of monks hanging on the highly decorated walls. For many, the chance to touch or kiss the tiny Virgin's dress in the *camarín* (chamber) behind the altar is the highlight of the tour. The 16th-century Gothic cloister has two tiers of horseshoe arches around an ornate central pavilion. The church, with a magnificent 16th-century iron grille partly forged from the chains of freed slaves, may be visited separately.

Environs

The surrounding **Sierra de las Villuercas** and **Los Ibores** sierras, where herbs were once picked for the monastery pharmacy, have good woodland walks. The road south also gives access to the pasturelands of **La Serena**, a vital breeding ground for the steppe (*see pp346–7*), and the huge reservoir of **Cíjara**, surrounded by a game reserve.

Monasterio de Guadalupe, overlooking the town

❾ Trujillo

Cáceres. 🚂 9,600. 🚌 ℹ️ Plaza Mayor, 927 32 26 77. 🚍 Thu. 🎭 Chíviri (Easter Sun), Feria del Queso (weekend of 1 May).
🌐 turismotrujillo.com

When the Plaza Mayor of the medieval hilltop town of Trujillo is floodlit at night, it is one of the most beautiful squares in Spain. By day, there is much to visit, including the **Iglesia de Santa María la Mayor**, on one of the town's winding streets, which contains various sarcophagi.

At the top of the hill is an 11th-century Islamic fortress, which defended the town against the Christian advance during the Reconquest *(see pp58–9)*; but in 1232 it was retaken by the forces of Fernando III. Trujillo

Statue of Francisco Pizarro in Trujillo's main square

was the birthplace of several conquistadors, most notably Francisco Pizarro, who conquered Peru *(see p62)*, of whom there is a statue in the main square. His brother, Hernando Pizarro,

founded the **Palacio del Marqués de la Conquista**, one of several palaces and convents built with New World wealth. It has an elaborate corner window with carved stone heads of the Pizarro brothers and their Inca wives. The beautiful 16th-century **Palacio de Juan Pizarro de Orellana** was built by descendants of Francisco de Orellana, the explorer of Ecuador and the Amazon.

In late April or early May, gourmets flock here for the four-day cheese fair.

🏛️ **Palacio del Marqués de la Conquista**
Plaza Mayor. **Closed** to the public.

🏛️ **Palacio de Juan Pizarro de Orellana**
Plaza de Don Juan Tena. **Tel** 927 32 11 58. **Open** 10am–dusk daily.

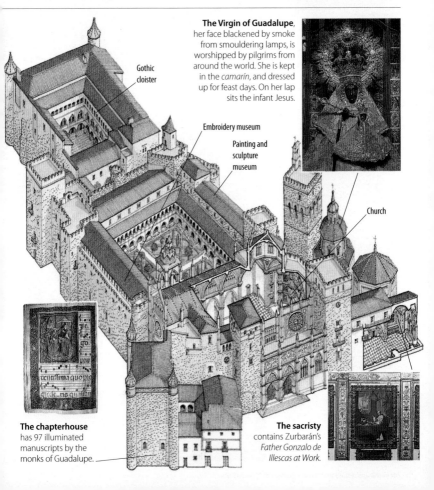

The Virgin of Guadalupe, her face blackened by smoke from smouldering lamps, is worshipped by pilgrims from around the world. She is kept in the *camarín*, and dressed up for feast days. On her lap sits the infant Jesus.

Gothic cloister

Embroidery museum

Painting and sculpture museum

Church

The chapterhouse has 97 illuminated manuscripts by the monks of Guadalupe.

The sacristy contains Zurbarán's *Father Gonzalo de Illescas at Work*.

⑩ Street-by-Street: Cáceres

After Alfonso IX of Leon conquered Cáceres in 1229, its growing prosperity as a free trade town attracted merchants, and later aristocracy, to settle here. They rivalled each other with stately homes and palaces fortified by watchtowers, most of which Isabel and Fernando, the reigning monarchs *(see pp60–61)*, ordered to be demolished in 1476 to halt the continual jostling for power. Today's serene Renaissance town dates from the late 15th and 16th centuries, after which economic decline set in. Untouched by the wars of the 19th and 20th centuries, Cáceres became Spain's first listed heritage city in 1949.

★ **Casa de los Golfines de Abajo**
The ornamental façade of this 16th-century mansion displays the shield of one of the town's leading families, the Golfines.

Casa y Torre de Carvajal
This typical Renaissance mansion has a 13th-century round Arab tower and a peaceful garden with a patio.

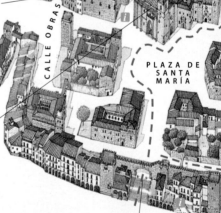

PIAS DE ROCO

CALLE DE LA AMARGURA

CUESTA DEL MARQUÉS

RINC

CALLE OBRAS

PLAZA DE SANTA MARÍA

CALLE INSTITU

PLAZA MAYOR

★ **Iglesia de Santa María**
Facing the Palacio Episcopal, this Gothic-Renaissance church has a beautiful cedarwood reredos and a 15th-century crucifix – the *Cristo Negro* (Black Christ).

The Torre de Bujaco is a 12th-century tower that visitors can climb for good views of Plaza Mayor.

Arco de la Estrella
This low-arched gateway was built by Manuel Churriguera in 1726. It leads through the city walls from the Plaza Mayor into the Old Town and is flanked by a 15th-century watchtower.

| 0 metres | 50 |
| 0 yards | 50 |

Key

— Suggested route

Barrio de San Antonio
This quaint old Jewish quarter, with narrow streets of whitewashed houses restored to their original condition, takes its name from the nearby hermitage of St Anthony.

VISITORS' CHECKLIST

Practical Information
Cáceres. 95,600. **Tel** 927 01 08 77. Plaza Mayor 3, 927 01 08 34. Wed. San Jorge (23 Apr), San Fernando (30 May). Museo de Cáceres: Open Tue–Sun. **turismo.ayto-caceres.es**

Transport
Juan Pablo II, 6, 902 32 03 20. C/ de Túnez 1, 927 23 25 50.

★ Museo de Cáceres
Housed in the Casa de las Veletas, this museum has contemporary art and archaeology from the region.

The Convento de San Pablo sells delicious *yemas* (candied egg yolks) made by the nuns.

Casa y Torre de las Cigüeñas
The slender, battlemented tower of the House of the Storks was allowed to remain after 1476 because of the owner's loyalty to Isabel. It is now owned by the army and not open to the public.

The Iglesia de San Mateo, built between the 14th and 17th centuries, is one of Cáceres' earliest churches.

Casa del Sol (Casa de los Solis)
The façade of this elegant Renaissance building, once home of the Solis family, is emblazoned with a sun (sol) motif.

For additional map symbols *see back flap*

⓫ Arroyo de la Luz

Cáceres. 🏠 6,300. 🚌 ℹ️ Plaza de la Constitución 21, 927 27 04 37, Wed–Sun. 🚍 Thu. 🎭 Día de la Luz (Easter Mon), Fiestas (15 Aug). 🌐 **arroyodelaluz.es**

Arroyo de la Luz is home to one of the artistic masterpieces of Extremadura. Its **Iglesia de la Asunción** contains a spectacular altarpiece, completed in 1565, which incorporates 20 paintings by the mystical religious painter Luis de Morales.

Environs
The area has a large population of white storks (see pp346–7). Nearby **Malpartida** is home to the largest colony, whose nests adorn the church roof. There are some good picnic spots in the surrounding countryside.

Alterpiece in the Iglesia de la Asunción, Arroyo de la Luz

⓬ Alcántara

Cáceres. 🏠 1,700. 🚌 ℹ️ Avenida de Mérida 21, 927 39 08 63. 🚍 Tue. 🎭 Classic Drama Festival (Aug), San Pedro (18–19 Oct). 🌐 **alcantara.es**

Alcantara has two important sights. One is the drystone **Roman bridge**, above the Tagus River, with its honorary arch and a temple. The other the restored **Convento de San Benito**. This was built as the headquarters of the Knights of the Order of Alcántara during the 16th century and was sacked by Napoleon. Its surviving treasures are in the **Iglesia de Santa María de Almocovar**.

Walls of the 16th-century Convento de San Benito, Alcántara

⓭ Valencia de Alcántara

Cáceres. 🏠 6,000. 🚌 🚌 ℹ️ Calle de Hernán Cortés, 927 58 21 84. 🚍 Mon. 🎭 San Isidro (15 May), San Bartolomé (24 Aug). 🌐 **valenciadealcantara.net**

The Gothic quarter of this hilltop frontier town is given an elegant air by its fountains and orange trees. The privately owned **Castillo de Piedra Buena** was built near the town by the Knights of the Order of Alcántara. On the town's outskirts are more than 40 dolmens, or megalithic burial sites.

Environs
Alburquerque, to the southeast, is sited on a rocky outcrop with a panoramic view from the ramparts and keep of its castle. Below is the Old Town and the 15th-century Iglesia de Santa María del Mercado.

⓮ Mérida

Badajoz. 🏠 58,100. 🚌 🚌 ℹ️ C/ José Álvarez Sáenz de Buruaga, 924 33 07 22. 🚍 Tue. 🎭 Easter Week, Classic Drama Festival (Jul–Aug), Feria (1–5 Sep). 🌐 **turismomerida.org**

Founded by Augustus in 25 BC, Augusta Emerita grew into the cultural and economic capital of Rome's westernmost province, Lusitania, but lost its eminence under the Moors. Though a small city, Mérida, the capital of Extremadura, has many fine Roman monuments.

The best approach is from the west of town, via the modern suspension bridge over the Río Guadiana, bringing you to the original entrance of the Roman city and Arab fortress.

The city's centrepiece is the **Roman theatre** (see pp54–5). One of the best-preserved Roman theatres anywhere, it is still used in summer for the city's drama festival and is part of a larger site with an **amphitheatre** (anfiteatro) and gardens. Nearby are the remains of a Roman house, the **Casa del Anfiteatro**, where there are underground galleries and large areas of well-preserved mosaics.

Opposite stands Rafael Moneo's stunning red-brick **Museo Nacional de Arte Romano**. The semicircular arches of its main hall are built to the same height as the city's Los Milagros aqueduct. Off this hall, which features sculptures from the Roman theatre, there are three galleries exhibiting ceramics, mosaics, coins and

Megalithic tomb on the outskirts of Valencia de Alcántara

Mérida's well-preserved Roman theatre, still used as a venue for classical drama

statuary. There is also an excavated Roman street. Near the museum are several other monuments, namely two villas with fine mosaics, and a racecourse.

A chapel in front of the 3rd-century **Iglesia de Santa Eulalia** is dedicated to the child saint who was martyred on this site in Roman times. Towards the centre of the town are the **Templo de Diana** (1st century AD), with tall, fluted

Sculpture of Emperor Augustus

columns, and the **Arco de Trajano**. The **Museo de Arte Visigodo** (Museum of Visigothic Art) is in the Convento de Santa Clara, off the main square. From the huge **Puente Romano** there is a good view of the massive walls of the **Alcazaba**, one of Spain's oldest Moorish buildings (AD 835), whose precinct includes towers, a cistern and Roman ruins. To the east

stands the **Casa del Mithraeo**, with its Pompeiian-style frescoes and fine mosaics.

The magnificent, ruined Los Milagros aqueduct, with its granite and brick arches, is off the N630 towards Cáceres.

🏛 Museo Nacional de Arte Romano
C/ José Ramón Mélida. **Tel** 924 31 16 90. **Open** Tue–Sun. **Closed** some pub hols. 🅿 (free Sat pm & Sun am). ♿
W mnar.es

🏛 Museo de Arte Visigodo
C/ Sta Julia. **Tel** 924 30 01 06. **Open** Tue–Sun. **Closed** some public hols.

Mérida Town Centre

① Iglesia de Santa Eulalia
② Museo Nacional de Arte Romano
③ Casa del Anfiteatro
④ Amphitheatre
⑤ Roman Theatre
⑥ Casa del Mithraeo
⑦ Alcazaba
⑧ Puente Romano
⑨ Museo de Arte Visigodo
⑩ Arco de Trajano
⑪ Templo de Diana

0 metres 250
0 yards 250

⑮ Badajoz

Badajoz. 🚗 152,500. ✈ 🚉 🚌
ℹ️ Pasaje de San Juan, 924 22 49 81.
🚌 Tue & Sun. 🎆 Feria (24 Jun).
🌐 **turismobadajoz.es**

Badajoz is a plain, modern city, though it retains traces of its former importance. It was a major city under the Moors but centuries of conflict robbed Badajoz of its former glories.

The Alcazaba now houses the **Museo Arqueológico**, which has over 15,000 pieces from around the province, as far back as Palaeolithic times. Nearby is the cathedral, dating from the 13th–18th centuries, with a stunning tiled cloister. The **MEAC** museum of contemporary Spanish and Latin American art is on Calle Museo, open Tuesday to Sunday.

🏛 **Museo Arqueológico**
Pl José Álvarez Saez de Buruaga.
Tel 924 00 19 08. **Open** Tue–Sun.

⑯ Olivenza

Badajoz. 🚗 12,000. 🚌 ℹ️ Plaza de
Santa María, 924 49 01 51. 🚌 Sat. 🎆
Muñecas de San Juan (23 Jun).

A Portuguese enclave until 1801, Olivenza has a lively character. Within the walled town are the medieval castle, housing the **Museo Etnográfico González Santana**, a museum of rural life, and three churches. **Santa María del Castillo** has a naive family tree of the Virgin Mary. **Santa María Magdalena** is a fine example of the 16th-century Portuguese Manueline style.

Interior of Santa María Magdalena church, Olivenza

The 16th-century **Santa Casa de Misericordia** has blue and white tiled friezes. In one, God is shown offering Adam and Eve 18th-century coats to cover their nakedness.

Off the main square **Pasteleria Fuentes** sells *Pécula Mécula* cake.

🏛 **Museo Etnográfico González Santana**
Plaza de Santa María. **Tel** 924 49 02 22.
Open Tue–Sun am. 🎆 ♿
🌐 **elmuseodeolivenza.com**

⑰ Cancho Roano

Zalamea de la Serena, EX114 (Carretera Zalamea-Quintana) km 3. **Tel** 629 23 52 79. **Open** daily (except Sun pm).
Closed some public hols.

This sanctuary-palace, which is thought to have been built under the civilization of Tartessus *(see p53)*, was discovered in the 1960s. Excavations on this small site (begun in 1978) have revealed a moated temple that was rebuilt three times – many of the walls and slate floors are still intact. Each temple was constructed on a grander scale than the previous one and then burned in the face of invasion during the 6th century BC.

Most of the artifacts unearthed from the site are on display in the archaeological museum at Badajoz.

Environs
A Roman funereal monument stands next to the church in nearby **Zalamea de la Serena**. The town comes alive during the August fiestas, when the townsfolk act out the classic 17th-century play, *The Mayor of Zalamea*, by Calderón de la Barca *(see p38)*, which was supposedly based on a local character. Shops in the town also sell *torta de la Serena*, a cheese made of sheep's milk.

Remains of the Tartessan sanctuary at Cancho Roano

⑱ Zafra

Badajoz. 🚗 16,700. 🚉 🚌 ℹ️ Plaza de España 8, 924 55 10 36. 🚌 Sun & last Sat of month. 🎆 San Miguel (Sep/Oct).
🌐 **turismoextremadura.com**

At the heart of this graceful town, nicknamed "little Seville" because of its similarity to the capital of Andalusia, are two arcaded squares. The **Plaza Grande**, the larger of the two, near the **Iglesia de la Candelaria**, was built in the 15th century. The older square is **Plaza Chica**, which used to be the marketplace. On Calle Sevilla

The colourful tiled cloister in the cathedral of Badajoz

Altarpiece by Zurbarán in the Iglesia de la Candelaria at Zafra

is the 15th-century Convento de Santa Clara. Nearby is the **Alcázar de los Duques de Feria**, now a parador with a patio of Herreriano style.

Environs
Some 25 km (16 miles) to the south, in **Fuente de Cantos**, is the house where painter Francisco de Zurbarán was born in 1598.

⑲ Jerez de los Caballeros

Badajoz. 🔼 10,000. 🚌 ℹ️ Plaza Constitución 4, 924 73 03 72. 🛒 Wed. 🎉 Easter week, Feria del Jamón (May). 🌐 **turismo.jerezdeloscaballeros.es**

The hillside profile of Jerez, broken by three Baroque church towers, is one of Extremadura's most picturesque. This small town is also historically important – Vasco Núñez de Balboa, who discovered the Pacific, was born here. In the **castle**, now laid out as gardens, knights of the Order of Knights Templar were beheaded in the Torre Sangrienta (Bloody Tower) in 1312. The old quarters of the town grew up around three churches: **San Bartolomé**, its façade studded with glazed ceramics; **San Miguel**, whose brick tower dominates the Plaza de España; and **Santa María de la Encarnación**.

Environs
Fregenal de la Sierra, 25 km (16 miles) to the south, is an attractive old town with a bullring and a castle.

⑳ Llerena

Badajoz. 🔼 6,000. 🚉 🚌 ℹ️ Calle Aurora 2, 924 87 05 51. 🛒 Thu. 🎉 Nuestra Señora de la Granada (1–15 Aug). 🌐 **llerena.org**

Extremadura's southeastern gateway to Andalusia, the town of Llerena, is a mixture of Mudéjar and Baroque buildings. In the pretty square, lined with palm trees, stands the arcaded, whitewash-and-stone church of **Nuestra Señora de la Granada**, its sumptuous interior reflecting the town's former importance as a seat of the Inquisition (see p278). At one end of the square is a fountain designed by Zurbarán, who lived here for 15 years. Also worth seeing is the 16th-century **Convento de Santa Clara**, on a street leading out of the main square.

Environs
At **Azuaga**, 30 km (20 miles) to the east, is the Iglesia de la Consolación, containing Renaissance and Mudéjar tiles.

㉑ Tentudía

Badajoz. 🚌 Calera de León. ℹ️ Calera de León, 924 584 084. Monasterio: **Open** Tue–Sun. 🎟️ 🎫 (for groups). 🌐 **turismoextremadura.com**

Where the Sierra Morena runs into Andalusia, fortified towns and churches founded by the medieval military orders stand among the wooded hills of Tentudía. Here, on a hilltop, stands the tiny **Monasterio de Tentudía**. Founded in the 13th century by the Order of Santiago, the monastery contains a superb Mudéjar cloister, and reredos with Seville *azulejos* (tiles).

Calera de León, just 6 km (4 miles) north of Tentudía, has a Renaissance convent, also founded by the Order of Santiago, with a Gothic church and a cloister on two floors.

Bullring at Fregenal de la Sierra

SOUTHERN SPAIN

Introducing Southern Spain   **420–429**

Seville   **430–450**

Seville Street Finder   **451–457**

Shopping in Seville   **458–459**

Entertainment in Seville   **460–461**

Andalusia   **462–505**

Southern Spain at a Glance

One large region – Andalusia – extends across the south of Spain. Its landscape varies from the deserts of Almería in the east, to the wetlands of Doñana National Park in the west; and from the snowcapped peaks of the Sierra Nevada to the beaches of the Costa del Sol. Three inland cities between them share the greatest of Spain's Moorish monuments: Granada, Córdoba and Seville, the capital, which stands on the banks of the Río Guadalquivir. Andalusia has many other historic towns as well as attractive, whitewashed villages, important nature reserves and the sherry-producing vineyards around Jerez de la Frontera.

Córdoba's Mezquita *(see pp484–5)* has a remarkable forest of arches in its interior and an exquisitely decorated mihrab (prayer niche) facing Mecca.

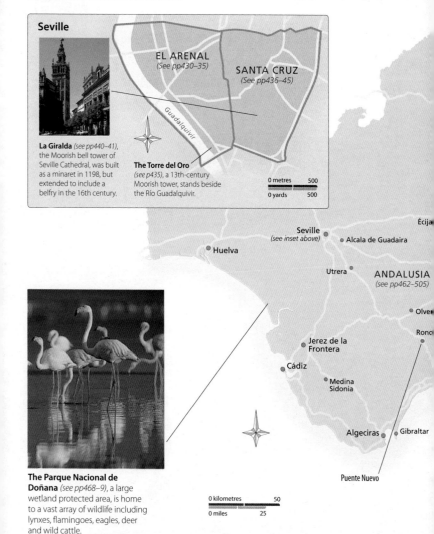

Seville

La Giralda *(see pp440–41)*, the Moorish bell tower of Seville Cathedral, was built as a minaret in 1198, but extended to include a belfry in the 16th century.

EL ARENAL
(See pp430–35)

SANTA CRUZ
(See pp436–45)

Guadalquivir

The Torre del Oro *(see p435)*, a 13th-century Moorish tower, stands beside the Río Guadalquivir.

| 0 metres | 500 |
| 0 yards | 500 |

Écija

Seville
(see inset above)

● Alcala de Guadaira

● Huelva

Utrera ●

ANDALUSIA
(see pp462–505)

● Olve

Rono

● Jerez de la
Frontera

● Cádiz

● Medina
Sidonia

Algeciras ● ● Gibraltar

Puente Nuevo

The Parque Nacional de Doñana *(see pp468–9)*, a large wetland protected area, is home to a vast array of wildlife including lynxes, flamingoes, eagles, deer and wild cattle.

| 0 kilometres | 50 |
| 0 miles | 25 |

◀ Beautiful *azulejos*, Moorish ceramic tiles, at the Real Alcázar, Seville

Above the city of Granada rises the famous Alhambra *(see pp494–5)*. The austere exterior of this great Moorish fortress-palace, built under the Nasrid dynasty, gives no hint of the sumptuous halls and enchanting courtyards and gardens contained within it.

The town hall *(see p502)*, or *ayuntamiento*, in the historic town of Baeza was built in the early Spanish Renaissance style, called Plateresque. Great attention to detail is displayed in the carving of this pillar at the entrance.

Villanueva del Arzobispo

Linares

Montoro

Baeza

Úbeda

-oba

Jaén

Huéscar

Vélez Rubio

Alcaudete

Baza

tepa

Guadix

Granada

Mojácar

Loja

Antequera

Tabernas

Málaga

Motril

Adra

Almeriá

The Puente Nuevo *(see p474)*, a bridge built in the 18th century, spans the Tagus gorge, which divides the old white town of Ronda from its newer districts.

bella

The Cabo de Gata nature reserve *(see p505)* is an area of steep cliffs and secluded coves, with a stretch of seabed that is rich in marine flora and fauna.

The Flavours of Southern Spain

Andalusia is vast, bordered on one side by the Mediterranean and on the other by the Atlantic. Inland are lofty mountains and undulating hills, endless olive groves and bright fields of sunflowers. The cuisine is as varied as the terrain, with a huge array of seafood, superb meat and game, and a harvest of sun-ripened fruit and vegetables. The *tapeo* (tapas-bar-hopping) is a regional institution and, around Granada, these little morsels are often still served free with drinks. Along the coast, especially the Costa del Sol, the influx of foreigners has brought glamorous international restaurants but, inland, traditional recipes are still the norm at old-fashioned inns.

Olives and olive oil

Diners choosing from a selection at a tapas bar

Tapas

The *tapeo*, or tapas crawl, is an intrinsic part of daily life in Andalusia. Each bar is usually known for a particular speciality: one might be well-known for its home-made *croquetas* (potato croquettes, usually filled with ham or cod), while another will serve exceptional hams, and yet another might make the best *albóndigas* (meatballs) in the

neighbourhood. Tapas are often accompanied by a glass of chilled, refreshing sherry, or perhaps a cold draught beer (*una caña*). Tapas were once free, but that tradition has largely died out.

Seafood

It's not surprising, given its extensive coastline, that Southern Spain offers every imaginable variety of seafood,

including cod, hake, prawns, crayfish, clams, razor clams, octopus, cuttlefish, sole and tuna. Almost every seaside resort will offer *pescaíto frito* (fried fish), originally a Malaga dish, made with the freshest catch of the day. In Cádiz, they are served appealingly in a paper cone, and in nearby Sanlúcar do not miss the sweet and juicy *langostinos* (king prawns).

Jamón iberico bellota — Morcilla with onion — Morcilla with rice — Salchichón iberico bellota — Chorizo rosario picante — Lomo embuchado

Selection of delicious Spanish *embutidos* (cured meats)

Regional Dishes and Specialities

Andalusia embodies many of the images most closely associated with Spain – the heady rhythms of flamenco, striking white villages and bullfighting. And tapas – in Andalusia, you can easily make a meal of these delectable treats, and every bar has an excellent range. Don't miss the mouthwatering hams from Jabugo and Trevélez which are famed throughout Spain, or the platters of freshly fried fish liberally doused with lemon juice. An ice-cold sherry (the word comes from Jérez, where most sherry is produced) is deliciously refreshing in the searing summer heat and is the most popular tipple at southern fiestas. While pork remains the most appreciated local meat, duck, beef and lamb are also favourites, subtly flavoured with aromatic bay leaves.

Pomegranates

Gazpacho This famous chilled soup is made with plump, ripe tomatoes, garlic and peppers.

Andalusian vegetable seller displaying fresh local produce

Meat and game

Pork and beef are the most popular meats in Andalusia. Glossy black bulls (some raised for bullfighting but most for meat) are a common sight, and one of the most popular local dishes is *rabo de toro* (bull's tail).

Prawns and sardines on display at the fish market

The famous hams of Jabugo (in the southwest) and Trevélez (near Granada) are among the finest produced in Spain, and are made with free-range, black-footed pigs fed on a diet of acorns. All kinds of cured meats are made here, often to traditional recipes which have remained unchanged for centuries. In the wild inland Sierras, you will find an abundance of game in season, along with the traditional country staples of lamb and rabbit.

Fruit and Vegetables

The undulating Andalusian fields and hillsides are densely covered with beautiful olive groves, and the best oils are graded as carefully as fine wines. Olive oil is liberally used in *andaluz* cuisine, and the typical southern breakfast is toasted country bread topped with thin slices of tomato and drizzled with olive oil – utterly delicious. The hot climate is perfect for fruit and vegetables, including luscious peaches, papayas, persimmons and mangoes, as well as tomatoes, asparagus, aubergines (eggplants) and artichokes. The chilled tomato soup, *gazpacho*, is a classic, but *salmorejo*, which is thicker and topped with a sprinkling of chopped boiled eggs and ham, is even tastier.

On the Menu

Chocos con habas Cuttlefish is cooked with beans, white wine and plenty of bay leaves.

Pato a la Sevillana Succulent duck, cooked slowly with onion, leeks, carrots, bay leaf and a dash of sherry, this is a speciality of Seville.

Rabo de Toro An *andaluz* classic, made with chunks of bull's tail, slowly braised with vegetables, bay leaf and a dash of sherry until tender.

Salmorejo Cordobés A creamy tomato dip thickened with breadcrumbs.

Torta de Camarones Delicious fritters filled with tiny, whole shrimp.

Tortilla del Sacromonte A speciality of Granada: omelette with brains, kidney or other offal, peppers and peas.

Huevos a la Flamenca Eggs are baked in a terracotta dish with vegetables, ham and chorizo sausage.

Pescaíto Frito A seaside favourite, this is a platter of small fish tossed in batter and fried in olive oil.

Tocino de Cielo This simple but delicious dessert consists of creamy egg custard with a caramel syrup topping.

Wines of Southern Spain

Andalusia is a land of fortified wines, and the best of these is *jerez* (sherry). Andalusians drink the light, dry fino and manzanilla styles of sherry as wines (they only have 15.5 per cent alcohol) – always chilled, and often as an accompaniment to tapas *(see pp578–9)*. The longer-aged, richer, yet still dry styles of amontillado and oloroso sherry go well with the cured *jamón serrano*. Other wines include fino, which may or may not be fortified, and Madeira-like Málaga.

Working the soil in Jerez

Tío Pepe is one of the finos of Jerez, which are noted for their bouquet of *flor* (yeast), pale colour and appetizing finish.

Wine Regions

The Jerez wine region covers the chalky downs between the towns of Jerez, Sanlúcar and El Puerto de Santa María. South of the Montilla-Moriles region are Málaga's vineyards, which have been reduced by urban development.

Montilla, softer in style than sherry, can make an excellent partner for Andalusia's regional cuisine.

Manzanilla is matured only in the town of Sanlúcar de Barrameda, which is situated where the Guadalquivir River meets the Atlantic Ocean. Like fino, it is bone dry, but has a distinctive salty tang.

Key

- Condado de Huelva
- Jerez-Xérès-Sherry
- Montilla-Moriles
- Málaga

0 kilometres 100
0 miles 50

Key Facts about Wines of Southern Spain

Location and Climate
The Jerez region has one of the sunniest climates in Europe – summer heat tempered by ocean breezes. The best type of soil is white, chalky *albariza*. In Montilla it is more clayey.

Grape Varieties
The best dry sherry is produced from the Palomino grape. Pedro Ximénez is used for the sweeter styles and is the main grape in Montilla and Málaga. Moscatel is also grown in Málaga.

Good Producers
Condado de Huelva: Manuel Sauci Salas (Riodiel), A.Villarán (Pedro Ximénez Villarán). *Jerez:* Barbadillo (Solear), Blázquez (Carta Blanca), Caballero (Puerto), Garvey (San Patricio), González Byass (Alfonso, Tío Pepe), Hidalgo (La Gitana, Napoleón), Lustau, Osborne (Quinta), Pedro Domecq (La Ina), Sandeman. *Montilla-Moriles:* Alvear (C.B., Festival), Gracia Hermanos, Pérez Barquero, Tomás García. *Málaga:* Scholtz Hermanos, López Hermanos.

How Sherry is Made

Sherry is mixed from two principal grape varieties: Palomino, which makes a drier, more delicate sherry; and Pedro Ximénez, which is made into a fuller, sweeter type of sherry.

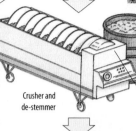

Grape-drying is only required for Pedro Ximénez grapes. They are laid on esparto mats to shrivel in the sun, concentrating the sugar.

Crusher and de-stemmer

Grape-picking takes place during the first three weeks in September. Palomino grapes are taken to the presses quickly to ensure freshness.

Grape-pressing and destalking, in cylindrical stainless-steel vats, is usually done at night to avoid the searing Andalusian heat.

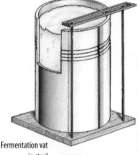

Fermentation vat in steel

Flor, a yeast, may form on the exposed surface of young wine in the fermentation vat, preventing oxidization and adding a delicate taste. If *flor* develops, the wine is a fino.

Fortification is the addition of pure grape spirit, raising the level of alcohol from around 11 per cent by volume to around 18 per cent for olorosos, and 15.5 per cent for finos.

The *solera* system

The youngest *solera* contains new wine.

Sherry for bottling is taken from the oldest *solera* on the bottom row.

The finished product

The *solera* system assures that the qualities of a sherry remain constant. The wine from the youngest *solera* is mixed with the older in the barrels below and as a result takes on its character.

Moorish Architecture

The first significant period of Moorish architecture arrived with the Cordoban Caliphate. The Mezquita was extended lavishly during this period and possesses all the enduring features of the Moorish style: arches, stucco work and ornamental use of calligraphy. Later, the Almohads imported a purer Islamic style, as can be seen in La Giralda *(see pp440–41)*. The Nasrids built the superbly crafted Alhambra *(see pp494–5)* and the Mudéjares *(see p59)* used their skill to create beautiful Moorish-style buildings such as the Palacio Pedro I in Seville's Real Alcázar *(see pp444–5)*.

Reflections in water, combined with an overall play of light, were central to Moorish architecture.

Moorish domes were frequently unadorned on the outside. Inside, an intricate lattice of stone ribs supported the dome's weight. Like this one in the Mezquita *(see pp484–5)*, they were inlaid with multicoloured mosaics featuring stylized flowers.

Defensive walls

Moorish gardens were often arranged around gently rippling pools and channels.

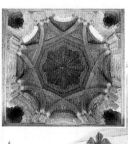

Pre-Caliphal era 710–929	Caliphal era 929–1031	Almoravid and Almohad era 1091–1248	Nasrid era c.1238–1492
	1031–91 *Taifa* period *(see p58)*		**c.1350** Alhambra palace

700	800	900	1000	1100	1200	1300	1400

	785 Mezquita in Córdoba begun	**1184** La Giralda in Seville begun	**c.1350** Palacio Pedro I
	936 Medina Azahara near Córdoba begun		**Mudéjar era,** after c.1215

Azulejos *(see p442)*, glazed tiles, often adorned walls in geometric patterns, as here in the Real Alcázar *(pp444–5)*.

Moorish Arches

The Moorish arch was developed from the horseshoe arch that the Visigoths used in the construction of churches. The Moors modified it and used it as the basis of great architectural endeavours, such as the Mezquita. Subsequent arches show more sophisticated ornamentation and the slow demise of the basic horseshoe shape.

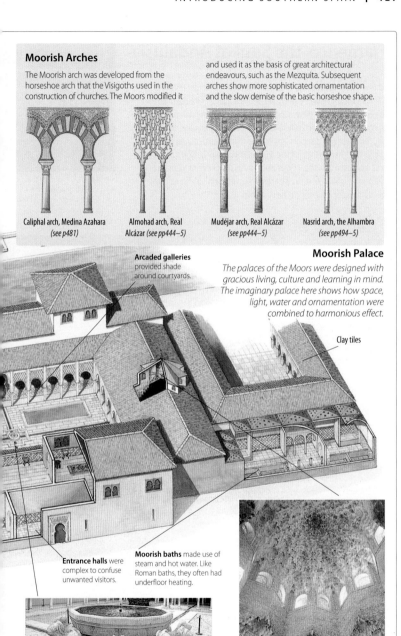

Caliphal arch, Medina Azahara
(see p481)

Almohad arch, Real Alcázar *(see pp444–5)*

Mudéjar arch, Real Alcázar
(see pp444–5)

Nasrid arch, the Alhambra
(see pp494–5)

Moorish Palace

The palaces of the Moors were designed with gracious living, culture and learning in mind. The imaginary palace here shows how space, light, water and ornamentation were combined to harmonious effect.

Arcaded galleries provided shade around courtyards.

Clay tiles

Entrance halls were complex to confuse unwanted visitors.

Moorish baths made use of steam and hot water. Like Roman baths, they often had underfloor heating.

Water cooled the Moors' elegant courtyards and served a contemplative purpose, as here in the Patio de los Leones in the Alhambra *(see p495).*

Elaborate stucco work typifies the Nasrid style of architecture. The Sala de los Abencerrajes in the Alhambra *(see p495)* was built using only the simplest materials, but it is nevertheless widely regarded as one of the most outstanding monuments of the period of the Moorish occupation.

Flamenco, the Soul of Andalusia

More than just a dance, flamenco is a forceful artistic expression of the sorrows and joys of life. Although it has interpreters all over Spain and even the world, it is a uniquely Andalusian art form, traditionally performed by gypsies. There are many styles of *cante* (song) from different parts of Andalusia, but no strict choreography – dancers improvise from basic movements, following the rhythm of the guitar and their feelings. Flamenco was neglected in the 1960s and 1970s, but recent years have seen a revival of serious interest in traditional styles and the development of exciting new forms.

Sevillanas, a folk dance favoured by Andalusians and strongly influenced by flamenco, is the official dance of Seville's April Fair.

At a *tablao* (flamenco club) there will be at least four people on stage, including the hand-clapper.

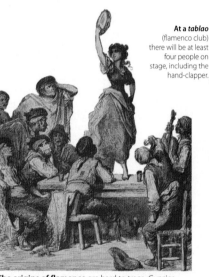

The origins of flamenco are hard to trace. Gypsies may have been the main creators of the art, mixing their own Indian-influenced culture with existing Moorish and Andalusian folklore, and with Jewish and Christian music. There were gypsies in Andalusia by the early Middle Ages, but only in the 18th century did flamenco begin to develop into its present form.

The Spanish Guitar

The guitar has a major role in flamenco, traditionally accompanying the singer. The flamenco guitar developed from the modern classical guitar, which evolved in Spain in the 19th century. Flamenco guitars have a lighter, shallower construction and a thickened plate below the soundhole, used to tap rhythms. Today, flamenco guitarists often perform solo. One of the greatest, Paco de Lucía, began by accompanying singers and dancers, before making his debut as a soloist in 1968. His inventive style, which combines traditional playing with Latin, jazz and rock elements, has influenced many musicians outside the realm of flamenco, such as the group Ketama, who play flamenco-blues.

Classical guitar

Legendary guitarist Paco de Lucía

Singing is an integral part of flamenco and the singer often performs solo. Camarón de la Isla (1950–92), a gypsy born near Cádiz, was among the most famous contemporary *cantaores* (flamenco singers). He began as a singer of expressive *cante jondo* (literally, "deep song"), from which he developed his own distinctive style. He has inspired many singers.

Where to Enjoy Flamento

Madrid has several good *tablaos*, flamenco venues (*see p325*). In Granada, Sacromonte's caves (*p493*) are an exciting location. In Seville, the Barrio de Santa Cruz (*pp436–45*) has good *tablaos*.

The proud yet graceful posture of the *bailaora* is suggestive of a restrained passion.

A harsh, vibrating voice is typical of the singer.

The *bailaora* (female dancer) is renowned for amazing footwork as well as intensive dance moments. Eva Yerbabuena and Sara Baras are both famous for their personal styles. Both lead their own acclaimed flamenco companies. Another flamenco star is Juana Amaya.

Traditional polka-dot dress

The *bailaor* (male dancer) plays a less important role than the *bailaora*. However, many have achieved fame, including Antonio Canales. He has introduced a new beat through his original foot movements.

The Flamenco Tablao

These days it is rare to come across spontaneous dancing at a tablao, *but if dancers and singers are inspired, an impressive show usually results. Artists performing with* duende *("magic spirit") will hear appreciative* olés *from the audience.*

Flamenco Rhythm

The unmistakable rhythm of flamenco is created by the guitar. Just as important, however, is the beat created by hand-clapping and by the dancer's feet in high-heeled shoes. The *bailaoras* may also beat a rhythm with castanets; Lucero Tena (born in 1938) became famous for her solos on castanets. Graceful hand movements are used to express the dancer's feelings of the moment – whether pain, sorrow, or happiness. Like the movements of the rest of the body, they are not choreographed, and the styles used vary from person to person.

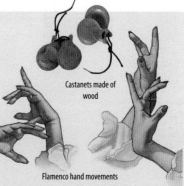

Castanets made of wood

Flamenco hand movements

EL ARENAL

Bounded by the Río Guadalquivir and guarded by the 13th-century Torre del Oro, El Arenal used to be a district of munitions stores and shipyards. Today this quarter is dominated by the dazzling white bullring, the Plaza de Toros de la Maestranza, where the Sevillians have been staging corridas for more than two centuries. The many bars and bodegas in the neighbouring streets are especially busy during the summer bullfighting season.

Once central to the city's life, the influence of the Guadalquivir declined as it silted up during the 17th century. By then El Arenal had become a notorious underworld haunt

clinging to the city walls. The river was converted into a canal in the early 20th century but restored to its former navigable glory in time for Expo '92. The east bank was transformed into a tree-lined promenade with excellent views of Triana and La Isla de la Cartuja across the water.

The Hospital de la Caridad testifies to the city's continuing love affair with the Baroque. Its church is filled with famous paintings by Murillo, and the story of the Seville School is told in the immaculately restored Museo de Bellas Artes further north. The city's stunning collection of art includes great works by Zurbarán, Murillo and Valdés Leal.

Sights at a Glance

Historic Buildings
❸ Plaza de Toros de la Maestranza
❹ Hospital de la Caridad
❺ Torre del Oro

Museums
❶ Museo de Bellas Artes
Churches
❷ Iglesia de la Magdalena

See also Seville Street Finder maps 1, 3, 5

0 metres   500
0 yards   500

◀ Stunning domed ceiling at the Museo de Bellas Artes, Seville

For map symbols *see back flap*

Street-by-Street: El Arenal

Once home to the port of Seville, El Arenal also
housed the ammunition works and the artillery
headquarters. Now its atmosphere is set by the
city's bullring, the majestic Plaza de Toros de la
Maestranza. During the bullfighting season *(see
p434)* the area's bars and restaurants are packed, but
for the rest of the year El Arenal's backstreets remain
quiet. The riverfront is dominated by one of Seville's
best-known monuments, the Moorish Torre del Oro,
while the long, tree-lined promenade beside the
Paseo de Cristóbal Colón is perfect for a slow,
romantic walk along the Guadalquivir.

❸ ★ **Plaza de Toros de la Maestranza**
Seville's 18th-century bullring, one of
Spain's oldest, has a Baroque façade in
white and ochre.

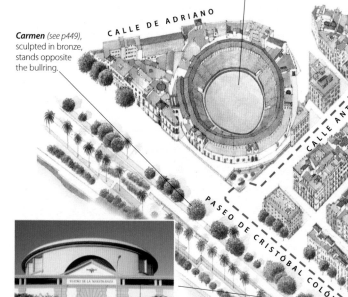

Carmen (see p449),
sculpted in bronze,
stands opposite
the bullring.

CALLE DE ADRIANO

CALLE ANTONIA DÍAZ

PASEO DE CRISTÓBAL COLÓN

Paseo Alcalde
Marqués de
Contadero

The Teatro de la Maestranza, a showpiece
theatre and opera house, was opened in
1991. Home of the Orquesta Sinfónica de
Sevilla, the theatre also features international
opera and dance companies.

| 0 metres | | 75 |
| 0 yards | | 75 |

The Guadalquivir used to cause catastrophic
inundations. Following floods in 1947, a barrage
was constructed. Today, tourists enjoy peaceful
boat trips, starting from the Torre del Oro.

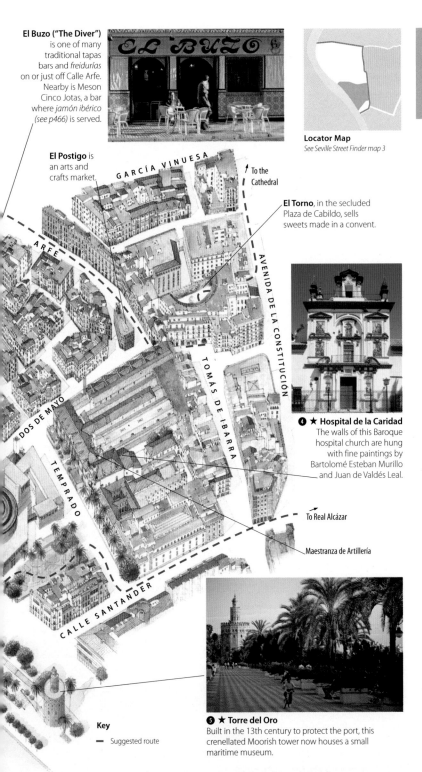

El Buzo ("The Diver") is one of many traditional tapas bars and *freidurías* on or just off Calle Arfe. Nearby is Meson Cinco Jotas, a bar where *jamón ibérico* (see p466) is served.

Locator Map
See Seville Street Finder map 3

El Postigo is an arts and crafts market.

GARCÍA VINUESA

To the Cathedral

El Torno, in the secluded Plaza de Cabildo, sells sweets made in a convent.

ARFE

AVENIDA DE LA CONSTITUCIÓN

TOMÁS DE IBARRA

DOS DE MAYO

TEMPRADO

❹ ★ **Hospital de la Caridad**
The walls of this Baroque hospital church are hung with fine paintings by Bartolomé Esteban Murillo and Juan de Valdés Leal.

To Real Alcázar

Maestranza de Artillería

CALLE SANTANDER

Key

— Suggested route

❺ ★ **Torre del Oro**
Built in the 13th century to protect the port, this crenellated Moorish tower now houses a small maritime museum.

Madonna and Child in the Baroque Iglesia de la Magdalena

❶ Museo de Bellas Artes

Plaza del Museo 9. **Map** 1 B5. **Tel** 95 554 29 42. 🚌 C5, 6, 13, 14, 27, 32, 43. **Open** 9am–7:30pm Tue–Sat, 9am–3:30pm Sun & public hols. 🎟 (free for EU citizens) 🚫 ♿ 🌐 **museosdeandalucia.es**

The Convento de la Merced Calzada houses one of the best art museums in Spain. Completed in 1612 by Juan de Oviedo, the building is designed around three patios. The Patio Mayor is the largest of these, remodelled by the architect Leonardo de Figueroa in 1724. The convent church is notable for its Baroque domed ceiling, painted by Domingo Martínez.

The museum's collection of Spanish art and sculpture, from the medieval to the modern, focuses on the work of Seville School artists. Among the star attractions is *La Servilleta*, a Virgin and Child (1665–8), which is said to be painted on a napkin (*servilleta*). One of Murillo's most popular works, it may be seen in the restored convent church.

The boisterous *La Inmaculada* (1672) by Juan de Valdés Leal is in a gallery devoted to the artist's forceful religious paintings. Several fine works by Zurbarán include *San Hugo en el*

San Jerónimo Penitente in the Museo de Bellas Artes

Refectorio (1655), which was painted for the monastery at La Cartuja (*see p450*).

❷ Iglesia de la Magdalena

Calle San Pablo 10. **Map** 3 B1. **Tel** 95 422 96 03. 🚇 Plaza Nueva. 🚌 43. **Open** 11am–1:30pm Tue–Thu. ✝ 7:30am–11am, 6:30–9pm Mon–Sat, 9am, 10:30am, noon, 1pm, 7pm, 8:15pm Sun.

This immense Baroque church by Leonardo de Figueroa, completed in 1709, is gradually being restored to its former glory. In its southwest corner stands the Capilla de la Quinta Angustia, a Mudéjar chapel with three cupolas. This chapel survived from an earlier church where the great Seville School painter Bartolomé Murillo was baptized in 1618. The font that was used for his baptism is now in the baptistry of the present building. The church's west front is topped by a belfry which is painted in vivid colours. Among the religious works in the church are a painting by Francisco de Zurbarán, *St Dominic in Soria*, housed in the Capilla Sacramental (to the right of the south door), and frescoes by Lucas Valdés over the sanctuary. On the wall of the north transept there is a cautionary fresco of a medieval *auto-da-fé (see p278)*.

❸ Plaza de Toros de la Maestranza

Paseo de Cristóbal Colón 12. **Map** 3 B2. **Tel** 95 422 45 77. 🚇 Puerta Jerez. 🚌 Archivo de Indias. **Open** 9:30am–7pm daily (Apr–Oct: to 9pm). **Closed** Good Friday, 25 Dec, from 3pm bullfight days. 🚫 📷 🌐 **realmaestranza.com**

Seville's famous bullring was built between 1761 and 1881.

The arcaded arena holds up to 14,000 spectators. Guided tours of this immense building start from the main entrance on Paseo de Cristóbal Colón. On the west side is the Puerta del Príncipe (Prince's Gate), through which the triumphant matadors are carried aloft by admirers from the crowd.

Just beyond the *enfermería* (emergency hospital) is a museum of portraits, posters and costumes, including a purple cape painted by Pablo Picasso. The tour continues on to the chapel where matadors pray for success, and then to the stables where the horses of the *picadores* (lance-carrying horsemen) are kept.

The bullfighting season starts on Easter Sunday and continues intermittently until October. Most *corridas* take place on Sunday evenings. Tickets can be bought from the *taquilla* (booking office) at the bullring.

A few doors from the Plaza de Toros is the Teatro de la Maestranza. Seville's opera house, designed by Luis Marín de Terán and Aurelio de Pozo, opened in 1991. Fragments of ironwork from the 19th-century ammunition works that first occupied the site adorn the river façade.

Arcaded arena of the Plaza de Toros de la Maestranza, begun in 1761

Finis Gloriae Mundi by Juan de Valdés Leal in the Hospital de la Caridad

❹ Hospital de la Caridad

Calle Temprado 3. **Map** 3 B2.
Tel 95 422 32 32. 🚍 🚇 Puerta Jerez.
🚌 C4. **Open** 9am–1pm, 3:30–7:30pm daily. 🅿 ♿

This charity hospital was founded in 1674 and it is still used today as a sanctuary for elderly and infirm people. In the gardens stands a statue of its benefactor, Miguel de Mañara, whose dissolute life before he joined a brotherhood is said to have inspired the story of Don Juan. The façade of the hospital church, with its whitewashed walls, reddish stonework and framed *azulejos*, provides a glorious example of Sevillian Baroque.

Inside are two square patios decorated with plants, 18th-century Dutch tiles, and fine fountains with Italian statues depicting Charity and Mercy. At their northern end a passage to the right leads to another patio, containing a 13th-century arch which survives from the city's shipyards.

Inside the church there are a number of original canvases by some of the leading painters of the 17th century, despite the fact that some of its greatest artworks were looted by Marshal Soult during the Napoleonic occupation of 1808–14 *(see p66)*. Directly above

the entrance is the ghoulish *Finis Gloriae Mundi* (The End of the World's Glory) by Juan de Valdés Leal, and opposite hangs his morbid *In Ictu Oculi* (In the Blink of an Eye). Many of the other works that can be seen are by Murillo, including *St John of God Carrying a Sick Man* and portraits of the Child Jesus and *St John the Baptist as a Boy*.

❺ Torre del Oro

Paseo de Cristóbal Colón. **Map** 3 B2.
Tel 95 422 24 19. 🚍 🚇 Puerta Jerez.
🚌 C3, C4. **Open** 9:30am–1:30pm Tue–Fri, 10:30am–1:30pm Sat & Sun.
Closed Aug & Mon. 🅿 (free Tue & for EU citizens). ♿

In Moorish Seville the Tower of Gold formed part of the walled defences, linking up with the Real Alcázar *(see pp444–5)*. It was built as a defensive lookout in 1220, with a companion tower on the opposite bank. A metal chain stretched between them to prevent hostile ships from sailing upriver. The turret was added in 1760. The gold in its name may be the gilded *azulejos* that once clad its walls, or treasures from the Americas unloaded here. The tower has had many uses, such as a chapel and a prison. Now, as the Museo Marítimo, it exhibits maritime maps and antiques.

The Torre del Oro, built by the Almohads

Seville's Fiestas

April Fair *(two weeks after Easter)*. Life in the city moves over the river to the fairground for a week. Here, members of clubs, trade unions and neighbourhood groups meet in *casetas* (entertainment booths) to drink and dance all night to the infectious rhythm of *sevillanas*. (Access to booths may be limited to private parties.) Every day, from around 1pm, elegant, traditionally dressed riders on horseback and mantilla-crowned women in open carriages show off their finest flamenco attire in parades. During the afternoons, bullfights are often staged in the Maestranza bullring.
Holy Week *(Mar/Apr)*. Over 100 gilded *pasos* (floats bearing religious images) are borne through the streets between Palm Sunday and Easter Day. Singers in the crowds often spontaneously burst into *saetas*, fragments of song in praise of Christ or the Virgin. Emotions are high in the early hours of Good Friday as the images of the Virgen de la Macarena and the Virgen de la Esperanza of Triana emerge from their churches.
Corpus Christi *(May/Jun)*. The *Seises*, boys dressed in Baroque costume, dance before the main altar of the cathedral *(see p441)*.

Float in Holy Week procession

SANTA CRUZ

Seville's old Jewish quarter, the Barrio de Santa Cruz, is a warren of white alleyways and patios that has long been the most picturesque corner of the city. Many of the best-known sights are located here: the cavernous Gothic cathedral with its landmark tower, La Giralda; the splendid Real Alcázar, with the royal palaces and lush gardens of Pedro I and Carlos V; and the Archivo de Indias, whose documents tell of Spain's exploration and conquest of the Americas.

Spreading northeast from these great monuments is an enchanting maze of whitewashed streets. The Golden Age artist Bartolomé Esteban Murillo lived here in the 17th century, while his contemporary, Juan de Valdés Leal, decorated the Hospital de los Venerables with superb Baroque frescoes. Further north is one of Seville's favourite shopping streets, the Calle de las Sierpes. The market squares around it, such as the charming Plaza del Salvador, provided backdrops for some of the stories of Cervantes. Nearby, the ornate façades and interiors of the Ayuntamiento (town hall) and the Casa de Pilatos, a gem of Andalusian architecture, testify to the great wealth that flowed into the city from the New World during the 16th century, much of it spent on art.

Sights at a Glance

Historic Buildings
2 Ayuntamiento
4 Casa de Pilatos
5 Hospital de los Venerables
6 Archivo de Indias
7 Real Alcázar pp444–5

Churches
1 Seville Cathedral and La Giralda
   pp440–41

Streets and Plazas
3 Calle de las Sierpes

See also Seville Street Finder maps 1–6

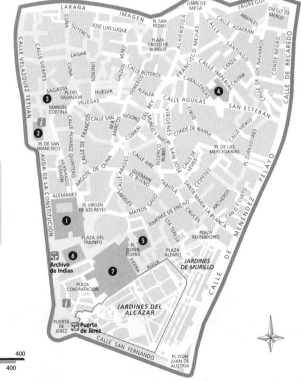

0 metres 400
0 yards 400

◀ Seville's landmark bell tower, La Giralda, illuminated at dusk

For map symbols *see back flap*

Street-by-Street: Santa Cruz

The maze of narrow streets to the east of Seville Cathedral and the Real Alcázar represents Seville at its most romantic and compact. As well as the expected souvenir shops, tapas bars and strolling guitarists, there are plenty of picturesque alleys, hidden plazas and flower-decked patios to reward the casual wanderer. Once a Jewish ghetto, its restored buildings, with characteristic window grilles, are now a harmonious mix of upmarket residences and tourist accommodation. Good bars and restaurants make the area well worth an evening visit.

Plaza Virgen de los Reyes is often lined by horse-drawn carriages. In the centre of the square is an early 20th-century fountain by José Lafita.

Palacio Arzobispal, the 18th-century Archbishop's Palace, is still used by Seville's clergy.

❶ ★ Cathedral and La Giralda
This huge Gothic cathedral and its Moorish bell tower are Seville's most popular sights.

Convento de la Encarnación

PLAZA DEL TRIUNFO

AVENIDA DE LA CONSTITUCIÓN

MATE

ROMERO MUR

SANTO TOMÁS

MIGUEL MANARA

❻ Archivo de Indias
Built in the 16th century as a merchants' exchange, the Archive of the Indies now houses documents relating to the Spanish colonization of the Americas.

Plaza del Triunfo has a Baroque column celebrating the city's survival of the great earthquake of 1755. In the centre is a modern statue of the Virgin Mary (Immaculate Conception).

For hotels and restaurants in this area see p572 and pp597–8

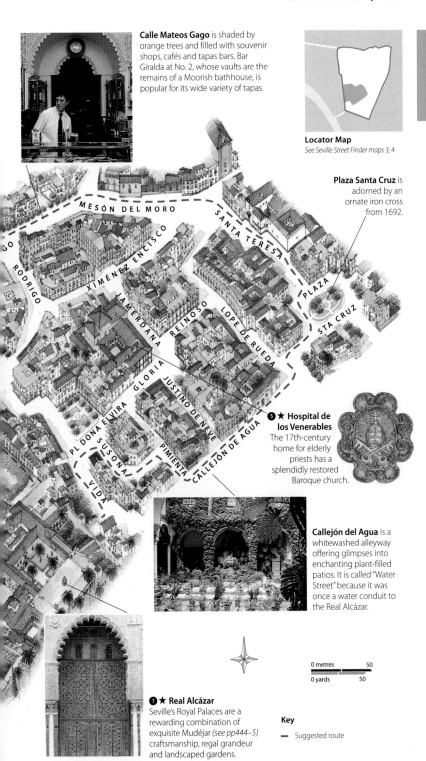

Calle Mateos Gago is shaded by orange trees and filled with souvenir shops, cafés and tapas bars. Bar Giralda at No. 2, whose vaults are the remains of a Moorish bathhouse, is popular for its wide variety of tapas.

Locator Map
See Seville Street Finder maps 3, 4

Plaza Santa Cruz is adorned by an ornate iron cross from 1692.

MESÓN DEL MORO

GO

RODRIGO

XIMÉNEZ ENCISCO

SANTA TERESA

JAMERDANA

REINOSO

LOPE DE RUEDA

PLAZA

STA CRUZ

GLORIA

JUSTINO DE NEVE

PL DOÑA ELVIRA

SUSONA

PIMIENTA

CALLEJÓN DE AGUA

VIDA

⑤ ★ Hospital de los Venerables
The 17th-century home for elderly priests has a splendidly restored Baroque church.

Callejón del Agua is a whitewashed alleyway offering glimpses into enchanting plant-filled patios. It is called "Water Street" because it was once a water conduit to the Real Alcázar.

0 metres   50
0 yards   50

⑦ ★ Real Alcázar
Seville's Royal Palaces are a rewarding combination of exquisite Mudéjar *(see pp444–5)* craftsmanship, regal grandeur and landscaped gardens.

Key

— Suggested route

❶ Seville Cathedral and La Giralda

Seville's cathedral occupies the site of a great mosque built by the Almohads *(see p58)* in the late 12th century. La Giralda, its bell tower, and the Patio de los Naranjos are a legacy of this Moorish structure. Work on the Christian cathedral, the largest in Europe, began in 1401 and took just over a century to complete. As well as enjoying its Gothic immensity and the works of art in its chapels and sacristy, visitors can climb La Giralda or visit the cathedral roof for stunning city views.

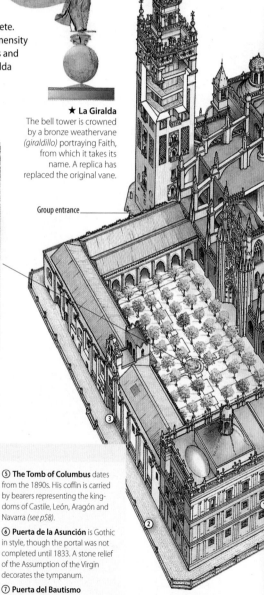

★ La Giralda
The bell tower is crowned by a bronze weathervane *(giraldillo)* portraying Faith, from which it takes its name. A replica has replaced the original vane.

Group entrance

★ Patio de los Naranjos
In Moorish times worshippers would wash their hands and feet in the fountain under the orange trees before praying.

KEY

① **Iglesia del Sagrario**, a large 17th-century chapel, is now used as a parish church.

② **Roman pillars** brought from Itálica *(see p480)* surround the cathedral steps.

③ **Puerta del Perdón** (exit)

④ **The Sacristía Mayor** houses many works of art, including paintings by Murillo.

⑤ **The Tomb of Columbus** dates from the 1890s. His coffin is carried by bearers representing the kingdoms of Castile, León, Aragón and Navarra *(see p58)*.

⑥ **Puerta de la Asunción** is Gothic in style, though the portal was not completed until 1833. A stone relief of the Assumption of the Virgin decorates the tympanum.

⑦ **Puerta del Bautismo**

Retablo Mayor
Santa María de la Sede, the cathedral's patron saint, sits at the high altar below a waterfall of gold. The 44 gilded relief panels of the reredos were carved by Spanish and Flemish sculptors between 1482 and 1564.

Main entrance

★ **Capilla Mayor**
Monumental iron grilles forged in 1518–32 enclose the main chapel, which is dominated by the overwhelming Retablo Mayor.

The Rise of La Giralda

The tower was built as a minaret in 1198. In the 14th century the bronze spheres at its top were replaced by Christian symbols. A new belfry was planned in 1557, but built to a more ornate design by Hernán Ruiz in 1568.

1198   1400   1557 (plan)   1568

Genoese fountain in the Mudéjar Patio Principal of the Casa de Pilatos

❷ Ayuntamiento

Plaza Nueva 1. **Map** 3 C1. **Tel** 95 547
12 16. 🚉 Plaza Nueva. **Open** tours
4:30pm & 7:30pm Mon–Thu.
Closed Aug. ✂ 🎥

Seville's City Hall stands
between the Plaza de San
Francisco, where *autos-da-fé*
(public trials of heretics) were
held, and the Plaza Nueva.
  Building was completed
between 1527 and 1534. The
side bordering the Plaza de San
Francisco is a fine example of
ornate Plateresque style *(see
p29)* favoured by the architect
Diego de Riaño. The west front
is Neo-Classical, built in 1891.
Sculpted ceilings survive in the
vestibule and the lower Casa
Consistorial (Council Meeting
Room), containing Velázquez's
*Imposition of the Chasuble on
St Ildefonso*. The upper Casa
Consistorial has a dazzling
coffered ceiling and paintings
by Zurbarán and Valdés Leal.

❸ Calle de las Sierpes

Map 3 C1. 🚌 C5, 10, 11, 12, 15, 16,
20, 24, 27, 32, 40, 41, 43. Casa de la
Condesa Lebrija. **Tel** 95 422 78 02.
🚉 Plaza Nueva. **Open** 10:30am–
7:30pm Mon–Fri, 10am–2pm, 4–6pm
Sat, 10am–2pm Sun; Jul & Aug: to 3pm
Mon–Fri, to 2pm Sat. **Closed** Sun in Jul
& Aug. 🎥 🌐 palaciodelebrija.com

Seville's main shopping
promenade, the "Street of the
Snakes", runs north from Plaza de
San Francisco. Long-established
stores selling hats, fans and
traditional *mantillas* (lace
headdresses) stand alongside

clothes and souvenir shops.
The parallel streets of Cuna and
Tetuán also offer some enjoyable
window-shopping. Halfway up
the road walking north, Calle
Jovellanos to the left leads to the
17th-century Capillita de San
José. Further on at the junction
with Calle Pedro Caravaca is the
Real Círculo de Labradores, a
men's club founded in 1856.
  Opposite – with its entrance
in Calle Cuna – is a 15th-century
private mansion, the **Casa de
la Condesa Lebrija**. Treasures
on display include a Roman
mosaic from the ruins of nearby
Itálica *(see p480)* and a
collection of *azulejos*.
  Right at the end of the
street is La Campana, Seville's
best-known *pastelería*.

❹ Casa de Pilatos

Plaza de Pilatos 1. **Map** 4 D1.
Tel 95 422 52 98. 🚌 C3, C4, C5, 21, 24,
27. **Open** 9am–6pm daily (to 7pm Jul
& Aug). ✂ 🎥 first floor. 🎥

Enraptured by by the architectural and decorative wonders
of High Renaissance Italy and
the Holy Land, the first Marquis
of Tarifa built the Casa de Pilatos.
So called because it was
thought to resemble Pontius
Pilate's home in Jerusalem,
today it is the residence of the
Dukes of Medinaceli and is one
of the finest palaces in Seville.
  Visitors enter through a marble
portal, commissioned by the
Marquis in 1529 from Genoese
craftsmen. Across the arcaded
Apeadero (carriage yard) is the
Patio Principal. This courtyard is
essentially Mudéjar *(see p59)* in
style and decorated with *azulejos*
and intricate plasterwork. In its
corners are three Roman statues,
depicting Minerva, a dancing
muse and Ceres, and a Greek
statue of Athena, dating from
the 5th century BC.
  In its centre is a fountain
which was imported from
Genoa. To the right, through
the Salón del Pretorio with its
coffered ceiling and marquetry,
is the Corredor de Zaquizamí.
The antiquities on display

Azulejos

Colourful *azulejos*, glazed ceramic tiles, are
a striking feature of Seville. The craft was
introduced to Spain by the Moors, who created
fantastic mosaics in sophisticated geometric patterns
for palace walls – the word *azulejo* derives from the Arabic for "little
stone". New techniques were introduced in the 16th century and later
mass production extended their use to decorative signs, shop
façades and advertising hoardings.

Azulejo billboard for Studebaker Motor Cars (1924), Calle Tetuán

Fresco by Juan de Valdés Leal in the Hospital de los Venerables

include sculptures of St Peter and St Ferdinand by Pedro Roldán, flanking the east door; and *The Apotheosis of St Ferdinand* by Lucas Valdés, top centre in the reredos of the main altar. Its frieze (inscribed in Greek) advises to "Fear God and Honour the Priest".

In the sacristy, the ceiling has an effective trompe l'oeil depicting *The Triumph of the Cross* by Juan de Valdés Leal.

❻ Archivo de Indias

Avda de la Constitución. **Map** 3 C2.
Tel 95 450 05 28. 🚌 C5,
Puerta Jerez. 🚇 Archivo de Indias.
Open 9:30am–4:45pm Mon–Sat
(to 2:30pm mid-Jun–mid-Sep),
10am–2pm Sun and public hols. ♿

The Archive of the Indies illustrates Seville's pre-eminent role in the colonization and exploitation of the New World. Built between 1584 and 1598 to designs by Juan de Herrera, co-architect of El Escorial *(see pp334–5),* it was originally a lonja (exchange), where merchants traded. In 1785, Carlos III had all Spanish documents relating to the "Indies" collected under one roof. Among the archive's 86 million handwritten pages and 8,000 maps and drawings are letters from Columbus, Cortés and Cervantes, and the correspondence of Felipe II.

Upstairs, the library rooms contain displays of drawings, maps and facsimile documents.

in adjacent rooms

in adjacent rooms include a bas-relief of *Leda and the Swan* and two Roman reliefs commemorating the Battle of Actium of 31 BC.

Coming back to the Patio Principal, you turn right into the Salón de Descanso de los Jueces. Beyond is a rib-vaulted Gothic chapel, with Mudéjar plasterwork walls and ceiling. On the altar is a copy of a 4th-century sculpture in the Vatican, *The Good Shepherd.* Left through the Gabinete de Pilatos, with its small central fountain, is the Jardín Grande.

Returning once more to the main patio, behind the statue of Ceres, a tiled staircase leads to the upper floor. It is roofed with a wonderful *media naranja* (half-orange) cupola built in 1537. There are Mudéjar ceilings in some rooms, full of family portraits and antiques.

❺ Hospital de los Venerables

Plaza de los Venerables 8. **Map** 3 C2.
Tel 95 456 26 96. 🚇 Archivo de Indias. **Open** 10am–1:30pm,
4–7:30pm daily. **Closed** 1 Jan,
Good Friday, 25 Dec. 🅿 ♿ 🚻

Set in the heart of the Barrio de Santa Cruz, this home for elderly priests was begun in 1675 and completed around 20 years later by Leonardo de Figueroa. It has now been restored as a cultural centre by FOCUS (Fundación Fondo de Cultura de Sevilla).

Stairs from the central, rose-coloured, sunken patio lead to the upper floors, which, along with the infirmary and cellar, are used as exhibition galleries.

The Hospital church, a showcase of Baroque splendours, has frescoes by both Juan de Valdés Leal and his son Lucas Valdés. Other highlights of the church

Façade of the Archivo de Indias by Juan de Herrera

❼ Real Alcázar

In 1364 Pedro I ordered the construction of a royal residence within the palaces which had been built by the city's Almohad *(see p58)* rulers. Within two years, craftsmen from Granada and Toledo had created a jewel box of Mudéjar patios and halls, the Palacio Pedro I, now at the heart of Seville's Real Alcázar. Later monarchs added their own distinguishing marks: Isabel I *(see p60)* dispatched navigators to explore the New World from her Casa de la Contratación, while Carlos I (the Holy Roman Emperor Charles V – *see p62*) had grandiose, richly decorated apartments built.

Gardens of the Alcázar
Laid out with terraces, fountains and pavilions, these gardens provide a delightful refuge from the heat and bustle of Seville.

★ **Charles V Rooms**
Vast tapestries and lively 16th-century *azulejos* decorate the vaulted halls of the apartments and chapel of Charles V.

Plan of the Real Alcázar

The complex has been the home of Spanish kings for almost seven centuries. The palace's upper floor is used by the royal family today.

Key

▢ Area illustrated above

▢ Gardens

★ **Patio de las Doncellas**
The Patio of the Maidens boasts plasterwork by the top craftsmen of Granada.

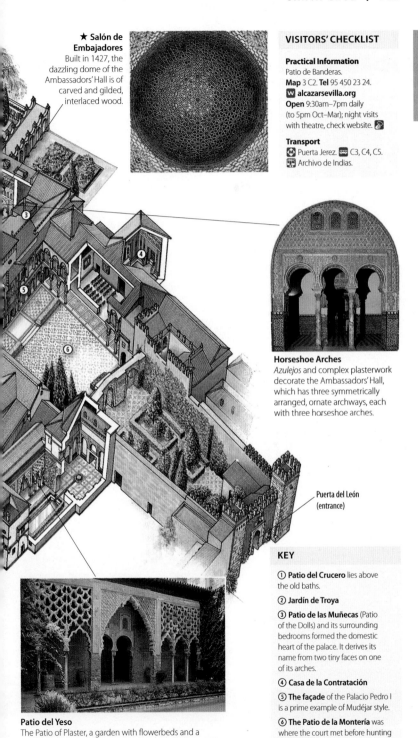

★ Salón de Embajadores
Built in 1427, the dazzling dome of the Ambassadors' Hall is of carved and gilded, interlaced wood.

VISITORS' CHECKLIST

Practical Information
Patio de Banderas.
Map 3 C2. **Tel** 95 450 23 24.
[W] alcazarsevilla.org
Open 9:30am–7pm daily
(to 5pm Oct–Mar); night visits
with theatre, check website.

Transport
Puerta Jerez. C3, C4, C5.
Archivo de Indias.

Horseshoe Arches
Azulejos and complex plasterwork decorate the Ambassadors' Hall, which has three symmetrically arranged, ornate archways, each with three horseshoe arches.

Puerta del León
(entrance)

KEY

① **Patio del Crucero** lies above the old baths.

② **Jardín de Troya**

③ **Patio de las Muñecas** (Patio of the Dolls) and its surrounding bedrooms formed the domestic heart of the palace. It derives its name from two tiny faces on one of its arches.

④ **Casa de la Contratación**

⑤ **The façade** of the Palacio Pedro I is a prime example of Mudéjar style.

⑥ **The Patio de la Montería** was where the court met before hunting expeditions.

Patio del Yeso
The Patio of Plaster, a garden with flowerbeds and a water channel, retains features of the earlier, 12th-century Almohad Alcázar.

FURTHER AFIELD

The north of Seville, La Macarena, is a characterful mix of decaying Baroque and Mudéjar churches, and old-style tapas bars. The place to visit here is the Basílica de la Macarena, a shrine to Seville's much-venerated Virgen de la Esperanza Macarena. Among the many convents and churches in the area, the Convento de Santa Paula offers a rare opportunity to peep behind the walls of an enclosed community.

The area south of the city is dominated by the extensive, leafy Parque María Luisa. A large part of the park originally formed the grounds of the Baroque Palacio de San Telmo. Many of the historic buildings in the park were erected for the Ibero-American Exposition of 1929. The grand five-star Hotel Alfonso XIII and the crescent-shaped Plaza de España are the most striking legacies of this upsurge of Andalusian pride. Nearby is the Royal Tobacco Factory, forever associated with the fictional gypsy heroine Carmen, who toiled in its sultry halls. Today, it is part of the Universidad, Seville's university. There is more to see across the river from the city centre. With its cobbled streets and shops selling ceramics, the Triana quarter retains the feel of old Seville. In the 15th century a Carthusian monastery, the Monasterio de Santa María de las Cuevas, was built north of Triana. Columbus resided there and the area around it, the Isla de la Cartuja, was chosen as the site for Expo '92. Today the site is home mainly to offices but the Isla Mágica amusement park and Teatro Central are also located here.

Sights at a Glance

Churches and Convents
❶ Basílica de la Macarena
❷ Convento de Santa Paula
❸ Iglesia de San Pedro

Historic Buildings
❺ Palacio de San Telmo
❻ Universidad
❿ Cámara Oscura, Torre de Los Perdigones

Historic Areas
❹ Metropol Parasol
❼ Parque María Luisa
❽ Triana
❾ Isla de la Cartuja

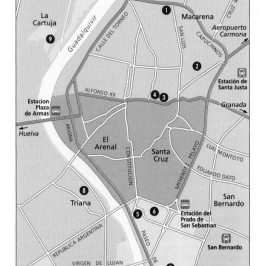

Key
▦ City centre
▢ Parks and open spaces
▭ Major road
═══ Minor road

St John the Baptist by Montañés in the Convento de Santa Paula

❶ Basílica de la Macarena

Calle Bécquer 1. **Map** 2 D3. **Tel** 95 437 01 95. 🚌 C1, C2, C3, C4, C5, 2, 10, 13, 14. **Open** 9:30am–1:30pm, 5–8:30pm daily. **Closed** Easter Fri. 🏛 for museum.

The Basílica de la Macarena was built in 1949 in the Neo-Baroque style by Gómez Millán as a new home for the much-loved Virgen de la Esperanza Macarena. It butts on to the 13th-century Iglesia de San Gil, where the image was housed until a fire in 1936.

The image of the Virgin, standing above the main altar amid waterfalls of gold and silver, has been attributed to Luisa Roldán (1656–1703), the most talented female artist of the Seville School. The wall-paintings, by Rafael Rodríguez Hernández, date from 1982.

The Virgin's magnificent processional gowns and jewels are held in the Treasury museum.

❷ Convento de Santa Paula

C/ Santa Paula 11. **Map** 2 E5. **Tel** 95 453 63 30. 🚌 C1, C2, C3, C4, C5, 10, 11. **Open** 10:30am–12:30pm Tue–Sun. 🏛 📷

Founded in 1475, Santa Paula is a working convent and home to 40 nuns. The museum consists of two galleries filled with religious artifacts and paintings.

The nave of the convent church has an elaborate wooden roof, dating from 1623. Among the statues in the church are St John the Evangelist and St John the Baptist, both the work of Juan Martínez Montañés.

❸ Iglesia de San Pedro

Plaza San Pedro. **Map** 2 D5. **Tel** 954 21 68 58. 🚌 10, 11, 12, 15, 16, 20, 24, 27, 32, C5. **Open** 9am, 11am & 8pm Mon–Sat, 10am, 11am, noon, 1pm Sun. 🏛

Diego Velázquez, the Golden Age painter *(see p36)*, was baptized in this church in 1599. It is built in a typically Sevillian mix of architectural styles. Mudéjar elements survive in the lobed brickwork of its tower, which is surmounted by a Baroque *(see p29)* belfry. The principal portal – facing the Plaza de San Pedro – is also Baroque, and was added by Diego de Quesada in 1613.

The poorly lit interior has a Mudéjar wooden ceiling. The vault of one of its chapels is decorated with exquisite geometric patterns of bricks.

Behind the church, in Calle Doña María Coronel, cakes are sold from a revolving drum in the wall of the 14th-century Convento de Santa Inés.

❹ Metropol Parasol

Plaza de la Encarnación. **Map** 2 D5. 🚌 C5, 10, 11, 12, 15, 16, 20, 24, 27, 32. Observation deck & walkways: **Tel** 95 456 15 12. **Open** 10am–11pm Sun–Thu, 10am–11:30pm Fri & Sat. 🏛 Museum: **Tel** 955 47 15 80. **Open** 10am–7:30pm Tue–Sat, 10am–1:30pm Sun & public hols. 🏛 ♿ 🌐 **setasdesevilla.com**

Referred to as *"Las Setas"* ("The Mushrooms") by locals, this ultramodern structure, designed by architect Jürgen Mayer H, opened in 2011. Its stunning latticed timber canopy spans the Plaza de la Encarnación on giant pillars. The complex includes an archaeological museum, a market and several bars and restaurants. An observation deck offers fabulous city views.

❺ Palacio de San Telmo

Avenida de Roma. **Map** 3 C3. **Tel** 955 00 10 10. 🚇 🚋 Puerta de Jerez. 🚌 C3, C4, C5, 3, 5, 6, 41. 🕐 Thu, Sat & Sun by appt. ♿ 📷

This imposing palace, named after the patron saint of navigators, was built in 1682 as a university to train ships' pilots, navigators and high-ranking officers. In 1849 it became the residence of the Dukes of Monpensier and until 1893 its grounds included what is now Parque María Luisa. Today it is the presidential headquarters of the Junta de Andalucía (the regional government).

❼ Parque María Luisa

Map 4 D4. 🚇 🚋 Prado de San Sebastián. 7 Museo Arqueológico: **Tel** 955 12 06 32. **Open** 9am–7:30pm Tue–Sat (9am–3:30pm Jun–mid-Sep), 9am–3:30pm Sun. **Closed** 1 & 6 Jan, 1 May, 24, 25 & 31 Dec. 🏛 (free for EU citizens). 🏛 Museo de Artes y Costumbres Populares: **Tel** 955 54 29 51. **Open** as above. 🏛 📷 ♿

Princess Maria Luisa donated part of the grounds of the Palacio de San Telmo to the city for this park in 1893. Landscaped by Jean

Plaza de España was built in a theatrical style by Aníbal González.

The Glorieta de Bécquer is an arbour with sculpted figures depicting the phases of love – a tribute to poet Gustavo Adolfo Bécquer.

The most striking feature of the Palacio de San Telmo is the exuberant Churrigueresque portal designed by Leonardo de Figueroa, and completed in 1734. Surrounding the Ionic columns are allegorical figures representing the Sciences and Arts. St Telmo, holding a ship and charts, is flanked by the sword-bearing St Ferdinand and St Hermenegildo, with a cross. On the north façade is ranged a row of sculptures of Sevillian celebrities, added by Susillo in 1895. Among them are artists such as Montañés, Murillo and Velázquez.

Opposite is Seville's most famous hotel, the Alfonso XIII, dating from the 1920s. Non-residents are welcome to visit the bar and the restaurant.

❻ Universidad

Calle San Fernando 4. **Map** 3 C3.
Tel 95 455 10 00. 🚇 Puerta de Jerez.
🚋 Puerta de Jerez or Prado de San Sebastian. 🚌 C1, C2, C3, C4, 5, 21, 22, 25, 26, 28, 29, 30, 31, 37, 38.
Open 8am–8:30pm Mon–Fri.
Closed public hols. 🆆 us.es

The former Real Fábrica de Tabacos (Royal Tobacco Factory) is now part of Seville University. In the 19th century, three-quarters of Europe's cigars were manufactured here, rolled by 10,000 *cigarreras* (female cigar-makers) – the inspiration for French author Mérimée's *Carmen*.

Built in 1728–71, the factory complex is the third-largest building in Spain. The moat and

Baroque fountain in one of the patios in the Universidad

watchtowers are evidence of the importance given to protecting the king's lucrative tobacco monopoly.

Forestier, director of the Bois de Boulogne in Paris, the park was the leafy setting for the 1929 Ibero-American Exposition. The legacies of this extravaganza are the Plaza de España, decorated with regional scenes on ceramic tiles, and the Plaza de América, both the work of Aníbal González. On the

latter, in the Pabellón Mudéjar, the Museo de Artes y Costumbres Populares displays traditional Andalusian folk arts. The Neo-Renaissance Pabellón de las Bellas Artes houses the provincial Museo Arqueológico. Exhibits include statues and fragments found at Itálica *(see p480)*.

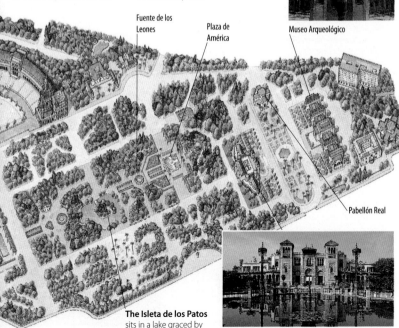

Fuente de los Leones

Plaza de América

Museo Arqueológico

Pabellón Real

The Isleta de los Patos sits in a lake graced by ducks and swans.

Museo de Artes y Costumbres Populares

Decorative tiles at Cerámica Santa Ana, a popular ceramics shop in Triana

❽ Triana

Map 3 A2. 🚇 Plaza de Cuba, Parque de los Príncipes. 🚌 C1, C2, C3.

This close-knit area, named after the Roman Emperor Trajan, was once Seville's gypsy quarter. Triana remains a traditional working-class district, with compact, flower-filled streets. For centuries it has been famous for its potteries. The best-known of its ceramics shops today is Cerámica Santa Ana at No. 31 Calle San Jorge.

A good way to approach Triana is across the Puente de Isabel II, leading to the Plaza del Altozano. The **Museo de la Inquisición**, in Castillo de San Jorge, avoids sensational images and concludes with a presentation on human rights today. Nearby is one of the characteristic streets of the area, the Calle Rodrigo de Triana, named after the Andalusian sailor who was the first to sight the shores of the New World on Columbus's voyage of 1492.

The Iglesia de Santa Ana, founded in the 13th century, is Triana's most popular church. In the baptistry is the Gypsy Font, believed to pass on the gift of flamenco song to the children of the faithful.

❾ Isla de la Cartuja

Map 1 B3. 🌐 caac.es 🚌 C1, C2. Monasterio de Santa María de las Cuevas: **Open** Tue–Sun. 🅿 ♿ Centro Andaluz de Arte Contemporáneo: **Tel** 95 503 70 70. **Open** Tue–Sun. 🅿 (free Tue for EU citizens). Isla Mágica: **Tel** 902 16 17 16. **Open** Apr: Sat & Sun; May: Thu, Sat & Sun; Jun & Jul: Tue–Sun; Aug–mid-Sep: daily; mid-Sep–Oct: Sat, Sun. **Closed** Nov–Feb. 🅿 ♿ 🌐 islamagica.es

The site of Expo '92 *(see pp72–3)*, this area has since been transformed into a sprawling complex of exhibition halls, museums and entertainment and leisure spaces.

The 15th-century Carthusian Monasterio de Santa María de las Cuevas was inhabited by monks until 1836. Columbus stayed and worked here, and it houses the Centro Andaluz de Arte Contemporáneo, which contains works by Andalusian artists, plus Spanish and international art.

The centrepiece of Expo, the Lago de España, is part of the Isla Mágica theme park. This re-creates the journeys and exploits of the explorers who left Seville in the 16th century for the New World. Isla Mágica also has a water park, the Agua Mágica.

❿ Cámara Oscura

Torre de los Perdigones, C/ Resolana. **Map** 2 D3. 🚌 C1, C2, C3, C4, C5, 2, 13, 14. **Tel** 95 490 93 53. **Open** noon–5pm Tue–Sun (closed when raining). 🅿

This huge camera obscura uses mirrors and magnifying lenses to display an image of the surrounding area. The Tower of Perdigones also offers scenic views of the city.

Main entrance of the Carthusian Monasterio de Santa María de las Cuevas, founded in 1400

For hotels and restaurants in this area see p572 and p598

SEVILLE STREET FINDER

The map references given with the sights described in the Seville section of the guide refer to the maps on the following pages. Map references are also given for Seville hotels *(see pp571–2)* and restaurants *(pp597–8)*. The schematic map below shows the area of Seville covered by the *Street Finder*. The symbols used for the sights and other features are listed in the key at the foot of the page.

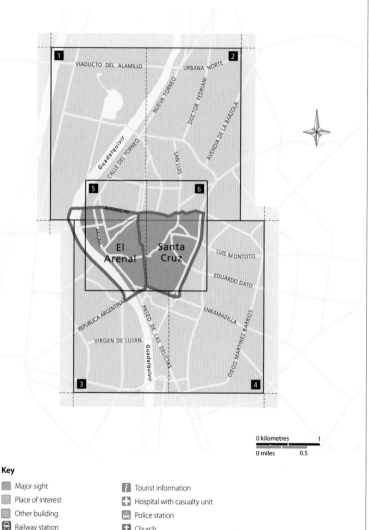

Key

- Major sight
- Place of interest
- Other building
- Railway station
- Metro station
- Tram stop
- Bus station
- River bus boarding point

- *i* Tourist information
- Hospital with casualty unit
- Police station
- Church
- Convent or monastery
- = Railway line
- Pedestrianized street

Scale of Map Pages

0 metres   250
0 yards   250

0 kilometres   1
0 miles   0.5

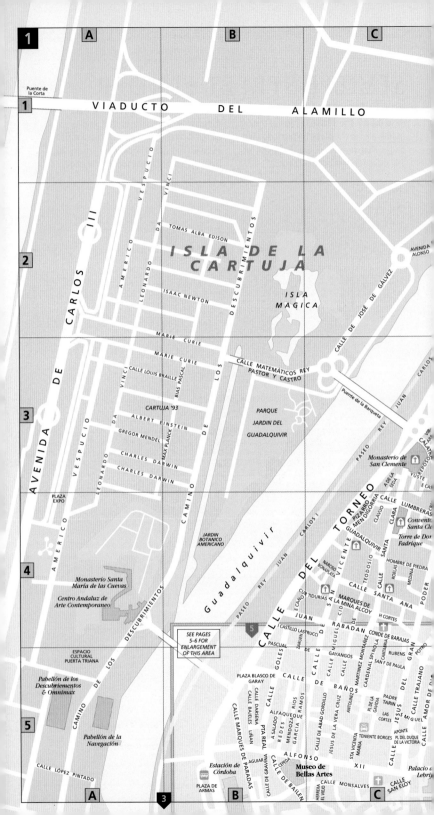

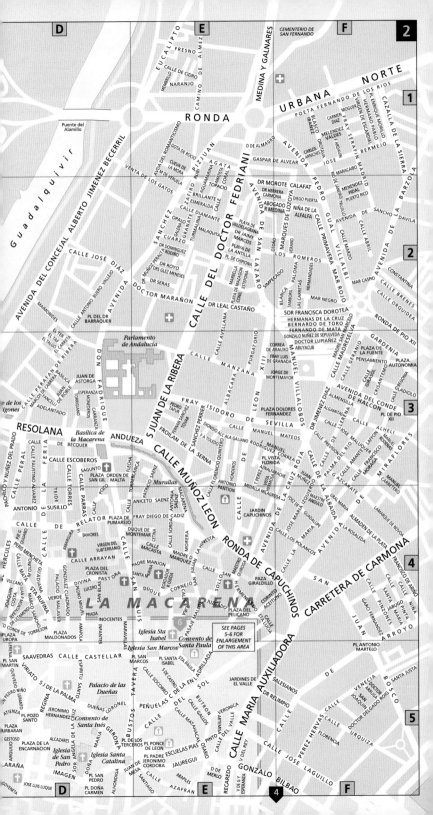

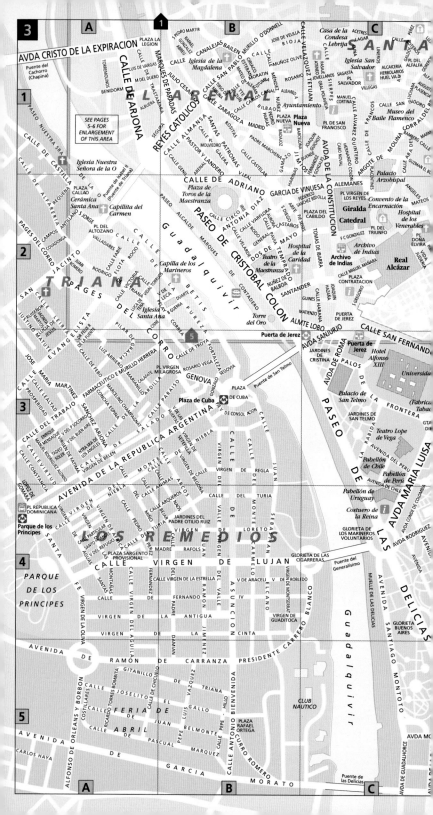

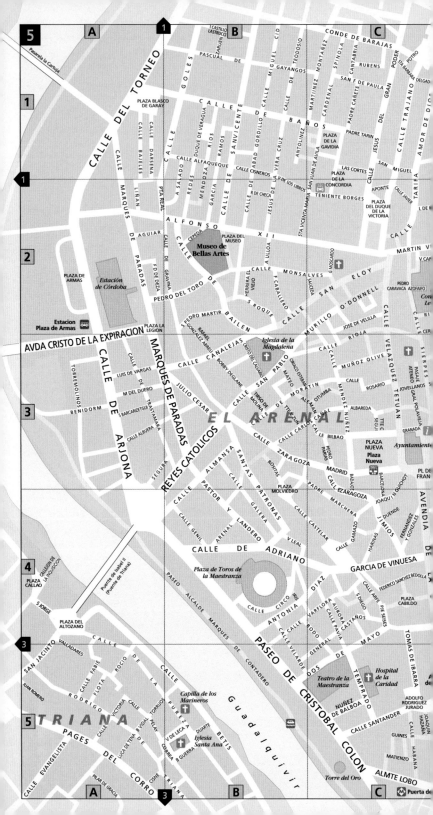

SHOPPING IN SEVILLE

The shopping experience in Seville is influenced by its culture – bustling with energy until the moment the siesta arrives, then relaxing over lunch before the frenzy begins again. Seville has a good mix of well-known chain stores and independently owned shops, and the stores in this vibrant city are as colourful and diverse as the people themselves. The main shopping district winds through Calle Tetuán and Calle Sierpes, and flows on towards Plaza Nueva and over to Plaza Alfalfa, where you will find a fantastic range of goods – anything from the latest fashions to unique Spanish arts and crafts. Yet more diverse items can be found while strolling along Amor de Dios towards Alameda de Hercules, where there are many wonderful Moroccan, Indian and African import shops to explore.

Specialist Shops

The streets of Calle Cuna, Calle Francos and Calle Lineros are lined with shops that capture the flamenco spirit. **Lina Boutique** has impeccably styled, unique dresses as well as accessories. **Calzados Mayo** sells flamenco dance shoes, while beautiful handmade shawls and intricate lace mantillas (veils) can be found at **Juan Foronda**. Handmade sombreros (hats), in addition to tasteful men's accessories, are available at **Maquedano**. For a fabulous range of leather goods and fashions, **El Caballo** is the place to shop.

To relive the spirit of Semana Santa (Easter Week), religious items can be bought at **Antigua Casa Rodríguez**. At **Poster Félix** you can find historical posters from festivals and bullfights of years gone by, and other vintage Spanish collectibles.

An array of fans at Díaz, Calle Sierpes, Seville

Department Stores and Galerias

El Corte Inglés, Spain's national department store, has two main locations in the centre – Plaza Duque de la Victoria and Plaza Magdalena. The larger building at Plaza Duque offers clothes, shoes, sporting goods, cosmetics, a gourmet shop and a supermarket; the smaller building stocks music, books and art supplies. The outlet in Plaza Magdalena sells fine china, kitchenware and appliances. It also houses a supermarket. El Corte Inglés is open Monday to Saturday until 10pm.

Plaza de Armas is the only shopping centre in the heart of town, with shops, bars, restaurants, a nightclub, cinema and a supermarket. Nervion Plaza, the largest shopping hub close to the city centre (and accessible by metro), is lined with shops, restaurants, bars, a cinema and a mall. Shopping centres are open from 10am to 10pm Monday to Saturday.

Open-Air Markets

The lively and colourful open-air markets feature a dazzling display of unique wares and are a great way to spend a leisurely morning. Distinctive accessories and clothing can be found in the markets of Plaza Duque de la Victoria and Plaza Magdalena, open all day (weather permitting) Thursday to Saturday.

The markets at Plaza Encarnación, El Arenal, Plaza del Altozano, in Triana, and Calle Fería (open mornings, Monday to Saturday) offer local produce, fish, meat and cheese, while the Thursday market at Calle Fería specializes in bric-a-brac. On Sunday mornings, stamps, coins and other collectibles are traded in Plaza del Cabildo, and the painters' market in Plaza del Museo has displays of local art.

Stylish handmade *sombreros*

Antiques and Crafts

Antique shops are scattered throughout the city centre, mainly in Barrio Santa Cruz and Alfalfa. **Antigüedades el Museo** has classic Spanish and European furnishings and art, while handmade goods can be found at **El Postigo**, an arts and crafts centre. **Sevillarte** boasts unique ceramics and functional artwork with Andalusian influences. Seville's great ceramic tradition is visible in the Triana district, which still has several operating ceramic workshops. Ceramic shops can also be found along Calle Sierpes and Calle Tetuán.

Food and Wine

To bring home some of Seville's gastronomic specialities or to prepare a nice picnic, visit **Latas y Botellas**. The gourmet shop **El Corte Inglés** has exquisite luxuries for the discerning palate, as well as an ample wine cellar. For general groceries try the supermarket downstairs. Every area has several small convenience stores. For out-of-hours shopping, **SuperCor** is open 8am–2am daily.

Fashion

The shops of Calle Tetuán and Calle Sierpes bustle with an exciting range of the latest fashions. **Luchi Cabrera** has exclusive women's clothes and accessories in a range of styles – from flamenco to formal and bridal wear. **Loewe** offers classic lines of clothing, luggage and accessories for both men and women, while **Zara** stocks all the latest high-street trends. **Adolfo Domínguez** offers high fashion for men, women and children. For unique and exotic accessories, head to the Alfalfa district, where several shops offer distinctive jewellery, handbags and other goods. **Esmeralda** has the biggest selection. For stylish baby clothes with Sevillian flair, head to **Larrana**.

The well-heeled of Seville shop at the vast array of shoe stores in the area as well as at the well-stocked "shoe street" of Calle Córdoba.

Books, Music and Souvenirs

Small bookshops are tucked into numerous corners of the city, but for the biggest selection of books in multiple

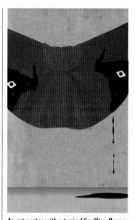
An art poster with a typical Sevillian flavour

languages, go to **Casa del Libro**. Music aficionados can find regional sounds of flamenco, Rock Andaluz and Semana Santa music, as well as international artists at **FNAC**, with its impressive collection of CDs, DVDs and books. Also, a large selection of musical instruments and equipment can be found at **Sevilla Musical**.

Typical souvenir shops are abundant along Avenida de la Constitución, Calle Mateos de Gago and all throughout Barrio Santa Cruz.

DIRECTORY

Specialist Shops

Antigua Casa Rodríguez
C/ Alcaicería de la Loza 10. **Map** 3 C1, 6 D3. **Tel** 954 21 24 27.

El Caballo
C/ Antonia Diaz 7. **Map** 3 B2, 5 B4. **Tel** 955 12 55 02.

Calzados Mayo
Pl Alfalfa 2. **Map** 3 C1, 6 D3. **Tel** 954 22 55 55.

Juan Foronda
C/ Sierpes 79. **Map** 3 C1, 5 C3. **Tel** 954 21 40 50.

Lina Boutique
C/ Lineros 17. **Map** 3 C1, 6 D3. **Tel** 954 21 24 23.

Maquedano
C/ Sierpes 40. **Map** 3 C1, 5 C3. **Tel** 954 56 47 71.

Poster Félix
Avda de la Constitución 26. **Map** 3 C2. **Tel** 954 218 026.

Department Stores and Galerias

El Corte Inglés
Pl Duque de la Victoria 8, 13B. **Map** 1 C5, 5 C2. **Tel** 954 59 70 00. *One of several branches.*

Antiques and Crafts

Antigüedades el Museo
Plaza del Museo 4. **Map** 1 C5, 5 B2. **Tel** 954 56 01 28.

El Postigo
C/ Arfe s/n. **Map** 3 B2, 5 C4. **Tel** 954 56 00 13.

Sevillarte
C/ Sierpes 66. **Map** 3 C1, 5 C3. **Tel** 954 21 28 36

Food and Wine

Latas y Botellas
Calle Regina 15. **Map** 2 D5, 6 D1. **Tel** 954 29 31 22.

SuperCor
Avda Carlos V, 16. **Map** 4 D3.

Fashion

Adolfo Domínguez
C/ Cuna 30 & Cerrajeria 2 (corner). **Map** 1 C5, 6 D2. **Tel** 608 11 08 90.

Esmeralda
C/ Alcaicería de la Loza 26. **Map** 3 C1, 6 D3. **Tel** 954 22 55 11.

Larrana
C/ Blanca de los Rios 4. **Map** 3 C1, 6 D3. **Tel** 954 21 55 28.

Loewe
Pl Nueva 12. **Map** 3 B1, 5 C3. **Tel** 954 22 52 53.

Luchi Cabrera
Pl El Salvador s/n. **Map** 3 C1, 6 D3. **Tel** 954 22 39 76.

Zara
C/ Rioja 10. **Map** 3 B1, 5 C2. **Tel** 954 21 10 58.

Books, Music and Souvenirs

Casa del Libro
C/ Velázquez Tetuan 8. **Map** 3 C1, 5 C3. **Tel** 902 02 64 10.

FNAC
Avda de la Constitución 8. **Map** 3 C1, 5 C4. **Tel** 902 10 06 32.

Sevilla Musical
C/ Cardinal Spinola 3. **Map** 1 C5, 5 C1 **Tel** 954 91 57 55.

ENTERTAINMENT IN SEVILLE

Seville is universally famed as being a city of celebration and vitality, and this is reflected in its two spring festivals, Semana Santa and Feria de Abril *(see p435)*. In fact, the city has a year-round programme of interesting cultural events. The modern Teatro de la Maestranza and Teatro Lope de Vega, along with a number of independent venues, host a range of dance, music, theatre and arts festivals, while the world's most important flamenco festival, the Bienal de Flamenco, takes place in the city. Seville also has an enviable selection of night spots, from the quiet, more relaxed area surrounding the cathedral to the buzzing bars of Calle Betis and the Alfalfa district. For sports fans, a local derby between Real Betis and Sevilla FC is an absolute must-see.

Decorative tile commemorating Seville's Real Betis football club

Seasons and Tickets

In Seville, the arts season usually starts in September, lasting until June–July. From April to the end of the summer, the streets and open-air stages also host shows.

Two of the city's biggest events – the Bienal de Flamenco and the Bienal de Arte Contemporáneo – are biannual and take place in the autumn in even-numbered years.

Tickets for major sports events, opera, concerts and festivals should be booked in advance – details can be provided by the city's tourist information offices. Football matches are very popular, so buy these in advance too.

Entertainment Guides

A monthly events guide, *El Giraldillo* (www.giraldillo.es) covers film, music, theatre, clubs, art, sport, books, gay life, travel and much more. *La Teatral*, a bimonthly publication, focuses on theatre and dance.

Flamenco

Flamenco embraces a broad range of dancing, singing and musical styles. One venue with high-quality performances is **Los Gallos**. For something really authentic, go to **La Anselma** in the Triana quarter – the traditional home of the gypsy community. **La Carbonería** is an informal bar where free flamenco shows are often performed by amateur artists.

Promoting semi-professional local artists, **Casa de la Memoria** in the Santa Cruz district presents varied shows daily. As the venue is quite small, it is recommended you buy tickets in advance, and show up early to get a seat. In Calle Betis, there are bars where the public can watch and join in with *sevillanas*, a popular Andalusian folk dance.

The **Museo del Baile Flamenco** is a good place to learn about the origins of the dance and current developments, as well as see performances.

Music and Dance

The setting of Bizet's *Carmen*, Rossini's *The Barber of Seville* and Mozart's *Don Giovanni* and *Figaro*, Seville is a city of opera lovers. Enjoy an opera-and-dinner show at **Sevilla de Opera**. International opera companies perform at the elegant **Teatro de la Maestranza** starting in December and lasting until May. This theatre is home to the Real Orquesta Sinfónica de Sevilla, whose performances are highly regarded. The annual programme of the theatre also includes chamber and classical music seasons. **Teatro Lope de Vega** and **Conservatorio Superior de Música Manuel Castillo** are

A live performance of flamenco at Los Gallos

Rosario Flores, the famous Andalusian singing star, performing at one of her concerts

two other remarkable venues for classical music.

The Maestranza and **Teatro Central** are the main venues hosting a wide range of national and international classical and contemporary dance performances.

Rock, Jazz and Blues

Few international rock stars make it to Seville, as Barcelona and Madrid tend to attract all the big names. However, large concerts are sometimes held at **Estadio Olímpico**. Some of Spain's most popular groups and singers in the flamenco pop genre, such as Niña Pastori and Rosario Flores, are from Andalusia. **Café Naima**

and **Sala Malandar Luxuria**, have live music from local bands, including jazz, folk and rock, but the highlight of the jazz calendar in Seville has to be the International Jazz Festival, held in November at the Teatro Central.

Nightlife

The nightlife of Seville offers an endless array of possibilities. Calle Betis, along the Triana side of the river, has many bars, restaurants and clubs. Alameda de Hércules is one of the liveliest areas, with **Café Habanilla** and **Café Central** as main bohemian hotspots. **Las Columnas** is the most popular tapas bar in Barrio de Santa Cruz district and **Bar Garlochi** is recommended for the first drink of the night. **La Terraza** at Eme Catedral Hotel is *the* place to see and be seen at (booking essential). The streets around Plaza de la Alfalfa overflow with youthful revellers.

Frequented by Spanish celebrities, **Antique** in Isla de la Cartuja is the place to dance till dawn. In summer, their outdoor terrace boasts two pools and fashion shows.

Bullfighting

The Maestranza Bullring *(see p434)* is mythical among fans of bullfighting. Some of the most important bullfights in Spain are held here during the Feria de Abril. The season runs from April to October. It is advisable to book in advance if the matadors are famous, and also if you want a seat in the *sombra* (shade). Tickets are sold at the *taquilla* (box office) at the bullring.

Amusement Parks

Isla Mágica re-creates the exploits of 16th-century New World explorers. The eight zones which visitors experience are Sevilla – Puerto de Indias, Mundo Maya, Puerta de América, Amazonia, La Guarida de los Piratas, La Fuente de Juventud, ElDorado and La Metrópolis de España. Fun for children of all ages.

DIRECTORY

Flamenco

La Anselma
C/ Pages del Corro 49.
Map 3 A2, 5 A5.

La Carbonería
C/ Levíes 18. **Map** 4 D1,
6 E3. **Tel** 954 56 37 49.

Casa de la Memoria
C/ Cuna 6. **Map** 3 C1,
6 D2. **Tel** 954 56 06 70.
W casadelamemoria.es

Los Gallos
Pl Santa Cruz 11.
Map 4 D2, 6 E4.
Tel 954 21 69 81.
W tablaolosgallos.com

Museo del Baile Flamenco
C/ Manuel Rojas Marcos 3.
Map 3 C1, 6 D3. **Tel** 954
34 03 11. W museodel
baileflamenco.com

Music and Dance

Conservatorio Superior de Música Manuel Castillo
C/ Baños 48. **Map** 1 C5,
5 B1. **Tel** 677 90 37 62.

Seville de Opera
Mercado del Arenal, Pastor y Landero, 8. **Map** 3 B1,
5 B4. **Tel** 955 29 46 61.
W sevilladeopera.com

Teatro Central
Av José Gálvez s/n, Isla de la Cartuja. **Map** 1 C2.
Tel 955 54 21 55.

Teatro de la Maestranza
Paseo de Colón 22. **Map** 3
B2, 5 C5. **Tel** 954 22 33 44.

Teatro Lope de Vega
Av María Luisa s/n.
Map 3 C3. **Tel** 955 47
28 22.

Rock, Jazz and Blues

Café Naima
C/ Trajano 47. **Map** 1 C5,
5 C1. **Tel** 954 38 24 85.

Estadio Olímpico
Isla de la Cartuja, s/n.
Map 1 B1. **Tel** 954 48 94 00.
W eosevilla.com

Sala Malandar Luxuria
Avda Torneo 43. **Map** 1 B4.
Tel 954 37 01 88.

Nightlife

Antique
Matemáticos Rey Pastor y Castro s/n. **Map** 1 B3.
Tel 954 46 22 07.

Bar Garlochi
C/ Boteros 26.
Map 3 C1, 6 E3.

Café Central
Pl Alameda de Hércules 64. **Map** 2 D4.
Tel 645 77 01 32.

Café Habanilla
Pl Alameda de Hércules 63. **Map** 2 D4.
Tel 954 90 27 18.

Las Columnas
C/ Rodrigo Caro 1.
Map 3 C2, 6 E4.

La Terraza
Eme Catedral Hotel,
C/ Alemanes 27.
Map 3 C2, 6 D4.
Tel 954 56 00 00.

Amusement Parks

Isla Mágica
Pabellón de España, Isla de la Cartuja. **Map** 1 C3.
Tel 902 16 17 16.
W islamagica.es

ANDALUSIA

*Huelva · Cádiz · Málaga · Gibraltar · Sevilla
Córdoba · Granada · Almería · Jaén*

Andalusia is where all Spain's stereotypes meet.
Bullfighters, beaches, flamenco, white villages, cave
houses, gaudy fiestas, religious processions, tapas and
sherry are all here in abundance. But each is part of a larger
whole, which includes great art and architecture, nature
reserves and an easy-going way of life.

The eight provinces of Andalusia stretch across Southern Spain from the deserts of Almería to the Portuguese border. One of Spain's longest rivers, the Guadalquivir, bisects the region. Andalusia is linked to the central tableland by a pass, the Desfiladero de Despeñaperros. The highest peaks on the Spanish mainland are in Andalusia's Sierra Nevada.

Successive invaders left their mark on Andalusia. The Romans built cities in this southern province, which they called Baetica, among them Córdoba, its capital, and the well-preserved Itálica near Seville. It was in Andalusia that the Moors lingered longest and left their greatest buildings – Córdoba's Mezquita and the splendid palace of the Alhambra in

Granada. Inevitably, perhaps, the most visited places are the great cities and the busy Costa del Sol, with Gibraltar, a geographical and historical oddity, at its western end. But there are many attractions tucked into other corners of the region. Many of the sights of Huelva province, bordering Portugal, are associated with Christopher Columbus, who set sail from here in 1492. Film directors have put to good use the atmospheric landscapes of Almería's arid interior, which are reminiscent of the Wild West or Arabia. Discreetly concealed among the countless olive groves that cover Jaén province, but not to be missed, are Andalusia's two lovely Renaissance towns, Úbeda and Baeza.

The city of Jaén surrounded by olive groves, seen from the Castillo de Santa Catalina

◄ Pedestrians strolling on the seaside promenade in Marbella, Costa del Sol

Exploring Andalusia

Andalusia is Spain's most varied region. It offers dramatic desert scenery at Tabernas, water sports on the Costa del Sol, skiing in the Sierra Nevada and sherry tasting in Jerez. Of the many nature reserves, the vast, watery Doñana teems with birdlife, while Cazorla is a rugged limestone massif. Granada and Córdoba are unmissable for their Moorish heritage; Úbeda and Baeza are Renaissance gems; and Ronda is one of dozens of superb white towns.

Key

═══ Motorway

▬▬▬ Major road

═══ Secondary road

─── Scenic route

═╪═ Main railway

─── Minor railway

▬▬▬ International border

─── Regional border

△ Summit

The smart marina at Sotogrande

For additional map symbols *see back flap*

0 kilometres   25

0 miles   25

Getting Around

Andalusia has a modern motorway network, with the principal NIV A4 (E5) from Madrid following the Guadalquivir Valley to Córdoba, Seville and Cádiz. The fast AVE train links Málaga, Seville and Córdoba with Madrid. Coaches cover most of the region. The main airports are Málaga, Seville, Jerez and Gibraltar.

Singers in festive spirit at a
village christening

Sights at a Glance

1. Sierra de Aracena
2. Huelva
3. Monasterio de la Rábida
4. Palos de la Frontera
5. El Rocío
6. *Parque Nacional de Doñana pp468–9*
7. Sanlúcar de Barrameda
8. Jerez de la Frontera
9. Cádiz
10. Costa de la Luz
11. Arcos de la Frontera
13. *Ronda pp474–5*
14. Algeciras
15. Gibraltar
18. Garganta del Chorro
19. El Torcal
20. Antequera

21. Osuna
22. Carmona
23. Itálica
24. Sierra Morena
25. Palma del Río
26. Écija
27. Medina Azahara
28. *Córdoba pp482–5*
29. Montilla
32. Nerja
34. Lanjarón
35. Las Alpujarras
36. Laujar de Andarax
37. Sierra Nevada
38. *Granada pp490–96*
39. La Calahorra
46. Vélez Blanco
48. Tabernas

49. Almería
50. Parque Natural de Cabo de Gata
Seville see pp430–61

Tours

12. Pueblos Blancos
16. Marbella
17. Málaga
30. Priego de Córdoba
31. Montefrío
33. Almuñécar
40. Guadix
41. Jaén
42. Andújar
43. *Baeza pp502–3*
44. Úbeda
45. Parque Natural de Cazorla
47. Mojácar

The famed *jamón ibérico* hanging in a bar in Jabugo, Sierra de Aracena

❶ Sierra de Aracena

Huelva. 🚉 El Repilado. 🚌 Aracena.
ℹ C/ Pozo de la Nieve s/n, Aracena,
663 93 78 76. 📅 Sat.

This wild mountain range is one of the most remote and least visited corners of Andalusia. On the hillside are the ruins of a Moorish fort. The hill is pitted with caverns and in one, the **Gruta de las Maravillas**, is a lake in a chamber hung with many stalactites.

The village of **Jabugo** is famed for its ham, *jamón ibérico*, or *pata negra (see p422)*.

Off the A471 are the giant opencast mines at Minas de Riotinto, where iron, copper and silver have been exploited since Phoenician times. The **Museo Minero** traces the history of the Rio Tinto Company.

🍴 Gruta de las Maravillas
Pozo de la Nieve. **Tel** 663 93 78 76
(for info about availability). **Open**
10am–1:30pm, 3–6pm. 🎫 🎫

🏛 Museo Minero
Plaza del Museo. **Tel** 959 59 00 25.
Open daily. **Closed** 1 & 6 Jan, 25 Dec.
🎫 ♿ 🎫 **W** parqueminero
deriotinto.es

❷ Huelva

Huelva. 🔺 130,000. 🚉 🚌 **ℹ** Calle
Jesús Nazareno 21, 959 65 02 00.
📅 Fri. 🎭 Las Columbinas (3 Aug).

Founded as Onuba by the Phoenicians, Huelva had its grandest days as a Roman port. It was almost wiped out in the great Lisbon earthquake of 1755. It is an industrial city today, sprawling around the quayside on the Río Odiel.

Columbus's departure for the New World *(see p60)* from Palos de la Frontera, across the Río Odiel estuary, is celebrated in the excellent **Museo Provincial**, which also charts the history of the Rio Tinto mines. To the east of the centre, the Barrio Reina Victoria is a bizarre example of English mock-Tudor suburban bungalows built by the Rio Tinto Company for its workers in the early 20th century. South of the town, at Punta del Sebo, the Monumento a Colón, a rather bleak statue of Columbus created by Gertrude Vanderbilt Whitney in 1929, dominates the Odiel estuary.

Bronze jug, Museo Provincial, Huelva

Environs
There are three resorts with sandy beaches near Huelva: **Punta Umbría**, on a promontory next to the bird-rich wetlands of the Marismas del Odiel; **Isla Cristina**, an important fishing port with excellent seafood restaurants; and **Mazagón** with miles of windswept dunes.

The hilly region east of Huelva known as **El Condado** produces many of Andalusia's finest wines, and Bollullos del Condado has the largest wine cooperative in the region. **Niebla**, nearby, has a Roman bridge. The town walls and 12th-century **Castillo de los Guzmanes** are both Moorish.

🏛 Museo Provincial
Alameda Sundheim 13. **Tel** 959 65
04 24. **Open** Tue–Sun. ♿

🏰 Castillo de los Guzmanes
C/ Campo Castillo, Niebla.
Tel 959 36 22 70. **Open** daily.

❸ Monasterio de la Rábida

Huelva. 🚌 from Huelva. **Tel** 959 35
04 11. **Open** Tue–Sun. ♿ 🎫 🎫

Four kilometres (2 miles) to the north of Palos de la Frontera is the Franciscan **Monasterio de la Rábida**, founded in the 15th century.

In 1491, a dejected Columbus sought refuge here after his plans to sail west to find the East Indies had been rejected by the Catholic Monarchs. Its prior, Juan Pérez, fatefully used his considerable influence as Queen Isabella's confessor to reverse the royal decision.

Inside, frescoes painted by Daniel Vásquez Díaz in 1930 glorify the explorer's life and discoveries. Also worth seeing are the Mudéjar cloisters, the flower-filled gardens and the beamed chapterhouse.

Frescoes depicting the life of Columbus at the Monasterio de la Rábida

❹ Palos de la Frontera

Huelva. 🏠 12,000. 🚌 ℹ️ Parque Botánico José Celestino Mutis Paraje de la Rábida, 959 35 03 11. 🏖️ Sat. 🎭 Santa María de la Rábida (3 & 16 Aug).

Columbus put to sea on 3 August 1492 from Palos, the home town of his two captains, the brothers Martín and Vicente Pinzón. Martín's former home, the **Casa Museo de Martín Alonso Pinzón**, is now a small museum of exploration, and his statue stands in the main square.

The 15th-century **Iglesia de San Jorge** has a fine portal, through which Columbus left after hearing Mass before boarding the *Santa María*. The pier is now silted up.

Environs

In the beautiful white town of **Moguer** are treasures such as the 16th-century hermitage of Nuestra Señora de Monte-mayor, and the Neo-Classical town hall. The **Monasterio de Santa Clara** houses the Museo Diocesano de Arte Sacro and has a pretty cloister.

🏛️ **Casa Museo de Martín Alonso Pinzón**
Calle Colón 24. **Tel** 959 10 00 41.
Open Mon–Fri.

🏛️ **Monasterio de Santa Clara**
Plaza de las Monjas. **Tel** 959 37 01 07.
Open Tue–Sun am. **Closed** public hols. 🎭 🎫

❺ El Rocío

Huelva. 🏠 2,500. 🚌 ℹ️ Avda de la Canaliega, 959 02 66 02. 🎭 Romería (May/Jun).

Bordering the Parque Nacional de Doñana (*see pp468–9*), El Rocío is famous for its annual *romería*, which sees almost a million people converge on the village. Many of the pilgrims travel from distant parts of Spain, some on gaudily decorated oxcarts, to visit the **Iglesia de Nuestra Señora del Rocío**. A statue of the Virgin in the church is believed to have performed miraculous healings since 1280. Early on the Monday morning of the festival, men from Almonte fight to carry the statue in procession, and the crowd clambers onto the float to touch the image.

Crowds following the image of the Virgin at El Rocío

Andalusia's Fiestas

Carnival (*Feb/Mar*), Cádiz. The whole city puts on fancy dress for one of Europe's largest and most colourful carnivals. Groups of singers practise for many months to perform ditties satirizing current fashions, celebrities and politicians.
Romería de la Virgen de la Cabeza (*last Sun in Apr*), Andújar (Jaén). A mass pilgrimage to a lonely sanctuary in the Sierra Morena.
Día de la Cruz (*first week in May*), Granada and Córdoba. Neighbourhood groups compete to create the most colourful crosses adorned with flowers on squares and street corners.
Córdoba Patio Fiesta (*mid-May*). Flower-decked patios in old Córdoba are opened to the public with displays of flamenco.
El Rocío (*May/Jun*). More than 70 brotherhoods of pilgrims arrive at the village of El Rocío to pay homage to the Virgen del Rocío.
Columbus Festival (*late Jul/early Aug*), Huelva. This celebration of Columbus's voyage is dedicated to the native music and dance of a different Latin American country every year.
Exaltación al Río Guadalquivir (*mid-Aug*), Sanlúcar de Barrameda (Cádiz). Horses are raced on the beach at the mouth of the Río Guadalquivir.

Iglesia de Nuestra Señora del Rocío, El Rocío

❻ Parque Nacional de Doñana

Doñana National Park is ranked among Europe's greatest wetlands. Together with its adjoining protected areas, the park covers in excess of 500 sq km (193 sq miles) of marshes and sand dunes. The area used to be a hunting ground *(coto)* belonging to the Dukes of Medina Sidonia. As the land was never suitable for human settlers, wildlife was able to flourish. In 1969, this large area became officially protected. In addition to a wealth of endemic species, thousands of migratory birds stop over in winter when the marshes become flooded again, after months of drought.

Shrub Vegetation
Backing the sand dunes is a thick carpet of lavender, rock rose and other low shrubs.

Prickly Juniper
This species of juniper *(Juniperus oxycedrus)* thrives in the wide dune belt, putting roots deep into the sand. The trees may get buried beneath the dunes.

Palacio del Acebrón

El Rocío

La Rocina

El Acebuche

Matalascañas

Palacio de Doñana

Laguna de Santa Olaya

Coastal Dunes
Softly rounded, white dunes, up to 30 m (100 ft) high, fringe the park's coastal edge. The dunes, ribbed by prevailing winds off the Atlantic, shift constantly.

Monte de Doñana, the wooded area behind the sand dunes, provides shelter for lynx, deer and boar.

The Interior
The number of visitors to the park's interior is strictly controlled to ensure minimal environmental impact. The only way to view the wildlife here is on officially guided day tours.

Key

    Marshes

    Dunes

••• Parque Nacional de Doñana

••• Parque Natural de Doñana

▬ Road

Deer
Fallow deer *(Dama dama)* and larger red deer *(Cervus elaphus)* roam the park. Stags engage in fierce contests in late summer as they prepare for breeding.

Wild cattle use the marshes as waterholes.

VISITORS' CHECKLIST

Practical Information
Huelva & Sevilla.
🌐 discoveringdonana.com
Marginal areas: **Open** daily.
Closed 1 & 6 Jan, Pentecost,
25 Dec. 🅸 La Rocina: **Tel** 959 43
95 69. 🅸 Palacio del Acebrón:
exhibition "Man and Doñana".
🅸 El Acebuche: reception,
exhibition, café & shop. **Tel** 959
50 61 22. Self-guided paths:
La Rocina & Charco de la Boca
(3.5 km); El Acebrón from Palacio
del Acebrón (1.5 km); Laguna
del Acebuche from Acebuche
(1.5 km). Inner park areas:
Open May–mid-Sep: Mon–Sat;
mid-Sep–Apr: Tue–Sun.
Guided tour only. Jeeps leave
El Acebuche at 8am & 3pm
(7pm in summer). Bookings
Tel 959 43 96 29. 🅿

Imperial Eagle
The imperial eagle *(Aquila adalberti)* is one of Doñana's rarest birds.

Río Guadiamar

José Antonio Valverde

Marisma de Iznalcázar

Marisma Gallega

Greater Flamingo
During the winter months, the salty lakes and marshes provide the beautiful, pink greater flamingo *(Phoenicopterus ruber)* with crustaceans, its main diet.

Río Guadalquivir

Sanlúcar de Barrameda

Fábrica de Hielo

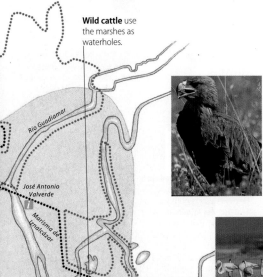

The Lynx's Last Refuge

The lynx is one of Europe's rarest mammals. In Doñana about 30 individual Spanish lynx *(Lynx pardellus)* have found a refuge. They have yellow-brown fur with dark brown spots and pointed ears with black tufts. Research is under way into this shy, nocturnal animal, which tends to stay hidden in scrub. It feeds mainly on rabbits and ducks, but might catch an unguarded fawn.

The elusive lynx, only glimpsed with patience

0 kilometres 5
0 miles 5

For additional map symbols *see back flap*

❼ Sanlúcar de Barrameda

Cádiz. 🚹 63,000. 🚌 ℹ️ Calzada del Ejército, 956 38 80 01. 🚍 Wed. 🎉 Exaltación al Río Guadalquivir and horse races (mid-Aug).

A fishing port at the mouth of the Río Guadalquivir, Sanlúcar is overlooked by a Moorish **castle**. This was the departure point for Columbus's third voyage in 1498 and also for Magellan's 1519 expedition to circumnavigate the globe.

Sanlúcar is best known for its light, dry manzanilla sherry made by, among other producers, **Bodegas Barbadillo**. Boats from the quay take visitors across the river to the Parque Nacional de Doñana (see pp468–9).

Environs
Chipiona, along the coast, is a lively little resort town with an excellent beach. The walled town of **Lebrija**, inland, enjoys views over vineyards. Its Iglesia de Santa María de la Oliva is a reconsecrated 12th-century Almohad mosque.

🏠 Bodegas Barbadillo
C/ Luis de Eguilaz 11. **Tel** 956 38 55 00. **Open** Tue–Sat. 🅿️ 🚻 ♿

Entrance to the Barbadillo bodega in Sanlúcar de Barrameda

❽ Jerez de la Frontera

Cádiz. 🚹 190,000. ✈️ 🚇 🚌 ℹ️ Plaza del Arenal s/n, Edificio Los Arcos, 956 33 88 74. 🚍 Mon. 🎉 Grape Harvest (Sep).

Jerez is the capital of sherry production (see pp424–5) and many bodegas can be visited. Among the well-known are **Pedro Domecq** and **González Byass**.

The city is also famous for its **Real Escuela Andaluza de Arte Ecuestre**, an equestrian school with public displays on Tuesdays and Thursdays. On other days you may be able to watch the horses being trained. The **Palacio del Tiempo**, nearby, has one of the largest clock collections in Europe. On the Plaza de San Juan, the 18th-century **Palacio de Penmartín** houses the Centro Andaluz de Flamenco, where exhibitions give a good introduction to this music and dance tradition (see pp428–9). The partially restored, 11th-century **Alcázar** encompasses a well-preserved mosque, now a church. Just to the north is the **cathedral**.

Environs
Not far from Jerez, the **Monasterio de la Cartuja Santa María de la Defensión** is considered one of the most beautiful in Spain. The port of **El Puerto de Santa María** has several bodegas that can be visited, including **Osborne**. The town also has a 13th-century castle and a large bullring.

🏇 Real Escuela Andaluza de Arte Ecuestre
Duque de Abrantes. **Tel** 956 31 96 35 (by appt). **Open** Mon–Fri. 🅿️ ♿ 🌐 realescuela.org

🏛️ Palacio del Tiempo
Calle Cervantes 3. **Tel** 956 18 21 00. **Open** Tue–Sun. 🅿️ ♿

🏇 Palacio de Penmartín
Plaza de San Juan 1. **Tel** 956 90 21 34. **Open** Mon–Fri. **Closed** public hols.

🏠 Alcázar
Alameda Vieja. **Tel** 650 80 01 00. **Open** daily. **Closed** 1 & 6 Jan, 25 Dec. 🅿️ ♿ 📷

🏠 Sherry Bodegas
Open phone for tour times. 🅿️ González Byass: C/ Manuel María González 12, Jerez. **Tel** 956 35 70 16. Pedro Domecq: C/ San Ildefonso 3, Jerez. **Tel** 956 15 15 00. Sandeman: C/ Pizarro 10, Jerez. **Tel** 675 64 71 77. Osborne: C/ de los Moros, Puerto de Santa María. **Tel** 956 86 91 00. Terry: C/ San Ildefonso 3, Jerez. **Tel** 956 15 15 00.

Real Escuela Andaluza de Arte Ecuestre, Jerez de la Frontera

⁹ Cádiz

Jutting out of the Bay of Cádiz, and almost entirely surrounded by water, Cádiz lays claim to being Europe's oldest city. Legend names Hercules as its founder, although history credits the Phoenicians with establishing the town of Gadir in 1100 BC. Occupied by the Carthaginians, Romans and Moors in turn, the city also prospered after the Reconquest *(see pp58–9)* on wealth taken from the New World. In 1587 Sir Francis Drake sacked the city in the first of many British attacks in the war for world trade. In 1812 Cádiz briefly became Spain's capital when the nation's first constitution was declared here *(see p67)*.

Exploring Cádiz

The joy of visiting Cádiz is to wander along the waterfront with its well-tended gardens and open squares before exploring the Old Town, which is full of narrow alleys busy with market and street life.

The pride of the city is its Carnival *(see p467)* – a riotous explosion of festivities, fancy dress, singing and drinking.

⛪ **Catedral**

Known as the Catedral Nueva (New Cathedral) and built on the site of an older one, this Baroque and Neo-Classical church, with its dome of golden-yellow tiles, is one of Spain's largest. In the crypt is the tomb of composer Manuel de Falla (1876–1946). The cathedral's treasures are stored in the Casa de la Contaduria, behind the cathedral.

🏛 **Museo de Cádiz**

Plaza de Mina. **Tel** 856 10 50 23.
Open 10am–8:30pm Tue–Sat
(9am–3:30pm Jun–mid-Sep);
10am–5pm Sun & public hols. ♿

The museum has archaeological exhibits charting the history of Cádiz and the largest art gallery in Andalusia, with works by Rubens, Zurbarán and Murillo. On the third floor is a collection of puppets made for village fiestas.

🏛 **Torre Tavira**

Calle Marqués del Real Tesoro 10.
Tel 956 21 29 10. **Open** daily.
Closed 1 Jan, 25 Dec. 📷 🎫

The city's official watchtower in the 18th century has now been converted into a camera obscura, and offers great views.

VISITORS' CHECKLIST

Practical Information
Cádiz. 🔺 155,000. ℹ️ Avenida José León de Carranza s/n, 956 28 56 01. 🚌 Mon. 🎭 Carnival (Feb/Mar). 🌐 **cadizturismo.com**

Transport
🚉 Plaza de Sevilla, **Tel** 902 24 02 02. 🚌 Plaza de la Hispanidad, **Tel** 902 19 92 08.

⛪ **Oratorio de San Felipe Neri**

Calle Santa Inés s/n. **Tel** 956 80 70 18.
Open 10:30am–2pm, 4:30–8pm (Jul & Aug: 5:30–8:30pm) Tue–Fri, 10:30am–2pm Sat, 10am–1pm (Jul & Aug: to noon) Sun.

In 1812, as Napoleon tightened his grip on Spain *(see pp66–7)*, a provisional government assembled at this 18th-century church to try to lay the foundations of Spain's first constitutional monarchy. The liberal constitution it declared was bold but ineffectual.

Zurbarán's *Saint Bruno in Ecstasy*, in the Museo de Cádiz

Cádiz Cathedral

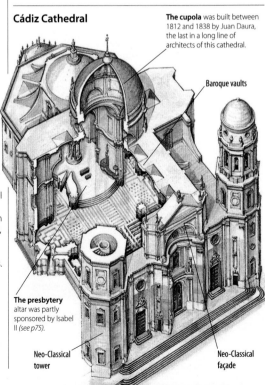

The cupola was built between 1812 and 1838 by Juan Daura, the last in a long line of architects of this cathedral.

Baroque vaults

The presbytery altar was partly sponsored by Isabel II *(see p75)*.

Neo-Classical tower

Neo-Classical façade

Fishing boats at the resort of Zahara de los Atunes on the Costa de la Luz

⑩ Costa de la Luz

Cádiz. 🚉 Cádiz. 🚌 Cádiz, Tarifa.
ℹ️ Paseo de la Alameda s/n, Tarifa,
956 68 09 93.

The Costa de la Luz (Coast of Light) between Cádiz and Tarifa, at Spain's southernmost tip, is an unspoiled, windswept stretch of coast characterized by strong, pure light – the source of its name. From the Sierra del Cabrito, to the west of Algeciras, it is often possible to see the outline of Tangier and the parched Moroccan landscape below the purple-tinged Rif mountains across the narrow Strait of Gibraltar.

Tarifa is named after an 8th-century Moorish commander, Tarif ben Maluk, who landed there with his forces during the Moorish conquest *(see pp56–7)*. Later, Tarifa and its 10th-century castle were defended by the legendary hero Guzmán during a siege by the Moors in 1292.

Tarifa has since become the windsurfing capital of Europe. The breezes that blow on to this coast also drive the numerous wind turbines on the hills.

Off the N340 (E5), at the end of a long, narrow road which strikes out across a wilderness of cacti, sunflowers and lone cork trees, is **Zahara de los Atunes**, a modest holiday resort with a few hotels. **Conil de la Frontera**, to the west, is busier and more built up.

The English admiral Nelson defeated a Spanish and French fleet off **Cabo de Trafalgar** in 1805, but died in the battle.

⑫ A Tour Around the Pueblos Blancos

Instead of settling on Andalusia's plains, where they would have fallen prey to bandits, some Andalusians chose to live in fortified hilltop towns and villages. These are known as *pueblos blancos* (white towns) because they are whitewashed in the Moorish tradition *(see p30)*. They are working agricultural towns today, but touring them will reveal a host of references to the past.

② Ubrique
Nestling at the foot of the Sierra de Ubrique, this *pueblo* is known for its flourishing leather industry.

↑ Sevilla

Cádiz, Jerez

① Arcos de la Frontera

Embalse de los Hurones

Charco de los Hurones

⑨ Jimena de la Frontera
Set amid hills, where wild bulls graze among cork and olive trees, this town has a ruined Moorish castle.

0 kilometres 10
0 miles 5

CA5221

CA503

A3

Key

▰▰ Tour route
═══ Other roads

La Sauceda

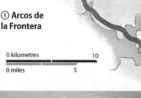

⑧ Gaucín
From here there are unsurpassed vistas over the Mediterranean, the Atlantic, the Rock of Gibraltar and across the strait to the Rif mountains of North Africa.

Tips for Drivers

Tour length: 205 km (127 miles).
Stopping-off points: There are places to stay and eat at all of these pueblos, but Ronda has the widest range of hotels and restaurants *(see p601)*. Arcos has a parador *(see p572)*.

⓫ Arcos de la Frontera

Cádiz. 🏠 30,000. 🚌 ℹ C/ Cuesta de Belén 5, 956 70 22 64. 🚌 Fri. 🎭 Toro del Domingo de Resurrección (last day of Easter), Velada de Nuestra Señora de las Nieves (4–6 Aug), Semana Santa, Feria de San Miguel (end of Sep).

Although legend has it that a son of Noah founded Arcos, it is more probable that it was the Iberians. It gained the name Arcobriga in the Roman era and, under the Caliphate of Córdoba (*see p56*), became the Moorish stronghold of Medina Arkosh. It is an archetypal white town, with a labyrinthine old quarter.

On the Plaza de España, at the top of the town, are the parador (*see p572*) and the **Iglesia de Santa María de la Asunción**, a Late Gothic-Mudéjar building noted for its choir stalls and altarpiece. The huge, Gothic **Iglesia de San Pedro**, perched on the edge of a cliff formed by the Río Guadalete, is a striking building. Nearby is the **Palacio del Mayorazgo**, which has an ornate Renaissance façade. The **town hall** (*ayuntamiento*) has a fine Mudéjar ceiling.

Environs

In the 15th-century the Guzmán family was granted the duke-dom of **Medina Sidonia**, a white west of Arcos de la Frontera. The area became one of the most important ducal seats in Spain. The Gothic Iglesia de Santa María la Coronada is the town's finest building. It contains a notable collection of Renaissance religious art.

🏛 **Palacio del Mayorazgo**
C/ San Pedro 2. **Tel** 956 70 30 13

Iglesia de Santa María de la Asunción in Arcos de la Frontera

(Casa de Cultura). **Open** 10am–2pm Mon–Fri. ♿

🏛 **Ayuntamiento**
Plaza del Cabildo. **Tel** 956 70 22 64. **Open** Mon–Fri. **Closed** public hols.

Embalse de Zahara

③

MA486
⑤

CA503

⑥

• **Benamahoma**

osque

④
A372
A376
⑦

Benaocaz•
A374

②
SIERRA DE UBRIQUE

PARQUE NATURAL DE LA SIERRA DE GRAZALEMA

La Cueva de la Pileta

Cortes de la Frontera
A369

A373

A373

arganta

Algatocín•

PARQUE NATURAL DE LOS ALCORNOCALES

Río Guadiaro

⑧

A369

A3331

Ronda ⑦
(*see pp474–5*)

⑨

③ **Zahara de la Sierr**
Fanning out below a castle ruin, this fine *pueblo blanco* has been declared a national monument.

④ **Grazalema**
This village in the Sierra de Grazalema has the highest rainfall in Spain.

⑤ **Ronda la Vieja**
Significant remains of the Roman town of Acinipo, including a theatre, can be visited.

⑥ **Setenil**
Some of the streets of this unusual white town, which climbs up the sides of a gorge, are covered by rock overhangs. The gorge was carved out of volcanic tufa rock by the Río Trejo.

⑬ Street-by-Street: Ronda

One of the most spectacularly located cities in Spain, Ronda sits on a massive rocky outcrop, straddling a precipitous limestone cleft. Because of its impregnable position this town was one of the last Moorish bastions, finally falling to the Christians in 1485. On the south side perches a classic Moorish *pueblo blanco (see pp472–3)* of cobbled alleys, window grilles and dazzling whitewash – most historic sights are in this part of the town. Located in El Mercadillo, the newer town, is one of the oldest bullrings in Spain.

★ Puente Nuevo
An impressive feat of 18th-century civil engineering, the "New Bridge" over the 100-m- (330-ft-) deep Tajo gorge joins old and new Ronda.

Convento de Santo Domingo was the local headquarters of the Inquisition *(see p278).*

To El Mercadillo, Plaza de Toros, parador and tourist information

Casa del Rey Moro
From this 18th-century mansion, built on the foundations of a Moorish palace, 365 steps lead down to the river.

Mirador El Campillo (viewpoint)

★ Palacio Mondragón
Much of this palace was rebuilt following the Reconquest *(see pp58–9),* but its arcaded patio is adorned with original Moorish mosaics and plasterwork.

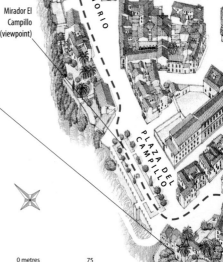

SANTO DOMIN

CALLE ARMIÑÁN

TENORIO

PLAZA DEL CAMPILLO

| 0 metres | | 75 |
| 0 yards | | 75 |

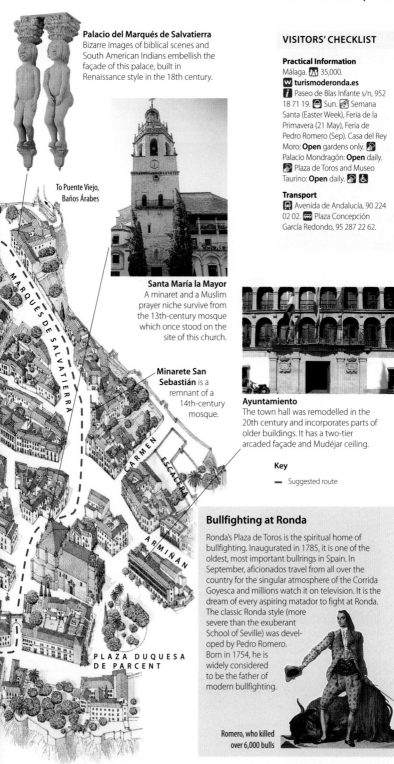

Palacio del Marqués de Salvatierra
Bizarre images of biblical scenes and South American Indians embellish the façade of this palace, built in Renaissance style in the 18th century.

To Puente Viejo, Baños Árabes

MARQUES DE SALVATIERRA

CARMEN

ESCALERA

ARMIÑAN

PLAZA DUQUESA DE PARCENT

Santa María la Mayor
A minaret and a Muslim prayer niche survive from the 13th-century mosque which once stood on the site of this church.

Minarete San Sebastián is a remnant of a 14th-century mosque.

VISITORS' CHECKLIST

Practical Information
Málaga. 🚉 35,000.
🌐 **turismoderonda.es**
ℹ️ Paseo de Blas Infante s/n, 952 18 71 19. 🚌 Sun. 🎭 Semana Santa (Easter Week), Feria de la Primavera (21 May), Feria de Pedro Romero (Sep). Casa del Rey Moro: **Open** gardens only. 🏛️ Palacio Mondragón: **Open** daily. 🏛️ Plaza de Toros and Museo Taurino: **Open** daily. 🏛️ ♿

Transport
🚉 Avenida de Andalucía, 90 224 02 02. 🚌 Plaza Concepción García Redondo, 95 287 22 62.

Ayuntamiento
The town hall was remodelled in the 20th century and incorporates parts of older buildings. It has a two-tier arcaded façade and Mudéjar ceiling.

Key
— Suggested route

Bullfighting at Ronda

Ronda's Plaza de Toros is the spiritual home of bullfighting. Inaugurated in 1785, it is one of the oldest, most important bullrings in Spain. In September, aficionados travel from all over the country for the singular atmosphere of the Corrida Goyesca and millions watch it on television. It is the dream of every aspiring matador to fight at Ronda. The classic Ronda style (more severe than the exuberant School of Seville) was developed by Pedro Romero. Born in 1754, he is widely considered to be the father of modern bullfighting.

Romero, who killed over 6,000 bulls

⑭ Algeciras

Cádiz. 🏛 200,000. 🚌 ℹ Paseo Río de la Miel s/n, 670 94 87 31. 🚌 Tue. 🎪 Feria Real (24 Jun–2 Jul).

From the industrial city of Algeciras, there are spectacular views of Gibraltar, 14 km (9 miles) away across its bay. The city is a major fishing port and Europe's main gateway for ferries to North Africa, especially Tangier and Spain's territories of Ceuta and Melilla.

⑮ Gibraltar

British Crown Colony. 🏛 35,000. 🚌 ℹ Duke of Kent House, Cathedral Square, (+35) 020 07 49 50. 🎪 Nat Day (10 Sep). 🌐 **gibraltar.gov.uk**

The high, rocky headland of Gibraltar was signed over to Britain "in perpetuity" at the Treaty of Utrecht in 1713 *(see p66)*. Today, about 4 million people stream across the border annually from La Línea de la Concepción in Spain.

Among the chief sights of Gibraltar are those testifying to its strategic military importance over the centuries. Halfway up the famous Rock are an 8th-century Moorish castle, whose **keep** was

St Michael's Cave, which served as a hospital during World War II

used as a prison until 2010, and 80 km (50 miles) of **siege tunnels** housing storerooms and barracks. **St Michael's Cave**, which served as a hospital during World War II, is now used for classical concerts.

The **Apes' Den**, near Europa Point, Gibraltar's southernmost tip, is home to the tailless apes. Legend says that the British will keep the Rock only as long as the apes remain there.

A cable car takes visitors to the **Top of the Rock**, at 450 m (1,475 ft). **Gibraltar Museum** charts the colony's history.

🏰 **The Keep, Siege Tunnels, St Michael's Cave, Apes' Den** Upper Rock Area. **Tel** (+35) 020 04 59 57. **Open** daily (except Siege Tunnels: Mon–Sat). **Closed** 1 Jan, 25 Dec. 🎫

🏛 **Gibraltar Museum** 18 Bombhouse Lane. **Tel** (+35) 020 07 42 89. **Open** Mon–Sat. **Closed** public hols. 🎫

The Costa del Sol

Thanks to its average of 300 days' sunshine a year and its varied coastline, the Costa del Sol, between Gibraltar and Málaga, offers a full range of beach-based holidays and water sports. Complementing the sophistication and luxury of Marbella are many other popular resorts aimed at the mass market. More than 30 of Europe's finest golf courses lie just inland.

Puerto Banús is Marbella's ostentatious marina. The expensive shops, restaurants and glittering nightlife reflect the wealth of its clientele.

Estepona's quiet evenings make it popular with families with young children. Behind the big hotels are old squares shaded by orange trees.

Marina at Sotogrande is an exclusive resort of luxury villas. The marina is fronted by good seafood restaurants.

San Pedro de Alcántara is a quiet resort with a modern marina and smart holiday developments.

San Pedro de Alcántara

Estepona
Atalaya
Ronda del Mar
Sabinillas
Rio Guadiaro
Punta de la Chullera
Sotogrande
Los Barrios
San Roque
La Línea de la Concepción
Algeciras
Bahía de Algeciras
GIBRALTAR (UK)
Gibraltar
Punta de Europa
Punta del Carnero
Tarifa

Yachts and motorboats in the exclusive marina of Marbella – the summer home of the international jet set

⑯ Marbella

Málaga. 🚗 120,000. 🚌 ℹ️ Glorieta de la Fontanilla, Paseo Marítimo, 95 277 14 42. 📅 Mon. 🎭 San Bernabé (Jun). 🌐 **marbella.es**

Marbella is one of Europe's most exclusive holiday resorts, frequented by royalty and film stars. There are 24 beaches, including Puerto Banus, Playa Rio Verde and Playa Nagueles. In winter, the major attraction is the golf. Among the delights of the old town, with its spotlessly clean alleys, squares, and smart shops and restaurants, is the **Iglesia de Nuestra Señora de la Encarnación**. The **Museo del Grabado Español Contemporáneo** displays some of Pablo Picasso's least-known work.

🏛️ **Museo del Grabado Español Contemporáneo**
C/ Hospital Bazan.
Tel 952 76 57 41. **Open** Mon–Sat.
Closed public hols. 🎫

Marbella is the Costa del Sol's most stylish resort. The Playa de Don Carlos is considered the best of its 24 beaches.

El Chapparal
Málaga
El Palo
La Capellania
Torremolinos
Benalmádena Costa
Marbella
Fuengirola   Torreblanca
Cabopino   Cala de   Punta de
Mijas   Calaburra
Rincón de la Victoria

Rincón de la Victoria is an unspoiled family beach, famous for its spit-roasted sardines.

Torremolinos, a high-rise holiday metropolis, is less brash than it used to be. Huge sums have been spent on new squares, a promenade, green spaces, and improving the beach with millions of tonnes of golden sand.

Cabopino, on a not-too-crowded stretch of coast, has areas that include nudist and gay beaches.

Benalmádena Costa caters almost exclusively for package holidays. Behind the rather rocky beaches and very large marina is a plethora of tourist attractions.

Fuengirola still has an active fishing port – as these boxes of fresh fish suggest – although it is better known today as a package-holiday resort with a chiefly British clientele. It has a spectacular backdrop of steep, ochre mountains.

0 kilometres   10
0 miles   10

The main façade of Málaga's cathedral, consecrated in 1588

⑰ Málaga

Málaga. 🗺 650,000. ✈ 🚆 🚌 🚢
🛈 Plaza de la Marina 11, 952 12 20 20. 🚌 Sun. 🎭 Carnival (Feb/Mar), Feria (second Sat–third Sun of Aug).
🌐 malagaturismo.com

Málaga, the second-largest city in Andalusia, is today a thriving port, just as it was in Phoenician times, and again under the Romans and then the Moors. It also flourished during the 19th century, when sweet Málaga wine (*see p424*) was one of Europe's most popular drinks – until phylloxera ravaged the area's vineyards in 1876.

The **cathedral** was begun in 1528 by Diego de Siloé, but it is a bizarre mix of styles. The half-built second tower, abandoned in 1765 when funds ran out, gave the cathedral its nickname: La Manquita ("the one-armed one").

Málaga's former Museo de Bellas Artes has been adapted to house a **Museo Picasso** displaying works by the native artist. The **Casa Natal de Picasso**, where the painter spent his early years, is now the Picasso Foundation.

Málaga's vast **Alcazaba** (*see p57*) was built between the 8th and 11th centuries. There is a partially excavated Roman amphitheatre by its entrance. A new city museum, **Museo de Malaga**, is being built and is due to open in 2016. It will display artifacts from the site.

On the hill directly behind the Alcazaba are the ruins of the **Castillo de Gibralfaro**, a 14th-century Moorish castle.

Environs
In the hills to the north and east of Málaga is the **Parque Natural de los Montes de Málaga**. Wildlife, such as eagles and wild boars, thrive here amid the scent of lavender and wild herbs. Walkers can follow a number of scenic marked trails. Going north on the C345 you can also visit **Ecomuseo Lagar de Torrijos**, a preserved winery of the 1840s.

🏛 **Museo Picasso**
Calle San Agustín 8. **Tel** 952 12 76 00. **Open** Tue–Sun. **Closed** 1 Jan, 25 Dec. 🅿

🏰 **Alcazaba**
Calle Alcazabilla. **Tel** 952 22 72 30. **Open** Tue–Sun.

⑱ Garganta del Chorro

Málaga. 🚆 El Chorro. 🚌 Parque Ardeles. 🛈 Avenida de la Constitución, Álora, 952 49 83 80.

Up the fertile Guadalhorce Valley, beyond the village of El Chorro, is one of the geographical wonders of Andalusia. The Garganta del Chorro is an immense chasm, 180 m (590 ft) deep and in places only 10 m (30 ft) wide, cut by the river through a limestone mountain. Downstream, a hydroelectric plant detracts from the wildness of the place.

The recently restored **Camino del Rey** is a catwalk clinging to the rock face which leads to a bridge across the gorge.

Environs
Álora, a classic white town (*see pp472–3*) with a ruined Moorish castle and an 18th-century church, lies 12 km (7 miles) down the valley.

Along the twisting MA441 from Álora is the village of **Carratraca**. In the 19th and early 20th centuries, Europe's highest society travelled here for the healing powers of the sulphurous springs. These days, Carratraca has a faded glory – water still gushes out at 700 litres (155 UK and 185 US gal) a minute and the outdoor baths remain open, but they are little used.

The Garganta del Chorro, rising high above the Guadalhorce River

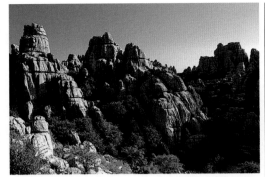
Weathered limestone formations in El Torcal

ⓘ El Torcal

Málaga. 🚉 Antequera. 🚌 Antequera.
ⓘ Antequera, 952 70 25 05. Parque
Natural del Torcal: **Tel** 952 24 33 24.
Open 10am–5pm daily (to 7pm Apr–
Sep). 🖳 **torcaldeantequera.com**

A massive exposed hump of
limestone upland, which has
been slowly weathered into
bizarre rock formations and
caves, the **Parque Natural del
Torcal** is popular with hikers.
Marked trails lead from a
visitors' centre.

The park is also a pleasure
for natural historians, with fox
and weasel populations, and
colonies of eagles, hawks and
vultures, as well as rare plants
and flowers like wild orchids.

⓴ Antequera

Málaga. 🏘 42,000. 🚉 🚌 ⓘ Pl San
Sebastián 7, 952 70 25 05. 🛒 Tue.
🎭 Ferias (end May & mid-Aug).
🖳 **antequera.es**

This busy market town was
strategically important first as
Roman Anticaria and later as
a Moorish border fortress
defending Granada.

Of its many churches, the
**Iglesia de Nuestra Señora del
Carmen**, with its vast Baroque
altarpiece, is not to be missed. At
the opposite end of the town is
the 19th-century **Plaza de Toros**,
with a museum of bullfighting.

The hilltop **castle** was built in
the 13th century on the site of
a Roman fort. Visitors can walk
round the castle walls by
approaching through the 16th-
century Arco de los Gigantes.

There are excellent views of
Antequera from the Torre del
Papabellotas on the best-
preserved part of the wall.

In the town below, the 18th-
century **Palacio de Nájera** is
the setting for the Municipal
Museum, the star exhibit of
which is a splendid Roman
bronze statue of a boy.

The massive **dolmens**, just
outside the town, are thought
to be the burial chambers of
tribal leaders and date from
around 2500–2000 BC.

Environs

Laguna de la Fuente de Piedra,
north of Antequera, teems with
bird life, including huge flocks of
flamingoes, which arrive to breed
after wintering in West Africa.
A road off the N334 leads to a
lakeside viewing point. There
is a visitors' centre in Fuente de
Piedra village. To the east, also off
the N334, is **Archidona**, with its
18th-century, octagonal Plaza

The triumphal, 16th-century Arco de los
Gigantes, Antequera

Ochavada built in French style,
but which also incorporates
traditional Andalusian features.

🏟 **Plaza de Toros**
Carretera de Sevilla. **Tel** 952 70 81 42.
Open Tue–Sun. Museo Taurino:
Open Sat, Sun, public hols.

🏛 **Palacio de Nájera**
Coso Viejo. **Tel** 952 70 83 00.
Open Tue–Sun. 🖼

Palacio del Marqués de la Gomera, in
Osuna, completed in 1770

⓴ Osuna

Sevilla. 🏘 17,500. 🚉 🚌 ⓘ Calle
Carrera 82, 954 81 57 32. 🛒 Mon.
🎭 San Alcadio (12 Jan), Virgen de
la Consolación (8 Sep).

Osuna was once a key Roman
garrison town. It rose again to
prominence in the 16th century
under the Dukes of Osuna, who
wielded immense power. In
the 1530s they founded the
Colegiata de Santa María, a
grand church with a Baroque
reredos and paintings by José
de Ribera. This was followed in
1548 by the **University**, a rather
severe building with a beautiful
patio. Some fine mansions,
among them the **Palacio del
Marqués de la Gomera**, also
reflect the town's former glory.

Environs

To the east lies **Estepa**, whose
modern-day fame rests on
its biscuits – *polvorones* and
mantecados. The Iglesia del
Carmen has a black and white,
Baroque façade.

Tomb of Servilia in the Roman necropolis in Carmona

❷ Carmona

Sevilla. 🏘 25,000. 🚌 ℹ Alcázar de la Puerta de Sevilla, 954 19 09 55. 🚆 Mon & Thu. 🎪 Feria (May), Fiestas Patronales (8–16 Sep). 🌐 turismo.carmona.org

Carmona is the first major town east of Seville, its old quarter built on a hill above the suburbs on the plain. Beyond the **Puerta de Sevilla**, a gateway in the Moorish city walls, is a dense cluster of mansions, Mudéjar churches, and winding streets.

The Plaza de San Fernando has a feeling of grandeur which is characterized by the Renaissance façade of the old **Ayuntamiento**. The present town hall, set just off the square, dates from the 18th century; in its courtyard are some Roman mosaics. Close by is the **Iglesia de Santa María la Mayor**. Built in the 15th century over a mosque, whose patio still survives, this is the finest of Carmona's churches.

Dominating the town are the ruins of the **Alcázar del Rey Pedro**, once a palace of Pedro I, known as Pedro the Cruel. Parts of it now form a parador (see p572).

Just outside Carmona is the **Necrópolis Romana**, the extensive remains of a Roman burial ground. A site museum displays some of the items found in the graves, including statues, glass and jewellery.

🏛 **Ayuntamiento**
Calle Salvador 2. **Tel** 95 414 00 11. **Open** Mon–Fri. **Closed** public hols.

🏛 **Necrópolis Romana**
Avenida Jorge Bonsor 9. **Tel** 600 14 36 32. **Open** Tue–Sun. **Closed** 1 Jan, 1 May & 25 Dec.

❸ Itálica

Sevilla. **Tel** 955 12 38 47. 🚌 from Sevilla. **Open** 9am–3:30pm Sun & public hols; Apr–mid-Jun & mid-Sep–Mar: 9am–5:30pm Tue–Sat; mid-Jun–mid-Sep: 9am–3:30pm Tue–Sat. 🅿

Itálica was founded in 206 BC by Scipio Africanus. One of the earliest Roman cities in Hispania (see pp54–5), it grew to become important in the 2nd and 3rd centuries AD. Emperor Hadrian, who was born in the city and reigned from AD 117–138, added marble temples and other grand buildings.

Archaeologists have speculated that the changing course of the Río Guadalquivir may have led to Itálica's later demise during Moorish times.

Next to the vast but crumbling **amphitheatre** is a display of finds from the site. More treasures are displayed in the Museo Arqueológico in Seville (see p449).

The traces of Itálica's streets and the mosaic floors of some villas can be seen. However, little remains of the city's temples or of its baths, as most of the stone and marble has been plundered over the centuries.

Roman mosaic from Itálica

Some well-preserved Roman baths and a theatre can be seen in **Santiponce**, a village just outside the site.

❹ Sierra Morena

Sevilla & Córdoba. 🚆 Cazalla, Constantina. 🚌 Constantina, Cazalla. ℹ Constantina (Sevilla): 955 88 12 97; Cazalla (Sevilla): 954 88 35 62; Córdoba: 957 64 11 40; El Robledo: 955 88 95 93.

The Sierra Morena, clad in oak and pine woods, runs across the north of the provinces of Sevilla and Córdoba. It forms a natural frontier between Andalusia and the plains of neighbouring Extremadura and La Mancha. Smaller sierras (ranges of hills) within the Sierra Morena chain are also named individually.

Fuente Obejuna, north of Córdoba, was immortalized by Lope de Vega (see p294) in his play about an uprising in 1476 against a local overlord. The Iglesia de San Juan Bautista in **Hinojosa del Duque** is a vast church in both Gothic and Renaissance styles. **Belalcázar** is dominated by the huge tower of a ruined 15th-century castle. Storks nest on the church towers of the plateau of **Valle de los Pedroches**, to the east.

Cazalla de la Sierra, the main town of the sierra north of Seville, is popular with young Sevillanos at weekends. Liquor de Guindas, a concoction of cherry liqueur and aniseed, is produced here. **Constantina**, to the east, is more peaceful with superb views of the countryside.

A cow grazing in the pastures of the Sierra Morena north of Seville

㉕ Palma del Río

Córdoba. 🚇 19,400. 🚌 🚍 **f** Calle
Santa Clara, 957 64 43 70. 🏛 Tue.
🎉 Ferias (19–21 May & 18–20 Aug).
w palmadelrio.es

The Romans sited a strategic
settlement here, on the road
between Córdoba and Itálica,
almost 2,000 years ago. The
remains of the 12th-
century city walls are a
reminder of the town's
frontier days under the
Almohads *(see p58)*.
The **Iglesia de la
Asunción**, a Baroque
church, dates from
the 18th century.
The **Monasterio de
San Francisco** is
now a hotel *(see
p574)*, and guests
can eat dinner in
the 15th-century
refectory of
the Franciscan
monks. Palma

Bell tower, La
Asunción

del Río is the
home town of El
Cordobés, one of
Spain's most famous matadors.
His biography, *Or I'll Dress You in
Mourning*, paints a vivid picture
of life in the town and of the
hardship which followed the
end of the Civil War.

Environs

One of the most dramatic
silhouettes in Southern Spain
breaks the skyline of **Almodóvar
del Río**. The Moorish castle –
parts of it dating from the 8th
century – stands on a hilltop
overlooking the whitewashed
town and fields of cotton.

🏰 **Castillo de Almodóvar del Río**
Tel 957 63 40 55. **Open** daily.
🎉 **Closed** 1 Jan, 25 Dec.

㉖ Écija

Sevilla. 🚇 40,000. 🚍 **f** C/ Elvira 1-A,
Palacio de Benamejí, 955 90 29 33.
🏛 Thu. 🎉 Feria (21–24 Sep).
w turismoecija.com

Écija is nicknamed "the frying
pan of Andalusia" owing to its
famously torrid climate. In the
searing heat, the palm trees on
the Plaza de España provide

blissful shade. An ideal place to
sit and observe daily life passing
by, this is also a spot for
evening strolls.

Écija has 11 Baroque church
steeples, many adorned with
gleaming *azulejos (see p442)*,
and together they make a very
impressive sight. The most florid
of these is the **Iglesia de Santa
María**, which overlooks the
Plaza de España. The **Iglesia
de San Juan**, with its exquisite,
brightly coloured bell tower,
is a very close rival.

Of the many mansions
along Calle Emilio Castelar, the
Baroque **Palacio de Peñaflor** is
worth a visit. Its pink marble
doorway is topped by twisted
columns, while an attractive
wrought-iron balcony runs
along the whole front façade.

🏛 **Palacio de Peñaflor**
C/ Emilio Castelar 26. **Tel** 954 83
02 73. **Closed** for refurbishment.

㉗ Medina Azahara

Córdoba. **Tel** 957 10 49 33. 🚍 Córdoba.
Open 9am–7:30pm (to 3:30pm mid-
Jun–mid-Sep, to 5:30pm mid-Sep–
Mar) Tue–Sat; 9am–3:30pm Sun &
public hols. 🎉

Just a few kilometres north of
Córdoba lies this once glorious
palace. Built in the 10th century
for Caliph Abd al Rahman III, it is
named after his favourite wife,

Detail of woodcarving in the main hall of
Medina Azahara

Azahara. He spared no expense,
employing more than 15,000
mules, 4,000 camels and 10,000
workers to bring building materials from as far as North Africa.

The palace is built on three
levels and includes a mosque,
the caliph's residence and fine
gardens *(see pp426–7)*. Marble,
ebony, jasper and alabaster once
adorned its many halls, and it is
believed that shimmering pools
of quicksilver added lustre.

The glory was short-lived. The
palace was sacked by Berber
invaders in 1010 and over
subsequent centuries it was
ransacked for its building materials. Now, the ruins give only
glimpses of its former beauty – a
Moorish main hall, for instance,
decorated with marble carvings
and a carved wood ceiling. The
palace is currently being restored.

Trompe l'oeil on the ornate Baroque façade of the Palacio de Peñaflor, Écija

㉘ Street-by-Street: Córdoba

The heart of Córdoba is the old Jewish quarter, situated to the west of the Mezquita's towering walls. A walk around this area gives the sensation that little has changed since the 10th century, when this was one of the greatest cities in the Western world. Wrought ironwork decorates cobbled streets too narrow for cars, where silversmiths create fine jewellery in their workshops. Most of the chief sights are here, while modern city life takes place some blocks north, around the Plaza de Tendillas. To the east of this square is the Plaza de la Corredera, a 17th-century arcaded square with a daily market.

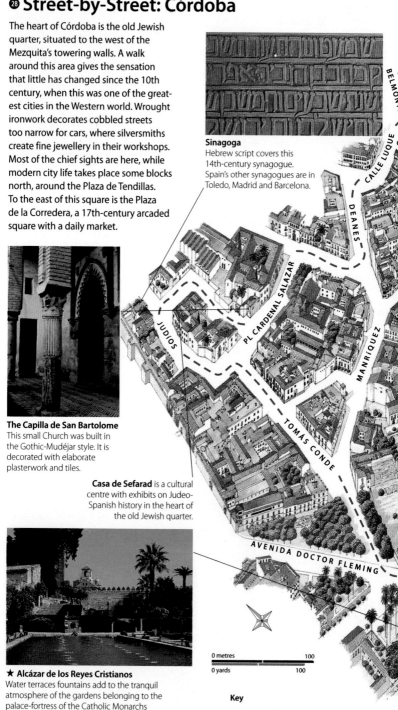

Sinagoga
Hebrew script covers this 14th-century synagogue. Spain's other synagogues are in Toledo, Madrid and Barcelona.

The Capilla de San Bartolome
This small Church was built in the Gothic-Mudéjar style. It is decorated with elaborate plasterwork and tiles.

Casa de Sefarad is a cultural centre with exhibits on Judeo-Spanish history in the heart of the old Jewish quarter.

★ Alcázar de los Reyes Cristianos
Water terraces fountains add to the tranquil atmosphere of the gardens belonging to the palace-fortress of the Catholic Monarchs (see pp60–61), built in the 14th century.

0 metres		100
0 yards		100

Key

— Suggested route

The Callejón de las Flores brims with colourful geraniums, which contrast with the whitewashed walls of this alley, leading to a tiny square.

The Palacio Episcopal now houses the tourist office.

Moorish bronze stag from Medina Azahara, Museo Arqueológico

Exploring Córdoba

Córdoba lies on a sharp bend in the Río Guadalquivir, which is spanned by a Roman bridge linking the 14th-century Torre de la Calahorra and the old town. One of the most atmospheric squares in Andalusia is the Plaza de los Capuchinos. With its haunting stone calvary, it is particularly evocative when seen by moonlight.

🏛 Museo de Bellas Artes
Plaza del Potro 2. **Tel** 957 10 36 59.
Open Tue–Sun.
Exhibits in a former charity hospital include sculptures by local artist Mateo Inurria (1867–1924) and works by Valdés Leal, Zurbarán and Murillo of the Seville School.

🏛 Museo Arqueológico
Plaza Jerónimo Páez 7.
Tel 957 35 55 29. **Open** Tue–Sat. 🗝
Located in a Renaissance mansion, displays include the remains of a Roman theatre found beneath the building, Roman pottery and impressive finds from the Moorish era.

🏛 Palacio de Viana
Plaza Don Gome 2. **Tel** 957 49 67 41.
Open Tue–Sun (am only Sun & public hols). 🗝 🎫
Furniture, tapestries, paintings and porcelain are displayed in the 17th-century former home of the Viana family.

🏛 Museo Romero de Torres
Plaza del Potro 1. **Tel** 957 47 03 56.
Open Tue–Sun. 🗝 (free Fri).
Julio Romero de Torres (1874–1930), who was born in this house, captured the soul of Córdoba in his paintings.

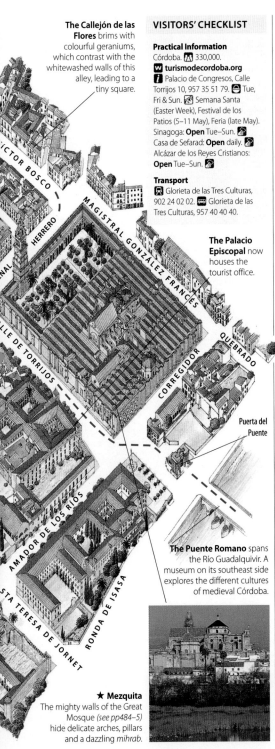

The Puente Romano spans the Río Guadalquivir. A museum on its southeast side explores the different cultures of medieval Córdoba.

Puerta del Puente

★ **Mezquita**
The mighty walls of the Great Mosque (see pp484–5) hide delicate arches, pillars and a dazzling *mihrab*.

Córdoba: the Mezquita

Córdoba's Great Mosque, dating back 12 centuries, embodied the power of Islam on the Iberian Peninsula. Abd al Rahman I *(see pp56–7)* built the original mosque between 785 and 787. The building evolved over the centuries, blending many architectural forms. In the 10th century al Hakam II made some of the most lavish additions, including the elaborate *mihrab* (prayer niche) and the *maqsura* (caliph's enclosure). During the 16th century a cathedral was built in the heart of the reconsecrated mosque, part of which was destroyed.

Patio de los Naranjos
Orange trees grow in the courtyard where the faithful washed before prayer.

KEY

① **Puerta de San Esteban** is set in a section of wall from an earlier Visigothic church.

② **The Puerta del Perdón** is a Mudéjar-style entrance gate, built during Christian rule in 1377. Penitents were pardoned here.

③ **Torre del Alminar**, a bell tower 93 m (305 ft) high, is built on the site of the original minaret. Steep steps lead to the top for a fine view of Córdoba.

④ **Capilla Mayor**

⑤ **The cathedral choir** has Churrigueresque stalls carved by Pedro Duque Cornejo in 1758.

⑥ **Capilla Real**

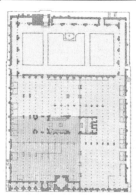

Expansion of the Mezquita

Abd al Rahman I built the original mosque. Extensions were added by Abd al Rahman II, al Hakam II and al Mansur.

Key to Additions

☐ Mosque of Abd al Rahman I

▨ Extension by Abd al Rahman II

▦ Extension by al Hakam II

☐ Extension by al Mansur

☐ Patio de los Naranjos

Cathedral
Part of the mosque was destroyed to accommodate the cathedral, started in 1523. Featuring an Italianate dome, it was designed chiefly by members of the Hernán Ruiz family.

VISITORS' CHECKLIST

Practical Information
C/ Torrijos 10.
Tel 957 47 05 12.
Open 10am–7pm Mon–Sat, 8:30–11:30am, 3–7pm Sun & pub hols (Nov–Feb: to 6pm Mon–Sat, 8:30–11:30am, 3–6pm Sun & pub hols). 🕌 ✝ 9:30am Mon–Sat; 11am, noon & 1:30pm Sun & hols.

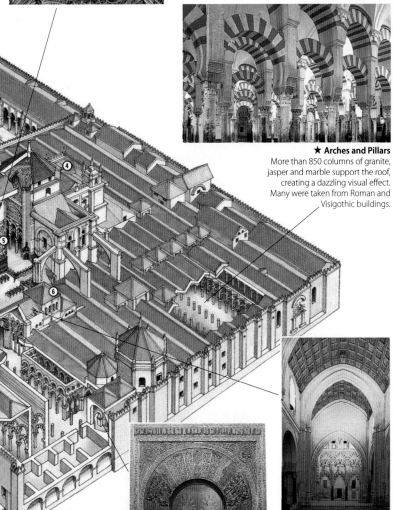

★ Arches and Pillars
More than 850 columns of granite, jasper and marble support the roof, creating a dazzling visual effect. Many were taken from Roman and Visigothic buildings.

★ Mihrab
This prayer niche, richly ornamented, held a gilt copy of the Koran. The worn flagstones indicate where pilgrims circled it seven times on their knees.

★ Capilla de Villaviciosa
The first Christian chapel was built in the mosque in 1371 by Mudéjar (see p59) craftsmen. Its multi-lobed arches are stunning.

Baroque statuary in the Fuente del Rey at Priego de Córdoba

㉙ Montilla

Córdoba. 🚗 23,000. 🚉 🚌 🅸 Capitán Alonso de Vargas 3, 957 65 24 62. 🗓 Fri. 🎉 Grape Harvest (late Aug).

Montilla is the centre of an important wine region that produces an excellent smooth white fino *(see p424)*. Unlike sherry, it is not fortified with alcohol. Several bodegas, including **Alvear** and **Pérez Barquero**, will show visitors around by prior arrangement.

The Mudéjar **Convento de Santa Clara** dates from 1512. The town library and tourist office is in the **Casa del Inca**, so named because Garcilaso de la Vega, who wrote about the Incas, lived there in the 1500s.

Environs
Aguilar, 13 km (8 miles) to the south, has the unusual, eight-sided Plaza de San José (built in 1810) and several seigneurial houses.

Baena, 40 km (25 miles) to the west of Montilla, has been famous for its olive oil since Roman times. On the Plaza de la Constitución is the Casa del Monte, an mansion dating from the 18th century. At Easter thousands of costumed drummers take to the streets.

🍷 **Bodega Alvear**
Avda María Auxiliadora 1. **Tel** 957 65 01 00. **Open** Mon–Fri. 🕐 12:30pm.

🍷 **Bodega Pérez Barquero**
Avda de Andalucía 27. **Tel** 957 65 05 00. **Open** Mon–Fri. **Closed** Aug. 🎟

㉚ Priego de Córdoba

Córdoba. 🚗 23,000. 🚌 🅸 Plaza de la Constitución 3, 957 70 06 25. 🗓 Sat. 🎉 Feria Real (1–5 Sep). 🌐 turismodepriego.com

Priego de Cordóba's claim to be the capital of Cordoban Baroque is borne out by the dazzling work of carvers, ironworkers and gilders in the many houses, and especially churches, built with wealth generated by a prosperous 18th-century silk industry.

A restored Moorish fortress stands in the whitewashed medieval quarter, the **Barrio de la Villa**. Close by is the outstanding **Iglesia de la Asunción**, converted from Gothic to Baroque style by Jerónimo Sánchez de Rueda. Its pièce de résistance is the sacristy, created in 1784 by local artist Francisco Javier Pedrajas. The main altar is Plateresque *(see p29)*.

At midnight every Saturday the brotherhood of another Baroque church, the **Iglesia de la Aurora**, parades the streets singing songs in praise of the Virgin.

Silk merchants built many of the splendid mansions that follow the curve around the Calle del Río. At the street's end is the Baroque Fuente del Rey (The King's Fountain). The 139 spouts splash water into three basins adorned with a riot of statuary.

La Asunción, Priego de Córdoba

Environs
Zuheros, perched on a crag in the limestone hills northwest of Priego, is one of Andalusia's prettiest villages. **Rute**, to the southwest, is known for its *anís (see p581)*.

Alcalá la Real, in the lowlands east of Priego, is overlooked by the hilltop ruins of a castle and a church. There are two handsome Renaissance buildings on its central square: the Fuente de Carlos V and the Palacio Abacia.

㉛ Montefrío

Granada. 🚗 7,000. 🚌 🅸 Plaza España 1, 958 33 60 04. 🗓 Mon. 🎉 Fiesta patronal (14–18 Aug).

The approach to Montefrío from the south offers wonderful views of tiled rooftops and pretty whitewashed houses. This archetypal Andalusian town is topped by the remains of its Moorish fortifications and the 16th-century Gothic **Iglesia de la Villa**. In the centre of town is the Neo-Classical **Iglesia de la Encarnación**, designed by Ventura Rodríguez (1717–85). The town is known for its chorizo, as well as its numerous stone crosses, thought to have been constructed in the 16th and 17th centuries.

Environs
Santa Fé was built by the Catholic Monarchs at the end of the 15th century. Their army

Barrels of Montilla, the sherry-like wine from the town of the same name

The castle overlooking the resort of Almuñécar on the Costa Tropical

camped here while laying siege to Granada, and this was the site of the formal surrender of the Moors in 1492 *(see pp60–61)*. A Moor's severed head, carved in stone, adorns the spire of the parish church.

Sited above a gorge, **Alhama de Granada** was named *Al hamma* (hot springs) by the Moors. Their baths, close to the spot where the hot water gushes from the ground just outside town, can be seen in the Hotel Balneario.

Loja, on the Río Genil, near Los Infiernos gorge, is known as "the city of water" because of its spring-fed fountains.

❸ Nerja

Málaga. 18,000. Calle Carmen 1, 952 52 15 31. Sun. Feria (9–12 Oct). **nerja.org**

This well-established resort, built on a cliff above sandy coves, lies at the foot of the beautiful Sierra de Almijara. There are sweeping views up and down the coast from the rocky promontory known as **El Balcón de Europa** (the Balcony of Europe). Along it runs a promenade lined with cafés and restaurants.

East of the town are the **Cuevas de Nerja**, a series of vast caverns which were discovered in 1959. Wall paintings found here are believed to be about 20,000 years old. Only a few of the many cathedral-sized chambers are open to public view. One of these has been converted into an impressive auditorium which has a capacity of several hundred people.

Environs
In **Vélez-Málaga**, the ruins of the Fortaleza de Belén, a Moorish fortress, dominate the medieval Barrio de San Sebastián.

Cuevas de Nerja
Carretera de las Cuevas de Nerja. **Tel** 952 52 95 20. **Open** daily. **Closed** 1 Jan, 15 May.

❸ Almuñécar

Granada. 22,000. Avda Europa, 958 63 11 25. Fri, 1st Sat of each month. Virgen de la Antigua (15 Aug). **almunecar.info**

Almuñécar lies on the Costa Tropical, so named because its climate allows the cultivation of exotic fruit. Inland, mountains rise to more than 2,000 m (6,560 ft). The Phoenicians founded the first settlement here, called Sexi, and the Romans constructed an aqueduct, the remains of which can be seen today. Almuñécar is now a popular holiday resort.

Above the Old Town is the **castle**, built by the Moors and altered in the 1500s. Below it is the **Parque Ornitológico**, which has an aviary and botanic gardens. The **Museo Arqueológico Cueva de Siete Palacios** displays a variety of Phoenician artifacts.

Environs
The ancient white town of **Salobreña** is set amid fields of sugar cane. Narrow streets lead up a hill to a restored Arab castle with fine views of the Sierra Nevada *(see p489)*.

Parque Ornitológico
Plaza de Abderraman. **Tel** 958 88 27 35. **Open** daily.

Museo Arqueológico Cueva de Siete Palacios
Casco Antiguo. **Tel** 607 86 54 66. **Open** Tue–Sun.

Castillo de Salobreña
Calle Andrés Segovia. **Tel** 958 61 27 33. **Open** daily. **Closed** public hols.

One of the succession of sandy coves that make up the resort of Nerja

The majestic peaks of the Sierra Nevada towering, in places, to over 3,000 m (9,800 ft) above sea level

㉞ Lanjarón

Granada. 🏘 24,000. 🚌 ℹ Avda de la Alpujarra s/n, 958 77 04 62. 🚍 Tue & Fri. 🎉 San Juan (24 Jun).

Scores of clear, snow-fed springs bubble from the slopes of the Sierra Nevada; their abundance at Lanjarón, on the southern side of this great range of mountains, has given the town a long history as a health spa. From June to October, visitors flock to take the waters for arthritic, dietary and nervous ailments. Bottled water from Lanjarón is sold all over the country.

A major festival begins on the night of 23 June and ends in an uproarious water battle in the early hours of 24 June, the Día de San Juan. Everyone in the streets gets doused.

The town is on the threshold of Las Alpujarras, a scenic upland area of dramatic landscapes, where steep, terraced hillsides and deep-cut valleys conceal remote, whitewashed villages. Roads to and from Lanjarón wind slowly and dizzily around the slopes.

㉟ A Tour of Las Alpujarras

The fertile, upland valleys of Las Alpujarras, clothed with chestnut, walnut and poplar trees, lie on the southern slopes of the Sierra Nevada. The architecture of the quaint white villages which cling to the hillsides – compact clusters of irregularly shaped houses with tall chimneys sprouting from flat, grey roofs – is unique in Spain. Local specialities are ham cured in the cold, dry air of Trevélez and brightly coloured, handwoven rugs.

④ Trevélez
Trevélez, in the shadow of Mulhacén, Spain's highest mountain, is famous for its cured ham.

② Poqueira Valley
Capileira, Bubión and Pampaneira are three villages typical of Las Alpujarras in this pretty river valley.

③ Fuente Agria
People come to this spring to drink the iron-rich, naturally carbonated waters.

① Orgiva
This is the largest town of the region, with a Baroque church in the main street and a lively Thursday market.

❸❻ Laujar de Andarax

Almería. 🏔 2,000. 🚌 ℹ Carretera C332 (A345), 950 51 35 48. 🗓 3 & 17 of each month. 🎭 San Vicente (22 Jan), San Marcos (25 Apr), Virgen de la Salud (19 Sep).

Laujar, in the arid foothills of the Sierra Nevada, looks southwards across the Andarax Valley towards the Sierra de Gádor.

Andarax was founded by one of the grandsons of Noah. In the 16th century, Abén Humeya, leader of the greatest Morisco rebellion (see p63), made his base here. The revolt was crushed by Christian troops and Abén Humeya was killed by his own followers. Inside Laujar's 17th-century church, **La Encarnación**, is a statue of the Virgin by Alonso Cano. Next to the Baroque **town hall** (ayuntamiento) is a fountain inscribed with some lines written by Francisco Villespesa, a dramatist and poet who was born in Laujar in 1877: "Six fountains has my pueblo/ He who drinks their waters/ will never forget them/so heavenly is their taste." El Nacimiento, a park to the east of Laujar, is a suitable place to have a picnic. You can accompany it with one of the area's hearty red wines. **Ohanes**, above the Andarax valley further to the east, is an attractive hill town of steep streets and whitewashed houses known for its crops of table grapes.

Painting, Iglesia de la Encarnación

❸❼ Sierra Nevada

Granada. 🚌 from Granada. ℹ Plaza de Andalucía, Cetursa Sierra Nevada, 902 70 89 00. 🌐 sierranevadaski.com

Fourteen peaks more than 3,000 m (9,800 ft) high crown the Sierra Nevada. The snow lingers until July and begins falling again in late autumn. One of Europe's highest roads, the A395, runs past **Solynieve**, an expanding ski resort at 2,100 m (6,890 ft), and skirts the two highest peaks, **Pico Veleta** at 3,398 m (11,149 ft) and **Mulhacén** at 3,482 m (11,420 ft).

The Sierra's closeness to the Mediterranean and its altitude account for the great diversity of the indigenous flora and fauna found on its slopes – the latter including golden eagles and some rare butterflies.

There are several mountain refuges for the use of serious hikers and climbers.

---

⑥ Yegen
A plaque marks the house where Gerald Brenan, the author of South from Granada, lived in the 1920s.

↑ Lacalahorra

⑧ Puerto de la Ragua
This pass, which leads across the mountains to Guadix, is nearly 2,000 m (6,560 ft) high and is often snowbound in winter.

⑦ Válor
Abén Humeya, leader of a rebellion by Moriscos in the 16th century, was born here. A commemorative battle between Moors and Christians is staged each year in mid-September.

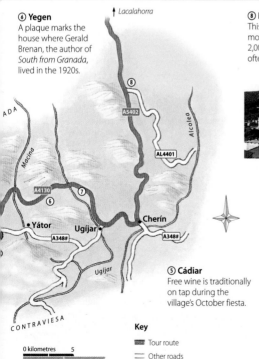

⑤ Cádiar
Free wine is traditionally on tap during the village's October fiesta.

Tips for Drivers

Tour length: 85 km (56 miles).
Stopping-off points: There are bars and restaurants in Orgiva, Capileira, Bubión (see p599) and Trevélez. Orgiva, Bubión and Trevélez have good hotels. Orgiva is the last petrol stop before Cádiar.

Key

▬▬ Tour route
═ Other roads
▲ Mountain peak

0 kilometres 5
0 miles 5

㊳ Granada

The guitarist Andrés Segovia (1893–1987) described Granada as a "place of dreams, where the Lord put the seed of music in my soul". It was first occupied by the Moors in the 8th century, and its golden period came during the rule of the Nasrid dynasty *(see pp58–9)* from 1238 to 1492, when artisans, merchants, scholars and scientists all contributed to the city's international reputation as a centre for culture. Under Christian rule, following its fall to the Catholic Monarchs in 1492 and the expulsion of the Moors *(see pp60–61)*, the city blossomed in Renaissance splendour. There was a period of decline in the 19th century, but Granada has been the subject of renewed interest and many efforts have been made to restore it to its past glory.

Entrance to the Moorish *mihrab* in the Palacio de la Madraza

Façade of Granada Cathedral

Exploring Granada

The old city centre around the cathedral is a maze of narrow one-way streets. It contains the Alcaicería – a reconstruction of a Moorish bazaar that burned down in 1843. Granada's two main squares are the Plaza Bib-Rambla, near the cathedral, and the Plaza Nueva. From the latter, Cuesta de Gomérez leads up to the city's two principal monuments: the Alhambra and the Generalife. On a hill opposite is the Albaicín district.

Churches well worth a visit are the Iglesia de San Juan de Dios, almost overwhelming in its wealth of Baroque decoration, and the Renaissance Iglesia de San Jerónimo.

⛪ Cathedral

C/ Gran Vía 5. **Tel** 958 22 29 59.
Open daily. 📷
On the orders of the Catholic Monarchs, work on the cathedral began in 1523 to plans in a Gothic style by Enrique de Egas. It continued under the Renaissance maestro, Diego de Siloé, who also designed the façade and the magnificent Capilla Mayor. Under its dome, 16th-century windows depict Juan del Campo's *The Passion*. The west front was designed by Alonso Cano, who was born in the city. His grave can be seen in the cathedral.

⛪ Capilla Real

C/ Oficios 3. **Tel** 958 22 92 39. **Open** daily. **Closed** Jan 1, Good Fri, Dec 25.
The Royal Chapel was built for the Catholic Monarchs between 1506 and 1521 by Enrique de Egas. A magnificent *reja* (grille) by Maestro Bartolomé de Jaén encloses the high altar and the Carrara marble figures of Fernando and Isabel, their daughter Juana la Loca (the Mad) and her husband Felipe el Hermoso (the Fair). Their coffins are in the crypt. In the sacristy there are art treasures, including paintings by Botticelli and Van der Weyden.

🏛 Palacio de la Madraza

Calle Oficios 14. **Tel** 958 99 63 50.
Open 9am–2pm, 5–8pm Mon–Fri.
Originally an Arab university (now part of Granada University), this building later became the city hall. The façade is 18th century. The Moorish hall has a finely decorated *mihrab* (prayer niche).

🏛 Corral del Carbón

Calle Mariana Pineda. **Tel** 958 22 59 90. **Open** 10:30am–1:30pm, 5–8pm Mon–Fri, 10:30am–2pm Sat. **Closed** public hols.

A relic of the Moorish era, this galleried courtyard was a theatre in Christian times. Today it houses a cultural centre.

🏛 Casa de los Tiros

Calle Pavaneras 19. **Tel** 600 143 175.
Open mid-Sep–May: 10am–8:30pm Tue–Sat, 10am–5pm Sun & pub hols; Jun–mid-Sep: 9am–3:30pm Tue–Sat, 10am–5pm Sun & pub hols.
Closed 1 Jan, 1 May, 25 Dec.

Built in Mudéjar style in the 1500s, this palace owes its name

Grille by Maestro Bartolomé de Jaén enclosing the altar of the Capilla Real

Cupola in the sanctuary of the Monasterio de la Cartuja

to the muskets projecting
from its battlements (*tiro* means
"shot"). It originally belonged
to the family that was awarded
the Generalife after the fall
of Granada. Among their possessions was a sword that had
belonged to Boabdil. This is
carved on the façade, along
with statues of Mercury,
Hercules and Jason.

🏛 Alhambra and Generalife
See pp494–6.

🏛 El Bañuelo
Carrera del Darro 31. **Tel** 958 02 78
00. **Open** 9:30am–2pm Tue–Sat.
Closed public hols.

These columnated Arab baths
were built in the 11th century.

🏛 Centro Cultural Caja Granada
Avenida de la Ciencia, 2. **Tel** 958 22 22
57. **Open** 9:30am–2pm Tue & Wed,
9:30am–2pm, 4–7pm Thu–Sat,
11am–3pm Sun, public hols. 🅟
W memoriadeandalucia.com

A cultural centre with a theatre,
restaurant and the superb
Memoria de Andalucia Museum.

🏛 Monasterio de la Cartuja
Paseo de la Cartuja. **Tel** 958 16 19 32.
Open daily.

Founded in 1516 by Christian
warrior, El Gran Capitán, this
monastery outside Granada
has a dazzling cupola by Antonio
Palomino, and a Churrigueresque *(see p29)* sacristy by Luis
de Arévalo and Luis Caballo.

Granada City Centre

① Cathedral
② Capilla Real
③ Palacio de la Madraza
④ Corral del Carbón
⑤ Casa de los Tiros
⑥ Alhambra
⑦ El Bañuelo
⑧ Centro Cultural
　Caja Granada

0 metres　250
0 yards　250

Street-by-Street: The Albaicín

This corner of the city, on the hillside opposite the Alhambra, is where one feels closest to Granada's Moorish ancestry. Now mostly pedestrianized, this was the site of the first fortress built in the 13th century, and there were also once over 30 mosques. Most of the city's churches were built over their sites. Along the cobbled alleys stand *cármenes*, villas with Moorish decoration and gardens, secluded from the world by high walls. In the jasmine-scented air of evening, stroll up to the Mirador de San Nicolás for a magical view over the rooftops of the Alhambra glowing in the sunset.

Street in the Albaicín
Steep and sinuous, the Albaicín's streets are truly labyrinthine. Many street names start with *Cuesta*, meaning "slope".

Real Chancillería
Built in 1530 by the Catholic Monarchs, the Royal Chancery has a beautiful Renaissance façade.

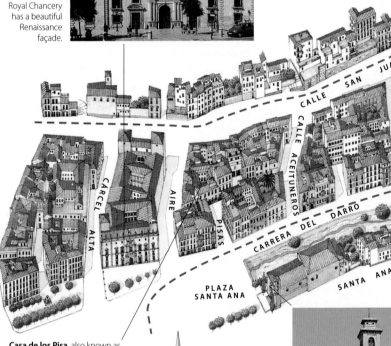

Casa de los Pisa, also known as Museo San Juan de Dios, displays works of art – some depicting St John of God, who died here in 1550.

★ **Iglesia de Santa Ana**
Just north of Plaza Nueva stands this 16th-century brick church in Mudéjar style. It has an elegant Plateresque portal and, inside, a coffered ceiling.

| 0 metres | | 50 |
| 0 yards | | 50 |

Carrera del Darro
The road along the Río Darro leads past crumbling bridges and the fine façades of ancient buildings, now all restored.

★ Museo Arqueológico
The ornate Plateresque carvings on the museum's façade include this relief of two shields. They show heraldic devices of the Nasrid kings of Granada, who were defeated by the Catholic Monarchs in 1492 (see pp60–61).

Key

— Suggested route

To Mirador de San Nicolás

DE LOS REYES

PLAZA CONCEPCIÓN

CARNERO

BANUELO

CONCEPCIÓN

CALLE ZAFRA

CALLE GLORIA

CARRETERA DEL SANTISIMO

→ To Sacromonte

CARRERA DEL DARRO

Río Darrio

The Convento de Santa Catalina was founded in 1521.

★ El Bañuelo
Star-shaped openings in the vaults let light into these well-preserved Moorish baths, which were built in the 11th century.

Sacromonte

Granada's gypsies formerly lived in the caves honeycombing this hillside. In the past, travellers would go there to enjoy spontaneous outbursts of flamenco. Today, virtually all the gypsies have moved away, but touristy flamenco shows of variable quality are still performed here in the evenings (see pp428–9). Sitting at the very top of the hill is the Abadía del Sacromonte, a Benedictine monastery. The ashes of St Cecilio, Granada's patron saint, are kept inside.

Gypsies dancing flamenco, 19th century

The Alhambra

A magical use of space, light, water and decoration characterizes this most sensual piece of architecture. It was built under Ismail I, Yusuf I and Muhammad V, caliphs when the Nasrid dynasty *(see pp58–9)* ruled Granada. Seeking to belie an image of waning power, they created their idea of paradise on Earth. Modest materials were used (plaster, timber and tiles), but they were superbly worked. Although the Alhambra suffered pillage and decay, including an attempt by Napoleon's troops to blow it up, in recent times it has undergone extensive restoration and its delicate craftsmanship still dazzles the eye.

★ **Salón de Embajadores**
The ceiling of this sumptuous throne room, built from 1334 to 1354, represents the seven heavens of the Muslim cosmos.

★ **Patio de Arrayanes**
This pool, set amid myrtle hedges and graceful arcades, reflects light into the surrounding halls.

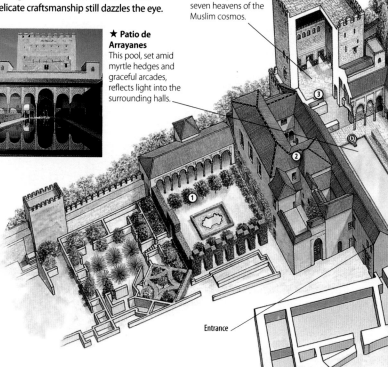

Entrance

KEY

① **Patio de Machuca**

② **Patio del Mexuar** was a council chamber where the reigning sultan listened to the petitions of his subjects and met with his ministers. It was completed in 1365.

③ **Sala de la Barca**

④ **Washington Irving's apartments**

⑤ **Jardín de Lindaraja**

⑥ **Baños Reales**

⑦ **Sala de las Dos Hermanas**, with its honeycomb dome, is regarded as the ultimate example of Spanish Islamic architecture.

⑧ **Sala de los Reyes**, a great banqueting hall, was used to hold extravagant parties and

sumptuous feasts. Beautiful ceiling paintings on leather, from the 14th century, depict tales of hunting and chivalry.

⑨ **Puerta de la Rawda**

⑩ **The Palace of Charles V** (1526) houses a collection of Spanish Islamic art, whose highlight is the Alhambra vase *(see p58)*.

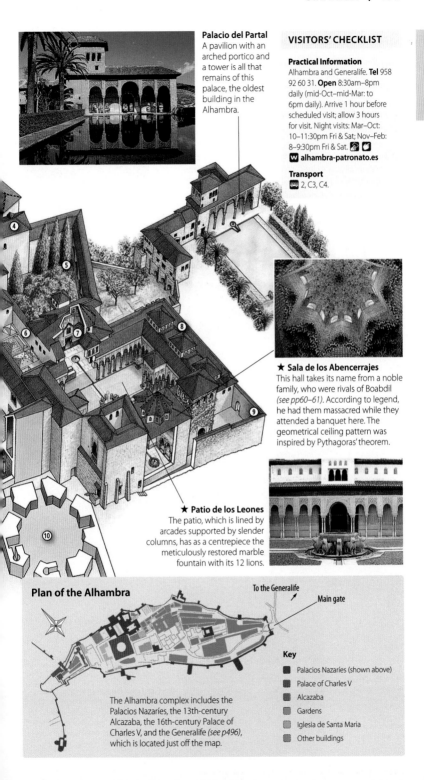

Palacio del Partal
A pavilion with an arched portico and a tower is all that remains of this palace, the oldest building in the Alhambra.

★ **Sala de los Abencerrajes**
This hall takes its name from a noble family, who were rivals of Boabdil (see pp60–61). According to legend, he had them massacred while they attended a banquet here. The geometrical ceiling pattern was inspired by Pythagoras' theorem.

★ **Patio de los Leones**
The patio, which is lined by arcades supported by slender columns, has as a centrepiece the meticulously restored marble fountain with its 12 lions.

Plan of the Alhambra

To the Generalife

Main gate

The Alhambra complex includes the Palacios Nazaríes, the 13th-century Alcazaba, the 16th-century Palace of Charles V, and the Generalife (see p496), which is located just off the map.

Key

■ Palacios Nazaríes (shown above)
■ Palace of Charles V
■ Alcazaba
■ Gardens
■ Iglesia de Santa Maria
■ Other buildings

Granada: Generalife

From the Alhambra's northern side, a footpath leads to the Generalife, the country estate of the Nasrid kings. Here, they could escape from palace intrigues and enjoy tranquillity high above the city, a little closer to heaven. The name Generalife, or Yannat al Arif, has various interpretations, perhaps the most pleasing being "the garden of lofty paradise". The gardens, begun in the 13th century, have been modified over the years. They originally contained orchards and pastures. The Generalife provides a magical setting for Granada's annual music and dance festival *(see p45)*.

The Patio de la Acequia is an enclosed Oriental garden built round a long central pool. Rows of water jets on either side make graceful arches above it.

Sala Regia

Jardines Altos
(Upper Gardens)

The Escalera del Agua is a staircase with water flowing gently down it.

The Patio de los Cipreses, otherwise known as the Patio de la Sultana, was the secret meeting place for Zoraya, wife of the Sultan Abu-l-Hasan, and her lover, the chief of the Abencerrajes.

Entrance

The Patio de Polo was the courtyard where palace visitors, arriving on horseback, would tether their steeds.

The Patio del Generalife lies just before the entrance to the Generalife. The walk from the Alhambra to the Generalife gardens passes first through the Jardines Bajos (lower gardens), before crossing this Moorish patio with its characteristically geometric pool.

The forbidding exterior of the castle above La Calahorra

❸ Castillo de La Calahorra

La Calahorra, Granada. **Tel** 958 67 70 98. 🚌 Guadix. **Open** 10am–1pm, 4–6pm Wed. 🐾

Grim, immensely thick walls and stout, cylindrical corner towers protect the castle on a hill above the village of La Calahorra. Rodrigo de Mendoza, son of Cardinal Mendoza, had the castle built for his bride: the work was carried out between 1509 and 1512 by Italian architects and craftsmen. Inside is an ornate, arcaded Renaissance courtyard over two floors with pillars and a Carrara marble staircase.

❹ Guadix

Granada. 🔼 20,100. 🚉 🚌
🏛 Avenida de la Constitución 15–18, 958 66 28 04. 🔔 Sat. 🎭 Fiesta & Feria (31 Aug–5 Sep). 🌐 guadix.es

The troglodyte quarter, with its 2,000 caves, is the town's most remarkable sight. The **Centro de Interpretación Cuevas de Guadix** and **Cueva-Museo Costumbres Populares** show how people live underground.

The **cathedral** was begun in 1594 and finished between 1701 and 1796. Relics of San Torcuato, who founded Spain's first Christian bishopric, are kept in the cathedral museum.

Near the Moorish **Alcazaba** is the fine Mudéjar-style **Iglesia de Santiago**.

🏛 Centro de Interpretación Cuevas de Guadix
C/ San Miguel 46. **Tel** 958 66 47 67. **Open** daily. 🐾

🏛 Cueva-Museo Costumbres Populares
Plaza de Ermita Nueva. **Tel** 958 66 55 69. **Open** Mon–Sat. 🐾

❺ Jaén

🔼 115,000. 🚉 🚌 🏛 Calle Maestra 18, 953 31 32 81. 🔔 Thu. 🎭 Nuestra Señora de la Capilla (11 Jun), San Lucas (18 Oct), Romería de Santa Catalina (25 Nov). 🌐 turjaen.org

The Moors called Jaén *Geen* – meaning "way station of caravans" – because of its strategic site on the road beween Andalusia and Castile. Their hilltop fortress was rebuilt as the **Castillo de Santa Catalina** after it was captured by King Fernando III in 1246. Part of it is now a parador *(see p573)*.

Andrés de Vandelvira, who was responsible for many of Úbeda's fine buildings *(see pp500–501)*, designed Jaén's **cathedral** in the 16th century. Later additions include two 17th-century towers that now flank the west front.

An old mansion, the **Palacio Villardompardo**, houses a museum of arts and crafts, and also gives access to the **Baños Árabes**, the 11th-century baths of Ali, a Moorish chieftain. These have horseshoe arches, ceilings with star-shaped windows and two ceramic vats in which bathers once immersed themselves. Tucked away in an alley is the **Capilla de San Andrés**, a Mudéjar chapel founded in the

16th century by Gutiérrez González who, as treasurer to Pope Leo X, was endowed with privileges. A gilded iron screen by Maestro Bartolomé de Jaén is the highlight of the chapel.

The **Real Monasterio de Santa Clara** was founded in the 13th century and has a lovely cloister dating from the late 16th century. Its church, which has a coffered ceiling, contains a bamboo image of Christ made in Ecuador.

The **Museo Provincial** displays Roman mosaics and sculptures, and Iberian, Greek and Roman ceramics.

🏰 Castillo de Santa Catalina
Ctra al Castillo. **Tel** 953 12 07 33. **Open** Tue–Sun. **Closed** 1 Jan, 24, 25 & 31 Dec.

🏛 Palacio Villardompardo
Plaza Santa Luisa de Marillac. **Tel** 953 24 80 68. **Open** Tue–Sun. **Closed** public hols.

🏛 Museo Provincial
Paseo de la Estación 29. **Tel** 953 10 13 66. **Open** Tue–Sun. **Closed** 1 Jan, 1 May, 25 Dec.

Horseshoe arches supporting the dome at the Baños Árabes, Jaén

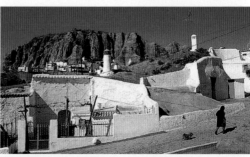

Whitewashed cave dwellings in the troglodyte quarter of Guadix

Roman bridge spanning the Guadalquivir at Andújar

❷ Andújar

Jaén. 🚹 40,000. 🚃 🚌 ℹ Pl Santa María. Torre del Reloj, 953 50 49 59. 🗓 Tue. 🎭 Romeria (last Sun of Apr).

Andújar is known for its olive oil and its pottery. It stands on the site of an Iberian town, Iliturgi, which was destroyed in the Punic Wars *(see p54)* by Scipio. The Roman conquerors built the 15-arched bridge spanning the Río Guadalquivir.

In the central square is the Gothic **Iglesia de San Miguel**, with paintings by Alonso Cano. The **Iglesia de Santa María** la Mayor has a Renaissance façade and a Mudéjar tower. Inside it is El Greco's *Christ in the Garden of Olives* (c.1605). A pilgrimage to the nearby **Santuario de la Virgen de la Cabeza** takes place in April.

Environs
The mighty fortress of **Baños de la Encina** has 15 towers and ramparts built by Caliph al Hakam II in AD 967. Further north, the road and railway between Madrid and Andalusia squeeze through a spectacular gorge in the eastern reaches of the Sierra Morena, the **Desfiladero de Despeñaperros**.

❸ Baeza

See pp502–3.

❹ Úbeda

Jaén. 🚹 35,000. 🚌 ℹ Palacio Marqués de Contadero, C/ Baja del Marqués 4, 953 77 92 04. 🗓 Fri. 🎭 San Miguel (28 Sep). 🌐 **andalucia.org**

Úbeda is a showcase of Renaissance magnificence, thanks to the patronage of some of Spain's most influential men of the 16th century, including such dignitaries as Francisco de los Cobos, secretary of state, and his greatnephew, Juan Vázquez de Molina, who gave his name to Úbeda's most historic square. The Old Town is contained within city walls that were first raised by the Moors in 852. The town was designated a UNESCO World Heritage Site in 2003.

Created on the orders of the Bishop of Jaén around 1562, the colossal former **Hospital de Santiago** was designed by Andrés de Vandelvira, who refined the Spanish Renaissance style into its more austere characteristics. The façade is flanked by square towers, one topped with a blue-and-white-tiled spire. Today the building is a conference centre. Sited in the 15th-century Casa Mudéjar, the

Úbeda City Centre

① Hospital de Santiago
② Museo Arqueológico
③ Iglesia de San Pablo
④ Capilla del Salvador
⑤ Parador de Úbeda
⑥ Palacio de las Cadenas
⑦ Santa María de los Reales Alcázares

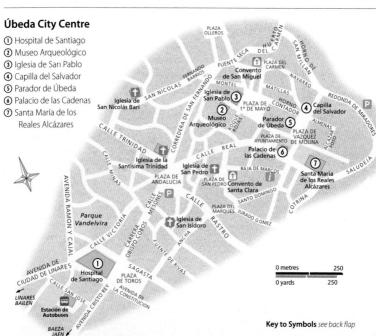

Key to Symbols *see back flap*

◀ Castle against a backdrop of snowcapped mountains, Sierra Nevada

Laguna de Valdeazores in the Parque Nacional de Cazorla

Museo Arqueológico exhibits artifacts from Neolithic to Moorish times.

The **Iglesia de San Pablo** has a 13th-century apse and a beautiful 16th-century chapel by Vandelvira. It is surmounted by a Plateresque tower that was completed in 1537.

A monument to the poet and mystic St John of the Cross (1549–91) stands in the **Plaza de Vázquez de Molina**. The **Capilla del Salvador**, on the square, was designed by three 16th-century architects – Diego de Siloé, Andrés de Vandelvira and Esteban Jamete – as the personal chapel of Francisco de los Cobos. Behind it stand Cobos' palace, with a Renaissance façade, and the Hospital de los Honrados Viejos (Hospital of the Honoured Elders), looking on to the Plaza de Santa Lucía. From here, the Redonda de Miradores follows the line of the city walls and offers views of the countryside.

Plaza Vázquez de Molina also holds Úbeda's **parador**. Built in the 16th century, but much altered in the 17th, it was the residence of Fernando Ortega Salido, dean of Málaga and chaplain of the Capilla del Salvador.

Úbeda's town hall and tourist office occupy the **Palacio de las Cadenas**, a mansion built for Vázquez de Molina by Vandelvira. It gets its name from the iron chains (cadenas) once attached to the columns supporting the main doorway.

Also on the square are the church of **Santa María de los Reales Alcazares**, which dates mainly from the 13th century, and the **Cárcel del Obispo** (Bishop's Jail), where nuns who had been punished by the bishop were confined.

🏥 Hospital de Santiago
Calle Obispo Cobos. **Tel** 953 75 08 42. **Open** Mon–Sat (Aug: Mon–Fri).

🏛 Museo Arqueológico
Casa Mudéjar, Calle Cervantes 6. **Tel** 953 10 86 23. **Open** Tue–Sun.

Capilla del Salvador, Úbeda, one of Spain's finest Renaissance churches

🔷 Parque Natural de Cazorla

Jaén. 🚌 Cazorla. 🛈 Plaza de Santa María, 953 71 01 02.

First-time visitors are amazed by the spectacular scenery of this 2150 sq-km- (830-sq-mile) nature reserve with thickly wooded mountains rising to peaks of 2,000 m (6,500 ft) and varied, abundant wildlife.

Access to the Parque Natural de Cazorla, Segura y Las Villas is via the town of Cazorla. Its imposing Moorish **Castillo de la Yedra** houses a folklore museum. A blues festival takes place in the town every July (see p45). From Cazorla, the road winds upwards beneath the ruins of the clifftop castle at **La Iruela**. After crossing a pass, it drops down to a crossroads (El Empalme del Valle) in the valley of the Río Guadalquivir. Roads lead to the river's source and to the quiet modern parador.

The main road through the park follows the river. The information centre at Torre del Vinagre is 17 km (11 miles) from the crossroads.

Environs
There is a well-restored Moorish castle at **Segura de la Sierra**, 30 km (19 miles) from the reserve's northern edge. Below it is an unusual rock-hewn bullring.

🏰 Castillo de la Yedra
Tel 953 10 14 02. **Open** Tue–Sun. **Closed** 1 Jan, 17 Sep, 24, 25 & 31 Dec. 🎫 (free for EU citizens).

Cazorla's Wildlife

More than 100 bird species live in this nature reserve, some very rare, such as the golden eagle and the griffon vulture. Cazorla is the only habitat in Spain, apart from the Pyrenees, where the lammergeier lives. Mammals in the park include the otter – active at dawn and dusk – mouflon and wild boar, and a small remaining population of Spanish ibex. The red deer was reintroduced in 1952. Among the flora supported by the limestone geology is the indigenous Viola cazorlensis.

Wild boar foraging for roots, insects and small mammals

⑬ Street-by-Street: Baeza

Nestling amid the olive groves that characterize much of Jaén province, beautiful Baeza is a small town, unusually rich in Renaissance architecture. Called Beatia by the Romans and later the capital of a Moorish fiefdom, Baeza is portrayed as a "royal nest of hawks" on its coat of arms. It was conquered by Fernando III in 1226 – the first town in Andalusia to be definitively won back from the Moors – and was then settled by Castilian knights. An era of medieval splendour followed, reaching a climax in the 16th century, when Andrés de Vandelvira's splendid buildings were erected. The town was designated a UNESCO World Heritage Site in 2003.

★ **Palacio de Jabalquinto**
An Isabelline-style (see p28) façade, flanked by elaborate, rounded buttresses, fronts this splendid Gothic palace.

Antigua Universidad
From 1542 until 1825, this Renaissance and Baroque building was one of Spain's first universities.

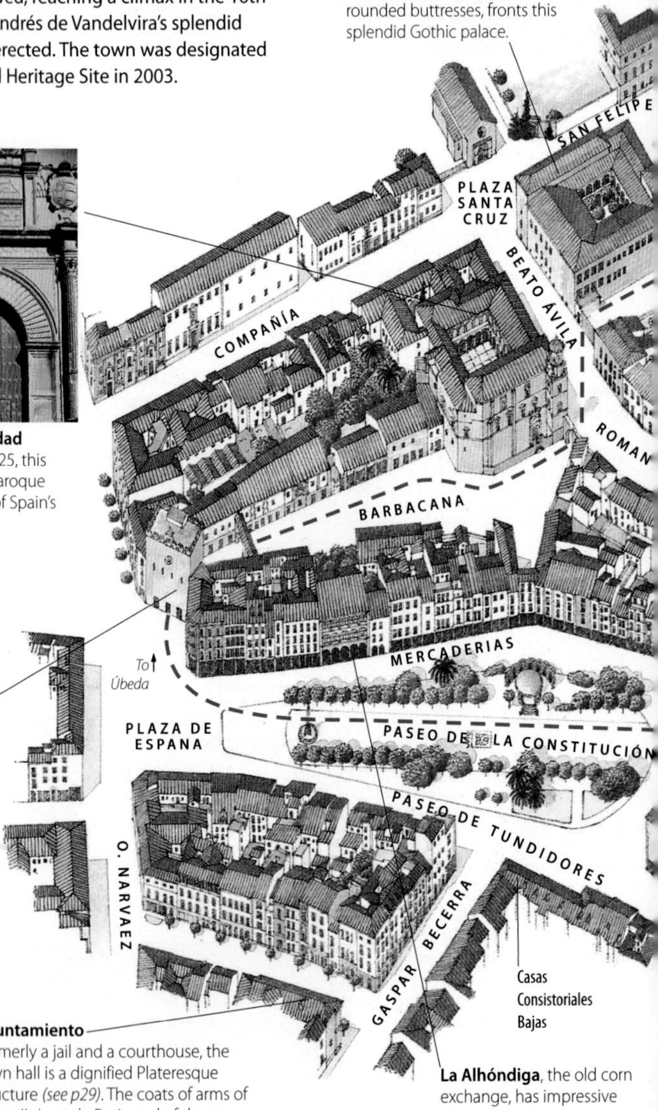

Torre de los Aliatares is a 1,000-year-old tower built by the Moors.

To Úbeda

PLAZA DE ESPANA

O. NARVAEZ

COMPAÑÍA

PLAZA SANTA CRUZ

SAN FELIPE

BEATO ÁVILA

ROMAN

BARBACANA

MERCADERIAS

PASEO DE LA CONSTITUCIÓN

PASEO DE TUNDIDORES

GASPAR BECERRA

Casas Consistoriales Bajas

Ayuntamiento
Formerly a jail and a courthouse, the town hall is a dignified Plateresque structure (see p29). The coats of arms of Felipe II, Juan de Borja and of the town of Baeza adorn its upper façade.

La Alhóndiga, the old corn exchange, has impressive triple-tier arches running along its front.

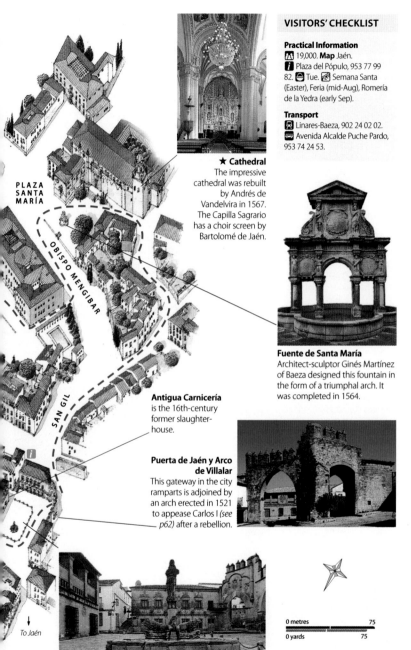

★ Cathedral
The impressive cathedral was rebuilt by Andrés de Vandelvira in 1567. The Capilla Sagrario has a choir screen by Bartolomé de Jaén.

VISITORS' CHECKLIST

Practical Information
🏠 19,000. **Map** Jaén.
ℹ️ Plaza del Pópulo, 953 77 99 82. 🚌 Tue. 🎭 Semana Santa (Easter), Feria (mid-Aug), Romería de la Yedra (early Sep).

Transport
🚆 Linares-Baeza, 902 24 02 02.
🚌 Avenida Alcalde Puche Pardo, 953 74 24 53.

Fuente de Santa María
Architect-sculptor Ginés Martínez of Baeza designed this fountain in the form of a triumphal arch. It was completed in 1564.

Antigua Carnicería
is the 16th-century former slaughter-house.

Puerta de Jaén y Arco de Villalar
This gateway in the city ramparts is adjoined by an arch erected in 1521 to appease Carlos I *(see p62)* after a rebellion.

PLAZA SANTA MARÍA

OBISPO MENGIBAR

SAN GIL

To Jaén

0 metres 75
0 yards 75

★ Plaza del Pópulo
The Casa del Pópulo, a fine Plateresque palace, now the tourist office, overlooks this square. In its centre is the Fuente de los Leones, a fountain with an Ibero-Roman statue flanked by lions.

Key
— Suggested route

For additional map symbols *see back flap*

Renaissance castle overlooking the village of Vélez Blanco

46 Vélez Blanco

Almería. 2,200. Vélez Rubio. Avenida Marqués de los Vélez, 950 41 95 85. Wed. Cristo de la Yedra (second Sun of Aug).

The mighty **Castillo de Vélez Blanco** was built between 1506 and 1513 by the first Marquis de Los Vélez. The Renaissance interiors are now displayed in the Metropolitan Museum in New York, but there is a reconstruction of one of the patios.

Just outside, the **Cueva de los Letreros** contains paintings from c.4000 BC. One depicts the Indalo, a figure holding a rainbow and believed to be a deity with magical powers, now adopted as the symbol of Almería.

Cueva de los Letreros
Camino de la Cueva de los Letreros. **Tel** 650 80 83 90. **Open** 4:30pm Wed, Sat, Sun & public hols (Jul & Aug: 7pm); book ahead.

47 Mojácar

Almería. 7,000. Calle Glorieta 1, 950 61 50 25. Wed, Sun. Moors and Christians (second weekend of Jun), San Agustín (28 Aug). **mojacar.es**

From a distance, Mojácar shimmers like the mirage of a Moorish citadel, its white houses cascading over a lofty ridge, 2 km (1 mile) inland from long, sandy beaches.

Following the Civil War *(see pp70–71)*, the village fell into ruin as most of its inhabitants emigrated, but in the 1960s it was discovered by tourists, which gave rise to a new era of prosperity. The old gateway in the walls still remains, but otherwise the village has been completely rebuilt, and holiday complexes have grown up along the nearby beaches. The coast south from Mojácar is among the least built up in Spain, with only small resorts and villages along its length.

48 Tabernas

Almería. 3,000. Carretera Nacional 340 km 464, 950 52 50 30. Wed. Virgen de las Angustias (11–15 Aug).

Tabernas is set in Europe's only desert. The town's Moorish fortress dominates the harsh surrounding scenery of cactus-dotted, rugged hills and dried-out riverbeds, which has provided the setting for many classic spaghetti westerns. Two film sets can be visited: **Mini-Hollywood** and **Fort**

Bravo Texas Hollywood, 1 km (1 mile) and 4 km (2 miles) from Tabernas respectively.

Not far from town is a solar energy research centre, where heliostats track the sun.

Environs
Sorbas sits on the edge of the chasm of the Río de Aguas. Its notable buildings are the 16th-century Iglesia de Santa María and a 17th-century mansion said to have been a summer retreat for the Duke of Alba.

Nearby is the karst scenery, honeycombed with hundreds of cave systems, of the **Yesos de Sorbas** nature reserve. Permission to explore them is required from Andalusia's environmental department.

Mini-Hollywood
Carretera N340. **Tel** 950 36 52 36. **Open** daily (Sat & Sun Nov–Easter). **oasys.playasenator.com**

Fort Bravo Texas Hollywood
Carretera N340, Tabernas. **Tel** 902 07 08 14. **Open** daily. **fortbravo.es**

Desert landscape around Tabernas, reminiscent of the Wild West

Spaghetti Westerns

Two Wild West towns lie off the N340 highway west of Tabernas. Here, visitors can re-enact classic film scenes or watch stuntmen performing bank hold-ups and saloon brawls. The *poblados del oeste* were built during the 1960s and early 1970s, when low costs and eternal sunshine made Almería the ideal location for spaghetti westerns. Sergio Leone, director of *The Good, the Bad and the Ugly*, built a ranch here and film sets sprang up in the desert. Local gypsies played Indians and Mexicans. The deserts and Arizona-style badlands are still used for television commercials and series, and by film directors such as Steven Spielberg.

Still from *For a Few Dollars More* by Sergio Leone

The 10th-century Alcazaba, which dominates Almería's old town

⑭ Almería

Almería. 🏔 170,000. ✈ 🚌 🚍 Estación Intermodal. 🛈 Parque Nicolás Salmerón, 950 17 52 20. 🎫 Tue, Fri & Sat. 🎪 Feria (last week of Aug). 🌐 turismoalmeria.com

Almería's colossal **Alcazaba**, dating from AD 995, is the largest fortress built by the Moors in Spain. The huge structure bears witness to the city's Golden Age, when it was an important port under the Caliphate of Córdoba (see pp56–7) exporting brocade, silk and cotton.

During the Reconquest, the Alcazaba withstood two major sieges before eventually falling to the armies of the Catholic Monarchs (see pp60–61) in 1489. The royal coat of arms can be seen on the Torre del Homenaje, built during their reign. The Alcazaba also has a Mudéjar chapel and gardens.

Adjacent to the Alcazaba is the old fishermen's and gypsy quarter of **La Chanca**, where some families live in caves with painted façades. This district is poor, and it is unwise to walk around here alone or at night.

Brightly coloured entrance to a gypsy cave in La Chanca district

Berber pirates from North Africa often raided Almería. Consequently, the **cathedral** looks almost like a castle, with its four towers, thick walls and small windows. The site was originally a mosque. This was converted into a church, but in 1522 it was destroyed in an earthquake. Work on the present building began in 1524 under the direction of Diego de Siloé, who designed the nave and high altar in Gothic style. The Renaissance façade and the carved walnut choir stalls are by Juan de Orea. Traces of Moorish Almería's most important mosque can be seen in the **Templo San Juan**. The **Plaza Vieja** is an attractive 17th-century arcaded square. On one side is the **town hall** (ayuntamiento), with a cream and pink façade (1899). In Calle Real, the Castillo de Tabernas Museo del Aceite de Oliva (tel 950 27 28 88) illustrates the fine art of making olive oil.

Environs
One of Europe's most import-ant examples of a Copper Age settlement is located at **Los Millares**, near Gádor, 17 km (11 miles) north of Almería. As many as 2,000 people may have occupied the site around 2500 BC.

🏛 **Alcazaba**
C/ Almanzor. **Tel** 950 80 10 08. **Open** Tue–Sun. **Closed** 1 Jan, 25 Dec. 🌐 museosdeandalucia.es

🏛 **Los Millares**
Santa Fé de Mondújar. **Tel** 677 90 34 04. **Open** Wed–Sun. **Closed** 1 Jan, 6 Jan, 25 Dec.

⑮ Parque Natural de Cabo de Gata

Almería. 🚌 San José. 🛈 Centro de Visitantes de las Amoladeras, Carretera Alp-202 km 7 (Retamar-Pujaire), 950 16 04 35. **Open** daily.

Towering cliffs of volcanic rock, sand dunes, salt flats and secluded coves characterize the 290-sq-km (110-sq-mile) Parque Natural de Cabo de Gata. Within its confines are a few fishing villages, and the small resort of San José. A lighthouse stands at the end of the cabo (cape), which can be reached by road from the village of Cabo de Gata. The park includes a stretch of seabed 2 km (1 mile) wide and the marine flora and fauna protected within it attract scuba divers and snorkellers.

The dunes and saltpans between the cape and the Playa de San Miguel are a habitat for thorny jujube trees. Many migrating birds stop here, and among the 170 or so bird species recorded are flamingos, avocets, griffon vultures and Dupont's larks.

Environs
Set amid citrus trees on the edge of the Sierra de Alhamilla, **Níjar's** fame stems from the pottery and the handwoven jarapas – blankets and rugs – that are made here. The barren plain between Níjar and the sea has been brought under cultivation using vast plastic greenhouses to conserve the scarce water.

The dramatic, dark volcanic rocks at Cabo de Gata, east of Almería

SPAIN'S ISLANDS

Introducing Spain's Islands   **508–509**

The Balearic Islands   **510–531**

The Canary Islands   **532–555**

Introducing Spain's Islands

Spain's two groups of islands lie in separate seas – the Balearics in the Mediterranean and the Canaries in the Atlantic, off the African coast. Both are popular package-tour destinations blessed with warm climates, good beaches and clear waters. But each has more to offer than high-rise hotels, fast-food restaurants and discos. The Balearics have white villages, wooded hills, caves and prehistoric monuments, while the extraordinary volcanic landscapes of the Canaries are unlike any other part of Spain. Four of Spain's national parks are in the Canary Islands.

Ibiza (see pp514–16) is the liveliest of the Balearic Islands. Ibiza town and Sant Antoni are the main tourist centres, offering world-famous nightlife and excellent beaches.

Eivissa (Ibiza)
• Ibiza

Formentera

CANARY ISLANDS
(see pp532–55)

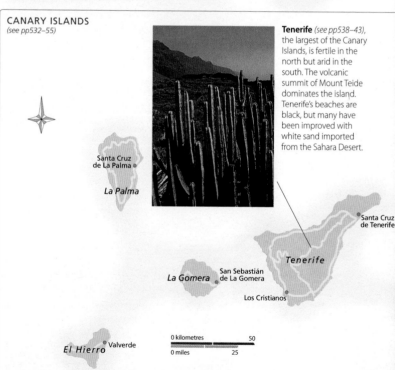

Tenerife (see pp538–43), the largest of the Canary Islands, is fertile in the north but arid in the south. The volcanic summit of Mount Teide dominates the island. Tenerife's beaches are black, but many have been improved with white sand imported from the Sahara Desert.

Santa Cruz de La Palma •
La Palma

° Santa Cruz de Tenerife

Tenerife

La Gomera ° San Sebastián de La Gomera

Los Cristianos °

| 0 kilometres | 50 |
| 0 miles | 25 |

El Hierro ° Valverde

◄ Yachts moored in Fornell harbour, Menorca

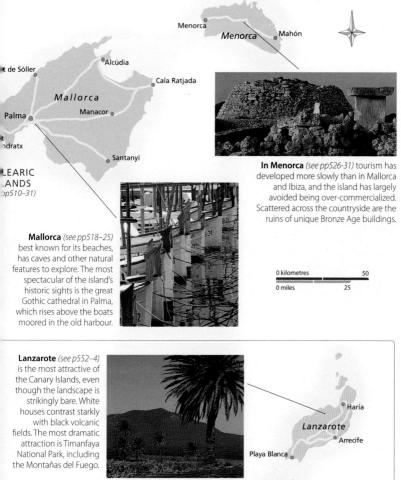

Menorca

Menorca　•Mahón

•Alcúdia

t de Sóller

Cala Ratjada

Mallorca

Palma　Manacor •

t

ndratx

•Santanyí

EARIC
ANDS
p510–31)

In Menorca *(see pp526-31)* tourism has developed more slowly than in Mallorca and Ibiza, and the island has largely avoided being over-commercialized. Scattered across the countryside are the ruins of unique Bronze Age buildings.

Mallorca *(see pp518–25)* best known for its beaches, has caves and other natural features to explore. The most spectacular of the island's historic sights is the great Gothic cathedral in Palma, which rises above the boats moored in the old harbour.

0 kilometres　　　　50

0 miles　　　25

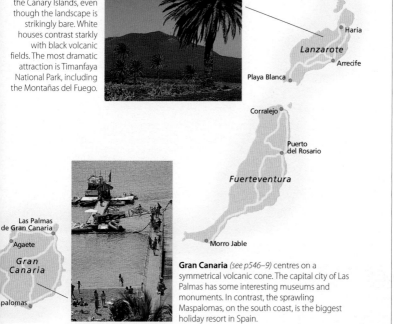

Lanzarote *(see p552–4)* is the most attractive of the Canary Islands, even though the landscape is strikingly bare. White houses contrast starkly with black volcanic fields. The most dramatic attraction is Timanfaya National Park, including the Montañas del Fuego.

•Haría

Lanzarote

•Arrecife

Playa Blanca •

Corralejo •

Puerto
del Rosario •

Fuerteventura

Las Palmas
de Gran Canaria •

•Agaete

*Gran
Canaria*

•Morro Jable

palomas •

Gran Canaria *(see p546–9)* centres on a symmetrical volcanic cone. The capital city of Las Palmas has some interesting museums and monuments. In contrast, the sprawling Maspalomas, on the south coast, is the biggest holiday resort in Spain.

THE BALEARIC ISLANDS

Ibiza · Formentera · Mallorca · Menorca

Chic resorts and attractive coves and beaches, combined with a climate which is hot but never uncomfortably so, have made tourism the mainstay of life along the coasts of the Balearic Islands. Inland, there is peace and quiet in abundance, and a great variety of sights to seek out: wooded hills, pretty white villages, monasteries, country churches, caves and prehistoric monuments.

Standing at a crossroads in the Mediterranean, the Balearic Islands have been plundered or colonized in turn by Phoenicians, Greeks, Carthaginians, Romans, Moors and Turks. In the 13th century Catalan settlers brought their language, a dialect of which is widely spoken today.

The islands can justifiably claim to cater for all tastes: from sunseekers on package holidays, for whom the larger resorts serve as brash fun factories, to jet-setters and film stars, who head for luxurious but discreet hideaways in the hills. The largest island, where tourism has been established the longest, is Mallorca. A massive Gothic cathedral stands near the waterfront of Palma, the capital.

The green countryside of Menorca is dotted with prehistoric monuments and its towns full of noble, historic mansions. The coast of Ibiza is notched by innumerable rocky coves. The island's hilly interior is characterized by brilliant white farmhouses and robust churches. On Formentera, small and relatively undeveloped, the pace of life is slow. The islets surrounding the four principal islands are mainly uninhabited; one of them, Cabrera (off Mallorca), is a national park.

View through the window of one of Ibiza's traditional, whitewashed farmhouses

◀ The dazzling turquoise water at Cala Salada, Ibiza

Exploring the Balearics

Though the Balearic islands are often associated with high-density, inexpensive package tourism, they offer enough variety to satisfy everyone's tastes. For those unattracted by the bustle of the coastal resorts and their beautiful beaches, the countryside and the old towns of Palma, Ibiza, Maó and Ciutadella are relatively undisturbed. Mallorca is by far the most culturally rich of the Balearics, with its distinguished collection of modern and traditional galleries, and interesting museums. Menorca is strong on Neolithic remains and Neo-Colonial architecture, while Ibiza is for lovers of clear, painterly light and rustic peasant houses; it also has some of the wildest nightclubs in Europe. Formentera – for many, the most alluring island – has crystal water, white sand, a pure, parched landscape and total tranquillity.

Poblat des Pescadors in the tourist village of Binibeca

Early-morning mist on the waters of Port de Pollença in Mallorca

MALLORCA SÓ
Dej
VALLDEMOSSA ⑨
Estellencs ⑧ LA
GF
ANDRATX ⑦ PALMA
Port d'Andratx
Palma Nova *Badí*
Palí
Cap

IBIZA
ELS AMUNTS
Sant Vicenç
④
SANT ANTONI ① ⑤ SANTA EULÀRIA
C731 C733
SANT JOSEP ② Jesús
Sa Talaiassa 475m ③ IBIZA (EIVISSA)
Ses Salines
Sant Francesc ⑥ FORMENTERA
Cala Saona Es Caló
Cap de Barbaria *Platja de Migjorn* *Punta Roja*

Getting Around

Nearly all foreign visitors to the Balearics arrive by plane – the no-frills airlines making it all the more popular. Mallorca, Menorca and Ibiza connect to major European cities as well as Madrid, Barcelona and Valencia. Several airlines fly to most other Spanish cities out of Son Sant Joan Airport in Palma. Another way of arriving is by boat from Barcelona, Valencia or Dénia. Between the islands there are regular ferry services, run by Transmediterranea, Balearia and Iscomar. Mallorca is the only island with rail services, which run between Palma and Inca (now extended to Sa Pobla and Manacor), and between Palma and Sóller. Roads vary from excellent to poor. The best way to get around is by car, except on Formentera, where cycling is best.

For hotels and restaurants in this region see pp574–5 and pp602–4

Sights at a Glance

1. Sant Antoni
2. Sant Josep
3. Ibiza (Eivissa)
4. Els Amunts
5. Santa Eulària
6. Formentera
7. Andratx
8. La Granja
9. Valldemossa
10. Alfàbia
11. Sóller
12. Santuario de Lluc
13. Pollença
14. *Palma pp522–5*
15. Puig de Randa
16. Capocorb Vell
17. Cabrera
18. Felanitx
19. Coves del Drac
20. Ciutadella
21. Ferreries
22. Es Mercadal
23. Maó
24. Cales Coves

A peaceful stroll on the sands of Ibiza's Sant Miquel beach

MENORCA

Cap de Cavalleria

Fornells

CIUTADELLA ㉒ ME1 FERRERIES ㉑ ㉒ ES MERCADAL

Cala Sta Galdana

Cap d' Artrutx

Alaior

㉓ MAÓ

CALES COVES ㉔

Binibeca

Sant Lluís

POLLENÇA ⑬ Port de Pollença

Cap de Formentor

Alcúdia

⑫ SANTUARIO DE LLUC

Sa Sóbra

rnalutx

Badia d'Alcúdia

Sa Pobla

.BIA

Inca

Sineu

Santa Margalida

Capdepera

Cala Rajada

Cap des Freu

Artà

Coves d'Artà

Son Servera

Petra

Montuïri

Manacor

Coves dels Hams

Portocristo

⑮ PUIG DE RANDA

Arenal

Llucmajor

⑲ COVES DEL DRAC

⑱ FELANITX

Campos

⑯ CAPOCORB VELL

Colònia Sant Jordi

Santanyí

Castell de Santueri

Portopetro

Cala Figuera

Cap de ses Salines

⑰ CABRERA

| 0 kilometres | 25 |
| 0 miles | 15 |

The rocky coast around the Coves d'Artà in Mallorca

Key

- ══ Motorway
- ▬ Major road
- ═ Secondary road
- ▬ Scenic route
- — Minor railway
- △ Summit

For additional map symbols *see back flap*

Ibiza

This small island, the nearest of the Balearics to the coast of Spain, was unknown and untouched by tourism until the 1960s, when it suddenly appeared in Europe's holiday brochures along with Benidorm and Torremolinos. There is still a curious, indefinable magic about Ibiza (Eivissa) and the island has not entirely lost its character. The countryside, particularly in the north, is a rural patchwork of groves of almonds, olives and figs, and wooded hills. Ibiza town retains the air of a 1950s Spanish provincial borough. At once package-tour paradise, hippie hideout and glamour hot spot, this is one of the Mediterranean's mythical destinations.

An Ibizan shepherdess

The bustling harbour of the resort of Sant Antoni

❶ Sant Antoni

Baleares. 🔼 17,500. 🚌 🚢
ℹ️ Passeig de Ses Fonts, 971 34 33 63. 🎎 Sant Antoni (17 Jan), Sant Bartolomé (24 Aug). 🆆 ibiza.travel

Ibiza's second town, Sant Antoni was known by the Romans as Portus Magnus because of its large natural harbour. Formerly a tiny fishing village, it has turned into a sprawling and exuberant resort. Although it was once notoriously over-commercialized, the town has undergone a dramatic face-lift. Nevertheless, the 14th-century parish church of Sant Antoni is practically marooned in a sea of modern high-rise hotels.

To the north of Sant Antoni, on the road to Cala Salada, is the chapel of **Santa Agnès**, an unusual early Christian temple (not to be confused with the village of the same name). When this catacomb-like chapel was discovered, in 1907, it contained Moorish weapons and fragments of pottery.

❷ Sant Josep

Baleares. 🔼 13,500. ℹ️ Sant Josep Airport, 971 80 91 18. 🎎 Sant Josep (19 Mar). 🆆 ibiza.travel

The village of Sant Josep, the administrative centre of south-west Ibiza, lies in the shadow of Ibiza's highest mountain. At 475 m (1,560 ft), Sa Talaiassa offers a panorama of all Ibiza, including the islet of **Es Vedrà**, rising from the sea like a rough-cut pyramid. For the most

The salt lakes of Ses Salines, a haven for many bird species

accessible view of this enormous rock, take the coastal road to the sandy cove of Cala d'Hort, where there are a number of good restaurants and a quiet beach.

Environs
Before tourism, salt was Ibiza's main industry, most of it coming from the salt flats at **Ses Salines** in the southeast corner of the island. Mainland Spain is the chief consumer of this salt, but much goes to the Faroe Islands and Scandinavia for salting fish. Ses Salines is also an important refuge for birds, including the flamingo. **Es Cavallet**, 3 km (2 miles) east, is an unspoiled stretch of soft, white sand. The Phoenician village of **Sa Caleta** is a UNESCO World Heritage Site.

❸ Ibiza

Baleares. 🔼 35,000. ✈️ 🚌 🚢
ℹ️ Plaza de la Catedral, 971 39 92 32. 🛒 Mon–Sat. 🎎 San Juan Bautista (24 Jun), Fiestas Patronales (1–8 Aug). 🆆 eivissa.es

The old quarter of Ibiza (Eivissa), known also as Dalt Vila, or upper town, is a miniature citadel guarding the mouth of the almost circular bay. The **Portal de ses Taules**, a magnificent gateway in the north wall of the 16th-century fortifications, carries the finely carved coat of arms of the kingdom of Aragón, to which the Balearic Islands belonged in the Middle Ages (see p231). Inside the walls is the 16th-century **Església de Santo Domingo** with its three red-tiled domes. The Baroque interior, with its barrel-vaulted ceiling and frescoed walls, has been restored to its former glory. Works of art by Erwin Bechtold, Barry Flanagan and other artists connected with Ibiza are on display in the **Museu d'Art Contemporani**, just inside the Portal de ses Taules. Crowning the whole Dalt Vila is the **cathedral**, a 13th-century Catalan Gothic building with 18th-century additions. The cathedral's Museo de la Sacristia houses assorted works of art.

Under the Carthaginians, the soil of Ibiza was considered holy. The citizens of Carthage deemed it an honour to be buried in the **Necrópolis Púnica del Puig des Molins**. Part of it can be visited by the public.

The crossroads village of **Jesús**, 3 km (2 miles) north, is worth a visit for its 16th-century church. Originally built as part of

A backstreet in the Sa Penya district of Ibiza town

a Franciscan monastery, it has a 16th-century altarpiece by Rodrigo de Osona the Younger.

Ⅲ Museu d'Art Contemporani
Ronda Narcís Puget s/n.
Tel 971 30 27 23. **Open** Tue–Sun.
Closed Mon & public hols.

☐ Necrópolis Púnica del Puig des Molins
Via Romana 31. **Tel** 971 30 17 71.
Open Tue–Sun. **Closed** Mon & public hols. **W maef.es**

❹ Els Amunts

Baleares. 🚍 Sant Miquel.
ℹ C/ Mariano Riquer Wallis 4, Santa Eulària d'es Riu, 971 33 07 28.

Els Amunts is the local name for the uplands of northern Ibiza, which stretch from Sant Antoni on the west coast to Sant Vicenç in the northeast. Though hardly a mountain range – Es Fornás is the highest point, at a mere 450 m (1,480 ft) – the area's

A view across the port towards Ibiza's upper town

inaccessibility has kept it unspoiled. There are few special sights here, apart from the land-scape: pine-clad hills sheltering fertile valleys whose rich red soil is planted with olive, almond and fig trees, and the occasional vineyard. Tourist enclaves are scarce, except for a handful of small resorts, such as Port de Sant Miquel, Portinatx and Sant Vicenç. Inland, villages like Sant Joan and Santa Agnès offer an insight into Ibiza's quiet, rural past.

The architectural high points of northern Ibiza are several beautiful white churches, like the one in **Sant Miquel**, which, on Thursdays in summer, is host to a display of Ibizan folk dancing. Outside Sant Llorenç is the tranquil, fortified hamlet of **Balàfia**, with flat-roofed houses, tiny whitewashed alleys, and a watchtower that was used as a fortress during raids by the Turks.

Ibiza's Hottest Spots

Ibiza's reputation for extraordinary summer nightlife is largely justified. The main action takes place in the Calle de la Virgen in the old harbour district, with its bars, fashion boutiques and restaurants; and the mega-discos out of town – Privilege, Pachá, Amnesia and Es Paradis. Some close as late as 7am, when the wildest club of them all, Space, is only just opening its doors. (Most clubs close during winter.) Ibiza has long been a magnet for the rich and famous. Celebrities seem to be more elusive of late, but well-known faces can still be glimpsed dining in Las Dos Lunas, being seen at Ocean Beach Club day or night, or soaking up the rays on the beach at Ses Salines.

Nightclubbers enjoying a bubble bath at Amnesia

One of the many beautiful beaches along the unspoiled shores of the island of Formentera

❺ Santa Eulària

Baleares. 28,000. 🚌 🚎 *i* Carrer Mariano Riquer Wallis 4, 971 33 07 28. 🛒 Wed & Sat. 🎉 Fiesta (12 Feb), Cala Llonga (14–15 Aug).

The town of Santa Eulària d'es Riu (Santa Eulalia del Río), on the island's only river, has managed to hold on to its character far more than many other Spanish resorts.

The 16th-century church, with its covered courtyard, and the surrounding old town, were built on the top of a little hill, the **Puig de Missa**, because this site was more easily defended in times of war than the shore below.

Adjacent to the church is the **Museo Etnológico de Ibiza y Formentera**, a folk museum housed in an Ibizan farmhouse. The exhibits (labelled in Catalan only) include traditional costumes, farming implements, toys and an olive press. A collection of photographs covering 50 years shows how Ibiza has changed.

The domed roof of Santa Eulària's 16th-century church

Two art and craft markets, Punta Arabí (Wed) and Las Dalias (Sat), feature hundreds of stalls.

🏛 Museo Etnológico de Ibiza y Formentera
Can Ros, Puig de Missa. **Tel** 971 33 28 45. **Open** Mon–Sat. **Closed** mid-Dec– mid-Jan. 🎫 🖾

❻ Formentera

Baleares. 7,000. 🚢 from Ibiza. *i* Estación Marítima, Puerto de La Savina, 971 32 20 57. 🛒 Sun. 🎉 Fiesta Sant Jaume (25 Jul). **ⓦ formentera.es**

An hour's boat ride from Ibiza will bring you to this largely unspoiled island where waters are blue and way of life is slow.

From the small port of La Savina, where the boat docks, there are buses to other parts of the island, or you can hire a car, moped or bicycle from one of the shops nearby.

Sant Francesc Xavier, Formentera's tiny capital, is situated 3 km (2 miles) from La Savina. Most of the island's amenities are in this town, plus a pretty 18th-century church in the main square, and a folk museum.

From Sant Francesc, a bumpy minor road leads for 9 km (6 miles) southwards, ending at Cap de Barbaria, the site of an 18th-century defensive tower and a lighthouse.

Formentera is entirely flat, apart from the small plateau of **La Mola**, which takes up the whole eastern end of the island.

From the fishing port of Es Caló the road winds upwards past the Restaurante Es Mirador, with its panoramic view, to the village of Nostra Senyora del Pilar de la Mola on top of the plateau. About 3 km (2 miles) to the east is a lighthouse, Far de la Mola, sited on the highest point of the island. Nearby stands a monument to Jules Verne (1828–1905), who used Formentera for the setting of one of his novels, *Hector Servadac*.

Although there are many purple road signs indicating places of cultural interest on Formentera, most lead only to disappointment. But one sight well worth seeking out is the megalithic sepulchre of **Ca Na Costa** (2000 BC) near Sant Francesc, the only one of its kind in the Balearics. This monument, a circle of upright stone slabs, predates the Carthaginians *(see pp52–3)*.

However, the island's great strength is its landscape, which has a delicate beauty and some of the Mediterranean's last unspoiled shorelines. More than 60 per cent of the island's landscape is protected by law. The finest beaches are, arguably, Migjorn and Cala Sahona, southwest of Sant Francesc. Nearly all beaches have nudist areas.

Illetes and Llevant are two beautiful beaches on either side of a long sandy spit in the far north of the island. To the north, between Formentera and Ibiza, is the island of **Espalmador**, with its natural springs.

The Flavours of the Balearics

This quartet of beautiful islands, strategically positioned on ancient trading routes, has been fought over for thousands of years. Each occupying force – Arabs, Catalans, French and British among them – has left its mark and the local cuisine reflects this. Mediterranean seafood, particularly spectacular lobster and crayfish, remains the most prominent local ingredient, but the islands are also known for their delicious pastries and desserts, like the feather-light *ensaimada* from Mallorca and the typical Ibizan *flaó*. Cured meats *(embutits)* and traditionally made cheeses are also local specialities.

Locally grown oranges

Seafood from the Mediterranean in a Mallorcan fish market

Mallorca and Menorca

Seafood predominates in the Balearic islands. Menorca is renowned for *caldereta de langosta* (spiny lobster stew), once a simple fishermen's dish but now an expensive delicacy. The classic Mallorcan dish is *pa amb oli*, a slice of toasted country bread rubbed with garlic and drizzled with local olive oil. Menorca's creamy garlic sauce *all i oli* is a delicious accompaniment to meat and seafood dishes, and the island also produces fine cheese, *formatge de Maó*.

Ibiza and Formentera

Seafood also reigns supreme on Ibiza and its quieter little sister, Formentera, especially in *calders* (stews) such as *borrida de rajada* (skate with potatoes, eggs and pastis), and *guisat de peix*. Pork is the staple meat. For a picnic, try *cocarrois*, pastries filled with meat, fish or vegetables and *formatjades*, soft-cheese-filled pastries flavoured with cinnamon. Delicious local desserts include *gató* (almond cake served with ice cream) and Ibizan *flaó*, made with creamy cheese and eggs, and flavoured with mint.

Cuscussó menorquin (bread pudding)

Flaó ibicenco

Galletas de alaior (aniseed biscuits)

Ensaimadas

Formatjades

El gató (almond tart)

Appetizing selection of delicious Balearic pastries

Regional Dishes and Specialities

All i oli

Fish and shellfish (particularly the revered local lobster) are omnipresent in the Balearics, particularly along the coast. Try them simply grilled to fully appreciate their freshness (many seaside restaurants have their own fishing boats), but you'll also find wonderful, slow-cooked stews which are bursting with flavour. The rugged inland regions provide mountain lamb and kid, along with pork, which is also used to make *embutits* including spicy Mallorcan *sobrassada* which is delicious with *pa amb oli*. The tourist industry hasn't killed off the long-standing farming tradition on the Balearics, which produce plentiful fruit and vegetables. Mallorca makes its own robust wines, particularly around the village of Binissalem, while Menorca, thanks to the long British occupation of the island, makes its own piquant gin.

Tumbet de peix A fish pie, made with layers of firm white fish, peppers, aubergine (eggplant) and sliced boiled egg.

Mallorca

Mallorca is often likened to a continent rather than simply an island. Its varied nature never fails to astonish, whether you are looking for landscape, culture or just entertainment. No other European island has a wider range of scenery, from the fertile plains of central Mallorca to the almost alpine peaks of the Tramuntana. The island's mild climate and lovely beaches have made it one of Spain's foremost package tour destinations but there is a wealth of culture, too, evident in sights like Palma Cathedral *(see pp524–5)*. Mallorca's appeal lies also in its charm as a living, working island: the cereal and fruit crops of the central plains, and the vineyards around Binissalem are vital to the island's economy.

Terraced orange grove in the Sierra Tramuntana

❼ Andratx

Baleares. 🏔 10,500. 🚌 *i* Avenida Mateo Bosch, 971 67 13 00. 🚌 Wed. 🎉 San Pedro (29 Jun).

This small town lies amid a valley of almond groves in the shadow of Puig de Galatzó, which rises to 1,026 m (3,366 ft). With its ochre and white shuttered houses and the old watchtowers perched high on a hill above the town, Andratx is a very pretty place.

The road southwest leads down to **Port d'Andratx** 5 km (3 miles) away. Here, in an almost totally enclosed bay, expensive yachts are moored in rows along the harbour and luxury holiday homes pepper the surrounding hillsides. In the past, Port d'Andratx's main role was as the fishing port and harbour for Andratx, but since the early 1960s it has gradually been transformed into an exclusive holiday resort for the rich and famous. When visiting Port d'Andratx, it is a good idea

to leave all thoughts of the real Mallorca behind and simply enjoy it for what it is – a chic and affluent resort.

❽ La Granja

Carretera de Esporlas. **Tel** 971 61 00 32. 🚌 **Open** daily; Feb–Oct: horse dressage shows 3–4:25pm Wed & Fri. 🎉 ♿ 🖥 **lagranja.net**

La Granja is a private estate, or *possessió*, near the little country town of Esporles. Formerly a Cistercian convent, it is now the property of the Seguí family, who have opened their largely unspoiled 18th-century house to the public as a kind of living museum. Peacocks roam the gardens, salt cod and hams hang in the kitchen, *The Marriage of Figaro* plays in the ballroom, and the slight air of chaos just adds to the charm of the place.

Bust of Frédéric Chopin at Valldemossa

❾ Valldemossa

Baleares. 🏔 1,800. 🚌 *i* Avenida Palma 7, 971 61 20 19. 🚌 Sun. 🎉 Santa Catalina Thomás (28 Jul), San Bartolomé (24 Aug).

This pleasant mountain town is linked with George Sand, the French novelist who stayed here in the winter of 1838–9 and later wrote unflatteringly of the island in *Un Hiver à Majorque*. Dearer to Mallorcans was the Polish composer Frédéric Chopin (1810–49), who stayed with Sand at the **Real Cartuja de Jesús de Nazaret**. "Chopin's cell", off the monastery's main courtyard, is where a few of his works were written, and still houses the piano on which he composed.

Nearby is a 17th-century pharmacy displaying outlandish medicinal preparations such as "powdered nails of the beast". In the cloisters is an art museum with works by Tàpies, Miró and the Mallorcan artist Juli Ramis (1909–90), and a series of Picasso illustrations, *The Burial of the Count of Orgaz*, inspired by the El Greco painting of the same name *(see p36)*.

🏛 **Real Cartuja de Jesús de Nazaret**

Plaça de la Cartuja de Valldemossa. **Tel** 696 40 59 92. **Open** daily. **Closed** 1 Jan, 25 Dec, Sun in Dec & Jan. 🎉 ♿ 🖥 **celdadechopin.es**

A view across the harbour of Port d'Andratx

⑩ Alfàbia

Carretera de Sóller km 17. **Tel** 971 61 31 23. 🚌 **Closed** Sat pm & Sun, Dec. ♿ 🇼 jardinesdealfabia.com

Very few *possessiós* in Mallorca are open to the public, which makes Alfàbia worth visiting. The house and garden are an excellent example of a typical Mallorcan aristocratic estate and exude a Moorish atmosphere. Very little remains of the original 14th-century architecture, so it is well worth looking out for the Mudéjar inscription on the ceiling of the entrance hall and the Hispano-Arabic fountains and pergola. The garden is a sumptuous 19th-century creation, making imaginative use of shade and the play of water.

⑪ Sóller

Baleares. 🅰 9,100. 🚉 🚌 ℹ Plaza España 15, 971 63 80 08. 🕒 Sat. 🎪 Sa Fira & Es Firó (2nd week May).

Soller is a little town grown fat on the produce of its olive groves and orchards, which climb up the slopes of the Sierra Tramuntana. In the 19th century Sóller traded its oranges and wine for French goods, and the town retains a faintly Gallic, bourgeois feel.

One of Sóller's best-known features is its delightfully old-fashioned narrow-gauge railway, complete with quaint wooden carriages. The town, whose station is in the Plaça d'Espanya, lies on a scenic route between Palma and the fishing village of Port de Sóller 5 km (3 miles) to the west.

Environs
From Sóller a road winds southwards along the spectacular west coast to **Deià** (Deyá). This village was once the home of Robert Graves (1895–1985), the English poet and novelist, who came to live here in 1929. His simple tombstone can be seen in the small cemetery. The **Museu Arqueològic**, curated by the archaeologist William Waldren, offers a glimpse into prehistoric Mallorca. Outside the village

Houses and trees crowded together on the hillside of Deià

is **Son Marroig**, the estate of Austrian Archduke Ludwig Salvator (1847–1915), who documented the Balearics in a series of books included in a display of his possessions.

🏛 Museu Arqueològic
Calle Teix 4, Es Clot Deià. **Tel** 971 63 90 01. **Open** Tue, Thu, Sun. 🎟

Statue of La Moreneta at the Santuario de Lluc

⑫ Santuario de Lluc

Lluc. 🚌 from Palma. **Tel** 971 87 15 25. **Open** Sun–Fri. 🏛 museum only. 🇼 lluc.net

High in the mountains of the Sierra Tramuntana, in the remote village of Lluc, is an institution regarded by many as the spiritual heart of Mallorca. The Santuario de Lluc was built mainly in the 17th and 18th centuries on the site of an ancient shrine. The monastery's Baroque church, with its imposing façade, contains the stone image of La Moreneta, the Black Virgin of Lluc, supposedly found by a young shepherd boy on a nearby hilltop in the 13th century. The altar and sanctuary of one chapel are by Catalan architect and designer Antoni Gaudí *(see pp144–5)*. Along the Camí dels Misteris, the paved walkway up to this hilltop, there are some bronze bas-reliefs by Pere Llimona. Just off the main Plaça dels Pelegrins are a café and bar, a pharmacy and a shop. The museum, situated on the first floor, includes Mallorcan paintings and medieval manuscripts. The monastery incorporates a guesthouse.

From Lluc, 13 km (8 miles) of tortuous road winds through the hills and descends towards the coast, ending at the beautiful rocky bay of **Sa Calobra**. From here, it is just 5 minutes' walk up the coast to the deep gorge of the Torrent de Pareis.

Sheer cliff face rising out of the sea at Sa Calobra

The cloisters of the Convent de Santo Domingo in Pollença

⑬ Pollença

Baleares. ⚑ 15,500. 🚌 ℹ Calle Santo Domingo 17, 971 53 50 77. 🛉 Sun. 🎉 Sant Antoni (17 Jan), Patron Saint (2 Aug).

Although Pollença has become one of Mallorca's most popular tourist spots, it still appears unspoiled. The town, with its ochre-coloured stone houses and winding lanes, is picturesquely sited on the edge of fertile farmland. The Plaça Major, with its bars frequented mainly by locals, has an old-world atmosphere.

Pollença has fine churches, including the 18th-century **Parròquia de Nostra Senyora dels Angels** and the Convent de Santo Domingo, containing the **Museu de Pollença**, with its displays of archaeology and art. It also holds Pollença's Classical Music Festival in July and August. A chapel on the hilltop, **El Calvari**, is reached either by road or a long climb of 365 steps. On the altar there is a Gothic Christ, carved in wood.

Environs

Alcúdia, 10 km (6 miles) to the east, is surrounded by 14th-century walls with two huge gateways. Near the town centre is the **Museu Monografico de Pollentia**, exhibiting statues, jewellery and other remains found in the Roman settlement of Pollentia, 2km (1 mile) south of Alcúdia.

🏛 **Museu de Pollença**
Calle Guillem Cife de Colonya 33. **Tel** 971 53 11 66. **Open** Tue–Sun. 🅿

🏛 **Museu Monografico de Pollentia**
Calle San Jaume 30, Alcúdia. **Tel** 971 54 70 04. **Open** Tue–Sun. 🅿

⑭ Palma de Mallorca

See pp522–5.

⑮ Puig de Randa

8 km (5 miles) northeast of Llucmajor. 🚌 to Llucmajor, then taxi. ℹ C/ Constitución 1, Llucmajor, 971 66 91 62.

In the middle of a fertile plain called the *pla* rises a mini-mountain 543 m (1,780 ft) high, the Puig de Randa. It is said that Mallorca's greatest son, the 14th-century theologian and mystic Ramon Llull, came to a hermitage on this mountain to meditate and write his religious treatise, *Ars Magna*. On the way up Puig de Randa there are two small monasteries, the 14th-century Santuari de Sant Honorat and the Santuari de Nostra Senyora de Gràcia. The latter, built on a ledge under an overhanging cliff, contains a 13th-century chapel with fine Valencian tiles inside.

On the mountaintop is the **Santuari de Cura**, built to commemorate Llull's time on the *puig*, and largely devoted to the study of his work. Its central courtyard is built in the typical beige stone of Mallorca. A small museum, housed in a 16th-century former school off the courtyard, contains some of Llull's manuscripts.

The philosopher Ramon Llull

⑯ Capocorb Vell

Carretera Llucmajor–Cap Blanc (MA-6014) km 23. **Tel** 971 18 01 55. 🚌 El Arenal. **Open** 10am–5pm Fri–Wed. 🅿
🌐 talaiotscapocorbvell.com

Mallorca is not as rich in megalithic remains as Menorca, but this *talaiotic* village *(see p531)* in the stony flatlands of the southern coast is worth seeing. The settlement, which dates back to around 1000 BC, originally consisted of five *talaiots* (stone tower-like structures with timbered roofs) and another 28 smaller dwellings. Little is known about its inhabitants and the uses for some of the rooms inside the buildings, such as the tiny underground gallery. Too small for living in, this room may have been used to perform magic rituals.

Part of the charm of this place lies in its surroundings among fields of fruit trees and dry-stone walls, a setting that somehow complements the ruins. Apart from a snack bar nearby, the site remains mercifully undeveloped and relatively peaceful.

One of the *talaiots* of Capocorb Vell

⑰ Cabrera

Baleares. 🚢 from Colònia Sant Jordi. 🛈 Calle Gabriel Roca s/n, Colònia Sant Jordi, 971 65 60 73.

From the beaches of Es Trenc and Sa Ràpita, on the south coast of Mallorca, Cabrera looms on the horizon. The largest island in an archipelago of the same name, it lies 18 km (11 miles) from the most southerly point of Mallorca. Cabrera is home to several rare plants, reptiles and seabirds, such as Eleonora's falcon. The waters are important for marine life. All this has resulted in it being declared a national park *(see pp34–5)*. For centuries Cabrera was used as a military base and it has a small population. On it stands a 14th-century castle.

A street in Felanitx

⑱ Felanitx

Baleares. 🟥 14,200. 🚌 🛈 Avenida Cala Marsas 15, 971 82 60 84. 🚍 Sun. 🎪 Sant Joan Pelós (24 Jun).

This bustling agricultural town is the birthplace of Renaissance architect Guillem Sagrera (1380–1456) and the 20th-century painter Miquel Barceló. Felanitx is visited mainly for three reasons: the imposing façade of the 13th-century church, the **Esglesia de Sant Miquel**; its *sobrassada de porc negre* (a spiced raw sausage made from the meat of the local black pig); and its lively religious fiestas including Sant Joan Pelós *(see p527)*.

About 5 km (3 miles) south-east is the **Castell de Santueri**, founded by the Moors but rebuilt in the 14th century by the kings of Aragón, who ruled Mallorca. Though a ruin, it is worth the detour for the views to the east and south from its vantage point, 400 m (1,300 ft) above the plain.

⑲ Coves del Drac

500 m (0.3 miles) south of Porto Cristo. 🚌 from Porto Cristo. **Tel** 971 82 07 53. **Open** daily. **Closed** 1 Jan, 25 Dec. 🎫 Ⓦ cuevasdeldrach.com

Mallorca has numerous caves, ranging from mere holes in the ground to cathedral-like halls. The four vast chambers of the Coves del Drac are reached by a steep flight of steps. At the bottom is the beautifully lit cave, "Diana's Bath". Another chamber holds the underground lake, Martel, 29 m (95 ft) below ground level and 177 m (580 ft) long. Music fills the air of the cave, played from boats plying the lake. Equally dramatic are the two remaining caves, charmingly named "The Theatre of the Fairies" and "The Enchanted City".

Environs

The **Coves d'Hams** is so called because some of its stalactites are shaped like hooks – *hams* in Mallorcan. The caves are 500 m (1,640 ft) long and contain the "Sea of Venice", an underground lake on which musicians sail.

The entrance to the **Coves d'Artà**, near Capdepera, is 40 m (130 ft) above sea level and affords a wonderful view. The caves' main attraction is a stalagmite 22 m (72 ft) high.

🕳 Coves d'Hams
Carretera Manacor–Porto Cristo, km 11.5. **Tel** 971 82 09 88. **Open** daily. **Closed** 1 Jan, 25 Dec. 🎫 Ⓦ cuevas-hams.com

🕳 Coves d'Artà
Carretera Canyamel. **Tel** 971 84 12 93. **Open** daily. **Closed** 1 Jan, 25 Dec. 🎫 Ⓦ cuevasdearta.com

The dramatically lit stalactites of the Coves d'Artà

⑭ Street-by-Street: Palma

On an island whose name has become synonymous with mass tourism, Palma surprises by its cultural richness. Under the Moors it was already a prosperous town of fountains and cool courtyards. After he had conquered it in 1229, Jaime I wrote, "It seemed to me the most beautiful city we had ever seen." Signs of Palma's past wealth are still evident in the sumptuous churches, grand public buildings and fine private mansions that crowd the old town. The hub of the city is the old-fashioned Passeig des Born, whose cafés invite you to try one of Mallorca's specialities, the *ensaimada*, a spiral of pastry dusted with icing sugar.

Plaça del Marqués de Palmer

The Fundació la Caixa, once the Gran Hotel, is now a cultural centre.

The Forn des Teatre is an old pastry shop noted for its *ensaimadas* and *gató* (almond cake).

Palau Reial de l'Almudaina
This palace belongs to the Spanish royal family and houses a museum, whose highlights include the chapel of Santa Ana, with its Romanesque portal, and the Gothic *tinell* or salon.

Key

— Suggested route

La Llotja is a beautiful 15th-century exchange with tall windows and delicate tracery.

CARRER UNIO

PLAÇA REI JOAN CARLES

PASSEIG DES BORN

CARRER JUAME II

CARRER DE PALAU REIAL

CARRER DE SANT PERE NO

CARRER MIRADOR

AVINGUDA D'ANTONI MAURA

PL.

To Castell de Bellver and Fundació Pilar i Joan Miró

Parc de la Mar

★ **Cathedral**
Built of golden limestone quarried from Santanyi, Palma's huge Gothic cathedral stands in a dramatic location near the waterfront.

For additional map symbols *see back flap*

To Plaça Espanya, bus
and train stations

| 0 metres | 100 |
| 0 yards | 100 |

VISITORS' CHECKLIST

Practical Information
Baleares. 380,000. Plaça
Reina 2, 971 17 39 90. Sat.
San Sebastián (20 Jan). **info
mallorca.net** Museu de Mallorca:
Tel 971 17 78 38. **Open** 10am–6pm
Mon–Fri, 11am–2pm Sat. Banys
Àrabs: **Open** daily. Palau de
l'Almudaina: **Open** Tue–Sun.

Transport
9 km (6 miles) east. Plaça
Espanya, 971 75 20 51. Plaça
Espanya, Calle Eusebi Estada, 971
17 77 77. Muelle de Peraires,
971 70 73 00 (Transmediterranea).

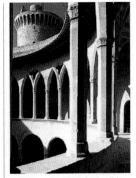

The circular walls of the Gothic Castell de
Bellver

★ **Basílica de Sant Francesc**
The church and cloister of St Francis
are in a refined Gothic style with a
Baroque altarpiece and rose window.

**The Museu
Diocesà**, housed in
the Bishop's Palace,
has a collection of
religious treasures.

Museu de Mallorca
The museum has
displays on local history,
art and architecture,
including this statue of
an ancient warrior.

Banys Àrabs
The 10th-century baths, with
their well-preserved arches, are
a remnant of the Balearic
Islands' Moorish culture.

Castell de Bellver
C/ Camilo José Cela 17. **Tel** 971 73
50 65. **Open** Tue–Sun.
About 5 km (3 miles) from
the city centre, 113 m (370 ft)
above sea level, is Palma's
Gothic castle. Commissioned by
Jaime II during the short-lived
Kingdom of Mallorca (1276–
1349) as a summer residence, it
soon after became a prison until
1915. Today the castle frequently
hosts concerts and plays.

Fundació Pilar i Joan Miró
Carrer Joan de Saridakis 29. **Tel** 971
70 14 20. **Open** mid-May–mid-Sep:
10am–7pm Tue–Sat; mid-Sep–mid-
May: 10am–6pm Tue–Sat; 10am–3pm
Sun all year. (free Sat).
miro.palmademallorca.es

When Joan Miró died in 1983,
his wife converted his former
studio and gardens into an
art centre. The building –
"the Alabaster Fortress" – was
designed by Navarrese architect
Rafael Moneo. It incorporates
Miró's original studio (complete
with unfinished paintings), a
permanent collection, a shop,
a library and an auditorium.

Palma Aquarium
C/ Manuela de los Herreros i Sorá 21.
Tel 902 70 29 02. **Open** daily.
palmaaquarium.com
Located a 15-minute drive from
the city centre, this aquarium
is home to a range of flora and
fauna from the Mediterranean
Sea and the Indian, Atlantic and
Pacific oceans. Visitors can see
recreated ecosystems featuring
700 species and 5 million litres
of seawater.

For hotels and restaurants in this region see pp574–5 and pp602–4

Palma Cathedral

According to legend, when Jaime I of Aragón was caught in a storm on his way to conquer Mallorca in 1229, he vowed that if God led him to safety he would build a great church in his honour. In the following years the old mosque of Medina Mayurqa was torn down and architect Guillem Sagrera (1380–1456) drew up plans for a new cathedral. The last stone was added in 1587, and in subsequent years the cathedral has been rebuilt, notably early last century when parts of the interior were remodelled by Antoni Gaudí *(see pp144–5)*. Today Palma Cathedral, or Sa Seu, as Mallorcans call it, is one of the most breathtaking buildings in Spain, combining vast scale with typically Gothic elegance *(see p28)*.

Bell Tower
This robust tower was built in 1389 and houses nine bells, the largest of which is known as N'Eloi, meaning "praise".

Palma Cathedral
One of the best-sited cathedrals anywhere, it is spectacularly poised high on the sea wall, above what was once Palma's harbour.

KEY

① **Portal Major**

② **19th-century tower**

③ **Flying buttresses**

④ **Cathedral Museum** contains one of the highlights of the beautifully displayed collection in the Old Chapterhouse, a 15th-century reliquary of the True Cross which is encrusted with jewels and precious metals.

⑤ **The Great Organ** was built with a Neo-Gothic case in 1795, and restored in 1993 by Gabriel Blancafort.

⑥ **The Capella Reial**, or Royal Chapel, was redesigned by Antoni Gaudí between 1904 and 1914.

⑦ **Choir stalls**

⑧ **Portal del Mirador**

Entrance to cathedral museum

★ **Great Rose Window**
The largest of seven rose windows looks down from above the High Altar like a gigantic eye. Built in 1370 with stained glass added in the 16th century, the window has a diameter of over 11 m (36 ft).

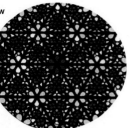

Capella de la Trinitat
This tiny chapel was built in 1329 as the mausoleum of Jaime II and III of Aragón. It contains their alabaster tombs.

Bishop's Throne
Built in 1269 and made of Carrara marble, the chair is embedded in a Gothic vaulted niche.

★ **Baldachino**
Gaudí's bizarre wrought-iron canopy above the altar incorporates lamps, tapestries and a multicoloured crucifix.

Nave
The magnificent ceiling, 44 m (144 ft) high, is held up by 14 slender pillars. At over 19 m (62 ft) wide, it is one of the broadest naves in the world.

Menorca

Menorca is the Balearic island furthest from the mainland and it is set apart from the rest of the country in many other ways. The coastline of Menorca is, arguably, more unspoiled than in any other part of Spain. Its countryside remains largely green and pleasant with cows roaming the meadows. The old towns of Maó – the island's capital – and Ciutadella are filled with noble, historic buildings and beautiful squares. Menorca also has abundant reminders of its more distant history: the island boasts a spectacular hoard of Bronze Age stone structures, which provide an invaluable insight into its prehistoric past. The Menorcans are often more inclined to drink the locally brewed gin *(ginebra)* than the wine which is favoured elsewhere in Spain.

Fishermen mending their nets in Ciutadella's harbour

The peaceful seafront of Ciutadella at twilight

⑳ Ciutadella

Baleares. 🏘 22,000. 🚌 🚢 **ℹ** Plaça des Born, 971 48 41 55. 🛒 Fri & Sat. 🎉 Sant Joan (23–24 Jun). 🌐 illesbalears.es

The key date in the history of Ciutadella is 1558. In that year the Turks, under Barbarossa, entered and decimated the city, consigning 3,495 of its citizens to the slave markets of Constantinople. Of Ciutadella's main public buildings, only the fine Catalan Gothic **Església Catedral de Menorca** managed to survive this fearsome onslaught in more or less its original condition, only later to be stripped of all its paintings, ornaments and other treasures by Republican extremists during the Civil War.

The nearby **Plaça des Born** was built as a parade ground for Moorish troops, and from 1558 was gradually rebuilt in Renaissance style. Today it is one of Spain's most impressive squares, containing pleasant cafés and bordered by shady palm trees. At the centre of the Plaça d'es Born is an obelisk which commemorates the "Any de sa Desgràcia" (Year of

The historic Plaça des Born in the centre of Ciutadella

Misfortune), when the Turks invaded the city. Around the square are the Gothic-style **town hall** *(ajuntament)*, the late 19th-century **Teatre Municipal d'es Born**, and a series of aristocratic mansions with Italianesque façades, the grandest of which is the early 19th-century **Palau de Torre-Saura**. From the northern end of the square there is a fine view over the small harbour.

If you walk up the Carrer Major d'es Born past the cathedral, you come to **Ses Voltes**, an alley lined on both sides by whitewashed arches. Turn right along the Carrer del Seminari for the Baroque **Església dels Socors** and the **Museu Diocesà** with its displays of ecclesiastical paraphernalia. In the narrow streets of the old town there are many impressive palaces, including the early 19th-century **Palau Salort**, on the Carrer Major d'es Born, which is closed to the public, though its exterior can be admired. The Art Nouveau **market** (1895), its ironwork painted in municipal dark green, stands nearby.

The peace of Ciutadella is disturbed every June by the Festa de Sant Joan, a spectacular ritual of horsemanship. During the festival the local gin *(ginebra)* is drunk copiously and the city grinds to a halt.

🏛 **Museu Diocesà**
Carrer del Seminari 7. **Tel** 971 48 12 97. **Open** May–Oct: Tue–Sat. 🎫 ♿ 📷

🏛 **Palau Salort**
Carrer Major d'es Born 9. **Closed** to the public.

㉑ Ferreries

Baleares. 3,100. 🚌 ℹ️ Carrer Sant Bartomeu 55, 971 37 30 03. 🚌 Tue, Fri, Sat. 🎭 Sant Bartomeu (23–25 Aug).

Ferreries lies in between Mercadal and Ciutadella and sprang up when a road was built to connect the two towns. Today Ferreries is an attractive village of white houses, built against the slope of a hill. The simple church, Sant Bartomeu, dates from 1770.

The bay of **Santa Galdana**, 10 km (6 miles) to the south, is even prettier. You can take a pleasant walk from the beach inland through the fertile river-bed of Barranc d'Algendar.

Courtyard in the Santuari del Toro

㉒ Es Mercadal

Baleares. 3,700. 🚌 ℹ️ Carrer Major 16, 971 37 50 02. 🚌 Sun. 🎭 Sant Martí (third Sun of Jul).

Es Mercadal is a small country town – one of the three, with Alaior and Ferreries, that are strung out along the main road from Maó to Ciutadella. The town is unremarkable in itself, but within reach of it are three places of interest.

El Toro, 3 km (2 miles) to the east, is Menorca's highest mountain, at 350 m (1,150 ft). It is also the spiritual heart of the island and at its summit is the Santuari del Toro, built in 1670, which is run by nuns.

About 10 km (6 miles) north of Es Mercadal, the fishing village of **Fornells** transforms itself every summer into an outpost of St Tropez. In the harbour, smart yachts jostle with fishing boats, and the local jet-set crowd into the Bar Palma. Fornells' main culinary speciality is the *caldereta de llagosta* (lobster casserole), but the quality varies and prices can be high.

The road-cum-dirt track to the **Cap de Cavalleria**, 13 km (8 miles) north of Es Mercadal, passes through one of the Balearics' finest landscapes. Cavalleria is a rocky promontory, whipped by the tramontana wind from the north. It juts out into a choppy sea which, in winter, looks more like the North Atlantic than the Mediterranean. At the western edge of the peninsula are the remains of Sanisera, a Phoenician village mentioned by Pliny in the 1st century AD. The road leads to a headland, with a lighthouse and cliffs 90 m (295 ft) high, where peregrine falcons, sea eagles and kites ride the wind.

Further west along the coast is a string of fine, unspoiled beaches, though with difficult access: Cala Pregonda, Cala del Pilar and La Vall d'Algaiarens are three of the most beautiful.

Horse rearing in the fiesta of Sant Lluís

The Balearic Islands' Fiestas

Sant Antoni Abat *(16–17 Jan)*, Mallorca. This fiesta is celebrated with parades and the blessing of animals all over Mallorca and in Sant Antoni in Ibiza.

Sant Joan *(24 Jun)*, Ciutadella (Menorca). The horse plays a major part in Menorca's festivals. In the streets and squares of Ciutadella on 24 June, the Day of St John the Baptist, elegantly dressed riders put their horses through ritualized medieval manoeuvres. The fiesta reaches a climax when the horses rear up on their hind legs and the jubilant crowds swarm around them trying to hold them up with their hands. Similarly, the annual fiesta in Sant Lluís, which takes place at the end of August, sees many of the locals taking to the streets on horseback.

Sant Joan Pelós *(24 Jun)*, Felanitx (Mallorca). As part of this fiesta, a man is dressed in sheepskins to represent John the Baptist.

Romeria de Sant Marçal *(30 Jun)*, Sa Cabeneta (Mallorca). A feature of this fiesta is a market selling *siurells*, primitive Mallorcan whistles.

Our Lady of the Sea *(16 Jul)*, Formentera. The island's main fiesta honours the Virgen del Carmen, patroness of fishermen, with a flotilla of fishing boats.

A quiet stretch of beach at Santa Galdana

The steep hillside of Maó running up from the harbour

㉓ Maó

Baleares. 🅰 24,000. ✈ 🚌 ⛴
ℹ Plaza Constitució 22, 971 36 37 90.
🚢 Tue, Sat. 🎆 Fiesta de Sant Antoni
(17 Jan), Fiestas de Gràcia (7–8 Sep).

The quietly elegant town of
Maó has lent its Spanish name,
Mahón, to mayonnaise. It was
occupied by the British three
times during the 18th century.
The legacy of past colonial rule
can be seen in sober Georgian
town houses, with their dark
green shutters and sash windows.
Maó's harbour is one of the
finest in the Mediterranean.
Taking the street leading from
the port to the upper town, the
S-shaped Costa de Ses Voltes,
you come to the 18th-century
Església del Carme, a former
Carmelite church whose cool
white cloister now houses an
attractive fruit and vegetable
market. Behind the market is
the **Col·lecció Hernández
Sanz y Hernández Mora**, which
houses Menorcan art and
antiques. The nearby Plaça
Constitució is overlooked by the
church of Santa Maria, which
has a huge organ. Next door is
the **town hall** (ajuntament) with
its Neo-Classical façade, into
which is mounted the famous
clock donated by Sir Richard
Kane (1660–1736), the first
British governor of Menorca.
Located at the end of the
Carrer Isabel II is the **Església de
Sant Francesc**, with an intriguing
Romanesque doorway and
Baroque façade. The church
houses the refurbished Museu
de Menorca, which is open daily
except Monday. Two minutes'
walk south of here will take you
to Maó's main square, the Plaça
de S'Esplanada, behind which
is the **Ateneu Científic Lliterat
Artistic**, a centre of Menorca-
related culture and learning.
Inside are collections of local
ceramics and maps, and a library.
It is advisable to obtain
permission before looking
around. On the north side of the
harbour is a mansion known as
Sant Antoni or the Golden Farm.
As Maó's finest example of
Palladian architecture, it has
an arched façade, painted plum
red, with white arches, in the
traditional Menorcan style.
Nelson, the British admiral, is
thought to have stayed here. The
house has a collection of Nelson
memorabilia and a fine library
but is closed to the public.

🏛 **Col·lecció Hernández Sanz
y Hernández Mora**
Claustre del Carme 5. **Tel** 971 35 05 97.
Open 10am–1pm Mon–Sat.

🏛 **Ateneu Científic
Literari i Artistic**
C/ Rovellada de Dalt 25. **Tel** 971 36
05 53. **Closed** Sun, public hols.

㉔ Cales Coves

Baleares. 🚌 Sant Climent, then
25 mins walk. **Tel** Maó, 971 36 37 90.

On either side of a pretty bay
can be found Cales Coves – the
site of Neolithic dwellings of up
to 9 m (30 ft) in length, hollowed
out of the rock face. The caves,
thought to have been inhabited
since prehistoric times, are today
occupied by a community of
people seeking an alternative
lifestyle. Some of the caves have
front doors, chimneys and even
butane cookers.
About 8 km (5 miles) west,
along the coast, lies Binibeca,
a tourist village built in a style
sympathetic to old Menorca.
The jumble of white houses and
tiny streets of the Poblat de
Pescadors, an imitation fishing
village, have the look of the
genuine article.

Modern sculpture outside one of the
dwellings at Cales Coves

Ancient Menorca

Menorca is exceptionally rich in prehistoric remains – the island has been described as an immense open-air museum. The majority of the sites are the work of the "talayot" people who lived between 2000 BC and 1000 BC and are named after the *talaiots* or huge stone towers that characterize the Menorcan landscape. There are hundreds of these Bronze Age villages and structures dotted around the island. Usually open to the public and free of charge, these sites provide an invaluable insight into the ancient inhabitants of the Balearics.

Huge *talaiot* amid the settlement of Trepucó

Different Structures

The ancient stone structures scattered around the countryside of Menorca and, to a lesser extent, Mallorca can be placed into three main categories: taulas, talaiots *and* navetas.

Taulas are two slabs of rock, one placed on top of the other, in a "T" formation. Suggestions as to their possible function range from a sacrificial altar to a roof support.

Talaiots are circular or square buildings that may have been used as meeting places and dwellings.

Navetas are shaped like upturned boats and apparently had a dual role as dwellings and burial quarters. At least ten of these remain in Menorca.

Spectacular *taula* at Talatí de Dalt, standing 3 m (10 ft) high

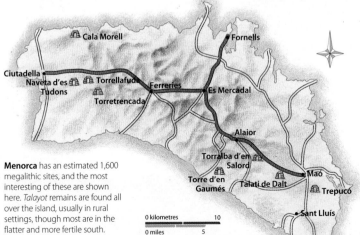

Cala Morell

Fornells

Ciutadella
Naveta d'es
Tudons
Torrellafuda
Ferreries
Es Mercadal
Torretrencada

Alaior

Torralba d'en
Salord
Torre d'en
Gaumés
Talatí de Dalt
Maó
Trepucó

Sant Lluís

Menorca has an estimated 1,600 megalithic sites, and the most interesting of these are shown here. *Talayot* remains are found all over the island, usually in rural settings, though most are in the flatter and more fertile south.

0 kilometres   10
0 miles   5

THE CANARY ISLANDS

La Palma · El Hierro · La Gomera · Tenerife
Gran Canaria · Fuerteventura · Lanzarote

Poised on the edge of the tropics west of Morocco, the Canaries enjoy a generous supply of sunshine, pleasantly tempered by the trade winds. Their scenery ranges from lava desert to primeval forest and from sand dunes to volcanic peaks. The old towns on the main islands have colonial centres, full of character.

Seven islands and half a dozen islets make up the Canary archipelago. They are the tips of hundreds of volcanoes that first erupted from the seabed 14 million years ago. Teneguía on La Palma last erupted in 1971.

In the 14th and 15th centuries, when navigators discovered the islands and claimed them for Spain, they were inhabited by the Guanches, who practised a stone culture. Sadly, little evidence of them remains.

Today the islands are divided into two provinces. The four western isles, making up the province of Santa Cruz de Tenerife, are all mountainous; Tenerife's colossal dormant volcano, Mount Teide, casts the world's biggest sea-shadow. La Palma, El Hierro and La Gomera, where Columbus stayed on his voyages, are all small, unspoiled islands, not yet developed for mass tourism.

The eastern islands belong to the province of Las Palmas. Forested Gran Canaria is the biggest and its capital, Las Palmas de Gran Canaria, is a colonial town. Lanzarote, by contrast, is flat, with lunar landscapes, while Fuerteventura has long, virgin beaches.

Protected area of sand dunes at Maspalomas, next to the busy Playa del Inglés, Gran Canaria

◀ Picturesque view of the stretch of golden sand at Playa de Las Teresitas, Tenerife

Exploring the Western Canary Islands

Tenerife has the widest range of holiday attractions of any of the Canary Islands. The province of Santa Cruz de Tenerife also includes the three tiny westerly islands of La Palma, La Gomera and El Hierro, which are scarcely developed for tourism and have no large resorts. Gradually, more visitors are discovering these peaceful, green havens. If you enjoy walking, wildlife and mountain scenery, visit one of these hideaways. All three islands have comfortable hotels, including paradors. But, compared with Gran Canaria and the eastern islands, there are fewer sandy beaches here, and little organized entertainment or sightseeing.

Las Teresitas artificial beach, Santa Cruz de Tenerife

LA PALMA

Los Sauces

Puntagorda

LP1

Caldera de Taburiente

LP1

Los Llanos de Aridane

Breña Alta

Santa Cruz de la Palma

El Paso

Tazacorte

LA PALMA

❶

LP2

LP206

Fuencaliente

Sights at a Glance

❶ La Palma
❷ El Hierro
❸ La Gomera
❹ Los Cristianos
❺ *Parque Nacional del Teide pp542–3*
❻ Puerto de la Cruz
❼ La Orotava
❽ Candelaria
❾ La Laguna
❿ Montes de Anaga
⓫ Santa Cruz de Tenerife

LA GOMI

Vallehermoso

Parqu de G

Valle Gran Rey   TF713

❸

LA GOME

Allajero

Sa

Roque Bonanza on the rocky east coast of El Hierro

EL HIERRO

Valverde

Ermita de los Reyes

Frontera

HI1

Puerto de la Estaca

❷

EL HIERRO

La Restinga

Key

═══ Motorway

━━━ Major road

═══ Secondary road

─── Scenic route

△ Summit

Terraced hillside, maximizing cultivation in the lush green Valle Gran Rey, in western La Gomera

0 kilometres   25
0 miles   10

TENERIFE

MONTES DE ANAGA ❿

LA LAGUNA ❾

Tacoronte

Playa de Las Teresitas

❶❶ SANTA CRUZ DE TENERIFE

PUERTO DE LA CRUZ

TF5

El Rosário

Buenavista del Norte   Garachico

Punta de Teno

LA OROTAVA ❼

❻

TF82

TF24   TF1

❽ CANDELARIA

Güimar

Pico del Teide 3718m

PARQUE NACIONAL DEL TEIDE ❺

TF38

Guia

TF21

Parador de Cañadas del Teide

TF28

Vilaflor

Punta de Abona

Adeje   TF21

Granadilla de Abona

Sebastián

Playa de las Américas   Arona

LOS CRISTIANOS ❹   TF1   El Médano

Punta de la Rasca   Costa del Silencio   Punta Roja

The wild landscape of Punta de Teno in western Tenerife

Getting Around

From mainland Spain there are flights *(see p626)* and ferries *(see p627)* to the Canary Islands. Transport to the small islands is mainly from Tenerife. La Gomera is easily reached by ferry or hydrofoil from Los Cristianos, or by plane from Gran Canaria or Tenerife. Airports on La Palma and El Hierro are served by regular flights from Tenerife's northern airport of Los Rodeos. Unless you take an organized coach trip, a car is essential to see the island scenery. Roads are improving, but great care is needed for mountain driving.

❶ La Palma

Santa Cruz de Tenerife. 🚹 80,000.
✈️ 🚢 Santa Cruz de la Palma.
ℹ️ Avenida Blas Pérez González s/n,
Santa Cruz de la Palma, 922 41 21 06.
🌐 **visitlapalma.es**

Reaching an altitude of 2,426 m (7,959 ft) on a land base of less than 706 sq km (280 sq miles), La Palma is the world's steepest island. It lies on the northwestern tip of the archipelago and has a cool, moist climate and lush vegetation. The mountainous interior is covered with forests of pine, laurel and giant fern.

The centre of the island is dominated by the **Caldera de Taburiente**, a volcano's massive crater, more than 8 km (5 miles) wide. National park status *(see pp34–5)* is an indication of its botanical and geological importance. The International Astrophysics Observatory crowns the summit. A couple of roads traverse La Palma's dizzy heights,

The Parque Nacional de la Caldera de Taburiente, La Palma

Pastel façades and delicate wooden balconies in Santa Cruz, La Palma

offering spectacular views of the craters of La Cumbrecita and Roque de los Muchachos.

Santa Cruz de la Palma, the island's main town and port, is an elegant place of old houses with balconies, some fine churches and several 16th-century buildings. In the cobbled street behind the seafront, Calle O'Daly (named after an Irish banana trader), are the Iglesia El Salvador, boasting a Mudéjar coffered ceiling, and the town hall *(ayuntamiento)*, which is housed in a cardinal's palace. A full-sized cement replica of the *Santa María*, Columbus's flagship, stands at the end of the Plaza Alameda.

The tortuous mountain road southwest of Santa Cruz winds over Las Cumbres mountains via Breña Alta to **El Paso** in the centre of the island. A relatively sizable community, the village is known for its silk production and hand-rolled cigars.

Among the almond terraces and vineyards of southern La Palma, solidified lava from the Teneguia volcano is a reminder of its recent activity *(see p555)*.

Craters on El Hierro, Spain's most western territory

❷ El Hierro

Santa Cruz de Tenerife. 🚹 10,500. ✈️
🚢 Puerto de la Estaca. ℹ️ C/ Doctor Quintero Magdaleno, 4, Valverde, 922 55 03 02. 🌐 **elhierro.travel**

Due to a dearth of sandy beaches, El Hierro has escaped tourist invasions. Instead it has caught the attention of naturalists, with its hilly landscape and unusual fauna and flora. El Hierro is the smallest of the Canaries, and the furthest west; it is the last place in Spain where the sun sets.

Valverde, the island's capital; stands inland at 600 m (2,000 ft) above sea level. Canary pines and peculiarly twisted juniper trees cover El Hierro's mountainous interior, best seen

La Gomera's Whistle Language

The problems of communication posed by La Gomera's rugged terrain produced an unusual language, known as *El Silbo*. This system of piercing whistles probably developed because its sounds carry across the great distances from one valley to the next. Its origins are mysterious, but it was allegedly invented by the Guanches *(see p551)*. Few young Gomerans have any use for *El Silbo* today, and the language would probably be dead if it were not for the demonstrations of it still held for interested visitors at the parador, and in the restaurant at Las Rosas.

El Silbo practised on La Gomera

from the many footpaths and scenic viewpoints along the roads. A ridge of woodland, curving east–west across the island, marks the edge of a volcano. The crater forms a fertile depression known as El Golfo.

In the far west is the **Ermita de los Reyes**, a place of pilgrimage and the starting point of the island's biggest fiesta, held in July every four years.

The turquoise seas off the south coast are popular with skin-divers, who base themselves in the small fishing village of **La Restinga**.

❸ La Gomera

Santa Cruz de Tenerife. ⚒ 21,400.
✈ 🚢 ℹ Calle Real 32, San Sebastián de la Gomera, 922 14 15 12.
🌐 **lagomera.travel**

La Gomera is the most accessible of the smaller western islands, only 40 minutes by hydrofoil from Los Cristianos on Tenerife (90 minutes by ferry), or by plane from Tenerife or Gran Canaria. Many come to La Gomera for a day only, taking a coach trip. Others hire a car and explore on their own: a scenic but exhausting drive for a single day as the terrain is intensely buckled, and the central plateau is deeply scored by dramatic ravines. Driving across these gorges involves negotiating countless dizzying hairpin bends.

The best way to enjoy the island is to stay a while and explore it at leisure, preferably doing some walking. On a

Terraced hillsides in the fertile Valle Gran Rey, La Gomera

fine day, La Gomera's scenery is glorious. Rock pinnacles jut above steep slopes studded with ferns while terraced hillsides glow with palms and flowering creepers. The best section, the **Parque Nacional de Garajonay**, is a UNESCO World Heritage Site.

San Sebastián, La Gomera's main town and ferry terminal, is situated on the east coast, a scattering of white buildings around a small beach. Among its sights are some places associated with Columbus *(see pp62–3)*, who topped up his water supplies here before

setting out on his adventurous voyages. A well in the customs house bears the grand words "With this water America was baptized". According to legend he also prayed in the Iglesia de la Asunción, and stayed at a local house.

Beyond the arid hills to the south lies **Playa de Santiago**, the island's only real resort, which has a grey pebble beach. **Valle Gran Rey**, in the far west, is a fertile valley of palms and staircase terraces. These days it is colonized by foreigners attempting alternative lifestyles. In the north, tiny roads weave a tortuous course around several pretty villages, plunging at intervals to small, stony beaches. **Las Rosas** is a popular stop-off for coach parties, who can enjoy the visitors' centre and a restaurant with a panoramic view.

The road towards the coast from Las Rosas leads through the town of **Vallehermoso**, dwarfed by the huge **Roque de Cano**, which is an impressive mass of solidified lava. Just off the north coast stands **Los Órganos**, a fascinating rock formation of crystallized basalt columns resembling the pipes of an organ.

Juniper trees on El Hierro, twisted and bent by the wind

Tenerife

In the language of its aboriginal Guanche inhabitants Tenerife means "Snowy Mountain", a tribute to its most striking geographical feature, the dormant volcano of Mount Teide, Spain's highest peak. The largest of the Canary Islands, Tenerife is a roughly triangular landmass rising steeply on all sides towards the cloud-capped summit that divides it into two distinct climatic zones: damp and lushly vegetated in the north, sunny and arid in the south. Tenerife offers a more varied range of attractions than any of the other Canary Islands, including its spectacular volcanic scenery, water sports and a vibrant atmosphere after dark. Its beaches, however, have unenticing black sand and are rather poor for swimming. The main resorts are crowded with high-rise hotels and apartments, offering nightlife but little peace and quiet.

Bananas in northern Tenerife

❶ Los Cristianos

Santa Cruz de Tenerife. 🅰 60,000. 🚍
🚢 ⓘ Paseo las Vistas 1, 922 78 70 11.
🚢 Sun. 🎭 Fiesta del Carmen (first Sun of Sep). 🅦 arona.org

The old fishing village of Los Cristianos, on Tenerife's south coast, has grown into a town spreading out along the foot of barren hills. Ferries and hydrofoils make regular trips from its little port to La Gomera and El Hierro (see pp536–7).

To the north lies the modern expanse of **Playa de las Américas**, Tenerife's largest development. It offers visitors a cheerful, relaxed, undemanding cocktail of sun and fun.

A brief sortie inland leads to the much older town of **Adeje** and to the **Barranco del Infierno**, a wild gorge with an attractive waterfall (2 hours' round walk from Adeje).

Along the coast to the east, the **Costa del Silencio** is a pleasant contrast to most of the other large resorts, with its bungalow developments surrounding fishing villages. Los Abrigos has lively fish restaurants lining its harbour.

Further east, **El Médano** shelters below an ancient volcanic cone. Its two beaches are popular with windsurfers.

❺ Parque Nacional del Teide

See pp542–3.

❻ Puerto de la Cruz

Santa Cruz de Tenerife. 🅰 27,500.
🚍 ⓘ C/ Las Lonjas s/n, 922 38 60 00.
🚢 Sat. 🎭 Carnival (Feb–Mar), Fiesta del Carmen (second Sun of Jul).

Puerto de la Cruz, the oldest resort in the Canaries, first sprang to prominence in 1706, when a volcanic eruption obliterated Tenerife's principal port of Garachico. Puerto de la Cruz took its place, later becoming popular with genteel English convalescents. The town's older buildings give it much of its present character.

The beautiful Complejo Costa Martiánez, designed by the Lanzarote architect César Manrique (see p552), compensates for a lack of good beaches with its seawater pools, palms and fountains. Other attractions include the tropical gardens of **Loro Parque**, where visitors can also see parrots and dolphins.

Outside town, the **Jardín de Orquídeas** is the oldest garden in Tenerife, and has a large orchid collection. **Icod de los Vinos**, a short drive west, has a spectacular ancient dragon tree.

🦜 **Loro Parque**
Avenida Loro Parque. **Tel** 922 37 38 41.
Open daily. 🈯 🅦 loroparque.com

🌺 **Jardín de Orquídeas**
Camino Sitio Litre s/n. **Tel** 922 38 24 17.
Open daily. 🈯
🅦 jardindeorquideas.com

The landscaped Lago Martiánez lido, Puerto de la Cruz

The Dragon Tree

The Canary Islands have many unusual plants, but the dragon tree (Dracaena draco) is one of the strangest. This primitive creature looks a little like a giant cactus, with swollen branches that sprout multiple tufts of spiky leaves. When cut, the trunk exudes a reddish sap once believed to have magical and medicinal properties. Dragon trees form no annual rings, so their age is a mystery. Some are thought to be hundreds of years old. The most venerable surviving specimen can be seen at Icod de los Vinos.

❼ La Orotava

Santa Cruz de Tenerife. 🏔 40,000.
🚌 ℹ C/ Calvario 4, 922 32 30 41.
🎭 Carnival (Feb/Mar), Corpus Christi
(May/Jun), Romería San Isidoro
Labrador (Jun).

A short distance from Puerto de
la Cruz, in the fertile hills above
the Orotava Valley, La Orotava
makes a popular excursion. The
old part of this historic town
clusters around the large **Iglesia
de Nuestra Señora de la
Concepción**. This domed
Baroque building with twin
towers was built in the late 18th
century to replace an earlier
church that was destroyed in
earthquakes at the beginning
of that century.

In the surrounding streets and
squares are many old churches,
convents and grand houses
with elaborate wooden
balconies. At **Casa de los
Balcones** and **Casa del Turista**
handicrafts and regional food
products can be purchased.

Nuestra Señora de la Candelaria, patron
saint of the Canary Islands

❽ Candelaria

Santa Cruz de Tenerife. 🏔 17,000. 🚌
ℹ Plaza del CIT, 922 50 04 15. 🚌 Sat,
Sun. 🎭 Nuestra Señora de la
Candelaria (14–15 Aug).

This coastal town is famous for
its shrine to **Nuestra Señora de
la Candelaria**, the Canary
Islands' patron saint, whose
image is surrounded by flowers
and candles in a modern church
in the main square. This gaudy
Virgin, supposedly washed
ashore in pagan times, was

Statue of a Guanche chief on the seafront of Candelaria

venerated before Christianity
reached the island. In 1826 a
tidal wave returned her to the
sea, but a replica draws pilgrims
to worship here every August.
Outside, stone effigies of
Guanche chiefs line the sea wall.

❾ La Laguna

Santa Cruz de Tenerife. 🏔 141,000..
🚌 ℹ C/ de la Carrera 7, 922 63 11
94. 🚌 daily. 🎭 San Benito (15 Jul),
Santísimo Cristo de la Laguna (14 Sep).

A bustling university town and
former island capital, La Laguna
is the second-largest settlement
on Tenerife and a UNESCO
World Heritage Site.

In its old quarter, best
explored on foot, there are
many atmospheric squares,
historic buildings and good
museums. Most of the sights lie
between the bell-towered
**Iglesia de Nuestra Señora de la
Concepción** (1502), and the
Plaza del Adelantado, on which
stand the town hall, a convent
and the **Palacio de Nava**.

❿ Montes de Anaga

Santa Cruz de Tenerife. 🚌 Santa Cruz
de Tenerife, La Laguna.

The rugged mountains north of
Santa Cruz are kept green and
lush by a cool, wet climate. They
abound with a wide variety of
interesting birds and plants,
including cacti, laurels and tree
heathers. Walking the mountain
trails is very popular, and maps
showing many of the best paths
are readily available from the
tourist office. A steep road with
marker posts climbs up from
the village of San Andrés by the
beautiful but artificial beach of
Las Teresitas. On clear days there
are marvellous vistas along the
paths, especially from the
viewpoints of Pico del Inglés
and Bailadero.

Winding down through the
laurel forests of Monte de las
Mercedes and the colourful
valley of Tejina you reach
Tacoronte, with its interesting
churches, an ethnographic
museum and a bodega, where
you can sample local wines.

The Canary Islands' Fiestas

Carnival *(Feb/Mar)*, Santa Cruz de Tenerife. One of Europe's biggest carnivals, this grand street party is a lavish spectacle of extravagant costumes and Latin American dance music to rival that of Rio de Janeiro. For years under the Franco regime, Carnival was suppressed for its irreverent frivolity. It begins with the election of a queen of the festivities and builds up to a climax on Shrove Tuesday, when there is a large procession. The "funeral" of an enormous mock sardine takes place on Ash Wednesday. Carnival is also celebrated on the islands of Lanzarote and Gran Canaria.

Revellers in Carnival outfits on Tenerife

Corpus Christi *(May/Jun)*, La Orotava (Tenerife). The streets of the town are filled with flower carpets in striking patterns, while the Plaza del Ayuntamiento is covered in copies of works of art, formed from coloured volcanic sands.

La Bajada de la Virgen de las Nieves *(Jul, every five years: 2015, 2020)* Santa Cruz de La Palma.

Romería de la Virgen de la Candelaria *(15 Aug)*, Candelaria (Tenerife). Pilgrims come here in their thousands to venerate the Canary Islands' patroness.

Fiesta del Charco *(7–11 Sep)*, San Nicolás de Tolentino (Gran Canaria). People leap into a large saltwater pond to catch mullet.

Large ships moored at the busy port of Santa Cruz de Tenerife

⑪ Santa Cruz de Tenerife

Santa Cruz de Tenerife. 🏘 220,000. 🚌 🚢 ℹ Plaza de España, 922 28 93 94. 🚢 Sun. 🎭 Carnival (Feb/Mar), Día de la Cruz (3 May). W **webtenerife.com**

Tenerife's capital city is an important regional port, with a deep-water harbour suitable for large ships. Its most attractive beach, **Las Teresitas**, lies 7 km (4 miles) to the north.

Completely artificial, it was created by importing millions of tonnes of golden Saharan sand and building a protective reef just offshore. Shaded by palms, backed by mountains and so far devoid of concrete hotel developments, the result improves on anything nature has bestowed on Tenerife.

Santa Cruz can boast many handsome historic buildings. The hub of the town is around the **Plaza de España**, situated near the harbour. Just off it is the Calle de Castillo, the main shopping street. Its two most noteworthy churches are the **Iglesia de Nuestra Señora de la Concepción**, with parts dating from 1500, and Baroque **Iglesia de San Francisco**.

Particularly interesting is the **Museo de la Naturaleza y el Hombre**, in the Palacio Insular, where Guanche mummies grin in glass cases. Inside the museum you can also see the cannon which is alleged to have removed the arm of the British admiral Nelson during an unsuccessful raid on the city in the late 18th century.

Other attractions include the **Museo de Bellas Artes**, which features old masters as well as modern works. Many of its paintings focus on local events and landscapes. Contemporary sculptures adorn the **Parque Municipal García Sanabria**, a pleasant park with shady paths, laid out in 1926.

In the morning, visit the **Mercado de Nuestra Señora de África**, which combines a bazaar with a food market. Outside stalls sell domestic goods; those inside offer an eclectic mix of regional produce spices and cut flowers. Santa Cruz is especially worth a visit during its flamboyant carnival.

🏛 **Museo de la Naturaleza y el Hombre**
Calle Fuentes Morales. **Tel** 922 53 58 16. **Open** daily. 🅿 ♿

🏛 **Museo de Bellas Artes**
Calle José Murphy 12. **Tel** 922 24 43 58. **Open** Tue–Sun.

The artificial beach of Las Teresitas in Santa Cruz

The Flavours of the Canary Islands

The exotic fruits and vegetables that grow in the subtropical Canaries climate, and the unusual fish that are caught in local waters, have led to a cuisine very different from that of the Iberian Peninsula. From the original inhabitants, the Guanche, culinary traditions survive in local staples like *gofio* (maize meal). Over the centuries, Spanish, Portuguese and North African influences have been incorporated into the local cuisine, but the underlying theme is always one of simplicity and a reliance on ultra-fresh local produce. All kinds of unusual delicacies are available, from sweet-fleshed parrotfish to succulent tropical fruits.

Maize (corn)

Fish straight from the ocean, being dried in the sun to preserve them

Seafood and Meat

The Canaries offer an incredible array of seafood, with varieties unknown on the Spanish mainland. Delicacies like *lapas* (limpets) are around only for a few months during the summer, and are usually served simply grilled (*a la plancha*). Other unusual varieties include wreckfish, damselfish, dentex and parrotfish. These, along with more common varieties, are usually fried, baked in a salt crust or dried in the sun.

Meats include standard Iberian favourites like pork, kid and beef, but they are often prepared according to ancient Guanche traditions.

Fruit and Vegetables

The mild, stable Canarian climate is perfect for growing luscious tropical fruits (the most famous crop of the islands being bananas). Exotic vegetables thrive, too, as well as potatoes and tomatoes, which were introduced here 500 years ago from the newly discovered Americas. The islands boast varieties of potato unknown elsewhere, and these feature in the local favourite *papas arrugadas* ("wrinkly potatoes"), which are made by boiling potatoes in their skins in very salty water – sometimes seawater.

Dates — Bananas — Pineapple — Papayas (paw paw)

Mangoes — Guavas

Mouthwatering fresh fruits from the Canary Islands

Canarian Dishes and Specialities

Almonds

The Greeks named the Canaries "the fortunate islands", and they are certainly blessed in terms of the freshness and abundance of the local produce. What ever you choose to eat, you can be sure of encoutering a bowl of the ubiquitous *mojo* sauce. This aromatic Canarian creation accompanies almost every dish, and appears in countless versions: the main ones are red *picón*, which is spiced up with pepper and paprika, and green *verde*, with parsley and coriander. The Canarian staple, *gofio* (roasted maize meal), is served for breakfast and used in local dishes such as *gofio de almendras*, a rich almond dessert. The islands are also known for delicious pastries like the honey-drizzled *bienmesabes* (meaning "tastes good to me") and traditional cheeses.

Sopa de pescados tinerfeña
This Tenerife fish soup of sea bass and potatoes is scented with saffron and cumin.

❺ Parque Nacional del Teide

Towering over Tenerife, Mount Teide, surrounded by a wild volcanic landscape, is an awesome sight. 180,000 years ago a much larger adjacent cone collapsed, leaving behind the devastation of Las Cañadas, a 16-km- (10-mile-) wide caldera, and the smaller volcano, Teide, on its northern edge. Today volcanic material forms a wilderness of weathered, mineral-tinted rocks, ash beds and lava streams. A single road crosses the plateau of Las Cañadas, passing a parador, cable car station, and visitors' centre. Follow the marked paths for unforgettable views of this unique, protected area.

Volcanic Landscapes
The eight-minute cable-car ride leaves you 160 m (525 ft) short of Teide's summit. Authorization must be given to climb up to the summit.

Los Roques de García
These flamboyantly shaped lava rocks near the parador are some of the most photographed in the whole park. The rocks of Los Azulejos, nearby, glitter blue-green because of the copper deposits within them.

Pico del Teide
3,718 m ②

Pico Viejo
3,414 m
①

↖*Chío*

↯ **Mirador de Chío**

Roques de García

C823

Mirador de La Ruleta ↯

Llano de Ucanca

↯ **Mirador de Boca Tauce**

Vilaflor ↯

C821 **Mirado Ucanca** ↯

Key

— Road
— Track
-- Footpath

0 kilometres   2
0 miles   1

KEY

① **Pico Viejo**, a volcanic cone also known as Montaña Chahorra, last erupted in the 18th century.

② **Pico del Teide**, which is still volcanically active, is Spain's highest summit.

③ **At El Portillo Visitors' Centre**, a video film and exhibition chart the origins of the park.

Wild Flowers

The inhospitable badlands of Las Cañadas are inhabited by some rare and beautiful plants. Many of these are unique to the Canary Islands. Most striking is the tall *Echium wildprettii*, a kind of viper's bugloss, whose red flowers reach 3 m (10 ft) in early summer. Other common plants include Teide broom, the Teide daisy, and a unique species of violet. The best time of year for flower-spotting is May to June. Displays housed in the visitors' centre will help identify them. Don't take any plants away with you: all vegetation within the park is strictly protected and must not be uprooted or picked.

For additional map symbols *see back flap*

La Caldera de Las Cañadas
A rim of fractured crags forms a pie-crust edge to the sides of this enormous caldera – a wide volcanic crater *(see p555)*. Now collapsed and intensely eroded, the perimeter of the caldera measures 45 km (28 miles).

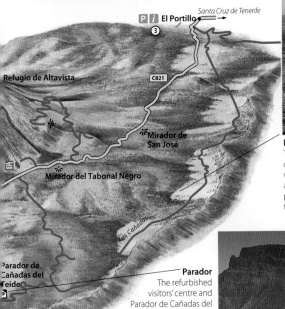

Santa Cruz de Tenerife

P i El Portillo
③

Refugio de Altavista

C821

Mirador de San José

Mirador del Tabonal Negro

Las Cañadas

Parador de Cañadas del Teide

Las Cañadas
The flat expanses of the seven *cañadas* (small sandy plateaus) were created by the collapse of ancient craters. Several colourful plants have managed to colonize this dusty, barren wasteland.

Parador
The refurbished visitors' centre and Parador de Cañadas del Teide are set in surreal scenery, and make an excellent base for those who want to explore the park thoroughly.

Canary mustard *(Descurainia bourgeauana)*

Teide wallflower *(Erysimum scoparium)*

Teide violet *(Viola cheiranthifolia)*

Teide viper's bugloss *(Echium wildpretii)*

Exploring the Eastern Canary Islands

The Eastern Province of the Canary Islands – Las Palmas – comprises the islands of Gran Canaria, Lanzarote and Fuerteventura. All feature unusual and spectacular scenery, plenty of sunshine and excellent sandy beaches, but each has a very different atmosphere. Gran Canaria boasts the only really large town, Las Palmas de Gran Canaria, which is also the administrative centre for the eastern islands. It also offers the biggest resort, Maspalomas, with its Playa del Inglés, which has a package-holiday feel. As a contrast, the white beaches of Fuerteventura have been left fairly undeveloped and it is still possible to find privacy among their sand dunes. Lanzarote has fine beaches, too, while its interior is dominated by a volcanic landscape which makes for great excursions.

Corralejo's beach, in the north of Fuerteventura

The marina at Puerto Rico, in southern Gran Canaria

Getting Around

Most people travel from mainland Spain to the eastern islands by air *(see p626)*. The alternative is a long sea crossing from Cádiz *(see p627)*. There are flights between all the islands, mainly from Gran Canaria. There are also regular inter-island ferries. Taxis and public transport are fine within resorts, but expensive over long distances. Cars can be hired on all the islands, usually at airports or ferry terminals. The main roads are well surfaced and fast on the flatter sections, though traffic in Gran Canaria can be heavy in places. A four-wheel drive Jeep is advisable to reach some remoter beaches.

Cenobio de Valerón
Gáldar
Arucas
AGAETE 🟡**15** Firgas
🟡**17** **LAS PALMAS DE GRAN CANARIA**
Teror
CRUZ 🟡**16** **TAFIRA**
San Nicolás **DE TEJEDA** 🟡**18** Vega de San Mateo
de Tolentino *Roque Nublo* Telde
Pico de las Nieves
1949m
Mogán Santa Lucía
PUERTO DE
MOGÁN 🟡**12** Agüimes
🟡**13** **PUERTO RICO**
🟡**14** **MASPALOMAS**

GRAN CANARIA

Key

═══ Motorway
▬▬▬ Major road
═══ Secondary road
▬▬▬ Scenic route
△ Summit

For additional map symbols *see back flap*

Sights at a Glance

⑫ Puerto de Mogán
⑬ Puerto Rico
⑭ Maspalomas
⑮ Agaete
⑯ Tafira
⑰ Las Palmas de
   Gran Canaria
⑲ Península de Jandía
⑳ Betancuria
㉑ Caleta de Fuste
㉒ Puerto del Rosario
㉓ Corralejo
㉔ Playa Blanca

㉕ Parque Nacional
   de Timanfaya
㉖ Puerto del Carmen
㉗ Arrecife
㉘ Costa Teguise
㉙ Teguise
㉚ Haría
㉛ Jameos del Agua

Tour

⑱ Cruz de Tejeda

Volcanoes of Montañas de Fuego in Parque Nacional de Timanfaya, Lanzarote

Gran Canaria

Gran Canaria is the most popular of the Canary Islands, with over 3 million holiday-makers visiting it each year. The island offers a surprising range of scenery, climate, resorts and attractions within its compact bounds. Winding roads follow the steep, ruggedly beautiful terrain which rises to a symmetrical cone at the centre of the island. Las Palmas, Gran Canaria's capital and port, is the largest city in the Canaries, and Maspalomas/Playa del Inglés, in the south, is one of the biggest resorts in Spain. Both tourist meccas are packed with high-rise hotels and villa complexes, but not far away there is some marvellous scenery to discover.

Holiday-makers on the golden sands of Puerto Rico beach

⑫ Puerto de Mogán

Las Palmas. 🗻 1,500. 🛈 Avenida de Mogán, Puerto Rico, 928 15 88 04. 🗓 Fri. 🕮 Virgen del Carmen (Jul). 🖥 **grancanaria.com**

Situated at the end of the verdant valley of Mogán, this is one of Gran Canaria's most appealing developments – an idyll to many visitors after the brash Playa del Inglés. Based around a small fishing port, it consists of a village-like complex of pretty, white, creeper-covered houses and a similarly designed hotel built around a marina. Boutiques, bars and restaurants add an ambience without any of the accompanying rowdiness.

The sandy beach, sheltered between the cliffs, is scarcely big enough for all visitors; a car is recommended to reach more facilities at Maspalomas. Ferries provide a leisurely way to get to nearby resorts.

Sun-worshippers in Puerto Rico

⑬ Puerto Rico

Las Palmas. 🗻 1,800. 🛈 Avenida de Mogán, 928 15 88 04. 🕮 María de Auxiliadora (May), San Antonio (13 Jun), Carmen (16 Jul).

The barren cliffs west of Maspalomas now sprout apartment complexes at every turn. Puerto Rico is an over-developed resort, but has one of the more attractive beaches on the island, a firm crescent of imported sand supplemented by lidos and excellent water-sports facilities. It is a great place to learn sailing, diving and windsurfing, or just to soak up the ultraviolet – Puerto Rico enjoys the best sunshine record in the whole of Spain.

⑭ Maspalomas

Las Palmas. 🗻 33,000. 🚍 🛈 Centro Comercial Anexo II, Playa del Inglés, 928 76 84 09. 🗓 Wed & Sat. 🕮 Santiago (25 Jul), San Bartolomé (24 Aug). 🖥 **grancanaria.com**

When the motorway from Las Palmas Airport first tips you into this bewildering mega-resort, it seems like a homogeneous blur, but gradually three separate communities emerge. **San Agustín**, the furthest east, is sedate compared with the others. It has a series of beaches of dark sand, attractively sheltered by low cliffs and landscaped promenades, and a casino.

The next exit off the coastal highway leads to **Playa del Inglés**, the largest and liveliest resort, a triangle of land jutting into a huge belt of golden sand. Developed from the end of the 1950s, the area is built up with giant blocks of flats linked by a maze of roads. Many hotels lack sea views, though most have spacious grounds with swimming pools. At night the area pulsates

Floral arches decorating a street of apartments in Puerto de Mogán

For hotels and restaurants in this region see p575 and pp604–5

with bright disco lights and flashing neon. There are more than 300 restaurants and over 50 discos.

West of Playa del Inglés the beach undulates into the **Dunas de Maspalomas**. A relieving contrast to the hectic surrounding resorts, these dunes form a nature reserve protected from further development. The western edge of the dunes (marked by a lighthouse) is occupied by a cluster of luxury hotels. Just behind the dunes lies a golf course encircled by bungalow estates.

Everything is laid on for the package holiday: water sports, excursions, fast food, as well as go-karts, camel safaris and funfairs. Best of these include **Palmitos Park**, with exotic birds in subtropical gardens, and **Sioux City**, a fun-packed Western theme park.

🎪 **Palmitos Park**
Barranco de los Palmitos.
Tel 928 79 70 70. **Open** daily. 🅿 ♿
🌐 palmitospark.es

🎪 **Sioux City**
Cañón del Águila. **Tel** 928 76 25 73.
Open Tue–Sun. 🅿 ♿ 🌐 siouxcity.es

⑮ Agaete

Las Palmas. 🏘 5,600. ℹ Avenida
Señora de las Nieves 1, 928 55 43 82.
🎉 Fiesta de las Nieves (5 Aug).
🌐 agaete.es

The cloudier northern side of the island is far greener and lusher than the arid south, and banana plantations take up most of the coastal slopes. Agaete, on the northwest coast,

The rocky shore and steep cliffs of the northeast coast near Agaete

a pretty scatter of white houses around a striking rocky bay, is growing into a small resort. Every August, Agaete holds the Fiesta de la Rama, a Guanche *(see p551)* rainmaking ritual which dates from long before the arrival of the Spanish. An animated procession of villagers bearing green branches heads from the hills above the town down to the coast and into the sea. The villagers beat the water to summon the rain.

The **Ermita de las Nieves** contains a 16th-century Flemish triptych and model sailing ships. Close by is the **Huerto de las Flores**, a botanical garden.

Environs

A brief detour inland up along the Barranco de Agaete takes you through a fertile valley of papaya, mango and citrus trees. North of Agaete are the towns of Guía and Gáldar. Though there is little to see here, both parish churches do contain examples of the religious statuary of the celebrated 18th-century sculptor, José Luján Pérez.

Nearby, towards the north coast, lies the **Cenobio de Valerón**. One of the most dramatic of the local Guanche sights, this cliff-face is pock-marked with nearly 300 caves beneath a basalt arch. These are believed to have been hideaways for Guanche priest-esses, communal grain stores and refuges from attack.

🌿 **Huerto de las Flores**
Calle Huertas. **Tel** 680 70 02 01.
Open Tue–Sat. 🅿 ♿ 🎴

Miles of wind-sculptured sand: the dunes at Maspalomas

⑯ Tafira

Las Palmas. 🚶 23,000. 🚌 🛈 Calle
Triana 93, Las Palmas, 928 21 96 00.
🎉 San Francisco (Oct).

The hills southwest of Las
Palmas have long been desirable
residential locations. A colonial air
still wafts around Tafira's patrician
villas. The **Jardín Canario**, a
botanical garden founded in
1952, is the main reason for a
visit. Plants from all of the Canary
Islands can be studied in their
own, re-created habitats.

Near La Atalaya lies one of
Gran Canaria's most impressive
natural sights – the **Caldera de la
Bandama**. This is a volcanic crater
1,000 m (3,300 ft) wide, best seen
from the Mirador de Bandama
where you gaze down into the
green depression about 200 m
(660 ft) deep. Some of the
inhabited caves in the **Barranco
de Guayadeque**, a valley of red
rocks to the south, were dug in
the late 15th century. A few of
them have electricity.

🌿 **Jardín Canario**
Carretera de Dragonal, Tafira. **Tel** 928
21 95 80. **Open** daily. **Closed** 1 Jan &
Good Fri. 🚻 🖥 jardincanario.org

⑰ Las Palmas de Gran Canaria

Las Palmas. 🚶 378,000. 🚌 ⛴
🛈 Calle Triana 93, 928 21 96 00.
🎉 Carnival (Feb/Mar).

Las Palmas is the largest city in
the Canary Islands. A bustling
seaport and industrial city, it sees
1,000 ships docking each month.
Las Palmas has faded somewhat

Palm trees in a natural setting in the Jardín Canario, Tafira

from the days when wealthy convalescents flocked here in winter
and glamorous liners called in
on transatlantic voyages. But it
remains a vibrant place to visit.

Las Palmas is a sprawling city
built around an isthmus. The
modern commercial shipping
area, Puerto de la Luz, takes
up the eastern side of the
isthmus, which leads to the
former island of La Isleta, a
sailors' and military quarter.
On the other side of the
isthmus is the crowded **Playa
de las Canteras**, a 3-km-
(2-mile-) long stretch
of golden beach. The
promenade behind has
been built up with bars,
restaurants and hotels.

The town centre
stretches along the
coast from the isthmus.
For a scenic tour, begin
in the **Parque Santa
Catalina**, near the port. This is a
popular, shady square of cafés
and newspaper kiosks. In the
leafy residential quarter of
Ciudad Jardín are the Parque

Doramas and the traditional
casino hotel of Santa Catalina.

The **Pueblo Canario** is a tourist
enclave where visitors can watch
folk dancing, and browse in the
craft shops and the small art
gallery. All this can be viewed
from above by walking uphill
towards the Altavista district and
the Paseo Cornisa. At the end
of town is the Barrio Vegueta,
an atmospheric quarter
which dates back to the
Spanish conquest. At its
heart stands the **Catedral
de Santa Ana**, begun
in 1500. The adjacent
**Museo Diocesano de
Arte Sacro** contains
works of religious art.
The square in front is
guarded by Canarian
dogs in bronze.

Nearby, the **Casa de
Colón** is a 15th-century
governor's residence
where Columbus stayed.
A museum dedicated to
his voyages displays charts,
models and diary extracts.

Early history can be seen
in the **Museo Canario**, which
contains Guanche mummies,
skulls, pottery and jewellery.

Bronze dog at Plaza
Santa Ana

🏛 **Museo Diocesano de
Arte Sacro**
Calle Espíritu Santo 20.
Tel 928 31 49 89. **Open** Mon–Sat. 🎫

🏛 **Casa de Colón**
Calle Colón 1. **Tel** 928 31 23 73.
Open daily. **Closed** 1 Jan, 24, 25 &
31 Dec. 📷

🏛 **Museo Canario**
Calle Doctor Verneau 2. **Tel** 928 33 68
00. **Open** daily. **Closed** 1 Jan, 25 Dec.
🎫 📷 🖥 elmuseocanario.com

The Casa de Colón museum, Las Palmas, dedicated to Columbus

For hotels and restaurants in this region see p575 and pp604–5

⑱ Tour of Cruz de Tejeda

Gran Canaria's mountainous interior makes for an ideal day tour, from any part of the island. Choose a fine day or the views may be obscured. The route from Maspalomas leads through dry ravines of bare rock and cacti, becoming more fertile with altitude. Roads near the central highlands snake steeply through shattered, tawny crags, past caves and pretty villages to panoramic viewpoints from which you can see Mount Teide (see pp542–3) on Tenerife. On the north side, the slopes are much lusher, growing citrus fruits and eucalyptus trees.

White farmhouses en route to Teror

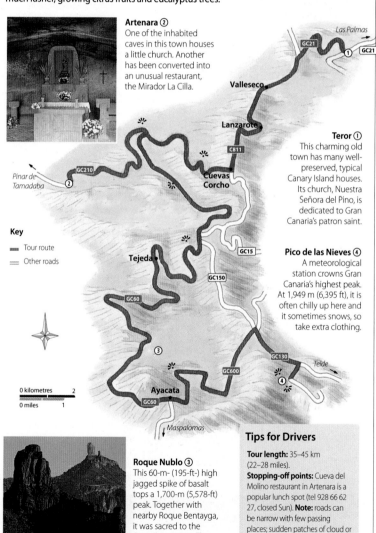

Artenara ②
One of the inhabited caves in this town houses a little church. Another has been converted into an unusual restaurant, the Mirador La Cilla.

Las Palmas

GC21

GC21

Valleseco

Lanzarote

C811

Teror ①
This charming old town has many well-preserved, typical Canary Island houses. Its church, Nuestra Señora del Pino, is dedicated to Gran Canaria's patron saint.

Pinar de Tamadaba

GC210

Cuevas Corcho

Pico de las Nieves ④
A meteorological station crowns Gran Canaria's highest peak. At 1,949 m (6,395 ft), it is often chilly up here and it sometimes snows, so take extra clothing.

GC15

Key

▬▬ Tour route

═══ Other roads

Tejeda

GC150

GC60

③

GC130   Telde

GC600   ④

0 kilometres   2

0 miles   1

Ayacata

GC60

→ Maspalomas

Roque Nublo ③
This 60-m- (195-ft-) high jagged spike of basalt tops a 1,700-m (5,578-ft) peak. Together with nearby Roque Bentayga, it was sacred to the Guanches. It's a stiff climb to the summit.

Tips for Drivers

Tour length: 35–45 km (22–28 miles).

Stopping-off points: Cueva del Molino restaurant in Artenara is a popular lunch spot (tel 928 66 62 27, closed Sun). **Note:** roads can be narrow with few passing places; sudden patches of cloud or mist may loom without warning.

Fuerteventura

Lying just 100 km (60 miles) off the Atlantic coast of Morocco, leaf-shaped Fuerteventura is continually battered by coastal winds – no doubt why, every summer the island hosts the Windsurfing & Kiteboarding World Cup. It is the second largest of the Canary Islands after Tenerife, and the most sparsely populated: its 69,500 inhabitants are outnumbered by goats. The island used to be densely wooded, but European settlers cut down the timber for shipbuilding; the dry climate (so dry, water has to be shipped over from the mainland) and the goats have since reduced the vegetation to parched scrub. The only significant revenue is tourism, which is still in its infancy. However, sun-lovers are beginning to flock to its more than 150 splendid beaches. The island is popular with water-sports fans and naturists alike.

A herd of goats near the airport on Fuerteventura

⓭ Península de Jandía

Las Palmas. 🚌 Costa Calma, Morro Jable. 🚢 (jetfoil) from Gran Canaria. ℹ️ Centro Comercial Cosmo, Bajo, 928 54 07 76.

Excellent beaches of pale sand fringe the Jandía Peninsula in the south of Fuerteventura. A string of *urbanizaciones* (residential developments) now takes up much of the peninsula's sheltered east coast (Sotavento).
Costa Calma, a burgeoning cluster of modern complexes, offers the most interesting beaches with long stretches of fine sand interrupted by low cliffs and coves. **Morro Jable**, a fishing village now swamped by new developments, lies at the southern end of a vast, glittering strand. Beyond Morro Jable, the access road dwindles away into a potholed track leading towards the lonely lighthouse at Punta de Jandía.

Expanses of deserted sand, accessible only by four-wheel drive vehicle, line the westerly, windward coast (Barlovento) – too exposed for all but the hardiest beach-lovers. Some of the island's best subtropical marine life can be found in this area, however, making it popular with skin divers.

From 1938 to the early 1960s, Jandía belonged to a German entrepreneur and was out of bounds to locals. Even today, rumours of spies, submarines and secret Nazi bases still circulate.

⓮ Betancuria

Las Palmas. 🔼 740. 🚌 ℹ️ C/ Juan de Bethancourt 6, 928 87 80 92. 🎉 San Buenaventura (14 Jul), Romería de La Peña (3rd Sat of Sep).

Inland, rugged peaks of extinct volcanoes, separated by wide plains, present a scene of austere grandeur. Scattered, stark villages and obsolete windmills occupy the lowlands, which are occasionally fertile enough to nurture a few crops or palm trees. Beyond, devoid of vegetation, the hills form stark outlines. From a distance they appear brown and grey, but up close the rocks glow with an astonishing range of mauves,

The gilded interior of the Iglesia Santa María in Betancuria

pinks and ochres. The richness of colour in this interior wilderness is at its most striking at sunset.

Betancuria, built in a valley surrounded by mountains in the centre of the island, is named after Jean de Béthencourt, Fuerteventura's 15th-century conqueror, who moved his capital inland to thwart pirates. Nestling in the mountains, this peaceful oasis is now the island's prettiest village. The **Iglesia de Santa María** contains gilded altars, decorated beams and sacred relics. The **Museo Arqueológico** houses many local artifacts.

Environs
To the south, the village of **Pájara** boasts a 17th-century church with a curiously decorated doorway. Its design of serpents and strange beasts is believed to be of Aztec influence. Inside, the twin aisles both contain statues: one of a radiant Madonna and Child in white and silver, the other a Virgen de los Dolores in black.

La Oliva, to the north, was the site of the Spanish military headquarters until the 19th century. The Casa de los Coroneles (House of the Colonels) is a faded yellow mansion with a grand façade and hundreds of windows. Inside it has coffered ceilings. The fortified church and the arts centre displaying works of Canary Island artists are also worth a visit.

🏛 **Museo Arqueológico**
Calle Roberto Roldán. **Tel** 646 97 22 01. **Open** Tue–Sat. ♿ ⬆

㉑ Caleta de Fuste

Las Palmas. ⚙ 1,600. 🚌 ℹ Calle Juan Ramón Soto Morales 10, El Castillo, 928 16 36 11. 🛍 Sat. 📅 Día del Carmen (16 Jul), Nuestra Señora de Antigua (8 Sep).

South of Puerto del Rosario about halfway down the eastern coast, lies Caleta de Fuste. The attractive low-rise, self-catering holiday centres surround a horseshoe bay of soft, gently shelving sand. The largest complex, El Castillo, takes its name from an 18th-century watchtower situated by the harbour.

There are many water-sports facilities, including diving and windsurfing schools, as well as the Pueblo Majorero, an attractive "village" of shops and restaurants around a central plaza near the beach. These features make Caleta de Fuste one of Fuerteventura's most relaxed and pleasant resorts.

Fishing boats on a beach on the Isla de Lobos, near Corralejo

㉒ Puerto del Rosario

Las Palmas. ⚙ 16,500. ✈ 🚌 🚢 ℹ Avenida Marítima s/n, 928 85 01 10. 📅 El Rosario (7 Oct). 🌐 turismo-puertodelrosario.org

Fuerteventura's administrative capital was founded in 1797. Originally known as Puerto de Cabras (Goats' Harbour), after a nearby gorge that was once used for watering goats, it was rechristened to smarten up its image in 1957. The only large port on Fuerteventura, Puerto del Rosario is the base for inter-island ferries and a busy fishing industry. The town is also enlivened by the presence of the Spanish army, which occupies large barracks once used by the Spanish Foreign Legion.

㉓ Corralejo

Las Palmas. ⚙ 7,200. 🚢 ℹ Avenida Marítima 2, 928 86 62 35. 🛍 Mon & Fri. 📅 Día del Carmen (16 Jul). 🌐 corralejograndesplayas.com

This much-expanded fishing village is now (together with the Jandía Peninsula) one of the island's two most impor-tant resorts. Its main attraction is a belt of glorious sand dunes stretching to the south, resembling the Sahara in places, and protected as a nature reserve – a designation that arrived too late to prevent the construction of two hotels right on the beach.

The rest of the resort, mostly consisting of apartments and hotels, spills out from the town centre. The port area is lively, with busy fish restaurants and an efficient 40-minute ferry service to Lanzarote.

Offshore is the tiny **Isla de Lobos**, named after the once abundant monk seals (lobos marinos). Today, scuba divers, snorkellers, sport fishers and surfers claim the clear waters. Glass-bottomed cruise boats take less adventurous excursionists to the island for barbecues and swimming trips.

The Guanches

When Europeans first arrived in the Canary Islands in the late 14th century, they discovered a tall, white-skinned race, who lived in caves and later in small settlements around the edges of barren lava fields. Guanche was the name of one tribe on Tenerife, but it came to be used as the European name for all the indigenous tribes on the islands, and it is the one that has remained. The origins of the Guanches are still unclear, but it is probable that they arrived on the islands in the 1st or 2nd century BC from Berber North Africa. Within 100 years of European arrival the Guanches had been subdued and virtually exterminated by the ruthless conquistadors. Very few traces of their culture remain today.

Reminders of the Guanches can be seen in many places in the Canaries. Specimens of their mummified dead, as well as baskets and stone and bone artifacts, are on display in several museums and there are statues of chiefs in Candelaria (see p539) on Tenerife.

Guanche bowl for preparing gofio (see p541)

A Guanche basket

Lanzarote

The easternmost and fourth largest of the Canary Islands is virtually treeless and relies on desalination plants for some of its water. Yet many visitors consider Lanzarote the most attractive of all the islands for the vivid shapes and contrasting colours of its volcanic landscapes. Despite low rainfall, carefully tended crops flourish in its black volcanic soil. Locals pride themselves on the way their island has been preserved from the worst effects of tourism; there are no garish billboards, overhead cables or high-rise buildings. Its present-day image owes much to the artist César Manrique. Touring the spectacular volcanic Timanfaya National Park is a favourite trip.

Wind turbines harnessing Lanzarote's winds for power

㉔ Playa Blanca

Las Palmas. 🏠 4,500. 🚌 🚢 ℹ Calle Varadero 3, 928 51 81 50. 🎉 Nuestra Señora del Carmen (16 Jul).
🌐 **turismolanzarote.com**

The fishing village origins of this resort are readily apparent around its harbour. Although it has expanded in recent years, Playa Blanca remains an agreeably

Las Coloradas beach near Playa Blanca in southern Lanzarote

family-oriented place with some character. It has plenty of cafés and restaurants, shops and bars, and several large hotels. However, the buildings are well dispersed and the resort is rarely noisy at night. Visitors converge here not for nightlife or contrived entertainment, but for relaxing beach holidays. There are one or two good stretches of sand near to the town, but the most entic- ing lie hidden around the rocky headlands to the east, where

the clear, warm sea laps into rocky coves, and clothes seem superfluous. **Playa de Papagayo** is the best known of these, but a diligent search will probably gain you one all to yourself. A four-wheel-drive vehicle is advisable to negotiate the narrow, unsurfaced roads which lead to these beaches.

㉕ Parque Nacional de Timanfaya

Las Palmas Yaiza. ℹ Ctra LZ–67, km 11.5, Mancha Blanca, 928 11 80 42. **Open** daily. 🌄

From 1730 to 1736, a series of volcanic eruptions took place on Lanzarote. Eleven villages were buried in lava, which eventually spread over 200 sq km (77 sq miles) of Lanzarote's most fertile land. Miraculously, no one was killed, though many islanders emigrated.

Today, the volcanoes that once devastated Lanzarote pro- vide one of its most lucrative and enigmatic attractions, aptly known as the **Montañas del Fuego** (Fire Mountains). They are part of the Parque Nacional de Timanfaya, established in 1974 to protect a fascinating and important geological record. The entrance to the park lies just north of the small village of **Yaiza**. Here you can pause and take a 15-minute camel ride up the volcanic slopes for wonderful views across the park. Afterwards, you pay the entrance fee and drive through haunting scenery of dark, barren lava cinders topped by brooding

César Manrique (1919–92)

Local hero César Manrique trained as a painter, and spent time in mainland Spain and New York before returning to Lanzarote in 1968. He campaigned for traditional and environ- mentally friendly development on the island for the remaining part of his life, setting strict building height limits and colour requirements. Dozens of tourist sites throughout the Canaries benefited from his talents and enthusiasm.

César Manrique in 1992

Camel rides from Yaiza across the Montañas de Fuego

red-black volcano cones. Finally, you will reach **Islote de Hilario**. You can park at El Diablo panoramic restaurant. From here, buses take visitors for exhilarating 30 minute tours of the desolate, lunar-like landscapes.

Afterwards, back at Islote de Hilario, guides will provide graphic demonstrations that this volcano is not extinct, but only dormant – brushwood pushed into a crevice bursts instantly into a ball of flame, while water poured into a sunken pipe shoots out in a scorching jet of steam.

The road from Yaiza to the coast leads to the **Salinas de Janubio**, where salt is extracted from the sea. At **Los Hervideros** the rough coast can create spectacular seas and further north, at **El Golfo**, is an eerie emerald-coloured lagoon.

㉖ Puerto del Carmen

Las Palmas. 🏔 13,700. 🚌 🚢
ℹ Avenida de la Playa, 928 51 33 51.
🎭 Nuestra Señora del Carmen
(16 Jul). 🖥 **turismolanzarote.com**

More than 60 per cent of Lanzarote's tourists stay in this resort, which stretches several kilometres along the seafront. The coastal road carves its way through a solid slab of holiday infrastructure, which is pleasantly designed and unoppressive, and offers easy access to a long golden beach, Playa Blanca, which in places is very wide. Another beach nearby is Playa de los Pocillos. To the north is the quaint village of Tías and **A Casa José Saramago**, the house-cum-museum where the Nobel Prize-winning writer

(1922–2010) lived his last 18 years in exile after the Portuguese government deemed his work religiously offensive.

Fishing boat in Arrecife port

㉗ Arrecife

Las Palmas. 🏔 46,900. ✈ 🚌
ℹ Calle Triana 38, 928 81 17 62.
🎭 San Ginés (25 Aug).

Arrecife, with its modern buildings and lively streets, is the commercial and administrative centre of the island. Despite its modern trappings, the capital retains

much of its old charm, with palm-lined promenades, a fine beach and two small forts. **Castillo San Gabriel** offers lovely views from a mezzanine, accessed via a stone walkway over the sea, crossing the Puente de Bolas. It also houses the Museo de Historia de Arrecife. The 18th-century **Castillo de San José** is now a museum of contemporary art and was renovated faithfully to the original interior by César Manrique. One of his paintings is on display here.

🏰 **Castillo San Gabriel**
Puerto de Naos. **Tel** 928 81 27 50.
Open 9am–1pm Mon–Fri.

🏰 **Castillo de San José**
Puerto de Naos. **Tel** 928 81 23 21.
Open daily. **Closed** 1 Jan, 25 Dec.

㉘ Costa Teguise

10 km (6 miles) north of Arrecife. 🚌
ℹ Avda Islas Canarias, Junto Pueblo Marinero, 928 59 25 42.

This resort, largely financed by a mining conglomerate, has transformed the arid, low-lying terrain north of Arrecife into an extensive cluster of time-share accommodation, leisure clubs and luxury hotels. The contrast between old town Teguise (see p554), Lanzarote's former capital, and the exclusive Costa Teguise is striking. Fake greenery and suburban lamps line boulevards amid barren ashlands. White villas line a series of small sandy beaches. The high level of investment has succeeded in attracting jet-set clientele. King Juan Carlos also has a villa here.

Umbrellas on the beach, Puerto del Carmen

Iglesia de San Miguel on the main
square in Teguise

㉙ Teguise

Las Palmas. 🏠 12,300. 🚌 🛈 Plaza
de la Constitución, 928 84 53 98.
🚢 Sun. 🎉 Día del Carmen (16 Jul),
Las Nieves (5 Aug).

Teguise, the island's capital until
1852, is a well-kept, old-fashioned
town with wide, cobbled streets
and patrician houses grouped
around the **Iglesia de San
Miguel**. Visit on a Sunday, when
there is a handicrafts market and
folk dancing. Outside Teguise, in
the castle of Santa Bárbara is the
Museo de la Piratería, which
tells the story of the pirates who
passed through here.

Environs
To see more of inland Lanzarote,
follow the central road south of
Teguise, through the strange
farmland of **La Geria**. Black
volcanic ash has been scooped
into protective, crescent-shaped
pits which trap moisture to
enable vines and other crops to
flourish. **Mozaga**, one of the
main villages in the area, is a
major centre of wine production.

Volcanic ash swept into crescent-shaped pits for farming, La Geria

On the roadside near Mozaga is
the *Monumento al Campesino*,
Manrique's *(see p552)* striking
modern sculpture dedicated to
Lanzarote's farmers.
　Between Teguise and Arrecife
is the **Fundación César
Manrique**. The former home of
the artist incorporates five lava
caves, some of his own work and
his contemporary art collection.

🏛 **Museo de la Piratería**
Montaña de Guanapay. **Tel** 928 84 50
01. **Open** daily. **Closed** 1 & 6 Jan, 25
Dec. 🚫 🌐 museodelapirateria.com

🏛 **Fundación César Manrique**
Taro de Tahíche. **Tel** 928 84 31 38.
Open daily. **Closed** 1 Jan. 🚫
🌐 fcmanrique.org

㉚ Haría

Las Palmas. 🏠 4,000. 🚌 🛈 Plaza
de la Constitución 1, 928 83 52 51.
🚢 Sat. 🎉 San Juan (24 Jun).

Palm trees and white, cube-
shaped houses distinguish this
picturesque village. It acts as a
gateway to excursions round
the northern tip of the island.
The road to the north gives
memorable views over exposed
cliffs, and the 609-m- (2,000-ft-)
high Monte Corona.

Environs
From Manrique's **Mirador del
Río** you can see La Graciosa,
and the northernmost of the
Canary Islands, Alegranza.
Orzola is a delightful fishing
village providing fish lunches as
well as boat trips to La Graciosa.
To the south are the Mala prickly
pear plantations, where
cochineal (crimson dye) is
extracted from the insects
which feed on the plants.

Nearby is the **Jardín de Cactus**,
a well-stocked cactus garden,
which has a smart restaurant,
again designed by Manrique.

🕌 **Mirador del Río**
Haría. **Tel** 928 52 65 48. **Open** daily. 🚫

🌵 **Jardín de Cactus**
Guatiza. **Tel** 928 52 93 97. **Open** daily. 🚫

Landscaped pool on top of the caves of
Jameos del Agua

㉛ Jameos del Agua

Las Palmas. **Tel** 928 84 80 20.
Open daily. 🚫

An eruption of the Monte Corona
volcano formed the Jameos del
Agua lava caves on Lanzarote's
northeast coast. In 1965–8,
these were landscaped by César
Manrique into an imaginative
subterranean complex
containing a restaurant, nightclub, a swimming pool edged
by palm trees, and gardens of
oleander and cacti. Steps lead
to a shallow seawater lagoon
where a rare species of blind
white crab, unique to Lanzarote,
glows softly in the dim light. An
exhibition on volcanology and
Canarian flora and fauna also
deserves a look. Folk-dancing
evenings are regularly held in
this unusual setting.

Environs
Another popular attraction is
the nearby **Cueva de los
Verdes**, a tube of solidifed lava
stretching 6 km (4 miles)
underground. Guided tours of
the caves are available.

🕳 **Cueva de los Verdes**
Haría. **Tel** 928 84 84 84.
Open daily. 🚫

Volcanic Islands

The volcanic activity which formed the Canary Islands has created a variety of scenery, from distinctive lava formations to enormous volcanoes crowned by huge, gaping craters. The islands are all at different stages in their evolution. Tenerife, Lanzarote, El Hierro and La Palma are still volcanically active; dramatic displays of flames and steam can be seen in Lanzarote's Montañas de Fuego *(see p552)*. The last eruption was on La Palma in 1971.

Origin of the Islands
The Canaries are situated above faults in the earth's crust, which is always thinner under the oceans than under the continents. When magma (molten rock) rises through these cracks, volcanoes are formed.

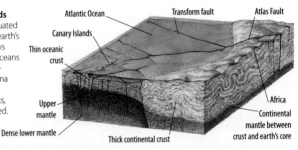

Atlantic Ocean · Canary Islands · Thin oceanic crust · Upper mantle · Dense lower mantle · Thick continental crust · Transform fault · Atlas Fault · Africa · Continental mantle between crust and earth's core

Evolution of the Canary Islands

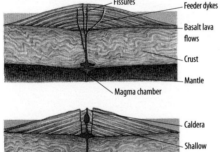

Fissures · Feeder dykes · Basalt lava flows · Crust · Mantle · Magma chamber

1 Lanzarote, El Hierro and La Palma are wide, gently sloping shield volcanoes standing on the sea floor. All of them are composed of basalt formed by a hot, dense magma. The flexible crust is pressed down by the weight of the islands.

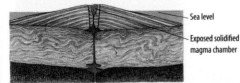

Caldera · Shallow magma chamber

2 An explosive eruption can empty the magma chamber, leaving the roof unsupported. This collapses under the weight of the volcano above to form a depression, or caldera, such as Las Cañadas on Tenerife. There are thick lava flows during this stage of the island's evolution.

Sea level · Exposed solidified magma chamber

3 If eruptions cease, a volcano will be eroded by the action of the sea, and by wind and rain. Gran Canaria's main volcano is in the early stages of erosion, while the volcano on Fuerteventura has already been deeply eroded, exposing chambers of solidified magma.

Rope lava near La Restinga, El Hierro *(see pp536–7)*

Pico Viejo crater, next to Mount Teide, Tenerife *(see p542)*

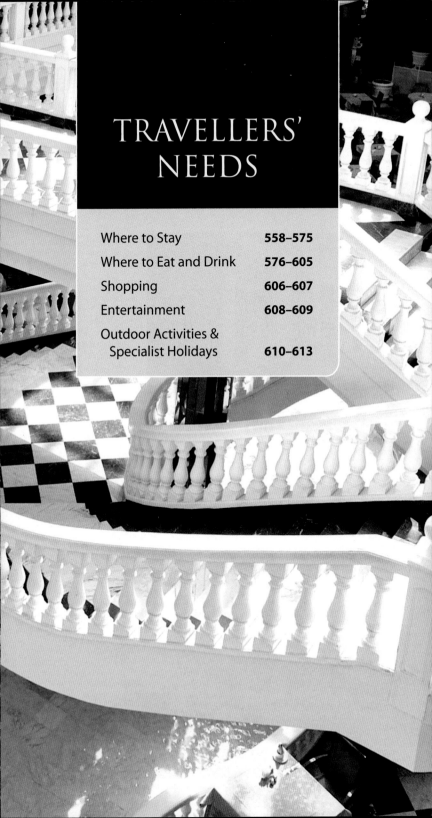

TRAVELLERS' NEEDS

Where to Stay   558–575

Where to Eat and Drink   576–605

Shopping   606–607

Entertainment   608–609

Outdoor Activities &
  Specialist Holidays   610–613

WHERE TO STAY

Medieval castles turned into luxury hotels and mansions converted into youth hostels typify the variety of places to stay in Spain. The tourists who sustain Spain's economy have over 10,000 establishments, offering over one and a half million beds, to choose from. Suites in once-royal palaces are at the top of the scale. Then there are luxury beach hotels on the Costa del Sol and in the Balearic and the Canary Islands. Visitors can also stay on remote farms, or in villas and old houses available for self-catering. For budget travel there are pensions, family-run *casas rurales*, guesthouses and camp sites, as well as refuges with stunning views for mountaineers. Some of the best hotels in all these categories and in every style and price range are listed on pages 562–75.

Entrance to Taberna del Alabardero in Seville *(see p571)*

Hotel Grading and Facilities

Spain's hotels are classified into categories and awarded stars by the country's regional tourist authorities. Hotels (indicated by an H on a blue plaque near the door) are awarded from one to five stars. *Hostals* (Hs) and *pensiones* (P) offer fewer comforts but are cheaper than hotels.

Spain's star-rating system reflects the number and range of facilities available rather than the quality of service. Most hotels have air-conditioning, and an increasing number provide amenities including Internet access, and have restaurants offering local fare.

Most hotels have restaurants that are open to non-residents. Although *hotel-residencias* (HR) and *hostal-residencias* (HsR) do not have dining rooms, some serve breakfast. Among Spain's largest hotel chains are **Meliá Hotels International**, **Grupo Riu** and **NH-Hotels**. Tour operators often book rooms in Spain's larger hotel groups.

Paradors

Paradors are government-run hotels, classified from three to five stars. Spain's first parador opened in the Sierra de Gredos in 1928; there is now a wide network of over 90, on the mainland and the Canary Islands. Most, and certainly the most historic, are located in the centre and the north of the mainland. The best are in former royal hunting lodges, castles, monasteries and other monuments; some modern paradors have been purpose-built, often in spectacular scenery or in towns of historic interest.

A parador is not necessarily the best hotel in town, but it can be counted on to deliver a high level of comfort and service. Each is furnished in its own individual style, and has a restaurant offering regional cuisine. They are generally well signposted.

If you plan to tour in high season or to stay in the smaller paradors, it is wise to reserve a room in advance. The paradors may be booked through the **Central de Reservas** in Madrid or through their London agent, **Keytel International**.

Prices

Spanish law requires all hotels to display their prices behind the reception and in each room. As a rule, the higher a hotel's star rating, the more you pay. Rates for a double room can be as little as €35–50 a night for a one-star *hostal*; a five-star hotel will cost more than €275 a night, but a room price higher than €350 a night is rare, especially outside Madrid or Barcelona.

Prices usually vary according to room, region and season. A suite or a room with a view, a balcony or other special feature may cost more than average. Rural and suburban hotels tend to be less expensive than those in the city centre. All the prices given on pages 562–75 are based on mid- or high-season rates. High season covers July and August, but in some areas it runs from April to October. In the Canary Islands the winter is high season.

A parador within a modern extension of a medieval castle

◀ Striking black-and-white floor and sweeping staircase at a luxury hotel in Tenerife

Many of Spain's city hotels charge especially inflated rates for their rooms during major fiestas – such as the April Fair in Seville *(see p435)*, Los Sanfermines in Pamplona *(see p136)*, Carnival in Santa Cruz de Tenerife *(see p540)* and Easter Week *(see p42)* – and major trade fairs.

Most hotels quote prices per room and meal prices per person without including VAT (IVA), which is 10 per cent on the mainland and 5 per cent on the Canary Islands.

Stylish lounge area at Hotel Arts, Barcelona *(see p565)*

Booking and Check-in

During the off-season period, especially in rural or small towns, there is no real need to book ahead; but if you plan to travel in high season, you should reserve a room by phone or email, on the Internet, or through a travel agent. You will need to reserve if you want a special room: one with a double bed (twin beds are the norm); on the ground floor; away from a noisy main road; or a room with a view.

The resort hotels often close from autumn to spring. It is advisable to check ahead that your preferred hotels will be open at that time of year.

You will normally be asked for your credit card details when you book a room. A deposit of 20–25 per cent may be requested if you book during a peak period or for a stay of more than a few nights. Send it by credit card or giro in Spain and

by credit card or banker's draft from outside the country. If you have to cancel, do so at least a week before the booking date or you may lose all or some of the deposit.

In most cases hotels will honour a booking only until 8pm unless business is poor. If you are delayed, call the hotel to assure them you are coming and to tell them when to expect you.

When you check in to a hotel you will be asked for your passport or identity card to comply with Spanish police regulations. It will normally be returned to you promptly as soon as your details have been copied.

You are expected to check out of your room by noon on the last day of your stay, or to pay for another night.

Paying

Most hotels accept major credit cards. In some large, busy hotels you may be asked for an authorization hold on your credit card until you check out. Make sure this is cancelled when you pay your bill.

Personal and travellers' cheques are not accepted in almost all Spanish hotels, even if backed by a cheque guarantee card or drawn on a Spanish bank. Many people pay cash, and in some cheap hotels this may be the only mode of payment accepted.

Tipping hotel staff such as porters and cleaners is left to the discretion of the guests.

View of the pretty beach from a Lanzarote hotel

Casas Rurales

The owners of some *casas rurales* (country houses) accept a few visitors, usually in high season. They are most numerous in Asturias, Navarra, Aragón and Catalonia (where they are called *cases de pagès*). They are also becoming common in Galicia and Cantabria (where they are called *casonas*), and in Andalusia.

Casas rurales range from manor houses to small, isolated farms. Some offer bed and breakfast; some an evening meal or full board; and others are self-catering. Do not expect hotel service or lots of facilities. You may, however, be given a friendly welcome and good home cooking, all at an afford-able price. You can book *casas rurales* directly or through regional associations, such as **RAAR** in Andalusia, **Ruralia** in Asturias, **Turismo Verde** in Huesca, Aragón, **Ruralverd** in Catalonia and **AGATUR** (Asociación Gallega de Turismo Rural) in Galicia.

Agroturisme Biniatram in Menorca, offering rooms in converted farm buildings *(see p575)*

Self-catering

Villas and holiday flats let by the week are plentiful along the Spanish coasts, and on the rise in the cities. In scenic country-side areas there are many *casas rurales* (farm and village houses) for rent by the day. For information about the *casas rurales*, contact their regional organizations *(see p559)*. They also take bookings. **Villas 4 You** is a UK organization that acts as an agent for owners of holiday houses and flats in Spain, as does **International Lodging Corporation** in the US. Other organizations and owners of holiday homes advertise in the travel sections of UK Sunday newspapers. Tour operators offer a range of self-catering accommodation.

The prices for self-catering accommodation vary according to the location, the property and the season. A four-person villa with a pool can cost under €350 for a week if it is inland and €1,200 a week or more if it is on the coast.

An apartment hotel (known as a *villa turística* in Andalusia) is another option. Half hotel, half holiday flat, it gives guests a choice between self-catering (all rooms have a kitchen) or eating in the hotel restaurant. Holiday villages are similar, often catering for specialist interests. One example is the village of Ainsa, in the mountain sports region of Aragón *(see p567)*, which offers a mix of camping and hostel accommodation, with restaurants and bars.

Camping site close to the beach, in Miami Platja, Catalonia

Youth Hostels and Mountain Refuges

To use the network of *albergues juveniles* (youth hostels) in Spain you need to show a YHA (Youth Hostel Association) card from your country or an international card, which you can buy from any hostel. Here, the prices per person for bed and breakfast are lower than hotel prices.

Youth hostels can be booked directly or via the **Red Española de Albergues Juveniles** (Spanish Network of Youth Hostels). Despite the name, there is no age limit.

Mountaineers heading for the more remote areas may use the *refugios* (refuges) – shelters with a dormitory, cooking facilities and heating. Some are huts with a few bunks; others are houses with up to 50 beds.

The *refugios* are marked on large-scale maps of mountain areas and national parks and administered by the regional mountaineering associations. The **Federación Española de Deportes de Montaña y**

Escalada (FEDME) and the local tourist offices can supply their addresses.

A mountain refuge providing shelter in unspoiled Asturias

Camp Sites

There are nearly 1,200 camp sites in Spain. Most are on the coasts, but some are also outside major cities, and in the popular countryside and moun-tain areas. Most have electricity and running water; some also have laundrettes, playgrounds, restaurants, shops or a pool. **Glamping Hub** offers a more upscale camping experience, with unparalleled access to nature. There is a variety of unique accommodation to choose from, including luxury treehouses, retro-style caravans, yurts, caves, tepees, eco-friendly domes, luxury tents and cabins all over Spain.

It is a good idea to carry a camping carnet with you. This can be used instead of a passport to check in at sites and it covers you for third-party insurance. Carnets are issued in the UK by

Youth hostel in rustic style on the edge of Cazorla nature reserve, Jaén

the AA, RAC and the **Camping and Caravanning Club**.

Every year, the *Guía Oficial de Campings* is published by Turespaña. More details are also available from the **Federación Española de Empresarios de Campings y Ciudades de Vacaciones**. In Spain, camping is only permitted on official sites.

Monasteries and Convents

If you have a taste for peace and austerity you may enjoy a night in one of Spain's 150 religious houses where guests are welcome. Most belong to the Benedictine and the Cistercian orders. Room prices are inexpensive. They are not hotels, however; you have to book ahead by writing or by phone; and few have private telephones or televisions. The guests may be asked to tidy their rooms, observe the same strict mealtimes as the monks or nuns and to help with the washing up. Some convents admit only women and some monasteries only men.

Travellers with Disabilities

Hotel managers will advise on access for people in wheelchairs, and the staff will help, but few hotels are well equipped for disabled guests, although some of the youth hostels are.

COCEMFE (the Confederación Coordinadora Estatal de Minusválidos Físicos de España) runs a hotel in Madrid for disabled people's groups. COCEMFE and Ilunion Viajes *(see p617)* advise on hotels for guests with special needs. Accessible holidays can be booked through **Can Be Done**, which has a list of accommodation on the coast and islands, including resorts and self-catering apartments.

Further Information

Turespaña (Spanish Tourist Office) has a useful website, which has a very comprehensive database of hotels, hostals, pensions and other accommodation in Spain. Bookings can be made via the website as well.

Wrought-iron gates adorn the entrance to Hotel Alma, Barcelona

Recommended Hotels

The hotels listed on pages 562–75 cover a range of themes and price categories, from simple B&Bs to luxury retreats. Listed by area, they all offer great value within their category. Certain entries are marked as DK Choice. These options offer something extra special. They may be set in beautiful surroundings, a historic palace or in a converted farmhouse where you're treated like a member of the family. Common to all is a second-to-none quality of service and atmosphere.

DIRECTORY

Hotel Grading & Facilities

Grupo Riu
Tel 902 40 05 02.
W riu.com

Meliá Hotels International
Tel 902 14 44 40.
W melia.com

NH-Hoteles
Tel 902 57 03 68.
W nh-hotels.com

Paradors

Central de Reservas
José Abascal 2, 28003 Madrid. Tel 902 54 79 79.
W parador.es

Keytel International
W keytel.co.uk

Casa Rurales

AGATUR
Recinto Ferial, Apdo 26, Silleda, 36540, Pontevedra.
Tel 986 57 70 00.
W agatur.org

RAAR
Sagunto 8, 04004, Almería. Tel 902 44 22 33.
W raar.es

Ruralia
C/ Centro de Empresas, oficina 3, 33500, Llanes (Asturias).
Tel 902 10 70 70.
W ruralia.com

Ruralverd
C/ del Pí 11, Principal 8, 08002, Barcelona.
Tel 93 304 37 74.
W ruralverd.es

Turismo Verde
C/ Miguel Servet 12, 22002, Huesca. Tel 902 29 41 41, or 974 242 098.
W turismoverde.es

Self-catering

International Lodging Corporation
W ilcweb.com

Villas 4 You
Tel 0800 096 3439.
W villas4you.co.uk

Youth Hostels & Mountain Refuges

Federación Española de Deportes de Montaña y Escalada
C/ Floridablanca 84, 08015, Barcelona.
Tel 93 426 42 67.
W fedme.es

Red Española de Albergues Juveniles
Tel 91 308 46 75.
W reaj.com

Camp Sites

Camping and Caravanning Club
Tel 0845 130 7633 in UK.
W campingand caravanningclub.co.uk

Federación Española de Empresarios de Campings y Ciudades de Vacaciones
C/ Valderribas 48, Esc 3, 1C, 28007, Madrid.
Tel 914 48 12 34.
W fedcamping.com

Glamping Hub
W glampinghub.com

Travellers with Disabilities

Can Be Done
Congress House, 14 Lyon Road, Harrow HA1 2EN, UK. Tel 020 8907 2400.
W canbedone.co.uk

COCEMFE
C/ Luis Cabrera 63, 28002, Madrid. Tel 917 44 36 00.
W cocemfe.es

Further Information

Spanish Tourist Office
Tel 0207 317 2011 in UK.
Tel 212 265 8822 in US.
W spain.info

Where to Stay

Galicia

A CORUÑA: Hotel Melia Maria Pita   €
Modern
Avenida Pedro Barrié de la Maza 1, 15003
Tel *981 20 50 00*
W melia.com
A family-friendly hotel with good service, kids' clubs and family suites. Beachfront location.

A CORUÑA: Hotel Hesperia Finisterre   €€
Luxury
Paseo del Parrote 2–4, 15001
Tel *981 20 54 00*
W hesperia.com
Harbour views and five-star facilities. An excellent base for exploring the area.

A GUARDA: Hotel Convento de San Benito   €
Historic
Plaza San Benito s/n, 36780
Tel *986 61 11 66*
W hotelsanbenito.es
Delightful hotel set in a restored medieval convent with sea views.

BAIONA: Parador de Baiona   €€€
Historic
Rua Arquitecto Jesus Valverde, 36300
Tel *986 35 50 00*
W parador.es
This walled medieval fortress, not far from the Old Town, boasts a spectacular location, surrounded by sea on three sides.

CAMBADOS: Parador de Cambados   €€
Historic
Paseo Calzada s/n, 36630
Tel *986 54 22 50*
W parador.es
This elegant 17th-century mansion is a great base for exploring the lush landscapes of the Rías Baixas.

LUGO: Hotel Rústico Vila do Val   €
Boutique
Plaza Santa María 2, 27770, Ferreira do Valadouro
Tel *982 57 16 53*
W hotelviladoval.com
A charming, rustic hotel tucked away 20 minutes from the coast.

O GROVE: Gran Hotel La Toja   €€
Luxury
Isla de La Toja s/n, 36991
Tel *986 73 00 25*
W granhotellatoja.com
Fabulous renovated spa hotel set on a tiny island off O Grove.

OURENSE: Monasterio de Santo Estevo   €
Historic
Monasterio de Santo Estevo s/n, 32162
Tel *988 01 01 10*
W parador.es
Modern comfort in a beautiful medieval parador.

PONTEVEDRA: Balneario de Mondariz   €€
Luxury
Avenida Enrique Peinador s/n, 36890
Tel *986 65 61 56*
W balneariomondariz.es
This hotel has a justly famous spa, kids' activities and a golf course.

RIBADEO: Hotel Rolle   €
Historic
C/ Ingeniero Schulz 6, 27700
Tel *982 12 06 70*
W hotelrolle.com
Set in an 18th-century town house, this hotel has charming, rustic rooms and friendly service.

SANTIAGO DE COMPOSTELA: San Miguel Hotel Gastronómico   €
Rooms with a View
Plaza de San Miguel dos Agros 9, 15704
Tel *981 55 57 79*
W sanmiguelsantiago.com
Views of the Old Town, chic rooms and an excellent restaurant.

SANTIAGO DE COMPOSTELA: San Francisco Hotel Monumento   €€
Historic
Campillo San Franciso 3, 15705
Tel *981 58 16 34*
W sanfranciscohm.com
Stylish, modern hotel set in a historic monastery. Indoor swimming pool and hot tub.

Monasterio de Santo Estevo in Ourense, boasting spectacular views

SANXENXO: Hotel Carlos I Silgar   €€
Luxury
Calle Vigo s/n, 36960
Tel *986 72 70 36*
W hotelcarlos.es
Spa facilities, seafront location and impeccable service.

DK Choice

VIGO: Gran Hotel Nagari   €€
Boutique
Plaza de Compostela 21, 36201
Tel *986 21 11 11*
W granhotelnagari.com
An extremely chic and luxurious hotel, with spacious, beautifully decorated rooms and all modern amenities. The spa offers a plethora of treatments to relax and indulge the senses.

Asturias and Cantabria

CABRANES: Hostería de Torazo   €€€
Luxury
Plaza de la Sierra 1, Torazo, 33535
Tel *985 89 80 99*
W hosteriadetorazo.com
Modern hotel with a plush spa, set in a pretty, traditional village.

CANGAS DE ONÍS: Parador de Cangas de Onís   €
Historic
Villanueva de Cangas, 33550
Tel *985 84 94 02*
W parador.es
Stunning 8th-century monastery on the banks of the River Sella.

COLUNGA: Palacio de Libardón   €
Historic
Lugar Barrio de Arriba 197, 33325
Tel *605 81 63 87*
W palaciodelibardon.com
A charming restored *palacio* with friendly hosts and excellent food.

COMILLAS: Hotel Josein   €
Rooms with a View
Calle Manuel Noriega 27, 39520
Tel *942 72 02 25*
W hoteljosein.com
Splendid location overlooking the beach. Comfortable rooms.

**CUDILLERO: Hotel Casona
Selgas** €
Historic
Avenida Selgas s/n, 33154
Tel *985 59 05 48*
W hotelcasonaselgas.com
A small, family-run hotel with
superb service and helpful hosts.

DK Choice

**FUENTE DÉ: Parador de
Fuente Dé** €
Historic
Crta de Espinama s/n, 39588
Tel *911 77 61 42*
W parador.es
This parador has all the usual
high standards and amenities,
but it's the truly spectacular
setting, surrounded by the
mountains of the Picos de
Europa, that sets it apart. Explore
or simply marvel at the views.

GIJÓN: Hotel Hernán Cortes €
Historic
Fernandez Vallin 5, 33205
Tel *985 34 60 00*
W hotelhernancortes.es
Comfortable rooms in a historic
casino. Central location near the
beach, bars and shops.

**LLANES: Hotel Rural
Cuartamenteru** €
Boutique
Barrio Anteji s/n, Poo de Llanes, 33509
Tel *985 40 32 76*
W cuartamenteru.com
This hotel has a tranquil setting
with mountain views.

MIESES: Posada el Bosque €
Boutique
*Crta Monastero de Santo.
Toribio, 39586*
Tel *942 73 01 27*
W posadaelbosque.com
A charming mountain hotel ideal
for a romantic getaway.

**OVIEDO: Castillo del Bosque
La Zoreda** €€
Boutique
*Bosque de La Zoreda s/n, 33170,
La Manjoya*
Tel *985 96 33 33*
W castillodelbosquedelazoreda.com
Five-star luxury hotel housed in
a fabulous 20th-century palace
surrounded by beautiful gardens.

**PECHÓN: Hotel Tinas de
Pechón** €€
Boutique
Barrio Quintana 64, 39594
Tel *942 71 73 36*
W tinasdepechon.com
Tinas is a stylish, contemporary
hotel close to the beach. All
rooms have kitchenettes.

Designer minimalism at Hotel Miró, Bilbao

**RIBADESELLA: Hotel Villa
Rosario I** €€
Historic
Dionisio Ruizsánche 6, 33560
Tel *985 86 00 90*
W hotelvillarosario.com
Renovated palace on the seafront
at Ribadesella. Sea and mountain
views, and excellent facilities.

**SAN VICENTE DE LA
BARQUERA: Hotel Villa de
San Vicente** €
Rooms with a View
Calle Fuente Nueva 1, 39540
Tel *942 71 21 38*
W hotelvsvicente.com
Clean, cosy and quiet rooms.
Lovely views of the castle.

**SANTANDER: Hostal Jardin
Secreto** €
B&B
C/ Cardenal Cisneros 37, 39007
Tel *942 07 07 14*
W jardinsecretosantander.com
Simple, tastefully decorated rooms,
with a garden on the terrace.

**SANTILLANA DEL MAR: Hotel
Casa del Marqués** €€
Historic
Calle del Cantón 26, 39330
Tel *942 81 88 88*
W hotelcasadelmarques.com
Once home to the first Marqués
of Santillana del Mar, this 500-
year-old building is now a hotel.

The Basque Country,
Navarra and La Rioja

**ANGUIANO: Abadía de
Valvanera** €
Historic
*Crta LR-113, km 24.6,
Monasterio de Valvanera*
Tel *941 37 70 44*
W abadiavalvanera.com

Simple, understated rooms
in an old Benedictine abbey
located in the beautiful Sierra
de la Demanda.

BERA: Hotel Churrut €€
Historic
Plaza de los Fueros 2, 31780
Tel *948 62 55 40*
W hotelchurrut.com
A converted, restored 17th-
century home. Cosy and stylish.
Excellent restaurant.

BILBAO: Hotel Carlton €€
Historic
Plaza de Federico Moyúa 2, 48009
Tel *944 16 22 00*
W hotelcarlton.es
This elegant 1926 hotel is a
city landmark. Rooms are
decorated in classical style.

BILBAO: Hotel Miró €€
Boutique
Alameda Mazarredo 77, 48009
Tel *946 61 18 80*
W mirohotelbilbao.com
Designed by Antonio Miró,
this minimalist luxury hotel is
a stone's throw away from the
Guggenheim Museum.

**BRIÑAS: Hospedería Señorío
de Briñas** €
Historic
Travesera de La Calle Real 3, 26290
Tel *941 30 42 24*
W hotelesconencantodelarioja.com
A historic palace amid bucolic
wine country. Complimentary
visits to the family-run wine cellar.

**DONAMARÍA: Donmaria'ko
Benta** €
Inn
Barrio Ventas 4, 31750
Tel *948 45 07 08*
W donamariako.com
Family-run place with a traditional
restaurant and garden views.

For more information on types of hotels *see page 561*

DK Choice
ELCIEGO: Hotel Marqés de Riscal €€€
Boutique
Calle Torrea 1, 01340
Tel 945 18 08 80
w hotel-marquesderiscal.com
This stunning hotel combines avant-garde design with an unbeatable location in the heart of the Basque wine country. Indulge in grape-based spa treatments, relax on the rooftop lounge or take a winery tour.

GETARIA: Hotel Rural Gaintza €
Rooms with a View
C/ San Prudentzio Auzoa 26, 20808
Tel 943 14 00 32
w txakoligaintza.com
Elegant, contemporary rooms in an old farmhouse with views of beautiful vineyards.

HARO: Los Agustinos €
Historic
San Agustín 2, 26200
Tel 941 31 13 08
w hotellosagustinos.com
This hotel was originally founded in 1373 as a convent. The rooms are set around impressive cloisters topped with a glass ceiling.

HONDARRIBIA: Parador de Hondarribia €€
Historic
Plaza de Armas 14, 20280
Tel 943 64 55 00
w parador.es
A 10th-century castle featuring original artifacts, courtyards and terraces. Impressive views as well.

LAGUARDIA: Hospedería Los Parajes €€
Boutique
Calle Mayor 46–48, 01300
Tel 945 62 11 30
w hospederiadelosparajes.com
This 15th-century stylish hotel features a spa with *hammam*. Each room is uniquely decorated.

LEKEITIO: Hotel Zubieta €
Historic
Atea s/n, 48280
Tel 946 84 30 30
w hotelzubieta.com
A 17th-century country house on the outskirts of the town. The hotel has pretty rooms that overlook the gardens.

LOGROÑO: Hotel Calle Mayor €
Historic
Marqués de San Nicolás 71, 26001
Tel 941 23 23 68
w hotelcallemayor.com
A former 16th-century mansion, this urban hotel blends modern design within historic walls.

MUNDAKA: Atalaya Hotel €
B&B
Itxaropen Kalea 1, 48360
Tel 946 17 70 00
w atalayahotel.es
Rooms with garden or sea views. A prime location for surfers and sun-worshippers.

OLITE: Parador de Olite €
Historic
Plaza de Teobaldos 2, 31390
Tel 948 74 00 00
w parador.es
Set in a majestic 15th-century castle, this parador is a national monument. Classical interiors.

PAMPLONA: Pamplona Catedral Hotel €
Boutique
C/ Dos de Mayo 4, 31001
Tel 948 22 66 88
w pamplonacatedralhotel.com
Designer rooms in a former convent in the historic centre.

PAMPLONA: Gran Hotel La Perla €€€
Historic
Plaza del Castillo 1, 31001
Tel 948 22 30 00
w granhotellaperla.com
Ernest Hemingway's favourite Pamplona haunt, the Gran Perla Hotel dates back to 1881. Rooms have historical themes.

RONCESVALLES: Hotel Roncesvalles €
Historic
Mayor s/n, 31650
Tel 948 76 01 05
w hotelroncesvalles.com
Once a medieval hospital, this chic hotel now hosts many pilgrims of the Camino de Santiago.

SAN SEBASTIÁN: Aida €
B&B
C/ Iztueta 9, 20001
Tel 943 32 78 00
w pensionesconencanto.com
Housed in a charming old building, this friendly guesthouse has cosy rooms and studios with kitchenettes.

SAN SEBASTIÁN: Hotel Maria Cristina €€€
Luxury
Paseo República Argentina 4, 20004
Tel 943 43 76 00
w hotel-mariacristina.com
A five-star hotel decorated in *belle époque* style and known for its excellent service. River views.

SANTO DOMINGO DE LA CALZADA: Parador de Santo Domingo €
Historic
Plaza del Santo 3, 26250
Tel 941 34 03 00
w parador.es
Dating from the 12th century, this parador was once a hospital for pilgrims on the Camino.

VITORIA: La Casa de los Arquillos €
Historic
Paseo de Los Arquillos 1–2, 01001
Tel 945 15 12 59
w lacasadelosarquillos.com
This 18th-century building was once a tailor's workshop. The rooms are bright and airy.

ZARAUTZ: Hotel KA €€
Boutique
Calle Mendilauta 13, 20800
Tel 943 13 00 00
w hotelka.com
The hotel is owned by famous Spanish chef Karlos Arguiñano. Located on the beach of Zarautz.

Barcelona
Old Town
Bonic Barcelona €
B&B **Map** 5 A3
Josep Anselm Clavé 9, 08002
Tel 626 05 34 34
w bonic-barcelona.com
A charming little B&B in the Gothic Quarter, with delightful staff and thoughtful extras.

Relaxed sophistication at Hotel Marqés de Riscal in Elciego

Hotel Banys Orientals €
Boutique **Map** 5 B3
C/ Argenteria 37, 08003
Tel 932 95 46 52
W hotelbanysorientals.com
Great value accommodation with
a choice of rooms or suites.

Duquesa de Cardona €€
Boutique **Map** 5 A3
Passeig Colom 12, 08002
Tel 932 68 90 90
W hduquesadecardona.com
Understated hotel with a
sublime roof terrace overlooking
Port Vell.

Hotel Barcelona Catedral €€
Boutique **Map** 5 A2
C/ Capellans 4, 08002
Tel 933 04 22 55
W barcelonacatedral.com
Elegant rooms, and a panoramic
roof terrace with a plunge pool.
Efficient service.

Hotel España €€
Historic **Map** 2 F3
Sant Pau 9–11, 08001
Tel 935 50 00 00
W hotelespanya.com
A beautifully restored 1859 gem
with a great restaurant and bar.

Hotel Yurbban €€
Boutique **Map** 5 B1
C/ Trafalgar 30, 08010
Tel 932 68 07 27
W yurbban.com
Chic, designer rooms, and a roof-
top sundeck and plunge pool.

Montecarlo €€
Historic **Map** 5 A2
La Rambla 124, 08002
Tel 934 12 04 04
W montecarlobcn.com
Comfortable, modern rooms at
surprisingly reasonable rates.

DK Choice

Hotel Mercer €€€
Luxury **Map** 5 B3
C/ Lledó 7, 08002
Tel 933 10 74 80
W mercerbarcelona.com
Exclusive and intimate, this hotel
occupies a sumptuous historic
mansion which incorporates a
section of ancient Roman walls.
Behind the old façade is a sleek,
contemporay interior as well as
a roof terrace with plunge pool.

Hotel Neri €€€
Boutique **Map** 5 A2
Sant Sever 5, 08002
Tel 933 04 06 55
W hotelneri.com
Enchanting hideaway in an 18th-
century palace. Superb restaurant.

The stylish rooftop terrace with plunge pool
at Hotel Mercer, Lledó

Ohla €€€
Luxury **Map** 5 B1
Via Laietana 49, 08003
Tel 933 41 50 50
W ohlahotel.com
A flamboyant five-star option with
a Michelin-starred restaurant.

Eixample

Close to Passeig de Gràcia B&B €
B&B **Map** 4 E5
Diputació 327, 08008
Tel 696 53 14 39
Charming, family-run B&B in an
exquisite Modernist building.

Hostal L'Antic Espai €
B&B **Map** 3 B5
Gran Via 660, 08010
Tel 933 04 19 45
Delightful B&B. Breakfast is served
on the flower-filled terrace.

Hotel Actual €€
Boutique **Map** 3 B3
Rosselló 238, 08008
Tel 935 52 05 50
W hotelactual.com
Minimalist rooms in monochro-
matic colours. Free Wi-Fi.

Hotel Jazz €€
Modern
Pelai 3, 08001
Tel 935 52 96 96
W hoteljazz.com
Spacious, modern rooms and a
rooftop plunge pool. Good value.

DK Choice

Alma €€€
Boutique **Map** 3 B4
Mallorca 271, 08008
Tel 932 16 44 90
W almabarcelona.com
Elegant Alma is famed for
its excellent service. Chic,
minimalist rooms and a lovely
secret courtyard and roof
terrace. Enjoy amenities such
as the spa and pool.

Hotel Omm €€€
Luxury **Map** 3 B3
Rosselló 265, 08008
Tel 934 45 40 00
W hotelomm.es
Modern, ultra-trendy hotel with a
fabulous restaurant, club and spa.

Mandarin Oriental Hotel €€€
Luxury **Map** 3 A4
Passeig de Gràcia 38–40, 08007
Tel 931 51 88 88
W mandarinoriental.com
Plush five-star hotel with white-
and-gold interiors and a superb
Michelin-starred restaurant.

Further Afield

ABaC €€€
Luxury
Avinguda Tibidabo 1, 08022
Tel 933 19 66 00
W abacbarcelona.com
Ultra-chic hotel attached to one
of the finest restaurants in Spain.

DK Choice

Hotel Arts €€€
Luxury **Map** 6 E4
Carrer de la Marina 19–21, 08005
Tel 932 21 10 00
W hotelartsbarcelona.com
A stunning, luxury hotel in a
glass skyscraper right on the
beach. Outstanding amenities
include a Six Senses Spa, a
wide selection of top-quality
restaurants and bars and a
fabulous collection of contemporary art. Excellent service.

Catalonia

BEGUR: Hotel Aiguaclara €€
Boutique
Sant Miquel 2, 17255
Tel 972 62 29 05
W hotelaiguaclara.com
Set in a beautiful village, with just
a handful of enchanting rooms.

BORREDÀ: El Querol Vell €€
Historic
C/ Manresa 75, 08619
Tel 938 23 98 10
W elquerolvell.com
Set in beautiful countryside, this
farmhouse has charming rooms,
plus a garden and a restaurant.

CADAQUÉS: Hotel Llané Petit €
Boutique
Platja Llane Petit s/n, 17488
Tel 972 25 10 20
W llanepetit.com
Charming beachfront option on
the edge of town, with crisp
blue-and-white rooms.

For more information on types of hotels *see page 561*

Sleek, contemporary exterior of Ciutat de Girona, Girona

CARDONA: Hotel Bremon €€
Historic
Cambres 15, 08261
Tel *938 68 49 02*
W hotelbremon.com
An elegantly converted convent, this hotel has stylish rooms and apartments. Superb restaurant.

DELTEBRE: Delta Hotel €
B&B
Avinguda del Canal, Camí de la Illeta s/n, 43580
Tel *977 48 00 46*
W deltahotel.net
Charming family-run rural hotel; a great base for exploring the beautiful Ebro Delta.

FIGUERES: Hotel Plaza Inn €
Inn
Pujada del Castell 14, 17600
Tel *972 51 45 40*
W plazainn.es
Close to the Dalí museum, this inn has Dalí-themed rooms and great service.

GIRONA: Ciutat de Girona €
Modern
Nord 2, 17001
Tel *972 48 30 38*
W hotelciutatdegirona.com
This stylish hotel has airy rooms and a great restaurant.

GRANOLLERS: Casa Fonda Europa €€
Historic
Anselm Clavé 1, 08402
Tel *938 70 03 12*
W casafondaeuropa.com
A classic, long-established inn with fine rooms and a smart restaurant serving Catalan cuisine.

LLAFRANC: El Far de Sant Sebastià €€
Boutique
Muntanya de Sant Sebastià, 17211
Tel *972 30 16 39*
W hotelelfar.com
Set on a clifftop overlooking a lovely stretch of the Costa Brava.

LLEIDA: Finca Prats €€
Luxury
N-240, 25198
Tel *902 44 56 66*
W fincaprats.com
Five-star hotel with 18-hole golf course and an impressive spa.

LLORET DE MAR: Sant Pere del Bosc Hotel & Spa €€€
Luxury
Paratge Sant Pere del Bosc s/n, 17310
Tel *972 36 16 36*
W santperedelboschotel.com
Lavish suites and a spectacular spa in a Modernist villa.

MONTBLANC: Fonda Cal Blasi €
Historic
Carrer Alenyá 11, 43400
Tel *977 86 13 36*
W santperedelboschotel.com
A cosy hotel in a 19th-century building. Wonderful restaurant.

MONTSENY: Hotel Can Cuch €€
Historic
Can Cuch de Muntanya 35, 08445
Tel *931 03 39 80*
W hotelcancuch.com
Stunning *masia* (farmhouse) in the hills with exquisite guestrooms.

MONTSERRAT: Abat Cisneros €€
Modern
Plaça de Montserrat s/n, 08199
Tel *938 77 77 01*
Comfortable rooms and splendid mountain views.

OLOT: Les Cols Pavelons €€
Luxury
Avinguda de les Cols 2, 17800
Tel *699 813 817*
W lescolspavellons.com
Stunning hotel with glassy cube pavilions in the garden, and an award-winning restaurant.

DK Choice

PLATJA D'ARO: Silken Park Hotel San Jorge €€
Boutique
Avenida Andorra 28, 17250
Tel *972 65 23 11*
W hoteles-silken.com
Friendly and relaxed, this elegant hotel in a fine clifftop location on the Costa Brava has pleasant rooms with balconies overlooking the sea. Steps lead down the cliff to a perfect little cove fringed with rocks and pine trees.

SANTA CRISTINA D'ARO: Mas Tapiolas €€€
Boutique
Crta C65, km 7, Veïnat de Solius s/n, 17246
Tel *932 83 70 17*
W hotelmastapiolas.es

Gorgeous hotel in a beautiful 18th-century farmhouse a short drive from the beaches. Lovely gardens and a fine restaurant.

SITGES: Hotel Galeon €
Boutique
Sant Francesc 46, 08870
Tel *938 94 13 79*
W hotelsitges.com
A friendly hotel with cosy rooms, many with terraces overlooking the sea, and a small pool.

TARRAGONA: Hotel Lauria €
B&B
Rambla Nova 20, 43004
Tel *977 23 67 12*
W dormicumhotels.com
Classically decorated rooms in this hotel, which is close to all the sights. On-site pool. Great value.

TORRENT: Mas de Torrent Hotel & Spa €€€
Historic
Afueras de Torrent, 17123
Tel *902 55 03 21*
W mastorrent.com
Refined rooms, good service and an excellent restaurant are to be found in this *masia* (farmhouse).

TOSSA DE MAR: Hotel Cap d'Or €
B&B
Passeig del Mar 1, 17320
Tel *972 34 00 81*
W hotelcapdor.com
This small, whitewashed hotel is set in an 18th-century building right on the seafront.

VIC: Parador de Turismo de Vic-Sau €€
Modern
Paraje el Bac de Sau. Crta de Tavèrnoles, Bv 5213, km 10, 08500
Tel *938 12 23 23*
This parador, modern but built in traditional style, has an idyllic setting in woods overlooking a serene lake. Lovely grounds and pool.

Plush furnishings at Mas de Torrent Hotel & Spa, Torrent

VIELHA: Hotel El Ciervo €€
Historic
Plaça de Sant Orenc 3, 25530
Tel *973 64 01 65*
W hotelelciervo.net
Family-run hotel with pretty
rooms. Welcoming owners.

Aragón

AINSA: Los Siete Reyes €
Boutique
Plaza Mayor s/n, 22330
Tel *974 50 06 81*
W lossietereyes.com
Rooms either have views of Ainsa's
old square or of the Pyrenees.

ALQUEZAR: Casa Alodia €
Boutique
C/ San Gregorio; C/ Arrabal s/n, 22145
Tel *626 35 18 16*
W casa-alodia.com
This hotel has two buildings: San
Gregorio's suits families, Arrabal is
good for a romantic break.

BAROS: Barosse €
B&B
Calle Estiras 4, 22712
Tel *974 36 05 82*
W barosse.com
Five beautiful rooms and a daily-
changing evening menu.

DK Choice

CALACEITE: Hotel Cresol €
Inn
Calle Santa Bárbara 16, 44610
Tel *609 90 81 90*
W hotelcresol.com
Set deep in olive country,
this inn is a beautifully
converted olive mill. Rooms are
furnished to a high standard;
contemporary artwork and
traditional furniture provide a
perfect balance between the
ancient and the modern.

**FUENTESPALDA: Mas de
la Serra** €€
Inn
Mas de la Serra, 44587
Tel *976 36 90 98*
W masdelaserra.com
A renovated farmhouse
surrounded by acres of almond
trees. Glorious views.

**MIRAMBEL: Las Moradas
del Temple** €€
Boutique
C/ Agustín Pastor 15, 44141
Tel *964 17 82 70*
W lasmoradasdeltemple.es
A romantic hotel with four-poster
beds, set in a charming stone inn
in Mirambel's historic centre.

Country-cottage style at Barosse B&B, Baros

**SALLENT DE GALLEGO: Hotel
Valle de Izas** €
Boutique
Calle Francia 26, 22640
Tel *974 48 85 08*
W hotelvalledeizas.com
Traditionally decorated wooden
bedrooms give this village hotel
a homely feel.

**SOS DEL REY CATÓLICO:
El Sueño de Virila** €
Boutique
Calle Coliseo 8, 50680
Tel *948 88 86 59*
W elsuenodevirila.com
Once a synagogue, El Sueño de
Virila is now a four-floor rural villa.

ZARAGOZA: Hotel Sauce €
Boutique
Calle Espoz y Mina 33, 50003
Tel *976 20 50 50*
W hotelsauce.com
Centrally located hotel with
tastefully designed rooms.

Valencia and Murcia

ALICANTE: Amerigo €€
Boutique
Calle Rafael Altamira 11, 03002
Tel *965 14 65 70*
W hospes.es
Amerigo is a Dominican convent
converted into a stylish hotel with
a health spa, bar and restaurant.

BOCAIRENT: Hotel L'Estació €€
Historic
Parc de l'Estació s/n, 46880
Tel *962 35 00 00*
W hotelestacio.com
This gorgeous country inn was
once a 19th-century train station.

CALABARDINA: Al Sur €
Inn
Torre al Cope 24, 30889
Tel *968 41 94 66*
W halsur.com

Intimate hotel with a soothing
decor. Great location, with enviable views of the unspoiled coast.

CALPE: Gran Hotel Sol y Mar €
Luxury
Calle Benidorm 3, 03710
Tel *965 87 50 55*
W granhotelsolymar.com
This charming, modern hotel is
close to both town and beach.
Spa on site.

**CARTAGENA: La Manga Club
Principe Felipe** €€
Luxury
La Manga Club, 30389
Tel *968 33 12 34*
W lamangaclub.com
An exclusive Spanish-village-style
hotel, La Manga Club is popular
with celebrities.

DÉNIA: Rosa €
Boutique
Calle Congre 3, Las Marinas 03700
Tel *965 78 15 73*
W hotelrosadenia.com
Delightful Mediterranean villa-style
hotel set in lovely seaside gardens.

ELX: Huerta del Cura €
Inn
Puerta de la Morera 14, 03203
Tel *966 61 00 11*
W hotelhuertodelcura.com
A lush palm tree oasis with
bungalow accommodation
and a variety of sports amenities.

DK Choice

FORTUNA: Balneario Leana €
Historic
Calle Balneario, 30630
Tel *902 44 44 10*
W balneariodeleanafortuna.com
Renowned as Murcia's oldest
hotel – it was founded in 1860 –
this atmospheric health spa
conjures up a unique aura of the
past, with Modernist details.

For more information on types of hotels *see page 561*

Stylish decor at Hostal Gala, Madrid

**LA VILA JOÍOSA: Hotel
Montiboli** €€
Luxury
Partida Montiboli, 03570
Tel *965 89 02 50*
ⓦ montiboli.com
Lovely clifftop hotel with rooms,
suites and bungalows. Sea views.

MURCIA: Arco de San Juan €
Historic
Plaza de Ceballos 10, 30003
Tel *968 21 04 55*
ⓦ arcosanjuan.com
A beautifully converted palace
with spacious rooms and a blend
of old and new furnishing styles.

OLIVA: Pensión San Vicente €
Inn
Plaza Ganguis 13, 46780
Tel *962 85 59 00*
ⓦ pensionsanvicente.es
An old-fashioned charmer
with friendly service. Located in
the historic centre of Oliva, on
the sprawling Costa del Azahar.

**ORIHUELA: Hotel Melia
Palacio Tudemir** €
Luxury/Boutique
Calle Afonso XIII 1, 03330
Tel *966 73 80 10*
ⓦ melia.com
Well-restored 18th-century palace
with contemporary touches.

**PENÍSCOLA: Hostería
del Mar** €€
Historic
Avinguda Papa Luna 18, 12598
Tel *964 48 06 00*
ⓦ hosteriadelmar.net
Beachfront hotel with modern
amenities. Minimum stay of seven
nights with half board in summer.

VALENCIA: Hostal Venecia €
Historic
Calle en Llop 5, 46002
Tel *963 52 42 67*
Well-run hotel in the heart of
the city, with functional modern
rooms and attentive service.

**VALENCIA: SH Inglés
Boutique** €€
Boutique
Calle Marqués de Dos Aguas 6, 46002
Tel *963 51 64 26*
ⓦ inglesboutique.com
Tastefully furnished rooms and
suites in a renovated palace.

VILAFAMÉS: El Jardin Vertical €€
Historic
Carrer Nou 15, 12192
Tel *964 32 99 38*
ⓦ eljardinvertical.com
Refurbished 17th-century red-
stone house set amid olive and
almond groves.

XÀBIA: Hotel Javea €
Boutique
C/ Pio X 5, 03730
Tel *965 79 54 61*
ⓦ hotel-javea.com
A charming hotel with simple,
stylish rooms and wonderful
port views. Panoramic views
from the restaurant.

XÀTIVA: Hostería Mont Sant €
Historic
Subida al Castillo, 46800
Tel *962 27 50 81*
ⓦ mont-sant.com
Beautiful mansion with citrus-
filled gardens, spa and restaurant.

Madrid
Old Madrid

Abracadabra €
B&B **Map** 3 C4
Calle Bailén 39, 28005
Tel *656 85 97 84*
ⓦ abracadabrabandb.com
Charming B&B with well furnished,
cosy rooms. Delicious breakfasts.

Chic & Basic Mayerling €
Modern **Map** 4 F3
Calle del Conde Ramanones 6, 28012
Tel *914 20 15 80*
ⓦ chicandbasic.com

Light-filled, cleverly designed
minimalist rooms. Excellent value.

DK Choice

Hostal Gala €
Boutique **Map** 4 E1
Costanilla de los Angeles 15, 28013
Tel *915 41 96 92*
ⓦ hostalgala.com
An excellent choice in the city
centre, this hostel has affordable
yet stylish rooms and apartments, many with balconies
overlooking a delightful square.
Warm, friendly service and
extras such as power showers
make this place stand out.

Hotel Plaza Mayor €
Historic **Map** 4 E3
Calle Atocha 2, 28012
Tel *913 60 06 06*
ⓦ h-plazamayor.com
Smart, modern rooms close to
the Plaza Mayor. Friendly staff.

Hotel Liabeny €€
Boutique **Map** 4 F1
Calle de la Salud 3, 28013
Tel *915 31 90 00*
ⓦ liabeny.es
A great central choice with a long
list of facilities – including a sauna
and restaurant – for the price.

Posada del León de Oro €€
Historic **Map** 4 E3
Calle Cava Baja 12, 28005
Tel *911 19 14 94*
ⓦ posadadelleondeoro.com
A 19th-century inn and
restaurant with stylish rooms
arranged around a traditional
courtyard.

Casa de Madrid €€€
Luxury **Map** 4 D2
Calle Arrieta 2 (2nd floor), 28013
Tel *915 59 57 91*
ⓦ casademadrid.com
Exquisite guesthouse with a hand-
ful of antique-furnished rooms.

Bourbon Madrid

Hotel One Shot 23 €
Boutique **Map** 7 B3
Calle del Prado 23, 28014
Tel *914 20 40 01*
ⓦ oneshothotels.com
Chic rooms, some with balconies,
in an enviable central location.

AC Palacio del Retiro €€
Boutique **Map** 8 D2
Calle Alfonso XII 14, 28014
Tel *915 23 74 60*
ⓦ ac-hotels.com
Gorgeous hotel with all the luxury
trimmings, set in an elegantly
renovated 19th-century mansion.

Hospes Madrid €€
Boutique **Map** 8 D1
Plaza de la Independencia 3, 28001
Tel *914 32 29 11*
W hospes.com
Exquisite rooms, a fabulous spa
and a gourmet restaurant.

Hotel Único €€
Boutique **Map** 6 E3
Calle Claudio Coello 67, 28001
Tel *917 81 01 73*
W unicohotelmadrid.com
An enchanting boutique hotel
with stylish guest rooms and a
wonderful restaurant with two
Michelin stars. Attentive service.

Me Madrid €€
Luxury **Map** 7 A3
Plaza de Santa Ana 14, 28012
Tel *902 14 44 40*
W memadrid.com
A fashionable hotel with stunning
rooms and suites, a rooftop bar
and a popular restaurant.

DK Choice

Hotel Ritz by Belmond €€€
Luxury **Map** 7 C2
Plaza de la Lealtad 5, 28014
Tel *917 01 67 67*
W ritzmadrid.com
Opulent *belle-époque*-style gem
set in gardens right next to the
Prado, Hotel Ritz by Belmond
boasts a gilded interior and the
rarefied air of another century –
the hotel still imposes a dress
code after 11am. Excellent
service and a splendid bar to
match, where luminaries like
Dalí and Lorca once held court.

Further Afield

Artrip Hotel €
Boutique
Calle Valencia 11, 28012
Tel *915 39 32 82*
W artriphotel.com
Modern hotel with exposed brick
walls and high ceilings.

Clement Barajas Hotel €€
Boutique
Avenida General 43, 28042
Tel *917 46 03 30*
W clementhoteles.com
This hotel has bright rooms.
Convenient for Barajas Airport,
with a regular shuttle service.

Silken Puerta América €€€
Luxury
Avenida de América 41, 28002
Tel *917 44 54 00*
W hoteles-silken.com
Each floor of this spectacular
hotel was designed by a different
celebrity architect.

Madrid Province

**CHINCHÓN: Condesa de
Chinchón** €
Boutique
Calle de los Huertos 26, 28370
Tel *918 93 54 00*
W condesadechinchon.com
Beautiful little hotel with modern
rooms and an excellent restaurant.

**SAN LORENZO DE EL ESCORIAL:
Hotel Posada Don Jaime** €
Historic
Calle San Anton 24, 28200
Tel *619 30 89 36*
W posadadonjaime.es
Traditionally decorated rooms
and a lovely, plant-filled terrace.

Castilla y León

AMPUDIA: Casa del Abad €
Boutique
*Plaza Francisco Martín
Gromaz 12, 34191*
Tel *979 76 80 08*
W casadelabad.com
Once an abbey, this iconic
building still retains its
original features.

**ÁVILA: Hostel Puerta
del Alcázar** €
B&B
Calle San Segundo 39, 05001
Tel *920 21 10 74*
W puertadelalcazar.com
In front of Ávila's city walls, with
a vista over the cathedral.

ÁVILA: Palacio de los Velada €€
Historic
Plaza de la Catedral 10, 05001
Tel *920 25 51 00*
W veladahoteles.com
Refurbished 16th-century palace
located close to the cathedral.
Excellent restaurant, El Tostado.

Lavish interiors of the sitting area
at the Hotel Ritz by Belmond

**BÉJAR: Hospedería Real
de Béjar** €
Boutique
Plaza de la Piedad 34, 37700
Tel *923 40 84 94*
W hospederiarealdebejar.com
Comfortable hotel located in
the city centre, near Plaza Mayor.
Modern amenities.

**BURGOHONDO: Posada Real
El Linar del Zaire** €
Boutique
Crta Avila-Casavieja 42B, 05113
Tel *920 28 40 91*
W ellinardelzaire.com
A great base for exploring the
Valle del Alberche.

BURGOS: Torre Berrueza €
Boutique
*Calle Nuño Rasura 5, 09560,
Espinosa de los Monteros*
Tel *610 34 23 04*
W torreberrueza.es
Housed in a medieval tower, this
hotel has a traditional restaurant.

**BURGOS: NH Collection
Palacio de Burgos** €€€
Historic
Calle de la Merced 13, 09002
Tel *947 47 99 00*
W nh-collection.com/es/hotel/nh-
collection-palacio-de-burgos
This centrally located, 16th-
century inn has exquisite rooms
and a lovely gourmet restaurant.

CANDELADA: El Mirlo Blanco €
B&B
*Crta Candelada a Madrigal de la
Vera, km 2, 1, 05480*
Tel *902 10 40 00*
W el-mirlo-blanco.com
A rural hideaway set amid
abundant countryside.

**CIRCO DE GREDOS: Refugio
de Elola** €
B&B
Laguna de Gredos s/n, 05634
Tel *920 20 75 76*
W refugioeloya.com
Basic dormitory accommodation
with spectacular mountain views.

LEÓN: NH Plaza Mayor €
Luxury
Plaza Mayor 15–17, 24000
Tel *987 34 43 57*
W nh-hotels.com
An ancient setting meets modern
design. Comfortable rooms.

LUYEGO: Hosteria Camino €
Boutique
*Calle Nuestra Señora de los
Remedios s/n, 24717*
Tel *987 60 17 57*
W hosteriacamino.com
Charming hotel with patios on
the Camino de Santiago.

For more information on types of hotels *see page 561*

MEDINACELI: Hotel Medina Salim €
Boutique
Calle Barranco 15, 42240
Tel *975 32 69 74*
W hotelmedinasalim.com
A modern building incorporating the town's old walls. Great views.

PEDRAZA: Hospedería de Santo Domingo €
Inn
Calle Matadero 3, 40172
Tel *921 50 99 71*
W hospederiadesantodomingo.com
This hotel in the Jewish Quarter offers superb views of the Sierra de Guadarrama and the aqueduct.

PONFERRADA: Hotel Aroi Bierzo Plaza €
Modern
Plaza del Ayuntamiento 4, 24001
Tel *987 40 90 01*
W aroihoteles.com
Well-equipped rooms and two cosy restaurants where visitors can try regional delicacies. Ideal for exploring El Bierzo.

PUEBLA DE SANABRIA: Posada de las Misas €
Boutique
Plaza Mayor 13, 49300
Tel *980 62 03 58*
W posadadelasmisas.com
Beautiful views from this well-located hotel. Guests have access to the library and galleries.

SALAMANCA: NH Puerto de la Catedral €
Luxury
Plaza Juan XXIII 5, 37008
Tel *923 28 08 29*
W nh-hotels.com
Elegant chain hotel with contemporary, well-appointed rooms.

DK Choice

SALAMANCA: Hotel Rector €€
Boutique
Paseo Rector Esperabé 10, 37008
Tel *923 21 84 82*
W hotelrector.com
Formerly the mansion of one of Salamanca's most distinguished families, this refined hotel oozes elegance but with a personal touch. The spotless rooms are cleaned twice daily, with a evening turn-down.

SANTA MARÍA DE MAVE: El Convento de Mave €
Historic
Calle Monasterio s/n, 34402
Tel *979 12 36 11*
W elconventodemave.com
A 12th-century monastery with a 21st-century makeover.

Entrance to one of the elegant and spotless rooms at Hotel Rector, Salamanca

SEGOVIA: Hotel Don Felipe €
Historic
Calle de Daoiz 7, 40001
Tel *921 46 60 95*
W hoteldonfelipe.es
Set in a mansion, this serene hotel offers modern facilities and has a peaceful garden.

SOMAÉN: Posada Real de Santa Quiteria €€
Historic
Barrio Alto 8, 42257
Tel *975 32 03 93*
W posadasantaquiteria.com
Rooms are beautifully decorated at this enchanting country inn.

SORIA: Hostería Solar de Tejada €
Boutique
Calle Claustrilla 1, 42002
Tel *975 23 00 53*
W hosteriasolardetejada.es
Located in the heart of town, with individually decorated rooms.

TOLBAÑOS: Molino de los Gamusinos €€
Boutique
Camino del Molino s/n, 05289
Tel *920 22 77 14*
W losgamusinos.com
This secluded hotel is an ideal retreat from where you can explore the area.

VALLADOLID: Hotel Marqués de la Ensenada €
Luxury
Avenida de Gijon 1, 47009
Tel *983 36 14 91*
W marquesdelaensenada.com
Five-star hotel in a converted riverside mill. Conviniently located near the city centre.

VALLADOLID: Meliá Recoletos Boutique Hotel €
Boutique
Calle Acera de Recoletos 13, 47004
Tel *902 14 44 40*
W melia.com

Refreshingly quiet chain hotel situated in the heart of the city.

ZAMORA: Parador de Zamora €€
Luxury
Plaza de Viriato 5, 49001
Tel *980 51 44 97*
W parador.es
Suits of armour and tapestries adorn the interior at this parador set in a medieval palace.

Castilla-La Mancha

ALARCÓN: Parador de Alarcón €€€
Luxury
Avda Amigos de los Castillos 3, 16214
Tel *969 33 03 15*
W parador.es
A medieval castle from the 8th century, perched on a cliff. Stunning views of the Júcar river.

ALBACETE: Hotel Santa Isabel €€
Luxury
Avenida Gregorio Arcos s/n, 02007
Tel *967 26 46 80*
W hotelsantaisabelalbacete.com
Stunning modern hotel with a vintage car collection in the garage. Free Wi-Fi.

ALMADÉN: Plaza de Toros de Almadén €
Historic
Plaza Waldo Ferrer s/n, 13400
Tel *926 26 43 33*
W hotelplazadetoros.com
Comfortable, rustic rooms. Located in a unique hexagonal bull ring.

ALMAGRO: Hotel Casa Grande Almagro €
Boutique
Calle Federico Relimpio 10, 13270
Tel *671 49 62 88*
W casagrandealmagro.com
A 16th-century property, close to Plaza Mayor and the famous medieval theatre.

ALMONACID DE TOLEDO: Villa Nazules €
Modern
Crta Almonacid a Chueca s/n, 45190
Tel *925 59 03 80*
W villanazules.com
Villa Nazules is a four-star hotel boasting an excellent spa and wellness facilities.

CUENCA: Convento del Giraldo €
Historic
Calle San Pedro 12, 16001
Tel *969 23 27 00*
W hotelconventodelgiraldo.com
This historic, charming building fuses 17th-century character with comforting modern touches.

CUENCA: Parador de Cuenca €€
Historic
Subida San Pablo s/n, 16001
Tel *969 23 23 20*
W parador.es
On the Hoz del Huécar gorge,
near Cuenca's hanging houses.

SIGUENZA: Casa el Castillo €€
Boutique
Calle Vigiles 9, 19250
Tel *949 39 16 13*
W casadelcastillo.com
Atmospheric little inn with friendly
owners. Pleasant rooms.

DK Choice

**SIGÜENZA: Molino de
Alcuneza** €€
Historic
Crta Alboreca, km 0.5, 19264
Tel *949 39 15 01*
W molinodealcuneza.com
This idyllic hotel is located
close to the medieval city of
Sigüenza. The building dates
from the 14th century and once
served as a mill. The modern spa
includes a *hammam*.

**TALAVERA DE LA REINA: Be
Smart Talavera** €
Luxury
Avenida de Toledo s/n, 45600
Tel *925 72 72 00*
W belivehotels.com
Central, four-star hotel with
elegantly designed rooms.

TOLEDO: Hotel Santa Isabel €
Boutique
Calle Santa Isabel 24, 45002
Tel *925 25 31 20*
W hotelsantaisabeltoledo.com
A two-star hotel in the 14th-
century abode of a local noble.

TOLEDO: Parador de Toledo €€
Luxury
Cerro del Emperador s/n, 45002
Tel *925 22 18 50*
W parador.es
Set on the hillside with excellent
views. Superb restaurant.

VALDEPEÑAS: Veracruz Plaza €
Boutique
Plaza Veracruz s/n, 13300
Tel *926 31 30 00*
W hotelveracruzplaza.com
Indulge at the amazing spa, with
steam room and a Turkish bath.

**VILLANUEVA DE LOS INFANTES:
La Morada de Juan de Vargas** €
Boutique
Calle Cervantes 3, 13320
Tel *926 36 17 69*
W lamoradadevargas.com
Lovely 16th-century property.
Rooms are individually decorated.

YESTE: Balneario de Tus €
Historic
Crta Yeste-Tus, km 13, 02485
Tel *967 43 68 17*
W balneariodetus.com
A spa destination since Roman
times. Contemporary treatments
include hot mud wraps.

Extremadura

ALANGE: Gran Hotel Aqualange €
Modern
Paseo de las Huertas 3, 06840
Tel *924 36 56 08*
W balneariodealange.com
Unwind at this hotel next to
the thermal Roman baths.

**BADAJOZ: NH Gran Hotel Casino
de Extremadura** €€
Luxury
Adolfo Diaz Ambrona 11, 06006
Tel *924 28 44 02*
W nh-hotels.com
Ultramodern hotel with all basic
amenities. Excellent city views.

**CÁCERES: Sercotel
Extremadura Hotel** €
Luxury
Avda Virgen de Guuadalupe 28, 10001
Tel *927 62 96 39*
W extremadurahotel.com
Enjoy the peaceful surroundings
at this hotel near the city centre.

**JARANDILLA DE LA VERA:
Parador de Jarandilla
de la Vera** €€
Historic
Avda García Prieto 1, 10450
Tel *927 56 01 17*
W parador.es
This 14th-century palace, once
the home of Charles V, has simple
rooms. Ideal for visiting Yuste and
the nearby villages of La Vera.

MÉRIDA: Hotel Adealba €
Boutique
Romero Leal 18, 06800
Tel *924 38 83 08*
W hoteladealba.com
Bright, modern hotel within
walking distance of Roman sights.

MÉRIDA: Parador de Mérida €€
Historic
Plaza de la Constitución 3, 06800
Tel *924 31 38 00*
W parador.es
Set in an 18th-century Franciscan
convent, with charming rooms.

**TRUJILLO: NH Palacio de
Santa Marta** €
Historic
Ballesteros 6, 10200
Tel *927 65 91 90*
W nh-hotels.com
A 16th-century palace, right in the
main square, blending traditional
features with modern comforts.

DK Choice

**ZAFRA: Casa Palacio Conde
de La Corte** €
Boutique
Plaza del Pilar Redondo 2, 06300
Tel *924 56 33 11*
W vivedespacio.com/
condedelacorte
This 19th-century palace, the
former residence of the sixth
Count Corte of Berrona, has been
elegantly restored to represent
the grandeur of that era. The
decor incorporates period
features with modern amenities.

Seville

El Arenal

Hispano Luz Confort €
B&B **Map** 3 C2
C/ Miguel Mañara 4, 41004
Tel *955 63 80 79*
W hispanoluzconfort.com
Simple rooms, some having
balconies with city views. Bike
rental on-site.

Taberna del Alabardero €€
Historic **Map** 5 B3
Calle Zaragoza 20, 41001
Tel *954 50 27 21*
W tabernadelalabardero.es
The rooms here boast antiques
and stylish fabrics. Cosy central
patio with stained-glass roof.

The warm-toned central courtyard of Taberna del Alabardero, Seville

For more information on types of hotels *see page 561*

Santa Cruz

DK Choice

Casa Numero Siete €€
Boutique **Map** 6 E3
Calle Virgenes 7, 41004
Tel *954 22 15 81*
W casanumero7.com
Discover luxury in a 19th-century
mansion in the heart of Seville's
evocative Old Quarter. The decor
at this small but immaculate
guesthouse includes antiques
and family heirlooms. Relax in
the elegant lounge and enjoy
the discreet but friendly service.

Las Casas del Rey de Baeza €€
Boutique **Map** 6 E2
Plaza Jesús de la Redención 2, 41003
Tel *954 56 14 96*
W hospes.com
Stylish hotel with chic bedrooms
and Colonial-style furniture.
Lovely open-air patio and spa.

EME Catedral Hotel €€
Luxury **Map** 6 D4
Calle Alemanes 27, 41004
Tel *954 56 00 00*
W emecatedralhotel.com
Two great restaurants, a terrace, a
pool and spa are the attractions
at this centrally located hotel.

Alfonso XIII €€€
Historic **Map** 3 C3
Calle San Fernando 2, 41004
Tel *954 91 70 00*
W hotel-alfonsoxiii-seville.com
A regal hotel with opulent
furnishings, crystal chandeliers
and marble columns.

Further Afield

Cervantes €
Boutique **Map** 6 D1
Calle Cervantes 10, 41004
Tel *954 90 02 80*
W hotel-cervantes.com
A charming hotel with coloured-
glass ceilings and a beautifully
tiled patio. Cosy rooms.

Patio de la Alameda €
B&B **Map** 2 D4
Alameda de Hercules 56, 41002
Tel *954 90 49 99*
W patiodelaalameda.com
Mosaic-tiled bathrooms and
Baroque mirrors in rooms set
around three courtyards.

Barcelo Renacimiento €€
Luxury **Map** 1 C2
Avenida Alvaro Alonso Barba,
Isla de la Cartuja, 41092
Tel *954 46 22 22*
W barcelo.com

Geared towards business users,
this hotel has avant-garde decor
and a spacious convention
centre with all amenities.

Casa Sacristia de Santa Ana €€
Historic **Map** 2 D4
Alameda de Hercules 22, 41002
Tel *954 91 57 22*
W hotelsacristia.com
Beautifully restored 18th-century
sacristy. Fine restaurant.

Andalusia

ARACENA: Finca Buen Vino €€
B&B
Crta N433, km 95, 21293
Tel *959 12 40 34*
W fincabuenvino.com
Established hilltop guesthouse
offering individually furnished
rooms and a rented cottage.

ARCOS DE LA FRONTERA:
Casa Grande €
Historic
Calle Maldonaldo 10, 11360
Tel *956 70 39 30*
W lacasagrande.net
A gleaming whitewashed 18th-
century mansion with splendid
views of the Andalusian country-
side. Good breakfast spread.

ARCOS DE LA FRONTERA:
Parador de Arcos
de la Frontera €
Historic
Plaza del Cabildo, 11630
Tel *956 70 05 00*
W parador.es
Spacious rooms, some with a
Jacuzzi. Traditional fountains and
tiled patios add to the charm.

CÁDIZ: Hotel Playa Victoria €€
Boutique
Glorieta Ingeniero La Cierva 4, 11010
Tel *956 20 53 40*
W palafoxhoteles.com
Ecofriendly seafront hotel with
avant-garde interior furnishings.

CAÑOS DE MECA: La Breña €€
Boutique
Avda Trafalgar 4, 11149
Tel *956 43 73 68*
W hotelbrena.com
Simple spacious rooms with sea
views. Excellent beach location.

DK Choice

CARMONA: Parador
de Carmona €€
Luxury
Calle Alcazar s/n, 41410
Tel *954 14 10 10*
W parador.es
Originally a Moorish fortress,
this parador has a stunning
hilltop location and majestic
interiors decorated with
tapestries and antiques. The
rooms are neat, stylish and
comfortable. Relax in the
outdoor swimming pool.
Warm and friendly service.

CASTELLAR DE LA FRONTERA:
Casa Convento La Almoraima €
Historic
Ctra Algeciras-Ronda s/n, Finca la
Almoraima, 11350
Tel *956 69 30 50*
W laalmoraimahotel.com
A former monastery converted
into a modern hotel.

CAZALLA DE LA SIERRA:
Cartuja de Cazalla €
Historic
Crta Cazalla-Constantina,
km 2.5, 41370
Tel *954 88 45 16*
W cartujadecazalla.com
A unique refuge, this Carthusian
monastery is popular with artists,
sculptors and families.

CAZORLA: Molino de la Farraga €
Historic
Camino de la Hoz, 23470
Tel *953 72 12 49*
W molinolafarraga.com
A restored 200-year-old mill set in
tranquil gardens. Spotless rooms.

View from the roof terrace at Casa Grande, Arcos de la Frontera

CAZORLA: Parador de Cazorla €€
Luxury
Calle Sierra de Cazorla s/n, 23470
Tel *953 72 70 75*
W parador.es
Vintage parador located in the heart of pine-forested Parque Natural de Cazorla. Ideal for nature-lovers. Spacious rooms.

CÓRDOBA: Casa Olea €
Inn
Crta CO-231/CO-7204
Tel *696 74 82 09*
W casaolea.com
A traditional Andalusian *cortijo* (farmhouse) with luxurious bedding and underfloor heating.

CÓRDOBA: Hotel Maestre €
Inn
Calle Romero Barros 4–6, 17003
Tel *957 47 24 10*
W hotelmaestre.com
A classic hotel with a flower-filled patio. Simple rooms and self-catering apartments on offer.

DK Choice

CÓRDOBA: Lola €€
Boutique
Calle Romero 3, 14001
Tel *957 20 03 05*
W hotelconencantolola.com/ html/hotel.html
Set in a lovingly restored 19th-century palace, this charming hotel is the most atmospheric and evocative place to stay in Córdoba's labyrinthine Judería quarter. There are eight period furnished rooms, named after Arab princesses. Enjoy panoramic city views from the roof terrace.

CÓRDOBA: Hospes Palacio de Bailio €€€
Boutique
Calle Ramirez de las Casas Deza 10–12, 14001
Tel *957 49 89 93*
W hospes.com
Magnificently restored 17th-century palace with elegant furnishings and beautiful gardens.

EL ROCIO: Hotel El Toruño €
Inn
Plaza Acebuchal 22, 21750
Tel *959 44 23 23*
W toruno.es
A homely, whitewashed villa in the Parque Nacional de Doñana. Prices double during the annual pilgrimage to the Virgen del Rocío.

GIBRALTAR: Rock Hotel €€
Historic
Europa Road 3, 30339
Tel *956 77 30 00*
W rockhotelgibraltar.com

A wood-pannelled ceiling and bed canopy adorn this room at La Bobadilla, Loja

A 70-year-old cliffside Colonial-style hotel with cosy rooms.

GRANADA: Posada del Toro €
Inn
Elvira 25, 18010
Tel *958 22 73 33*
W posadadeltoro.com
Renovated 19th-century inn blending old charm and modern comforts. Wi-Fi in all rooms.

GRANADA: Parador de Granada €€€
Luxury
Calle Real de la Alhambra, 18009
Tel *958 22 12 40*
W parador.es
Incomparable location inside the grounds of the Alhambra Palace. Elegantly appointed rooms.

GRAZALEMA: Hotel Fuerte Grazalema €
Inn
Baldio de los Alamillos, Crta A372, km 53, 11610
Tel *956 13 30 00*
W fuertehoteles.com
A comfortable rural hotel located inside the Grazalema Nature Reserve. Ideal for outdoor types.

JAÉN: Parador de Jaén €€
Historic
Castillo de Santa Catalina s/n, 23002
Tel *953 23 00 00*
W parador.es
Hilltop parador with traditional Arabic decor and lavish rooms with panoramic views.

LOJA: La Bobadilla €€€
Luxury
Crta Salinas–Villanueva de Tapia (A-333), km 65.5, Finca Bobadillo, 18300
Tel *958 32 18 61*
W barcelolabobadilla.com
All rooms and suites in this plush hotel have a unique decor. Huge pools and facilities for sports.

MÁLAGA: Salles Hotel €€
Luxury
Calle Marmoles 6, 29007
Tel *952 07 02 16*
W salleshotel.com
Well-appointed hotel in the heart of Málaga. Rooftop pool.

MARBELLA: Marbella Club Hotel €€€
Luxury
Bulevar Príncipe Alfonso von Hohenlohe, 29600
Tel *952 82 22 11*
W marbellaclub.com
Deluxe beachside hotel with lush gardens, pools, world-class golf course and spa.

MAZAGÓN: Parador de Mazagón €€
Luxury
Crta San Juan-Matalascañas, km 30, 21120
Tel *959 53 63 00*
W parador.es
Comfortable parador set amid pinewoods. Pool and Jacuzzi.

MIJAS: Hotel Hacienda Puerta del Sol €
Luxury
Crta Fuengirola-Mijas, km 4, 29650
Tel *952 48 64 00*
W hotelfuengirolamijas.com
Stylish hotel with tennis courts, gym and open-air swimming pools.

MONACHIL: La Almunia del Valle €
Boutique
Camino de la Umbria, 18193
Tel *958 30 80 10*
W laalmuniadelvalle.com
Small and friendly retreat high in the Sierra Nevada. Pretty gardens and open-air pool.

NERJA: El Carabeo €
Boutique
C/ Hernando de Carabeo 34, 29780
Tel *952 52 54 44*
W hotelcarabeo.com
Artwork and antique decor in rooms. Book-filled lounge.

OJEN: Posada del Angel €
Inn
Calle Mesones 21, 29610
Tel *952 88 18 08*
W laposadadelangel.net
Traditional Andalusian hostelry with individually decorated rooms.

ORGIVA: Taray Botanico €
B&B
Crta A348 Tablete-Abuñol, 18400
Tel *958 78 45 25*
W hoteltaray.com
Lovely whitewashed rural hotel with olive- and orange-filled garden. Facilities available for guests with disabilities.

For more information on types of hotels *see page 561*

Spectacular old-world setting at Hotel La Residencia in Deià, Mallorca

PALMA DEL RIO: Monasterio de San Francisco €
Historic
Avda del Pio XII 35, 14700
Tel 957 71 01 83
W intergrouphoteles.com
Authentic, converted 15th-century Franciscan monastery. Some rooms are refurbished monks' cells with hand-painted sinks.

PECHINA: Hotel Balneario de Sierra de Alhamilla €
Historic
C/ Los Baños s/n, 04259
Tel 950 31 74 13
W balneariosierraalhamilla.es
Well-restored 18th-century spa hotel that has a thermal pool with underwater jets.

PUERTO DE SANTA MARIA: Monasterio de San Miguel €€
Historic
Calle Virgen de los Milagros 27, 11500
Tel 956 54 04 40
W sanmiguelhotelmonasterio.com
This former Capuchin monastery offers simple rooms, spacious gardens and lush public areas for contemplation.

SAN JOSÉ: Cortijo el Sotillo €€
Historic
Crta San Jose, 04118
Tel 950 61 11 00
W cortijoelsotillo.es
Relaxed 18th-century farmhouse set in the Cabo de Gata natural park. Good restaurant.

SEVILLA: Exe Gran Hotel Solucar €
Modern
Crta Nac. Sevilla–Huelva A472 s/n, Sanlucar la Mayor, 41800
Tel 955 70 34 08
W exegranhotelsolucar.com
Bright, airy rooms with basic amenities. Guests can enjoy breakfast at the lovely poolside courtyard.

TARIFA: Hurricane Hotel €€
Boutique
Crta. N-340, km 78, 11380
Tel 956 68 49 19
W hotelhurricane.com
The Hurricane is a laid-back Moorish-style hotel with lush gardens, two pools, a gym, a sauna and massage facilities.

ÚBEDA: Zenit El Postigo €
Inn
Calle El Postigo 5, 23400
Tel 953 75 00 00
W elpostigo.zenithoteles.com
Comfortable modern hostelry with amenities including a cosy winter fireplace and refreshing summer pool.

VEJER DE LA FRONTERA: La Casa del Califa €
Boutique
Plaza de España 16, 11150
Tel 956 44 77 30
W lacasadelcalifa.com
The perfect balance of comfort and style combined with superb views and excellent service.

The Balearic Islands

FORMENTERA, ES CALO: Hotel Entre Pinos €€
B&B
Crta La Mola, km 12.3, 07872
Tel 971 32 70 19
W hotelentrepinos.es
A relaxed, family-run hotel close to two stunning beaches. Spa services available.

FORMENTERA, LA SAVINA: Hostal La Savina €
B&B
Avenida Mediterránea 20–40, 07870
Tel 971 63 60 46
W hostal-lasavina.com
Charming family-run hotel with simple, whitewashed rooms. Sea views.

IBIZA, IBIZA CITY: Mirador de Dalt Vila €€€
Historic
Plaza España 4, 07800
Tel 971 30 30 45
W hotelmiradoribiza.com
Sumptuous 19th-century palace with elegant rooms and suites.

IBIZA, PORTINATX: Marconfort El Greco €€
Luxury
Cala Portinatx s/n, 07810
Tel 971 32 05 70
W marconfort.com
All-inclusive resort with a great location in Portinatx Bay. Water park, pool and buffet restaurant.

IBIZA, SANT JOAN DE LABRITJA: The Giri Residence €€€
Boutique
Calle Principal 3–5, 07810
Tel 971 33 33 45
W thegiri.com
A fashionable getaway combining Moroccan interiors with a relaxed Mediterranean ambience.

MALLORCA, DEIÁ: Hotel La Residencia €€€
Luxury
Son Canals s/n, 07179
Tel 971 63 90 11
W hotel-laresidencia.com
A renowned art hotel housed in two splendidly restored 16th- and 18th-century manors.

MALLORCA, PALMA: Hotel Feliz €€€
Boutique
Avinguda Joan Miró 74, 07015
Tel 971 28 88 47
W hotelfeliz.com
This bright hotel has an eclectic 1970s-inspired decor. Sea views.

MALLORCA, POLLENÇA: Hotel Posada de Lluc €
Boutique
Roser Vell 11, 07460
Tel 971 53 52 20
W posadalluc.com
A 15th-century building with rooms featuring original stone walls and beamed ceilings.

DK Choice

MALLORCA, POLLENÇA: Son Brull €€€
Boutique
Crta Palma- Pollença PM 220, km 49.8, 07460
Tel 971 53 53 53
W sonbrull.com
A sophisticated, family-run spa-hotel converted from an old farmstead, Son Brull is surrounded by a beautiful natural environment. Each of the rooms is tastefully decorated with subtle Mallorcan touches. Excellent restaurant.

MALLORCA, PORTIXOL: Portixol €€€
Boutique
Calle Sirena, 07006
Tel 971 27 18 00
W portixol.com
One of the island's most stylish hotels, with a Scandinavian vibe.

MAÓ AND AROUND: Sant Joan de Binissaida €€
Boutique
Camí de Binissaida 108, 07720
Tel 971 35 55 98
W binissaida.com

Beautiful hotel in an 18th-century farmhouse. Famed restaurant.

MENORCA, CALA MORELL:
Agroturisme Biniatram   €
B&B
Crta Cala Morell, km 1, 07760
Tel *971 38 31 13*
w biniatram.com
A small, rustic B&B with light, airy apartments in modernized farm buildings. Great outside pool.

MENORCA, MAHÓN:
Hostal La Isla   €
B&B
Santa Caterina 4, 07701
Tel *971 36 64 92*
w hostal-laisla.com
This family-run guesthouse offers clean, comfortable rooms and attentive service. Very good value.

MENORCA, SAN LUIS:
Biniaroca Hotel Rural   €€
Boutique
Camí Vell 57, 07710
Tel *971 15 00 59*
w biniarroca.com
A charming, private cottage with antiques and a pretty garden. Perfect for single travellers.

The Canary Islands

EL HIERRO, SABINOSA: Pozo de la Salud   €
Rooms with a View
El Pozo de la Salud s/n, 38911
Tel *922 55 95 61*
Relax with the sound of the Atlantic Ocean at this hotel.

EL HIERRO, VALVERDE: Parador de El Hierro   €€
Luxury
Las Playas 15, 38910
Tel *922 55 80 36*
w parador.es
A tranquil, modern hotel with a garden featuring coconut palms. Ask for a room with a sea view.

FUERTEVENTURA, CORRALEJO:
Gran Hotel Atlantis Bahia Real €€
Luxury
Avenida Grandes Playas s/n, 35660
Tel *928 53 64 44*
w bahiarealresort.com
Five-star hotel located right on the seafront. Stunning views of the Isla de Lobos and Lanzarote.

FUERTEVENTURA, VILLAVERDE:
Hotel Rural Mahoh   €
B&B
Sitio de Juan Bello, 35660
Tel *928 86 80 50*
w mahoh.com
Housed in a property fashioned out of volcanic stone and wood.

DK Choice

GRAN CANARIA, ARGUINEGUÍN:
Radisson Blu Resort   €€
Luxury
Barranco de la Verga s/n, 35120
Tel *928 15 04 00*
w radissonblu.com
Located on the top of a cliff, this is one of Gran Canaria's most effortlessly stylish hotels. Enjoy sweeping views of the Atlantic from the rooms, restaurants and pools. Relax on the beaches nearby or in the on-site bijou spa.

GRAN CANARIA, MARZAGAN:
Hotel El Mondalón   €
Boutique
Crta de los Hoyos, GC–801 1800pk, 35017
Tel *928 35 57 58*
w hotelruralmondalon.es
This countryside hotel features a games room, heated outdoor pool and a children's play area.

LA GOMERA, PLAYA DE SANTIAGO: Jardín Tecina   €
Luxury
Lomada de Tecina s/n, 38811
Tel *922 14 58 50*
w jardin-tecina.com
Handily placed for the airport, the Jardín Tecina has a large garden full of lush vegetation. Each room has a private terrace with a view.

LA GOMERA, SAN SEBASTIÁN:
Parador de la Gomera   €
Luxury
Lomo de la Horca s/n, 38800
Tel *922 87 11 00*
w parador.es
Traditional Canarian building with views of the neighbouring Tenerife, including Mount Teide.

LA PALMA, BREÑA BAJA:
Hacienda San Jorge   €
Boutique
Playa de Los Cancajos 22, 38712
Tel *922 18 10 66*
w hsanjorge.com

Take a dip on Los Cancajos' black-sand beach or in the hotel's seawater pool, shaped like a lake. All rooms are self-catering.

LA PALMA, TAZACORTE: Hotel Hacienda de Abajo   €€
Boutique
Calle Miguel de Unamuno 11, 38770
Tel *922 40 60 00*
w hotelhaciendadeabajo.com
An opulently renovated 17th-century sugar estate furnished with antiques.

LANZAROTE, ARRIETA: Finca de Arrieta   €
Boutique
Diseminado Arrieta 1, 35542
Tel *928 82 67 20*
w lanzaroteretreats.com
Quirky eco retreat featuring all modern comforts. Accommodation includes villas and yurts.

LANZAROTE, COSTA TEGUISE:
Sands Beach Resort   €
Modern
Avenida Islas Canarias 18, 35508
Tel *928 82 60 95*
w sandsbeach.eu
Self-catering apartments with a resort full of amenities and a spa.

TENERIFE, GARACHICO: Hotel San Roque   €€
Historic
Calle Esteban de Ponte 32, 38450
Tel *922 13 34 35*
w hotelsanroque.com
A lovingly restored 18th-century manor house offering elegantly furnished rooms.

TENERIFE, PUERTO DE LA CRUZ:
Hotel Botanico   €€
Luxury
Avenida Richard J. Yeoward 1, 38400
Tel *922 38 14 00*
w hotelbotanico.com
A plush five-star hotel offering a variety of luxury suites, restaurants and leisure facilities. Or simply lose yourself and all track of time in the Oriental Spa Garden.

Agroturisme Biniatram's stunning pool and landscaped gardens in Cala Morell, Menorca

For more information on types of hotels *see page 561*

WHERE TO EAT AND DRINK

One of the joys of eating out in Spain is the sheer sociability of the Spanish. Family and friends, often with children in tow, can be seen eating out from early in the day until after midnight. The country's food has a highly regional bias and traditional restaurants will typically serve dishes based on local produce. Spain also has its fair share of top-quality gourmet restaurants, notably in the Basque Country. The restaurants listed on pages 582–605 have been selected for their food and conviviality. Pages 578–81 illustrate some of the best tapas and drinks on offer; and the book's five regional sections include features on each area's unique food and wines.

An elaborately decorated bar, with a variety of drinks on offer, Barcelona

Restaurants and Bars

The cheapest and quickest places to eat are the bars and cafés that serve tapas. Some bars, however, especially pubs (late-opening bars for socializing) serve no food. Family-run *bar-restaurantes*, *ventas*, *posadas*, *mesones* and *fondas* – all old words for the different types of inns – serve inexpensive, sit-down meals. *Chiringuitos* are beachside bars that open only during the summer season.

Most restaurants close one day a week, some for lunch or dinner only, and most for an annual holiday. Away from the tourist areas, a few also close on some public holidays. It is always worth calling the restaurant ahead to check.

Eating Hours in Spain

The Spanish often have two breakfasts (*desayunos*). The first is a light meal of biscuits or toast with olive oil or butter and jam and *café con leche* (milky coffee). A more substantial breakfast may follow between 10 and 11am, perhaps in a café. This may consist of a savoury snack, such as a *bocadillo* (sandwich) with sausage, ham or cheese, or a thick slice of *tortilla de patatas* (potato omelette). Fruit juice, coffee or beer are the usual accompaniments.

From about 1pm at weekends people will stop in the bars for a beer or a *copa* (glass) of wine with tapas. During the week, those who can will have arrived home from work by 2pm for *la comida* (lunch), which is the main meal of the day. Others may dine in a restaurant. The cafés, *salones de té* (tearooms) and *pastelerías* (pastry shops) fill up by about 5:30 or 6pm for *la merienda* (tea) of sandwiches, pastries or cakes, with coffee, tea or juice. Snacks like *churros* (fried batter sticks) can also be bought from stalls. By 7pm, bars are crowded with people having tapas with sherry, wine or beer. In Spain *la cena* (dinner or supper) begins at about 9 or 10pm. Restaurants sometimes begin their evening service earlier for tourists. In summer, however, Spanish families and groups of friends often do not sit down to eat until as late as midnight. At weekend lunchtimes, especially in summer, you may find that restaurants are filled by large and noisy family gatherings.

Decorative lamp in a bar

How to Dress

A jacket and tie are rarely required, but the Spanish dress smartly, especially for city restaurants. Day dress is casual in beach resorts, but shorts are frowned upon in the evenings.

Reading the Menu

Aside from tapas, perhaps the cheapest eating options in Spanish restaurants are the *platos combinados* (meat or fish with vegetables and, usually, chips) and the fixed-price *menú*

Designer tapas bar in Barcelona

Dining alfresco at tables on a café terrace

del día. A *plato combinado* is only offered by cheaper establishments. Most restaurants offer an inexpensive, fixed-price *menú del día* at lunchtime, normally of three courses, but with little choice. Some restaurants offer a *menú de degustación* consisting of a choice of six or seven of the head chef's special dishes.

The Spanish word for menu is *la carta*. It starts with *sopas* (soups), *ensaladas* (salads), *entremeses* (hors d'oeuvres), *huevos y tortillas* (eggs and omelettes) and *verduras y legumbres* (vegetable dishes).

Main courses are *pescados y mariscos* (fish and shellfish) and *carnes y aves* (meat and poultry). Daily specials are chalked on a board or clipped to menus. Paella and other rice dishes may be served as the first course. A useful rule is to follow rice with meat, or start with serrano ham or salad and then follow with a paella.

Desserts are called *postres* in Spanish. These can include fruit, *natillas* (custard) and *flan* (crème caramel). Gourmet restaurants have more creative choices.

In big cities such as Madrid there's an increasing number of good vegetarian restaurants. Most menus have at least one vegetable or egg dish. A good number of places welcome children.

Wine Choices

Dry fino wines go with shellfish, serrano ham, olives, soups and most first courses. Main courses are usually accompanied by wines from Ribera del Duero, Rioja, Navarra or Penedès. A bar might serve wines from Valdepeñas or the local vineyards. Oloroso wines *(see p581)* are often ordered as a digestif.

Prices and Paying

If you order from *la carta* in a restaurant, your bill can soar way above the price of the *menú del día*, especially if you order pricey items such as fresh seafood, fish or *jamon ibérico* *(see p422)*. If there is an expensive fish such as sole or swordfish on the menu at a bargain price, it will be frozen. Sea bass and shellfish such as large prawns, lobster and crab, are priced by weight as a rule. The price ranges given in this guide apply to the regular menu, but if you have tapas it is usually cheaper.

La cuenta (the bill) includes service and perhaps a small cover charge. Prices on menus do not always include VAT (IVA), so 10 per cent may be added to the total bill. The Spanish hardly ever tip restaurant waiters more than 5 per cent, often just rounding up the bill.

Cheques are never used in Spain. The major credit cards and international direct debit cards are accepted in most restaurants, but sometimes not in smaller places like tapas bars, cafés or *bodegas*.

Smoking

Smoking is banned inside all bars and restaurants. However, it is permitted on outside terraces.

Wheelchair Access

New restaurants are designed for wheelchairs, but phone in advance to check on access to tables and toilets.

Recommended Restaurants

The restaurants in this guide have been selected for a variety of criteria including good food, service and location. They range from down-to-earth tapas bars to coastal places specializing in seafood and inland locales featuring country fare, to sophisticated establishments with tasting menus prepared by leading chefs. Places serving Modern Spanish food offer contemporary versions of traditional classics, whereas places we have decribed as Traditional Spanish serve more conventional fare, such as stews and fish dishes.

Any entry highlighted as DK Choice offers something that distinguishes it from the masses, be it a celebrity chef, sensational food, unusual location or unique menu.

Extensive choice of wine on show at a restaurant in Santander

Choosing Tapas

Tapas, sometimes called *pinchos*, are small snacks that originated in Andalusia in the 19th century to accompany sherry. Stemming from a bartender's practice of covering a glass with a saucer or *tapa* (cover) to keep out flies, the custom progressed to a chunk of cheese or bread being used, and then to a few olives being placed on a platter to accompany a drink. Once free of charge, tapas are usually paid for nowadays, and a selection makes a delicious light meal. Choose from a range of appetizing varieties, from cold meats to elaborately prepared hot dishes of meat, seafood or vegetables.

Mixed green olives

Patatas bravas is a piquant dish of fried potatoes with a spicy red sauce.

Albóndigas (meatballs) are a hearty *tapa*, often served with a spicy tomato sauce.

Almendras fritas are fried, salted almonds.

Banderillas are canapés skewered on toothpicks. The entire canapé should be eaten at once.

Calamares fritos are squid rings and tentacles which have been dusted with flour before being deep-fried in olive oil. They are usually served garnished with a piece of lemon.

Jamón serrano is salt-cured ham dried in mountain (*serrano*) air.

On the Tapas Bar

Almejas Clams

Berberechos Steamed cockles

Berenjenas al horno Roasted aubergines (eggplants)

Boquerones Anchovies

Boquerones al natural Fresh anchovies in garlic and olive oil

Buñuelos de bacalao Salted cod fritters

Butifarra Catalonian sausage

Calabacín rebozado Battered courgettes (zucchini) (Catalan)

Calamares a la romana Fried squid rings

Callos Tripe

Caracoles Snails

Champiñones al ajillo Mushrooms fried in white wine with garlic

Chistorra Spicy sausage

Chopitos Cuttlefish fried in batter

Chorizo al vino Chorizo sausage cooked in red wine

Chorizo diablo Chorizo served flamed with brandy

Costillas Spare ribs

Criadillas Bulls' testicles

Croquetas Croquettes of ham, cod or chicken

Empanada Pastry filled with tomato, onion and meat or fish

Ensaladilla rusa Potatoes, carrots, red peppers, peas, olives, boiled egg, tuna and mayonnaise

Gambas al pil pil Spicy, garlicky fried king prawns (shrimp)

Longaniza roja Spicy red pork sausage from Aragón (*Longaniza blanca* is paler and less spicy)

Magro Pork in a paprika and tomato sauce

Tapas Bars

Even a small village will have at least one bar where the locals go to enjoy drinks, tapas and conversation with friends. On Sundays and holidays, favourite places are packed with whole families enjoying the fare. In larger towns it is customary to move from bar to bar, sampling the specialities of each. A *tapa* is a single serving, whereas a *ración* is similar to an entrée-sized portion. Tapas are usually eaten standing or perching on a stool at the bar rather that sitting at a table, for which a surcharge is usually made.

Diners make their choice at a busy tapas bar

Chorizo, a popular sausage flavoured with paprika and garlic, may be eaten cold or fried and served hot.

Salpicón de mariscos is a luxurious cold salad of assorted fresh seafood in a zesty vinaigrette.

Gambas a la plancha is a simple but flavourful dish of grilled prawns (shrimp).

Tortilla española is the ubiquitous Spanish omelette of onion and potato bound with egg.

Pollo al ajillo consists of small pieces of chicken (often wings) sauted and then simmered with a garlic sauce.

Queso manchego is a sheep's-milk cheese from La Mancha.

Manitas de cerdo Pig's trotters

Mejillones Mussels

Morcilla Black (blood) pudding

Muslitos del mar Crab-meat croquettes, on a claw skewer

Navajas Grilled razor-shells

Orejas de cerdo Pig's ears

Pa amb tomàquet Bread rubbed with olive oil and tomatoes (Catalan)

Pan de ajo Garlic bread

Patatas a lo pobre Potato chunks sautéd with onions and red and green peppers

Patatas alioli Potato chunks in a garlic mayonnaise

Pescadito fritos Small fried fish

Pimientos de padrón Small green peppers which are occasionally hot

Pimientos rellenos Stuffed peppers

Pinchos morunos Pork skewers

Pisto Thick ratatouille of diced tomato, onion and courgette

Pulpitos Baby octopus

Rabo de toro Oxtail

Revueltos Scrambled eggs with asparagus or mushrooms

Sepia a la plancha Grilled cuttlefish

Sesos Brains, usually lamb or calf

Surtido de Ibéricos Assortment of cold cuts/charcuterie

Tabla de quesos A range of Spanish cheeses

Tortilla riojana Ham, sausage and red pepper omelette

Tostas Bread with various toppings such as tuna or Brie

Verdura a la plancha Grilled vegetables

What to Drink in Spain

Spain is one of the world's largest wine-producing countries and many fine wines are made here, particularly reds in La Rioja and sherry in Andalusia. Many other beverages – alcoholic and non-alcoholic – are served in bars and cafés, which provide an important focus for life in Spain. The Spanish are also great coffee drinkers. In the summer, a tempting range of cooling drinks is on offer, in addition to beer, which is always available. Brandy and a variety of liqueurs, such as *anís*, are drunk as apéritifs and *digestifs*, as is chilled pale gold fino sherry.

Customers enjoying a drink at a terrace café in Seville

A plate of *churros* (batter sticks)

Hot chocolate

Café con leche

Camomile   Lime flower

Hot Drinks

Café con leche is a large half-and-half measure of milk and espresso coffee; *café cortado* is an espresso with a splash of milk; *café solo* is a black coffee. Hot chocolate is also popular and is often served with *churros* (batter sticks). Herbal teas include *manzanilla* (camomile) and *tila* (lime flower).

Cold Drinks

In most Spanish towns and cities it is safe to drink the tap water, but people generally prefer to buy bottled mineral water, either still *(sin gas)* or sparkling *(con gas)*. Besides soft drinks, a variety of other thirst-quenching summer beverages is available, including *horchata (see p257)*, a sweet, milky drink made from ground *chufas* (earth almonds). Another popular refreshing drink is *leche merengada* (lemon and cinnamon flavoured milk ice cream). *Gaseosa*, fizzy lemonade, can be drunk either on its own or as a mixer, usually with wine. *Zumo de naranja natural* (freshly squeezed orange juice) is an excellent thirst quencher.

Sparkling and still mineral water

Horchata, made from *chufas*

Spanish Wine

Wine has been produced in Spain since pre-Roman times and there is a great variety on offer today, including famous types such as Rioja. The key standard for the industry is the *Denominación de Origen* (DO) classification, a guarantee of a wine's origin and quality. *Vino de la Tierra* is a classification of wines below that of DO in which over 60 per cent of the grapes come from a specified region. *Vino de Mesa*, the lowest category, covers basic unclassified wines. For more detailed information on Spain's principal wine-producing regions, refer to the following pages: Northern Spain *(see pp82–3)*, Eastern Spain *(see pp206–7)*, Central Spain *(see pp344–5)*, and Southern Spain *(see pp424–5)*.

Penedès white wine

Rioja red wine   Sparkling wine (cava)

Spirits and Liqueurs

Spanish brandy, which comes mainly from the sherry bodegas in Jerez, is known as *coñac*. Most bodegas produce at least three different labels and price ranges. Magno is a good middle-shelf brandy; top-shelf labels are Cardenal Mendoza and Duque de Alba. *Anís*, which is flavoured with aniseed, is popular. *Pacharán*, made from sloes, is sweet and also tastes of aniseed. Licor 43 is a vanilla liqueur. Ponche is brandy that has been aged and flavoured with herbs.

Anís *Pacharán* Licor 43 Ponche

Sherry

Sherry, or fino, is produced in bodegas in Jerez de la Frontera (Andalusia) and in nearby towns El Puerto de Santa María and Sanlúcar de Barrameda *(see pp424–5)*. Although not officially called sherry, similar kinds of wine are produced in Montilla near Córdoba. Pale fino is dry and light and excellent as an apéritif. Amber amontillado (aged fino) has a strong, earthy taste while oloroso is full-bodied and ruddy.

Two brands of fino sherry

Beer

Most Spanish beer *(cerveza)* is bottled lager, although you can almost always find it on draught. Popular brands include Moritz, Alhambra, San Miguel, Cruzcampo Mahou and Estrella. In Barcelona a glass of beer is called *una caña*; in Madrid, *un tercio*. Alcohol-free lager *(cerveza sin alcohol)* is available.

Bottled beers

Red wine and lemonade

Mixed Drinks

Sangria is a refreshing mixture of red wine, *gaseosa* (lemonade) and other ingredients including chopped fruit and sugar. Wine diluted with lemonade is called *vino con gaseosa*, also known as *tinto de verano* in the south. Another favourite drink is *Agua de Valencia*, a refreshing blend of *cava* (sparkling wine) and orange juice. Young people will often order the popular gin and tonic.

Sangria

How to Read a Wine Label

If you know what to look for, the label will provide a key to the wine's flavour and quality. It will bear the name of the wine and its producer or bodega, its vintage if there is one, and show its *Denominación de Origen* (DO) if applicable. Wines labelled *joven* are recent vintages and the least expensive, while *crianza* and *reserva* wines are aged a minimum of three years – part of that time in oak casks – and therefore more expensive. Table wine *(vino de mesa)*, the lowest quality, may be *tinto* (red), *blanco* (white) or *rosado* (rosé). Cava is a sparkling wine made by the *méthode champenoise* in specified areas of origin.

Brand name Company's crest

Capacity of the bottle 13% Alc.

Estate-bottled rather than cooperative

MARQUÉS DE MURRIETA
Embotellado por: BODEGAS MARQUÉS DE MURRIETA, S.A. – YGAY

Vinos de Rioja

The wine's *Denominación de Origen*

YGAY .

(LOGROÑO)

RESERVA
COSECHA 1970

The vintage Symbol for region

Where to Eat and Drink

Galicia

A CORUÑA: Cúrcuma　€
Tapas
Marconi 4, 15002
Tel *646 14 66 42*　**Closed** *Mon*
This small, popular tapas bar is a
great-value option. Book ahead.

**A CORUÑA: Restaurante Comer
y Picar**　€
Tapas
Calle Coandante Fontanes 1, 15003
Tel *981 28 52 20*　**Closed** *Mon &
Sun dinner*
Family-run place next to Riazor
beach. *Zamburiñas* (scallops) and
pulpo (octopus) are specialities.

A CORUÑA: Domus　€€
Modern Spanish
Casa del Hombre, 15002
Tel *981 20 11 36*　**Closed** *Mon, Tue
dinner, Wed & Sun*
An architectural gem with
spectacular sea views. Modern
Spanish fare, with friendly service.

A CORUÑA: Taberna Gaioso　€€
Fine Dining
Plaza España 15, 15001
Tel *981 21 33 55*　**Closed** *Mon*
The sophisticated dining room
and *bodega* perfectly match the
cuisine. Tapas and à la carte menu.

BAIONA: Tapería San Xoán　€
Tapas
Calle San Xoan 19, 36300 (Pontevedra)
Tel *638 89 62 40*　**Closed** *Mon &
Tue in winter*
Excellent, varied tapas served in a
stone-built bar-restaurant. Good-
value and a lively atmosphere.

BETANZOS: La Penela　€
Traditional Spanish
Rúa Ferradores 21, 15300
Tel *981 77 31 27*

Fine dining and wine in the elegant Yayo
Daporta, Cambados

Home-cooked, traditional
Gallegan food in a central,
convenient location. It's popular
with locals and gets busy at
peak times, so get there early.

**BETANZOS: Vega Comer
y Picar**　€
Traditional Spanish
Calle los Angeles 3, 15300
Tel *981 77 32 54*
Quality, local fare. Go for the
tortilla – the town's signature dish.

DK Choice

**CAMBADOS: Yayo
Daporta**　€€€
Fine Dining
Calle del Hospital 7, 36630
Tel *986 52 60 62*　**Closed** *Mon,
Sun dinner, 14–28 Nov*
Haute cuisine served in an
elegant, intimate atmosphere
in a 16th-century building.
Faultless, innovative cooking
underpinned by the finest,
freshest ingredients, and
accompanied by a selection
of wines that guests pick themselves from the bodega. A well-
deserved Michelin star holder.

CEDEIRA: Villa Vella Cedeira　€€
Traditional Spanish
Paseo Arriba da Ponte 19, 15350
Tel *981 48 07 64*　**Closed** *Mon*
Choose between a variety of
pintxos in the tapas bar or the
superb seafood in the dining
room at this convivial restaurant.

FISTERRA: O Centelo　€€
Seafood
Avenida del Puerto s/n, 15155
Tel *981 74 04 52*
Enjoy fresh seafood while taking
in wonderful views over the port,
especially at sunset. There is also
an inexpensive tapas bar on the
ground floor.

LUGO: Paprica　€
Mediterranean
Calle Noreas 10, 27001
Tel *982 25 58 24*　**Closed** *Mon, Sun*
This intimate restaurant is
decorated on an attractive,
modern style. Innovative food at
surprisingly competitive prices.

LUGO: Taberna do Labrego　€
Traditional Spanish
Camino Real 32, 27372, Pacios-Begonte
Tel *982 39 82 62*　**Closed** *Mon*
This hidden gem offers great-
value Gallegan cuisine in a
quaint setting. Also noted for
its excellent gin and tonics.

Price Guide
Prices are based on a three-course
evening meal for one including a half
bottle of house wine, service and taxes.

€	up to €40
€€	€40 to €55
€€€	over €55

MALPICA: As Garzas　€€€
Fine Dining
Porto Barizo, 15113
Tel *981 72 17 65*
A modern take on traditional
Spanish cuisine earned
As Garzas its Michelin star.
Huge windows showcase
its beachfront setting.

**O GROVE: Marisquerias
Solaina**　€€
Seafood
Avenida de Benimar s/n, 36980
Tel *986 73 29 69*　**Closed** *Tue*
Top-quality seafood at a
decent price. Match it with
a glass of white wine for the
perfect accompaniment.

ORTIGUEIRA: Club Naútico　€€
Mediterranean
Calle Cuiña s/n, 15330
Tel *629 84 02 76*
Delicious seafood served in smart
surroundings overlooking the
marina. Good, inexpensive tapas
as well.

OURENSE: A Taberna　€
Traditional Spanish
C/ Julio Prieto 32, 32005
Tel *988 24 33 32*　**Closed** *Mon*
This delightfully old-fashioned
restaurant serves excellent,
home-cooked local cuisine.
It has a gourmet shop, too.

OURENSE: La Table　€
French
*Plaza de la Capela 29, O Pereiro de
Aguiar, 32710*
Tel *988 25 96 77*
Small, but top-quality restaurant
serving tasty French dishes.
Impeccable service.

**PONTEVEDRA: Restaurante
Mare e Monti**　€
Italian
Rio de Camiño de Ferro, 36003
Tel *886 21 48 94*
Lovely Italian restaurant. Stone-
baked pizzas and traditional
pastas feature on the menu.

RIBADEO: Casa Villaronta　€
Seafood
Calle de San Francisco 9, 27700
Tel *982 12 86 09*
Villaronta is reputed to serve the
best *pulpo* (octopus) in the world.

SAN SALVADOR DE POIO: Casa Solla €€€
Fine Dining
Avenida de Sineiro 7, 36005
Tel *986 87 28 84* **Closed** *Mon, Thu & Sun dinner; mid-Dec–early Jan; Semana Santa*
One of the best restaurants in Spain. Innovative cooking in a remote setting.

SANTA COMBA: Fogón Retiro da Costiña €€
Fine Dining
Avenida de Santiago 12, 15840
Tel *981 88 02 44*
Traditional fare elevated to haute cuisine status by a creative chef. The bodega provides perfect accompaniments to superb meals.

SANTIAGO DE COMPOSTELA: Abastos 2.0 €
Modern Spanish
Plaza de Abastos s/n, Casetas 13–18, 15704
Tel *654 01 59 37* **Closed** *Mon, Sun*
An appealing contemporary approach to traditional cuisine using fresh, local produce.

SANTIAGO DE COMPOSTELA: O Dezaseis €
Tapas
Calle de San Pedro 16, 15703
Tel *981 56 48 80* **Closed** *Sun*
A stylish, rustically decorated bar serving a choice of traditional and creative tapas, plus a fantastic set lunch *(menú del día)*.

SANTIAGO DE COMPOSTELA: O Gato Negro €
Seafood
Rúa Raiña s/n, 15702
Tel *981 58 31 05*
Quintessentially authentic seafood bar and restaurant. Excellent tapas and main dishes.

SANTIAGO DE COMPOSTELA: Casa Marcelo €€€
Fusion
Rúa Hortas 1, 15705
Tel *981 55 85 80* **Closed** *Mon, Sun*
Watch the chef preparing Asian-fusion delights in the open kitchen at this charming restaurant.

SANXENXO: La Taberna de Rotilio €€
Traditional Spanish
Avenida del Puerto 7–9, 36960
Tel *986 72 02 00* **Closed** *Mon, Sun dinner, mid-Dec–mid-Jan*
All the regional classics in generous portions. Friendly service.

VERÍN: Casa Zapatillas €
Traditional Spanish
Avenida Luis Espada 34, 32600
Tel *988 41 07 29*

Impeccable style at El Corral del Indianu, Arriondas

Classic Spanish cuisine, great tapas and a phenomenal selection of Galician wines make this traditional eatery a local favourite.

VIGO: Tapas Areal €
Tapas
Calle de México 36, 36204
Tel *986 41 86 43*
Varied selection of tapas. Leave room for a home-made dessert.

VIGO: Tapeame €
Tapas
Plaza de Compostela 2, 32601
Tel *986 22 88 02*
A modern restaurant offering a contemporary, diverse tapas menu. Good for vegetarians.

VIVEIRO: Restaurante Nito €€
Traditional Spanish
Hotel Ego, Playa de Area 1, 27850
Tel *982 56 09 87*
Located in Hotel Ego, this lovely spot combines great seafood with glorious views.

Asturias and Cantabria

AMPUERO: Restaurante Solana €€
Fine dining
La Bien Aparecida No 11, 39849
Tel *942 67 67 18* **Closed** *Mon, Sun dinner, 15 days in Nov*
Michelin-starred hilltop restaurant. Worth the journey for its creative cuisine and great views.

ARRIONDAS: El Corral del Indianu €€
Modern Spanish
Avenida de Europa 14, 33540
Tel *985 84 10 72* **Closed** *Thu*
Elaborate cooking with the finest ingredients is what earned chef José Antonio Campoviejo a Michelin star at this chic restaurant. The *menú de degustación* has 12 courses of gastronomic delights.

DK Choice

ARRIONDAS: Casa Marcial €€€
Fine Dining
La Salgar 10, Parres, 33540
Tel *985 84 09 91* **Closed** *Mon*
Set in the rolling countryside, Casa Marcial was the childhood home of renowned chef Nacho Manzano and is now host to his inspired cooking and two Michelin stars. The menu offers modern twists on Spanish classics complemented by an impressive wine list – all served in elegant surroundings.

CANGAS DE ONÍS: Sidrería Los Ramos €
Traditional Spanish
La Venta s/n, 33550
Tel *608 14 59 97* **Closed** *Jan–Feb*
Delicious, regional home-cooked food. A solid choice, always popular with the locals.

CASTRO URDIALES: Mesón El Segoviano €
Seafood
Correría 19, 39700
Tel *942 86 18 59* **Closed** *Mon & Sun lunch*
Classic restaurant right on the port. Serves fresh, local seafood as well as meat dishes.

CUDILLERO: La Curuxina €
Traditional Spanish
Calle Riofrio 5, 33150
Tel *985 59 11 41*
Popular for tasty local dishes such as *fabada asturiana* (pork and bean stew) or octopus cooked with shellfish.

GIJÓN: Sidrería La Galana €
Tapas
Plaza Mayor 10, 33201
Tel *985 17 24 29*
Great location on the bustling Plaza Mayor in Old Town. Superb tapas, vibrant atmosphere.

For more information on types of restaurants *see page 577*

GIJÓN: Ciudadela €€
Mediterranean
Calle Capua 7, 33202
Tel *985 34 77 32*   **Closed** *Sun*
The dishes from the constantly changing menu of this inviting restaurant are served with style. The two dining areas include a romantic, candlelit grotto.

LAREDO: La Marina Company €
Seafood
Calle Zamanillo, 39770
Tel *942 60 63 35*
Simple, well-executed traditional fare with excellent-value set menu options. In the Old Town.

LASTRES: El Barrigón de Bertín €€
Fine Dining
Calle San Jose, 33330
Tel *985 85 04 45*   **Closed** *Wed*
Multi-award-winning chef with an haute cuisine take on classic Asturian cooking. Uses the finest and freshest local ingredients.

LLANES: Sidrería El Rubiu €
Traditional Spanish
Lugar Vidiago, s/n, 33597
Tel *985 41 14 18*   **Closed** *Mon & Tue dinner*
Stone-built restaurant serving hearty Asturian food. The *fabada* (bean stew) is a must-try.

NOJA: Restaurante Sambal €€
Fine Dining
Calle el Arenal, 39180
Tel *942 63 15 31*   **Closed** *Sun–Thu dinner in winter*
Gourmet dining accompanied by fine views. Terrace for good weather. Excellent wine list.

NOREÑA: Sidrería Casa El Sastre €
Traditional Spanish
Calle de Fray Ramon 27, 33180
Tel *985 74 12 52*   **Closed** *Mon*
Home-cooked regional fare and delicious desserts. Wash it all down with a local cider.

OVIEDO: El Raítan €
Modern Spanish
Plaza Trascorrales 6, 33009
Tel *985 21 42 18*   **Closed** *Sun–Thu dinner*
This stylish restaurant has a delightful little terrace. It serves a delicious *fabada* (bean stew) as well as other traditional local dishes and tapas.

OVIEDO: Casa Fermín €€€
Fine Dining
Calle de San Francisco 8, 33003
Tel *985 21 64 52*   **Closed** *Sun*
With a well-deserved reputation for excellence, the high prices reflect the quality. Modern decor.

The dining area located by the sea at Annua, San Vicente de la Barquera

PONTEJOS: La Atalaya €
Traditional Spanish
Carretera Pedrosa 52, 39618
Tel *942 50 39 06*   **Closed** *Mon–Wed in winter, Mon & Sun dinner in summer*
Consistently delivers exceptional food and service in a tasteful dining room. Economical set and tasting menus are available. Popular with the locals.

POTES: Casa Cayo €
Traditional Spanish
Calle de la Cantabra, 6, 39570
Tel *942 73 01 50*
Hearty, regional fare. Perfect after a day's hiking in the mountains.

RIBADESELLA: Restaurante Güeyu Mar €€€
Seafood
Playa de Vega 84, 33560
Tel *985 86 08 63*
This fine seafood restaurant's terrace overlooks Vega beach.

SAN VICENTE DE LA BARQUERA: Annua €€€
Fine Dining
Paseo de la Barquera s/n, 39540
Tel *942 71 50 50*   **Closed** *Mon*
Michelin-starred restaurant with breathtaking views over the sea. Impeccable cooking, creative menus and a superb wine list.

SANTA EULALIA DE OSCOS: Mesón La Cerca €
Traditional Spanish
La Villa, 33776
Tel *985 62 60 41*
Located in a quaint building with outdoor tables under a *horreo* (stilted grain store). Famous for the empanadas.

SANTANDER: La Bombi €
Traditional Spanish
Calle de Casimiro Sáinz 15, 39003
Tel *942 21 30 28*
Brilliantly executed northern Spanish food in a beautifully decorated dining room.

SANTANDER: Trattoria Florida €
Italian
Calle de la Florida 14, 39001
Tel *942 04 84 54*   **Closed** *Mon*
This authentic Italian restaurant serves a wide range of pizzas, pastas and vegetarian options.

SANTANDER: Cañadio €€
Tapas
Calle de Gómez Oreña, 15, 39003
Tel *942 31 41 49*   **Closed** *Sun*
This long-established restaurant, with a branch in Madrid, is a classy joint. Excellent, varied tapas in a fun atmosphere.

SANTANDER: El Marucho €€
Seafood
Calle de Tetuán 21, 39004,
Tel *942 27 30 07*   **Closed** *Tue*
Bite into fresh fish and seafood at this simple, rustic bar-restaurant. Lively atmosphere and a good-value option.

SANTILLANA DEL MAR: Casa Uzquiza €
Traditional Spanish
Calle del Escultor Jesús Otero 5, 39330
Tel *942 81 80 70*
Enjoy tasty local cuisine in the stone-walled dining room, or out on the pretty terrace in summer.

SANTILLANA DEL MAR: Los Blasones €
Traditional Spanish
Plaza de la Gandara, 8, 39330
Tel *942 81 80 70*   **Closed** *Thu in winter; mid-Dec–mid-Mar*
Authentic regional cuisine with an emphasis on local ingredients. Charming, rustic vibe.

VILLAVICIOSA: El Verano €€
Seafood
Calle Agüero 3, 33300
Tel *985 89 24 65*
This appealingly unpretentious restaurant in the tiny hamlet of Agüero, about 8 km (5 miles) from Villaviciosa, serves some of the finest seafood in Asturias.

The Basque Country, Navarra & La Rioja

AOIZ: Beti Jai €
Traditional Navarran
Santa Águeda 2, 31430
Tel *948 33 60 52* **Closed** *Sun dinner*
Set in a Basque rural hotel. Serves classic Navarran fare, but with new culinary twists and flavours.

CINTRUÉNIGO: Maher €€
Fine Dining
Ribera 19, 31592
Tel *948 81 11 50* **Closed** *Sun dinner; Mon; mid-Dec–mid-Jan*
Time-honoured recipes are given a contemporary twist at this elegant restaurant, using seasonal products sourced from Ribera.

ESTELLA: Navarra €
Traditional Navarran
Calle Gustavo de Maeztu, 31200
Tel *948 55 00 40* **Closed** *Sun dinner; Mon; Jan*
Set in an old Navarran house decked out in medieval decor. Specialities include lamb and stuffed asparagus.

EZCARAY: El Portal de Echaurren €
Modern Riojan
Héroes de Alcázar 2, 26280
Tel *941 35 40 47* **Closed** *Sun dinner; Mar–Jul: Mon & Tue*
The first restaurant in La Rioja's history to receive a Michelin star. Run alongside a gastronomic hotel. Delicious seafood.

EZCARAY: El Rincón del Vino €
Traditional Riojan
C/ Jesús Nazareno 2, 26280
Tel *941 35 43 75* **Closed** *winter: Mon–Thu dinner; Sep–Jun: Wed*
Suckling lamb and other grilled specialities at the weekend. The adjacent wine shop has thousands of Riojan labels.

HARO: Las Duelas €
Modern Riojan
San Agustín 2, 26200
Tel *941 30 44 63* **Closed** *Jan*

Set in a monastery, Las Duelas offers a wide variety of Riojan dishes. Flawless balance between traditional and creative cuisine.

LOGROÑO: Bar Soriano €
Tapas
Travesía del Laurel 2, 26001
Tel *941 22 88 07* **Closed** *Wed*
Each tapas bar has a different speciality on this popular street: here you'll find succulent *champis* (button mushrooms), served *pintxo*-style on French bread.

LOGROÑO: Mesón Egües €
Traditional Riojan
Campa 3, 26005
Tel *941 22 86 03* **Closed** *Sun*
Uses the highest-quality ingredients to create simple but hearty grilled dishes. Try the braised oxtail and *chuleta* (chop).

OLITE: Casa Zanito €
Traditional Navarran
Rua Mayor 16, 31390
Tel *948 74 00 02* **Closed** *Mon & Tue; 18 Dec–24 Jan*
A charming hotel-restaurant located in medieval Olite. Go for the fixed-price Menú Labrit.

PAMPLONA: Ansoleaga 33 €
Fine Dining
Florencio de Ansoleaga 33, 31001
Tel *948 04 48 60*
Nibble on Navarran food while admiring the views of the old town from the dining room.

PAMPLONA: Café Bar Gaucho €
Pintxos
Calle de Espoz y Mina 7, 31002
Tel *948 22 50 73*
This small, buzzing place is one of Pamplona's best *pintxo* bars, with a huge variety of flavoursome dishes. Cash only.

PAMPLONA: Europa €€
Fine Dining
Espoz y Mina 11, 31002
Tel *948 22 18 00* **Closed** *Sun*
Situated in Hotel Europa in the heart of town. Try the chocolate mousse with orange confit.

SAN SEBASTIÁN: Urbano €
Traditional Basque
31 de Agosto Kalea 17, 20003
Tel *943 42 04 34* **Closed** *Wed & Sun dinner*
The senses will be awakened here as the chef aims to embrace aromas, textures and flavours. The duck confit is superb.

SAN SEBASTIÁN: Zeruko €
Pintxos
Pescadería 10 (Old Town)
Tel *943 42 34 51* **Closed** *Mon*
Whipping up creative *pintxos*, trendy Zeruko is a hugely popular destination in San Sebastián's "*pintxo*-crawl" scene.

DK Choice

SAN SEBASTIÁN: Akelarre €€€
Modern Basque
Padre Orkolaga 56, 20008
Tel *943 31 12 09* **Closed** *Sun dinner; Mon; Jan–Jun: Tue; Feb & early Oct*
One of Spain's most highly regarded restaurants, Akelarre offers inventive Basque cuisine rooted in tradition. The dining room's sweeping views of the Atlantic set the perfect stage for an unforgettable meal. Order the *menú de degustación* to sample the best of the season.

SAN SEBASTIÁN: Arzak €€€
Modern Basque
Alcalde José Elosegui 273, 20016
Tel *943 278 465/34 943 285 593*
Closed *Sun & Mon; mid-Jun–early Jul & Nov*
Dine at this iconic Basque eatery by living legend Juan Mari Arzak, and his daughter Elena, who was voted the World's Best Female Chef in 2012.

SAN VICENTE DE LA SONSIERRA: Casa Toni €
Traditional Riojan
Zumalacárregui 27, 26338
Tel *941 33 40 01* **Closed** *Sun & Mon dinner; 2 wks Jul & Sep*
Traditional Riojan food with a modern twist. Go for the special, four-course Menú el Rocio for €25.

SANTO DOMINGO DE LA CALZADA: El Rincón de Emilio €
Traditional Riojan
Plaza de Bonifacio Gil 7, 26250
Tel *941 34 09 90* **Closed** *Tue dinner; Feb*
Dedicated to traditional Riojan cuisine for more than 30 years. Riojan cod is the house speciality. The stuffed piquillo peppers are worth a try, too.

Views of the Atlantic from Akelarre's dining room, San Sebastián

For more information on types of restaurants *see page 577*

TAFALLA: Túbal   €€€
Traditional Navarran
Plaza de Navarra 4, 31300
Tel *948 70 08 52*   **Closed** *Sun & Tue dinner; Mon*
Vegetables from the restaurant's own garden are the stars. Tables on balconies overlook the square.

TUDELA: Restaurante 33   €
Fine Dining
C/ Capuchinos 7, 31500
Tel *948 82 76 06*   **Closed** *Sun–Wed dinner*
The food is big on flavour at this award-winning establishment. Most products are from the restaurant's own garden.

URDÁNIZ: El Molino de Urdániz   €€€
Fine Dining
Crta Francia por Zubiri (Na-135) km 16.5, 31698
Tel *948 30 41 09*   **Closed** *Mon; Tue, Wed & Sat dinner*
A rustic stone-built house serving dishes that combine traditional food from the Pyrenees with cutting-edge execution and complex flavours.

VIANA: Borgia   €€
Fine Dining
C/ Serapio Urra, 1 31230
Tel *948 64 57 81*   **Closed** *Sun–Thu dinner, all day Sun in Aug*
Modern decor and authentic food of the highest quality. Specializes in steaks – try the beef cheek with blood-orange sauce.

VITORIA: El Clarete   €
Modern Basque
Cercas Bajas 18, 01008
Tel *945 26 38 74*   **Closed** *Mon–Wed dinner; Sun*
Food deeply rooted in Basque tradition with an innovative twist. Go for the *marmitako* (tuna stew) with lobster or suckling pig with a mango cream. Great tapas bar as well.

VITORIA: Zaldiaran   €€
Modern Basque
Avenida Gasteiz 21, 01008
Tel *945 13 48 22*   **Closed** *Sun & Tue dinner*
Zaldiaran is regarded as Vitoria's best restaurant. Relish creative fare made with elaborate techniques and flavours.

Barcelona
Old Town

La Báscula   €
Vegetarian   **Map** 5 C3
Flassaders 30, 08003
Tel *933 19 98 66*

A charming café in a renovated old chocolate factory serving vegetarian and vegan dishes, plus great cakes and pastries.

Bodega la Plata   €
Tapas   **Map** 5 A3
Mercé 28, 08002
Tel *933 15 10 09*
A miniature, old-fashioned bodega serving wine straight from the barrel along with a small selection of tapas. The freshly fried sardines are a huge hit.

DK Choice

Café de L'Acadèmia   €
Modern Catalan   **Map** 5 B3
Lledó 1, Plaça Sant Just, 08002
Tel *933 19 82 53*   **Closed** *Sat & Sun; 3 wks Aug*
A long-established favourite, Café de L'Acadèmia serves fresh, modern Catalan cuisine in a brick-lined dining room and out on a candlelit terrace overlooking an enchanting Gothic square. The menu changes regularly according to what is freshly available on the market.

Can Culleretes   €
Traditional Catalan   **Map** 5 A3
Quintana 5, 08002
Tel *933 17 30 22*   **Closed** *Mon, Sun dinner*
Barcelona's oldest restaurant, Can Culleretes is great for classics such as *botifarra amb seques* (country sausage with beans) and seafood stew.

Kaiku   €
Mediterranean   **Map** 5 B3
Plaça del Mar 1, 08003
Tel *932 21 90 82*   **Closed** *Mon, Sun dinner; Aug*

Old-world charm meets new-world tapas at Suculent, Barcelona

Deceptively simple-looking, serving fantastic dishes prepared with smoked rice and home-grown vegetables. The excellent desserts are served on a platter.

Lo de Flor   €
Mediterranean   **Map** 2 E2
Carretes 18, 08001
Tel *934 42 38 53*   **Closed** *lunch; Tue; 2 wks Aug*
Romantic, rustic restaurant with minimalist decor. Short but well-chosen wine list.

Mam i Teca   €
Modern Catalan   **Map** 2 F2
Carrer de la Lluna 4, 08001
Tel *934 41 33 35*   **Closed** *Tue, Sat lunch*
Tiny space serving Catalan dishes made with local produce.

La Paradeta   €
Seafood   **Map** 5 C3
Comercial 7, 08009
Tel *932 68 19 39*   **Closed** *Mon*
Fish and chips, Barcelona-style. Choose your fish and watch it being cooked. No reservations.

Quimet i Quimet   €
Tapas Bar   **Map** 2 D3
Poeta Cabanyes 25, 08004
Tel *934 42 31 42*   **Closed** *Sun, Sat dinner; Aug*
A small, bottle-lined tapas bar with delicious cheeses, canapés and other treats.

Senyor Parellada   €
Mediterranean   **Map** 5 B3
Argenteria 37, 08003
Tel *933 10 50 94*
Elegant yet relaxed restaurant for modern fare in a handsome 19th-century town house.

DK Choice

Suculent   €
Tapas   **Map** 2 F3
Rambla del Raval 43, 08001
Tel *934 43 65 79*   **Closed** *Mon; Sun dinner*
This pretty old bodega has been reinvented as a trendy gastro bar by a trio of celebrity chefs, while retaining its original essence. It offers a range of creative tapas, platters of carefully selected cheeses and cured meats as well as more substantial fare such as lamb chops and rice dishes.

Teresa Carles   €
Vegetarian   **Map** 5 A1
Carrer de Jovellanos 2, 08001
Tel *933 17 18 29*
This elegant family-run place with wooden interiors is one of the city's best vegetarian restaurants.

Dos Palillos' colourful decor matches its inventive menu, Barcelona

Zim €
Tapas Map 5 B2
C/ Daqueria 20, 08002
Tel 934 12 65 48 **Closed** lunch
Miniature bar serving wines by the
glass along with simple tapas, with
a focus on fine Catalan cheeses.

Gravin €€
Italian Map 5 B3
Rera Palau 3–5, 08003
Tel 932 68 46 28 **Closed** Mon & Tue
lunch
Sophisticated Italian food from
the Puglia region in an elegant
dining room with exposed brick
walls and tiled floors.

La Mar Salada €€
Mediterranean Map 5 B5
Passeig Joan Borbó 58–59, 08003
Tel 932 21 10 15 **Closed** Tue
Bright and modern setting, with
a fantastic set lunch. Great for
seafood lovers with dishes such as
cod pilpil with honey and spinach.

Pla €€
Fusion Map 5 A3
Bellafila 5,08002
Tel 934 12 65 52 **Closed** lunch
Hidden down a narrow street,
this reliably good option offers
deftly prepared fusion cuisine.

Dos Palillos €€€
Tapas Map 2 F2
Elisabets 9, 08001
Tel 933 04 05 13 **Closed** Sun &
Mon; Tue & Wed dinner
Ultra-chic yet relaxed tapas bar
with a Michelin star, serving
spectacular Asian fusion tapas.

Koy Shunka €€€
Japanese Map 5 B3
C/ Copons 7, 08002
Tel 934 12 79 39 **Closed** Mon;
Sun dinner; Aug
A Michelin star supports its
claim to being the best Japanese
restaurant in the city, with an
adventurous menu.

Eixample

Bar Calders €
Café Map 2 D2
Parlament 25, 08015
Tel 933 29 93 49
A pretty terrace, perfect for a
vermut (vermouth) and delicious
tapas, hummus and salads.
Named after Catalan writer Pere
Calders, it stocks his books as well.

Fábrica Moritz €
Tapas Map 2 E1
Ronda de Sant Antoni 41, 08011
Tel 934 26 00 50
A huge bar and restaurant in
a sumptuous, beautifully
renovated Modernista building.

Tapas 24 €
Tapas Map 3 A5
Diputació 269, 08007
Tel 934 88 09 77 **Closed** Sun
Inventive selection of everyday
to fantastic creative tapas by the
chef Carles Abellan.

Boca Grande €€
Seafood Map 3 A3
Passatge de la Concepció 12, 08003
Tel 934 67 51 49
This trendy restaurant dishes
out delicious fresh seafood in
spectacular surroundings. It also
has a lovely terrace, oyster bar,
winery and cocktail bar.

Caldeni €€
Modern Catalan Map 3 C4
València 452, 08013
Tel 932 32 58 11 **Closed** Sun & Mon
Fantastic, contemporary cuisine
from Dani Lechuga, a rising
young star in the culinary scene.

Ikibana €€
Fusion Map 2 D2
Avinguda del Paral.lel 148, 08015
Tel 934 42 46 48
A striking interior and Japanese-
Brazilian fusion cuisine make
Ikibana one of Barcelona's most
stylish restaurants.

Petit Comitè €€
Modern Catalan Map 3 A3
Passatge de la Concepció 13, 08008
Tel 935 50 06 20 **Closed** Mon
Modern Catalan fare with a dash
of French aplomb can be found
at this smart restaurant.

Tickets €€
Tapas Map 1 C2
Avinguda Paral·lel 164, 08015
Closed lunch (except Sat); Mon & Sun
Imaginative tapas and a funfair-
themed interior in this restaurant.
A truly wonderful experience.

DK Choice

La Xalada €€
Mediterranean Map 2 D2
Carrer del Parlament 1, 08013
Tel 931 29 43 31 **Closed** Mon &
Tue; Wed lunch
One of the trendiest eateries
on Carrer del Parlament,
La Xalada serves delectable
Catalan cuisine, prepared with
a deft, modern touch and the
very best seasonal produce.
There are a few tables out on
the small terrace, or you can
eat in the delightfully retro
interior, with gilded columns
and artfully mismatched
furnishings and china.

Moments €€€
Modern Catalan Map 3 A5
Passeig de Gràcia 38–40, 08007
Tel 931 51 87 81 **Closed** Sun & Mon
Set in the Mandarian Oriental
Hotel, the inventive, mouth-
watering cuisine served here has
earned Moments many awards
including a Michelin star.

Further Afield

Casa de Tapes Cañota €
Tapas Map 1 B2
Lleida 7, 08004
Tel 933 25 91 71 **Closed** Mon, Sun
dinner; mid-Aug–early Sep
This big and bustling joint serves
gourmet tapas such as succulent
beef with garlic.

DK Choice

Gut €
Mediterranean Map 3 B2
C/ del Perill 13, Gràcia, 08012
Tel 931 86 63 60
Arrive early for a seat at this
charming restaurant, where
tasty, healthy food, including
vegetarian and gluten-free
options, is prepared daily with
market-fresh ingredients. Also,
don't miss the delicious, home-
made cakes.

For more information on types of restaurants see page 577

Cafè Godot   €€
Mediterranean   **Map** 3 B2
C/ de Sant Domènec 19, Gràcia, 08012
Tel 933 68 20 36
Stylish modern café serving
bistro-style food with a
contemporary twist, including
a great brunch on weekends.

Kuai Momos   €€
Tapas   **Map** 3 B2
C / Martínez de la Rosa 71, Gràcia,
08012
Tel 932 18 53 27   **Closed** Sun
A chic, lively restaurant serving
Asian tapas such as gyoza
(Japanese dumplings), salads,
curries and rice dishes.

Wagokoro   €€
Japanese   **Map** 3 A1
Regàs 35, 08006
Tel 935 01 93 40 **Closed** Sun & Mon,
Tue dinner; 1 wk Aug
Outstanding, authentic
Japanese food is served in this
simple dining room run by a
warm and welcoming Catalan-
Japanese couple.

ABaC   €€€
Modern Catalan
Ave Tibidabo 1, 08022
Tel 933 19 66 00 **Closed** Sun & Mon
Exceptional cuisine from chef
Jordi Cruz, who, in 2004, became
the youngest Spanish chef to earn
a Michelin star at just 25. His
creations at ABaC have earned
two of the coveted gongs.

Botafumeiro   €€€
Seafood   **Map** 3 A2
Gran de Gràcia 81, 08012
Tel 932 18 42 30
A large, traditional restaurant
with white-aproned waiters
bearing ultra-fresh seafood
platters to the crowded tables
at this popular local.

Catalonia

ANGLÈS: L'Aliança d'Anglès €€
Modern Catalan
Carrer Jacint Verdaguer 3, 17160
Tel 972 42 01 56 **Closed** Mon; Sun,
Tue & Wed dinner
Look no further than L'Aliança
D'Anglès for fantastic, creative
cuisine in an elegant early 20th-
century villa set in gardens.

ARTIES: Casa Irene   €€
Traditional Catalan
C/ Major 3, 25599
Tel 973 64 43 64   **Closed** Mon
This elegant restaurant, offering
quality fare, resides in a stone-
built traditional house; perfect
after a day on the ski slopes.

Tables with a picturesque view at El Motel, Figueres

BANYOLES: Ca L'Arpa   €€€
Modern Catalan
Passeig Industria 5, 17820
Tel 972 57 23 53   **Closed** Mon, Tue
lunch, Sun dinner
Part of a chic hotel, this restaurant
specializing in modern Catalan
cuisine can be found in Banyoles'
charming historic quarter.

BEGUR: Fonda Caner   €€
Traditional Catalan
Pi i Ralló 10, Costa Brava, 17255
Tel 972 62 23 91   **Closed** Nov–Mar
A traditional restaurant, with lots
of old-fashioned charm, tucked
away in Begur's old quarter.
Organic and seasonal cuisine.

BEGUR: Restaurant Rostei €€
Mediterranean
Concepció Pi 8, Costa Brava, 17255
Tel 972 62 42 15 **Closed** Sun–Thu, Fri
& Sat lunch in winter; Mon, Tue–Sat
lunch in summer
A romantic restaurant in Begur's
historic quarter, Restaurant Rostei
serves delicious seafood and
fantastic desserts.

BESALÚ: Cúria Reial   €€
Traditional Catalan
Plaça de la Llibertat 14, 17850
Tel 972 59 02 63   **Closed** Tue
Traditional Catalan cuisine served
under stone vaults. Try the duck
with foie gras.

CADAQUÉS: Compartir   €€€
Modern Catalan
Riera Sant Vicenç s/n, 17488
Tel 972 25 84 82
A trio of Catalunya's top chefs offer
highly imaginative dishes such as
sardines marinated in orange,
olives and mint, or asparagus
served with a piquant foam.

CALDES D'ESTRAC: Marola €€
Seafood
Passeig dels Anglesos 6, 08393
Tel 937 91 32 00   **Closed** Tue; Sun,
Mon, Wed & Thu dinner

A modest yet charming spot with
a beachfront setting – perfect for
fresh seafood and paella.

CAMBRILS: Can Bosch   €€€
Seafood
Rambla Jaume I 19, 43850
Tel 977 36 00 19   **Closed** Mon, Sun
dinner; late Dec–Jan
There is delectable seafood to
be had here, overlooking the
port at Cambrils. The restaurant
has held a coveted Michelin star
since 1984.

ESCUNHAU: El Niu   €
Traditional Catalan
Deth Pònt 1, 25539
Tel 973 64 14 06 **Closed** Sun dinner;
late Jun–late Jul
Traditional mountain inn with
a roaring fireplace. The menu
features tasty grilled meats. The
dining room has a hunting-
inspired decor.

FIGUERES: El Motel   €€€
Traditional Catalan
Avinguda Salvador Dalí 170, 17600
Tel 972 50 05 62
This elegant restaurant enjoys
a reputation for serving fine
regional cuisine. It also has an
extensive wine list.

GARRAF: La Cúpula   €€
Seafood
Platja de Garraf, 08871
Tel 936 32 00 15 **Closed** Mon & Tue;
Sun, Wed & Thu dinner
With a splendid clifftop setting,
La Cúpula is a perfect place for
a seafood lunch.

GIRONA: Divinum   €€
Tapas
Albereda 7, 17004
Tel 872 08 02 18   **Closed** Sun;
Mon dinner
Divinum is an elegant,
contemporary tapas restaurant
with an excellent wine list to
accompany the petite dishes.

DK Choice

GIRONA: El Celler de Can Roca €€€
Modern Catalan
C/ de Can Sunyer 48, 17007
Tel 972 22 21 57 **Closed** Sun & Mon; 1 wk Aug; Easter
One of the world's top restaurants, this temple to molecular gastronomy boasts three Michelin stars. It is run by the three Roca brothers: Joan is head chef, Jordi is dessert chef and Josep is the sommelier. Expect innovative dishes such as oysters with champagne and caramelized olives served on a bonsai tree. You must reserve 11 months in advance.

HORTA DE SANT JOAN: Mas del Cigarrer €
Traditional Catalan
Crta Horta de Sant Joan a Bot s/n, 43596
Tel 977 43 51 53 **Closed** mid-Sep-June: Sun & Mon, Tue-Thu dinner
Famous for calçots (barbecued leek-like vegetable) and cargolades (feasts of calçots and wild snails).

L'AMETLLA DE MAR: L'Alguer €€
Seafood
Trafalgar 21, 43860
Tel 977 45 61 24 **Closed** Mon; mid-Dec-mid-Jan
Fresh seafood served in a dining room with door-to-ceiling glass windows, right on the seafront.

L'ESPLUGA DE FRANCOLÍ: Hostal del Senglar €€
Traditional Catalan
Plaça Montserrat Canals 1, 43440
Tel 977 87 04 11 **Closed** Mon
Excellent for flame-grilled meats and hearty country dishes.

LLAGOSTERA: Els Tinars €€€
Modern Catalan
Crta de Sant Feliu a Girona, km 7, 17240
Tel 972 83 06 26 **Closed** Mon, Sun dinner
First-rate contemporary cuisine with a focus on seasonal local produce. Good value set menus.

LLEIDA: L'Estel de la Mercè €€
Modern Catalan
C/ Cardenal Cisneros 30, 25002
Tel 973 28 80 08 **Closed** Mon, Sun dinner
A bright hotel-restaurant serving fresh, contemporary Catalan cuisine. A gastro tapas bar, too.

PERALADA: Cal Sagristà €€
Traditional Catalan
Rodona 2, 17491
Tel 972 53 83 01 **Closed** Tue, Mon dinner; 3 wks Feb & Nov

Fresh, delicious Catalan cuisine in a charmingly restored old convent; save room for dessert.

RIPOLL: Reccapolis €€
Traditional Catalan
Crta de Sant Joan 68, 17500
Tel 972 70 21 06 **Closed** Wed, Sun-Thu dinner; mid-Aug-mid-Sep
Comforting country favourites in a handsome century-old house; excellent set lunch.

ROSES: Rafa's €€
Seafood
Carrer Sant Sebastià 56, 17480
Tel 972 25 40 03 **Closed** Sun, Mon; Dec-mid-Jan
Informal, convivial and hugely popular seafood restaurant with expertly cooked fish.

ROSES: Els Brancs €€€
Modern Catalan
Av. de José Díaz Pacheco 26, 17480
Tel 972 25 62 00 **Closed** lunch; Mon; Oct-Mar
An award-winning gastronomic restaurant serving creative Catalan cuisine. Amazing terrace over the cliff, perfect for sunset views of Roses Bay.

SANT CARLES DE LA RÀPITA: Miami Can Pons €€
Seafood
Passeig Marítim 18-20, 43540
Tel 977 74 05 51 **Closed** Sun
Classic seafront restaurant in the Hotel Miami Mar. Attentive service and excellent value.

SANT FELIU DE GUÍXOLS: Cau Del Pescador €€
Seafood
Carrer Sant Doménec 11, 17220
Tel 972 32 40 52 **Closed** Mon; Tue in winter
A smart restaurant in an old fisherman's cottage. Sample the justly famed suquet (seafood stew).

The white-on-blonde, luxurious dining room at El Celler de Can Roca, Girona

SANT FELIU DE GUÍXOLS: Villa Más €€€
Traditional Catalan
Passeig de Sant Pol 95, 17220
Tel 972 82 25 26 **Closed** Mon except Jun-Aug; early Dec-early Jan
Enchanting 19th-century villa overlooking the Sant Pol beach. Outstanding Catalan cuisine and a fine selection of wines.

SANT FRUITÓS DE BAGES: L'Ó €€€
Modern Catalan
Camí de Sant Benet de Bages, 08272
Tel 938 75 94 29 **Closed** Mon-Wed, Sun dinner
Minimalist dining room in a medieval monastery. Inventive Catalan cuisine by Michelin-starred chef Jordi Llobet.

SANT JOAN DE LES ABADESSES: La Teulería €€
Traditional Catalan
Crta C-38, km 1.5, 17860
Tel 972 72 05 01 **Closed** Wed; Sun dinner; last wk Aug
An elegant restaurant offering such regional dishes as roasted lamb from the Ripollès area. Very good-value gastronomic menu.

SANT POL DE MAR: Sant Pau €€€
Modern Catalan
Carrer Nou 10, 08395
Tel 937 60 06 62 **Closed** Sun & Mon, Thu lunch; 3 wks May & Nov
Carme Ruscalleda, one of the world's best chefs, works her magic here at one of Spain's finest restaurants.

SANT SADURNÍ D'ANOIA: La Cava d'en Sergi €€
Modern Catalan
Carrer de València 17, 08770
Tel 938 91 16 16 **Closed** Mon, Sun dinner (all day last Sun of the month); 3 wks Aug
Stylish restaurant serving modernized Catalan classics with a wonderful range of local wines.

SANTA CRISTINA D'ARO: Can Roquet €€
Mediterranean
Plaça de l'Església, Romanyà de la Selva, 17246
Tel 972 83 30 81
Tasty modern French and Catalan cuisine, and a lovely terrace overlooking fields and woods.

SITGES: Cinnamon €
Fusion
Passeig de Pujades 2, Vallpineda, 08750
Tel 938 94 71 66 **Closed** Mon & Tue; Wed, Thu & Sun dinner
Delicious Asian fusion cuisine in a lovely old farmhouse. Hosts DJ sessions and other events.

For more information on types of restaurants see page 577

SITGES: El Pou €
Tapas
Sant Pau 5, 08770
Tel *931 28 99 21* **Closed** *Tue; Mon, Wed & Thu lunch in winter*
In the old centre, this relaxed restaurant offers a great selection of classic and modern tapas.

TARRAGONA: La Cuineta €
Mediterranean
Baixada del Patriarca 2, 43003
Tel *977 22 61 01* **Closed** *dinner; Sun*
A delightful little restaurant in the historic quarter serving fresh Mediterranean dishes. Great-value lunch menu for €15.

TARRAGONA: Aq €€
Modern Catalan
Carrer Les Coques 7, 43003
Tel *977 21 59 54* **Closed** *Sun & Mon*
Exciting contemporary cuisine by chef Ana Ruiz is served up in this smart dining room. The lunch menu is great value.

TARRAGONA: Sol-Ric €€
Mediterranean
Avenida Via Augusta 227, 43007
Tel *977 23 20 32* **Closed** *Mon; Sun dinner*
Divine seafood and other regional fare in an elegant setting with a great summer terrace.

TARRAGONA: Les Coques €€€
Traditional Catalan
Carrer Sant Llorenç 15, 43003
Tel *977 22 83 00* **Closed** *Sun*
A long-established favourite in the old city serving sophisticated regional dishes.

TORTOSA: Sant Carles €
Traditional Catalan
Rambla de Felip Pedrell 13, 43500
Tel *977 44 10 48* **Closed** *Sun*
Family-run restaurant with hearty, home-made Catalan cuisine. The menu focuses on seafood.

Outdoor seating at Restaurant Canteré in Hecho

VALLGORGUINA: Can Barrina €€
Traditional Catalan
Crta de Palautordera E, 08469
Tel *938 47 30 65*
Beautiful country hotel and restaurant in Montseny Natural Park. Delicious food, splendid views and a charming terrace.

VIC: D. O. Vic €€
Modern Catalan
Sant Miquel de Sants 16, 08500
Tel *938 83 23 96* **Closed** *Mon & Sun; 2 wks Aug*
Small, minimalist restaurant serving outstanding Catalan cuisine with a creative touch.

Aragón

AÍNSA: Restaurante Bodegón de Mallacán €
Regional Spanish
Plaza Mayor 6, 22330
Tel *974 50 09 77*
Hotel Posada Real's restaurant offers a taste of medieval times. The wild boar marinated in red wine is a must-try.

AÍNSA: Callizo €€
Modern Spanish
Plaza Mayor, 22330
Tel *974 40 03 85*
Refined, beautifully presented and imaginative cuisine served in this elegant restaurant on the main square.

ALBARRACÍN: Rincón del Chorro €
Regional Spanish
C/ Chorro 15, 44100
Tel *978 71 01 12* **Closed** *Mon, Sun dinner; winter: Mon–Thu & Fri–Sun dinner*
Mega portions are piled high on your plate at this Albarracín staple. Oxtail stew is a popular choice to get your teeth into.

ANCILES: Restaurante Ansils €
Regional Spanish
C/ General Ferraz 6, 22469
Tel *974 55 11 50* **Closed** *Mon–Fri lunch in winter*
Nestled in a picturesque Pyrenees village, this place specializes in local Valle de Benasque cuisine. Avant-garde decor.

CATALAYUD: Mesón de La Dolores €
Regional Spanish
C/ Sancho y Gil 4, 50300
Tel *976 88 90 55*
The staff wear period costumes at this hotel-restaurant. Relaxed mood and informal atmosphere.

DARACO: Restaurante Ruejo €
Modern Spanish
C/ Mayor 88, 50360
Tel *976 54 50 71*
This classy joint has an inventive menu, featuring octopus salad and cheese and honey ice cream.

ESQUEDES: Venta del Sotón €€
Regional Spanish
Carretera A-132 Huesca-Puente la Reina km 14, 22810
Tel *974 27 02 41* **Closed** *Mon; Sun & Tue dinner*
Sample the tasting menu at this ivy-clad, slate-roofed establishment. The large circular chimney is typical of Pyrenean properties.

FRAGA: +Billauba €€
Regional Spanish
Avenida de Aragón 41E, 22520
Tel *974 47 41 67* **Closed** *Sun; Mon–Thu dinner; 1 wk Jan, 2 wks Aug*
Every season marks a new menu with dishes crafted from freshly sourced ingredients.

GRAUS: Restaurante El Criticón €
Traditional Spanish
Hotel Palacio del Obispo, Plaza Coreche, 222430
Tel *974 54 59 00* **Closed** *Sun–Thu dinner*
A temple to classic Spanish food named for a book by Baltasar Gracían, who lived in Graus.

HECHO: Restaurante Canteré €
Modern Spanish
C/ Aire 1, 22720
Tel *974 37 52 14*
Enjoy the popular bar at ground level before moving up to this cutting-edge restaurant with thematic seasonal menus.

DK Choice

HUESCA: El Origen €
Modern Spanish
Plaza de la Justicia 4, 22001
Tel *974 22 97 45*
Old meets new at this central Huesca spot, which, although commited to Aragonese cuisine, whips up some delightful dishes from across the country. Opt for the fixed-price tasting menu. Vegetarians are well catered for here. There is a children's playground to keep the kids amused as well.

JACA: La Tasca de Ana €
Tapas
C/ Ramiro I 3, 22700
Tel *974 36 47 26* **Closed** *2 wks May & Sep; winter: Mon–Fri lunch*
Efficient waiters serve a variety of tapas treats at this reasonably priced bar.

Contemporary, sleek dining room at Saboya 21, Tarazona

SOS DEL REY CATÓLICO:
La Cocina del Principal €€
Spanish
C/ Fernando El Católico 13, 50680
Tel *948 88 83 48*
Fresh, locally sourced fruit
and vegetables are used at this
establishment, located in the
centre of the medieval village.
Classic Spanish meat dishes.

TARAZONA: Saboya 21 €€
Traditional Spanish
C/ Marrodán 34, 50500
Tel *976 64 35 15* **Closed** *Mon*
Light, bright dining room boasts
a menu to match its decor. Local
meat, seafood and vegetable
dishes on offer.

TERUEL: Restaurante Yain €
Traditional Spanish
Plaza de la Judería 9, 44001
Tel *978 62 40 76* **Closed** *Mon & Sun;*
Tue–Thu dinner
Located in the town's Jewish
quarter, this establishment
prides itself on the excellence of
its sommellier. It takes its name
from the Hebrew word for wine.

TERUEL: Restaurante Rufino €€
Traditional Spanish
C/ Ronda Ambeles 36, 44001
Tel *978 60 55 26* **Closed** *Sun &*
Mon dinner
This small, stylish restaurant
specializing in truffles draws
large crowds.

ZARAGOZA: Palomeque €
Tapas
C/ Agustín Palomeque 11, 50004
Tel *976 21 40 82* **Closed** *Sun*
Come here for tapas in the
morning and more substantial
meals during lunch and dinner.
Presentation is sheer artistry.

ZARAGOZA: La Rinconada
de Lorenzo €€
Modern Spanish
Calle La Salle 3, 50006
Tel *976 55 51 08*

Award-winning tapas and choice
traditional recipes at this long-
established local favourite.

ZARAGOZA: El Chalet €€€
Modern Spanish
C/ Santa Teresa de Jesús 25, 50006
Tel *976 56 91 04* **Closed** *Mon,*
Sun dinner
This two-floor converted villa,
just around the corner from Real
Zaragoza's home ground, has a
striking glass canopy. Tasty,
creatively presented dishes.

Valencia and Murcia

ALICANTE: Rincón Gallego €€
Seafood
Plaza del Ayuntamiento 7, 03002
Tel *965 14 00 14* **Closed** *Mon*
Galician restaurant serving tapas
and regional dishes such as *pulpo
a la gallega* (steamed octopus)
and *percebes* (goose barnacles).

BENIMANTELL: L'Obrer €
Traditional Spanish
Crta de Alcoi 25, 03516
Tel *965 88 50 88* **Closed** *Sun;*
dinner (except Fri & Sat in Aug)
Elegant restaurant with charming
decor serving classic Spanish fare.

CARAVACA DE LA CRUZ:
El Casón de los Reyes €
Traditional Spanish
Crta Granada 11, 30400
Tel *968 72 22 47*
A welcoming place with tasty
tapas, meals featuring local recipes
and a great-value set lunch.

FORCALL: Mesón de la Villa €
Traditional Spanish
Plaza Mayor 8, 12310
Tel *964 17 11 25* **Closed** *Mon*
Vaulted restaurant located in
16th-century cellars below the
town hall. Great-value dishes,
plus a choice of home-made
desserts and wines.

LORCA: Paredes €€
Traditional Spanish
C/ de Granada 588, 30800
Tel *626 27 77 25* **Closed** *Mon;*
Tue–Fri dinner
Small, welcoming restaurant
serving tasty Spanish cuisine.
Good meat and seafood dishes.

DK Choice

MORELLA: Casa Roque €
Fusion
Calle Cuesta de San Juan 1, 12300
Tel *964 16 03 36* **Closed** *Mon*
(except Aug); Sun dinner
This widely sought-after eating
spot is located in an old stone
mansion high in the wild
Mestrat region of inland
Castellón. The eclectic range
of dishes includes such
gastronomic delights as steak
with truffles in puff pastry. With
a superb *menú de degustación*
and a good-value menu of
the day.

ONDARA: Casa Pepa €€€
Traditional Spanish
Partida de Pamís 7–30, 03760
Tel *965 76 66 06* **Closed** *Mon;*
Jul & Aug: lunch
Enjoy Michelin-star food in a
pleasant old mansion amid orange
and olive trees. Expect well-
executed, sophisticated dishes.

VALENCIA: L'Estimat €€
Seafood
*Avenida de Neptuno 16, Playa de las
Arenas*
Tel *963 71 10 18* **Closed** *Tue;*
Mon & Sun dinner
Perhaps the best seafood spot on
the entire Valencia beachfront.
Wide selection of set menus and
an excellent à la carte choice.

VALENCIA: La Salita €€
Modern Spanish
Calle Séneca 12, 46021
Tel *963 81 75 16* **Closed** *Sun*
Well-presented contemporary
cuisine from top chef Begoña
Rodrigo, who changes the menu
every fortnight in order to feature
the best seasonal produce.

Madrid
Old Madrid

Casa Revuelta €
Tapas **Map** 4 E3
*C/ Latoneros 3 (off Plaza Puerta
Cerrada), 28005*
Tel *915 21 45 16*
This long-established classic
boasts a colourfully tiled interior
and serves tasty local dishes.

Bright and quirky interior at Delic, Madrid

La Ciudad Invisible €
Café **Map** 4 E1
Costanilla de los Ángeles 7, 28013
Tel *915 42 25 40* **Closed** *Mon*
Do a spot of reading at this stylish yet relaxed travel book-shop and café-bar. It offers a variety of light meals, tapas and wine, and regularly features changing art exhibitions.

DK Choice

Delic €
Café **Map** 4 D3
Plaza de la Paja s/n, 28005
Tel *913 64 54 50* **Closed** *Mon lunch*
A hip favourite on a charming square, Delic is perfect for a lazy breakfast or a tasty light lunch – try the leek tart or the Japanese dumplings. With wonderful tarts, muffins and brownies, it is also a great stop for tea and cakes in the afternoons. Later on, come for cocktails and occasional live music.

Emma y Julia €
Italian **Map** 4 E3
Calle Cava Baja 19, 28005
Tel *913 66 10 23*
Actors, artists and even the royal family are regulars at this popular restaurant that had the first gluten-free menu in the city. Serves some of the best pizzas, too.

Le Petit Bistrot €
French **Map** 7 A3
Plaza de Matute 5, 28012
Tel *914 29 62 55* **Closed** *Mon*
Le Petit Bistrot is a charming place with wooden tables that serves classics such as French onion soup and duck *magret* (breast). Great-value set lunch.

El Abrazo de Vergara €€
Modern Spanish **Map** 4 D2
C/ Vergara 10, 28013
Tel *915 42 00 62* **Closed** *Mon*

Choose the rice with wild mushrooms and truffles or a selection of goumet tapas – perhaps spider crab croquettes or cherry *gazpacho* – in this sleek, modern restaurant.

La Bola €€
Traditional Spanish **Map** 4 D1
C/ de la Bola 5, 28013
Tel *913 54 02 07*
Cocido (local stew) cooked in a charcoal grill has been served here in traditional clay pots since 1870. Classic Castilian dishes served in an old-fashioned atmosphere.

La Camarilla €€
Tapas **Map** 4 E3
C/ Cava Baja 21, 28005
Tel *913 54 02 07*
La Camarilla has reinvented tapas in Madrid. Try the acclaimed cheek of Iberian pork with minestrone, in their renovated, bright dining room.

Casa Jacinto €€
Traditional Madrileño **Map** 4 D1
C/ Reloj 20, 28013
Tel *915 42 67 25* **Closed** *Sun*
Hidden behind a humble exterior, Casa Jacinto serves the best *cocido* (local stew) in town.

Casa Lucio €€
Traditional Spanish **Map** 4 E3
C/ Cava Baja 35, 28005
Tel *913 65 32 52*
Since 1974, Lucio's *huevos estrellados* (slummed eggs) are a speciality of this eatery. Just across the street, Lucio's gastro-bar serves tapas and *pintxos*.

La Gastroteca de Santiago €€
Modern Spanish **Map** 4 D2
Plazuela de Santiago 1, 28013
Tel *915 48 07 07*
This place has elaborate dishes and an excellent wine list. Leave space for the artisanal desserts. Fancy atmosphere, charming terrace.

Julián de Tolosa €€
Spanish **Map** 4 D3
C/ Cava Baja 18, 28005
Tel *913 65 82 10* **Closed** *Sun dinner*
A handsome restaurant with exposed brick walls, famous for its huge, succulent steaks cooked on a charcoal brazier.

Naïa €€
Modern Spanish **Map** 4 D3
Plaza de la Paja 3, 28005
Tel *913 66 27 83* **Closed** *Mon*
This chic but relaxed bistro is popular with the boho actor and artist type. Dishes might include a spicy monkfish and scallop stew, or cod with orange and black olives.

Botín €€€
Traditional Madrileño **Map** 4 E3
C/ Cuchilleros 17, 28005
Tel *913 66 42 17*
Listed by the *Guinness Book of Records* as the world's oldest restaurant, Botín is set in a series of rustic interconnected dining rooms and is justly lauded for its superb *cochinillo* (roast suckling pig).

Dstage €€€
Fine Dining **Map** 5 B5
C/ Regueros 8, 28004
Tel *917 02 15 86*
Highly acclaimed chef Diego Guerrero has garnered a string of awards for his stunning cuisine. There is a choice of degustation menus, each with around 12 artistically presented and ever-evolving courses.

La Terraza del Casino €€€
Modern Spanish **Map** 7 A2
C/ Alcalá 15, 28014
Tel *915 32 12 75* **Closed** *Mon*
Dazzling decor and a stunning terrace are matched by impressive adventurous fare by an award-winning chef.

Bourbon Madrid

Café del Círculo de Bellas Artes €
Café **Map** 7 B2
C/ Marqués de Casa Riera 2, 28014
Tel *913 60 54 00*
This airy Art Deco café is located in a beautiful cultural centre, and is worth coming for everything from coffee to a tasty lunch, to evening cocktails.

Lateral Gastrobar €
Tapas **Map** 7 A3
Plaza de Santa Ana 12, 28012
Tel *914 20 15 82*
One of Madrid's best terraces. Offers variety of *pintxos*, which use quality products and merge traditional and avant-garde recipes.

Ainhoa €€
Basque **Map** 5 C5
C/ Bárbara de Braganza 12, 28004
Tel 913 08 27 26
Grilled spring lamb chops and stuffed peppers are some of what's on offer at this classic Basque restaurant. Good-value midweek dinner menu.

Bar Tomate €€
Mediterranean **Map** 5 C4
C/ Fernando el Santo 26, 28010
Tel 917 02 38 70
A fashionable spot for market-fresh dishes like tuna tartare with guacamole or hake with olives and tomatoes. The airy, loft-style interior has big wooden tables, perfect for groups.

Le Cabrera €€
Gastro-bar
Paseo de Recoletos 2, 28001
Tel 913 19 94 57
A gorgeous, designer gastro-bar, Le Cabrera serves exquisite gourmet tapas as well as fabulous cocktails in its retro-plush interior.

Café Gijón €€
Café **Map** 6 D5
C/ Paseo de Recoletos 21, 28004
Tel 915 21 54 25
One of Madrid's famous literary cafés, established in 1887, Gijón serves the classics in a wood-panelled dining room or on the large terrace.

La Casa del Abuelo €€
Tapas **Map** 7 A2
C/ Victoria 12, 28012
Tel 915 21 23 19
La Casa del Abuelo (Grandfather's House) has been in the same family for a century, and the family specializes in delicious prawns served with a local sweet wine and a range of tasty tapas.

Cien Llaves €€
Modern Spanish **Map** 7 C1
C/ Paseo de Recoletos 2, 28001
Tel 915 77 59 55
Located in the old kitchens of the Palacio de Linares. The terrace, a unique outdoor setting in downtown Madrid, has a magical atmosphere, surrounded by greenery. Try the *gazpacho*.

Estado Puro €€
Tapas **Map** 7 A3
C/ San Sebastián 2 (in the Hotel NH Palacio de Tepa), 28012
Tel 913 89 64 90
Super-stylish, with gourmet tapas by celebrated chef Paco Roncero, who takes classic recipes such as *buñuelos de bacalao* (cod puffs) and reinvents them brilliantly.

Taberna del Chato €€
Tapas **Map** 4 F3
C/ Cruz 35, 28012
Tel 915 23 16 29
Exquisite wines, beautifully presented gourmet tapas from ham croquettes to *nidos de langostinos* (langoustine nests) have made this a local favourite.

Palacio Cibeles €€€
Modern Spanish **Map** 7 C1
Plaza Cibeles 1, 6th floor, 28014
Tel 915 23 14 54
The spectacular, Neo-Gothic former post office, now the city hall, houses a modern restaurant on the 6th floor, with fabulous views complementing its contemporary cuisine.

Further Afield

A 2 Velas €
Café **Map** 2 F4
C/ San Vicente Ferrer 16, 28004
Tel 914 46 18 63
Fresh, unusual salads and tasty international dishes, from blinis with smoked salmon to Vietnamese spring rolls, are on offer at this charming, relaxed cafe.

Bodegas La Ardosa €
Tapas **Map** 5 A5
C/ Colón 13, 28004
Tel 915 21 49 79
An old-fashioned tapas bar where you can enjoy *salmorejo cordobés* (a chilled tomato and almond soup) and other staples.

La Pescadería €
Modern Spanish **Map** 4 F1
C/ de la Ballesta 32, 28004
Tel 915 23 90 51
Fancy yet friendly atmosphere. Try the salmon tartar, baby cuttlefish and tuna belly millefeuille.

Le Cabrera's Art-Deco-inspired backlit bar and polished-chrome bar stools, Madrid

Naif Madrid €€
International **Map** 5 A5
C/ San Joaquín 16, 28004
Tel 910 07 20 71
A boho-chic, loft-style restaurant with tasty gourmet burgers, fancy sandwiches and inspired salads. Good for lunch, afternoon coffee and cake, and evening cocktails.

La Tasquita de Enfrente €€
Modern Spanish **Map** 4 F1
C/ Ballesta 6, 28004
Tel 915 32 54 49
There's no menu here: you'll be offered a selection based whatever was freshest at the market. What you can be sure of is authentic Spanish recipes given a modern twist using locally sourced produce. The wines are selected for you that best pair with each dish.

Santceloni €€€
Modern Spanish
Paseo de la Castellana 57, 28046
Tel 912 10 88 40
The late great chef Santi Santamaria is mourned, but his legacy lives on in this spectacular award-winning restaurant. Classic Spanish dishes are reinterpreted with flair and imagination. Impeccable service.

Madrid Province

ALCALÁ DE HENARES:
Hostería del Estudiante €
Traditional Spanish
Calle Colegios 3, 28801
Tel 918 88 03 30
The regional delicacies here have become an institution. Try the famous *migas* (fried breadcrumbs with garlic) and *duelos y quebrantos* (traditional Manchegan dish with scrambled eggs, chorizo and bacon).

DK Choice

ARANJUEZ: Casa José €€€
Modern Spanish
C/ Abastos 32
Tel 918 91 14 88
Casa José is an enchanting restaurant, in a beautifully restored mansion, with sophisticated dishes like leek with broccoli foam and sea anemone, or marinated grouper. Local produce is used wherever possible, and the extensive wine list features more than 250 labels, including interesting boutique wines.

For more information on types of restaurants *see page 577*

CHINCHON: Mesón Cuevas del Vino €
Traditional Spanish
C/ Benito Hortelano 1, 28370
Tel *918 94 02 06* **Closed** *Sun dinner*
A 17th-century mill, now a rustically decorated restaurant, Mesón Cuevas del Vino is a good bet for classic dishes like lamb chops.

EL ESCORIAL: Montia €
Modern Spanish
C/ Calvario 4, 28200
Tel *911 33 69 88* **Closed** *Mon*
This Michelin-starred restaurant serves creative dishes made using organic regional products.

NAVACERRADA: El Rumba €
Modern Spanish
Plaza del Doctor Gereda, 28491
Tel *918 56 04 05* **Closed** *Mon & Tue in winter*
El Rumba does wonderful charcoal-grilled local meats, and a sprinkling of modern dishes like scallops with citrus and *salmorejo*.

SAN LORENZO DE EL ESCORIAL: Casa Zaca €€
Traditional Spanish
C/ Embajadores 6, San Ildefonso, 28200
Tel *921 47 00 87*
A former coaching inn now boasts the town's most elegant restaurant, featuring classic fare, such as *cocido* (chickpea stew), *callos* (beef tripe stew) and a delicious lamb stew.

TOLEDO: Adolfo €€
Modern Spanish
C/ Hombre de Palo 7, 45001
Tel *925 22 73 21*
Dine under a splendid *artesanado* ceiling at Adolfo, where sophisticated versions of Toledano dishes are accompanied by excellent wines.

TOLEDO: El Palacete €€
Traditional Spanish
C/ Soledad 2, 45001
Tel *925 22 53 75*
Housed in an exquisite 11th-century mansion, El Palacete serves the usual Spanish tapas alongside famed local dishes such as roast partridge and duck confit.

Castilla y León

AMPUDIA: El Arambol de Casa del Abad €
Traditional Spanish
Plaza Francisco Martín Gromaz 12, 34191
Tel *979 76 85 00*

Tuck in to substantial dishes like a medieval friar in the old cellar and winepress of San Miguel de Ampudia's residence.

ARANDA DE DUERO: Mesón El Pastor €
Regional Spanish
Plaza de la Virgencilla 11, 09400
Tel *947 50 04 28* **Closed** *Tue lunch*
A prominent wood-burning brick oven takes pride of place, where the regional speciality *lechazo asado* (roasted milk-fed-only lamb) is prepared.

ARÉVALO: Asador Siboney €
Regional Spanish
C/ Figones 4, 05200
Tel *920 30 15 23*
This is one fancy grill housed in a colonial mansion with many works of art. Their signature dish is *cochinillo* (piglet).

ASTORGA: Las Termas €
Regional Spanish
Calle Santiago 1, 24700
Tel *987 60 22 12* **Closed** *Mon*
Suitable for those with big appetites, because the portions are generous. The rare *cocido maragato* (local stew with cabbage, chickpeas and seven different meats) is a speciality.

ATAPUERCA: Comosapiens €
Regional Spanish
Camino de Santiago 24–26, 09199
Tel *947 43 05 01* **Closed** *Wed*
This refurbished straw loft has a menu that brings Castilian-Leonese tradition up to speed.

ÁVILA: Alcaravea €
Regional Spanish
Plaza Catedral 15, 05001
Tel *920 22 66 00* **Closed** *Sun dinner*
The menu here features local staples that have been passed down over the years.

Mesón Cuevas del Vino in Chinchon, for classic fare in a rustic setting

BENAVENTE: El Ermitaño €
Regional Spanish
Carretera Benavente-León km 1, 2, 49600
Tel *980 63 22 13* **Closed** *Mon*
You'll struggle to tell the colour of the crockery at this out-of-the-way restaurant as portions are generous to overflowing.

BURGOS: Cardamomo Vegetariano €
Vegetarian
C/ Jesús María Ordoño 3, 09004
Tel *947 05 21 52* **Closed** *Mon & Sun*
Burgos may be famous for its cheese, but the menu at this central spot is virtually vegan.

BURGOS: La Favorita €
Pinchos
C/ Avellanos 8, 09003
Tel *947 20 59 49*
Delve into tasty snacks at this urban tavern. Plenty of vegetarian-friendly options.

CANEDO: Prada a Tope-Palacio de Canedo €
Regional Spanish
C/ La Iglesia s/n, 24546
Tel *987 56 33 66*
Hearty fare for the hungry includes chorizo sausages marinated in wine.

CARRIÓN DE LOS CONDES: La Corte €€
Regional Spanish
C/ Santa María 36, 34120
Tel *979 88 01 38* **Closed** *Fri (except Aug); mid-Oct–mid-Apr*
Refuel while walking the Camino de Santiago at this hostel restaurant, specializing in filling Castilian cuisine. Open for breakfast, lunch and dinner.

COVARRUBIAS: Casa Galin €
Regional Spanish
Plaza Doña Urraca 4, 09346
Tel *974 36 47 26* **Closed** *Tue, Sun dinner*
Indulge in Castilian-style fare here, with salty *sopa castellana* (garlic soup) and the classic *olla podrida* (a pork and bean stew).

EL BURGO DE OSMA: Virrey Palafox €
Traditional Spanish
C/ Universidad 7, 42300
Tel *975 34 13 11* **Closed** *Mon & Sun*
Hotel restaurant boasts suckling roast piglet as its signature dish.

GUIJUELO: El Pernil Ibérico €
Traditional Spanish
C/ Chinarral 62, 37770
Tel *923 58 14 02*
Enjoy excellent cold meats at this tavern. If you don't leave full enough, you can buy them, too.

Elegant place settings at El Rincon de Antonio, Zamora

LEÓN: La Gitana €
Regional Spanish
C/ de las Carnicerías 7, 24003
Tel *987 21 51 71* **Closed** *Thu*
In the pedestrianized Húmedo neighbourhood, La Gitana is a relaxed place – you can use bread to mop up your plate.

LEÓN: Cocinandos €€
Modern Spanish
C/ Campanillas 1, 24008
Tel *987 07 13 78* **Closed** *Mon & Sun*
Marrying style with substance, this Michelin-starred gem offers a sophisticated take on traditional Castilian recipes.

LEÓN: Delirios €€
Modern Spanish
C/ Ave María 2 Bajo, 24007
Tel *987 23 76 99* **Closed** *Mon & Sun dinner (all day Sun in summer)*
This central restaurant, around the corner from the cathedral, is a temple to modern gastronomy. Innovative cuisine, emphasizing the use of local products.

PALENCIA: Asador La Encina €
Regional Spanish
C/ de Casañe 2, 34002
Tel *979 71 09 36* **Closed** *Sun dinner*
Famous for its *tortilla de patata* (Spanish omelette), this modern grill does the simple things well.

PALENCIA: La Traserilla €€
Regional Spanish
C/ de San Marcos 12, 34001
Tel *979 74 54 21*
Also known as Casa de Comidas (House of Food), the old exterior contrasts with the modern decor. Big on meat and vegetables.

SALAMANCA: La Cocina de Toño €
Modern Spanish
C/ de la Gran Vía 20, 37001
Tel *923 26 39 77* **Closed** *Mon lunch, Sun dinner (all day Sun in summer)*

Michelin-starred establishment doing Nouveau Castilian cuisine with a Basque twist.

SALAMANCA: iPan iVino €
Tapas
Calle Felipe Espino 10, 37002
Tel *923 26 86 77*
Colourful wine bar with creative tapas and probably the best wine menu in the city.

SALAMANCA: Zazu Bistro €€
Mediterranean
Plaza de la Libertad 8, 37002
Tel *923 26 16 90*
This stylish restaurant pays tribute to Mediterranean cuisine with nods to classic French and Italian recipes. Wine list to match.

SEGOVIA: El Bernandino €
Traditional Spanish
C/ Cervantes 2, 40001
Tel *921 46 24 77*
Updated Castillian cuisine with traditional roots, served up in a graceful town house. The town's star dish, roast suckling pig, is the house speciality.

SEGOVIA: Cueva de San Esteban €
Traditional Spanish
C/ de Valdeláguila 15, 40001
Tel *921 46 09 82*
The *jamón* hanging from the ceiling gives you an idea how traditional this restaurant is.

SEGOVIA: Restaurante José María €€
Regional Spanish
C/ Cronista Lecea 11, 40001
Tel *921 46 11 11*
Chef José María Ruiz Benito combines Segovian staples with the latest gastronomic fashions.

SIGUENZA: El Doncel €€
Modern Spanish
Paseo de la Alameda 3
Tel *949 39 00 01*

A beautiful 18th-century mansion provides a sublime setting for exciting contemporary cuisine. Extensive wine list.

SORIA: Baluarte €
Modern Spanish
C/ Caballeros 14, 42002
Tel *975 21 36 58* **Closed** *Mon*
Enjoy a fine gastronomic experience during the mushroom and black truffle season.

TORDESILLAS: Bar-Restaurante Figón €
Traditional Spanish
Plaza Pepe Zorita 22, 47100
Tel *983 77 13 98* **Closed** *Wed dinner*
Octopus salad is a popular dish at this laid-back local. A greater menu selection than elsewhere.

VALLADOLID: La Parrilla de San Lorenzo €
Traditional Spanish
C/ Pedro Niño 1, 47001
Tel *983 33 50 88*
Located in the basement of a monastery, this grill is a treasure trove of antiques. The menu is just as traditional with family recipes handed down through generations.

DK Choice

ZAMORA: El Rincón de Antonio €€
Regional Spanish
C/ de la Rúa de los Francos 6, 49001
Tel *980 53 70*
Housed in a 19th-century mansion in medieval Zamora, the kitchen utilizes local products to recreate the food of Zamora of old. There are bite-sized tapas offerings at the bar. Choose from a cellar offering 800 different vintages, along with cava, liqueurs and spirits.

Castilla-La Mancha

DK Choice

ALBACETE: Álvarez €
Regional Spanish
C/ Salamanca 12, 02001
Tel *967 21 82 69* **Closed** *Mon*
If you grew up in Castilla-La Mancha, a meal here would be a nostalgic experience. For this is food Mama used to make. There are croquettes of various stuffings, *gazpacho manchego* (meat-based stew) and *cordero asado* (roast lamb). Desserts include a ricotta and almond flan.

ALBACETE: Nuestro Bar €
Regional Spanish
C/ Alcalde Conangla 102, 02002
Tel 967 24 33 73
Part bar, part restaurant, part
museum. Traditional agricultural
equipment and antique cooking
utensils adorn the walls.

**ALBACETE: Restaurante
Don Gil** €€
Modern Spanish
C/ Baños 2, 02004
Tel 967 23 97 85 **Closed** Mon
Located alongside the Mercado
de Villacerrada, this is where
Albacete's in crowd come to eat.

ALCOCER: Casa Goyo €
Regional Spanish
C/ Mayor, 58, 19125
Tel 949 35 50 03 **Closed** Mon
Hostal España's in-house
restaurant is a rustic affair. Make
sure you go with an appetite
because the portions are huge.

ALMAGRO: El Corregidor €
Regional Spanish
Calle de Jerónimo Ceballos 2, 13270
Tel 926 86 06 48 **Closed** Mon
Housed in an 18th-century
palace, there are different dining
rooms that surround a traditional
patio. Classic Manchegan cuisine.

**CIUDAD REAL: Pago del
Vicario** €€
Traditional Spanish
Carretera Ciudad Real–Porzuna, km
16, 13196
Tel 926 66 60 27
Overlooking the barrel room and
the vineyard, this place offers a
fusion cuisine. The Manchegan
roast lamb goes superbly with
the wines from one of the best
wine cellars of the region.

CUENCA: Raff €
Tapas
C/ Federico García Lorca 3, 16004
Tel 969 69 08 55 **Closed** Sun

The stylish, contemporary
ambience is in contrast to
the traditional tapas and raciónes
on offer.

CUENCA: El Secreto €
Regional Spanish
Calle Alfonso VIII, 81, 16001
Tel 678 61 13 01 **Closed** Wed,
Tue dinner
Feast off the à la carte menu
or share the mouthwatering
tapas. Special set menus
for vegetarians.

CUENCA: Figón de Huécar €€
Spanish
C/ Julián Romero 6, 16001
Tel 629 06 33 66 **Closed** Mon
The erstwhile family residence of
a famous local singer enjoys
spectacular views over Huécar
Gorge. Its terrace is lit up at night.

**GUADALAJARA: Amparito
Roca** €€€
Modern Spanish
C/ de Toledo 19, 19002
Tel 949 21 46 39 **Closed** Sun dinner
Tiled floor, wooden walls and a
flower on every table makes
eating at this experimental
restaurant feel like an event.

ILLESCAS: El Bohío €€€
Modern Spanish
Avenida Castilla-La Mancha 81, 45200
Tel 925 51 11 26
Chef Pepe Rodríguez has been
awarded a Michelin star for the
traditional yet inventive menu
at El Bohío.

**MARCHAMALO: Restaurante
Las Llaves** €€
Modern Spanish
Plaza Mayor 16, 19180
Tel 949 25 04 85 **Closed** Mon
Pass through the grand portal
of a 16th-century building
to discover a suitably elegant
interior. Foie gras features on
the menu.

OCAÑA: Restaurante Palio €€
Regional Spanish
C/ Mayor 12, 45300
Tel 925 13 00 45 **Closed** Mon
This restaurant prides itself on its
attention to detail – its home-
made bread uses stone-ground
organic flour.

OROPESA: Tierra €€€
Modern Spanish
C/ de la Oropesa 9, 45572
Tel 925 45 75 34
Gourmet dishes can be found in
this Michelin-starred restaurant,
located in the luxurious Hotel
Valdepalacios. Its name, meaning
"land", refers to the area's richness
of culture, agriculture and
cuisine. Warm atmosphere.

**SAN PEDRO: Restaurante
Montecristo** €
Regional Spanish
C/ de la Libertad, 14, 03360 (Albacete)
Tel 967 36 44 55 **Closed** Tue
Red meat and fresh fish
dominate the menu at this
established riverside restaurant.

**TALAVERA DE LA REINA:
Taberna Mingote** €
Tapas
Plaza Federico García Lorca 5, 45600
Tel 925 82 56 33 **Closed** Wed
Small tables give this tavern a
lively atmosphere, even when
it's not packed. Tapas options
change during the week.

**TALAVERA DE LA REINA:
Penalty** €€
Seafood
C/ de la Cabeza del Moro 5, 45600
Tel 987 23 76 99 **Closed** Mon
Ensuring the highest quality of
ingredients, Penalty imports its
fish and shellfish from Galicia,
one of Spain's most noted areas
for seafood.

**TARANCÓN: Restaurante
Hospedería, Finca La Estacada** €€
Regional Spanish
Carretera Nnal 400 km 103, 16400
Tel 969 32 71 88
Housed in a luxury complex
which includes a hotel, spa and
vineyard, this restaurant offers
excellent views of the vines
which produce its highly
regarded wines.

TOLEDO: Casa Aurelio €
Regional Spanish
Plaza del Ayuntamiento 8, 45002
Tel 925 22 77 16 **Closed** Tue
Dishes to make your mouth
water at this Toledo institution
include the delectable crêpe de
bacalao con crema de cigala and
pâté de sardinas (cod crepe with
lobster cream and sardine pâté).

The elegant Restaurante Hospedería, Finca La Estacada, Tarancón

TOLEDO: Madre Tierra €
Vegetarian
Bajada de Tripería 2, 45001
Tel *925 22 35 71*　　**Closed** *Tue, Mon dinner*
Enjoy the fruits (and vegetables) of Mother Earth at Toledo's first vegetarian restaurant, complemented with extensive tea and wine lists.

TOLEDO: Restaurante Locum €€
Regional Spanish
C/ de Locum 6, 45001
Tel *925 22 32 35*　　**Closed** *Tue*
A short walk from Toledo's cathedral you'll find a traditional restaurant featuring the likes of *rabo del toro* (stewed bull tail).

TOLEDO: Adolfo €€€
Modern Spanish
C/ del Hombre de Palo 7, 45001
Tel *925 22 73 21*　　**Closed** *Sun dinner*
The pleasant roof terrace offers panoramic views of the city below. Wine is sourced from the restaurant's private vineyard.

VALDEPEÑAS: La Fonda de Alberto €
Modern Spanish
C/ del Cristo 67, 13300
Tel *926 31 61 76*　　**Closed** *Mon*
Cold soups and salads are the highlights of summer menus while hearty red meat dishes feature in winter. Along with a wine list 300+ strong.

VALDEPEÑAS: Venta del Comendador de la Villa de Valdepeñas €
Regional Spanish
C/ de Bernardo Balbuena 2, 13300
Tel *926 31 22 26*
Food like grandmother used to make: fine breads with thyme, rosemary and mint flavours. Good, central location.

Extremadura

ALANGE: Meson Trinidad €
Regional Spanish
Encomienda 51, 06840
Tel *924 36 50 66*　　**Closed** *Tue*
This family-run inn serves authentic local dishes in a friendly atmosphere with spectacular views of the castle.

CÁCERES: El Figón de Estaquio €
Regional Spanish
Plaza de San Juan 12–14, 10003
Tel *927 24 43 62*
In the heart of the historic centre, this long-standing and resolutely old-fashioned restaurant has been preparing tasty local dishes since 1947.

CÁCERES: Torre de Sande €
Modern Spanish
Calle de los Condes 3, 10003
Tel *927 21 11 47*　　**Closed** *Mon*
On the historic main square, this modern restaurant offers a wide range of tapas and à la carte dishes based on local recipes.

CÁCERES: Atrio €€€
Regional Spanish
Plaza de San Mateo 1, 10003
Tel *927 24 29 28*
One of the finest restaurants in Spain, with two Michelin stars, Atrio serves modern cuisine with sterling service.

GUADALUPE: Hospedería del Real Monasterio €
Regional Spanish
Plaza de Juan Carlos I s/n, 10140
Tel *927 36 70 00*
Located in a Plateresque cloister and run by Franciscans, this place is popular for its traditional roasted lamb.

MERIDA: Merida Palace €€
Regional Spanish
Plaza España 19, 06800
Tel *924 38 38 00*
This restaurant, in a 16th-century palace-cum-hotel, offers elegant dining in relaxed surroundings.

TRUJILLO: Corral del Rey €
Regional Spanish
Plazuela Corral del Rey 2 (Plaza Mayor), 10200
Tel *927 32 30 71*　　**Closed** *winter: Sun & Wed dinner; summer: all day Sun*
Specializing in roasted meat and fish with an extensive wine & cigar menu. Off the main square.

TRUJILLO: La Troya €
Regional Spanish
Plaza Mayor 10, 10200
Tel *927 32 13 64*
On the main square, this 16th-century *mesón* serves typical Spanish cuisine in hearty portions – the lamb stew is recommended.

ZAFRA: Ramirez €
Regional Spanish
Avenida San Miguel 18, 06300 Zafra
Tel *924 55 51 38*
Lively lunchtime or relaxed evening dining in this centrally located diner which offers an extensive range of local cuisine.

ZAFRA: Parador €€
Regional Spanish
Plaza Corazon de Maria 7, 06300
Tel *924 55 45 40*
Soak up the surroundings at this 15th-century castle while tasting tapas or dining from the à la carte menu.

The warm red-and-white coloured interior of Restaurante Palio, Ocaña

Seville

El Arenal

Bodeguita Casablanca €
Tapas　　**Map** 3 C2
C/ Adolfo Rodriguez Jurado 12, 41002
Tel *954 22 41 14*　　**Closed** *Sun; Sat dinner*
Family-run tapas bar with a no-frills decor of tiles and barrel tables. Popular with locals.

La Brunilda Tapas €
Tapas　　**Map** 3 B1
C/ Galera 5, 41001
Tel *954 22 04 81*　　**Closed** *Sun dinner*
Bright, modern bar with excellent tapas, such as succulent ox sirloin with thyme potatoes and chicken breast with polenta and wild mushrooms.

Santa Cruz

Casa Plácido €
Tapas　　**Map** 6 E4
Mesón del Moro 5, 41004
Tel *954 56 39 71*　　**Closed** *Thu*
Diminutive tapas bar in heart of the old quarter. Traditional decor of tiles and bullfight posters, plus hanging hams. Fino from the barrel. Excellent tortillas.

DK Choice

La Albahaca €€
Traditional Spanish **Map** 4 D2
Plaza de Santa Cruz 12, 41004
Tel *954 22 07 14*
If you want to splash out and savour a gourmet meal in a truly lavish eating spot, then look no further than La Albahaca. Located in a stately 1920s renovated mansion in the heart of the historic Santa Cruz quarter, it has four opulent, individually decorated dining rooms. Quality French-Basque specialities include sea bass with plum and raisins.

For more information on types of restaurants *see page 577*

Casa Robles €€
Traditional Spanish   Map 3 C1
C/ Alvarez Quintero 58, 41001
Tel 954 56 32 72
Prize-winning eating spot with
stunning decor of paintings,
statues and coloured tiles.
Great fish and shellfish selection.
Cathedral views from the
restaurant terrace and the best
wine list in Seville.

Don Raimundo €€
Traditional Spanish   Map 3 C1
C/ Argote de Molina 26, 41004.
Tel 954 22 33 55
Ex-17th-century convent with
stone walls, ceiling beams and
huge chandeliers. Serves
splendid *jabali al horno* (oven-
cooked wild boar).

Doña Elvira €€
Traditional Spanish   Map 3 C2
Plaza de Doña Elvira 6, 41004
Tel 954 29 36 98
Legendary Don Juan has links
with this traditional Sevillan
restaurant. Dine indoors or
alfresco, on the open-air terrace.
Known for excellent *gazpachos*
and paellas.

Further Afield

Bar Antojo €
Fusion   Map 1 C3
Calatrava 44, 41002
Tel 955 42 53 37
A unique bar with mismatched
furniture, bookshelves and a
relaxed atmosphere, Bar Antojo
offers creative takes on regional
comfort food, with a bit of
international fusion thrown in for
good measure.

Con Tenedor €
Mediterranean   Map 2 E4
C/ San Luis 50, 41003
Tel 954 91 63 33   **Closed** Mon–Thu
lunch

Top-value spot with friendly
service, serving dishes made
from fresh market produce. Also
hosts art exhibitions on Mondays
and Saturdays.

Espacio Eslava €
Seafood   Map 1 C4
C/ Eslava 3, 41002
Tel 954 90 65 68   **Closed** Mon;
Sun dinner
Simple, unadorned eating spot
featuring creative Andalusian
cuisine. First-rate seafood and
salads and inventive choice of
tapas. Hugely popular.

Mesón Guadalquivir €
Traditional Spanish   Map 4 E3
C/ Camilo José Cela 1, 41018
Tel 954 92 41 39   **Closed** Sun
High-standard, reasonably priced
Andalusian cuisine in a chic-yet-
traditional city favourite.
Exceptional *chipiron a la plancha*
(freshly grilled squid with rice)
and home-made lemon sorbet.

Torre de los Perdigones €
Fusion   Map 2 D3
C/ Resolana s/n, 41009
Tel 954 90 93 53
Restaurant quietly set in tower
amid parklands. Dishes include
tuna *tataki* (seared, marinated
tuna) and wild mushroom and
asparagus risotto. Summer
terrace with live music.

DK Choice

Vega 10 €
Fusion   Map 3 B3
Rosario Vega 10, 41011
Tel 955 23 77 48   **Closed** Sun
Vega 10 offers creative dishes
that change according to
season, using fresh, high-quality
ingredients. The tapas menu
changes daily as well. Also
boasts a good wine selection.

Abades Triana €€€
Seafood   Map 3 B3
C/ Betis 69, 41010
Tel 954 28 64 59
Fabulous riverside establishment
with stunning vierws. Windowed
El Cubo section has "floating
glass" floor. Superb international
and Mediterranean cuisine. Also
exquisite tasting menus.

Andalusia

ALGECIRAS: Montes €
Seafood
C/ Juan Morrison 27, 11201
Tel 956 65 42 07
Simple, unpretentious place with
good choice of vegetarian and
seafood rice dishes. Great *sopa de
picadillo* (ham, onion and potato
broth). Popular with locals.

ALGECIRAS: La Cabaña €€
Traditional Spanish
Avenida Agua Marina 5, 11203
Tel 956 66 73 79   **Closed** Mon
Warm, traditional restaurant with
indoor and terrace dining.
Offerings include Galician style
octopus and charcoal-grilled
sirloin steaks.

ALMERÍA: Casa Sevilla €
Seafood
C/ Rueda López s/n, 04001
Tel 950 23 58 19   **Closed** Sun
Sociable family restaurant serving
fresh seafood dishes. Monthly
wine tastings.

**ALMERÍA: Rincón de Juan
Pedro** €
Traditional Spanish
C/ Federico Castro 2, 04003
Tel 950 23 58 19
Almeria town tapas favourite
with larger *raciónes* for the extra-
hungry. Serves pungent hams,
chorizos and cheeses, plus local
specialities like *trigo a la cortijera*
(wheat berry and sausage stew).

ALMERÍA: Valentin €
Seafood
C/ Tenor Iribarne 19, 04001
Tel 950 26 44 75   **Closed** Mon; Sep
Popular *marisqueria* (restaurant
specializing in shellfish) in central
Almeria. Everything is market-fresh.

ALMERÍA: Club de Mar €€
Seafood
Playa de Almadrabillas 1, 04007
Tel 950 23 50 48   **Closed** Tue
Swish restaurant in Almeria's
prestigious yacht club. Seafront
terrace. Renowned for its
bouillabaisse and fried fish
platters. The restaurant does not
accept credit cards.

Abades Triana seafood restaurant in Seville

Key to Price Guide *see page 582*

DK Choice

ALMONTE: Aires de Doñana (La Choza del Rocio) €
Traditional Spanish
Avenida de la Canaliega 1
Tel *959 44 22 89*   **Closed** *Mon*
This converted *choza* (large thatched hut) is typical of the Doñana park in which it's located. Beautifully decorated, it enjoys splendid terrace views across woods and waterways. The creative Andalusian cuisine offers specialities like *revuelto marismeño* (scrambled eggs with local herbs).

ALMONTE: El Tamborilero €
Traditional Spanish
C/ Unamuno 15, 21730
Tel *959 40 69 55*   **Closed** *Sun, 1–15 Jul*
Former bodega with traditional decor. The chef invites you into the kitchen to choose from their selections of the day.

ALMUÑECAR: By Larius €€
Traditional Spanish
Paseo de Velilla 9, 18690
Tel *958 63 93 58*   **Closed** *Mon & Sun lunch*
Located by the beach. Exquisitely prepared traditional favourites include duck breast, turbot and grilled lamb chops and tenderloin.

BAEZA: Casa Juanito €
Traditional Spanish
Av del Alcalde Puché Pardo 57, 23440
Tel *953 74 00 40*
Cosy family-run place in a historical town. Divine home-made desserts.

BAEZA: El Sarmiento €€
Traditional Spanish
Plaza del Arcediano 10, 23440
Tel *953 74 03 23*   **Closed** *Mon*
Tucked away between the city wall and cathedral, this place offers abundant plates of fresh vegetables and a variety of meats.

BENALMADENA: La Fuente €
Traditional Spanish
Plaza de España 9, 29639
Tel *952 56 94 66*   **Closed** *Mon*
Charming restaurant with tables on the square. Try the king prawns in a mild chilli, ginger and coriander butter with rice.

BUBION: Teide €
Traditional Spanish
C/ Carretera s/n,18412
Tel *958 76 30 37*   **Closed** *2nd half Jun*
Elegant stone-built restaurant in Alpujarran village. The simple menu includes *migas* (fried breadcrumbs with garlic) and *choto asado* (roast kid).

Appetizing tapas at El Molino de la Romera, Carmona

CÁDIZ: Balandro €
Seafood
Alameda Apodaca 22, 11004
Tel *956 22 09 92*
Restaurant in converted 18th-century mansion overlooking the bay. Superb seafood, plus a good selection of meat dishes.

CÁDIZ: Freiduria Cervecería Las Flores €
Seafood
Plaza Topete 4, 11001
Tel *956 22 61 12*
Down-to-earth restaurant specializing in shellfish and fried fish platters. See your choice cooked on the spot.

CÁDIZ: Ventorillo del Chato €€
Seafood
Via Augusta Julia, 11011
Tel *956 25 00 25*   **Closed** *Sun dinner (except Aug)*
This 18th-century seaside inn specializes in fresh fish. Try the *corvino al vapor* (steamed sea bass).

CARBONERAS: El Cabo €€
Seafood
Paseo Marítimo 67, 04140
Tel *950 13 06 24*   **Closed** *Mon*
This friendly beachside restaurant close to Cabo de Gata National Park does imaginative seafood.

CARMONA: Goya €
Traditional Spanish
C/ Prlm 2, 41410
Tel *954 14 30 60*
Typical Sevillan establishment off the city's main square.

CARMONA: El Molino de la Romera €
Traditional Spanish
C/ Sor Angela de la Cruz 8, 41410
Tel *954 14 20 00*   **Closed** *Mon*
Converted from a 15th-century Moorish olive oil mill and granary,

this evocative place serves quality regional dishes, such as succulent venison in red wine.

CARMONA: Parador Alcazar del Rey Don Pedro €
Traditional Spanish
C/ del Alcazar s/n, 41410
Tel *954 14 10 10*
Stylish, traditional parador restaurant with Moorish patio and vaulted, antique-furnished dining room.

CAZORLA: Meson Leandro €
Traditional Spanish
C/ Hoz 3, 23470
Tel *953 72 06 32*   **Closed** *Wed, 2nd half Jun*
Michelin-recommended, in lovely Jaén village bordering a National Park. Famed for its meat dishes.

CÓRDOBA: La Boqueria €
Traditional Spanish
C/ Maria la Judia s/n, 14011
Tel *957 40 25 62*
Gourmet café-restaurant serving market-fresh dishes, such as rice with lobster and Jabugo ham.

CÓRDOBA: Casa Pepe de la Juderia €
Traditional Spanish
C/ Romero 1, 14003
Tel *957 20 07 44*   **Closed** *Sun*
Enduring favourite since 1928. Dine indoors or on the flower-filled patio.

CÓRDOBA: Regadera €
Traditional Spanish
C/ de la Cruz de Rastro 2, 14002
Tel *957 10 14 00*   **Closed** *Mon*
Just steps from the riverfront, Regadera has a fresh appeal and excellent-value menu of the day.

CÓRDOBA: La Almudaina €€
Traditional Spanish
Campo Santo de los Mártires 1, 14004
Tel *957 47 43 42*   **Closed** *Sun dinner*
Located in a former bishop's palace. Dishes include *solomillo al foie* (pork sirloin with foie).

CÓRDOBA: San Miguel €€
Traditional Spanish
Plaza San Miguel 1, 14002
Tel *957 47 83 28*   **Closed** *Sun*
Sterling family-run spot. Specialities include Iberian cured meats, *pisto* (ratatouille) and *manitas de cerdo* (pig's trotters).

EL ROCIO: Restaurante Toruño €
Traditional Spanish
Plaza Acebuchal 22, 21750
Tel *959 44 24 22*
Inviting restaurant with lovely terrace and excellent views. Try one of the rice dishes.

For more information on types of restaurants *see page 577*

FUENGIROLA: Vegetalia €
Vegetarian
C/ Santa Isabel 8, Los Boliches 29640
Tel *952 58 60 31* **Closed** *Sun,*
Jul–Aug
Finnish-owned vegetarian
restaurant with a bargain self-
service lunchtime buffet.
Delicious home-made desserts.

GERENA: Casa Salvi Tapas €
Tapas
Miguel de Cervantes 46, 41860
Tel *955 78 32 72*
Don't let the traditional decor
fool you: the vast selection of
tapas and plates, excellent grilled
meats, wide range of seafood,
and fresh vegetables and
seasonal game.

GIBRALTAR: The Waterfront €€
International
Queensway Quay, Marina Bay
Tel *350 2004 5666* **Closed** *Tue*
A romantic spot with lovely
sunset views, Waterfront offers
a wide choice of food that
includes Cajun chicken, steaks,
fish and vegetarian dishes.

GIBRALTAR: Rib Room €€€
Traditional Spanish
Rock Hotel, Europa Road
Tel *350 2007 3000*
Iconic restaurant in one of
Gibraltar's most distinguished
hotels, serving modern British
cuisine with Iberian and
Moroccan influences.

**GRANADA: Antigua Bodega
Castañeda** €
Traditional Spanish
C/ Elvira 5, 18010
Tel *958 21 54 64*
Archetypal tapas bar with barrels,
beams and colourful tiles. Feast
on Trevélez mountain ham, squid
and sardines and enjoy a chilled
fino on the side.

DK Choice

**GRANADA: Mirador de
Mirayma** €
Traditional Spanish
C/ Pianista Gracia Carrillo 2, 18010
Tel *958 22 82 90* **Closed** *Sun*
dinner
Even in Granada few restaurants
offer such a winning com-
bination of idyllic setting and
quality cuisine. Located beside
the secluded patio of a private
house right inside the Albaicin
it enjoys marvellous city views.
The authentic Andaluz food
includes fresh *remojón* (salad
with salt cod, olives and orange)
and *salmorejo* (thicker version
of *gazpacho*).

Picturesque views from the Rib Room,
Gibraltar

GRANADA: Ruta del Veleta €
Fusion
*Crta Sierra Nevada 136, km 5, 4,
Cenes de la Vega, 18190*
Tel *958 48 61 34* **Closed** *Sun dinner*
Popular regional eating spot on
the old road to Sierra Nevada.
Alpujarran decor and hearty
dishes like roast kid. Seasonal
game and good seafood choice.

**GRANADA: Carmen del San
Miguel** €€
Traditional Spanish
Plaza Torres Bermejas 3, 18009
Tel *958 22 67 23* **Closed** *Sun dinner;
all day Sun in summer*
Attractive restaurant overlooking
the Alhambra, with traditional
dishes, such as rabbit and quail.

GRANADA: Chikito €€
Traditional Spanish
Plaza del Campillo 9, 18009
Tel *958 22 33 64* **Closed** *Wed*
Attractive tapas bar-restaurant.
Try their delicious broad beans
with ham or be brave and dig
into the *tortilla Sacromonte* –
omelette with marrow, brains,
herbs and bull's testicles!

HUELVA: Terranova €
Traditional Spanish
Calle San Sebastian 19, 21004
Tel *959 26 15 07*
Modern environment with an
ample selection of fresh seafood,
fish, meat and vegetables,
impeccably prepared with
innovative twists.

**HUERCAL ALMERIA, VIATOR:
Cueva Blanca** €€€
Fusion
C/ Churre 13, 04240
Tel *950 30 51 37* **Closed** *Mon & Sun*

Cosy cave-restaurant just north
of Almería. Creative dishes include
salmon en sidra (salmon in cider).

JABUGO: Meson Cinco Jotas €
Traditional Spanish
Crta San Juan del Puerto, 21290
Tel *959 12 10 71* **Closed** *Mon*
Unpretentious restaurant in the
birthplace of Spain's greatest
jamón. Home-cured *Jabugo* and
cod with prawns and olives are
among the best dishes.

JAÉN: Taberna Don Sancho €
Traditional Spanish
Avenida de Andalucia 17, 23005
Tel *953 27 51 21*
Friendly, lively tavern with
imaginative versions of
traditional dishes.

JAÉN: Casa Antonio €€
Traditional Spanish
C/ Fermin Palma 3, 23008
Tel *953 27 02 62* **Closed** *Mon; Sun
dinner; Aug*
Elegant restaurant with modern
decor and contemporary
versions of traditional dishes.
Menu changes regularly.

**JEREZ DE LA FRONTERA: Reino
de Leon Gastrobar** €
Fusion
C/ Latorre 8, 11402
Tel *956 32 29 15*
Chic restaurant with dishes such
as mini kebabs of tandoori
Masala chicken, and sea-bass
fillets with champagne cream,
apple slivers and passionfruit.

LA LINEA: La Marina €€
Seafood
*Paseo Maritimo, La Atunara s/n,
11300*
Tel *956 17 15 31* **Closed** *Mon*
Large seaside eating spot with
nautical decor. Great views of bay
and Gibraltar. Delicious *chirlas
marinera* (clams).

LA RINCONADA: El Pela €
Traditional Spanish
Plaza de Rodriguez Montes 2, 41300
Tel *954 79 77 03* **Closed** *Wed*
Down-to-earth Sevillan
restaurant. Try the *arroz negro*
(black rice). Breakfast is served
with *pan prieto de la Algaba*
(local speciality bread).

**LOS BARRIOS: Mesón El
Copo** €€
Seafood
C/ La Almadraba 2 (Palmones), 11369
Tel *956 67 77 10* **Closed** *Sun*
Top beachside seafood eating
spot. Try the fresh local *urta*
(sea bream) and *gallineta*
(Atlantic red fish). Good
home-made desserts.

MÁLAGA: Antigua Casa de la Guardia €
Traditional Spanish
Alameda Principal 18, 29015
Tel *952 21 46 80* **Closed** *Sun*
Vintage 19th-century wine cellar and bar on Málaga's central avenue. Their speciality tipple is dark, rich Pedro Ximénez wine served directly from the barrel.

MÁLAGA: Mesón Astorga €
Traditional Spanish
C/ Gerona 11, 29006
Tel *952 34 25 63* **Closed** *Sun*
Classical Malagueno restaurant with dishes prepared from fresh market produce. Try the fried aubergine with sugar-cane honey.

MÁLAGA: Mesón Cortijo de Pepe €
Traditional Spanish
Plaza de la Merced 2, 29012
Tel *952 22 40 71* **Closed** *Tue*
Popular Andalusian tapas bar in emblematic square adjoining Picasso's birthplace. Good calamari and prawn dishes.

DK Choice

MÁLAGA: El Tintero €
Seafood
Playa del Dedo s/n (El Palo), 29018
Tel *952 20 68 26*
This is without doubt the noisiest restaurant on the Costa del Sol, but don't let that put you off. Its beachside location, sweeping views across the bay and magnificent choice of fish dishes more than compensate. There's no menu. You simply point at the dish you want as waiters vociferously pass by announcing them. Except for lobster they're all more or less the same price. Staff count the plates when you're done to calculate your bill.

MÁLAGA: Café de Paris €€
Fusion
C/ Velez Málaga s/n, 29016
Tel *952 22 50 43* **Closed** *Sun & Mon*
Stylish restaurant serving modern Spanish-Mediterranean dishes including black truffles and *arroz au parmesan* (parmesan rice). Superb *menú de degustación*.

MARBELLA: Altamirano €
Seafood
Plaza Altamirano 3, 29600
Tel *952 82 49 32* **Closed** *Wed, early Jan–mid-Feb*
Good-value family restaurant with garden for alfresco dining. Specialities range from *fritura malagueno* (fried fish platter) to *besugo a la brasa* (barbecued sea bream).

MARBELLA: El Portalón €€€
Traditional Spanish
Crta de Cádiz, km 178, 29600
Tel *952 82 72 80* **Closed** *Sun dinner*
Sumptuously traditional restaurant. Try the *lubina con verduras frescas* (sea bass with fresh vegetables) or *lechona al horno de leña* (suckling pig baked in a wood-fired oven).

MARBELLA: Skina €€€
Fusion
C/ Aduar 12, 29601 **Closed** *Sun, Mon, early Dec, early Jan–early Feb*
Tel *952 76 52 77*
Chic, intimate, old town eating spot with eclectic fusion of dishes from rabbit terrine to sole with artichokes and tomato. Superlative tasting menu.

ORGIVA: El Limonero €
Traditional Spanish
C/ Yanez 27, 18400
Tel *958 78 51 57*
Popular Alpujarran joint serving healthy traditional dishes like *dorada al horno* (oven-baked sea bream). Great salads and pastas.

OSUNA: Doña Guadalupe €
Traditional Spanish
Plaza de Guadalupe 6–8, 41640
Tel *954 81 05 58* **Closed** *Mon, Sun dinner, 2 wks Aug*
Family-run restaurant with outdoor terrace dining. Classic regional fare includes *faisan con arroz* (pheasant and wild rice).

OSUNA: El Mesón del Duque €
Traditional Spanish
Plaza de la Duquesa 1, 41640
Tel *954 81 28 45* **Closed** *Wed*
Fine establishment with terrace overlooking a church. Good choice of Andalusian specialities including home-made meatballs.

PALMA DEL RIO: El Refectorio (Monasterio de San Francisco) €€
Traditional Spanish
Avenida Pio XII 35, 14700
Tel *957 71 01 83*

Dine out in the old rectory of a converted 15th-century monastery. Traditional dishes include game in winter. In summer, dining on the candlelit patio is a must.

PUERTO DE SANTA MARIA: Casa Flores €€
Traditional Spanish
Ribera del Rio 9, 11500
Tel *956 54 35 12*
This stalwart has traditional tiles and bullfight motif decor to go with the traditional menu.

RONDA: Tragatapas €
Traditional Spanish
C/ Nueva 4, 29400
Tel *952 87 72 09*
Cosy unassuming locale in the town centre, with inventive tapas like asparagus and goat's cheese, marinated salmon and sautéed mushrooms. Excellent value.

RONDA: Pedro Romero €€
Traditional Spanish
C/ Virgen de la Paz 18, 29400
Tel *952 87 11 10*
Named after a 17th-century matador, this restaurant serves excellent *rabo de toro* (braised bull's tail) and *perdiz con alubias* (partridge with kidney beans).

RONDA: Tragabuches €€
Traditional Spanish
C/ Jose Aparicio 1, 29400
Tel *952 19 02 91* **Closed** *Mon, Sun dinner*
Try the chef's supreme *ajo blanco* (cold summer almond and garlic soup) at this Michelin-starred restaurant. Scintillating *menú de degustación*; impeccable service.

ROQUETAS DE MAR: Alejandro €
Seafood
Avenida Antonio Machado 32, 04740
Tel *950 32 24 08* **Closed** *Mon; Sun dinner*
Ultra-smart establishment specializing in exquisite seafood fusion dishes. Splash out on the *degustación con marisco* (tasting menu with shellfish).

Traditional Spanish dining room given a modern twist at Tragabuches, Ronda

For more information on types of restaurants *see page 577*

SANLÚCAR DE BARRAMEDA:
Casa Bigote €
Seafood
C/ Pórtico Bajo de Guía 10, 11540
Tel *956 36 26 96* **Closed** *Sun*
Set beside the Gudalquivir
estuary, Casa Bigote is a largely
traditional marine restaurant
serving fresh seafood and
regional hams. Exceptional *lomo
de atún* (tuna steak) and
langostinos (king prawns).

TORREMOLINOS: Frutos €
Traditional Spanish
Avenida de la Riviera 80, 29620
Tel *952 38 15 40* **Closed** *Sun dinner*
One of the grand old Costa del
Sol restaurants, Frutos serves first-
rate traditional dishes like
judiones a la Granja (Castilian-
style white beans), roast suckling
pig and fresh fish. Make sure to
visit the well-stocked basement
wine cellar.

DK Choice

TORREMOLINOS: Nuevo
Lanjarón €
Traditional Spanish
C/ Europa 10, 29620
Tel *952 38 87 74* **Closed** *Mon*
This long-established place is
probably the best value
restaurant on the Costa del Sol.
Located in a neat white and
ochre building in Torremolinos'
old Calvario quarter, it offers a
variety of inexpensive set
menus that include well-
prepared fish and meat dishes.
Try the *estofado de ternera* (veal
stew) followed by home-made
flan. Wonderful service.

TORREMOLINOS: Yate El
Cordobés €
Seafood
Paseo Maritimo s/n (Bajondillo) 29620
Tel *952 38 49 56* **Closed** *lunch
(Feb & Dec)*
Located right on Bajondillo
Beach, the local seafood dishes at
Yate El Cordobés range from
espetos de sardinas (charcoal
cooked fresh sardines) to *mero en
adobo* (grouper with garlic
mayonnaise sauce) and home-
spun desserts.

ÚBEDA: El Seco €
Traditional Spanish
C/ Corazon de Jesus 8, 23400
Tel *953 79 14 52*
A family-run restaurant in
Úbeda, El Seco has a cosy dining
room. Its home-cooked dishes
include *bacalao* El Seco (cod in
cream sauce) and *paletilla de
cordero al horno* (oven-baked
shoulder of lamb).

DK Choice

ÚBEDA: Parador Condestable
Davalos €€
Traditional
Plaza Vázquez de Molina, 23400
Tel *953 75 03 45*
If you want to dine out in style
in Úbeda, then don't miss this
magnificent, sumptuous
restaurant located in the old
quarter's grand 16th-century
parador. The setting is historic,
the decor traditional and the
atmosphere homely. Its wealth
of gourmet offerings include an
outstanding cold *ajo blanco*
(garlic and almond soup) and
mouthwatering game, such as
stewed kid with pine nuts.

VERA: Terrazza Carmona €
Traditional Spanish
C/ del Mar 1, 04620
Tel *950 39 07 60* **Closed** *Mon*
Terrazza Carmona is an award-
winning roadside restaurant
specializing in regional dishes like
seasonal wild boar with olives.
Indulge in a *tarta borracha*
(drunken tart!) for dessert.

The Balearic Islands

DK Choice

FORMENTERA, CALÓ DE
SANT AGUSTI: Es Calo €€
Seafood
*C/ Vicari Joan Mari 14, Es Calo de
Sant Agusti*
Tel *971 32 73 11* **Closed** *Nov–
mid-Apr*
Es Calo offers seafront dining
with the freshest fish, seafood,
rice, paellas and meat dishes.
Try the *bogavante frito con
huevos de payés* (fried lobster
with peasant eggs), but be sure
to save room for the home-
made desserts.

FORMENTERA, EL PILAR DE LA
MOLA: Pequeña Isla €
Regional Spanish
Avenida El Pilar, 101 El Pilar de la Mola
Tel *971 32 70 68* **Closed** *Nov–Apr*
In the hilltop village of La Mola,
the menu at Pequeña Isla
includes local dishes such as fish
stew and roasted lamb.

FORMENTERA, SAN FERRAN:
Blue Bar €
Café
*Carretera San Ferran–La Mola, km 7.
9, Platja Migjorn, 07871*
Tel *971 18 70 11* **Closed** *mid-Oct–Apr*

Beachfront dining at Yate El Cordobes in
Torremolinos

One of the original 1960s hippie
beach bars, Blue Bar on
Formentera serves decent salads,
pasta dishes, fish and vegetarian
options.

IBIZA, IBIZA TOWN: Sa Nansa €€
Seafood
Avenida 8 de Agosto 27, 07800
Tel *971 31 87 50* **Closed** *Mon;
Sun dinner*
Sa Nansa offers simply the best
seafood, whether it is grilled,
stewed or included in one of
their fabulously tasty rice or
noodle dishes.

IBIZA, IBIZA TOWN: El Olivo €€€
French
Pza de Vila 7–9, 07800
Tel *971 30 06 80* **Closed** *Mon;
mid-Oct–mid-Apr*
The menu at the popular El Olivo
restaurant in fashionable Dalt Vila
is Ibizan-French with a *nueva
cocina* edge. Get a table on the
trendy terrace.

IBIZA, SAN ANTONIO: Villa
Mercedes €€€
Mediterranean
Paseo del Mar, Puerto de San Antonio
Tel *971 34 85 43* **Closed** *Mon;
Jan & Feb*
Villa Mercedes is a romantic
restaurant with a lovely garden
terrace and Moroccan-themed
chill-out lounge.

IBIZA, SAN CARLOS:
Anita's Bar €
Tapas
Lugar Barri San Carlos s/n, 07850
Tel *971 33 50 90* **Closed** *Mon*
An institution, Anita's has played
a major role in Ibiza's counter-
culture, and it remains a
favourite. It features memorable
wall art.

DK Choice

IBIZA, SAN LORENZO:
La Paloma €€
Mediterranean
C/ Can Pou 4, 07812
Tel *971 32 55 43* **Closed** *Mon (Oct–Jun)*
A labour of love undertaken by two families, La Paloma is a postcard-pretty garden restaurant that serves home-made dishes using organic, local ingredients. Situated in a renovated finca and surrounded by fruit orchards, a small range of delicious Italian inspired dishes are served with genuine care.

IBIZA, SAN RAFAEL:
El Ayoun €€€
Moroccan
C/ Isidor Macabich 6, 07816
Tel *971 19 83 35* **Closed** *lunch*
This is as authentic as a Moroccan restaurant gets in Ibiza: couscous and rich tajine dishes, with some spicy starters.

IBIZA, SANT CARLES:
El Bigotes €
Seafood
Cala Mastella. Sant Carles, 07850
Tel *650 79 76 33* **Closed** *Nov–Mar*
Perched on a crystalline cove, El Bigotes serves fresh fish in a simple rustic outdoor setting.

DK Choice

MALLORCA, LLOSETA:
Santi Taura €€
Regional Spanish
C/ Joan Carles I 48, 07360
Tel *656 73 82 14* **Closed** *Mon lunch; Tue; Sun dinner*
Local chef Santi Taura reinterprets old recipes from the islands in this smart restaurant in Lloseta. Tasting menus are accompanied by an oration of the history and culture of what's on your plate.

MALLORCA, PALMA: Café L'Antiquari €
Tapas
C/ Arabi 5, 07003
Tel *871 57 23 13* **Closed** *Sun*
A relaxed neighbourhood place with a quirky decor and friendly hippie vibe. Good brunches.

MALLORCA, PALMA: Club Nautico Cala Gamba €
Seafood
Passeig Cala Gamba s/n, 07007
Tel *971 26 23 72* **Closed** *Mon*
The decor is nautical in theme and large windows overlook

the marina. The menu is sustainably weighted towards locally caught fish.

MALLORCA, PALMA: Forn de Sant Joan €
Mediterranean
C/ Sant Joan 4, 07012
Tel *971 72 84 22*
One of Palma's best creative restaurants, set in an old bakery.

MALLORCA, PALMA: Gran Café Cappuccino €
Café
C/ de Sant Miquel, 53, 07002
Tel *971 71 97 64* **Closed** *Sun*
This is a stylish spot for morning coffee, light lunches and evening drinks in the heart of Palma.

MALLORCA, PALMA: Misa €
Mediterranean
C/ Can Maçanet 1, 07003
Tel *971 59 53 01* **Closed** *Sun*
French-inspired bistro fare using top-quality ingredients. Reserve a table in advance.

MALLORCA, PALMA: Tasca de Blanquerna €
Tapas
C/ Blanquerna 6, 07003
Tel *971 29 01 08* **Closed** *Sun; Mon dinner*
The chef here creates tasty small plates with Asian and Meditteranean influences.

MALLORCA, PALMA: Wine Garage €
Tapas
C/ Montenegro 10, 07001
Tel *971 72 44 83* **Closed** *Sun*
Attractive wine bar with innovative tapas, ever changing with the seasons. Wine menu presented on an iPad.

DK Choice

MALLORCA, PALMA:
Simply Fosh €€€
Modern
C/ de la Missió 7A, 07003
Tel *971 72 01 14* **Closed** *Sun*
British chef Marc Fosh has garnered a well-deserved reputation as one of the island's finest chefs; Simply Fosh is where he shows off his artistry. Situated inside the hyper-hip Convent de la Missió hotel, his original cuisine using local ingredients delights without being too challenging.

MALLORCA, PORTIXOL:
Can Punta €
Greek
C/ Vicari Joaquim Fuster 105, 07006
Tel *971 27 73 64* **Closed** *Mon in summer*
Located on the waterfront, this delightful place dishes out fresh Greek-inspired salads and tapas. Relaxed atmosphere.

MALLORCA, PORTIXOL:
Fibonacci Pan €
Café
C/ Vicario Joaquin Fuster 95, 07006
Tel *971 24 99 61*
This Scandinavian-style bakery serves appetizing sandwiches, moist cakes, flaky croissants, and invigorating salads and soups.

MENORCA, ALAIOR: Es Forn de Torre Soli Nou €
Grill
Urb. Torre Solí Nou, 07730
Tel *971 37 28 98*
Focusing on meat and poultry *a la brasa* (barbecued), the best tables are on the breezy terrace.

The upmarket Simply Fosh in Palma, Mallorca

For more information on types of restaurants *see page 577*

MENORCA, CALA EN PORTER:
Sa Paissa €
Café/Bistro
Av Central 54, 07730
Tel *971 37 73 89*
Located in a hostel of the same
name. Breakfast, lunch and dinner.

MENORCA, CALA´N BOSCH:
Es Tast de na Silvia €
Mediterranean
Passeig Portixol 21, 07760
Tel *971 38 78 95* **Closed** *Wed*
The best option in a crowd of
touristy restaurants. Top-notch,
Mediterranean cuisine in a
romantic, welcoming restaurant.

MENORCA, CIUTADELLA:
Cas Ferrer de Sa Font €
Regional Spanish
C/ Sa Font 16, 07760
Tel *971 48 07 84* **Closed** *Apr, May,*
Sep & Oct: Mon, Sun dinner; Jun–
Aug: Sun lunch
Laid out in three rooms of an
imposing 17th-century town
mansion, Cas Ferrer serves a
small but good selection of
traditional island dishes.

MENORCA, CIUTADELLA:
Es Tastet €
Mediterranean
C/ Carnisseria 9, 07760
Tel *971 38 47 97* **Closed** *Sun lunch*
A great little owner-run place
that serves breakfast and tapas,
as well as pasta and fish dishes,
all using fresh market produce.

MENORCA, ES CASTELL:
Son Granot €
Regional Spanish
Carretera Sant Felip, 07720
Tel *971 35 55 55* **Closed** *Sun (mid-*
Jul–mid-Sep)
Located on a hilltop, and part of
a rural hotel, this place serves
traditional Menorcan cuisine.

Place settings at Son Granot in Es
Castell, Menorca

MENORCA, FERRERIES:
Meson de Gallo €
Regional Spanish
Crta Cala Santa Galdana, km 1.5, 07750
Tel *971 37 30 39* **Closed** *Mon;*
Dec & Jan
The signature dish here is rooster
(*el gallo*) paella. It's also famed for
its steaks with Mallorcan cheese.

DK Choice

MENORCA, MAHÓN:
Ses Forquilles €
Tapas
Rovellada de Dalt 20, 07703
Tel *971 35 27 11* **Closed** *Mon;*
Sun in winter
An inviting crowd-pleaser.
Creative gourmet tapas and
entrées made with the finest of
local produce. Tapas bar on
ground floor; restaurant above.

MENORCA, SA MESQUIDA:
Cap Roig €€
Seafood
Carretera Sa Mesquida 13, 07701
Tel *971 18 83 83* **Closed** *Mon;*
Oct–Mar
Named after the star of its menu,
Cap Roig ("scorpion fish") is
highly recommended for its
caldereta de llagosta (lobster stew).

The Canary Islands

EL HIERRO, LA RESTINGA:
Restaurante El Refugio €
Seafood
C/ La Lapa 2, 38911
Tel *922 55 70 29* **Closed** *Mon*
Family restaurant has a *"del la*
barca del plato" (from the boat to
the plate) ethos.

EL HIERRO, VALVERDE:
La Mirada Profunda €
Modern Spanish
C/ Santiago 25, 38900
Tel *922 55 17 87*
A taste of Barcelona's avant-
garde gastronomy. The wine
list includes local vintages.

EL HIERRO, VALVERDE:
El Secreto €
Tapas
C/ Quintero Ramos 2, 38900
Tel *922 55 06 58* **Closed** *Mon*
The secret here is a refreshingly
simple take on tapas.

FUERTEVENTURA, EL COTILLO:
La Vaca Azul €
Seafood
C/ Requena 9, 35660
Tel *928 53 86 85*
The famous Blue Cow is more
surf than turf, with the Atlantic

Ocean providing the majority of
the star ingredients on your plate.

FUERTEVENTURA, MORRO DE
JABLE: La Laja €
Seafood
Av da Tomás Grau Gurrea 1, 35625
Tel *928 54 20 54*
Fresh fish doesn't come much
fresher than at this coastal
restaurant. Rice and pasta dishes
will suit vegetarians.

GRAN CANARIA, ARTENARA:
Restaurante Mirador La Cilla €
Regional
Camino de La Cilla 9, 35350
Tel *928 62 75 37*
A tunnel leads to a sun terrace
offering panoramic views, where
you can linger over Canarian
regional specialities.

GRAN CANARIA, BAÑADEROS:
Restaurante Terraza El Puertillo €
Seafood
Paseo Marítimo El Puertillo 12, 35414
Tel *928 62 70 28*
The Hormigas make you feel part
of the family at their beachside
restaurant. They do a great paella.

GRAN CANARIA, EL
MADRONAL: Casa Martell €
Regional
Carretera del Centro Km 18.2, 35308
Tel *928 64 12 83*
There are specialities of the house
to enjoy but you won't find them
on any menu. Home-grown
organic vegetables feature heavily.

GRAN CANARIA, LAS PALMAS:
Cho Zacarias €
Mediterranean
C/ Audiencia 7, 35001
Tel *928 33 13 74* **Closed** *Mon;*
Sun dinner
Old-world Vegueta houses a
modern, forward-thinking
restaurant which reimagines its
location as the French Riviera
with a menu to match.

GRAN CANARIA, LAS PALMAS:
Samsara €
Fusion
CC La Charca, Avenida del Oasis 30,
35100
Tel *928 14 27 36* **Closed** *Mon*
Stylish place which spices up
traditional Spanish ingredients
such as *solomillo* (sirloin) and
cordero (lamb) with the likes of
curry and teriyaki.

LA GOMERA, ARURE:
Restaurante Mirador César
Manrique €
Regional Spanish
Carretera General Valle Gran Rey-
Arure, 38870
Tel *922 80 70 45* **Closed** *Mon*

With one of the best views on the island, dine while looking out over the Valle Gran Rey.

DK Choice

LA GOMERA, LAS HAYAS: Restaurante La Montaña-Casa Efigenia €
Vegetarian
Plaza Eucaliptos, 38869
Tel *922 80 42 48*
Outside, eucalyptus trees guard the entrance to this celebrated hamlet restaurant, part of a rural accommodation complex. Inside, matriarch Efigenia traditionally spoonfeeds you your first taste of the restaurant's only main course, a hearty vegetable stew served with *gofio* (roasted maize). The freshest salads and *almogrote* (a cheesy dip) are perfect accompaniments.

LA GOMERA, SAN SEBASTIÁN DE LA GOMERA: Restaurante El Charcón €
Regional Spanish
Playa de la Cueva, 38800
Tel *922 14 18 98* **Closed** *Sun & Mon*
You'll eat what they've caught and be darned happy about it at this 10-table-small restaurant housed in a natural cave. As well as fish, they utilize market-fresh vegetables in their meal preparation.

LA PALMA, FUENCALIENTE: La Casa del Volcan €
Regional Spanish
C/ de los Volcanes 23, 38740
Tel *922 44 44 27* **Closed** *Mon*
Local cheese, goat and rabbit are some of the fixtures on the menu at this traditional restaurant, which specializes in Canarian food.

LA PALMA, GARAFIA: Kiosko Briesta €
Traditional Spanish
Carretera General Las Tricias, km 6, 38787
Tel *922 40 02 10* **Closed** *Tue*
Charming family-run restaurant that has a tree growing through it and a fireplace for chilly winter days. Serves a good variety of meat, including lamb and rabbit.

LA PALMA, SANTA CRUZ DE LA PALMA: Restaurante Parrilla Las Nieves €
Regional Spanish
Plaza de las Nieves 2, 38700
Tel *922 41 66 00* **Closed** *Thu*
Go local in an establishment where tourists are conspicuous by their absence. A daily menu offers a gateway to an appreciation of authentic Canarian cuisine.

Tables on the terrace at Rincón de Juan Carlos, Tenerife

LANZAROTE, LA GERIA: Bodega El Chupadero €
Regional Spanish
La Geria 3, 35570
Tel *928 17 31 15* **Closed** *Mon*
Simple, hearty fare can be had at this rustic restaurant attached to a bodega in Lanzarote's volcanic wine region.

LANZAROTE, NAZARET: Lagomar €
Modern Spanish
C/ los Loros 2, 35539
Tel *928 84 56 65* **Closed** *Mon*
Lagomar is housed in a stunning property, built into the cliffs. Creative, well-executed dishes include pork steak over sweet potato parmentier and paprika sauce.

LANZAROTE, TEGUISE: La Cantina €
Tapas
C/ León y Castillo 8, 35530
Tel *928 84 55 36*
Located in picturesque Teguise, which was once the island's capital, this is a restaurant specializing in tapas which also includes an art gallery and deli on its premises.

LANZAROTE, TIMANFAYA: Restaurante El Diablo €
Regional Spanish
Parque Nacional de Timanfaya, Charco Prieto, s/n, 35560
Tel *928 84 00 56*
Brace yourself for a truly unique dining experience at El Diablo: the food is grilled directly over a live volcanic crater, which billows out sulphuric steam.

TENERIFE, COSTA ADEJE: El Molino Blanco €€
International
Avenida Austria 5, 38660
Tel *922 79 62 82*

A meat-heavy menu, though vegetarians will be looked after on request. The place transforms into a music venue after sunset.

TENERIFE, EL SAUZAL: Terrazas del Sauzal €
International
Pasaje Sierva de Dios 9, 38360
Tel *922 57 14 91* **Closed** *Mon, Tue*
It boasts an international menu, but eating here is really about the 10,000 sq m of surrounding gardens that makes for a picturesque setting.

TENERIFE, LOS GIGANTES: El Rincón de Juan Carlos €€
Modern Spanish
Acantilado de Los Gigantes, Pasaje Jacaranda, 2, 38683
Tel *922 86 80 40* **Closed** *Sun*
Juan Carlos Padron is Tenerife's only celebrity chef. Paired with his brother Jonathan, a renowned pastry chef, their tasting menus are inspired. Outstanding food, excellent wine and service to match.

TENERIFE, PUERTO DE LA CRUZ: Tambo €
Seafood
C/ Añaterve 1, Punta Brava, 38400
Tel *922 37 62 62* **Closed** *Mon*
The fruits of the sea dominate the menu at Tambo, with the mussels and squid particularly recommended.

TENERIFE, SANTA CRUZ DE TENERIFE: Anocheza €
Modern Spanish
C/ Santa Teresita 3, 38004
Tel *922 29 16 73* **Closed** *Mon, Sun*
Chef Eduardo Cáceres opened his own restaurant after starring in the kitchens of some of Tenerife's finest hotels. Try the duck marinated in hoisin sauce stuffed with shitake mushrooms.

For more information on types of restaurants *see page 577*

SHOPPING IN SPAIN

Spain has a thriving shopping culture, with many unique, family-run boutiques as well as a few reliable chain stores and big department stores. Good buys include leather, fashion, wine and ceramics, though these days it is possible to find anything you are looking for, from traditional gifts to designer clothes. Spain has its own rules of etiquette when it comes to shopping. In small shops, most merchandise is behind the counter, and the clerk will retrieve whatever you need, making for a time-consuming, but friendly, way to shop. It is polite to greet the shop owner and fellow shoppers with a "buenos días" or "buenas tardes" as you enter, and to say "adiós" as you leave.

Fresh produce in a market in Pollença (Mallorca)

Opening Hours

Most shops in Spain, barring some supermarkets or department stores, close at midday. Small shops are open Monday to Saturday (10am–2pm and 5–8pm). Service-related shops such as dry cleaners usually open an hour earlier and close an hour later. Nearly all shops are closed on Sunday and holidays, except during the Christmas season and sales.

Payment Methods

Cash is still the payment of choice in Spain. Cheques are rarely accepted, and credit cards may not be accepted in small shops or markets. Even in large stores, there may be a minimum purchase required for credit card users.

ATMs are widely available throughout the country, even in small towns, so getting cash should not be a problem.

VAT

Value added tax (VAT), known as *IVA* in Spanish, is included in the price of nearly everything in Spain. However, non-EU residents are eligible for a VAT refund (*see p616*). If you buy goods worth a total of €90.15 or more, request a VAT refund form from the shop-keeper, then get it stamped at a Spanish customs office before you check your bags in at the airport. Present the stamped form at an affiliated bank or office in the airport, or mail it for the refund to be credited to your credit card.

Sales

Spain's twice-annual *rebajas* (sales) are a fantastic oppor-tunity to find good deals on everything from shoes and clothes to linens, electronics and household goods. Most stores offer a reduction of 50 per cent or more.

The first *rebajas* of the year begin on 7 January (the day after Three Kings Day) and continue until mid-February.

Summer *rebajas* start on 1 July each year and last until the end of August.

Markets

A visit to a Spanish market is a great lesson in local culture. Every town, large or small, has at least one fresh market, where you can buy local produce, Spanish cheeses and sausages and other foods.

Markets in the cities follow regular store opening hours, but in smaller towns they may only be open in the morning, or on certain days of the week.

Speciality markets for antiques, arts and crafts are popular in Spain, as are the *rastros* (flea markets). These are usually open only at weekends, though the times vary across markets and towns.

The country's most celebrated market is El Rastro (*see p306*), a massive flea market in Madrid, which has been running for many generations. It is frequented by locals and tourists alike. Watch out for pickpockets.

Display of hand-painted ceramics in Toledo

Shopping in Barcelona pp190–93; in Madrid pp320–23; in Seville pp458–9

Regional Products

Spain has a strong artisan heritage, and the best places to buy authentic traditional items are the artisan markets and speciality shops. All over Spain, you'll find great pottery and ceramics. Spain's pottery is sturdy and colourful and each region puts its own spin on the traditional forms. Andalusia, El Bisbal in Catalonia, Paterna and Manises near Valencia and Talavera de la Reina in Castilla-La Mancha are the main centres for ceramic production.

Leather goods are another traditional craft. Reasonably priced shoes, wallets and accessories are available almost everywhere.

In Toledo, filigree metalwork and swords are sold on almost every street corner. Other sought-after products include guitars, traditional fans, Lladró porcelain figures and lacework.

Food and Drink

Basketware, sold in all parts of Spain

Spain is second only to Italy in wine production, and Spanish wine is rated to be of the best value in Europe. Major wine regions are Penedès (reds, whites and *cava*), Priorat (reds), Rías Baixas (whites), Ribera del Duero (reds), Rioja (reds) and Toro (whites). Sherry from Jerez is another popular Spanish drink.

A gourmet's paradise, Spain is great for food shopping. Olives and olive oil are always a good buy. Prominent olive-growing areas include Andalusia, Aragón and southern Catalonia. You can also buy Spain's famous *Jamón Ibérico* (Iberian cured ham), or one of the many region-specific sausages such as Catalan *butifarra* and Castilian *morcilla*.

Gourmet chocolate shops are becoming popular now, especially in the cities. Escribà in Barcelona has a good reputation for producing exquisite confectionery.

A Madrid branch of the fashionable Camper shoe store

One-Stop Shopping

Small family-run shops are quaint, but when you're in a hurry department stores and one-stop shops are more convenient. Spain's most famous department store, El Corte Inglés, is found in every major city in Spain, sometimes with multiple branches. This megastore sells everything from clothes and sports goods, to furniture and food.

Other one-stop shops include hypermarkets such as Carrefour (the Walmart of Europe), Alcampo and Hipercor.

American-style malls, called *centros comerciales* in Spain, are gaining popularity and can be found on the outskirts of most large cities.

Fashion

Spain has a long textile history, so it's no surprise to find good-quality clothing here. In large cities such as Madrid and Barcelona, you'll find boutiques of major Spanish labels, including Antonio Miro, Lydia Delgado, Josep Font, Adolfo Dominguez and Loewe. Spanish fashion may not be on par with Paris or Milan yet, but designers here are increasingly gaining a reputation for quality and originality.

For something trendy and a bit easier on the wallet, Spanish-owned chains such as Zara, Mango and Massimo Dutti are great places to shop.

Mallorca is a good place to buy shoes, home to Spain's most famous shoe company, Camper. Along with branded shoes, *espadrilles* (traditional Spanish rope-soled shoes) are a good informal option.

Size Chart

Women's dresses, coats and skirts

European	36	38	40	42	44	46	48
British	10	12	14	16	18	20	22
American	8	10	12	14	16	18	20

Women's shoes

European	36	37	38	39	40	41
British	3	4	5	6	7	8
American	5	6	7	8	9	10

Men's suits

European	44	46	48	50	52	54	56	58 (size)
British	34	36	38	40	42	44	46	48 (inches)
American	34	36	38	40	42	44	46	48 (inches)

Men's shirts (collar size)

European	36	38	39	41	42	43	44	45 (cm)
British	14	15	15½	16	16½	17	17½	18 (inches)
American	14	15	15½	16	16½	17	17½	18 (inches)

Men's shoes

European	39	40	41	42	43	44	45	46
British	6	7	7½	8	9	10	11	12
American	7	7½	8	8½	9½	10½	11	11½

ENTERTAINMENT IN SPAIN

Spain has always been known for its vibrant, colourful culture – wherever you are, there is usually a fiesta going on somewhere nearby, or some impromptu celebration taking place in the street. So, while there's usually no need to seek out formal entertainment, those who do want to plan a day or night out will find plenty of choice, ranging from raucous cabarets to live flamenco and highbrow cultural events. Although Madrid, Barcelona and, to a lesser extent, Seville have the widest selection of programmes, the other regional capitals are not far behind. The coastal resorts also witness a lot of action in the summer months. Regular annual events in various parts of Spain are detailed on pages 42–3.

Preparing for a dressage display at the equestrian school in Jerez

Traditional Music and Dance

Spain's rich musical heritage is marked by typical regional instruments, musical styles and dance forms. The *txistu*, a small wind instrument is typical to the Basque Country, Galicia and Asturias lilt to the notes of the *gaita* (bagpipes), while Valencia is proud of its countless brass bands.

Andalusia is the home of flamenco, while Aragón's rhythm comes from the hop-step of its folk dance, *jota*. In Catalonia, the famous *sardana* *(see p229)* is accompanied by a *flabiol* (flute), *tabal* (drum) and *gralla* (a type of oboe).

Jazz, Rock and Pop

Television talent shows tend to dominate the Spanish pop industry, but many creative bands fail to get international recognition only because they sing in Spanish. At the cultural crossroads of southern Europe, the Spanish music scene is also enriched by influences from South America and Africa.

The Benicassim festival in July and the Sonar festival in June in Barcelona are the preferred live events for those in search of new music. An international blues festival is held every July in Cazorla *(see p45)*, with big international jazz artists playing in small town stadiums and even bullrings.

The Spanish music channel RNE 3 broadcasts an eclectic selection of Spanish as well as international music.

Flamenco

Flamenco *(see pp428–9)* is a traditional art form that combines song, music and dance. Infused with sensuality and emotion, it originated in Andalusia but is performed all over Spain. It is a highly varied musical form, and acts can range from spontaneous performances in gypsy patios to international spectacles in major concert halls.

Shows are often adapted to tourists' tastes. To see and hear flamenco that even purists admire, try the smaller venues or catch a performance during an Andalusian fiesta, particularly in the provinces of Seville and Jerez.

Córdoba hosts the National Flamenco Competition in November every third year. The next two are being held in 2016 and 2019.

Classical Music, Opera and Ballet

Opera, classical music and ballet are performed in all the major cities in concert halls. The best-known venues include the Auditorio Nacional de Música and Teatro Real in Madrid *(see p326)*, Palau de la Música in Valencia *(see p256)*, Teatro de la Maestranza in Seville *(see p460)* and Gran Teatre del Liceu and L'Auditori *(see p195)* in Barcelona.

For a more unusual concert setting, look out for performances in Spain's spectacular caves, such as those found in Nerja *(see p487)*, Drac *(see p521)* and the Cuevas of Canelobre

Palau de la Música, Valencia

Entertainment in Barcelona pp194–9; in Madrid pp324–9; in Seville pp460–61

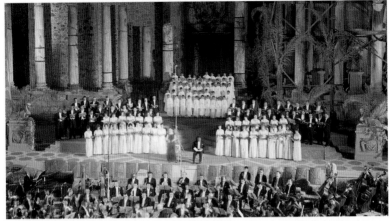

A performance at the beautifully preserved Roman theatre in Mérida, Extremadura

near Alicante. Sacred music can still be heard in some of Spain's monasteries. Montserrat *(see p222–3)* is famous for its all-boy choir. In Leyre monastery *(see p139)*, the Gregorian plainchant is performed during Mass.

Theatre

Spain has a great repertoire of classical theatre and, although most performances are in Spanish, it may be worth going to a show for the venue alone.

Corral de Comedias in Almagro *(see p403)* is a perfectly preserved 17th-century Golden Age theatre. Mérida's stunning Roman theatre *(see pp58–9 and pp414–5)* serves as the splendid backdrop for an annual summer festival of classical theatre.

Cinema

Spain's thriving film scene has certainly gained international exposure. The country makes around 100 feature films a year with directors such as Pedro Almodóvar and Alejandro Amenábar.

Most foreign-language films are dubbed in Spanish, but select cinemas in university cities and areas with a number of foreign residents show films in their original language. San Sebastián hosts an acclaimed international film festival *(see p127)* in September, and the Sitges Film Festival takes place in October.

The open-air summer cinemas in some coastal resorts are an experience in themselves, but do remember to carry a mosquito repellent.

Nightlife

Spain's prodigious nightlife starts later than in most other countries, with 11pm considered an early start for most revellers. The idea is to spend the first part of the evening in pubs or *bares de copas*: sparsely decorated drinking dens, usually with loud music blaring. Then move on to the clubs and discos, often located out of town, where the noise will not bother anyone.

You can enjoy a floorshow while dining out at coastal package-holiday resorts such as Lloret del Mar on the Costa Brava, Maspalomas on Gran Canaria, Torremolinos on the Costa del Sol and Benidorm on the Costa Blanca.

Spectator Sports

Football is Spain's favourite sport and is centred on the battle between the two top teams, Real Madrid and Barcelona. Other teams with large followings include Real Betis from Seville, Deportivo La Coruña, FC Valencia and Real Zaragoza. Cycling, tennis, basketball and golf are also popular.

Bullfighting

For an authentic spectacle of Spain's most recognized traditional sport *(see pp40–41)*, watch a bullfight in a large arena – Madrid *(see p310)*, Seville *(see p434)*, Valencia, Bilbao and Zaragoza have the best bullrings. All bullfights start in the early evening at around 5pm. Tickets should be bought directly at the venue. Bullfighting is now banned in Catalonia.

Entertainment for Children

Spain's big theme parks are Port Aventura on the Costa Daurada *(see p228)* and Terra Mítica outside Benidorm *(see p264)*. Other amusements suitable for kids include the cowboys of Mini-Hollywood *(see p504)* and the dancing horses of Jerez *(see p470)*.

Rollercoaster ride at Port Aventura on the Costa Daurada

OUTDOOR ACTIVITIES & SPECIALIST HOLIDAYS

Spain is one of Europe's most geographically varied countries, with mountain ranges, woodlands and river deltas suitable for scenic tours and sports holidays. The options are endless and include sailing on the Mediterranean or surfing in the Atlantic, mountain climbing in the Pyrenees or rambling through the plains of Castille, snow skiing in the Sierra Nevada or water-skiing off the coast of Mallorca. To focus on just one activity, sign up for a specialist holiday. Weekend or week-long holidays, featuring everything from yoga to horse riding, are gaining popularity in Spain. Local tourist offices can provide information on outdoor activities.

Walking and Trekking

Spain offers exciting choices for a challenging week-long trek through the Pyrenees, or a gentle walk along the coast. Look out for the wide, well-marked GR (*Grandes Recorridos* meaning "long-distance") trails, which crisscross Spain. Though most people usually choose to walk only a small portion of each GR trail, long-distance trekkers use them to traverse all the way across the country.

Nearly 8 per cent of Spain's total terrain is protected parkland, and the countless natural parks and 13 large national parks are the most popular and attractive hiking options. Some of the best parks for walking include Aragón's Parque Nacional de Ordesa *(see pp236–7)*, Catalunya's Parque Nacional d'Aigüestortes *(see p215)*, and Asturias' Parque Nacional de los Picos de Europa *(see pp112–13)*. For details about trails in the parks, contact the **Environment Ministry of Spain**.

For information on other trails, contact the **Federación Española de Deportes de Montaña y Escalada**.

Air Sports

The best way to take in Spain's landscape is to view it from above. Options for thrilling aerial views include hot-air ballooning, skydiving, paragliding and hang-gliding. One of the well-known hot-air balloon companies is **Kon-Tiki**, which began flying in rural Catalonia and now covers the whole country. **Glovento Sur** operates in Southern Spain. Standard rides start from €165 per person, depending on the trip's length.

For those who have forever been fascinated by the birds' ability to fly, paragliding and hang-gliding are two excellent options. The **Real Federación Aeronáutica Española** can provide information on schools and outfitters across Spain. Contact them for further details.

When it comes to a real thrill, nothing surpasses skydiving. Reputable companies offering skydiving courses or tandem jumps include **Skydive Empuriabrava** in Catalonia and **Skydive Lillo** near Toledo. Expect a single tandem jump (a jump made while attached to a qualified instructor) to cost between €180 and €320.

Water Sports

Spain is virtually surrounded by water, so it is little surprise that sailing is popular here. The country's most celebrated yacht ports are those of upscale resorts including Palma de Mallorca and Marbella, and in 2007 and 2010 the port of Valencia hosted the prestigious America's Cup sailing tournament. Mooring a private yacht or sailboat in a top-notch marina is expensive and often impossible. A much easier alternative is to rent a sailboat by the day or week, or to sign up for a half- or full-day sailing excursion. Most other seaside towns also have small recreational ports offering sailboats and yacht charters which can be rented by providing a sailing licence. For details, contact the **Real Federación Española de Vela**.

Scuba diving is available up and down the coast of Spain and on nearly all the islands. However, the best places for underwater exploration are around the Canary Islands. Just off the island of El Hierro are the warm, calm waters of the Mar de las Calmas, which is full

Paragliding above the Vall d'Aran in the eastern Pyrenees

Whitewater rafting in the Spanish Pyrenees

of colourful coral and dozens of marine species. In the Mediterranean, head to the Balearic Islands or to the Illes Medes, seven tiny islets off the Costa Brava that are home to some of the most diverse marine life in all the Mediterranean. The local Illes Medes information office, **Estació Nàutica**, will provide detailed information about area outfitters.

Surfing and windsurfing are other popular sports. On mainland Spain the best places for either kind of surfing are the Basque coast (especially towns such as Zarautz and Mundaka) and Tarifa, which is also good for kitesurfing, on the Costa de la Luz. In the Canary islands, try Lanzarote or Fuerteventura for surfing and El Médano (Tenerife) for windsurfing. El Médano's **Surf Center Playa Sur** has information. Sea kayaking is becoming very

popular and kayak rental is now available in many Mediterranean resort towns. Since rentals are cheap and little prior experience is necessary, kayaking is a great option for boating novices who might want to spend some time out on the water.

Adventure Sports

Since Spain is Europe's second-most-mountainous country after Switzerland, mountain climbing is a natural sport here. Head to the Aragón Pyrenees or the Catalan Pyrenees for a wide range of challenging rock faces. Other popular spots include the mountain of Montserrat in Catalonia, the Parque Natural de los Cañones y Sierra de Guara in Aragón, the Sierra Nevada in Andalusia and the Picos de Europa in Asturias. For more information, contact the **Federación Española de Deportes de Montaña y Escalada**.

If mere mountain climbing doesn't sound interesting enough, go for *barranquismo* (canyoning), a thrilling adventure sport that lets you explore canyons, cliffs and rivers with a combination of hiking, climbing, rappelling and swimming.

The undisputed capital of canyoning is Parque Natural de la Sierra y los Cañones de Guara, a park and natural area in central Aragón that is home to dozens of "wet" and "dry" canyons. Outfitters such as **Camping Lecina** provide

wetsuits and experienced guides – a must for novices – for €45 per person. Most services and lodging are in, or near, the pretty town of Alquezar.

Another fun way to explore rivers is whitewater rafting. Although Spain is not known for its raging rivers, there are a few places where some white water can be found. Head for the rivers: Noguera Pallaresa in Catalunya, the Carasa in Asturias or the Miño in Galicia. Late spring and early summer are the best times for rafting, since run-off from melted snow ensures a good deal of water and big rapids.

Fly-fishing in the rivers of Castilla y León, famous for their trout

Fishing

Deep-sea fishing excursions are offered all along Spain's coasts. Fishing in the Mediterranean or the Atlantic is unregulated except for marine reserves and some parks. Trout fishing in lakes and streams is possible; some of the best trout rivers are in Asturias, Rioja and Castilla y León. It is challenging to fish in the narrow, tree-lined streams of the Pyrenees.

It is essential to acquire a seasonal or a daily permit specifying if the fishing area is *sin muerte* (catch and release). Bring your own equipment, as only a few companies offer guided trips. For details on fishing sites and regulations, contact **Federación Española de Pesca y Casting**.

Windsurfing off Fuerteventura in the Canary Islands

Cycling

Road biking and mountain biking are both popular in Spain. Helmets are recommended while cycling, especially on highways, where extreme caution should be exercised. Drivers here are not accustomed to sharing the road and accidents on highways are not uncommon. The **Real Federación Española de Ciclismo** will provide useful information as well as advice on how to plan a safe cycling excursion.

Mountain bikers will find plenty of trails to keep them busy pedalling in Spain. Several walking paths are also suitable for mountain biking, which are referred to as "BTT" (Bici Todo Terreno or all-terrain bikes; www.centrosbtt.es). Throughout Catalunya, Centros BTT are set up to inform bikers about trails and conditions. In other regions, where this service is not available, trail information and maps can be found at tourist offices.

For young or inexperienced cyclers, *vias verdes* (rail trails) are a fantastic option. These flat, long-distance trails follow the paths of discontinued rail lines, ideal for those who want lovely views without making an effort. Many *vias verdes* cut through historic towns, making interesting pit stops along the way. The **Fundación de los Ferrocarriles Españoles** has detailed information about routes.

Golf

Golf is popular throughout Spain, though most courses can be found near the coasts and coastal resort areas. There are too many important golfing areas to highlight just one; the **Real Federación Española de Golf** has detailed information on all the courses. Some of the golf courses offer activities for non-golfers as well. For year-round golf, head to the island of Tenerife, where nearly a dozen courses, including the beautifully situated **Golf Las Américas**, are huddled in the southern corner of the island.

Skiing and Winter Sports

Spain's mountainous terrain makes it an excellent place for skiing, and resorts here are often cheaper than those in the Alps or other places in Europe. The top ski resorts are the Sierra Nevada in Granada and Baqueira-Beret, in the Pyrenean Val d'Aran. It is also possible to ski in the Sierra de Guadarrama, just north of Madrid, and in a handful of other high-altitude areas. Details are available through the **Real Federación Española de Deportes de Invierno**. For more ski resorts visit www.esquiweb.com.

Birdwatching

Spain's mild climate attracts a huge variety of fowl year-round. In winter, one can observe birds native to northern Europe; in spring, native Mediterranean species come to nest. There are numerous natural parks working to conserve Spain's diverse bird population. The top bird-watching site is Extremadura's Parque Natural Monfragüe, where big birds of prey can be seen swooping and hunting. Other excellent places to observe birds in their natural habitat are Andalusia's Parque Nacional de Doñana, Guadalquivir Delta and Laguna de Fuente de Piedra, and Delta de l'Ebre in southern Catalonia.

Spas

Health and wellness spas, or *balnearios*, are nothing new in Spain. As far back as Roman times residents here were enjoying the healthy benefits of mineral-rich waters along the Mediterranean or in the interior. Day spas offering a range of beauty and therepeutic treatments are popular as well, especially in cities and resorts. The **Asociación Nacional de Estaciones Termales** website (National Association of Thermal Resorts) has details on reputable spas throughout the country.

Naturism

Specially designated nudist, or naturist, beaches are not hard to find in Spain. Contact the various coastal tourist offices for details of nudist beaches. Alternatively, log on to the official website of the **Federación Española de Naturismo (FEN)**, which has a comprehensive list.

Specialist Holidays

A weekend or week-long specialist holiday provides the luxury of practising a favourite hobby, or probably learning a new one.

Food and wine holidays are more popular than ever in Spain, with its varied cuisine and excellent wines. A growing number of companies – many of them owned by expat British – have opened in recent years, offering everything from tours of well-known wine regions to the chance to harvest grapes or olives. For upscale, made-to-order tours of wine regions all over Spain, contact the Madrid-based company **Cellar Tours**. For daily cooking classes and an in-depth look at local Spanish cuisines and customs, try a cooking holiday like those offered by the Priorat-based **Catacurian** or the Málaga-based **Cooking Holiday Spain**.

The scenic landscapes of Spain are a wonderful inspiration to indulge the artistic temperament. A painting holiday offers the chance to escape to the quiet countryside and paint. Companies including **Andalucian Adventures** offer multi-day holidays for artists of all levels. Holidays include instruction with an experienced painter as well as practising independently. Sculpture or drawing classes are often available too.

Activity-focused holidays are a great option as well. Spain's pleasant weather is particularly favourable for walking, biking, water-skiing or horseback riding. The holiday company **On Foot in Spain** offers a variety of walking holidays in Northern

Spain, while **Switchbacks Mountain Bike Vacations** has cycling holidays for all levels in Andalusia. For water-sports enthusiasts, **Xtreme Gene** specializes in water skiing holidays. Those interested in dance can try **Club Dance**, a London-based company offering dancing holidays. **Fantasia Adventure Holidays** specializes in horseback riding holidays in Southern Spain.

To relax, a yoga holiday may be ideal. There are some great alternatives for getting away from the stress of daily life, such as **Kaliyoga**, which offers yoga instruction in a pristine setting. A healthy menu and ample free time for hiking or meditating add to the general feel-good factor of a yoga holiday.

A specialist holiday is also a great opportunity to learn Spanish. Language holidays are available in many parts of Spain, where the Spanish language can be learned in the best way possible – by immersing oneself completely in the country's culture. Language holidays provide the chance to observe the Spanish way of life from close quarters, for an extended period of time.

The **Instituto Cervantes** has information on schools and classes across Spain.

DIRECTORY

Walking and Trekking

Environment Ministry of Spain
Pl Infanta Isabel I, Madrid.
Tel 915 97 65 77.
w mma.es

Federación Española de Deportes de Montaña y Escalada
C/ Floridablanca 84, Barcelona. **Tel** 934 26 42 67. **w** fedme.es

Air Sports

Glovento Sur
Placeta Nevot 4 1°A, Granada. **Tel** 958 29 03 16. **w** gloventosur.com

Kon-Tiki
Igualada, Barcelona.
Tel 93 515 60 60.
w globuskontiki.com

Real Federación Aeronáutica Española
Carretera de la Fortuna, Madrid. **Tel** 915 08 29 50.
w rfae.org

Skydive Empuriabrava
Costa Brava, Catalonia.
Tel 972 45 01 11.
w skydive empuriabrava.com

Skydive Lillo
Aeródromo Don Quijote, Lillo. **Tel** 902 36 62 09.
w skydivelillo.com

Water Sports

Estació Náutica
C/ de la Platja 10–12, L'Estartit. **Tel** 972 75 06 99.
w enestartit.com

Real Federación Española de Vela
C/ Luis de Salazar 9, Madrid. **Tel** 915 19 50 08.
w rfev.es

Surf Center Playa Sur
El Médano, Tenerife.
Tel 922 17 66 88.
w surfcenter.el-medano.com

Adventure Sports

Camping Lecina
Lecina, Sierra de Guara.
Tel 974 31 83 86.
w campinglecina.com

Federación Española de Deportes de Montaña y Escalada
See Walking and Trekking.

Fishing

Federación Española de Pesca y Casting
Madrid. **Tel** 915 32 83 52.
w fepyc.es

Cycling

Fundación de los Ferrocarriles Españoles
Madrid.
w viasverdes.com

Real Federación Española de Ciclismo
Madrid. **Tel** 915 40 08 41.
w rfec.com

Golf

Golf Las Américas
Playa de las Américas, Tenerife. **Tel** 922 75 20 05.
w golflasamericas.com

Real Federación Española de Golf
Arroyo del Monte 5, Madrid. **Tel** 915 55 26 82.
w rfegolf.es

Skiing and Winter Sports

Real Federación Española de Deportes de Invierno
C/ Benisoda 3, Madrid.
Tel 913 76 99 31.
w rfedi.es

Spas

Asociación Nacional de Estaciones Termales
C/ Rodriguez San Pedro 56, Madrid.
Tel 902 11 76 22.
w balnearios.org

Naturism

Federación Española de Naturismo (FEN)
w naturismo.org

Specialist Holidays

Andalucian Adventures
Bonds Mill, Bristol Rd, Stonehouse, Glos (UK).
Tel 00 44 (0)1453 823328.
w andalucian-adventures.co.uk

Catacurian
C/ Progrés 2, El Masroig, Tarragona. **Tel** 977 82 50 85. **w** catacurian.com

Cellar Tours
C/ Zurbano 45, 1°, Madrid.
Tel 911 43 65 53.
w cellartours.com

Club Dance Holidays
108 New Bond Street, London (UK).
Tel 00 44 (0)20 7099 4816.
w clubdanceholidays.com

Cooking Holiday Spain
Urb. Torremar, C/ Roma 9, Benalmadena, Málaga.
Tel 637 80 27 43.
w cookingholidayspain.com

Fantasia Adventure Holidays
C/ Luis Braille P21–3A, Barbate, Cadiz.
Tel 610 94 36 85.
w fantasiaadventureholidays.com

Instituto Cervantes
C/ Alcalá 49, Madrid.
Tel 914 36 76 00.
w cervantes.es

Kaliyoga
Orgiva, Granada.
Tel 858 99 58 90 or 00 44 (0)1373 814663 (UK).
w kaliyoga.com

On Foot in Spain
Ribeira, A Coruña.
Tel 686 99 40 62.
w onfootinspain.com

Switchbacks Mountain Bike Vacations
Barrio La Ermita s/n, Bubion, Granada.
Tel 660 62 33 05.
w switch-backs.com

Xtreme Gene
C/ Rosario 5, Almodovar del Río, Córdoba.
Tel 957 05 70 10.
w xtreme-gene.com

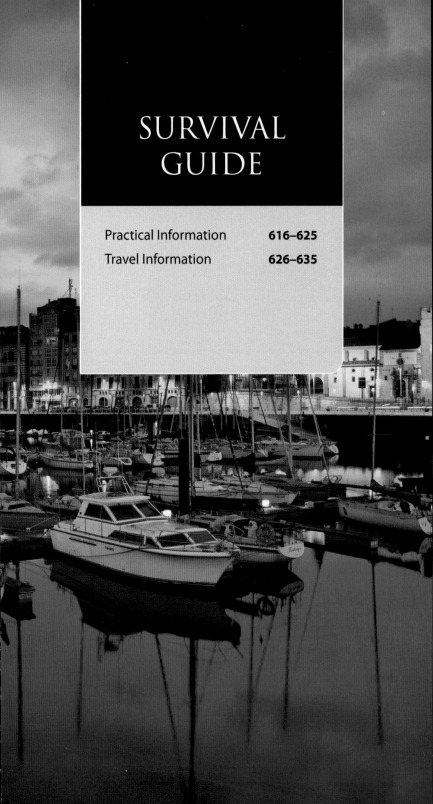

SURVIVAL
GUIDE

Practical Information   **616–625**

Travel Information   **626–635**

PRACTICAL INFORMATION

Spain has a highly developed and diverse tourist industry that caters to a wide variety of travellers – from eco-friendly backpacking and cultural visits to some of Europe's most impressive heritage sites, to sunseeking at resorts for all ages and budgets. Information on accommo-dation, restaurants and leisure activities can be found at the *oficinas de turismo* in all major towns. In addition, Spanish people are naturally open and welcoming to outsiders, so the best information often comes from the locals themselves.

Relaxing on a sandy Spanish beach in summer

When to Go

August is traditionally Spain's main holiday month. Many businesses close for the entire month, and traffic is very heavy at the beginning and end of this period. At any time of year, try to find out in advance if your visit coincides with local *fiestas* – although these are exciting attractions, they often entail wide-spread closures and high prices.

Visas and Passports

Spain is part of the Schengen Agreement, which establishes a common border for various countries in the European Union. Visitors from other participating countries will not be asked for identification upon arrival. However, it is recommended that you carry identification in any case. A valid passport must be shown upon arrival from a non-Schengen country, including the UK.

Visas are not required for citizens of EU countries, Iceland, Norway and Switzerland. A list of entry requirements, available from Spanish embassies, specifies more than 40 other countries, including the USA, Canada, Australia, New Zealand and Japan, whose nationals do not need to apply for a visa if they are visiting Spain for a period of up to 90 days. Those who are planning longer visits than this may apply to the *Gobierno Civil* (a form of local government office) for an extension. You will also need to provide proof of employment or proof of sufficient funds to support yourself during a longer stay. All visitors from countries other than those listed above are legally required to obtain a visa before travelling to Spain.

Student visas are available from the country of origin and give the holder permission to stay until the end of their course.

If you are intending to stay for a long time, it is recommended that you contact your nearest Spanish embassy several months in advance.

Tax-Free Goods Information

Non-EU residents can claim back *IVA* (VAT) on single items worth over €90.15 bought in shops displaying a "Tax Free for Tourists" sign. (Bear in mind that food, drink, tobacco, cars, motorbikes and medicines are exempt from this.) You pay the full price and ask the sales assistant for a *formulario* (tax-exemption form). On leaving Spain, before you check your bags, ask customs officials to stamp your *formulario*; this must be done within three months of the purchase. You should then receive the refund, either by mail or alternatively from some banks and bureaux de change at the airport (La Caixa bank in Barcelona; and Global Refund at Terminals 1 and 4 of Madrid Airport), either in cash or as a refund to your credit card.

Tax-free goods sign

Tourist Information

All major cities and towns have *oficinas de turismo*. They will provide tourists with town plans, lists of hotels and restaurants, information about the locality, and details of leisure activities and events.

Several large cities abroad have a Spanish National Tourist Office; you can also visit www.spain.info, the official website of the Spanish Tourist Board.

OFICINA DE TURISMO
Spanish tourist office sign, featuring the distinctive "i" logo

Social Customs and Etiquette

The Spanish greet and say goodbye to strangers at bus stops and in lifts, shops and other public places. They often talk to people they do not know. Men shake hands when introduced and subsequently whenever they meet, and it is customary for men to greet women with a kiss on each cheek – even when first introduced. Friends and family members embrace or kiss upon meeting. In cities and towns it is considered bad manners to wear shorts or vests in the streets, and you may be asked to cover up to enter churches and other monuments.

ERRESERBATUA

BIZKAIKO FORU ALDUNDIA

RESERVADO DIPUTACION FORAL DE BIZKAIA

A bilingual Basque/Castilian reserved parking sign

Language

The main language of Spain, *Castellano* (Castilian), is spoken by almost everyone throughout the country. There are three main regional languages: Catalan, spoken in Catalonia; *Gallego* (Galician) in Galicia; and *Euskara* (Basque) in the Basque Country. Variants of Catalan are spoken in the Valencia region and also in the Balearic Islands. Learning a few courtesy phrases in Catalan can be a good way to win over the locals in these areas.

Places that deal with tourists – hotels, information offices, restaurants – usually employ people who speak English.

Admission Prices

Admission fees are charged for most museums and monuments, and prices vary within different regions, and depending on the importance of the sight. Some public museums are free on Sundays. Most museums have free admission coinciding with national or regional holidays. Check the individual museums' websites for more detailed information.

Opening Hours

Most museums in Spain close on Sunday afternoon and all day Monday. It is wise to check opening times in advance, since they can vary depending on the time of year. Many museums often close from 2pm to 5pm; some reopen from 5pm to 8pm. Churches may follow these hours, or they may only be open to the public for services.

In some smaller towns in Spain, it is not uncommon for churches, castles and other sights popular with tourists to be kept locked. The key, which is available to visitors on request, will be lodged with a caretaker in a neighbouring house, in the town hall or, sometimes, kept for safekeeping at the local bar.

Taxes and Tipping

There is a relaxed attitude to tipping in Spain, and tips in bars and taxis are usually just the change left over or rounded up to the nearest euro. A small service charge is generally added to restaurant bills, particularly in tapas bars. A tip of 5 or 10 per cent, depending on the level of service and the overall price of the meal, is the norm in restaurants. VAT of 10 per cent is added to the bill, but this is often included in the price of the dishes (this must be stipulated on the menu). VAT of 10 per cent is also added to the hotel bill at the end of your stay.

Travellers with Special Needs

Spain offers a number of options for travellers with special needs. The national association for the disabled, the Confederación Coordinadora Estatal de Minusválidos Físicos de España (COCEMFE), publishes useful guides to facilities in Spain and will help plan a holiday to suit individual needs (see p561).

If you need metro maps and other informative leaflets in Braille, these are available from the Spanish national organization for the blind, the Organización Nacional de Ciegos (ONCE). You will find that tourist offices and the social services departments of town halls are worth investigating as they can also provide useful up-to-date information on local conditions and facilities suitable for disabled travellers.

COCEMFE logo

Ilunion Viajes is a travel agency that specializes in package and organized holidays for people with limited mobility. The UK-based Tourism For All (www.tourismforall.org.uk) offers information on facilities for the disabled in a selection of Spanish resorts. The Society for the Advancement of Travel for the Handicapped (SATH) publishes similar information on a number of destinations for travellers from the US.

Conversion Chart

Imperial to metric
1 inch = 2.54 centimetres
1 foot = 30 centimetres
1 mile = 1.6 kilometres
1 ounce = 28 grams
1 pound = 454 grams
1 pint = 0.6 litre
1 gallon = 4.6 litres

Metric to imperial
1 millimetre = 0.04 inch
1 centimetre = 0.4 inch
1 metre = 3 feet 3 inches
1 kilometre = 0.6 mile
1 gram = 0.04 ounce
1 kilogram = 2.2 pounds
1 litre = 1.8 pints

Children catching small fish with nets, Cala Gracio, Ibiza

Travelling with Children

Spain is a famously child-friendly country, and travellers with kids will find that their offspring are usually welcome in bars, restaurants and hotels.

It is recommended that you take a few sensible precautions when travelling with children, especially in the summer months. Avoid being out and about in the hottest hours of the day (noon–3pm); apply sunscreen with a high protection factor on your children's skin regularly and liberally; always ensure they wear a sunhat with a wide brim; and take frequent breaks for refreshments. Visit www.travelforkids.com for a list of travel agents specializing in child-friendly family holidays.

All large hospitals in Spain provide a paediatrics service, and pharmacy attendants are trained to provide basic treatment for minor health complaints. Visit www.spain-expat.com/spain/information/doctors_in_spain for a list of English-speaking doctors. All public health-care facilities have access to interpreters, whether in person or via the phone.

PLAZA DE /AN MIGUEL

Tiled street sign

Senior Travellers

There are plenty of options for both leisurely and more active holidays for senior travellers in Spain.

Health spas have become increasingly popular throughout the country, and they combine relaxation with specific treatments using thermal waters (www.balnearios.org). Walking tours suitable for senior travellers can be found along the country's network of green paths (www.viasverdes.com).

It is always worth enquiring about senior discounts as some of the larger hotels offer special rates.

Gay and Lesbian Travellers

Attitudes to gay and lesbian people vary greatly between urban and rural areas in Spain. All major cities have thriving gay scenes, with Madrid and Barcelona boasting gay-friendly areas of town (Chueca and "Gayxample") with hotels, restaurants and services aimed at gay and lesbian travellers. The Federación Estatal de Lesbianas, Gays, Transexuales y Bisexuales (FELGTB) (www.felgtb.org) provides information for travellers online and at its local offices in most Spanish towns.

The Gay Pride parades (www.cogam.org) have become major events and are a good place to meet people. A law allowing gays and lesbians to marry, adopt children and enjoy the same rights as heterosexuals was passed in June 2005.

Travelling on a Budget

Travellers looking for budget accommodation should keep an eye out for the sign Hostal or Pensión, which indicates clean and comfortable rooms at a fraction of the cost of a hotel (see also www.hostelworld.com). Most restaurants in Spain offer a menú del día – three courses with wine for as little as €10, and tapas can be another cheap and filling option (they even come free with drinks in some areas).

The Spanish train service is relatively cheap (see pp628–9). Prices can vary on popular lines (for example, the Barcelona–Madrid) depending on the type and speed of train, so check in advance (www.renfe.es). The cheapest, and sometimes the quickest, way to get around is on the excellent network of coaches. Different companies serve different regions, so check timetables and prices online (www.alsa.es) or at the tourist office before travelling. Hitchhiking is common in rural areas and on the Balearic Islands, but avoid hitchhiking alone.

The best and cheapest spectacles in Spain are often found on the streets, especially during the *fiesta* mayor of the various regions and cities, which often include processions and dancing (see pp42–3).

Hostal sign indicating budget accommodation

Student Information

Holders of the International Student Identity Card (ISIC) are entitled to various benefits in Spain, such as discounted accommodation and travel fares as well as reduced entrance charges to museums, galleries and other attractions.

Information for student travellers from overseas is available from national student organizations and, in Spain, from the local government-run **Centros de Información Juvenil (CIJ)** in large towns. The company **Turismoy Viajes Educativos (TIVE)** offers specialist travel services for students.

ISIC student card

Spanish Time

In winter, Spain is one hour ahead of Greenwich Mean Time (GMT) and in summer an hour ahead of British Summer Time (BST). The Canary Islands are on GMT in winter and an hour ahead in summer.

La madrugada refers to the small hours. *Mañana* (morning) lasts until about 2pm and *mediodía* (midday) is the part of the day from about 1pm to 4pm. *La tarde* is the afternoon and *la noche* the evening.

Electrical Adaptors

Spain's electricity supply is 220 volts. Plugs have two round pins. A three-tier standard travel converter enables you to use appliances from abroad. Most hotels can lend you an adaptor. If you come from the USA make sure that your electrical equipment works at this voltage.

Responsible Travel

After several decades of rapid construction that saw much of the country's coastline buried under concrete, Spain has taken big steps to encourage a more sustainable approach to tourism. A series of laws prohibits any construction up to 100 m (328 ft) from the coastline. Tourism, an important source of income, has also become more strictly regulated.

Casas rurales, private country homes that cater to small groups of tourists in a welcoming family atmosphere, offer a perfect option for green travel. Visit www. ecoturismorural.com for more details. The Blue Flag Programme, owned and run by the non-profit Foundation for Environmental Education (FEE), lists 550 beaches and 97 marinas in Spain that comply with their strict environmental criteria. Spain has a delicate ecosystem and several areas that are still barely developed for travellers – take extra care when visiting these spots.

Visitors to Spain can encourage sustainable tourism by using locally owned shops and businesses. Cities are legally obliged to have markets in each district. Elsewhere, go to family-owned shops or buy products at source: most towns have weekend food markets that draw local farmers.

DIRECTORY

Embassies

United Kingdom
Torre Espacio, Paseo de la Castellana 259D, 28046 Madrid.
Tel 91 714 63 00.
W gov.uk/government/world.spain.es

United States
Calle Serrano 75, 28006 Madrid.
Tel 91 587 22 00.
W madrid.usembassy.gov

Spanish Tourist Offices

Australia (consulate)
Level 24, St Martin's Tower, 31 Market St, Sydney NSW 2000.
Tel 29 261 2433.

Barcelona
Plaça de Catalunya 17, 08002 Barcelona.
Tel 93 285 38 34.
W spain.info

Madrid
Plaza de Colón, 28013 Madrid.
Tel 91 454 44 10.
W spain.info

Seville
Plaza San Francisco 19, 41004 Seville.
Tel 95 459 52 88.
W andalucia.org

United Kingdom
6th Floor, 64 North Row, London W1K 7DE. **Tel** 00 44 (0)20 7317 2011. W spain.info

United States
60 East 42nd St, Suite 5300 New York NY 10165.
Tel 00 1 (212) 265 8822.
W spain.info

Disabled Travel

Ilunion Viajes
Calle Pechuán 1, 28002 Madrid.
Tel 91 323 10 29.
W viajes.ilunion.com

Student Travel

CIJ
Paseo de Recoletos 14 1, 28004 Madrid. **Tel** 912 767 444.
W injuve.es

TIVE
Calle Fernando el Católico 88, 28015 Madrid.
Tel 91 543 74 12.
W madrid.org/inforjoven

Students enjoy reduced admission fees to many museums and galleries

Personal Security and Health

In Spain, as in most European countries, rural areas are generally safe, but certain parts of cities are subject to petty crime. Carry cards and money in a belt, and never leave anything visible in your car. Taking out medical insurance cover is advisable, but pharmacists are good sources of assistance for minor health problems. If you lose your documents, contact the local police first to make a claim, then your consulate. Emergency phone numbers vary *(see box opposite)*.

Spanish Police

There are three types of police in Spain. The *Guardia Civil* (National Guard) police mainly rural areas. Their uniform is olive green, but there are local and regional variations. They impose fines for traffic offences outside the cities and police the borders.

The *Policía Nacional*, who mainly wear a blue uniform, operate in towns with a population of more than 30,000. They have been replaced with a regional force, the *Ertzaintza*, in the Basque Country, and with the *Mossos d'Esquadra* in Catalonia. These can be recognized by their respective red and blue berets.

The *Policía Local*, also called *Policía Municipal* or *Guardia Urbana*, dress in blue. They operate independently in each town and also have a separate branch for city traffic control. All three services will direct you to the relevant authority in the event of an incident requiring police help.

Personal Security and Property

Violent crime is rare in Spain, but visitors should avoid walking alone in poorly lit areas. Wear bags and cameras across your body, not on your shoulder.

Holiday insurance is there to protect you financially from the loss or theft of your property, but it is always best to take obvious precautions.

What to Be Aware Of

Be aware of street scams in large cities, including unexpected offers to help with bags, to clean stains off your clothes or to participate in impromptu football games. Never leave a bag or handbag unattended anywhere, and do not place your purse or handbag on the tabletop in a café. Take particular care at markets, tourist sights and stations. Be especially careful of pickpockets when getting on or off a crowded train or metro.

The moment you discover a loss or theft, report it to the local police station. To claim insurance you must do this immediately, since many companies give you only 24 hours. Ask for a *denuncia* (written statement), which you need to make a claim. If your passport is stolen, or if you lose it, report it to your consulate, too.

While tourists remain targets for petty crime in Spanish cities, remember that it is common for Spanish people to approach you and strike up a conversation, and you should not let normal precautions stop you from interacting with the locals.

Men occasionally make complimentary remarks *(piropos)* to women in public, particularly in the street. This is an old custom and is not intended to be intimidating.

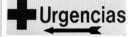

Sign identifying a *Cruz Roja* (Red Cross) emergency treatment centre

In an Emergency

The *Policía Nacional* operate a nationwide emergency phone number (091). Local emergency numbers are listed in telephone directories under *Servicios de Urgencia*; they also appear on tourist maps and leaflets.

For emergency medical treatment, call the emergency services or an ambulance, or go straight to the nearest hospital casualty department *(Urgencias)*.

Visit www.jointcommission.org for a list of hospitals vetted by the US-based NGO Joint Commission.

Pharmacies

Spanish pharmacists have wide responsibilities. They can advise and, in some cases, prescribe

Guardia Civil

Policía Nacional

Policía Local

without consulting a doctor. In a non-emergency, a *farmacéutico* is a good option. It is easy to find one who speaks English.

The *farmacia* sign is a green or red illuminated cross. Those open at night are listed in the windows of all the local pharmacies. Note that *perfumerías* sell toiletries only.

Spanish pharmacy sign

Medical Treatment

In general, the Spanish health system is modern and efficient, and it can be relied on for emergency treatment. There are two kinds of hospitals in Spain: public hospitals (*públicos*) and private clinics (*clínicas privadas*). For emergency treatment, go straight to *Urgencias* at any hospital; for less serious problems, head to a *Centro de Atención Primaria* or *Ambulatorio* and ask for the *médico de urgencias*.

If you have private health insurance, you can go to a private clinic for normal medical complaints.

Legal Assistance

Some insurance policies cover legal costs, for instance after an accident. If you are in need of assistance and are not covered, telephone your nearest consulate. The *Colegio de Abogados* (lawyers' association) of the nearest city can also advise you on where to obtain legal advice or representation locally.

If you need an interpreter, consult the local *Páginas Amarillas* (Yellow Pages) under *Traductores* or *Intérpretes*. Both *Traductores Oficiales* and *Traductores Jurados* are qualified to translate legal and official documents.

Travel and Health Insurance

All EU nationals are entitled to short-term free emergency health-care cover. To claim, you must obtain the European Health Insurance Card (EHIC) from the UK Department of Health or a post office before you travel. The card gives you free health cover at all public Spanish hospitals. It comes with a booklet explaining exactly what health care you are entitled to and how to claim. You may have to pay and claim the money back later. Not all treatments are covered, so for more peace of mind, arrange medical cover in advance.

There is a wide range of medical insurance available for travellers to Spain. Shop around before deciding because prices vary greatly, as do the levels of cover offered, with some including aspects like emergency travel back home or the cost of relatives joining you. Many credit cards also offer limited health insurance for their users.

Public Conveniences

Public pay-toilets are rare in Spain. Try department stores, or bars and restaurants where you are a customer. You may have to ask for a key (*la llave*), and it is best to bring your own tissues. There are also toilets at service stations on motorways. Toilets are most commonly known as *los servicios*.

Outdoor Hazards

Every summer Spain is prey to forest fires fanned by winds and fuelled by bone-dry vegetation. Be sensitive to fire hazards and use car ashtrays. Broken glass can also start a fire, so take your empty bottles away with you.

Patrol car of the *Policía Nacional*, Spain's main urban police force

Policía Local patrol car, mainly seen in small towns

Cruz Roja (Red Cross) ambulance

The sign *coto de caza* in woodland areas identifies a hunting reserve where you must follow the country codes. *Toro bravo* means "fighting bull" – do not approach. A *camino particular* sign indicates a private driveway. Do not approach dogs that are protecting country properties.

If you are climbing or hill-walking, make sure that you are properly equipped and let someone know when you expect to return.

DIRECTORY

Emergency Numbers

Emergency: all services
Tel 112 (nationwide).

Policía Nacional
Tel 091 (nationwide).

Fire Brigade
(*Bomberos*)
Tel 080 (in most major cities).

Ambulance
Tel 112 or 061.
For other cities' emergency services, consult the local telephone directory.

Banking and Local Currency

You may enter Spain with any amount of money, but if you intend to export more than €10,000, you should declare it. Travellers' cheques may be exchanged at banks, *cajas de cambio* (foreign currency exchanges), some hotels and some shops. Banks generally offer the best exchange rates. The cheapest exchange may be offered on your credit or direct debit card, which you can use in cash dispensers (automated teller machines, ATMs) displaying the appropriate sign.

A 24-hour cash dispenser

Banking Hours

Spanish banks are beginning to extend their opening times, but expect extended hours only at large central branches in the big cities.

Banks are open from 8am to 2pm during the week. Some open until 1pm on Saturdays. All close on Saturdays in July and August; in some areas, they also close on Saturdays from May to September.

Changing Money

Most banks have a foreign exchange desk with the sign *Cambio* or *Extranjero*, which will accept travellers' cheques and cash. Always take your passport as identification to effect any transaction.

You can draw up to €300 on major credit cards at a bank. It is worth mentioning your travel plans to your bank and credit card company before you go away, so that your card is not blocked by their fraud prevention system.

Bureaux de change, with the sign *Caja de Cambio* or "Change", may state that they charge no commission, but their exchange rates are invariably less favourable than those found at banks. One benefit is that they are often open outside normal banking hours. They are usually located in popular tourist areas, as well as at airports and mainline rail stations. *Cajas de Ahorro* (savings banks) also exchange money. They open from 8:30am to 2pm on weekdays and also on Thursday afternoons from 4:30pm to 7:45pm.

Cheques and Cards

The use of travellers' cheques is declining and it is not always easy to find places to cash the cheques. Banks also need 24 hours' notice to cash cheques larger than €3,000.

Prepaid VISA and MasterCard credit cards are a convenient way to pay, as are Travel Money Cards. These cards work like debit cards. They are available in several currencies from most banks, and can be reloaded through their websites.

The most widely accepted cards are **VISA**, and **MasterCard**, although **American Express** is also used. The major banks will allow cash withdrawals on credit cards. All cash dispensers accept most foreign cards, and they will often give you a choice of several languages, including English. Most, however, only operate with cards that have an electronic chip. Also, the level of commission charged on your withdrawal will depend on your own bank, and some credit cards may charge an additional fee.

When you pay with a card, cashiers pass it through a card-reading machine and you usually need to provide a pin number. In shops you will always be asked for additional photo ID. Since leaving your passport in the hotel safe is preferable, make sure you have an alternative original document on hand (photocopies will rarely do), such as a driver's licence.

As with the rest of Europe, cards are not always accepted in smaller bars and restaurants, so take some cash with you.

BBVA

Logo for BBVA, the Banco Bilbao Vizcaya Argentaria

Cash Dispensers

If your card is linked to your home bank account, you can use it with your PIN to withdraw money from cash dispensers. All take VISA and MasterCard.

When you enter your PIN, instructions are displayed in English, French, German and Spanish. Many dispensers are inside buildings and to gain access you will have to run your card through a door-entry system.

Cards with the Cirrus and Maestro logos can also be widely used to withdraw money from cash machines.

DIRECTORY

Foreign Banks

Barclays Bank
C/ Velázquez 68, 28001 Madrid.
Tel 901 14 14 14.

Citibank
C/ Velázquez 31, 28001 Madrid.
Tel 914 26 07 82.

Lloyds TSB
C/ Serrano 90, 28006 Madrid.
Tel 901 10 90 00.

Lost Cards and Travellers' Cheques

American Express
Tel 900 81 00 29.

Diners Club
Tel 902 40 11 12.

MasterCard
Tel 900 97 12 31 (toll-free from landlines only).

VISA
Tel 900 99 11 24 (toll-free from landlines only).

The Euro

Spain was one of the 12 countries adopting the euro in 2002, with its original currency, the peseta, phased out in the course of the same year.

EU countries using the euro as sole official currency are known as the Eurozone. Several EU members have opted out of joining this common currency.

Euro notes are identical throughout the Eurozone countries, each one including designs of fictional architectural structures and monuments. The coins, however, have one identical side (the value side), and one side with an image unique to each country. Both notes and coins are exchangeable in each of the participating euro countries.

Banknotes

Euro banknotes, each a different colour and size, come in seven denominations. The €5 note (grey in colour) is the smallest, followed by the €10 note (pink), €20 note (blue), €50 note (orange), €100 note (green), €200 note (yellow) and €500 note (purple).

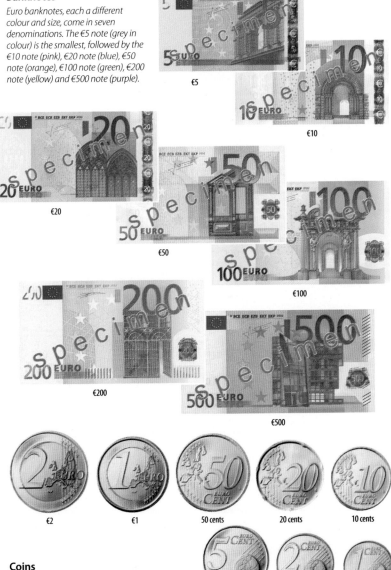

€5

€10

€20

€50

€100

€200

€500

Coins

The euro has eight coin denominations: €2 and €1 (silver and gold); 50 cents, 20 cents and 10 cents (gold); and 5 cents, 2 cents and 1 cent (bronze).

€2

€1

50 cents

20 cents

10 cents

5 cents

2 cents

1 cent

Communications and Media

The telecommunications company Movistar dominates the industry in Spain, but companies like Orange, Yoigo and Vodafone also compete for the mobile phone market. Public telephones are easy to find; most require a phone card. International calls tend to be expensive. The postal service, Correos, is identified by a blue crown logo on a yellow background. Registered post and telegrams can be sent from Correos offices. They also sell stamps, but most people buy them from *estancos* (tobacconists).

Telephoning in Spain

When calling from a fixed line, there are four charge bands for international calls: EU countries; non-EU countries and Northwest Africa; North and South America; and the rest of the world. International calls can be quite expensive, especially when made from a hotel, which may add a surcharge. Though now harder to find, a call from a phone booth, or *cabina*, costs 35 per cent more than from a private phone, though using phonecards, available at tobacconists, supermarkets and newsstands, gives much cheaper rates. Most reverse-charge calls must be made through the operator. When telephoning Spain from abroad, first dial the international code for Spain (34) followed by the area code.

Mobile Phones

Roaming costs to use your mobile phone in Spain vary greatly among the different providers; however, mobile phones have now become a more reasonable option if your operator offers a special

The logo of Spain's main telecom company

fixed rate. The EU has tried to standardize the cost of using a mobile phone within its borders.

If you are planning to make a lot of calls, the best option is to buy a Spanish top-up SIM card, or a handset with a top-up SIM card, at a department store or specialist phone shop. The most popular providers in Spain are Movistar and Vodafone; each have their own shops with experts who can give you advice. For a simple handset, plus SIM card (allowing free incoming calls in Spain), expect to pay in the region of €50–€60.

To add more credit to your phone card, purchase a scratch card from shops and supermarkets. Alternatively, you can do it automatically with your credit card by dialling a number from your phone – check with your service provider. Mobile phone top-ups are also available at most ATMs.

Internet and Email

Wireless hot spots are available in all airports, hotels and conference centres throughout Spain, although the majority are not free. Credit can be bought online with a major credit card.

The number of Internet cafés (*cibercafés*) in most cities and resorts is dwindling. *Locutorios* (privately owned call centres) often provide cheap Internet access. Also, free Internet access can be found in public libraries, some public areas (such as Madrid's Plaza Mayor), universities and most restaurants, bars and cafés offering Wi-Fi service.

Newspapers and Magazines

Newsagents in tourist-oriented town centres often stock periodicals in languages other than Spanish. The English-language daily newspapers available on publication day are the *International Herald Tribune*, the *Financial Times*, the *Guardian International* and the *Sun*, which is printed in the south of Spain.

A selection of Spanish newspapers

Useful Spanish Dialling Codes

- When calling within a city, within a province, or to call another province, dial the entire number. The province is indicated by the initial digits: Barcelona numbers, for example, start with 93; Girona with 972; and Tarragona 977.
- To make an international call, dial 00, then dial the country code, the area code and the number.
- Country codes are: UK 44; Eire 353; France 33; USA and Canada 1; Australia 61; New Zealand 64. It may be necessary to omit the initial digit of the destination's area code.

- For operator/directory service, dial 11888.
- For international directories, dial 11825.
- To make a reverse-charge (collect) call to the UK only, dial 900 961 682. Inexpensive international calls can be made in *locutorios*, or call centres. These can be found in most cities and towns. Cheap phone cards can also be purchased there.
- To report technical faults, dial 1002 (Movistar only).
- For the speaking clock and for a wake-up call, dial 1212 (from Movistar landlines only).

Several other English-language and European titles are also on the stands, but usually only the day after publication. The most widely read Spanish papers are *El País*, *El Mundo*, *ABC*, *La Razón* and *La Vanguardia* (in Catalonia).

Popular weekly news magazines such as *Time*, *Newsweek* and *The Economist* are readily available throughout the country.

Weekly listings magazines for local arts, entertainment and events are published in Barcelona *(see p194)*, Madrid *(see p324)* and Seville *(see p460)*. Several other Spanish cities also have their own listings magazines.

A number of foreign-language periodicals are published by expatriates in Madrid and in the country's other main tourist areas. Some examples in English include *Metropolitan* in Barcelona, *Sur* on the Costa del Sol, the *Costa Blanca News* and the *Mallorca Daily Bulletin*.

Television and Radio

Televisión Española, Spain's state television company, broadcasts on two channels, TVE1 and TVE2, which run 24 hours a day.

Several of the *comunidades* have their own publicly owned television channels, which broadcast in the language of the region. In addition, there are a few national television stations: Antena 3, Tele-5 (Telecinco), La Sexta and Cuatro.

Digital TV in Spain is offered by two companies, Canal+ and Imagenio. This provides access to dozens of local channels and the possibility of watching programmes in their original language or with subtitles.

Radio is very popular throughout Spain and there are a number of English-language radio stations based mainly in the south, including Talk Radio Europe, which is the largest network, (88.2 FM, 88.9 FM, 105.1 FM, 92.7 FM, 103.9 FM and

104.6 FM) and Wave96FM (96 FM) from Malagá on the Costa del Sol. All of these stations can also be listened to online and are a good source of local and international news in English.

Postal Service

Correos is Spain's postal service. Mail sent within the same city usually takes a day to arrive. Deliveries between cities take two to three days. Urgent or important post can be sent by *urgente* (express) or *certificado* (registered) mail. For fast delivery, use the Correos Postal Express Service or a private courier.

Post can be registered, and telegrams sent from all Correos offices. However, it is much easier to buy stamps from an *estanco* (tobacconist). Postal rates fall into three price bands: Spain; Europe and North Africa; and the rest of the world. Parcels must be weighed and stamped at Correos offices.

Spanish postbox

The main Correos offices open 8:30am–9:30pm Monday to Friday and 9:30am–1pm on Saturday; outside the cities they close by 1–2pm on weekdays.

Letters sent from a post office usually arrive more quickly than if posted in a postbox *(buzón)*. In cities, postboxes are yellow pillar boxes; elsewhere they are small, wall-mounted postboxes. *Poste restante* letters should be addressed care of the *Lista de Correos* and the town, and collected from main offices.

To send and receive money by post, ask for a *giro postal*.

Addresses

In Spanish addresses, the house number follows the name of the street. The floor of a block of flats comes after a hyphen. Therefore 4-2° means a flat on the second floor of number four. All postcodes in Spain have five digits, the first two being the province number.

Local Government

Spain is one of Europe's most decentralized states. Many powers have been devolved to the 17 regions, also known as *comunidades autónomas*, which have their own elected parliaments. These regions have varying degrees of independence from Madrid, with the Basques and Catalans enjoying the most autonomy. The *comunidades* provide some services – such as the promotion of tourism – that were once carried out by the central government.

The country is subdivided into 50 provinces, each with its *diputación* (council). The affairs of each of the Balearic and Canary islands are run by an island council.

Every town, or group of villages, is administered by an *ayuntamiento* (town council – the word also means "town hall"), which is then supervised by an elected *alcalde* (mayor) and a team of councillors.

Murcia's town hall *(ayuntamiento or casa consistorial)*

TRAVEL INFORMATION

Spain has invested heavily in its transport infrastructure since 2005, creating new motorways and high-speed rail networks to connect much of the country. Madrid Airport is an important international travel hub, and new terminals at Malaga and Barcelona Airports have been built to cater for the huge influx of passengers. Intercity rail services are reliable and efficient, but coaches are a faster and more frequent option between smaller towns. In much of rural Spain, public transport is limited, and a car is the most practical option for getting about. Spain boasts some beautiful back roads to hidden areas of the country. Ferries connect mainland Spain with the UK, Italy, North Africa and the Balearic and Canary islands.

Green Travel

Public transport in larger cities has adopted a green focus, and most buses now run on clean fuel. Services are generally excellent, and reasonably priced. With the opening of the long-awaited Madrid–Barcelona high-speed rail link (the AVE), Spain now boasts one of Europe's best railway infrastructures. There are plans for added links to the Basque region and Galicia, and from Northern Spain into France. Prices on the AVE vary depending on the days you want to travel, and they are much lower if you buy your tickets online.

Some areas of Spain are still best accessed by road. Car users should consider renting hybrid vehicles, now available from major car rental firms. Local and environmentally friendly bus services reach most areas.

Aircraft at Ibiza's airport

Arriving by Air

Spain is served by most international airlines and by many budget airlines. Its national airline **Iberia** offers flights from most European capitals. **British Airways** flies to Madrid and Barcelona, as do US airlines **Delta**, **United** and **American Airlines**. Iberia has a wide-ranging service from the USA.

International Airports

The most regular international services operate from Madrid and Barcelona. Palma de Mallorca, Tenerife Sur, Las Palmas de Gran Canaria, Ibiza, Málaga, Lanzarote, Alicante, Fuerteventura and Menorca handle a lot of tourists, especially in the summer.

Tickets and Fares

Air fares vary by season and demand. Special deals, particularly for city breaks, often run in winter. Look out for Iberia's reduced fares and for low-cost carriers, such as **easyJet** and **Ryanair** (UK). **Vueling** offers low-cost flights from Spain to other European countries.

Airport	Information	Distance to City Centre	Taxi Fare to City Centre	Public Transport Time to City Centre
Alicante (Alacant)	902 40 47 04	10 km (6 miles)	€28	Bus: 20 mins
Barcelona	902 40 47 04	14 km (9 miles)	€35	Rail: 35 mins Bus: 25 mins
Bilbao	902 40 47 04	12 km (7 miles)	€26	Bus: 30 mins
Madrid	902 40 47 04	16 km (10 miles)	€35	Bus: 20 mins Metro: 30–40 mins
Málaga	902 40 47 04	8 km (5 miles)	€24	Rail: 15 mins Bus: 20 mins
Palma de Mallorca	902 40 47 04	9 km (5.5 miles)	€25	Bus: 15 mins
Las Palmas de Gran Canaria	902 40 47 04	18 km (11 miles)	€31	Bus: 60 mins
Santiago de Compostela	902 40 47 04	10 km (6 miles)	€28	Bus: 20–30 mins
Seville	902 40 47 04	10 km (6 miles)	€22–€30	Bus: 25–30 mins
Tenerife Sur – Reina Sofía	902 40 47 04	64 km (40 miles) to Santa Cruz	€80	Bus: 60 mins
Valencia	902 40 47 04	9 km (5.5 miles)	€20–€25	Bus: 20 or 60 mins

The departures concourse at Seville Airport

Internal Flights

In the past, the majority of domestic flights were operated by Iberia, but now there are other main carriers, such as **Air Europa** and Vueling. The most frequent shuttle service is the Puente Aéreo, run between Barcelona and Madrid by Iberia every 15 minutes at peak times, and half-hourly or hourly at other times. The flight generally takes 50 minutes. Vueling and Air Europa services between Madrid and the regional capitals are not as frequent as the Puente Aéreo, but they are usually cheaper; book early to take advantage of lower fares. Flights between the Canary Islands are operated by **Binter**. Some flights from domestic airports are billed as international flights and stop over at major Spanish cities en route.

Acciona Trasmediterránea logo

Arriving by Sea

Ferries connect the Spanish mainland to the Balearic and Canary islands, and to North Africa, Italy and the UK. All the important routes are served by car ferries. Always make an advance booking, especially in summer.

Three routes link Spain with the UK. **Brittany Ferries** sails between Plymouth in the UK and Santander in Cantabria. There are also routes linking Portsmouth with Santander, and Portsmouth with Bilbao in the Basque Country. The crossings take over 24 hours. Each ship has cabins, chairs to sleep on, restaurants, cafés and cinemas. The Italian

Grimaldi Lines has overnight journeys to Rome, Livorno and Sardinia.

Ferries to the Islands

Frequent crossings run from Barcelona and Valencia to the three main Balearic islands. **Acciona Trasmediterránea** ferries take from four hours (using the fast ferry from Barcelona) to eight hours. The same company also operates frequent inter-island services, while small operators take day-trippers (passengers only) from Ibiza to Formentera. **Balearia** also sails to the Balearic Islands from Barcelona and Valencia.

Acciona Trasmediterránea operates a weekly service from Cádiz to the main ports of the Canary Islands, which normally takes 32 hours. Car ferries link the various islands. There are also passengers-only services between the islands of Gran Canaria, Tenerife and Fuerteventura, and between Tenerife and La Gomera.

Ferries to the islands have cabins, cafés, restaurants, bars, shops, cinemas, pools and sunbathing decks. They also have facilities for people with special needs. Entertainment is provided on mainland crossings to the Canary Islands.

Ferries to Africa

Acciona Trasmediterránea has daily services to the Spanish territories in North Africa: from Málaga and Almería to Melilla, and from Algeciras to Ceuta, as well as from Algeciras and Tarifa to Tangier. Balearia also sails to Ceuta and Tangier from Algeciras. It maybe worth checking the website for up-to-date offers.

Balearia car ferry sailing to the Balearic Islands

Travelling by Train

The Spanish state railway, RENFE (*Red Nacional de Ferrocarriles Españoles*), operates a service that is continually improving, particularly between cities. The fastest intercity services are called TALGO and AVE – these names are acronyms for the high-speed luxury trains that run on these routes. *Largo recorrido* (long-distance) and *regionales y cercanías* (regional and local) trains are notoriously slow, many stopping at every station on the way. They are much cheaper than the high-speed trains, but journey times can be hours longer.

Arriving by Train

There are several routes to Spain from France. The main western route runs from Paris through Hendaye in the Pyrenees to San Sebastián. The eastern route from Paris runs via Cerbère and Port Bou to Barcelona. The trains from London, Brussels, Amsterdam, Geneva, Zurich and Milan all reach Barcelona via Cerbère. At Cerbère there are also connections with the TALGO and the long-distance services to Valencia, Alicante, Girona and Murcia. If you book a sleeper on the TALGO from Paris, you travel to your destination without having to change trains. There are direct trains to Madrid and Barcelona from Paris, and to Barcelona from Milan, Geneva and Zurich.

Exploring by Train

Spain offers many options for train travellers. The introduction of high-speed services has made it possible to travel the long distances between the main cities extremely quickly. Ticket prices compare favourably with the cost of high-speed train fares in many other countries in Europe. Efficient high-speed AVE rail services link Madrid with Seville in two and a half hours, and with Barcelona in three hours. The AVE from Madrid to Zaragoza takes one and a half hours; to Málaga two hours and 40 minutes; and to Valladolid only 50 minutes. AVE routes also link Barcelona with

AVE high-speed trains at Estación de Santa Justa in Seville

Seville and with Málaga – both trips take five and a half hours.

The *largo recorrido* (long-distance) trains are so much slower that you usually need to travel overnight. You can choose between a *cochecama* (a compartment with two or four *camas*, or beds) or a *litera*, one of six seats in a compartment that converts into a bunk bed. You reserve these when booking and pay a supplement. Book at least a month in advance. *Regionales y cercanías* (the regional and local services) are frequent and cheap.

In Madrid the major stations for regional and long-distance trains are Atocha and Chamartín. The AVE runs from Atocha, and the TALGO from both. Sants and Passeig de Gràcia are Barcelona's two main stations. In Seville Santa Justa is the only

Logo for the high-speed rail service AVE

DIRECTORY

National Enquiries and Reservations

Luxury Train Club
Benwell House, Preston, Chippenham, Wiltshire SN15 4DX, UK. **Tel** 00 44124 989 0205.
W luxurytrainclub.com

RENFE
Tel 902 32 03 20; for information on disabled access call 902 24 05 05. **W** renfe.es

Regional Railways

ET
Tel 902 54 32 10.
W euskotren.es

FGC
Tel 932 05 15 15.
W fgc.net

FGV
Tel 961 92 40 00.
W fgv.es

station for regional and international services. Major train terminals pass luggage through scanners; allow extra time for this.

Fares

Fares for rail travel in Spain are structured according to the speed and quality of the service. Tickets for the TALGO and AVE trains cost the most.

Interrail tickets for people under 26 and Eurail tickets for non-EU residents are available from major travel agencies in Europe and from **RENFE** ticket offices in Spain. Always take proof of your identity when booking.

Holidays onboard Spain's luxury train (*see opposite*) are expensive but offer high standards of comfort.

Regional Railways

Three of the *comunidades autónomas* have regional rail companies. Catalonia and Valencia each has its own *Ferrocarrils de la Generalitat* – respectively, the **FGC** and the

Spain's Principal RENFE Network

Spain's rail network operates a wide variety of services. Consult a RENFE brochure or train time-table before buying your ticket.

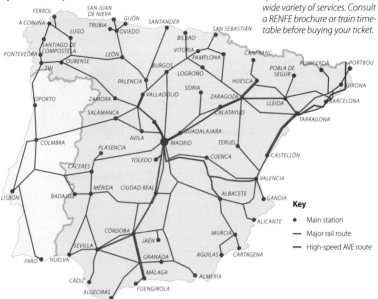

Key

● Main station
— Major rail route
— High-speed AVE route

FGV; and the Basque Country has the **ET** (*Eusko Trenbideak*).

Tickets for Spain's luxury train, similar to the Orient Express, can be obtained from travel agents. El Transcantábrico, run by the **Luxury Train Club**, travels the 1,000 km (620 miles) of Spain's north coast between San Sebastián and Santiago de Compostela. Passengers travel in style for eight days in 14 restored period carriages that were all built between 1900 and 1930.

The regional tourist offices publicize unusual rail services in their local areas, such as the narrow-gauge lines to Inca and Sóller in Mallorca *(see p519)*.

Booking Tickets

Tickets for TALGO, AVE and any other *largo recorrido* travel may be bought at any of the major railway stations from the *taquilla* (ticket office). They are also sold by all travel agents in Spain, who will charge a commission. RENFE tickets are sometimes sold by travel agents in other countries. Telephone reservations may be made directly to all RENFE ticket offices with a credit card. Tickets can also

Ticket machine for local and regional lines

be bought via the RENFE website, which has some cheaper fares, and printed out. Tickets for local and regional services are purchased from the station *taquilla*. In larger stations, they can be bought from ticket machines. Tickets for *cercanías* (local services) cannot be reserved. For a one-way journey, ask for *ida*, and for a return, ask for *ida y vuelta*. Return tickets are cheaper.

Timetables

RENFE timetables change in May and October each year. Your travel agent will be able to provide the correct times for your train journey. Timetables can also be accessed in English via the RENFE website. In Spain, timetables are available from RENFE offices. Most come as leaflets and are broken down into the various types of journey: intercity, *largo recorrido* and *regionales*. *Cercanías* time-tables are posted on boards at local railway stations.

Atocha, one of Madrid's largest mainline railway stations

Travelling by Road

Spain's fastest roads are its *autopistas*. They are normally dual carriageways and are subsidized by *peajes* (tolls). *Autovías* are similar but have no tolls. The *carretera nacional* is the countrywide network of main roads or highways with the prefix N. Smaller minor roads are generally less well kept, but they are often a more leisurely and enjoyable way to see rural areas of Spain.

Cambio de sentido (slip road) 300 m (330 yards) ahead

Arriving by Car

Many people drive to Spain via the French motorways. The most direct routes across the Pyrenees, using the motorways, pass through Hendaye on the western flank and Port Bou in the east. Other, rather more tortuous routes may be used, from Toulouse through the Vall d'Aran, for instance. From the UK, there are car ferries from Plymouth to Santander and from Portsmouth to Santander and Bilbao in northern Spain *(see p627)*.

What to Take

A Green Card from your motor insurance company is needed in order to extend your comprehensive cover to Spain. The RAC, AA and Europ Assistance have rescue and recovery policies with European cover. Spanish law requires you to carry your vehicle's registration document, a valid insurance certificate and your driving licence at all times. You must always be able to show a passport or a national identity card as ID. You must also display a sticker on the back of the car showing its country of registration. The headlights of right-hand drive vehicles need to be adjusted or deflected. Stickers for this are available at ferry ports and on ferries. You risk on-the-spot fines if you do not carry a red warning triangle and a reflective jacket. In winter, carry chains if you intend to drive in mountain areas. In summer, take drinking water when travelling in remote areas.

Buying Petrol

In Spain *gasolina* (petrol) and *gasóleo* (diesel) are priced by the litre. *Gasolina sin plomo* (unleaded petrol) is available everywhere. All three cost more at the *autopista* service stations. Self-service stations, where you fill up yourself, are common. Modern petrol pumps in Spain are sometimes operated by credit card. You should run your card through the machine, press the buttons to indicate the amount of petrol you want in euros, and then serve yourself.

You must wait for service if there are attendants at the station. They will ask *¿cuánto?* (how much?); you should reply *lleno* (fill the tank), or specify an amount in euros: *diez euros, por favor*. If you do use your credit card to pay at a motorway service station, you will be asked to show your passport or another form of identification. Gibraltar and Andorra have tax-free, cheap petrol, so it is worth filling up before entering Spain.

Speed limit 50 km/h (31 mph)

Pedestrian crossing sign

Rules of the Road

Most traffic regulations and warnings to motorists are represented on signs by easily recognized symbols. However, a few road rules and signs may be unfamiliar to some drivers from other countries.

To turn left at a busy junction or across oncoming traffic, you may have to turn right first and cross a main road, often by way of traffic lights, a bridge or an underpass. If you are accidentally going the wrong way on a motorway or a main road with a solid white line, you can turn round at a sign for a *cambio de sentido*. At crossings, give way to the right unless a sign indicates otherwise. You must wear seat belts in both front and rear seats.

Oncoming drivers may flash their headlights to mean "you go", "danger", "your lights are on unnecessarily" or "speed trap ahead".

A filling station run by a leading chain with branches throughout Spain

Speed Limits and Fines

Speed limits for cars without trailers on the roads in Spain are as follows:
• 120 km/h (75 mph) on *autopistas* (toll motorways);
• 100 km/h (62 mph) on *autovías* (non-toll motorways);
• 90 km/h (56 mph) on *carreteras nacionales* (main roads) and *carreteras comarcales* (secondary roads);
• 40 km/h (31 mph) in built-up areas.

Speeding fines are imposed on the spot and are determined by the speed at which you are driving; fines range from €6.50 to €12 per kilometre over the limit. Fines for other traffic offences (such as turning the wrong way into a one-way street) depend on the severity of the offence and often on the whim of the police officer.

Tests for drink-driving and fines for drivers over the blood alcohol legal limit, which is 30 mg per ml, are now imposed frequently throughout the country. If driving, it is best not to drink any alcohol at all.

Motorways

Spain has more than 2,900 km (1,800 miles) of *autopistas*, and many more are planned. These are generally toll roads and can be expensive to use. You can establish whether a motorway is toll-free by the letters that prefix the number of the road: A = free motorway, AP = toll motorway.

The long-distance tolls are calculated per kilometre, and the rate varies from region to region. Among the busiest and most expensive are the AP7 along the south coast from Barcelona to Alicante and the AP68 Bilbao–Zaragoza *autopista*.

There are service stations every 40 km (25 miles) or so along the *autopistas*, and they are marked by a blue and white parking sign (P) or a sign indicating the services available. As you approach a service station, a sign will indicate the distance to the next one and will also list its services. Most will have a petrol station, toilets, a shop and a café.

Driving through the Sierra Nevada along one of Europe's highest roads

Emergency telephones occur every 2 km (1.2 miles) along the *autopistas*.

Using Autopista Tolls

If you are travelling on an *autopista*, you pick up a ticket from a tollbooth *(peaje)* as you drive on to it and give it up at a booth as you exit. Your toll will be calculated according to the distance you have covered. Over some short stretches of motorways near the cities a fixed price is charged.

Tolls can be paid either in cash or by credit card. You must join one of three channels at the *peaje* leading to different booths. Do not drive into *telepago*, a credit system for which a chip on your windscreen is required. *Tarjetas* has machines for you to pay by credit card, while in *manual* an attendant will take your ticket and your money.

Autopista toll booths ahead

Other Roads

Carreteras nacionales, Spain's main roads, have black-and-white signs and are designated N (*Nacional*) plus a number. Those with Roman numerals (NIII) start at the Puerta del Sol in Madrid. The distance from the Kilometre Zero mark in the Puerta del Sol (*see p276*) appears on kilometre markers. Those with ordinary numbers (N6) have kilometre markers giving the distance from the provincial capital. Some *carreteras nacionales* are dual carriageways, but most are single-lane roads and can be slow. They tend to be least busy from 2pm to 5pm.

Autovías are roads built in recent years to motorway standard to replace N roads. They have blue signs similar to *autopista* signs. Because they have no tolls, they are busier than *autopistas*.

Carreteras comarcales, secondary roads, have a number preceded by the letter C. Other minor roads have numbers preceded by letters representing the name of the province, such as the LE1313 in Lleida. In winter, watch out for signs indicating whether a mountain pass ahead is open (*abierto*) or closed (*cerrado*).

The *peaje manual* channel, with attendant

Car Hire

The most popular car-hire companies in Spain are **Europcar**, **Avis** and **Hertz**. All have offices at airports and major train stations, as well as in the large cities.

In addition to the international car-hire companies, a few Spanish firms, such as **Atesa**, operate nationwide. There is also a growing number of low-cost hire firms like **easyCar**, **pepecar** and **hispacar**, although you may need to pick up your car some distance from the airport.

You can often get the best deals by booking in advance online. There are also fly-drive and other package deals including car hire available. Fly-drive, an option for two or more travellers, can be arranged by travel agents and tour operators.

If you wish to hire a car locally for around a week or less, you will be able to arrange it with a local travel agent. A car for hire is called a *coche de alquiler*.

For chauffeur-driven cars in Spain, Avis offers deals from major cities. Car-hire prices and conditions vary according to the region and locality.

Some of the leading car-hire companies operating in Spain

Maps

Fold-out road maps can be obtained at airports, on the ferries and from tourist offices. The Spanish Ministry of Transport publishes a comprehensive road map in book form, the *Mapa Oficial de Carreteras*. The oil company Repsol publishes the **Guía Repsol**, a road map and restaurant guide conveniently in one book and also available for iPhone and iPad. **Michelin** publishes a useful series of maps

City taxis queuing for fares outside an airport

(440–448, with orange covers) at a scale of 1:400,000 (1 cm:4 km), sold at bookshops and petrol stations. Websites www.guiarepsol.com and www.viamichelin.com allow you to plan your route, providing information on roads, weather and toll fees.

A series of more detailed maps at 1:200,000 for cycling and walking is published by Plaza y Janés. Military maps at scales of 1:50,000 and 1:100,000 are available from **Stanfords** in London and from some local and specialist bookshops in Spain, such as **Altaïr** in Barcelona. Tourist offices usually have free street maps.

You can find detailed street maps of central Barcelona on *pp184–9*, of Madrid on *pp312–19* and of Seville on *pp452–7* of this guide.

Parking

The arrival of resident-only parking schemes means that street parking is increasingly hard to come by in major cities.

As a rule, you may not park where the pavement edge is painted yellow or where a "no parking" sign is displayed. Occasionally there is a "no parking" sign on both sides of a city street, one saying "1–15" and the other "16–30". This means that you can park on one side of the street only for the fortnight indicated on the sign.

In the cities, non-metered on-street parking is rare, but there are blue pay-and-display parking spaces. To use them, buy a ticket from the machine

No parking at any time of day

and display it on the inside of your windscreen. The cost averages about €1–€3 per hour. You can usually park for up to two hours. Major cities have many underground car parks. You collect a ticket when you enter and either pay the attendant as you drive out, or pay at a machine which returns your ticket so you can deposit it in another machine at the exit.

Taxis

Every city and/or region has its own taxi design and tariffs, but all taxis will display a green light if they are free. All are metered; when you set off, a minimum fee will be shown. In smaller villages, the taxi may be a resident driving an unmetered private car – ask at your hotel or in a shop for the number of a recommended local driver.

Road Conditions and Weather Forecasts

For recorded road and traffic information, call the national toll-free number for **Información de Tráfico de Carreteras**. This service is in Spanish only. Ask at your hotel reception if you need a translation. The RAC offers route-planning services tailored to individual requirements; these may include current road conditions.

The weather information service, **Agencia Estatal de Metereología**, gives forecasts for each region, as well as the national and international weather. It also gives details on maritime and mountain conditions.

Arriving by Coach

Often the cheapest way to reach and travel around Spain is by coach. **Eurolines** operates various routes throughout Europe and runs daily services to Barcelona. Check out the website for available offers.

Coaches from the UK depart from London Victoria Coach Station. Tickets may be bought from **National Express**, the sister company of Eurolines, or travel agents. The journey takes about 24 hours.

Alsa, a regional coach service

Travelling Around Spain by Coach

There is no Spanish national coach company, but private regional companies operate routes around the country. The largest coach company is **Alsa**, which runs in all regions and has routes and services that cover most of the country. Other companies operate in

Cycling

Cycling is popular in Spain, and there are bicycles for hire in most tourist spots. However, there are few cycle lanes outside the cities. Bicycles may be carried on *cercanías* trains after 2pm on Fridays until the last train on Sunday night; on any *regional* train with a goods compartment; and

Cycle touring, a popular holiday activity

on all long-distance overnight trains. If you need to take your bicycle long-distance at other times, check it in an hour before the train departs. You may have to send it as luggage and pay a baggage charge based on its weight. It might not travel with you, so you will have to collect it when it arrives.

particular regions – Alsina Graells, for instance, covers most of the south and east of Spain. Tickets and information for long-distance travel are available at all main coach stations as well as from travel agents, but note that it is not always possible to book tickets in advance.

In Madrid the biggest coach stations are Estación Sur and Intercambiador de Autobuses. Always check which coach station your bus is due to leave from when you purchase your ticket.

Indicators for Seville's circular bus routes

Local Buses

Local bus routes and time-tables are posted at bus termini and stops. You pay on the bus or buy a card with preloaded trips called an *abono* from *estancos* (tobacconists).

DIRECTORY

Car Hire

Atesa
Tel 902 10 01 01.
w atesa.es

Avis
Tel 0808 284 0014 in UK.
Tel 902 18 08 54 in Spain.
w avisworld.com
w avis.es

easyCar
w easycar.com

Europcar
Tel 0870 607 5000 in UK.
Tel 913 43 45 12 in Spain.
w europcar.com
w europcar.es

Hertz
Tel 0207 026 00 77 in UK.
Tel 915 09 73 00 in Spain.
w hertz.co.uk
w hertz.es

hispacar
w hispacar.com

pepecar
w pepecar.com

Maps

Altaïr
Gran Vía 616, 08007
Barcelona.
Tel 93 342 71 71.

Guía Repsol
w guiarepsol.com

Michelin
w viamichelin.es

Stanfords
12–14 Long Acre,
London WC2E 9LP.
Tel 020 7836 1321.
w stanfords.co.uk

Weather Forecasts

Agencia Estatal de Meteorología
w aemet.es

Traffic and Road Conditions

Información de Tráfico de Carreteras
Tel 011 from a landline.
w dgt.es/es/el-trafico

Coach Operators

Alsa
Tel 902 42 22 42.
w alsa.es

Eurolines
Tel 08717 81 81 78 in UK.
Tel 902 40 50 40 in Spain.
w eurolines.com

National Express
w nationalexpress.com

Coach Stations

Barcelona
Estació del Nord, Calle Ali Bei 80. Tel 902 26 06 06.
w barcelonanord.com

Madrid
Estación Sur, Calle Méndez Álvaro 83.
Tel 91 468 42 00.
w estacionauto busesmadrid.com
Intercambiador de Autobuses, Avenida de América 9.

Seville
Estación Plaza de Armas, Calle Cristo de la Expiración.
Tel 902 45 05 50.
w autobusesplaza dearmas.es

Getting Around Cities

Sightseeing and getting around in Spain's cities is best done on foot and by public transport – try to avoid driving a car into the city centres. Barcelona, Valencia and Madrid all have efficient underground (metro) systems, as well as overground railways that link up with the suburbs and airports. Madrid also has a metro service from the airport to the city. Good city maps are available from tourist offices, or they can be printed out from the Internet. Municipal websites (www.bcn.es for Barcelona; www.munimadrid.com for Madrid; www.valencia.es for Valencia; and www.sevilla.org for Seville) provide up-to-the-minute information in English on travelling in the cities.

Walking on Las Ramblas, Barcelona

Metro

The best way to see Barcelona over a couple of days is to buy a T10 ticket. Once you validate a T10, you can make combined journeys on the metro, buses, trams and local trains for 90 minutes. The more expensive T-2Dies gives you unlimited transport for 1–5 days until the end of service. The Barcelona metro run by **Transports Metropolitans de Barcelona** is open from 5am to midnight on weekdays and Sundays (and until 2am on Fridays) and for 24 hours every Saturday.

Metro de Madrid is the third-oldest system in Europe (1919) after London and Paris. Its 13 lines serve the whole city and are divided into various zones depending on different areas of the city and surrounding area. You can buy a single ticket for Zona A or a ten-journey ticket; this allows travel on both metro and buses. Tourist tickets providing between one and seven days' unlimited travel can

be purchased at train stations or at the airport. The metro runs every day from 6am to 2am.

The **Metro de Valencia**, operated by Ferrocarrils de la Generalitat Valenciana (FGV), is best used to get to and from the beach, since it does not go near the town centre. It also tends to skip other important destinations, such as the City of Arts and Sciences. The metro will also get you to many places around Valencia, beyond the city centre. A metro ticket to any station within the city limits is the same price.

Metro de Sevilla's first line opened in 2009, linking the centre with the city's outlying suburbs, and as such it is of relatively little relevance to

visitors – these areas contain little of interest for tourists. Three more lines are planned in the coming years.

Buses and Trams

Buses in Spain can sometimes follow an erratic timetable and many do not run after 10pm, although there are some night buses.

In Barcelona the T10 and T-2Dies tickets are valid on buses and trams, on the metro and on trains to the airport.

Bus, tram and metro tickets in Madrid, including tourist tickets, are interchangeable. If you do not have a ticket, you can pay the driver directly. Most buses run from 6am until 11pm. Night buses (called *buhos*) run less frequently and always pass by the Plaza de Cibeles. The price is the same as for day tickets.

Valencia has a good bus network, and buses are the preferred way of travelling for locals. If you are out and about a lot during the day, get a ten-journey *bono* (voucher). You can view a map of the routes on the EMT website (www.emtvalencia. es). The tram runs from the Pont de Fusta (Wooden Bridge), near the Serrano Towers, around the city and to the beaches at Las Arenas and La Malvarrosa.

Buses are the easiest and cheapest way to get around Seville and to the main sights. The bus network is comprised of circular (C-1, C-2, C-3, C-4, C-5 buses) and line routes (north, south, east and west).

Trains

If you are heading out of Barcelona to nearby beaches or mountains, you can take a train from Plaça Catalunya, Passeig de Gràcia, Estació de França or Estació de Sants. The local overland train services are run by **Ferrocarrils de la Generalitat de Catalunya (FGC)** and the main line trains are run by RENFE *(see p628)*. T10 and T-2Dies tickets can also be used on local trains within the city area.

One of Barcelona's taxis

Madrid bus

Madrid's rail system is comfortable, economical and efficient. The 13 lines all leave from or pass through Atocha station, and trains run daily from 6am until midnight every 15–30 minutes. **Consorcio Regional de Transportes de Madrid** provide helpful information on routes, fares and tourist tickets.

Taxis

Barcelona's distinctive yellow-and-black taxi cabs can be relied upon for a good and reasonably priced service, although it is rare to find a driver who speaks English. The meter begins running with a set fee and will rise every kilometre. Be aware that the tariff rises at night and on Saturdays, Sundays and public holidays. There are supplements added to your taxi fare when arriving at or leaving the airport, port or train station; for each piece of luggage; and also after 10pm on Fridays, Saturdays and holidays.

The taxis in Madrid are white with a diagonal red band on the front doors. A lit green light on top of the taxi indicates that it is available. Finding a taxi in the downtown area of Madrid is relatively simple and should take only a few minutes. The taxi meter starts its fare with a flat fee, the *bajada de bandera* (lowering of the flag). After that, the meter runs according to the distance covered, the urban area, the day of the week (higher fares apply on holidays) and the pick-up point (there are higher fares for pick-ups in bus stations, train stations and the airport). The night fare is always higher than the day fare. All additional fares should be indicated on informational signs on the back windows. There is an extra charge for pick-ups and drop-offs at Barajas Airport, but there is no extra charge for luggage.

Taxis are a good option for short journeys in Valencia. There is a minimum fee during the day and fares are higher at night; extra fees apply for trips to the airport.

Seville's taxis provide a viable way of getting into town, although much of the city centre is difficult to access by car because of heavy traffic, especially during the Feria de Abril or Semana Santa *fiestas*. As elsewhere, the tariff is higher for journeys at night.

Walking

Barcelona is an excellent city to explore on foot. The Old Town (Ciutat Vella), near the port and up to the Plaza Catalunya, consists of narrow medieval streets and winding alleyways. It is easy to get lost in this area, and care should be taken here at night. Las Ramblas is one of the world's most famous walkways and offers a vibrant slice of Mediterranean street life. The Eixample area is also good for walking, with large boulevards in a grid pattern. If you need to get your bearings, simply ask a local which direction is *mar* (sea, to the south) and which is *montaña* (mountain, to the north).

Distances are considerable in Madrid, and it is advisable to combine walking with public transport to make more efficient use of your time in the city. The most popular areas to visit on foot are those around the emblematic Plaza Mayor and the city's most famous park, El Retiro, which is also near the most well-known museums.

Most sights in the centre of Seville are best reached on foot. The popular Barrio Santa Cruz should be visited with a map. During late spring and

the summer, shade is highly prized. In summer months the city government stretches tarpaulins across the buildings in the centre so that many of the streets are in the shade.

Cycling

Cycling tours are a popular way of seeing Barcelona, and its cycle lanes provide safe access to most of the city. Visit www.bikerentalbarcelona.com or contact the tourist office to hire bikes.

For those wishing to explore Madrid, www.bravobike.com offer a wide variety of city bicycle tours, some of which include the surrounding areas.

There are many cycle lanes in Valencia, and cycling tours provide a great way of seeing all the major sights. More information can be found at www.doyoubike.com.

Seville is home to Sevici, a fleet of bicycles that can be hired on subscription. Visit www.sevici.es for details. (For more on cycling *see p633*.)

DIRECTORY

Metro

Transports Metropolitans de Barcelona
Tel 932 98 70 00.
W tmb.cat

Metro de Madrid
Tel 902 44 44 03.
W metromadrid.es

Metro de Valencia
Tel 900 46 10 46.
W metrovalencia.es

Metro de Sevilla
Tel 902 36 49 85.
W metro-sevilla.es

Public transport

FGC (Barcelona)
Tel 932 05 15 15.
W fgc.net

Consorcio Regional de Transportes de Madrid
Tel 915 80 42 60, or 012 from Madrid.
W ctm-madrid.es

General Index

Page numbers in **bold** refer to main entries.

A

Abd al Rahman I, Caliph 56, 57, 484
Abd al Rahman II, Caliph 56, 484
Abd al Rahman III, Caliph 481
Los Abrigos 538
Abu-l-Hasan, Sultan 496
Accessories shops 192, 193
Madrid 322, 323
Accident or Self-Portrait (Ponce de León) 302
Acebo 408
Aceúche, fiestas 409
Acueducto de los Arcos (Teruel) 245
Addresses, postcodes 625
Adeje 538
Admission prices 617
The Adoration of the Magi (Campaña) 358
The Adoration of the Shepherds (El Greco) 296
Adrian of Utrecht 62
Adventure sports 611, 613
Africa, ferries 627
Agaete **547**
Agres 263
Agriculture **32–3**
New World crops 63
Agüero **238**
Aguilar 17, 486
Aguilar, Marquises of 373
Aguilar de Campoo **373**
Águilas 267
Aigüestortes, Parc Nacional d' 34, 211, **215**
Aínsa **235**
hotels 567
restaurants 590
Air sports 610, 613
Air travel 626–7
Airlines 626–7
Airports 626
Ajuntament (Barcelona) 148, **151**
Alacant *see* Alicante
Alaior, restaurants 603
Alange
hotels 571
restaurants 597
Alarcón **399**
hotels 570
Álava 119
Alba, Duchess of 290
Alba, Dukes of 365, 504
Alba family 308
Alba de Tormes 365
Albacete **400**
hotels 570
restaurants 595–6
Albacete province 383
Albaicín (Granada) **492–3**

Albarracín 200–201, **245**
restaurants 590
La Alberca 360
Albornoz, Alonso Carrillo de 396
L'Albufera 248, **258**
Albuquerque 414
Alcalá de Henares **336–7**
restaurants 593
Alcalá del Júcar 384, **399**
Alcalá la Real 486
Alcalá de la Selva 244
Alcañiz **243**
Alcántara 55, **414**
Alcanyis 256
Alcaraz **400–401**
La Alcarria **386–7**
Alcazaba (Almería) 505
Alcazaba (Málaga) **56–7**, 478
Alcázar (Jerez de la Frontera) 470
Alcázar (Segovia) **348–9**, 350
Alcázar (Toledo) 393, **394**
Alcázar de los Duques de Feria (Zafra) 417
Alcázar de los Reyes Cristianos (Córdoba) 17, **482**
Alcázar de San Juan 398
Los Alcázares 266
Alcocer, restaurants 596
Alcoi 247, **263**
festivals 42, 44, 259
Alcossebre 251
Alcoy *see* Alcoi
Alcúdia 520
Alella wine region 206–7
Alemán, Rodrigo 361
Alexander VI, Pope 258–9
Alfàbia **519**
Alfonso I, King of Aragón 386
Alfonso I, King of Asturias 56
Alfonso II, King of Aragón
captures Teruel 244
Monasterio de Piedra 242
Puigcerdà 216
Santiago de Compostela cathedral 96
tomb of 226
unites Catalonia and Aragón 58
Alfonso III, the Great, King of Asturias
casket of 356
Zamora city walls 360
Alfonso VI, King of Castile
captures Toledo 58
and El Cid 374
and Madrid 374
Puerta Antigua de Bisagra (Toledo) 395
Alfonso VIII, King of Castile
Alarcón 399
Battle of Las Navas de Tolosa 58
La Caballada (Atienza) 391
Real Monasterio de Huelgas (Burgos) 375

Alfonso IX, King of León
captures Cáceres 412
Universidad (Salamanca) 364
Alfonso X the Learned, King of Castile
Cantigas 59
and the Castilian language 38
Ciudad Real 403
poetry 334
Alfonso XI, King of Castile, Monasterio de Santa Clara (Tordesillas) 370
Alfonso XII, King of Spain 75
portrait 68
statue 301
Alfonso XIII, King of Spain
abdication 68, 69
Hotel Ritz by Belmond (Madrid) 290
marriage 294
Palacio Real (Madrid) 280
portrait 75
and Primo de Rivera 69
Santander summer palace 117
Algeciras **476**
restaurants 598
Algorta 123
Alhama de Granada 487
Alhambra (Granada) 10, 17, 28, 58, 421, 426–7, 463, **494–5**
Alhóndiga (Bilbao) 122
Ali ben Yusuf 279
Alicante (Alacant) 11, 16, 262, **264–5**
airport 626
hotels 567
restaurants 591
Alicante province 247
Alicante wine region 206–7
All Saints' Day 43, 46, 47
Allariz 102
Almadén 403
hotels 570
Almagro **403**
festivals 45
hotels 570
restaurants 596
Almansa 400
Almansa wine region 344–5
Almería **505**
restaurants 598
Almería province 463
Almodóvar, Pedro 25, 26
Women on the Verge of a Nervous Breakdown 309
Almodóvar del Río 481
Almohads 58
architecture 426–7
Almonacid del Marquesado, fiestas 47, 391
Almonacid de Toledo, hotels 570
Almond trees 33
Almonte, restaurants 599

Almoravids 58
  architecture 426
Almuñécar **487**
Alonso, Fernando 26
Alonso Martínez (Madrid), nightlife
  328–9
Álora 478
Alpuente 252
Las Alpujarras **488–9**
Alquézar **239**
  hotels 567
Altamira Caves *see* Cuevas de
  Altamira
Altea 262, 264
Alto Campoo **115**
Alto Turia **252**
Álvarez family 391
Amadeo I, King of Savoy 67, 75
Amandi 111
Amargós, Josep 159
Amaya, Juana 429
Ambulances 620, 621
Amenabar, Alejandro 25
L'Ametlla de Mar, restaurants 589
Amposta 229
Ampudia
  hotels 569
  restaurants 594
Ampuero, restaurants 583
Ampurdán-Costa Brava wine region
  206–7
Ampurias *see* Empúries
Amusement parks
  Tibidabo (Barcelona) **182**, 196, 197
  see also Theme parks; Water parks
Anarchism 51, **68–9**, 71
Anaya, Diego de, tomb of 364
Anciles, restaurants 590
Al Andalus 51, **56–7**
  Reconquest 58–9
Andalusia **462–505**
  climate 48
  fiestas 467
  food and drink 422–3
  hotels 572–4
  Madrid and Moorish Spain:
  Granada, Córdoba and Seville 10,
  17
  map 464–5
  restaurants 598–602
Andorra 211, **216**
Andorra la Vella 216
Andratx **518**
Andújar **500**
  fiestas 467
Aneto 235
Angelico, Fra, *The Annunciation* 297
Anglès, restaurants 588
Anguiano
  fiestas 136
  hotels 563
Anís 581
The Annunciation (Fra Angelico) 297

Año Nuevo 47
Ansó 234
Antequera **479**
Antique shops
  Barcelona 192, 193
  Madrid 321, 323
  Seville 459
Anual, Battle of (1921) 69
Aoiz, restaurants 585
Apartment hotels 560
Apes' Den (Gibraltar) 476
April Fair (Seville) 44, 435
Aquariums
  Oceanografic (Valencia) 16,
  257
  Palma Aquarium **523**
  San Sebastián **126**
Aqueduct (Segovia) 55, 368, **369**
Aqüeducte de les Ferreres 229
Arabs 56
Aracena, hotels 572
Aracena, Sierra de **466**
Aragón **230–45**
  climate 49
  fiestas 243
  food and drink 204–5
  hotels 567
  map 232–3
  restaurants 590–91
Aragón, River 139
Aranda de Duero 381
  restaurants 594
Aranjuez, restaurants 593
Aranjuez, Palacio Real de **337**
Arantza 138
Arantzazu 128
Arazas, River 236
Arc de Berà 229
Arc del Triomf (Barcelona) **158**
Arce, Martín Vázquez de 386
Arches, Moorish 427
Archidona 479
Architecture **28–31**
  castles of Castile 348–9
  Modernisme 144–5
  Moorish 426–7
  Mudéjar 59
  Romanesque churches 87
Archivo de Indias (Seville) 13, 438,
  443
ARCO (Madrid) 47
Arco de Santa María (Burgos) 374
Arcos de la Frontera 472, **473**
  hotels 572
El Arenal (Seville) **430–35**
  area map 431
  hotels 571
  restaurants 597
  street-by-street map 432–3
Ares del Maestre 250
Arévalo 369
  restaurants 594
Arévalo, Luis de 491

El Argar civilization 52
Argüelles (Madrid), nightlife
  328–9
Arguineguín, hotels 575
Arias, Eugenio 332
Arias, Rodrigo 365
Arizkun 138
Armada 63, 93
Arnedillo 133
Arrecife **553**
Arrieta, hotels 575
Arriondas, restaurants 583
Arroyo de la Luz **414**
Arroyuelo 115
Art **36–7**
Art holidays 612, 613
Art Nouveau 29
  Barcelona 163
  Modernisme 144–5
Art shops
  Barcelona 192, 193
  Madrid 321
Artenara 549
  restaurants 604
Arties 214
  restaurants 588
Artium (Vitoria) 130
Arts, performing 25–6
  see also Cinema; Dance; Music;
  Theatre
Arure, restaurants 604–5
Assumption Day 43, 45, 47
Astorga **356**
  restaurants 594
  The Road to Santiago 86
Astún 234
Asturias and Cantabria 104–17
  climate 48
  fiestas 114
  food and drink 80
  hotels 562–3
  map 106–7
  restaurants 583–4
  Wild Spain: Cantabria, Asturias and
  Galicia 11, **15**
Atapuerca, restaurants 594
Ateneo de Madrid **295**
Atienza **386**
  fiestas 391
ATMs 622
Augustus, Emperor
  captures Cantabria and Asturias
  54
  and Lugo 103
  Mérida 414, 415
Ausetan tribe 224
Auto-da-fé in the Plaza Mayor (Ricci)
  278
Autol 133
Autumn Landscape in Oldenburg
  (Schmidt-Rottluff) 293
Autumn in Spain 46
  fiestas 43

Ávila 12, **366–7**
  hotels 569
  restaurants 594
Ávila province 351
Avilés **109**
Ayllón 369
Ayna 401
Ayub 242
Ayuntamiento 625
Ayuntamiento (Arcos de la Frontera) 473
Ayuntamiento (Carmona) 480
Ayuntamiento (Seville) **442**
Azahar, Costa del *see* Costa del Azahar
Azca (Madrid), nightlife 329
Aztecs 62
Azuaga 417
Azulejos (ceramic tiles) 28, 426, **442**

B

Bacon, Francis 122
Badajoz **416**
  hotels 571
Badajoz province 405
Baena 486
Baetica (Roman province) 54
Baeza 421, **502–3**
  restaurants 599
  street-by-street map 502–3
Bagur *see* Begur
Baiona (Bayona) **100**
  hotels 562
  restaurants 582
La Bajada de la Virgen de las Nieves (Santa Cruz de la Palma) 540
Bakio 123
Balàfia 515
Balboa, Vasco Núñez de 417
El Balcón de Europa 487
Balcón de Mediterráneo (Benidorm) 264
Balearic Islands 508–9, **510–31**
  climate 49
  ferries 627
  fiestas 527
  hotels 574–5
  Ibiza (Eivissa) 514–16
  Mallorca 518–25
  map 508–9
  maps 512–13
  Menorca 526–31
  regional food 517
  restaurants 602–4
Ballet 608
Balloons, hot-air 610
Bañaderos, restaurants 604
Banderilleros 41
Banks 622
Baños Árabes (Jaén) 497
Baños de Cerrato 372
Baños de la Encina 500
Baños de Montemayor 408
El Bañuelo (Granada) 491, **493**
Banyoles, restaurants 588

Banyoles, lake 217
Banys Àrabs (Palma) 523
Baqueira-Beret **215**
Baras, Sara 429
Barbarossa 526
Barbastro 239
Barceló, Miquel 521
Barcelona **140–99**
  2 Days in Barcelona **12–13**
  Barcelona and the Mediterranean Coast by Train 11, **16**
  Barri Gòtic **148–9**
  cathedral 143, 148, **152–3**
  coach stations 633
  Eixample **162–71**
  entertainment **194–9**
  exhibitions 68, 69
  fiestas 44, 45, 46, 161, 194, 196
  Further Afield **178–82**
  hotels 564–5
  Introducing Barcelona 142–3
  Jewish community **150**
  Montjuïc **172–7**
  nightlife 198–9
  Old Town **146–61**
  Olympic Games 27, 73
  Picasso in **157**
  El Prat Airport 626
  Quadrat d'Or **164–5**
  Las Ramblas 143, **154–5**
  restaurants 586–8
  Sagrada Família **170–71**
  shopping **190–93**
  Spanish Civil War 70
  Street Finder 183–9
  street-by-Street map: Barri Gòtic 148–9
  street-by-Street map: Montjuïc 174–5
  street-by-Street map: Quadrat d'Or 164–5
  transport 634–5
  transport map *see* inside back cover
Barcelona Football Club 180, **181**
Barcelona province 211
Barceloneta (Barcelona) 12, **160**
Bárcena Mayor 105, 106, **115**
Bárdenas Reales 134
Baroja, Pío 39, **68**
Baroque architecture 29, 67
Baros, hotels 567
Barranc d'Algendar 527
Barranco de Guayadeque 548
Barranco del Infierno 538
Barri Gòtic (Barcelona) 11, 12, **148–9**
  nightlife 198, 199
  street-by-street map 148–9
Barri Xinès (Barcelona) 154
Los Barrios, restaurants 600
Barruera 215
Bars 576
  Barcelona 198–9
  Madrid 324–5, 327, 328–9
  Seville 461
  tapas bars 579

Bartolomé de Jaén, Maestro 490, 497
Basílica de la Macarena (Seville) **448**
Basílica de Nuestra Señora del Pilar (Zaragoza) 240–41
Basílica Pontificia de San Miguel (Madrid) 274
Basilica de Sant Francesc (Palma) 523
Basílica de Santa María (San Sebastián) 14, 126
Basílica de Santa Maria del Mar (Barcelona) **157**
Basílica de la Virgen de los Desamparades (Valencia) **254**
Basketball 26
Basque Country, Navarra and La Rioja **118–39**
  Bilbao and the Basque Lands 11, **14**
  climate 49
  Communist demonstrations 68–9
  fiestas 136
  food and drink 81
  hotels 563–4
  Kingdom of Navarra 134
  map 120–21
  restaurants 585–6
Basques 23, 119
  culture **129**
  ETA 71, 72
  Guernica-Lumo 122–3
  independence movement 27
  language 119, 617
  literature 38
Bassá, Ferrer 181
  Virgin and Child 36
Battle of the Flowers (Laredo) 114
Las Batuecas 360
Bayeu, Francisco 306
  tapestry designs 310
Bayona *see* Baiona
Bayonne Treaty (1386) 59
Beaches
  Costa Blanca 262
  Costa Brava 221
  Costa del Sol 476–7
Bears, brown **108**
Beatus of Liébana, St 114, 216, 219
Becerra, Gaspar 356
Bechtold, Erwin 515
Bécquer, Gustavo Adolfo 448
Bed and breakfast 559, 561
Beech forests 84
Beer 581
Begur (Bagur) 221
  hotels 565
  restaurants 588
Béjar 361
  hotels 568
Belaguer, José María Escrivá de 239
Belalcázar 480
Belchite 243
Belén, Ana 73
Belmonte 348, **398–9**

Benalmádena Costa 477
  restaurants 599
Benasque **235**
Benavente, restaurants 594
Benedict XIII, Pope 251
Benedictine order
  accommodation 561
  Monastir de Montserrat 222–3
Benet, Joan 39
Benicarló 251
Benicàssim 251
Benidorm **264**
  beach 262
Benimantell, restaurants 591
Bera (Vera) 138
  hotels 563
Berbers 56, 57
Berceo, Gonzalo de 38
Berenguer, Francesc 182
Berga, fiestas 225
Berlanga de Duero 381
Bermejo, Bartolomé 36
  St Dominic of Silos Enthroned as
  Abbot 298
Bermeo 123
Berruguete, Alonso, *Natividad* 371
Berruguete, Pedro de 36, 298
Besalú **217**
  restaurants 588
Betancuria **550**
Betanzos **92**
  restaurants 582
Béthencourt, Jean de 550
Beuys, Joseph 177
Biasteri *see* Laguardia
Biblioteca de Catalunya (Barcelona)
  154
Biblioteca Nacional de España
  (Madrid) **291**
Bicycle hire 633
Bielsa 237
  fiestas 243
Bienal de Arte Flamenco (Seville) 46
Bienvenida, Antonio 310
El Bierzo **354**
Bierzo wine region 344–5
Bigarny, Philippe de 372, 377
Bilbao (Bilbo) **122**
  airport 626
  Bilbao and the Basque Lands 11, **14**
  festivals 45
  hotels 563
  Museo Guggenheim **124–5**
Bilbao (Madrid), nightlife 328–9
Binibeca 512, 530
Birds
  L'Albufera 258
  birdwatching 612
  Central Spain 346–7
  Delta de l'Ebre 229
  Lagunas de Ruidera 401
  Parque Natural de Cabo de Gata
  505
  Parque Natural de Monfragüe 410
  Tablas de Damiel 403

Bizkaia *see* Vizcaya
Blai, Pere 151
Blanca of Navarra 133
Blancafort, Gabriel 524
Blanes **220**
Blay, Miquel 217
  St George 156
Blues Cazorla 45
Boabdil 60, 61, 491, 495
Bocairent 263
  hotels 567
Bodas de Isabel de Segura (Teruel)
  245
Bodega Alvear (Montilla) 486
Bodega Pérez Barquero (Montilla)
  486
Bodegas 577
Bodegas Barbadillo (Sanlúcar de
  Barrameda) 470
Bofill, Guillem 218–19
Bofill, Ricardo 160, 177
Bolnuevo 267
Bonaparte, Joseph *see* José I
Bonastre, Maestro de 256
Bookshops
  Barcelona 192, 193
  Madrid 322, 323
  Seville 459
La Boqueria (Barcelona) 190
Borges, José Luis 39
Borgoña, Juan de 397
Borja, Cesare 370
Borja, Juan de 502
Borja, St Francis 259
Borja (Borgia) family 258–9
El Born (Barcelona) **157**
Borrassa, Luis 36
Borredà, hotels 565
Bort, Jaime 266
Bosch, Hieronymus 256
  The Garden of Delights 296
  Prado (Madrid) 299
Bossòst 214
Botticelli, Sandro 299, 490
Bourbon dynasty 65, **66**, 68, 74
  Castell de Montjuïc 177
  restoration of 75
Bourbon Madrid **286–303**
  area map 287
  hotels 568–9
  restaurants 592–3
Bous en la Mar (Dénia) 259
Breakfast 576
Breña Baja, hotels 575
Brenan, Gerald 489
Brihuega 387
Briñas, hotels 563
Briviesca **373**
Bronze Age 52
Brown bears **108**
Brueghel, Pieter the Elder 285, 299
Bubión, restaurants 599
Budget travel 618
Buen Amor, castle of 365
Buigas, Carles 175, 177

Buigas, Gaietà 160
Buitrago del Lozoya **332**
Bullfighting 25, 26, **40–41**, 609
  Bullfighting Museum (Antequera)
  479
  Museo Taurino (Madrid) 310
  Plaza de Toros (Antequera) 479
  Plaza de Toros de la Maestranza
  (Seville) 432, **434**, 461
  Plaza de Toros de Las Ventas
  (Madrid) 304, **310**, 325, 327
  Ronda 475
Bullrunning (Pamplona) 136
Bulnes 112
Buñol, fiestas 252–3, 259
Buñuel, Luis 360, 408
El Burgo de Osma **381**
  restaurants 594
Burgohondo, hotels 569
Burgos **374–7**
  cathedral 341, 376–7
  hotels 569
  map 375
  restaurants 594
Burgos province 351
"Burgos trials" 71
The Burial of the Count of Orgaz (El
  Greco) 36, 392, 394
Buses 633, 634
Butterflies, Vall d'Aran 214
El Buzo (Seville) 433

C

Ca Na Costa 516
La Caballada (Atienza) 391
Caballé, Montserrat 26, 195
Caballero Bonald, José Manuel 39
Caballo, Luis 491
El Cabañal beach (Valencia) 257
Cabañeros National Park 35, 391
Sa Cabaneta, fiestas 527
Cable cars
  Fuente Dé 113
  Parque Nacional del Teide 542–3
Cabo Fisterra 89, **93**
Cabo de Gata, Parque Natural de
  421, **505**
Cabo de Palos 267
Cabo Tinoso 267
Cabo de Trafalgar 472
Cabopino 477
Cabranes, hotels 562
Cabrera 511, **521**
Cabrera, Archipiélago de 34, 521
Cabuérniga, Valle de *see* Valle de
  Cabuérniga
Cáceres 405, **412–13**
  hotels 571
  restaurants 597
  street-by-street map 412–13
Cáceres province 405
Cadalso 115
Cadaqués 211, **220**, 221
  hotels 565
  restaurants 588

Cadí-Moixeró 216
Cádiar 489
Cádiz **471**
  festivals 43, 47, 467
  history 53
  hotels 572
  restaurants 599
Cádiz province 463
Caesar, Julius 54
Café Gijón (Madrid) **295**, 324, 325
Cafés
  Madrid 324–5, 327, 328–9
  Seville 461
La Caixa 244
CaixaForum (Barcelona) **177**
CaixaForum (Zaragoza) 241
Cala 'n Bosch, restaurants 604
Cala Morell, hotels 575
Cala en Porter, restaurants 604
Cala Salada (Ibiza) 510
Calabardina, hotels 567
Calaceite, hotels 567
La Calahorra (Elx) 265
La Calahorra, Castillo de (Andalusia) **497**
Calatañazor 381
Calatayud **242**
  wine region 206–7
Calatrava, Santiago 257
Calatrava la Nueva **402–3**
Caldera de la Bandama 548
Caldera de Taburiente National Park 35, 536
Calderón, Rodrigo 277
Calderón de la Barca, Pedro 38, 64, 65, 416
Caldes de Boí 215
Caldes d'Estrac, restaurants 588
Calera de León 417
Cales Coves 528–9, **530**
Sa Caleta 514
Caleta de Fuste **551**
Calle Mateos Gago (Seville) 439
Calle de Serrano (Madrid) **300**
Calle de las Sierpes (Seville) **442**
Callejón del Agua (Seville) 439
Callosa D'en Sarria, fiestas 46
Es Caló 516
  hotels 574
Caló de Sant Agusti, restaurants 602
Sa Calobra 519
Calp (Calpe) 263
  hotels 567
The Calvary (van der Weyden) 335
Cámara Oscura (Seville) **450**
Camariñas 93
Cambados 99
  hotels 562
  restaurants 582
Cambrils 228
  restaurants 588
Camino del Rey (Garganta del Chorro) 478
Camp Nou (Barcelona) **180**
Camp sites 561

Campaña, Pedro de, The Adoration of the Magi 358
Campin, Robert 299
Campisábalos 386
Campo, Juan del 490
Campo del Agua 354
Campo de Borja wine region 206–7
Campo de Criptana 383, **398**
Campo del Moro (Madrid) 272, **279**
Camprodon 217
Canalejas, José 69, 276
Canales, Antonio 429
Canary Islands 508–9, **532–55**
  climate 49
  ferries 627
  fiestas 540
  Fuerteventura 550–51
  Gran Canaria 546–9
  hotels 575
  International Music Festival 47
  Lanzarote 552–4
  map 508–9
  map: Eastern Islands 544–5
  map: Western Islands 534–5
  maps 19, 21
  regional food 541
  restaurants 604–5
  Tenerife 538–43
  volcanoes 555
Cancho Roano **416**
Candas 108
Candela, Felix 257
Candelada, hotels 569
Candelaria **539**
  fiestas 540
Candelario 361
Canedo, restaurants 594
Cañete 387
Cangas de Onís 15, **111**
  fiestas 114
  hotels 562
  restaurants 583
Cano, Alonso 308, 489, 490, 500
Caños de Meca, hotels 572
Cánovas del Castillo, Antonio 68, 290
Cantabria see Asturias and Cantabria
Cantabrian mountains 115
El Cantar del Mío Cid 38, 374
Cantavieja 250
Canyoning 611
Cap de Cavalleria 527
Cáparra 408
Capek, Karel 38
Capilla Real (Granada) 17, **490**
Capocorb Vell **520–21**
El Capricho (Comillas) **115**, 145
Car hire 632
Carantoñas (Aceúche) 409
Caravaca de la Cruz **267**
  restaurants 591
Caravaggio 298
  David Victorious over Goliath 299
Caravans 561
Carboneras, restaurants 599

Carbonero, José Moreno 39
Cardona **224**
  hotels 566
Cardona, Dukes of 224
Carducho, Vicente 284, 333
Cares, River 112
Cariñena 243
Cariñena wine area 206–7
Carlist Wars 66, 67, 68
Carlos I, King of Spain see Charles V
Carlos II, King of Spain
  death 65
  portrait 74, 110
Carlos III, King of Spain 66, 75
  Archivo de Indias (Seville) 443
  becomes king 67
  expels Jesuits 66, 276
  Illa de Tabarca 265
  Museo del Prado (Madrid) 296
  Palacio Real (Madrid) 280, 281
  Paseo de la Castellana (Madrid) 310
  Paseo del Prado (Madrid) 288
  Plaza Cánovas del Castillo (Madrid) 290
  Plaza Mayor (Madrid) 277
  portraits 299
  Puerta de Alcalá (Madrid) 291
  Puerta del Sol (Madrid) 276
  Real Jardín Botánico (Madrid) 301
  statue of 301
  tomb of 137
Carlos III the Noble, King of Navarra 134
Carlos IV, King of Spain 66, 243
  The Family of King Charles IV (Goya) 37
  Palacio Real (Madrid) 280
  Palacio Real de Aranjuez 337
  portraits 75, 280
Carlos V, Emperor see Charles V, Emperor
Carlos de Viana, Prince 134
Carmen, statue of 432
Carmona (Andalusia) 10, 13, 17, **480**
  hotels 572
  restaurants 599
Carmona (Cantabria) 105, **115**
Carnival **43**, 47
  Bielsa 243
  Cádiz 467
  Santa Cruz de Tenerife 540
Carracedo del Monasterio 355
Carratraca 478
Carreño, Juan 110
Carrer Montcada (Barcelona) **158**
Carrera del Darro (Granada) 493
Carreras, José 26, 195
Carrero Blanco, Admiral 71
Carrión de los Condes 372
  restaurants 594
Cars 630–32
  see also Tours by car
Cartagena 11, 16, **267**
  hotels 567

Carthaginians 51, 52, 53, 267
Cartuja de Miraflores (Burgos) 375
Casa de l'Ardiaca (Barcelona) 148,
  150
Casa Batlló (Barcelona) 13, 144, 145,
  168
Casa de Campo (Madrid) **306**
Casa de Cervantes (Valladolid) **371**
Casa de Colón (Las Palmas de Gran
  Canaria) 548
Casa de las Conchas (Salamanca)
  28, 362, **365**
Casa de la Condesa Lebrija (Seville)
  442
Casa de Dulcinea (El Toboso) 398
Casa de los Golfines de Abajo
  (Caceres) 412
A Casa José Saramago (Lanzarote)
  553
Casa Milà "La Pedrera" (Barcelona)
  13, 29, 142, 144, 162, 165, 166–7,
  169
Casa Modernista (Novelda) 264
Casa de las Muertes (Salamanca)
  365
Casa-Museo de Cervantes (Alcalá de
  Henares) 337
Casa-Museo de Lope de Vega
  (Madrid) **294**
Casa-Museo de Martín Alonso
  Pinzón (Palos de la Frontera) 467
Casa de Pilatos (Seville) 13, **442–3**
Casa Terrades (Barcelona) 165, **169**
Casa de los Tiros (Granada) **490–91**
Casa Vicens (Barcelona) 145, 168
Casals, Pau 195
  Museu Pau Casals (El Vendrell) 228
Casas, Father Bartolomé de las 62
Casas rurales 559, 560
Cash dispensers 622
Casino, Murcia 266
Casón del Buen Retiro (Prado) 301
Castelao, Alfonso 98
Castelar, Emilio 68
Es Castell, restaurants 604
Castell dels Tres Dragons
  (Barcelona) **159**
Castellar de la Frontera, hotels 572
Castelló de la Plana **251**
  fiestas 44
Castellón 247
Castile, Kingdom of 58
Castile and León, Kingdom of 58, 59
Castilian *see* Spanish language
Castilla y León **350–81**
  castles of Castile 348–9
  climate 48
  fiestas 372
  food and drink 342–3
  hotels 569–70
  map 352–3
  restaurants 594–5
Castilla-La Mancha **382–403**
  climate 49
  fiestas 391

Castilla-La Mancha (cont.)
  food and drink 343
  hotels 570–71
  map 384–5
  restaurants 595–7
Castles
  Alarcón 399
  Alcalá de la Selva 244
  Alcañiz 243
  Alcazaba (Almería) 505
  Alcazaba (Málaga) **56–7**, 478
  Alcázar del Rey Pedro (Carmona)
    480
  Alcázar (Jerez de la Frontera) 470
  Alcázar (Segovia) **348–9**, 350, 368,
    369
  Alcázar (Toledo) 393, **394**
  Almodóvar del Rio 481
  Almuñécar 487
  Antequera 479
  Arévalo 369
  Bellver (Palma) **523**
  Belmonte 348, 398
  Berlanga de Duero 381
  Buen Amor 365
  Buitrago del Lozoya 332
  La Calahorra 497
  Calatañazor 381
  Calatrava la Nueva 402–3
  Caravaca de la Cruz 267
  Castell del Papa Luna (Peníscola)
    251
  Castile 348–9
  Castillo de la Concepción
    (Cartagena) 267
  Castillo de Gibralfaro (Málaga) 478
  Castillo de los Guzmanes (Niebla)
    466
  Castillo de la Mota (Medina del
    Campo) 348, **370**
  Castillo San Gabriel (Arrecife) 553
  Castillo de San José (Arrecife) 553
  Castillo de Santa Bárbara (Alicante)
    16, **264**, 265
  Castillo de Santa Catalina (Jaén)
    497
  Castillo de Santa Cruz de la Mota
    (San Sebastián) 126
  Castillo de la Yedra (Cazorla) 501
  Chinchilla de Monte Aragón 400
  Citadel (Jaca) 235
  Citadel (Pamplona) 137
  Coca 348, **369**
  Dénia 259
  Guadalest 263
  Hondarribia 127
  Javier **139**
  Jerez de los Caballeros 417
  Keep (Gibraltar) 476
  Loarre **238–9**
  Manzanares el Real 336
  Medina de Pomar 373
  Monterrey (Verín) 101
  Montjuïc (Barcelona) 142, **177**
  Onda 252

Castles (cont.)
  Oropesa 391
  Palacio Real de Olite 135
  Pedraza de la Sierra 369
  Peñafiel 349, 371
  Peñaranda de Duero 353, 380
  Ponferrada 355
  Sagunt 253
  Salobreña 487
  Salvatierra 403
  Sanlúcar de Barrameda 470
  Santueri (Felanitx) 521
  Simancas 371
  Tarifa 472
  Valderrobres 244
  Valencia de Alcántara 414
  Vélez Blanco 504
  Xàtiva 258
  see also Palaces
Castrillo de Murcia, fiestas 372
Castro, Rosalia de, Museo Rosalia de
  Castro (Padrón) 98
Castro de Coaña **108**
Castro Urdiales 15, **117**
  restaurants 583
Castropol 15, **108**
Catalan independence movement
  27, 70
Catalan language **216**, 617
Catalans 23
Catalayud, restaurants 590
Catalonia (Catalunya) **210–29**
  climate 49
  fiestas 225
  food and drink 204
  hotels 565–7
  map 212–13
  restaurants 588–90
Cathedrals
  Albacete 400
  Albarracín 245
  Almería 505
  Astorga 356
  Ávila 366–7
  Badajoz 416
  Baeza 503
  Barcelona 12, 143, 146, 148, **152–3**
  Bilbao 122
  El Burgo de Osma 381
  Burgos 341, 374, **376–7**
  Cádiz **471**
  Ciudad Rodrigo 361
  Ciutadella 526
  Córdoba 485
  Coria 409
  Cuenca 389
  Girona **218–19**
  Granada 17, **490**
  Guadalajara 387
  Guadix 497
  Huesca 239
  Ibiza 515
  Jaca 235
  Jaén 497
  Jerez de la Frontera 470

Cathedrals (cont.)
León 28, 61, 340, **358–9**
Lleida 224
Logroño 133
Lugo 103
Madrid (de la Almudena) **279**
Málaga 478
Mondoñedo 92
Murcia 16, 202, **266**
Orihuela 265
Ourense 102
Oviedo 15, **110**
Palencia 372
Palma 522, **524–5**
Las Palmas de Gran Canaria 548
Pamplona 136–7
Plasencia 409
Roda de Isábena 240
Salamanca 362, **364**
Santander 117
Santiago de Compostela 15, 89, 95, **96–7**
Santo Domingo de la Calzada 132
Segovia 368
La Seu d'Urgell 216
Seville 13, 438, **440–41**
Sigüenza 386
Soria 381
Tarazona 233, 240
Tarragona 229
Teruel 59, 244, **245**
Toledo 341, 393, **396–7**
Tortosa 229
Tudela 134
Tui 100–101
Valencia 16, **254–5**
Valladolid **371**
Vic 224
Vitoria 14, **130**
Zamora 360
Zaragoza 241
Catholic Church 25
Inquisition 278
religious art 36
Catholic Monarchs *see* Fernando II, King of Aragón; Isabel I, Queen of Castile
Cava 580, 581
Es Cavallet 514
cave dwellings 31
Caves
Albarracín 245
Cales Coves 528–9, **530**
Coves d'Artà 513, 521
Coves del Drac **521**
Coves dels Hams 521
Coves de Sant Josep **252**
Les Covetes dels Moros 263
Cueva del Buxu 111
Cueva de El Monte Castillo 116
Cueva de los Letreros 504
Cueva de Montesinos 401
Cueva de Tito Bustillo 111
Cueva de Valporquero **356**

Caves (cont.)
Cueva de los Verdes (Jameos del Agua) 554
Cuevas de Águila 366
Cuevas de Altamira 11, 15, 52, 53, **116**
Cuevas de Nerja 487
Cuevas de Santimamiñe 123
Gruta de las Maravillas 466
Guadix 497
Ramales de la Victoria 117
St Michael's Cave (Gibraltar) 476
Yesos de Sorbas 504
Cazalla de la Sierra 480
hotels 572
Cazorla
festivals 45
hotels 572–3
Parque Natural de **501**
restaurants 599
O Cebreiro (O Cabreiro) **103**
The Road to Santiago 86
Cedeira 92
restaurants 582
Cehegín 267
Cela, Camilo José 39, 386
Celanova **101**
Cella 245
Celts 52
Castro de Coaña 108
Monte de Santa Tecla 100
O Cebreiro 103
Cenobio de Valerón 547
Central Spain **338–417**
birds 346–7
Castilla y León 350–81
Castilla-La Mancha 382–403
Extremadura 404–17
map 340–41
regional food 342–3
wines 344–5
Centre de Cultura Contemporània (Barcelona) 154
Centre Excursionista de Catalunya (Barcelona) 149
Cercedilla 333
Cercle de Pessons 216
Cerdà i Sunyer, Ildefons 144, 163
Cerdanya valley 216
Cereal farming 32
Cerler 235
Cermeño, Juan Martín de 160
Ceroni, Juan Antonio 364
Cerralbo, 17th Marquis of, Museo Cerralbo (Madrid) 308
Certamen Internacional de Habaneras y Polifonía (Torrevieja) 45
Cervantes, Miguel de **337**
Archivo de Indias (Seville) 443
Casa de Cervantes (Valladolid) 371
Casa-Museo de Cervantes (Alcalá de Henares) 337
Don Quixote 38, 64, 398, **399**
statue of 284

Cervatos 115
Cervera de Pisuerga 373
Césareo de Arles, San 133
Chagall, Marc 220
La Chanca (Almería) 505
Charco, Fiesta del (San Nicolás de Tolentino) 540
Charlemagne, Emperor
Battle of Roncesvalles 56, 138
Girona cathedral 219
Charles V, Emperor (Carlos I) **63**, 309
Alcázar (Toledo) 393, 394
and Baeza 503
coronation 62
empire 62
El Escorial 335
homage to Tarazona 240
illegitimate son 161
Monasterio de Yuste 409
Palace of Charles V, Alhambra (Granada) 494–5
Palacio Real (Madrid) 281
portrait 74
Real Alcázar (Seville) 444
Simancas castle 371
Charles Martel, King of the Franks 56
Cheeses
Manchego 342, 579
Northern Spain 80
Chelva 252
Cheques 622
Chestnut forests 85
Children
entertainment 609
travelling with 618
Chillida, Eduardo 123
The Comb of the Winds 126
Toki-Egin 303
Chillón 403
Chinchilla de Monte Aragón 400
Chinchón **337**
fiestas 294
hotels 569
restaurants 594
Chipiona 470
Chopin, Frédéric 518
Christianity 55
Reconquest **58–9**
Christmas **43**, 47
Christus, Petrus, *The Virgin of the Dry Tree* 292
Chueca (Madrid), nightlife 328–9
Churches
opening hours 617
Romanesque architecture 87
see also Cathedrals; Convents; *individual towns and cities*; Monasteries
Churriguera brothers 29, 362
Arco de la Estrella (Cáceres) 412
Iglesia-Convento de San Esteban (Salamanca) 364
Medina de Rioseco altarpiece 371
Plaza Mayor (Salamanca) 364

Churriguera brothers (cont.)
Real Academia de Bellas Artes de
San Fernando (Madrid) 285
San Cayetano (Madrid) 306
Churrigueresque architecture 29
El Cid **374**
captures Alpuente 252
captures Valencia 58
epic poems 38
Puerta Antigua de Bisagra
(Toledo) 395
statue of 374
tomb of 377
and Valencia 254
Cider Festival (Nava) 45
Cigales wine region 344–5
Cíjara 410
Cinco Villas 234
Las Cinco Villas del Valle de Bidasoa
138
Cinema 25, 609
Barcelona 196, 197
Madrid 326, 327
San Sebastián Film Festival 46, **127**
Spaghetti Westerns **504**
Cintruénigo, restaurants 585
Ciraqui 135
Circo de Gredos, hotels 569
Cisneros, Cardinal 61, 277, 337
Cistercian Order 103, 561
"Cistercian triangle" 225, 226
Ciudad Encantada 387
Ciudad Real 403
Ciudad Real province 383
Ciudad Rodrigo **361**
restaurants 596
Ciudad de Vascos 391
Ciutadella (Ciudadela) **526**
fiestas 527
restaurants 604
Ciutat de les Arts i de les Ciències
(Valenica) 16, **257**
Ciutat Flamenco festival (Barcelona)
196
Clarín, Leopoldo Alas 39, 110
Classical music 608–9
Barcelona 195, 197
Madrid 326, 327
Seville 460–61
Classical Theatre Festival (Mérida)
45
Claude Lorrain 299
Clavé, Josep Anselm 156
Clement X, Pope 259
Climate 48–9
Climbing 611
The Clothed Maja (Goya) 297
Clothes
in restaurants 576
size chart 607
Clothes shops 607
Barcelona 191–2, 193
Madrid 322, 323
Seville 459
Cloud and Chair (Tàpies) 164

Clubs
Barcelona 198–9
Madrid 328–9
Seville 461
Coach travel 633
Cobos, Francisco de los 500, 501
Coca, Castillo de 348, **369**
Cocido madrileño 342
Cock and hen of St Dominic 132
Coello, Claudio 37, 285, 364
Coffee 580
Cola de Caballo 237
El Colacho (Castrillo de Murcia) 372
La Colegiata (Santillana del Mar) 116
Colegiata Real (Roncesvalles) 138
Colegiata de San Isidoro (León) 357
Colegiata de San Isidro (Madrid)
275, **276**
Colegiata de Santa María (Toro) 360,
361
Colegio de Fonseca or de los
Irlandeses (Salamanca) **365**
Colegio del Patriarca (Valencia) **255**
Colegio de San Ildefonso (Alcalá de
Henares) 336–7
Coll 215
Collage (Miró) 37
Collet, Charles 223
Colmenar Viejo 336
Colossus of Rhodes (Dalí) 37
Columbus, Christopher 148, 410
Archivo de Indias (Seville) 443
Barcelona Cathedral 152
Burgos 374
Casa de Colón (Las Palmas de
Gran Canaria) 548
death 370
explorations 51, 60, **61**
festival (Huelva) 467
and Huelva 466
Monasterio de la Rábida 466
Monasterio de Santa María de las
Cuevas (Seville) 450
Monument a Colón (Barcelona)
154, **160**
and Palos de la Frontera 467
Pinta 100
Plaza de Colón (Madrid) 300
return to Spain 150
San Sebastián (La Gomera) 537
Sanlúcar de Barrameda 470
Santa María 536
statues of 142, 466
tomb of 13, 440
Colunga, hotels 562
The Comb of the Winds (Chillida) 126
Combarro 99
Comendador-Leroux, Pérez, Museo
Pérez Comendador-Leroux
(Hervás) 408
Comillas **114–15**
hotels 562
Communications 624–5
Communist Party 68, 71, 72
Companys, Lluís 177

Complejo Costa Martiánez (Puerto
de la Cruz) 538
Compostela see Santiago de
Compostela
Comunidad de Madrid (Madrid
province) 270, 331
Comunidad Valenciana 245, 247
Comunidades 625
Conca de Barberà wine region
206–7
El Condado 466
Condado de Huelva wine region 424
The Condesa Mathieu de Noailles
(Zuloaga) 122
Congosto de Ventamillo 235
Congreso de los Diputados (Madrid)
288, **295**
Conil de la Frontera 472
Conquistadors 62–3
Constable, John 309
Constantina 480
Constantine I, Emperor 55
Constitution Day 47
Consuegra 25, 31, **398**
festivals 46
Convents
accommodation in 561
Convento de las Dueñas
(Salamanca) 363, **365**
Convento de Regina Coeli
(Santillana del Mar) 107
Convento de San Domingos de
Bonaval (Santiago de
Compostela) 88, 94
Convento de Santa Paula (Seville)
448
Convento de Santa Teresa (Ávila)
367
Convento de las Úrsulas
(Salamanca) **365**
Conversion chart 617
Copa del Rey MAPFRE 45
Córdoba 13, **482–5**
fiestas 45, 46, 467
hotels 573
Madrid and Moorish Spain:
Granada, Córdoba and Seville 10,
17
Mezquita 57, 420, 463, 483, **484–5**
Moors 56
restaurants 599
street-by-street map 482–3
Córdoba province 463
El Cordobés 481
Coria **409**
Cornejo, Pedro Duque 484
Corpus Christi 42, 102
La Orotava 540
Seville 435
Toledo 391
Corral, Jerónimo del 371
Corral del Carbón (Granada) 17, **490**
Corral de Comedias (Almagro) 403
Corralejo 544, **551**
hotels 575

Cortes (parliament) 295
Cortés, Hernán 62, 443
Corullón 355
A Coruña (La Coruña) **93**
 hotels 562
 restaurants 582
A Coruña province 89
Cosmocaixa - Museu de la Ciència (Barcelona) **182**
Costa Adeje, restaurants 605
Costa del Azahar **251**
Costa Blanca 203, 247, **262**
Costa Brava 13, 203, 211, **221**
Costa Cálida **267**
Costa Calma 550
Costa Daurada (Costa Dorada) **228**
Costa de la Luz **472**
Costa da Morte **93**
Costa del Silencio 538
Costa del Sol **476–7**
Costa Teguise **553**
 hotels 575
 restaurants 605
Costa Tropical 487
Costa Vasca 11, 14, **123**
Costa Verde 11, 15, 104, **108–9**
Costers del Segre wine region 206–7
El Cotillo, restaurants 604
Counter-Reformation, and literature 38
Covadonga 15, 105, **112**, 113
 fiestas 114
Covarrubias **374**
 restaurants 594
Covarrubias, Alonso de 387
Coves d'Artà 513, 521
Coves del Drac **521**
Coves d'Hams 521
Coves de Sant Josep **252**
Les Covetes dels Moros 263
Craft shops
 Madrid 322, 323
 Seville 459
Cranach, Lucas 299
Credit cards 622
 in hotels 559
 in restaurants 577
 in shops 606
Crime 620
Los Cristianos **538**
Cro-Magnon people 52, 129
Cruz, Penélope 25
Cruz de Tejeda, tour of **549**
Cuacos de Yuste 409
Cuban War of Independence 69
Cubero, José 310
Cudillero 15, 108
 hotels 563
 restaurants 583
Cuenca 341, 382, **388–9**
 festivals 44
 hotels 570–71
 restaurants 596
 street-by-street map 388–9

Cuenca, Serranía de see Serranía de Cuenca
Cuenca province 383
Cuervo, River 387
Cueva de Brujas 138
Cueva del Buxu 111
Cueva de los Letreros 504
Cueva de Montesinos 401
Cueva de Tito Bustillo 111
Cueva de Valporquero **356**
Cueva de los Verdes (Jameos del Agua) 554
Cuevas de Águila 366
Cuevas de Altamira 11, 15, 52, 53, **116**
Cuevas de Nerja 487
Cuevas de Santimamiñe 123
Currency 622–3
Customs information 616
Cycling 612, 613, 633
 in cities 635

D

Dagli Orti, Gianni, *Pier in the Prince's Garden at Aranjuez Castle* 8–9
Daimau, Luis 36
Dairy farming 32
Dalí, Salvador **219**, 265, 285
 Cadaqués 220
 Casa Museu Salvador Dalí (Cadaqués) 220
 Colossus of Rhodes 37
 Landscape at Cadaqués 302
 Rainy Taxi 219
 Tarot cards 131
 Teatro-Museo Dalí (Figueres) 219
La Dama de Elche **52**, 53, 265, 300
Dance 608
 Barcelona **194–5**, 196, 197
 flamenco **428–9**, 608
 Madrid 325, 327
 Sardana **229**
 Seville 460–61
 specialist holidays 613
Dance of Death (Verges) 225
Danza de los Zancos (Anguiano) 136
Daoíz y Torres, Luis 308
Daroca 231, **242**
 restaurants 590
David Victorious over Goliath (Caravaggio) 299
de Kooning, Willem 124
Degrain, Antonio Muñoz 256
Deià (Deyá) 519
 hotels 574
Delaunay, Robert 122
Delgado, Alvaro 39
Delta de l'Ebre 34, **229**
Deltebre 229
 hotels 566
Dénia 249, **259**, 262
 fiestas 43, 259
 hotels 567
The Denuding of Christ (El Greco) 396

Department stores 607
 Barcelona 191, 193
 Madrid 321, 323
 Seville 458, 459
The Descent from the Cross (van der Weyden) 299
Descent of the River Miño 101
Descent of the River Sella 45
Desfiladero de los Beyos 112
Desfiladero de Despeñaperros 500
Desfiladero de la Hermida 114
Desfiladero del Río Cares 112
Design shops
 Barcelona 192, 193
 Madrid 322, 323
Designer labels, Barcelona 191, 193
Deyá see Deià
Día de la Constitución 47
Día de la Cruz (Granada and Córdoba) 467
Día de la Hispanidad 46, 47
Día del Pilar (Zaragoza) 46, 243
Día de Sant Ponç (Barcelona) 161
Día de los Tres Reyes 47
La Diada (Barcelona) 161
Dialling codes 624
Díaz, Daniel Vásquez 466
Dinosaur footprints 133
Dios, Juan de 492
Disabled travellers **617**, 619
 in hotels 561
 in restaurants 577
Discounts
 railway 628
 students 618–19
Diving and snorkelling 610–11
Domènech i Montaner, Lluís 144
 Casa de l'Ardiaca (Barcelona) 150
 Casa Lleó Morera (Barcelona) 164, **168**
 Castell dels Tres Dragons (Barcelona) 159
 Fundacío Tàpies (Barcelona) 164, **168**
 Hospital de la Santa Creu i de Sant Pau (Barcelona) 163, **169**
 Palau de la Música Catalana (Barcelona) 156
 Universidad Pontificia (Comillas) 115
Domènech i Roura, Pere 177
Domingo, Plácido 26
Domínguez, Adolfo 300
Dominic, St **132**
 tomb of 380
Don Quixote see Cervantes
Doña i Ocell (Miró) 180
Donamaria, hotels 563
Doñana National Park 34, 420, **468–9**
El Doncel, tomb of (Sigüenza) 60, 386
Donostia see San Sebastiàn
Dos de Mayo (Madrid) 44, 294
Dragon tree 538

Drake, Sir Francis 471
Drassanes (Barcelona) 161
Drinks *see* Food and drink
Dumas, Alexandre 38
Dunas de Maspalomas 547
Duratón, River 369
Dürer, Albrecht 299
Durro 215
Durruti, Buenaventura 290

E

Easter **42**, 47, 294, 372, 435
Eastern Spain **200–67**
  Aragón 230–45
  Barcelona and the Mediterranean
    Coast by Train 11, **16**
  Catalonia 210–29
  flowers of the *matorral* 208–9
  map 202–3
  regional food 204–5
  Valencia and Murcia 246–67
  wildlife of the *matorral* 209
  wines 206–7
Ebro, River 115, 229, 231
Ecce Homo (Juanes) 256
Echagüe, Antonio Ortiz 127
Echalar *see* Etxalar
Écija 10, 13, 17, **481**
Economy 26, 27
Edificio Metrópolis (Madrid) 288
Egas, Enrique de 490
Eiffel, Gustave 101
Eivissa *see* Ibiza
Eixample (Barcelona) 13, **162–71**
  area map 163
  hotels 565
  nightlife 198, 199
  restaurants 587
Ejea de los Caballeros 234
El Puig, Monasterio de **253**
Elche *see* Elx
Elciego, hotels 564
Electrical adaptors 619
Elizabeth, Empress of Austria 265
Elizondo **138**
Eljas 408
Els Amunts **515**
Elx (Elche) **265**
  fiestas 42, 45, 259
  hotels 567
Embalse de El Grado 239
Embalse de Puentes Viejas 332
Embassies 619
Emergencies 620–21
Emilian, St 133
Los Empelaos (Valverde de la Vera)
  409
Empúries (Ampurias) 55, **220**
La Encamisá (Torrejoncillo) 409
Encants Vell (Barcelona) 190
Enciso **133**
La Endiablada (Almonacid del
  Marquesado) 47, 391
Enlightenment 39, 51, **66**
Enrique IV, King of Castile 60, 398

Enrique, Prince of Asturias 373
Entertainment **608–9**
  Barcelona 194–9
  Madrid 324–9
  Seville 460–61
Epiphany 43, 47
Ercina, Lago de la 105, 112
Erill-la-Vall 215
Ermita 31
Ermita de los Reyes (El Hierro) 537
Ermita de San Antonio de la Florida
  (Madrid) **307**
Ermita de San Lorenzo 399
Ermita de San Marcial 127
Ermita de la Virgen del Prado
  (Talavera de la Reina) 390
L'Escala 221
Los Escobazos (Jarandilla de la Vera)
  409
El Escorial (Madrid) 63, 270, **334–5**
Escunhau 214
  restaurants 588
Espartero, General 67, 75
L'Espluga de Francolí, restaurants 589
Esquedas, restaurants 590
Estación de Atocha (Madrid) **301**
Estación del Norte (Valencia) **256**
Estadi Olímpic de Montjuïc
  (Barcelona) **177**
Estadio Bernabéu 310, 325
L'Estartit 221
Estella (Lizarra) **136**
  restaurants 585
Estepa 479
Estepona 476
ETA 27, 71, 72, 73
Etiquette 617
Etxalar (Echalar) **138**
Eulalia, St 152
  sarcophagus 153
Eunate 135
The Euro 623
European Union 27, 72
Euskadi *see* Basque Country
Euskera language 119, 617
Exaltación al Río Guadalquivir
  (Sanlúcar de Barrameda) 467
Expo '92 (Seville) 27, **72–3**, 450
Extremadura **404–17**
  climate 48
  fiestas 409
  food and drink 343
  hotels 571
  map 406–7
  restaurants 597
Ezcaray, restaurants 585

F

Fabada 80
Fairs, annual, Madrid 321
The Fall of Granada (Pradilla) 60–61
Falla, Manuel de, tomb of 471
Las Fallas (Valencia) 44, 259, 260–
  61
Falqués, Pere 164

The Family of King Charles IV (Goya)
  37
Family life 24–5
Farming *see* Agriculture
Fashion shops 607
  Barcelona 191–2, 193
  Madrid 322, 323
  Seville 459
Father Gonzalo de Illescas at Work
  (Zurbarán) 411
Faust, Karl 220
FC Barcelona 180, 181
Felanitx **521**
  fiestas 527
Felipe II, King of Spain 74, 502
  Archivo de Indias (Seville) 443
  Armada 93
  armour 63
  birthplace 370
  El Escorial 334–5
  empire 62
  Illescas 390
  Madrid 273
  marriage 62
  Palacio Real (Madrid) 281
Felipe III, King of Spain 74, 380
  expels Moriscos 64
  Iglesia de San Antonio de los
    Alemanes (Madrid) 308
  statue of 277
Felipe IV, King of Spain 65, 74
  Monasterio de las Descalzas
    Reales (Madrid) 285
  Parque del Retiro (Madrid) 301
  statue of 279
Felipe V, King of Spain
  abdication 66, 75
  becomes king 65
  Biblioteca Nacional de España
    (Madrid) 291
  Castell de Montjuïc 177
  and Catalan language 216
  Cinco Villas 234
  La Granja de San Ildefonso 367
  Lleida Cathedral 224
  Palacio Real (Madrid) 280
  Parc de la Ciutadella 158
  Plaza Mayor (Salamanca) 364
  portraits 66, 74
  Real Fábrica de Tapices 310
  siege of Barcelona 66
  and Xàtiva 258
Felipe VI, King of Spain 27, 45, 73, 74,
  75
Felipe el Hermoso (the Fair) 490
Felix, St, tomb of 218
Feria del Caballo (Jerez de la
  Frontera) 44
Feria Nacional del Queso (Trujillo) 44
Fernán Gómez, Fernando 300
Fernández, Gregorio 284, 371
Fernández de Moratín, Leandro 39
Fernando I of Castilla-León
  ivory crucifix 300
  unites Castile and León 58

Fernando II of Aragón (the Catholic) **60–61**
and Almería 505
birthplace 234
and Cáceres 412
and Columbus 150
Granada 490
Inquisition 278
marriage 231, 370
Monasterio de San Juan de los Reyes (Toledo) 395
and Orihuela 265
Real Chancillería (Granada) 492
Santa Fé 486–7
unification of Spain 51, **74**
Fernando II of Castile 391
annexes Navarra 134
Fernando III of Castile 497
Burgos cathedral 376
conquers Baeza 502
reunites Castile and León 59
and Trujillo 411
and Yeste 400
Fernando VI, King of Spain 75
Arnedillo 133
death 67
Fernando VII, King of Spain 75
Colegiata de San Isidro (Madrid) 276
Ferrer, Pere 151
Ferrer, St Vincent 250
Ferreries (Ferrerias) **527**
restaurants 604
Ferries 627
Ferrol 92
Festa Major (Barcelona) 161
Festivals see Fiestas and festivals
Fiestas and festivals **42–7**
Andalusia 467
Aragón 243
Asturias and Cantabria 114
Balearic Islands 527
Barcelona 161, 197
Basque Country, Navarra and La Rioja 136
Canary Islands 540
Castilla y León 372
Castilla-La Mancha 391
Catalonia 225
Extremadura 409
Galicia 102
Madrid 294
Seville 435
Valencia and Murcia 259
see also individual towns and festivals by name
Figueras (Asturias) 108
Figueres (Figueras) (Catalonia) **219**
hotels 566
restaurants 588
Figueroa, Leonardo de 449
Convento de la Merced Calzada (Seville) 434
Hospital de los Venerables (Seville) 443
Iglesia de la Magdalena (Seville) 434

Films see Cinema
Fines, driving 631
Finis Gloriae Mundi (Valdés Leal) 435
Finisterre see Fisterra
Fire brigade 621
Fire hazards 621
Fire-walking fiesta (San Pedro Manrique) 372
First Republic 66, **68**, 75
Fish and seafood, Northern Spain 80
Fishing 611, 613
Fishing industry **101**
Fisterra (Finisterre) 93
restaurants 582
Fitero 134
Fiveller, Joan 151
Flame in Space and Naked Woman (Miró) 176
Flamenco **428–9**, 608
Barcelona 196, 197
festivals 46
Madrid 325, 327
Seville 13, 22, 460, 461
Flanagan, Barry 515
Flandes, Juan de 372
Florentino, Nicolás 364
Flores, Rosario 461
Floridablanca, Count of 66
Flower pavements (Ponteareas) 102
Flowers
matorral 208–9
Parque Nacional del Teide 542–3
Fluvià, River 217
Foix, Counts of 216
Folguera, Françesc 222
La Folía (San Vicente de la Barquera) 114
Fonseca, Alonso de 372
tomb of 365
Font de Canaletes (Barcelona) 155
Font i Carreras 177
Font Màgica (Barcelona) 172, 173, 175
Fontíbre 115
Fontseré, Josep 159
Food and drink
Andalusia 422–3
Aragón 204–5
Asturias and Cantabria 80
Balearic Islands 517
Basque Country, Navarra and La Rioja 136
Canary Islands 541
Castilla y León 342–3
Castilla-La Mancha 343
Catalonia (Catalunya) 204
Central Spain 342–3
Eastern Spain 204–5
Extremadura 343
Galicia 80
Horchata **257**
Madrid 342
Northern Spain 80–81
Sherry **425**
shops 607
shops in Barcelona 190–91, 193

Food and drink (cont.)
shops in Madrid 320–21, 323
shops in Seville 459
Southern Spain 422–3
specialist holidays 612, 613
Valencia and Murcia 205
what to drink in Spain 580–81
wines of Central Spain 344–5
wines of Eastern Spain 206–7
wines of Northern Spain 82–3
wines of Southern Spain 424–5
see also Restaurants
Football 26, 609
Barcelona 195
Barcelona v Real Madrid **181**
Camp Nou (Barcelona) **180**
Madrid 325, 327
Forcall 250
restaurants 591
Foreign exchange 622
Forestier, Jean 159, 448–9
Forests, Northern Spain 84–5
Forment, Damià 227, 239
Formentera 511, **516**
fiestas 527
food and drink 517
hotels 574
restaurants 602
El Formigal 234
Fornells 506–7, 527
Fort Bravo Texas Hollywood (Tabernas) 504
Fortuna, hotels 567
Foster, Sir Norman 122, 181
Fournier, Heraclio 131
Foz 92
Fraga, restaurants 590
Francés, Juan 396
Francés, Nicolás 358
Franco, General Francisco 51, **70–71**, 75
Asturian miners' revolt 69
birthplace 92
bombing of Gernika-Lumo 14, 122
Burgos 374
death 27, 71, 72
Palacio de El Pardo 336
Santa Cruz del Valle de los Caídos 333
Spanish Civil War 70–71
François I, King of France 276
Franks 55
Fray Pedro Machado (Zurbarán) 285
Fregenal de la Sierra 417
Freud, Lucian, Portrait of Baron Thyssen-Bornemisza 292
Frías 373
Frómista **372–3**
Fruit
Canary Islands 541
Southern Spain 423
Fuencaliente 403
Fuendetodos **242–3**
Fuengirola 477
restaurants 600

Fuente Agria 488
Fuente de Cantos 417
Fuente de Cibeles (Madrid) 290
Fuente Dé
  cable car 113
  hotels 563
Fuente de Neptuno (Madrid) 288, 290
Fuente Obejuna 480
Fuenterrabbía see Hondarribia
Fuentespalda, hotels 567
Fuerteventura 509, **550–51**
  hotels 575
  map 545
  restaurants 604
Fugger brothers 403
Fundació Antoni Tàpies (Barcelona)
  164, **168**
Fundació Joan Miró (Barcelona) 175,
  176
Funfairs see Amusement parks;
  Theme parks

G
Gainsborough, Thomas 309
Gáldar 547
Galdiano, Lázaro, Museo Lázaro
  Galdiano (Madrid) 309
Galerías
  Barcelona 191, 193
  Seville 458, 459
Galicia **88–103**
  climate 48
  fiestas 43, 102
  food and drink 80
  hotels 562
  map 90–91
  restaurants 582–3
  Wild Spain: Cantabria, Asturias and
  Galicia 11, **15**
Gallego, Fernando 298
Gallego language 89, 617
Galleons 62–3
Galleries see Museums and galleries
Galters, Charles 152, 153
Ganchegui, Luis Peña 180
Gandesa 213
Gandia **258–9**, 262
Gañinas 372
Garachico, hotels 575
Garafia, restaurants 605
Garajonay, Parque Nacional 35, 537
García Lorca, Federico 39, **71**, 295
  on bullfighting 40
García Márquez, Gabriel 39
García, Purificación 300
Garcilaso de la Vega 486
The Garden of Delights (Bosch) 296
Gardens see Parks and gardens
Gargallo, Pablo (Pau) 156, 169
  Museu Pablo Gargallo (Zaragoza)
  241
Garganta de Añisclo 237
Garganta del Chorro **478**
Garganta de los Infiernos 409
Garganta de la Yecla 380

Garona, River (Garonne) 214
Garraf, restaurants 588
Gasparini, Matteo 280
Gasteiz see Vitoria
Gata 408
The Gathering at Pombo Café
  (Solana) 303
Gaucín 472
Gaudí, Antoni 11, **144–5, 168**, 176
  El Capricho (Comillas) 115, 145
  Casa Batlló (Barcelona) 13, 144,
  145, **168**
  Casa de Botines (León) 357
  Casa Milà (Barcelona) 13, 29, 144,
  162, 165, 166–7, **169**
  Casa-Museu Gaudí (Barcelona) 182
  Casa Vicens (Barcelona) 145, 168
  materials 145
  Modernisme **144–5**
  Palacio Episcopal (Astorga) 356
  Palau Güell (Barcelona) **144–5**, 155
  Palma Cathedral 524, 525
  Parc de la Ciutadella (Barcelona)
  159
  Parc Güell (Barcelona) 145, **182**
  Plaça Reial lampposts (Barcelona)
  155
  Sagrada Família (Barcelona) 13,
  143, 144, 145, 163, 168, **170–71**
  Santuario de Lluc 519
Gauguin, Paul, Mata Mua 293
Gazpacho 422
Gehry, Frank 14, 124
Generalife (Granada) 17, **496**
Generation of 27 39
Generation of 1898 68
Gerena, restaurants 600
La Geria 554
  restaurants 605
Gernika-Lumo (Guernica) 11, 14,
  122–3
Gerona see Girona
Getaria (Guetaria) 14, 123
  hotels 564
Getxo, fiestas 45
Giaquinto, Corrado 281
Gibraltar 463, **476**
  hotels 573
  restaurants 600
Gift shops
  Barcelona 192, 193
  Madrid 322
  Seville 459
Los Gigantes, restaurants 605
Gijón 11, 15, **109**
  hotels 563
  restaurants 583–4
Gin, Balearic Islands 517
Giordano, Luca 299
  The Glory of the Spanish Monarchy
  335
  Iglesia de San Antonio de los
  Alemanes (Malasaña) frescoes
  308

Giovanni de Bologna 277
Gipuzkoa see Guipúzcoa
La Giralda (Seville) 10, 13, 420, 426,
  436, 437, 438, **440–41**
Giralte, Francisco 306
Girona (Gerona) 13, **218–19**
  hotels 566
  map 218
  restaurants 588–9
Girona province 211
The Glory of the Spanish Monarchy
  (Giordano) 335
The Godoy, Manuel 66, 285
Goicoa, José 126
Goldblatt, David 154
Golden Age 64–5
Golf 612, 613
Golfines family 412
El Golfo 553
Golondrinas (Barcelona) **161**
La Gomera 534, 535, **537**
  hotels 575
  restaurants 605
  whistle language 536
Góngora, Luis de 38
González, Anibal 448, 449
González, Felipe 27, 72, **73**
González, Fernán, tomb of 374
González, Gutiérrez 497
González, Julio 256
Good Friday 47, 259, 372
El Gordo 47
Gormaz 381
Gothic architecture 28, 61
Gothic Quarter (Barcelona) see Barri
  Gòtic
Government, local 625
Goya, Francisco de 36, **243**, 256
  altar painting (Chinchón) 337
  Casa-Museo de Goya
  (Fuendetodos) 242–3
  The Clothed Maja 297
  Ermita de San Antonio de la
  Florida (Madrid) 307
  The Family of King Charles IV 37
  Museo Camón Aznar (Zaragoza)
  241
  Museo de Navarra (Pamplona)
  137
  The Naked Maja 263, 297
  Palacio de Liria (Madrid) 308
  Palacio Real (Madrid) 280
  Prado (Madrid) 298
  The Procession of the Flagellants
  278
  Queen María Luisa 66
  Real Accademia de Bellas Artes de
  San Fernando (Madrid) 285
  San Francisco el Grande (Madrid)
  306
  Saturn Devouring One of his Sons
  298
  Self-Portrait 243
  statue of 294
  tapestry designs 310, 336

Goya, Francisco de (cont.)
  The Third of May 66–7, 298
  tomb of 307
Gràcia (Barcelona), nightlife 199
Gran Canaria 509, 546–9
  hotels 575
  map 544
  restaurants 604
El Gran Capitán 491
Gran Teatre del Liceu (Barcelona)
  155, 195
Gran Vía (Madrid) 12, 268–9, 282–3,
  284–5
Granada **490–96**
  Alhambra 58, 421, **494–5**
  fiestas 42, 45, 467
  Generalife 496
  hotels 573
  Madrid and Moorish Spain:
  Granada, Córdoba and Seville 10,
  17
  map 491
  Reconquest 60–61
  restaurants 600
  street-by-street map: Albaicín
  492–3
Granada province 463
Grandas de Salime 108
La Granja **518**
La Granja de San Ildefonso **367**
Granollers, hotels 566
Grape Harvest (Jerez de la Frontera)
  46
Graus **240**
  restaurants 590
Graves, Robert 519
Grazalema 473
  hotels 573
Grec Arts Festival (Barcelona) 45, 194
El Greco 127, 256, 285, **395**
  The Adoration of the Shepherds 296
  The Burial of the Count of Orgaz 36,
  392, 394
  The Denuding of Christ 396
  Hospital de la Caridad (Illescas)
  390
  Iglesia de San Miguel (Andújar)
  500
  Museo Cerralbo (Madrid) 308
  Museo del Greco (Toledo) **395**
  *The Nobleman with his Hand on his
  Chest* 298
  *The Virgin of the Immaculate
  Conception* 394
Gredos, Sierra de *see* Sierra de
  Gredos
Greek colonizers 51, 52, 53
Green travel 626
Gregorian plainchant 333, **380**, 609
Gregory I, Pope 380
Grimau, Julián 276
Gris, Juan, *Jug and Glass* 37
O Grove (El Grove) 98
  hotels 562
  restaurants 582

Gruta de las Maravillas 466
Gruta de San José *see* Coves de Sant
  Josep
Guadalajara **387**
  restaurants 596
Guadalajara province 383
Guadalest **263**
Guadalhorce, River 478
Guadalquivir, River 432, 480
Guadalupe **410–11**
  restaurants 597
Guadamur 391
Guadarrama mountains 12
Guadiela, River 387
Guadix **497**
Guanches 53, **551**
A Guarda (La Guardia) 53, **100**
  hotels 562
Guardamar del Segura 262
La Guardia *see* (A) Guarda
Güas, Juan 371, 395
Güell, Count Eusebi 145, 182
Guernica *see* Gernika-Lumo
Guernica (Picasso) 12, **70–71**, 122,
  303
Guetaria *see* Getaria
Guía 547
Guifré el Pélos (Wilfred the Hairy)
  216, 217
Guijuelo, restaurants 594
Guipúzcoa (Gipuzkoa) 119
Guitar Festival (Córdoba) 45
Guitars 428
Guzmán 472
Guzmán family 473
Gypsies 428, 493

H

Ha-Leví, Samuel 395
Habsburg dynasty 51, 64, 74
Hadrian, Emperor 480
Al Hakam II, Caliph 484, 500
Hams, Southern Spain 423
Hang-gliding 610
Hanging Houses (Cuenca) 382, **389**
Hannibal 54, 253
Haría **554**
Harlequin with a Mirror (Picasso) 292
Haro 11, 14, 82, **132**
  fiestas 136
  hotels 564
  restaurants 585
Hat shops, Barcelona 192, 193
Las Hayas, restaurants 605
Hayedo de Montejo de la Sierra
  332
Hayedo de Tejera Negra 386
Health 620–21
Hecho 234
  restaurants 590
Hemingway, Ernest 38, 136
Hercules 471
Hermosilla, José 290
Hernández, Rafael Rodríguez 448
Hernani 127

Herrera, Juan de 277
  Archivo de Indias (Seville) 443
  El Escorial 335
  Oropesa Castle 391
  Valladolid Cathedral 371
Herrería de Compludo 354
Hervás **408**
Los Hervideros 553
El Hierro 534, **536–7**
  hotels 575
  restaurants 604
  volcanoes 555
Hinojosa del Duque 480
Hio 99
La Hiruela 332
Hisham II, Caliph 56
Hispania 54
History **51–75**
Hitler, Adolf 70
HM the King's International Cup
  (Palma de Mallorca) 45
Holanda, Cornelis de 102
Holidays, public 47
Holm oak 209
The Holy Children with the Shell
  (Murillo) 37
Holy Grail 238, 255
Holy Week (Seville) 435
Homo erectus 52
Hondarribia (Fuenterrabía) **127**
  hotels 564
Hopper, Edward, *Hotel Room* 292
Horchata **257**
Hórreo 31, 89
Horse riding 613
  Real Escuela Andaluza de Arte
  Ecuestre (Jerez de la Frontera) 470
Horta de Sant Joan, restaurants 589
Hospital de la Caridad (Illescas) 390
Hospital de la Caridad (Seville) 433,
  435
Hospital de la Santa Creu i de Sant
  Pau (Barcelona) 13, 163, **169**
Hospital de Santiago (Úbeda) 500, 501
Hospital de los Venerables (Seville)
  13, 439, **443**
Hostal de los Reyes Católicos
  (Santiago de Compostela) 94
Hostal de San Marcos (León) 29, 357
Hostels, youth 560, 561
Hotel Ritz by Belmond (Madrid) 289,
  290
Hotel Room (Hopper) 292
Hotels **558–75**
  Andalusia 572–4
  Aragón 567
  Asturias and Cantabria 562–3
  Balearic Islands 574–5
  Barcelona 564–5
  Basque Country, Navarra and La
  Rioja 563–4
  booking and check-in 559
  Canary Islands 575
  casas rurales 559
  Castilla y León 569–70

Hotels (cont.)
Castilla-La Mancha 570–71
Catalonia 565–7
disabled travellers 561
Extremadura 571
Galicia 562
grading and facilities 558
hotel chains 558, 561
Madrid 568–9
Madrid Province 569
monasteries and convents 561
mountain refuges 560
paradors 558, 561
paying 559
prices 558–9
self-catering 560
Seville 571–2
Valencia and Murcia 567–8
youth hostels 560
Hoz de Arbayún 139
Hoz de Beteta 387
Hoz de Júcar 399
Hoz de Lumbier 139
Huelva **466**
fiestas 46, 467
restaurants 600
Huelva province 463
Huércal Almería, restaurants 600
Huertas (Madrid), nightlife 328–9
Huerto del Cura (Elx) 265
Huerto de las Flores (Agaete) 547
Huesca **239**
restaurants 590
Huesca province 231
Huguet, Jaume 150
Human towers (Catalonia) 225
Humeya, Abén 489
Las Hurdes **408**
Hurtado, Francisco de 333
Hypermarkets 607

I
Iberian tribes 52
Ibiza (Eivissa) 508, 511, **514–16**
food and drink 517
hotels 574
map 512
nightlife 515
restaurants 602–3
Ibiza Town **514–15**
hotels 574
restaurants 602
Los Ibores, Sierra de 410
Icod de los Vinos 538
Igantzi (Yanci) 138
Iglesia de la Magdalena (Seville)
434
Iglesia de Nuestra Señora del Rocío
(El Rocío) 467
Iglesia de San Antolín (Tordesillas)
370
Iglesia de San Jerónimo el Real
(Madrid) **294**
Iglesia de San Juan Bautista (Baños
de Cerrato) 372

Iglesia de San Miguel de Escalada
(León) 357
Iglesia de San Nicolás de Bari
(Madrid) **279**
Iglesia de San Pedro (Seville) **448**
Iglesia de Santa Ana (Granada) 492
Iglesia de Santa María (Caceres) 412
Iglesia de Santa María de Eunate
(near Puente la Reina) 135
Iglesia de Santiago del Arrabal
(Toledo) **395**
Iglesia de Santo Tomé (Toledo) 392,
394
Iglesia-Convento de San Esteban
(Salamanca) 363, **364**
Ignatius of Loiola, St
Jesuit Order 128
Santiario de Loiola 128
Illa de la Discòrdia (Barcelona) 164,
168
Illa de Tabarca 262, **265**
Illas Cíes 99
Illes Medes (Islas Medes) 221
Illescas **390**
restaurants 596
Incas 62
Infantado, Dukes of 336
Inmaculada Concepción 47
Inquisition 60, **278**
Palau Reial (Barcelona) 150
Institut Amatller d'Art Hispanic 168
Insurance
car 630
holiday 621
Interior design shops
Barcelona 192, 193
Madrid 322, 323
International Classical Theatre
Festival (Almagro) 45
International Exhibition, Barcelona
(1929) 173, 174, 175, 176, 177
International Festival of Music and
Dance (Granada) 45
International Festival of Santander
45
International Jazz Festivals 45
International Vintage Car Rally 44
Internet 624
Interpreters 621
Inurria, Mateo 483
Irache 136
Iranzu 136
Irati, Selva de 139
Iregua Valley 133
La Iruela 501
Iruña see Pamplona
Irving, Washington 494
Isaba 139
Isabel I, Queen of Castile (the
Catholic) **60–61**
and Almería 505
Arévalo castle 369
Battle of Toro 361
and Cáceres 412, 413
and Columbus 150, 466

Isabel I, Queen of Castile (the
Catholic (cont.)
and Granada 490
Iglesia de San Jerónimo el Real
(Madrid) 294
Inquisition 278
Madrigal de las Altas Torres 370
marriage 370
Medina del Campo 370
Monasterio de San Juan de los
Reyes (Toledo) 395
and Orihuela 265
Real Alcázar (Seville) 444
Real Chancillería (Granada) 492
Santa Fé 486–7
unification of Spain 51, **74**
Isabel II, Queen of Spain
abdication 67
Museo Arqueológico Nacional
(Madrid) 300
portraits 75
Teatro Real (Madrid) 279
Isabel Clara Eugenia, Princess 285
Isabel of Portugal, tomb of 375
Isidore, St 275, 276, 277
Isla 108
Isla de la Cartuja (Seville) **450**
Isla Cristina 466
Isla Mágica (Seville) 450, 461
Isla Perdiguera 266
Isla Vedra see (Es) Vedrá
Islands **506–55**
Balearic Islands 510–31
Canary Islands 532–55
Introducing Spain's Islands 508–9
Islas Canarias see Canary Islands
Islote de Hilario 553
Ismail I 494
Isozaki, Irata 177
Itálica 55, **480**
Itineraries **10–17**
2 Days in Barcelona **12–13**
2 Days In Seville **13**
2 Days in Madrid **12**
Barcelona and the Mediterranean
Coast by Train 11, **16**
Bilbao and the Basque Lands 11,
14
Madrid and Moorish Spain 10, **17**
Wild Spain: Cantabria, Asturias and
Galicia 11, **15**

J
Jabugo 466
restaurants 600
Jaca **235**
festivals 45
restaurants 590
Jaén 463, **497**
hotels 573
restaurants 600
Jaén, Bartolomé de 503
Jaén province 463
Jaime (Jaume) I, King of Aragón
Monasterio de El Puig 253

Jaime (Jaume) I, King of Aragón (cont.)
and Palma 522, 524
statue of 151
and Valencia 243, 254
Jaime II, King of Aragón
Barcelona cathedral 152, 153
Castell de Bellver (Palma) 523
tomb of 225, 525
Jaime III, King of Aragón, tomb 525
Jameos del Agua **554**
James, St 59
and Padrón 98
The Road to Santiago **86–7**, 89
Santiago de Compostela 96–7
statue of 133
tomb of 56, 95, 97
Jamete, Esteban 501
Jandía, Península de **550**
Jarama, River 333
Jarandilla de la Vera
fiestas 409
hotels 571
Jardí Botànic Mar i Murtra (Blanes) 220
Jardín de Cactus (Guatiza) 554
Jardín Canario (Tarifa) 548
Jardín de Orquídeas (Puerto de la Cruz) 538
Jardines del Río Turia (Valencia) **256**
Játiva see Xàtiva
Jávea see Xàbia
Javier, Castillo de **139**
Jazz 608
Barcelona 196, 197
Madrid 326, 327
Seville 461
Jerez de los Caballeros **417**
Jerez de la Frontera **470**
festivals 44, 46
restaurants 600
Jerez-Xérès-Sherry wine region 424–5
Jesuit Order **128**
Carlos III expels 66
Colegiata de San Isidro (Madrid) 276
Jesús 515
Jewellery shops
Barcelona 192, 193
Madrid 322, 323
Jews
in Barcelona **150**
forced conversions 60
Girona 218
Jiloca, River 245
Jimena de la Frontera 472
Jiménez, Juan Ramón 39
Joan, Pere 229
Jordaens, Jakob 299
Jorquera 399
José I (Joseph Bonaparte) 67, 75, 279
José Tomás 41

Jovellanos, Gaspar Melchor de 109
Júcar (Xúquer), River 252, 387, 399
Juan I, King of Aragón 373
Juan II, King of Aragón, tomb of 226
Juan II, King of Castile, tomb of 375
Juan, King of Portugal 59
Juan, Prince, tomb of 367
Juan de Austria, Don 161
Juan Carlos I, King of Spain 27, 75
abdication 73
and attempted coup d'état 72
coronation 294
Costa Teguise 553
as Franco's successor 71
Juan de la Cruz, San see John of the Cross, St
Juana, Doña 285
Juana la Beltraneja 60, 365
Juana la Loca (the Mad), Queen of Castile 61, 74
Capilla Real (Granada) 490
Castillo de la Mota (Medina del Campo) 370
Juanes, Juan de, Ecce Homo 256
Jug and Glass (Gris) 37
Jujol, Josep Maria
Casa Milà (Barcelona) 169
Plaça d'Espanya fountain (Barcelona) 177
Juliana, St, tomb of 116
Julióbriga 115
Jumilla wine region 206–7
Juni, Juan de 371, 381
Jürgen Mayer H 448

K

Kane, Sir Richard 530
Kayaking 611
Ketama 428
Kingdom of Castile 58
Kingdom of Castile and León 58, 59
Kingdom of Navarra **134**
Kite surfing 611
Knick-knack shops, Barcelona 192, 193
The Knight's Dream (Pereda) 64–5
Knights Hospitallers 398
Knights of Montesa 250
Knights of the Order of Alcántara 414
Knights of the Order of Toisón del Oro 152
Knights Templar
Castell del Papa Luna (Peñíscola) 251
Castro Urdiales 117
Iglesia del Crucifijo (Puente la Reina) 135
Jerez de los Caballeros castle 417
El Maestrat 250
Ponferrada Castle 355
Kokoschka, Oskar 122
Kolbe, Georg 174
Morning 177

Koons, Jeff 14, 125
Kursaal (San Sebastián) **127**

L

La Isla, Camarón de 429
Labels, wine 581
Labour Day 47
Laga 123
Lagartera 391
Lago de Carucedo 354
Lago de Sanabria 355
Laguardia (Biasteri) **131**
hotels 564
La Laguna **539**
Laguna de la Fuente de Piedra 479
Laguna Negra de Urbión 381
Lagunas de Peñalara 333
Lagunas de Ruidera **401**
Laida 123
Lalique, René 365
Landscape at Cadaqués (Dalí) 302
Language **617**
Basque (Euskara) 119
Catalan **216**
Gallego 89
La Gomera's whistle language 536
phrase book 671–2
specialist holidays 613
Valenciano dialect 247
Lanjarón **488**
Lanzarote 509, **552–4**
hotels 575
map 545
restaurants 605
volcanoes 555
Laredo 15, **117**
fiestas 114
restaurants 584
Larouco 46
Larra 39
Lastres 108
restaurants 584
Latin American Film Festival (Huelva) 46
La Latina (Madrid) **306**
nightlife 329
Laujar de Andarax **489**
Lavapiés (Madrid), nightlife 329
Laza, fiestas 102
El Lazarillo de Tormes 38
Leather goods, Madrid 322, 323
Lebrija 470
Ledesma 365
Legal assistance 621
Léger, Fernand 122
Lekeitio (Lequeitio) 14, **123**
hotels 564
León **357–9**
Cathedral 28, 61, 340, **358–9**
hotels 569
restaurants 595
The Road to Santiago 86
León, Fray Luis de 399
León province 351
see also Castilla y León

Leonardo da Vinci 291, 298, 309
Leone, Sergio 504
Leonor, Queen 137
Lepanto, Battle of (1571) 63
Lequeitio *see* Lekeitio
Lérida *see* Lleida
Lerma **380**
Lerma, Duke of 64, 380
Lesaka 138
Letur 401
Leyre, Monasterio de 79, **139**
Lichtenstein, Roy 160
Liétor 401
Linares, Marquis of 290
Linares de Mora 244
La Linea, restaurants 600
Liqueurs 581
Literature **38–9**
Lizarra *see* Estella
Llafranc 221
  hotels 566
Llagostera, restaurants 589
Llamazares, Julio 39
Llanes 109
  hotels 563
  restaurants 584
Lleida (Lérida) **224–5**
  hotels 566
  restaurants 589
Lleida (Lérida) province 211
Llerena **417**
Llívia 216
Lloret de Mar 211, 221
  hotels 563
Lloseta, restaurants 603
La Llotja (Barcelona) **156**
Llull, Ramon 520
Llúria, Roger de, statue of 203
Local government 625
Logroño **133**
  hotels 564
  restaurants 585
Loiola, St Ignatius *see* Ignatius of
  Loiola, St
Loja 487
  hotels 573
La Lonja (Valencia) **255**
Lope de Vega, Félix 38, 64, 337
  Casa-Museo de Lope de Vega
  (Madrid) **294**
  Fuente Obejuna 480
López, Antonio López y 114
López, Vicente 127
Lorca **267**
  fiestas 259
  restaurants 591
Loro Parque (Puerto de la Cruz) 538
Los Vélez, Marquis of 504
Lost property 620
Louis XIV, King of France 65
Lovers of Teruel **245**
Lozoya 333
Luarca 15, 108
Lucan 38
Lucía, Paco de 428

Ludwig Salvator, Archduke 519
Lugo 11, 15, 55, **103**
  hotels 562
  restaurants 582
Lugo province 89
Luis I, King of Spain 66, 75
Luis de León, Fray 364
Luke, St 223
Lupiana 387
Lusitania (Roman province) 54
Luyego, hotels 569
Lynx **469**

M

Maceo, Antonio 69
Machado, Antonio 39, 381
Machuca, Pedro 298
Madrid **268–329**
  2 Days in Madrid **12**
  Barajas Airport 626
  Bourbon Madrid 286–303
  climate 48
  coach stations 633
  Dos de Mayo 44, 294
  entertainment 324–9
  fiestas and festivals 44, 47, 294
  food and drink 342
  French occupation 67
  hotels 568–9
  Introducing Madrid 270–71
  Madrid and Moorish Spain 10, **17**
  Museo del Prado 296–9
  Museo Nacional Centro de Arte
  Reina Sofia 271, 302–3
  Museo Thyssen-Bornemisza
  292–3
  nightlife 328–9
  Old Madrid 272–85
  Palacio Real 270, 280–81
  Paseo del Prado 288–9
  restaurants 591–3
  shopping 320–23
  Street Finder 311–19
  street-by-street map: Old Madrid
  274–5
  street-by-street map: Paseo del
  Prado 288–9
  transport 634–5
  transport map *see* inside back
  cover
Madrid Province **330–37**
  hotels 569
  restaurants 593–4
Madrigal de la Altas Torres 370
El Madroñal, restaurants 604
El Maestrat **250**
Magazines 624–5
Magellan, Ferdinand 62, 470
Os Magostos 46
Mahón *see* Maó
Majorca *see* Mallorca
Málaga **478**
  airport 626
  Alcazaba 56–7
  festivals 42

Málaga (cont.)
  hotels 573
  restaurants 601
Málaga province 463
Málaga wine region 424
Malasaña (Madrid) 12, **308**
  nightlife 328–9
Maldonado, Rodrigo 365
Mallorca (Majorca) 509, 511, **518–25**
  fiestas 527
  food and drink 517
  hotels 574
  map 512–13
  restaurants 603
Malpartida 414
Malpica 93
  restaurants 582
La Malvarrosa beach (Valencia) 257
Mañara, Miguel de 435
Mañas, José Ángel 39
La Mancha *see* Castilla-La Mancha
La Mancha wine region 344–5
Manchego cheese 342, 579
Manises 257
Mannerists 298
Manolete 41, 310
Manrique, César 538, **552**, 553
  Fundación César Manrique
  (Teguise) 554
  Jameos del Agua 554
  Monumento al Campesino 554
Al Mansur 57, 381, 484
Manzanares, River 280
Manzanares el Real **336**
Maó (Mahón) **530**
  hotels 575
  restaurants 604
Maps
  Las Alpujarras tour 488–9
  Ancient Menorca 531
  Andalusia 464–5
  Aragón 232–3
  Asturias and Cantabria 106–7
  Baeza 502–3
  Balearic Islands 508–9, 512–13
  Barcelona 142–3
  Barcelona: Barri Gòtic 148–9
  Barcelona: Eixample 163
  Barcelona: Further Afield 179
  Barcelona: Montjuïc 173, 174–5
  Barcelona: Old Town 147
  Barcelona: Quadrat d'Or 164–5
  Barcelona: Las Ramblas 155
  Barcelona: Street Finder 183–9
  Barcelona: transport map *see*
  inside back cover
  Barcelona transport *see* inside
  back cover
  Basque Country, Navarra and La
  Rioja 120–21
  birds of Central Spain 346
  broad-leaved forests 85
  Burgos 375
  Cáceres 412–13
  Canary Islands 21, 508–9

Maps (cont.)
Canary Islands: Eastern Islands 544–5
Canary Islands: Western Islands 534–5
Castilla y León 352–3
Castilla-La Mancha 384–5
Castles of Castilla y León 349
Catalonia 212–13
Central Spain 340–41
climate of Spain 48–9
Córdoba 482–3
Costa Blanca 262
Costa del Sol 476–7
Cruz de Tejeda tour 549
Cuenca 388–9
Eastern Spain 202–3
Extremadura 406–7
Galicia 90–91
Girona 218
Granada: Albaicín 492–3
Granada: city centre 491
Itineraries 10–11
legacy of Spanish colonization 68
Madrid 270–71
Madrid: Bourbon Madrid 287
Madrid: Further Afield 305
Madrid: Old Madrid 273, 274–5
Madrid: Paseo del Prado 288–9
Madrid: Street Finder 311–19
Madrid: transport map *see* inside back cover
Madrid Province 270, **331**
Madrid transport *see* inside back cover
Mérida 415
national parks 35
Northern Spain 78–9
Palma 522–3
Pamplona 137
Parque Nacional de Doñana 468–9
Parque Nacional de Ordesa 236–7
Parque Nacional de Picos de Europa 112–13
Parque Nacional del Teide 542–3
prehistoric Spain 52
Pueblos Blancos tour 472–3
railways 629
Regional Spain 20–21
Rías Baixas 99
road maps 632
The Road to Santiago 86–7
Roman Spain 54
Ronda 474–5
Salamanca 362–3
Santiago de Compostela 94–5
Segovia 368
Seville: El Arenal 431, 432–3
Seville: Further Afield 447
Seville: Santa Cruz 437, 438–9
Seville: Street Finder 451–7
Sierra de Alcaraz 400–401
Sierra de Francia and Sierra de Bejar tour 360–61
Southern Spain 420–21

Maps (cont.)
Spain 18–19
Spain in 1714 66
Spain in July 1936 70
Spain today 72
Spain's exploration of the New World 60
Spanish Empire in 1580 62
Spanish Empire in 1647 64
Toledo 392–3
Úbeda 500
Valencia 255
Valencia and Murcia 248–9
Vitoria 130
Wines of Central Spain 344–5
Wines of Eastern Spain 206–7
Wines of Northern Spain 82–3
Wines of Southern Spain 424–5
Zaragoza 241
Mar de Castillo 386–7
Mar Menor 16, **266**
Maragatos **357**
Marbella 462, **477**
hotels 573
restaurants 601
Marchamalo, restaurants 596
Marcilla, Diego de 245
Marès i Deulovol, Frederic 227
Museu Frederic Marès 149
Museu Frederic Marès (Barcelona) **150**
Margaret of Austria 284, 291
María Cristina, Queen
Palacio Miramar 126
regency 67, 75
María Luisa, Princess 448
María Luisa, Queen **66**, 243
María Teresa, Queen of France 65
Marías, Javier 39
Markets 606
Barcelona 155, 158, 190, 193
Madrid 306, 320–21, 323
Seville 458, 459
Valencia 255
Vic 224
Marsé, Juan 39
Martí the Humanist 150
Martial 38
Martínez, Domingo 434
Martínez, Ginés 503
Martorell, Bernat 36
Transfiguration 153
Martorell, Joan 114–15
The Martyrdom of St Philip (Ribera) 296
Mary Tudor, Queen of England 62
Marzagan, hotels 575
Maspalomas 533, **546–7**
Mata Mua (Gauguin) 293
Matadors 40–41
Matarana, Bartolomé 255
Mateo, Maestro 96
Mateu, Pau 151
Matorral
flowers 208–9
wildlife 209

The Matter of Time (Richard) 124, 125
Matxitxaco 123
Maundy Thursday 47
Mauricio, Bishop 376
Mayonnaise 530
Mazagón 466
hotels 573
El Médano 538
Media 624–5
Medical treatment 621
Medina Azahara 57, 427, **481**
Medina del Campo 348, **370**
Medina de Pomar 373
Medina de Rioseco **371**
Medina Sidonia, Dukes of 468, 473
Medinaceli **381**
hotels 570
Medinaceli, Dukes of 442
Las Médulas 354
Megaliths, Menorca 531
Meier, Richard 154
Mendizábal, Juan Álvarez 67, 332
Mendoza, Cardinal 394, 497
Mendoza, Rodrigo de 497
Mendoza family 387
Mengs, Anton Raffael 299
Las Meninas (Picasso) 36, 157
Las Meninas (Velázquez) 12, **36–7**, 298
Menorca (Minorca) 509, 511, **526–31**
Ancient Menorca 53, **531**
fiestas 527
food and drink 517
hotels 574–5
map 513
restaurants 603–4
Méntrida wine region 344–5
Menus 576–7
Es Mercadal **527**
Mercado Central (Valencia) **255**
Mercado de San Miguel (Madrid) 12, **274**
Mercat del Born (Barcelona) **158**
Mercat de San Josep (Barcelona) 155
Mercè, Festival de la (Barcelona) 46, 161, 194
Mérida 407, **414–15**
festivals 45
history 54
hotels 571
map 415
restaurants 597
Roman Theatre 54–5
Mérimée, Prosper 449
Sa Mesquida, restaurants 604
Metro systems 634, 635
see also inside back cover
Metropol Parasol (Seville) **448**
Mezquita (Córdoba) 10, 17, 420, 426, 483, **484–5**
Midsummer's Eve (Catalonia) 225
Mies van der Rohe, Ludwig, Pavelló Mies van der Rohe (Barcelona) 174, **177**

Mieses, hotels 563
Mijas, hotels 573
Milà, Casa (Barcelona) **169**
Milà family 169
Millán, Gómez 448
Los Millares 52, 505
Mini-Hollywood (Tabernas) 504, 609
Minorca *see* Menorca
Mirador del Río 554
Mirambel 250
    hotels 567
Miranda del Castañar 361
Miró, Joan 174, 265
    Collage 37
    Doña i Ocell 180
    Flame in Space and Naked Woman 176
    Fundació Joan Miró (Barcelona) 175, **176**
    Fundació Pilar y Joan Miró (Palma) 523
    Plaça de la Boqueria mosaic (Barcelona) 155
    Portrait II 302
Misteri d'Elx 45, 259
Mitjans, Francesc 180
Mobile phones 624
Modernisme (Modernismo) 29, **144–5**
    Barcelona 163
    Illa de la Discòrdia (Barcelona) 168
Moguer 467
Mojácar **504**
Molina de Aragón **386**
Mombeltrán 366
Monachil, hotels 573
Monasteries
    accommodation in 561
    Carracedo del Monasterio 355
    Cartuja de Miraflores (Burgos) 375
    Monasterio de la Cartuja (Granada) 67, **491**
    Monasterio de las Descalzas Reales (Madrid) **285**
    Monasterio de la Encarnación (Ávila) 367
    Monasterio de la Encarnación (Madrid) **284**
    Monasterio de Guadalupe **410–11**
    Monasterio de Iranzu 136
    Monasterio de Leyre 79, **139**
    Monasterio de Nuestra Señora de Irache 136
    Monasterio de La Oliva **134**
    Monasterio de Oseira **103**
    Monasterio de Piedra **242**
    Monasterio de El Puig **253**
    Monasterio de la Rábida **466**
    Monasterio de Ribas de Sil 90, **102**
    Monasterio de San Juan de Duero 378–9, 381
    Monasterio de San Juan de la Peña **238**, 255
    Monasterio de San Juan de los Reyes (Toledo) **395**

Monasteries (cont.)
    Monasterio de San Martiño Pinaro 94
    Monasterio de San Millán de Suso 133
    Monasterio de San Millán de Yuso 133
    Monasterio de San Salvador (Celanova) 101
    Monasterio de Santa Clara (Moguer) 467
    Monasterio de Santa Clara (Olite) 135
    Monasterio de Santa Clara (Tordesillas) 370
    Monasterio de Santa María (A Guarda) 100
    Monasterio de Santa María (Fitero) 134
    Monasterio de Santa María (Ripoll) 216
    Monasterio de Santa María (Valdediós) 11
    Monasterio de Santa María de las Cuevas (Seville) 450
    Monasterio de Santa María de El Paular **332–3**
    Monasterio de Santa María de Huerta 381
    Monasterio de Santa María la Real 133
    Monasterio de Santo Domingo de Silos **380**
    Monasterio Sobrado de los Monjes 103
    Monasterio de Tentudía 417
    Monasterio de Uclés **390**
    Monasterio de Veruela **240**
    Monasterio de Yuste **409**
    Monestir de Montserrat 211, **222–3**
    Monestir de Poblet 203, 211, **226–7**
    Monestir de Santa Maria de Pedralbes (Barcelona) **181**
    Monestir de Santes Creus **225**
    Real Monasterio de Huelgas (Burgos) 375
    Real Monasterio de Santo Tomás (Ávila) 367
    San Paio de Antealtares (Santiago de Compostela) 95
    Sant Joan de les Abadesses 217
Moncloa (Madrid), nightlife 328–9
Mondoñedo **92**
Moneo, Rafael 127, 296, 523
Monestir *see* Monasteries
Money 622–3
Monfragüe, Parque Natural de **410**
Monpensier, Dukes of 448
Monreal del Campo 242
Montalbán 391
Montañas del Fuego 545, 552, 555
Montañés, Juan Martínez 65, 448
Montblanc (Montblanch) **225**
    hotels 566

El Monte Castillo 116
Monte Igueldo 126
Monte de Santa Tecla 100
Monte Ulía 126
Monte Urgull 14, **126**
Montefrío 17, **486–7**
Montejo de la Sierra 332
Montes de Anaga **539**
Montes de León 354
Montes de Málaga, Parque Natural de los 478
Montes de Toledo 385, **391**
Montes Universales 245
Montgolfier brothers 66
Montilla 10, 17, **486**
Montilla-Moriles wine region 424
Montjuïc (Barcelona) **172–7**
    area map 173
    nightlife 198–9
    street-by-street map 174–5
Montseny, hotels 566
Montserrat
    hotels 566
    Monestir de 211, **222–3**
Monturiol i Estarriol, Narcís, statue of 219
Monument a Colom (Barcelona) **160**
Monument del Dos de Mayo (Madrid) 289
Moor, Antonis 299
Moore, Henry 123
Moore, Sir John 93
Moorish architecture 28, **426–7**
Moors 51
    converts 63
    expulsion from Spain 60–61
    expulsion of Moriscos 64, 65
    Granada 490
    history 56–7
    Reconquest **58–9**, 105
Moors and Christians (Alcoi) 44, 259
Moors and Christians (Callosa d'en Sarria) 46
Mora de Rubielos **244**
Mora, Juan Gómez de
    Monasterio de la Encarnación (Madrid) 284
    Plaza Mayor (Madrid) 277
    Plaza de la Villa (Madrid) 277
Morales, Luis de 298, 365, 414
Moratalla 267
Morella **250**
    restaurants 591
Moriscos 63
    expulsion of 64, 65
Morning (Kolbe) 177
Morro Jable 550
    restaurants 604
Mosques
    Mezquita (Córdoba) 420, 426, 463, **484–5**
    Mezquita del Cristo de la Luz (Toledo) 393
Mosteiro de Oseira *see* Monasterio de Oseira

Mosteiro de San Estevo de Rivas do Sil *see* Monasterio de Ribas del Sil
La Mota Castle (Medina del Campo) 348, **370**
Mota del Cuervo 398
Motorways 631
Mountain refuges 560
Mountain sports 611
Mountains 34
La movida 309
Movies *see* Cinema
Moya 387
Mozaga 554
Mozarabic architecture 28, 357
Mudéjar architecture 28, 59, 426
Muela de Cortes 252
Muhammad II al Nasir 58
Muhammad V 494
Muhammad ben Abd al Rahman 273
Mulhacén 489
Mundaka 123
   hotels 564
Mundo, River 400
Muñoz Molina, Antonio 39
Muralla Bizantina (Cartagena) 267
Murat, Marshal 67
Murcia 11, 16, **266**
   Cathedral 202, 266
   festivals 42
   hotels 568
Murcia province *see* Valencia and Murcia
Murillo, Bartolomé Esteban 256, 285, 440
   baptism 434
   The Holy Children with the Shell 37
   Hospital de la Caridad (Seville) 433, 435
   Museo de Bellas Artes (Seville) 434
   San Diego de Alcalá Giving Food to the Poor 65
Muros 99
Museums and galleries
   admission charges 617
   opening hours 617
   Artium (Vitoria) 130
   Ateneu Científic Literari i Artístic (Maó) 530
   Bullfighting Museum (Antequera) 479
   CaixaForum (Barcelona) **177**
   CaixaForum (Zaragoza) 241
   Camp Nou Experience Tour & Museum (Barcelona) **180**
   Casa de l'Ardiaca (Barcelona) 148, **150**
   Casa de Cervantes (Valladolid) **371**
   Casa de Colón (Las Palmas de Gran Canria) 548
   A Casa José Saramago (Lanzarote) 553
   Casa de Juntas (Gernika-Lumo) 123

Museums and galleries (cont.)
   Casa Lis Museo Art Nouveau y Art Deco (Salamanca) **365**
   Casa de Sefarad (Córdoba) 482
   Casa-Museo de Cervantes (Alcalá de Henares) 337
   Casa-Museo Gaudí (Barcelona) 182
   Casa-Museo de Goya (Fuendetodos) 242–3
   Casa-Museo de Lope de Vega (Madrid) **294**
   Casa-Museo de Martín Alonso Pinzón (Palos de la Frontera) 467
   Casa-Museu Salvador Dalí (Cadaqués) 220
   Casa-Museo de Unamuno (Salamanca) 365
   Casa Natal de Picasso (Málaga) 478
   Castillo de la Yedra (Cazorla) 501
   Castro de Coaña 108
   Cathedral Museum (Murcia) 266
   Cathedral Museum (Palma) 524
   Cathedral Museum (Santiago de Compostela) 96
   Centre de Cultura Contemporània (Barcelona) 154
   Centro Andaluz de Arte Contemporaneo (Seville) 450
   Centro Cultural Caja Granada **491**
   Centro de Interpretación Cuevas de Guadix 497
   Ciutat de les Arts i de les Ciències (Valencia) 16, **257**
   Collecío Hernández Sanz y Hernández Mora (Maó) 530
   Conjunt Monumental de la Plaça del Rei (Barcelona) 12, 149, **150–51**
   Cosmocaixa - Museu de la Ciència (Barcelona) **182**
   Cueva-Museo Costumbres Populares (Guadix) 497
   Eco-Museo (Deltebre) 229
   Ecomuseo Lagar de Torrijos 478
   Espacio Cultural Ignacio Zuloaga (Zumaia) 123
   Fundació Antoni Tàpies (Barcelona) 164, **168**
   Fundació Joan Miró (Barcelona) **176**
   Fundació Pilar i Joan Miró (Palma) **523**
   Fundación César Manrique (Teguise) 554
   Gibraltar Museum (Gibraltar) 476
   Herrería de Compludo (El Bierzo) 354
   Iglesia de San Antolín (Tordesillas) 370
   Instituto Valenciano de Arte Moderno (IVAM, Valencia) **256**
   León Cathedral 358
   MEAC (Badajoz) 416
   Monasterio de El Puig 253

Museums and galleries (cont.)
   Monastery of Montserrat 222
   Museo de Albacete 400
   Museo de América (Madrid) **307**
   Museo de Armería (Vitoria) **131**
   Museo de Arqueología y de Naipes (BIBAT) (Vitoria) **131**
   Museo de Arqueología y de Naipes (Vitoria) 14
   Museo Arqueológico (Badajoz) 416
   Museo Arqueológico (Betancuria) 550
   Museo Arqueológico (Córdoba) **483**
   Museo Arqueológico (Granada) 493
   Museo Arqueológico (Oviedo) 110, 111
   Museo Arqueológico (Seville) 449
   Museo Arqueológico (Úbeda) 501
   Museo Arqueológico Cueva de Siete Palacios (Almuñécar) 487
   Museo Arqueológico Nacional (Madrid) **300**
   Museo de Arte Abstracto (Cuenca) 388
   Museo de Arte Contemporáneo (Alicante) 265
   Museo de Arte Contemporáneo de Castilla y León (MUSAC) (León) 357
   Museo de Arte Contemporáneo de Vilafamés 251
   Museo de Arte Público de Madrid 300
   Museo de Arte Sacro (Vitoria) **131**
   Museo de Arte Visigodo (Mérida) 415
   Museo de Artes y Costumbres Populares (Seville) 449
   Museo de Bellas Artes (Bilbao) 14, **122**
   Museo de Bellas Artes (Castelló de la Plana) 251
   Museo de Bellas Artes (Córdoba) **483**
   Museo de Bellas Artes (Oviedo) 110, 111
   Museo de Bellas Artes (Santa Cruz de Tenerife) 540
   Museo de Bellas Artes (Santander) 117
   Museo de Bellas Artes (Seville) 13, 430, **434**
   Museo de Bellas Artes (Valencia) **256**
   Museo de Burgos 375
   Museo de Cáceres 413
   Museo de Cádiz **471**
   Museo Camón Aznar (Zaragoza) 241
   Museo Canario (Las Palmas de Gran Canaria) 548
   Museo Cerralbo (Madrid) **308**

Museums and galleries (cont.)
Museo de Ciencias Naturales El
Carmen (Onda) 252
Museo de Cuenca 388
Museo Diocesà (Palma) 523
Museo Diocesano (Cuenca) 389
Museo Diocesano (Mondoñedo)
92
Museo Diocesano (Santillana del
Mar) 116
Museo Diocesano de Arte Sacro
(Las Palmas de Gran Canaria) 548
Museo Etnográfico (Grandas de
Salime) 108
Museo Etnográfico (O Cebreiro)
103
Museo Etnográfico Gonzalez
Santana (Olivenza) 416
Museo Etnográfico y Textil Pérez
Enciso (Plasencia) 409
Museo Etnològic de Ibiza y
Formentera (Santa Eulària) 516
Museo Etnológico de la Huerta de
Murcia (Murcia) 266
Museo de la Evolución Humana
(Burgos) 375
Museo del Grabado Español
Contemporáneo (Marbella) 477
Museo del Greco (Toledo) **395**
Museo Guggenheim (Bilbao) 11,
14, 122, **124–5**
Museo de Historia de Arrecife 553
Museo de Historia de Madrid 29,
308–9
Museo de Historia de Valencia **257**
Museo de Huesca 239
Museo de la Inquisición (Seville)
450
Museo Interactivo da Historia de
Lugo 103
Museo Lázaro Galdiano (Madrid)
309
Museo de León 357
Museo de Málaga 478
Museo Marítimo (Santander) 117
Museo Martorell (Barcelona) **159**
Museo de Microminiaturas
(Guadalest) 263
Museo Minero (Riotinto) 466
Museo de Monte de Santa Tecla (A
Guarda) 100
Museo Municipal (Xàtiva) 258
Museo Nacional Arqueología
Marítima (Cartagena) 267
Museo Nacional de Arte Romano
(Mérida) 340, 414–15
Museo Nacional de Artes
Decorativas (Madrid) 289, **291**
Museo Nacional Centro de Arte
Reina Sofía (Madrid) 12, 271,
302–3
Museo Nacional de Céramica
Gonzalez Martí (Valencia) **255**
Museo Nacional de Escultura
(Valladolid) **371**

Museums and galleries (cont.)
Museo de la Naturaleza y el
Hombre (Santa Cruz de Tenerife)
540
Museo de Navarra 137
Museo Numantino (Soria) 381
Museo Pablo Gargallo (Zaragoza)
241
Museo Pérez Comendador-Leroux
(Hervás) 408
Museo del Pescador (Bermeo) 123
Museo Picasso (Buitrago del
Lozoya) 332
Museo de Picasso (Málaga) 478
Museo de la Piratería (Teguise) 554
Museo de Pontevedra 98
Museo del Prado (Madrid) 12, 271,
296–9
Museo de Prehistoria y
Arqueología (Santander) 117
Museo Provincial (Huelva) 466
Museo Provincial (Jaén) 497
Museo Provincial (Lugo) 103
Museo Provincial (Teruel) 245
Museo Reina Sofía see Museo
Nacional Centro de Arte Reina
Sofía
Museo de Ricas Telas (Burgos) 375
Museo Romero de Torres
(Córdoba) **483**
Museo Rosalia de Castro (Padrón)
98
Museo Ruiz de Luna (Talavera de
la Reina) 390
Museo de San Gil (Atienza) 386
Museo San Juan de Dios
(Granada) 492
Museo San Juan de Dios
(Orihuela) 265
Museo de San Telmo (San
Sebastián) 14, **127**
Museo de Santa Cruz (Toledo)
393, **394**
Museo Sefardí (Toledo) **395**
Museo de Semana Santa (Zamora)
360
Museo Sorolla (Madrid) **309**
Museo Taurino (Madrid) 310
Museo del Teatro Romano
(Cartagena) 267
Museo Thyssen-Bornemisza
(Madrid) 271, 288, **292–3**
Museo Vasco (Bilbao) 122
Museo del Vino (Valdepeñas) 402
Museo de Zaragoza 241
Museu Arqueològic (Barcelona)
175, **176**
Museu Arqueològic (Sóller) 519
Museu d'Art (Girona) **219**
Museu d'Art Contemporani
(Barcelona) **154**
Museu d'Art Contemporani (Ibiza)
515
Museu d'Automates (Barcelona)
182

Museums and galleries (cont.)
Museu Blau (Barcelona) **181**
Museu Cau Ferrat (Sitges) 228
Museu de Cera (Barcelona) 155
Museu Comarcal de la Conca de
Barberà (Montblanc) 225
Museu Comarcal de la Garrotxa
(Olot) 217
Museu dels Cultures del Món
(Barcelona) 158
Museu Diocesà (Ciutadella) 526
Museu Diocesà (La Seu d'Urgell)
216
Museu Diocesà i Comarcal
(Solsona) 224
Museu Episcopal de Vic 224
Museu Etnològic (Barcelona) 175
Museu Frederic Marès (Barcelona)
149, **150**
Museu d'Història de Barcelona 12,
149, **150–51**
Museu d'Història de Girona **219**
Museu d'Història dels Jueus
(Girona) **218**
Museu d'Idees i Invents Barcelona
(MIBA) **151**
Museu del Joguet (Figueres) 219
Museu de Mallorca (Palma) 523
Museu Marítim and Drassanes
(Barcelona) **161**
Museu Monografico de Pollentia
(Alcúdia) 520
Museu Municipal (Tossa del Mar)
220
Museu Nacional Arqueològic
(Tarragona) 228–9
Museu Nacional d'Art de
Catalunya (Barcelona) 174, **176**
Museu Olímpic i de l'Esport
(Barcelona) 177
Museu Pau Casals (El Vendrell) 228
Museu Picasso (Barcelona) **157**
Museu de Pollença 520
Museu dera Vall d'Aran (Vielha) 214
Museu de la Xocolata (Barcelona)
158
Museum of Art (El Escorial) 335
Necropolis de Puig d'es Molins
(Ibiza) 515
Palacio Episcopal (Astorga) 356
Palacio de Nájera (Antequera) 479
Patio Herreriano Museo de Arte
Contemporáneo Español
(Valladolid) **371**
Pretori i Circ Romans (Tarragona)
228, 229
Real Academia de Bellas Artes de
San Fernando (Madrid) **285**
Salón de Reinos (Madrid) 289, **291**
Teatre-Museu Dalí (Figueres) 219
Tesoro de Villena (Villena) 264
Villa Romana la Olmeda (Pedrosa
de la Vega) 373
Vinseum (Vilafranca del Penedès)
225

Music 608–9
  Barcelona 195–7
  flamenco **428–9**, 608
  Gregorian plainchant **380**
  Madrid 325–7
  Seville 460–61
Music shops
  Barcelona 192, 193
  Madrid 322, 323
  Seville 459
Muslim Spain 56–7
Mussolini, Benito 70

N

Nacimento del Río Cuervo 387
Nadal, Rafael 26
Nagel, Andrés 180
Nàjera **133**
The Naked Maja (Goya) 263, 297
Napoleon I, Emperor 51
  and Alcántara 414
  and the Alhambra (Granada) 494
  and Guadalupe 410
  invasion of Madrid 243
  occupation of Spain 67
  War of Independence 471
Naranjo de Bulnes 112
Narcissus, St, tomb of 218
Nasrid architecture 426–7
Nasrid dynasty 494, 496
National Day 47
National Flamenco Competition
  (Córdoba) 46
National parks **34–5**
  Parc Nacional d'Aigüestortes 34,
    211, **215**
  Parque Nacional de Cabañeros 35,
    391
  Parque Nacional de la Caldera de
    Taburiente (La Palma) 35, 536
  Parque Nacional de Doñana 34,
    420, **468–9**
  Parque Nacional de Garajonay 35,
    537
  Parque Nacional de Ordesa 34,
    202, 231, **236–7**
  Parque Nacional de los Picos de
    Europa 11, 15, 34, **112–13**
  Parque Nacional de Las Tablas de
    Daimiel 34, **403**
  Parque Nacional del Teide 35,
    542–3, 555
  Parque Nacional de Timanfaya 35,
    545, **552–3**
  walking in 610
Nationalists, Spanish Civil War 70–71
Natividad (Berruguete) 371
NATO 72
Nature reserves
  Font Roja 263
  Laguna de Gallocanta 242
  Parc Natural del Delta de l'Ebre 229
  Parque Natural del Alto Tajo 386
  Parque Natural de Cabo de Gata
    421, **505**

Nature reserves (cont.)
  Parque Natural de Cazorla **501**
  Parque Natural de las Hoces del
    Duratón 369
  Parque Natural de Moncayo 240
  Parque Natural de Monfragüe **410**
  Parque Natural de los Montes de
    Málaga 478
  Parque Natural de Somiedo 109
  Parque Natural del Torcal 479
  Reserva Nacional de los Ancares
    Leoneses 354
  Reserva Nacional de Fuentes
    Carrionas 373
  Reserva Nacional de Gredos 366
Naturism 612, 613
Nava, festivals 45
Navacerrada 333
  restaurants 594
Navarra *see* Basque Country, Navarra
  and La Rioja Navarra wine region
Navarra wine region 82–3
Las Navas de Tolosa, Battle of (1212)
  58–9, 138
La Naveta d'es Tudons 53
Nazaret, restaurants 605
Nazis 70
Neanderthal man 52
Necropolis de Puig d'es Molins
  (Ibiza) 515
Necrópolis Romana (Carmona) 480
Nelson, Admiral 66, 67, 472, 530
Neolithic era 52
Nerja **487**
  hotels 573
New Year **43**, 47, 294
Newspapers 624–5
Nicolau, Pere 36, 256
Niebla 466
Nightlife 609
  Barcelona 198–9
  Ibiza 515
  Madrid 328–9
  Seville 461
Níjar 505
Noche Buena (Christmas Eve) 47
Noche Vieja (New Year's Eve) 47
Noia (Noya) 98, 99
Noja, restaurants 584
Noreña, restaurants 584
North Africa, ferries 627
Northern Spain **76–139**
  Asturias and Cantabria 104–17
  Basque Country, Navarra and La
    Rioja 118–39
  forests 84–5
  Galicia 88–103
  map 78–9
  regional food 80–81
  The Road to Santiago 86–7
  wines 82–3
Novelda **264**
Nudism 612
Nuestra Señora de Covadonga 114
Numantia 381

O

O Cabreiro *see* Cebreiro
Oak forests 85
Ocaña 398
  restaurants 596
Ochagavia 139
Ohanes 489
Oia, fiestas 102
Ojen, hotels 573
Old Madrid **272–85**
  area map 273
  hotels 568
  restaurants 591–2
  street-by-street map 274–5
Old Town (Barcelona) **146–61**
  hotels 564–5
  restaurants 586–7
Olite (Herriberri) **134–5**
  hotels 564
  restaurants 585
La Oliva 550
Oliva, hotels 568
Oliva, Abbot 224
Olivares, Count-Duke 64, 308
Oliveira, Juan José 100
Olivenza **416**
Olives and olive oil 33, 422
Olleros de Pisuerga 373
La Olmeda 373
Olot **217**
  hotels 566
Olympic Games, Barcelona (1992)
  27, 73, 160, 177
Oña 373
Oñati (Oñate) 14, **128**
Onda **252**
Ondara, restaurants 591
Ondarroa 123
Opening hours **617**
  banks 622
  restaurant 576
  shops 320, 606
Opera 25–6, 608
  Barcelona 195, 197
  Madrid 326, 327
  Seville 460
Opus Dei 239
Oranges 33, 205
Oratorio de San Felipe Neri (Cádiz)
  471
Order of Calatrava 58
  Alcañiz 243
  Almagro 403
  Calatrava la Nueva 402–3
Order of Santiago
  Casa de las Conchas (Salamanca)
    365
  Hostal de San Marcos (León) 357
  Monasterio de Tentudía 417
  Monasterio de Uclés 390
  Vilar de Donas 103
  Yeste 400
Ordesa, Parque Nacional de 34, 202,
  231, **236–7**
Ordoño II 358

Orea, Juan de 505
Orellana, Francisco de 411
Orense see Ourense
Los Órganos 537
Orgaz 391
Orgiva 488
  hotels 573
  restaurants 601
Ori, Monte 139
Orihuela (Oriola) **265**
  hotels 568
Oropesa 251, **391**
  restaurants 596
La Orotava **539**
  fiestas 540
Orreaga see Roncesvalles
Ortega, Gómez 301
Ortigueira (Galicia) 92
  restaurants 582
Ortigueira, Ría de 92
Ortiguera (Asturias) 108
Orzola 554
Los Oscos 108
Oseira, Monasterio de **103**
Osona, Rodrigo de (the Younger)
  515
Osuna **479**
  restaurants 601
Osuna, Dukes of 479
Our Lady of the Sea (Formentera) 527
Ourense (Orense) **102**
  hotels 562
  restaurants 582
Ourense (Orense) province 89
Outdoor activities **610–13**
Outdoor hazards 621
Oviedo 15, 78, **110–11**
  hotels 563
  restaurants 584
Oviedo, Juan de 434

P

Pacheco, Francisco 65
Padilla, Juan de, tomb of 375
Padilla, María de 370
Padrón **98**
Paella 205
Paintings 36–7
El País 73
Pájara 550
Palaces
  Alcázar de los Reyes Cristianos
    (Córdoba) 17, **482**
  Alfajería (Zaragoza) 230, 241
  Alhambra (Granada) 10, 17, 28, 58,
    421, 426–7, 463, **494–5**
  El Escorial (Madrid) 270, **334–5**
  La Granja de San Ildefonso **367**
  Medina Azahara 57, 427, **481**
  Moorish architecture 427
  Palacio Arzobispal (Seville) 438
  Palacio de Avellaneda (Peñaranda
    de Duero) 380–81
  Palacio de las Cadenas (Úbeda) 29,
    501

Palaces (cont.)
  Palacio de los Condes de Gómara
    (Soria) 381
  Palacio del Cordón (Zamora) 360
  Palacio de Cristal (Madrid) 301
  Palacio de los Duques del
    Infantado (Guadalajara) 387
  Palacio Episcopal (Astorga) 356
  Palacio de Jabalquinto (Baeza) 502
  Palacio de Juan Pizarro de
    Orellana (Trujillo) 411
  Palacio de Linares (Madrid) 290
  Palacio de Liria (Madrid) **308**
  Palacio de la Madraza (Granada)
    490
  Palacio de la Magdalena
    (Santander) 117
  Palacio del Marqués de Gomera
    (Osuna) 479
  Palacio del Marqués de la
    Conquista (Trujillo) 411
  Palacio del Mayorazgo (Arcos de la
    Frontera) 473
  Palacio Miramar (San Sebastián)
    126
  Palacio de los Momos (Zamora)
    360
  Palacio Mondragón (Ronda) 474
  Palacio de Monterrey (Salamanca)
    362
  Palacio de la Música y Congresos
    Euskalduna (Bilbao) 122
  Palacio de Nájera (Antequera) 479
  Palacio de Navarra (Pamplona)
    137
  Palacio de El Pardo **336**
  Palacio Pedro I (Seville) 426, 444
  Palacio de Peñaflor (Écija) 481
  Palacio de Penmartín (Jerez de la
    Frontera) 470
  Palacio Real (Madrid) 270, **280–81**
  Palacio Real de Aranjuez **337**
  Palacio de Revillagigedo/Centro
    Cultural Cajastur (Gijón) 109
  Palacio de Riofrío 368–9
  Palacio de Sada (Sos del Rey
    Católico) 234
  Palacio de San Telmo (Seville)
    448–9
  Palacio de Santa Cruz 275
  Palacio Sobrellano (Comillas) 114–15
  Palacio del Tiempo (Jerez de la
    Frontera) 470
  Palacio de Velázquez (Madrid) 301
  Palacio de Viana (Córdoba) **483**
  Palacio Villardompardo (Jaén) 497
  Palacio del Viso (Viso del Marqués)
    402
  Palau Baro de Quadras (Barcelona)
    165
  Palau Ducal (Gandia) 259
  Palau de la Generalitat (Barcelona)
    148, **151**
  Palau de la Generalitat (Valencia)
    254

Palaces (cont.)
  Palau Güell (Barcelona) **144–5**,
    154, 155
  Palau Moja (Barcelona) 155
  Palau de la Música (Valencia) 256
  Palau de la Música Catalana
    (Barcelona) **156**, 195
  Palau Nacional (Barcelona) 142
  Palau Reial (Barcelona) 149, 150–51
  Palau Reial de l'Almudaina (Palma)
    522
  Palau Salort (Ciutadella) 526
  Palau de la Virreina (Barcelona)
    155
  Real Alcázar (Seville) 10, 13, 418–19,
    426, 427, 439, **444–5**
  see also Castles
Palacio, León Gill de 309
Palacios, Antonio 100
Palaeolithic era 52
Palamós 221
Palau see Palaces
Palencia **372**
  restaurants 595
Palencia province 351
Palloza 354
Palm Sunday processions 42
La Palma 534, **536**
  festivals 47
  hotels 575
  restaurants 605
  volcanoes 555
Palma de Mallorca **522–5**
  airport 626
  Cathedral 524–5
  festivals 45
  hotels 574
  restaurants 603
  street-by-street map 522–3
Palma del Río **481**
  hotels 574
  restaurants 601
Las Palmas de Gran Canaria **548**
  airport 626
  restaurants 604
Palmitos Park (Maspalomas) 547
Palomino, Antonio 491
Palos de la Frontera **467**
Pamplona (Iruña) **136–7**
  bull run 79
  fiestas 24, 43, 136
  hotels 564
  map 137
  restaurants 585
  The Road to Santiago 87
Pantaleon, St 284
Panteón Real (León) 357
Panxón 99
Paradores 558, 561
Paragliding 610
Paris School 37
Parking 632
Parks and gardens
  Alcázar de los Reyes Cristianos
    (Córdoba) 482

Parks and gardens (cont.)
Balcón de Mediterráneo (Benidorm) 264
Campo del Moro (Madrid) **279**
Casa de Campo (Madrid) 306
Generalife (Granada) 17, **496**
La Granja de San Ildefonso **367**
Huerto del Cura (Elx) 265
Huerto de las Flores (Agaete) 547
Jardí Botànic Mar i Murtra (Blanes) 220
Jardín de Cactus (Guatiza) 554
Jardín Canario (Tarifa) 548
Jardín de Orquídeas (Puerto de la Cruz) 538
Jardines del Río Turia (Valencia) **256**
Loro Parque (Puerto de la Cruz) 538
Moorish gardens 426
Palacio Miramar (San Sebastián) 126
Palacio Real de Aranjuez **337**
Palmitos Park (Maspalomas) 547
Parc de la Ciutadella (Barcelona) 143, **158–9**
Parc de l'Espanya Industrial (Barcelona) **180**
Parc de Joan Miró (Barcelona) **180**
Park Güell (Barcelona) 140–41, 145, **182**
Parque de l'Aigüera (Benidorm) 264
Parque de El Capricho (Madrid) **310**
Parque María Luisa (Seville) 13, **448–9**
Parque Municipal García Sanabria (Santa Cruz de Tenerife) 540
Parque del Oeste (Madrid) 307
Parque Ornitológico (Almuñécar) 487
Parque Regional de Calblanque 266
Parque del Retiro (Madrid) 271, 286, 287, **301**
Real Alcázar (Seville) 444
Real Jardín Botánico (Madrid) **301**
Tibidabo (Barcelona) **182**
Zoo de Barcelona **159**
see also Amusement parks; National parks; Nature reserves; Theme parks; Water parks
Pas Valley 116
Pasaia Donibane 127
Pasarela Cibeles (Madrid) 47
Paseo de la Castellana (Madrid) **310**
Paseo del Prado (Madrid), street-by-street map **288–9**
El Paso 536
Passeig de Gràcia (Barcelona) 13, **164**
The Passion (Chinchon) 294
Passports 616
lost/stolen 620

Pastor, Fiesta del (Cangas de Onís) 114
Pastori, Niña 461
Pastrana 387
Patio Fiesta (Córdoba) 467
Patones 332
La Patum (Berga) 225
Paul III, Pope 128
Pavelló Mies van der Rohe (Barcelona) 174, **177**
Pazo de Oca 98
Pazos 89
Pechina, hotels 574
Pechón, hotels 563
Pedrajas, Francisco Javier 486
Pedraza de la Sierra **369**
hotels 570
La Pedrera see Casa Milà
La Pedriza 336
Pedro I the Cruel, King of Castile 395
Alcázar del Rey Pedro (Carmona) 480
Monasterio de Santa Clara (Tordesillas) 370
Real Alcázar (Seville) 444
Pedro II, King of Aragón 58
Pedro de Osma, San, tomb of 381
Pelayo 56, 111, 112, **113**
Pelayo, Marcelino Menéndez 295
Os Peliqueiros (Laza) 102
Peña Cortada 252
La Peña de Francia 360
Peñafiel 24, 349, 371
Peñalba de Santiago 355
Peñaranda de Duero 353, **380–81**
Peñarroya 244
Peñas de San Pedro, fiestas 391
Penedès wine region 206–7
Península de Jandía **550**
Peninsular War see War of Independence
Peñíscola 11, 16, 246, **251**
hotels 568
Peñón de Ifach see Penyal d'Ifac
Pensions 558
Penyal d'Ifac **263**
Peratallada **220**
Perdido, Monte 237
Pere the Ceremonious 219, 226
Pereda, Antonio de, The Knight's Dream 64–5
Perelada, restaurants 589
Pérez, José Luján 547
Pérez, Juan 466
Pérez de Andrade, Count Fernán 92
Pérez Galdós, Benito 39
Pero Palo (Villanueva de la Vera) 409
Personal security 620–21
Peter, St 223
Peter of Aragón 239
Petrol 630
Petronila of Aragón 58
Pharmacies 620–21
Phoenicians 51, 52, 53

Phone cards 624
Phrase book 671–2
Picadores 40
Picasso, Pablo 36, 37, **69**, 265
in Barcelona **157**
Casa Natal de Picasso (Málaga) 478
Guernica 12, **70–71**, 122, **303**
Harlequin with a Mirror 292
in Madrid 285
matador's cape 434
Las Meninas 36, 157
Museo Picasso (Buitrago del Lozoya) 332
Museo Picasso (Málaga) 478
Museu Picasso (Barcelona) **157**
Self-Portrait 157
Valdemossa 518
Woman in Blue 302
Pico de las Nieves 549
Pico del Remedio 252
Pico de Tres Mares 115
Pico Veleta 489
Pico Viejo 555
Picos de Europa 78, 105, 106
Parque Nacional de Picos de Europa 15, 34, **112–13**
Piedra, Monasterio de **242**
Pier in the Prince's Garden at Aranjuez Castle (dagli Orti) 8–9
El Pilar de la Mola, restaurants 602
Pilgrims, The Road to Santiago **86–7**
Pinazo, Ignacio 256
Piños, Elisenda de Montcada de 181
Pinzón, Martín, Casa Museo de Martín Alonso Pinzón (Palos de la Frontera) 467
Pinzón, Vicente 467
Pizarro, Francisco 62, 411
Pizarro, Hernando 411
Plaça de la Boqueria (Barcelona) 155
Plaça d'Espanya (Barcelona) **177**
Plaça Reial (Barcelona) 155
Plainchant, Gregorian 333, **380**, 609
Planetariums, El Planetari (Castelló de la Plana) 251
Plasencia **409**
Plateresque architecture 29
La Platja d'Aro (Playa de Aro) 221
hotels 566
Platja de Sant Joan (Playa de San Juan) 262
Playa de las Américas 538
Playa d'Aro see La Platja d'Aro
Playa Blanca **552**
Playa del Camello (Santander) 106
Playa de las Canteras 548
Playa de la Concha (San Sebastián) 14, **126**
Playa del Inglés 546–7
Playa de Ondarreta (San Sebastián) 121, 126
Playa Papagayo 552
Playa de San Juan see Platja de Sant Joan

Playa de Santiago 537
  hotels 575
Playa de Zurriola (San Sebastián) 126
La Plaza 109
Plaza de Cánovas del Castillo (Madrid) 288
Plaza Cánovas del Castillo (Madrid) **290**
Plaza de Cibeles (Madrid) 2–3, 271, 289, **290**
Plaza de Colón (Madrid) **300**
Plaza de la Constitución (San Sebastián) 126
Plaza de España (Madrid) **284**
Plaza de España (Seville) 446, 448
Plaza de los Fueros (Tudela) 134
Plaza mayor 31
Plaza Mayor (Cuenca) 389
Plaza Mayor (Madrid) 12, 65, 270, 274, **277**
Plaza Mayor (Salamanca) 363, **364**
Plaza de Oriente (Madrid) **279**
Plaza de la Paja (Madrid) **306**
Plaza del Pópulo (Baeza) 503
Plaza de Toros (Antequera) 479
Plaza de Toros de la Maestranza (Seville) 40, 431, 432, **434**
Plaza de Toros de Las Ventas (Madrid) 304, **310**, 325
Plaza del Triunfo (Seville) 438
Plaza de la Villa (Madrid) 274, **276–7**
Plaza Virgen de los Reyes (Seville) 438
Plentzia 123
Poble Espanyol (Barcelona) 174, **177**
Poble Sec (Barcelona), nightlife 199
Poblet, Monestir de 203, 211, **226–7**
Poetry 38
Police 620
Politics 27
Pollença (Pollensa) **520**
  hotels 574
Pompey 54
Ponce de León, Alfonso, *Accident or Self-Portait* 302
Ponferrada **355**
  hotels 570
Ponteareas, fiestas 102
Pontedeume (Puentedeume) 92
Pontejos, restaurants 584
Pontevedra 90, 91, **98**, 99
  festivals 45
  hotels 562
  restaurants 582
Pontevedra province 89
Pop music 608
Poqueira Valley 488
Port d'Andratx 518
Port Aventura 228, 609
Port Olímpic (Barcelona) **160**
  nightlife 198, 199
Port de Pollença (Pollensa) 512
Port Vell (Barcelona) 12, **160**
  nightlife 198, 199

Pórtico da Gloria (Santiago de Compostela) 96
Portinatx 515
  hotels 574
Portixol, restaurants 603
Portrait II (Miró) 302
Portrait of Baron Thyssen-Bornemisza (Freud) 292
Posets 235
Postal services 625
Potes **114**
  restaurants 584
Poussin, Nicolas, *St Cecilia* 299
Pozo, Aurelio de 434
Pradilla, Francisco, *The Fall of Granada* 60–61
Prado, Museo del (Madrid) 12, 271, **296–9**
Praza do Obradoiro (Santiago de Compostela) 94
Pre-Romanesque architecture 28, 110
Prehistoric Spain **52–3**
  Cales Coves 530
  Capocorb Vell **520–21**
  Cueva de El Monte Castillo 116
  Cuevas de Altamira 116
  Menorca 531
  Los Millares 505
Priego de Córdoba 10, 17, **486**
Prim, General 67, 159
Primo de Rivera, José Antonio 68, 333
  military coup 69
  resignation 69
Priorato wine region 206–7
The Procession of the Flagellants (Goya) 278
Provinces 625
PSOE (Socialist Workers' Party) 72, 73
Public conveniences 621
Public holidays 47
Public transport 634–5
Pubs 576
Puebla de Sanabria **355**
  hotels 570
Puebla de la Sierra 332
Pueblo Canario (Las Palmas de Gran Canaria) 548
Pueblo Nuevo del Bullaque 391
Pueblos Blancos, tour of **472–3**
El Puente del Arzobispo 391
Puente Colgante (Bilbao) 122
Puente Internacional (Tui) 101
Puente Nuevo (Ronda) 421, **474**
Puente la Reina **135**
  The Road to Santiago 87
Puente Romano (Córdoba) 483
Puente Romano (Salamanca) 362
El Puente de Sanabria, hotels 569
Puente Seco (Coria) 409
Puente Viesgo 116
Puentedeume *see* Pontedeume
Puerta de Alcalá (Madrid) 289, **291**
Puerta Antigua de Bisagra (Toledo) **395**

Puerta de Europa (Madrid) 310
Puerta del Sol (Madrid) 275, **276**
Puerto Banús 476
Puerto del Carmen **553**
Puerto de la Cruz **538**
  hotels 575
  restaurants 605
Puerto Lápice 398
Puerto de Mazarrón 267
Puerto de Mogán **546**
Puerto de la Ragua 489
Puerto Rico 544, **546**
Puerto del Rosario **551**
El Puerto de Santa María 470
  hotels 574
  restaurants 601
Puerto de Somport 232, **234**
Puig i Cadafalch, Josep 144
  CaixaForum (Barcelona) 177
  Casa Amatller (Barcelona) 168
  Casa Terrades (Barcelona) 165, **169**
  Palau Baro de Quadras (Barcelona) 165
Puig de Missa 516
Puig de Randa 520
Puigcerdà **216**
Punta de Teno 535
Punta Umbria 466
Pyrenees
  Folklore Festival (Jaca) 45
  Parque Nacional de Ordesa 236–7
  wildlife 236
Pyrenees, Peace of the (1659) 65

Q

Quadrat d'Or (Barcelona), street-by-street map **164–5**
Quesada, Diego de 448
Quevedo, Francisco de 38, 402
Quintanilla de la Viñas 374
Quixote, Don *see* Cervantes

R

Rábida, Monasterio de la **466**
Radio 625
Rail travel 628–9
  Barcelona and the Mediterranean Coast by Train 11, **16**
  in cities 634–5
Raimat wine estate 207
Rainfall 48–9
Rainy Taxi (Dalí) 219
Rajoy, Mariano 73
Ramales de la Victoria 117
Las Ramblas (Barcelona) 12, 143, **154–5**
Ramiro I, King of Aragón 110
Ramiro II, King of Aragón 239
Ramis, Julie 518
Ramon Berenguer I, King of Catalonia 153
Ramon Berenguer IV, King of Catalonia 58
  Monestir de Poblet 226
  Monestir de Santes Creus 225

Ranc, Jean 299
A Rapa das Bestas (Oia, Pontevedra) 45, 102
Raphael 285, 299
Rascafría 333
El Rastro (Madrid) **306**, 321
El Raval (Barcelona) **154**
  nightlife 198, 199
Real Academia de Bellas Artes de San Fernando (Madrid) **285**
Real Academia de la Historia (Madrid) **295**
Real Alcázar (Seville) 10, 13, 418–19, 426, 427, 439, **444–5**
Real Cartuja de Jesús de Nazaret (Valldemossa) 518
Real Chancillería (Granada) 492
Real Escuela Andaluza de Arte Ecuestre (Jerez de la Frontera) 470
Real Fábrica de Tapices (Madrid) **310**
Real Jardín Botánico (Madrid) **301**
Real Madrid 181, 310, 325
Real Monasterio de Huelgas (Burgos) 375
Real Monasterio de Santo Tomás (Ávila) 367
Rebull, Joan, *Three Gypsy Boys* 148
Reccared, King 55
Recceswinth, King 371
Reconquest 58–9, 105
Refuges, mountain 560
Reial Acadèmia de Ciènces i Arts (Barcelona) 155
La Reineta 122
Reinosa 115
Religion 25
Religious art 36
Religious Music Week (Cuenca) 44
Rembrandt 299, 308
Renaissance architecture 29
Republicans **68–9**, 70
Requena 252
Reserva Nacional de los Ancares Leoneses 354
Reserva Nacional de Fuentes Carrionas 373
Reserva Nacional de Gredos 366
Responsible travel 619
Restaurants **576–605**
  Andalusia 598–602
  Aragón 590–91
  Asturias and Cantabria 583–4
  Balearic Islands 602–4
  Barcelona 586–8
  bars 576
  Basque Country, Navarra and La Rioja 585–6
  Canary Islands 604–5
  Castilla y León 594–5
  Castilla-La Mancha 595–7
  Catalonia 588–90
  dress in 576
  eating hours 576
  Extremadura 597
  Galicia 582–3

Restaurants (cont.)
  in hotels 558
  Madrid 591–3
  Madrid Province 593–4
  prices and paying 577
  reading the menu 576–7
  Seville 597–8
  smoking in 577
  tapas 578–9
  Valencia and Murcia 591
  what to drink in Spain 580–81
  wheelchair access 577
  wine choices 577
  see also Food and drink
La Restinga 537
  restaurants 604
Retiro Park (Madrid) 271, 286, 287, **301**
Reus 229
Reynés, Josep 158
Reynolds, Joshua 309
Riaño, Diego de 442
Rías Altas **92**
Rías Baixas (Rías Bajas) 78, **99**
  wine region 82–3
Ribadavia 102
Ribadeo
  hotels 562
  restaurants 582
Ribadeo, Ría de 92
Ribadesella **111**
  hotels 563
  restaurants 584
Ribalta, Francisco 36, 255, 256
  Christ Embracing St Bernard 298
Ribas de Sil, Monasterio de 90, **102**
Ribeiro wine region 82–3
Ribera, José de 284, 285, 298, 479
  The Martyrdom of St Philip 296
  The Saviour 36
Ribera, Pedro de
  Cuartel del Conde-Duque (Madrid) 308
  Museo de Historia de Madrid 308–9
  San Cayetano (Madrid) 306
Ribera Sacra wine region 82
Ribero del Duero wine region 344–5
Ricci, Francisco de, *Auto-da-fé in the Plaza Mayor* 278
Rice growing 33
Rincón de Ademuz **245**
Rincón de la Victoria 477
La Rinconada, restaurants 600
Río Cárdenas Valley 120
Rio Tinto Company 466
Riofrío 368–9
La Rioja *see* Basque Country, Navarra and La Rioja
Rioja wine region 82–3
Ripoll **216**
  restaurants 589
Road to Santiago **86–7**

Road travel 630–33
  road conditions and weather forecasts 632
El Rocío **467**
  festivals 42
  hotels 573
  restaurants 599
Rock of Gibraltar 476
Rock music 608
  Barcelona 196, 197
  Madrid 326, 327
  Seville 461
Rocroi, Battle of (1643) 64
Roda de Isábena 240
Rodrigo, Joaquín 337
Rodríguez, Ventura
  Basílica de Nuestra Señora del Pilar (Zaragoza) 241
  Colegiata de San Isidro 276
  Iglesia de la Encarnación (Montefrío) 486
  Monasterio de la Encarnación (Madrid) 284
  Monasterio de Santo Domingo de Silos 380
  Palacio de Liria (Madrid) 308
  Plaza Cánovas del Castillo (Madrid) 290
  Plaza de Cibeles (Madrid) 290
Rogers, Richard 177
Roig i Soler 159
Rojas, Fernando de 38
Roldán, Luisa 448
Roldán, Pedro 443
Romanesque architecture 28
  churches 87
Romans 51, **54–5**
  Alcántara 414
  Barcelona 151
  Carmona 480
  Cartagena 267
  Empúries 220
  Itálica 480
  Julióbriga 115
  Lugo 103
  Mérida 414–15
  Sagunt 253
  Segóbriga 390
  Segovia 55, 368, 369
  Tarragona 228–9
Romanticism 39
Romería del Cristo del Sahúco (Peñas de San Pedro) 391
Romería de Sant Marçal (Sa Cabaneta) 527
Romería de Santa Orosia (Yerba de Basa) 243
Romería de la Virgen de la Cabeza (Andújar) 467
Romería de la Virgen de la Candelaria 540
Romerías 42
Romero, Pedro 475
Romero de Torres, Julio, Museo Romero de Torres (Córdoba) 483

Roncal 138, 139
Roncesvalles (Orreaga) **138**
 Colegiata Real stained-glass 58–9
 hotels 564
Ronda 421, 473, **474–5**
 bullfighting 475
 restaurants 601
Ronda la Vieja 473
Roque Bonanza (El Hierro) 534
Roque de Cano 537
Roque Nublo 549
Roquetas de Mar, restaurants 601
Las Rosas 537
Roses 221
 restaurants 589
Rothko, Mark 124
Rubens, Peter Paul 285, 299, 308,
 471
 The Three Graces 297
 Venus and Cupid 293
Rubielos de Mora 244
Rueda, Jerónimo Sánchez de 486
Rueda, Lope de 295
Rueda wine region 344–5
Ruidera, Lagunas de **401**
Ruiz, Hernán 441, 485
Ruiz, Juan 38
Ruiz de Luna, Juan 390
Rulers 74–5
Rural architecture 31
Rusiñol, Santiago 228
Rute 486

S

Sábada 234
Sabartes, Jaime 157
Sabatini, Francesco 301
 Palacio de El Pardo (Madrid) 336
 Palacio Real (Madrid) 281
 Puerta de Alcalá (Madrid) 291
Sabinosa, hotels 575
Sacromonte (Granada) 17, **493**
Safety 620–21
Saffron (*azafrán*) 343
 Saffron Festival (Consuegra) 46
Safont, Marc 151
Sagnier, Enric 182
Sagrada Família (Barcelona) 13, 143,
 144, 145, 163, 168, **170–71**
Sagrera, Guillem 521, 524
Sagunt (Sagunto) **253**
Sahagún 357
Sailing 610
St Agatha's Day (Zamarramala) 372
Saint Bruno in Ecstasy (Zubarán) 471
St Casilda (Zurbarán) 293
St Cecilia (Poussin) 299
*St Dominic of Silos Enthroned as
 Abbot* (Bermejo) 298
St George's Day (Catalonia) 225
St James's Day (Santiago de
 Compostela) 102
St John of the Cross 38, 367, 501
St Michael's Cave (Gibraltar) 476
Saja 115

Salamanca 340, **362–5**
 hotels 570
 restaurants 595
 street-by-street map 362–3
 University 59, 364
Salamanca province 351
Salardú 214
Sales 606
Salido, Fernando Ortega 501
Salinas de Añana 131
Salinas de Janubio 553
Sallent de Gállego 234
 hotels 567
Salobreña 487
 restaurants 602
Salón de Reinos (Madrid) **291**, 301
Salou 228
Salzillo, Francisco 266
San Agustín (Sant Agustí) 546
San Andrés de Teixido 92
San Antonio *see* Sant Antoni
San Carlos, restaurants 602
San Carlos del Valle 402
San Clemente 399
*San Diego de Alcalá Giving Food to
 the Poor* (Murillo) 65
San Ferran, restaurants 602
San Francisco *see* Sant Françesc
San Isidro (Madrid) 294
San Isidro, Fiestas de (Madrid) 44
San José, hotels 574
San Juan de la Cruz *see* St John of
 the Cross
San Juan de Gaztelugatxe 123
San Juan de la Peña, Monasterio de
 238, 255
San Julián de los Prados 111
San Lorenzo, restaurants 603
San Lorenzo de El Escorial
 hotels 569
 restaurants 594
San Luís, hotels 575
San Martín de Castañeda 355
San Martín de Frómista 87
San Martín de Oscos 108
San Miguel de Escalada 357
San Miguel de Lillo 111
San Miguel de las Victorias 387
San Millán de la Cogolla 120, **133**
San Nicolás de Tolentino, fiestas
 540
San Pedro, restaurants 596
San Pedro de Alcántara 476
San Pedro de Arlanza 374
San Pedro Manrique, fiestas 372
San Pedro de la Nave 360–61
San Rafael, restaurants 603
San Salvador de Poyo, restaurants
 583
San Sebastián (Donostia) 11, 14, 79,
 126–7
 festivals 45, 47
 Film Festival 46, **127**
 hotels 564
 restaurants 585

San Sebastián (La Gomera) 537
 hotels 575
 restaurants 605
San Vicente de la Barquera 115
 fiestas 114
 hotels 563
 restaurants 584
San Vicente de la Sonsierra,
 restaurants 585
Sancho I, King of Aragón 239
Sancho I, King of Navarra 57
Sancho I Garcés, King of Pamplona
 134
Sancho II, King of Castilla y León 374
 death 360, 374
Sancho III the Great, King of Navarra
 134, 139
Sancho VI the Wise, King of Navarra
 134
Sancho VII the Strong, King of
 Navarra 58, 59
 tomb of 138
Sand, George 518
Los Sanfermines (Pamplona) 24, 136
Sangria 581
Sangüesa (Zangotxo) **139**
Sanjeno *see* Sanxenxo
Sanlúcar de Barrameda **470**
 fiestas 467
 restaurants 602
Sant Agustí *see* San Agustín
Sant Antoni (San Antonio) **514**
 restaurants 602
Sant Antoni Abat 527
Sant Carles de la Ràpita 229
 restaurants 589
Sant Feliu de Guíxols, restaurants
 589
Sant Francesc Xavier 516
Sant Fruitós de Bages, restaurants
 589
Sant Joan (Ciutadella) 527
Sant Joan de les Abadesses **217**
 restaurants 589
Sant Joan de Binissaida, hotels 575
Sant Joan de Labritja, hotels 574
Sant Joan Pelós (Felanitx) 527
Sant Josep (San José) **514**
Sant Martí (La Cortinada) 216
Sant Miquel (San Miguel) 513, **515**
Sant Pol de Mar, restaurants 589
Sant Sadurní 225
 restaurants 589
Sant Vincenç 515
Santa Ana (Madrid), nightlife 328–9
Santa Comba de Bande 101
 restaurants 583
Santa Cristina d'Aro
 hotels 566
 restaurants 589
Santa Cruz (Seville) 13, **436–45**
 area map 437
 hotels 572
 restaurants 597–8
 street-by-street map 438–9

Santa Cruz, Marquis of 402
Santa Cruz de la Palma **536**
  fiestas 540
  restaurants 605
Santa Cruz de Tenerife 534, **540**
  fiestas 43, 47, 540
  restaurants 605
Santa Cruz del Valle de los Caídos **333**
Santa Eulalia 103
Santa Eulalia de Oscos, restaurants 584
Santa Eulària d'es Riu (Santa Eulalia del Río) **516**
Santa Fé 486–7
Santa Galdana 527
Santa María de Melque 391
Santa María de Huerta 381
Santa María de Lebeña 114
Santa María de Mave, hotels 570
Santa María del Naranco **110–11**
Santa María de El Paular, Monasterio de **332–3**
Santa Pola 262
Santander 11, 15, 105, 106, **117**
  festivals 45
  hotels 563
  restaurants 584
Santes Creus **225**
Santiago de Compostela 11, 15, 78, **94–7**
  airport 626
  cathedral 89, 95, **96–7**
  fiestas 102
  hotels 562
  pilgrimages 89
  restaurants 583
  The Road to Santiago **86–7**
  street-by-street map 94–5
Santiago de la Ribera 266
Santillana del Mar 11, 15, 79, 105, **116**
  hotels 563
  restaurants 584
Santiponce 480
Santo Domingo de la Calzada **132**
  hotels 564
  restaurants 585
  The Road to Santiago 87
Santo Domingo de Silos **380**
Santo Toribio de Liébana 114
Santos Inocentes 47
Santuario de Arantzazu 11, 14, **128**
Santuario de Lluc **519**
Santuario de Loiola 11, 14, **128**
Santuario de Torreciudad **239**
Santuario de la Vera Cruz (Caravaca de la Cruz) 267
Santuario de la Virgen de la Cabeza (Andújar) 500
Sanxenxo (Sangenjo)
  hotels 562
  restaurants 583
Saportella, Francesca 181
Saramago, José 553

Sardana **229**
El Sardinero (Santander) 117
Saturn Devouring One of his Sons (Goya) 298
Saturrarán 123
Saura, Antonio 37
El Sauzal, restaurants 605
La Savina 516
  hotels 574
The Saviour (Ribera) 36
Scams 620
Schmidt-Rottluff, Karl, *Autumn Landscape in Oldenburg* 293
Scipio Africanus 54, 480, 500
Sea kayaking 611
Sea travel 627
Seafood
  Canary Islands 541
  Southern Spain 422
Second Republic **68–9**, 75
Second-hand fashion, Barcelona 192, 193
Segóbriga **390**
Segovia 12, 341, **368–9**
  Alcázar **348–9**, 350
  aqueduct 55, 368, **369**
  hotels 570
  map 368
  restaurants 595
  Roman remains 55
Segovia, Andrés 490
Segovia province 351
Seguí family 518
Segura, Isabel de 245
Segura, River 266
Segura de la Sierra 501
Self-catering accommodation 560, 561
Self-Portrait (Goya) 243
Self-Portrait (Picasso) 157
Sella, River 45, 112
Selva de Irati 139
Semana Santa *see* Easter
Semana Trágica, Barcelona (1909) 69
Semanas Grandes 45
Sempere, Eusebio 265
Seneca 38, 54
Senior travellers 618
Septembrina Revolution (1868-70) 75
Sepúlveda **369**
La Serena 410
Serna, Ramón Gómez de la 309
Serra, Jaume 36
Serra, Richard, *The Matter of Time* 124, 125
Serranía de Cuenca **387**
Sert, Josep Lluís, Fundacío Joan Miró (Barcelona) 175, **176**
Sert, Josep Maria
  Casa de la Ciutat (Barcelona) murals 151
  Murals of Basque Life 127
  Vic cathedral murals 224

Ses Salines (Las Salinas) 514
Setenil 473
La Seu d'Urgell 212, **216**
Seville **430–61**
  2 Days in Seville **13**
  airport 626
  El Arenal 430–35
  Cathedral 438, **440–41**
  coach stations 633
  entertainment **460–61**
  exhibitions 69
  Expo '92 72–3
  fiestas and festivals 42, 44, 46, 435
  flamenco 13, 22, 460, 461
  Further Afield 447–50
  La Giralda 420, 436, 437, 438, **440–41**
  hotels 571–2
  Madrid and Moorish Spain: Granada, Córdoba and Seville 10, **17**
  nightlife 461
  Real Alcázar 444–5
  restaurants 597–8
  Santa Cruz 436–45
  shopping **458–9**
  Street Finder 451–7
  street-by-street map: El Arenal 432–3
  street-by-street map: Santa Cruz 438–9
  transport 634–5
Seville province 463
Seville School 65, 448, 483
Shakespeare, William 337
Sheep farming 32
Sherry **425**, 581
  Jerez de la Frontera 470
  Montilla 486
Shoes
  shops 607
  shops in Barcelona 192, 193
  shops in Madrid 322, 323
  size chart 607
Shops **606–7**
  Barcelona 190–93
  Madrid 320–23
  opening hours 320, 606
  payment 606
  sales 606
  Seville 458–9
Siege Tunnels (Gibraltar) 476
Sierra de Alcaraz **400–401**
Sierra de Aracena **466**
Sierra de Béjar **360–61**
Sierra Centro de Guadarrama 330, **333**
Sierra de la Demanda 380
Sierra de Francia **360–61**
Sierra de Gata **408**
Sierra de Gredos **366**
Sierra de Gúdar **244**
Sierra de Mariola 263
Sierra Morena **480**

Sierra Nevada 34, 488, **489**, 498–9
Sierra Norte **332**
Sigüenza **386**
  hotels 571
  restaurants 595
Sil, River 102
El Silbo (whistle language) 536
Silió, festivals 114
Siloé, Diego de 371
  Almería Cathedral 505
  Burgos Cathedral 376
  Capilla del Salvador (Úbeda) 501
  Granada Cathedral 490
  Málaga Cathedral 478
Siloé, Gil de 372
  altarpieces 375, 376
  Covarrubias 374
  tomb of Juan de Padilla 375
Simancas 371
Simon of Cologne 372, 374
Siresa 234
Sitges 11, 16, 213, **228**
  festivals 44
  hotels 566
  restaurants 589–90
Size chart 607
Skiing 612, 613
Skydiving 610
Smoking, in restaurants 577
Sobrado de los Monjes, Monasterio 103
Social customs 617
Socialist Workers' Party (PSOE) 72, 73
Solán de Cabras 387
Solana, José Gutiérrez, *The Gathering at Pombo Café* 303
Solano, Susana 154
Soler, Frederic 159
Solis family 413
Sóller **519**
Solsona **224**
Solynieve 489
Somaén, hotels 570
Somiedo, Parque Natural de 109
Somontano wine region 206–7
Son Marroig 519
Sorbas 504
Soria **381**
  hotels 570
  restaurants 595
Soria province 351
Sorolla, Joaquín 37, 256, 257
  Museo Sorolla (Madrid) 309
Sos del Rey Católico **234**
  hotels 567
  restaurants 591
Sotogrande 464, 476
Soult, Marshal 435
Southern Spain **418–505**
  Andalusia 462–505
  Flamenco 428–9
  map 420–21
  Moorish architecture 426–7

Southern Spain (cont.)
  regional food 422–3
  Seville 430–61
  wines 424–5
Souvenir shops, Seville 459
Spaghetti Westerns **504**
Spanish Armada 63
Spanish Civil War 51, **70–71**
  Santa Cruz del Valle de los Caídos 333
Spanish Formula One Grand Prix (Barcelona) 44
Spanish Inquisition *see* Inquisition
Spanish language 617
Spanish Motorcycle Grand Prix (Jerez de la Frontera) 44
Spanish Socialist Party 73
Spanish Tourist Office 561
Spanish-American War 68
Spas 612, 613
Special needs, travellers with 617
Specialist holidays 612–13
Speed limits 631
Spirits 581
Sports 26, **610–13**
  Barcelona 197
  spectator 609
Sports fashion, Barcelona 191, 193
Spring in Spain 44
  fiestas 42
Stained glass, León Cathedral 359
Still Life with Four Vessels (Zurbarán) 298
Stone Age 52
Storks **347**
Student information 618–19
Suárez, Adolfo 72
Subirachs, Josep Maria 170
Summer in Spain 45
  fiestas 42–3
Sunshine 48–9
Surfing 611
Surrealism 176, 219
Surrender of Breda (Velázquez) 65
Susillo 449
Synagogues
  Barcelona 150
  Córdoba 482
  Sinagoga de Santa María la Blanca (Toledo) 59, **395**
  Sinagoga del Tránsito (Toledo) **395**

T

Tabarca island *see* Illa de Tabarca
Tabernas **504**
Tablas de Daimiel National Park 34, **403**
Tacca, Pietro
  statue of Felipe III 277
  statue of Felipe IV 279
Tacoronte 539
Tafalla, restaurants 586
Tafira **548**
Tagus (Tajo), River 337, 390

Talavera, Battle of (1809) 67
Talavera de la Reina **390**
  hotels 571
  restaurants 596
Talayots 531
Las Tamboradas (Teruel province) 243
La Tamborrada (San Sebastián) 47
Tapas **578–9**
  Andalusia 422
Tapia de Casariego 108
Tàpies, Antoni 37, 518
  Cloud and Chair 164
  Fundació Antoni Tàpies 164, **168**
Taramundi **108**
Tarancón, restaurants 596
Tarantino, Quentin 127
Tarazona 233, **240**
  restaurants 591
Tarif ben Maluk 472
Tarifa 472
  hotels 574
Tarifa, Marquis of 442
Tariq 56
Tarraconensis (Roman province) 54
Tarragona 11, 16, 55, 203, **228–9**
  hotels 566
  restaurants 590
Tarragona province 211
Tarragona wine region 206–7
Tartessus 53
Taüll 28, 215
Tauste 234
Tax-free goods 616
Taxis 632, 635
Tazacorte, hotels 575
Teatre Grec (Barcelona) 175
Teatre Nacional de Catalunya 195
Teatro Español (Madrid) **295**
Teatro de la Maestranza (Seville) 432, 460, 461
Teguise **554**
  restaurants 605
Teide, Mount 35, **542–3**
Teide, Parque Nacional del **542–3**, 555
Teito 31
Tejero, Colonel Antonio 72, 295
Telephones 624
Television 26, 625
Tembleque **398**
Temperatures 48–9
Templo de Debod (Madrid) **307**
Tena, Lucero 429
Tenerife 508, 532, **538–43**
  airport 626
  hotels 575
  map 535
  restaurants 605
  volcanoes 555
Tentudía **417**
Terán, Luis Marín de 434
Teresa de Ávila, St **367**
  Ávila 367
  tomb of 365

Las Teresitas (Santa Cruz de Tenerife) 532, 534, **540**
Teror 549
Terra Alta wine region 206–7
Terra Mítica 609
Terrorism 73
Teruel **244–5**
  cathedral 59
  fiestas 243
  Lovers of Teruel 245
  restaurants 591
Teruel province 231
Teverga **109**
Texeiro, Pedro 309
Theatre 609
  Barcelona 194–5, 197
  Madrid 326, 327
  see also Teatre; Teatro
Theft 620
Theme parks 609
  Fort Bravo Texas Hollywood (Tabernas) 504
  Isla Mágica (Seville) 450, 461
  Mini-Hollywood (Tabernas) 504, 609
  Port Aventura 228
  Sioux City (Maspalomas) 547
  see also Amusement parks; Water parks
The Third of May (Goya) **66–7**, 298
Thirty Years War 65
The Three Graces (Rubens) 297
Three Gypsy Boys (Rebull) 148
Thyssen-Bornemisza, Hans Heinrich 292
Thyssen-Bornemisza, Baron Heinrich 292
  portrait 292
Tibaldi, Pellegrino 334
Tibidabo (Barcelona) 178, **182**, 196, 197
  nightlife 199
Tickets
  Entertainment, Barcelona 194, 197
  Entertainment, Madrid **324**, 327
  Entertainment, Seville 460
  railways 629
Tiepolo, Giovanni Battista 299
Tiermes 369
Tierra de Campos 351
Tiles, azulejos 28, 426, **442**
Timanfaya, Parque Nacional de 35, 545, **552–3**
  restaurants 605
Time zones 618
Timetables, railway 629
Tintoretto 299, 395
Tipping
  in hotels 559
  in restaurants 577
Titian 285, 299, 308
El Toboso **398**

Todos los Santos 47
Toilets 621
La Toja see (A) Toxa
Toki-Egin (Chillida) 303
Tolbanos, hotels 570
Toledan School 395
Toledo 59, 338–9, **392–7**
  Cathedral 341, 393, **396–7**
  fiestas 42, 391
  hotels 571
  restaurants 594, 596–7
  street-by-street map 392–3
Toledo, Juan Bautista de 335
Toledo, Montes de see Montes de Toledo
Toledo province 383
Tolls, motorway 631
La Tomatina (Buñol) **252–3**, 259
Tomé, Narciso 370, 397
El Torcal **479**
Torcal, Parque Natural del 479
Torcuato, San 497
Tordesillas **370**
  restaurants 595
Tordesillas, Treaty of (1494) 61
Torla 236
Toro 360, 361
El Toro 527
Toro, Benicio del 127
Toro wine region 344–5
Toros de Guisando 366
Torquemada, Tomás de 60, 240
  tomb of 367
Torre del Clavero (Salamanca) 363, **365**
Torre de Collserola (Barcelona) **181**
Torre de Hércules (A Coruña) 93
Torre del Infantado (Potes) 114
Torre de los Lujanes (Madrid) 274, 276, 277
Torre Mangana (Cuenca) 388
Torre del Oro (Seville) 433, **435**
Torre Palacio de los Varona (Villanañe) **131**
Torre de Picasso (Madrid) **29**, 310
Torre Tavira (Cádiz) **471**
Torrejoncillo, fiestas 409
Torremolinos 477
  restaurants 602
Torrent, hotels 566
Torres de Serranos (Valencia) **256**
Torrevieja (Torrevella) 262, **265**
  festivals 45
Tortosa **229**
  restaurants 590
Tossa de Mar 27, 210, **220**, 221
  hotels 566
Tourism 27, **73**
Tourist information **616**, 619
  Madrid 327
Tourist season 616
Tours by car
  Las Alpujarras 488–9
  Cruz de Tejeda 549
  Pueblos Blancos 472–3

Tours by car (cont.)
  Sierra de Alcaraz 400–401
  Sierra de Francia and Sierra de Bejar 360–61
A Toxa (La Toja) **98**
Trafalgar, Battle of (1805) 66, 67
Traffic regulations 630
Trains see Rail travel
Trajan, Emperor 54, 450
Trams 634
Transfiguration (Martorell) 153
Travel **626–35**
  air 626–7
  Andalusia 464
  Aragón 233
  Asturias and Cantabria 107
  Balearic Islands 512
  Basque Country, Navarra and La Rioja 121
  bus 633, 634
  Canary Islands: Eastern Islands 544
  Canary Islands: Western Islands 535
  Castilla y León 353
  Castilla-La Mancha 385
  Catalonia 212
  coach 633
  cycling 633
  Extremadura 407
  ferries 627
  Galicia 91
  getting around cities 634–5
  golondrinas (Barcelona) 161
  rail 628–9
  regional Spain 20
  road 630–33
  taxis 632, 635
  Valencia and Murcia 248
Travellers' cheques 622
Trekking 610, 613
Trepucó 531
Els Tres Tombs (Barcelona) 161
Trevélez 488
Triana (Seville) 13, **450**
The Triumph of Bacchus (Velázquez) 296
The Triumph of the Cross (Valdés Leal) 443
Trofeo Conde de Godó (Barcelona) 44
Trujillo **411**
  fiestas 44
  hotels 571
  restaurants 597
Tudela (Tutera) **134**
  restaurants 586
Tuesta 131
Tui (Tuy) **100–101**
Turégano 369
Turia, River 252, 254, 258
Turner, J M W 309
Turner, Lana 46
Tutera see Tudela
Tuy see Tui
Txakoli (chacolí) 82
Txakoli de Guetaria wine region 82–3

U

Úbeda **500–501**
   hotels 574
   map 500
   restaurants 602
Ubrique 472
Uclés, Monasterio de **390**
Ujué **134**
Ulla, River 98
Unamuno, Miguel de 39, 365
Uncastillo 234
UNESCO 182, 537
Unification of Spain 74
United Nations 71
Universal Exhibition, Barcelona
   (1888) 68, 69, 158, 159, 160
Universidad (Baeza) 502
Universidad (Salamanca) 362, **364**
Universidad (Seville) **449**
Universidad Pontificia (Comillas) 115
Universidad de Sancti Spiritus
   (Oñati) 128
Urda 398
Urdániz, restaurants 586
Urraca de Navarra, Doña 58
   tomb of 372
Utiel-Requena wine region 206–7
Utrecht, Treaty of (1713) 66, 476

V

Valdediós **111**
Valdelinares 244
Valdepeñas **402**
   hotels 571
   restaurants 597
Valdepeñas wine region 344–5
Valderrobres **244**
Valdés, Lucas 434, 443
Valdés Leal, Juan de 483
   Ayuntamiento (Seville) paintings
      442
   Finis Gloriae Mundi 435
   Hospital de la Caridad (Seville)
      433, 435
   Museo de Bellas Artes (Seville) 434
   The Triumph of the Cross 443
Valencia 11, 16, 202, 247, **254–7**
   airport 626
   beaches 257
   festivals 42, 44, 259, 260–61
   horchata 257
   hotels 568
   map 255
   restaurants 591
   transport 634–5
Valencia and Murcia **246–67**
   climate 49
   fiestas 259
   food and drink 205
   hotels 567–8
   map 248–9
   restaurants 591
Valencia de Alcántara **414**
Valencia de Don Juan 357
Valencia wine region 206–7

Valenciano dialect 247
Valencina de la Concepción, hotels
   574
Vall d'Aran (Valle de Arán) **214**
   butterflies 214
Vall de Boí **215**
Valladolid 29, **370–71**
   fiestas 42, 372
   history 64
   hotels 570
   restaurants 595
Valladolid province 351
Valldemossa **518**
Valle de Alcudia **403**
Valle del Amboz 406
Valle de Arán *see* Vall d'Aran
Valle de Bohí *see* Vall de Boí
Valle de Cabuérniga **115**
Valle de los Caídos, Santa Cruz del
   333
Valle de la Fuenfría 333
Valle Gran Rey 535, 537
Valle de Ordesa 236
Valle de los Pedroches 480
Valle de Roncal **138–9**
Valle de Salazar 139
Valle de Silencio 355
Valle-Inclán, Ramón María del 39
Vallehermoso 537
Los Valles **234**
Valley of the Fallen *see* Valle de los
   Caídos
Vallgorguina, restaurants 590
Vallmitjana, Agapit 223
Valmaseda, Juan de 372
Válor 489
Valporquero, Cueva de *see* Cueva de
   Valporquero
Valverde 536
   hotels 575
   restaurants 604
Valverde de Fresno 408
Valverde de la Vera, fiestas 409
Van der Weyden, Rogier 490
   The Calvary 335
   The Descent from the Cross 299
Van Dyck, Anthony 256, 285, 299
Van Gogh, Vincent 160
Van Loo, Louis-Michel 299
Vandals 55
Vandelvira, Andrés de
   Baeza 502, 503
   Capilla del Salvador (Úbeda) 501
   Hospital de Santiago (Úbeda) 500
   Iglesia de San Pablo (Úbeda) 501
   Jaén Cathedral 497
   Palacio de las Cadenas (Úbeda) 501
Vasarely, Viktor 122
VAT 606, 616
   in restaurants 577
Vayreda, Joaquim 217
Vázquez de Molina, Juan 500, 501
Es Vedrá (Isla Vedra) 514
Vega de Pas 116
Véjer de la Frontera, hotels 574

Velarde y Santillán, Pedro 308
Velázquez, Diego de **36**, 64, 65, 285,
   291
   Ayuntamiento (Seville) 442
   baptism 448
   Las Meninas 12, **36–7**, 157, 298
   Museo de Bellas Artes (Valencia) 256
   Orihuela Cathedral 265
   statue of Felipe IV 279
   Surrender of Breda 65
   The Triumph of Bacchus 296
Velázquez Bosco, Ricardo 301
Vélez Blanco **504**
Vélez-Málaga 487
El Vendrell 228
Ventana del Diablo 387
Ventas con Peña Aguilera 391
Venus and Cupid (Rubens) 293
Vera (Andalusia), restaurants 602
Vera (Basque Country) *see* Bera
Veral, River 234
Verdaguer, Jacint 216
Vergara, Ignacio 255
Verges, fiestas 225
Verín **101**
   restaurants 583
Vernacular architecture **30–31**
Verne, Jules 516
Veronese, Paolo 299
Veruela, Monasterio de **240**
Vespasian, Emperor 54
Vespucci, Amerigo 161
Vía de la Plata 356
Viana, restaurants 586
Viana family 483
Vic (Vich) **224**
   hotels 566
   restaurants 590
Victoria Eugenia, Queen 294
Vielha (Viella) **214**
   hotels 567
Vigo **100**
   hotels 562
   restaurants 583
La Vijanera (Silió) 114
La Vila Joiosa (Villajoyosa) 264
   hotels 568
Vilafamés **251**
   hotels 568
Vilafranca del Penedès **225**
Vilagarcía de Arousa 99
Vilar de Donas **103**
Vilaseca i Casanovas, Josep 158
Villa Romana la Olmeda (Pedrosa de
   la Vega) 373
Villacarriedo 116
Villaescusa de Haro 399
Villafranca del Bierzo **354–5**
Villajoyosa *see* La Vila Joiosa
Villamiel 408
Villanueva 109
Villanueva, Juan de 277
   Museo del Prado (Madrid) 296
   Real Academia de la Historia
      (Madrid) 295

Villanueva, Juan de (cont.)
  Real Jardín Botánico 301
  Teatro Español (Madrid) 295
Villanueva de Alcolea, festivals 43
Villanueva de los Infantes **402**
  hotels 571
Villanueva de la Vera, fiestas 409
El Villar de Álava 82
Villar i Lozano, Francesc de Paula 171
Villareal de San Carlos 410
Villaverde, hotels 575
Villaviciosa 111
  restaurants 584
Villena, Juan Pacheco, Marquis of
  348, 398, 399
Villena Treasure **52–3**, 264
Villespesa, Francisco 489
Villuercas, Sierra de 410
Vinaròs 251
Vincent, St, tomb of 367
Vinos de Madrid wine region 344–5
Vintage fashion, Barcelona 192, 193
La Virgen Blanca Vitoria (Vitoria) 136
Virgen de la Hoz 386
Virgin and Child (Bassá) 36
The Virgin of the Dry Tree (Christus) 292
Virgin of Guadalupe 25, **411**
*The Virgin of the Immaculate
  Conception* (El Greco) 394
Virgin of Montserrat 222, **223**
Las Virtudes 402
Visas 616
Visigoths 51, 54, **55**, 56
  architecture 427
Viso del Marqués **402**
Vitoria (Gasteiz) 11, 14, **130–31**
  fiestas 136
  hotels 564
  map 130
  restaurants 586
Viveiro (Vivero) 92
  restaurants 583
Vizcaya (Bizkaia) 119
Volcanic islands (Canary Islands) 35,
  555
Vuelta Ciclista a España 46

W

Waldren, William 519
Walking 610, 613
  in cities 635
  in national parks 610
  Ordesa National Park 237
Wamba 371
War of Independence 66, 67
War of the Spanish Succession 66,
  74
Water, drinking 580
Water parks, Agua Mágica (Seville)
  450
Water sports 610–11, 613
Watteau, Antoine 292, 299
Weather 48–9
  forecasts 632
Weights and measures 617

Wellington, Duke of
  siege of Ciudad Rodrigo 361
  War of Independence 67, 130
Wetlands 34
Wheelchair access *see* Disabled
  travellers
Whistle language, La Gomera 536
Whitewater rafting 611
Whitney, Gertrude Vanderbilt 466
Wildlife 34–5
  L'Albufera 258
  Birds of Central Spain 346–7
  brown bears 108
  Butterflies of the Vall d'Aran 214
  Delta de l'Ebre 229
  Forests of Northern Spain 84–5
  Lagunas de Ruidera 401
  matorral 209
  Parque Nacional de Doñana 468–9
  Parque Natural de Cabo de Gata 505
  Parque Natural de Cazorla 501
  Parque Natural de Monfragüe 410
  Pyrenees 236
  Tablas de Daimiel 403
  see also National parks; Nature
  reserves; Zoos
Windmills 31, 383, 398
Windsurfing 611
Wine
  Balearic Islands 517
  Central Spain 344–5
  Eastern Spain 206–7
  labels 581
  Northern Spain 82–3
  in restaurants 577
  Sherry **425**
  shopping for 607
  Southern Spain 424–5
  specialist holidays 612, 613
  vineyards 33
  What to Drink in Spain 580
Wine Battle (Haro) 136
Winter in Spain 47
  fiestas 43
Winter sports 612, 613
Woman in Blue (Picasso) 302
Women travellers 620
Woods and forests 35
World Cup 72
World Music, Madrid 326, 327
World War II 70
Wornum, Selden 126

X

Xàbia (Jávea) 249, **259**, 262
  hotels 568
Xàtiva **258**
  hotels 568
Xavier, St Francis 139
Xúquer, River *see* Júcar, River

Y

Yacimientos de Atapuerca 375
Yanci *see* Igantzi
Yáñez de la Almedina, Fernando 298

Los Yébenes 391
Yecla wine region 206–7
Yegen 489
Yemas 343, 367
Yerba de Basa, fiestas 243
Yerbabuena, Eva 429
Yesos de Sorbas 504
Yeste 400
  hotels 571
Youth hostels 560, 561
Yuste, Monasterio de **409**
Yusuf I 494

Z

Zafón, Carlos Ruiz 39
Zafra **416–17**
  hotels 571
  restaurants 597
Zahara de los Atunes 472
Zahara de la Sierra 473
Zalamea de la Serena 416
Zamarramala, fiestas 43, 372
Zamora **360–61**
  hotels 570
  restaurants 595
Zamora province 351
Zangotza *see* Sangüesa
Zapatero, José Luis Rodríguez **73**
Zaragoza 202, **240–41**
  fiestas 46, 243
  hotels 567
  map 241
  restaurants 591
Zaragoza province 231
Zarautz 14, **123**
  hotels 564
Zarco, Doña Ana Martínez 398
Zarzuela 326, 327
Zoos, Zoo de Barcelona **159**
Zoraya 496
Zorita 250
Zorrilla, José 39, 370
Zuázola, Bishop of Ávila 128
Zuheros 486
Zuloaga, Ignacio 127
  The Condesa Mathieu de Noailles
  122
  Espacio Cultural Ignacio Zuloaga
  (Zumaia) 123
  Pedraza de la Sierra 369
Zumaia (Zumaya) 14, **123**
Zurbarán, Francisco de 36, 65, 251
  Ayuntamiento (Seville) paintings 442
  birthplace 417
  Father Gonzalo de Illescas at Work 411
  fountain (Llerena) 417
  Fray Pedro Machado 285
  Iglesia de la Magdalena (Seville) 434
  Monasterio de Guadalupe 410,
  411
  Museo de Bellas Artes (Seville) 434
  Saint Bruno in Ecstasy 471
  St Casilda 293
  Still Life with Four Vessels 298
  Zafra altarpiece 417

Acknowledgments

Dorling Kindersley would like to thank the following people whose contributions and assistance made preparation of this book possible.

Main Contributors

John Ardagh is a journalist and writer, and the author of several books on modern Europe,

David Baird, resident in Andalusia from 1971 to 1995, is the author of *Inside Andalusia.*

Vicky Hayward, a writer, journalist and editor, lives in Madrid, and has travelled extensively in Spain.

Adam Hopkins is an indefatigable travel writer and author of *Spanish Journeys: A Portrait of Spain.*

Lindsay Hunt has travelled widely and has contributed to several Eyewitness Travel Guides.

Nick Inman writes regularly on Spain for books and magazines.

Paul Richardson is the author of *Not Part of the Package,* a book on Ibiza, where he lives.

Martin Symington is a regular contributor to the *Daily Telegraph.* He also worked on the *Eyewitness Travel Guide to Great Britain.*

Nigel Tisdall, contributor to the *Eyewitness Travel Guide to France,* is the author of the *Insight Pocket Guide to Seville.*

Roger Williams has contributed to Insight Guides on Barcelona and Catalonia, and was the main contributor to the *Eyewitness Travel Guide to Provence.*

Additional Contributors

Mary Jane Aladren, Sarah Andrews, Pepita Aris, Emma Dent Coad, Rebecca Doulton, Harry Eyres, Josefina Fernández, Anne Hersh, Nick Rider, Mercedes Ruiz Ochoa, David Stone, Clara Villanueva, Christopher Woodward, Patricia Wright.

Additional Illustrations

Arcana Studio, Richard Bonson, Louise Boulton, Martine Collings, Brian Craker, Jared Gilbey (Kevin Jones Associates), Paul Guest, Steven Gyapay, Claire Littlejohn.

Additional Photography

David Cannon, Tina Chambers, Geoff Dann, Phillip Dowell, Mike Dunning, Neil Fletcher, Steve Gorton, Heidi Grassley, Frank Green-away, Derek Hall, Colin Keates, Alan Keohane, Dave King, Ella Milroy, D Murray, Cyril Laubsouer, Ian O'Leary, Stephen Oliver, Alex Robinson, Rough Guides/Demetrio Carrasco, J Selves, Rough Guides/Ian Aitken, Colin Sinclair, Tony Souter, Mathew Ward, P Wojcik.

Cartography

Lovell Johns Ltd (Oxford), ERA-Maptec Ltd.

Revisions Team

Sam Atkinson, Pilar Ayerbe, Rosemary Bailey, Vicky Barber, Teresa Barea, Claire Baranowski, Cristina Barrallo, Fran Bastida, Lynette McCurdy Bastida, Jill Benjamin, Marta Bescos, Vandana Bhagra, Sonal Bhatt, Julie Bond, Chris Branfield, Gretta Britton, Daniel Campi, Paula Canal (Word on Spain), Maria Victoria Cano, Lola Carbonell, Peter Casterton, Elspeth Collier, Carey Combe, Jonathan Cox, Martin Cropper, Neha Dhingra, Linda Doyle, Nicola Erdpresser, Bernat Fiol, Emer FitzGerald, Anna Freiberger,

Rhiannon Furbear, Mary-Ann Gallagher, Candela Garcia Sanchez-Herrera, Aruna Ghose, Elena González, Lydia Halliday, Des Hemsley, Matthew Hirtes, Tim Hollis, Claire Jones, Juliet Kenny, Sumita Khatwani, Priya Kukadia, Priyanka Kumar, Rahul Kumar, Michael Lake, Erika Lang, Maite Lantaron, Jude Ledger, Rebecca Lister, Shobhna Iyer, Hayley Maher, Sarah Martin, Lynnette McCurdy Bastida, Alison McGill, Caroline Mead, Sam Merrell, Kate Molan, Jane Oliver, Simon Oon, Mary Ormandy, Mike Osborn, Malcolm Parchment, Helen Partington, Susie Peachey, Elizabeth Pitt, Pollyanna Poulter, Anna Pirie, Tom Prentice, Rada Radojicic, Mani Ramaswamy, Lucy Ratcliffe, Erin Richards, Ellen Root, Sands Publishing Solutions, Sue Sharp, Neil Simpson, Rituraj Singh, Sadie Smith, Peter Stone, Anna Streiffert, Leah Tether, Helen Townsend, Suzanne Wales, Jennifer Walker, Catherine Waring, Andy Wilkinson, Hugo Wilkinson, Robert Zonenblick.

Proofreader

Huw Hennessy, Nikky Twyman, Stewart J Wild.

Indexer

Helen Peters.

Special Assistance

Dorling Kindersley would like to thank the regional and local tourist offices, *ayuntamientos,* shops, hotels, restaurants and other organizations in Spain for their invaluable help. Particular thanks also to Dr Giray Ablay (University of Bristol); María Eugenia Alonso and María Dolores Delgado Peña (Museo Thyssen-Bornemisza); Ramón Álvarez (Consejería de Educación y Cultura, Castilla y León); Señor Ballesteros (Santiago de Compostela Tourist Office); Carmen Brieva, Javier Campos and Luis Esteruelas (Spanish Embassy, London); Javier Caballero Arranz; Fernando Cañada López; The Club Taurino of London; Consejería de Turismo, Castilla-La Mancha; Consejería de Turismo and Consejería de Cultura, Junta de Extremadura; Mònica Colomer and Montse Planas (Barcelona Tourist Office); María José Docal and Carmen Cardona (Patronato de Turismo, Lanzarote); Edilesa; Klaus Ehrlich; Juan Fernández, Lola Moreno and others at *El País-Aguilar;* Belén Galán (Centro de Arte Reina Sofía); Amparo Garrido; Adolfo Díaz Gómez (Albacete Tourist Office); Professor Nigel Glendinning (Queen Mary and Westfield College, University of London); Pedro Hernández; Insituto de Cervantes, London; Victor Jolín (SOTUR); Joaquim Juan Cabanilles (Servicio de Investigación Prehistórica, Valencia); Richard Kelly; Mark Little (*Lookout* Magazine); Carmen López de Tejada and Inma Felipe (Spanish National Tourist Office, London); Caterine López and Ana Roig Mundi (ITVA); Julia López de la Torre (Patrimonio Nacional, Madrid); Lovell Johns Ltd (Oxford); Josefina Maestre (Ministerio de Agricultura, Pesca y Alimentación); Juan Malavia García and Antonio Abarca (Cuenca Tourist Office); Mario (Promoción Turismo, Tenerife); Janet Mendel; Javier Morata (Acanto Arquitectura y Urbanismo. Madrid); Juan Carlos Murillo; Sonia Ortega and Bettina Krücken (Spain Gourmetour); Royal Society for the Protection of Birds (UK); Alícia Ribas Sos; Katusa Salazar-Sandoval (Fomento de Turismo, Ibiza); María Ángeles Sánchez and Marcos; Ana Sarrieri (Departamento de Comercio, Consumo y Turismo, Gobierno Vasco); Klaas Schenk; María José Sevilla (Foods From Spain); The Sherry Institute of Spain (London); Anna Skidmore (Fomento de Turismo, Mallorca); Philip Sweeney; Rupert Thomas; Mercedes

Trujillo and Antonio Cruz Caballero (Patronato de Turismo, Gran Canaria); Gerardo Uarte (Gobierno de Navarra); Fermín Unzue (Dirección General de Turismo, Cantabria); Puri Villanueva.

Artwork Reference

Sr Joan Bassegoda, Catedral Gaudí (Barcelona); José Luis Mosquera Muller (Mérida); Jorge Palazón, Paisajes Españoles (Madrid).

Photography Permissions

The Publisher would like to thank the following for their kind assistance and permission to photograph at their establishments: © Patrimonio Nacional, Madrid; Palacio de la Almudaina, Palma de Mallorca; El Escorial, Madrid; La Granja de San Ildefonso; Convento de Santa Clara, Tordesillas; Las Huelgas Reales, Burgos; Palacio Real, Madrid; Monasterio de las Descalzas; Bananera "El Guanche S.L."; Museo Arqueológico de Tenerife-OACIMC del Excmo, Cavildo Insular de Tenerife; Asociación de Encajeras de Acebo-Cáceres; Museo de Arte Abstracto Español, Cuenca; Fundación Juan March; Pepita Alia Lagartera; Museo Naval de Madrid; © Catedral de Zamora; Museo de Burgos; Claustro San Juan de Duero, Museo Numantino, Soria; San Telmo Museoa Donostia-San Sebastián; Hotel de la Reconquista, Oviedo; Catedral de Jaca; Museo de Cera, Barcelona; Museu D'Història de la Ciutat, Barcelona; © Capitol Catedral de Lleida; Jardí Botànic Marimurtra, Estació Internacional de Biologia Mediterrània, Girona; Museo Arqueológico Sagunto (Teatro Romano-Castillo); Museo Municipal y Ermita de San Antonio de la Florida, Madrid. Also all the other churches, museums, hotels, restaurants, shops, galleries and sights too numerous to thank individually.

Picture Credits

Key: a=above; b=below/bottom; c=centre; f=far; l=left; r=right; t=top.

Works of art have been published with the permission of the following copyright holders: *Dona i Ocell* Joan Miró © Succession Miró/ADAGP, Paris & DACS, London 2011 180tl; *Guernica* Pablo Ruiz Picasso 1937 © Succession Picasso/DACS, London 2011 303crb; *Morning* George Kolbe © DACS London 2011 174tr, 177tl; *Peine de los Vientos* Eduardo Chillida © DACS, London 2011 126b; Various works by Joaquín Sorolla © DACS, London 2011 309tr; *Rainy Taxi* Salvador Dalí © Kingdom of Spain, Gala - Salvador Dalí Foundation, DACS, London 2011 219tr; *Tapestry of the Foundation* Joan Miró 1975 © Succession Miró/ADAGP, Paris & DACS, London 175crb; *Three Gypsy Boys* ©°Joan Rebull 1976 148bl.

The publisher would like to thank the following individuals, companies and picture libraries for their kind permission to reproduce their photographs:

6 TOROS 6: 41cb.

Abades Triana: 598bl; **Ace Photo Agency**: Bob Masters 30bl; Mauritius 27t; Bill Wassman 324br; **AISA Archivo Iconografico, Barcelona**: 26tl, 40bc, 50, 52cla, 52clb, 53bl, 53br, 54cra, 54clb, 55tl, 56cla, 56bl(d), 58bl, 58br, 58cla, 58–9, 59c, 59cra, 59bl, 60bl, 65bc 69tr, 71tl, 71bc, 307b, 359bl, 427bl, 427br, 428cl, 493br; Biblioteca Nacional, Madrid *Felipe V* Luis Meléndez 75bl; Catedral de Sevilla *Ignacio de Loyola* Alonso Vázquez 128br(d); *Camilo José Cela* Álvaro Delgado 1916 © DACS, London 2011 39br (d); *La Tertulia del Pombo* José Gutiérrez Solana 1920 © DACS, London 2011 303tl; Museo de América, Madrid *Vista de Sevilla* Alonso Sánchez Coello 62clb; Museo de Bellas Artes, Seville *Sancho Panza y El Rucio* Moreno Carbonero 64cla; Museo de Bellas Artes, Valencia *Ecce Homo* Juan de Juanes 256bl; Museo Frankfurt *La Armada* 63tl; Museo de Historia de México *Hernán Cortés* S E Colane 62bl(d); Museo Histórico Militar, San Sebastián *Guerra Carlista* 67br(d); Museo Lázaro Galdiano, Madrid *Lope de Vega* Caxes 294tr; Museo Nacional del Teatro *Poster for "Yerma"* (FG Lorca) Juan Antonio Morales y José Caballero © DACS, London 2011 39tr; Museo del Prado, Madrid *La Rendición de Breda* Diego Velázquez 65crb, *El Tres de Mayo de 1808 en Madrid* Francisco de Goya y Lucientes 66–7(d), La Reina María Luisa *María* Francisco de Goya 66cl, *Carlos IV* Francisco de Goya 75bc, *Los Borrachos* Diego de Velázquez 296tr, *Saturno devorando a un hijo* Francisco de Goya 298tr, *El Descendimiento* Van der Weyden 299bl; Real Academia de Bellas Artes de San Fernando, Madrid *El Sueño del Caballero* Antonio de Pereda 64–5(d); **Agroturismo Biniatram**: 559br, 575bc; **Akelarre**: 585bl; **AKG**, London: 71cr; **Alamy Images**: The Art Archive 8–9; Paul Hardy Carter 204cla; Michelle Chaplow 460bl; China Span/Keren Su 338–9; Ian Dagnall 15br; Expuesto/Nicholas Randall 608br; Mike Finn-Kelcey 629c; Robert Harding Picture Library 423cl, 608cla; Eric James 137t; Russell Kord 350; paulbourdice 517cla; PjrTravel 625c; Prisma Bildagentur AG 178; Profimedia. CZ s.r.o. 541cla; Alex Segre 81tl, 579tr; Richard Sowley 673cr; Peter Titmuss 205tl; travelstock44 158bl; Renaud Visage 422cla; Ken Welsh 602tr, 619bl; **Allsport**: Stephen Munday 46cr; **Alsa Group S.L.L.C.**: 633cl; **Annua**: 584tr; **Aquila**: Adrian Hoskins 214cl, 214clb, 214bl; Mike Lane 347clb; James Pearce 209bl; **ARCAID**: Paul Raftery 124bl; **Arxiu Mas**: 40br, 41bl, 55crb, 58tl, 61clb, 61br, 57br(d); Museo del Prado, Madrid *Felipe II* Sánchez Coello 74br(d); Patrimonio Nacional 63c, 63b(d); **The Art Archive**: Museo del Prado Madrid/Dagli Orti (A) *St Cecilia Patron Saint of Music* Nicolas Poussin (1594–1665) 299cr.

Balearia: 627bl; **Barosse**: 567tr; **Belmond Ltd.**: 569bc; **Biofotos**: Heather Angel 84cla, 84bl; **La Bobadilla**: 573tc; **Bridgeman Art Library**: *St Dominic Enthroned as Abbot* Bartolomé Bermejo 298cla; Index/ Museo del Prado, Madrid *Auto-da-fé in the Plaza Mayor* Francisco Rizi 278c; Musée des Beaux-Artes, Berne *Colossus of Rhodes* Salvador Dalí 1954 © Kingdom of Spain, Gala – Salvador Dalí Foundation, DACS, London 2011 37tr; Museo del Prado, Madrid *Charles IV and his Family* Francisco de Goya y Lucientes 37cb, *The Adoration of the Shepherds* El Greco 296clb, *The Annunciation* Fra Angelico 297br, *The Clothed Maja* Francisco de Goya y Lucientes 297cra, *The Naked Maja* Francisco de Goya y Lucientes 297cr, *The Three Graces* Peter Paul Rubens 297br, *The Martydom of St Philip* José de Ribera 296cl; Museo Picasso, Barcelona *Las Meninas, Infanta Margarita* Pablo Ruiz Picasso 1957 © Succession Picasso/DACS, London 2011 36ca; **Michael Busselle**: 211r, 213b, 214t.

Le Cabrera: 593bc; **Camper Store**, Madrid: 607tr; **Casa Grande**: 572br; **El Celler de Can Roca**: 589bc; **Centro de Arte Reina Sofía**: *Bertsolaris* Zubiaurre © DACS, London 2011 129clb, *Paisaje de Cadaqués* Salvador Dalí 1923 © Kingdom of Spain, Gala – Salvador Dalí Foundation, DACS, London 2011 302cb, *Accidente Ponce de León* 302bl, *Toki-Egin (Homenaje a San Juan de la Cruz)* Eduardo Chillida 1952 © DACS, London 2011 303bl; **Cephas**: Mick Rock 33bl, 46t, 82tr, 206tr, 206cla, 344tr, 424tr, 425br, 425cr; Roy Stedall 425tr; **Cinc Sentits**: 576br; **Ciutat de Girona**: 566tl; **Grupo Codorniu**: 207tl; **Bruce Coleman**: Eric Crichton 208tr; José Luis González Grande 209cra; Werner Layer

347tl; Andy Purcell 35c; Hans Reinhard 84crb; Norbert Schwirtz 209cla; Colin Varndell 209crb; **Dee Conway:** 429ca, 429cr; **Comerç 24:** 603br; **Corbis:** Owen Franken 81c, 205c, 342cl, 343c, 423tl; Hemis/Hughes Herve 230; Michael Jenner 260–61; Jean-Pierre Lescourret 12tr; Massimo Listri 13b; Claude Medale 127bc; Caroline Penn 343tl; Jose Fuste Raga 12bl, 14b, 378–9; Robert Harding World Imagery/Marco Cristofori 2–3; Splash News/LOTE 27c; Rudy Sulgan 272; Westend61/Mel Stuart 506–7; **Joe Cornish:** 32cla, 368br, 376tr; **El Corral del Indianu:** 583tr **Giancarlo Costa:** 41bc; **Cover:** Genin Andrada 44bl, 47bl; Austin Catalan 72bl; Juan Echeverria 35cra, 45br, 549bl; Pepe Franco 190cla; Quim Llenas 129cra, 321tl; Matías Nieto 47cr; F J Rodríguez 129bl; **Cuidad de las Artes y las Ciencas (CACSA):** Javier Yaya Tur 257t; **Cocomfe:** 617b.

J D Dallet: 73tr, 468tl, 605br; **Delic:** 592tl; **El Deseo:** Pedro Almodóvar 309bc; **Dos Patillos:** 587tr; **Dreamstime.com:** Davidmartyn 104; Deymos 14tr, Evgeniy_p 175tl; Matej Kastelic 268–9; Marlee 210; Matthi 16tr; Luciano Mortula 140–41; Juan Moyano 10bl, 532; Nanisub 79bl; Rawlways 560cr; Tomas Sereda 330; Slava296 556–7; Jose I. Soto 88; Studiobarcelona 276tl; Typhoonski 560tr; Maria Vazquez 275tl; Robert Zehetmayer 304.

Edex: 55bl, 409b; **Edilesa:** 356b; **Elephant Club:** 576cr; **Paco Elvira:** 34crb; **EMI:** Hispavox 380bc; **Equipo 28:** 429tl; **L'Estartit Tourist Board:** 221c; **ET Archive:** 56br; **Europa Press:** 73ca; **Mary Evans Picture Library:** 60cla, 67bl, 278bl, 475br; **Eye Ubiquitous:** James Davis Travel Photography 25tr, 222br.

Firo Foto: 161cr; 537tr; **Flamencocool:** Seville, 459tr; **Grupo Freixenet:** 207tr; **Fundación César Manrique:** 552br; **Fundación Colección Thyssen-Bornemisza:** *Madonna of Humility* Fra Angelico 181tc, *La Virgen del Árbol* Petrus Christus 292tr, *Mata Mua* Paul Gauguin 1892 293br, *Harlequin with a Mirror* Pablo Ruiz Picasso 1923 © Succession Picasso/DACS, London 2011 292bl, *Hotel Room* © Edward Hopper 1931 292cla, *Portrait of Baron H H Thyssen-Bornemisza* © Lucian Freud 1981–82 292br, *Venus y Cupido* Peter Paul Rubens (after 1629) 293tl, *Santa Casilda* Francisco de Zurbarán 1640–1645 293cr, *Autumn Landscape in Oldenburg* Karl Schmidt-Rottluff 1907 © DACS, London 2011 293bl; **Fundació Joan Miró, Barcelona:** *Flama en l'Espai i Dona Nua* Joan Miró 1932 © Succession Miró/ADAGP, Paris and DACS, London, 2011 176tl.

Getty Images: Gonzalo Azumendi 404, 614–15; Baloulumix/Julien Fourniol 446; California CPA 200–1; Alan Copson 418–19; R Duran (rduranmerino@gmail.com) 436; Krzysztof Dydynski 286; Michele Falzone 510; Iconica/Don Klumpp 618tl; Israel Gutiérrez Photography 76–7; Domingo Leiva 382; I. Lizarraga 118; Peter Macdiarmid 73br; Conor MacNeill 146; marck from belgium 172; Meinrad Riedo 246; Ferran Traite Soler 162; Visions of Our Land 166–7; Ken Welsh 462, 498–9; Terry Williams 616cla; zzafrankha – foodholic telling stories about food 528–9; **Godo Foto:** 224bl, 225tr, 229t, 253b, 259t, 337bl; **Ronald Grant Archive:** *For a Few Dollars More* © United Artists 504bl; © **FMGB Guggenheim Bilbao Museoa.** Erica Barahona Ede. All rights reserved. Partial or total reproduction is prohibited 124tr, *The Matter of Time* Richard Serra © ARS, NY and DACS, London 2011 124br, 125t. **Robert Harding Picture Library:** 145cra, 164cla, 176br, 253tl,

307tl, 515br; Nigel Blythe 23b, 153cr; Bob Cousins 30clb; Robert Frerck 467tr; James Strachan 284tl; **María Victoria Hernández:** 537bl; **Hostal Gala, Madrid:** 568tl; **Hotel Alma:** 561tr; **Hotel Arts Barcelona:** 559cl; **Hotel Marqes de Riscal:** 564bl; **Hotel Mercer:** 565tc; **Hotel Miró:** 563tr; **Hotel Rector:** 570tl; **Hulton Deutsch Collection:** 70br, 395br.

The Image Bank, London: Mark Romanelli 144bl; Mathew Weinreb 165br; **Images Colour Library:** AGE Fotostock 32tr, 33tr, 34cra, 34ca, 34br, 40tr, 41ca, 44cr, 46cl, 126b, 191tr, 191br, 215br, 237cra, 237br, 325br, 339c, 347cla, 353tr, 425cl, 428br, 470bl, 501tl, 535t, 611cr, 611bl; Horizon International 40–41, 144clb; **Incafo:** J A Fernández & C De Noriega 79bl, 129br; Juan Carlos Muñoz 400b, 501br; A Ortega 34bl; **Index:** 52c, 52b, 53cr, 53crb, 58cra, 60br (d), 63tr, *Los Moriscos Suplicando al Rey Felipe III* 65cr, 68–9, 69bc, 71cb, *Carlos I* 74tc, 74clb, 75br; Bridgeman, London 62cra; CCJ 27br; *Garrote Vil* José Gutiérrez Solana 1931 © DACS, London 2011 69clb(d); Galería del Ateneo, Madrid *Lucio Anneo Seneca* Villodas 54cla(d); Galeria Illustres Catalonia, Barcelona *Joan Prim I Prats* J Cusachs 67cra(d); Image *José Zorilla* 39cb; Instituto Valencia de Don Juan, Madrid *Carlos V* Simón Bening 63crb; Iranzo 60cra; Mithra 56clb, 62br(d), Museo de América, Madrid *Indio Yumbo y Frutas Tropicales* 63cra; Museo Lázaro Galdiano, Madrid *Lope de Vega* Anonymous 38tr, *Félix Lope de Vega* Francisco Pacheco 64br(d); Museo Municipal, Madrid *Fiesta en la Plaza Mayor de Madrid* Juan de la Corte 65tl; Museo del Prado, Madrid *Ascensión de un Globo Montgolfier en Madrid* Antonio Carnicero 66ca(d), *José Moreño Conde de Floridablanca* Francisco de Goya 66br(d), *Flota del Rey Carlos III de España* A Joli 67tl(d); National Maritime Museum, Greenwich *Batalla de Trafalgar* Chalmers 66clb; A Noé 60cb; Palacio del Senado, Madrid *Alfonso X "El Sabio"* Matías Moreno 38b(d), *Rendición de Granada* Francisco Pradilla 60–1(d); Patrimonio Nacional 55br; Private Collection, Madrid *Pedro Calderón de la Barca* Antonio de Pereda 65bl(d); Real Academia de Bellas Artes de San Fernando, Madrid *San Diego de Alcalá Dando de Comer a los Pobres* Bartolomé Esteban Murillo 65cra(d), *Fernando VII* Francisco de Goya 75tl(d); *Isabel II* 75tc, *Self-Portrait* Francisco de Goya 243b; A Tovy 73crb; **Nick Inman:** 208bc, 257tr, 624tr, 629b; **Institut Turístic Valencià:** 249br.

César Justel: 357bc.

Anthony King: 295tl.

Life File Photographic: 221c; Tony Abbott 346cla; Xavier Catalan 145crb; Emma Lee 145cr, 633tr; **Andrzej Lisowski:** 626c; **Neil Lukas:** 468cb, 468bl.

Magnum: S Franklin 72cb; Jean Gaumy 73tl; **MARKA,** Milan: Sergio Pitamitz 158tl; Imagen Mas, Leon: 359tr; **Miguel Torres, SA:** 207c; **John Miller:** 509cb, 533b, 542cl, 547bl, 552cla, 553br; **Mas de Torrent Hotel & Spa:** 566br; **Meson Cuevas Del Vino:** 594bc; **El Molino de la Romera:** 599tc; **El Motel – Hotel Empordà:** 588tl; **Museo Arqueológic de Barcelona:** 175c; **Museo Arqueológico de Villena:** 52–3; **Museo Arqueológico Nacional:** 300tl; **Museu de Ciencies Naturals de Barcelona:** 159tc; **Museo Nacional del Prado:** *El Jardín de las Delicias* 296bl; **Museu Picasso,** Barcelona: *Auto Retrato* Pablo Ruiz Picasso 1899–1900 © Succession Picasso/DACS, London 2011 157bl.

Natural Science Photos: Nigel Charles 112tl; C Dani & I Jeske 347br; Richard Revels 346br; Brian Sutton 346bl; P & S Ward 236bc; **Naturpress:** Oriol Alamany 35bl; J L Calvo & J R Montero 347crb; José Luis Grande 469bc; Walter Kwaternik 34clb, 35crb, 346cra, 347cra; Francisco Márquez 469crb, 420bl; Aurelio Martín 35br, Sebastián Martín 347bc; José A Martínez 84tr, 211b, 346clb, 346crb; © **National Maritime Museum:** 62–3; **Network:** Bilderberg/W Kunz 425tl; **NHPA:** Laurie Campbell 84cra; Stephen Dalton 85clb; Vicente García Canseco 35cla, 469ca; Manfred Daneggar 84br, 85br.

Omega Foto:114tl, Manuel Pinilla 46bl; **Oronoz:** 4, 37br, 40cl, 41br, 51b, 51t, 54b, 57tl, 57cb, 57crb, 58clb, 59tl, 59bc, 63tl, 62cl, 64clb, 69tl, 72cla, 74crb, 116tl, 309cr, 359br, 367br, 374bc, 438bl, 445bl, 482cl, 483tr, 493bl, 609t; Biblioteca Nacional, Madrid *Isabel la Católica* Luis Madrazo 74tl(d); Iglesia Santo Tomé, Toledo *El Entierro del Conde de Orgaz* El Greco 36cl; *Portrait II* Joan Miró 1938 © Succession Miró/ADAGP, Paris and DACS, London 302tr; Monasterio Santa Maria, Barcelona *Virgen con Niño* Ferrer Bassa 36bl(d); Museo de Bellas Artes, Cádiz *San Bruno en Éxtasis* Zurbarán 471tr; Museo Casa Gredo, Toledo *Carlos II* Miranda Correño 74tr(d); Museo Municipal de Bellas Artes, Tenerife *Retrato de Boabdil o Abu Abdala* 61tr(d); Museo Nacional de Escultura, Valladolid *Natividad* Berruguete 371tc; Museo Naval, Madrid *Desembarco de Colón* José Garnelo 61tl; Museo Naval Laminas, Madrid *Carabelas de Colón* Monleón 61bl(d); Museo del Prado, Madrid *El Salvador* José de Ribera 36crb, *Las Meninas o Familia de Felipe V* Diego Velázquez 36–7, *Felipe III* Pedro A Vidal 64bl, *Felipe V* 66bl, *Guernica* Pablo Ruiz Picasso 1937 © Succession Picasso/DACS, London 2011, 70–71, *Felipe IV* Diego Velázquez 70bc(d), *Bodegón* Zurbarán 298bl, *David Vencedor de Goliat* Caravaggio 299tc; Palacio Moncloa *Interior de la Catedral de Santiago* Villaamil Pérez 86–7, *Mujer en Azul* Pablo Ruiz Picasso 1901 © Succession Picasso/DACS, London 2011 302cla; Private Collection, Palma *Oleo Sobre Lienzo* Joan Miró 1932 © Succession Miró/ADAGP, Paris and DACS, London, 2011 37ca; Real Academia de Bellas Artes de San Fernando *Fray Pedro Machado* Zurbarán 285tr.

José M Pérez de Ayala: 34cr, 468tr, 468cla, 469tl, 469ca; **The Photographers Library:** 527tr; **Pictures Colour Library:** 26b, 34tr, 262b, 420cl; **PRISMA:** 68cla, 68bl, 69crb, 70cla, 70clb, 71tr, 101tr, 144tl, 243c, 254cl, 325tl, 463b, 520crb, 534clb, 536cl, 543clb, 543bc, 543br, 543bl, 547tr, 555bl, 555br; *Franco* Aguiar 75tr; *El Ingenioso Hidalgo Don Quixote de la Mancha* 1605 Ricardo Balaca 399br; Domènech & Azpiliqueta 122tl; Albert Heras 190br; Marcel Jaquet 534clb, 545b; Hans Lohr 487br; *Los Niños de la Concha* Bartolomé Esteban Murillo 37bl(d); Museo de Arte Moderno, Barcelona *Pío Baroja* Ramón Casas 68cb(d); Museo de Bellas Artes, Bilbao *Condesa Mathieu de Noailles* Ignacio Zuloaga y Zubaleta © DACS, London 2011 122bl; Museo de Bellas Artes, Zaragoza *Príncipe de Viana* José Moreno Carbonero 134b (d); Mateu 195cr; Palacio del Senado, Madrid *Alfonso XIII* Aquino © DACS,

London 2011 75crb; Patrimonio Nacional Palacio de Riofrío, Segovia: 68bc; *Auto Retrato* Pablo Ruiz Picasso 1907 © Succession Picasso/DACS, London 2011 69ca; Real Academia de Bellas Artes de San Fernando, Madrid *Las Bodas de Camacho* José Moreno Carbonero 39tl(d), *Procession of the Flagellants* Francisco de Goya 278br(d); **Pure Espana:** Port Aventura 609br.

Restaurant Canteré: 590bl; **Restaurante Hospedería, Finca la Estacada:** 596bl; **Restaurante Palio:** 597tr; **Rex Features:** Sipa Press 219cb; **Rib Room:** 600tc; **El Rincon de Antonio:** 595tl; **El Rincon de Juan Carlos:** 605tr; © **Royal Museum of Scotland:** Michel Zabé 51t; **José Lucas Ruiz:** 444br, 460cl.

Saboya 21: 591tl; **María Ángeles Sánchez:** 42tr, 43bl, 47tl, 83t, 102tl, 294cla, 308bl, 391c, 409tr, 536tr, 536cr, 536bc, 540cl, 551tr; **El Serbal:** 577br; **Simply Fosh:** 603tr; **Son Granot:** 604bc; **Spanish Tourist Board:** 259c; **Spectrum Colour Library:** 144tr; **STA Travel Group:** 619ca; **Stockphotos:** Madrid: Campillo 611tl; Heinz Hebeisen 45bl; Mikael Helsing 610bl, David Hornback 25b; Javier Sánchez 336tl; **Suculent:** 586bc; **James Strachan:** 295bc, 306tr, 306c, 308tr; **Tony Stone Worldwide:** Doug Armand 24bl; Jon Bradley 320bl; Robert Everts 444ca; **Superstock:** age fotostock/ Massimo Pizzotti 282–3, 306bl, LatitudeStock 22; Pixtal 80cl.

Taberna del Alabardero: 558cl, 571br; **Telefónica:** 624ca; **Tragabuches:** 601br.

Denominación de Origen Utiel-Requena: 207cb.

Vinas del Vero, S.A: 206cra; **Vinos de Jumilla:** 207bc; **Visions of Andalucía:** Michelle Chaplow 428–9; J D Dallet 401tr; **VU:** Christina García Rodero 24c, 42bl, 43cr, 43tr, 136cl, 372cl, 435cr.

Werner Forman Archive: National Maritime Museum, Greenwich 56cr; **Alan Williams:** 82bl; **Peter Wilson:** 340cr, 472b, 473cr, 479tl, 485tl; **World Pictures:** 321br, 516t.

Yayo Daporta: 582bl.

Front endpaper: All special photography except **Alamy Images:** Russell Kord ltc; **Corbis:** Hemis/Hughes Herve rtc; **Dreamstime.com:** Davidmartyn Ltr; Matej Kastelic lc; Marlee rtr; Luciano Mortula Rca; Juan Moyano Rcb; Jose I. Soto ltl; Gonzalo Azumendi lcl; Michele Falzone rcrb; Domingo Leiva lbl; I. Lizarraga Rtl; Meinrad Riedo rbl; Ken Welsh lbr..

Jacket: *Front and Spine:* **AWL Images:** Alan Copson.

All other images © Dorling Kindersley.
For further information see www.DKimages.com

Phrase Book

In an Emergency

Help!	Socorro	soh-**koh**-roh
Stop!	!Pare!	**pah**-reh
Call a doctor!	¡Llame a un médico!	**yah**-meh ah oon meh-dee-koh
Call an ambulance!	¡Llame a una ambulancia!	**yah**-meh ah **oonah** ahm-boo-**lahn**-thee-ah
Call the police!	¡Llame a la policía!	**yah**-meh ah lah poh-lee-**thee**-ah
Call the fire brigade!	¡Llame a los bomberos!	**yah**-meh ah lohs bohm-**beh**-rohs
Where is the nearest telephone?	¿Dónde está el teléfono más próximo?	**dohn**-deh ehs-**tah** ehl teh-**leh**-foh-noh mahs prohx-ee-moh
Where is the nearest hospital?	¿Dónde está el hospital más próximo?	**dohn**-deh ehs-**tah** ehl ohs-pee-**tahl** mahs prohx-ee-moh

Communication Essentials

Yes	Sí	see
No	No	noh
Please	Por favor	pohr fah-**vohr**
Thank you	Gracias	**grah**-thee-ahs
Excuse me	Perdone	pehr-**doh**-neh
Hello	Hola	**oh**-lah
Goodbye	Adiós	ah-dee-**ohs**
Goodnight	Buenas noches	**bweh**-nahs **noh** chehs
Morning	La mañana	lah mah-**nyah**-nah
Afternoon	La tarde	lah **tahr**-deh
Evening	La tarde	lah **tahr**-deh
Yesterday	Ayer	ah-**yehr**
Today	Hoy	oy
Tomorrow	Mañana	mah-**nyah**-nah
Here	Aquí	ah-**kee**
There	Allí	ah-**yee**
What?	¿Qué?	keh
When?	¿Cuándo?	**kwahn**-doh
Why?	¿Por qué?	pohr-**keh**
Where?	¿Dónde?	**dohn**-deh

Useful Phrases

How are you?	¿Cómo está usted?	**koh**-moh ehs-**tah** oos-**tehd**
Very well, thank you.	Muy bien, gracias.	mwee bee-**ehn grah**-thee-ahs
Pleased to meet you.	Encantado de conocerle.	ehn-kahn-**tah**-doh deh koh-noh-**thehr**-leh
See you soon.	Hasta pronto.	ahs-tah **prohn**-toh
That's fine.	Está bien.	ehs-**tah** bee-**ehn**
Where is/are …?	¿Dónde está/están …?	**dohn**-deh ehs-**tah**/ehs-**tahn**
How far is it to …?	Cuántos metros/kilómetros hay de aquí a …?	**kwahn**-tohs meh-trohs/kee-**loh**-meh-trohs **eye** deh ah-**kee** ah
Which way to …?	¿Por dónde se va a …?	pohr **dohn**-deh seh **bah** ah
Do you speak English?	¿Habla inglés?	**ah**-blah een-**glehs**
I don't understand	No comprendo	noh kohm-**prehn**-doh
Could you speak more slowly, please?	¿Puede hablar más despacio, por favor?	pweh-deh ah-**blahr** mahs dehs-pah-thee-oh pohr fah-**vohr**
I'm sorry.	Lo siento.	loh see-**ehn**-toh

Useful Words

big	grande	**grahn**-deh
small	pequeño	peh-**keh**-nyoh
hot	caliente	kah-lee-**ehn**-teh
cold	frío	**free**-oh
good	bueno	**bweh**-noh
bad	malo	**mah**-loh
enough	bastante	bahs-**tahn**-the
well	bien	bee-**ehn**
open	abierto	ah-bee-**ehr**-toh
closed	cerrado	thehr-**rah**-doh
left	izquierda	eeth-key-**ehr**-dah
right	derecha	deh-**reh**-chah
straight on	todo recto	toh-doh **rehk**-toh
near	cerca	**thehr**-kah
far	lejos	**leh**-hohs
up	arriba	ah-**ree**-bah
down	abajo	ah-**bah**-hoh
early	temprano	tehm-**prah**-noh
late	tarde	**tahr**-deh
entrance	entrada	ehn-**trah**-dah
exit	salida	sah-**lee**-dah
toilet	lavabos, servicios	lah-**vah**-bohs, sehr-**bee**-thee-ohs
more	más	mahs
less	menos	**meh**-nohs

Shopping

How much does this cost?	¿Cuánto cuesta esto?	**kwahn**-toh kwehs-tah ehs-toh
I would like …	Me gustaría …	meh goos-ta-**ree**-ah
Do you have…?	¿Tienen…?	tee-**yeh**-nehn
I'm just looking, thank you.	Sólo estoy mirando, gracias.	soh-loh ehs-**toy** mee-**rahn**-doh **grah**-thee-ahs
Do you take credit cards?	¿Aceptan tarjetas de crédito?	ah-**thep**-tahn tahr-**heh**-tahs deh **kreh**-dee-toh
What time do you open?	¿A qué hora abren?	ah keh oh-rah **ah**-brehn
What time do you close?	¿A qué hora cierran?	ah keh oh-rah thee-**eh**-rahn
This one.	Éste.	**ehs**-the
That one.	Ése.	**eh**-she
expensive	caro	**kahr**-oh
cheap	barato	bah-**rah**-toh
size, clothes	talla	**tah**-yah
size, shoes	número	no**ø**-mehr-oh
white	blanco	**blahn**-koh
black	negro	**neh**-groh
red	rojo	**roh**-hoh
yellow	amarillo	ah-mah-**ree**-yoh
green	verde	**behr**-deh
blue	azul	ah-**thool**
antiques shop	la tienda de antigüedades	lah tee-**ehn**-dah deh ahn-tee-gweh-**dah**-dehs
bakery	la panadería	lah pah-nah-deh-**ree**-ah
bank	el banco	ehl **bahn**-koh
book shop	la librería	lah lee-breh-**ree**-ah
butcher's	la carnicería	lah kahr-nee-theh-**ree**-ah
cake shop	la pastelería	lah pahs-teh-leh-**ree**-ah
chemist's	la farmacia	lah fahr-**mah**-thee-ah
fishmonger's	la pescadería	lah pehs-kah-deh-**ree**-ah
greengrocer's	la frutería	lah froo-teh-**ree**-ah
grocer's	la tienda de comestibles	lah tee-**yehn**-dah deh koh-mehs-**tee**-blehs
hairdresser's	la peluquería	lah peh-loo-keh-**ree**-ah
market	el mercado	ehl mehr-**kah**-doh
newsagent's	el kiosko de prensa	ehl kee-**ohs**-koh deh **prehn**-sah
post office	la oficina de correos	lah oh-fee-**thee**-nah deh koh-**reh**-ohs
shoe shop	la zapatería	lah thah-pah-teh-**ree**-ah
supermarket	el supermercado	ehl soo-pehr-mehr-**kah**-doh
tobacconist	el estanco	ehl ehs-**tahn**-koh
travel agency	la agencia de viajes	lah ah-**hehn**-thee-ah deh bee-**ah**-hehs

Sightseeing

art gallery	el museo de arte	ehl moo-**seh**-oh deh **ahr**-the
cathedral	la catedral	lah kah-teh-**drahl**
church	la iglesia	lah ee-**gleh**-see-ah
	la basílica	lah bah-**see**-lee-kah
garden	el jardín	ehl hahr-**deen**
library	la biblioteca	lah bee-blee-oh-**teh**-kah
museum	el museo	ehl moo-**seh**-oh
tourist information office	la oficina de turismo	lah oh-fee-**thee**-nah deh too-**rees**-moh
town hall	el ayuntamiento	ehl ah-yoon-tah-mee-**ehn**-toh
closed for holiday	cerrado por vacaciones	thehr-**rah**-doh pohr bah-kah-cee-**oh**-nehs
bus station	la estación de autobuses	lah ehs-tah-ee-**ohn** deh owtoh-**boo**-sehs
railway station	la estación de trenes	lah ehs-tah-thee-**ohn** deh **treh**-nehs

Staying in a Hotel

Do you have a vacant room?	¿Tienen una habitación libre?	tee-**eh**-nehn **oo**-nah ah-bee-tah-thee-**ohn** lee-breh
double room	habitación doble	ah-bee-tah-thee-**ohn doh**-bleh
with double bed	con cama de matrimonio	kohn **kah**-mah deh mah-tree-**moh**-nee-oh
twin room	habitación con dos camas	ah-bee-tah-thee-**ohn** kohn dohs **kah**-mahs
single room	habitación individual	ah-bee-tah-thee-**ohn** een-dee-vee-doo-**ahl**
room with a bath	habitación con baño	ah-bee-tah-thee-**ohn** kohn **bah**-nyoh
shower	ducha	**doo**-chah
porter	el botones	ehl boh-**toh**-nehs
key	la llave	lah **yah**-veh
I have a reservation.	Tengo una habitación reservada.	tehn-goh **oo**-na ah-bee-tah-thee-**ohn** reh-sehr-**bah**-dah

Eating Out

Have you got a table for …?	¿Tienen mesa para …?	tee-**eh**-nehn meh-**sah** pah-**rah**
I want to reserve a table.	Quiero reservar una mesa.	kee-eh-roh reh-sehr-**bahr oo**-nah meh-sah
The bill, please.	La cuenta, por favor.	lah **kwehn**-tah pohr fah-**vohr**
I am a vegetarian	Soy vegetariano/a	soy beh-heh-tah-ree-**ah**-no/na
waitress/ waiter	camarera/ camarero	kah-mah-**reh**-rah/ kah-mah-**reh**-roh
menu	la carta	lah **kahr**-tah
fixed-price menu	menú del día	meh-**noo** dehl **dee**-ah
wine list	la carta de vinos	lah **kahr**-tah deh **bee**-nohs
glass	un vaso	oon **bah**-soh
bottle	una botella	oo-nah boh-**teh**-yah
knife	un cuchillo	oon koo-**chee**-yoh
fork	un tenedor	oon teh-neh-**dohr**
spoon	una cuchara	oo-nah koo-**chah**-rah
breakfast	el desayuno	ehl deh-sah-**yoo**-noh
lunch	la comida/ el almuerzo	lah koh-**mee**-dah/ ehl ahl-**mwehr**-thoh
dinner	la cena	lah **then**-nah
main course	el segundo plato	ehl pree-**mehr plah**-toh
starters	los primeros	lohs ehn-treh **meh**-sehs
dish of the day	el plato del día	ehl **plah**-toh dehl **dee**-ah
coffee	el café	ehl kah-**feh**
rare	poco hecho	**poh**-koh eh-choh
medium	medio hecho	**meh**-dee-oh **eh**-choh
well done	muy hecho	mwee **eh**-choh

Menu Decoder

asado	ah-**sah**-doh	roast
el aceite	ah-**thee-eh**-teh	oil
las aceitunas	ah-theh-**toon**-ahs	olives
el agua mineral	**ah**-gwa mee-neh-**rahl**	mineral water
sin gas/con gas	seen gas/kohn gas	still/sparkling
el ajo	**ah**-hoh	garlic
el arroz	ahr-**rohth**	rice
el azúcar	ah-**thoo**-kahr	sugar
la carne	**kahr**-neh	meat
la cebolla	theh-**boh**-yah	onion
la cerveza	thehr-**beh**-thah	beer
el cerdo	**therh**-doh	pork
el chocolate	choh-koh-**lah**-teh	chocolate
el chorizo	choh-**ree**-thoh	red sausage
el cordero	kohr-**deh**-roh	lamb
el fiambre	fee-**ahm**-breh	cold meat
frito	**free**-toh	fried
la fruta	**froo**-tah	fruit
los frutos secos	froo-tohs **seh**-kohs	nuts
las gambas	**gahm**-bahs	prawns
el helado	eh-**lah**-doh	ice cream
al horno	ahl **ohr**-noh	baked
el huevo	oo-**eh**-voh	egg
el jamón serrano	hah-**mohn** sehr-**rah**-noh	cured ham
el jerez	heh-**rehz**	sherry

la langosta	lahn-**gohs**-tah	lobster
la leche	**leh**-cheh	milk
el limón	lee-**mohn**	lemon
la limonada	lee-moh-**nah**-dah	lemonade
la mantequilla	mahn-teh-**kee**-yah	butter
la manzana	mahn-**thah**-nah	apple
los mariscos	mah-**rees**-kohs	seafood
la menestra	meh-**nehs**-trah	vegetable stew
la naranja	nah-**rahn**-hah	orange
el pan	pahn	bread
el pastel	pahs-**tehl**	cake
las patatas	pah-**tah**-tahs	potatoes
el pescado	pehs-**kah**-doh	fish
la pimienta	pee-mee-**yehn**-tah	pepper
el plátano	**plah**-tah-noh	banana
el pollo	**poh**-yoh	chicken
el postre	**pohs**-treh	dessert
el queso	**keh**-soh	cheese
la sal	sahl	salt
las salchichas	sahl-**chee**-chahs	sausages
la salsa	**sahl**-sah	sauce
seco	**seh**-koh	dry
el solomillo	soh-loh-**mee**-yoh	sirloin
la sopa	**soh**-pah	soup
la tarta	**tahr**-tah	pie/cake
el té	teh	tea
la ternera	tehr-**neh**-rah	beef
las tostadas	tohs-**tah**-dahs	toast
el vinagre	bee-**nah**-greh	vinegar
el vino blanco	**bee**-noh **blahn**-koh	white wine
el vino rosado	**bee**-noh roh-**sah**-doh	rosé wine
el vino tinto	**bee**-noh **teen**-toh	red wine

Numbers

0	cero	**theh**-roh
1	uno	**oo**-noh
2	dos	dohs
3	tres	trehs
4	cuatro	**kwa**-troh
5	cinco	**theen**-koh
6	seis	says
7	siete	see-**eh**-the
8	ocho	**oh**-choh
9	nueve	**nweh**-veh
10	diez	dee-**ehth**
11	once	**ohn**-theh
12	doce	**doh**-theh
13	trece	**treh**-theh
14	catorce	kah-**tohr**-theh
15	quince	**keen**-theh
16	dieciséis	dee-eh-thee-**seh-ees**
17	diecisiete	dee-eh-thee-see-**eh**-the
18	dieciocho	dee-eh-thee-**oh**-choh
19	diecinueve	dee-eh-thee-**nweh**-veh
20	veinte	**beh**-een-the
21	veintiuno	beh-een-tee-**oo**-noh
22	veintidós	beh-een-tee-**dohs**
30	treinta	**treh**-een-tah
31	treinta y uno	treh-een-tah ee **oo**-noh
40	cuarenta	kwah-**rehn**-tah
50	cincuenta	theen-**kwehn**-tah
60	sesenta	seh-**sehn**-tah
70	setenta	seh-**tehn**-tah
80	ochenta	oh-**chehn**-tah
90	noventa	noh-**vehn**-tah
100	cien	thee-**ehn**
101	ciento uno	thee-**ehn**-toh **oo**-noh
102	ciento dos	thee-**ehn**-toh dohs
200	doscientos	dohs-thee-**ehn**-tohs
500	quinientos	khee-nee-**ehn**-tohs
700	setecientos	seh-teh-thee-**ehn**-tohs
900	novecientos	noh-veh-thee-**ehn**-tohs
1,000	mil	meel
1,001	mil uno	meel **oo**-noh

Time

one minute	un minuto	oon mee-**noo**-toh
one hour	una hora	**oo**-na **oh**-rah
half an hour	media hora	**meh**-dee-a **oh**-rah
Monday	lunes	**loo**-nehs
Tuesday	martes	**mahr**-tehs
Wednesday	miércoles	mee-**ehr**-koh-lehs
Thursday	jueves	hoo-**weh**-vehs
Friday	viernes	bee-**ehr**-nehs
Saturday	sábado	**sah**-bah-doh
Sunday	domingo	doh-**meen**-goh

Barcelona Transport Map

Barcelona's metro runs 5am–midnight Mon–Thu; 5am–2am Fri; and until midnight Sun. The lines are identified by number and colour; platform signs display the name of the last station on the line. A multi-journey (for example a T-10) card allows travellers to interchange between different modes of transport. The Barcelona Card, available in one-day to five-day values offers unlimited travel on metro and bus. Tickets for the interconnecting FF CC suburban rail network, which runs to Barcelona's environs, and for the funiculars, must be purchased separately if the final destination is outside of area 1.

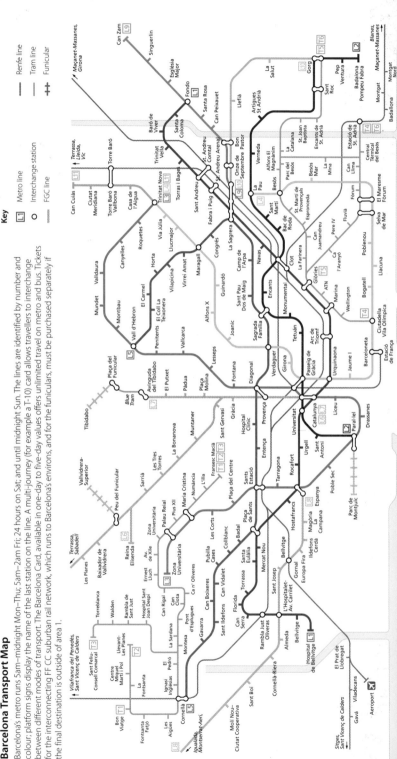

Key

☐ Metro line
○ Interchange station
FGC line
—— Renfe line
—— Tram line
—+—+— Funicular